Oxford-Duden Pictorial English Dictionary with English-Arabic Index

English-Arabic Index prepared by
Moustafa Gabr

Great Clarendon Street, Oxford OX2 6DP

Oxford University Press is a department of the University of Oxford
it furthers the University's objective of excellence in research, scholarship
and education by publishing worldwide in

Oxford New York

Auckland Bangkok Buenos Aires Cape Town Chennai
Dar es Salaam Delhi Hong Kong Istanbul Karachi Kolkata
Kuala Lumpur Madrid Melbourne Mexico City Mumbai Nairobi
São Paulo Shanghai Singapore Taipei Tokyo Toronto

Published in the United States
by Oxford University Press Inc., New York

British Library Cataloguing in Publication Data
Data available

Library of Congress Cataloging in Publication Data
Data available

ISBN 0 19 860201 4 (hardback)
ISBN 0 19 860703 2 (paperback)

32p6T

Pictorial English Dictionary edited by Michael Clark and Bernadette Mohan.
Illustrations by Jochen Schmidt, Mannheim.
Co-ordinating editors of the second edition: Michael Clark, Oxford and
Werner Scholze-Stubenrecht, Mannheim.
English-Arabic Index prepared by Moustafa Gabr

Printed in Hong Kong

CONTENTS

Guide to using the dictionary

The Pictorial English Dictionary, English-Arabic index, and Contents are ordered thematically under the following topic headings:

- The Atom, the Universe, and the Earth
- Man and his Social environment
- Nature as Environment, Agriculture, and Forestry
- Trades, Crafts, and Industry
- Printing Industry
- Transport, Communications, and Information Technology
- Office, Bank, and Stock Exchange
- Community
- Recreation, Games, and Sport
- Entertainment, Culture, and Art
- Animals and Plants

To find the Arabic translation for a vocabulary item, first browse the subject areas listed in the Contents (pp. 6–9); select your relevant subject area, and locate its corresponding number in the Dictionary (numbers are at the top corner of each page). When you have found your vocabulary item, go to the relevant entry in the Index.

Abbreviations

Am.	*American usage*
c.	*castrated (animal)*
coll.	*colloquial*
f.	*female (animal)*
form.	*formerly*
joc.	*jocular*
m.	*male (animal)*
poet.	*poetic*
sg.	*singular*
sim.	*similar*
y.	*young (animal)*

OXFORD-DUDEN
PICTORIAL ENGLISH
DICTIONARY

قاموس أوكسفورد ـ دودن
الإنجليزي المصور

Contents

The arabic numerals are the numbers of the pictures

Office, Bank, Stock Exchange

Community

Recreation, Games, Sport

Entertainment, Culture, and Art

Animals and Plants

1 Atom I

1-8 atom models
1 model of the hydrogen (H) atom
2 atomic nucleus, a proton
3 electron
4 electron spin
5 model of the helium (He) atom
6 electron shell
7 Pauli exclusion principle (exclusion principle, Pauli principle)
8 complete electron shell of the Na atom (sodium atom)
9-14 molecular structures (lattice structures)
9 crystal of sodium chloride (of common salt)
10 chlorine ion
11 sodium ion
12 crystal of cristobalite
13 oxygen atom
14 silicon atom
15 energy level diagram (term diagram, possible quantum jumps) of the hydrogen atom
16 atomic nucleus (proton)
17 electron
18 ground state level
19 excited state
20-25 quantum jumps (quantum transitions)
20 Lyman series
21 Balmer series
22 Paschen series
23 Brackett series
24 Pfund series
25 free electron
26 Bohr-Sommerfeld model of the H atom
27 electron orbits of the electron
28 spontaneous decay of radioactive material
29 atomic nucleus
30, 31 alpha (α) particle (alpha ray, helium nucleus)
30 neutron
31 proton
32 beta (β) particle (beta ray, electron)
33 gamma (γ) ray, a hard X-ray
34 nuclear fission
35 heavy atomic nucleus
36 neutron bombardment
37, 38 fission fragments
39 released neutron
40 gamma (γ) ray
41 chain reaction
42 incident neutron
43 nucleus prior to fission
44 fission fragment
45 released neutron
46 repeated fission
47 fission fragment
48 controlled chain reaction in a nuclear reactor
49 atomic nucleus of a fissionable element
50 neutron bombardment
51 fission fragment (new atomic nucleus)
52 released neutron
53 absorbed neutrons
54 moderator, a retarding layer of graphite
55 extraction of heat (production of energy)
56 X-ray
57 concrete and lead shield
58 bubble chamber for showing the tracks of high-energy ionizing particles
59 light source
60 camera
61 expansion line
62 path of light rays
63 magnet
64 beam entry point
65 reflector
66 chamber

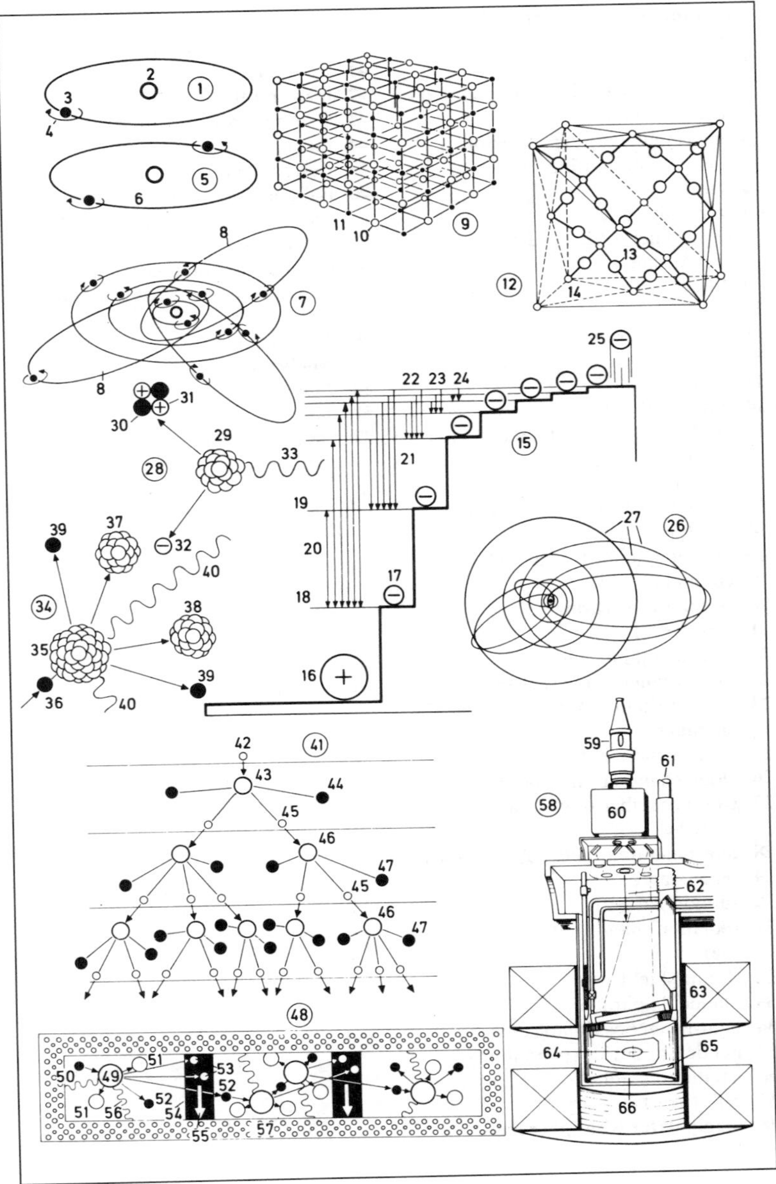
1
2
3
4
5
6
7
8
9
10
11
12
13
14
15
16
17
18
19
20
21
22
23
24
25
26
27
28
29
30
31
32
33
34
35
36
37
38
39
40
41
42
43
44
45
46
47
48
49
50
51
52
53
54
55
56
57
58
59
60
61
62
63
64
65
66

2 Atom II

1-23 radiation detectors (radiation meters)
1 radiation monitor
2 ionization chamber (ion chamber)
3 central electrode
4 measurement range selector
5 instrument housing
6 meter
7 zero adjustment
8-23 dosimeter (dosemeter)
8 film dosimeter
9 filter
10 film
11 film-ring dosimeter
12 filter
13 film
14 cover with filter
15 pocket meter (pen meter, pocket chamber)
16 window
17 ionization chamber (ion chamber)
18 clip (pen clip)
19 Geiger counter (Geiger-Müller counter)
20 counter tube casing
21 counter tube
22 instrument housing
23 measurement range selector
24 Wilson cloud chamber (Wilson chamber)
25 compression plate
26 cloud chamber photograph
27 cloud chamber track of an alpha particle
28 **telecobalt unit** (*coll.* cobalt bomb)
29 pillar stand
30 support cables
31 radiation shield (radiation shielding)
32 sliding shield
33 bladed diaphragm
34 light-beam positioning device
35 pendulum device (pendulum)
36 irradiation table
37 rail (track)
38 **manipulator with sphere unit**
39 handle
40 safety catch (locking lever)
41 wrist joint
42 master arm
43 clamping device (clamp)
44 tongs
45 slotted board
46 radiation shield (protective shield, protective shielding), a lead shielding wall [section]
47 grasping arm of a pair of manipulators (of a master/slave manipulator)
48 dust shield
49 **synchrotron**
50 danger zone
51 magnet
52 pumps for emptying the vacuum chamber

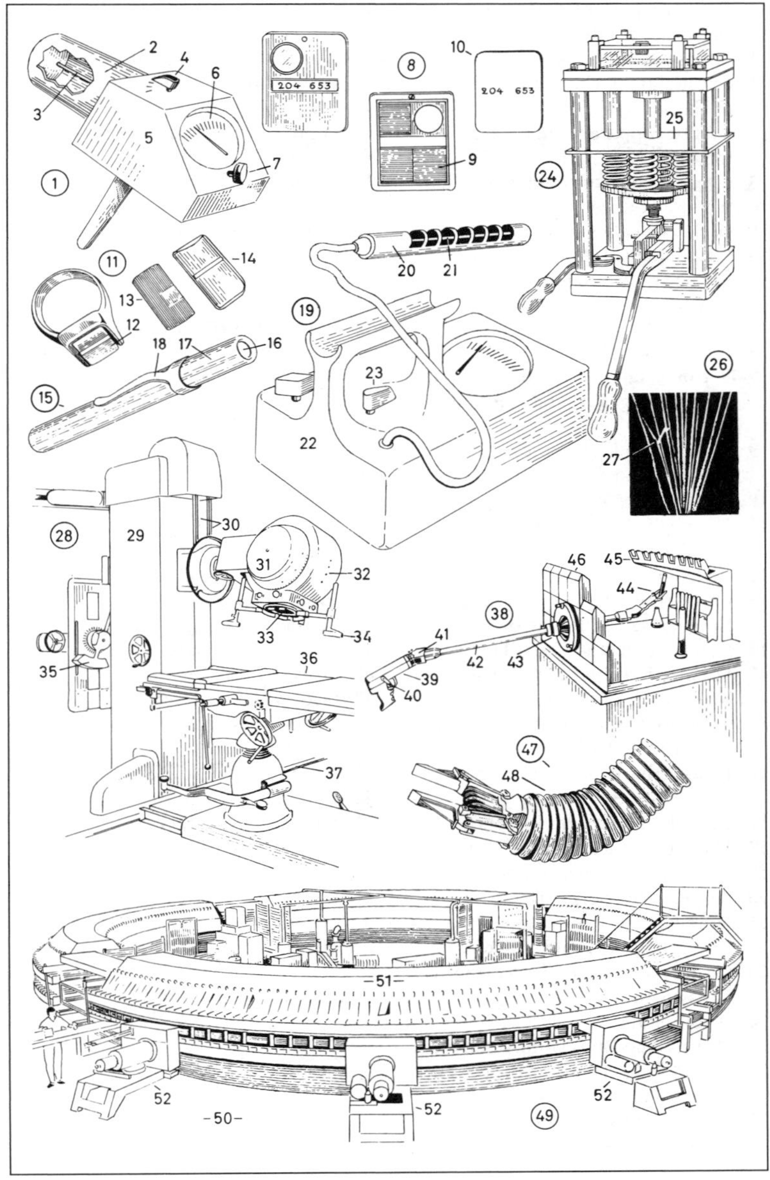
1
2
3
4
5
6
7
204 653
8
9
10
204 653
11
12
13
14
15
16
17
18
19
20
21
22
23
24
25
26
27
28
29
30
31
32
33
34
35
36
37
38
39
40
41
42
43
44
45
46
47
48
49
50
51
52

3 Astronomy I

1-35 star map of the northern sky (northern hemisphere)
1-8 divisions of the sky
1 celestial pole with the Pole Star (Polaris, the North Star)
2 ecliptic (apparent annual path of the sun)
3 celestial equator (equinoctial line)
4 tropic of Cancer
5 circle enclosing circumpolar stars
6, 7 equinoctial points (equinoxes)
6 vernal equinoctial point (first point of Aries)
7 autumnal equinoctial point
8 summer solstice
9-48 constellations (grouping of fixed stars into figures) **and names of stars**
9 Aquila (the Eagle) with Altair the principal star (the brightest star)
10 Pegasus (the Winged Horse)
11 Cetus (the Whale) with Mira, a variable star
12 Eridamus (the Celestial River)
13 Orion (the Hunter) with Rigel, Betelgeuse and Bellatrix
14 Canis Major (the Great Dog, the Greater Dog) with Sirius (the Dog Star), a star of the first magnitude
15 Canis Minor (the Little Dog, the Lesser Dog) with Procyon
16 Hydra (the Water Snake, the Sea Serpent)
17 Leo (the Lion) with Regulus
18 Virgo (the Virgin) with Spica
19 Libra (the Balance, the Scales)
20 Serpens (the Serpent)
21 Hercules
22 Lyra (the Lyre) with Vega
23 Cygnus (the Swan, the Northern Cross) with Deneb
24 Andromeda
25 Taurus (the Bull) with Aldebaran
26 The Pleiades (Pleiads, the Seven Sisters), an open cluster of stars
27 Auriga (the Wagoner, the Charioteer) with Capella
28 Gemini (the Twins) with Castor and Pollux
29 Ursa Major (the Great Bear, the Greater Bear, the Plough, Charles's Wain, *Am.* the Big Dipper) with the double star (binary star) Mizar and Alcor
30 Boötes (the Herdsman) with Arcturus
31 Corona Borealis (the Northern Crown)
32 Draco (the Dragon)
33 Cassiopeia
34 Ursa Minor (the Little Bear, Lesser Bear, *Am.* Little Dipper) with the Pole Star (Polaris, the North Star)
35 the Milky Way (the Galaxy)
36-48 the southern sky
36 Capricorn (the Goat, the Sea Goat)
37 Sagittarius (the Archer)
38 Scorpio (the Scorpion)
39 Centaurus (the Centaur)
40 Triangulum Australe (the Southern Triangle)
41 Pavo (the Peacock)
42 Grus (the Crane)
43 Octans (the Octant)
44 Crux (the Southern Cross, the Cross)
45 Argo (the Celestial Ship)
46 Carina (the Keel)
47 Pictor (the Painter)
48 Reticulum (the Net)

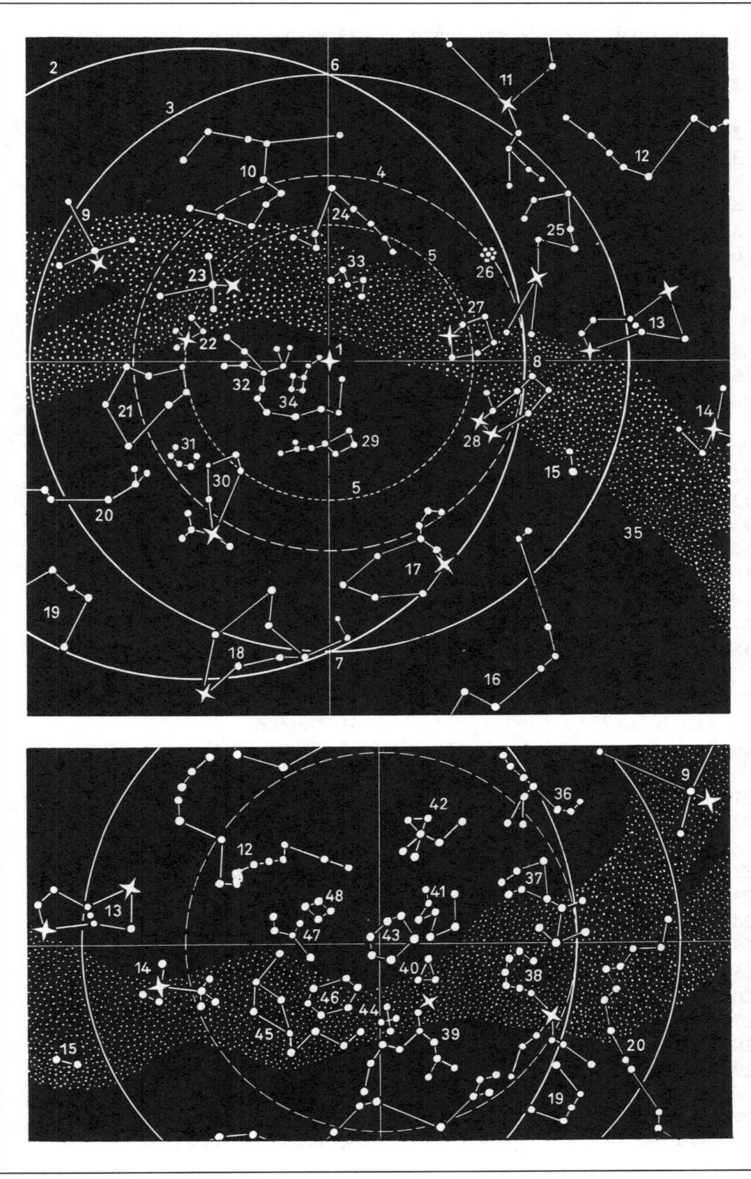
2
6
3
11
12
10
4
9
24
25
33
5
26
23
27
13
22
1
8
32
34
21
14
28
31
29
30
15
5
20
35
17
19
18
7
16
9
36
42
12
37
41
48
13
47
43
14
40
38
46
44
45
39
15
20
19

4 Astronomy II

1-9 the moon
1 moon's path (moon's orbit round the earth)
2-7 lunar phases (moon's phases) (lunation)
2 new moon
3 crescent (crescent moon, waxing moon)
4 half-moon (first quarter)
5 full moon
6 half-moon (last quarter, third quarter)
7 crescent (crescent moon, waning moon)
8 the earth (terrestrial globe)
9 direction of the sun's rays
10-21 apparent path of the sun at the beginning of the seasons
10 celestial axis
11 zenith
12 horizontal plane
13 nadir
14 east point
15 west point
16 north point
17 south point
18 apparent path of the sun on 21 December
19 apparent path of the sun on 21 March and 23 September
20 apparent path of the sun on 21 June
21 border of the twilight area
22-28 rotary motions of the earth's axis
22 axis of the ecliptic
23 celestial sphere
24 path of the celestial pole [precession and nutation]
25 instantaneous axis of rotation
26 celestial pole
27 mean axis of rotation
28 polhode
29-35 solar and lunar eclipse [not to scale]
29 the sun
30 the earth
31 the moon
32 solar eclipse
33 area of the earth in which the eclipse appears total
34, 35 lunar eclipse
34 penumbra (partial shadow)
35 umbra (total shadow)
36-41 the sun
36 solar disc (disk) (solar globe, solar sphere)
37 sunspots
38 cyclones in the area of sunspots
39 corona (solar corona), observable during total solar eclipse or by means of special instruments
40 prominences (solar prominences)
41 moon's limb during a total solar eclipse
42-52 planets (planetary system, solar system) [not to scale] and planet symbols
42 the sun
43 Mercury
44 Venus
45 Earth, with the moon, a satellite
46 Mars, with two moons
47 asteroids (minor planets)
48 Jupiter
49 Saturn
50 Uranus
51 Neptune
52 Pluto, with the moon Charon
53-64 signs of the zodiac (zodiacal signs)
53 Aries (the Ram)
54 Taurus (the Bull)
55 Gemini (the Twins)
56 Cancer (the Crab)
57 Leo (the Lion)
58 Virgo (the Virgin)
59 Libra (the Balance, the Scales)
60 Scorpio (the Scorpion)
61 Sagittarius (the Archer)
62 Capricorn (the Goat, the Sea Goat)
63 Aquarius (the Water Carrier, the Water Bearer)
64 Pisces (the Fish)

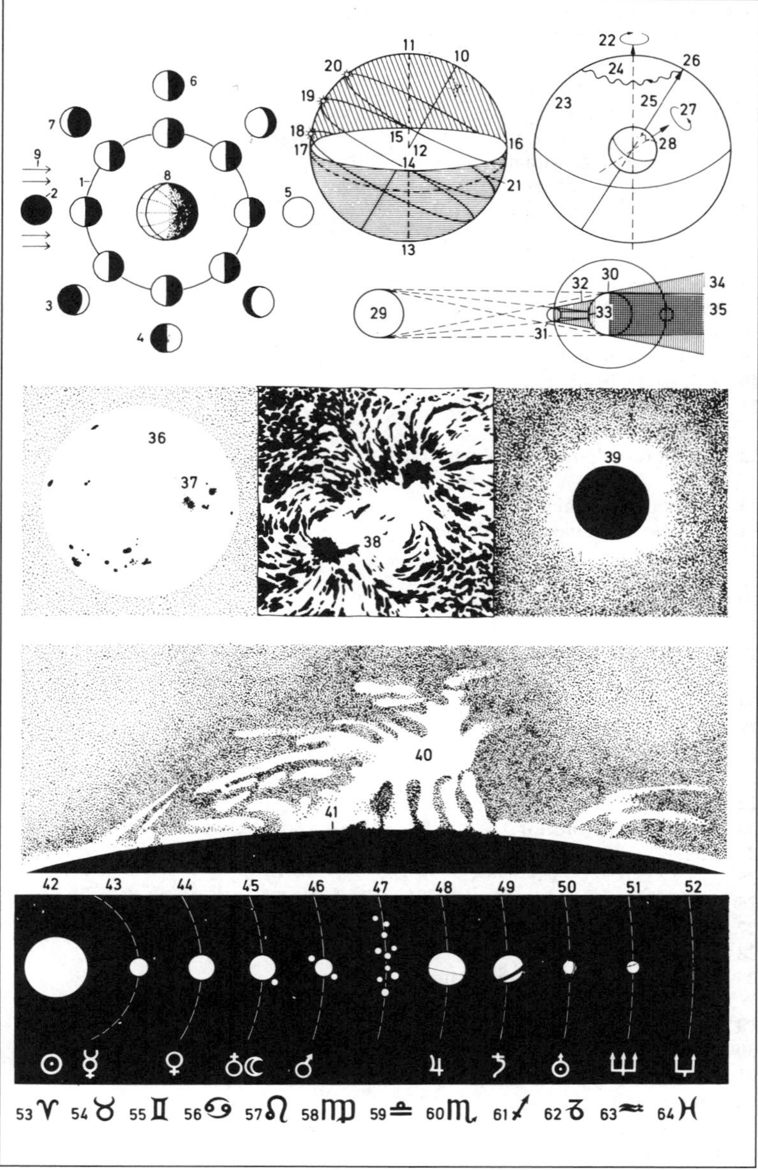
1
2
3
4
5
6
7
8
9
10
11
12
13
14
15
16
17
18
19
20
21
22
23
24
25
26
27
28
29
30
31
32
33
34
35
36
37
38
39
40
41
42
43
44
45
46
47
48
49
50
51
52
53 ♈
54 ♉
55 ♊
56 ♋
57 ♌
58 ♍
59 ♎
60 ♏
61 ♐
62 ♑
63 ♒
64 ♓

5 Astronomy III

1-16 the European Southern Observatory (ESO) on *Cerro la Silla, Chile,* an observatory [section]
1 primary mirror (main mirror) with a diameter of 3.6 m (144 inches)
2 prime focus cage with mounting for secondary mirrors
3 flat mirror for the coudé ray path
4 Cassegrain cage
5 grating spectrograph
6 spectrographic camera
7 hour axis drive
8 hour axis
9 horseshoe mounting
10 hydrostatic bearing
11 primary and secondary focusing devices
12 observatory dome, a revolving dome
13 observation opening
14 vertically movable dome shutter
15 wind screen
16 siderostat
17-28 the *Stuttgart* Planetarium [section]
17 administration, workshop, and store area
18 steel scaffold
19 glass pyramid
20 revolving arched ladder
21 projection dome
22 light stop
23 planetarium projector
24 well
25 foyer
26 theatre (*Am.* theater)
27 projection booth
28 foundation pile
29-33 the *Kitt Peak* solar observatory near *Tucson, Ariz.* [section]
29 heliostat
30 sunken observation shaft
31 water-cooled windshield
32 concave mirror
33 observation room housing the spectrograph

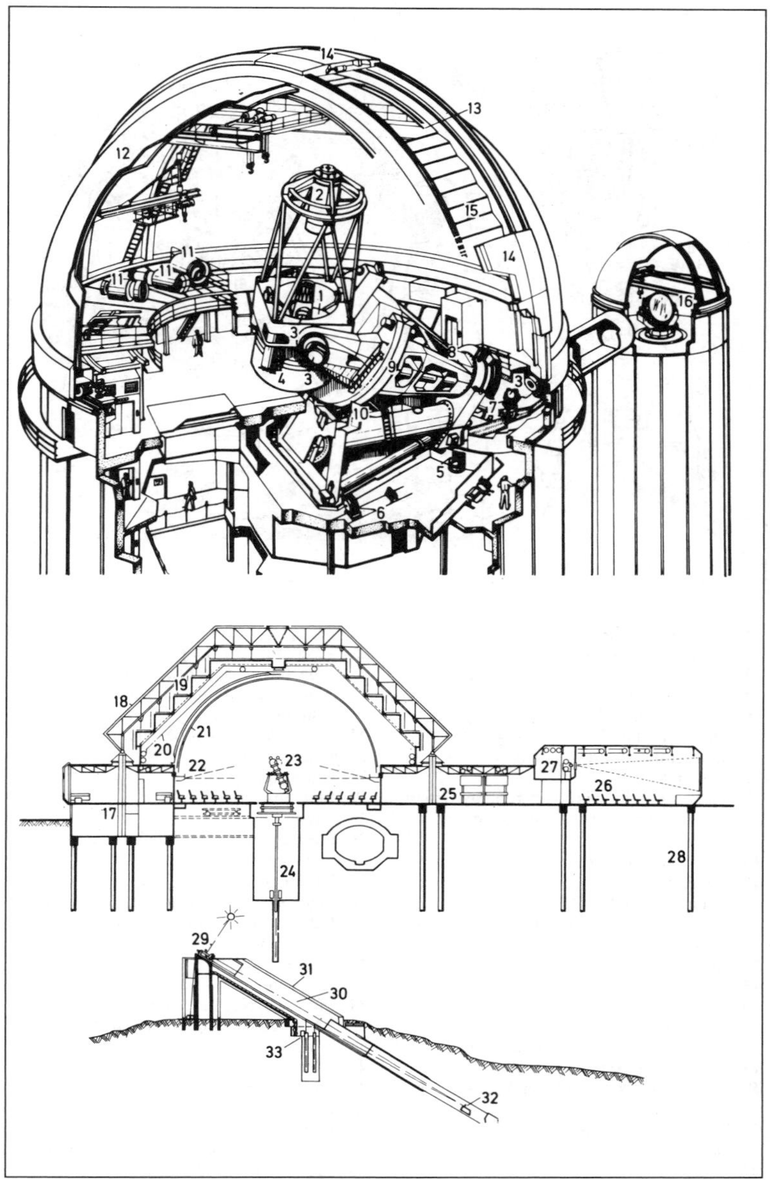
14
13
12
2
15
14
11
11
11
1
16
3
8
9
3
4
3
3
7
10
5
6
19
18
21
20
22
23
27
26
25
17
24
28
29
31
30
33
32

6 Moon Landing

1 Apollo spacecraft
2 service module (SM)
3 nozzle of the main rocket engine
4 directional antenna
5 manoeuvring (*Am.* maneuvering) rockets
6 oxygen and hydrogen tanks for the spacecraft's energy system
7 fuel tank
8 radiators of the spacecraft's energy system
9 command module (Apollo space capsule)
10 entry hatch of the space capsule
11 astronaut
12 lunar module (LM)
13 moon's surface (lunar surface), a dust-covered surface
14 lunar dust
15 piece of rock
16 meteorite crater
17 the earth
18-27 space suit (extra-vehicular suit)
18 emergency oxygen apparatus
19 sunglass pocket [with sunglasses for use on board]
20 life support system (life support pack), a backpack unit
21 access flap
22 space suit helmet with sun filters
23 control box of the life support pack
24 penlight pocket
25 access flap for the purge valve
26 tube and cable connections for the radio, ventilation, and water-cooling systems
27 pocket for pens, tools, etc.
28-36 descent stage
28 connector
29 fuel tank
30 engine
31 mechanism for unfolding the legs
32 main shock absorber
33 landing pad
34 ingress/egress platform (hatch platform)
35 ladder to platform and hatch
36 cardan mount for engine
37-47 ascent stage
37 fuel tank
38 ingress/egress hatch (entry/exit hatch)
39 LM manoeuvring (*Am.* maneuvering) rockets
40 window
41 crew compartment
42 rendezvous radar antenna
43 inertial measurement unit
44 directional antenna for ground control
45 upper hatch (docking hatch)
46 inflight antenna
47 docking target recess

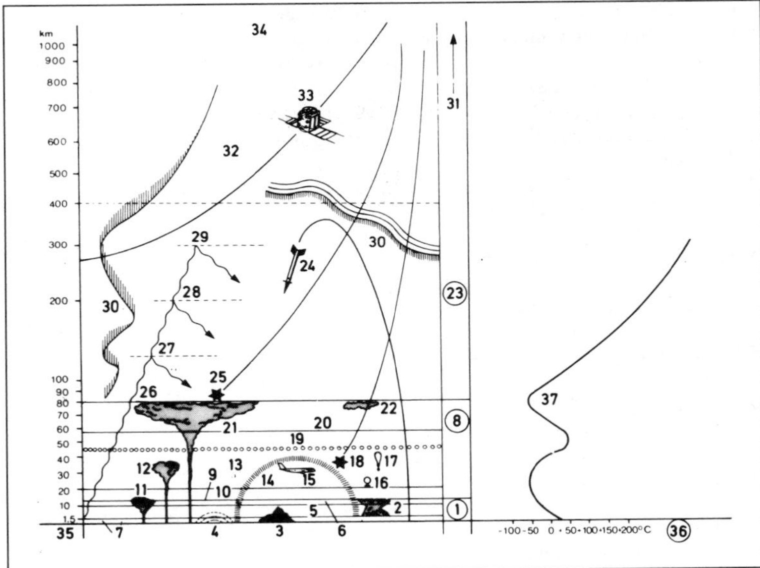

1 **the troposphere**
2 thunderclouds
3 the highest mountain, *Mount Everest* [8,882 m]
4 rainbow
5 jet stream level
6 zero level [inversion of vertical air movement]
7 ground layer (surface boundary layer)
8 **the stratosphere**
9 tropopause
10 separating layer (layer of weaker air movement)
11 atomic explosion
12 hydrogen bomb explosion
13 ozone layer
14 range of sound wave propagation
15 stratosphere aircraft
16 manned balloon
17 sounding balloon
18 meteor
19 upper limit of ozone layer
20 zero level
21 eruption of Krakatoa
22 luminous clouds (noctilucent clouds)
23 **the ionosphere**
24 range of research rockets
25 shooting star
26 short wave (high frequency)
27 E-layer (Heaviside-Kennelly Layer)
28 F_1-layer
29 F_2-layer
30 aurora (polar light)
31 **the exosphere**
32 atom layer
33 range of satellite sounding
34 fringe region
35 altitude scale
36 temperature scale (thermometric scale)
37 temperature graph

8 Meteorology I

1-19 clouds and weather

1-4 clouds found in homogeneous air masses

1 cumulus (woolpack cloud), a heap cloud; *here:* cumulus humilis (fair-weather cumulus), a flat-based heap cloud

2 cumulus congestus, a heap cloud with more marked vertical development

3 stratocumulus, a layer cloud (sheet cloud) arranged in heavy masses

4 stratus (high fog), a thick, uniform layer cloud (sheet cloud)

5-12 clouds found at warm fronts

5 warm front

6 cirrus, a high to very high ice-crystal cloud, thin and assuming a wide variety of forms

7 cirrostratus, an ice-crystal cloud veil

8 altostratus, a layer cloud (sheet cloud) of medium height

9 altostratus praecipitans, a layer cloud (sheet cloud) with precipitation in its upper parts

10 nimbostratus, a rain cloud, a layer cloud (sheet cloud) of very large vertical extent which produces precipitation (rain or snow)

11 fractostratus, a ragged cloud occurring beneath nimbostratus

12 fractocumulus, a ragged cloud like 11 but with billowing shapes

13-17 clouds at cold fronts

13 cold front

14 cirrocumulus, thin fleecy cloud in the form of globular masses; *covering the sky:* mackerel sky

15 altocumulus, a cloud in the form of large globular masses

16 altocumulus castellanus and altocumulus floccus, species of 15

17 cumulonimbus, a heap cloud of very large vertical extent, to be classified under 1-4 in the case of tropical storms

18-19 types of precipitation

18 steady rain or snow covering a large area, precipitation of uniform intensity

19 shower, scattered precipitation

black arrow = cold air　　white arrow = warm air

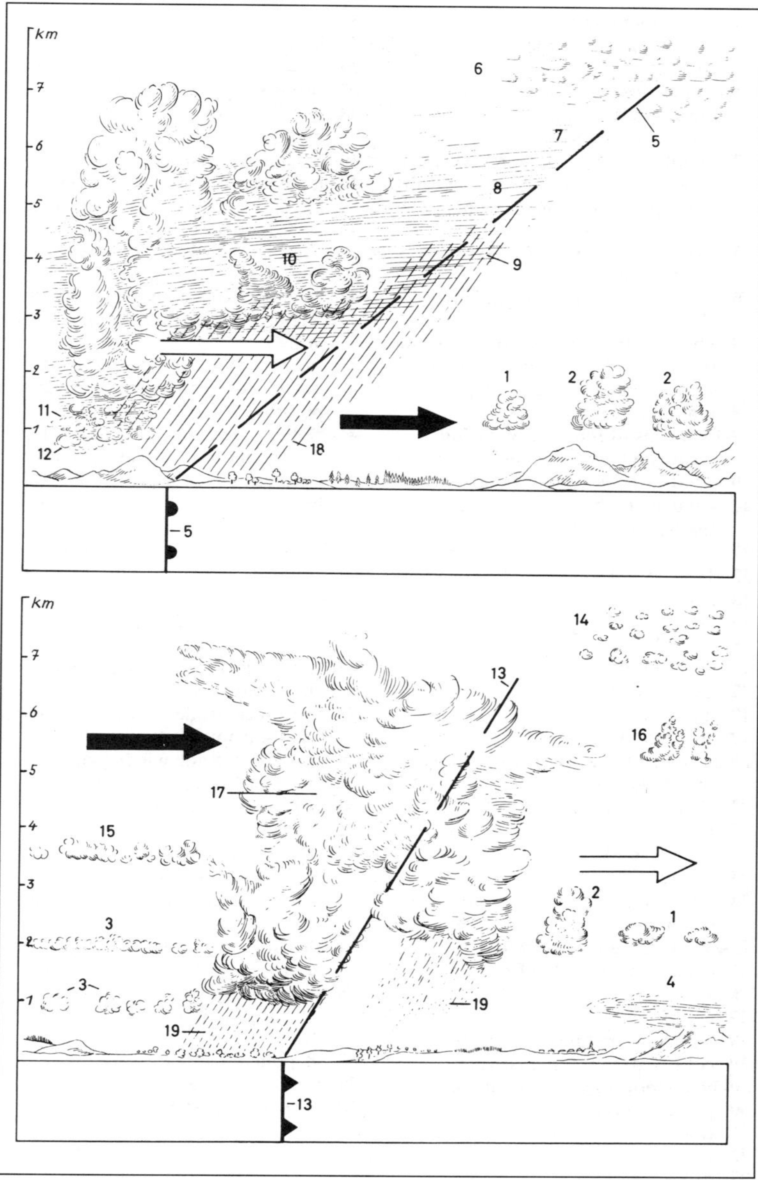
km
7
6
5
4
3
2
1
6
7
5
8
9
10
1
2
2
11
12
18
5
km
7
6
5
4
3
2
1
14
13
16
17
15
3
2
1
3
4
3
19
19
13

9 Meteorology II and Climatology

1-39 weather chart (weather map, surface chart, surface synoptic chart)
1 isobar (line of equal or constant atmospheric or barometric pressure at sea level)
2 pleiobar (isobar of over 1,000 mb)
3 meiobar (isobar of under 1,000 mb)
4 atmospheric (barometric) pressure given in millibars
5 low-pressure area (low, cyclone, depression)
6 high-pressure area (high, anticyclone)
7 observatory (meteorological watch office, weather station) or ocean station vessel (weather ship)
8 temperature
9-19 means of representing wind direction (wind-direction symbols)
9 wind-direction shaft (wind arrow)
10 wind-speed barb (wind-speed feather) indicating wind speed
11 calm
12 1-2 knots (1 knot = 1.852 kph)
13 3-7 knots
14 8-12 knots
15 13-17 knots
16 18-22 knots
17 23-27 knots
18 28-32 knots
19 58-62 knots
20-24 state of the sky (distribution of the cloud cover)
20 clear (cloudless)
21 fair
22 partly cloudy
23 cloudy
24 overcast (sky mostly or completely covered)
25-29 fronts and air currents
25 occlusion (occluded front)
26 warm front
27 cold front
28 warm airstream (warm current)
29 cold airstream (cold current)
30-39 meteorological phenomena
30 precipitation area
31 fog
32 rain
33 drizzle
34 snow
35 ice pellets (graupel, soft hail)
36 hail
37 shower
38 thunderstorm
39 lightning
40-58 climatic map
40 isotherm (line connecting points having equal mean temperature)
41 0 ° C (zero) isotherm (line connecting points having a mean annual temperature of 0 ° C)
42 isocheim (line connecting points having equal mean winter temperature)
43 isothere (line connecting points having equal mean summer temperature)
44 isohel (line connecting points having equal duration of sunshine)
45 isohyet (line connecting points having equal amounts of precipitation)
46-52 atmospheric circulation (wind systems)
46-47 calm belts
46 equatorial trough (equatorial calms, doldrums)
47 subtropical high-pressure belts (horse latitudes)
48 north-east trade winds (north-east trades, tropical easterlies)
49 south-east trade winds (south-east trades, tropical easterlies)
50 zones of the variable westerlies
51 polar wind zones
52 summer monsoon
53-58 earth's climates
53 equatorial climate: tropical zone (tropical rain zone)
54 the two arid zones (equatorial dry zones): desert and steppe zones
55 the two temperate rain zones
56 boreal climate (snow forest climate)
57, 58 polar climates
57 tundra climate
58 perpetual frost climate

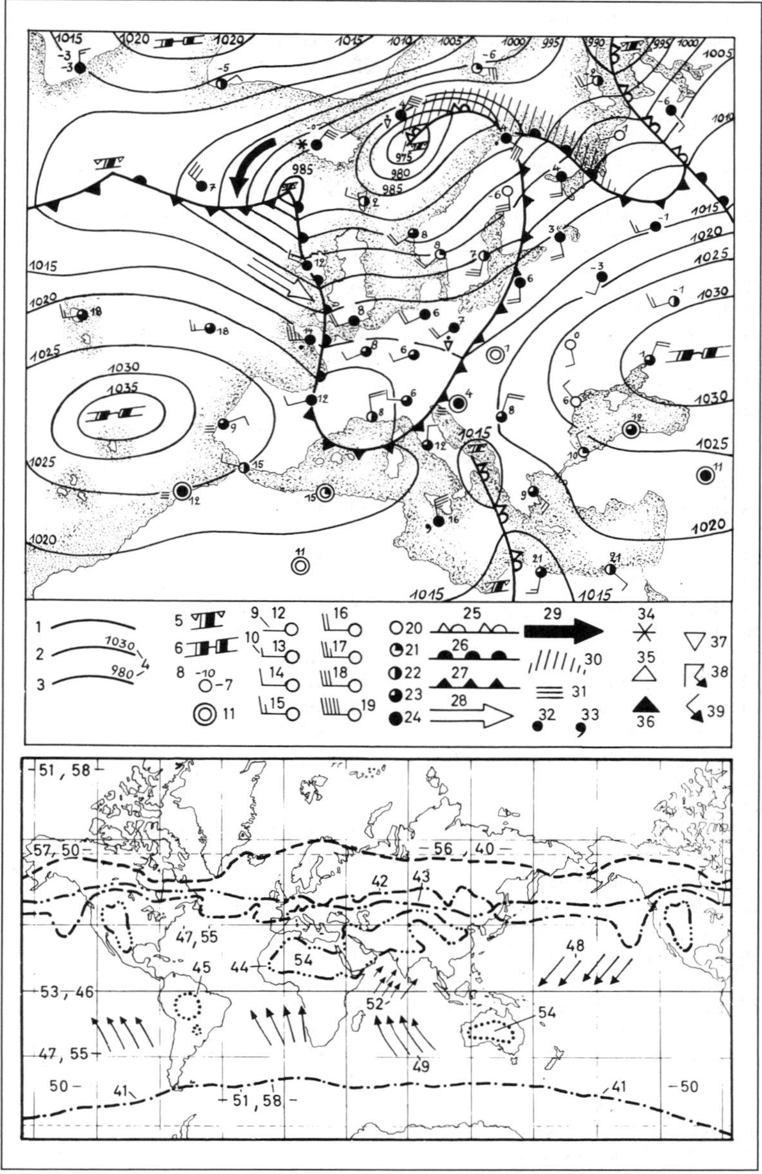
51, 58
57, 50
56, 40
42
43
47, 55
45
44
54
48
53, 46
52
54
47, 55
49
50
41
51, 58
41
50

10 Meteorological Instruments

1 mercury barometer, a siphon barometer, a liquid-column barometer
2 mercury column
3 millibar scale, a millimetre (*Am.* millimeter) scale
4 barograph, a self-registering aneroid barometer
5 drum (recording drum)
6 bank of aneroid capsules (aneroid boxes)
7 recording arm
8 hygrograph
9 hygrometer element (hair element)
10 reading adjustment
11 amplitude adjustment
12 recording arm
13 recording pen
14 change gears for the clockwork drive
15 off switch for the recording arm
16 drum (recording drum)
17 time scale
18 case (housing)
19 thermograph
20 drum (recording drum)
21 recording arm
22 sensing element
23 silver-disc (silver-disk) pyrheliometer, an instrument for measuring the sun's radiant energy
24 silver disc (disk)
25 thermometer
26 wooden insulating casing
27 tube with diaphragm (diaphragmed tube)
28 wind gauge (*Am.* gage) (anemometer)
29 wind-speed indicator (wind-speed meter)
30 cross arms with hemispherical cups
31 wind-direction indicator
32 wind vane
33 aspiration psychrometer
34 dry bulb thermometer
35 wet bulb thermometer
36 solar radiation shielding
37 suction tube
38 recording rain gauge (*Am.* gage)
39 protective housing (protective casing)
40 collecting vessel
41 rain cover
42 recording mechanism
43 siphon tube
44 precipitation gauge (*Am.* gage) (rain gauge)
45 collecting vessel
46 storage vessel
47 measuring glass
48 insert for measuring snowfall
49 thermometer screen (thermometer shelter)
50 hygrograph
51 thermograph
52 psychrometer (wet and dry bulb thermometer)
53, 54 thermometers for measuring extremes of temperature
53 maximum thermometer
54 minimum thermometer
55 radiosonde assembly
56 hydrogen balloon
57 parachute
58 radar reflector with spacing lines
59 instrument housing with radiosonde [a short-wave transmitter] and antenna
60 transmissometer, an instrument for measuring visibility
61 recording instrument (recorder)
62 transmitter
63 receiver
64 weather satellite (ITOS satellite)
65 temperature regulation flaps
66 solar panel
67 television camera
68 antenna
69 solar sensor (sun sensor)
70 telemetry antenna
71 radiometer

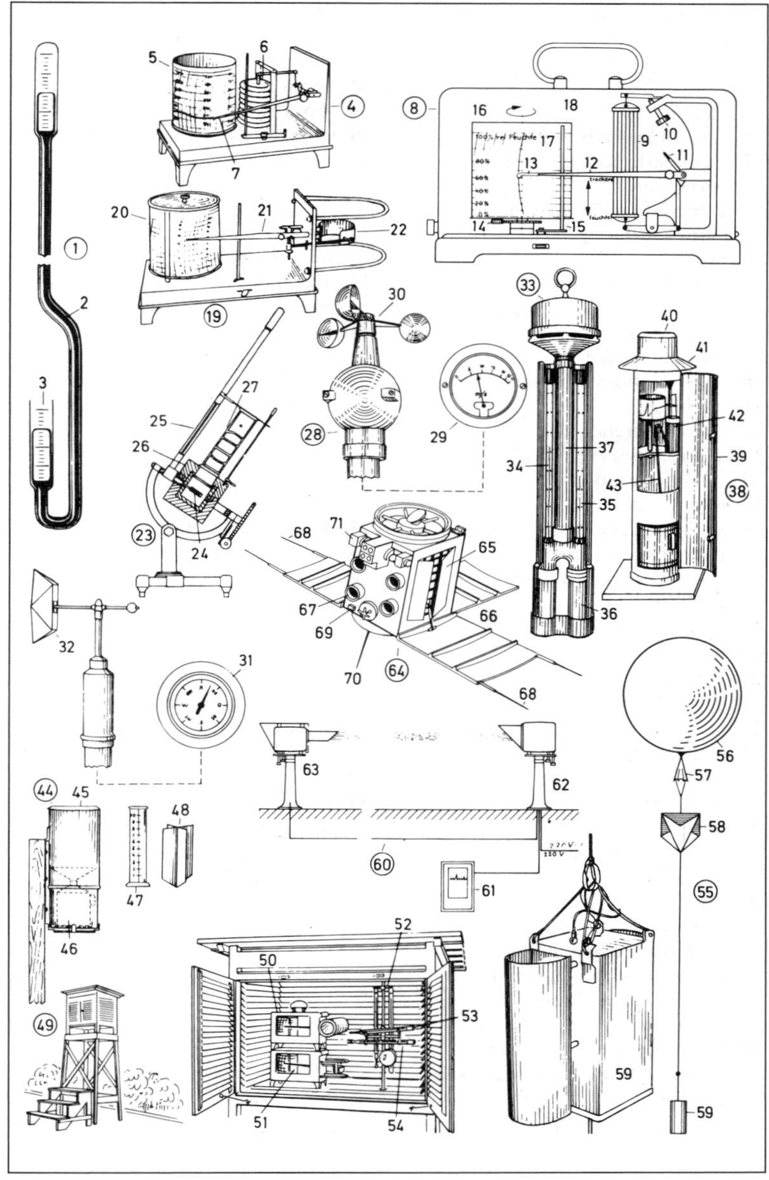
1
2
3
4
5
6
7
8
9
10
11
12
13
14
15
16
17
18
100% rel Feuchte
80%
60%
40%
20%
0%
trocken
feucht
19
20
21
22
23
24
25
26
27
28
29
30
31
32
33
34
35
36
37
38
39
40
41
42
43
44
45
46
47
48
49
50
51
52
53
54
55
56
57
58
59
60
220 V
110 V
61
62
63
64
65
66
67
68
69
70
71

11 Physical Geography I

1-5 layered structure of the earth
1 earth's crust (outer crust of the earth, lithosphere, oxysphere)
2 hydrosphere
3 mantle
4 sima (intermediate layer)
5 core (earth core, centrosphere, barysphere)
6-12 hypsographic curve of the earth's surface
6 peak
7 continental mass
8 continental shelf (continental platform, shelf)
9 continental slope
10 deep-sea floor (abyssal plane)
11 sea level
12 deep-sea trench
13-28 volcanism (vulcanicity)
13 shield volcano
14 lava plateau
15 active volcano, a stratovolcano (composite volcano)
16 volcanic crater (crater)
17 volcanic vent
18 lava stream
19 tuff (fragmented volcanic material)
20 subterranean volcano
21 geyser
22 jet of hot water and steam
23 sinter terraces (siliceous sinter terraces, fiorite terraces, pearl sinter terraces)
24 cone
25 maar (extinct volcano)
26 tuff deposit
27 breccia
28 vent of extinct volcano
29-31 plutonic magmatism
29 batholite (massive protrusion)
30 lacolith, an intrusion
31 sill, an ore deposit
32-38 earthquake (*kinds:* tectonic quake, volcanic quake) **and seismology**
32 earthquake focus (seismic focus, hypocentre, *Am.* hypocenter)
33 epicentre (*Am.* epicenter), point on the earth's surface directly above the focus
34 depth of focus
35 shock wave
36 surface waves (seismic waves)
37 isoseismal (line connecting points of equal intensity of earthquake shock)
38 epicentral area, an area of macroseismic vibration
39 **horizontal seismograph** (seismometer)
40 electromagnetic damper
41 adjustment knob for the period of free oscillation of the pendulum
42 spring attachment for the suspension of the pendulum
43 mass
44 induction coils for recording the voltage of the galvanometer
45-54 effects of earthquakes
45 waterfall (cataract, falls)
46 landslide (rockslide, landslip, *Am.* rock slip)
47 talus (rubble, scree)
48 scar (scaur, scaw)
49 sink (sinkhole, swallowhole)
50 dislocation (displacement)
51 solifluction lobe (solifluction tongue)
52 fissure
53 tsunami (seismic sea wave) produced by seaquake (submarine earthquake)
54 raised beach

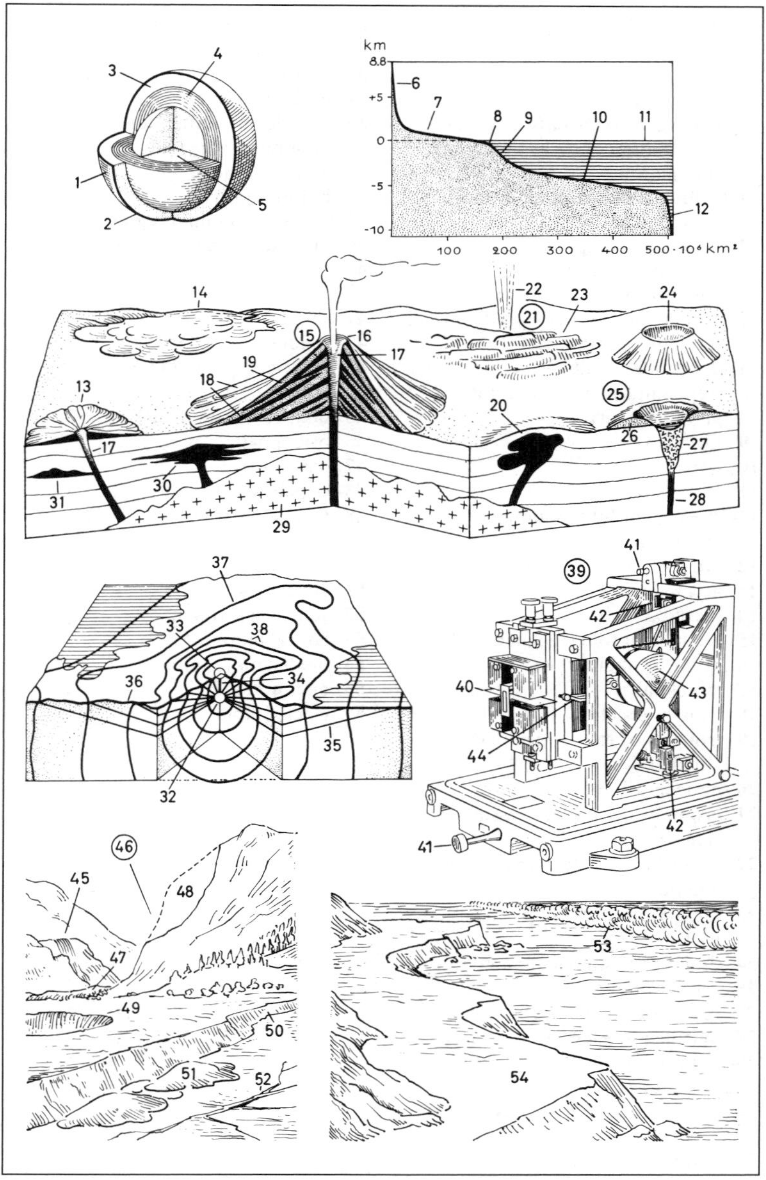
1
2
3
4
5
km
8,8
+5
0
-5
-10
6
7
8
9
10
11
12
100
200
300
400
500 · 10⁶ km²
13
14
15
16
17
18
19
20
21
22
23
24
25
26
27
28
29
30
31
32
33
34
35
36
37
38
39
40
41
42
43
44
45
46
47
48
49
50
51
52
53
54

12 Physical Geography II

1-33 geology
1 stratification of sedimentary rock
2 strike
3 dip (angle of dip, true dip)
4-20 orogeny (orogenis, tectogenis, deformation of rocks by folding and faulting)
4-11 fault-block mountain (block mountain)
4 fault
5 fault line (fault trace)
6 fault throw
7 normal fault (gravity fault, normal slip fault, slump fault)
8-11 complex faults
8 step fault (distributive fault, multiple fault)
9 tilt block
10 horst
11 graben
12-20 range of fold mountains (folded mountains)
12 symmetrical fold (normal fold)
13 asymmetrical fold
14 overfold
15 recumbent fold (reclined fold)
16 saddle (anticline)
17 anticlinal axis
18 trough (syncline)
19 trough surface (trough plane, synclinal axis)
20 anticlinorium
21 groundwater under pressure (artesian water)
22 water-bearing stratum (aquifer, aquafer)
23 impervious rock (impermeable rock)
24 drainage basin (catchment area)
25 artesian well
26 rising water, an artesian spring
27 petroleum reservoir in an anticline
28 impervious stratum (impermeable stratum)
29 porous stratum acting as reservoir rock
30 natural gas, a gas cap
31 petroleum (crude oil)
32 underlying water
33 derrick
34 mountainous area
35 rounded mountain top
36 mountain ridge (ridge)
37 mountain slope
38 hillside spring
39-47 high-mountain region
39 mountain range, a massif
40 summit (peak, top of the mountain)
41 shoulder
42 saddle
43 rock face (steep face)
44 gully
45 talus (scree, detritus)
46 bridle path
47 pass (col)
48-56 glacial ice
48 firn field (firn basin, nevé)
49 valley glacier
50 crevasse
51 glacier snout
52 subglacial stream
53 lateral moraine
54 medial moraine
55 end moraine
56 glacier table

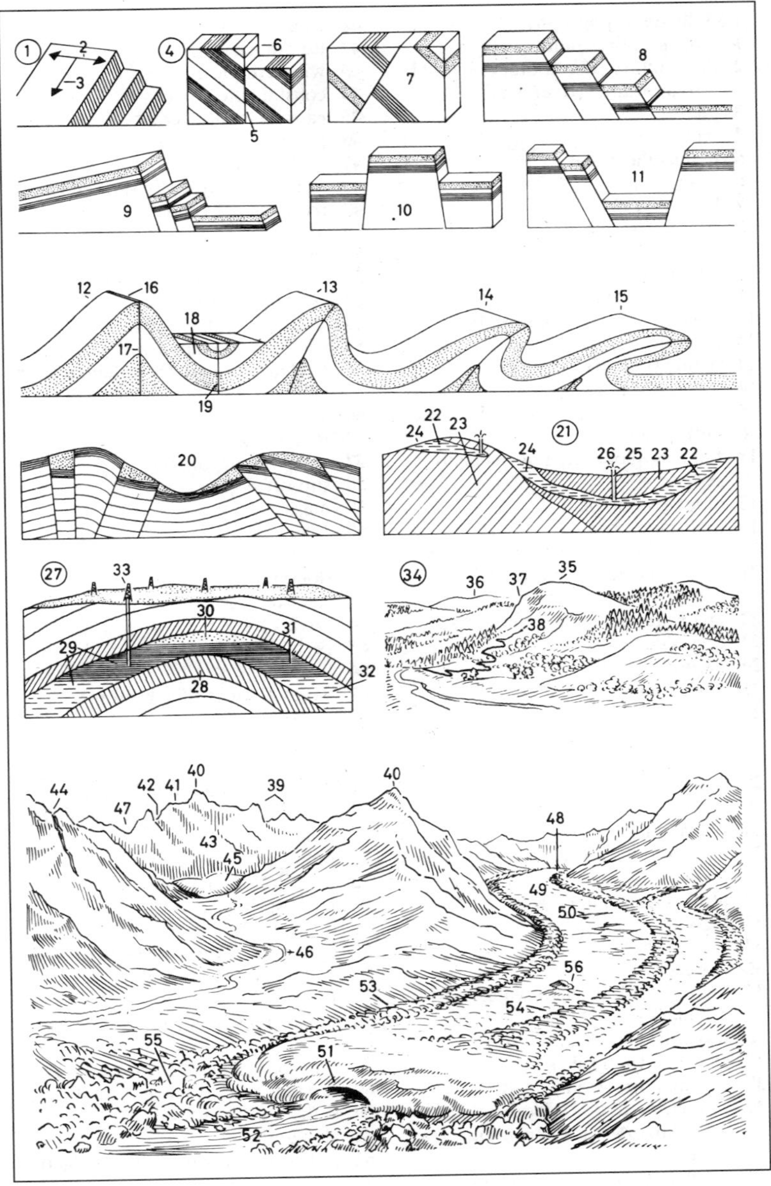
1
2
3
4
5
6
7
8
9
10
11
12
13
14
15
16
17
18
19
20
21
22
23
24
25
26
27
28
29
30
31
32
33
34
35
36
37
38
39
40
41
42
43
44
45
46
47
48
49
50
51
52
53
54
55
56

13 Physical Geography III

1-13 fluvial topography
1 river mouth, a delta
2 distributary (distributary channel), a river branch (river arm)
3 lake
4 bank
5 peninsula (spit)
6 island
7 bay (cove)
8 stream (brook, rivulet, creek)
9 levee
10 alluvial plain
11 meander (river bend)
12 meander core (rock island)
13 meadow
14-24 bog (marsh)
14 low-moor bog
15 layers of decayed vegetable matter
16 entrapped water
17 fen peat [consisting of rush and sedge]
18 alder-swamp peat
19 high-moor bog
20 layer of recent sphagnum mosses
21 boundary between layers (horizons)
22 layer of older sphagnum mosses
23 bog pool
24 swamp
25-31 cliffline (cliffs)
25 rock
26 sea (ocean)
27 surf
28 cliff (cliff face, steep rock face)
29 scree
30 [wave-cut] notch
31 abrasion platform (wave-cut platform)
32 atoll, a ring-shaped coral reef
33 lagoon
34 breach (hole)
35-44 beach
35 high-water line (high-water mark, tidemark)
36 waves breaking on the shore
37 groyne (*Am.* groin)
38 groyne (*Am.* groin) head
39 wandering dune (migratory dune, travelling, *Am.* traveling, dune), a dune
40 barchan (barchane, barkhan, crescentic dune)
41 ripple marks
42 hummock
43 wind cripple
44 coastal lake
45 **canyon** (cañon, coulee)
46 plateau (tableland)
47 rock terrace
48 sedimentary rock (stratified rock)
49 river terrace (bed)
50 joint
51 canyon river
52-56 types of valley [cross section]
52 gorge (ravine)
53 V-shaped valley (V-valley)
54 widened V-shaped valley
55 U-shaped valley (U-valley, trough valley)
56 synclinal valley
57-70 river valley
57 scarp (escarpment)
58 slip-off slope
59 mesa
60 ridge
61 river
62 flood plain
63 river terrace
64 terracette
65 pediment
66 hill
67 valley floor (valley bottom)
68 riverbed
69 sediment
70 bedrock
71-83 karst formation in limestone
71 dolina, a sink (sinkhole, swallowhole)
72 polje
73 percolation of a river
74 karst spring
75 dry valley
76 system of caverns (system of caves)
77 water level (water table) in a karst formation
78 impervious rock (impermeable rock)
79 limestone cave (dripstone cave)
80, 81 speleothems (cave formations)
80 stalactite (dripstone)
81 stalagmite
82 linked-up stalagmite and stalactite
83 subterranean river

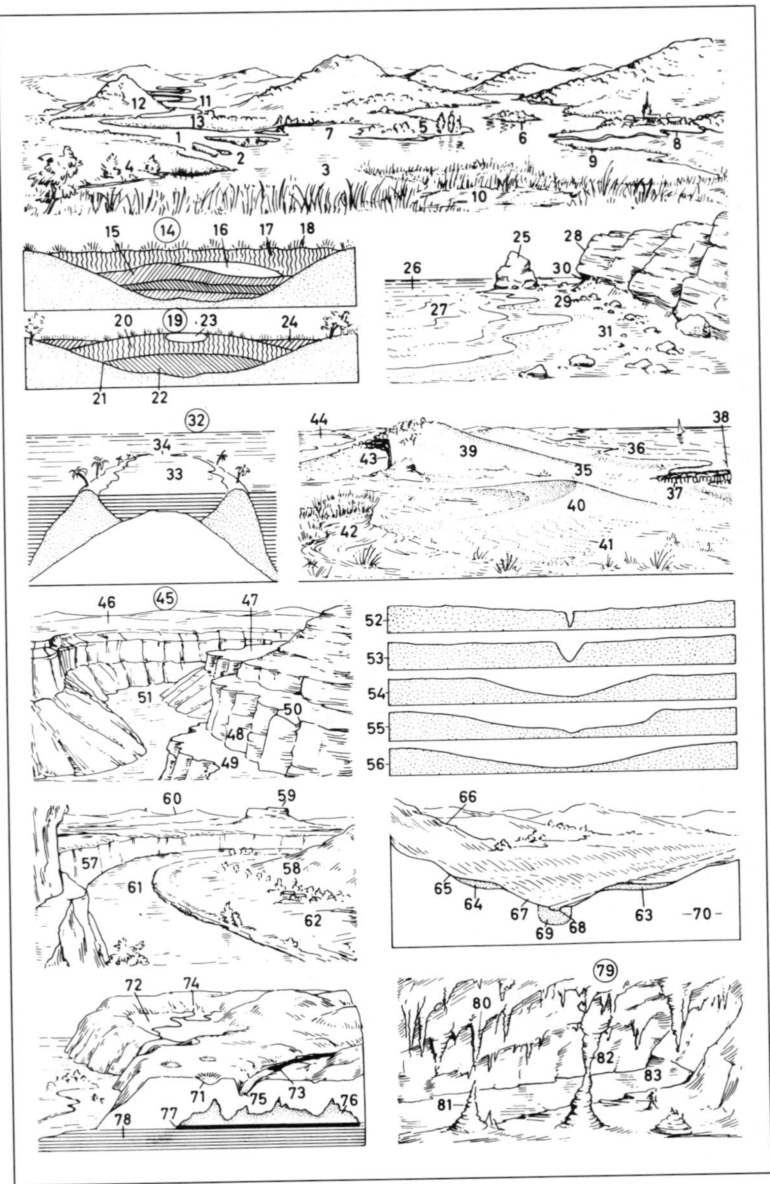
1
2
3
4
5
6
7
8
9
10
11
12
13
14
15
16
17
18
19
20
21
22
23
24
25
26
27
28
29
30
31
32
33
34
35
36
37
38
39
40
41
42
43
44
45
46
47
48
49
50
51
52
53
54
55
56
57
58
59
60
61
62
63
64
65
66
67
68
69
70
71
72
73
74
75
76
77
78
79
80
81
82
83

14 Map I

1-7 graticule of the earth (network of meridians and parallels on the earth's surface)
1 equator
2 line of latitude (parallel of latitude, parallel)
3 pole (North Pole or South Pole), a terrestrial pole (geographical pole)
4 line of longitude (meridian of longitude, meridian, terrestrial meridian)
5 Standard meridian (Prime meridian, Greenwich meridian, meridian of Greenwich)
6 latitude
7 longitude
8, 9 map projections
8 conical (conic) projection
9 cylindrical projection (Mercator projection, Mercator's projection)
10-45 map of the world
10 tropics
11 polar circles
12-18 continents
12, 13 America
12 North America
13 South America
14 Africa
15, 16 Europe and Asia
15 Europe
16 Asia
17 Australia
18 Antarctica (Antarctic Continent)
19-26 ocean (sea)
19 Pacific Ocean
20 Atlantic Ocean
21 Arctic Ocean
22 Antarctic Ocean (Southern Ocean)
23 Indian Ocean
24 Strait of Gibraltar, a sea strait
25 Mediterranean (Mediterranean Sea, European Mediterranean)
26 North Sea, a marginal sea (epeiric sea, epicontinental sea)
27-29 key (explanation of map symbols)
27 cold ocean current
28 warm ocean current
29 scale
30-45 ocean (oceanic) currents (ocean drifts)
30 Gulf Stream (North Atlantic Drift)
31 Kuroshio (Kuro Siwo, Japan Current)
32 North Equatorial Current
33 Equatorial Countercurrent
34 South Equatorial Current
35 Brazil Current
36 Somali Current
37 Agulhas Current
38 East Australian Current
39 California Current
40 Labrador Current
41 Canary Current
42 Peru Current
43 Benguela (Benguella) Current
44 West Wind Drift (Antarctic Circumpolar Drift)
45 West Australian Current
46-62 surveying (land surveying, geodetic surveying, geodesy)
46 levelling (*Am.* leveling) (geometrical measurement of height)
47 graduated measuring rod (levelling, *Am.* leveling, staff)
48 level (surveying level, surveyor's level), a surveyor's telescope
49 triangulation station (triangulation point)
50 supporting scaffold
51 signal tower (signal mast)
52-62 theodolite, an instrument for measuring angles
52 micrometer head
53 micrometer eyepiece
54 vertical tangent screw
55 vertical clamp
56 tangent screw
57 horizontal clamp
58 adjustment for the illuminating mirror
59 illuminating mirror
60 telescope
61 spirit level
62 circular adjustment
63-66 photogrammetry (phototopography)
63 air survey camera for producing overlapping series of pictures
64 stereoscope
65 pantograph
66 stereoplanigraph

1
2
3
4
5
6
7
8
9
11
21
40
26
15
16
12
39
30
24
31
10
10
41
25
32
32
14
32
33
33
33
1
36
34
34
34
20
33
13
23
10
19
42
35
43
34
17
37
45
38
44
5
44
11
18
22
27
29
28
63
46
47
48
49
51
50
58
59
52
60
53
54
61
55
56
57
62
64
65
66

15 Map II

1-114 map signs (map symbols, conventional signs) on a 1: 25 000 map
1 coniferous wood (coniferous trees)
2 clearing
3 forestry office
4 deciduous wood (non-coniferous trees)
5 heath (rough grassland, rough pasture, heath and moor, bracken)
6 sand or sand hills
7 beach grass
8 lighthouse
9 mean low water
10 beacon
11 submarine contours
12 train ferry
13 lightship
14 mixed wood (mixed trees)
15 brushwood
16 motorway with slip road (*Am.* freeway with on-ramp, freeway with acceleration lane)
17 trunk road
18 grassland
19 marshy grassland
20 marsh
21 main line railway (*Am.* trunk line)
22 road over railway
23 branch line
24 signal box (*Am.* switch tower)
25 local line
26 level crossing
27 halt
28 residential area
29 water gauge (*Am.* gage)
30 good, metalled road
31 windmill
32 thorn house (graduation house, salina, salt-works)
33 broadcasting station (wireless or television mast)
34 mine
35 disused mine
36 secondary road (B road)
37 works
38 chimney
39 wire fence
40 bridge over railway
41 railway station (*Am.* railroad station)
42 bridge under railway
43 footpath
44 bridge for footpath under railway
45 navigable river
46 pontoon bridge
47 vehicle ferry
48 mole
49 beacon
50 stone bridge
51 town or city
52 market place (market square)
53 large church with two towers
54 public building
55 road bridge
56 iron bridge
57 canal
58 lock
59 jetty
60 foot ferry (foot passenger ferry)
61 chapel (church) without tower or spire
62 contours
63 monastery or convent
64 church landmark
65 vineyard
66 weir
67 aerial ropeway
68 view point
69 dam
70 tunnel
71 triangulation station (triangulation point)
72 remains of a building
73 wind pump
74 fortress
75 ox-bow lake
76 river
77 watermill
78 footbridge
79 pond
80 stream (brook, rivulet, creek)
81 water tower
82 spring
83 main road (A road)
84 cutting
85 cave
86 lime kiln
87 quarry
88 clay pit
89 brickworks
90 narrow-gauge (*Am.* narrow gage) railway
91 goods depot (freight depot)
92 monument
93 site of battle
94 country estate, a demesne
95 wall
96 stately home
97 park
98 hedge

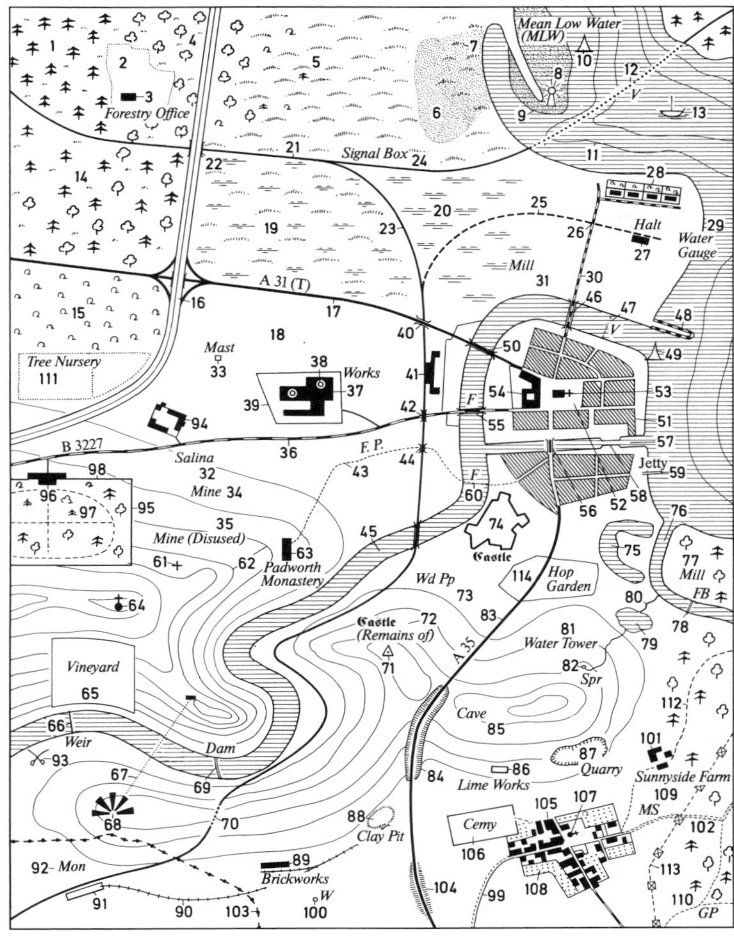

99 poor or unmetalled road
100 well
101 farm
102 unfenced path (unfenced track)
103 district boundary
104 embankment
105 village
106 cemetery
107 church or chapel with spire
108 orchard
109 milestone
110 guide post
111 tree nursery
112 ride (aisle, lane, section line)
113 electricity transmission line
114 hop garden

16 Man I

1-54 the human body
1-18 head
1 vertex (crown of the head, top of the head)
2 occiput (back of the head)
3 hair
4-17 face
4-5 forehead
4 frontal eminence (frontal protuberance)
5 superciliary arch
6 temple
7 eye
8 zygomatic bone (malar bone, jugal bone, cheekbone)
9 cheek
10 nose
11 nasolabial fold
12 philtrum
13 mouth
14 angle of the mouth (labial commissure)
15 chin
16 dimple (fossette) in the chin
17 jaw
18 ear
19-21 neck
19 throat
20 hollow of the throat
21 nape of the neck
22-41 trunk
22-25 back
22 shoulder
23 shoulderblade (scapula)
24 loins
25 small of the back
26 armpit
27 armpit hair
28-30 thorax (chest)
28-29 breasts (breast, mamma)
28 nipple
29 areola
30 bosom
31 waist
32 flank (side)
33 hip
34 navel
35-37 abdomen (stomach)
35 upper abdomen
36 abdomen
37 lower abdomen
38 groin
39 pudenda (vulva)
40 seat (backside, *coll.* bottom)
41 anal groove (anal cleft)
42 gluteal fold (gluteal furrow)
43-54 limbs
43-48 arm
43 upper arm
44 crook of the arm
45 elbow
46 forearm
47 hand
48 fist (clenched fist, clenched hand)
49-54 leg
49 thigh
50 knee
51 popliteal space
52 shank
53 calf
54 foot

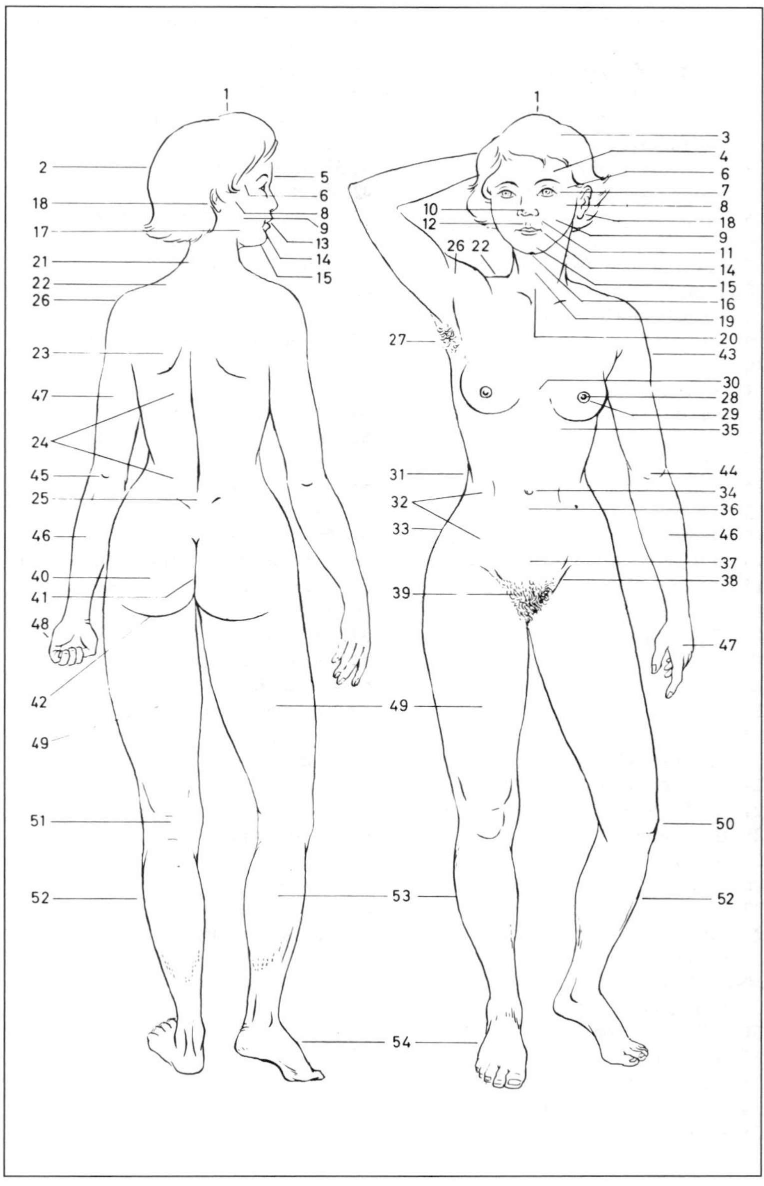
1
1
2
3
4
5
6
6
7
18
8
8
10
12
18
9
17
13
9
11
21
14
14
26 22
15
15
22
16
26
19
20
27
23
43
30
47
28
29
24
35
45
31
44
25
34
32
36
33
46
46
37
40
38
41
39
48
47
42
49
49
49
51
50
52
53
52
54

17 Man II

1-29 skeleton (bones)
1 skull
2-5 vertebral column (spinal column, spine, backbone)
2 cervical vertebra
3 dorsal vertebra (thoracic vertebra)
4 lumbar vertebra
5 coccyx (coccygeal vertebra)
6, 7 shoulder girdle
6 collarbone (clavicle)
7 shoulderblade (scapula)
8-11 thorax (chest)
8 breastbone (sternum)
9 true ribs
10 false ribs
11 costal cartilage
12-14 arm
12 humerus
13 radius
14 ulna
15-17 hand
15 carpus
16 metacarpal bone (metacarpal)
17 phalanx (phalange)
18-21 pelvis
18 ilium (hip bone)
19 ischium
20 pubis
21 sacrum
22-25 leg
22 femur (thigh bone, thigh)
23 patella (kneecap)
24 fibula (splint bone)
25 tibia (shinbone)
26-29 foot
26 tarsal bones (tarsus)
27 calcaneum (heelbone)
28 metatarsus
29 phalanges
30-41 skull
30 frontal bone
31 left parietal bone
32 occipital bone
33 temporal bone
34 external auditory canal
35 lower jawbone (lower jaw, mandible)
36 upper jawbone (upper jaw, maxilla)
37 zygomatic bone (cheekbone)
38 sphenoid bone (sphenoid)
39 ethmoid bone (ethmoid)
40 lachrimal (lacrimal) bone
41 nasal bone
42-55 head [section]
42 cerebrum (great brain)
43 pituitary gland (pituitary body, hypophysis cerebri)
44 corpus callosum
45 cerebellum (little brain)
46 pons (pons cerebri, pons cerebelli)
47 medulla oblongata (brain stem)
48 spinal cord
49 oesophagus (esophagus, gullet)
50 trachea (windpipe)
51 epiglottis
52 tongue
53 nasal cavity
54 sphenoidal sinus
55 frontal sinus
56-65 organ of equilibrium and hearing
56-58 external ear
56 auricle
57 ear lobe
58 external auditory canal
59-61 middle ear
59 tympanic membrane
60 tympanic cavity
61 auditory ossicles: hammer, anvil, and stirrup (malleus, incus, and stapes)
62-64 inner ear (internal ear)
62 labyrinth
63 cochlea
64 auditory nerve
65 eustachian tube

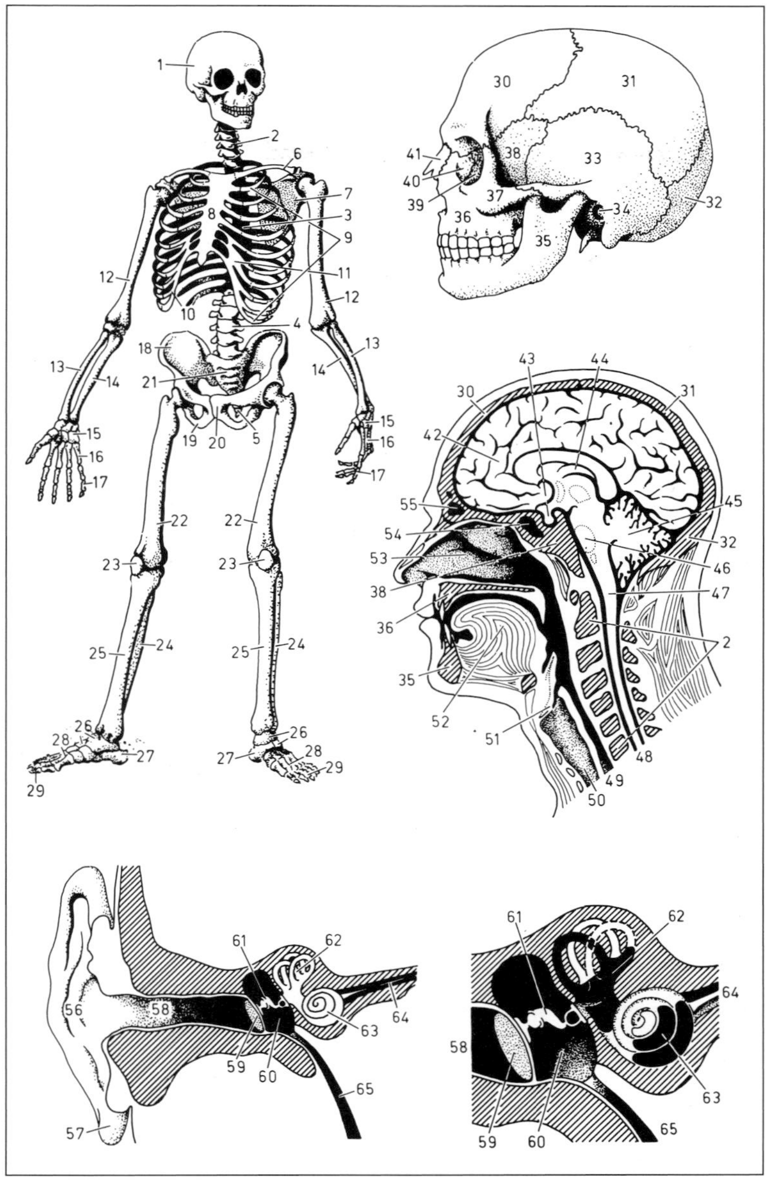
1
2
6
7
3
8
9
11
12
10
4
18
13
14
21
15
19
20
5
16
17
22
23
25
24
26
28
27
29
30
31
41
38
33
40
37
39
36
34
32
35
43
44
42
55
45
54
53
46
47
36
2
35
52
51
48
49
50
56
58
61
62
64
63
59
60
65
57

18 Man III

1-21 blood circulation (circulatory system)
1 common carotid artery, an artery
2 jugular vein, a vein
3 temporal artery
4 temporal vein
5 frontal artery
6 frontal vein
7 subclavian artery
8 subclavian vein
9 superior vena cava
10 arch of the aorta (aorta)
11 pulmonary artery [with venous blood]
12 pulmonary vein [with arterial blood]
13 lungs
14 heart
15 inferior vena cava
16 abdominal aorta (descending portion of the aorta)
17 iliac artery
18 iliac vein
19 femoral artery
20 tibial artery
21 radial artery
22-33 nervous system
22 cerebrum (great brain)
23 cerebellum (little brain)
24 medulla oblongata (brain stem)
25 spinal cord
26 thoracic nerves
27 brachial plexus
28 radial nerve
29 ulnar nerve
30 great sciatic nerve [lying posteriorly]
31 femoral nerve (anterior crural nerve)
32 tibial nerve
33 peroneal nerve
34-64 musculature (muscular system)
34 sternocleidomastoid muscle (sternomastoid muscle)
35 deltoid muscle
36 pectoralis major (greater pectoralis muscle, greater pectoralis)
37 biceps brachii (biceps of the arm)
38 triceps brachii (triceps of the arm)
39 brachioradialis
40 flexor carpi radialis (radial flexor of the wrist)
41 thenar muscle
42 serratus anterior
43 obliquus externus abdominis (external oblique)
44 rectus abdominis
45 sartorius
46 vastus lateralis and vastus medialis
47 tibialis anterior
48 tendo calcanaeus (Achilles' tendon)
49 abductor hallucis (abductor of the hallux), a foot muscle
50 occipitalis
51 splenius of the neck
52 trapezius
53 infraspinatus
54 teres minor (lesser teres)
55 teres major (greater teres)
56 extensor carpi radialis longus (long radial extensor of the wrist)
57 extensor communis digitorum (common extensor of the digits)
58 flexor carpi ulnaris (ulnar flexor of the wrist)
59 latissimus dorsi
60 gluteus maximus
61 biceps femoris (biceps of the thigh)
62 gastrocnemius, medial and lateral heads
63 extensor communis digitorum (common extensor of the digits)
64 peroneus longus (long peroneus)

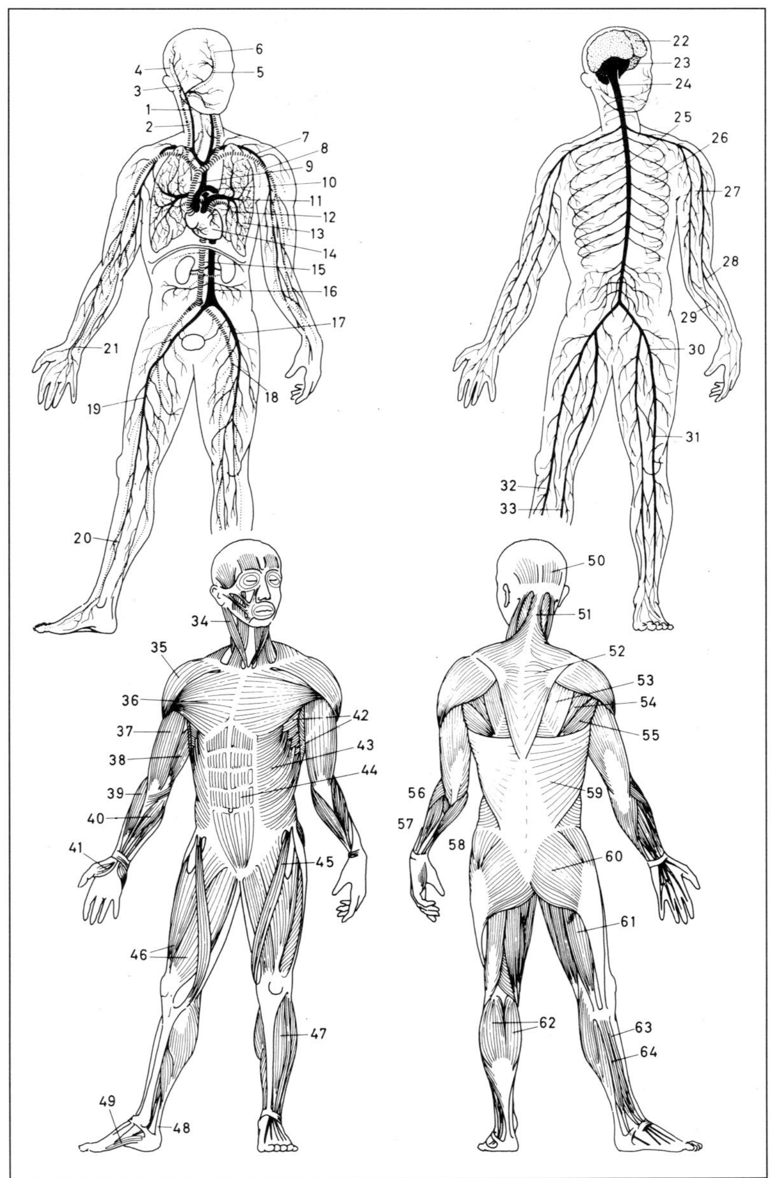
1
2
3
4
5
6
7
8
9
10
11
12
13
14
15
16
17
18
19
20
21
22
23
24
25
26
27
28
29
30
31
32
33
34
35
36
37
38
39
40
41
42
43
44
45
46
47
48
49
50
51
52
53
54
55
56
57
58
59
60
61
62
63
64

19 Man IV

1-13 head and neck
1 sternocleidomastoid muscle (sternomastoid muscle)
2 occipitalis
3 temporalis (temporal, temporal muscle)
4 occipito frontalis (frontalis)
5 orbicularis oculi
6 muscles of facial expression
7 masseter
8 orbicularis oris
9 parotid gland
10 lymph node (submandibular lymph gland)
11 submandibular gland (submaxillary gland)
12 muscles of the neck
13 Adam's apple (laryngeal prominence) [in men only]
14-37 mouth and pharynx
14 upper lip
15 gum
16-18 teeth (set of teeth)
16 incisors
17 canine tooth (canine)
18 premolar (bicuspid) and molar teeth (premolars and molars)
19 angle of the mouth (labial commissure)
20 hard palate
21 soft palate (velum palati, velum)
22 uvula
23 palatine tonsil (tonsil)
24 pharyngeal opening (pharynx)
25 tongue
26 lower lip
27 upper jaw (maxilla)
28-37 tooth
28 periodontal membrane (periodontium, pericementum)
29 cement (dental cementum, crusta petrosa)
30 enamel
31 dentine (dentin)
32 dental pulp (tooth pulp, pulp)
33 nerves and blood vessels
34 incisor
35 molar tooth (molar)
36 root (fang)
37 crown
38-51 eye
38 eyebrow (supercilium)
39 upper eyelid (upper palpebra)
40 lower eyelid (lower palpebra)
41 eyelash (cilium)
42 iris
43 pupil
44 eye muscles (ocular muscles)
45 eyeball
46 vitreous body
47 cornea
48 lens
49 retina
50 blind spot
51 optic nerve
52-63 foot
52 big toe (great toe, first toe, hallux, digitus I)
53 second toe (digitus II)
54 third toe (digitus III)
55 fourth toe (digitus IV)
56 little toe (digitus minimus, digitus V)
57 toenail
58 ball of the foot
59 lateral malleolus (external malleolus, outer malleolus, malleolus fibulae)
60 medial malleolus (internal malleolus, inner malleolus, malleolus tibulae, malleolus medialis)
61 instep (medial longitudinal arch, dorsum of the foot, dorsum pedis)
62 sole of the foot
63 heel
64-83 hand
64 thumb (pollex, digitus I)
65 index finger (forefinger, second finger, digitus II)
66 middle finger (third finger, digitus medius, digitus III)
67 ring finger (fourth finger, digitus anularis, digitus IV)
68 little finger (fifth finger, digitus minimus, digitus V)
69 radial side of the hand
70 ulnar side of the hand
71 palm of the hand (palma manus)
72-74 lines of the hand
72 life line (line of life)
73 head line (line of the head)
74 heart line (line of the heart)
75 ball of the thumb (thenar eminence)
76 wrist (carpus)
77 phalanx (phalange)
78 finger pad
79 fingertip
80 fingernail (nail)
81 lunule (lunula) of the nail
82 knuckle
83 back of the hand (dorsum of the hand, dorsum manus)

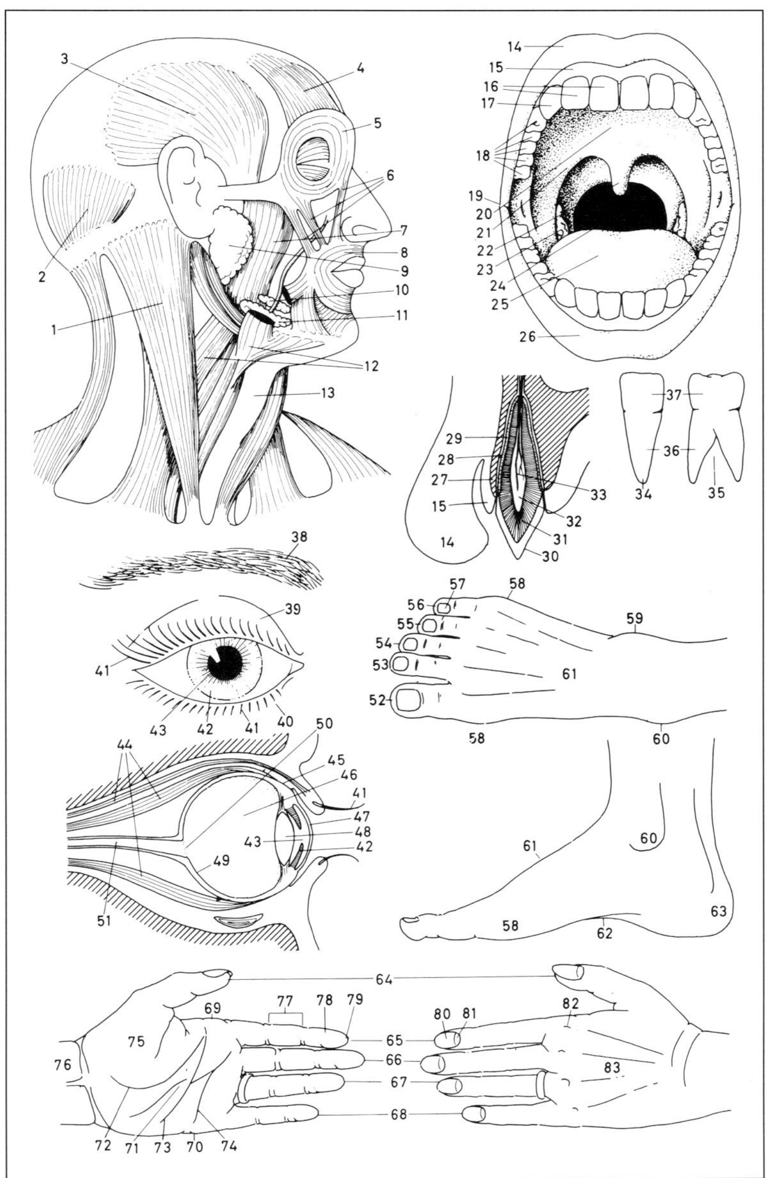
1
2
3
4
5
6
7
8
9
10
11
12
13
14
15
16
17
18
19
20
21
22
23
24
25
26
27
28
29
30
31
32
33
34
35
36
37
38
39
40
41
42
43
44
45
46
47
48
49
50
51
52
53
54
55
56
57
58
59
60
61
62
63
64
65
66
67
68
69
70
71
72
73
74
75
76
77
78
79
80
81
82
83

20 Man V

1-57 internal organs [front view]
1 thyroid gland
2, 3 larynx
2 hyoid bone (hyoid)
3 thyroid cartilage
4 trachea (windpipe)
5 bronchus
6, 7 lung
6 right lung
7 upper pulmonary lobe (upper lobe of the lung) [section]
8 heart
9 diaphragm
10 liver
11 gall bladder
12 spleen
13 stomach
14-22 intestines (bowel)
14-16 small intestine (intestinum tenue)
14 duodenum
15 jejunum
16 ileum
17-22 large intestine (intestinum crassum)
17 caecum (cecum)
18 appendix (vermiform appendix)
19 ascending colon
20 transverse colon
21 descending colon
22 rectum
23 oesophagus (esophagus, gullet)
24, 25 heart
24 auricle
25 anterior longitudinal cardiac sulcus
26 diaphragm
27 spleen
28 right kidney
29 suprarenal gland
30, 31 left kidney [longitudinal section]
30 calyx (renal calyx)
31 renal pelvis
32 ureter
33 bladder
34, 35 liver [from behind]
34 falciform ligament of the liver
35 lobe of the liver
36 gall bladder
37, 38 common bile duct
37 hepatic duct (common hepatic duct)
38 cystic duct
39 portal vein (hepatic portal vein)
40 oesophagus (esophagus, gullet)
41, 42 stomach
41 cardiac orifice
42 pylorus
43 duodenum
44 pancreas
45-57 heart [longitudinal section]
45 atrium
46, 47 valves of the heart
46 tricuspid valve (right atrioventricular valve)
47 bicuspid valve (mitral valve, left atrioventricular valve)
48 cusp
49 aortic valve
50 pulmonary valve
51 ventricle
52 ventricular septum (interventricular septum)
53 superior vena cava
54 aorta
55 pulmonary artery
56 pulmonary vein
57 inferior vena cava
58 peritoneum
59 sacrum
60 coccyx (coccygeal vertebra)
61 rectum
62 anus
63 anal sphincter
64 perineum
65 pubic symphisis (symphisis pubis)
66-77 male sex organs [longitudinal section]
66 penis
67 corpus cavernosum and spongiosum of the penis (erectile tissue of the penis)
68 urethra
69 glans penis
70 prepuce (foreskin)
71 scrotum
72 right testicle (testis)
73 epididymis
74 spermatic duct (vas deferens)
75 Cowper's gland (bulbourethral gland)
76 prostate (prostate gland)
77 seminal vesicle
78 bladder
79-88 female sex organs [longitudinal section]
79 uterus (matrix, womb)
80 cavity of the uterus
81 fallopian tube (uterine tube, oviduct)
82 fimbria (fimbriated extremity)
83 ovary
84 follicle with ovum (egg)
85 os uteri externum
86 vagina
87 lip of the pudendum (lip of the vulva)
88 clitoris

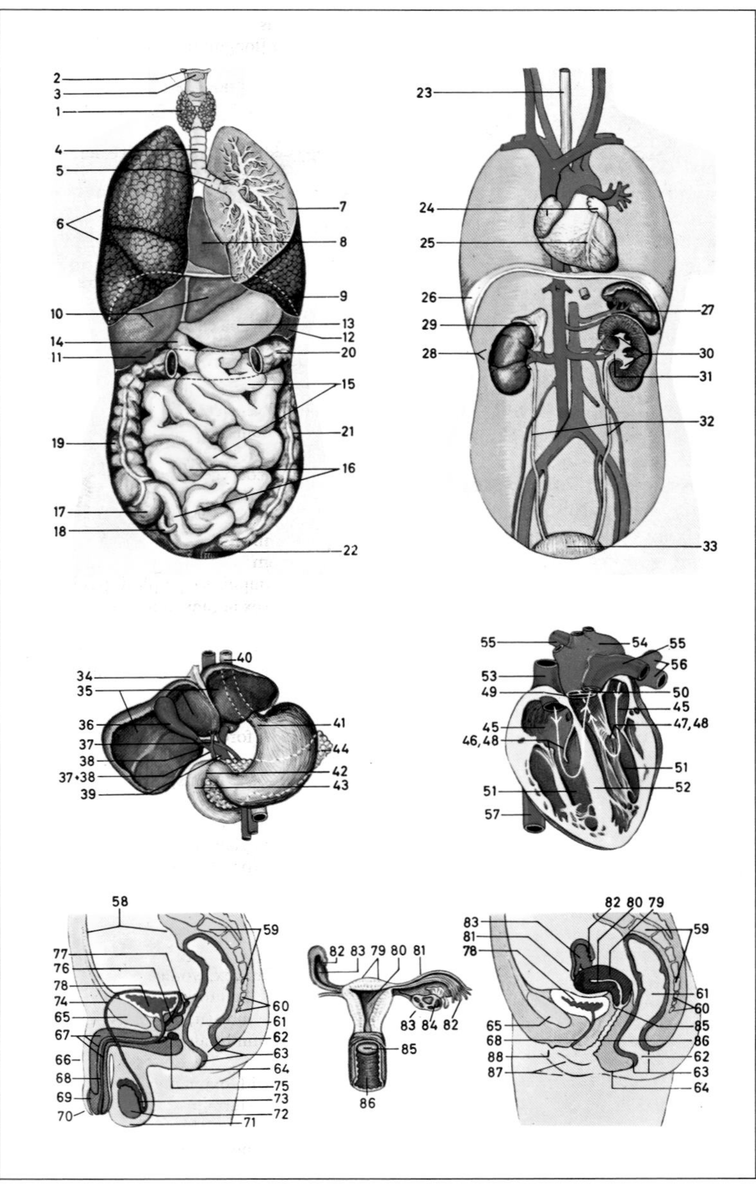
2
3
1
4
5
6
7
8
9
10
13
12
14
11
20
15
21
19
16
17
18
22
23
24
25
26
27
29
28
30
31
32
33
34
35
36
37
38
37+38
39
40
41
44
42
43
55
54
55
56
53
49
50
45
45
47,48
46,48
51
51
52
57
58
59
77
76
78
74
65
67
66
68
69
70
60
61
62
63
64
75
73
72
71
82 83 79 80 81
83 84 82
85
86
82 80 79
83
81
78
59
61
60
65
85
68
86
88
62
87
63
64

21 First Aid

1-13 emergency bandages
1 arm bandage
2 triangular cloth used as a sling (an arm sling)
3 head bandage (capeline)
4 first aid kit
5 first aid dressing
6 sterile gauze dressing
7 adhesive plaster (sticking plaster)
8 wound
9 bandage
10 emergency splint for a broken limb (fractured limb)
11 fractured leg (broken leg)
12 splint
13 headrest
14-17 measures for stanching the blood flow (tying up (ligature) of a blood vessel)
14 pressure points of the arteries
15 emergency tourniquet on the thigh
16 walking stick used as a screw
17 compression bandage
18-23 rescue and transport of an injured person
18 Rautek grip (for rescue of a car accident victim)
19 helper
20 injured person (casualty)
21 chair grip
22 carrying grip
23 emergency stretcher of sticks and a jacket
24-27 positioning of an unconscious person and artificial respiration (resuscitation)
24 coma position
25 unconscious person
26 mouth-to-mouth resuscitation (*variation:* mouth-to-nose resuscitation)
27 resuscitator (respiratory apparatus, resuscitation apparatus), a respirator (artificial breathing device)
28-33 methods of rescue in ice accidents
28 person who has fallen through the ice
29 rescuer
30 rope
31 table (or similar device)
32 ladder
33 self-rescue
34-38 rescue of a drowning person
34 method of release (release grip, release) to free rescuer from the clutch of a drowning person
35 drowning person
36 lifesaver
37, 38 towing (tows)
37 double shoulder tow
38 head tow

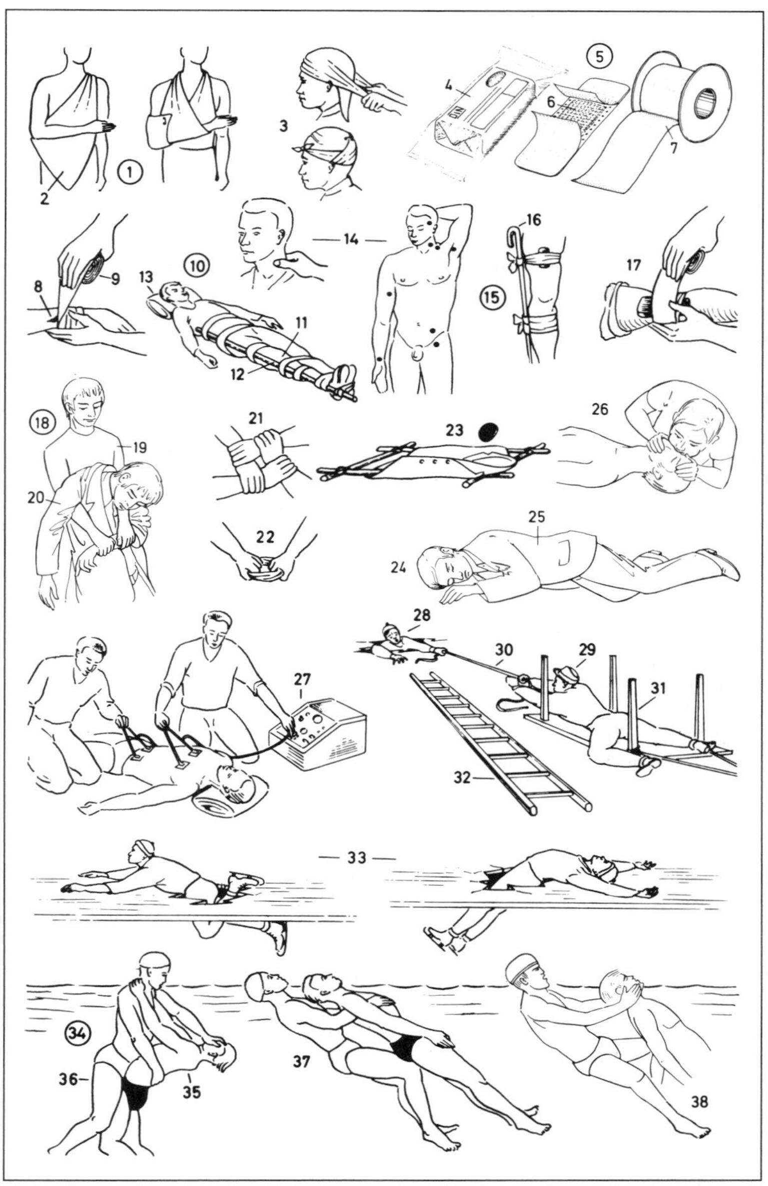
1
2
3
4
5
6
7
8
9
10
11
12
13
14
15
16
17
18
19
20
21
22
23
24
25
26
27
28
29
30
31
32
33
34
35
36
37
38

22 Doctor I

1-74 general practice (*Am.* physician's office)
1 waiting room
2 patient
3 patients with appointments (for a routine check-up or renewal of prescription)
4 magazines [for waiting patients]
5 reception
6 patients file
7 eliminated index cards
8 medical record (medical card)
9 health insurance certificate
10 advertising calendar (publicity calendar)
11 appointments book
12 correspondence file
13 automatic telephone answering and recording set (telephone answering device)
14 radiophone
15 microphone
16 illustrated chart
17 wall calendar
18 telephone
19 [doctor's] assistant
20 prescription
21 telephone index
22 medical dictionary
23 pharmacopoeia (list of registered medicines)
24 franking machine (*Am.* postage meter)
25 stapler
26 diabetics file
27 dictating machine
28 paper punch
29 doctor's stamp
30 ink pad
31 pencil holder
32-74 surgery
32 chart of eyegrounds
33 doctor's bag (doctor's case)
34 intercom
35 medicine cupboard
36 swab dispenser

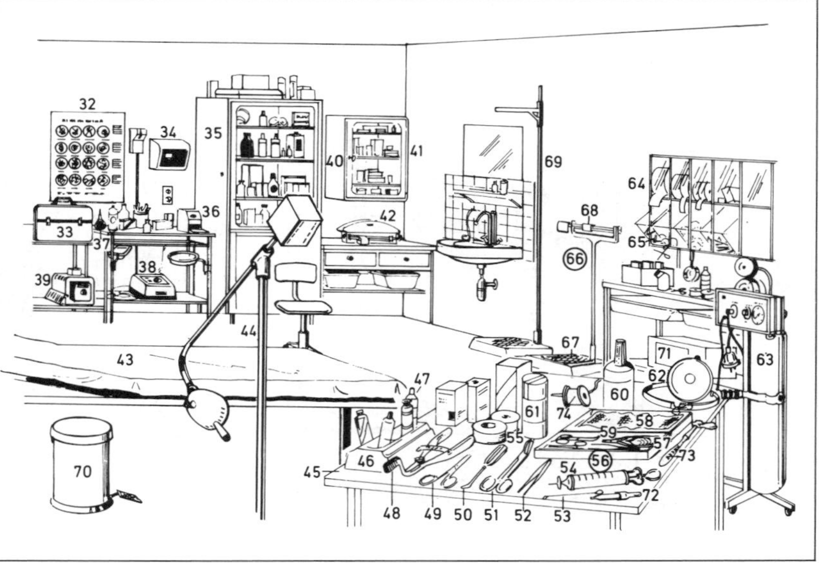

37 inflator (Politzer bag)
38 electrotome
39 steam sterilizer
40 cabinet
41 medicine samples (from the pharmaceutical industry)
42 baby scales
43 examination couch
44 directional lamp
45 instrument table
46 tube holder
47 tube of ointment
48-50 instruments for minor surgery
48 mouth gag
49 Kocher's forceps
50 scoop (curette)
51 angled scissors
52 forceps
53 olive-pointed (bulb-headed) probe
54 syringe for irrigations of the ear or bladder
55 adhesive plaster (sticking plaster)
56 surgical suture material
57 curved surgical needle
58 sterile gauze
59 needle holder
60 spray for disinfecting the skin
61 thread container
62 ophthalmoscope
63 freezer for cryosurgery
64 dispenser for plasters and small pieces of equipment
65 disposable hypodermic needles and syringes
66 scales, sliding-weight scales
67 weighing platform
68 sliding weight (jockey)
69 height gauge (*Am.* gage)
70 waste bin (*Am.* trash bin)
71 hot-air sterilizer
72 pipette
73 percussor
74 aural speculum (auriscope, aural syringe)

23 Doctor II

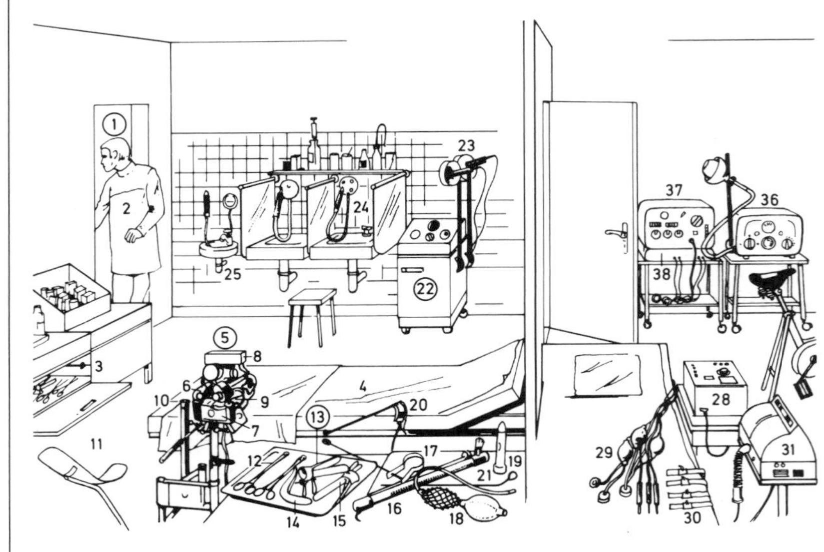

1 consulting room
2 general practitioner
3-21 instruments for gynaecological and proctological examinations
3 warming the instruments up to body temperature
4 examination couch
5 colposcope
6 binocular eyepiece
7 miniature camera
8 cold light source
9 cable release
10 bracket for the leg support
11 leg support (leg holder)
12 holding forceps (sponge holder)
13 vaginal speculum
14 lower blade of the vaginal speculum
15 platinum loop (for smears)
16 rectoscope
17 biopsy forceps used with the rectoscope (proctoscope)
18 insufflator for proctoscopy (rectoscopy)
19 proctoscope (rectal speculum)
20 urethroscope
21 guide for inserting the proctoscope
22 diathermy unit (short-wave therapy apparatus)
23 radiator
24 inhaling apparatus (inhalator)
25 basin [for sputum]
26-31 ergometry
26 bicycle ergometer
27 monitor (for visual display of the ECG and of pulse and respiratory rates when performing work)
28 ECG (electrocardiograph)
29 suction electrodes
30 strap-on electrodes for the limbs
31 spirometer (for measuring respiratory functions)
32 measuring blood pressure
33 sphygmomanometer
34 inflatable cuff
35 stethoscope
36 microwave treatment unit

37 faradization unit (for applying low-frequency currents with different pulse shapes)
38 automatic tuner
39 short-wave therapy apparatus
40 timer
41-59 laboratory
41 medical laboratory technician
42 capillary tube stand for blood sedimentation
43 measuring cylinder
44 automatic pipette
45 kidney dish
46 portable ECG machine for emergency use
47 automatic pipetting device
48 constant temperature water bath
49 tap with water jet pump
50 staining dish (for staining blood smears, sediments, and other smears)
51 binocular research microscope
52 pipette stand for photometry
53 computer and analyser for photometry
54 photometer
55 potentiometric recorder
56 transforming section
57 laboratory apparatus (laboratory equipment)
58 urine sediment chart
59 centrifuge

24 Dentist

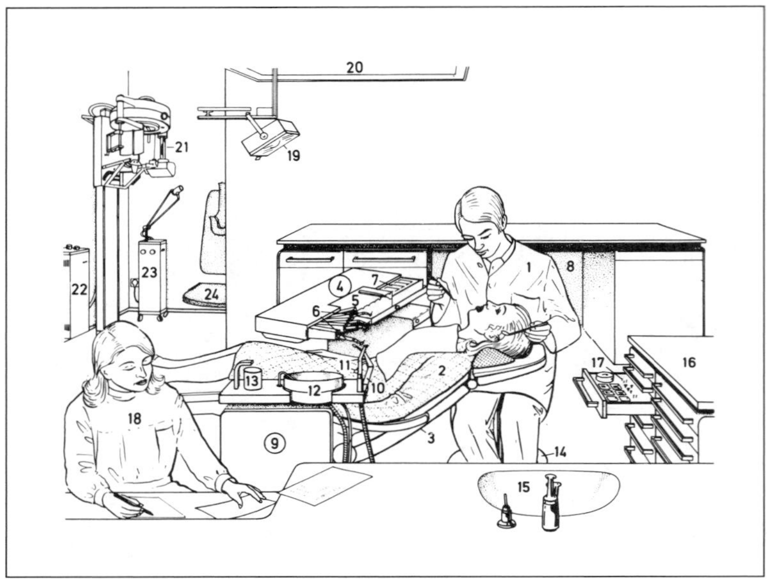

1 dentist (dental surgeon)
2 patient
3 dentist's chair
4 dental instruments
5 instrument tray
6 drills with different handpieces
7 medicine case
8 storage unit (for dental instruments)
9 assistant's unit
10 multi-purpose syringe (for cold and warm water, spray, or air)
11 suction apparatus
12 basin
13 water glass, filled automatically
14 stool
15 washbasin
16 instrument cabinet
17 drawer for drills
18 dentist's assistant
19 dentist's lamp
20 ceiling light
21 X-ray apparatus for panoramic pictures
22 X-ray generator
23 microwave treatment unit, a radiation unit
24 seat
25 denture (set of false teeth)
26 bridge (dental bridge)
27 prepared stump of the tooth
28 crown (*kinds:* gold crown, jacket crown)
29 porcelain tooth (porcelain pontic)
30 filling
31 post crown
32 facing
33 diaphragm
34 post
35 carborundum disc (disk)
36 grinding wheel
37 burs
38 flame-shaped finishing bur
39 fissure burs

40 diamond point
41 mouth mirror
42 mouth lamp
43 cautery
44 platinum-iridium electrode
45 tooth scalers
46 probe
47 extraction forceps
48 tooth-root elevator
49 bone chisel
50 spatula
51 mixer for filling material
52 synchronous timer
53 hypodermic syringe for injection of local anaesthetic
54 hypodermic needle
55 matrix holder
56 impression tray
57 spirit lamp

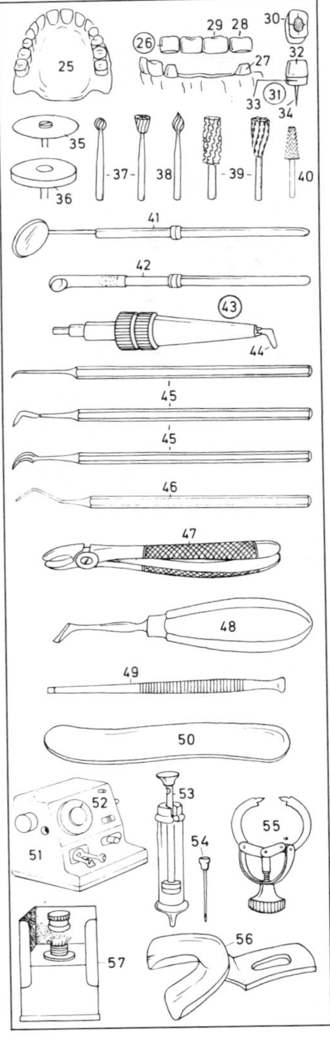

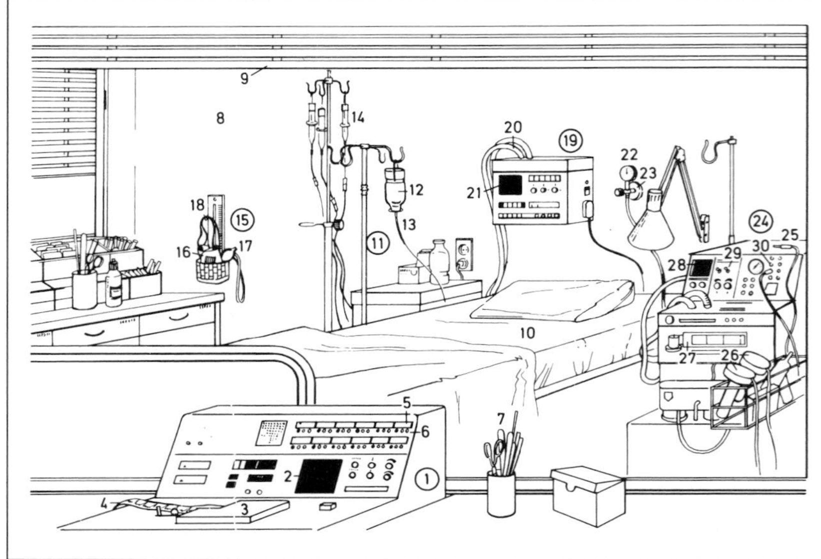

1-30 intensive care unit

1-9 control room

1 central control unit for monitoring heart rhythm (cardiac rhythm) and blood pressure

2 electrocardiogram monitor (ECG monitor)

3 recorder

4 recording paper

5 patient's card

6 indicator lights (with call buttons for each patient)

7 spatula

8 window (observation window, glass partition)

9 blind

10 bed (hospital bed)

11 stand for infusion apparatus

12 infusion bottle

13 tube for intravenous drips

14 infusion device for water-soluble medicaments

15 sphygmomanometer

16 cuff

17 inflating bulb

18 mercury manometer

19 bed monitor

20 connecting lead to the central control unit

21 electrocardiogram monitor (ECG monitor)

22 manometer for the oxygen supply

23 wall connection for oxygen treatment

24 mobile monitoring unit

25 electrode lead to the short-term pacemaker

26 electrodes for shock treatment

27 ECG recording unit

28 electrocardiogram monitor (ECG monitor)

29 control switches and knobs (controls) for adjusting the monitor

30 control buttons for the pacemaker unit

31 **pacemaker** (cardiac pacemaker)

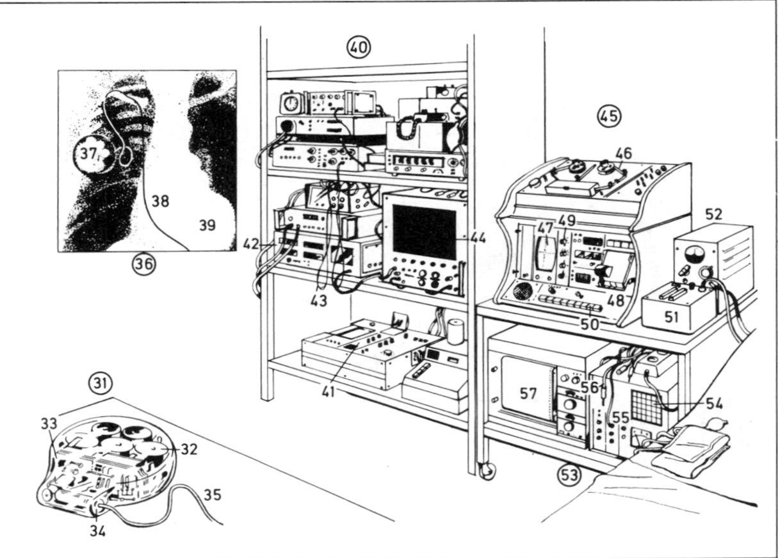

32 mercury battery
33 programmed impulse generator
34 electrode exit point
35 electrode
36 implantation of the pacemaker
37 internal cardiac pacemaker (internal pacemaker, pacemaker)
38 electrode inserted through the vein
39 cardiac silhouette on the X-ray
40 **pacemaker control unit**
41 electrocardiograph (ECG recorder)
42 automatic impulse meter
43 ECG lead to the patient
44 monitor unit for visual monitoring of the pacemaker impulses
45 long-term ECG analyser
46 magnetic tape for recording the ECG impulses during analysis
47 ECG monitor
48 automatic analysis on paper of the ECG rhythm
49 control knob for the ECG amplitude
50 program selector switches for the ECG analysis
51 charger for the pacemaker batteries
52 battery tester
53 pressure gauge (*Am.* gage) for the right cardiac catheter
54 trace monitor
55 pressure indicator
56 connecting lead to the paper recorder
57 paper recorder for pressure traces

26 Hospital II

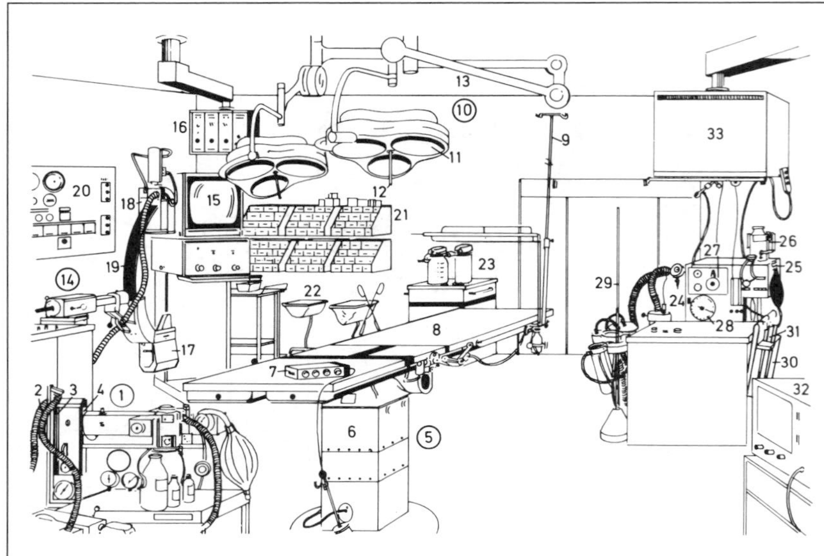

1-54 surgical unit

1-33 operating theatre (*Am.* theater)

1 anaesthesia and breathing apparatus (respiratory machine)

2 inhalers (inhaling tubes)

3 flowmeter for nitrous oxide

4 oxygen flow meter

5 pedestal operating table

6 table pedestal

7 control device (control unit)

8 adjustable top of the operating table

9 stand for intravenous drips

10 swivel-mounted shadow-free operating lamp

11 individual lamp

12 handle

13 swivel arm

14 mobile fluoroscope

15 monitor of the image converter

16 monitor [back]

17 tube

18 image converter

19 C-shaped frame

20 control panel for the air-conditioning

21 surgical suture material

22 mobile waste tray

23 containers for unsterile (unsterilized) pads

24 anaesthesia and respiratory apparatus

25 respirator

26 fluothane container (halothane container)

27 ventilation control knob

28 indicator with pointer for respiratory volume

29 stand with inhalers (inhaling tubes) and pressure gauges (*Am.* gages)

30 catheter holder

31 catheter in sterile packing

32 sphygmograph

33 monitor

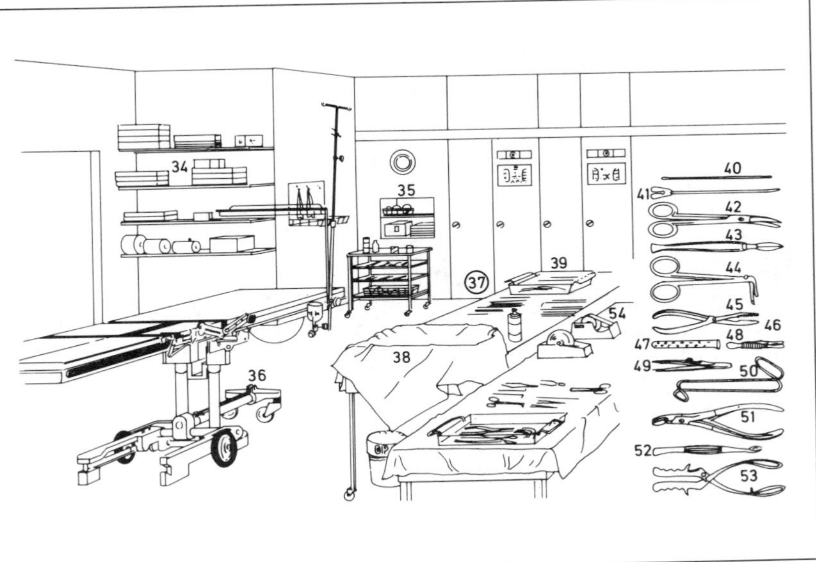

34-54 preparation and sterilization room

34 dressing material
35 small sterilizer
36 carriage of the operating table
37 mobile instrument table
38 sterile cloth
39 instrument tray

40-53 surgical instruments

40 olive-pointed (bulb-headed) probe
41 hollow probe
42 curved scissors
43 scalpel (surgical knife)
44 ligature-holding forceps
45 sequestrum forceps
46 jaw
47 drainage tube
48 surgeon's tourniquet
49 artery forceps
50 blunt hook
51 bone nippers (bone-cutting forceps)
52 scoop (curette) for erasion (curettage)
53 obstetrical forceps
54 roll of plaster

27 Hospital III

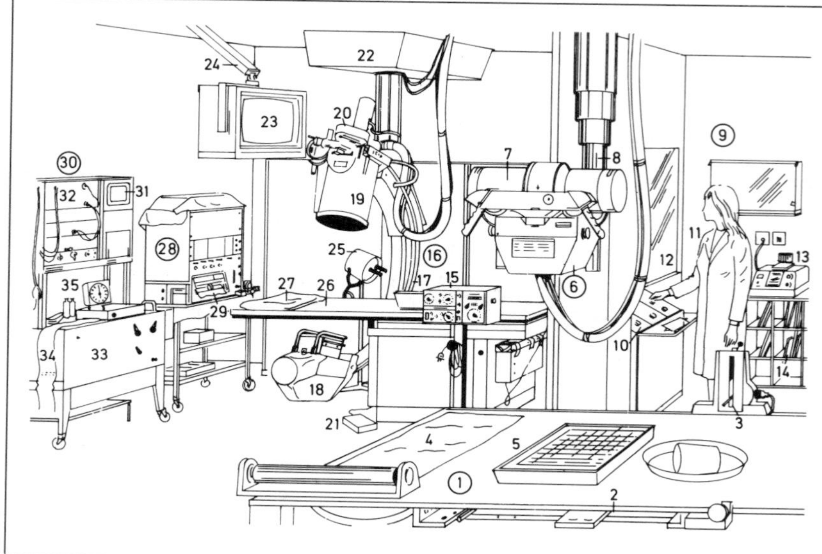

1-35 X-ray unit

1 X-ray examination table
2 support for X-ray cassettes
3 height adjustment of the central beam for lateral views
4 compress for pyelography and cholecystography
5 instrument basin
6 X-ray apparatus for pyelograms
7 X-ray tube
8 telescopic X-ray support
9 central X-ray control unit
10 control panel (control desk)
11 radiographer (X-ray technician)
12 window to the angiography room
13 oxymeter
14 pyelogram cassettes
15 contrast medium injector
16 X-ray image intensifier
17 C-shaped frame
18 X-ray head with X-ray tube
19 image converter with converter tube
20 film camera
21 foot switch
22 mobile mounting
23 monitor
24 swivel-mounted monitor support
25 operating lamp
26 angiographic examination table
27 pillow
28 eight-channel recorder
29 recording paper
30 catheter gauge (*Am.* gage) unit for catheterization of the heart
31 six-channel monitor for pressure graphs and ECG
32 slide-in units of the pressure transducer
33 paper recorder unit with developer for photographic recording
34 recording paper
35 timer

36-50 spirometry

36 spirograph for pulmonary function tests

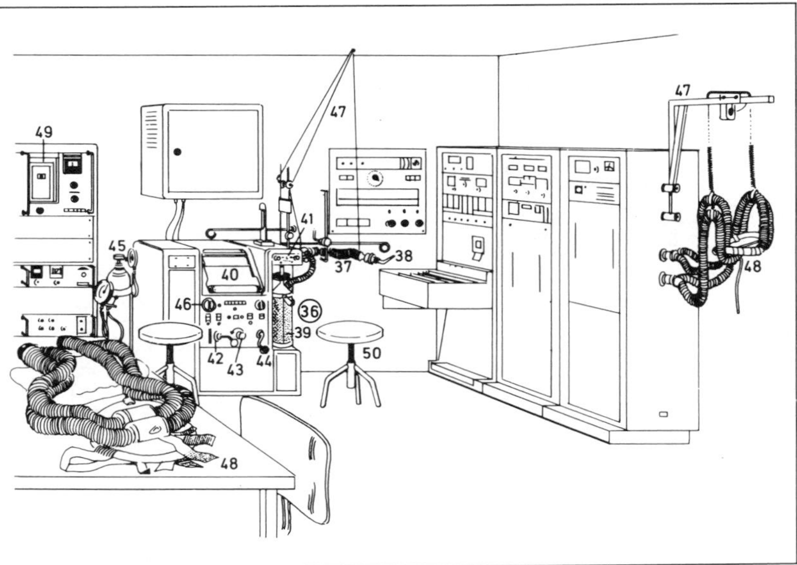

37 breathing tube
38 mouthpiece
39 soda-lime absorber
40 recording paper
41 control knobs for gas supply
42 O_2 stabilizer
43 throttle valve
44 absorber attachment
45 oxygen cylinder
46 water supply
47 tube support
48 mask
49 CO_2 consumption meter
50 stool for the patient

28 Infant Care and Layette

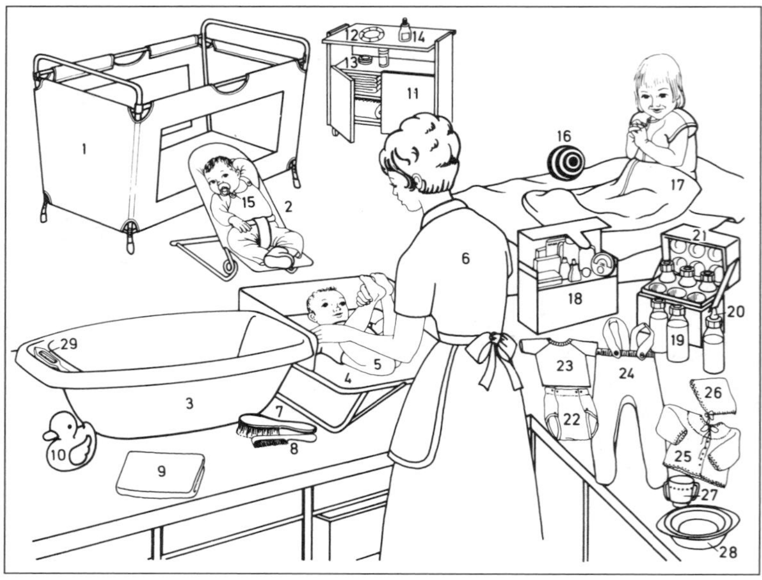

1 collapsible cot
2 bouncing cradle
3 baby bath
4 changing top
5 baby (new-born baby)
6 mother
7 hairbrush
8 comb
9 hand towel
10 toy duck
11 changing unit
12 teething ring
13 cream jar
14 box of baby powder
15 dummy
16 ball
17 sleeping bag
18 layette box
19 feeding bottle
20 teat
21 bottle warmer
22 rubber baby pants for disposable nappies (*Am.* diapers)
23 vest
24 leggings
25 baby's jacket
26 hood
27 baby's cup
28 baby's plate, a stay-warm plate
29 thermometer

30 bassinet, a wicker pram
31 set of bassinet covers
32 canopy
33 baby's high chair, a folding chair
34 pram (baby-carriage) [with windows]
35 folding hood
36 window
37 pushchair (*Am.* stroller)
38 foot-muff (*Am.* foot-bag)
39 play pen
40 floor of the play pen
41 building blocks (building bricks)
42 small child
43 bib
44 rattle (baby's rattle)
45 bootees
46 teddy bear
47 potty (baby's pot)
48 carrycot
49 window
50 handles

29 Children's Clothes

1-12 baby clothes
1 pram suit
2 hood
3 pram jacket (matinée coat)
4 pompon (bobble)
5 bootees
6 sleeveless vest
7 envelope-neck vest
8 wrapover vest
9 baby's jacket
10 rubber baby pants
11 playsuit
12 two-piece suit
13-30 infants' wear
13 child's sundress, a pinafore dress
14 frilled shoulder strap
15 shirred top
16 sun hat
17 one-piece jersey suit
18 front zip (*Am.* zipper)
19 catsuit (playsuit)
20 motif (appliqué)
21 romper
22 playsuit (romper suit)
23 coverall (sleeper and strampler)
24 dressing gown (bath robe)
25 children's shorts
26 braces (*Am.* suspenders)
27 children's T-shirt
28 jersey dress (knitted dress)
29 embroidery
30 children's ankle socks
31-47 school children's wear
31 raincoat
32 leather shorts (lederhosen)
33 staghorn button
34 braces (*Am.* suspenders)
35 flap
36 girl's dirndl
37 cross lacing
38 snow suit (quilted suit)
39 quilt stitching (quilting)
40 dungarees (bib and brace)
41 bib skirt (bib top pinafore)
42 tights
43 sweater (jumper)
44 pile jacket
45 leggings
46 girl's skirt
47 child's jumper
48-68 teenagers' clothes
48 girl's overblouse (overtop)
49 slacks
50 girl's skirt suit
51 jacket
52 skirt
53 knee-length socks
54 girl's coat
55 tie belt
56 girl's bag
57 woollen (*Am.* woolen) hat
58 girl's blouse
59 culottes
60 boy's trousers
61 boy's shirt
62 anorak
63 inset pockets
64 hood drawstring (drawstring)
65 knitted welt
66 parka coat (parka)
67 drawstring (draw cord)
68 patch pockets

1
2
3
4
5
6
7
8
9
10
11
12
13
14
15
16
17
18
19
20
21
22
23
24
25
26
27
28
29
30
31
32
33
34
35
36
37
38
39
40
41
42
43
44
45
46
47
48
49
50
51
52
53
54
55
56
57
58
59
60
61
62
63
64
65
66
67
68

30 Ladies' Wear I (Winter Wear)

1 mink jacket
2 cowl neck jumper
3 cowl collar
4 knitted overtop
5 turndown collar
6 turn-up (turnover) sleeve
7 polo neck jumper
8 pinafore dress
9 blouse (with revers collar)
10 shirt-waister dress, a button-through dress
11 belt
12 winter dress
13 piping
14 cuff
15 long sleeve
16 quilted waistcoat
17 quilt stitching (quilting)
18 leather trimming
19 winter slacks
20 striped polo jumper
21 boiler suit (dungarees, bib and brace)
22 patch pocket
23 front pocket
24 bib
25 wrapover dress (wrap-around dress)
26 shirt
27 peasant-style dress
28 floral braid
29 tunic (tunic top)
30 ribbed cuff
31 quilted design
32 pleated skirt
33 two-piece knitted dress
34 boat neck, a neckline
35 turn-up
36 kimono sleeve
37 knitted design
38 lumber-jacket
39 cable pattern
40 shirt-blouse
41 loop fastening
42 embroidery
43 stand-up collar
44 cossack trousers
45 two-piece combination (shirt top and long skirt)
46 tie (bow)
47 decorative facing
48 cuff slit
49 side slit
50 tabard
51 inverted pleat skirt
52 godet
53 evening gown
54 pleated bell sleeve
55 party blouse
56 party skirt
57 trouser suit (slack suit)
58 suede jacket
59 fur trimming
60 fur coat (*kinds:* Persian lamb, broadtail, mink, sable)
61 winter coat (cloth coat)
62 fur cuff (fur-trimmed cuff)
63 fur collar (fur-trimmed collar)
64 loden coat
65 cape
66 toggle fastenings
67 loden skirt
68 poncho-style coat
69 hood

1
2
3
4
5
6
7
8
9
10
11
12
13
14
15
16
17
18
19
20
21
22
23
24
25
26
27
28
29
30
31
32
33
34
35
36
37
38
39
40
41
42
43
44
45
46
47
48
49
50
51
52
53
54
55
56
57
58
59
60
61
62
63
64
65
66
67
68
69

31 Ladies' Wear II (Summer Wear)

1 skirt suit
2 jacket
3 skirt
4 inset pocket
5 decorative stitching
6 dress and jacket combination
7 piping
8 pinafore dress
9 summer dress
10 belt
11 two-piece dress
12 belt buckle
13 wrapover (wrap-around) skirt
14 pencil silhouette
15 shoulder buttons
16 batwing sleeve
17 overdress
18 kimono yoke
19 tie belt
20 summer coat
21 detachable hood
22 summer blouse
23 lapel
24 skirt
25 front pleat
26 dirndl (dirndl dress)
27 puffed sleeve
28 dirndl necklace
29 dirndl blouse
30 bodice
31 dirndl apron
32 lace trimming (lace), cotton lace
33 frilled apron
34 frill
35 smock overall
36 house frock (house dress)
37 poplin jacket
38 T-shirt
39 ladies' shorts
40 trouser turn-up
41 waistband
42 bomber jacket
43 stretch welt
44 Bermuda shorts
45 saddle stitching
46 frill collar
47 knot
48 culotte
49 twin set
50 cardigan
51 sweater
52 summer (lightweight) slacks
53 jumpsuit
54 turn-up
55 zip (*Am.* zipper)
56 patch pocket
57 scarf (neckerchief)
58 denim suit
59 denim waistcoat
60 jeans (denims)
61 overblouse
62 turned-up sleeve
63 stretch belt
64 halter top
65 knitted overtop
66 drawstring waist
67 short-sleeved jumper
68 V-neck (vee-neck)
69 turndown collar
70 knitted welt
71 shawl

Ladies' Wear II (Summer Wear) 31

32 Underwear, Nightwear

1-15 ladies' underwear (ladies' underclothes, lingerie)
1 brassière (bra)
2 pantie-girdle
3 pantie-corselette
4 longline brassière (longline bra)
5 stretch girdle
6 suspender
7 vest
8 pantie briefs
9 ladies' knee-high stocking
10 long-legged (long leg) panties
11 long pants
12 tights (pantie-hose)
13 slip
14 waist slip
15 bikini briefs
16-21 ladies' nightwear
16 nightdress (nightgown, nightie)
17 pyjamas (*Am.* pajamas)
18 pyjama top
19 pyjama trousers
20 housecoat
21 vest and shorts set [for leisure wear and as nightwear]
22-29 men's underwear (men's underclothes)
22 string vest
23 string briefs
24 front panel
25 sleeveless vest
26 briefs
27 trunks
28 short-sleeved vest
29 long johns
30 braces (*Am.* suspenders)
31 braces clip
32-34 men's socks
32 knee-length sock
33 elasticated top
34 long sock
35-37 men's nightwear
35 dressing gown
36 pyjamas (*Am.* pajamas)
37 nightshirt
38-47 men's shirts
38 casual shirt
39 belt
40 cravat
41 tie
42 knot
43 dress shirt
44 frill (frill front)
45 cuff
46 cuff link
47 bow-tie

1
2
3
4
5
6
7
8
9
10
11
12
13
14
15
16
17
18
19
20
21
22
23
24
25
26
27
28
29
30
31
32
33
34
35
36
37
38
39
40
41
42
43
44
45
46
47

33 Men's Wear

1-67 men's fashion
1 single-breasted suit, a men's suit
2 jacket
3 suit trousers
4 waistcoat (vest)
5 lapel
6 trouser leg with crease
7 dinner dress, an evening suit
8 silk lapel
9 breast pocket
10 dress handkerchief
11 bow-tie
12 side pocket
13 tailcoat (tails), evening dress
14 coat-tail
15 white waistcoat (vest)
16 white bow-tie
17 casual suit
18 pocket flap
19 front yoke
20 denim suit
21 denim jacket
22 jeans (denims)
23 waistband
24 beach suit
25 shorts
26 short-sleeved jacket
27 tracksuit
28 tracksuit top with zip
29 tracksuit bottoms
30 cardigan
31 knitted collar
32 men's short-sleeved pullover (men's short-sleeved sweater)
33 short-sleeved shirt
34 shirt button
35 turn-up
36 knitted shirt
37 casual shirt
38 patch pocket
39 casual jacket
40 knee-breeches
41 knee strap
42 knee-length sock
43 leather jacket
44 bib and brace overalls
45 adjustable braces (*Am.* suspenders)
46 front pocket
47 trouser pocket
48 fly
49 rule pocket
50 check shirt
51 men's pullover
52 heavy pullover
53 knitted waistcoat (vest)
54 blazer
55 jacket button
56 overall
57 trenchcoat
58 coat collar
59 coat belt
60 poplin coat
61 coat pocket
62 fly front
63 car coat
64 coat button
65 scarf
66 cloth coat
67 glove

1
2
3
4
5
6
7
8
9
10
11
12
13
14
15
16
17
18
19
20
21
22
23
24
25
26
27
28
29
30
31
32
33
34
35
36
37
38
39
40
41
42
43
44
45
46
47
48
49
50
51
52
53
54
55
56
57
58
59
60
61
62
63
64
65
66
67

34 Hairstyles and Beards

1-25 men's beards and hairstyles (haircuts)
1 long hair worn loose
2 allonge periwig (full-bottomed wig), a wig; *shorter and smoother:* bob wig, toupet
3 curls
4 bag wig (purse wig)
5 pigtail wig
6 queue (pigtail)
7 bow (ribbon)
8 handlebars (handlebar moustache, *Am.* mustache)
9 centre (*Am.* center) parting
10 goatee (goatee beard), chintuft
11 closely-cropped head of hair (crew cut)
12 whiskers
13 Vandyke beard (stiletto beard, bodkin beard), with waxed moustache (*Am.* mustache)
14 side parting
15 full beard (circular beard, round beard)
16 tile beard
17 shadow
18 head of curly hair
19 military moustache (*Am.* mustache) (English-style moustache)
20 partly bald head
21 bald patch
22 bald head
23 stubble beard (stubble, short beard bristles)
24 side-whiskers (sideboards, sideburns)
25 clean shave
26 Afro look (for men and women)
27-38 ladies' hairstyles (coiffures, women's and girls' hairstyles)
27 ponytail
28 swept-back hair (swept-up hair, pinned-up hair)
29 bun (chignon)
30 plaits (bunches)
31 chaplet hairstyle (Gretchen style)
32 chaplet (coiled plaits)
33 curled hair
34 shingle (shingled hair, bobbed hair)
35 pageboy style
36 fringe (*Am.* bangs)
37 earphones
38 earphone (coiled plait)

1
2
3
4
5
6
7
8
9
10
11
12
13
14
15
16
17
18
19
20
21
22
23
24
25
26
27
28
29
30
31
32
33
34
35
36
37
38

35 Headgear

1-21 ladies' hats and caps

1 milliner making a hat
2 hood
3 block
4 decorative pieces
5 sombrero
6 mohair hat with feathers
7 model hat with fancy appliqué
8 linen cap (jockey cap)
9 hat made of thick candlewick yarn
10 woollen (*Am.* woolen) hat (knitted hat)
11 mohair hat
12 cloche with feathers
13 large men's hat made of sisal with corded ribbon
14 trilby-style hat with fancy ribbon
15 soft felt hat
16 Panama hat with scarf
17 peaked mink cap
18 mink hat
19 fox hat with leather top
20 mink cap
21 slouch hat trimmed with flowers

22-40 men's hats and caps
22 trilby hat (trilby)
23 loden hat (Alpine hat)
24 felt hat with tassels (Tyrolean hat, Tyrolese hat)
25 corduroy cap
26 woollen (*Am.* woolen) hat
27 beret
28 German sailor's cap ('Prinz Heinrich' cap)
29 peaked cap (yachting cap)
30 sou'wester (southwester)
31 fox cap with earflaps
32 leather cap with fur flaps
33 musquash cap
34 astrakhan cap, a real or imitation astrakhan cap
35 boater
36 (grey, *Am.* gray, or black) top hat made of silk taffeta; *collapsible:* crush hat (opera hat, claque)
37 sun hat (lightweight hat) made of cloth with small patch pocket
38 wide-brimmed hat
39 toboggan cap (skiing cap, ski cap)
40 workman's cap

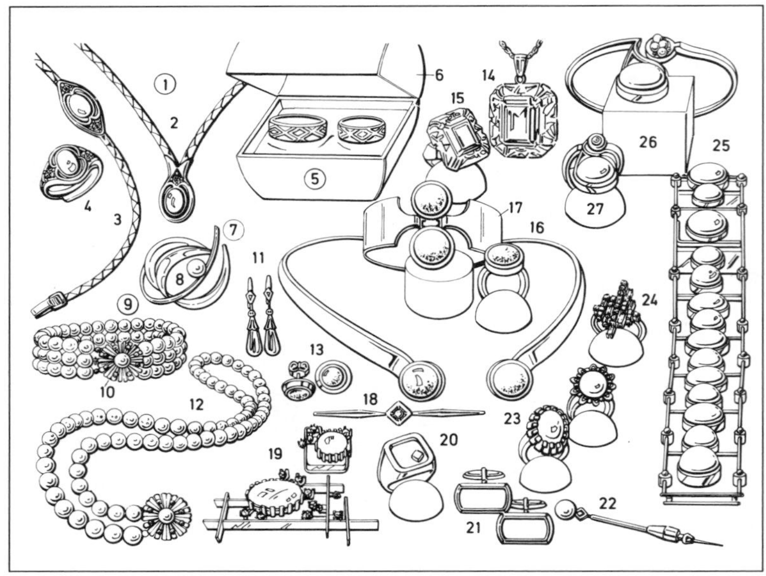

1 set of jewellery (*Am.* jewelry)
2 necklace
3 bracelet
4 ring
5 wedding rings
6 wedding ring box
7 brooch, a pearl brooch
8 pearl
9 cultured pearl bracelet
10 clasp, a white gold clasp
11 pendant earrings (drop earrings)
12 cultured pearl necklace
13 earrings
14 gemstone pendant
15 gemstone ring
16 choker (collar, neckband)
17 bangle
18 diamond pin
19 modern-style brooches
20 man's ring
21 cuff links
22 tiepin
23 diamond ring with pearl
24 modern-style diamond ring
25 gemstone bracelet
26 asymmetrical bangle
27 asymmetrical ring
28 ivory necklace
29 ivory rose
30 ivory brooch
31 jewel box (jewel case)
32 pearl necklace
33 bracelet watch
34 coral necklace
35 charms
36 coin bracelet
37 gold coin
38 coin setting
39 link
40 signet ring
41 engraving (monogram)
42-86 cuts and forms

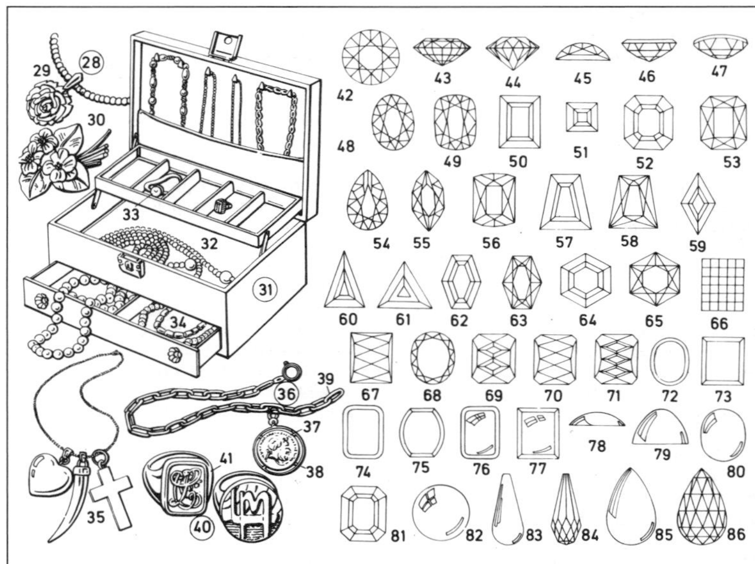

42-71 faceted stones
42, 43 standard round cut
44 brilliant cut
45 rose cut
46 flat table
47 table en cabochon
48 standard cut
49 standard antique cut
50 rectangular step-cut
51 square step-cut
52 octagonal step-cut
53 octagonal cross-cut
54 standard pear-shape (pendeloque)
55 marquise (navette)
56 standard barrel-shape
57 trapezium step-cut
58 trapezium cross-cut
59 rhombus step-cut
60, 61 triangular step-cut
62 hexagonal step-cut
63 oval hexagonal cross-cut
64 round hexagonal step-cut
65 round hexagonal cross-cut
66 chequer-board cut
67 triangle cut
68-71 fancy cuts
72-77 ring gemstones
72 oval flat table
73 rectangular flat table
74 octagonal flat table
75 barrel-shape
76 antique table en cabochon
77 rectangular table en cabochon
78-81 cabochons
78 round cabochon (simple cabochon)
79 high dome (high cabochon)
80 oval cabochon
81 octagonal cabochon
82-86 spheres and pear-shapes
82 plain sphere
83 plain pear-shape
84 faceted pear-shape
85 plain drop
86 faceted briolette

37 Types of Dwelling

1-53 detached house
1 basement
2 ground floor (*Am.* first floor)
3 upper floor (first floor, *Am.* second floor)
4 loft
5 roof, a gable roof (saddle roof, saddleback roof)
6 gutter
7 ridge
8 verge with bargeboards
9 eaves, rafter-supported eaves
10 chimney
11 gutter
12 swan's neck (swan-neck)
13 rainwater pipe (downpipe, *Am.* downspout, leader)
14 vertical pipe, a cast-iron pipe
15 gable (gable end)
16 glass wall
17 base course (plinth)
18 balcony
19 parapet
20 flower box
21 French window (French windows) opening on to the balcony
22 double casement window
23 single casement window
24 window breast with window sill
25 lintel (window head)
26 reveal
27 cellar window
28 rolling shutter
29 rolling shutter frame
30 window shutter (folding shutter)
31 shutter catch
32 garage with tool shed
33 espalier
34 batten door (ledged door)
35 fanlight with mullion and transom
36 terrace
37 garden wall with coping stones
38 garden light
39 steps
40 rockery (rock garden)
41 outside tap (*Am.* faucet) for the hose
42 garden hose
43 lawn sprinkler
44 paddling pool
45 stepping stones
46 sunbathing area (lawn)
47 deck-chair
48 sunshade (garden parasol)
49 garden chair
50 garden table
51 frame for beating carpets
52 garage driveway
53 fence, a wooden fence

54-57 housing estate (housing development)
54 house on a housing estate (on a housing development)
55 pent roof (penthouse roof)
56 dormer (dormer window)
57 garden

58-63 terraced house [one of a row of terraced houses], **stepped**
58 front garden
59 hedge
60 pavement (*Am.* sidewalk, walkway)
61 street (road)
62 street lamp (street light)
63 litter bin (*Am.* trash bin)

64-68 house divided into two flats (*Am.* house divided into two apartments, duplex house)
64 hip (hipped) roof
65 front door
66 front steps
67 canopy
68 flower window (window for house plants)

69-71 pair of semi-detached houses divided into four flats (*Am.* apartments)
69 balcony
70 sun lounge (*Am.* sun parlor)
71 awning (sun blind, sunshade)

72-76 block of flats (*Am.* apartment building, apartment house) with access balconies
72 staircase
73 balcony
74 studio flat (*Am.* studio apartment)
75 sun roof, a sun terrace
76 open space

77-81 multi-storey block of flats (*Am.* multistory apartment building, multistory apartment house)
77 flat roof
78 pent roof (shed roof, lean-to roof)
79 garage
80 pergola
81 staircase window
82 high-rise block of flats (*Am.* high-rise apartment building, high-rise apartment house)
83 penthouse

84-86 weekend house, a timber house
84 horizontal boarding
85 natural stone base course (natural stone plinth)
86 strip windows (ribbon windows)

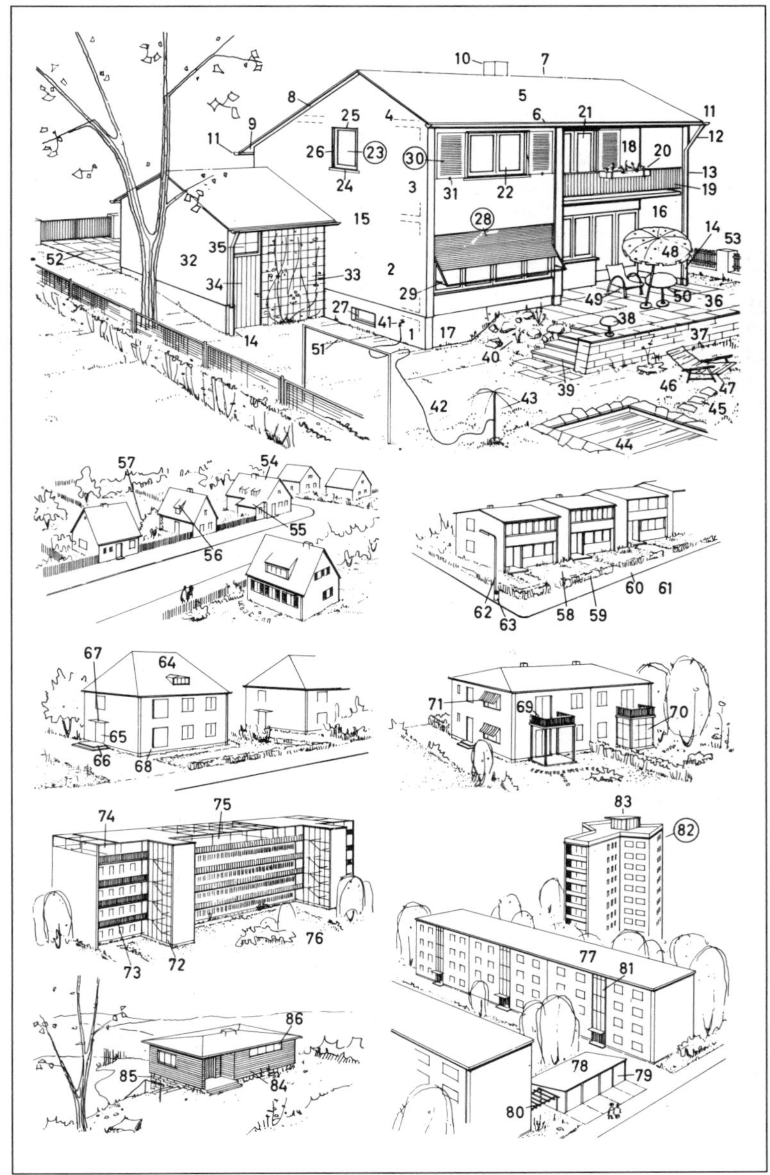
1
2
3
4
5
6
7
8
9
10
11
12
13
14
15
16
17
18
19
20
21
22
23
24
25
26
27
28
29
30
31
32
33
34
35
36
37
38
39
40
41
42
43
44
45
46
47
48
49
50
51
52
53
54
55
56
57
58
59
60
61
62
63
64
65
66
67
68
69
70
71
72
73
74
75
76
77
78
79
80
81
82
83
84
85
86

38 Roof and Boiler Room

1-29 attic
1 roof cladding (roof covering)
2 skylight
3 gangway
4 cat ladder (roof ladder)
5 chimney
6 roof hook
7 dormer window (dormer)
8 snow guard (roof guard)
9 gutter
10 rainwater pipe (downpipe, *Am.* downspout, leader)
11 eaves
12 pitched roof
13 trapdoor
14 hatch
15 ladder
16 stile
17 rung
18 loft (attic)
19 wooden partition
20 lumber room door (boxroom door)
21 padlock
22 hook [for washing line]
23 clothes line (washing line)
24 expansion tank for boiler
25 wooden steps and balustrade
26 string (*Am.* stringer)
27 step
28 handrail (guard rail)
29 baluster
30 lightning conductor (lightning rod)
31 **chimney sweep** (*Am.* chimney sweeper)
32 brush with weight
33 shoulder iron
34 sack for soot
35 flue brush
36 broom (besom)
37 broomstick (broom handle)
38-81 **hot-water heating system,** full central heating
38-43 **boiler room**
38 coke-fired central heating system
39 ash box door (*Am.* cleanout door)
40 flueblock
41 poker
42 rake
43 coal shovel
44-60 **oil-fired central heating system**
44 oil tank
45 manhole
46 manhole cover
47 tank inlet
48 dome cover
49 tank bottom valve
50 fuel oil (heating oil)
51 air-bleed duct
52 air vent cap
53 oil level pipe
54 oil gauge (*Am.* gage)
55 suction pipe
56 return pipe
57 central heating furnace (oil heating furnace)
58-60 **oil burner**
58 fan
59 electric motor
60 covered pilot light
61 charging door
62 inspection window
63 water gauge (*Am.* gage)
64 furnace thermometer
65 bleeder
66 furnace bed
67 control panel
68 hot water tank (boiler)
69 overflow pipe (overflow)
70 safety valve
71 main distribution pipe
72 lagging
73 valve
74 flow pipe
75 regulating valve
76 radiator
77 radiator rib
78 room thermostat
79 return pipe (return)
80 return pipe [in two-pipe system]
81 smoke outlet (smoke extract)

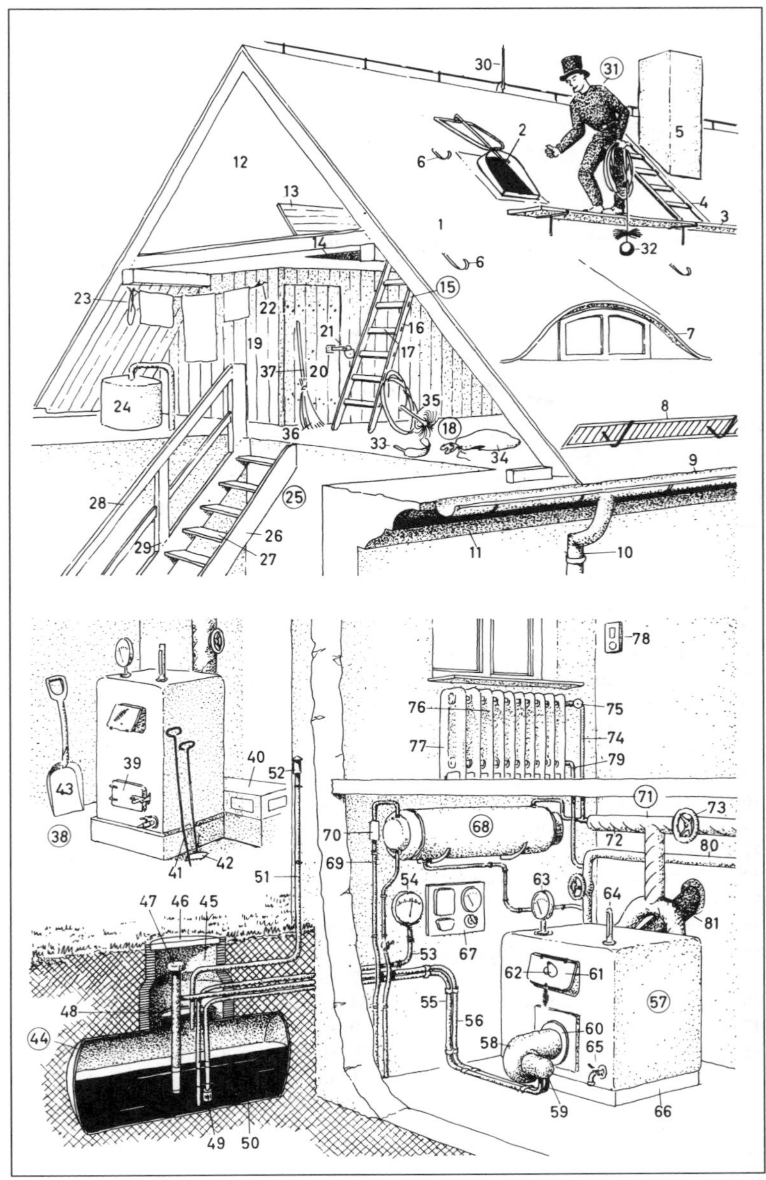
30
31
2
5
6
12
13
4
3
1
14
32
23
22
15
21
16
19
17
7
37
20
35
24
8
18
36
33
34
9
25
28
26
29
27
11
10
78
76
75
77
74
40
79
39
52
43
71
73
38
70
68
72
41
42
80
69
51
54
63
64
47
46
45
81
53
67
62
61
48
55
56
57
60
44
58
65
59
66
49
50

39 Kitchen

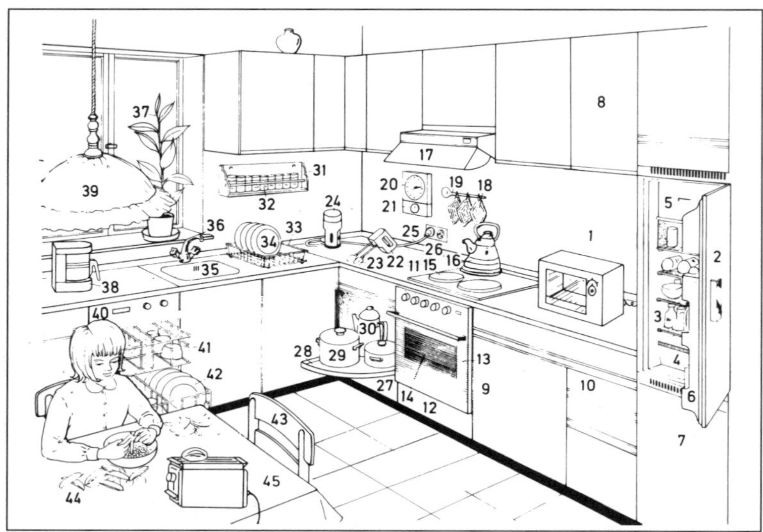

1 microwave oven (microwave)
2 refrigerator (fridge, *Am.* icebox)
3 refrigerator shelf
4 salad drawer
5 freezing compartment
6 bottle rack (in storage door)
7 upright freezer
8 wall cupboard, a kitchen cupboard
9 base unit
10 cutlery drawer
11 work surface (worktop)
12-17 cooker unit
12 electric cooker (*also:* gas cooker)
13 oven
14 oven window
15 hotplate, an automatic high-speed plate
16 kettle (whistling kettle)
17 cooker hood
18 pot holder
19 pot holder rack
20 kitchen clock
21 timer
22 hand mixer
23 whisk
24 electric coffee grinder (with rotating blades)
25 lead
26 wall socket
27 corner unit
28 revolving shelf
29 pot (cooking pot)
30 jug
31 spice rack
32 spice jar
33-36 sink unit
33 dish drainer
34 tea plate
35 sink
36 water tap (*Am.* faucet); *here:* mixer tap (*Am.* mixing faucet)
37 pot plant, a foliage plant
38 coffee maker
39 kitchen lamp
40 dishwasher (dishwashing machine)
41 dish rack
42 dinner plate
43 kitchen chair
44 kitchen table
45 toaster

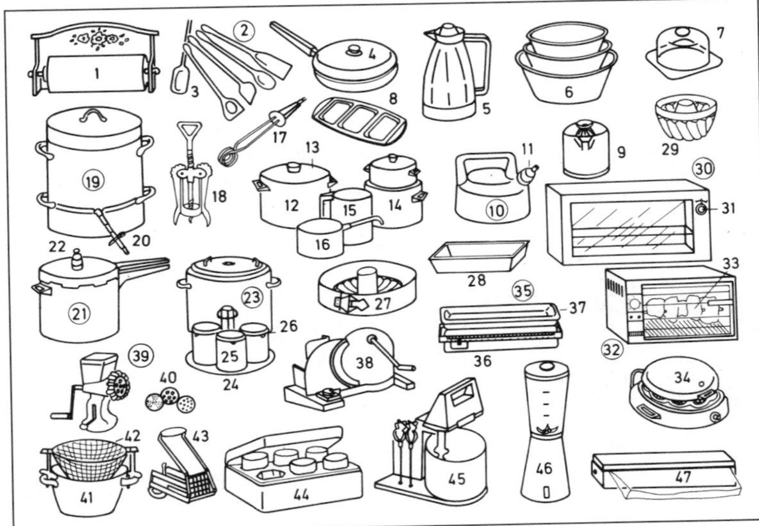

1 general-purpose roll holder with kitchen roll (paper towels)
2 set of wooden spoons
3 mixing spoon
4 frying pan
5 Thermos jug
6 set of bowls
7 cheese dish with glass cover
8 three-compartment dish
9 lemon squeezer
10 whistling kettle
11 whistle
12-16 pan set
12 pot (cooking pot)
13 lid
14 casserole dish
15 milk pot
16 saucepan
17 immersion heater
18 corkscrew [with levers]
19 juice extractor
20 tube clamp (tube clip)
21 pressure cooker
22 pressure valve
23 fruit preserver
24 removable rack
25 preserving jar
26 rubber ring
27 spring form
28 cake tin
29 cake tin
30 microwave oven (microwave)
31 timer
32 rotisserie
33 spit
34 electric waffle iron
35 sliding-weight scales
36 sliding weight
37 scale pan
38 food slicer
39 mincer (*Am.* meat chopper)
40 blades
41 chip pan
42 basket
43 potato chipper
44 yoghurt maker
45 mixer
46 blender
47 bag sealer

41 Hall

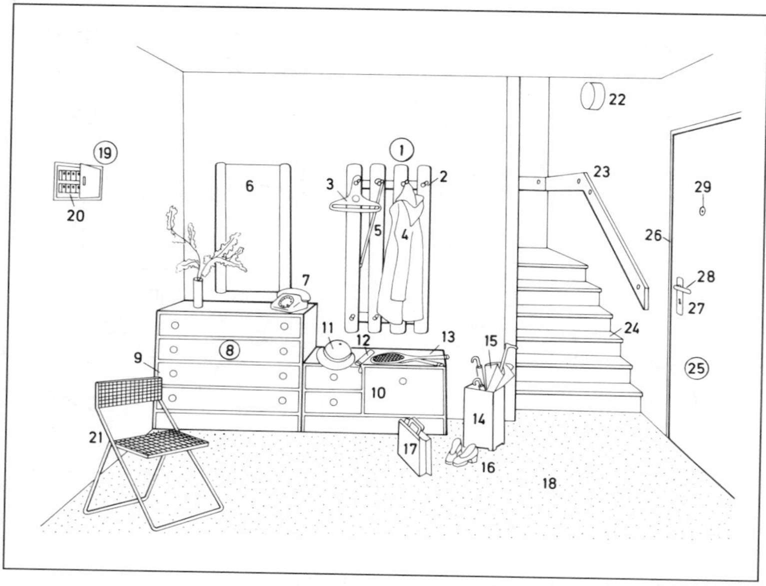

1-29 hall (entrance hall)
1 coat rack
2 coat hook
3 coat hanger
4 rain cape
5 walking stick
6 hall mirror
7 telephone
8 chest of drawers for shoes, etc.
9 drawer
10 seat
11 ladies' hat
12 telescopic umbrella
13 tennis rackets (tennis racquets)
14 umbrella stand
15 umbrella
16 shoes
17 briefcase
18 fitted carpet
19 fuse box
20 miniature circuit breaker
21 tubular steel chair
22 stair light
23 handrail
24 step
25 front door
26 door frame
27 door lock
28 door handle
29 spyhole

1-20 wall units (shelf units)
2 side wall
3 bookshelf
4 row of books
5 display cabinet unit
6 cupboard base unit
7 cupboard unit
8 television set (TV set)
9 stereo system (stereo equipment)
10 speaker (loudspeaker)
11 pipe rack
12 pipe
13 globe
14 brass kettle
15 telescope
16 mantle clock
17 bust
18 encyclopaedia [in several volumes]
19 room divider
20 drinks cupboard
21-26 upholstered suite (seating group)
21 armchair
22 arm
23 seat cushion (cushion)
24 settee
25 back cushion
26 [round] corner section
27 scatter cushion
28 coffee table
29 ashtray
30 tray
31 whisky (whiskey) bottle
32 soda water bottle (soda bottle)
33-34 dining set
33 dining table
34 chair
35 net curtain
36 indoor plants (houseplants)

43 Bedroom

1 wardrobe (*Am.* clothes closet)
2 linen shelf
3 cane chair
4-13 double bed (*sim.:* double divan)
4-6 bedstead
4 foot of the bed
5 bed frame
6 headboard
7 bedspread
8 duvet, a quilted duvet
9 sheet, a linen sheet
10 mattress, a foam mattress with drill tick
11 [wedge-shaped] bolster
12, 13 pillow
12 pillowcase (pillowslip)
13 tick
14 bookshelf [attached to the headboard]
15 reading lamp
16 electric alarm clock
17 bedside cabinet
18 drawer
19 bedroom lamp
20 picture
21 picture frame
22 bedside rug
23 fitted carpet
24 dressing stool
25 dressing table
26 perfume spray
27 perfume bottle
28 powder box
29 dressing-table mirror (mirror)

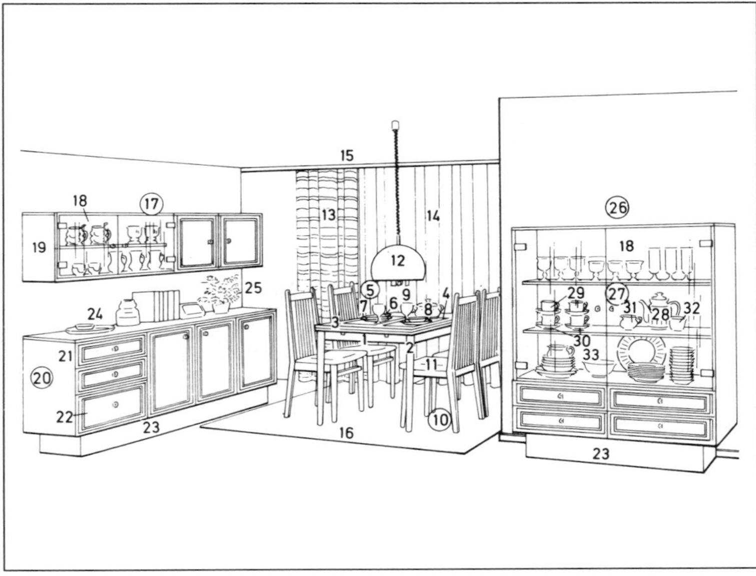

1-11 dining set
1 dining table
2 table leg
3 table top
4 place mat
5 place (place setting, cover)
6 soup plate (deep plate)
7 dinner plate
8 soup tureen
9 wineglass
10 dining chair
11 seat
12 lamp (pendant lamp)
13 curtains
14 net curtain
15 curtain rail
16 carpet
17 wall unit
18 glass door
19 shelf
20 sideboard
21 cutlery drawer
22 linen drawer
23 base
24 round tray
25 pot plant
26 china cabinet (display cabinet)
27 coffee set (coffee service)
28 coffee pot
29 coffee cup
30 saucer
31 milk jug
32 sugar bowl
33 dinner set (dinner service)

45 Tableware and Cutlery

1 dining table
2 tablecloth, a damask cloth
3-12 place (place setting, cover)
3 bottom plate
4 dinner plate
5 deep plate (soup plate)
6 dessert plate (dessert bowl)
7 knife and fork
8 fish knife and fork
9 serviette (napkin, table napkin)
10 serviette ring (napkin ring)
11 knife rest
12 wineglasses
13 place card
14 soup ladle
15 soup tureen (tureen)
16 candelabra
17 sauceboat (gravy boat)
18 sauce ladle (gravy ladle)
19 table decoration
20 bread basket
21 roll
22 slice of bread
23 salad bowl
24 salad servers
25 vegetable dish
26 meat plate (*Am.* meat platter)
27 roast meat (roast)
28 fruit dish
29 fruit bowl
30 fruit (stewed fruit)
31 potato dish
32 serving trolley
33 vegetable plate (*Am.* vegetable platter)
34 toast
35 cheeseboard
36 butter dish
37 open sandwich
38 filling
39 sandwich
40 fruit bowl
41 almonds (*also:* potato crisps, peanuts)
42 oil and vinegar bottle
43 ketchup (catchup, catsup)
44 sideboard
45 electric hotplate
46 corkscrew
47 crown cork bottle opener (crown cork opener), a bottle opener

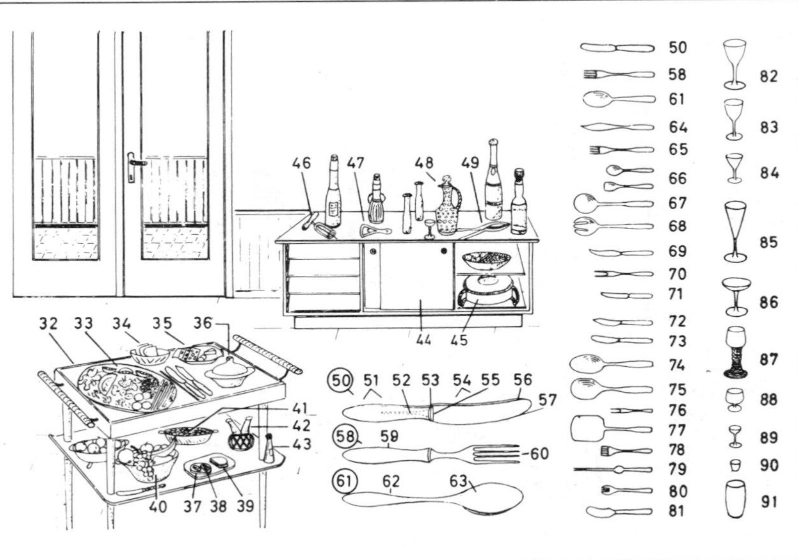

48 liqueur decanter
49 nutcrackers (nutcracker)
50 knife
51 handle
52 tang (tongue)
53 ferrule
54 blade
55 bolster
56 back
57 edge (cutting edge)
58 fork
59 handle
60 prong (tang, tine)
61 spoon; *here:* dessert spoon, soup spoon
62 handle
63 bowl
64 fish knife
65 fish fork
66 dessert spoon (fruit spoon)
67 salad spoon
68 salad fork
69, 70 carving set (serving cutlery)
69 carving knife
70 serving fork
71 fruit knife
72 cheese knife
73 butter knife
74 vegetable spoon, a serving spoon
75 potato server (serving spoon for potatoes)
76 cocktail fork
77 asparagus server (asparagus slice)
78 sardine server
79 lobster fork
80 oyster fork
81 caviare knife
82 white wine glass
83 red wine glass
84 sherry glass (madeira glass)
85, 86 champagne glasses
85 tapered glass
86 champagne glass, a crystal glass
87 rummer
88 brandy glass
89 liqueur glass
90 spirit glass
91 beer glass

46 Flat (Apartment)

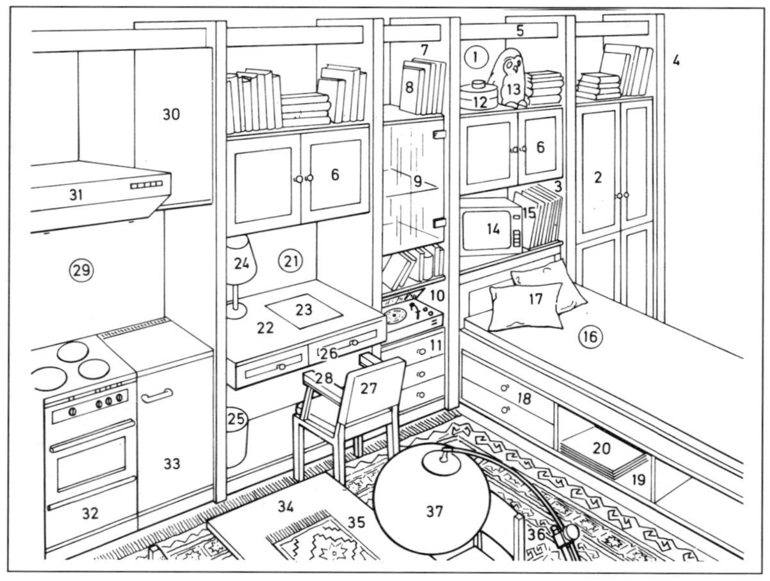

1 wall units (shelf units)
2 wardrobe door (*Am.* clothes closet door)
3 body
4 side wall
5 trim
6 two-door cupboard unit
7 bookshelf unit (bookcase unit) [with glass door]
8 books
9 display cabinet
10 record player
11 drawer
12 decorative biscuit tin
13 soft toy animal
14 television set (TV set)
15 records (discs)
16 bed unit
17 scatter cushion
18 bed unit drawer
19 bed unit shelf
20 magazines
21 desk unit (writing unit)
22 desk
23 desk mat (blotter)
24 table lamp
25 wastepaper basket
26 desk drawer
27 desk chair
28 arm
29 kitchen unit
30 wall cupboard
31 cooker hood
32 electric cooker
33 refrigerator (fridge, *Am.* icebox)
34 dining table
35 table runner
36 oriental carpet
37 standard lamp

1 children's bed, a bunk bed
2 storage box
3 mattress
4 pillow
5 ladder
6 soft toy elephant, a cuddly toy animal
7 soft toy dog
8 cushion
9 fashion doll
10 doll's pram
11 sleeping doll
12 canopy
13 blackboard
14 counting beads
15 toy horse for rocking and pulling
16 rockers
17 children's book
18 compendium of games
19 ludo
20 chessboard
21 children's cupboard
22 linen drawer
23 drop-flap writing surface
24 notebook (exercise book)
25 school books
26 pencil (*also:* crayon, felt tip pen, ballpoint pen)
27 toy shop
28 counter
29 spice rack
30 display
31 assortment of sweets (*Am.* candies)
32 bag of sweets (*Am.* candies)
33 scales
34 cash register
35 toy telephone
36 shop shelves (goods shelves)
37 wooden train set
38 dump truck, a toy lorry (toy truck)
39 tower crane
40 concrete mixer
41 large soft toy dog
42 dice cup

48 Kindergarten (Day Nursery)

1-20 pre-school education (nursery education)
1 nursery teacher
2 nursery child
3 handicraft
4 glue
5 watercolour (*Am.* watercolor) painting
6 paintbox
7 paintbrush
8 glass of water
9 jigsaw puzzle (puzzle)
10 jigsaw puzzle piece
11 coloured (*Am.* colored) pencils (wax crayons)
12 modelling (*Am.* modeling) clay (Plasticine)
13 clay figures (Plasticine figures)
14 modelling (*Am.* modeling) board
15 chalk (blackboard chalk)
16 blackboard
17 counting blocks
18 felt pen (felt tip pen)
19 shapes game
20 group of players
21-32 toys
21 building and filling cubes
22 construction set
23 children's books
24 doll's pram, a wicker pram
25 baby doll
26 canopy
27 building bricks (building blocks)
28 wooden model building
29 wooden train set
30 rocking teddy bear
31 doll's pushchair
32 fashion doll
33 child of nursery school age
34 cloakroom

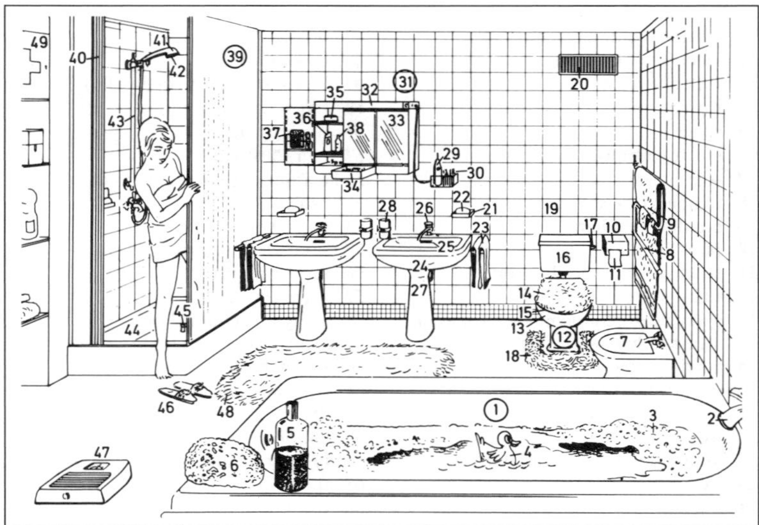

1 bath
2 mixer tap (*Am.* mixing faucet) for hot and cold water
3 foam bath (bubble bath)
4 toy duck
5 bath salts
6 bath sponge (sponge)
7 bidet
8 towel rail
9 terry towel
10 toilet roll holder (*Am.* bathroom tissue holder)
11 toilet paper (*coll.* loo paper, *Am.* bathroom tissue)
12 toilet (lavatory, W.C., *coll.* loo)
13 toilet pan (toilet bowl)
14 toilet lid with terry cover
15 toilet seat
16 cistern
17 flushing lever
18 pedestal mat
19 tile
20 ventilator (extraction vent)
21 soap dish
22 soap
23 hand towel
24 washbasin
25 overflow
26 hot and cold water tap
27 washbasin pedestal with trap (anti-syphon trap)
28 tooth glass (tooth mug)
29 electric toothbrush
30 detachable brush heads
31 mirrored bathroom cabinet
32 fluorescent lamp
33 mirror
34 drawer
35 powder box
36 mouthwash
37 electric shaver
38 aftershave lotion
39 shower cubicle
40 shower curtain
41 adjustable shower head
42 shower nozzle
43 shower adjustment rail
44 shower base
45 waste pipe
46 bathroom mule
47 bathroom scales
48 bath mat
49 medicine cabinet

50 Household Appliances and Utensils

1-20 irons
1 electric ironing machine
2 electric foot switch
3 roller covering
4 ironing head
5 sheet
6 electric iron (lightweight iron)
7 sole-plate
8 temperature selector
9 handle (iron handle)
10 pilot light
11 steam, spray, and dry iron
12 filling inlet
13 spray nozzle for damping the washing
14 steam hole (steam slit)
15 ironing table
16 ironing board (ironing surface)
17 ironing-board cover
18 iron well
19 aluminium (*Am.* aluminum) frame
20 sleeve board
21 linen bin
22 dirty linen
23-34 washing machines and driers
23 automatic washing machine
24 washing drum
25 safety latch (safety catch)
26 program selector control
27 front soap dispenser [with several compartments]
28 tumble drier
29 drum
30 front door with ventilation slits
31 worktop
32 airer
33 clothes line (washing line)
34 extending airer
35 stepladder (steps), an aluminium (*Am.* aluminum) ladder
36 stile
37 prop
38 tread (rung)
39-43 shoe care utensils
39 tin of shoe polish
40 shoe spray, an impregnating spray
41 shoe brush
42 brush for applying polish
43 tube of shoe polish
44 clothes brush
45 carpet brush
46 broom
47 bristles
48 broom head
49 broomstick (broom handle)
50 screw thread
51 washing-up brush
52 pan (dustpan)
53-86 floor and carpet cleaning
53 brush
54 bucket (pail)
55 floor cloth (cleaning rag)
56 scrubbing brush
57 carpet sweeper
58 upright vacuum cleaner
59 changeover switch
60 swivel head
61 bag-full indicator
62 dust bag container
63 handle
64 tubular handle
65 flex hook
66 wound-up flex
67 all-purpose nozzle
68 cylinder vacuum cleaner
69 swivel coupling
70 extension tube
71 floor nozzle (*sim.:* carpet beater nozzle)
72 suction control
73 bag-full indicator
74 sliding fingertip suction control
75 hose (suction hose)
76 combined carpet sweeper and shampooer
77 electric lead (flex)
78 plug socket
79 carpet beater head (*sim.:* shampooing head, brush head)
80 all-purpose vacuum cleaner (wet and dry vacuum cleaner)
81 castor
82 motor unit
83 lid clip
84 coarse dirt hose
85 special accessory (special attachment) for coarse dirt
86 dust container
87 shopper (shopping trolley)

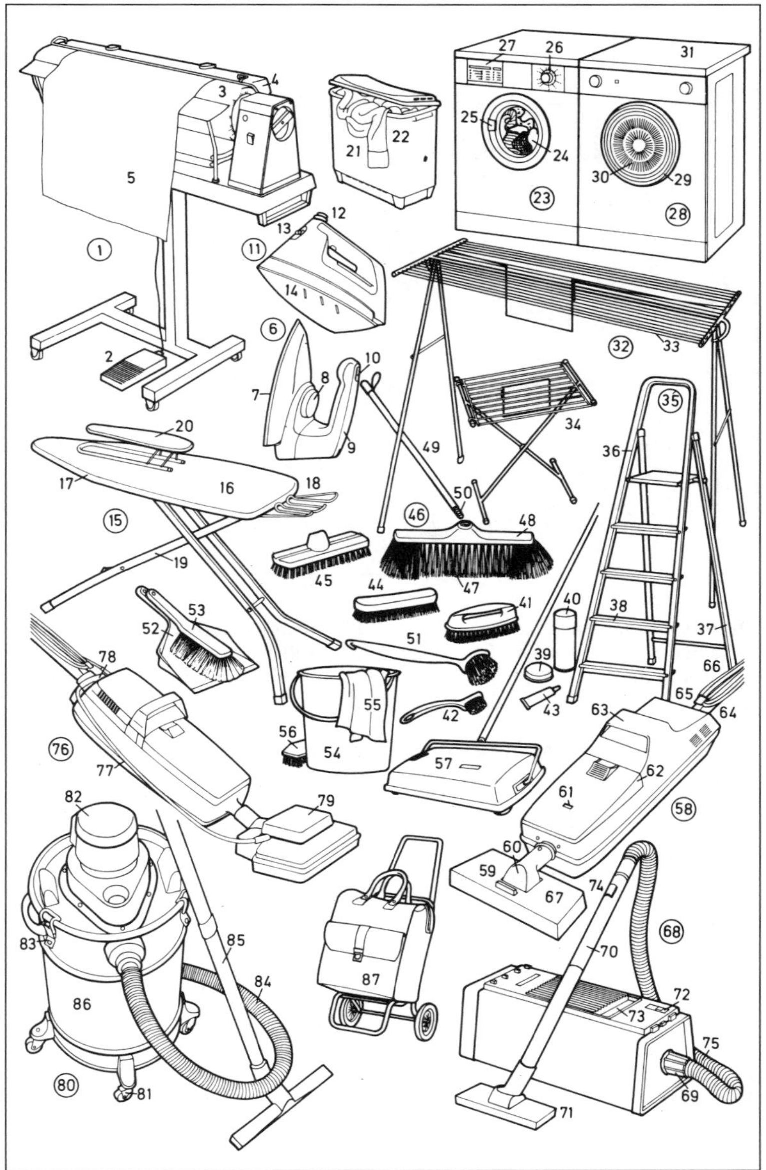
1
2
3
4
5
6
7
8
9
10
11
12
13
14
15
16
17
18
19
20
21
22
23
24
25
26
27
28
29
30
31
32
33
34
35
36
37
38
39
40
41
42
43
44
45
46
47
48
49
50
51
52
53
54
55
56
57
58
59
60
61
62
63
64
65
66
67
68
69
70
71
72
73
74
75
76
77
78
79
80
81
82
83
84
85
86
87

51 Flower Garden

1-35 flower garden

1 pergola

2 deck-chair

3 lawn rake (wire-tooth rake)

4 garden rake

5 Virginia creeper (American ivy, woodbine), a climbing plant (climber, creeper)

6 rockery (rock garden)

7 rock plants; *varieties:* stonecrop (wall pepper), houseleek, dryas, aubretia

8 pampas grass

9 garden hedge

10 blue spruce

11 hydrangeas

12 oak (oak tree)

13 birch (birch tree)

14 garden path

15 edging

16 garden pond

17 flagstone (stone slab)

18 water lily

19 tuberous begonias

20 dahlias

21 watering can (*Am.* sprinkling can)

22 weeding hoe

23 lupin

24 marguerites (oxeye daisies, white oxeye daisies)

25 standard rose

26 gerbera

27 iris

28 gladioli

29 chrysanthemums

30 poppy

31 blazing star

32 snapdragon (antirrhinum)

33 lawn

34 dandelion

35 sunflower

1-32 allotment (fruit and vegetable garden)
1, 2, 16, 17, 29 dwarf fruit trees (espaliers, espalier fruit trees)
1 quadruple cordon, a wall espalier
2 vertical cordon
3 tool shed (garden shed)
4 water butt (water barrel)
5 climbing plant (climber, creeper, rambler)
6 compost heap
7 sunflower
8 garden ladder (ladder)
9 perennial (flowering perennial)
10 garden fence (paling fence, paling)
11 standard berry tree
12 climbing rose (rambling rose) on the trellis arch
13 bush rose (standard rose tree)
14 summerhouse (garden house)
15 Chinese lantern (paper lantern)
16 pyramid tree (pyramidal tree, pyramid), a free-standing espalier
17 double horizontal cordon
18 flower bed, a border
19 berry bush (gooseberry bush, currant bush)
20 concrete edging
21 standard rose (standard rose tree)
22 border with perennials
23 garden path
24 allotment holder
25 asparagus patch (asparagus bed)
26 vegetable patch (vegetable plot)
27 scarecrow
28 runner bean (*Am.* scarlet runner), a bean plant on poles (bean poles)
29 horizontal cordon
30 standard fruit tree
31 tree stake
32 hedge

53 Indoor Plants (Houseplants)

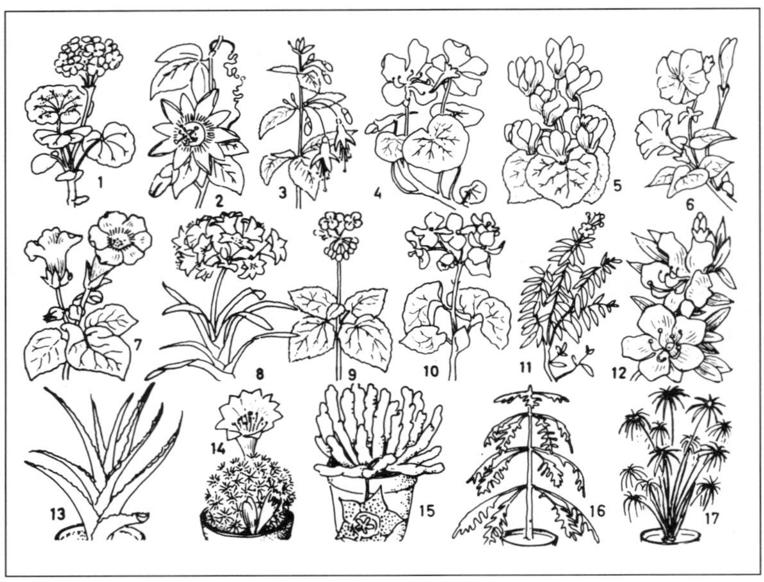

1 pelargonium (crane's bill), a geranium
2 passion flower (Passiflora), a climbing plant (climber, creeper)
3 fuchsia, an anagraceous plant
4 nasturtium (Indian cress, tropaeolum)
5 cyclamen, a primulaceous herb
6 petunia, a solanaceous herb
7 gloxinia (Sinningia), a gesneriaceous plant
8 Clivia minata, an amaryllis (narcissus)
9 African hemp (Sparmannia), a tiliaceous plant, a linden plant
10 begonia
11 myrtle (common myrtle, Myrtus)
12 azalea, an ericaceous plant
13 aloe, a liliaceous plant
14 globe thistle (Echinops)
15 stapelia (carrion flower), an asclepiadaceous plant
16 Norfolk Island Pine (an araucaria grown as an ornamental)
17 galingale, a cyperacious plant of the sedge family

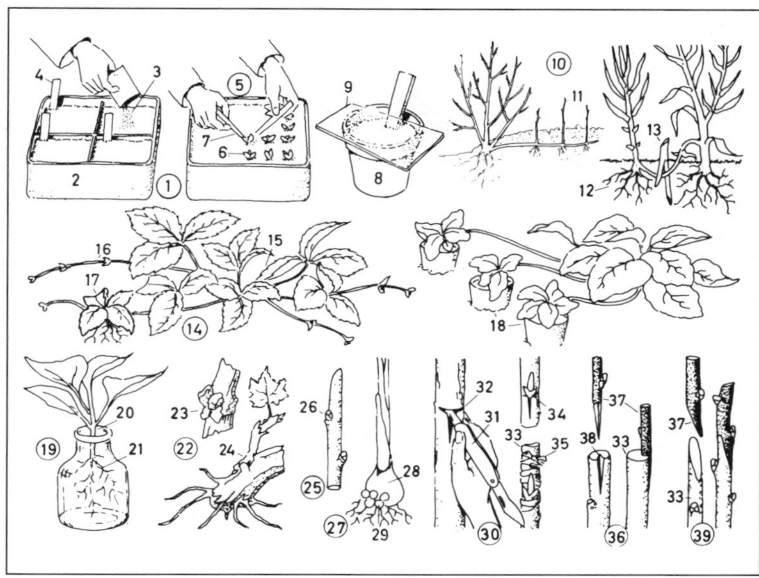

1 seed sowing (sowing)
2 seed pan
3 seed
4 label
5 pricking out (pricking off, transplanting)
6 seedling (seedling plant)
7 dibber (dibble)
8 flower pot (pot)
9 sheet of glass
10 propagation by layering
11 layer
12 layer with roots
13 forked stick used for fastening
14 propagation by runners
15 parent (parent plant)
16 runner
17 small rooted leaf cluster
18 setting in pots
19 cutting in water
20 cutting (slip, set)
21 root
22 bud cutting on vine tendril
23 scion bud, a bud
24 sprouting (shooting) cutting
25 stem cutting (hardwood cutting)
26 bud
27 propagation by bulbils (brood bud bulblets)
28 old bulb
29 bulbil (brood bud bulblet)
30-39 **grafting** (graftage)
30 budding; *here:* shield budding
31 budding knife
32 T-cut
33 support (stock, rootstock)
34 inserted scion bud
35 raffia layer (bast layer)
36 side grafting
37 scion (shoot)
38 wedge-shaped notch
39 splice grafting

55 Market Garden (*Am.* Truck Garden, Truck Farm)

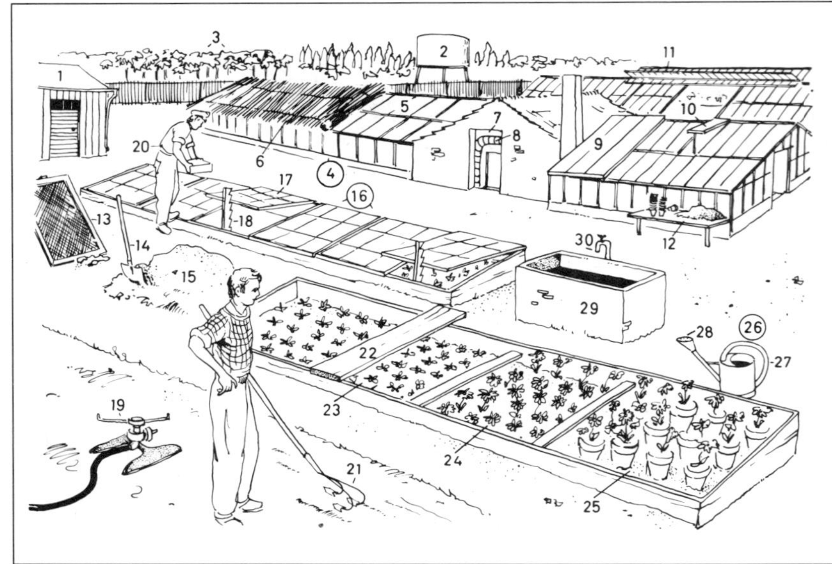

1-51 market garden (*Am.* truck garden, truck farm)
1 tool shed
2 water tower (water tank)
3 market garden (*Am.* truck garden, truck farm), a tree nursery
4 hothouse (forcing house, warm house)
5 glass roof
6 [roll of] matting (straw matting, reed matting, shading)
7 boiler room (boiler house)
8 heating pipe (pressure pipe)
9 shading panel (shutter)
10, 11 ventilators (vents)
10 ventilation window (window vent, hinged ventilator)
11 ridge vent
12 potting table (potting bench)
13 riddle (sieve, garden sieve, upright sieve)
14 garden shovel (shovel)
15 heap of earth (composted earth, prepared earth, garden mould, *Am.* mold)
16 hotbed (forcing bed, heated frame)
17 hotbed vent (frame vent)
18 vent prop
19 sprinkler (sprinkling device)
20 gardener (nursery gardener, grower, commercial grower)
21 cultivator (hand cultivator, grubber)
22 plank
23 pricked-out seedlings (pricked-off seedlings)
24 forced flowers [forcing]
25 potted plants (plants in pots, pot plants)
26 watering can (*Am.* sprinkling can)
27 handle
28 rose
29 water tank
30 water pipe

31 bale of peat
32 warm house (heated greenhouse)
33 cold house (unheated greenhouse)
34 wind generator
35 wind wheel
36 wind vane
37 shrub bed, a flower bed
38 hoop edging
39 vegetable plot
40 plastic tunnel (polythene greenhouse)
41 ventilation flap
42 central path
43 vegetable crate
44 tomato plant
45, 46 nursery hand
47 tub plant
48 tub
49 orange tree
50 wire basket
51 seedling box

56 Garden Tools

1 dibber (dibble)
2 spade
3 lawn rake (wire-tooth rake)
4 rake
5 ridging hoe
6 trowel
7 combined hoe and fork
8 sickle
9 gardener's knife (pruning knife, billhook)
10 asparagus cutter (asparagus knife)
11 tree pruner (long-handled pruner)
12 semi-automatic spade
13 three-pronged cultivator
14 tree scraper (bark scraper)
15 lawn aerator (aerator)
16 pruning saw (saw for cutting branches)
17 battery-operated hedge trimmer
18 motor cultivator
19 electric drill
20 gear
21 cultivator attachment
22 fruit picker
23 tree brush (bark brush)
24 sprayer for pest control
25 lance
26 hose reel (reel and carrying cart)
27 garden hose
28 motor lawn mower (motor mower)
29 grassbox
30 two-stroke motor
31 electric lawn mower (electric mower)
32 electric lead (electric cable)
33 cutting unit
34 hand mower
35 cutting cylinder
36 blade
37 riding mower
38 brake lock
39 electric starter
40 brake pedal
41 cutting unit
42 tip-up trailer
43 revolving sprinkler, a lawn sprinkler
44 revolving nozzle
45 hose connector
46 oscillating sprinkler
47 wheelbarrow
48 grass shears
49 hedge shears
50 secateurs (pruning shears)

1
2
3
4
5
6
7
8
9
10
11
12
13
14
15
16
17
18
19
20
21
22
23
24
25
26
27
28
29
30
31
32
33
34
35
36
37
38
39
40
41
42
43
44
45
46
47
48
49
50

57 Vegetables (Vegetable Plants)

1-11 leguminous plants (Leguminosae)
1 pea, a plant with a papilionaceous corola
2 pea flower
3 pinnate leaf
4 pea tendril, a leaf tendril
5 stipule
6 legume (pod), a seed vessel (pericarp, legume)
7 pea [seed]
8 bean plant (bean), a climbing plant (climber, creeper); *varieties:* broad bean (runner bean, *Am.* scarlet runner), climbing bean (climber, pole bean), scarlet runner bean; *smaller:* dwarf French bean (bush bean)
9 bean flower
10 twining beanstalk
11 bean [pod with seeds]
12 tomato
13 cucumber
14 asparagus
15 radish
16 white radish
17 carrot
18 stump-rooted carrot
19 parsley
20 horse-radish
21 leeks
22 chives
23 pumpkin (*Am.* squash); *sim.:* melon
24 onion
25 onion skin
26 kohlrabi
27 celeriac
28-34 brassicas (leaf vegetables)
28 chard (Swiss chard, seakale beet)
29 spinach
30 Brussels sprouts (sprouts)
31 cauliflower
32 cabbage (round cabbage, head of cabbage), a brassica; *cultivated races (cultivars):* green cabbage, red cabbage
33 savoy (savoy cabbage)
34 kale (curly kale, kail), a winter green
35 scorzonera (black salsify)
36-40 salad plants
36 lettuce (cabbage lettuce, head of lettuce)
37 lettuce leaf
38 corn salad (lamb's lettuce)
39 endive (endive leaves)
40 chicory (succory, salad chicory)
41 globe artichoke
42 sweet pepper (Spanish paprika)

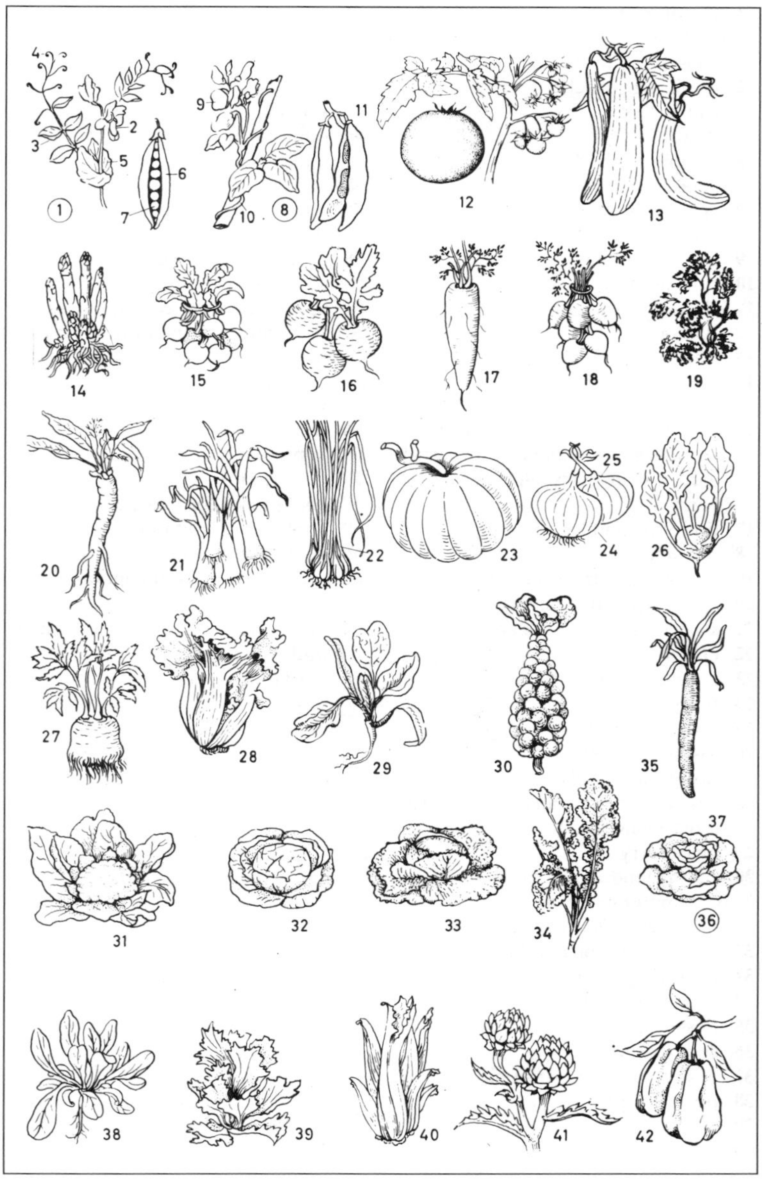
1
2
3
4
5
6
7
8
9
10
11
12
13
14
15
16
17
18
19
20
21
22
23
24
25
26
27
28
29
30
31
32
33
34
35
36
37
38
39
40
41
42

58 Soft Fruit and Pomes

1-30 soft fruit (berry bushes)
1-15 Ribes
1 gooseberry bush
2 flowering gooseberry cane
3 leaf
4 flower
5 magpie moth larva
6 gooseberry flower
7 epigynous ovary
8 calyx (sepals)
9 gooseberry, a berry
10 currant bush
11 cluster of berries
12 currant
13 stalk
14 flowering cane of the currant
15 raceme
16 strawberry plant; *varieties:* wild strawberry (woodland strawberry), garden strawberry, alpine strawberry
17 flowering and fruit-bearing plant
18 rhizome
19 ternate leaf (trifoliate leaf)
20 runner (prostrate stem)
21 strawberry, a pseudocarp
22 epicalyx
23 achene (seed)
24 flesh (pulp)
25 raspberry bush
26 raspberry flower
27 flower bud (bud)
28 fruit (raspberry), an aggregate fruit (compound fruit)
29 blackberry
30 thorny tendril
31-61 pomiferous plants
31 pear tree; *wild:* wild pear tree
32 flowering branch of the pear tree
33 pear [longitudinal section]
34 pear stalk (stalk)
35 flesh (pulp)
36 core (carpels)
37 pear pip (seed), a fruit pip
38 pear blossom
39 ovules
40 ovary
41 stigma
42 style
43 petal
44 sepal
45 stamen
46 quince tree
47 quince leaf
48 stipule
49 apple-shaped quince [longitudinal section]
50 pear-shaped quince [longitudinal section]
51 apple tree; *wild:* crab apple tree
52 flowering branch of the apple tree
53 leaf
54 apple blossom
55 withered flower
56 apple [longitudinal section]
57 apple skin
58 flesh (pulp)
59 core (apple core, carpels)
60 apple pip, a fruit pip
61 apple stalk (stalk)
62 codling moth (codlin moth)
63 burrow (tunnel)
64 larva (grub, caterpillar) of a small moth
65 wormhole

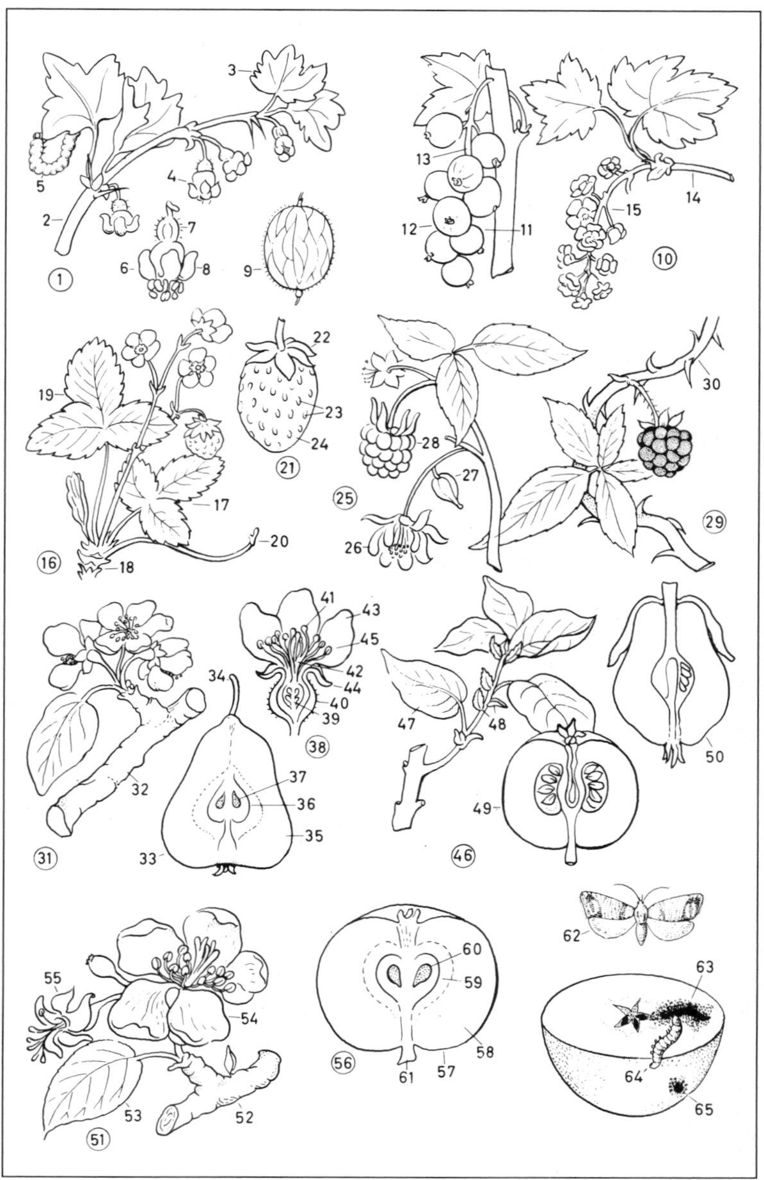
3
5
4
2
7
6
8
9
1
13
14
15
12
11
10
22
19
23
24
21
28
27
17
25
20
26
16
18
30
29
41
43
45
42
44
40
39
38
34
32
37
36
35
31
33
47
48
49
46
50
62
60
59
58
56
61
57
63
64
65
55
54
53
52
51

59 Drupes and Nuts

1-36 drupes (drupaceous plants)
1-18 cherry tree
1 flowering branch of the cherry tree (branch of the cherry tree in blossom)
2 cherry leaf
3 cherry flower (cherry blossom)
4 peduncle (pedicel, flower stalk)
5 cherry; *varieties:* sweet cherry (heart cherry), wild cherry (bird cherry), sour cherry, morello cherry (morello)
6-8 cherry (cherry fruit) [cross section]
6 flesh (pulp)
7 cherry stone
8 seed
9 flower (blossom) [cross section]
10 stamen
11 petal
12 sepal
13 pistil
14 ovule enclosed in perigynous ovary
15 style
16 stigma
17 leaf
18 nectary (honey gland)
19-23 plum tree
19 fruit-bearing branch
20 oval, black-skinned plum
21 plum leaf
22 bud
23 plum stone
24 greengage
25 mirabelle (transparent gage), a plum
26-32 peach tree
26 flowering branch (branch in blossom)
27 peach flower (peach blossom)
28 flower shoot
29 young leaf (sprouting leaf)
30 fruiting branch
31 peach
32 peach leaf
33-36 apricot tree
33 flowering apricot branch (apricot branch in blossom)
34 apricot flower (apricot blossom)
35 apricot
36 apricot leaf
37-51 nuts
37-43 walnut tree
37 flowering branch of the walnut tree
38 female flower
39 male inflorescence (male flowers, catkins with stamens)
40 alternate pinnate leaf
41 walnut, a drupe (stone fruit)
42 soft shell (cupule)
43 walnut, a drupe (stone fruit)
44-51 hazel tree (hazel bush), an anemophilous shrub (a wind-pollinating shrub)
44 flowering hazel branch
45 male catkin
46 female inflorescence
47 leaf bud
48 fruit-bearing branch
49 hazelnut (hazel, cobnut, cob), a drupe (stone fruit)
50 involucre (husk)
51 hazel leaf

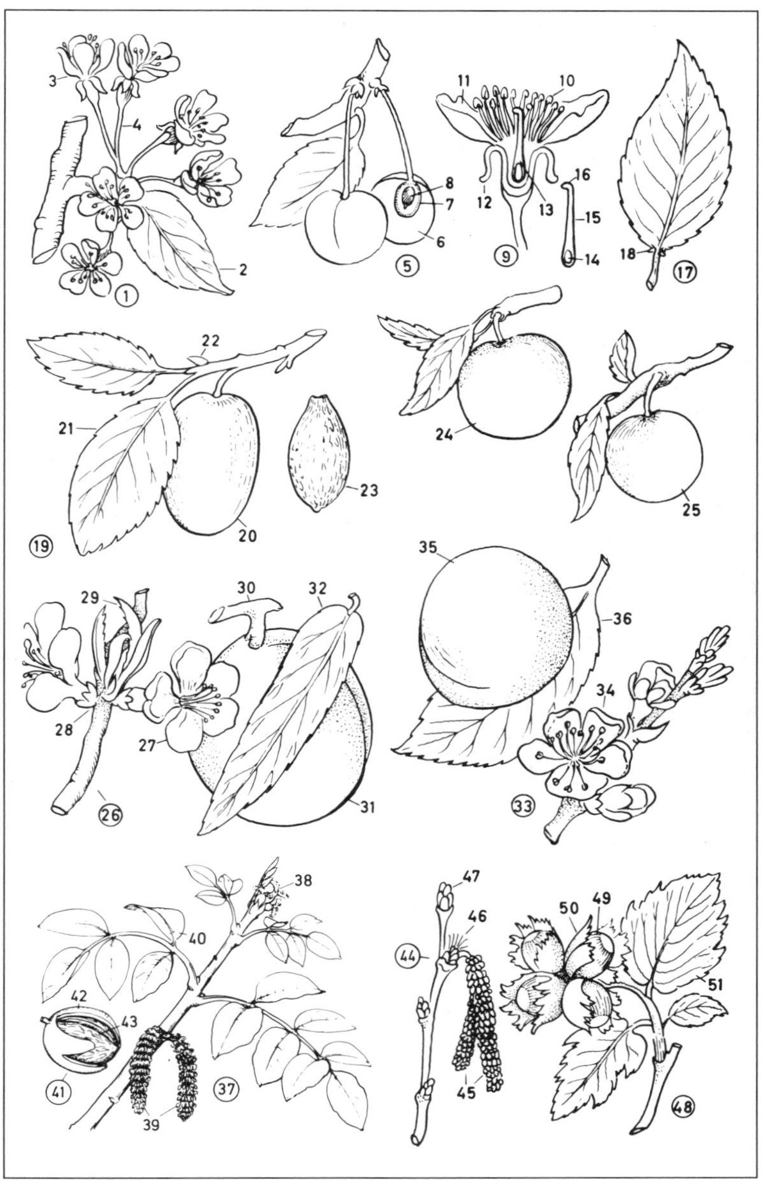
1
2
3
4
5
6
7
8
9
10
11
12
13
14
15
16
17
18
19
20
21
22
23
24
25
26
27
28
29
30
31
32
33
34
35
36
37
38
39
40
41
42
43
44
45
46
47
48
49
50
51

60 Garden Flowers

1 snowdrop (spring snowflake)
2 garden pansy (heartsease pansy), a pansy
3 trumpet narcissus (trumpet daffodil, Lent lily), a narcissus
4 poet's narcissus (pheasant's eye, poet's daffodil); *sim.:* polyanthus narcissus
5 bleeding heart (lyre flower), a fumariaceous flower
6 sweet william (bunch pink), a carnation
7 gillyflower (gilliflower, clove pink, clove carnation)
8 yellow flag (yellow water flag, yellow iris), an iris
9 tuberose
10 columbine (aquilegia)
11 gladiolus (sword lily)
12 Madonna lily (Annunciation lily, Lent lily), a lily
13 larkspur (delphinium), a ranunculaceous plant
14 moss pink (moss phlox), a phlox
15 garden rose (China rose)
16 rosebud, a bud
17 double rose
18 rose thorn, a thorn
19 gaillardia
20 African marigold (tagetes)
21 love-lies-bleeding, an amaranthine flower
22 zinnia
23 pompon dahlia, a dahlia

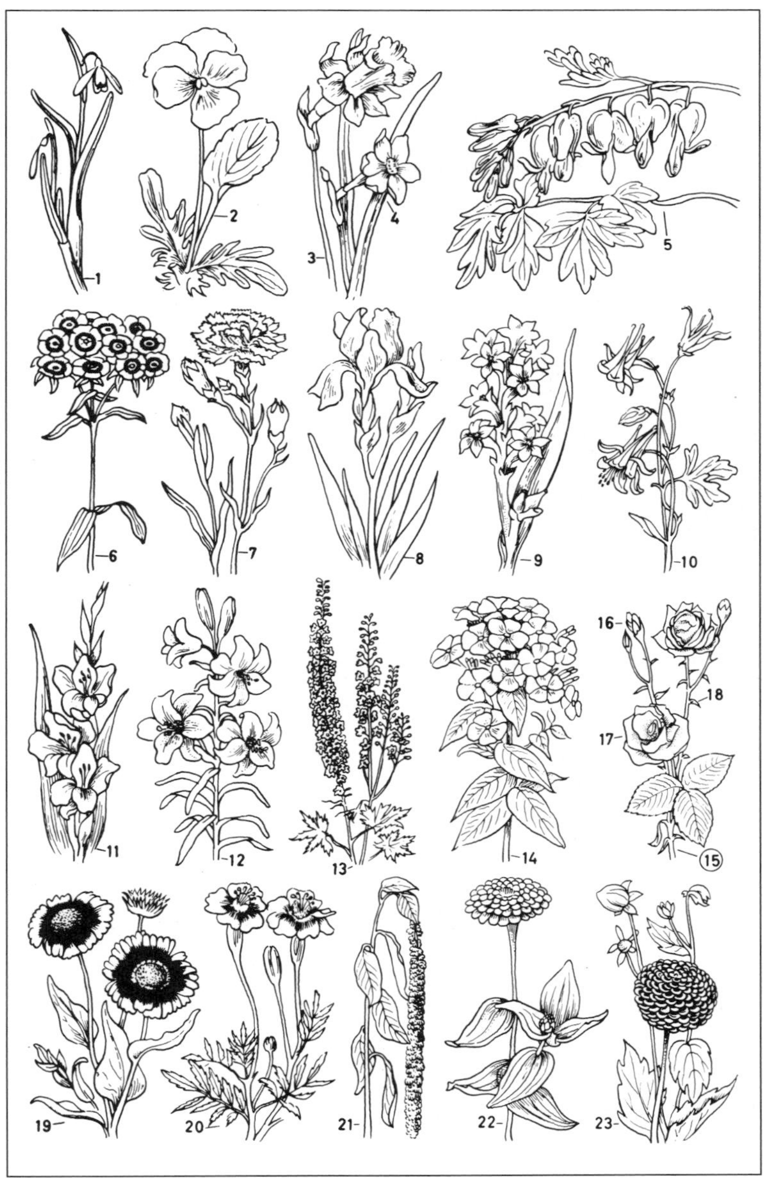
1
2
3
4
5
6
7
8
9
10
11
12
13
14
15
16
17
18
19
20
21
22
23

61 Weeds

1 corn flower (bluebottle), a centaury
2 corn poppy (field poppy), a poppy
3 bud
4 poppy flower
5 seed capsule containing poppy seeds
6 corn cockle (corn campion, crown-of-the-field)
7 corn marigold (field marigold), a chrysanthemum
8 corn camomile (field camomile, camomile, chamomile)
9 shepherd's purse
10 flower
11 fruit (pouch-shaped pod)
12 common groundsel
13 dandelion
14 flower head (capitulum)
15 infructescence
16 hedge mustard, a mustard
17 stonecrop
18 wild mustard (charlock, runch)
19 flower
20 fruit, a siliqua (pod)
21 wild radish (jointed charlock)
22 flower
23 fruit (siliqua, pod)
24 common orache (common orach)
25 goosefoot
26 field bindweed (wild morning glory), a bindweed
27 scarlet pimpernel (shepherd's weatherglass, poor man's weather-glass, eye-bright)
28 wild barley (wall barley)
29 wild oat
30 common couch grass (couch, quack grass, quick grass, quitch grass, scutch grass, twitch grass, witch-grass); *sim.:* bearded couch grass, sea couch grass
31 gallant soldier
32 field eryngo (Watling Street thistle), a thistle
33 stinging nettle, a nettle

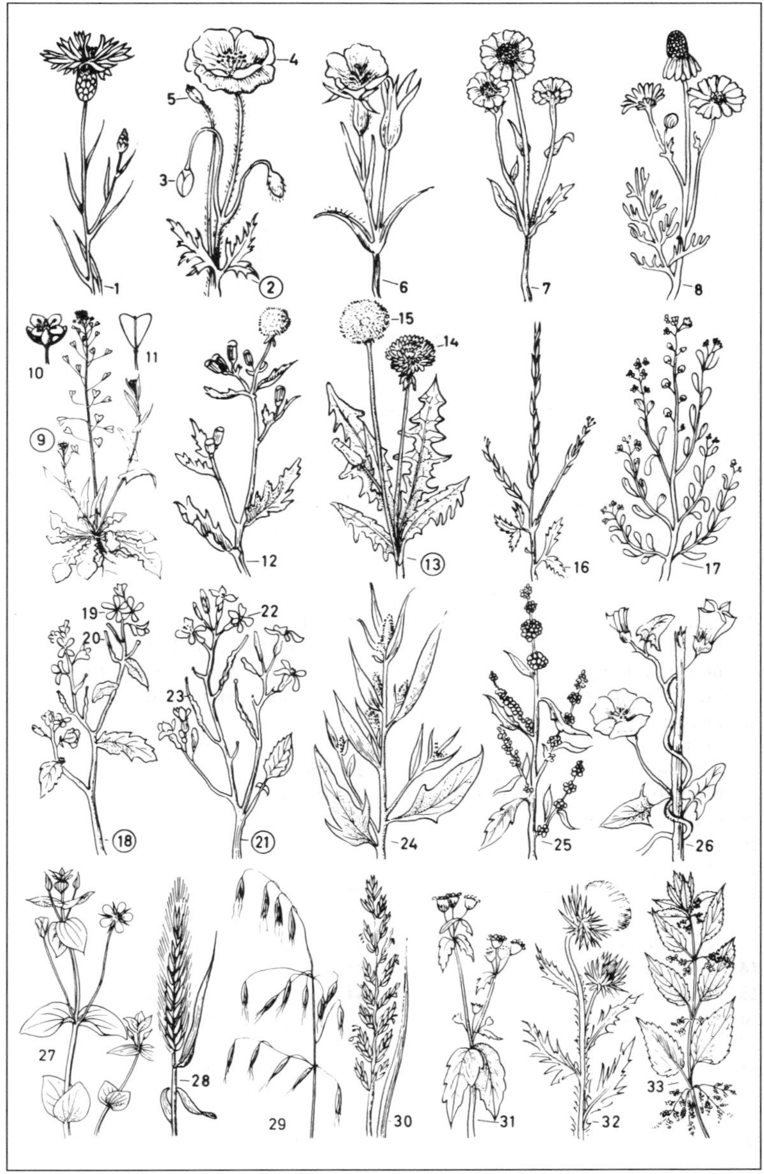
1
2
3
4
5
6
7
8
9
10
11
12
13
14
15
16
17
18
19
20
21
22
23
24
25
26
27
28
29
30
31
32
33

62 Farm Buildings (*Am.* Farmstead)

1 house
2 stable
3 house cat (cat)
4 farmer's wife
5 broom
6 farmer
7 cowshed
8 pigsty (sty, *Am.* pigpen, hogpen)
9 outdoor trough
10 pig
11 above-ground silo (fodder silo)
12 silo pipe (standpipe for filling the silo)
13 liquid manure silo
14 outhouse
15 machinery shed
16 sliding door
17 door to the workshop
18 three-way tip-cart, a transport vehicle
19 tipping cylinder
20 shafts
21 manure spreader (fertilizer spreader, manure distributor)
22 spreader unit (distributor unit)
23 spreader cylinder (distributor cylinder)
24 movable scraper floor
25 side planking (side board)
26 wire mesh front
27 sprinkler cart
28 sprinkler stand
29 sprinkler, a revolving sprinkler
30 sprinkler hoses
31 farmyard
32 watchdog
33 calf
34 dairy cow (milch-cow, milker)
35 farmyard hedge
36 chicken
37 cock (*Am.* rooster)
38 tractor
39 tractor driver
40 all-purpose trailer

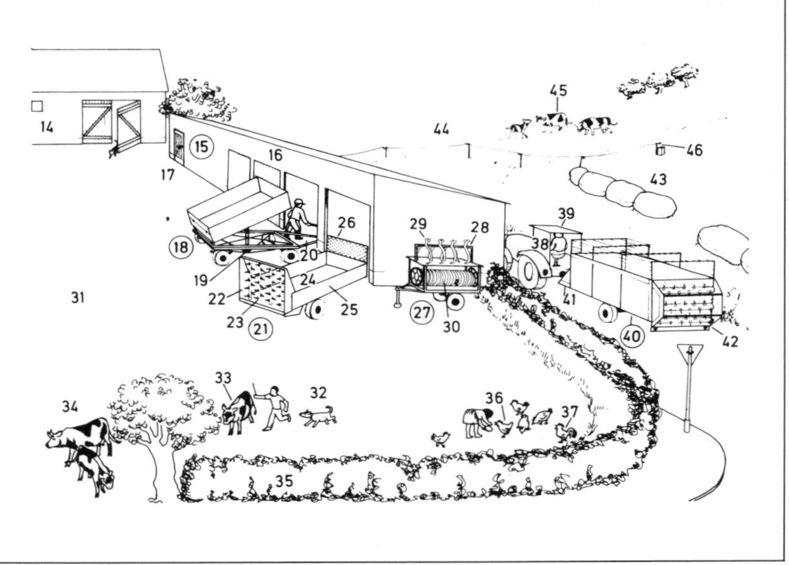

41 [folded] pick-up attachment
42 unloading unit
43 polythene silo, a fodder silo
44 meadow
45 grazing cattle
46 electrified fence

63 Agriculture (Farming)

1-41 work in the fields
1 fallow (fallow field, fallow ground)
2 boundary stone
3 boundary ridge, a balk (baulk)
4 field
5 swingletree (*Am.* whiffletree, whippletree)
6 plough (*Am.* plow)
7 clod
8 furrow
9 stone
10-12 sowing
10 sower
11 seedlip
12 seed corn (seed)
13 field guard
14 chemical fertilizer (artificial fertilizer); *kinds:* potash fertilizer, phosphoric acid fertilizer, lime fertilizer, nitrogen fertilizer
15 cartload of manure (farmyard manure, dung)
16 oxteam (team of oxen, *Am.* span of oxen)
17 fields (farmland)
18 farm track (farm road)
19-30 **hay harvest** (haymaking)
19 rotary mower with swather (swath reaper)
20 connecting shaft (connecting rod)
21 power take-off (power take-off shaft)
22 meadow
23 swath (swathe)
24 tedder (rotary tedder)
25 tedded hay
26 rotary swather
27 trailer with pick-up attachment
28 fence rack (rickstand), a drying rack for hay
29 rickstand, a drying rack for hay
30 hay tripod
31-41 grain harvest and seedbed preparation
31 combine harvester
32 cornfield
33 stubble field
34 bale of straw
35 straw baler (straw press), a high-pressure baler
36 swath (swathe) of straw (windrow of straw)
37 hydraulic bale loader
38 trailer
39 manure spreader
40 four-furrow plough (*Am.* plow)
41 combination seed-harrow

1
2
3
4
5
6
7
8
9
10
11
12
13
14
15
16
17
18
19
20
21
22
23
24
25
26
27
28
29
30
31
32
33
34
35
36
37
38
39
40
41

64 Agricultural Machinery I

1-33 combine harvester (combine)
1 divider
2 grain lifter
3 cutter bar
4 pick-up reel, a spring-tine reel
5 reel gearing
6 auger
7 chain and slat elevator
8 hydraulic cylinder for adjusting the cutting unit
9 stone catcher (stone trap)
10 awner
11 concave
12 threshing drum (drum)
13 revolving beater [for freeing straw from the drum and preparing it for the shakers]
14 straw shaker (strawwalker)
15 fan for compressed-air winnowing
16 preparation level
17 louvred-type sieve
18 sieve extension
19 shoe sieve (reciprocating sieve)
20 grain auger
21 tailings auger
22 tailings outlet
23 grain tank
24 grain tank auger
25 augers feeding to the grain tank unloader
26 grain unloader spout
27 observation ports for checking tank contents
28 six-cylinder diesel engine
29 hydraulic pump with oil reservoir
30 driving axle gearing
31 driving wheel tyre (*Am.* tire)
32 rubber-tyred (*Am.* rubber-tired) wheel on the steering axle
33 driver's position
34-39 self-propelled forage harvester (self-propelled field chopper)
34 cutting drum (chopper drum)
35 corn head
36 cab (driver's cab)
37 swivel-mounted spout (discharge pipe)
38 exhaust
39 rear-wheel steering system
40-45 rotary swather
40 cardan shaft
41 running wheel
42 double spring tine
43 crank
44 swath rake
45 three-point linkage
46-58 rotary tedder
46 tractor
47 draw bar
48 cardan shaft
49 power take-off (power take-off shaft)
50 gearing (gears)
51 frame bar
52 rotating head
53 tine bar
54 double spring tine
55 guard rail
56 running wheel
57 height adjustment crank
58 wheel adjustment
59-84 potato harvester
59 control levers for the lifters of the digger and the hopper and for adjusting the shaft
60 adjustable hitch
61 drawbar
62 drawbar support
63 cardan shaft connection
64 press roller
65 gearing (gears) for the hydraulic system
66 disc (disk) coulter (*Am.* colter) (rolling coulter)
67 three-bladed share
68 disc (disk) coulter (*Am.* colter) drive
69 open-web elevator
70 agitator
71 multi-step reduction gearing
72 feeder
73 haulm stripper (flail rotor)
74 rotary elevating drum
75 mechanical tumbling separator
76 haulm conveyor with flexible haulm strippers
77 haulm conveyor agitator
78 haulm conveyor drive with V-belt
79 studded rubber belt for sorting vines, clods and stones
80 trash conveyor
81 sorting table
82 rubber-disc (rubber-disk) rollers for presorting
83 discharge conveyor
84 endless-floor hopper
85-96 beet harvester
85 topper
86 feeler
87 topping knife
88 feeler support wheel with depth adjustment
89 beet cleaner
90 haulm elevator
91 hydraulic pump
92 compressed-air reservoir
93 oil tank (oil reservoir)
94 tensioning device for the beet elevator
95 beet elevator belt
96 beet hopper

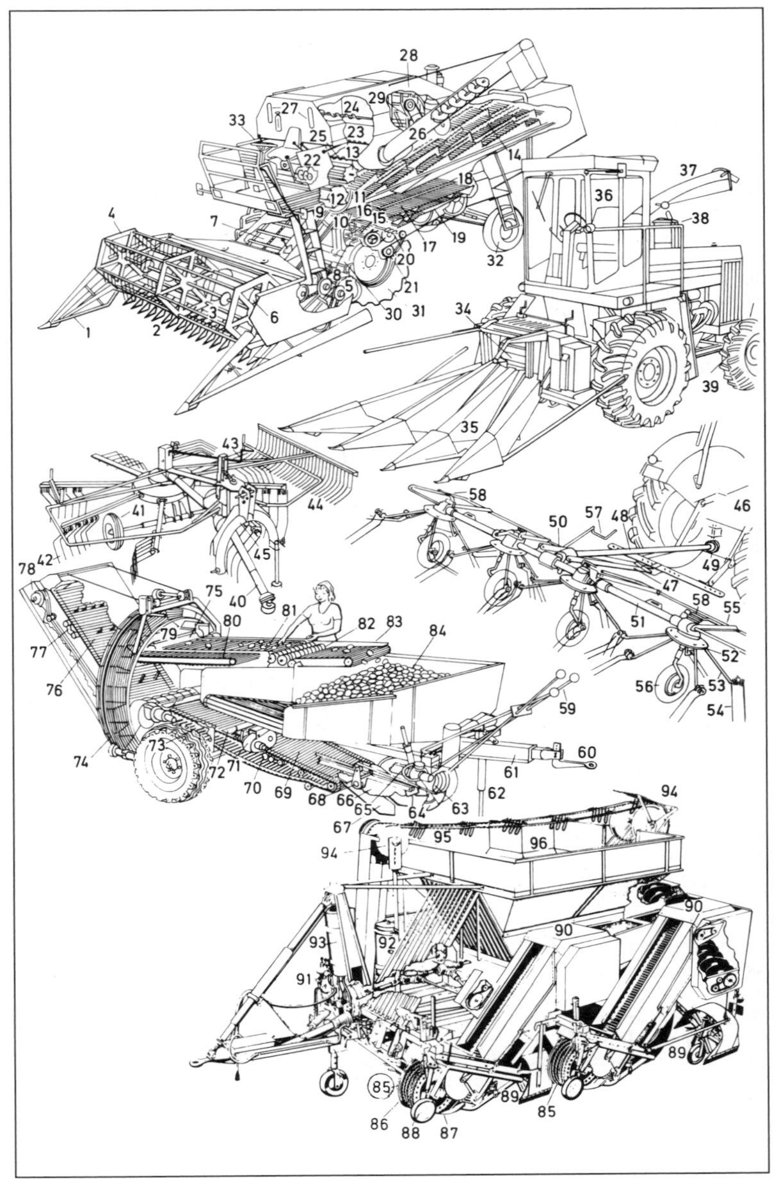
1
2
3
4
5
6
7
8
9
10
11
12
13
14
15
16
17
18
19
20
21
22
23
24
25
26
27
28
29
30
31
32
33
34
35
36
37
38
39
40
41
42
43
44
45
46
47
48
49
50
51
52
53
54
55
56
57
58
59
60
61
62
63
64
65
66
67
68
69
70
71
72
73
74
75
76
77
78
79
80
81
82
83
84
85
86
87
88
89
90
91
92
93
94
95
96

65 Agricultural Machinery II

1 **wheel plough** (*Am.* plow), a single-bottom plough *[form.]*
2 handle
3 plough (*Am.* plow) stilt (plough handle)
4-8 **plough (*Am.* plow) bottom**
4 mouldboard (*Am.* moldboard)
5 landside
6 sole (slade)
7 ploughshare (share, *Am.* plowshare)
8 frog (frame)
9 beam (plough beam, *Am.* plowbeam)
10 knife coulter (*Am.* colter), a coulter
11 skim coulter (*Am.* colter)
12 guide-chain crossbar
13 guide chain
14-19 **forecarriage**
14 adjustable yoke
15 land wheel
16 furrow wheel
17 hake chain
18 draught beam (drawbar)
19 hake
20 **tractor** (general-purpose tractor)
21 cab frame (roll bar)
22 seat
23 power take-off gear-change (gearshift)
24-29 **power lift**
24 ram piston
25 lifting rod adjustment
26 drawbar frame
27 top link
28 lower link
29 lifting rod
30 drawbar coupling
31 live power take-off (live power take-off shaft, take-off shaft)
32 differential gear (differential)
33 floating axle
34 torque converter lever
35 gear-change (gearshift)
36 multi-speed transmission
37 fluid clutch (fluid drive)
38 power take-off gear
39 main clutch
40 power take-off gear-change (gearshift) with power take-off clutch
41 hydraulic power steering and reversing gears
42 fuel tank
43 float lever
44 four-cylinder diesel engine
45 oil sump and pump for the pressure-feed lubrication system
46 fresh oil tank
47 track rod (*Am.* tie rod)
48 front axle pivot pin
49 front axle suspension
50 front coupling (front hitch)
51 radiator
52 fan
53 battery
54 oil bath air cleaner (oil bath air filter)
55 **cultivator** (grubber)
56 sectional frame
57 spring tine
58 share, a diamond-shaped share (*sim.:* chisel-shaped share)
59 depth wheel
60 depth adjustment
61 coupling (hitch)
62 **reversible plough** (*Am.* plow), a mounted plough
63 depth wheel
64-67 **plough** (*Am.* plow) **bottom,** a general-purpose plough bottom
64 mouldboard (*Am.* moldboard)
65 ploughshare (share, *Am.* plowshare), a pointed share
66 sole (slade)
67 landside
68 skim coulter (*Am.* colter)
69 disc (disk) coulter (*Am.* colter) (rolling coulter)
70 plough (*Am.* plow) frame
71 beam (plough beam, *Am.* plowbeam)
72 three-point linkage
73 swivel mechanism
74 **drill**
75 seed hopper
76 drill coulter (*Am.* colter)
77 delivery tube, a telescopic tube
78 feed mechanism
79 gearbox
80 drive wheel
81 track indicator
82 **disc (disk) harrow,** a semimounted implement
83 discs (disks) in X-configuration
84 plain disc (disk)
85 serrated-edge disc (disk)
86 quick hitch
87 **combination seed-harrow**
88 three-section spike-tooth harrow
89 three-section rotary harrow
90 frame

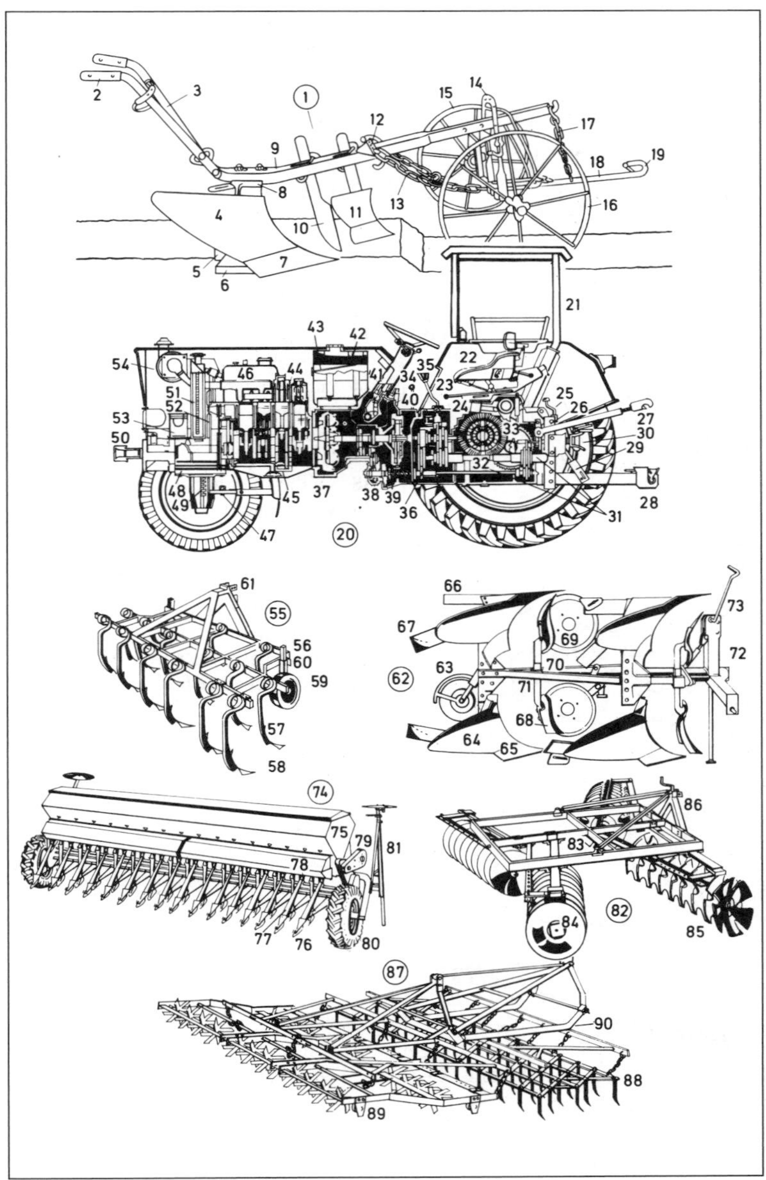
1
2
3
4
5
6
7
8
9
10
11
12
13
14
15
16
17
18
19
20
21
22
23
24
25
26
27
28
29
30
31
32
33
34
35
36
37
38
39
40
41
42
43
44
45
46
47
48
49
50
51
52
53
54
55
56
57
58
59
60
61
62
63
64
65
66
67
68
69
70
71
72
73
74
75
76
77
78
79
80
81
82
83
84
85
86
87
88
89
90

66 Agricultural Implements

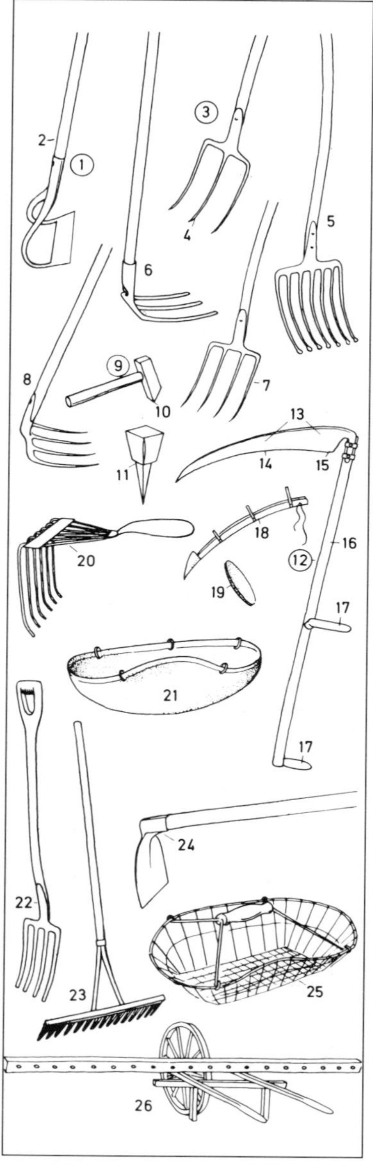

1 draw hoe (garden hoe)
2 hoe handle
3 three-pronged (three-tined) hay fork (fork)
4 prong (tine)
5 potato fork
6 potato hook
7 four-pronged (four-tined) manure fork (fork)
8 manure hoe
9 whetting hammer [for scythes]
10 peen (pane)
11 whetting anvil [for scythes]
12 scythe
13 scythe blade
14 cutting edge
15 heel
16 snath (snathe, snead, sneath)
17 handle
18 scythe sheath
19 whetstone (scythestone)
20 potato rake
21 potato planter
22 digging fork (fork)
23 wooden rake (rake, hayrake)
24 hoe (potato hoe)
25 potato basket, a wire basket
26 clover broadcaster

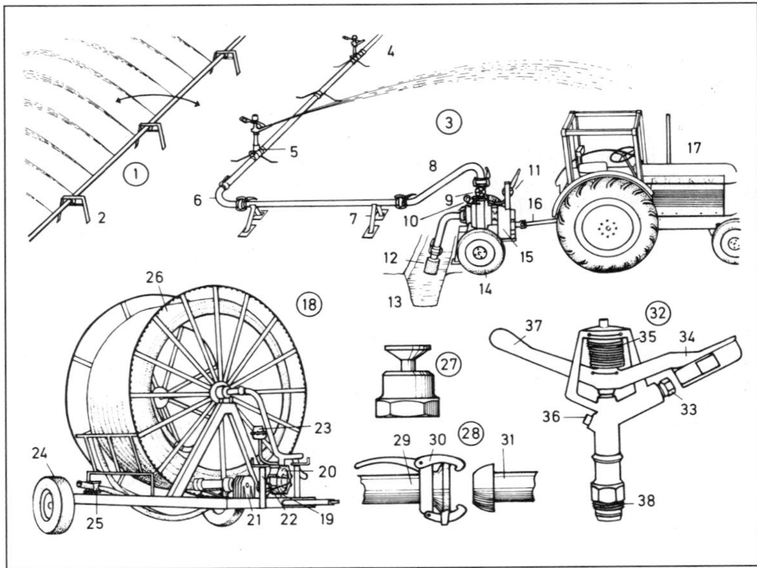

1 oscillating spray line
2 stand (steel chair)
3 portable irrigation system
4 revolving sprinkler
5 standpipe coupler
6 elbow with cardan joint (cardan coupling)
7 pipe support (trestle)
8 pump connection
9 delivery valve
10 pressure gauge (*Am.* gage) (manometer)
11 centrifugal evacuating pump
12 basket strainer
13 channel
14 chassis of the p.t.o.-driven pump (power take-off-driven pump)
15 p.t.o.-driven (power take-off-driven) pump
16 cardan shaft
17 tractor
18 long-range irrigation unit
19 drive connection
20 turbine
21 gearing (gears)
22 adjustable support
23 centrifugal evacuating pump
24 wheel
25 pipe support
26 polyester pipe
27 sprinkler nozzle
28 quick-fitting pipe connection with cardan joint
29 M-cardan
30 clamp
31 V-cardan
32 revolving sprinkler, a field sprinkler
33 nozzle
34 breaker
35 breaker spring
36 stopper
37 counterweight
38 thread

68 Arable Crops

1-47 arable crops (agricultural produce, farm produce)
1-37 varieties of grain (grain, cereals, farinaceous plants, bread-corn)
1 rye (*also:* corn, 'corn' often meaning the main cereal of a country or region; in Northern Germany: rye; in Southern Germany and Italy: wheat; in Sweden: barley; in Scotland: oats; in North America: maize; in China: rice)
2 ear of rye, a spike (head)
3 spikelet
4 ergot, a grain deformed by fungus [shown with mycelium]
5 corn stem after tillering
6 culm (stalk)
7 node of the culm
8 leaf (grain leaf)
9 leaf sheath (sheath)
10 spikelet
11 glume
12 awn (beard, arista)
13 seed (grain, kernel, farinaceous grain)
14 embryo plant
15 seed
16 embryo
17 root
18 root hair
19 grain leaf
20 leaf blade (blade, lamina)
21 leaf sheath
22 ligule (ligula)
23 wheat
24 spelt
25 seed; *unripe:* green spelt, a soup vegetable
26 barley
27 oat panicle, a panicle
28 millet
29 rice
30 rice grain
31 maize (Indian corn, *Am.* corn); *varieties:* popcorn, dent corn, flint corn (flint maize, *Am.* Yankee corn), pod corn (*Am.* cow corn, husk corn), soft corn (*Am.* flour corn, squaw corn), sweet corn
32 female inflorescence
33 husk (shuck)
34 style
35 male inflorescence (tassel)
36 maize cob (*Am.* corn cob)
37 maize kernel (grain of maize)
38-45 root crops
38 potato plant (potato), a tuberous plant; *varieties:* round, round-oval (pear-shaped), flat-oval, long, kidney-shaped potato; *according to colour:* white (*Am.* Irish), yellow, red, purple potato
39 seed potato (seed tuber)
40 potato tuber (potato, tuber)
41 potato top (potato haulm)
42 flower
43 poisonous potato berry (potato apple)
44 sugar beet, a beet
45 root (beet)
46 beet top
47 beet leaf

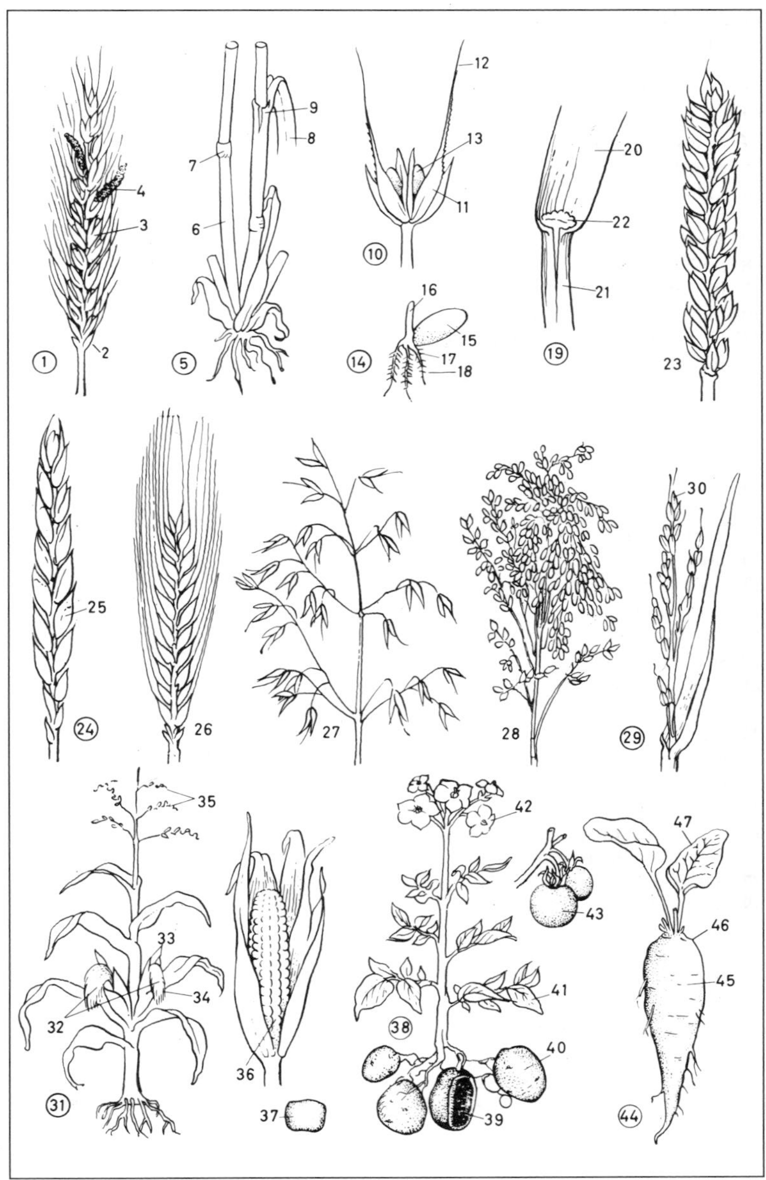

1
2
3
4
5
6
7
8
9
10
11
12
13
14
15
16
17
18
19
20
21
22
23
24
25
26
27
28
29
30
31
32
33
34
35
36
37
38
39
40
41
42
43
44
45
46
47

69 Fodder Plants (Forage Plants)

1-28 fodder plants (forage plants) for tillage

1 red clover (purple clover)
2 white clover (Dutch clover)
3 alsike clover (alsike)
4 crimson clover
5 four-leaf (four-leaved) clover
6 kidney vetch (lady's finger, lady-finger)
7 flower
8 pod
9 lucerne (lucern, purple medick)
10 sainfoin (cock's head, cockshead)
11 bird's foot (bird-foot, bird's foot trefoil)
12 corn spurrey (spurrey, spurry), a spurrey (spurry)
13 common comfrey, one of the borage family (Boraginaceae)
14 flower (blossom)
15 field bean (broad bean, tick bean, horse bean)
16 pod
17 yellow lupin
18 common vetch
19 chick-pea
20 sunflower
21 mangold (mangelwurzel, mangold-wurzel, field mangel)
22 false oat (oat-grass)
23 spikelet
24 meadow fescue grass, a fescue
25 cock's foot (cocksfoot)
26 Italian ryegrass; *sim.:* perennial ryegrass (English ryegrass)
27 meadow foxtail, a paniculate grass
28 greater burnet saxifrage

1
2
3
4
5
6
7
8
9
10
11
12
13
14
15
16
17
18
19
20
21
22
23
24
25
26
27
28

70 Breeds of Dog

1-14 mastiffs
1 bulldog
2 ear, a rose-ear
3 muzzle
4 nose
5 foreleg
6 forepaw
7 hind leg
8 hind paw
9 pug (pug dog)
10 boxer
11 withers
12 tail, a docked tail
13 collar
14 Great Dane
15-18 terriers
15 wire-haired fox terrier
16 bull terrier
17 Scotch terrier (Scottish terrier)
18 Bedlington terrier
19 Pekinese (Pekingese, Pekinese dog, Pekingese dog)
20-22 spitzes
20 spitz (Pomeranian)
21 chow (chow-chow)
22 husky
23, 24 greyhounds (*Am.* grayhounds)
23 Afghan (Afghan hound)
24 greyhound (*Am.* grayhound), a courser
25 Alsatian (German sheepdog, *Am.* German shepherd), a police dog, watch dog, and guide dog
26 flews (chaps)
27 Dobermann terrier

28 dog brush
29 dog comb
30 lead (dog lead, leash); *for hunting:* leash
31 muzzle
32 feeding bowl (dog bowl)
33 bone
34 Newfoundland dog
35 schnauzer
36 poodle; *sim. and smaller:* pygmy (pigmy) poodle
37 St. Bernard (St. Bernard dog)
38-43 hunting dogs
38 cocker spaniel
39 dachshund, a terrier
40 German pointer
41 English setter
42 trackhound
43 pointer, a trackhound

71 Horse I

1-6 equitation (high school riding, haute école)
1 piaffe
2 walk
3 passage
4 levade (pesade)
5 capriole
6 courbette (curvet)
7-25 harness
7-13, 25 bridle
7-11 headstall (headpiece, halter)
7 noseband
8 cheek piece (cheek strap)
9 browband (front band)
10 crownpiece
11 throatlatch (throatlash)
12 curb chain
13 curb bit
14 hasp (hook) of the hame (*Am.* drag hook)
15 pointed collar, a collar
16 trappings (side trappings)
17 saddle-pad
18 girth
19 backband
20 shaft chain (pole chain)
21 pole
22 trace
23 second girth (emergency girth)
24 trace
25 reins (*Am.* lines)
26-36 breast harness
26 blinker (*Am.* blinder, winker)
27 breast collar ring
28 breast collar (Dutch collar)
29 fork
30 neck strap
31 saddle-pad
32 loin strap
33 reins (rein, *Am.* line)
34 crupper (crupper-strap)
35 trace
36 girth (belly-band)
37-49 saddles
37-44 stock saddle (*Am.* western saddle)
37 saddle seat
38 pommel horn (horn)
39 cantle
40 flap (*Am.* fender)
41 bar
42 stirrup leather
43 stirrup (stirrup iron)
44 blanket
45-49 English saddle (cavalry saddle)
45 seat
46 cantle
47 flap
48 roll (knee roll)
49 pad
50, 51 spurs
50 box spur (screwed jack spur)
51 strapped jack spur
52 curb bit
53 gag bit (gag)
54 currycomb
55 horse brush (body brush, dandy brush)

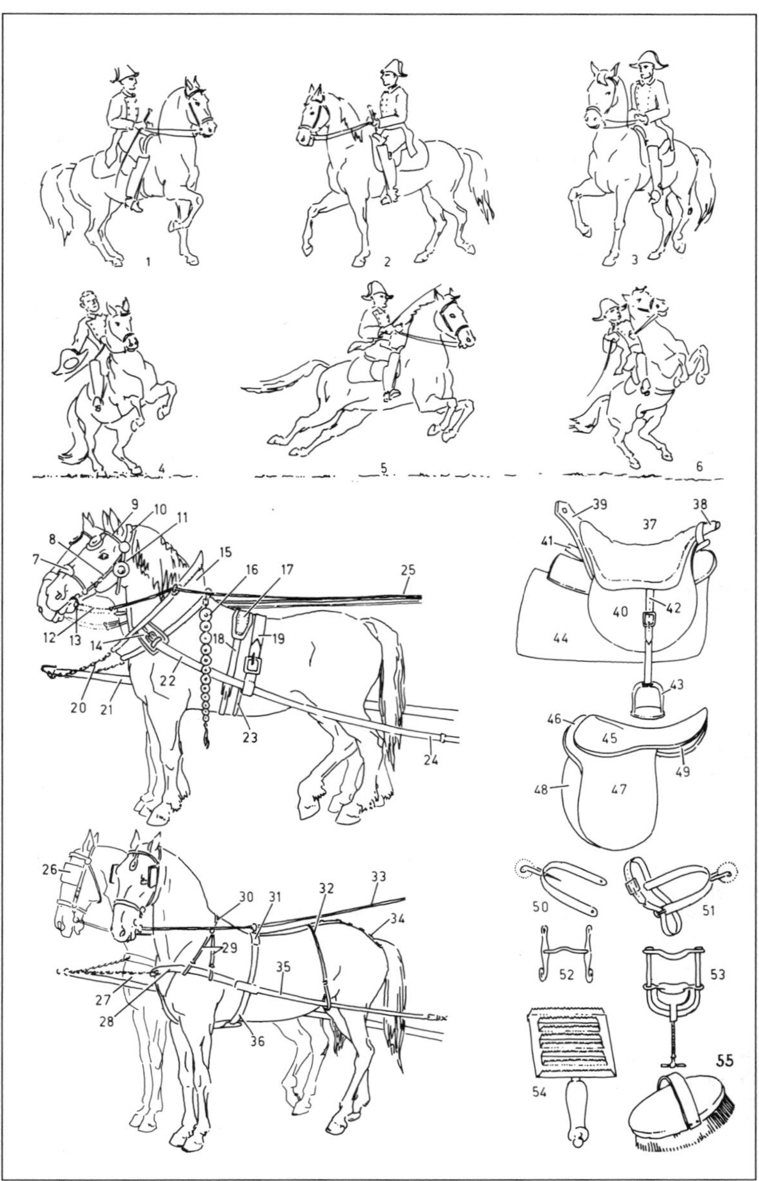
1
2
3
4
5
6
7
8
9
10
11
12
13
14
15
16
17
18
19
20
21
22
23
24
25
26
27
28
29
30
31
32
33
34
35
36
37
38
39
40
41
42
43
44
45
46
47
48
49
50
51
52
53
54
55

72 Horse II

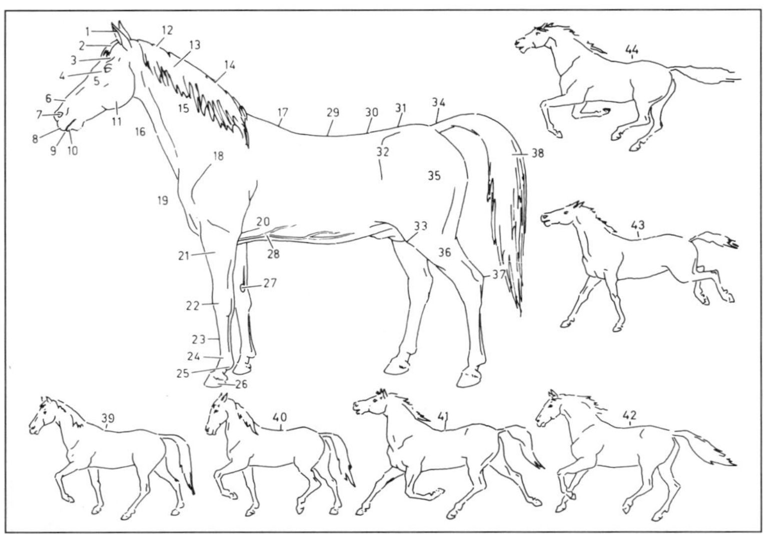

1-38 points of the horse
1-11 head (horse's head)
1 ear
2 forelock
3 forehead
4 eye
5 face
6 nose
7 nostril
8 upper lip
9 mouth
10 underlip (lower lip)
11 lower jaw
12 crest (neck)
13 mane (horse's mane)
14 crest (horse's crest)
15 neck
16 throat (*Am.* throatlatch, throat-lash)
17 withers
18-27 forehand
18 shoulder
19 breast
20 elbow
21 forearm
22-26 forefoot
22 knee (carpus, wrist)
23 cannon
24 fetlock
25 pastern
26 hoof
27 chestnut (castor), a callosity
28 spur vein
29 back
30 loins (lumbar region)
31 croup (rump, crupper)
32 hip
33-37 hind leg
33 stifle (stifle joint)
34 root (dock) of the tail
35 haunch
36 gaskin
37 hock
38 tail
39-44 gaits of the horse
39 walk
40 pace
41 trot
42 canter (hand gallop)
43, 44 full gallop
43 full gallop at the moment of descent on to the two forefeet
44 full gallop at the moment when all four feet are off the ground

Abbreviations:
m. = male; *c.* = castrated;
f. = female; *y.* = young

1-8 cattle and horses
1 cow, a ruminant; *m.* bull; *c.* ox; *f.* cow; *y.* calf
2 horse; *m.* stallion; *c.* gelding; *f.* mare; *y.* foal
3 donkey
4 pack saddle (carrying saddle)
5 pack (load)
6 tufted tail
7 tuft
8 mule, a cross between a male donkey and a mare
9 pig, a cloven-hoofed animal; *m.* boar; *f.* sow; *y.* piglet
10 pig's snout (snout)
11 pig's ear
12 curly tail
13 sheep; *m.* ram; *c.* wether; *f.* ewe; *y.* lamb
14 goat
15 goat's beard
16 dog, a Leonberger; *m.* dog; *f.* bitch; *y.* pup (puppy, whelp)
17 cat, an Angora cat (Persian cat); *m.* tom (tom cat)
18-36 small domestic animals
18 rabbit; *m.* buck; *f.* doe
19-36 poultry (domestic fowl)
19-26 chicken
19 hen
20 crop (craw)
21 cock (*Am.* rooster); *c.* capon
22 cockscomb (comb, crest)
23 lap
24 wattle (gill, dewlap)
25 falcate (falcated) tail
26 spur
27 guinea fowl
28 turkey; *m.* turkey cock (gobbler); *f.* turkey hen
29 fan tail
30 peacock
31 peacock's feather
32 eye (ocellus)
33 pigeon; *m.* cock pigeon
34 goose; *m.* gander; *y.* gosling
35 duck; *m.* drake; *y.* duckling
36 web (palmations) of webbed foot (palmate foot)

74 Poultry Farming (Poultry Keeping), Egg Production

1-27 poultry farming (intensive poultry management)
1-17 straw yard (strawed yard) **system**
1 fold unit for growing stock (chick unit)
2 chick
3 brooder (hover)
4 adjustable feeding trough
5 pullet fold unit
6 drinking trough
7 water pipe
8 litter
9 pullet
10 ventilator
11-17 broiler rearing (rearing of broiler chickens)
11 chicken run (*Am.* fowl run)
12 broiler chicken (broiler)
13 mechanical feeder (self-feeder, feed dispenser)
14 chain
15 feed supply pipe
16 mechanical drinking bowl (mechanical drinker)
17 ventilator
18 battery system (cage system)
19 battery (laying battery)
20 tiered cage (battery cage, stepped cage)
21 feeding trough
22 egg collection by conveyor
23-27 mechanical feeding and dunging (manure removal, droppings removal)
23 rapid feeding system for battery feeding (mechanical feeder)
24 feed hopper
25 endless-chain feed conveyor (chain feeder)
26 water pipe (liquid feed pipe)
27 dunging chain (dunging conveyor)
28 setting and hatching machine
29 ventilation drum [for the setting compartment]
30 hatching compartment (hatcher)
31 metal trolley for hatching trays
32 hatching tray
33 ventilation drum motor
34-53 egg productions
34 egg collection system (egg collection)
35 multi-tier transport
36 collection by pivoted fingers
37 drive motor
38 sorting machine
39 conveyor trolley
40 fluorescent screen
41 suction apparatus (suction box) for transporting eggs
42 shelf for empty and full egg boxes
43 egg weighers
44 grading
45 egg box
46 fully automatic egg-packing machine
47 radioscope box
48 radioscope table
49-51 feeder
49 suction transporter
50 vacuum line
51 supply table
52 automatic counting and grading
53 packing box dispenser
54 leg ring
55 wing tally (identification tally)
56 bantam
57 laying hen
58 hen's egg (egg)
59 eggshell, an egg integument
60 shell membrane
61 air space
62 white [of the egg] (albumen)
63 chalaza (*Am.* treadle)
64 vitelline membrane (yolk sac)
65 blastodisc (germinal disc, cock's tread, cock's treadle)
66 germinal vesicle
67 white
68 yolk

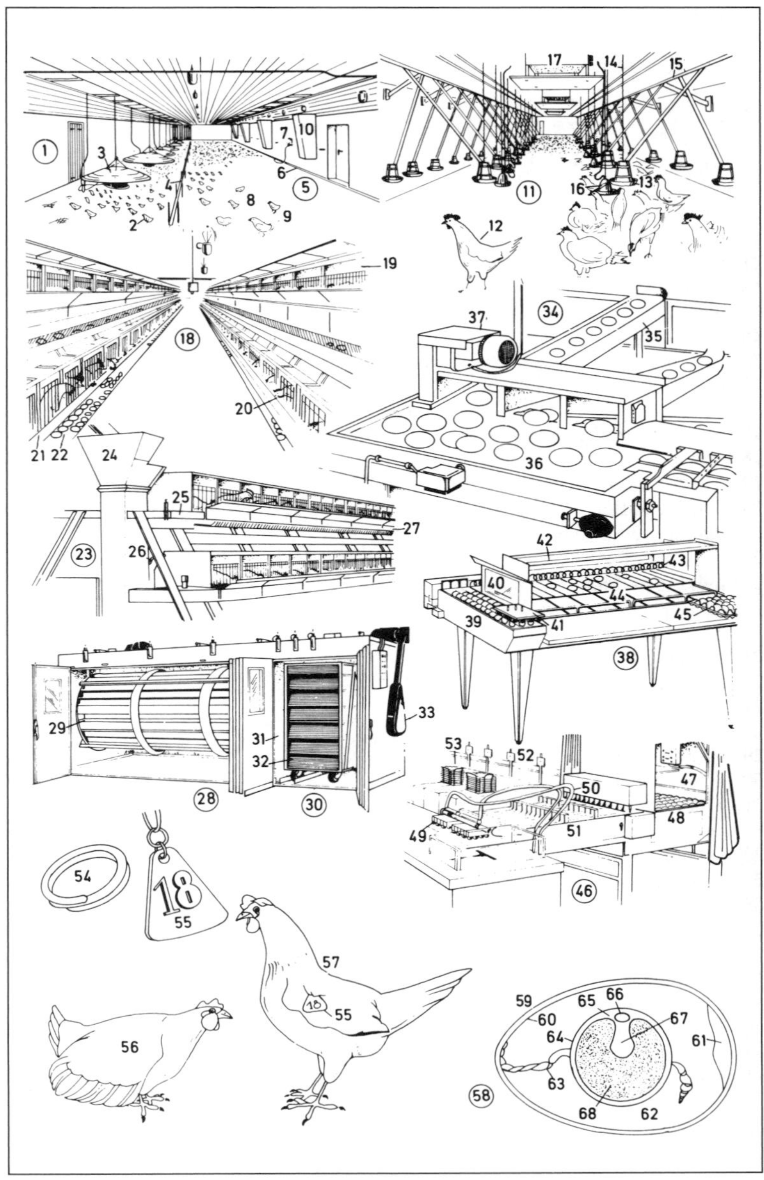
1
2
3
4
5
6
7
8
9
10
11
12
13
14
15
16
17
18
19
20
21
22
23
24
25
26
27
28
29
30
31
32
33
34
35
36
37
38
39
40
41
42
43
44
45
46
47
48
49
50
51
52
53
54
18
55
56
57
55
58
59
60
61
62
63
64
65
66
67
68

75 Rearing (*Am.* Raising) of Livestock

1 **stable**
2 horse stall (stall, horse box, box)
3 feeding passage
4 pony
5 bars
6 litter
7 bale of straw
8 ceiling light
9 **sheep pen**
10 mother sheep (ewe)
11 lamb
12 double hay rack
13 hay
14 **dairy cow shed**
15-16 tether
15 chain
16 rail
17 dairy cow (milch-cow, milker)
18 udder
19 teat
20 manure gutter
21 manure removal by sliding bars
22 short standing
23 **milking parlour** (*Am.* parlor), a herringbone parlour
24 working passage
25 milker (*Am.* milkman)
26 teat cup cluster
27 milk pipe
28 air line
29 vacuum line
30 teat cup
31 window
32 pulsator
33 release phase
34 squeeze phase
35 **pigsty** (*Am.* pigpen, hogpen)
36 pen for young pigs
37 feeding trough
38 partition
39 pig, a young pig
40 farrowing and store pen
41 sow
42 piglets (*Am.* shoats, shotes) (sucking pigs [for first 8 weeks])
43 farrowing rails
44 liquid manure channel

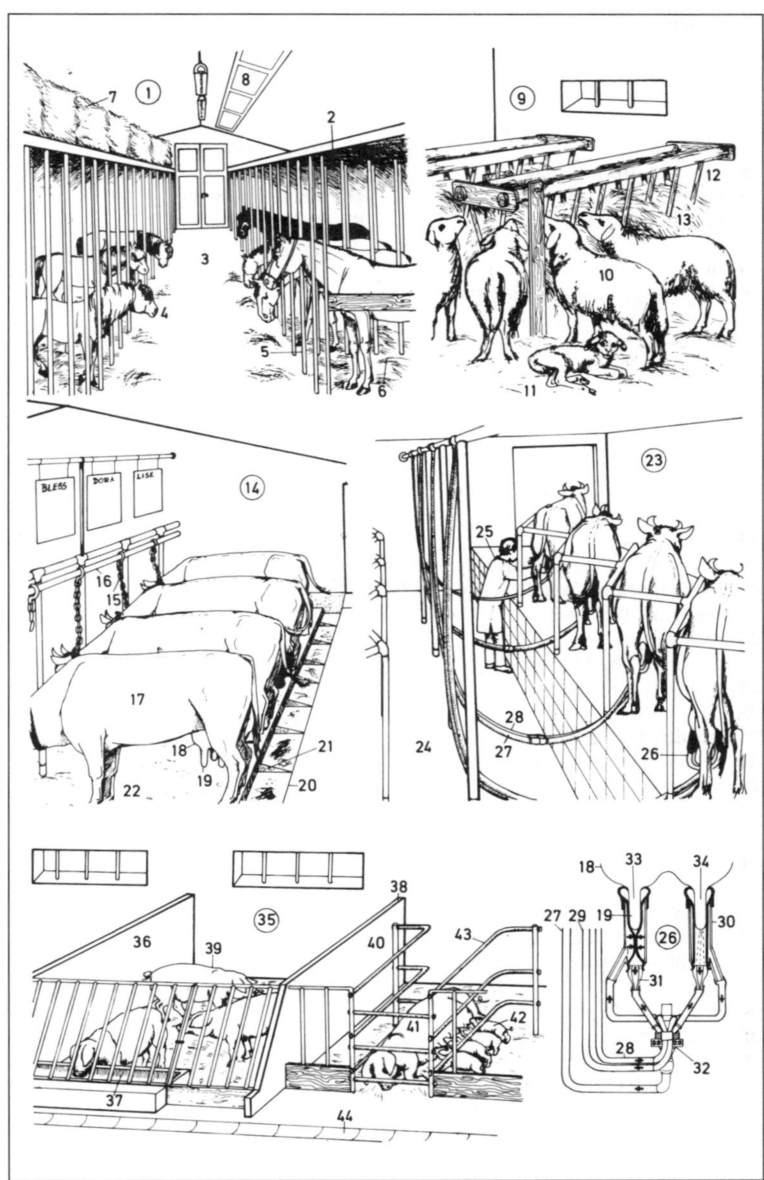
1
2
3
4
5
6
7
8
9
10
11
12
13
14
BLESS
DORA
LISE
15
16
17
18
19
20
21
22
23
24
25
26
27
28
35
36
37
38
39
40
41
42
43
44
18
33
34
27
29
19
26
30
31
28
32

1-48 dairy (dairy plant)
1 milk reception
2 milk tanker
3 raw milk pump
4 flowmeter, an oval (elliptical) gear meter
5 raw milk storage tank
6 gauge (*Am.* gage)
7 central control room
8 chart of the dairy
9 flow chart (flow diagram)
10 storage tank gauges (*Am.* gages)
11 control panel
12-48 milk processing area
12 sterilizer (homogenizer)
13 milk heater; *sim.:* cream heater
14 cream separator
15 fresh milk tanks
16 tank for sterilized milk
17 skim milk (skimmed milk) tank
18 buttermilk tank
19 cream tank
20 fresh milk filling and packing plant
21 filling machine for milk cartons; *sim.:* milk tub filler
22 milk carton
23 conveyor belt (conveyor)
24 shrink-sealing machine
25 pack of twelve in shrink foil
26 ten-litre filling machine
27 heat-sealing machine
28 plastic sheets
29 heat-sealed bag
30 crate
31 cream maturing vat
32 butter shaping and packing machine
33 butter churn, a creamery butter machine for continuous butter making
34 butter supply pipe
35 shaping machine
36 packing machine
37 branded butter in 250 g packets
38 plant for producing curd cheese (curd cheese machine)
39 curd cheese pump
40 cream supply pump
41 curds separator
42 sour milk vat
43 stirrer
44 curd cheese packing machine
45 packeted curd cheese
46 bottle-capping machine (capper)
47 cheese machine
48 rennet vat

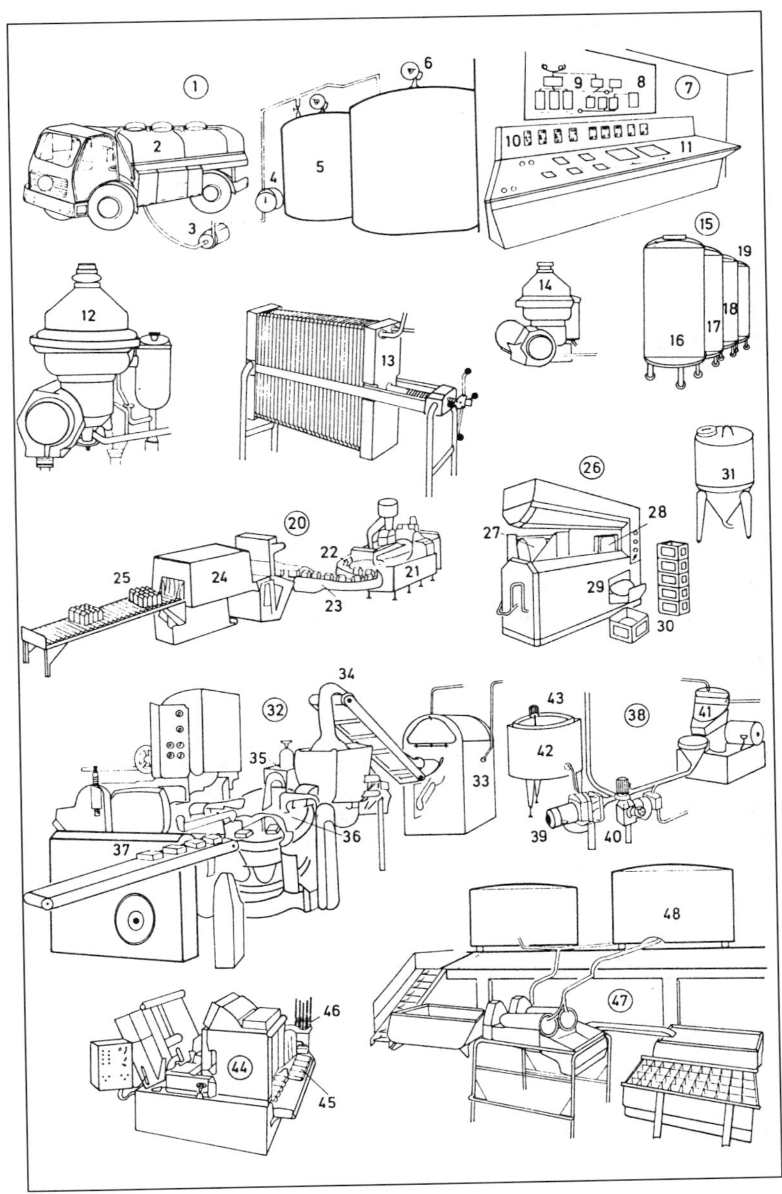
1
2
3
4
5
6
7
8
9
10
11
12
13
14
15
16
17
18
19
20
21
22
23
24
25
26
27
28
29
30
31
32
33
34
35
36
37
38
39
40
41
42
43
44
45
46
47
48

77 Bees and Beekeeping (Apiculture)

1-25 bee (honey-bee, hive-bee)
1, 4-5 castes (social classes) of bees
1 worker (worker bee)
2 three simple eyes (ocelli)
3 load of pollen on the hind leg
4 queen (queen bee)
5 drone (male bee)
6-9 left hind leg of a worker
6 pollen basket
7 pollen comb (brush)
8 double claw
9 suctorial pad
10-19 abdomen of the worker
10-14 stinging organs
10 barb
11 sting
12 sting sheath
13 poison sac
14 poison gland
15-19 stomachic-intestinal canal
15 intestine
16 stomach
17 contractile muscle
18 honey bag (honey sac)
19 oesophagus (esophagus, gullet)
20-24 compound eye
20 facet
21 crystal cone
22 light-sensitive section
23 fibre (*Am.* fiber) of the optic nerve
24 optic nerve
25 wax scale
26-30 cell
26 egg
27 cell with the egg in it
28 young larva
29 larva (grub)
30 chrysalis (pupa)
31-43 honeycomb
31 brood cell
32 sealed (capped) cell with chrysalis (pupa)
33 sealed (capped) cell with honey (honey cell)
34 worker cells
35 storage cells, with pollen
36 drone cells
37 queen cell
38 queen emerging from her cell
39 cap (capping)
40 frame
41 distance piece
42 [artificial] honeycomb
43 septum (foundation, comb foundation)
44 queen's travelling (*Am.* traveling) box
45-50 beehive, a frame hive (movable-frame hive, movable-comb hive)
45 super (honey super) with honeycombs
46 brood chamber with breeding combs
47 queen-excluder
48 entrance
49 flight board (alighting board)
50 window
51 old-fashioned bee shed
52 straw hive (skep), a hive
53 swarm (swarm cluster) of bees
54 swarming net (bag net)
55 hooked pole
56 apiary (bee house)
57 beekeeper (apiarist, *Am.* beeman)
58 bee veil
59 bee smoker
60 natural honeycomb
61 honey extractor (honey separator)
62-63 strained honey (honey)
62 honey pail
63 honey jar
64 honey in the comb
65 wax taper
66 wax candle
67 beeswax
68 bee sting ointment

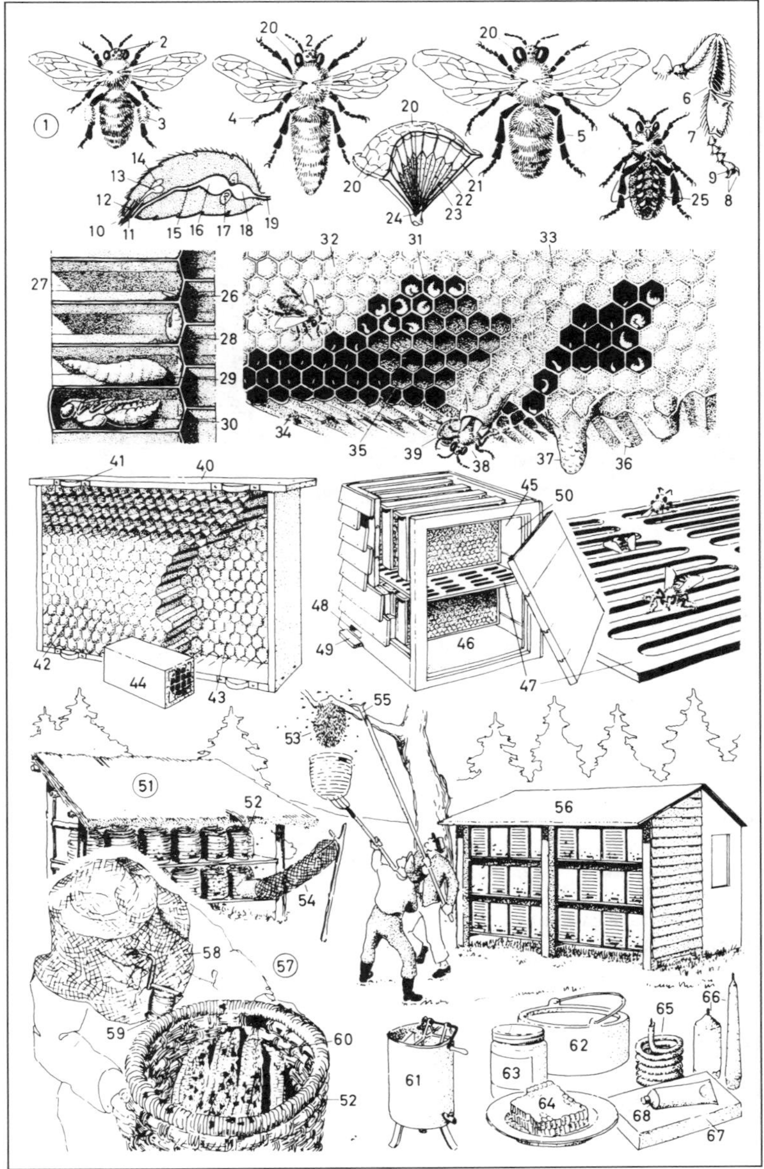
1
2
3
4
5
6
7
8
9
10
11
12
13
14
15
16
17
18
19
20
21
22
23
24
25
26
27
28
29
30
31
32
33
34
35
36
37
38
39
40
41
42
43
44
45
46
47
48
49
50
51
52
53
54
55
56
57
58
59
60
61
62
63
64
65
66
67
68

78 Wine Growing (Viniculture, Viticulture)

1-21 vineyard area

1 vineyard using wire trellises for training vines

2-9 vine (*Am.* grapevine)

2 vine shoot

3 long shoot

4 vine leaf

5 bunch of grapes (cluster of grapes)

6 vine stem

7 post (stake)

8 guy (guy wire)

9 wire trellis

10 tub for grape gathering

11 grape gatherer

12 secateurs for pruning vines

13 wine grower (viniculturist, viticulturist)

14 dosser carrier

15 dosser (pannier)

16 crushed grape transporter

17 grape crusher

18 hopper

19 three-sided flap extension

20 platform

21 vineyard tractor, a narrow-track tractor

1-22 wine cellar (wine vault)
1 vault
2 wine cask
3 wine vat, a concrete vat
4 stainless steel vat (*also:* vat made of synthetic material)
5 propeller-type high-speed mixer
6 propeller mixer
7 centrifugal pump
8 stainless steel sediment filter
9 semi-automatic circular bottling machine
10 semi-automatic corking machine
11 bottle rack
12 cellarer's assistant
13 bottle basket
14 wine bottle
15 wine jug
16 wine tasting
17 head cellarman
18 cellarman
19 wineglass
20 inspection apparatus [for spot-checking samples]
21 horizontal wine press
22 humidifier

80 Garden and Field Pests

1-19 fruit pests
1 gipsy (gypsy) moth
2 batch (cluster) of eggs
3 caterpillar
4 chrysalis (pupa)
5 small ermine moth, an ermine moth
6 larva (grub)
7 tent
8 caterpillar skeletonizing a leaf
9 fruit-surface-eating tortrix moth (summer fruit tortrix moth)
10 appleblossom weevil, a weevil
11 punctured, withered flower (blossom)
12 hole for laying eggs
13 lackey moth
14 caterpillar
15 eggs
16 winter moth, a geometrid
17 caterpillar
18 cherry fruit fly, a borer
19 larva (grub, maggot)
20-27 vine pests
20 downy mildew, a mildew, a disease causing leaf drop
21 grape affected with downy mildew
22 grape-berry moth
23 first-generation larva of the grape-berry moth (*Am.* grape worm)
24 second-generation larva of the grape-berry moth (*Am.* grape worm)
25 chrysalis (pupa)
26 root louse, a grape phylloxera
27 root gall (knotty swelling of the root, nodosity, tuberosity)
28 brown-tail moth
29 caterpillar
30 batch (cluster) of eggs
31 hibernation cocoon
32 woolly apple aphid (American blight), an aphid
33 gall caused by the woolly apple aphid
34 woolly apple aphid colony
35 San-José scale, a scale insect (scale louse)
36 larvae (grubs) [*male* elongated, *female* round]
37-55 field pests
37 click beetle, a snapping beetle (*Am.* snapping bug)
38 wireworm, larva of the click beetle
39 flea beetle
40 Hessian fly, a gall midge (gall gnat)
41 larva (grub)
42 turnip moth, an earth moth
43 chrysalis (pupa)
44 cutworm, a caterpillar
45 beet carrion beetle
46 larva (grub)
47 large cabbage white butterfly
48 caterpillar of the small cabbage white butterfly
49 brown leaf-eating weevil, a weevil
50 feeding site
51 sugar beet eelworm, a nematode (a threadworm, hairworm)
52 Colorado beetle (potato beetle)
53 mature larva (grub)
54 young larva (grub)
55 eggs

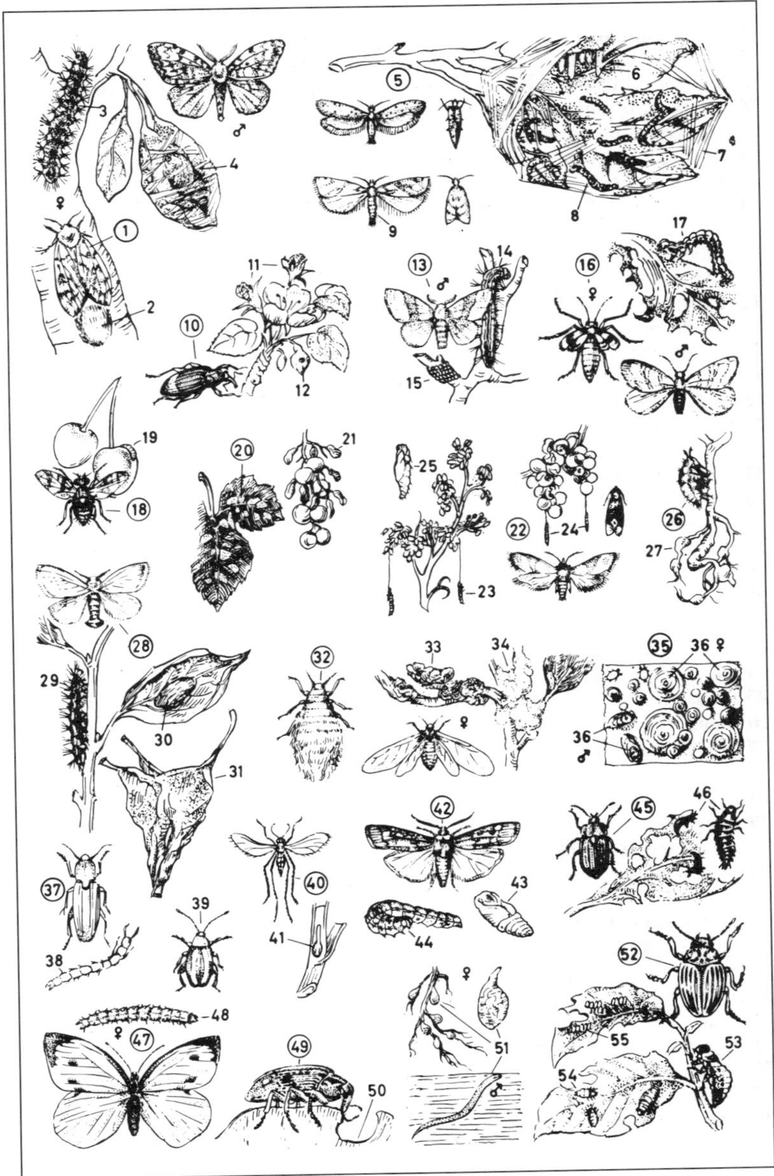
3
♂
4
5
6
7
8
9
♀
1
2
11
10
12
13
♂
14
15
16
♀
17
♂
19
18
20
21
25
22
24
23
26
27
28
29
30
31
32
33
34
♀
35
36 ♀
36
♂
37
38
39
40
41
42
43
44
45
46
52
48
♀ 47
49
50
♀
51
♂
55
53
54

81 House Insects, Food Pests, and Parasites

1-14 house insects
1 lesser housefly
2 common housefly
3 chrysalis (pupa, coarctate pupa)
4 stable fly (biting housefly)
5 trichotomous antenna
6 wood louse (slater, *Am.* sow bug)
7 house cricket
8 wing with stridulating apparatus (stridulating mechanism)
9 house spider
10 spider's web
11 earwig
12 caudal pincers
13 clothes moth, a moth
14 silverfish (*Am.* slicker), a bristletail
15-30 food pests (pests to stores)
15 cheesefly
16 grain weevil (granary weevil)
17 cockroach (black beetle)
18 meal beetle (meal worm beetle, flour beetle)
19 spotted bruchus
20 larva (grub)
21 chrysalis (pupa)
22 leather beetle (hide beetle)
23 yellow meal beetle
24 chrysalis (pupa)
25 cigarette beetle (tobacco beetle)
26 maize billbug (corn weevil)
27 one of the Cryptolestes, a grain pest
28 Indian meal moth
29 Angoumois grain moth (Angoumois moth)
30 Angoumois grain moth caterpillar inside a grain kernel
31-42 parasites of man
31 round worm (maw worm)
32 female
33 head
34 male
35 tapeworm, a flatworm
36 head, a suctorial organ
37 sucker
38 crown of hooks
39 bug (bed bug, *Am.* chinch)
40 crab louse (a human louse)
41 clothes louse (body louse, a human louse)
42 flea (human flea, common flea)
43 tsetse fly
44 malaria mosquito

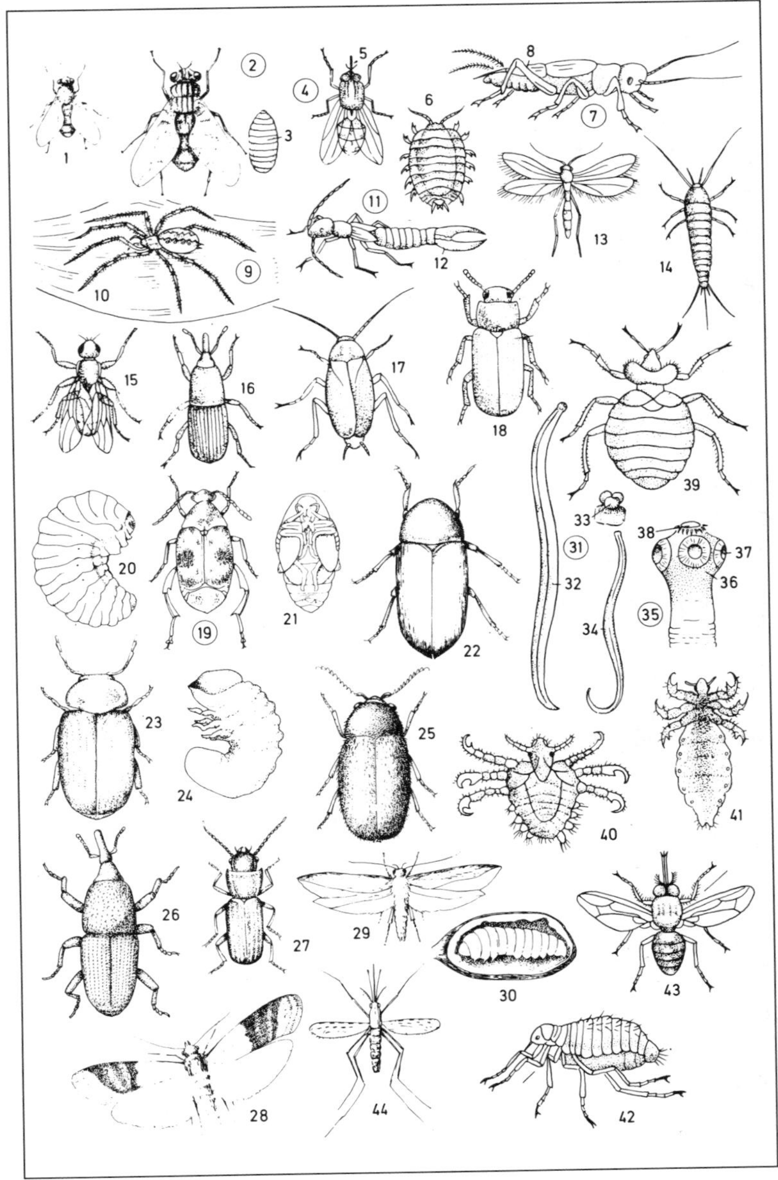
1
2
3
4
5
6
7
8
9
10
11
12
13
14
15
16
17
18
39
20
19
21
22
33
31
32
38
37
36
35
34
23
24
25
40
41
26
27
29
30
43
28
44
42

82 Forest Pests

1 cockchafer (May bug), a lamellicorn
2 head
3 antenna (feeler)
4 thoracic shield (prothorax)
5 scutellum
6-8 legs
6 front leg
7 middle leg
8 back leg
9 abdomen
10 elytron (wing case)
11 membranous wing
12 cockchafer grub, a larva
13 chrysalis (pupa)
14 processionary moth, a nocturnal moth (night-flying moth)
15 moth
16 caterpillars in procession
17 nun moth (black arches moth)
18 moth
19 eggs
20 caterpillar
21 chrysalis (pupa) in its cocoon
22 typographer beetle, a bark beetle
23-24 galleries under the bark
23 egg gallery
24 gallery made by larva
25 larva (grub)
26 beetle
27 pine hawkmoth, a hawkmoth
28 pine moth, a geometrid
29 male moth
30 female moth
31 caterpillar
32 chrysalis (pupa)
33 oak-gall wasp, a gall wasp
34 oak gall (oak apple), a gall
35 wasp
36 larva (grub) in its chamber
37 beech gall
38 spruce-gall aphid
39 winged aphid
40 pineapple gall
41 pine weevil
42 beetle (weevil)
43 green oak roller moth (green oak tortrix), a leaf roller
44 caterpillar
45 moth
46 pine beauty
47 caterpillar
48 moth

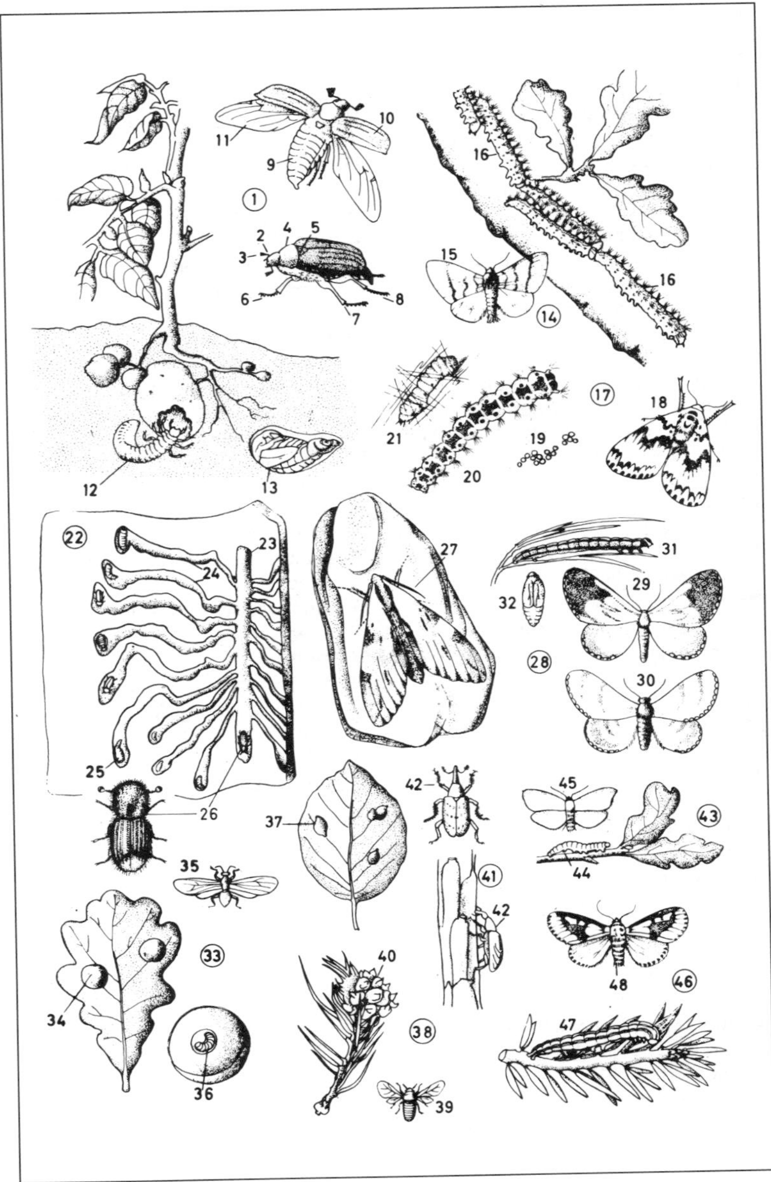
1
2
3
4
5
6
7
8
9
10
11
12
13
14
15
16
16
17
18
19
20
21
22
23
24
25
26
27
28
29
30
31
32
33
34
35
36
37
38
39
40
41
42
42
43
44
45
46
47
48

83 Pest Control

1 area spraying
2 tractor-mounted sprayer
3 spray boom
4 fan nozzle
5 spray fluid tank
6 foam canister for blob marking
7 spring suspension
8 spray
9 blob marker
10 foam feed pipe
11 vacuum fumigator (vacuum fumigation plant) of a tobacco factory
12 vacuum chamber
13 bales of raw tobacco
14 gas pipe
15 mobile fumigation chamber for fumigating nursery saplings, vine layers, seeds, and empty sacks with hydrocyanic (prussic) acid
16 gas circulation unit
17 tray
18 spray gun
19 twist grip (control grip, handle) for regulating the jet
20 finger guard
21 control lever (operating lever)
22 spray tube
23 cone nozzle
24 hand spray
25 plastic container
26 hand pump
27 pendulum spray for hop growing on slopes
28 pistol-type nozzle
29 spraying tube
30 hose connection
31 tube for laying poisoned bait
32 fly swat
33 soil injector (carbon disulphide, *Am.* carbon disulfide, injector) for killing the vine root louse
34 foot lever (foot pedal, foot treadle)
35 gas tube
36 mousetrap
37 vole and mole trap
38 mobile orchard sprayer, a wheelbarrow sprayer (carriage sprayer)
39 spray tank
40 screw-on cover
41 direct-connected motor-driven pump with petrol motor
42 pressure gauge (*Am.* gage) (manometer)
43 plunger-type knapsack sprayer
44 spray canister with pressure chamber
45 piston pump lever
46 hand lance with nozzle
47 semi-mounted sprayer
48 vineyard tractor
49 fan
50 spray fluid tank
51 row of vines
52 dressing machine (seed-dressing machine) for dry-seed dressing (seed dusting)
53 dedusting fan (dust removal fan) with electric motor
54 bag filter
55 bagging nozzle
56 dedusting screen (dust removal screen)
57 water canister [containing water for spraying]
58 spray unit
59 conveyor unit with mixing screw
60 container for disinfectant powder with dosing mechanism
61 castor
62 mixing chamber

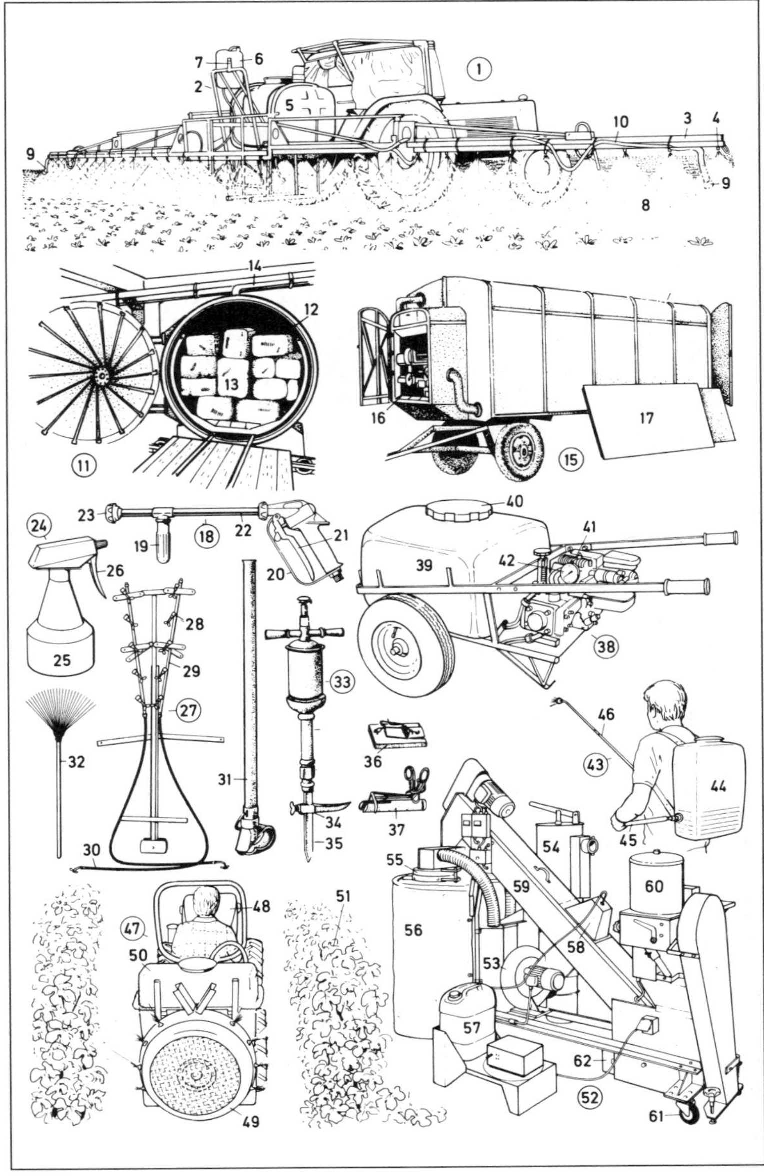
1
2
3
4
5
6
7
8
9
9
10
11
12
13
14
15
16
17
18
19
20
21
22
23
24
25
26
27
28
29
30
31
32
33
34
35
36
37
38
39
40
41
42
43
44
45
46
47
48
49
50
51
52
53
54
55
56
57
58
59
60
61
62

1-34 forest, a wood
1 ride (aisle, lane, section line)
2 compartment (section)
3 wood haulage way, a forest track
4-14 clear-felling system
4 standing timber
5 underwood (underbrush, undergrowth, brushwood, *Am.* brush)
6 seedling nursery, a tree nursery
7 deer fence (fence), a wire netting fence (protective fence for seedlings); *sim.:* rabbit fence
8 guard rail
9 seedlings
10, 11 young trees
10 tree nursery after transplanting
11 young plantation
12 young plantation after brashing
13 clearing
14 tree stump (stump, stub)

15-37 wood cutting (timber cutting, tree felling, *Am.* lumbering)

15 timber skidded to the stack (stacked timber, *Am.* yarded timber)

16 stack of logs, one cubic metre (*Am.* meter) of wood

17 post (stake)

18 forest labourer (woodsman, *Am.* logger, lumberer, lumberjack, lumberman, timberjack) turning (*Am.* canting) timber

19 bole (tree trunk, trunk, stem)

20 feller numbering the logs

21 steel tree calliper (caliper)

22 power saw (motor saw) cutting a bole

23 safety helmet with visor and ear pieces

24 annual rings

25 hydraulic felling wedge

26 protective clothing [orange top, green trousers]

27 felling with a power saw (motor saw)

28 undercut (notch, throat, gullet, mouth, sink, kerf, birdsmouth)

29 back cut

30 sheath holding felling wedge

31 log

32 free-cutting saw for removing underwood and weeds

33 circular saw (or activated blade) attachment

34 power unit (motor)

35 canister of viscous oil for the saw chain

36 petrol canister (*Am.* gasoline canister)

37 felling of small timber (of small-sized thinnings) (thinning)

85 Forestry II

1 axe (*Am.* ax)
2 edge (cutting edge)
3 handle (helve)
4 felling wedge (falling wedge) with wood insert and ring
5 riving hammer (cleaving hammer, splitting hammer)
6 lifting hook
7 cant hook
8 barking iron (bark spud)
9 peavy
10 slide calliper (caliper) (calliper square)
11 billhook, a knife for lopping
12 revolving die hammer (marking hammer, marking iron, *Am.* marker)
13 power saw (motor saw)
14 saw chain
15 safety brake for the saw chain, with finger guard
16 saw guide
17 accelerator lock
18 snedding machine (trimming machine, *Am.* knotting machine, limbing machine)
19 feed rolls
20 flexible blade
21 hydraulic arm
22 trimming blade
23 debarking (barking, bark stripping) of boles
24 feed roller
25 cylinder trimmer
26 rotary cutter
27 short-haul skidder
28 loading crane
29 log grips
30 post
31 Ackermann steering system
32 log dump
33 number (identification number)
34 skidder
35 front blade (front plate)
36 crush-proof safety bonnet (*Am.* safety hood)
37 Ackermann steering system
38 cable winch
39 cable drum
40 rear blade (rear plate)
41 boles with butt ends held off the ground
42 haulage of timber by road
43 tractor (tractor unit)
44 loading crane
45 hydraulic jack
46 cable winch
47 post
48 bolster plate
49 rear bed (rear bunk)

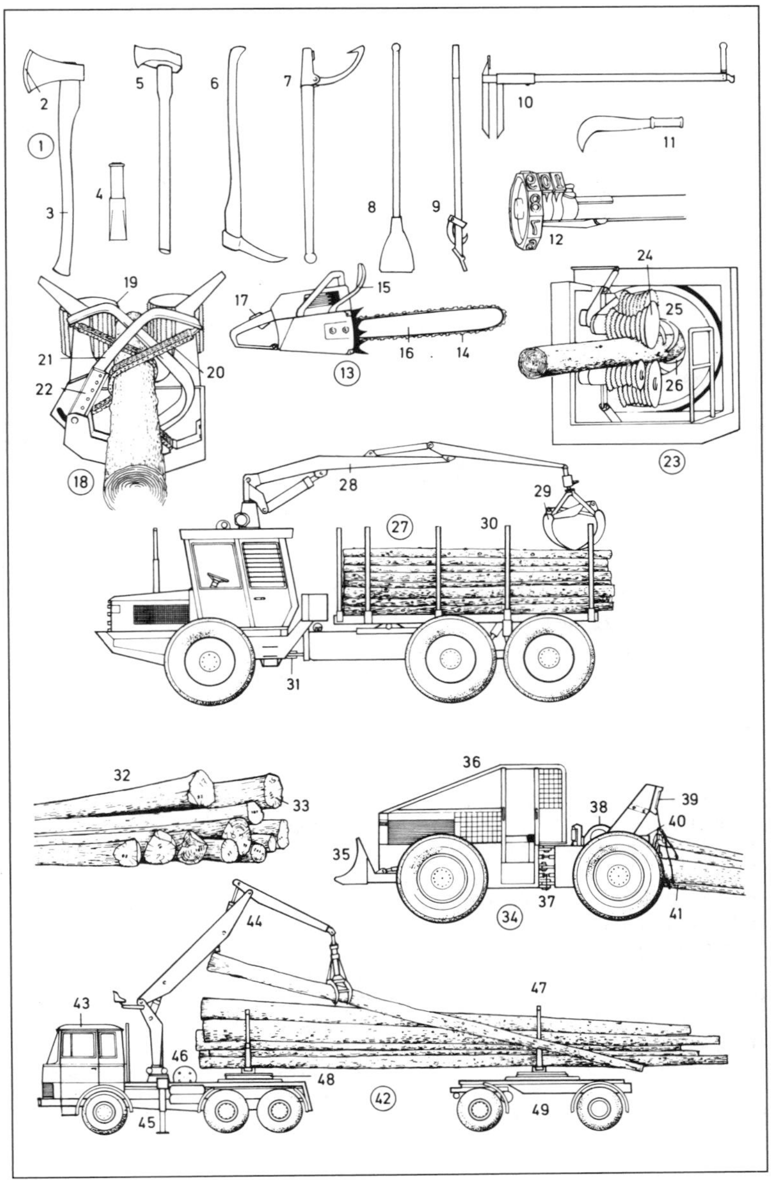
1
2
3
4
5
6
7
8
9
10
11
12
13
14
15
16
17
18
19
20
21
22
23
24
25
26
27
28
29
30
31
32
33
34
35
36
37
38
39
40
41
42
43
44
45
46
47
48
49

86 Hunting

1-52 kinds of hunting

1-8 stalking (deer stalking, *Am.* still-hunting) in the game preserve

1 huntsman (hunter)
2 hunting clothes
3 knapsack
4 sporting gun (sporting rifle, hunting rifle)
5 huntsman's hat
6 field glasses, binoculars
7 gun dog
8 track (trail, hoofprints)

9-12 hunting in the rutting season and the pairing season

9 hunting screen (screen, *Am.* blind)
10 shooting stick (shooting seat, seat stick)
11 blackcock, displaying
12 rutting stag
13 hind, grazing

14-17 hunting from a raised hide (raised stand)

14 raised hide (raised stand, high seat)
15 herd within range
16 game path (*Am.* runway)
17 roebuck, hit in the shoulder and killed by a finishing shot
18 phaeton

19-27 types of trapping

19 trapping of small predators
20 box trap (trap for small predators)
21 bait
22 marten, a small predator
23 ferreting (hunting rabbits out of their warrens)
24 ferret
25 ferreter
26 burrow (rabbit burrow, rabbit hole)
27 net (rabbit net) over the burrow opening

28 feeding place for game (winter feeding place)
29 poacher
30 carbine, a short rifle
31 boar hunt
32 wild sow (sow, wild boar)
33 boarhound (hound, hunting dog; *collectively:* pack, pack of hounds)
34-39 beating (driving, hare hunting)
34 aiming position
35 hare, furred game (ground game)
36 retrieving
37 beater
38 bag (kill)
39 cart for carrying game
40 waterfowling (wildfowling, duck shooting, *Am.* duck hunting)
41 flight of wild ducks, winged game
42-46 falconry (hawking)
42 falconer
43 reward, a piece of meat
44 falcon's hood
45 jess
46 falcon, a hawk, a male hawk (tiercel) swooping (stooping) on a heron
47-52 shooting from a butt
47 tree to which birds are lured
48 eagle owl, a decoy bird (decoy)
49 perch
50 decoyed bird, a crow
51 butt for shooting crows or eagle owls
52 gun slit

87 Hunting Weapons, Hunting Equipment

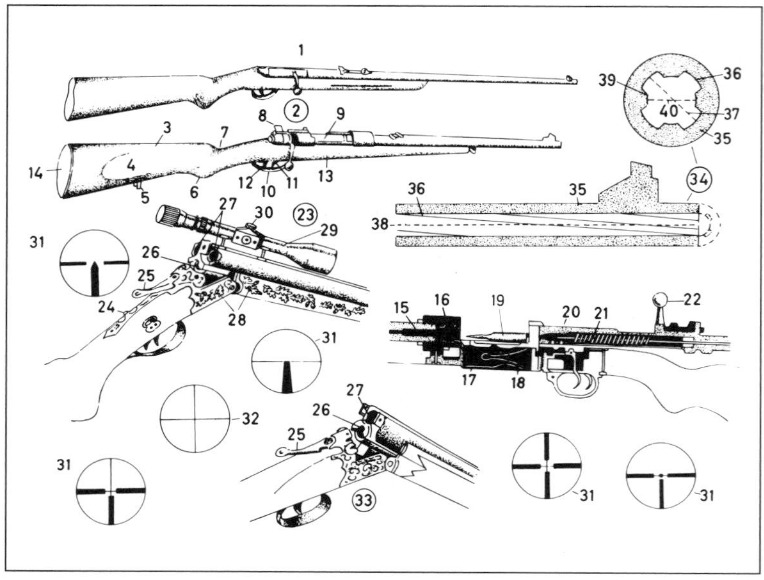

1-40 sporting guns (sporting rifles, hunting rifles)
1 single-loader (single-loading rifle)
2 repeating rifle, a small-arm (firearm), a repeater (magazine rifle, magazine repeater)
3, 4, 6, 13 stock
3 butt
4 cheek [on the left side]
5 sling ring
6 pistol grip
7 small of the butt
8 safety catch
9 lock
10 trigger guard
11 second set trigger (firing trigger)
12 hair trigger (set trigger)
13 foregrip
14 butt plate
15 cartridge chamber
16 receiver
17 magazine
18 magazine spring
19 ammunition (cartridge)
20 chamber
21 firing pin (striker)
22 bolt handle (bolt lever)
23 triple-barrelled (triple-barreled) rifle, a self-cocking gun
24 reversing catch; *in various guns:* safety catch
25 sliding safety catch
26 rifle barrel (rifled barrel)
27 smooth-bore barrel
28 chasing
29 telescopic sight (riflescope, telescope sight)
30 graticule adjuster screws
31-32 graticule (sight graticule)
31 various graticule systems
32 cross wires (*Am.* cross hairs)
33 over-and-under shotgun
34 rifled gun barrel
35 barrel casing
36 rifling
37 rifling calibre (*Am.* caliber)
38 bore axis
39 land
40 calibre (bore diameter, *Am.* caliber)

41-48 hunting equipment
41 double-edged hunting knife
42 [single-edged] hunting knife
43-47 calls for luring game (for calling game)
43 roe call
44 hare call
45 quail call
46 stag call
47 partridge call
48 bow trap (bow gin), a jaw trap
49 small-shot cartridge
50 cardboard case
51 small-shot charge
52 felt wad
53 smokeless powder (*different kind:* black powder)
54 cartridge
55 full-jacketed cartridge
56 soft-lead core
57 powder charge
58 detonator cap
59 percussion cap
60 hunting horn
61-64 rifle cleaning kit
61 cleaning rod
62 cleaning brush
63 cleaning tow
64 pull-through (*Am.* pull-thru)
65 sights
66 notch (sighting notch)
67 back sight leaf
68 sight scale division
69 back sight slide
70 notch [to hold the spring]
71 front sight (foresight)
72 bead
73 ballistics
74 azimuth
75 angle of departure
76 angle of elevation
77 apex (zenith)
78 angle of descent
79 ballistic curve

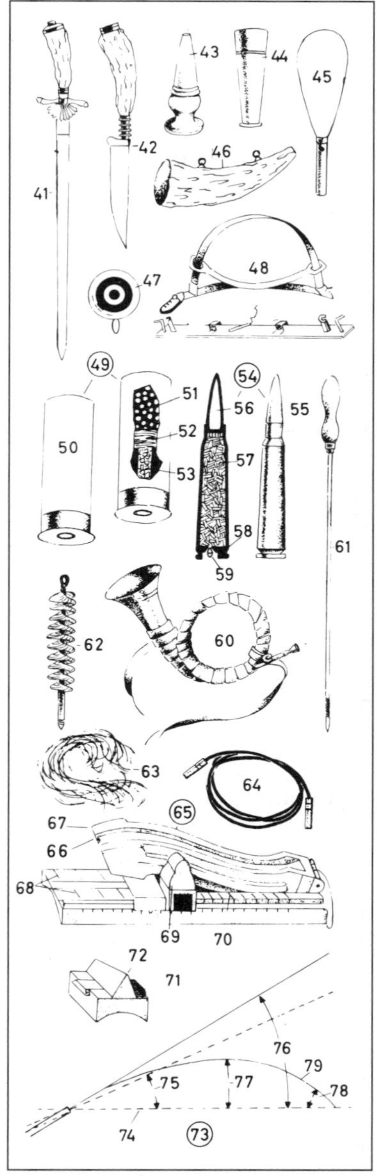

88 Game

1-27 red deer
1 hind (red deer), a young hind or a dam; *collectively:* antlerless deer, *(y.)* calf
2 tongue
3 neck
4 rutting stag
5-11 antlers
5 burr (rose)
6 brow antler (brow tine, brow point, brow snag)
7 bez antler (bay antler, bay, bez tine)
8 royal antler (royal, tray)
9 surroyal antlers (surroyals)
10 point (tine)
11 beam (main trunk)
12 head
13 mouth
14 larmier (tear bag)
15 eye
16 ear
17 shoulder
18 loin
19 scut (tail)
20 rump
21 leg (haunch)
22 hind leg
23 dew claw
24 hoof
25 foreleg
26 flank
27 collar (rutting mane)
28-39 roe (roe deer)
28 roebuck (buck)
29-31 antlers (horns)
29 burr (rose)
30 beam with pearls
31 point (tine)
32 ear
33 eye
34 doe (female roe), a female fawn or a barren doe
35 loin
36 rump
37 leg (haunch)
38 shoulder
39 fawn, *(m.)* young buck, *(f.)* young doe
40-41 fallow deer
40 fallow buck, a buck with palmate (palmated) antlers, *(f.)* doe
41 palm
42 red fox, *(m.)* dog, *(f.)* vixen, *(y.)* cub
43 eyes
44 ear
45 muzzle (mouth)
46 pads (paws)
47 brush (tail)
48 badger, *(f.)* sow
49 tail
50 paws
51 wild boar, *(m.)* boar, *(f.)* wild sow (sow), *(y.)* young boar
52 bristles
53 snout
54 tusk
55 shield
56 hide
57 dew claw
58 tail
59 hare, *(m.)* buck, *(f.)* doe
60 eye
61 ear
62 scut (tail)
63 hind leg
64 foreleg
65 rabbit
66 blackcock
67 tail
68 falcate (falcated) feathers
69 hazel grouse (hazel hen)
70 partridge
71 horseshoe (horseshoe marking)
72 wood grouse (capercaillie)
73 beard
74 axillary marking
75 tail (fan)
76 wing (pinion)
77 common pheasant, a pheasant, *(m.)* cock pheasant (pheasant cock), *(f.)* hen pheasant (pheasant hen)
78 plumicorn (feathered ear, ear tuft, ear, horn)
79 wing
80 tail
81 leg
82 spur
83 snipe
84 bill (beak)

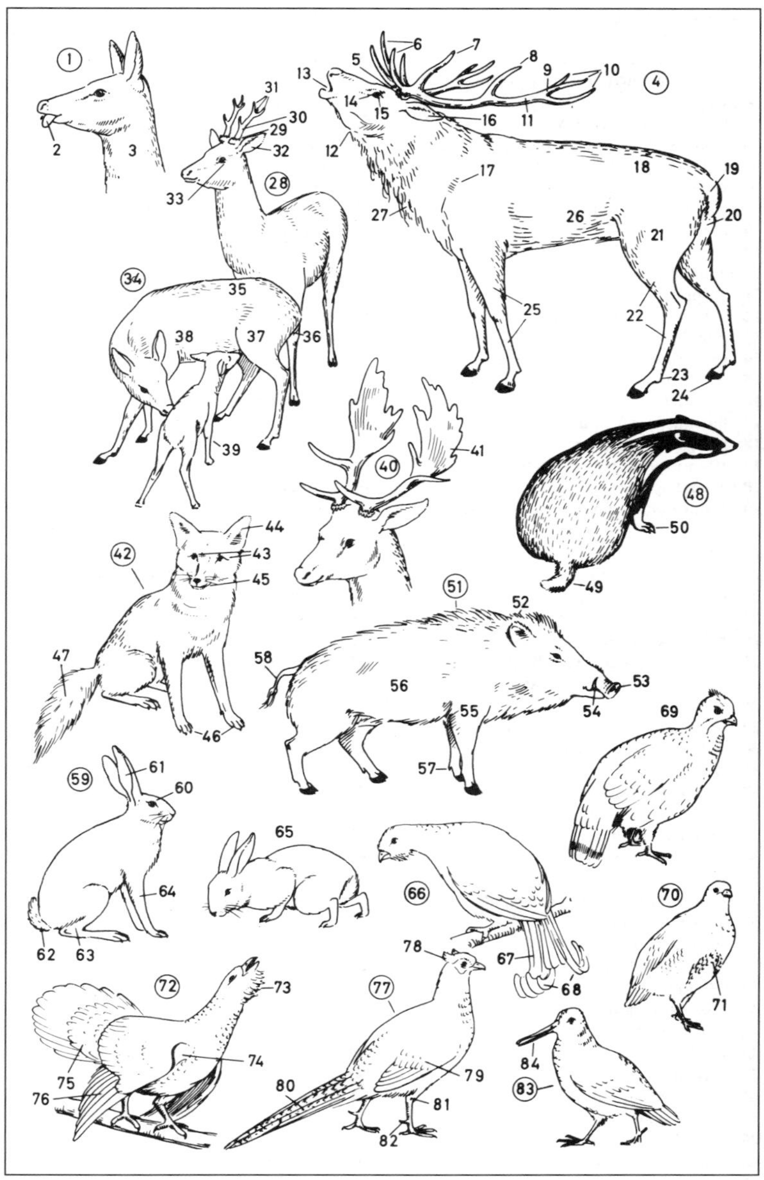
1
2
3
4
5
6
7
8
9
10
11
12
13
14
15
16
17
18
19
20
21
22
23
24
25
26
27
28
29
30
31
32
33
34
35
36
37
38
39
40
41
42
43
44
45
46
47
48
49
50
51
52
53
54
55
56
57
58
59
60
61
62
63
64
65
66
67
68
69
70
71
72
73
74
75
76
77
78
79
80
81
82
83
84

89 Fish Farming (Fish Culture, Pisciculture) and Angling

1-19 fish farming (fish culture, pisciculture)
1 cage in running water
2 hand net (landing net)
3 semi-oval barrel for transporting fish
4 vat
5 trellis in the overflow
6 trout pond; *sim.:* carp pond, a fry pond, fattening pond, or cleansing pond
7 water inlet (water supply pipe)
8 water outlet (outlet pipe)
9 monk
10 screen
11-19 hatchery
11 stripping the spawning pike (seed pike)
12 fish spawn (spawn, roe, fish eggs)
13 female fish (spawner, seed fish)
14 trout breeding (trout rearing)
15 Californian incubator
16 trout fry
17 hatching jar for pike
18 long incubation tank
19 Brandstetter egg-counting board
20-94 angling
20-31 bottom fishing (coarse fishing)
20 line shooting
21 coils
22 cloth (rag) or paper
23 rod rest
24 bait tin
25 fish basket (creel)
26 fishing for carp from a boat
27 rowing boat (fishing boat)
28 keep net
29 drop net
30 pole (punt pole, quant pole)
31 casting net
32 two-handed side cast with fixed-spool reel
33 initial position
34 point of release
35 path of the rod tip
36 trajectory of the baited weight
37-94 fishing tackle
37 fishing pliers
38 filleting knife
39 fish knife
40 disgorger (hook disgorger)
41 bait needle
42 gag
43-48 floats
43 sliding cork float
44 plastic float
45 quill float
46 polystyrene float
47 oval bubble float
48 lead-weighted sliding float
49-58 rods
49 solid glass rod
50 cork handle (cork butt)
51 spring-steel ring
52 top ring (end ring)
53 telescopic rod
54 rod section
55 bound handle (bound butt)
56 ring
57 carbon-fibre rod; *sim.:* hollow glass rod
58 all-round ring (butt ring for long cast), a steel bridge ring
59-64 reels
59 multiplying reel (multiplier reel)
60 line guide
61 fixed-spool reel (stationary-drum reel)
62 bale arm
63 fishing line
64 controlling the cast with the index finger
65-76 baits
65 fly
66 artificial nymph
67 artificial earthworm
68 artificial grasshopper
69 single-jointed plug (single-jointed wobbler)
70 double-jointed plug (double-jointed wobbler)
71 round wobbler
72 wiggler
73 spoon bait (spoon)
74 spinner
75 spinner with concealed hook
76 long spinner
77 swivel
78 cast (leader)
79-87 hooks
79 fish hook
80 point of the hook with barb
81 bend of the hook
82 spade (eye)
83 open double hook
84 limerick
85 closed treble hook (triangle)
86 carp hook
87 eel hook
88-92 leads (lead weights)
88 oval lead (oval sinker)
89 lead shot
90 pear-shaped lead
91 plummet
92 sea lead
93 fish ladder (fish pass, fish way)
94 stake net

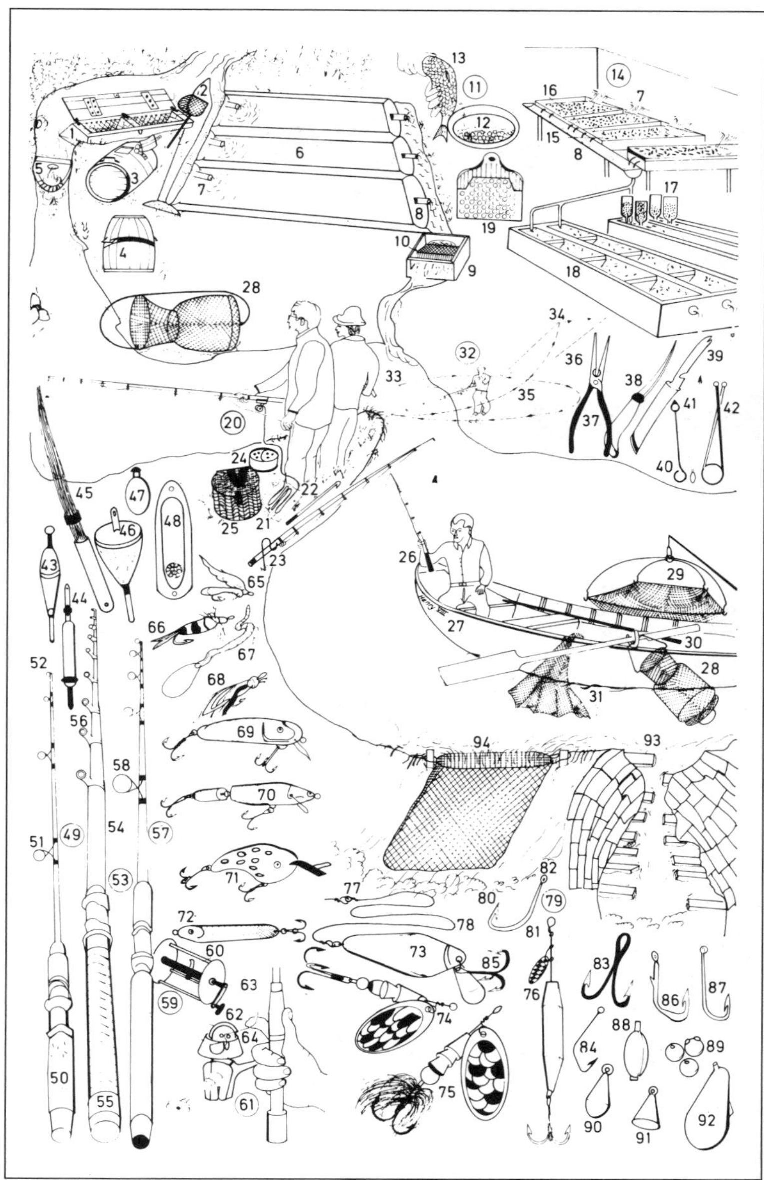
1
2
3
4
5
6
7
8
9
10
11
12
13
14
7
15
16
8
17
18
19
20
21
22
23
24
25
26
27
28
29
30
31
28
32
33
34
35
36
37
38
39
40
41
42
43
44
45
46
47
48
49
50
51
52
53
54
55
56
57
58
59
60
61
62
63
64
65
66
67
68
69
70
71
72
73
74
75
76
77
78
79
80
81
82
83
84
85
86
87
88
89
90
91
92
93
94

90 Sea Fishing

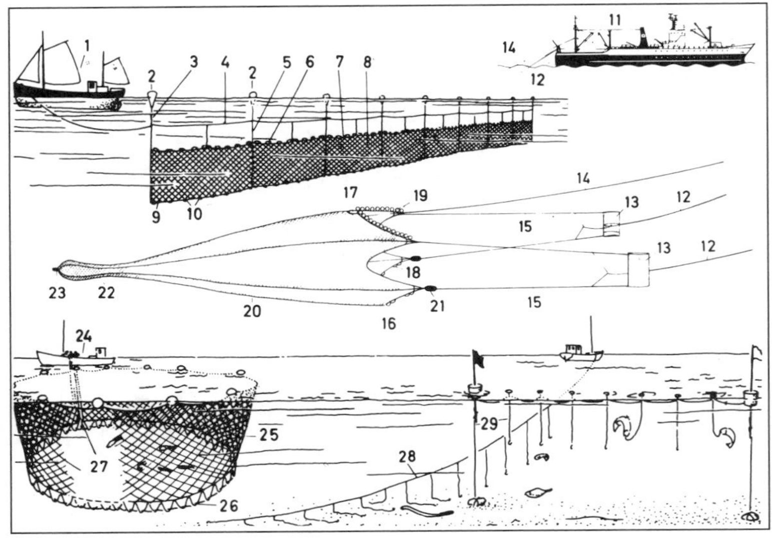

1-23 deep-sea fishing
1-10 drift net fishing
1 herring lugger (fishing lugger, lugger)
2-10 herring drift net
2 buoy
3 buoy rope
4 float line
5 seizing
6 wooden float
7 headline
8 net
9 footrope
10 sinkers (weights)
11-23 trawl fishing (trawling)
11 factory ship, a trawler
12 warp (trawl warp)
13 otter boards
14 net sonar cable
15 wire warp
16 wing
17 net sonar device
18 footrope
19 spherical floats
20 belly
21 1,800 kg iron weight
22 cod end (cod)
23 cod line for closing the cod end
24-29 inshore fishing
24 fishing boat
25 ring net cast in a circle
26 cable for closing the ring net
27 closing gear
28-29 long-line fishing (long-lining)
28 long line
29 suspended fishing tackle

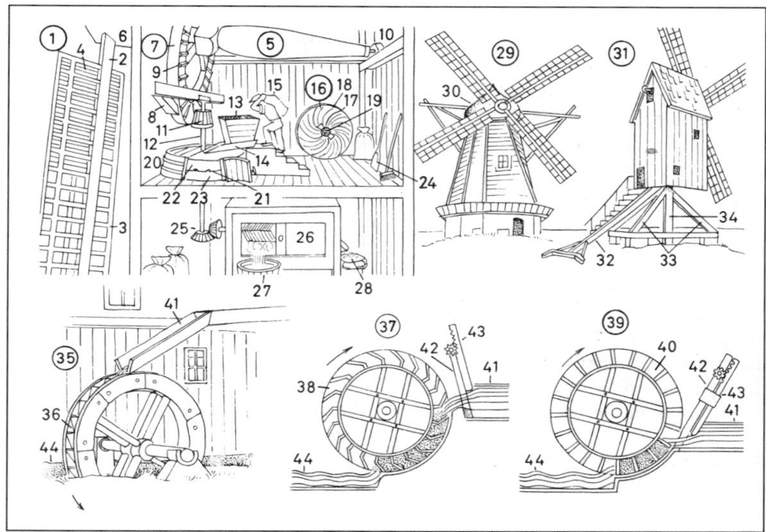

1-34 windmill
1 windmill vane (windmill sail, windmill arm)
2 stock (middling, back, radius)
3 frame
4 shutter
5 wind shaft (sail axle)
6 sail top
7 brake wheel
8 brake
9 wooden cog
10 pivot bearing (step bearing)
11 wallower
12 mill spindle
13 hopper
14 shoe (trough, spout)
15 miller
16 millstone
17 furrow (flute)
18 master furrow
19 eye
20 hurst (millstone casing)
21 set of stones (millstones)
22 runner (upper millstone)
23 bed stone (lower stone, bedder)
24 wooden shovel
25 bevel gear (bevel gearing)
26 bolter (sifter)
27 wooden tub (wooden tun)
28 flour
29 smock windmill (Dutch windmill)
30 rotating (revolving) windmill cap
31 post windmill (German windmill)
32 tailpole (pole)
33 base
34 post

35-44 watermill
35 overshot mill wheel (high-breast mill wheel), a mill wheel (waterwheel)
36 bucket (cavity)
37 middleshot mill wheel (breast mill wheel)
38 curved vane
39 undershot mill wheel
40 flat vane
41 headrace (discharge flume)
42 mill weir
43 overfall (water overfall)
44 millstream (millrace, *Am.* raceway)

92 Malting and Brewing I

1-41 preparation of malt (malting)
1 malting tower (maltings)
2 barley hopper
3 washing floor with compressed-air washing unit
4 outflow condenser
5 water-collecting tank
6 condenser for the steep liquor
7 coolant collecting plant
8 steeping floor (steeping tank, dressing floor)
9 cold water tank
10 hot water tank
11 pump room
12 pneumatic plant
13 hydraulic plant
14 ventilation shaft (air inlet and outlet)
15 exhaust fan
16-18 kilning floors
16 drying floor
17 burner ventilator
18 curing floor
19 outlet duct from the kiln
20 finished malt collecting hopper
21 transformer station
22 cooling compressors
23 green malt (germinated barley)
24 turner (plough)
25 central control room with flow diagram
26 screw conveyor
27 washing floor
28 steeping floor
29 drying kiln
30 curing kiln
31 barley silo
32 weighing apparatus
33 barley elevator
34 three-way chute (three-way tippler)
35 malt elevator
36 cleaning machine
37 malt silo
38 corn removal by suction
39 sacker
40 dust extractor
41 barley reception
42-53 mashing process in the mashhouse
42 premasher (converter) for mixing grist and water
43 mash tub (mash tun) for mashing the malt
44 mash copper (mash tun, *Am.* mash kettle) for boiling the mash
45 dome of the tun
46 propeller (paddle)
47 sliding door
48 water (liquor) supply pipe
49 brewer (master brewer, masher)
50 lauter tun for settling the draff (grains) and filtering off the wort
51 lauter battery for testing the wort for quality
52 hop boiler (wort boiler) for boiling the wort
53 ladle-type thermometer (scoop thermometer)

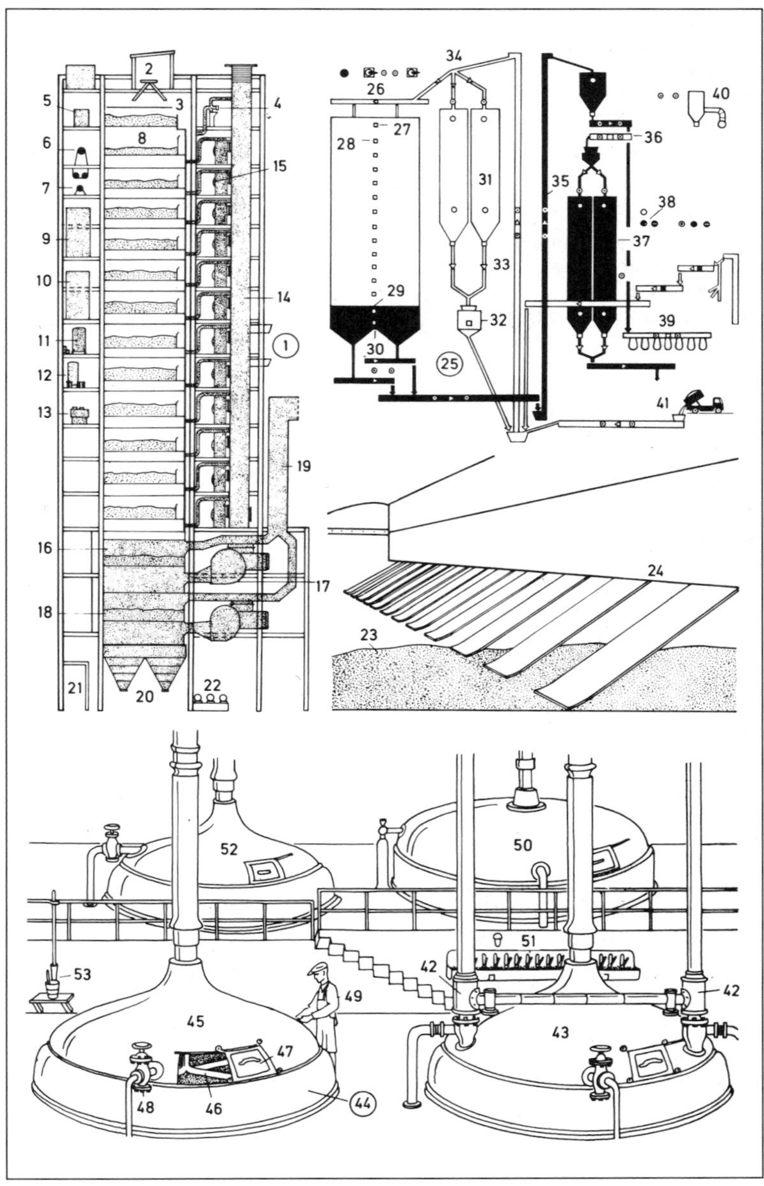
1
2
3
4
5
6
7
8
9
10
11
12
13
14
15
16
17
18
19
20
21
22
23
24
25
26
27
28
29
30
31
32
33
34
35
36
37
38
39
40
41
42
43
44
45
46
47
48
49
50
51
52
53

93 Brewing II

1-31 brewery (brewhouse)
1-5 wort cooling and break removal (trub removal)
1 control desk (control panel)
2 whirlpool separator for removing the hot break (hot trub)
3 measuring vessel for the kieselguhr
4 kieselguhr filter
5 wort cooler
6 pure culture plant for yeast (yeast propagation plant)
7 fermenting cellar
8 fermentation vessel (fermenter)
9 fermentation thermometer (mash thermometer)
10 mash
11 refrigeration system
12 lager cellar
13 manhole to the storage tank
14 broaching tap
15 beer filter
16 barrel store
17 beer barrel, an aluminium (*Am.* aluminum) barrel
18 bottle-washing plant
19 bottle-washing machine (bottle washer)
20 control panel
21 cleaned bottles
22 bottling
23 forklift truck (fork truck, forklift)
24 stack of beer crates
25 beer can
26 beer bottle, a Eurobottle with bottled beer; *kinds of beer:* light beer (lager, light ale, pale ale or bitter), dark beer (brown ale, mild), Pilsener beer, Munich beer, malt beer, strong beer (bock beer), porter, ale, stout, Salvator beer, wheat beer, small beer
27 crown cork (crown cork closure)
28 disposable pack (carry-home pack)
29 non-returnable bottle (single-trip bottle)
30 beer glass
31 head

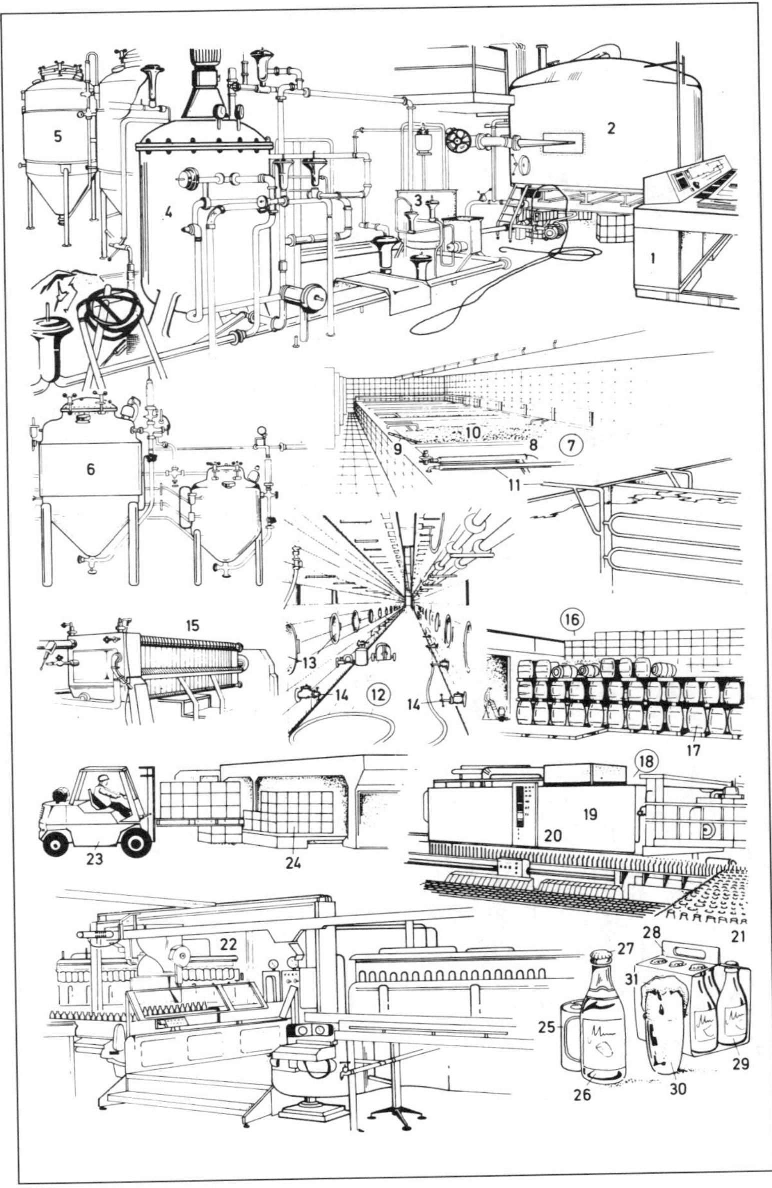
1
2
3
4
5
6
7
8
9
10
11
12
13
14
14
15
16
17
18
19
20
21
22
23
24
25
26
27
28
29
30
31

94 Slaughterhouse (Abattoir)

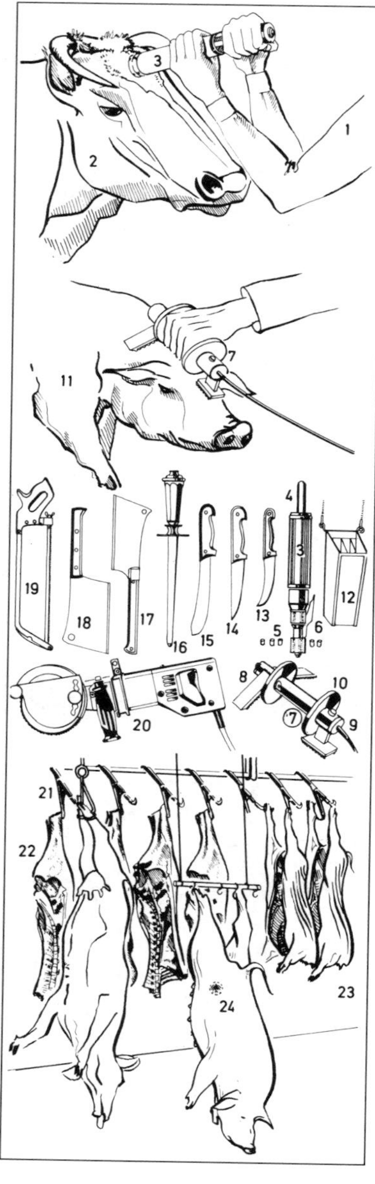

1 slaughterman (*Am.* slaughterer, killer)
2 animal for slaughter, an ox
3 captive-bolt pistol (pneumatic gun), a stunning device
4 bolt
5 cartridges
6 release lever (trigger)
7 electric stunner
8 electrode
9 lead
10 hand guard (insulation)
11 pig (*Am.* hog) for slaughter
12 knife case
13 flaying knife
14 sticking knife (sticker)
15 butcher's knife (butcher knife)
16 steel
17 splitter
18 cleaver (butcher's cleaver, meat axe (*Am.* meat ax))
19 bone saw (butcher's saw)
20 meat saw for sawing meat into cuts

21-24 cold store (cold room)

21 gambrel (gambrel stick)
22 quarter of beef
23 side of pork
24 meat inspector's stamp

Meat Joints 95

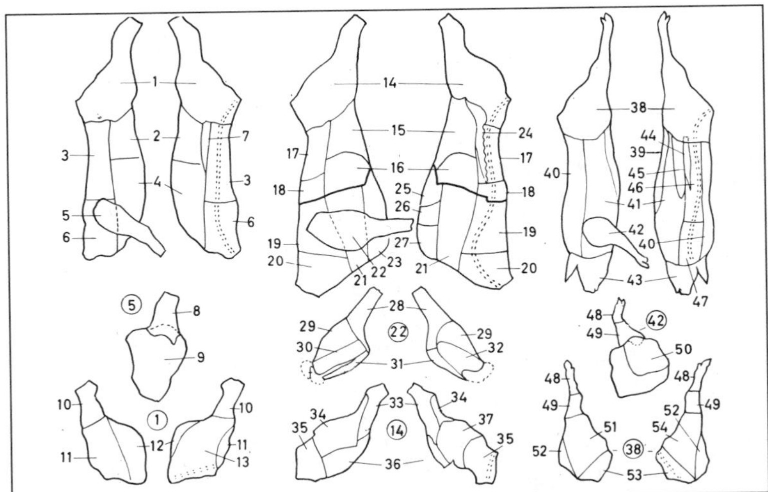

left: meat side;
right: bone side

1-13 *animal:* **calf;** *meat:* **veal**
1 leg with hind knuckle
2 flank
3 loin and rib
4 breast (breast of veal)
5 shoulder with fore knuckle
6 neck with scrag (scrag end)
7 best end of loin (of loin of veal)
8 fore knuckle
9 shoulder
10 hind knuckle
11 roasting round (oyster round)
12 cutlet for frying or braising
13 undercut (fillet)
14-37 *animal:* **ox;** *meat:* **beef**
14 round with rump and shank
15-16 flank
15 thick flank
16 thin flank
17 sirloin
18 prime rib (fore ribs, prime fore rib)
19 middle rib and chuck
20 neck
21 flat rib
22 leg of mutton piece (bladebone) with shin
23 brisket (brisket of beef)
24 fillet (fillet of beef)
25 hind brisket
26 middle brisket
27 breastbone
28 shin
29 leg of mutton piece
30 bladebone [meat side]
31 part of top rib
32 bladebone [bone side]
33 shank
34 silverside
35 rump
36 thick flank
37 top side
38-54 *animal:* **pig;** *meat:* **pork**
38 leg with knuckle and trotter
39 ventral part of the belly
40 back fat
41 belly
42 bladebone with knuckle and trotter
43 head (pig's head)
44 fillet (fillet of pork)
45 leaf fat (pork flare)
46 loin (pork loin)
47 spare rib
48 trotter
49 knuckle
50 butt
51 fore end (ham)
52 round end for boiling
53 fat end
54 gammon steak

96 Butcher's Shop

1-30 butcher's shop
1-4 meat
1 ham on the bone
2 flitch of bacon
3 smoked meat
4 piece of loin (piece of sirloin)
5 lard
6-11 sausages
6 price label
7 mortadella
8 scalded sausage; *kinds:* Vienna sausage (Wiener), Frankfurter sausage (Frankfurter)
9 collared pork (*Am.* headcheese)
10 ring of [Lyoner] sausage
11 pork sausages; *also:* beef sausages
12 cold shelves
13 meat salad (diced meat salad)
14 cold meats (*Am.* cold cuts)
15 pâté
16 mince (mincemeat, minced meat)
17 knuckle of pork
18 basket for special offers
19 price list for special offers
20 special offer
21 freezer
22 pre-packed joints
23 deep-frozen ready-to-eat meal
24 chicken
25 canned food
26 can
27 canned vegetables
28 canned fish
29 salad cream
30 soft drinks

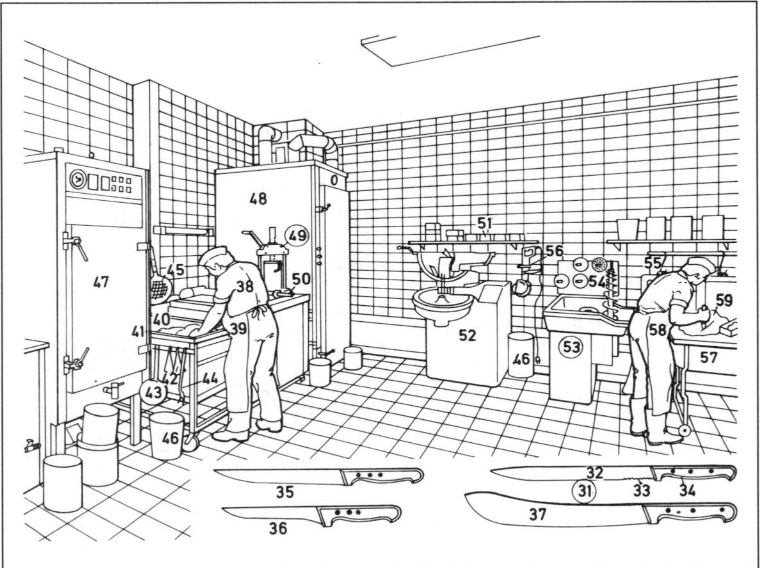

31-59 manufacture of sausages
31-37 butcher's knives
31 slicer
32 knife blade
33 saw teeth
34 knife handle
35 carver (carving knife)
36 boning knife
37 butcher's knife (butcher knife)
38 butcher (master butcher)
39 butcher's apron
40 meat-mixing trough
41 sausage meat
42 scraper
43 skimmer
44 sausage fork
45 scalding colander
46 waste bin (*Am.* trash bin)
47 cooker, for cooking with steam or hot air
48 smoke house
49 sausage filler (sausage stuffer)
50 feed pipe (supply pipe)
51 containers for vegetables
52 mincing machine for sausage meat
53 mincing machine (meat mincer, mincer, *Am.* meat grinder)
54 plates (steel plates)
55 meathook (butcher's hook)
56 bone saw
57 chopping board
58 butcher, cutting meat
59 piece of meat

97 Bakery

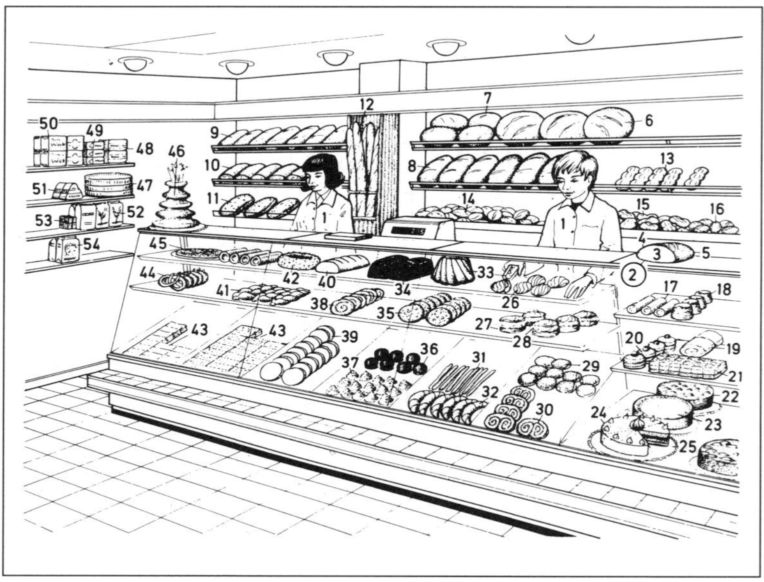

1-54 baker's shop
1 shop assistant (*Am.* salesgirl, saleslady)
2 bread (loaf of bread, loaf)
3 crumb
4 crust (bread crust)
5 crust (*Am.* heel)
6-12 kinds of bread (breads)
6 round loaf, a wheat and rye bread
7 small round loaf
8 long loaf (bloomer), a wheat and rye bread
9 white loaf
10 pan loaf, a wholemeal rye bread
11 yeast bread (*Am.* stollen)
12 French loaf (baguette, French stick)
13-16 rolls
13 brown roll
14 white roll
15 finger roll
16 rye-bread roll
17-47 cakes (confectionery)
17 cream roll
18 vol-au-vent, a puff pastry (*Am.* puff paste)
19 Swiss roll (*Am.* jelly roll)
20 tartlet
21 cream slice
22-24 flans (*Am.* pies) **and gateaux** (torten)
22 fruit flan (*kinds:* strawberry flan, cherry flan, gooseberry flan, peach flan, rhubarb flan)
23 cheesecake
24 cream cake (*Am.* cream pie) (*kinds:* butter-cream cake, Black Forest gateau)
25 cake plate
26 meringue
27 cream puff
28 whipped cream
29 doughnut (*Am.* bismarck)
30 Danish pastry
31 saltstick (Salzstange) (*also:* caraway roll, caraway stick)
32 croissant (crescent roll, *Am.* crescent)

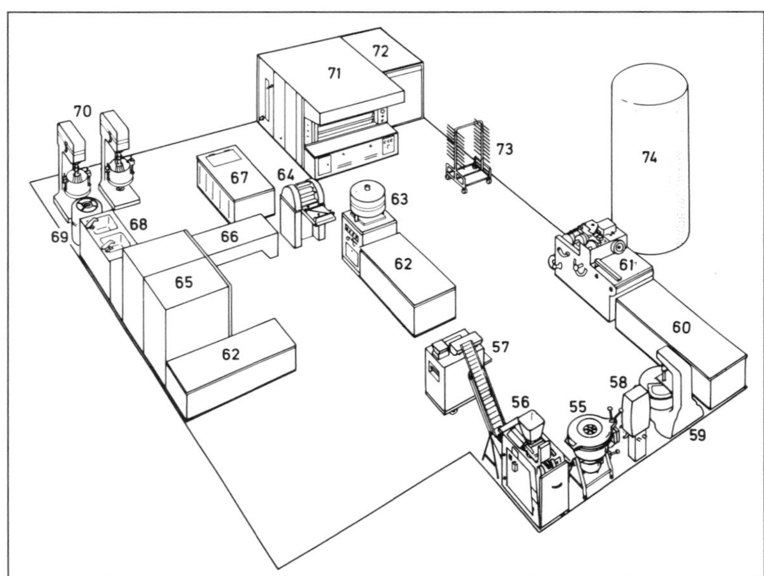

33 ring cake (gugelhupf)
34 slab cake with chocolate icing
35 streusel cakes
36 marshmallow
37 coconut macaroon
38 pastry whirl
39 iced bun
40 sweet bread
41 plaited bun (plait)
42 Frankfurter garland cake
43 slices (*kinds:* streusel slices, sugared slices, plum slices)
44 pretzel
45 wafer (*Am.* waffle)
46 tree cake (baumkuchen)
47 flan case
48-50 wrapped bread
48 wholemeal bread (*also:* wheatgerm bread)
49 pumpernickel (wholemeal rye bread)
50 crispbread
51 gingerbread (*Am.* lebkuchen)
52 flour (*kinds:* wheat flour, rye flour)
53 yeast (baker's yeast)
54 rusks (French toast)
55-74 bakery (bakehouse)
55 kneading machine (dough mixer)
56-57 bread unit
56 divider
57 moulder (*Am.* molder)
58 premixer
59 dough mixer
60 workbench
61 roll unit
62 workbench
63 divider and rounder (rounding machine)
64 crescent-forming machine
65 freezers
66 oven [for baking with fat]
67-70 confectionery unit
67 cooling table
68 sink
69 boiler
70 whipping unit [with beater]
71 reel oven (oven)
72 fermentation room
73 fermentation trolley
74 flour silo

98 Grocer's Shop (*Am.* Grocery Store)

1-87 grocer's shop (grocer's, delicatessen shop, *Am.* grocery store, delicatessen store), a retail shop (*Am.* retail store)
1 window display
2 poster (advertisement)
3 cold shelves
4 sausages
5 cheese
6 roasting chicken (broiler)
7 poulard, a fattened hen
8-11 baking ingredients
8 raisins; *sim.:* sultanas
9 currants
10 candied lemon peel
11 candied orange peel
12 computing-scale, a rapid scale
13 shop assistant (*Am.* salesclerk)
14 goods shelves (shelves)
15-20 canned food
15 canned milk
16 canned fruit (cans of fruit)
17 canned vegetables
18 fruit juice
19 sardines in oil, a can of fish
20 canned meat (cans of meat)
21 margarine
22 butter
23 coconut oil, a vegetable oil
24 oil; *kinds:* salad oil, olive oil, sunflower oil, wheatgerm oil, groundnut oil
25 vinegar
26 stock cube
27 bouillon cube
28 mustard
29 pickled gherkin
30 soup seasoning
31 shop assistant (*Am.* salesgirl, saleslady)
32-34 pastas
32 spaghetti
33 macaroni
34 noodles
35-39 cereal products
35 pearl barley
36 semolina
37 rolled oats (porridge oats, oats)
38 rice
39 sago
40 salt
41 grocer (*Am.* groceryman), a shopkeeper (tradesman, retailer, *Am.* storekeeper)

42 capers
43 customer
44 receipt (sales check)
45 shopping bag
46-49 wrapping material
46 wrapping paper
47 adhesive tape
48 paper bag
49 cone-shaped paper bag
50 blancmange powder
51 whole-fruit jam (preserve)
52 jam
53-55 sugar
53 cube sugar
54 icing sugar (*Am.* confectioner's sugar)
55 refined sugar in crystals
56-59 spirits
56 whisky (whiskey)
57 rum
58 liqueur
59 brandy (cognac)
60-64 wine in bottles (bottled wine)
60 white wine
61 Chianti
62 vermouth
63 sparkling wine
64 red wine
65-68 tea, coffee, etc.
65 coffee (pure coffee)
66 cocoa
67 coffee
68 tea bag
69 electric coffee grinder
70 coffee roaster
71 roasting drum
72 sample scoop
73 price list
74 freezer
75-86 confectionery (*Am.* candies)
75 sweet (*Am.* candy)
76 drops
77 toffees
78 bar of chocolate
79 chocolate box
80 chocolate, a sweet
81 nougat
82 marzipan
83 chocolate liqueur
84 Turkish delight
85 croquant
86 truffle
87 soda water

99 Supermarket

1-96 supermarket, a self-service food store
1 shopping trolley
2 customer
3 shopping bag
4 entrance to the sales area
5 barrier
6 sign (notice) banning dogs
7 dogs tied by their leads
8 basket
9 **bread and cake counter** (bread counter, cake counter)
10 display counter for bread and cakes
11 kinds of bread (breads)
12 rolls
13 croissants (crescent rolls, *Am.* crescents)
14 round loaf
15 gateau
16 pretzel [made with yeast dough]
17 shop assistant (*Am.* salesgirl, saleslady)
18 customer
19 sign listing goods
20 fruit flan
21 slab cake
22 ring cake
23 **cosmetics gondola,** a gondola (sales shelves)
24 canopy
25 hosiery shelf
26 stockings (nylons)
27-35 **toiletries** (cosmetics)
27 jar of cream (cream; *kinds:* moisturising cream, day cream, night-care cream, hand cream)
28 packet of cotton wool
29 talcum powder
30 packet of cotton wool balls
31 toothpaste
32 nail varnish (nail polish)
33 shaving cream
34 bath salts
35 sanitary articles
36, 37 pet foods
36 complete dog food
37 packet of dog biscuits
38 bag of cat litter
39 **cheese counter**
40 whole cheese
41 Swiss cheese (Emmental cheese) with holes
42 Edam cheese, a round cheese
43 gondola for dairy products
44 long-life milk; *also:* pasteurized milk, homogenized milk)
45 plastic milk bag

46 cream
47 butter
48 margarine
49 box of cheeses
50 box of eggs
51 **fresh meat counter** (meat counter)
52 ham on the bone
53 meat (meat products)
54 sausages
55 ring of pork sausage
56 ring of blood sausage
57 freezer
58-61 **frozen food**
58 poulard
59 turkey leg (drumstick)
60 boiling fowl
61 frozen vegetables
62 **gondola for baking ingredients and cereal products**
63 wheat flour
64 sugar loaf
65 packet of noodles
66 salad oil
67 packet of spice
68-73 **tea, coffee, etc.**
68 coffee
69 packet of tea
70 instant coffee
71 **drinks gondola**
72 soft drinks
73 can of beer
74 bottle of fruit juice
75 can of fruit juice
76 bottle of wine
77 bottle of Chianti
78 bottle of champagne
79 emergency exit
80 **fruit and vegetable counter**
81 vegetable basket
82 tomatoes
83 cucumbers
84 cauliflower
85 pineapple
86 apples
87 pears
88 scales for weighing fruit
89 grapes (bunches of grapes)
90 bananas
91 can
92 **checkout**
93 cash register
94 cashier
95 chain
96 assistant departmental manager

100 Shoemaker (Bootmaker)

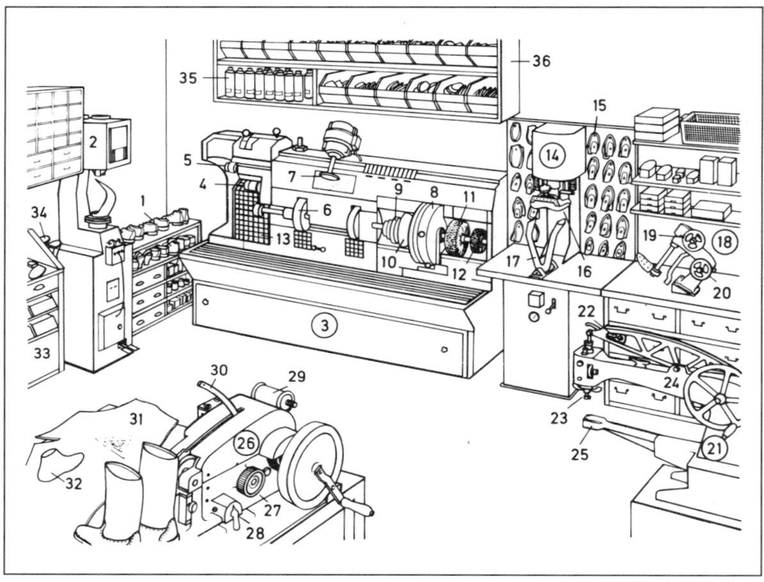

1-68 shoemaker's workshop (bootmaker's workshop)
1 finished (repaired) shoes
2 auto-soling machine
3 finishing machine
4 heel trimmer
5 sole trimmer
6 scouring wheel
7 naum keag
8 drive unit (drive wheel)
9 iron
10 buffing wheel
11 polishing brush
12 horsehair brush
13 extractor grid
14 automatic sole press
15 press attachment
16 pad
17 press bar
18 stretching machine
19 width adjustment
20 length adjustment
21 stitching machine
22 power regulator (power control)
23 foot
24 handwheel
25 arm
26 sole stitcher (sole-stitching machine)
27 foot bar lever
28 feed adjustment (feed setting)
29 bobbin (cotton bobbin)
30 thread guide (yarn guide)
31 sole leather
32 [wooden] last
33 workbench
34 last
35 dye spray
36 shelves for materials

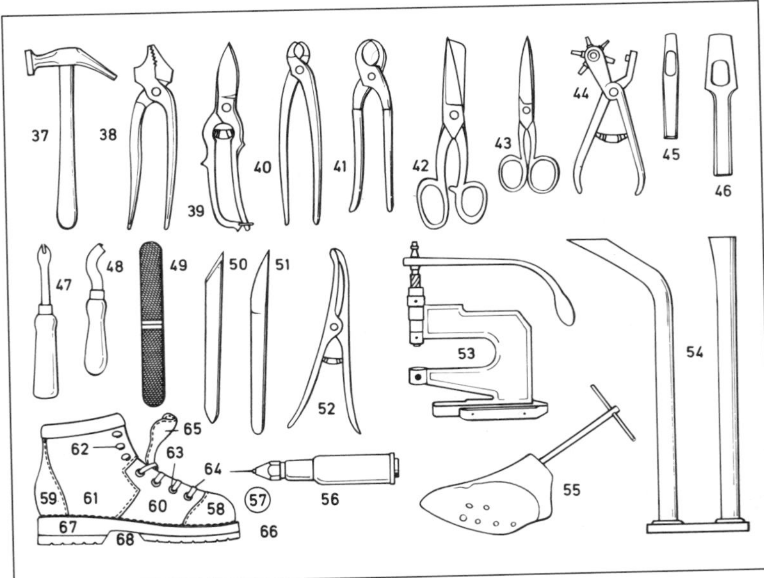

37 shoemaker's hammer
38 shoemaker's pliers (welt pincers)
39 sole-leather shears
40 small pincers (nippers)
41 large pincers (nippers)
42 upper-leather shears
43 scissors
44 revolving punch (rotary punch)
45 punch
46 punch with handle
47 nail puller
48 welt cutter
49 shoemaker's rasp
50 cobbler's knife (shoemaker's knife)
51 skiving knife (skife knife, paring knife)
52 toecap remover
53 eyelet, hook, and press-stud setter
54 stand (with iron lasts)
55 width-setting tree
56 nail grip
57 boot
58 toecap
59 counter
60 vamp
61 quarter
62 hook
63 eyelet
64 lace (shoelace, bootlace)
65 tongue
66 sole
67 heel
68 shank (waist)

101 Shoes (Footwear)

1 winter boot
2 PVC sole (plastic sole)
3 high-pile lining
4 nylon
5 men's boot
6 inside zip (*Am.* zipper)
7 men's high leg boot
8 platform sole (platform)
9 Western boot (cowboy boot)
10 pony-skin boot
11 cemented sole
12 ladies' boot
13 men's high leg boot
14 seamless PVC waterproof wellington boot
15 natural-colour (*Am.* natural-color) sole
16 toecap
17 tricot lining (knitwear lining)
18 hiking boot
19 grip sole
20 padded collar
21 tie fastening (lace fastening)
22 open-toe mule
23 terry upper
24 polo outsole
25 mule
26 corduroy upper
27 evening sandal (sandal court shoe)
28 high heel (stiletto heel)
29 court shoe (*Am.* pump)
30 moccasin
31 shoe, a tie shoe (laced shoe, Oxford shoe, *Am.* Oxford)
32 tongue
33 high-heeled shoe (shoe with raised heel)
34 casual
35 trainer (training shoe)
36 tennis shoe
37 counter (stiffening)
38 natural-colour (*Am.* natural-color) rubber sole
39 heavy-duty boot (*Am.* stogy, stogie)
40 toecap
41 slipper
42 woollen (*Am.* woolen) slip sock
43 knit stitch (knit)
44 clog
45 wooden sole
46 soft-leather upper
47 sabot
48 toe post sandal
49 ladies' sandal
50 surgical footbed (sock)
51 sandal
52 shoe buckle (buckle)
53 sling-back court shoe (*Am.* sling pump)
54 fabric court shoe
55 wedge heel
56 baby's first walking boot

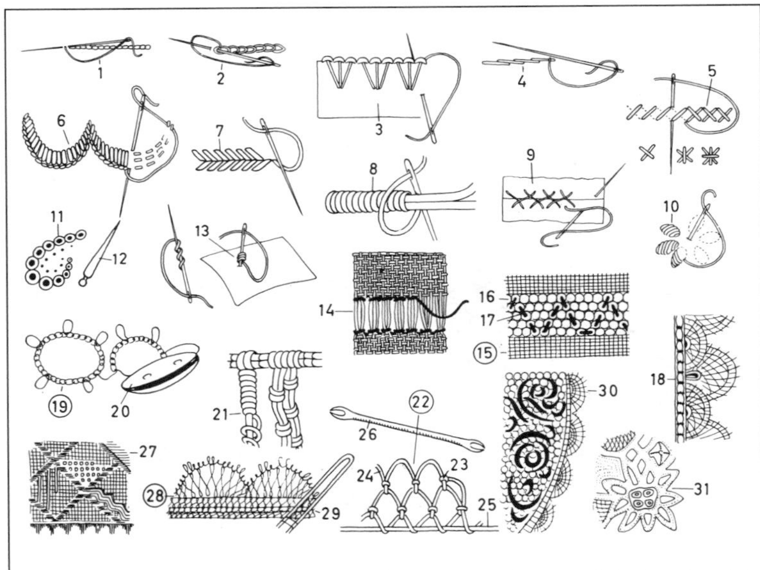

1 backstitch seam
2 chain stitch
3 ornamental stitch
4 stem stitch
5 cross stitch
6 buttonhole stitch (button stitch)
7 fishbone stitch
8 overcast stitch
9 herringbone stitch (Russian stitch, Russian cross stitch)
10 satin stitch (flat stitch)
11 eyelet embroidery (broderie anglaise)
12 stiletto
13 French knot (French dot, knotted stitch, twisted knot stitch)
14 hem stitch work
15 tulle work (tulle lace)
16 tulle background (net background)
17 darning stitch
18 pillow lace (bobbin lace, bone lace); *kinds:* Valenciennes, Brussels lace
19 tatting
20 tatting shuttle (shuttle)
21 knotted work (macramé)
22 filet (netting)
23 netting loop
24 netting thread
25 mesh pin (mesh gauge)
26 netting needle
27 open work
28 gimping (hairpin work)
29 gimping needle (hairpin)
30 needlepoint lace (point lace, needlepoint); *kinds:* reticella lace, Venetian lace, Alençon lace; *sim.:* with metal thread: filigree work
31 braid embroidery (braid work)

103 Dressmaker

1-27 dressmaker's workroom

1 dressmaker
2 tape measure (measuring tape), a metre (*Am.* meter) tape measure
3 cutting shears
4 cutting table
5 model dress
6 dressmaker's model (dressmaker's dummy, dress form)
7 model coat
8 sewing machine
9 drive motor
10 drive belt
11 treadle
12 sewing machine cotton (sewing machine thread) [on bobbin]
13 cutting template
14 seam binding
15 button box
16 remnant
17 movable clothes rack
18 hand-iron press
19 presser (ironer)
20 steam iron
21 water feed pipe
22 water container
23 adjustable-tilt ironing surface
24 lift device for the iron
25 steam extractor
26 foot switch controlling steam extraction
27 pressed non-woven woollen (*Am.* woolen) fabric

1-32 tailor's workroom
1 triple mirror
2 lengths of material
3 suiting
4 fashion journal (fashion magazine)
5 ashtray
6 fashion catalogue
7 workbench
8 wall shelves (wall shelf unit)
9 cotton reel
10 small reels of sewing silk
11 hand shears
12 combined electric and treadle sewing machine
13 treadle
14 dress guard
15 band wheel
16 bobbin thread
17 sewing machine table
18 sewing machine drawer
19 seam binding
20 pincushion
21 marking out
22 tailor
23 shaping pad
24 tailor's chalk (French chalk)
25 workpiece
26 steam press (steam pressing unit)
27 swivel arm
28 pressing cushion (pressing pad)
29 iron
30 hand-ironing pad
31 clothes brush
32 pressing cloth

105 Ladies' Hairdresser

1-39 ladies' hairdressing salon and beauty salon (*Am.* beauty parlor, beauty shop)

1-16 hairdresser's tools

1 bowl containing bleach
2 detangling brush
3 bleach tube
4 curler [used in dyeing]
5 curling tongs (curling iron)
6 comb (back comb, side comb)
7 haircutting scissors
8 thinning scissors (*Am.* thinning shears)
9 thinning razor
10 hairbrush
11 hair clip
12 roller
13 curl brush
14 curl clip
15 dressing comb
16 stiff-bristle brush
17 adjustable hairdresser's chair
18 footrest
19 dressing table
20 salon mirror (mirror)
21 electric clippers
22 warm-air comb
23 hand mirror (hand glass)
24 hairspray (hair-fixing spray)
25 drier, a swivel-mounted drier
26 swivel arm of the drier
27 round base
28 shampoo unit
29 shampoo basin
30 hand spray (shampoo spray)
31 service tray
32 shampoo bottle
33 hair drier (hand hair drier, hand-held hair drier)
34 cape (gown)
35 hairdresser
36 perfume bottle
37 bottle of toilet water
38 wig
39 wig block

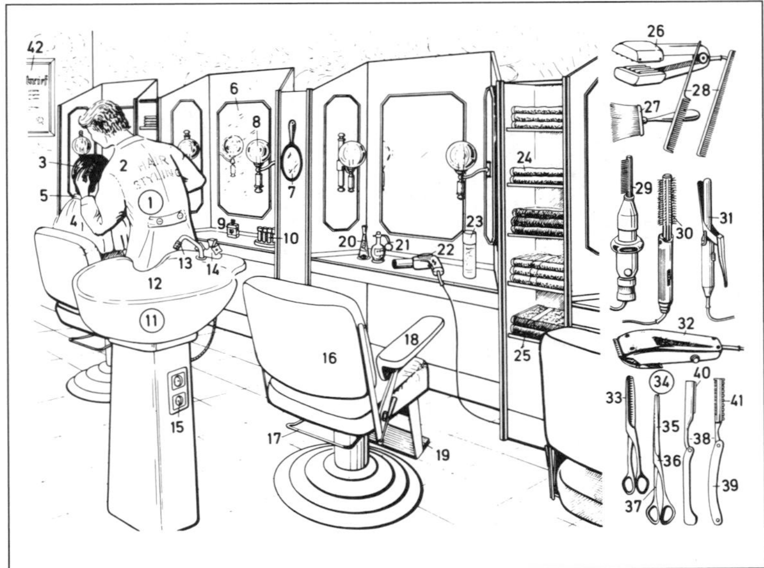

1-42 men's salon (men's hairdressing salon, barber's shop, *Am.* barbershop)

1 hairdresser (barber)
2 overalls (hairdresser's overalls)
3 hairstyle (haircut)
4 cape (gown)
5 paper towel
6 salon mirror (mirror)
7 hand mirror (hand glass)
8 light
9 toilet water
10 hair tonic
11 shampoo unit
12 shampoo basin
13 hand spray (shampoo spray)
14 mixer tap (*Am.* mixing faucet)
15 sockets, e.g. for hair drier
16 adjustable hairdresser's chair (barber's chair)
17 height-adjuster bar (height adjuster)
18 armrest
19 footrest
20 shampoo
21 perfume spray
22 hair drier (hand hair drier, hand-held hair drier)
23 setting lotion in a spray can
24 hand towels for drying hair
25 towels for face compresses
26 crimping iron
27 neck brush
28 dressing comb
29 warm-air comb
30 warm-air brush
31 curling tongs (hair curler, curling iron)
32 electric clippers
33 thinning scissors (*Am.* thinning shears)
34 haircutting scissors; *sim.:* styling scissors
35 scissor-blade
36 pivot
37 handle
38 open razor (straight razor)
39 razor handle
40 edge (cutting edge, razor's edge, razor's cutting edge)
41 thinning razor
42 diploma

107 Tobacco and Smoking Requisites

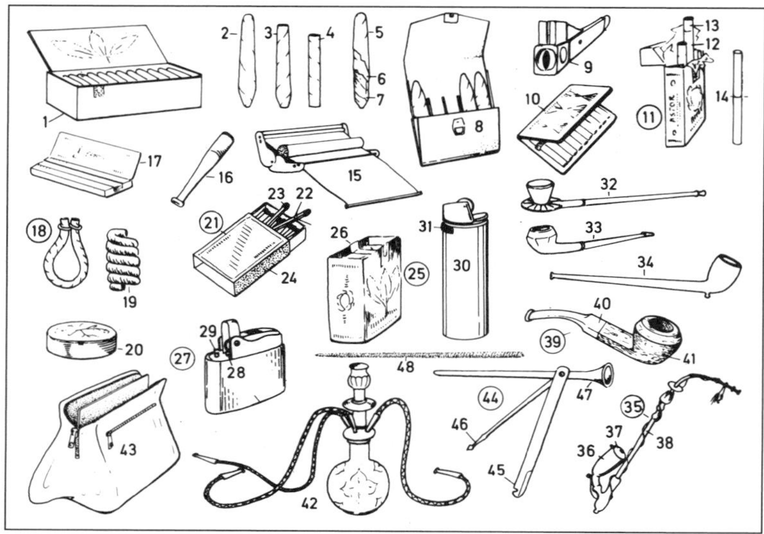

1 cigar box
2 cigar; *kinds:* Havana cigar (Havana), Brazilian cigar, Sumatra cigar
3 cigarillo
4 cheroot
5 wrapper
6 binder
7 filler
8 cigar case
9 cigar cutter
10 cigarette case
11 cigarette packet (*Am.* pack)
12 cigarette, a filter-tipped cigarette
13 cigarette tip; *kinds:* cork tip, gold tip
14 Russian cigarette
15 cigarette roller
16 cigarette holder
17 packet of cigarette papers
18 pigtail (twist of tobacco)
19 chewing tobacco; *a piece:* plug (quid, chew)
20 snuff box, containing snuff
21 matchbox
22 match
23 head (match head)
24 striking surface
25 packet of tobacco; *kinds:* fine cut, shag, navy plug
26 revenue stamp
27 petrol cigarette lighter (petrol lighter)
28 flint
29 wick
30 gas cigarette lighter (gas lighter), a disposable lighter
31 flame regulator
32 chibonk (chibonque)
33 short pipe
34 clay pipe (Dutch pipe)
35 long pipe
36 pipe bowl (bowl)
37 bowl lid
38 pipe stem (stem)
39 briar pipe
40 mouthpiece
41 sand-blast finished or polished briar grain
42 hookah (narghile, narghileh), a water pipe
43 tobacco pouch
44 smoker's companion
45 pipe scraper
46 pipe cleaner
47 tobacco presser
48 pipe cleaner

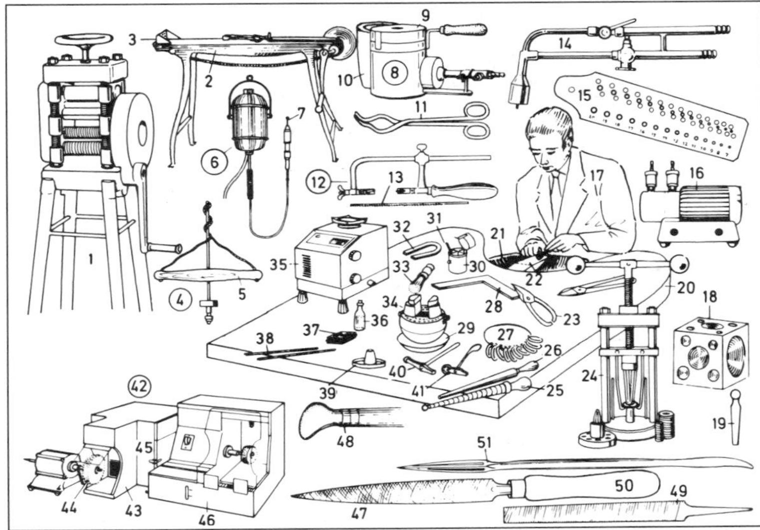

1 wire and sheet roller
2 drawbench (drawing bench)
3 wire (gold or silver wire)
4 archimedes drill (drill)
5 crossbar
6 suspended (pendant) electric drilling machine
7 spherical cutter (cherry)
8 melting pot
9 fireclay top
10 graphite crucible
11 crucible tongs
12 piercing saw (jig saw)
13 piercing saw blade
14 soldering gun
15 thread tapper
16 blast burner (blast lamp) for soldering
17 goldsmith
18 swage block
19 punch
20 workbench (bench)
21 bench apron
22 needle file
23 metal shears
24 wedding ring sizing machine
25 ring gauge (*Am.* gage)
26 ring-rounding tool
27 ring gauge (*Am.* gage)
28 steel set-square
29 (circular) leather pad
30 box of punches
31 punch
32 magnet
33 bench brush
34 engraving ball (joint vice, clamp)
35 gold and silver balance (assay balance), a precision balance
36 soldering flux (flux)
37 charcoal block
38 stick of solder
39 soldering borax
40 shaping hammer
41 chasing (enchasing) hammer
42 polishing and burnishing machine
43 dust exhauster (vacuum cleaner)
44 polishing wheel
45 dust collector (dust catcher)
46 buffing machine
47 round file
48 bloodstone (haematite, hematite)
49 flat file
50 file handle
51 polishing iron (burnisher)

109 Watchmaker, Clockmaker

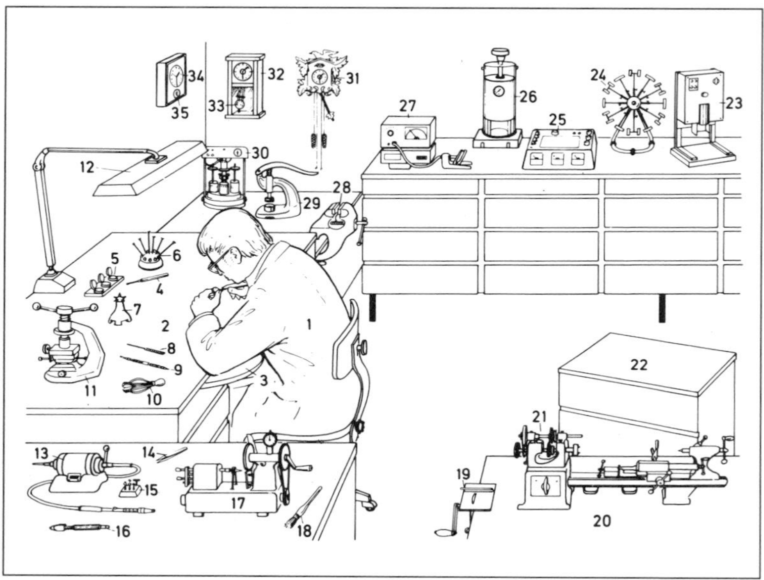

1 watchmaker; *also:* clockmaker
2 workbench
3 armrest
4 oiler
5 oil stand
6 set of screwdrivers
7 clockmaker's anvil
8 broach, a reamer
9 spring pin tool
10 hand-removing tool
11 watchglass-fitting tool
12 workbench lamp, a multi-purpose lamp
13 multi-purpose motor
14 tweezers
15 polishing machine attachments
16 pin vice (pin holder)
17 burnisher, for burnishing, polishing, and shortening of spindles
18 dust brush
19 cutter for metal watch straps
20 precision bench lathe (watchmaker's lathe)
21 drive-belt gear
22 workshop trolley for spare parts
23 ultrasonic cleaner
24 rotating watch-testing machine for automatic watches
25 watch-timing machine for electronic components
26 testing device for waterproof watches
27 electronic timing machine
28 vice (*Am.* vise)
29 watchglass-fitting tool for armoured (*Am.* armored) glasses
30 [automatic] cleaning machine for conventional cleaning
31 cuckoo clock (Black Forest clock)
32 wall clock (regulator)
33 compensation pendulum
34 kitchen clock
35 timer

1 electronic wristwatch
2 digital display (a light-emitting diode (LED) display; *also:* a liquid crystal display, LCD)
3 hour and minute button (on 6, also for setting the analogue (*Am.* analog) display)
4 date and second button
5 strap (watch strap)
6 multifunction electronic watch
7 analogue (*Am.* analog) display
8 alarm button
9 stopwatch button
10 rotating bezel (time-lapse indicator ring)
11 calendar clock (alarm clock)
12 digital display with flip-over numerals
13 alarm indicator
14 stop button
15 forward and backward wind knob
16 grandfather clock
17 face
18 clock case
19 pendulum
20 striking weight
21 time weight
22 sundial
23 hourglass (egg timer)
24-35 components of an automatic watch (automatic wristwatch, self-winding watch)
24 weight (rotor)
25 stone (jewel, jewelled bearing) a synthetic ruby
26 click
27 click wheel
28 clockwork (clockwork mechanism)
29 bottom train plate
30 spring barrel
31 balance wheel
32 escape wheel
33 crown wheel
34 winding crown
35 drive mechanism
36 principle of the electronic quartz watch
37 quartz
38 power source (a button cell)
39 hour hand
40 minute hand
41 wheels
42 stepping motor (stepper motor)
43 frequency divider (integrated circuit)
44 decoder

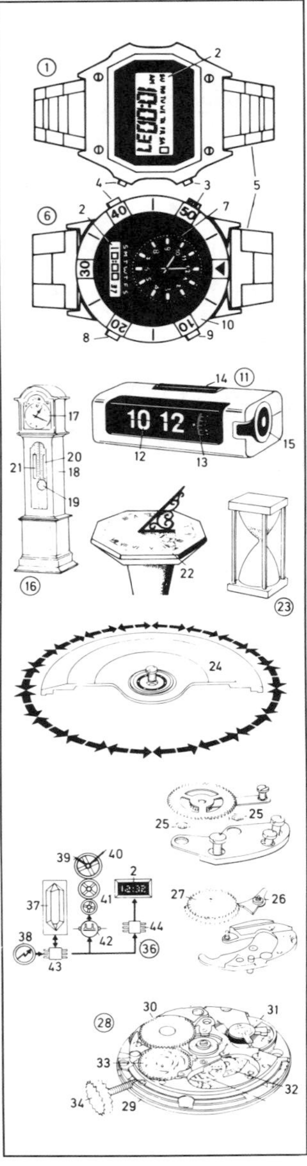

111 Optician

1-19 sales premises

1-4 spectacle fitting

1 optician
2 customer
3 trial frame
4 mirror
5 stand with spectacle frames (display of frames, range of spectacles)
6 sunglasses (sun spectacles)
7 metal frame
8 tortoiseshell frame (shell frame)
9 spectacles (glasses)

10-14 spectacle frame

10 fitting (mount) of the frame
11 bridge
12 pad bridge
13 side
14 side joint
15 spectacle lens, a bifocal lens
16 hand mirror (hand glass)
17 binoculars
18 monocular telescope (tube)
19 microscope

20-47 optician's workshop

20 workbench

21 universal centring (centering) apparatus

22 centring (centering) suction holder

23 sucker

24 edging machine

25 formers for the lens edging machine

26 inserted former

27 rotating printer

28 abrasive wheel combination

29 control unit

30 machine part

31 cooling water pipe

32 cleaning fluid

33 focimeter (vertex refractionometer)

34 metal-blocking device

35 abrasive wheel combination and forms of edging

36 roughing wheel for preliminary surfacing

37 fining lap for positive and negative lens surfaces

38 fining lap for special and flat lenses

39 plano-concave lens with a flat surface

40 plano-concave lens with a special surface

41 concave and convex lens with a special surface

42 convex and concave lens with a special surface

43 ophthalmic test stand

44 phoropter with ophthalmometer and optometer (refractometer)

45 trial lens case

46 collimator

47 acuity projector

1 laboratory and research microscope, *Leitz system*
2 stand
3 base
4 coarse adjustment
5 fine adjustment
6 illumination beam path (illumination path)
7 illumination optics
8 condenser
9 microscope (microscopic, object) stage
10 mechanical stage
11 objective turret (revolving nosepiece)
12 binocular head
13 beam-splitting prisms
14 transmitted-light microscope with camera and polarizer, *Zeiss system*
15 stage base
16 aperture-stop slide
17 universal stage
18 lens panel
19 polarizing filter
20 camera
21 focusing screen
22 discussion tube arrangement
23 wide-field metallurgical microscope, a reflected-light microscope (microscope for reflected light)
24 matt screen (ground glass screen, projection screen)
25 large-format camera
26 miniature camera
27 base plate
28 lamphouse
29 mechanical stage
30 objective turret (revolving nosepiece)
31 surgical microscope
32 pillar stand
33 field illumination
34 photomicroscope
35 miniature film cassette
36 photomicrographic camera attachment for large-format or television camera
37 surface-finish microscope
38 light section tube
39 rack and pinion
40 zoom stereomicroscope
41 zoom lens
42 dust counter
43 measurement chamber
44 data output
45 analogue (*Am.* analog) output
46 measurement range selector
47 digital display (digital readout)
48 dipping refractometer for examining food
49 microscopic photometer
50 photometric light source
51 measuring device (photomultiplier, multiplier phototube)
52 light source for survey illumination
53 remote electronics
54 universal wide-field microscope
55 adapter for camera or projector attachment
56 eyepiece focusing knob
57 filter pick-up
58 handrest
59 lamphouse for incident (vertical) illumination
60 lamphouse connector for transillumination
61 wide-field stereomicroscope
62 interchangeable lenses (objectives)
63 incident (vertical) illumination (incident top lighting)
64 fully automatic microscope camera, a camera with photomicro mount adapter
65 film cassette
66 universal condenser for research microscope 1
67 universal-type measuring machine for photogrammetry (phototheodolite)
68 photogrammetric camera
69 motor-driven level, a compensator level
70 electro-optical distance-measuring instrument
71 stereometric camera
72 horizontal base
73 one-second theodolite

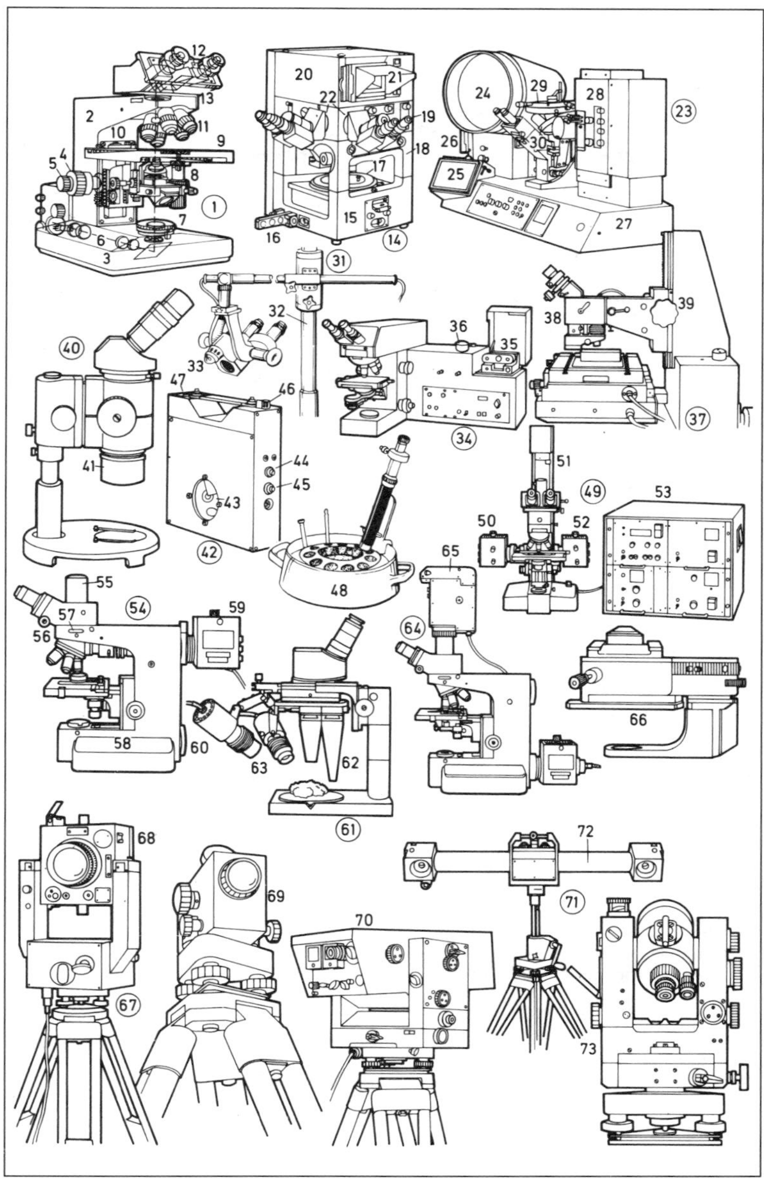
1
2
3
4
5
6
7
8
9
10
11
12
13
14
15
16
17
18
19
20
21
22
23
24
25
26
27
28
29
30
31
32
33
34
35
36
37
38
39
40
41
42
43
44
45
46
47
48
49
50
51
52
53
54
55
56
57
58
59
60
61
62
63
64
65
66
67
68
69
70
71
72
73

113 Optical Instruments II

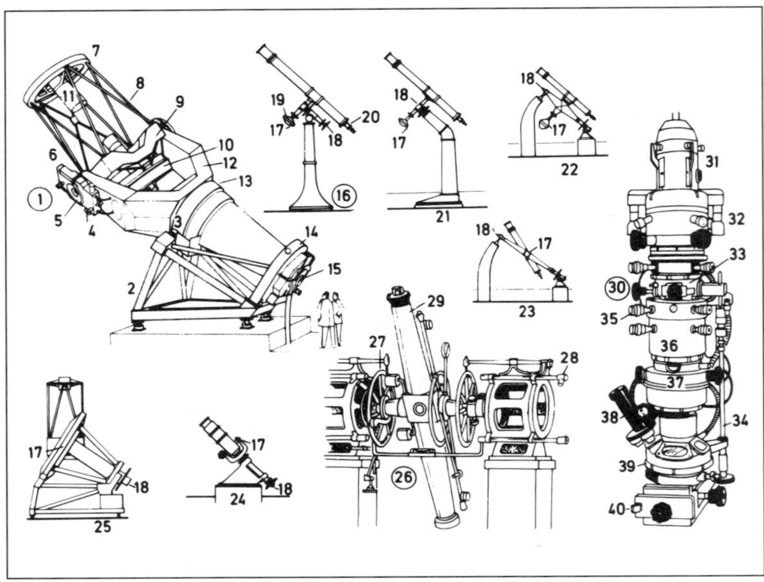

1 **2.2 m reflecting telescope** (reflector)
2 pedestal (base)
3 axial-radial bearing
4 declination gear
5 declination axis
6 declination bearing
7 front ring
8 tube (body tube)
9 tube centre (*Am.* center) section
10 primary mirror (main mirror)
11 secondary mirror (deviation mirror, corrector plate)
12 fork mounting (fork)
13 cover
14 guide bearing
15 main drive unit of the polar axis
16-25 **telescope mountings** (telescope mounts)
16 refractor (refracting telescope) on a German-type mounting
17 declination axis
18 polar axis
19 counterweight (counterpoise)
20 eyepiece
21 knee mounting with a bent column
22 English-type axis mounting (axis mount)
23 English-type yoke mounting (yoke mount)
24 fork mounting (fork mount)
25 horseshoe mounting (horseshoe mount)
26 meridian circle
27 divided circle (graduated circle)
28 reading microscope
29 meridian telescope
30 electron microscope
31-39 microscope tube (microscope body, body tube)
31 electron gun
32 condensers
33 specimen insertion air lock
34 control for the specimen stage adjustment
35 control for the objective apertures
36 objective lens
37 intermediate image screen
38 telescope magnifier
39 final image tube
40 photographic chamber for film and plate magazines

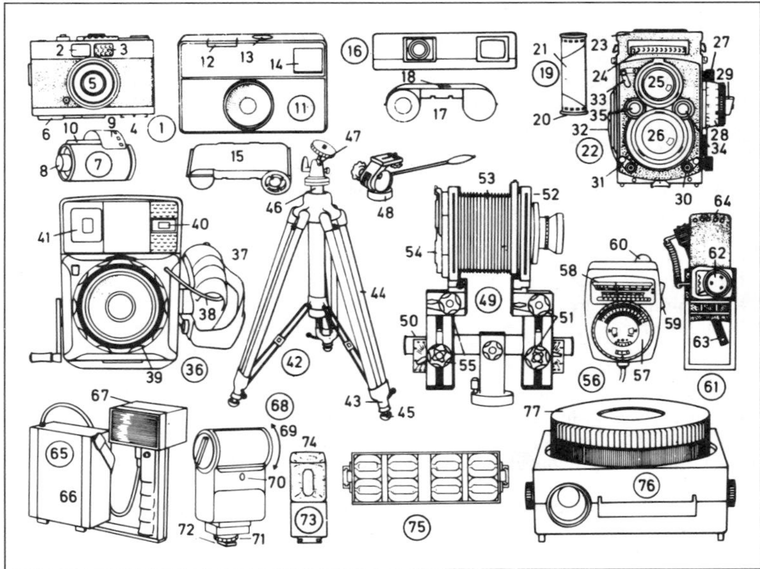

1 miniature camera (35 mm camera)
2 viewfinder eyepiece
3 meter cell
4 accessory shoe
5 flush lens
6 rewind handle (rewind, rewind crank)
7 miniature film cassette (135 film cassette, 35 mm cassette)
8 film spool
9 film with leader and perforations
10 cassette slit (cassette exit slot)
11 cartridge-loading camera
12 shutter release (shutter release button)
13 flash cube contact
14 rectangular viewfinder
15 126 cartridge (instamatic cartridge)
16 pocket camera (subminiature camera)
17 110 cartridge (subminiature cartridge)
18 film window
19 120 rollfilm
20 rollfilm spool
21 backing paper
22 twin-lens reflex camera
23 folding viewfinder hood (focusing hood)
24 meter cell
25 viewing lens
26 object lens
27 spool knob
28 distance setting (focus setting)
29 exposure meter using needle-matching system
30 flash contact
31 shutter release
32 film transport (film advance, film wind)
33 flash switch
34 aperture-setting control
35 shutter speed control
36 large-format hand camera (press camera)
37 grip (handgrip)
38 cable release
39 distance-setting ring (focusing ring)
40 rangefinder window
41 multiple-frame viewfinder (universal viewfinder)
42 tripod
43 tripod leg
44 tubular leg
45 rubber foot
46 central column
47 ball and socket head
48 cine camera pan and tilt head
49 large-format folding camera
50 optical bench
51 standard adjustment
52 lens standard
53 bellows
54 camera back
55 back standard adjustment
56 hand-held exposure meter (exposure meter)
57 calculator dial
58 scales (indicator scales) with indicator needle (pointer)
59 range switch (high/low range selector)
60 diffuser for incident light measurement
61 probe exposure meter for large-format cameras
62 meter
63 probe
64 dark slide
65 battery-portable electronic flash (battery-portable electronic flash unit)
66 power pack unit (battery)
67 flash head
68 single-unit electronic flash (flashgun)
69 swivel-mounted reflector
70 photodiode
71 foot
72 hot-shoe contact
73 flash cube unit
74 flash cube
75 flash bar (AGFA)
76 slide projector
77 rotary magazine

115 Photography II

1-24 system camera (fully automatic miniature single-lens reflex camera)
1 main switch
2 function adjustment button (to set exposure adjustment value, drive mode, and focus area)
3 exposure mode button
4 accessory shoe
5 program reset button
6 data panel (data monitor, data display)
7 card on/off key
8 function selector key
9 chip program card
10 card door
11 card window
12 battery chamber
13 remote control terminal
14 shutter release (shutter release button)
15 autofocus (AF) illuminator and self-timer light
16 manual shutter control [up/down control]
17 reflex mirror
18 autofocus sensor, a CCD image converter (image sensor)
19 bayonet mounting ring
20 aperture setting button
21 lens release
22 focus-mode switch (to switch to manual focusing)
23 autofocus zoom lens, a $\times$ 3 zoom lens (35–105 mm)
24 aperture and autofocus contacts
25-35 viewfinder screen (focusing screen, matt screen), a micro-honeycombed focusing screen
25 flash-on signal
26 flash-ready signal
27 focus signals
28 wide focus area
29 shutter speed display
30 manual-exposure compensation-value indicator
31 aperture or exposure adjustment indicator
32 spot metering indicator
33 spot metering area
34 centre focus area
35 focus area indicator
36-42 LCD data panel (data monitor)
36 program exposure-mode indicator
37 frame counter
38 function indicators
39 aperture or exposure adjustment indicator
40 shutter speed or film speed (film sensitivity) indicator
41 film transport indicator
42 function pointer
43 interchangeable lenses (autofocus lenses, AF lenses)
44 fisheye lens (fisheye)
45 wide-angle lens (short focal-length lens)
46 standard lens
47 medium focal-length lens
48 telephoto lens (long focal-length lens), a zoom lens (variable focus lens, varifocal lens)
49 long-focus lens
50 mirror lens
51 tele converter
52 data back
53 ten-metre (*Am.* ten-meter) film back (magazine back)
54-74 accessories for close-up and macro shots
54 extension tube
55 adapter ring
56 reversing ring
57 lens in retrofocus position
58 bellows unit (extension bellows, close-up bellows attachment)
59 focusing stage
60 slide-copying attachment
61 slide-copying adapter
62 cable release
63 copying stand (copy stand)
64 arm of the copying stand (copy stand)
65 rifle grip
66 table(-top) tripod (mini tripod)
67 ever-ready case
68 lens case
69 soft-leather lens pouch
70 camera bag, of metallic construction: aluminium (*Am.* aluminum) case
71 film container
72 filter case
73 second body
74 ring flash for macro shots

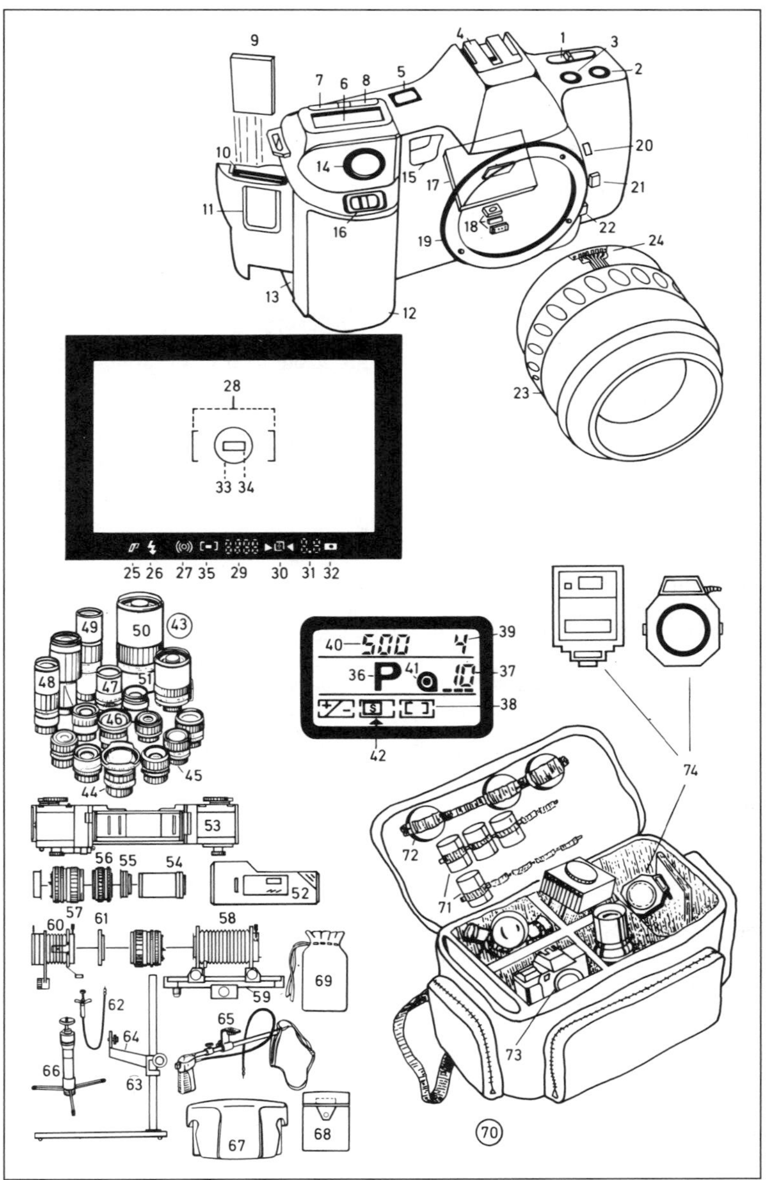
9
4
1
3
2
7
6
8
5
10
14
15
17
20
21
11
16
18
22
19
24
13
12
28
23
33 34
25 26 27 35 29 30 31 32
49
50
43
48
47
51
46
45
44
40
500
4
39
36
P
41
10
37
38
42
74
53
56 55 54
52
72
71
57 61 58
60
69
59
62
65
64
66
63
73
67
68
70

1-60 darkroom equipment
1 developing tank
2 spiral (developing spiral, tank reel)
3 multi-unit developing tank
4 multi-unit tank spiral
5 daylight-loading tank
6 loading chamber
7 film transport handle
8 developing tank thermometer
9 collapsible bottle for developing solution
10 chemical bottles for first developer, stop bath, colour developer, bleach-hardener, stabilizer
11 measuring cylinders
12 funnel
13 tray thermometer (dish thermometer)
14 film clip
15 wash tank (washer)
16 water supply pipe
17 water outlet pipe
18 laboratory timer (timer)
19 automatic film agitator
20 developing tank
21 darkroom lamp (safelight)
22 filter screen
23 film drier (drying cabinet)
24 exposure timer
25 developing dish (developing tray)
26 enlarger
27 baseboard
28 angled column
29 lamphouse (lamp housing)
30 negative carrier
31 bellows
32 lens
33 friction drive for fine adjustment
34 height adjustment (scale adjustment)
35 masking frame (easel)
36 colour (*Am.* color) analyser
37 colour (*Am.* color) analyser lamp
38 probe lead
39 exposure time balancing knob
40 colour (*Am.* color) enlarger
41 enlarger head
42 column
43-45 colour-mixing (*Am.* color-mixing) knob
43 magenta filter adjustment (minus green filter adjustment)
44 yellow filter adjustment (minus blue filter adjustment)
45 cyan filter adjustment (minus red filter adjustment)
46 red swing filter
47 print tongs
48 processing drum
49 squeegee
50 range (assortment) of papers
51 colour (*Am.* color) printing paper, a packet of photographic printing paper
52 colour (*Am.* color) chemicals (colour processing chemicals)
53 enlarging meter (enlarging photometer)
54 adjusting knob with paper speed scale
55 probe
56 semi-automatic thermostatically controlled developing dish
57 rapid print drier (heated print drier)
58 glazing sheet
59 pressure cloth
60 automatic processor (machine processor)

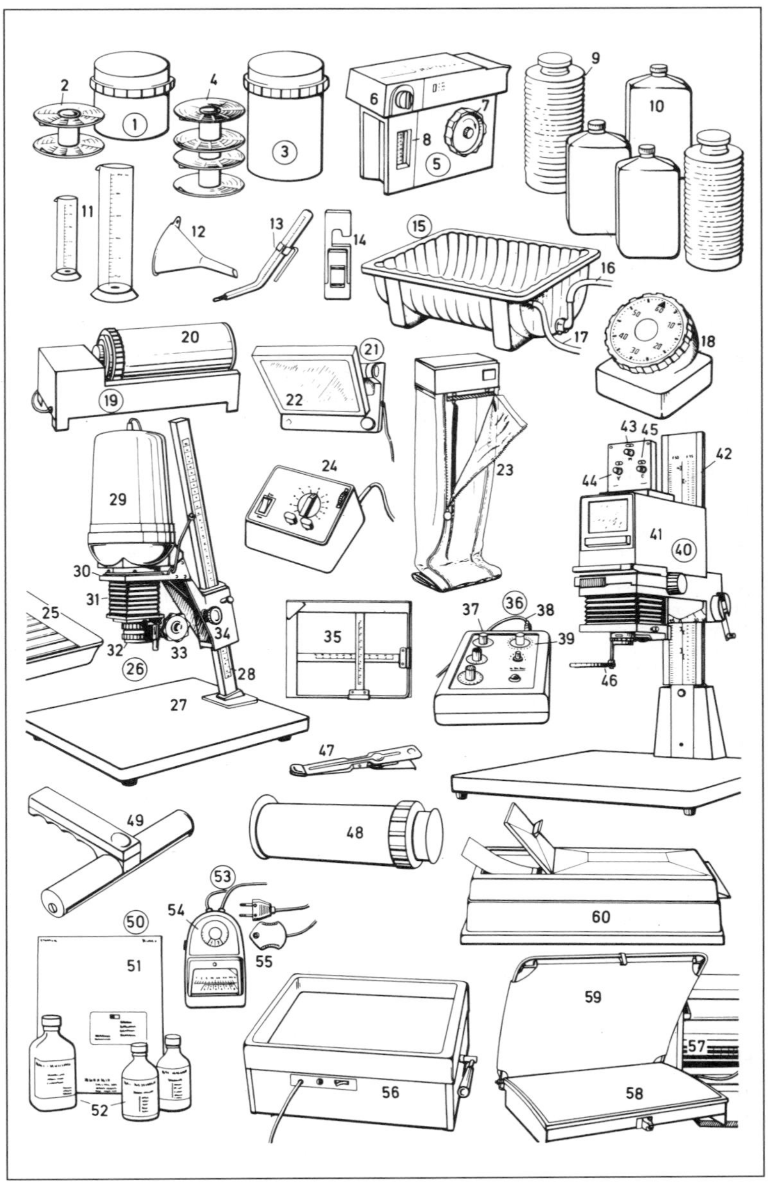
1
2
3
4
5
6
7
8
9
10
11
12
13
14
15
16
17
18
19
20
21
22
23
24
25
26
27
28
29
30
31
32
33
34
35
36
37
38
39
40
41
42
43
44
45
46
47
48
49
50
51
52
53
54
55
56
57
58
59
60

117 Cine Film

1 **cine camera,** a Super-8 sound camera
2 interchangeable zoom lens (variable focus lens, varifocal lens)
3 distance setting (focus setting) and manual focal length setting
4 aperture ring (aperture-setting ring, aperture control ring) for manual aperture setting
5 handgrip with battery chamber
6 shutter release with cable release socket
7 pilot tone or pulse generator socket for the sound recording equipment (with the dual film-tape system)
8 sound connecting cord for microphone or external sound source (in single-system recording)
9 remote control socket (remote control jack)
10 headphone socket (*sim.:* earphone socket)
11 autofocus override switch
12 filming speed selector
13 sound recording selector switch for automatic or manual operation
14 eyepiece with eyecup
15 diopter control ring (dioptric adjustment ring)
16 recording level control (audio level control, recording sensitivity selector)
17 manual/automatic exposure control switch
18 film speed setting
19 power zooming arrangement
20 automatic aperture control
21 **sound track system**
22 sound camera
23 telescopic microphone boom
24 microphone
25 microphone connecting lead (microphone connecting cord)
26 **mixing console** (mixing desk, mixer)
27 inputs from various sound sources
28 output to camera
29 **Super-8 sound film cartridge**
30 film gate of the cartridge
31 feed spool
32 take-up spool
33 recording head (sound head)
34 transport roller (capstan)
35 rubber pinch roller (capstan idler)
36 guide step (guide notch)
37 exposure meter control step
38 conversion filter step (colour, *Am.* color, conversion filter step)
39 **single-8 cassette**
40 film gate opening
41 unexposed film
42 exposed film
43 **16 mm camera**
44 reflex finder (through-the-lens reflex finder)
45 magazine
46-49 lens head
46 lens turret (turret head)
47 telephoto lens
48 wide-angle lens
49 normal lens (standard lens)
50 winding handle
51 **compact Super-8 camera**
52 footage counter
53 macro zoom lens
54 zooming lever
55 macro lens attachment (close-up lens)
56 macro frame (mount for small originals)
57 **underwater housing** (underwater case)
58 direct-vision frame finder
59 measuring rod
60 stabilizing wing
61 grip (handgrip)
62 locking bolt
63 control lever (operating lever)
64 porthole
65 **synchronization start** (sync start)
66 professional press-type camera
67 cameraman
68 camera assistant (sound assistant)
69 handclap marking sync start
70 **dual film-tape recording using a tape recorder**
71 pulse-generating camera
72 pulse cable
73 cassette recorder
74 microphone
75 **dual film-tape reproduction**
76 tape cassette
77 synchronization unit
78 cine projector
79 film feed spool
80 take-up reel (take-up spool), an automatic take-up reel (take-up spool)
81 **sound projector**
82 sound film with magnetic stripe (sound track, track)
83 automatic-threading button
84 trick button
85 volume control
86 reset button
87 fast and slow motion switch
88 forward, reverse, and still projection switch
89 splicer for wet splices
90 hinged clamping plate
91 **film viewer** (animated viewer editor)
92 foldaway reel arm
93 rewind handle (rewinder)
94 viewing screen
95 film perforator (film marker)
96 **six-turntable film and sound cutting table** (editing table, cutting bench, animated sound editor)
97 monitor
98 control buttons (control well)
99 film turntable
100 first sound turntable, e.g. for live sound
101 second sound turntable for post-sync sound
102 film and tape synchronizing head

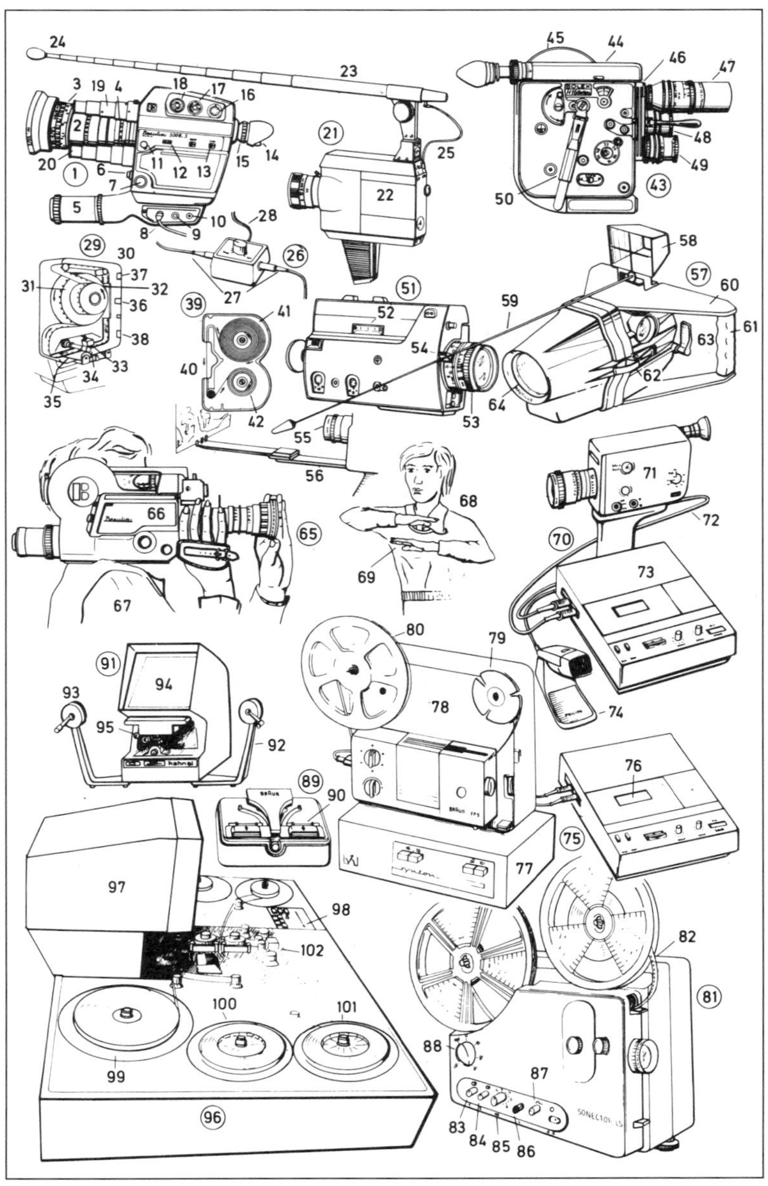
24 23
3 19 4 18 17 16
2 21
14 25
20 1 6 11 12 13 15
7 22
5
10 28
8 9
29 30 26
37 32 31 36
27 51
39 41 52 59
38
40 54
33 34
35 42 53
45 44 46 47
48
49
50 43
58
57 60
61 63 62 64
55
56
68
66
65
67
69
71
72
70
73
80 79
91
94
93
95
92
78
74
76
89 90
75
77
97
98
102
82
81
100 101
88
99
87
96
83 84 85 86

118 Building Site (Construction Site) I

1-49 carcase (carcass, fabric) [house construction, carcassing]
1 basement of tamped (rammed) concrete
2 concrete base course
3 cellar window (basement window)
4 outside cellar steps
5 utility room window
6 utility room door
7 ground floor (*Am.* first floor)
8 brick wall
9 lintel (window head)
10 reveal
11 jamb
12 window ledge (window sill)
13 reinforced concrete lintel
14 upper floor (first floor, *Am.* second floor)
15 hollow-block wall
16 concrete floor
17 work platform (working platform)
18 bricklayer (*Am.* brickmason)
19 bricklayer's labourer (*Am.* laborer); *also:* builder's labourer
20 mortar trough
21 chimney
22 cover (boards) for the staircase
23 scaffold pole (scaffold standard)
24 platform railing
25 angle brace (angle tie) in the scaffold
26 ledger
27 putlog (putlock)
28 plank platform (board platform)
29 guard board
30 scaffolding joint with chain or lashing or whip or bond
31 builder's hoist
32 mixer operator
33 concrete mixer, a gravity mixer
34 mixing drum
35 feeder skip
36 concrete aggregate [sand and gravel]
37 wheelbarrow
38 hose (hosepipe)
39 mortar pan (mortar trough, mortar tub)
40 stack of bricks
41 stacked shutter boards (lining boards)
42 ladder
43 bag of cement
44 site fence, a timber fence
45 signboard (billboard)
46 removable gate
47 contractors' name plates
48 site hut (site office)
49 building site latrine

50-57 bricklayer's (*Am.* brickmason's) **tools**
50 plumb bob (plummet)
51 thick lead pencil
52 trowel
53 bricklayer's (*Am.* brickmason's) hammer (brick hammer)
54 mallet
55 spirit level
56 laying-on trowel
57 float

58-68 masonry bonds
58 brick (standard brick)
59 stretching bond
60 heading bond
61 racking (raking) back
62 English bond
63 stretching course
64 heading course
65 English cross bond (Saint Andrew's cross bond)
66 chimney bond
67 first course
68 second course

69-82 excavation
69 profile (*Am.* batterboard) [fixed on edge at the corner]
70 intersection of strings
71 plumb bob (plummet)
72 excavation side
73 upper edge board
74 lower edge board
75 foundation trench
76 navvy (*Am.* excavator)
77 conveyor belt (conveyor)
78 excavated earth
79 plank roadway
80 tree guard
81 mechanical shovel (excavator)
82 shovel bucket (bucket)

83-91 plastering
83 plasterer
84 mortar trough
85 screen

86-89 ladder scaffold
86 standard ladder
87 boards (planks, platform)
88 diagonal strut (diagonal brace)
89 railing
90 guard netting
91 rope-pulley hoist

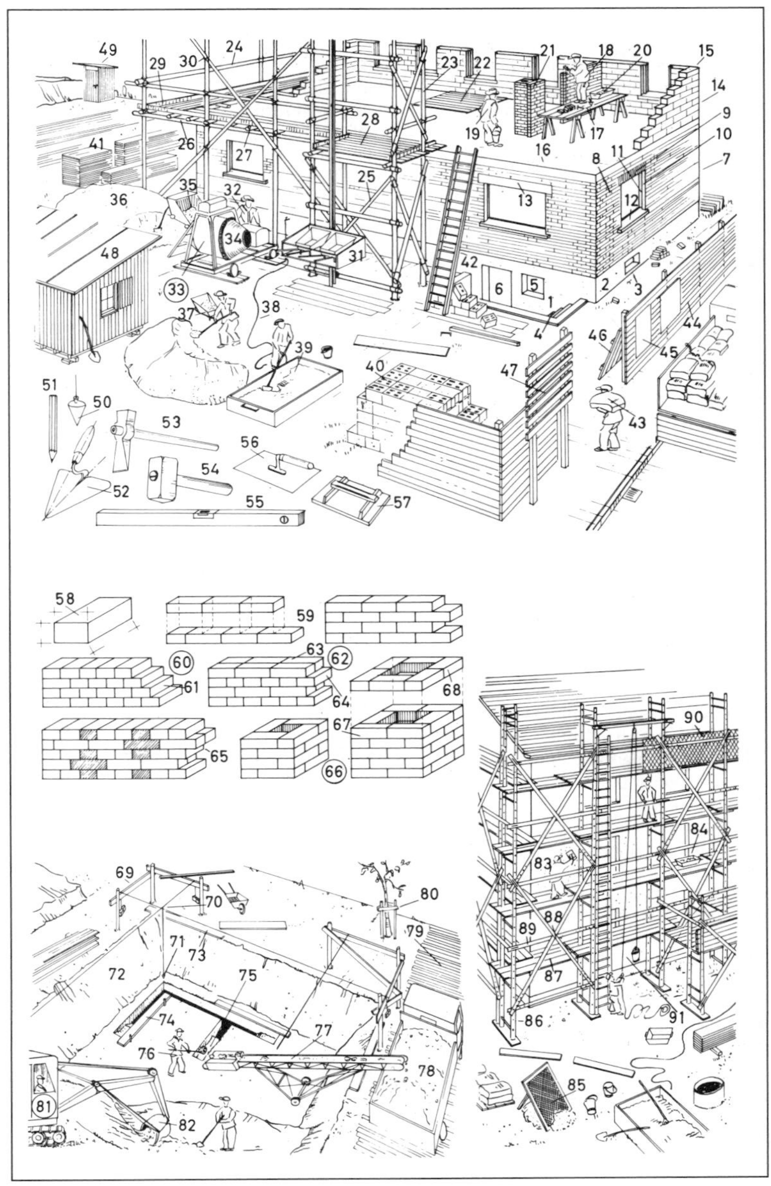
1
2
3
4
5
6
7
8
9
10
11
12
13
14
15
16
17
18
19
20
21
22
23
24
25
26
27
28
29
30
31
32
33
34
35
36
37
38
39
40
41
42
43
44
45
46
47
48
49
50
51
52
53
54
55
56
57
58
59
60
61
62
63
64
65
66
67
68
69
70
71
72
73
74
75
76
77
78
79
80
81
82
83
84
85
86
87
88
89
90
91

119 Building Site (Construction Site) II

1-89 reinforced concrete (ferroconcrete) construction
1 reinforced concrete (ferroconcrete) skeleton construction
2 reinforced concrete (ferroconcrete) frame
3 inferior purlin
4 concrete purlin
5 ceiling joist
6 arch (flank)
7 rubble concrete wall
8 reinforced concrete (ferroconcrete) floor
9 concreter (concretor), flattening out
10 projecting reinforcement (*Am.* connection rebars)
11 column box
12 joist shuttering
13 shuttering strut
14 diagonal bracing
15 wedge
16 board
17 sheet pile wall (sheet pile, sheet piling)
18 shutter boards (lining boards)
19 circular saw (buzz saw)
20 bending table
21 bar bender (steel bender)
22 hand steel shears
23 reinforcing steel (reinforcement rods)
24 pumice concrete hollow block
25 partition wall, a timber wall
26 concrete aggregate [gravel and sand of various grades]
27 crane track
28 tipping wagon (tipping truck)
29 concrete mixer
30 cement silo
31 tower crane (tower slewing crane)
32 bogie (*Am.* truck)
33 counterweight
34 tower
35 crane driver's cabin (crane driver's cage)
36 jib (boom)
37 bearer cable
38 concrete bucket
39 sleepers (*Am.* ties)
40 chock
41 ramp
42 wheelbarrow
43 safety rail
44 site hut
45 canteen
46 tubular steel scaffold (scaffolding)
47 standard
48 ledger tube
49 tie tube
50 shoe
51 diagonal brace
52 planking (platform)
53 coupling (coupler)

54-76 formwork (shuttering) **and reinforcement**
54 bottom shuttering (lining)
55 side shutter of a purlin
56 cut-in bottom
57 cross beam
58 cramp iron (cramp, dog)
59 upright member, a standard
60 strap
61 cross piece
62 stop fillet
63 strut (brace, angle brace)
64 frame timber (yoke)
65 strap
66 reinforcement binding
67 cross strut (strut)
68 reinforcement
69 distribution steel
70 stirrup
71 projecting reinforcement (*Am.* connection rebars)
72 concrete (heavy concrete)
73 column box
74 bolted frame timber (bolted yoke)
75 nut (thumb nut)
76 shutter board (shuttering board)

77-89 tools
77 bending iron
78 adjustable service girder
79 adjusting screw
80 round bar reinforcement
81 distance piece (separator, spacer)
82 Torsteel
83 concrete tamper
84 mould (*Am.* mold) for concrete test cubes
85 concreter's tongs
86 sheeting support
87 hand shears
88 immersion vibrator (concrete vibrator)
89 vibrating cylinder (vibrating head, vibrating poker)

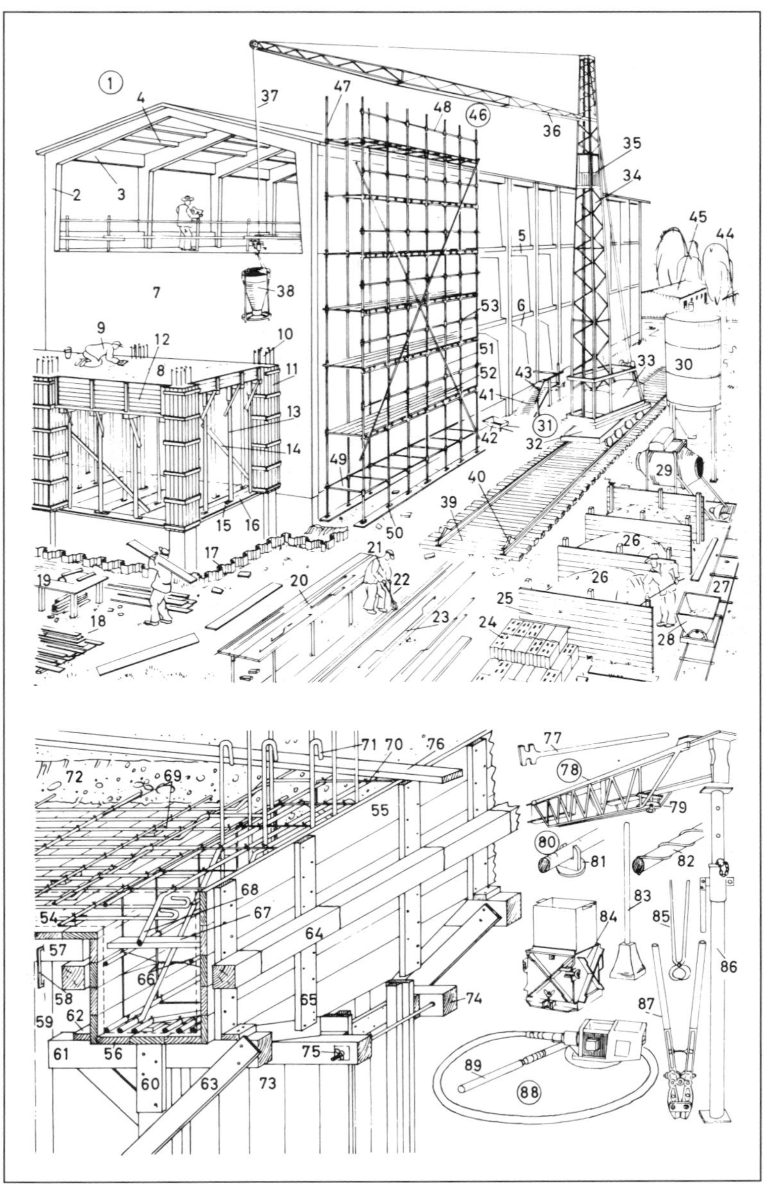
1
2
3
4
5
6
7
8
9
10
11
12
13
14
15
16
17
18
19
20
21
22
23
24
25
26
26
27
28
29
30
31
32
33
34
35
36
37
38
39
40
41
42
43
44
45
46
47
48
49
50
51
52
53
54
55
56
57
58
59
60
61
62
63
64
65
66
67
68
69
70
71
72
73
74
75
76
77
78
79
80
81
82
83
84
85
86
87
88
89

120 Carpenter

1-59 carpenter's yard
1 stack of boards (planks)
2 long timber (*Am.* lumber)
3 sawing shed
4 carpenter's workshop
5 workshop door
6 handcart
7 roof truss
8 tree [used for topping out ceremony], with wreath
9 timber wall
10 squared timber (building timber, scantlings)
11 drawing floor
12 carpenter
13 safety helmet
14 cross-cut saw, a chain saw
15 chain guide
16 saw chain
17 mortiser (chain cutter)
18 trestle (horse)
19 beam mounted on a trestle
20 set of carpenter's tools
21 electric drill
22 dowel hole
23 mark for the dowel hole
24 beams
25 post (stile, stud, quarter)
26 corner brace
27 brace (strut)
28 base course (plinth)
29 house wall (wall)
30 window opening
31 reveal
32 jamb
33 window ledge (window sill)
34 cornice
35 roundwood (round timber)
36 floorboards
37 hoisting rope
38 ceiling joist (ceiling beam, main beam)
39 wall joist
40 wall plate
41 trimmer (trimmer joist, *Am.* header, header joist)
42 dragon beam (dragon piece)
43 false floor (inserted floor)
44 floor filling of breeze, loam, etc.
45 fillet (cleat)
46 stair well (well)
47 chimney
48 framed partition (framed wall)
49 wall plate
50 girt
51 window jamb, a jamb
52 corner stile (corner strut, corner stud)
53 principal post
54 brace (strut) with skew notch
55 nogging piece
56 sill rail
57 window lintel (window head)
58 head (head rail)
59 filled-in panel (bay, pan)

60-82 carpenter's tools
60 hand saw
61 bucksaw
62 saw blade
63 compass saw (keyhole saw)
64 plane
65 auger (gimlet)
66 screw clamp (cramp, holdfast)
67 mallet
68 two-handed saw
69 try square
70 broad axe (*Am.* broadax)
71 chisel
72 mortise axe (mortice axe, *Am.* mortise ax)
73 axe (*Am.* ax)
74 carpenter's hammer
75 claw head (nail claw)
76 folding rule
77 carpenter's pencil
78 iron square
79 drawknife (drawshave, drawing knife)
80 shaving
81 bevel
82 mitre square (*Am.* miter square, miter angle)

83-96 building timber
83 undressed timber (*Am.* rough lumber)
84 heartwood (duramen)
85 sapwood (sap, alburnum)
86 bark (rind)
87 baulk (balk)
88 halved timber
89 wane (waney edge)
90 quarter baulk (balk)
91 plank (board)
92 end-grained timber
93 heartwood plank (heart plank)
94 unsquared (untrimmed) plank (board)
95 squared (trimmed) board
96 slab (offcut)

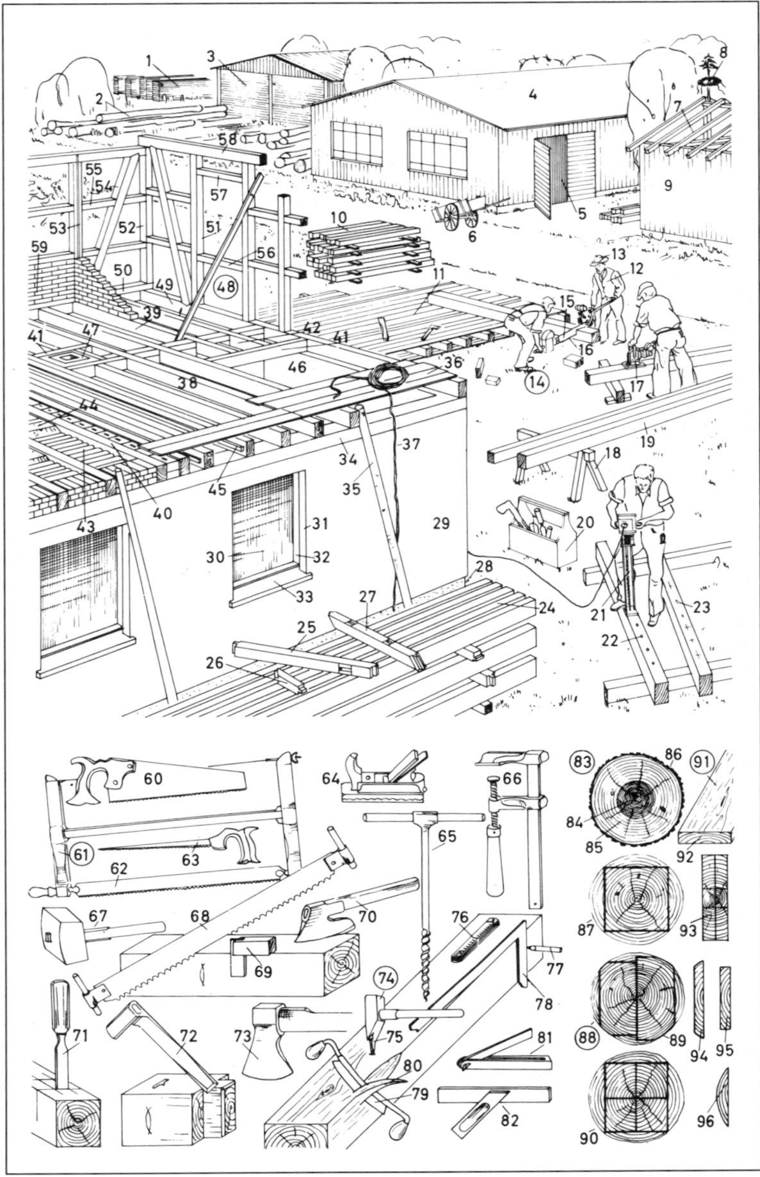
1
2
3
4
5
6
7
8
9
10
11
12
13
14
15
16
17
18
19
20
21
22
23
24
25
26
27
28
29
30
31
32
33
34
35
36
37
38
39
40
41
42
43
44
45
46
47
48
49
50
51
52
53
54
55
56
57
58
59
60
61
62
63
64
65
66
67
68
69
70
71
72
73
74
75
76
77
78
79
80
81
82
83
84
85
86
87
88
89
90
91
92
93
94
95
96

121 Roof, Timber Joints

1-26 styles and parts of roofs
1 gable roof (saddle roof, saddleback roof)
2 ridge
3 verge
4 eaves
5 gable
6 dormer window (dormer)
7 pent roof (shed roof, lean-to roof)
8 skylight
9 fire gable
10 hip (hipped) roof
11 hip end
12 hip (arris)
13 hip (hipped) dormer window
14 ridge turret
15 valley (roof valley)
16 hipped-gable roof (jerkin head roof)
17 partial-hip (partial-hipped) end
18 mansard roof (*Am.* gambrel roof)
19 mansard dormer window
20 sawtooth roof
21 north light
22 broach roof
23 eyebrow
24 conical broach roof
25 imperial dome (imperial roof)
26 weather vane
27-83 roof structures of timber
27 rafter roof
28 rafter
29 roof beam
30 diagonal tie (cross tie, sprocket piece, cocking piece)
31 arris fillet (tilting fillet)
32 outer wall
33 beam head
34 collar beam roof (trussed rafter roof)
35 collar beam (collar)
36 rafter
37 strutted collar beam roof structure
38 collar beams
39 purlin
40 post (stile, stud)
41 brace
42 unstrutted (king pin) roof structure
43 ridge purlin
44 inferior purlin
45 rafter head (rafter end)
46 purlin roof with queen post and pointing sill
47 pointing sill
48 ridge beam (ridge board)
49 simple tie
50 double tie
51 purlin
52 purlin roof structure with queen post
53 tie beam
54 joist (ceiling joist)
55 principal rafter
56 common rafter
57 angle brace (angle tie)
58 brace (strut)
59 ties
60 hip (hipped) roof with purlin roof structure
61 jack rafter
62 hip rafter
63 jack rafter
64 valley rafter
65 queen truss
66 main beam
67 summer (summer beam)
68 queen post (truss post)
69 brace (strut)
70 collar beam (collar)
71 trimmer (*Am.* header)
72 solid-web girder
73 lower chord
74 upper chord
75 boarding
76 purlin
77 supporting outer wall
78 roof truss
79 lower chord
80 upper chord
81 post
82 brace (strut)
83 support
84-98 timber joints
84 mortise (mortice) and tenon joint
85 forked mortise (mortice) and tenon joint
86 halving (halved) joint
87 simple scarf joint
88 oblique scarf joint
89 dovetail halving
90 single skew notch
91 double skew notch
92 wooden nail
93 pin
94 clout nail (clout)
95 wire nail
96 hardwood wedges
97 cramp iron (timber dog, dog)
98 bolt

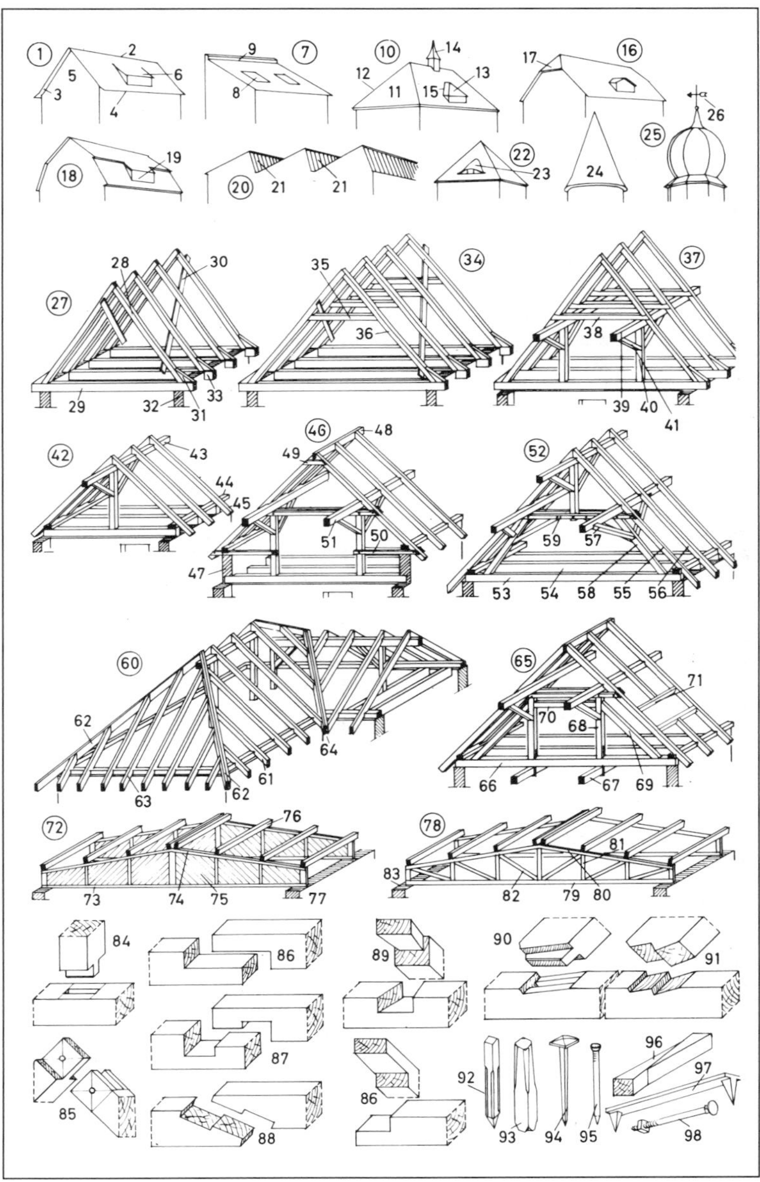
1
2
3
4
5
6
7
8
9
10
11
12
13
14
15
16
17
18
19
20
21
21
22
23
24
25
26
27
28
29
30
31
32
33
34
35
36
37
38
39
40
41
42
43
44
45
46
47
48
49
50
51
52
53
54
55
56
57
58
59
60
61
62
62
63
64
65
66
67
68
69
70
71
72
73
74
75
76
77
78
79
80
81
82
83
84
85
86
86
87
88
89
90
91
92
93
94
95
96
97
98

122 Roof and Roofer

1 tiled roof
2 plain-tile double-lap roofing
3 ridge tile
4 ridge course tile
5 under-ridge tile
6 plain (plane) tile
7 ventilating tile
8 ridge tile
9 hip tile
10 hipped end
11 valley (roof valley)
12 skylight
13 chimney
14 chimney flashing, made of sheet zinc
15 ladder hook
16 snow guard bracket
17 battens (slating and tiling battens)
18 batten gauge (*Am.* gage)
19 rafter
20 tile hammer
21 lath axe (*Am.* ax)
22 hod
23 hod hook
24 opening (hatch)
25 gable (gable end)
26 toothed lath
27 soffit
28 gutter
29 rainwater pipe (downpipe)
30 swan's neck (swan-neck)
31 pipe clip
32 gutter bracket
33 tile cutter
34 scaffold
35 safety wall
36 eaves
37 outer wall
38 exterior rendering
39 frost-resistant brickwork
40 inferior purlin
41 rafter head (rafter end)
42 eaves fascia
43 double lath (tilting lath)
44 insulating boards
45-60 tiles and tile roofings
45 split-tiled roof
46 plain (plane) tile
47 ridge course
48 slip
49 eaves course
50 plain-tiled roof
51 nib
52 ridge tile
53 pantiled roof
54 pantile
55 pointing
56 Spanish-tiled roof (*Am.* mission-tiled roof)
57 under tile
58 over tile
59 interlocking tile
60 flat interlocking tile
61-89 slate roof
61 roof boards (roof boarding, roof sheathing)
62 roofing paper (sheathing paper); *also:* roofing felt (*Am.* rag felt)
63 cat ladder (roof ladder)
64 coupling hook
65 ridge hook
66 roof trestle
67 trestle rope
68 knot
69 ladder hook
70 scaffold board
71 slater
72 nail bag
73 slate hammer
74 slate nail, a galvanized wire nail
75 slater's shoe, a bast or hemp shoe
76 eaves course (eaves joint)
77 corner bottom slate
78 roof course
79 ridge course (ridge joint)
80 gable slate
81 tail line
82 valley (roof valley)
83 box gutter (trough gutter, parallel gutter)
84 slater's iron
85 slate
86 back
87 head
88 front edge
89 tail
90-103 asphalt-impregnated paper roofing and corrugated asbestos cement roofing
90 asphalt-impregnated paper roof
91 width [parallel to the gutter]
92 gutter
93 ridge
94 join
95 width [at right angles to the gutter]
96 felt nail (clout nail)
97 corrugated asbestos cement roof
98 corrugated sheet
99 ridge capping piece
100 lap
101 wood screw
102 rust-proof zinc cup
103 lead washer

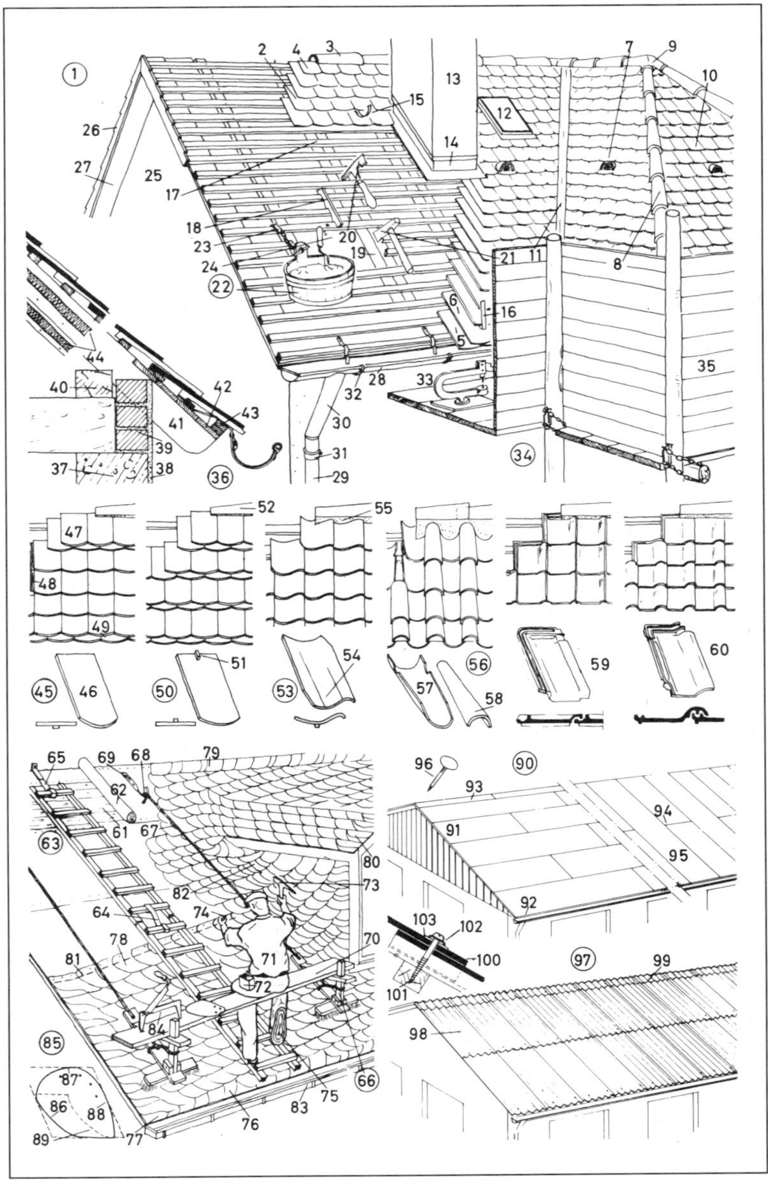
1
2
3
4
5
6
7
8
9
10
11
12
13
14
15
16
17
18
19
20
21
22
23
24
25
26
27
28
29
30
31
32
33
34
35
36
37
38
39
40
41
42
43
44
45
46
47
48
49
50
51
52
53
54
55
56
57
58
59
60
61
62
63
64
65
66
67
68
69
70
71
72
73
74
75
76
77
78
79
80
81
82
83
84
85
86
87
88
89
90
91
92
93
94
95
96
97
98
99
100
101
102
103

123 Floor, Ceiling, Staircase Construction

1 basement wall, a concrete wall
2 footing (foundation)
3 foundation base
4 damp course (damp-proof course)
5 waterproofing
6 rendering coat
7 brick paving
8 sand bed
9 ground
10 shuttering
11 peg
12 hardcore
13 oversite concrete
14 cement screed
15 brickwork base
16 basement stairs, solid concrete stairs
17 block step
18 curtail step (bottom step)
19 top step
20 nosing
21 skirting (skirting board, *Am.* mopboard, washboard, scrub board, base)
22 balustrade of metal bars
23 ground-floor (*Am.* first-floor) landing
24 front door
25 foot scraper
26 flagstone paving
27 mortar bed
28 concrete ceiling, a reinforced concrete slab
29 ground-floor (*Am.* first-floor) brick wall
30 ramp
31 wedge-shaped step
32 tread
33 riser
34-41 landing
34 landing beam
35 ribbed reinforced concrete floor
36 rib
37 steel-bar reinforcement
38 subfloor (blind floor)
39 level layer
40 finishing layer
41 top layer (screed)
42-44 dog-legged staircase, a staircase without a well
42 curtail step (bottom step)
43 newel post (newel)
44 outer string (*Am.* outer stringer)
45 wall string (*Am.* wall stringer)
46 staircase bolt
47 tread
48 riser
49 wreath piece (wreathed string)
50 balustrade
51 baluster
52-62 intermediate landing
52 wreath
53 handrail (guard rail)
54 head post
55 landing beam
56 lining board
57 fillet
58 lightweight building board
59 ceiling plaster
60 wall plaster
61 false ceiling
62 strip flooring (overlay flooring, parquet strip)
63 skirting board (*Am.* mopboard, washboard, scrub board, base)
64 beading
65 staircase window
66 main landing beam
67 fillet (cleat)
68, 69 false ceiling
68 false floor (inserted floor)
69 floor filling (plugging, pug)
70 laths
71 lathing
72 ceiling plaster
73 subfloor (blind floor)
74 parquet floor with tongued-and-grooved blocks
75 quarter-newelled (*Am.* quarter-neweled) staircase
76 winding staircase (spiral staircase) with open newels (open-newel staircase)
77 winding staircase (spiral staircase) with solid newels (solid-newel staircase)
78 newel (solid newel)
79 handrail

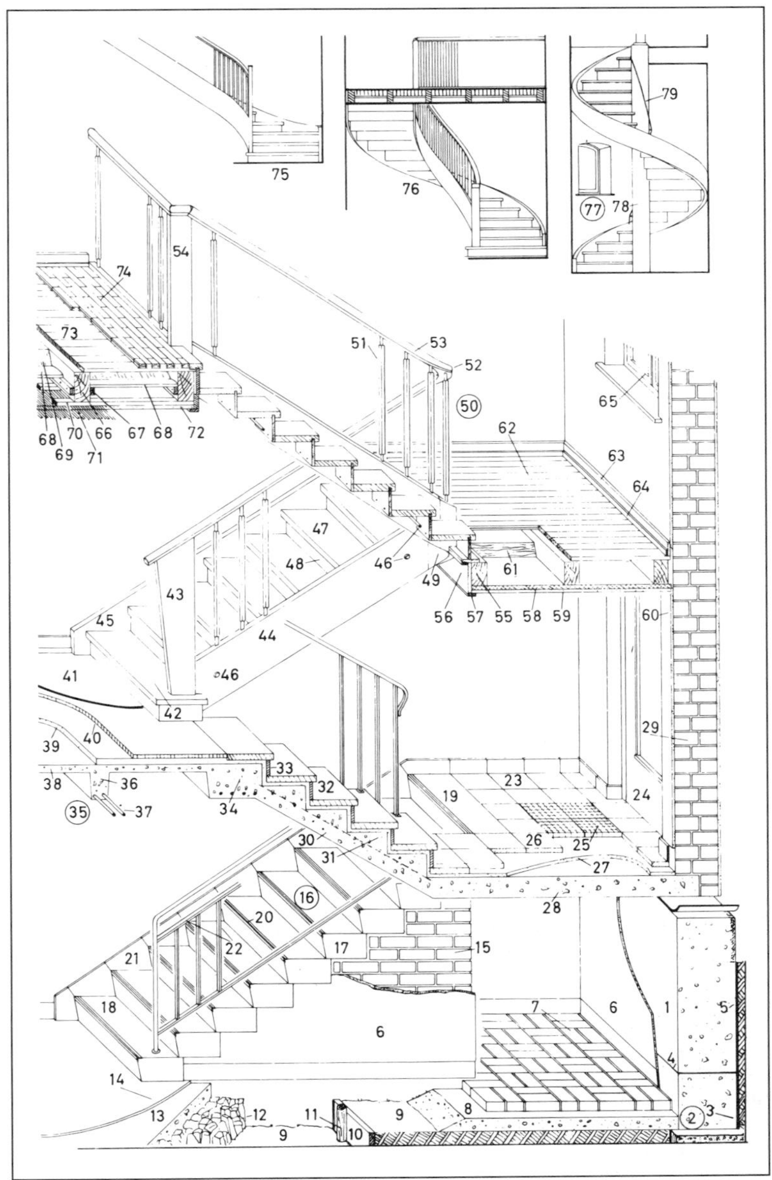
75
76
79
77
78
54
74
73
51
53
52
50
65
68
70
66
67
68
72
69
71
62
63
64
47
48
46
61
49
43
56
57
55
58
59
60
45
44
41
46
42
39
40
29
33
23
38
36
32
19
24
35
37
34
26
25
30
31
27
16
28
20
22
17
15
21
7
6
1
5
18
6
4
14
8
9
11
13
12
3
2
9
10

124 Glazier

1 glazier's workshop
2 frame wood samples (frame samples)
3 frame wood
4 mitre joint (mitre, *Am.* miter joint, miter)
5 sheet glass; *kinds:* window glass, frosted glass, patterned glass, crystal plate glass, thick glass, milk glass, laminated glass (safety glass, shatterproof glass)
6 cast glass; *kinds:* stained glass, ornamental glass, raw glass, bull's-eye glass, wired glass, line glass (lined glass)
7 mitring (*Am.* mitering) machine
8 glassworker (e.g. building glazier, glazier, decorative glass worker)
9 glass holder
10 piece of broken glass
11 lead hammer
12 lead knife
13 came (lead came)
14 leaded light
15 workbench
16 pane of glass
17 putty
18 glazier's hammer
19 glass pliers
20 glazier's square
21 glazier's rule
22 glazier's beam compass
23 eyelet
24 glazing sprig
25, 26 glass cutters
25 diamond glass cutter
26 steel-wheel (steel) glass cutter
27 putty knife
28 pin wire
29 panel pin
30 mitre (*Am.* miter) block (mitre box) [with saw]
31 mitre (*Am.* miter) shoot (mitre board)

1 metal shears (tinner's snips, *Am.* tinner's shears)
2 elbow snips (angle shears)
3 gib
4 lapping plate
5-7 propane soldering apparatus
5 propane soldering iron, a hatchet iron
6 soldering stone, a sal-ammoniac block
7 soldering fluid (flux)
8 beading iron for forming reinforcement beading
9 angled reamer
10 workbench (bench)
11 beam compass (trammel, *Am.* beam trammel)
12 electric hand die
13 hollow punch
14 chamfering hammer
15 beading swage (beading hammer)
16 abrasive-wheel cutting-off machine
17 plumber
18 mallet
19 mandrel
20 socket (tinner's socket)
21 block
22 anvil
23 stake
24 circular saw (buzz saw)
25 flanging, swaging, and wiring machine
26 sheet shears (guillotine)
27 screw-cutting machine (thread-cutting machine, die stocks)
28 pipe-bending machine (bending machine, pipe bender)
29 welding transformer
30 bending machine (rounding machine) for shaping funnels

126 Plumber, Gas Fitter, Heating Engineer

1 gas fitter and plumber
2 stepladder
3 safety chain
4 stop valve
5 gas meter
6 bracket
7 service riser
8 distributing pipe
9 supply pipe
10 pipe-cutting machine
11 pipe repair stand
12-25 gas and water appliances
12, 13 geyser, an instantaneous water heater
12 gas water heater
13 electric water heater
14 toilet cistern
15 float
16 bell
17 flush pipe
18 water inlet
19 flushing lever (lever)
20 radiator
21 radiator rib
22 two-pipe system
23 flow pipe
24 return pipe
25 gas heater
26-37 plumbing fixtures
26 trap (anti-syphon trap)
27 mixer tap (*Am.* mixing faucet) for washbasins
28 hot tap
29 cold tap
30 extendible shower attachment
31 water tap (pillar tap) for wash-basins
32 spindle top
33 shield
34 draw-off tap (*Am.* faucet)
35 supatap
36 swivel tap
37 flushing valve
38-52 fittings
38 joint with male thread
39 reducing socket (reducing coupler)
40 elbow screw joint (elbow coupling)
41 reducing socket (reducing coupler) with female thread
42 screw joint
43 coupler (socket)
44 T-joint (T-junction joint, tee)
45 elbow screw joint with female thread
46 bend
47 T-joint (T-junction joint, tee) with female taper thread
48 ceiling joint
49 reducing elbow
50 cross
51 elbow joint with male thread
52 elbow joint
53-57 pipe supports
53 saddle clip
54 spacing bracket
55 plug
56 pipe clips
57 two-piece spacing clip
58-86 plumber's tools, gas fitter's tools
58 gas pliers
59 footprints
60 combination cutting pliers
61 water pump pliers
62 flat-nose pliers
63 nipple key
64 round-nose pliers
65 pincers
66 adjustable S-wrench
67 screw wrench
68 shifting spanner
69 screwdriver
70 compass saw (keyhole saw)
71 hacksaw frame
72 hand saw
73 soldering iron
74 blowlamp (blowtorch) [for soldering]
75 sealing tape
76 tin-lead solder
77 club hammer
78 hammer
79 spirit level
80 steel-leg vice (*Am.* vise)
81 pipe vice (*Am.* vise)
82 pipe-bending machine
83 former (template)
84 pipe cutter
85 hand die
86 screw-cutting machine (thread-cutting machine)

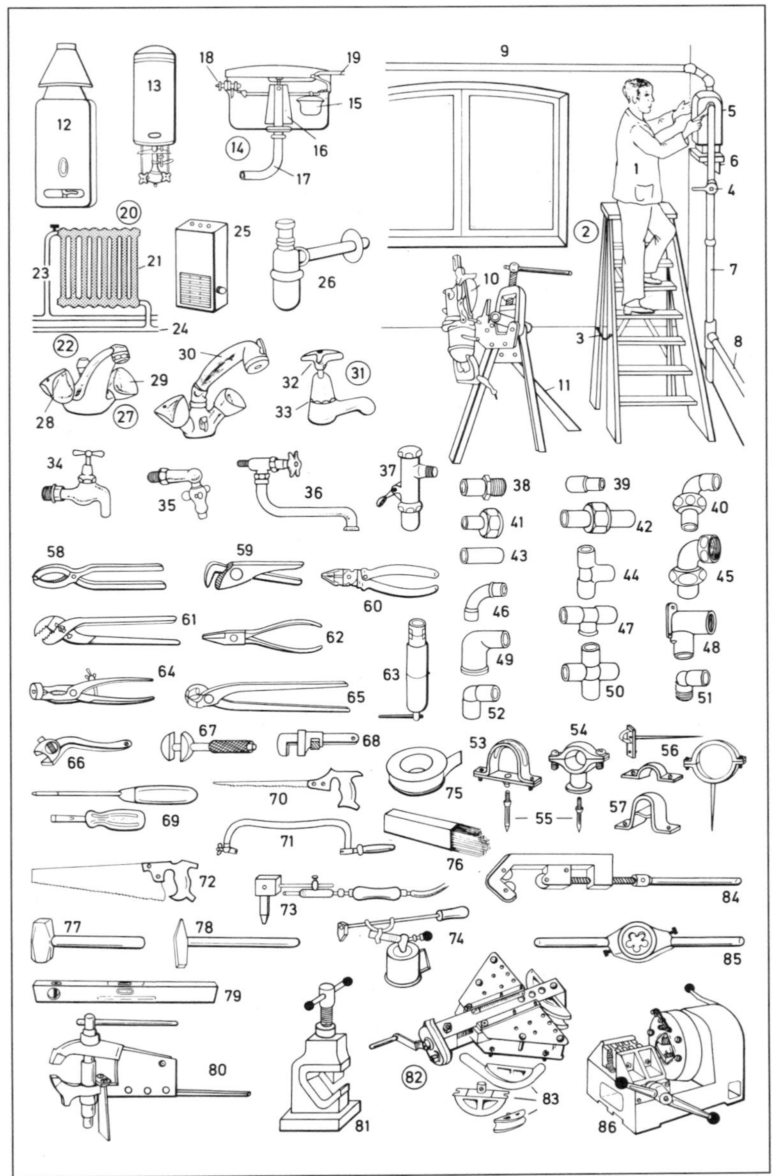
1
2
3
4
5
6
7
8
9
10
11
12
13
14
15
16
17
18
19
20
21
22
23
24
25
26
27
28
29
30
31
32
33
34
35
36
37
38
39
40
41
42
43
44
45
46
47
48
49
50
51
52
53
54
55
56
57
58
59
60
61
62
63
64
65
66
67
68
69
70
71
72
73
74
75
76
77
78
79
80
81
82
83
84
85
86

127 Electrician

1 electrician (electrical fitter, wireman)
2 bell push (doorbell) for low-voltage safety current
3 house telephone with call button
4 [flush-mounted] rocker switch
5 [flush-mounted] earthed socket (wall socket, plug point, *Am.* wall outlet, convenience outlet, outlet)
6 [surface-mounted] earthed double socket (double wall socket, double plug point, *Am.* double wall outlet, double convenience outlet, double outlet)
7 switched socket (switch and socket)
8 four-socket (four-way) adapter
9 earthed plug
10 extension lead (*Am.* extension cord)
11 extension plug
12 extension socket
13 surface-mounted three-pole earthed socket [for three-phase circuit] with neutral conductor
14 three-phase plug
15 electric bell (electric buzzer)
16 pull-switch (cord-operated wall switch)
17 dimmer switch [for smooth adjustment of lamp brightness]
18 drill-cast rotary switch
19 miniature circuit breaker (screw-in circuit breaker, fuse)
20 resetting button
21 set screw [for fuses and miniature circuit breakers]
22 underfloor mounting (underfloor sockets)
23 hinged floor socket for power lines and communication lines
24 sunken floor socket with hinged lid (snap lid)
25 surface-mounted socket outlet (plug point) box
26 pocket torch, a torch (*Am.* flashlight)
27 dry cell battery
28 contact spring
29 strip of thermoplastic connectors
30 steel draw-in wire (draw wire) with threading key, and ring attached
31 electricity meter cupboard
32 electricity meter
33 miniature circuit breakers (miniature circuit breaker consumer unit)
34 insulating tape (*Am.* friction tape)
35 fuse holder
36 circuit breaker (fuse), a fuse cartridge with fusible element
37 colour (*Am.* color) indicator [showing current rating]
38, 39 contact maker
40 cable clip
41 universal test meter (multiple meter for measuring current and voltage)
42 thermoplastic moisture-proof cable
43 copper conductor
44 three-core cable
45 electric soldering iron
46 screwdriver
47 water pump pliers
48 shock-resisting safety helmet
49 tool case
50 round-nose pliers
51 cutting pliers
52 junior hacksaw
53 combination cutting pliers
54 insulated handle
55 continuity tester
56 electric light bulb (general service lamp, filament lamp)
57 glass bulb (bulb)
58 coiled-coil filament
59 screw base
60 lampholder
61 fluorescent tube
62 bracket for fluorescent tubes
63 electrician's knife
64 wire strippers
65 bayonet fitting
66 three-pin socket with switch
67 three-pin plug
68 fuse carrier with fuse wire
69 light bulb with bayonet fitting

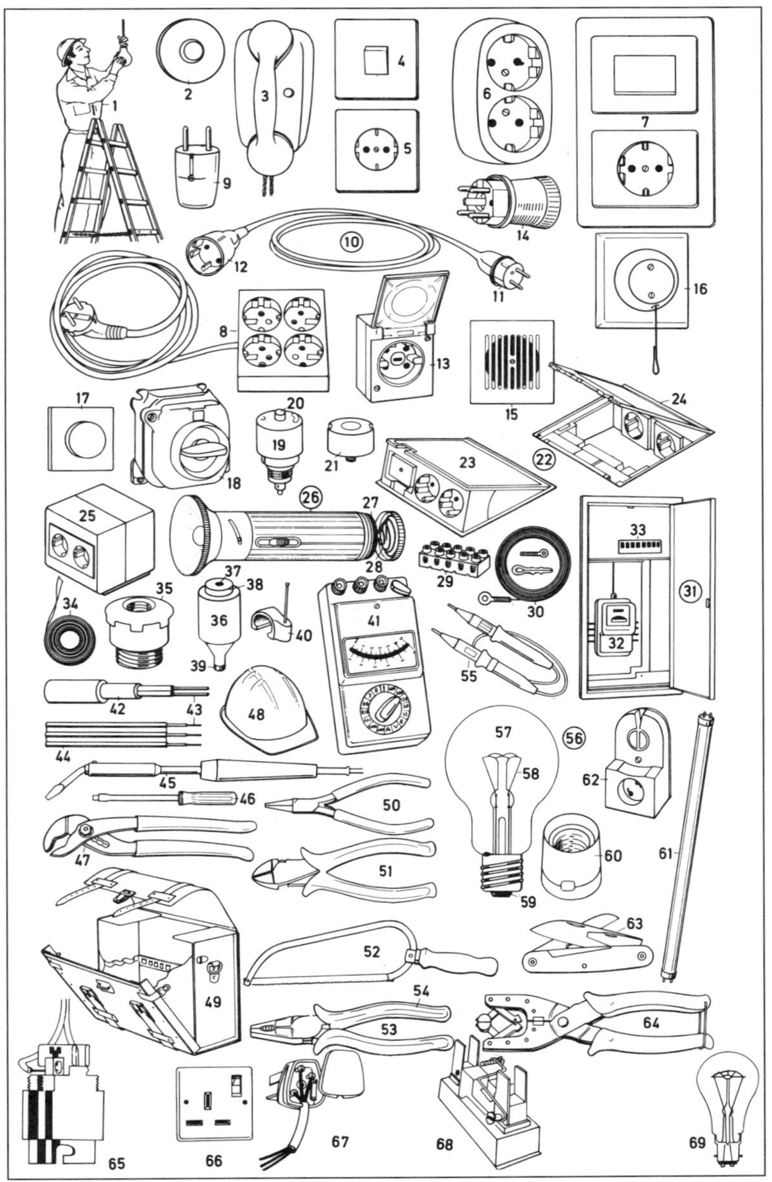
1
2
3
4
5
6
7
8
9
10
11
12
13
14
15
16
17
18
19
20
21
22
23
24
25
26
27
28
29
30
31
32
33
34
35
36
37
38
39
40
41
42
43
44
45
46
47
48
49
50
51
52
53
54
55
56
57
58
59
60
61
62
63
64
65
66
67
68
69

128 Paperhanger

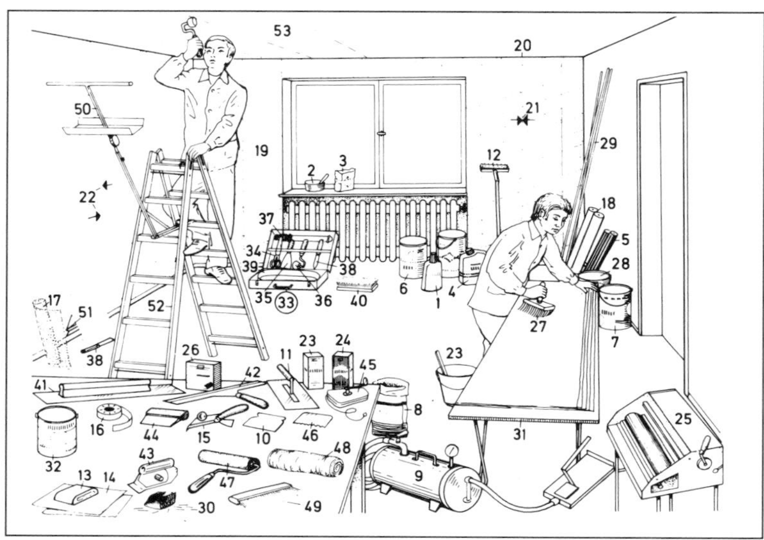

1-17 preparation of surfaces
1 wallpaper-stripping liquid (stripper)
2 plaster (plaster of Paris)
3 filler
4 glue size (size)
5 lining paper, a backing paper
6 primer
7 fluate
8 shredded lining paper
9 wallpaper-stripping machine (stripper)
10 scraper
11 smoother
12 perforator
13 sandpaper block
14 sandpaper
15 stripping knife
16 masking tape
17 strip of sheet metal [on which wallpaper is laid for cutting]

18-53 wallpapering (paper hanging)
18 wallpaper (*kinds:* wood pulp paper, wood chip paper, fabric wallhangings, synthetic wallpaper, metallic paper, natural (*e.g.* wood or cork) paper, tapestry wallpaper)
19 length of wallpaper
20 butted paper edges
21 matching edge
22 non-matching edge
23 wallpaper paste
24 heavy-duty paste
25 pasting machine
26 paste [for the pasting machine]
27 paste brush
28 emulsion paste
29 picture rail
30 beading pins
31 pasteboard (paperhanger's bench)
32 gloss finish
33 paperhanging kit
34 shears (bull-nosed scissors)
35 filling knife
36 seam roller
37 hacking knife
38 knife (trimming knife)
39 straightedge
40 paperhanging brush
41 wallpaper-cutting board
42 cutter
43 trimmer
44 plastic spatula
45 chalked string
46 spreader
47 paper roller
48 flannel cloth
49 dry brush
50 ceiling paperhanger
51 overlap angle
52 paperhanger's trestles
53 ceiling paper

1 **painting**
2 painter
3 paintbrush
4 emulsion paint (emulsion)
5 stepladder
6 can (tin) of paint
7, 8 cans (tins) of paint
7 can (tin) with fixed handle
8 paint kettle
9 drum of paint
10 paint bucket
11 paint roller
12 grill [for removing excess paint from the roller]
13 stippling roller
14 **varnishing**
15 oil-painted dado
16 canister for thinner
17 flat brush for larger surfaces (flat wall brush)
18 stippler
19 fitch
20 cutting-in brush
21 radiator brush (flay brush)
22 paint scraper
23 scraper
24 putty knife
25 sandpaper
26 sandpaper block
27 floor brush
28 **sanding and spraying**
29 grinder
30 sander
31 pressure pot
32 spray gun
33 compressor (air compressor)
34 flow coating machine for flow coating radiators, etc.
35 hand spray
36 airless spray unit
37 airless spray gun
38 efflux viscometer
39 seconds timer
40 **lettering and gilding**
41 lettering brush (signwriting brush, pencil)
42 tracing wheel
43 stencil knife
44 oil gold size
45 gold leaf
46 outline drawing
47 mahlstick
48 pouncing
49 pounce bag
50 gilder's cushion
51 gilder's knife
52 sizing gold leaf
53 filling in the letters with stipple paint
54 gilder's mop

130 Cooper and Tank Construction Engineer

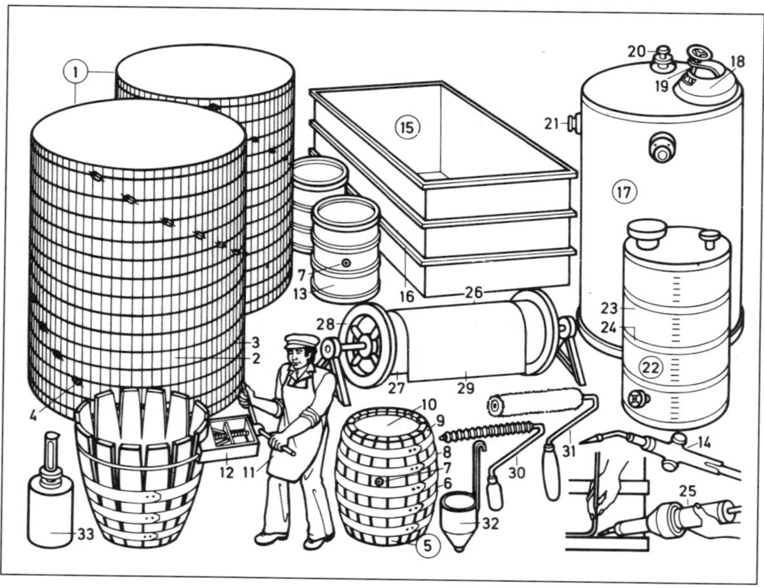

1-33 cooper's and tank construction engineer's workshops
1 tank
2 circumference made of staves (staved circumference)
3 iron rod
4 turnbuckle
5 barrel (cask)
6 body of barrel (of cask)
7 bunghole
8 band (hoop) of barrel
9 barrel stave
10 barrelhead (heading)
11 cooper
12 trusser
13 drum
14 gas welding torch
15 staining vat, made of thermoplastics
16 iron reinforcing bands
17 storage container, made of glass fibre (*Am.* glass fiber) reinforced polyester resin
18 manhole
19 manhole cover with handwheel
20 flange mount
21 flange-type stopcock
22 measuring tank
23 shell (circumference)
24 shrink ring
25 hot-air gun
26 roller made of glass fibre (*Am.* glass fiber) reinforced synthetic resin
27 cylinder
28 flange
29 glass cloth
30 grooved roller
31 lambskin roller
32 ladle for testing viscosity
33 measuring vessel for hardener

1-25 furrier's workroom
1 furrier
2 steam spray gun
3 steam iron
4 beating machine
5 cutting machine for letting out furskins
6 uncut furskin
7 let-out strips (let-out sections)
8 fur worker
9 fur-sewing machine
10 blower for letting out
11-21 furskins
11 mink skin
12 fur side
13 leather side
14 cut furskin
15 lynx skin before letting out
16 let-out lynx skin
17 fur side
18 leather side
19 let-out mink skin
20 lynx fur, sewn together (sewn)
21 broadtail
22 fur marker
23 fur worker
24 mink coat
25 ocelot coat

132 Joiner I

1-73 joiner's workshop
1-28 joiner's tools
1 wood rasp
2 wood file
3 compass saw (keyhole saw)
4 saw handle
5 [square-headed] mallet
6 try square
7-11 chisels
7 bevelled-edge chisel (chisel)
8 mortise (mortice) chisel
9 gouge
10 handle
11 framing chisel (cant chisel)
12 glue pot in water bath
13 glue pot (glue well), an insert for joiner's glue
14 handscrew
15-28 planes
15 smoothing plane
16 jack plane
17 toothing plane
18 handle (toat)
19 wedge
20 plane iron (cutter)
21 mouth
22 sole
23 side
24 stock (body)
25 rebate (rabbet) plane
26 router plane (old woman's tooth)
27 spokeshave
28 compass plane
29-37 woodworker's bench
29 foot
30 front vice (*Am.* vise)
31 vice (*Am.* vise) handle
32 vice (*Am.* vise) screw
33 jaw
34 bench top
35 well
36 bench stop (bench holdfast)
37 tail vice (*Am.* vise)
38 cabinet maker (joiner)
39 trying plane
40 shavings
41 wood screw
42 saw set
43 mitre (*Am.* miter) box
44 tenon saw
45 thicknesser (thicknessing machine)
46 thicknessing table with rollers
47 kick-back guard
48 chip-extractor opening
49 chain mortising machine (chain mortiser)
50 endless mortising chain
51 clamp (work clamp)
52 knot hole moulding (*Am.* molding) machine
53 knot hole cutter
54 quick-action chuck
55 hand lever
56 change-gear handle
57 sizing and edging machine
58 main switch
59 circular-saw (buzz saw) blade
60 height (rise and fall) adjustment wheel
61 V-way
62 framing table
63 extension arm (arm)
64 trimming table
65 fence
66 fence adjustment handle
67 clamp lever
68 board-sawing machine
69 swivel motor
70 board support
71 saw carriage
72 pedal for raising the transport rollers
73 blockboard

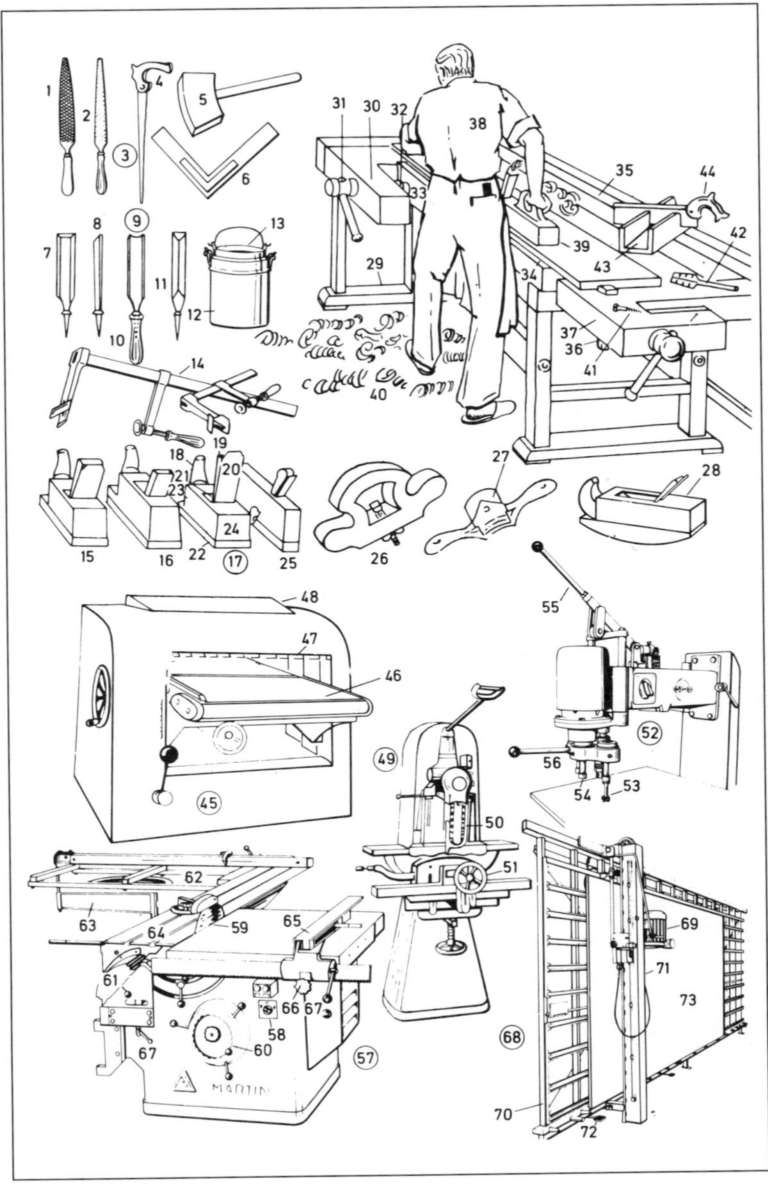
1
2
3
4
5
6
7
8
9
10
11
12
13
14
15
16
17
18
19
20
21
22
23
24
25
26
27
28
29
30
31
32
33
34
35
36
37
38
39
40
41
42
43
44
45
46
47
48
49
50
51
52
53
54
55
56
57
58
59
60
61
62
63
64
65
66
67
67
67
68
69
70
71
72
73
MARTIN

133 Joiner II

1 veneer-peeling machine (peeling machine, peeler)
2 veneer
3 veneer-splicing machine
4 nylon-thread cop
5 sewing mechanism
6 dowel hole boring machine (dowel hole borer)
7 boring motor with hollow-shaft boring bit
8 clamp handle
9 clamp
10 clamping shoe
11 stop bar
12 edge sander (edge-sanding machine)
13 tension roller with extension arm
14 sanding belt regulator (regulating handle)
15 endless sanding belt (sand belt)
16 belt-tensioning lever
17 canting table (tilting table)
18 belt roller
19 angling fence for mitres (*Am.* miters)
20 opening dust hood
21 rise adjustment of the table
22 rise adjustment wheel for the table
23 clamping screw for the table rise adjustment
24 console
25 foot of the machine
26 edge-veneering machine
27 sanding wheel
28 sanding dust extractor
29 splicing head
30 single-belt sanding machine (single-belt sander)
31 belt guard
32 band wheel cover
33 extractor fan (exhaust fan)
34 frame-sanding pad
35 sanding table
36 fine adjustment
37 fine cutter and jointer
38 saw carriage with chain drive
39 trailing cable hanger (trailing cable support)
40 air extractor pipe
41 rail
42 frame-cramping (frame-clamping) machine
43 frame stand
44 workpiece, a window frame
45 compressed-air line
46 pressure cylinder
47 pressure foot
48 frame-mounting device
49 rapid-veneer press
50 bed
51 press
52 pressure piston

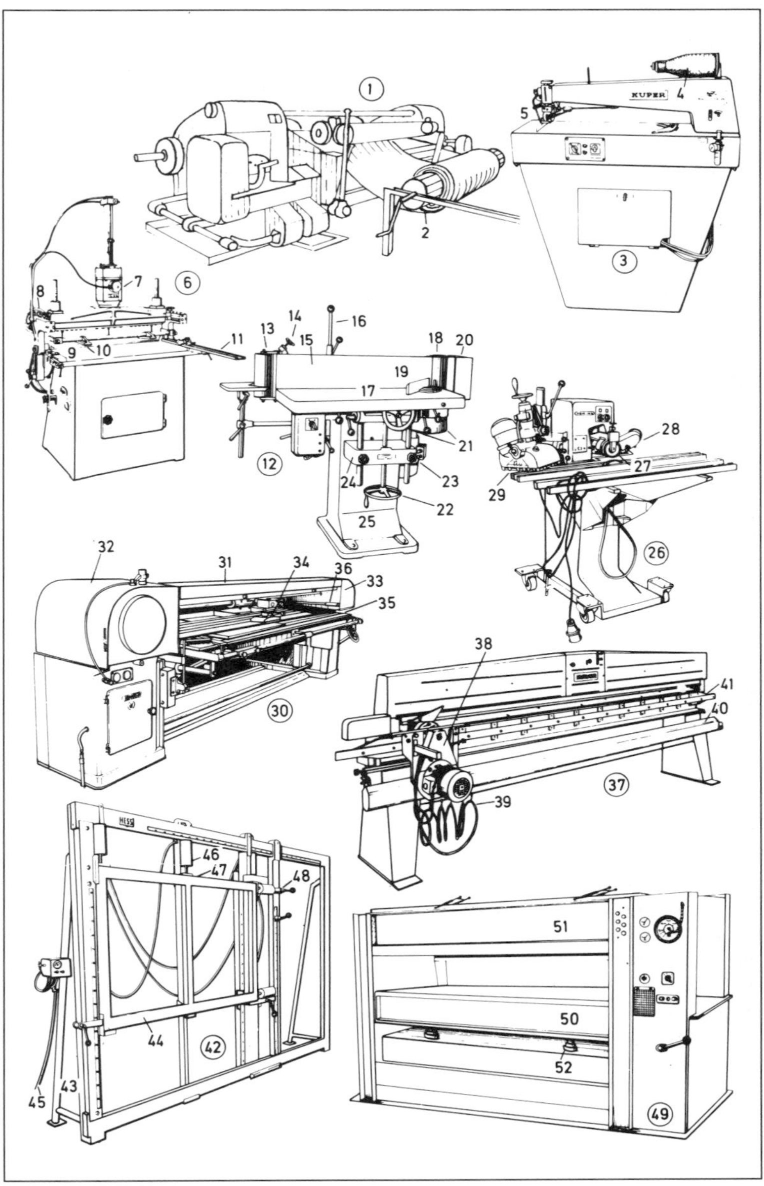
1
2
3
KUPER
4
5
6
7
8
9
10
11
12
13
14
15
16
17
18
19
20
21
22
23
24
25
26
27
28
29
30
31
32
33
34
35
36
37
38
39
40
41
42
43
44
45
HESS
46
47
48
49
50
51
52

134 Do-it-yourself

1-34 tool cupboard (tool cabinet) for do-it-yourself work
1 smoothing plane
2 set of fork spanners (fork wrenches, open-end wrenches)
3 hacksaw
4 screwdriver
5 cross-point screwdriver
6 saw rasp
7 hammer
8 wood rasp
9 roughing file
10 small vice (*Am.* vise)
11 corner pipe wrench
12 water pump pliers
13 pincers
14 all-purpose wrench
15 wire stripper and cutter
16 electric drill
17 hacksaw
18 plaster cup
19 soldering iron
20 tin-lead solder wire
21 lamb's wool polishing bonnet
22 rubber backing disc (disk)
23 grinding wheel
24 wire wheel brush
25 sanding discs (disks)
26 try square
27 hand saw
28 universal cutter
29 spirit level
30 firmer chisel
31 centre (*Am.* center) punch
32 nail punch
33 folding rule (rule)
34 storage box for small parts
35 tool box
36 woodworking adhesive
37 stripping knife
38 adhesive tape
39 storage box with compartments for nails, screws, and plugs
40 machinist's hammer
41 collapsible workbench (collapsible bench)
42 jig
43 electric percussion drill (electric hammer drill)
44 pistol grip
45 side grip
46 gearshift switch
47 handle with depth gauge (*Am.* gage)
48 chuck
49 twist bit (twist drill)
50-55 attachments for an electric drill
50 combined circular saw (buzz saw) and bandsaw
51 wood-turning lathe
52 circular saw attachment
53 orbital sanding attachment (orbital sander)
54 drill stand
55 hedge-trimming attachment (hedge trimmer)
56 soldering gun
57 soldering iron
58 high-speed soldering iron
59 upholstery, upholstering an armchair
60 fabric (material) for upholstery
61 do-it-yourself enthusiast

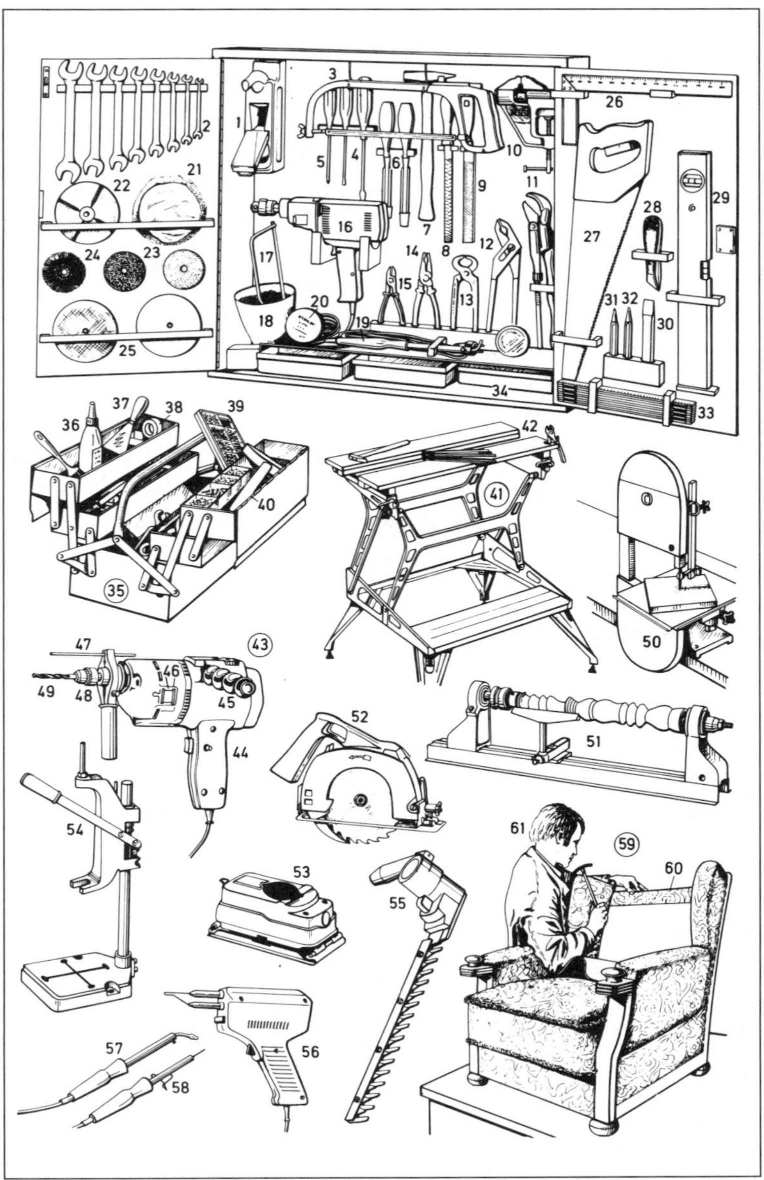
1
2
3
4
5
6
7
8
9
10
11
12
13
14
15
16
17
18
19
20
21
22
23
24
25
26
27
28
29
30
31
32
33
34
35
36
37
38
39
40
41
42
43
44
45
46
47
48
49
50
51
52
53
54
55
56
57
58
59
60
61

135 Turner

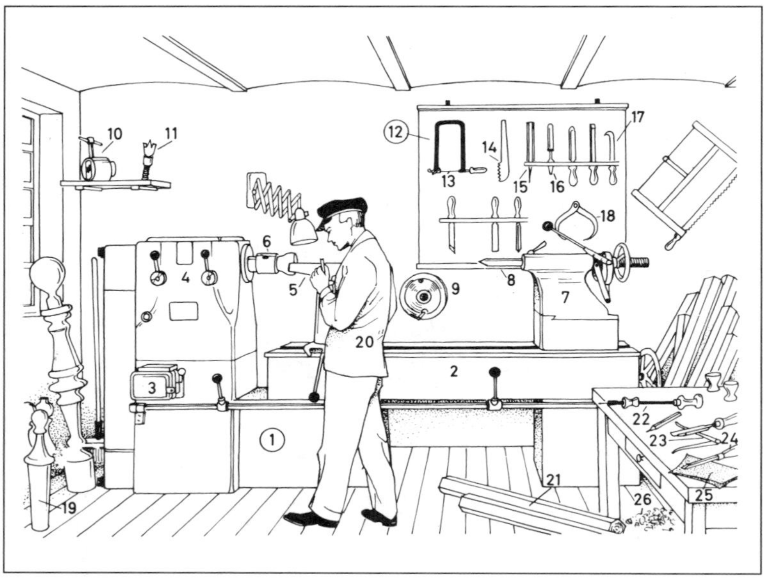

1-26 turnery (turner's workshop)
1 wood-turning lathe (lathe)
2 lathe bed
3 starting resistance (starting resistor)
4 gearbox
5 tool rest
6 chuck
7 tailstock
8 centre (*Am.* center)
9 driving plate with pin
10 two-jaw chuck
11 live centre (*Am.* center)
12 fretsaw
13 fretsaw blade
14, 15, 24 turning tools
14 thread chaser, for cutting threads in wood
15 gouge, for rough turning
16 spoon bit (shell bit)
17 hollowing tool
18 outside calliper (caliper)
19 turned work (turned wood)
20 master turner (turner)
21 [piece of] rough wood
22 drill
23 inside calliper (caliper)
24 parting tool
25 glass paper (sandpaper, emery paper)
26 shavings

1-40 basket making (basketry, basketwork)

1-4 weaves (strokes)

1 randing

2 rib randing

3 oblique randing

4 randing, a piece of wickerwork (screen work)

5 weaver

6 stake

7 workboard: *also:* lapboard

8 screw block

9 hole for holding the block

10 stand

11 chip basket (spale basket)

12 chip (spale)

13 soaking tub

14 willow stakes (osier stakes)

15 willow rods (osier rods)

16 basket, a piece of wickerwork (basketwork)

17 border

18 woven side

19 round base

20 woven base

21 slath

22-24 covering a frame

22 frame

23 end

24 rib

25 upsett

26 grass; *kinds:* esparto grass, alfalfa grass

27 rush (bulrush, reed mace)

28 reed

29 raffia (bast)

30 straw

31 bamboo cane

32 rattan (ratan) chair cane

33 basket maker

34 bending tool

35 cutting point (bodkin)

36 rapping iron

37 pincers

38 picking knife

39 shave

40 hacksaw

137 Blacksmith (Smith) I

1-8 hearth (forge) with blacksmith's fire
1 hearth (forge)
2 shovel (slice)
3 swab
4 rake
5 poker
6 blast pipe (tue iron)
7 chimney (cowl, hood)
8 water trough (quenching trough, bosh)
9 power hammer
10 ram (tup)
11-16 anvil
11 anvil
12 flat beak (beck, bick)
13 round beak (beck, bick)
14 auxiliary table
15 foot
16 upsetting block
17 swage block
18 tool-grinding machine (tool grinder)
19 grinding wheel
20 block and tackle
21 workbench (bench)
22-39 blacksmith's tools
22 sledge hammer
23 blacksmith's hand hammer
24 flat tongs
25 round tongs
26 parts of the hammer
27 peen (pane, pein)
28 face
29 eye
30 haft
31 cotter punch
32 hardy (hardie)
33 set hammer
34 sett (set, sate)
35 flat-face hammer (flatter)
36 round punch
37 angle tongs
38 blacksmith's chisel (scaling hammer, chipping hammer)
39 moving iron (bending iron)

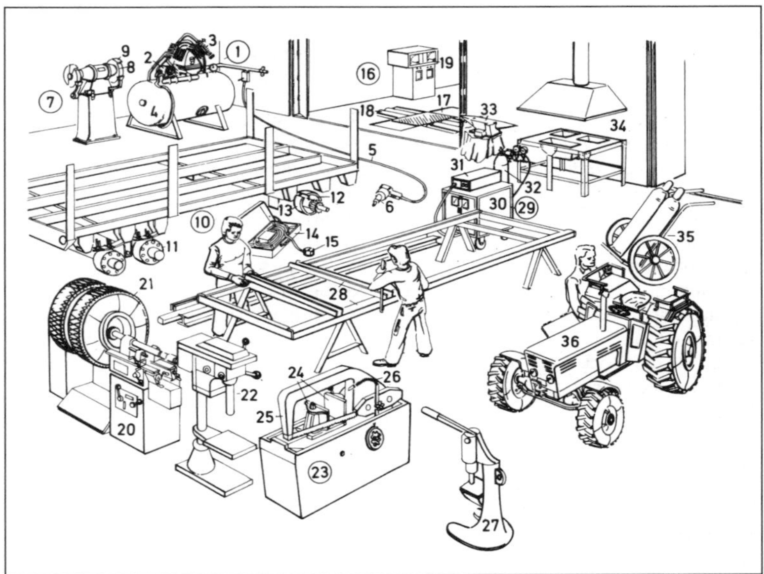

1 compressed-air system
2 electric motor
3 compressor
4 compressed-air tank
5 compressed-air line
6 percussion screwdriver
7 pedestal grinding machine (floor grinding machine)
8 grinding wheel
9 guard
10 trailer
11 brake drum
12 brake shoe
13 brake lining
14 testing kit
15 pressure gauge (*Am.* gage)
16 brake-testing equipment, a rolling road
17 pit
18 braking roller
19 meter (recording meter)
20 precision lathe for brake drums
21 lorry wheel
22 boring mill
23 power saw, a hacksaw (power hacksaw)
24 vice (*Am.* vise)
25 saw frame
26 coolant supply pipe
27 riveting machine
28 trailer frame (chassis) under construction
29 inert-gas welding equipment
30 rectifier
31 control unit
32 CO_2 cylinder
33 anvil
34 hearth (forge) with blacksmith's fire
35 trolley for gas cylinders
36 vehicle under repair, a tractor

139 Hammer Forging (Smith Forging) and Drop Forging

1 continuous furnace with grid hearth for annealing of round stock
2 discharge opening (discharge door)
3 gas burners
4 charging door
5 counterblow hammer
6 upper ram
7 lower ram
8 ram guide
9 hydraulic drive
10 column
11 short-stroke drop hammer
12 ram (tup)
13 upper die block
14 lower die block
15 hydraulic drive
16 frame
17 anvil
18 forging and sizing press
19 standard
20 table
21 disc (disk) clutch
22 compressed-air pipe
23 solenoid valve
24 air-lift gravity hammer (air-lift drop hammer)
25 drive motor
26 hammer (tup)
27 foot control (foot pedal)
28 preshaped (blocked) workpiece
29 hammer guide
30 hammer cylinder
31 anvil
32 mechanical manipulator to move the workpiece in hammer forging
33 dogs
34 counterweight
35 hydraulic forging press
36 crown
37 cross head
38 upper die block
39 lower die block
40 anvil
41 hydraulic piston
42 pillar guide
43 rollover device
44 burden chain (chain sling)
45 crane hook
46 workpiece
47 gas furnace (gas-fired furnace)
48 gas burner
49 charging opening
50 chain curtain
51 vertical-lift door
52 hot-air duct
53 air preheater
54 gas pipe
55 electric door-lifting mechanism
56 air blast

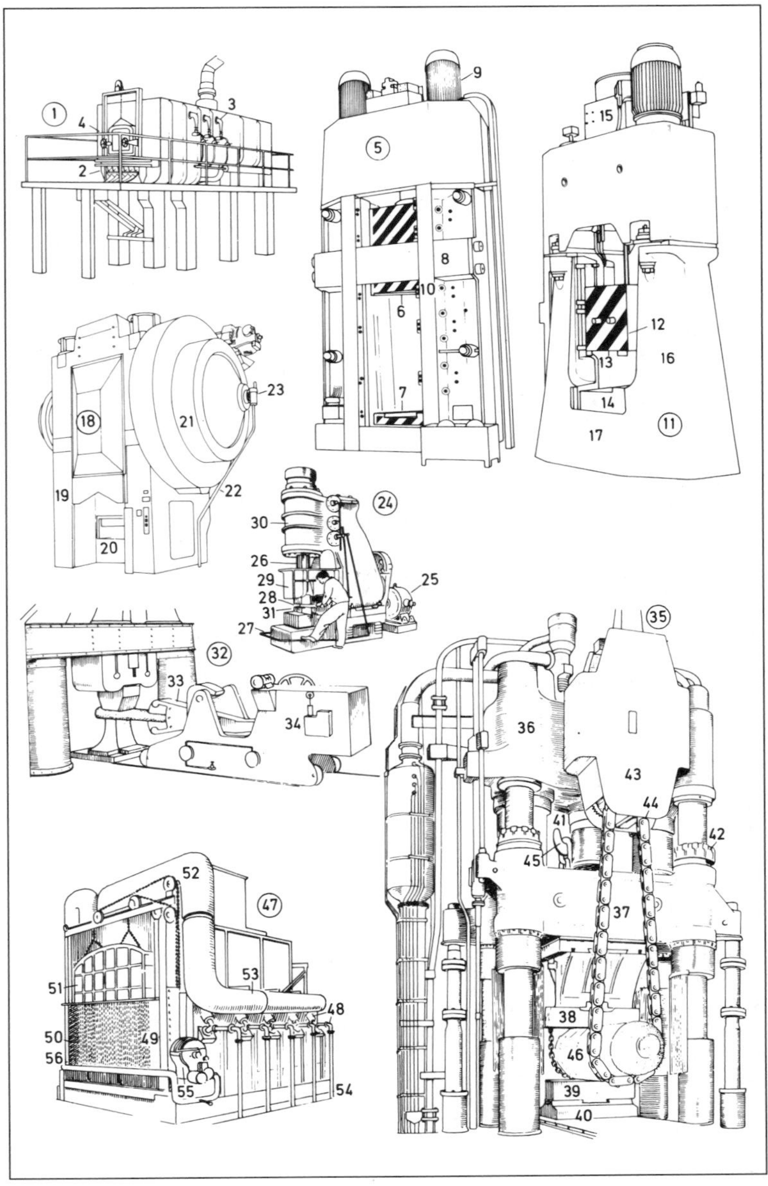
1
2
3
4
5
6
7
8
9
10
11
12
13
14
15
16
17
18
19
20
21
22
23
24
25
26
27
28
29
30
31
32
33
34
35
36
37
38
39
40
41
42
43
44
45
46
47
48
49
50
51
52
53
54
55
56

140 Metalworker

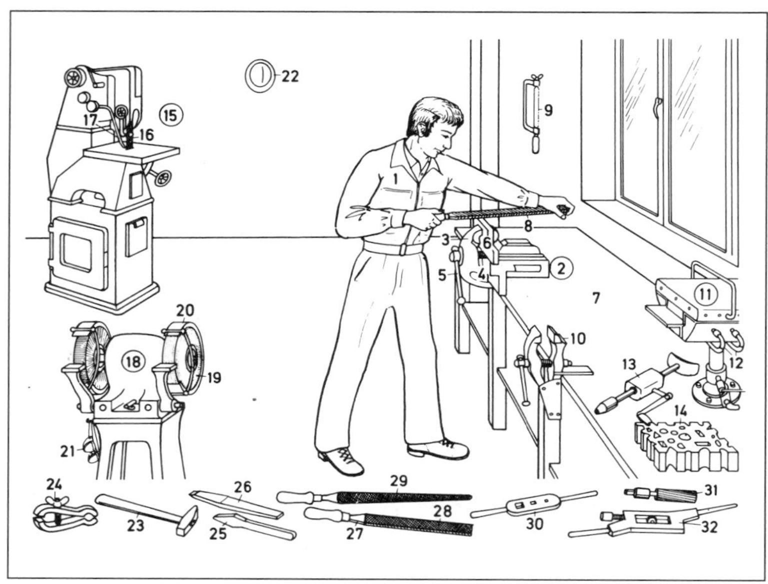

1-22 metalwork shop (mechanic's workshop, fitter's workshop, locksmith's workshop)

1 metalworker (*e.g.* mechanic, fitter, locksmith; *form. also:* wrought-iron craftsman)

2 parallel-jaw vice (*Am.* vise)

3 jaw

4 screw

5 handle

6 workpiece

7 workbench (bench)

8 files (*kinds:* rough file, smooth file, precision file)

9 hacksaw

10 leg vice (*Am.* vise), a spring vice

11 muffle furnace, a gas-fired furnace

12 gas pipe

13 hand brace (hand drill)

14 swage block

15 filing machine

16 file

17 compressed-air pipe

18 grinding machine (grinder)

19 grinding wheel

20 guard

21 goggles (safety glasses)

22 safety helmet

23 machinist's hammer

24 hand vice (*Am.* vise)

25 cape chisel (cross-cut chisel)

26 flat chisel

27 flat file

28 file cut (cut)

29 round file (*also:* half-round file)

30 tap wrench

31 reamer

32 die (die and stock)

33-35 key
33 stem (shank)
34 bow
35 bit
36-43 door lock, a mortise (mortice) lock
36 back plate
37 spring bolt (latch bolt)
38 tumbler
39 bolt
40 keyhole
41 bolt guide pin
42 tumbler spring
43 follower, with square hole
44 cylinder lock (safety lock)
45 cylinder (plug)
46 spring
47 pin
48 safety key, a flat key
49 lift-off hinge
50 hook-and-ride band
51 strap hinge
52 vernier calliper (caliper) gauge (*Am.* gage)
53 feeler gauge (*Am.* gage)
54 vernier depth gauge (*Am.* gage)
55 vernier
56 straightedge
57 square
58 breast drill
59 twist bit (twist drill)
60 screw tap (tap)
61 halves of a screw die
62 screwdriver
63 scraper (*also:* pointed triangle scraper)
64 centre (*Am.* center) punch
65 round punch
66 flat-nose pliers
67 detachable-jaw cut nippers
68 gas pliers
69 pincers

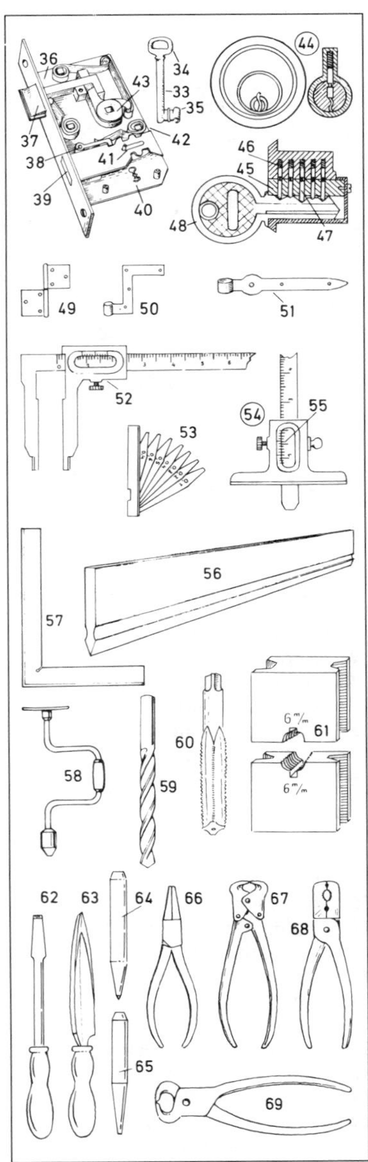

141 Gas Welder

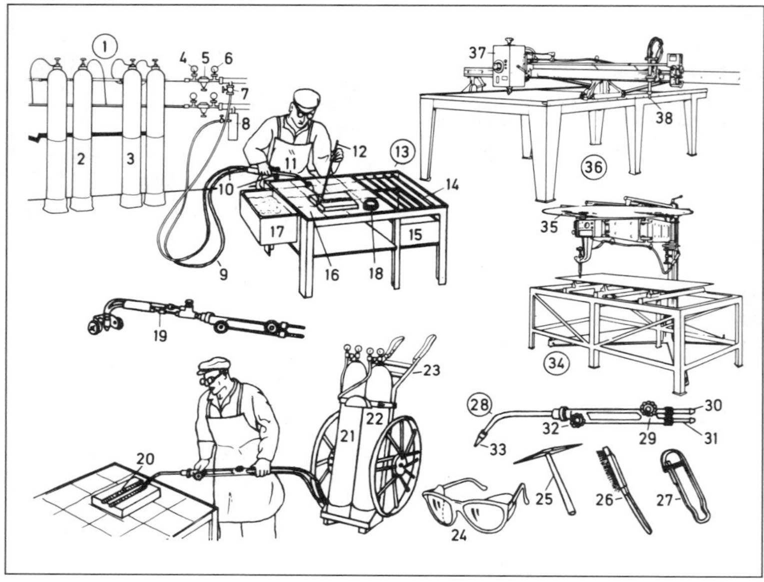

1 gas cylinder manifold
2 acetylene cylinder
3 oxygen cylinder
4 high-pressure manometer
5 pressure-reducing valve (reducing valve, pressure regulator)
6 low-pressure manometer
7 stop valve
8 hydraulic back-pressure valve for low-pressure installations
9 gas hose
10 oxygen hose
11 welding torch (blowpipe)
12 welding rod (filler rod)
13 welding bench
14 grating
15 scrap box
16 bench covering of chamotte slabs
17 water tank
18 welding paste (flux)
19 welding torch (blowpipe) with cutting attachment and guide tractor
20 workpiece
21 oxygen cylinder
22 acetylene cylinder
23 cylinder trolley
24 welding goggles
25 chipping hammer
26 wire brush
27 torch lighter (blowpipe lighter)
28 welding torch (blowpipe)
29 oxygen control
30 oxygen connection
31 gas connection (acetylene connection)
32 gas control (acetylene control)
33 welding nozzle
34 cutting machine
35 circular template
36 universal cutting machine
37 tracing head
38 cutting nozzle

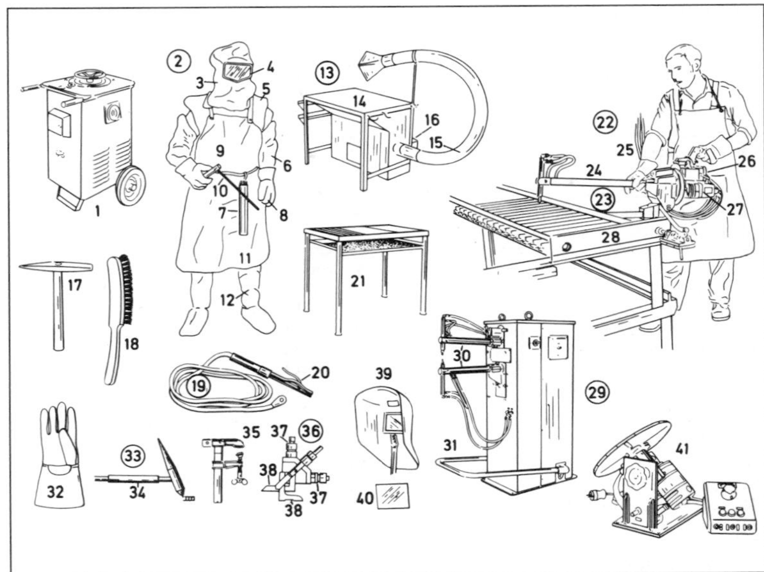

1 welding transformer
2 **arc welder**
3 arc welding helmet
4 flip-up window
5 shoulder guard
6 protective sleeve
7 electrode case
8 three-fingered welding glove
9 electrode holder
10 electrode
11 leather apron
12 shin guard
13 **welding table with fume extraction equipment**
14 table top
15 movable extractor duct
16 extractor support
17 chipping hammer
18 wire brush
19 welding lead
20 electrode holder
21 welding bench
22 **spot welding**
23 spot welding electrode holder
24 electrode arm
25 power supply (lead)
26 electrode-pressure cylinder
27 welding transformer
28 workpiece
29 foot-operated spot welder
30 welder electrode arms
31 foot pedal for welding pressure adjustment
32 five-fingered welding glove
33 inert-gas torch for inert-gas welding (gas-shielded arc welding)
34 inert-gas (shielding-gas) supply
35 work clamp (earthing clamp)
36 fillet gauge (*Am.* gage) (weld gauge) [for measuring throat thickness]
37 micrometer
38 measuring arm
39 arc welding helmet
40 filter lens
41 small turntable

143 Sections, Bolts, and Machine Parts

[material: steel, brass, aluminium (*Am.* aluminium), plastics, etc.; in the following, steel was chosen as an example]
1 angle iron (angle)
2 leg (flange)
3-7 steel girders
3 T-iron (tee-iron)
4 vertical leg
5 flange
6 H-girder (H-beam)
7 E-channel (channel iron)
8 round bar
9 square iron (*Am.* square stock)
10 flat bar
11 strip steel
12 iron wire
13-50 screws and bolts
13 hexagonal-head bolt
14 head
15 shank
16 thread
17 washer
18 hexagonal nut
19 split pin
20 rounded end
21 width of head (of flats)
22 stud
23 point (end)
24 castle nut (castellated nut)
25 hole for the split pin
26 cross-head screw, a sheet-metal screw (self-tapping screw)
27 hexagonal socket head screw
28 countersunk-head bolt
29 catch
30 locknut (locking nut)
31 bolt (pin)
32 collar-head bolt
33 set collar (integral collar)
34 spring washer (washer)
35 round nut, an adjusting nut
36 cheese-head screw, a slotted screw
37 tapered pin
38 screw slot (screw slit, screw groove)
39 square-head bolt
40 grooved pin, a cylindrical pin
41 T-head bolt
42 wing nut (fly nut, butterfly nut)
43 rag bolt
44 barb
45 wood screw
46 countersunk head
47 wood screw thread
48 grub screw
49 pin slot (pin slit, pin groove)
50 round end
51 nail (wire nail)
52 head
53 shank
54 point
55 roofing nail
56 riveting (lap riveting)
57-60 rivet
57 set head (swage head, die head), a rivet head
58 rivet shank
59 closing head
60 pitch of rivets
61 shaft
62 chamfer (bevel)
63 journal
64 neck
65 seat
66 keyway
67 conical seat (cone)
68 thread
69 ball bearing, an antifriction bearing
70 steel ball (ball)
71 outer race
72 inner race
73, 74 keys
73 sunk key (feather)
74 gib (gib-headed key)
75, 76 needle roller bearing
75 needle cage
76 needle
77 castle nut (castellated nut)
78 split pin
79 casing
80 casing cover
81 grease nipple (lubricating nipple)
82-96 gear wheels, cog wheels
82 stepped gear wheel
83 cog (tooth)
84 space between teeth
85 keyway (key seat, key slot)
86 bore
87 herringbone gear wheel
88 spoke (arm)
89 helical gearing (helical spur wheel)
90 sprocket
91 bevel gear wheel (bevel wheel)
92, 93 spiral toothing
92 pinion
93 crown wheel
94-96 epicyclic gear (planetary gear)
94 planet wheels
95 internal gear
96 sun wheel (sun gear)
97-107 absorption dynamometer
97 shoe brake (check brake, block brake)
98 brake pulley
99 brake shaft (brake axle)
100 brake block (brake shoe)
101 pull rod
102 brake magnet
103 brake weight
104 band brake
105 brake band
106 brake lining
107 adjusting screw, for even application of the brake

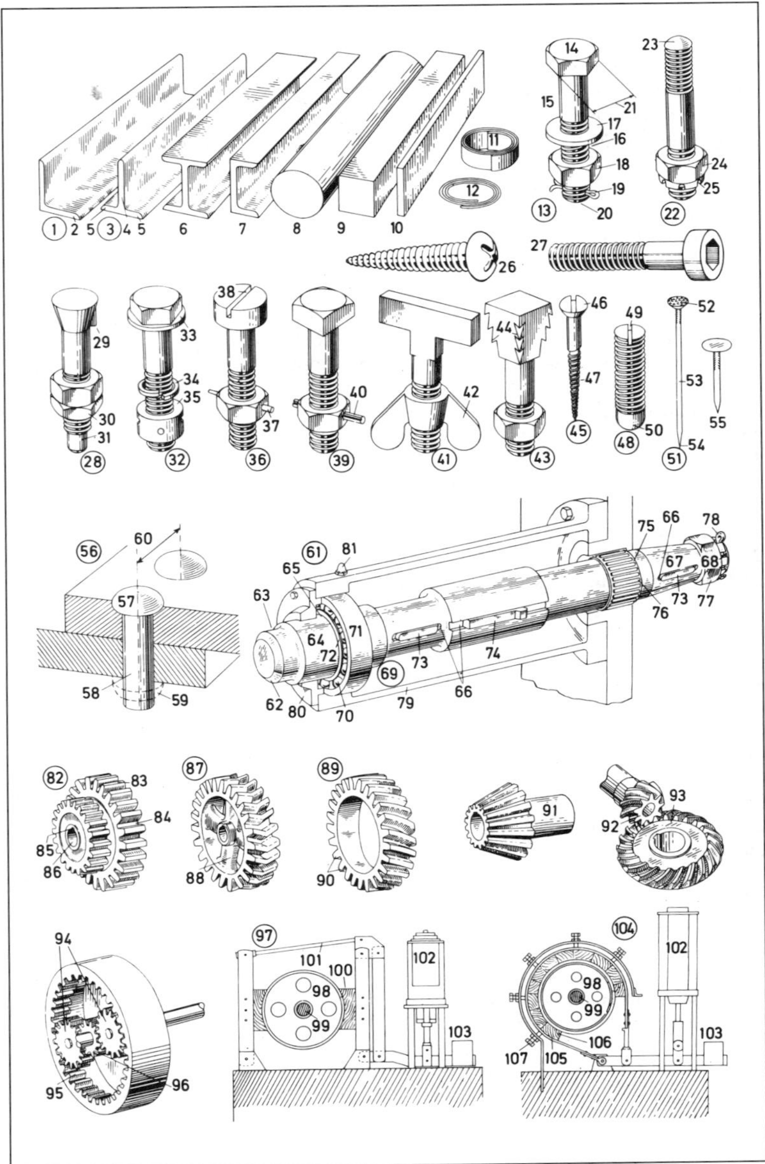
1
2
5
3
4
5
6
7
8
9
10
11
12
13
14
15
16
17
18
19
20
21
22
23
24
25
26
27
28
29
30
31
32
33
34
35
36
37
38
39
40
41
42
43
44
45
46
47
48
49
50
51
52
53
54
55
56
57
58
59
60
61
62
63
64
65
66
67
68
69
70
71
72
73
74
75
76
77
78
79
80
81
82
83
84
85
86
87
88
89
90
91
92
93
94
95
96
97
98
99
100
101
102
103
104
105
106
107

144 Coal Mine

1-51 coal mine (colliery, pit)
1 pithead gear (headgear)
2 winding engine house
3 pithead frame (head frame)
4 pithead building
5 processing plant
6 sawmill
7-11 coking plant
7 battery of coke ovens
8 larry car (larry, charging car)
9 coking coal tower
10 coke-quenching tower
11 coke-quenching car
12 gasometer
13 power plant (power station)
14 water tower
15 cooling tower
16 mine fan
17 depot
18 administration building (office building, offices)
19 tip heap (spoil heap)
20 cleaning plant
21-51 underground workings (underground mining)
21 ventilation shaft
22 fan drift
23 cage-winding system with cages
24 main shaft
25 skip-winding system
26 winding inset
27 staple shaft
28 spiral chute
29 gallery along seam
30 lateral
31 cross-cut
32 tunnelling (*Am.* tunneling) machine
33-37 longwall faces
33 horizontal ploughed longwall face
34 horizontal cut longwall face
35 vertical pneumatic pick longwall face
36 diagonal ram longwall face
37 goaf (gob, waste)
38 air lock
39 transportation of men by cars
40 belt conveying
41 raw coal bunker
42 charging conveyor
43 transportation of supplies by monorail car
44 transportation of men by monorail car
45 transportation of supplies by mine car
46 drainage
47 sump (sink)
48 capping
49 [layer of] coal-bearing rock
50 coal seam
51 fault

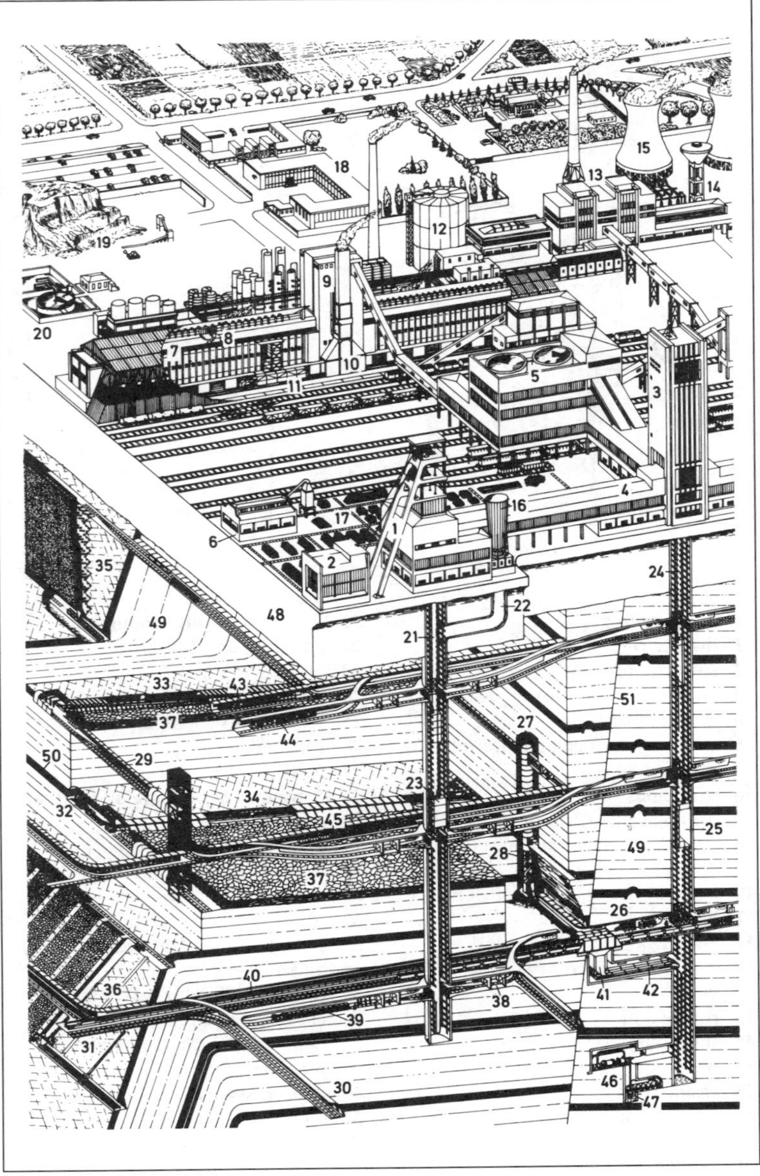
1
2
3
4
5
6
7
8
9
10
11
12
13
14
15
16
17
18
19
20
21
22
23
24
25
26
27
28
29
30
31
32
33
34
35
36
37
38
39
40
41
42
43
44
45
46
47
48
49
50
51

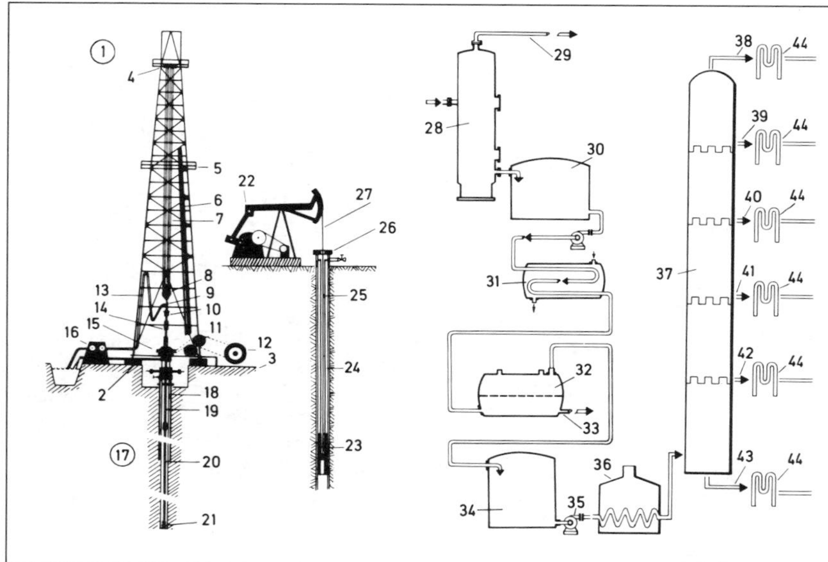

1-21 oil drilling
1 drilling rig
2 substructure
3 crown safety platform
4 crown blocks
5 working platform, an intermediate platform
6 drill pipes
7 drilling cable (drilling line)
8 travelling (*Am.* traveling) block
9 hook
10 [rotary] swivel
11 hoist
12 engine
13 standpipe and rotary hose
14 kelly
15 rotary table
16 slush pump (mud pump)
17 well
18 casing
19 drilling pipe
20 tubing
21 drilling bit; *kinds:* fishtail (blade) bit, rock (*Am.* roller) bit, core bit

22-27 oil (crude oil) production
22 pumping unit (pump)
23 plunger
24 tubing
25 sucker rods (pumping rods)
26 stuffing box
27 polish (polished) rod

28-35 treatment of crude oil [diagram]
28 gas separator
29 gas pipe (gas outlet)
30 wet oil tank (wash tank)
31 water heater
32 water and brine separator
33 salt water pipe (salt water outlet)
34 oil tank
35 trunk pipeline for oil [to the refinery or transport by tanker lorry (*Am.* tank truck), oil tanker or pipeline]

36-64 processing of crude oil [diagram]
36 oil furnace (pipe still)
37 fractionating column (distillation column) with trays
38 top gases (tops)

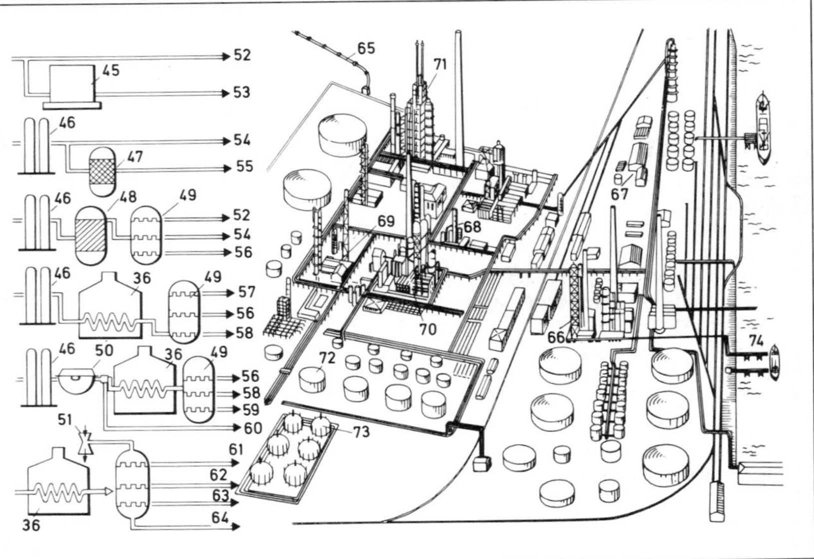

39 light distillation products
40 heavy distillation products
41 petroleum
42 gas oil component
43 residue
44 condenser (cooler)
45 compressor
46 desulphurizing (desulphurization, *Am.* desulfurizing, desulfurization) plant
47 reformer (hydroformer, platformer)
48 catalytic cracker (cat cracker)
49 distillation column
50 de-waxing (wax separation)
51 vacuum equipment
52-64 oil products
52 fuel gas
53 liquefied petroleum gas (liquid gas)
54 regular grade petrol (*Am.* gasoline)
55 super grade petrol (*Am.* gasoline)
56 diesel oil
57 aviation fuel
58 light fuel oil
59 heavy fuel oil
60 paraffin (paraffin oil, kerosene)
61 spindle oil
62 lubricating oil
63 cylinder oil
64 bitumen
65-74 oil refinery
65 pipeline (oil pipeline)
66 distillation plants
67 lubricating oil refinery
68 desulphurizing (desulphurization, *Am.* desulfurizing, desulfurization) plant
69 gas-separating plant
70 catalytic cracking plant
71 catalytic reformer
72 storage tank
73 spherical tank
74 tanker terminal

1-39 drilling rig (oil rig)
1-37 drilling platform
1 power station
2 generator exhausts
3 revolving crane (pedestal crane)
4 piperack
5 turbine exhausts
6 materials store
7 helicopter deck (heliport deck, heliport)
8 elevator
9 production oil and gas separator
10 test oil and gas separators (test separators)
11 emergency flare stack
12 derrick
13 diesel tank
14 office building
15 cement storage tanks
16 drinking water tank
17 salt water tank
18 jet fuel tanks
19 lifeboats
20 elevator shaft
21 compressed-air reservoir
22 pumping station
23 air compressor
24 air lock
25 seawater desalination plant
26 inlet filters for diesel fuel
27 gas cooler
28 control panel for the separators
29 toilets (lavatories)
30 workshop
31 pig trap [the 'pig' is used to clean the oil pipeline]
32 control room
33 accommodation modules (accommodation)
34 high-pressure cementing pumps
35 lower deck
36 middle deck
37 top deck (main deck)
38 substructure
39 mean sea level

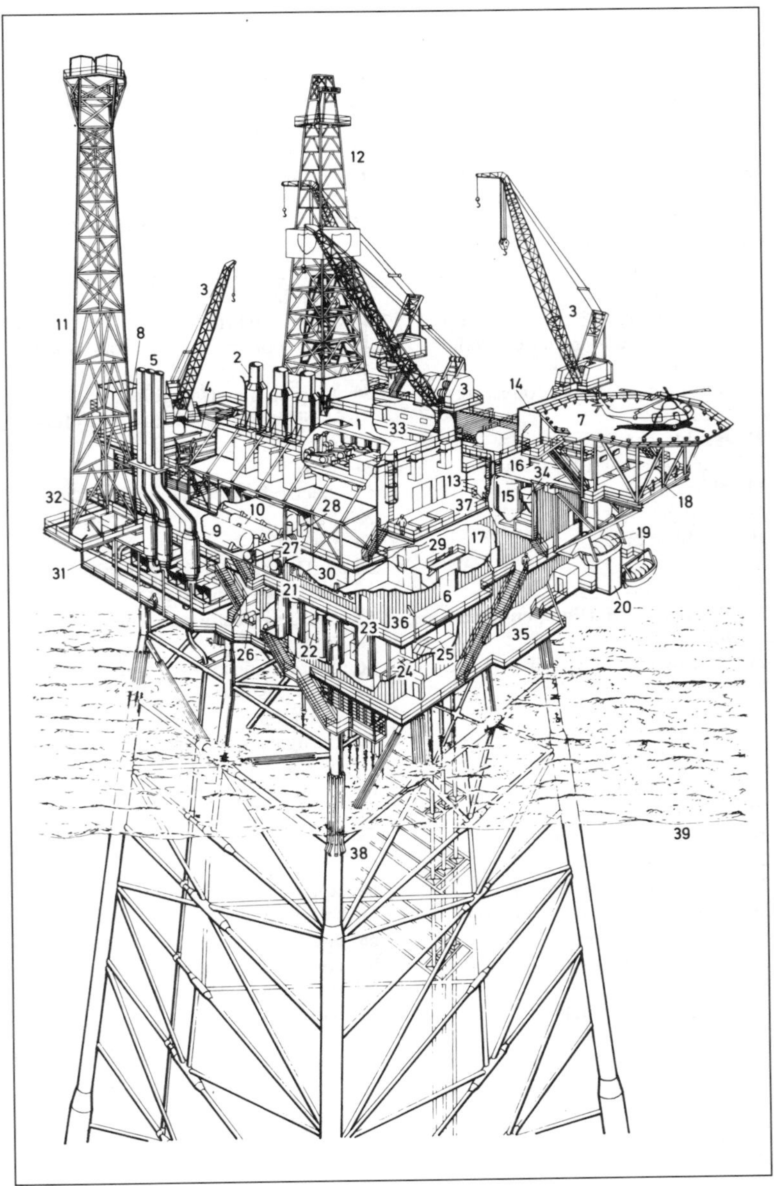
11
12
3
3
3
8
5
2
4
1
33
14
7
16
34
13
18
32
10
28
37
15
9
29
17
19
27
31
30
21
6
20
23
36
35
22
26
25
24
39
38

147 Iron and Steel Works

1-20 blast furnace plant
1 blast furnace, a shaft furnace
2 furnace incline (lift) for ore and flux or coke
3 skip hoist
4 charging platform
5 receiving hopper
6 bell
7 blast furnace shaft
8 smelting section
9 slag escape
10 slag ladle
11 pig iron (crude iron, iron) runout
12 pig iron (crude iron, iron) ladle
13 downtake
14 dust catcher, a dust-collecting machine
15 hot-blast stove
16 external combustion chamber
17 blast main
18 gas pipe
19 hot-blast pipe
20 tuyère
21-69 steelworks
21-30 Siemens-Martin open-hearth furnace
21 pig iron (crude iron, iron) ladle
22 feed runner
23 stationary furnace
24 hearth
25 charging machine
26 scrap iron charging box
27 gas pipe
28 gas regenerator chamber
29 air feed pipe
30 air regenerator chamber
31 [bottom-pouring] steel-casting ladle with stopper
32 ingot mould (*Am.* mold)
33 steel ingot
34-44 pig-casting machine
34 pouring end
35 metal runner
36 series (strand) of moulds (*Am.* molds)
37 mould (*Am.* mold)
38 catwalk
39 discharging chute
40 pig
41 travelling (*Am.* traveling) crane
42 top-pouring pig iron (crude iron, iron) ladle
43 pouring ladle lip
44 tilting device (tipping device, *Am.* dumping device)
45-50 oxygen-blowing converter (L-D converter, Linz-Donawitz converter)
45 conical converter top
46 mantle
47 solid converter bottom
48 fireproof lining (refractory lining)
49 oxygen lance
50 tapping hole (tap hole)
51-54 Siemens electric low-shaft furnace
51 feed
52 electrodes [arranged in a circle]
53 bustle pipe
54 runout
55-69 Thomas converter (basic Bessemer converter)
55 charging position for molten pig iron
56 charging position for lime
57 blow position
58 discharging position
59 tilting device (tipping device, *Am.* dumping device)
60 crane-operated ladle
61 auxiliary crane hoist
62 lime bunker
63 downpipe
64 tipping car (*Am.* dump truck)
65 scrap iron feed
66 control desk
67 converter chimney
68 blast main
69 wind box

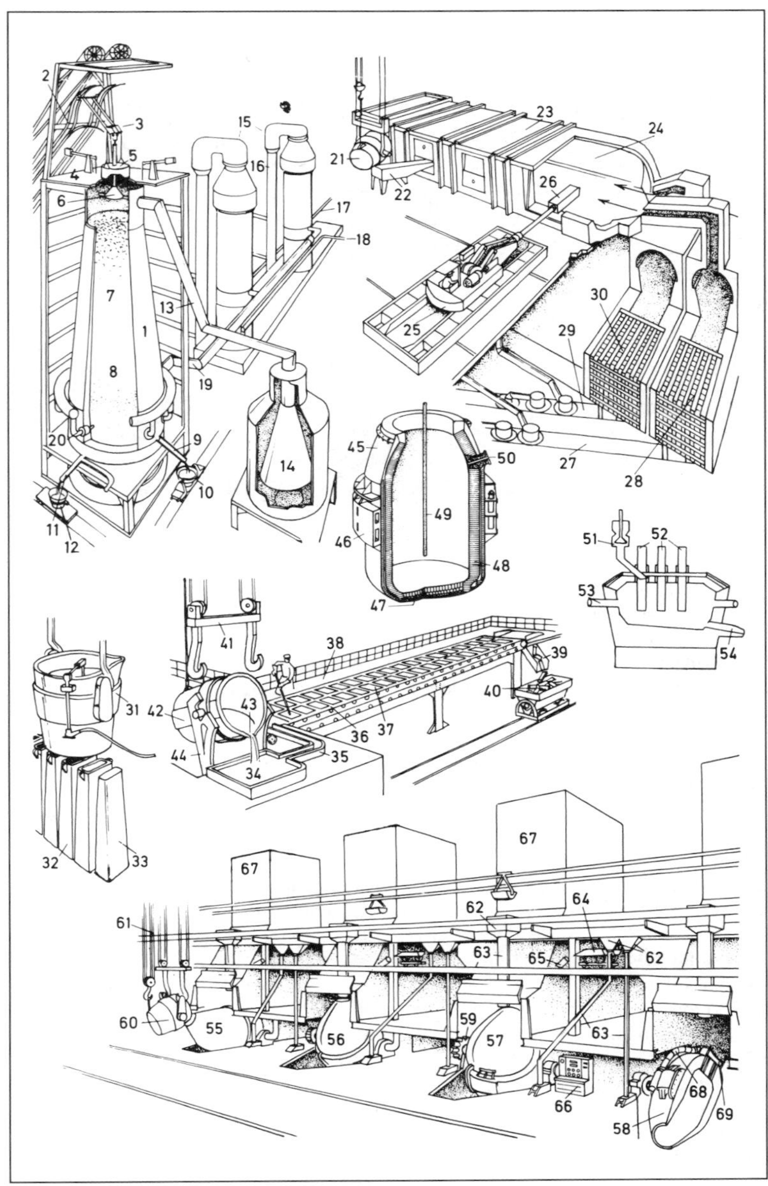
1
2
3
4
5
6
7
8
9
10
11
12
13
14
15
16
17
18
19
20
21
22
23
24
25
26
27
28
29
30
31
32
33
34
35
36
37
38
39
40
41
42
43
44
45
46
47
48
49
50
51
52
53
54
55
56
57
58
59
60
61
62
63
64
65
66
67
68
69

148 Iron Foundry and Rolling Mill

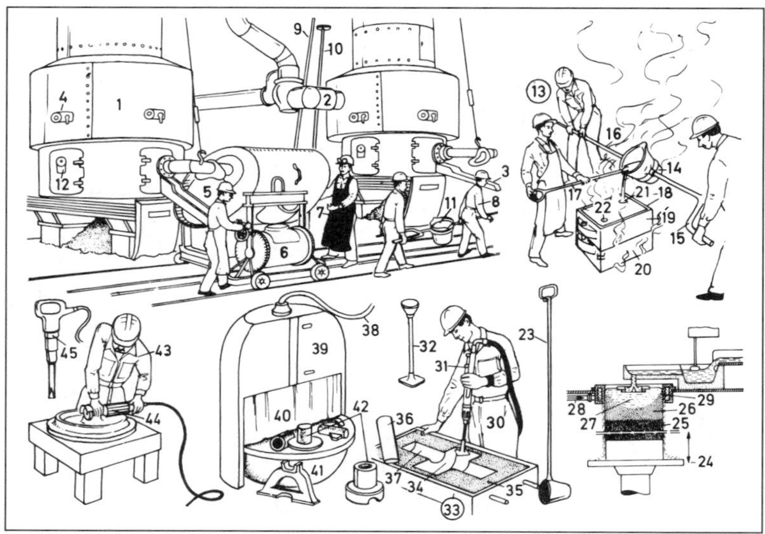

1-45 iron foundry

1-12 melting plant

1 cupola furnace (cupola), a melting furnace

2 blast main (blast inlet, blast pipe)

3 tapping spout

4 spyhole

5 tilting-type [hot-metal] receiver

6 mobile drum-type ladle

7 melter

8 founder (caster)

9 tap bar (tapping bar)

10 bott stick (*Am.* bot stick)

11 molten iron

12 slag spout

13 casting team

14 hand shank

15 double handle (crutch)

16 carrying bar

17 skimmer rod

18 closed moulding (*Am.* molding) box

19 upper frame (cope)

20 lower frame (drag)

21 runner (runner gate, down-gate)

22 riser (riser gate)

23 hand ladle

24-29 continuous casting

24 sinking pouring floor

25 solidifying pig

26 solid stage

27 liquid stage

28 water-cooling system

29 mould (*Am.* mold) wall

30-37 moulding (*Am.* molding) **department** (moulding shop)

30 moulder (*Am.* molder)

31 pneumatic rammer

32 hand rammer

33 open moulding (*Am.* molding) box

34 pattern

35 moulding (*Am.* molding) sand

36 core

37 core print

38-45 cleaning shop (fettling shop)

38 steel grit or sand delivery pipe

39 rotary-table shot-blasting machine

40 grit guard

41 revolving table

42 casting

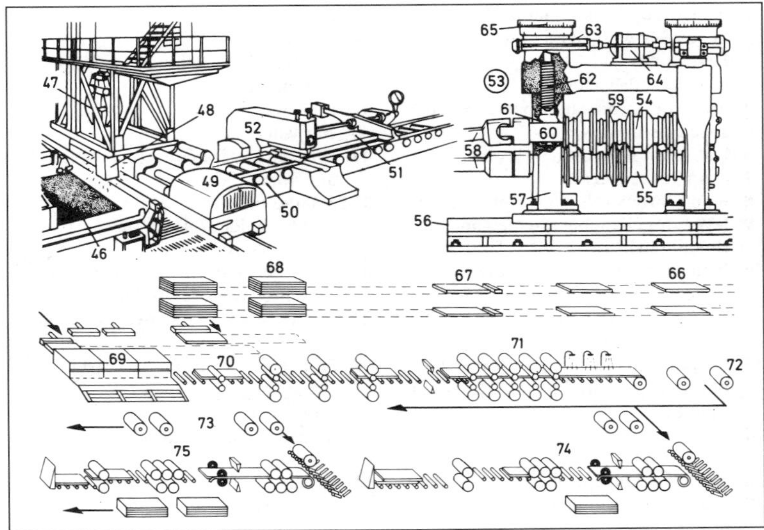

43 fettler
44 pneumatic grinder
45 pneumatic chisel
46-75 rolling mill
46 soaking pit
47 soaking pit crane
48 ingot
49 ingot tipper
50 roller table
51 workpiece
52 bloom shears
53 two-high mill
54-55 set of rolls (set of rollers)
54 upper roll (upper roller)
55 lower roll (lower roller)
56-60 roll stand
56 base plate
57 housing (frame)
58 coupling spindle
59 groove
60 roll bearing
61-65 adjusting equipment
61 chock
62 main screw
63 gear
64 motor
65 indicator for rough and fine adjustment
66-75 continuous rolling mill train for the manufacture of strip [diagram]
66-68 processing of semi-finished product
66 semi-finished product
67 gas cutting installation
68 stack of finished steel sheets
69 continuous reheating furnaces
70 blooming train
71 finishing train
72 coiler
73 stock of coils for sale
74 5 mm shearing train
75 10 mm shearing train

149 Machine Tools I

1 **centre** (*Am.* center) **lathe**
2 headstock with gear control (geared headstock)
3 reduction drive lever
4 lever for normal and coarse threads
5 speed change lever
6 leadscrew reverse-gear lever
7 change-gear box
8 feed gearbox (Norton tumbler gear)
9 levers for changing the feed and thread pitch
10 feed gear lever (tumbler lever)
11 switch lever for right or left hand action of main spindle
12 lathe foot (footpiece)
13 leadscrew handwheel for traversing of saddle (longitudinal movement of saddle)
14 tumbler reverse lever
15 feed screw
16 apron (saddle apron, carriage apron)
17 lever for longitudinal and transverse motion
18 drop (dropping) worm (feed trip, feed tripping device) for engaging feed mechanisms
19 lever for engaging half nut of leadscrew (lever for clasp nut engagement)
20 lathe spindle
21 tool post
22 top slide (tool slide, tool rest)
23 cross slide
24 bed slide
25 coolant supply pipe
26 tailstock centre (*Am.* center)
27 barrel (tailstock barrel)
28 tailstock barrel clamp lever
29 tailstock
30 tailstock barrel adjusting handwheel
31 lathe bed
32 leadscrew
33 feed shaft
34 reverse shaft for right and left hand motion and engaging and disengaging
35 four-jaw chuck (four-jaw independent chuck)
36 gripping jaw
37 three-jaw chuck (three-jaw self-centring, *Am.* self-centering, chuck)
38 **turret lathe**
39 cross slide
40 turret
41 combination toolholder (multiple turning head)
42 top slide
43 star wheel
44 coolant tray for collecting coolant and swarf
45-53 lathe tools
45 tool bit holder (clamp tip tool) for adjustable cutting tips
46 adjustable cutting tip (clamp tip) of cemented carbide or oxide ceramic
47 shapes of adjustable oxide ceramic tips
48 lathe tool with cemented carbide cutting edge
49 tool shank
50 brazed cemented carbide cutting tip (cutting edge)
51 internal facing tool (boring tool) for corner work
52 general-purpose lathe tool
53 parting (parting-off) tool
54 lathe carrier
55 driving (driver) plate
56-72 measuring instruments
56 plug gauge (*Am.* gage)
57 'GO' gauging (*Am.* gaging) member (end)
58 'NOT GO' gauging (*Am.* gaging) member (end)
59 calliper (caliper, snap) gauge (*Am.* gage)
60 'GO' side
61 'NOT GO' side
62 micrometer
63 measuring scale
64 graduated thimble
65 frame
66 spindle (screwed spindle)
67 vernier calliper (caliper) gauge (*Am.* gage)
68 depth gauge (*Am.* gage) attachment rule
69 vernier scale
70 outside jaws
71 inside jaws
72 vernier depth gauge (*Am.* gage)

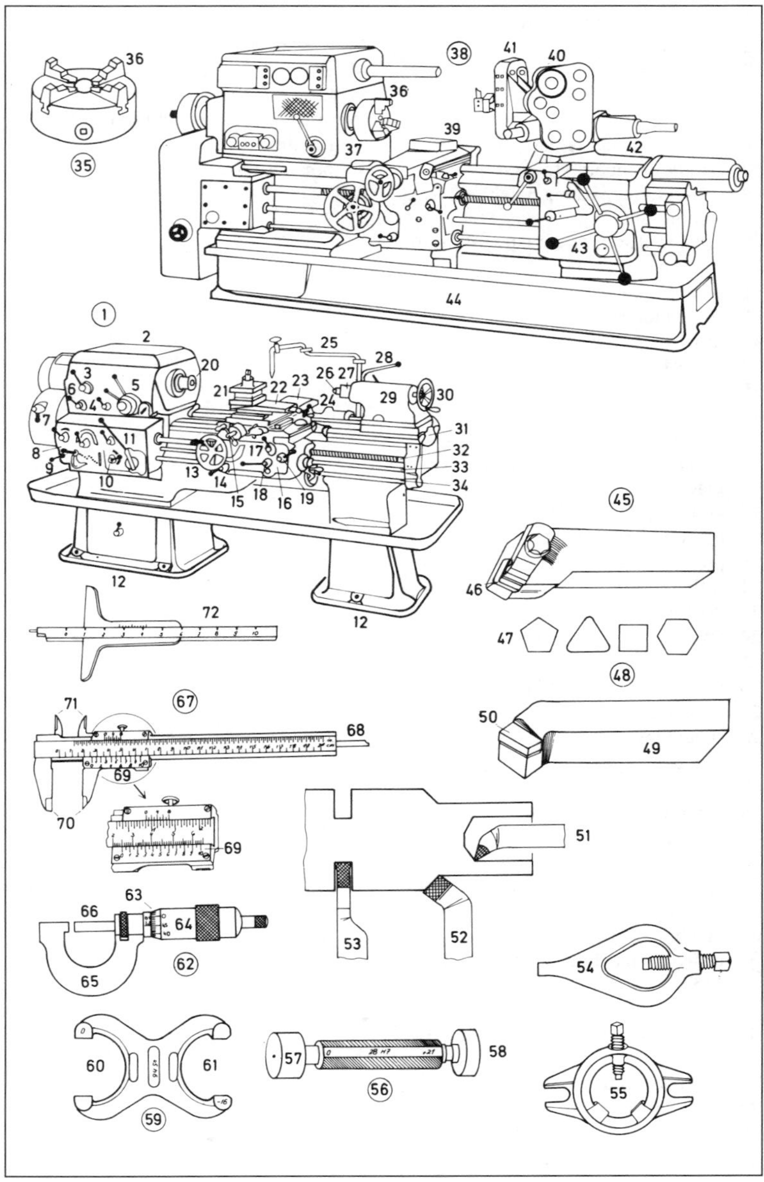

1
2
3
4
5
6
7
8
9
10
11
12
13
14
15
16
17
18
19
20
21
22
23
24
25
26
27
28
29
30
31
32
33
34
35
36
37
38
39
40
41
42
43
44
45
46
47
48
49
50
51
52
53
54
55
56
57
58
59
60
61
62
63
64
65
66
67
68
69
70
71
72

1 **universal grinding machine**
2 headstock
3 wheelhead slide
4 grinding wheel
5 tailstock
6 grinding machine bed
7 grinding machine table
8 **two-column planing machine** (two-column planer)
9 drive motor, a direct current motor
10 column
11 planer table
12 cross slide (rail)
13 tool box
14 **hacksaw**
15 clamping device
16 saw blade
17 saw frame
18 **radial** (radial-arm) **drilling machine**
19 bed (base plate)
20 block for workpiece
21 pillar
22 lifting motor
23 drill spindle
24 arm
25 **universal milling machine**
26 milling machine table
27 table feed drive
28 switch lever for spindle rotation speed
29 control box (control unit)
30 vertical milling spindle
31 vertical drive head
32 horizontal milling spindle
33 end support for steadying horizontal spindle
34 machine tap
35 **articulated robot,** an industrial robot
36 base plate
37 rotating column (base rotating axis)
38 shoulder joint
39 upper arm
40 elbow joint
41 tubular forearm
42 wrist joint
43 gripper mounting flange
44 gripper
45 fingers
46 upright robot (linear-axis robot, rectilinear robot)
47 portal robot (gantry robot)

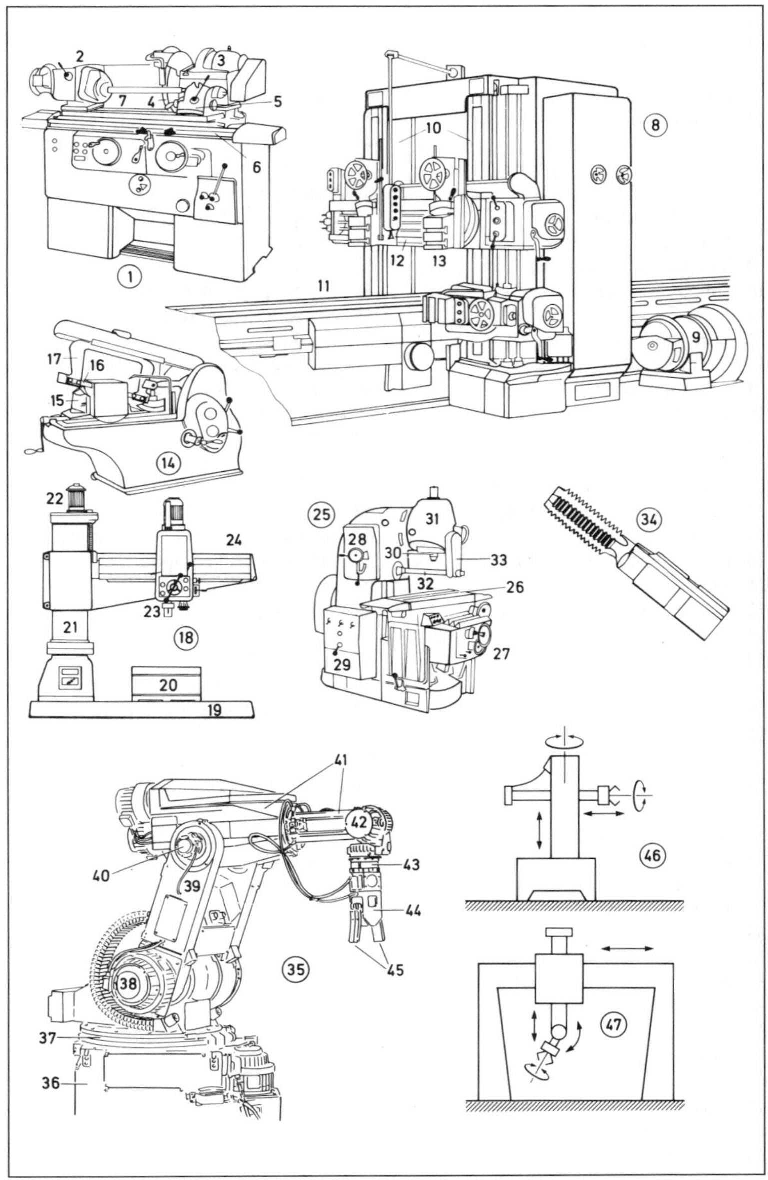
2
3
7
4
5
6
1
10
8
12
13
11
9
17
16
15
14
22
24
23
21
18
20
19
25
31
28
30
33
32
26
29
27
34
41
42
40
43
39
44
45
35
38
37
36
46
47

151 Drawing Office

1 drawing board
2 drafting machine with parallel motion
3 adjustable knob
4 drawing head (adjustable set square)
5 drawing board adjustment
6 drawing table
7 set square (triangle)
8 triangle
9 T-square (tee-square)
10 rolled drawing
11 diagram
12 time schedule
13 paper stand
14 roll of paper
15 cutter
16 technical drawing (drawing, design)
17 front view (front elevation)
18 side view (side elevation)
19 plan
20 surface not to be machined
21 surface to be machined
22 surface to be superfinished
23 visible edge
24 hidden edge
25 dimension line
26 arrow head
27 section line
28 section A–B
29 hatched surface
30 centre (*Am.* center) line
31 title panel (title block)
32 technical data
33 ruler (rule)
34 triangular scale
35 erasing shield
36 drawing ink cartridge
37 holders for tubular drawing pens
38 set of tubular drawing pens
39 hygrometer
40 cap with indication of nib size
41 pencil-type eraser
42 eraser
43 erasing knife
44 erasing knife blade
45 clutch-type pencil
46 pencil lead (refill lead, refill, spare lead)
47 glass eraser
48 glass fibres (*Am.* fibers)
49 ruling pen
50 cross joint
51 index plate
52 compass with interchangeable attachments
53 compass head
54 needle point attachment
55 pencil point attachment
56 needle
57 lengthening arm (extension bar)
58 ruling pen attachment
59 pump compass (drop compass)
60 piston
61 ruling pen attachment
62 pencil attachment
63 drawing ink container
64 spring bow (rapid adjustment, ratchet-type) compass
65 spring ring hinge
66 spring-loaded fine adjustment for arcs
67 right-angle needle
68 tubular ink unit
69 stencil lettering guide (lettering stencil)
70 circle template
71 ellipse template

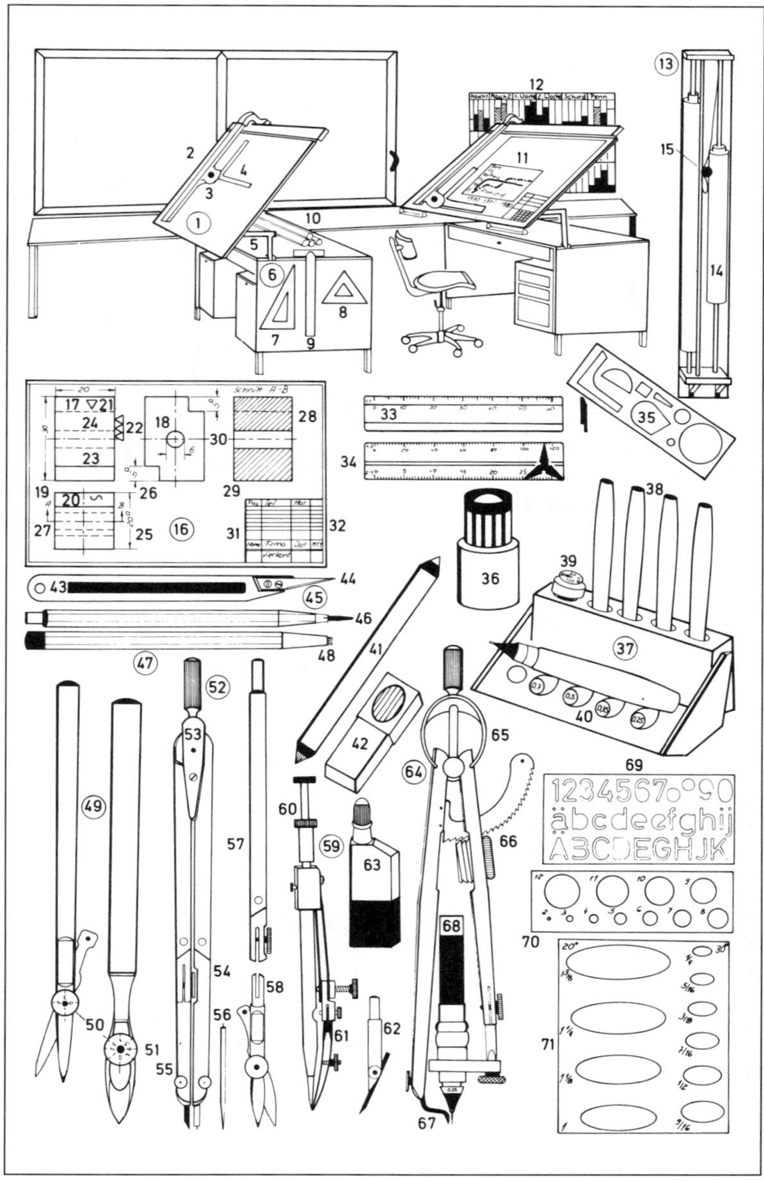
1
2
3
4
5
6
7
8
9
10
11
12
13
14
15
16
17
18
19
20
21
22
23
24
25
26
27
28
29
30
31
32
33
34
35
36
37
38
39
40
41
42
43
44
45
46
47
48
49
50
51
52
53
54
55
56
57
58
59
60
61
62
63
64
65
66
67
68
69
70
71
schnitt A-B
Firma
Dat.
1234567890
abcdeefghij
ABCDEGHJK

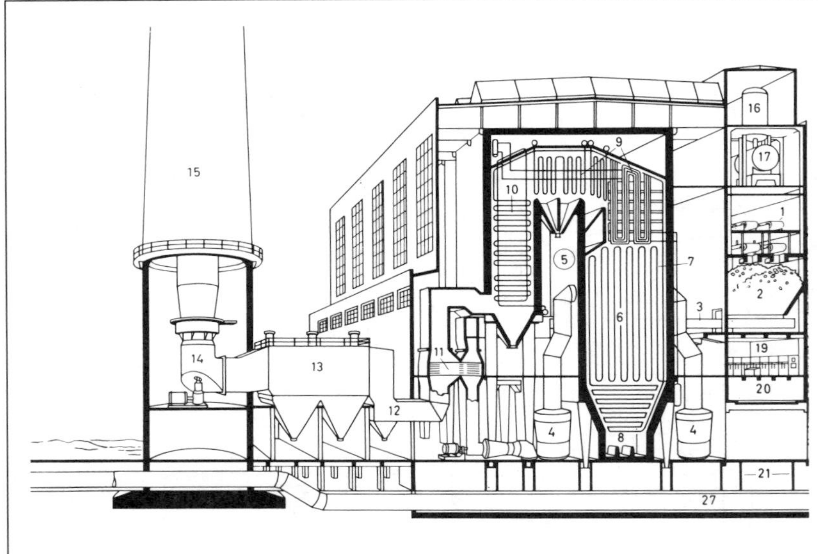

1-28 steam-generating station, an electric power plant

1-21 boiler house

1 coal conveyor

2 coal bunker

3 travelling-grate (*Am.* traveling-grate) stoker

4 coal mill

5 steam boiler, a water-tube boiler (radiant-type boiler)

6 burners

7 water pipes

8 ash pit (clinker pit)

9 superheater

10 water preheater

11 air preheater

12 gas flue

13 electrostatic precipitator

14 induced-draught (*Am.* induced-draft) fan

15 chimney (smokestack)

16 de-aerator

17 feedwater tank

18 boiler feed pump

19 control room

20 cable tunnel

21 cable vault

22 turbine house

23 steam turbine with alternator

24 surface condenser

25 low-pressure preheater

26 high-pressure preheater (economizer)

27 cooling water pipe

28 control room

29-35 outdoor substation, a substation

29 busbars

30 power transformer, a mobile (transportable) transformer

31 stay poles (guy poles)

32 high-voltage transmission line

33 high-voltage conductor

34 air-blast circuit breaker (circuit breaker)

35 surge diverter (*Am.* lightning arrester, arrester)

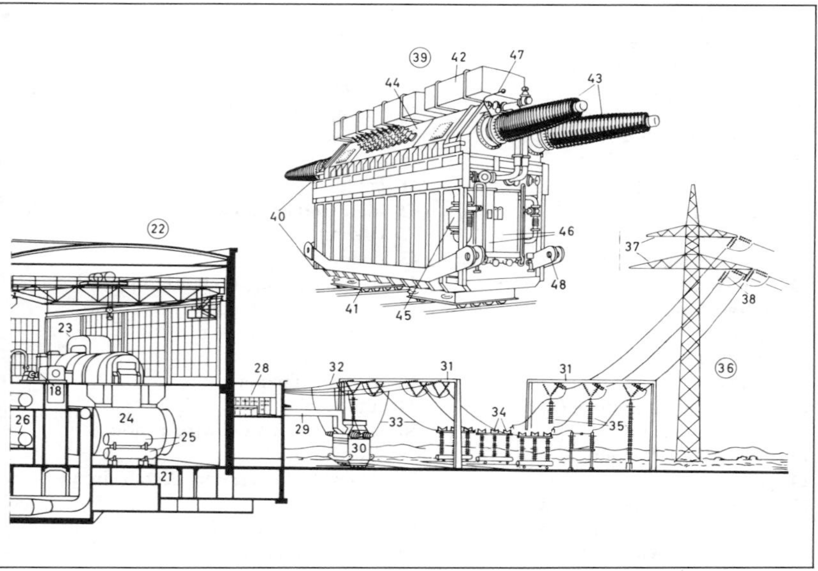

36 overhead line support, a lattice steel tower
37 cross arm (traverse)
38 strain insulator
39 **mobile (transportable) transformer** (power transformer, transformer)
40 transformer tank
41 bogie (*Am.* truck)
42 oil conservator
43 primary voltage terminal (primary voltage bushing)
44 low-voltage terminals (low-voltage bushings)
45 oil-circulating pump
46 oil cooler
47 arcing horn
48 transport lug

153 Power Plant (Power Station) II

1-8 control room
1-6 control console (control desk)
1 control board (control panel) for the alternators
2 master switch
3 signal light
4 feeder panel
5 monitoring controls for the switching systems
6 controls
7 revertive signal panel
8 matrix mimic board
9-18 transformer
9 oil conservator
10 breather
11 oil gauge (*Am.* gage)
12 feed-through terminal (feed-through insulator)
13 on-load tap changer
14 yoke
15 primary winding (primary)
16 secondary winding (secondary, low-voltage winding)
17 core
18 tap (tapping)
19 transformer connection
20 star connection (star network, Y-connection)
21 delta connection (mesh connection)
22 neutral point
23-30 steam turbine, a turbogenerator unit
23 high-pressure cylinder
24 medium-pressure cylinder
25 low-pressure cylinder
26 three-phase generator (generator)
27 hydrogen cooler
28 leakage steam path
29 jet nozzle
30 turbine monitoring panel with measuring instruments
31 automatic voltage regulator
32 synchro
33 cable box
34 conductor
35 feed-through terminal (feed-through insulator)
36 core
37 casing
38 filling compound (filler)
39 lead sheath
40 lead-in tube
41 cable
42 high voltage cable, for three-phase current
43 conductor
44 metallic paper (metallized paper)
45 tracer (tracer element)
46 varnished-cambric tape
47 lead sheath
48 asphalted paper
49 jute serving
50 steel tape or steel wire armour (*Am.* armor)
51-62 air-blast circuit breaker, a circuit breaker
51 compressed-air tank
52 control valve (main operating valve)
53 compressed-air inlet
54 support insulator, a hollow porcelain supporting insulator
55 interrupter
56 resistor
57 auxiliary contacts
58 current transformer
59 voltage transformer (potential transformer)
60 operating mechanism housing
61 arcing horn
62 spark gap

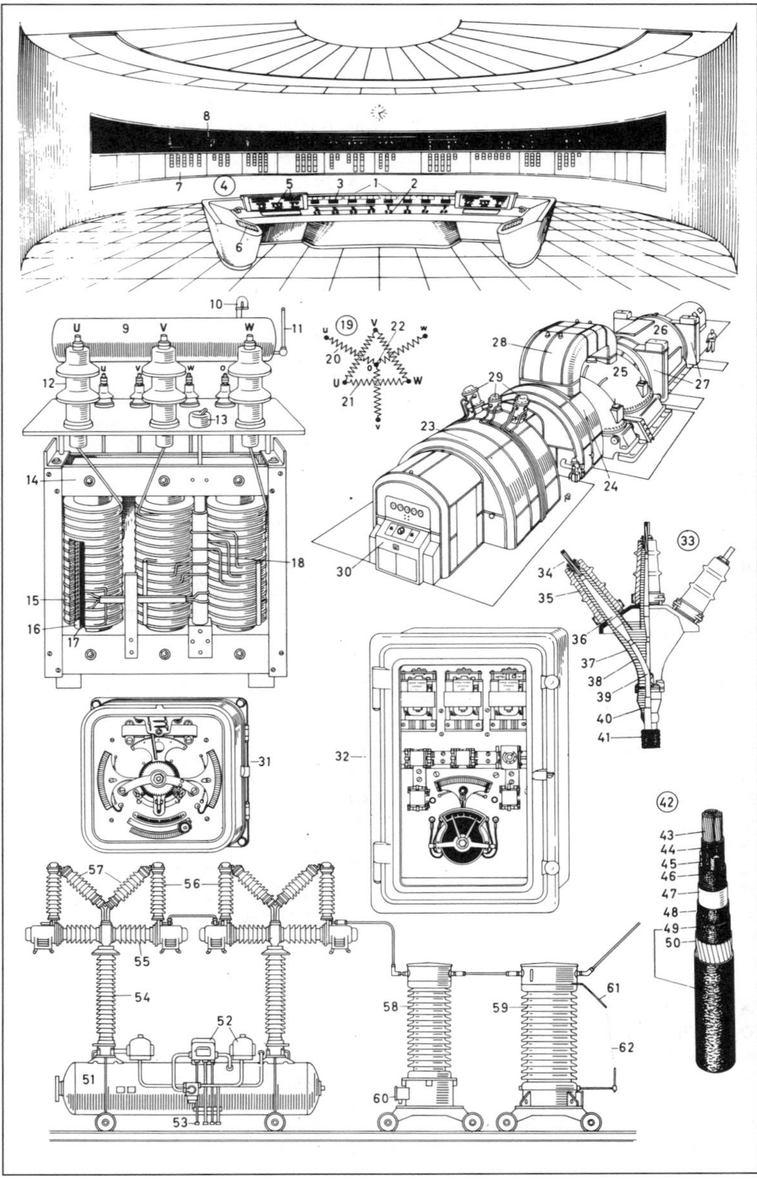
8
7
4
5
3
1
2
6
10
9
11
U
V
W
u
v
w
o
12
13
14
15
16
17
18
19
20
21
22
23
24
25
26
27
28
29
30
31
32
33
34
35
36
37
38
39
40
41
42
43
44
45
46
47
48
49
50
51
52
53
54
55
56
57
58
59
60
61
62

154 Nuclear Energy

1 **fast-breeder reactor** (fast breeder) [diagram]
2 primary circuit (primary loop, primary sodium system)
3 reactor
4 fuel rods (fuel pins)
5 primary sodium pump
6 heat exchanger
7 secondary circuit (secondary loop, secondary sodium system)
8 secondary sodium pump
9 steam generator
10 cooling water flow circuit
11 steam line
12 feedwater line
13 feed pump
14 steam turbine
15 generator
16 transmission line
17 condenser
18 cooling water
19 **nuclear reactor,** a pressurized-water reactor (nuclear power plant, atomic power plant)
20 concrete shield (reactor building)
21 steel containment (steel shell) with air extraction vent
22 reactor pressure vessel
23 control rod drive
24 control rods
25 primary coolant pump
26 steam generator
27 fuel-handling hoists
28 fuel storage
29 coolant flow passage
30 feedwater line
31 prime steam line
32 manway
33 turbogenerator set
34 turbogenerator
35 condenser
36 service building
37 exhaust gas stack
38 polar crane
39 cooling tower, a dry cooling tower
40 pressurized-water system
41 reactor
42 primary circuit (primary loop)
43 circulation pump (recirculation pump)
44 heat exchanger (steam generator)
45 secondary circuit (secondary loop, feedwater steam circuit)
46 steam turbine
47 generator
48 cooling system
49 boiling water system [diagram]
50 reactor
51 steam and recirculation water flow paths
52 steam turbine
53 generator
54 circulation pump (recirculation pump)
55 coolant system (cooling with water from river)
56 **radioactive waste storage** in salt mine
57-68 geological structure of abandoned salt mine converted for disposal of radioactive waste (nuclear waste)
57 Lower Keuper
58 Upper Muschelkalk
59 Middle Muschelkalk
60 Lower Muschelkalk
61 Bunter downthrow
62 residue of leached (lixiviated) Zechstein (Upper Permian)
63 Aller rock salt
64 Leine rock salt
65 Stassfurt seam (potash salt seam, potash salt bed)
66 Stassfurt salt
67 grenzanhydrite
68 Zechstein shale
69 shaft
70 minehead buildings
71 storage chamber
72 storage of medium-active waste in salt mine
73 511 m level
74 protective screen (anti-radiation screen)
75 lead glass window
76 storage chamber
77 drum containing radioactive waste
78 television camera
79 charging chamber
80 control desk (control panel)
81 upward ventilator
82 shielded container
83 490 m level

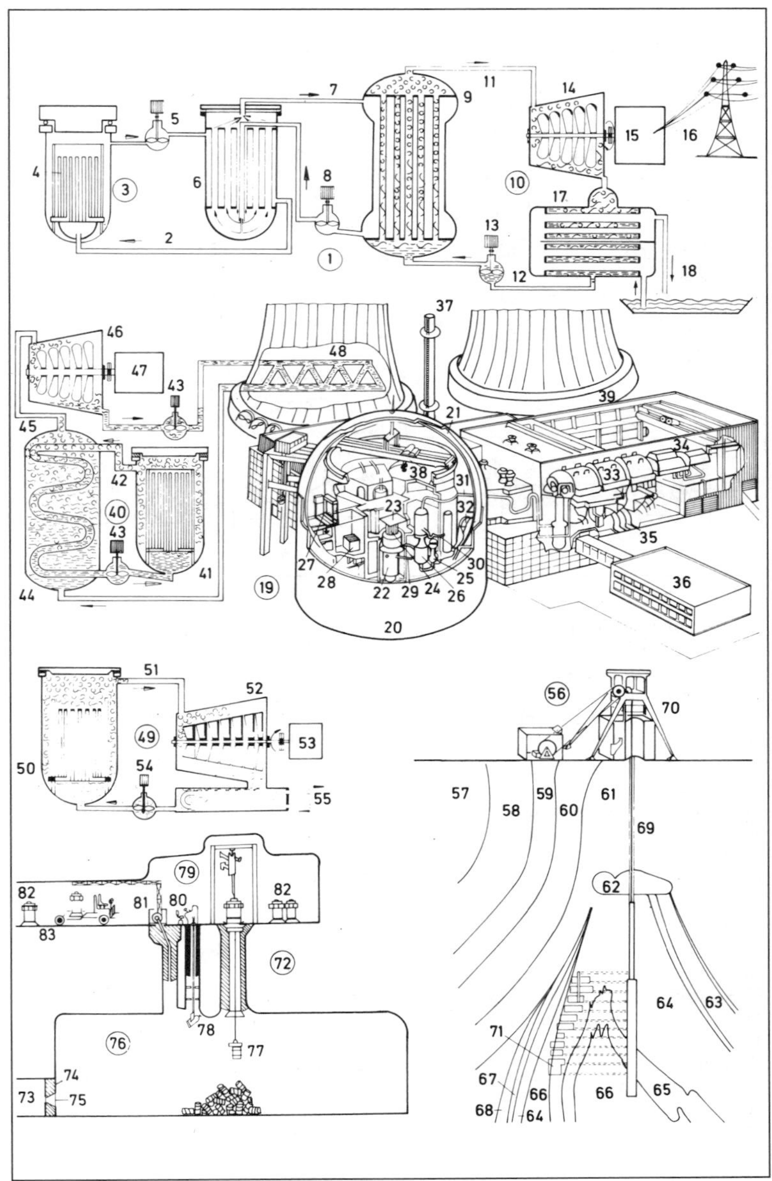
1
2
3
4
5
6
7
8
9
10
11
12
13
14
15
16
17
18
19
20
21
22
23
24
25
26
27
28
29
30
31
32
33
34
35
36
37
38
39
40
41
42
43
44
45
46
47
48
49
50
51
52
53
54
55
56
57
58
59
60
61
62
63
64
65
66
67
68
69
70
71
72
73
74
75
76
77
78
79
80
81
82
83

155 Modern Sources of Energy

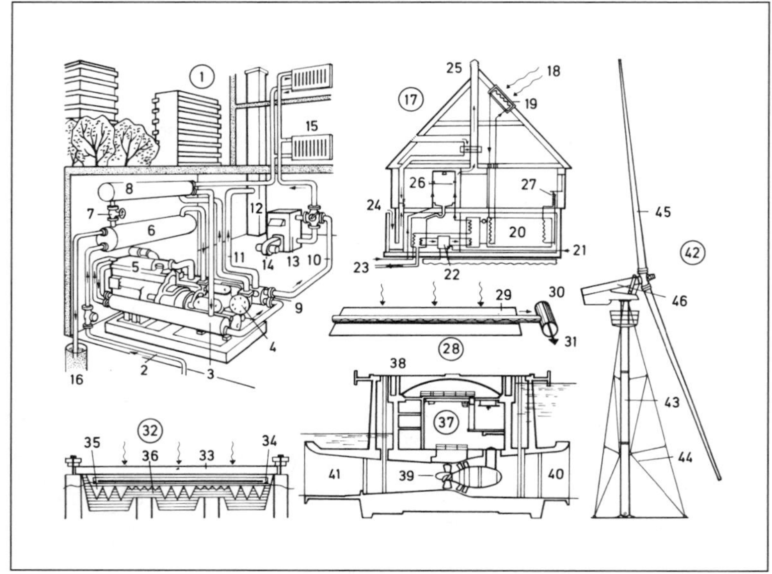

1 **heat pump system**
2 source water inlet
3 cooling water heat exchanger
4 compressor
5 natural-gas or diesel engine
6 evaporator
7 pressure release valve
8 condenser
9 waste-gas heat exchanger
10 flow pipe
11 vent pipe
12 chimney
13 boiler
14 fan
15 radiator
16 sink
17-36 utilization of solar energy
17 solar (solar-heated) house
18 solar radiation (sunlight, insolation)
19 collector
20 hot reservoir (heat reservoir)
21 power supply
22 heat pump
23 water outlet
24 air supply
25 flue
26 hot water supply
27 radiator heating
28 flat plate solar collector
29 blackened receiver surface with asphalted aluminium (*Am.* aluminum) foil
30 steel tube
31 heat transfer fluid
32 flat plate solar collector, containing solar cell
33 glass cover
34 solar cell
35 air ducts
36 insulation
37 **tidal power plant** [section]
38 dam
39 reversible turbine
40 turbine inlet for water from the sea
41 turbine inlet for water from the basin
42 **wind power plant** (wind generator aerogenerator)
43 truss tower
44 guy wire
45 rotor
46 generator with variable pitch for power regulation

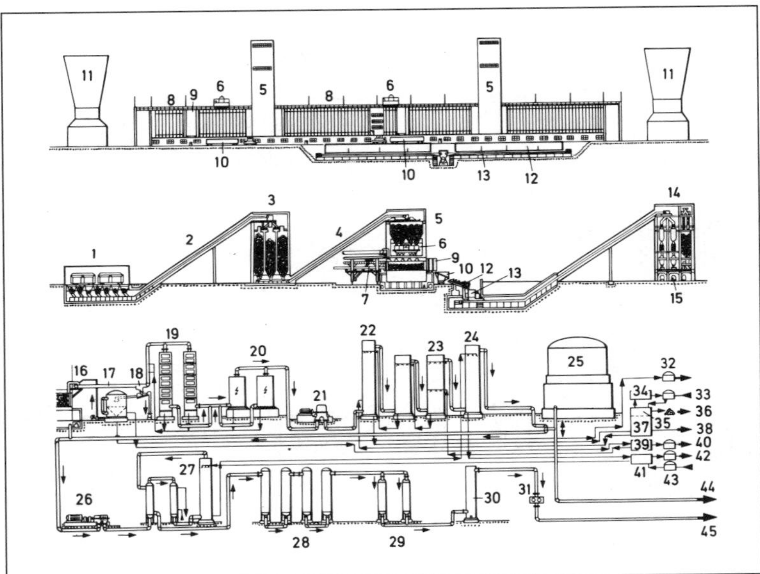

1-15 coking plant
1 dumping of coking coal
2 belt conveyor
3 blending bunker
4 service bunker conveyor
5 service bunker
6 larry car (larry, charging car)
7 pusher ram
8 battery of coke ovens
9 coke guide
10 quenching car, with engine
11 quenching tower
12 coke loading bay (coke wharf)
13 coke wharf conveyor
14 screening of coke and breeze
15 coke loading

16-45 coke-oven gas processing
16 discharge (release) of gas from the coke ovens
17 gas-collecting main
18 coal tar extraction
19 gas cooler
20 electrostatic precipitator
21 gas extractor
22 hydrogen sulphide (*Am.* hydrogen sulfide) scrubber (hydrogen sulphide wet collector)
23 ammonia scrubber (ammonia wet collector)
24 benzene (benzol) scrubber
25 gas holder
26 gas compressor
27 debenzoling by cooler and heat exchanger
28 desulphurization (*Am.* desulfurization) of pressure gas
29 gas cooling
30 gas drying
31 gas meter
32 crude tar tank
33 sulphuric acid (*Am.* sulfuric acid) supply
34 production of sulphuric acid (*Am.* sulfuric acid)
35 production of ammonium sulphate (*Am.* ammonium sulfate)
36 ammonium sulphate (*Am.* ammonium sulfate)
37 recovery plant for recovering the scrubbing agents
38 waste water discharge
39 phenol extraction from the gas water
40 crude phenol tank
41 production of crude benzol (crude benzene)
42 crude benzol (crude benzene) tank
43 scrubbing oil tank
44 low-pressure gas main
45 high-pressure gas main

157 Sawmill

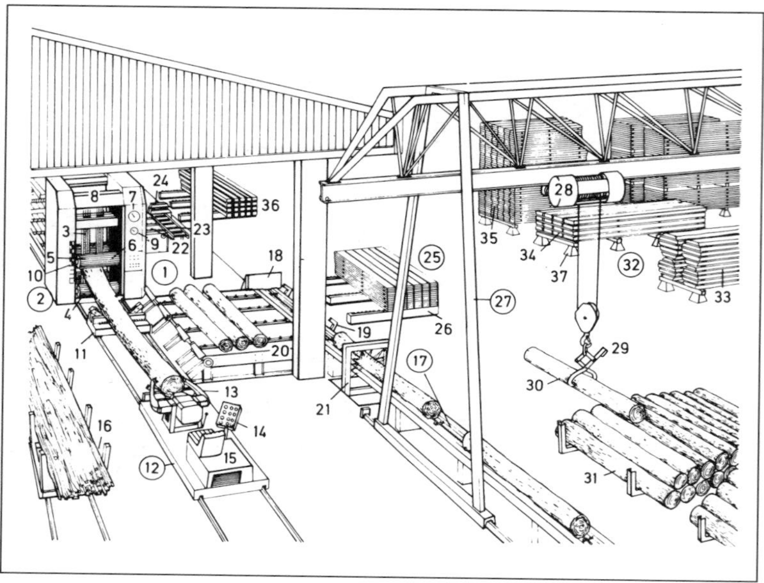

1 **sawmill**
2 vertical frame saw (*Am.* gang mill)
3 saw blades
4 feed roller
5 guide roller
6 fluting (grooving, grooves)
7 oil pressure gauge (*Am.* gage)
8 saw frame
9 feed indicator
10 log capacity scale
11 auxiliary carriage
12 carriage
13 log grips
14 remote control panel
15 carriage motor
16 truck for splinters (splints)
17 endless log chain (*Am.* jack chain)
18 stop plate
19 log-kicker arms
20 cross conveyor
21 washer (washing machine)
22 cross chain conveyor for sawn timber
23 roller table
24 undercut swing saw
25 piling
26 roller trestles
27 gantry crane
28 crane motor
29 pivoted log grips
30 roundwood (round timber)
31 log dump
32 squared timber store
33 sawn logs
34 planks
35 boards (planks)
36 squared timber
37 stack bearer

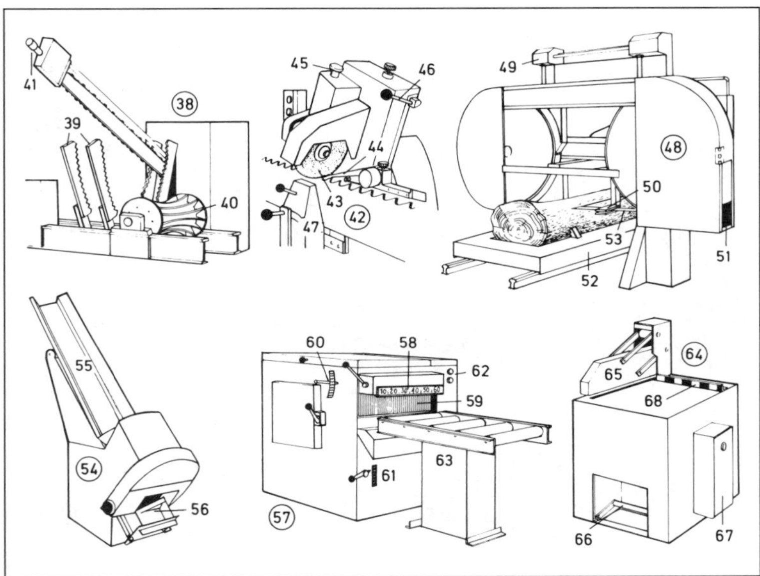

38 automatic cross-cut chain saw
39 log grips
40 feed roller
41 chain-tensioning device
42 saw-sharpening machine
43 grinding wheel (teeth grinder)
44 feed pawl
45 depth adjustment for the teeth grinder
46 lifter (lever) for the grinder chuck
47 holding device for the saw blade
48 horizontal bandsaw for sawing logs
49 height adjustment
50 chip remover
51 chip extractor
52 carriage
53 bandsaw blade
54 automatic blocking saw
55 feed channel
56 discharge opening
57 twin edger (double edger)
58 breadth scale (width scale)
59 kick-back guard (plates)
60 height scale
61 in-feed scale
62 indicator lamps
63 feed table
64 undercut swing saw
65 automatic hold-down with protective hood
66 foot switch
67 distribution board (panelboard)
68 length stop

158 Quarry

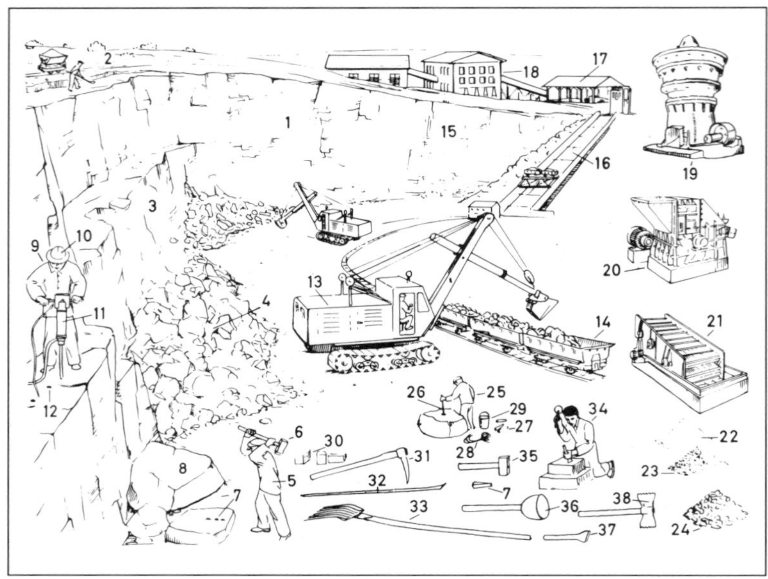

1 **quarry,** an open-cast working
2 overburden
3 working face
4 loose rock pile (blasted rock)
5 quarryman (quarrier), a quarry worker
6 sledge hammer
7 wedge
8 block of stone
9 driller
10 safety helmet
11 hammer drill (hard-rock drill)
12 borehole
13 universal excavator
14 large-capacity truck
15 rock face
16 inclined hoist
17 primary crusher
18 stone-crushing plant
19 coarse rotary (gyratory) crusher; *sim.:* fine rotary (gyratory) crusher
20 hammer crusher (impact crusher)
21 vibrating screen
22 screenings (fine dust)
23 stone chippings
24 crushed stone
25 shot firer
26 measuring rod
27 blasting cartridge
28 fuse (blasting fuse)
29 plugging sand (stemming sand) bucket
30 dressed stone
31 pick
32 crowbar (pinch bar)
33 fork
34 stonemason

35-38 stonemason's tools

35 stonemason's hammer
36 mallet
37 drove chisel (drove, boaster, broad chisel)
38 dressing axe (*Am.* ax)

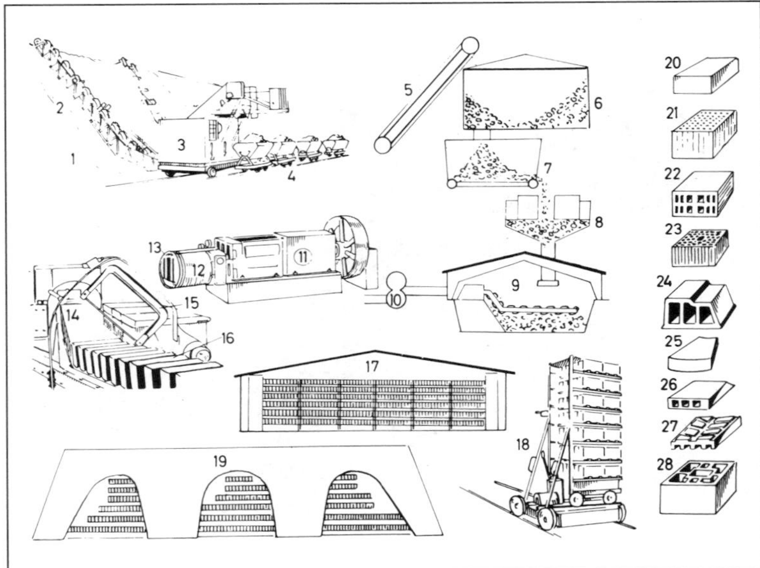

1 clay pit
2 loam, an impure clay (raw clay)
3 overburden excavator, a large-scale excavator
4 narrow-gauge (*Am.* narrow-gage) track system
5 inclined hoist
6 souring chambers
7 box feeder (feeder)
8 edge runner mill (edge mill, pan grinding mill)
9 rolling plant
10 double-shaft trough mixer (mixer)
11 extrusion press (brick-pressing machine)
12 vacuum chamber
13 die
14 clay column
15 cutter (brick cutter)
16 unfired brick (green brick)
17 drying shed
18 mechanical finger car (stacker truck)
19 circular kiln (brick kiln)
20 solid brick (building brick)
21, 22 perforated bricks and hollow blocks
21 perforated brick with vertical perforations
22 hollow clay block with horizontal perforations
23 hollow clay block with vertical perforations
24 floor brick
25 compass brick (radial brick, radiating brick)
26 hollow flooring block
27 paving brick
28 cellular brick [for fireplaces] (chimney brick)

160 Cement Works (Cement Factory)

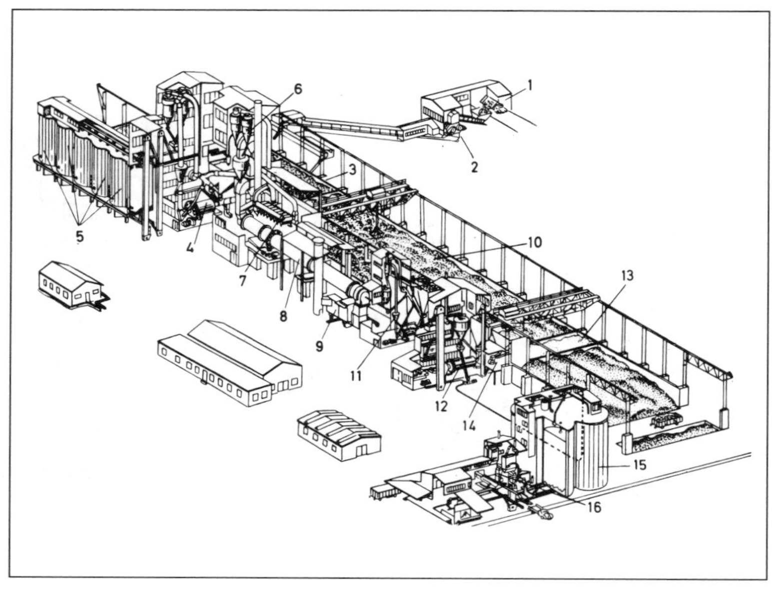

1. raw materials (limestone, clay and marl)
2. hammer crusher (hammer mill)
3. raw material store
4. raw mill for simultaneously grinding and drying the raw materials with exhaust gas from the heat exchanger
5. raw meal silos
6. heat exchanger (cyclone heat exchanger)
7. dust collector (an electrostatic precipitator) for the heat exchanger exhaust from the raw mill
8. rotary kiln
9. clinker cooler
10. clinker store
11. primary air blower
12. cement-grinding mill
13. gypsum store
14. gypsum crusher
15. cement silo
16. cement-packing plant

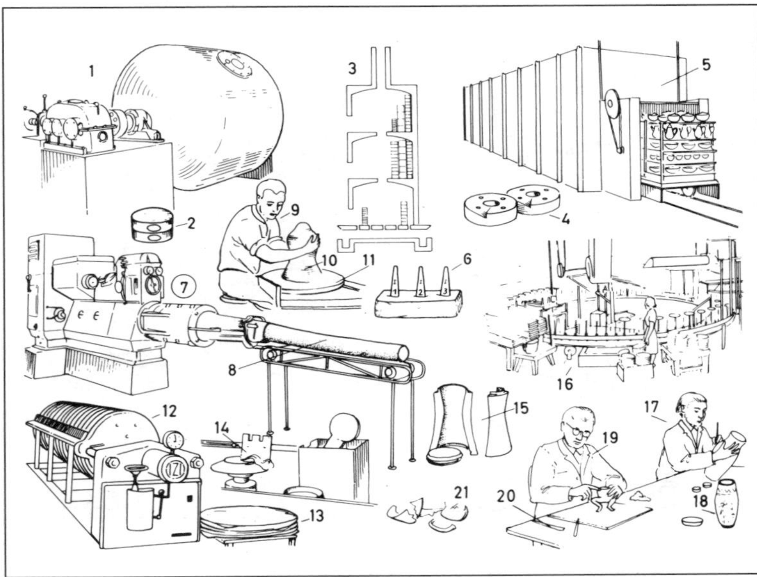

1 grinding cylinder (ball mill) for the preparation of the raw material in water
2 sample sagger (saggar, seggar), with aperture for observing the firing process
3 bottle kiln (beehive kiln) [diagram]
4 firing mould (*Am.* mold)
5 tunnel kiln
6 Seger cone (pyrometric cone, *Am.* Orton cone) for measuring high temperatures
7 de-airing pug mill (de-airing pug press), an extrusion press
8 clay column
9 thrower throwing a ball (bat) of clay
10 slug of clay
11 turntable; *sim.:* potter's wheel
12 filter press
13 filter cake
14 jiggering, with a profiling tool; *sim.:* jollying
15 plaster mould (*Am.* mold) for slip casting
16 turntable glazing machine
17 porcelain painter (china painter)
18 hand-painted vase
19 repairer
20 pallet (modelling, *Am.* modeling, tool)
21 shards (sherds, potsherds)

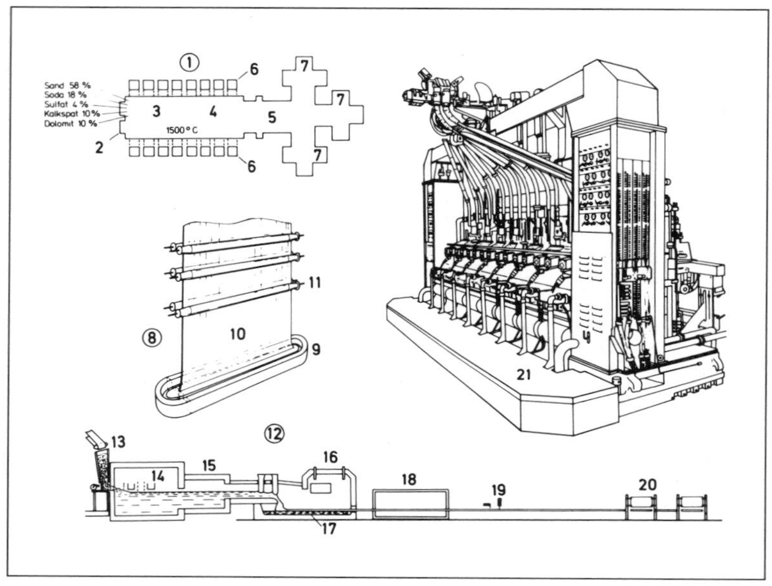

1-20 sheet glass production (flat glass production)
1 glass furnace (tank furnace) for the Fourcault process [diagram]
2 filling end, for feeding in the batch (frit)
3 melting bath
4 refining bath (fining bath)
5 working baths (working area)
6 burners
7 drawing machines
8 Fourcault glass-drawing machine
9 slot
10 glass ribbon (ribbon of glass, sheet of glass) being drawn upwards
11 rollers (drawing rolls)
12 float glass process
13 batch (frit) feeder (funnel)
14 melting bath
15 cooling tank
16 float bath in a protective inert-gas atmosphere
17 molten tin
18 annealing lehr
19 automatic cutter
20 stacking machines
21 IS (individual-section) machine, a bottle-making machine
22-37 blowing processes
22 blow-and-blow process
23 introduction of the gob of molten glass
24 first blowing
25 suction
26 transfer from the parison mould (*Am.* mold) to the blow mould (*Am.* mold)
27 reheating
28 blowing (suction, final shaping)
29 delivery of the completed vessel
30 press-and-blow process
31 introduction of the gob of molten glass
32 plunger

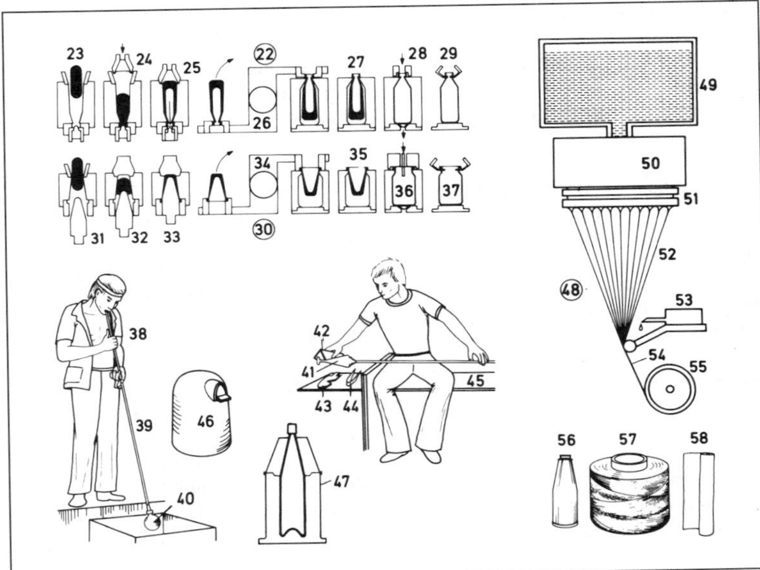

33 pressing
34 transfer from the press mould (*Am.* mold) to the blow mould (*Am.* mold)
35 reheating
36 blowing (suction, final shaping)
37 delivery of the completed vessel
38-47 glassmaking (glassblowing, glassblowing by hand, glass forming)
38 glassmaker (glassblower)
39 blowing iron
40 gob
41 hand-blown goblet
42 clappers for shaping the base (foot) of the goblet
43 trimming tool
44 tongs
45 glassmaker's chair (gaffer's chair)
46 covered glasshouse pot
47 mould (*Am.* mold), into which the parison is blown
48-55 production of glass fibre (*Am.* glass fiber)
48 continuous filament process
49 glass furnace
50 bushing containing molten glass
51 bushing tips
52 glass filaments
53 sizing
54 strand (thread)
55 spool
56-58 glass fibre (*Am.* glass fiber) **products**
56 glass yarn (glass thread)
57 sleeved glass yarn (glass thread)
58 glass wool

163 Cotton Spinning I

1-13 supply of cotton
1 ripe cotton boll
2 full cop (cop wound with weft yarn)
3 compressed cotton bale
4 jute wrapping
5 steel band
6 identification mark of the bale
7 bale opener (bale breaker)
8 cotton-feeding brattice
9 cotton feed
10 dust extraction fan
11 duct to the dust-collecting chamber
12 drive motor
13 conveyor brattice
14 **double scutcher** (machine with two scutchers)
15 lap cradle
16 rack head
17 starting handle
18 handwheel, for raising and lowering the rack head
19 movable lap-turner
20 calender rollers
21 cover for the perforated cylinders
22 dust escape flue (dust discharge flue)
23 drive motors (beater drive motors)
24 beater driving shaft
25 three-blade beater (Kirschner beater)
26 grid [for impurities to drop]
27 pedal roller (pedal cylinder)
28 control lever for the pedal roller, a pedal lever
29 variable change-speed gear
30 cone drum box
31 stop and start levers for the hopper
32 wooden hopper delivery roller
33 hopper feeder
34 **carding machine** (card, carding engine)
35 card can (carding can), for receiving the coiled sliver
36 can holder
37 calender rollers
38 carded sliver (card sliver)
39 vibrating doffer comb
40 start-stop lever
41 grinding-roller bearing
42 doffer
43 cylinder
44 flat clearer
45 flats
46 supporting pulleys for the flats
47 scutcher lap (carded lap)
48 scutcher lap holder
49 drive motor with flat belt
50 main drive pulley (fast-and-loose drive pulley)
51 principle of the card (of the carding engine)
52 fluted feed roller
53 licker-in (taker-in, licker-in roller)
54 licker-in undercasing
55 cylinder undercasing
56 **combing machine** (comber)
57 drive gearbox (driving gear)
58 laps ready for combing
59 calender rollers
60 comber draw box
61 counter
62 coiler top
63 principle of the comber
64 lap
65 bottom nipper
66 top nipper
67 top comb
68 combing cylinder
69 plain part of the cylinder
70 needled part of the cylinder
71 detaching rollers
72 carded and combed sliver

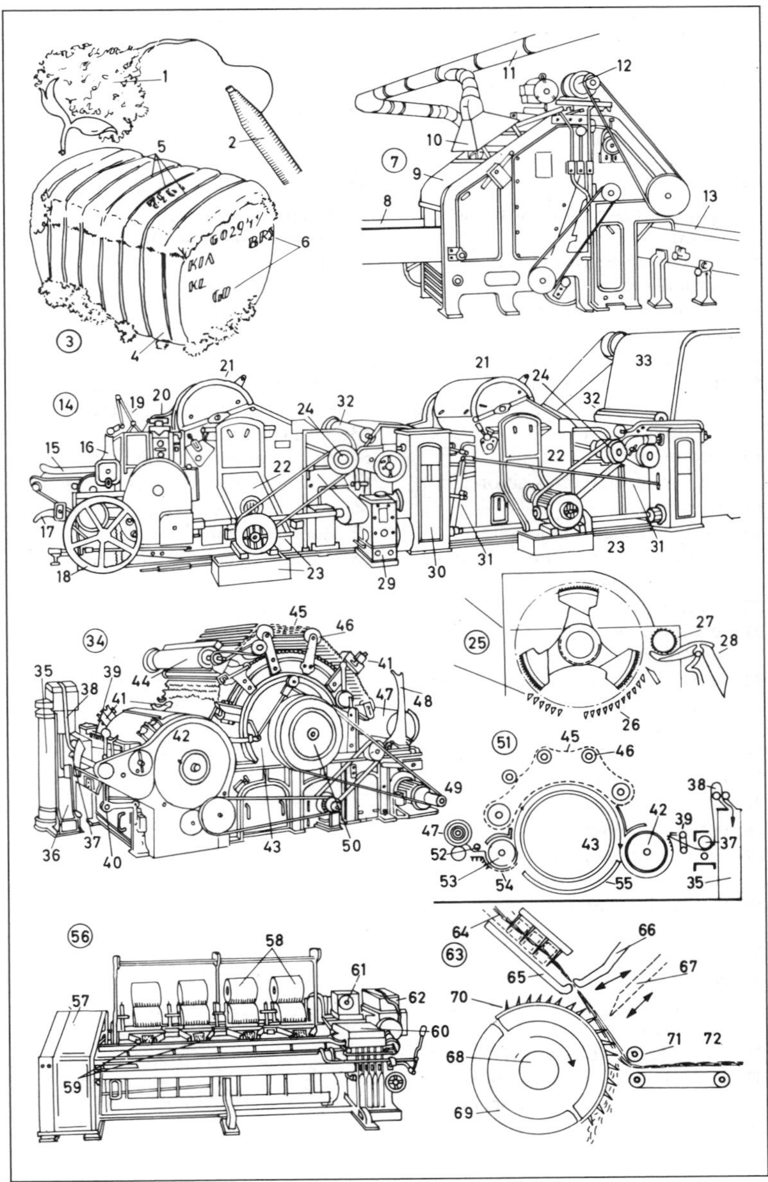

1
2
3
4
5
6
G02941
BRX
KIA
KL
7
8
9
10
11
12
13
14
15
16
17
18
19
20
21
22
23
24
25
26
27
28
29
30
31
32
33
34
35
36
37
38
39
40
41
42
43
44
45
46
47
48
49
50
51
52
53
54
55
56
57
58
59
60
61
62
63
64
65
66
67
68
69
70
71
72

164 Cotton Spinning II

1 **draw frame**
2 gearbox with built-in motor
3 sliver cans
4 broken thread detector roller
5 doubling of the slivers
6 stopping handle
7 draw frame cover
8 indicator lamps (signal lights)
9 simple four-roller draw frame [diagram]
10 bottom rollers (lower rollers), fluted steel rollers
11 top rollers (upper rollers) covered with synthetic rubber
12 doubled slivers before drafting
13 thin sliver after drafting
14 high-draft system (high-draft draw frame) [diagram]
15 feeding-in of the sliver
16 leather apron (composition apron)
17 guide bar
18 light top roller (guide roller)
19 high-draft speed frame (fly frame, slubbing frame)
20 sliver cans
21 feeding of the slivers to the drafting rollers
22 drafting rollers with top clearers
23 roving bobbins
24 fly frame operator (operative)
25 flyer
26 frame end plate
27 intermediate yarn-forming frame
28 bobbin creel (creel)
29 roving emerging from the drafting rollers
30 lifter rail (separating rail)
31 spindle drive
32 stopping handle
33 gearbox, with built-on motor
34 **ring frame** (ring spinning frame)
35 three-phase motor
36 motor base plate (bedplate)
37 lifting bolt [for motor removal]
38 control gear for spindle speed
39 gearbox
40 change wheels for varying the spindle speed [to change the yarn count]
41 full creel
42 shafts and levers for raising and lowering the ring rail
43 spindles with separators
44 suction box connected to the front roller underclearers
45 **standard ring spindle**
46 spindle shaft
47 roller bearing
48 wharve (pulley)
49 spindle catch
50 spindle rail
51 ring and traveller (*Am.* traveler)
52 top of the ring tube (of the bobbin)
53 yarn (thread)
54 ring fitted into the ring rail
55 traveller (*Am.* traveler)
56 yarn wound onto the bobbin
57 **doubling frame**
58 creel, with cross-wound cheeses
59 delivery rollers
60 bobbins of doubled yarn

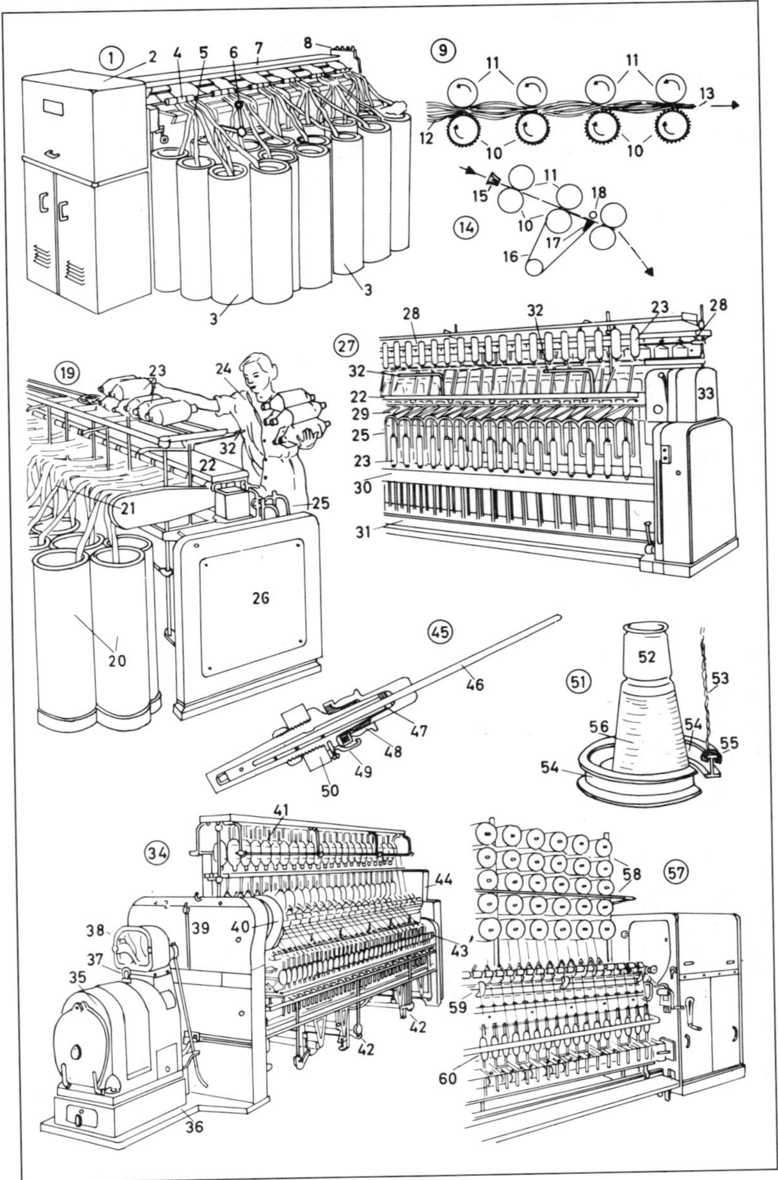
1
2
3
4
5
6
7
8
9
10
11
12
13
14
15
16
17
18
19
20
21
22
23
24
25
26
27
28
29
30
31
32
33
34
35
36
37
38
39
40
41
42
43
44
45
46
47
48
49
50
51
52
53
54
55
56
57
58
59
60

165 Weaving I

1-57 processes preparatory to weaving
1 cone-winding frame
2 travelling (*Am.* traveling) blower
3 guide rail, for the travelling (*Am.* traveling) blower
4 blowing assembly
5 blower aperture
6 superstructure for the blower rail
7 full-cone indicator
8 cross-wound cone
9 cone creel
10 grooved cylinder
11 guiding slot for cross-winding the threads
12 side frame, housing the motor
13 tension and slub-catching device
14 off-end framing with filter
15 yarn package, a ring tube or mule cop
16 yarn package container
17 starting and stopping lever
18 self-threading guide
19 broken thread stop motion
20 thread clearer
21 weighting disc (disk) for tensioning the thread
22 warping machine
23 fan
24 cross-wound cone
25 creel
26 adjustable comb
27 warping machine frame
28 yarn length recorder
29 warp beam
30 beam flange
31 guard rail
32 driving drum (driving cylinder)
33 belt drive
34 motor
35 release for starting the driving drum
36 screw for adjusting the comb setting
37 drop pins, for stopping the machine when a thread breaks
38 guide bar
39 drop pin rollers
40 indigo dying and sizing machine
41 take-off stand
42 warp beam
43 warp
44 wetting trough
45 immersion roller
46 squeeze roller (mangle)
47 dye liquor padding trough
48 air oxidation passage
49 washing trough
50 drying cylinders for pre-drying
51 tension compensator (tension equalizer)
52 sizing machine
53 drying cylinders
54 *for cotton:* stenter; *for wool:* tenter
55 beaming machine
56 sized warp beam
57 rollers

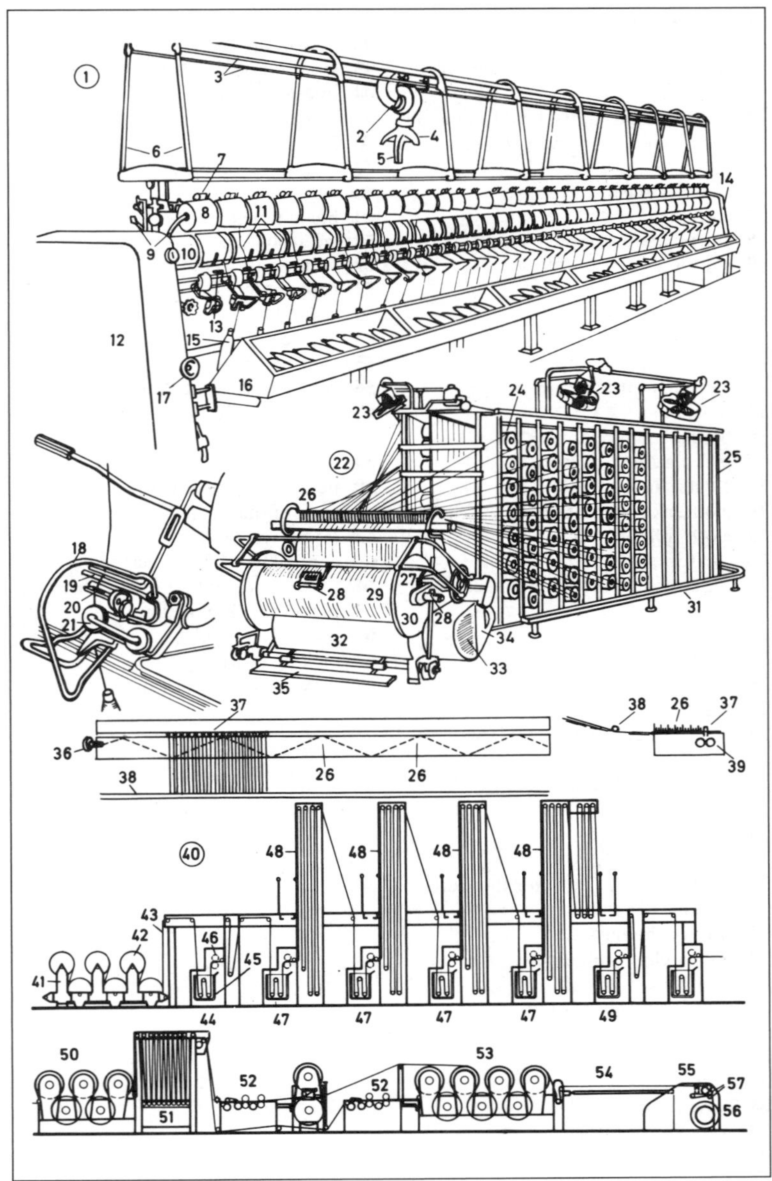

166 Weaving II

1 **weaving machine** (automatic loom)
2 pick counter (tachometer)
3 shaft (heald shaft, heald frame) guide
4 shafts (heald shafts, heald frames)
5 rotary battery for weft replenishment
6 sley (slay) cap
7 weft pirn
8 starting and stopping handle
9 shuttle box, with shuttles
10 reed
11 selvedge (selvage)
12 cloth (woven fabric)
13 temple (cloth temple)
14 electric weft feeler
15 flywheel
16 breast beam board
17 picking stick (pick stick)
18 electric motor
19 cloth take-up motion
20 cloth roller (fabric roller)
21 can for empty pirns
22 lug strap, for moving the picking stick
23 fuse box
24 loom framing
25 metal shuttle tip
26 shuttle
27 heald (heddle, wire heald, wire heddle)
28 eye (eyelet, heald eyelet, heddle eyelet)
29 eye (shuttle eye)
30 pirn
31 metal contact sleeve for the weft feeler
32 slot for the feeler
33 spring-clip pirn holder
34 drop wire
35 weaving machine (automatic loom) [side elevation]
36 heald shaft guiding wheels
37 backrest
38 lease rods
39 warp (warp thread)
40 shed
41 sley (slay)
42 race board
43 stop rod blade for the stop motion
44 bumper steel
45 bumper steel stop rod
46 breast beam
47 cloth take-up roller
48 warp beam
49 beam flange
50 crankshaft
51 crankshaft wheel
52 connector
53 sley (slay)
54 lam rods
55 camshaft wheel
56 camshaft (tappet shaft)
57 tappet (shedding tappet)
58 treadle lever
59 let-off motion
60 beam motion control
61 rope of the warp let-off motion
62 let-off weight lever
63 control weight [for the treadle]
64 picker with leather or bakelite pad
65 picking stick buffer
66 picking cam
67 picking bowl
68 picking stick return spring

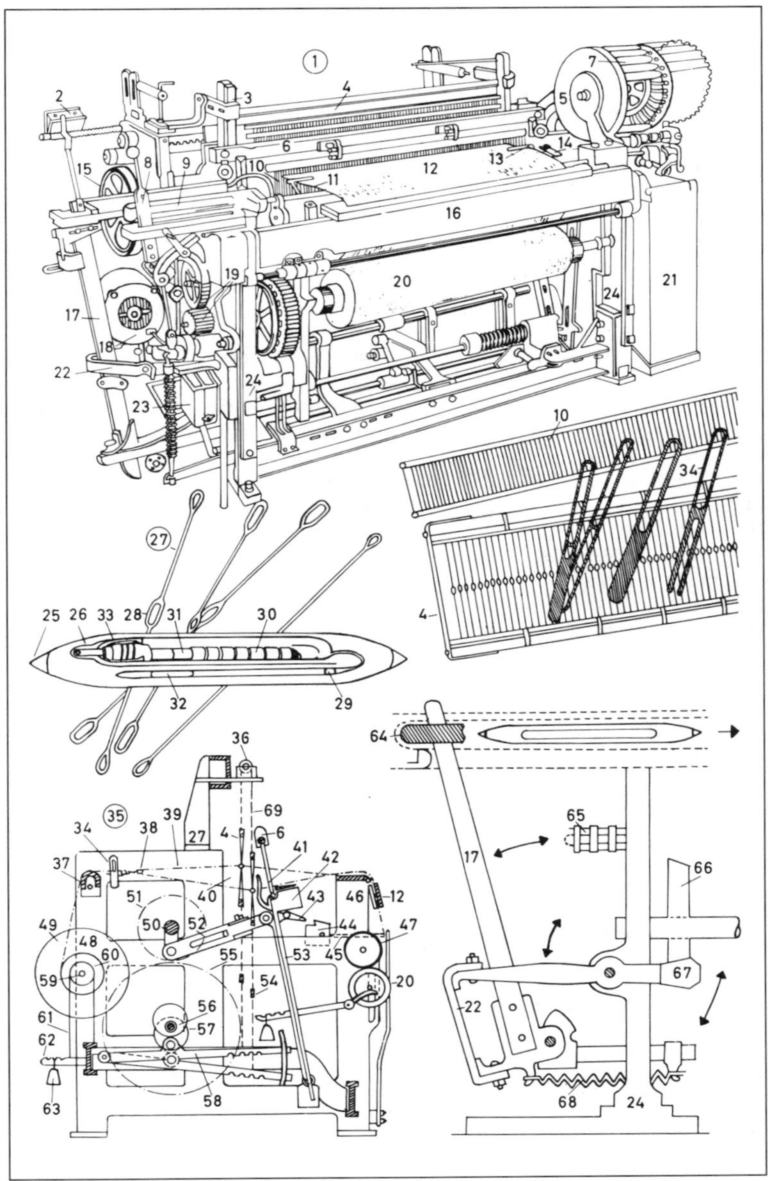
1
2
3
4
5
6
7
8
9
10
11
12
13
14
15
16
17
18
19
20
21
22
23
24
24
10
34
4
27
25 26 33 28 31 30
32
29
36
35
69
34 38 39
27 4 6
37
41 42
40
51
46 12
43
50 52
44
47
49
48
45
60
55
53
59
20
54
56
61
57
62
58
63
64
65
17
66
67
22
68 24

167 Knitting

1-66 hosiery mill
1 circular knitting machine for the manufacture of tubular fabric
2 yarn guide support post (thread guide support post)
3 yarn guide (thread guide)
4 bottle bobbin
5 yarn-tensioning device
6 yarn feeder
7 handwheel for rotating the machine by hand
8 needle cylinder (cylindrical needle holder)
9 tubular fabric
10 fabric drum (fabric box, fabric container)
11 needle cylinder (cylindrical needle holder) [section]
12 latch needles arranged in a circle
13 cam housing
14 needle cams
15 needle trick
16 cylinder diameter (*also:* diameter of tubular fabric)
17 thread (yarn)
18 Cotton's patent flat knitting machine for ladies' fully-fashioned hose
19 pattern control chain
20 side frame
21 knitting head
22 starting rod
23 Raschel warp-knitting machine
24 warp (warp beam)
25 yarn-distributing (yarn-dividing) beam
26 beam flange
27 row of needles
28 needle bar
29 fabric (Raschel fabric) [curtain lace and net fabrics] on the fabric roll
30 handwheel
31 motor drive gear
32 take-down weight
33 frame
34 base plate
35 hand flat (flat-bed) knitting machine
36 thread (yarn)
37 return spring
38 support for springs
39 carriage
40 feeder-selecting device
41 carriage handles
42 scale for regulating size of stitches
43 course counter (tachometer)
44 machine control lever
45 carriage rail
46 back row of needles
47 front row of needles
48 knitted fabric
49 tension bar
50 tension weight
51 needle bed showing knitting action
52 teeth of knock-over bit
53 needles in parallel rows
54 yarn guide (thread guide)
55 needle bed
56 retaining plate for latch needles
57 guard cam
58 sinker
59 needle-raising cam
60 needle butt
61 latch needle
62 loop
63 pushing the needle through the fabric
64 yarn guide (thread guide) placing yarn in the needle hook
65 loop formation
66 casting off of loop

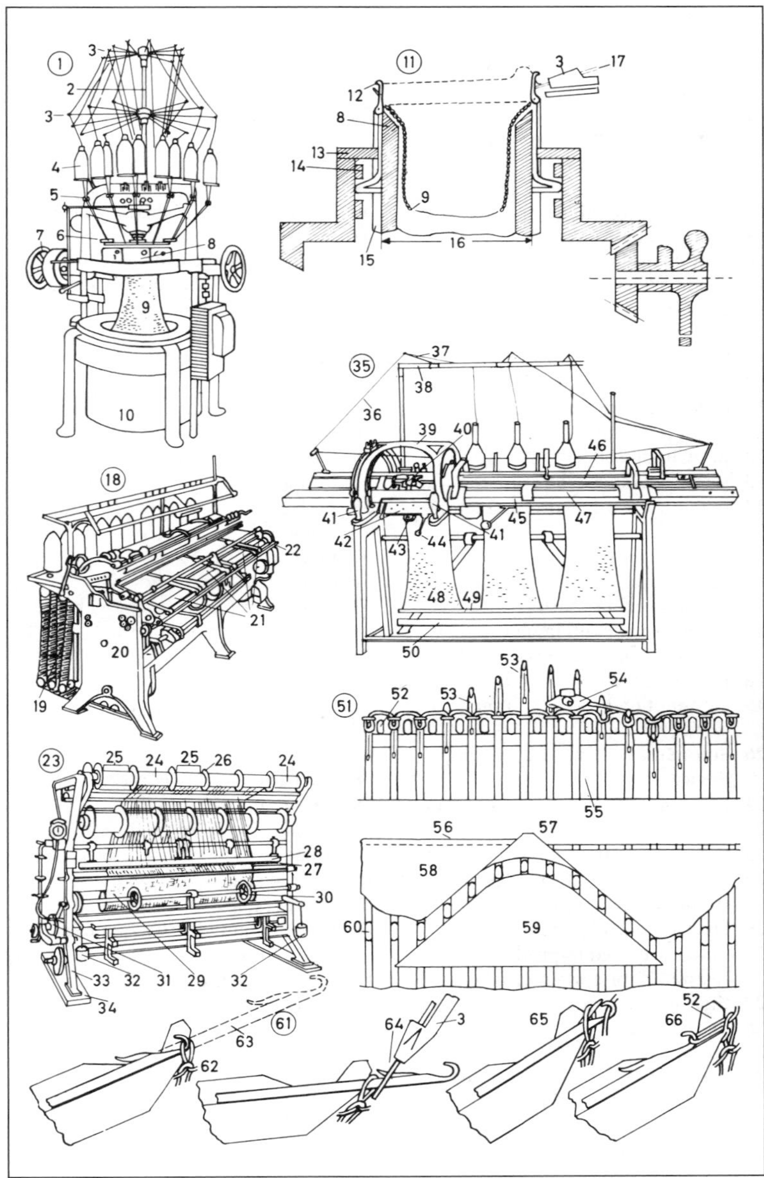
1
2
3
4
5
6
7
8
9
10
11
12
13
14
15
16
17
18
19
20
21
22
23
24
25
26
27
28
29
30
31
32
33
34
35
36
37
38
39
40
41
42
43
44
45
46
47
48
49
50
51
52
53
54
55
56
57
58
59
60
61
62
63
64
65
66

1-65 finishing
1 rotary milling (fulling) machine for felting the woollen (*Am.* woolen) fabric
2 pressure weights
3 top milling roller (top fulling roller)
4 drive wheel of bottom milling roller (bottom fulling roller)
5 fabric guide roller
6 bottom milling roller (bottom fulling roller)
7 draft board
8 open-width scouring machine for finer fabrics
9 fabric being drawn off the machine
10 drive gearbox
11 water inlet pipe
12 drawing-in roller
13 scroll-opening roller
14 pendulum-type hydro-extractor (centrifuge), for extracting liquors from the fabric
15 machine base
16 casing over suspension
17 outer casing containing rotating cage (rotating basket)
18 hydro-extractor (centrifuge) lid
19 stop-motion device (stopping device)
20 automatic starting and braking device
21 *for cotton:* stenter; *for wool:* tenter
22 air-dry fabric
23 operator's (operative's) platform
24 feeding of fabric by guides onto stenter (tenter) pins or clips
25 electric control panel
26 initial overfeed to produce shrink-resistant fabric when dried
27 thermometer
28 drying section
29 air outlet
30 plaiter (fabric-plaiting device)
31 wire-roller fabric-raising machine for producing raised or nap surface
32 drive gearbox
33 unraised cloth
34 wire-covered rollers
35 plaiter (cuttling device)
36 raised fabric
37 plaiting-down platform
38 rotary press (calendering machine), for press finishing
39 fabric
40 control buttons and control wheels
41 heated press bowl
42 rotary cloth-shearing machine
43 suction slot, for removing loose fibres (*Am.* fibers)
44 doctor blade (cutting cylinder)
45 protective guard
46 rotating brush
47 curved scray entry
48 treadle control
49 [non-shrinking] decatizing (decating) fabric-finishing machine
50 perforated decatizing (decating) cylinder
51 piece of fabric
52 cranked control handle
53 ten-colour (*Am.* ten-color) roller printing machine
54 base of the machine
55 drive motor
56 blanket [of rubber or felt]
57 fabric after printing (printed fabric)
58 electric control panel (control unit)
59 screen printing
60 mobile screen frame
61 squeegee
62 pattern stencil
63 screen table
64 fabric gummed down on table ready for printing
65 screen printing operator (operative)

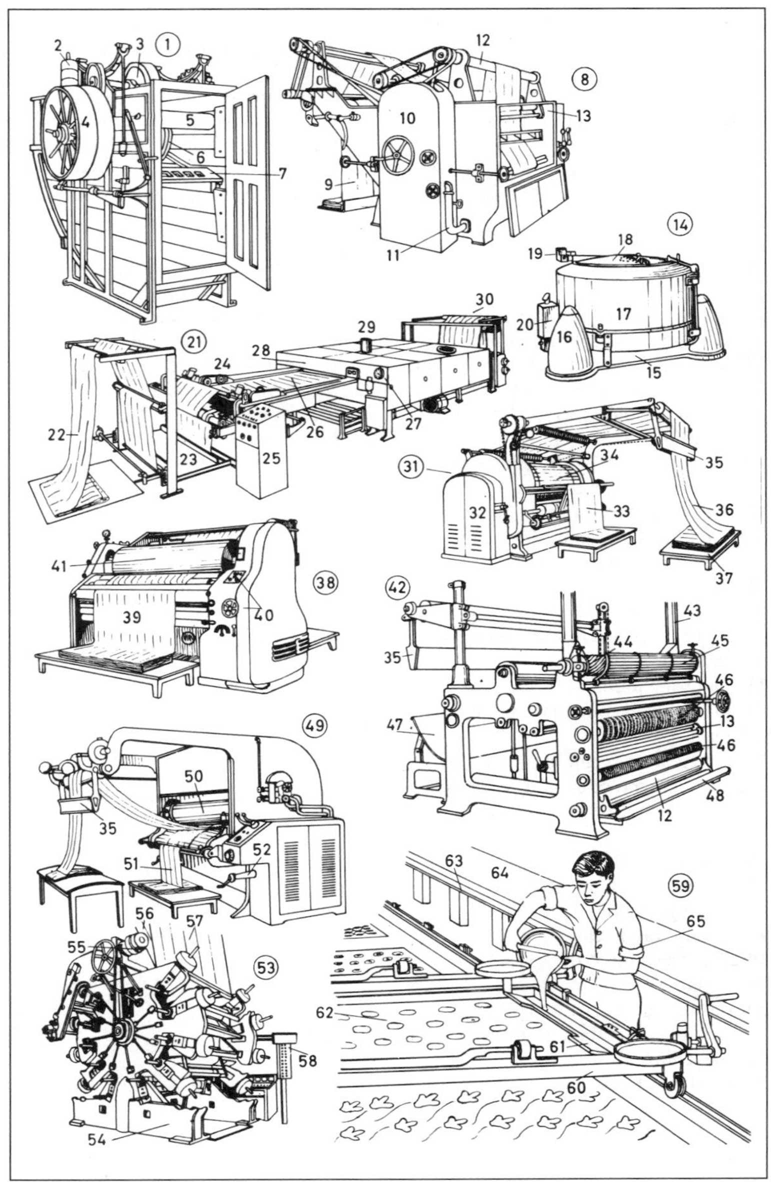
1
2
3
4
5
6
7
8
9
10
11
12
13
14
15
16
17
18
19
20
21
22
23
24
25
26
27
28
29
30
31
32
33
34
35
36
37
38
39
40
41
42
43
44
45
46
47
48
49
50
51
52
53
54
55
56
57
58
59
60
61
62
63
64
65

169 Synthetic (Man-made) Fibres (*Am.* Fibers) I

1-34 manufacture of **continuous filament and staple fibre** (*Am.* fiber) **viscose rayon yarns** by means of the viscose process
1-12 from raw material to viscose rayon
1 basic material [beech and spruce cellulose in form of sheets]
2 mixing cellulose sheets
3 caustic soda
4 steeping cellulose sheets in caustic soda
5 pressing out excess caustic soda
6 shredding the cellulose sheets
7 maturing (controlled oxidation) of the alkali-cellulose crumbs
8 carbon disulphide (*Am.* carbon disulfide)
9 conversion of alkali-cellulose into cellulose xanthate
10 dissolving the xanthate in caustic soda for the preparation of the viscose spinning solution
11 vacuum ripening tanks
12 filter presses
13-27 from viscose to viscose rayon thread
13 metering pump
14 multi-holed spinneret (spinning jet)
15 coagulating (spinning) bath for converting (coagulating) viscose (viscous solution) into solid filaments
16 Godet wheel, a glass pulley
17 Topham centrifugal pot (box) for twisting the filaments into yarn
18 viscose rayon cake
19-27 processing of the cake
19 washing
20 desulphurizing (desulphurization, *Am.* desulfurizing, desulfurization)
21 bleaching
22 treating of cake to give filaments softness and suppleness
23 hydro-extraction to remove surplus moisture
24 drying in heated room
25 winding yarn from cake into cone form
26 cone-winding machine
27 viscose rayon yarn on cone ready for use
28-34 from viscose spinning solution to viscose rayon staple fibre (*Am.* fiber)
28 filament tow
29 overhead spray washing plant
30 cutting machine for cutting filament tow to desired length
31 multiple drying machine for cut-up staple fibre (*Am.* fiber) layer (lap)
32 conveyor belt (conveyor)
33 baling press
34 bale of viscose rayon ready for dispatch (despatch)

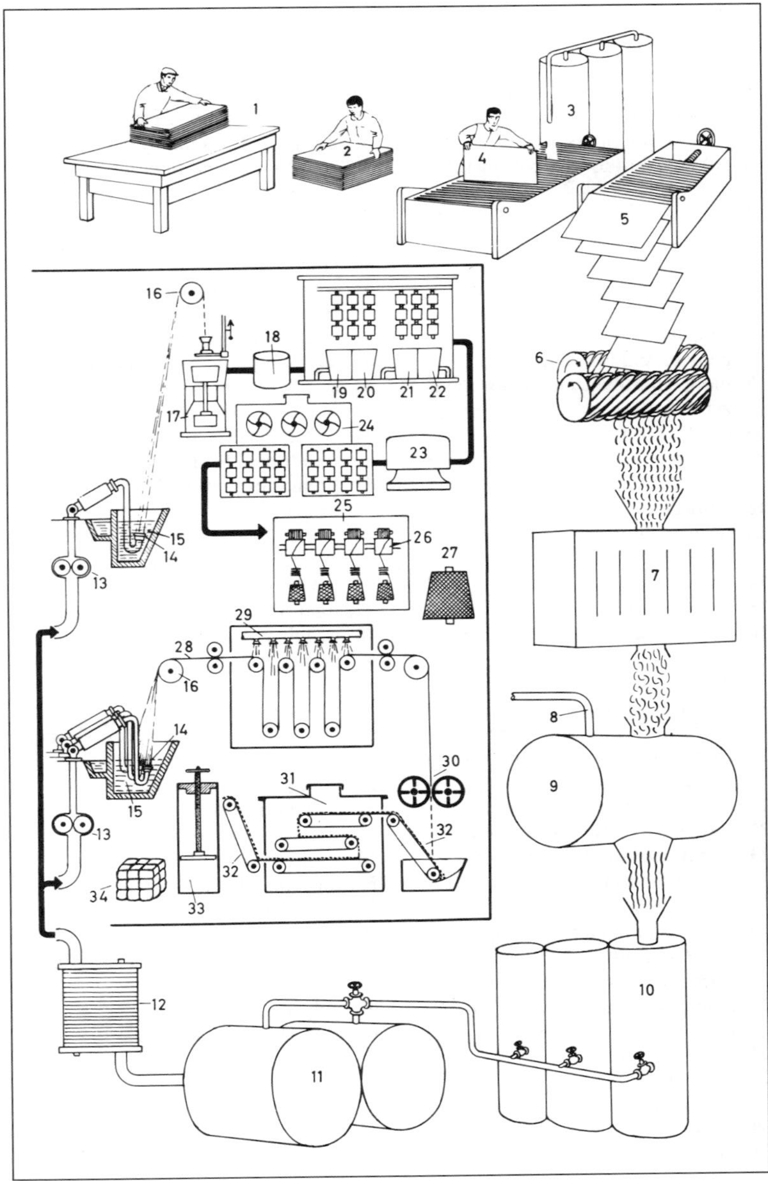
1
2
3
4
5
6
7
8
9
10
11
12
13
14
15
16
17
18
19
20
21
22
23
24
25
26
27
28
29
30
31
32
33
34

1-62 manufacture of **polyamide** (nylon 6, perlon) **fibres** (*Am.* fibers)
1 coal [raw material for manufacture of polyamide (nylon 6, perlon) fibres (*Am.* fibers)]
2 coking plant for dry coal distillation
3 extraction of coal tar and phenol
4 gradual distillation of tar
5 condenser
6 benzene extraction and dispatch (despatch)
7 chlorine
8 benzene chlorination
9 monochlorobenzene (chlorobenzene)
10 caustic soda solution
11 evaporation of chlorobenzene and caustic soda
12 autoclave
13 sodium chloride (common salt), a by-product
14 phenol (carbolic acid)
15 hydrogen inlet
16 hydrogenation of phenol to produce raw cyclohexanol
17 distillation
18 pure cyclohexanol
19 oxidation (dehydrogenation)
20 formation of cyclohexanone (pimehinketone)
21 hydroxylamine inlet
22 formation of cyclohexanoxime
23 addition of sulphuric acid (*Am.* sulfuric acid) to effect molecular rearrangement
24 ammonia to neutralize sulphuric acid (*Am.* sulfuric acid)
25 formation of caprolactam oil
26 ammonium sulphate (*Am.* ammonium sulfate) solution
27 cooling cylinder
28 caprolactam
29 weighing apparatus
30 melting pot
31 pump
32 filter
33 polymerization in the autoclave
34 cooling of the polyamide
35 solidification of the polyamide
36 vertical lift (*Am.* elevator)
37 extractor for separating the polyamide from the remaining lactam oil
38 drier
39 dry polyamide chips
40 chip container
41 top of spinneret for melting the polyamide and forcing it through spinneret holes (spinning jets)
42 spinneret holes (spinning jets)
43 solidification of polyamide filaments in the cooling tower
44 collection of extruded filaments into thread form
45 preliminary stretching (preliminary drawing)
46 stretching (cold-drawing) of the polyamide thread to achieve high tensile strength
47 final stretching (final drawing)
48 washing of yarn packages
49 drying chamber
50 rewinding
51 polyamide cone
52 polyamide cone ready for dispatch (despatch)
53 mixer
54 polymerization under vacua
55 stretching (drawing)
56 washing
57 finishing of tow for spinning
58 drying of tow
59 crimping of tow
60 cutting of tow into normal staple lengths
61 polyamide staple
62 bale of polyamide staple

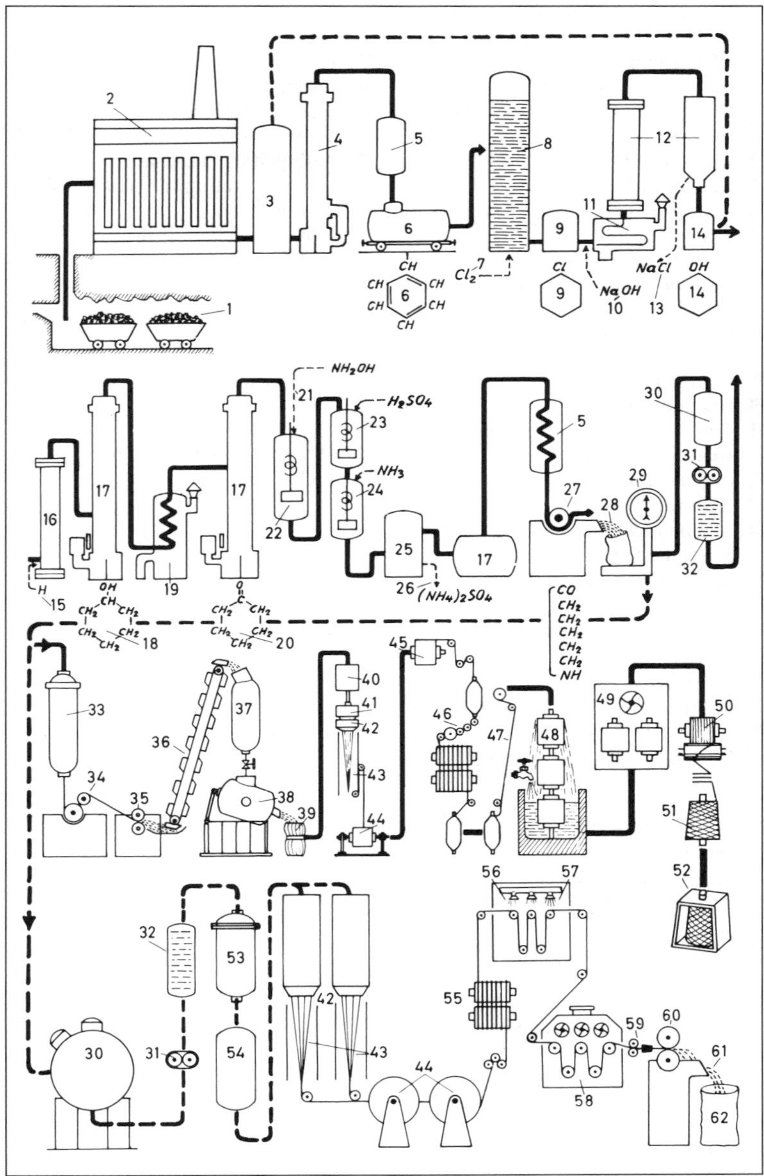
1
2
3
4
5
6
CH
CH
CH
6
CH
CH
CH
Cl_2 7
8
9
Cl
9
11
$NaOH$
10
12
$NaCl$
13
14
OH
14
16
H
15
17
OH
CH
CH_2 CH_2
CH_2 CH_2
CH_2
18
19
17
O
C
CH_2 CH_2
CH_2 CH_2
CH_2
20
NH_2OH
21
22
H_2SO_4
23
NH_3
24
25
26
$(NH_4)_2SO_4$
5
27
17
28
29
CO
CH_2
CH_2
CH_2
CH_2
CH_2
NH
30
31
32
33
34
35
36
37
38
39
40
41
42
43
44
45
46
47
48
49
50
51
52
32
53
30
31
54
42
43
44
55
56
57
58
59
60
61
62

1-29 weaves [black squares: warp thread raised, weft thread lowered; white squares: weft thread raised, warp thread lowered]
1 plain weave (tabby weave) [weave viewed from above]
2 warp thread
3 weft thread
4 draft (point paper design) for plain weave
5 threading draft
6 denting draft (reed-threading draft)
7 raised warp thread
8 lowered warp thread
9 tie-up of shafts in pairs
10 treadling diagram
11 draft for basket weave (hopsack weave, matt weave)
12 pattern repeat
13 draft for warp rib weave
14 section of warp rib fabric, a section through the warp
15 lowered weft thread
16 raised weft thread
17 first and second warp threads [raised]
18 third and fourth warp threads [lowered]
19 draft for combined rib weave
20 selvedge (selvage) thread draft (additional shafts for the selvedge)
21 draft for the fabric shafts
22 tie-up of selvedge (selvage) shafts
23 tie-up of fabric shafts
24 selvedge (selvage) in plain weave
25 section through combination rib weave
26 thread interlacing of reversible warp-faced cord
27 draft (point paper design) for reversible warp-faced cord
28 interlacing points
29 weaving draft for honeycomb weave in the fabric
30-48 basic knits
30 loop, an open loop
31 head
32 side
33 neck
34 head interlocking point
35 neck interlocking point
36 closed loop
37 mesh [with inlaid yarn]
38 diagonal floating yarn (diagonal floating thread)
39 loop interlocking at the head
40 float
41 loose floating yarn (loose floating thread)
42 course
43 inlaid yarn
44 tuck and miss stitch
45 pulled-up tuck stitch
46 staggered tuck stitch
47 2×2 tuck and miss stitch
48 double pulled-up tuck stitch

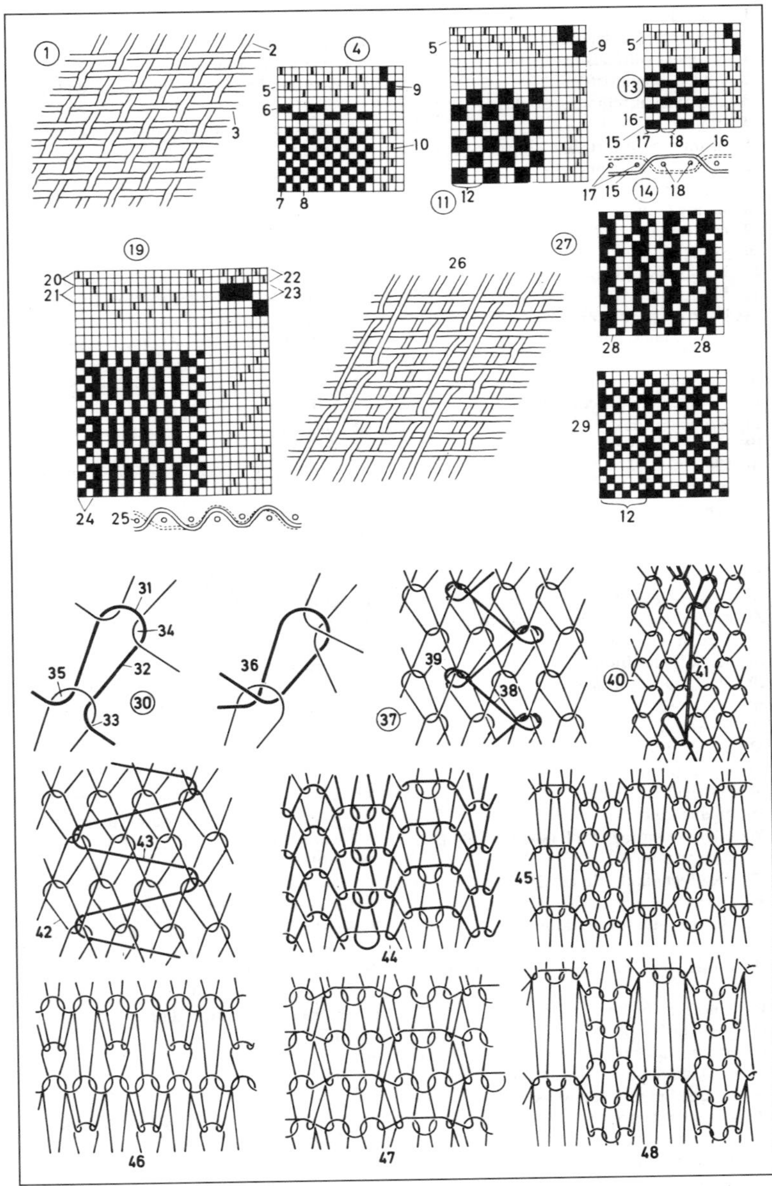
1
2
3
4
5
6
7
8
9
10
11
12
13
14
15
16
17
18
19
20
21
22
23
24
25
26
27
28
29
30
31
32
33
34
35
36
37
38
39
40
41
42
43
44
45
46
47
48

1-52 sulphate (*Am.* sulfate) pulp mill (kraft pulp mill) [in diagram form]
1 chippers with dust extractor
2 rotary screen (riffler)
3 chip packer (chip distributor)
4 blower
5 disintegrator (crusher, chip crusher)
6 dust-settling chamber
7 digester
8 liquor preheater
9 control tap
10 swing pipe
11 blow tank (diffuser)
12 blow valve
13 blow pit (diffuser)
14 turpentine separator
15 centralized separator
16 jet condenser (injection condenser)
17 storage tank for condensate
18 hot water tank
19 heat exchanger
20 filter
21 presorter
22 centrifugal screen
23 rotary sorter (rotary strainer)
24 concentrator (thickener, decker)
25 vat (chest)
26 collecting tank for backwater (low box)
27 conical refiner (cone refiner, Jordan, Jordan refiner)
28 black liquor filter
29 black liquor storage tank
30 condenser
31 separators
32 heaters (heating elements)
33 liquor pump
34 heavy liquor pump
35 mixing tank
36 salt cake storage tank (sodium sulphate storage tank)
37 dissolving tank (dissolver)
38 steam heater
39 electrostatic precipitator
40 air pump
41 storage tank for the uncleared green liquor
42 concentrator (thickener, decker)
43 green liquor preheater
44 concentrator (thickener, decker) for the weak wash liquor (wash water)
45 storage tank for the weak liquor
46 storage tank for the cooking liquor
47 agitator (stirrer)
48 concentrator (thickener, decker)
49 causticizing agitators (causticizing stirrers)
50 classifier
51 lime slaker
52 reconverted lime
53-65 groundwood mill (mechanical pulp mill) [diagram]
53 continuous grinder (continuous chain grinder)
54 strainer (knotter)
55 pulp water pump
56 centrifugal screen
57 screen (sorter)
58 secondary screen (secondary sorter)
59 rejects chest
60 conical refiner (cone refiner, Jordan, Jordan refiner)
61 pulp-drying machine (pulp machine)
62 concentrator (thickener, decker)
63 waste water pump (white water pump, pulp water pump)
64 steam pipe
65 water pipe
66 continuous grinder (continuous chain grinder)
67 feed chain
68 groundwood
69 reduction gear for the feed chain drive
70 stone-dressing device
71 grinding stone (grindstone, pulpstone)
72 spray pipe
73 conical refiner (cone refiner, Jordan, Jordan refiner)
74 handwheel for adjusting the clearance between the knives (blades)
75 rotating bladed cone (rotating bladed plug)
76 stationary bladed shell
77 inlet for unrefined cellulose (chemical wood pulp, chemical pulp) or groundwood pulp (mechanical pulp)
78 outlet for refined cellulose (chemical wood pulp, chemical pulp) or groundwood pulp (mechanical pulp)
79-86 stuff (stock) preparation plant [diagram]
79 conveyor belt (conveyor) for loading cellulose (chemical wood pulp, chemical pulp) or groundwood pulp (mechanical pulp)
80 pulper
81 dump chest
82 cone breaker
83 conical refiner (cone refiner, Jordan, Jordan refiner)
84 refiner
85 stuff chest (stock chest)
86 machine chest (stuff chest)

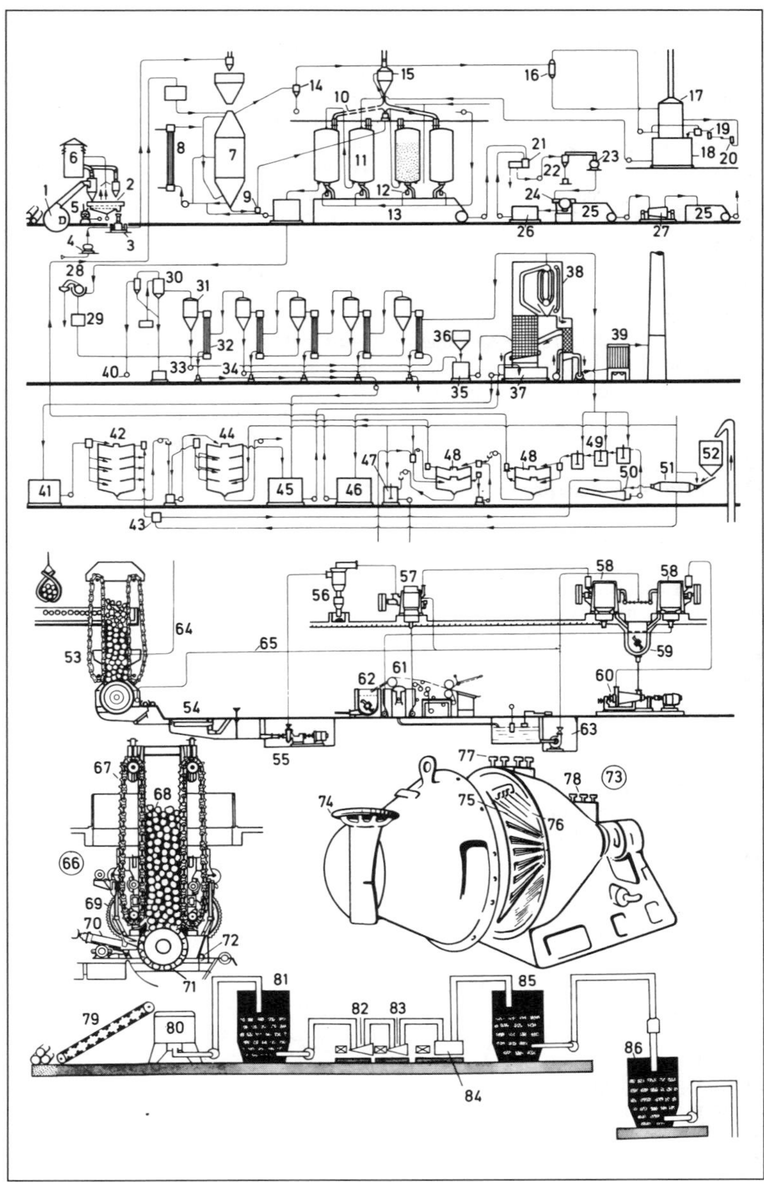
1
2
3
4
5
6
7
8
9
10
11
12
13
14
15
16
17
18
19
20
21
22
23
24
25
26
27
28
29
30
31
32
33
34
35
36
37
38
39
40
41
42
43
44
45
46
47
48
49
50
51
52
53
54
55
56
57
58
59
60
61
62
63
64
65
66
67
68
69
70
71
72
73
74
75
76
77
78
79
80
81
82
83
84
85
86

173 Papermaking II

1 stuff chest (stock chest, machine chest), a mixing chest for stuff (stock)
2-10 laboratory apparatus (laboratory equipment) for analysing stuff (stock) and paper
2 Erlenmeyer flask
3 volumetric flask
4 measuring cylinder
5 Bunsen burner
6 tripod
7 petri dish
8 test tube rack
9 balance for measuring basis weight
10 micrometer
11 centrifugal cleaners ahead of the breastbox (headbox, stuff box) of a paper machine
12 standpipe
13-28 paper machine (production line) [diagram]
13 feed-in from the machine chest (stuff chest) with sand table (sand trap, riffler) and knotter
14 wire (machine wire)
15 vacuum box (suction box)
16 suction roll
17 first wet felt
18 second wet felt
19 first press
20 second press
21 offset press
22 drying cylinder (drier)
23 dry felt (drier felt)
24 size press
25 cooling roll
26 calender rolls
27 machine hood
28 delivery reel
29-35 blade coating machine (blade coater)
29 raw paper (body paper)
30 web
31 coater for the top side
32 infrared drier
33 heated drying cylinder
34 coater for the underside (wire side)
35 reel of coated paper
36 calender (super-calender)
37 hydraulic system for the press rolls
38 calender roll
39 unwind station
40 lift platform
41 rewind station (rewinder, re-reeler, reeling machine, re-reeling machine)
42 roll cutter
43 control panel
44 cutter
45 web
46-51 papermaking by hand
46 vatman
47 vat
48 mould (*Am.* mold)
49 coucher (couchman)
50 post ready for pressing
51 felt

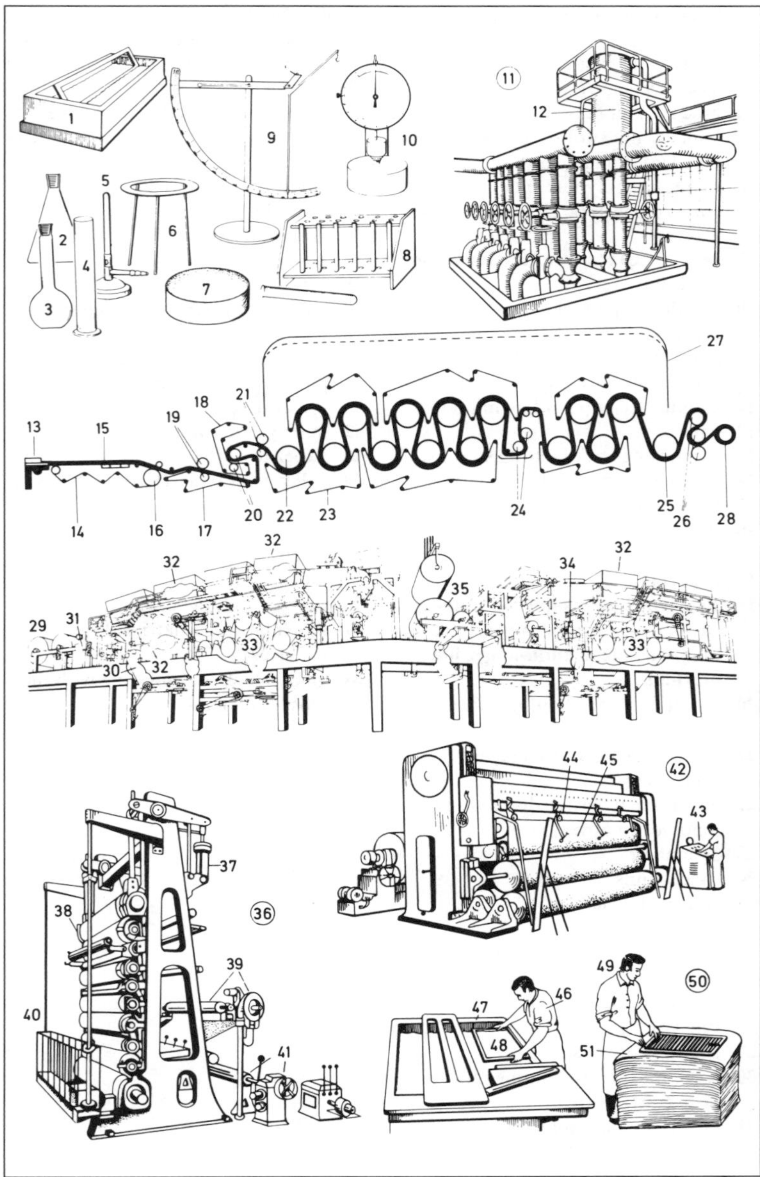
1
2
3
4
5
6
7
8
9
10
11
12
13
14
15
16
17
18
19
20
21
22
23
24
25
26
27
28
29
30
31
32
33
34
35
36
37
38
39
40
41
42
43
44
45
46
47
48
49
50
51

174 Typesetting Room (Composing Room) I

1 **hand-setting room** (hand-composing room)
2 composing frame
3 case (typecase)
4 case cabinet (case rack)
5 hand compositor (compositor, typesetter, maker-up)
6 manuscript (typescript)
7 sorts (types, type characters, characters)
8 rack (case) for furniture (spacing material)
9 standing type rack (standing matter rack)
10 storage shelf (shelf for storing formes, *Am.* forms)
11 standing type (standing matter)
12 galley
13 composing stick (setting stick)
14 composing rule (setting rule)
15 type (type matter, matter)
16 page cord
17 bodkin
18 tweezers
19 **Linotype line-composing (line-casting, slug-composing, slug-casting) machine, a multi-magazine machine**
20 distributing mechanism (distributor)
21 type magazines with matrices (matrixes)
22 elevator carrier for distributing the matrices (matrixes)
23 assembler
24 spacebands
25 casting mechanism
26 metal feeder
27 machine-set matter (cast lines, slugs)
28 matrices (matrixes) for hand-setting (sorts)
29 Linotype matrix
30 teeth for the distributing mechanism (distributor)
31 face (type face, matrix)
32-45 **monotype single-unit composing** (typesetting) **and casting machine** (monotype single-unit composition caster)
32 monotype standard composing (typesetting) machine (keyboard)
33 paper tower
34 paper ribbon
35 justifying scale
36 unit indicator
37 keyboard
38 compressed-air hose
39 monotype casting machine (monotype caster)
40 automatic metal feeder
41 pump compression spring (pump pressure spring)
42 matrix case (die case)
43 paper tower
44 galley with types (letters, characters, cast single types, cast single letters)
45 electric heater (electric heating unit)
46 matrix case (die case)
47 type matrices (matrixes) (letter matrices)
48 guide block for engaging with the cross-slide guide

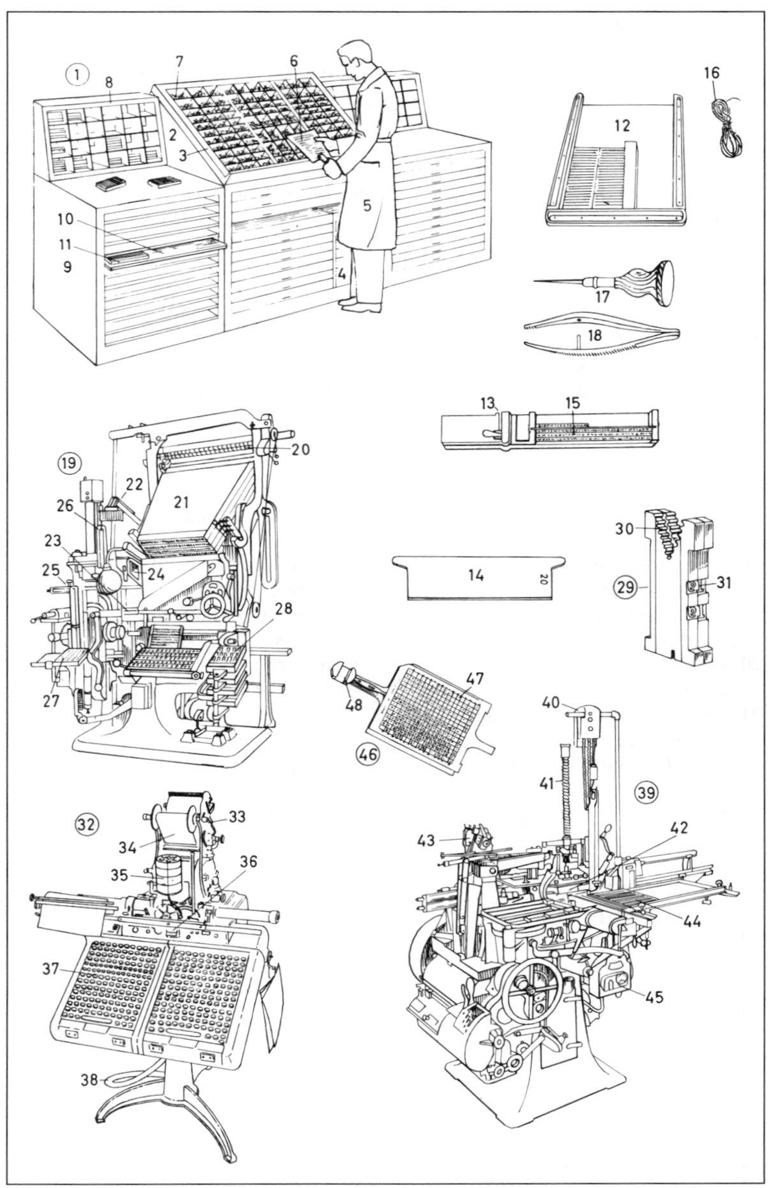
1
2
3
4
5
6
7
8
9
10
11
12
13
14
15
16
17
18
19
20
21
22
23
24
25
26
27
28
29
30
31
32
33
34
35
36
37
38
39
40
41
42
43
44
45
46
47
48

175 Typesetting Room (Composing Room) II

1-17 composition (type matter, type)
1 initial (initial letter)
2 bold type (bold, boldfaced type, heavy type, boldface)
3 semibold type (semibold)
4 line
5 space
6 ligature (double letter)
7 italic type (italics)
8 light face type (light face)
9 extra bold type (extra bold)
10 bold condensed type (bold condensed)
11 majuscule (capital letter, capital, upper case letter)
12 minuscule (small letter, lower case letter)
13 letter spacing (interspacing)
14 small capitals
15 break
16 indention
17 space
18 **type sizes** [one typographic point = 0.376 mm (Didot system), 0.351 mm (Pica system)]
19 six-to-pica (2 points)
20 half nonpareil (four-to-pica) (3 points)
21 brilliant (4 points); *sim.:* diamond ($4^1/_2$ points)
22 pearl (5 points); *sim.:* ruby (*Am.* agate) ($5^1/_2$ points)
23 nonpareil (6 points); *sim.:* minionette ($6^1/_2$ points)
24 minion (7 points)
25 brevier (8 points)
26 bourgeois (9 points)
27 long primer (10 points)
28 pica (12 points)
29 English (14 points)
30 great primer (two-line brevier, *Am.* Columbian) (16 points)
31 paragon (two-line primer) (20 points)
32-37 typefounding (type casting)
32 punch cutter
33 graver (burin, cutter)
34 magnifying glass (magnifier)
35 punch blank (die blank)
36 finished steel punch (finished steel die)
37 punched matrix (stamped matrix, strike, drive)
38 **type** (type character, character)
39 **head**
40 shoulder
41 counter
42 face (type face)
43 type line (bodyline)
44 height to paper (type height)
45 height of shank (height of shoulder)
46 body size (type size, point size)
47 nick
48 set (width)
49 **matrix-boring machine** (matrix-engraving machine), a special-purpose boring machine
50 stand
51 cutter (cutting head)
52 cutting table
53 pantograph carriage
54 V-way
55 pattern
56 pattern table
57 follower
58 pantograph
59 matrix clamp
60 cutter spindle
61 drive motor

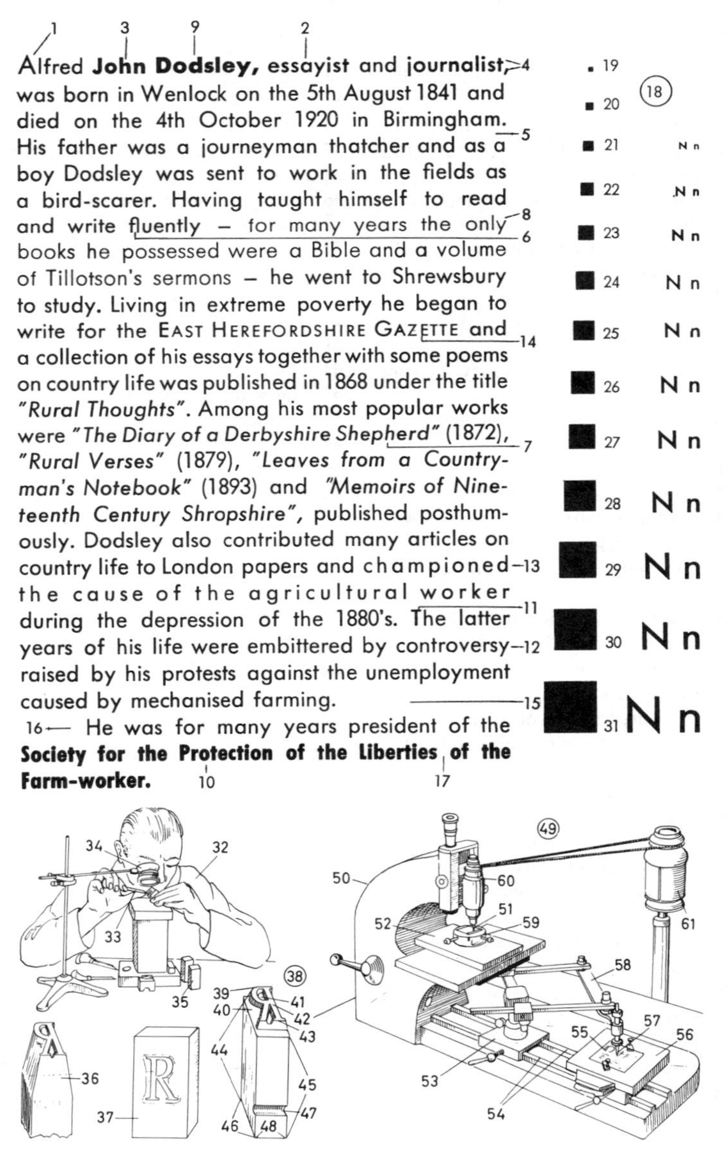
1 3 9 2
Alfred John Dodsley, essayist and journalist, 4
was born in Wenlock on the 5th August 1841 and
died on the 4th October 1920 in Birmingham.
His father was a journeyman thatcher and as a 5
boy Dodsley was sent to work in the fields as
a bird-scarer. Having taught himself to read
and write fluently – for many years the only 8
6
books he possessed were a Bible and a volume
of Tillotson's sermons – he went to Shrewsbury
to study. Living in extreme poverty he began to
write for the EAST HEREFORDSHIRE GAZETTE and 14
a collection of his essays together with some poems
on country life was published in 1868 under the title
"Rural Thoughts". Among his most popular works
were "The Diary of a Derbyshire Shepherd" (1872), 7
"Rural Verses" (1879), "Leaves from a Country-
man's Notebook" (1893) and "Memoirs of Nine-
teenth Century Shropshire", published posthum-
ously. Dodsley also contributed many articles on
country life to London papers and championed 13
the cause of the agricultural worker
11
during the depression of the 1880's. The latter
years of his life were embittered by controversy 12
raised by his protests against the unemployment
caused by mechanised farming. 15
16 He was for many years president of the
Society for the Protection of the Liberties of the
Farm-worker.
10 17
19
20
18
21 N n
22 N n
23 N n
24 N n
25 N n
26 N n
27 N n
28 N n
29 N n
30 N n
31 N n
34
32
33
35
38
39
40
41
42
43
44
45
46
47
48
36
37
R
49
50
60
51
52
59
61
58
57
55
56
53
54

176 Typesetting Room III (Phototypesetting, Photocomposition, Photosetting)

1-21 phototypesetting **configurations**
1 off-line configuration
2, 3 data capture
2 terminal for keying unformatted text
3 text capture and correction terminal
4 layout terminal (page-layout terminal)
5 data carrier, a diskette (floppy disk)
6 (photo)typesetting unit (phototypesetter)
7 on-line configuration
8 make-up terminal (page make-up terminal)
9 central processing unit (typesetting computer)
10 magnetic tape unit (magnetic tape drive)
11 disk store
12 printer, a laser printer
13 phototypesetting machine (phototypesetter)
14 text capture (text-capture terminal)
15 typesetter (keyboarder or typographer)
16 screen (monitor)
17 floppy disk drive
18 computer and memory unit with central processing unit and hard disk
19 mouse, an input device
20 mouse mat
21 keyboard, an input device
22 **direct-entry phototypesetter**
23-33 **desktop publishing** (DTP)
23 diskette (floppy disk) with text, layout, and graphics programs
24 scanner (flat-bed scanner)
25 personal computer (PC) or workstation
26 printout (computer printout)
27 raster image processor (RIP)
28 laser phototypesetter
29 proof
30 high-resolution graphics screen, a large-format colour monitor
31 display window
32 typographic parameters
33 (typographic) command window
34 film copier
35-46 **cathode ray tube** (CRT) **typesetter**
35 scanning system
36 scan-generating (scanning) cathode ray tube (CRT)
37 lens
38 character grid (matrix case)
39 condenser lens
40 photomultiplier
41 output system
42 video amplifier
43 character-generating tube (CRT character generator)
44 exposure plane
45 matrix case
46 guide claw

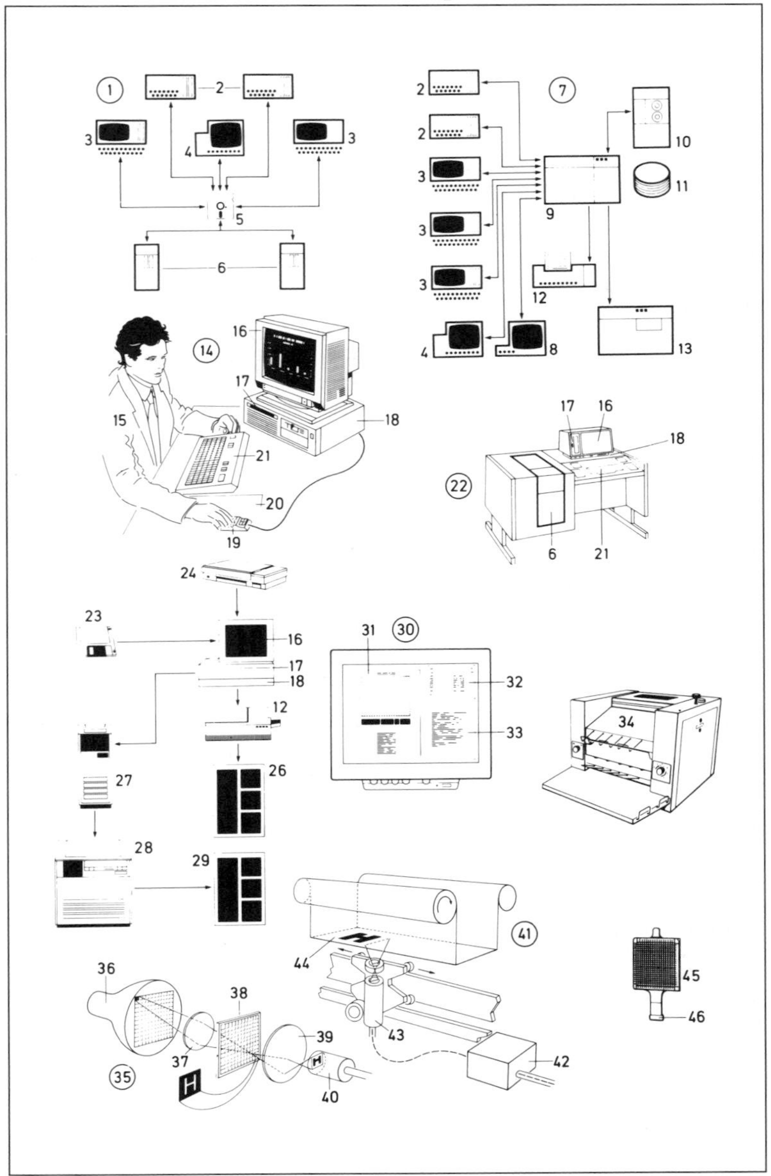
1
2
3
4
3
5
6
7
2
2
3
3
3
4
8
9
10
11
12
13
14
15
16
17
18
19
20
21
22
17
16
18
6
21
24
23
16
17
18
12
27
26
28
29
31
30
32
33
34
41
44
36
38
37
35
H
39
40
43
42
45
46

177 Photomechanical Reproduction

1 overhead process camera (overhead copying camera)
2 focusing screen (ground glass screen)
3 hinged screen holder
4 graticule
5 control console
6 hinged bracket-mounted control panel
7 percentage focusing charts
8 vacuum film holder
9 screen magazine
10 bellows
11 standard
12 register device
13 overhead gantry
14 copyboard
15 copyholder
16 lamp bracket
17 xenon lamp
18 copy (original)
19 retouching and stripping desk
20 illuminated screen
21 height and angle adjustment
22 copyboard
23 linen tester, a magnifying glass
24 universal process and reproduction camera
25 camera body
26 bellows
27 lens carrier
28 angled mirror
29 stand
30 copyboard
31 halogen lamp
32 vertical process camera, a compact camera
33 camera body
34 focusing screen (ground glass screen)
35 vacuum back
36 control panel
37 flash lamp
38 mirror for right-reading images
39 scanner (colour, *Am.* color, correction unit)
40 base frame
41 lamp compartment
42 xenon lamp housing
43 feed motors
44 transparency arm
45 scanning drum
46 scanning head
47 mask-scanning head
48 mask drum
49 recording space
50 daylight cassette
51 colour (*Am.* color) computer with control unit and selective colour correction
52 engraving machine
53 seamless engraving adjustment
54 drive clutch
55 clutch flange
56 drive unit
57 machine bed
58 equipment carrier
59 bed slide
60 control panel
61 bearing block
62 tailstock
63 scanning head
64 copy cylinder
65 centre (*Am.* center) bearing
66 engraving system
67 printing cylinder
68 cylinder arm
69 electronics (electronic) cabinet
70 computers
71 program input
72 automatic film processor for scanner films

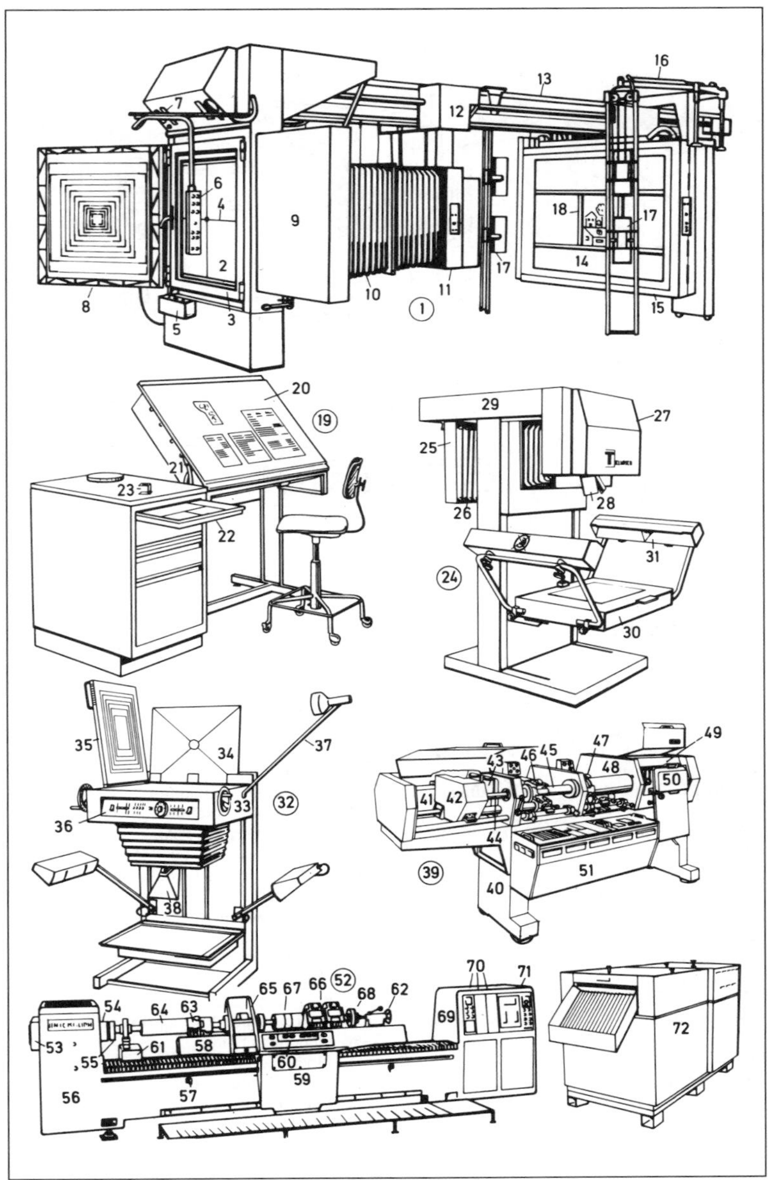
1
2
3
4
5
6
7
8
9
10
11
12
13
14
15
16
17
18
19
20
21
22
23
24
25
26
27
28
29
30
31
32
33
34
35
36
37
38
39
40
41
42
43
44
45
46
47
48
49
50
51
52
53
54
55
56
57
58
59
60
61
62
63
64
65
66
67
68
69
70
71
72

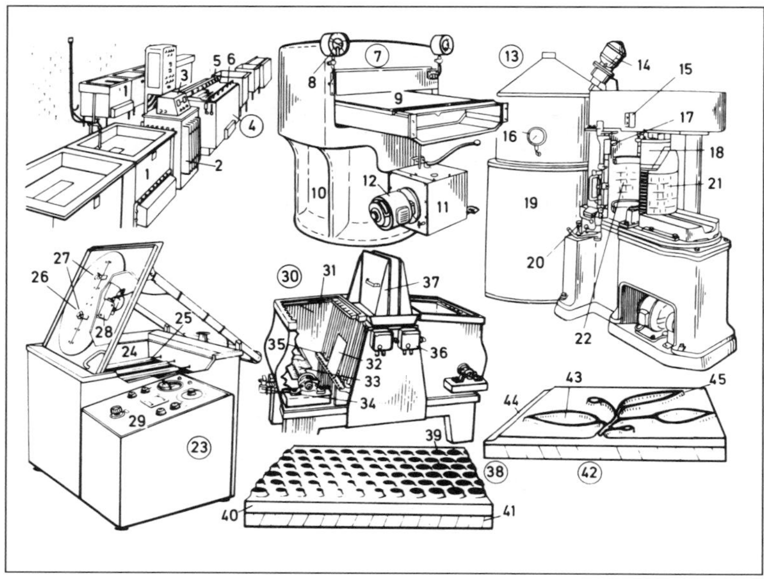

1-6 electrotyping plant
1 cleaning tank
2 rectifier
3 measuring and control unit
4 electroplating tank (electroplating bath, electroplating vat)
5 anode rod (with copper anodes)
6 plate rod (cathode)
7 **hydraulic moulding** (*Am.* molding) **press**
8 pressure gauge (*Am.* gage) (manometer)
9 apron
10 round base
11 hydraulic pressure pump
12 drive motor
13 **curved plate casting machine** (curved electrotype casting machine)
14 motor
15 control knobs
16 pyrometer
17 mouth piece
18 core
19 melting furnace
20 starting lever
21 cast curved plate (cast curved electrotype) for rotary printing
22 fixed mould (*Am.* mold)
23 **etching machine**
24 etching tank with etching solution (etchant, mordant) and filming agent (film former)
25 paddles
26 turntable
27 plate clamp
28 drive motor
29 control unit
30 **twin etching machine**
31 etching tank (etching bath) [in section]
32 photoprinted zinc plate
33 paddle
34 outlet cock (drain cock, *Am.* faucet)
35 plate rack
36 control switches
37 lid
38 **halftone photoengraving** (halftone block, halftone plate), a block (plate, printing plate)
39 dot (halftone dot), a printing element
40 etched zinc plate
41 block mount (block mounting, plate mount, plate mounting)
42 **line block** (line engraving, line etching, line plate, line cut)
43 non-printing, deep-etched areas
44 flange (bevel edge)
45 sidewall

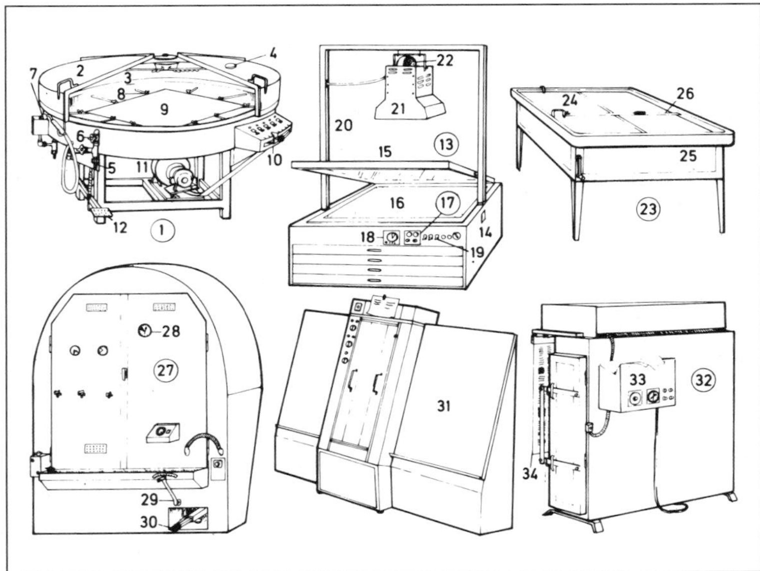

1 plate whirler (whirler, plate-coating machine) for coating offset plates
2 sliding lid
3 electric heater
4 temperature gauge (*Am.* gage)
5 water connection for the spray unit
6 spray unit
7 hand spray
8 plate clamps
9 zinc plate (*also:* magnesium plate, copper plate)
10 control panel
11 drive motor
12 brake pedal
13 vacuum printing frame (vacuum frame, printing-down frame)
14 base of the vacuum printing frame (vacuum frame, printing-down frame)
15 plate glass frame
16 coated offset plate
17 control panel
18 exposure timer
19 vacuum pump switches
20 support
21 point light exposure lamp, a quartz-halogen lamp
22 fan blower
23 stripping table (make-up table) for stripping films
24 crystal glass screen
25 light box
26 straightedge rules
27 vertical plate-drying cabinet
28 hygrometer
29 speed control
30 brake pedal
31 processing machine for presensitized plates
32 burning-in oven for glue-enamel plates (diazo plates)
33 control box (control unit)
34 diazo plate

1 four-colour (*Am.* four-color) rotary offset press (rotary offset machine, web-offset press)
2 roll of unprinted paper (blank paper)
3 reel stand (carrier for the roll of unprinted paper)
4 forwarding rolls
5 side margin control (margin control, side control, side lay control)
6-13 inking units (inker units)
6, 8, 10, 12 inking units (inker units) in the upper printing unit
6, 7 perfecting unit (double unit) for yellow
7, 9, 11, 13 inking units (inker units) in the lower printing unit
8, 9 perfecting unit (double unit) for cyan
10, 11 perfecting unit (double unit) for magenta
12, 13 perfecting unit (double unit) for black
14 drier
15 folder (folder unit)
16 control desk
17 sheet
18 four-colour (*Am.* four-color) rotary offset press (rotary offset machine, web-offset press) [diagram]
19 reel stand
20 side margin control (margin control, side control, side lay control)
21 inking rollers (ink rollers, inkers)
22 ink duct (ink fountain)
23 damping rollers (dampening rollers, dampers, dampeners)
24 blanket cylinder
25 plate cylinder
26 route of the paper (of the web)
27 drier
28 chilling rolls (cooling rollers, chill rollers)
29 folder (folder unit)
30 four-colour (*Am.* four-color) sheet-fed offset machine (offset press) [diagram]
31 sheet feeder (feeder)
32 feed table (feed board)
33 route of the sheets through swing-grippers to the feed drum
34 feed drum
35 impression cylinder
36 transfer drums (transfer cylinders)
37 blanket cylinder
38 plate cylinder
39 damping unit (dampening unit)
40 inking unit (inker unit)
41 printing unit
42 delivery cylinder
43 chain delivery
44 delivery pile
45 delivery unit (delivery mechanism)
46 single-colour (*Am.* single-color) offset press (offset machine)
47 pile of paper (sheets, printing paper)
48 sheet feeder (feeder), an automatic pile feeder
49 feed table (feed board)
50 inking rollers (ink rollers, inkers)
51 inking unit (inker unit)
52 damping rollers (dampening rollers, dampers, dampeners)
53 plate cylinder, a zinc plate
54 blanket cylinder, a steel cylinder with rubber blanket
55 pile delivery unit for the printed sheets
56 gripper bar, a chain gripper
57 pile of printed paper (printed sheets)
58 guard for the V-belt (vee-belt) drive
59 single-colour (*Am.* single-color) offset press (offset machine) [diagram]
60 inking unit (inker unit) with inking rollers (ink rollers, inkers)
61 damping unit (dampening unit) with damping rollers (dampening rollers, dampers, dampeners)
62 plate cylinder
63 blanket cylinder
64 impression cylinder
65 delivery cylinders with grippers
66 drive wheel
67 feed table (feed board)
68 sheet feeder (feeder)
69 pile of unprinted paper (blank paper, unprinted sheets, blank sheets)
70 small sheet-fed offset press
71 inking unit (inker unit)
72 suction feeder
73 pile feeder
74 instrument panel (control panel) with counter, pressure gauge (*Am.* gage), air regulator, and control switch for the sheet feeder (feeder)
75 flat-bed offset press (offset machine) ('Mailänder' proofing press, proof press)
76 inking unit (inker unit)
77 inking rollers (ink rollers, inkers)
78 bed (press bed, type bed, forme bed, *Am.* form bed)
79 cylinder with rubber blanket
80 starting and stopping lever for the printing unit
81 impression-setting wheel (impression-adjusting wheel)

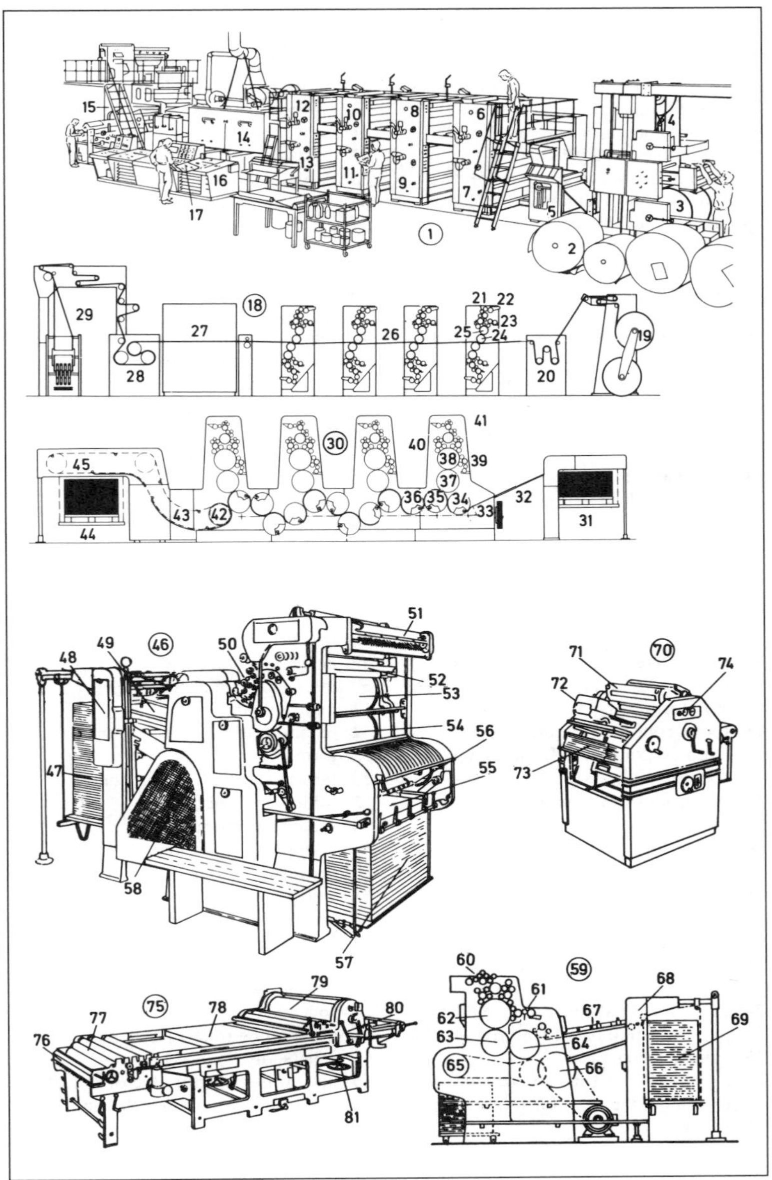
15
12
10
8
6
14
4
13
11
9
7
16
17
5
3
1
2
29
18
21 22
23
27
26
25
24
19
28
20
41
30
40
38
39
45
37
32
36
35
34
43
42
33
31
44
51
49
46
50
48
52
53
54
56
55
47
58
57
71
70
74
72
73
60
59
79
61
68
78
80
77
67
69
62
63
64
76
65
66
81
75

181 Letterpress Printing

1-65 presses (machines) for letterpress printing (letterpress printing machines)
1 **two-revolution flat-bed cylinder press**
2 impression cylinder
3 lever for raising or lowering the cylinder
4 feed table (feed board)
5 automatic sheet feeder (feeder) [operated by vacuum and air blasts]
6 air pump for the feeder and delivery
7 inking unit (inker unit) with distributing rollers (distributor rollers, distributors) and forme rollers (*Am.* form rollers)
8 ink slab (ink plate) inking unit (inker unit)
9 delivery pile for printed paper
10 sprayer (anti set-off apparatus, anti set-off spray) for dusting the printed sheets
11 interleaving device
12 foot pedal for starting and stopping the press
13 **platen press** (platen machine, platen) [in section]
14 paper feed and delivery (paper feeding and delivery unit)
15 platen
16 toggle action (toggle-joint action)
17 bed (type bed, press bed, forme bed, *Am.* form bed)
18 forme rollers (*Am.* form rollers) (forme-inking, *Am.* form-inking, rollers)
19 inking unit (inker unit) for distributing the ink (printing ink)
20 **stop-cylinder press** (stop-cylinder machine)
21 feed table (feed board)
22 feeder mechanism (feeding apparatus, feeder)
23 pile of unprinted paper (blank paper, unprinted sheets, blank sheets)
24 guard for the sheet feeder (feeder)
25 pile of printed paper (printed sheets)
26 control mechanism
27 forme rollers (*Am.* form rollers) (forme-inking, *Am.* form-inking, rollers)
28 inking unit (inker unit)
29 [Heidelberg] **platen press** (platen machine, platen)
30 feed table (feed board) with pile of unprinted paper (blank paper, unprinted sheets, blank sheets)
31 delivery table
32 starting and stopping lever
33 delivery blower
34 spray gun (sprayer)
35 air pump for vacuum and air blasts
36 **locked-up forme** (*Am.* form)
37 type (type matter, matter)
38 chase
39 quoin
40 length of furniture
41 **rotary letterpress press** (rotary letterpress machine, web-fed letterpress machine) for newspapers of up to 16 pages
42 slitters for dividing the width of the web
43 web
44 impression cylinder
45 jockey roller (compensating roller, compensator, tension roller)
46 roll of paper
47 automatic brake
48 first printing unit
49 perfecting unit
50 inking unit (inker unit)
51 plate cylinder
52 second printing unit
53 former
54 tachometer with sheet counter
55 folder (folder unit)
56 folded newspaper
57 **inking unit** (inker unit) for the rotary press (web-fed press) [in section]
58 web
59 impression cylinder
60 plate cylinder
61 forme rollers (*Am.* form rollers) (forme-inking, *Am.* form-inking, rollers)
62 distributing rollers (distributor rollers, distributors)
63 lifter roller (ductor, ductor roller)
64 duct roller (fountain roller, ink fountain roller)
65 ink duct (ink fountain)

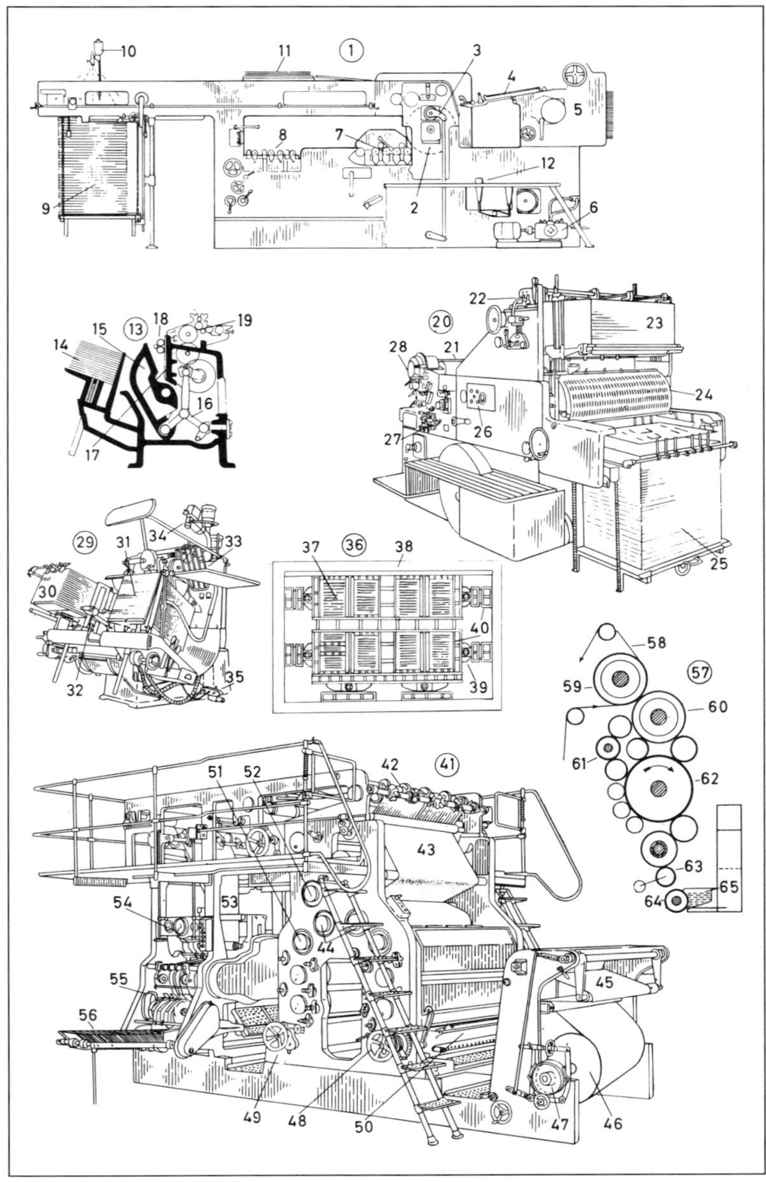
1
2
3
4
5
6
7
8
9
10
11
12
13
14
15
16
17
18
19
20
21
22
23
24
25
26
27
28
29
30
31
32
33
34
35
36
37
38
39
40
41
42
43
44
45
46
47
48
49
50
51
52
53
54
55
56
57
58
59
60
61
62
63
64
65

182 Photogravure (Gravure Printing, Intaglio Printing)

1 exposure of the carbon tissue (pigment paper)
2 vacuum frame
3 exposing lamp, a bank of quartz-halogen lamps
4 point source lamp
5 heat extractor
6 carbon tissue transfer machine (laydown machine, laying machine)
7 polished copper cylinder
8 rubber roller for pressing on the printed carbon tissue (pigment paper)
9 cylinder-processing machine
10 gravure cylinder coated with carbon tissue (pigment paper)
11 developing tank
12 staging
13 developed cylinder
14 retoucher painting out (stopping out)
15 etching machine
16 etching tank with etching solution (etchant, mordant)
17 printed gravure cylinder
18 gravure etcher
19 calculator dial
20 timer
21 revising (correcting) the cylinder
22 etched gravure cylinder
23 ledge
24 multicolour (*Am.* multicolor) rotogravure press
25 exhaust pipe for solvent fumes
26 reversible printing unit
27 folder (folder unit)
28 control desk
29 newspaper delivery unit
30 conveyor belt (conveyor)
31 bundled stack of newspapers

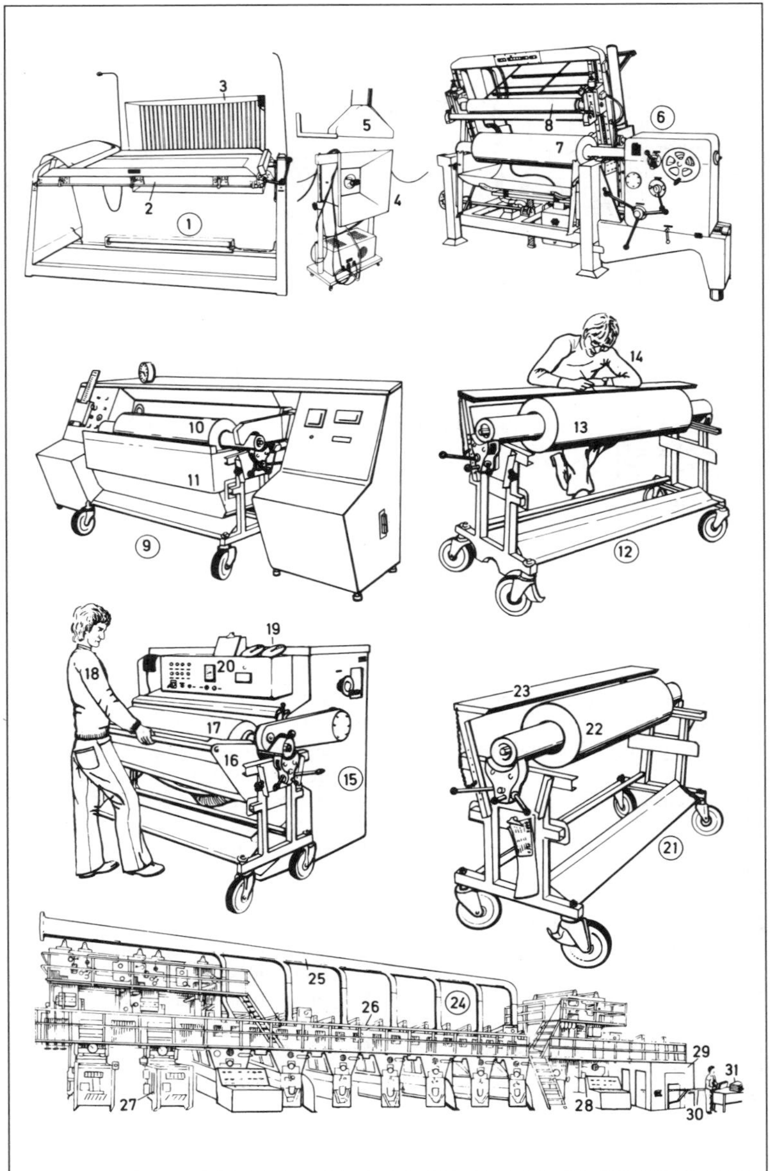
1
2
3
4
5
6
7
8
9
10
11
12
13
14
15
16
17
18
19
20
21
22
23
24
25
26
27
28
29
30
31

183 Bookbinding I

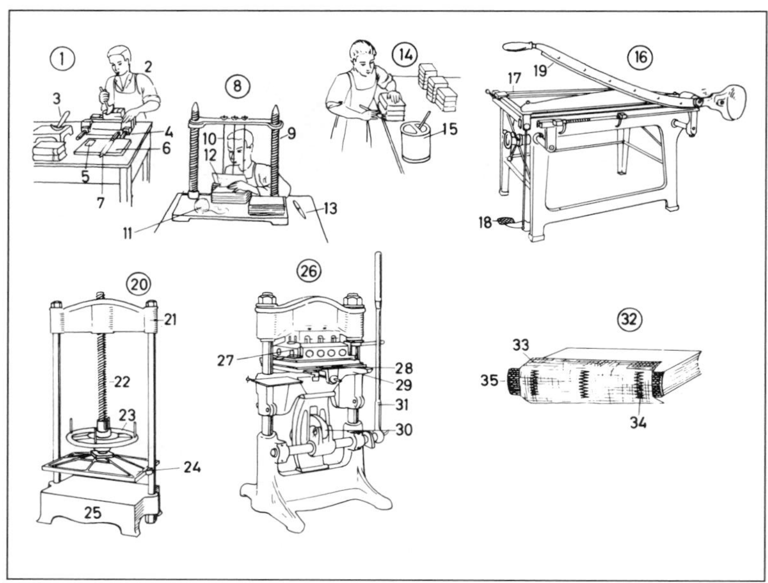

1-35 hand bookbindery (hand bindery)
1 gilding the spine of the book
2 gold finisher (gilder), a bookbinder
3 fillet
4 holding press (finishing press)
5 gold leaf
6 gold cushion
7 gold knife
8 sewing (stitching)
9 sewing frame
10 sewing cord
11 ball of thread (sewing thread)
12 section (signature)
13 bookbinder's knife
14 gluing the spine
15 glue pot
16 board cutter (guillotine)
17 back gauge (*Am.* gage)
18 clamp with foot pedal
19 cutting blade
20 standing press, a nipping press
21 head piece (head beam)
22 spindle
23 handwheel
24 platen
25 bed (base)
26 gilding (gold blocking) and embossing press, a hand-lever press; *sim.:* toggle-joint press (toggle-lever press)
27 heating box
28 sliding plate
29 embossing platen
30 toggle action (toggle-joint action)
31 hand lever
32 book sewn on gauze (mull, scrim) (book block)
33 gauze (mull, scrim)
34 sewing (stitching)
35 headband

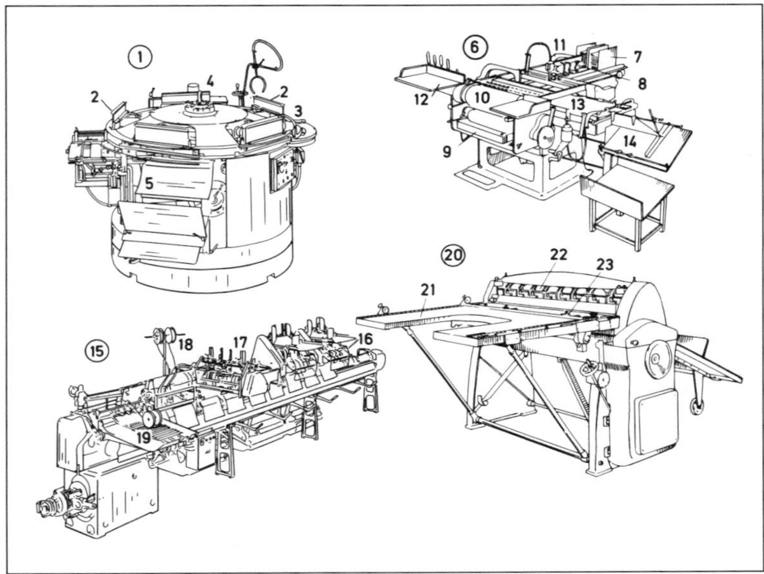

1-23 bookbinding machines

1 **adhesive binder** (perfect binder) for short runs

2 manual feed station

3 cutoff knife and roughing station

4 gluing mechanism

5 delivery (book delivery)

6 **case maker** (case-making machine)

7 board feed hoppers

8 pick-up suckers

9 glue tank

10 cover cylinder

11 picker head

12 feed table for covering materials [linen, paper, leather]

13 pressing mechanism

14 delivery table

15 **gang stitcher** (gathering and wire-stitching machine, gatherer and wire stitcher)

16 sheet feeder (sheet-feeding station)

17 folder-feeding station

18 stitching wire feed mechanism

19 delivery table

20 **rotary board cutter** (rotary board-cutting machine)

21 feed table with cut-out section

22 rotary cutter

23 feed guide

185 Bookbinding III

1-35 bookbinding machines
1 guillotine (guillotine cutter, automatic guillotine cutter)
2 control panel
3 clamp
4 back gauge (*Am.* gage)
5 calibrated pressure adjustment [to clamp]
6 illuminated cutting scale
7 single-hand control for the back gauge (*Am.* gage)
8 combined buckle and knife folding machine (combined buckle and knife folder)
9 feed table (feed board)
10 fold plates
11 stop for making the buckle fold
12 cross fold knives
13 belt delivery for parallel-folded signatures
14 third cross fold unit
15 delivery tray for cross-folded signatures
16 sewing machine (book-sewing machine)
17 spool holder
18 thread cop (thread spool)
19 gauze roll holder (mull roll holder, scrim roll holder)
20 gauze (mull, scrim)
21 needle cylinders with sewing needles
22 sewn book
23 delivery
24 reciprocating saddle
25 sheet feeder (feeder)
26 feed hopper
27 casing-in machine
28 joint and side pasting attachment
29 blade
30 preheater unit
31 gluing machine for whole-surface, stencil, edge, and strip gluing
32 glue tank
33 glue roller
34 feed table
35 delivery

36 book
37 dust jacket (dust cover, book jacket, wrapper), a publisher's wrapper
38 jacket flap
39 blurb
40-42 binding
40 cover (book cover, case)
41 spine (backbone, back)
42 tailband (footband)
43-47 preliminary matter (prelims, front matter)
43 half-title
44 half-title (bastard title, fly title)
45 title page
46 full title (main title)
47 subtitle
48 publisher's imprint (imprint)
49 fly leaf (endpaper, endleaf)
50 handwritten dedication
51 bookplate (ex libris)
52 open book
53 page
54 fold
55-58 margin
55 back margin (inside margin, gutter)
56 head margin (upper margin)
57 fore edge margin (outside margin, fore edge)
58 tail margin (foot margin, tail, foot)
59 type area
60 chapter heading
61 asterisk
62 footnote
63 page number
64 double-column page
65 column
66 running title (running head)
67 caption
68 marginal note (side note)
69 signature (signature code)
70 attached bookmark (attached bookmarker)
71 loose bookmark (loose bookmarker)

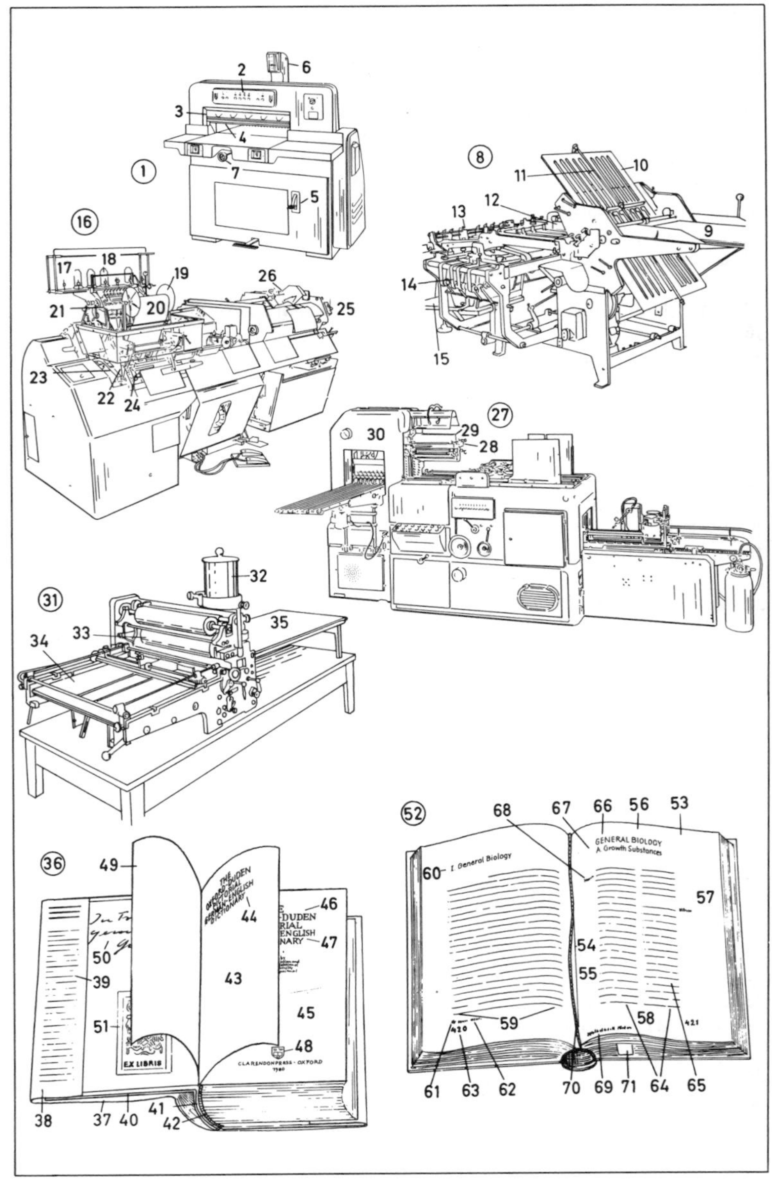
1
2
3
4
5
6
7
8
9
10
11
12
13
14
15
16
17
18
19
20
21
22
23
24
25
26
27
28
29
30
31
32
33
34
35
36
37
38
39
40
41
42
43
44
45
46
47
48
49
50
51
52
53
54
55
56
57
58
59
60
61
62
63
64
65
66
67
68
69
70
71
EX LIBRIS
CLARENDON PRESS · OXFORD
I. General Biology
GENERAL BIOLOGY
A Growth Substances
420
421

1-54 carriages (horse-drawn vehicles)
1-3, 26-39, 45, 51-54 carriages and coaches (coach wagons)
1 berlin
2 wagonette; *larger:* brake (break)
3 coupé; *sim.:* brougham
4 front wheel
5 coach body
6 dashboard (splashboard)
7 footboard
8 coach box (box, coachman's seat, driver's seat)
9 lamp (lantern)
10 window
11 door (coach door)
12 door handle (handle)
13 footboard (carriage step, coach step, step, footpiece)
14 fixed top
15 spring
16 brake (brake block)
17 back wheel (rear wheel)
18 dogcart, a one-horse carriage
19 shafts (thills, poles)
20 lackey (lacquey, footman)
21 livery
22 braided (gallooned) collar
23 braided (gallooned) coat
24 braided (gallooned) sleeve
25 top hat
26 hackney carriage (hackney coach, cab, growler, *Am.* hack)
27 stableman (groom)
28 coach horse (carriage horse, cab horse, thill horse, thiller)
29 hansom cab (hansom), a cabriolet, a one-horse chaise (one-horse carriage)
30 shafts (thills, poles)
31 reins (rein, *Am.* line)
32 coachman (driver) with inverness
33 covered char-a-banc (brake, break), a pleasure vehicle
34 gig (chaise)
35 barouche
36 landau, a two-horse carriage; *sim.:* landaulet, landaulette
37 omnibus (horse-drawn omnibus)
38 phaeton
39 Continental stagecoach (mailcoach, diligence); *also:* road coach
40 mailcoach driver
41 posthorn
42 hood
43 post horses (relay horses, relays)
44 tilbury
45 troika (Russian three-horse carriage)
46 leader
47 wheeler (wheelhorse, pole horse)
48 English buggy
49 American buggy
50 tandem
51 vis-à-vis
52 collapsible hood (collapsible top)
53 mailcoach (English stagecoach)
54 covered (closed) chaise

1
2
3
4
5
6
7
8
9
10
11
12
13
14
15
16
17
18
19
20
21
22
23
24
25
26
27
28
29
30
31
32
33
34
35
36
37
38
39
40
41
42
43
44
45
46
47
48
49
50
51
52
53
54

187 Bicycle

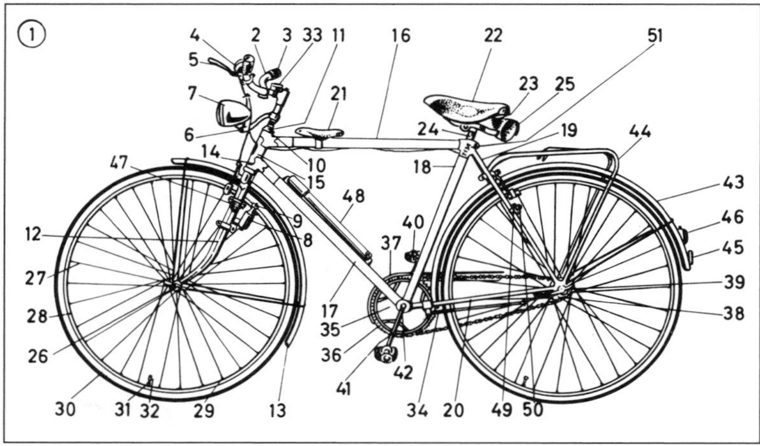

1 bicycle (cycle, *coll.* bike, *Am.* wheel), a gent's bicycle, a touring bicycle (touring cycle, roadster)
2 handlebar (handlebars), a touring cycle handlebar
3 handlebar grip (handgrip, grip)
4 bicycle bell
5 hand brake (front brake), a rim brake
6 lamp bracket
7 headlamp (bicycle lamp)
8 dynamo
9 pulley
10-12 front forks
10 handlebar stem
11 steering head
12 fork blades (fork ends)
13 front mudguard (*Am.* front fender)
14-20 bicycle frame
14 steering tube (fork column)
15 head badge
16 crossbar (top tube)
17 down tube
18 seat tube
19 seat stays
20 chain stays
21 child's seat (child carrier seat)
22 bicycle saddle
23 saddle springs
24 seat pillar
25 tool bag
26-32 wheel (front wheel)
26 hub
27 spoke
28 rim (wheel rim)
29 spoke nipple (spoke flange, spoke end)
30 tyre (*Am.* tire) (pneumatic tyre, high-pressure tyre); *inside:* tube (inner tube); *outside:* tyre (outer case, cover)
31 valve, a tube valve with valve tube or a patent valve with ball
32 valve sealing cap
33 bicycle speedometer with milometer
34 kick stand (prop stand)
35-42 bicycle drive (chain drive)
35-39 chain transmission
35 chain wheel
36 chain, a roller chain
37 chain guard
38 sprocket wheel (sprocket)
39 wing nut (fly nut, butterfly nut)
40 pedal
41 crank
42 bottom bracket bearing

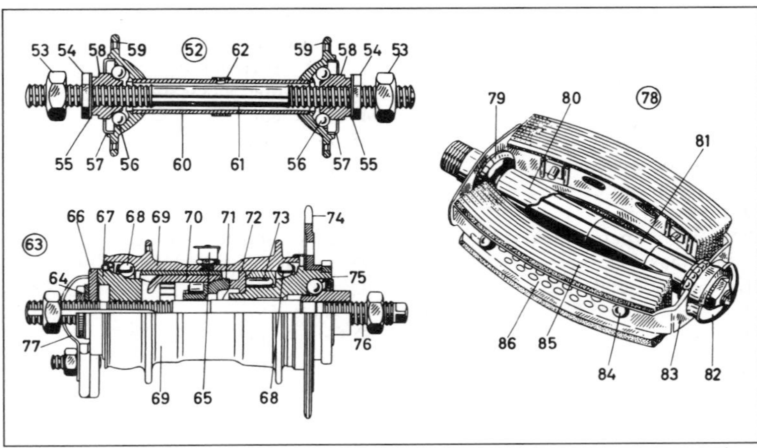

43 rear mudguard (*Am.* rear fender)
44 luggage carrier (carrier)
45 reflector
46 rear light (rear lamp)
47 footrest
48 bicycle pump
49 bicycle lock, a wheel lock
50 patent key
51 cycle serial number (factory number, frame number)
52 front hub (front hub assembly)
53 wheel nut
54 locknut (locking nut)
55 washer (slotted cone adjusting washer)
56 ball bearing
57 dust cap
58 cone (adjusting cone)
59 centre (*Am.* center) hub
60 spindle
61 axle
62 clip covering lubrication hole (lubricator)
63 free-wheel hub with back-pedal brake (with coaster brake)
64 safety nut
65 lubricator
66 brake arm
67 brake arm cone
68 bearing cup with ball bearings in ball race
69 hub shell (hub body, hub barrel)
70 brake casing
71 brake cone
72 driver
73 driving barrel
74 sprocket
75 thread head
76 axle
77 bracket
78 bicycle pedal (pedal, reflector pedal)
79 cup
80 spindle
81 axle
82 dust cap
83 pedal frame
84 rubber stud
85 rubber block (rubber tread)
86 glass reflector

1 folding bicycle
2 hinge (*also:* locking lever)
3 adjustable handlebar (handlebars)
4 adjustable saddle
5 stabilizers
6 motor-assisted bicycle
7 air-cooled two-stroke engine
8 telescopic forks
9 tubular frame
10 fuel tank (petrol tank, *Am.* gasoline tank)
11 semi-rise handlebars
12 two-speed gear-change (gearshift)
13 high-back polo saddle
14 swinging-arm rear fork
15 upswept exhaust
16 heat shield
17 drive chain
18 crash bar (roll bar)
19 speedometer (*coll.* speedo)
20 battery-powered moped, an electrically-powered vehicle
21 swivel saddle
22 battery compartment
23 wire basket
24 touring moped (moped)
25 pedal crank (pedal drive, starter pedal)
26 single-cylinder two-stroke engine
27 spark-plug cap
28 fuel tank (petrol tank, *Am.* gasoline tank)
29 moped headlamp (front lamp)
30-35 handlebar fittings
30 twist grip throttle control (throttle twist grip)
31 twist grip (gear-change, gearshift)
32 clutch lever
33 hand brake lever
34 speedometer (*coll.* speedo)
35 rear-view mirror (mirror)
36 front wheel drum brake (drum brake)
37 Bowden cables (brake cables)
38 stop and tail light unit
39 light motorcycle with kickstarter
40 housing for instruments with speedometer and electronic rev counter (revolution counter)
41 telescopic shock absorber
42 twin seat
43 kickstarter
44 pillion footrest, a footrest
45 handlebar (handlebars)
46 chain guard
47 motor scooter (scooter)
48 removable side panel
49 tubular frame
50 metal fairings
51 prop stand (stand)
52 foot brake
53 horn (hooter)
54 hook for handbag or briefcase
55 foot gear-change control (foot gearshift control)
56 high-riser; *sim.:* Chopper
57 high-rise handlebar (handlebars)
58 imitation motorcycle fork
59 banana saddle
60 chrome bracket

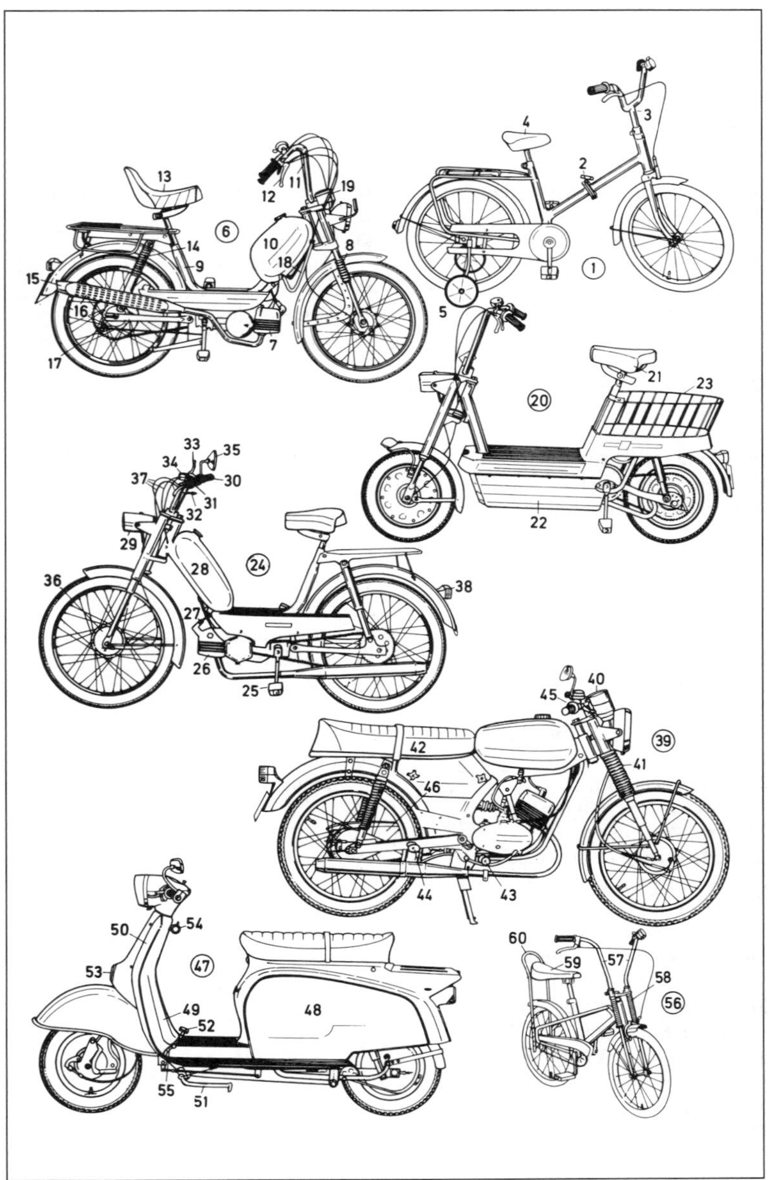
1
2
3
4
5
6
7
8
9
10
11
12
13
14
15
16
17
18
19
20
21
22
23
24
25
26
27
28
29
30
31
32
33
34
35
36
37
38
39
40
41
42
43
44
45
46
47
48
49
50
51
52
53
54
55
56
57
58
59
60

189 Motorcycle

1 lightweight motorcycle (light motorcycle) [50 cc]
2 fuel tank (petrol tank, *Am.* gasoline tank)
3 air-cooled single-cylinder four-stroke engine (with overhead camshaft)
4 carburettor (*Am.* carburetor)
5 intake pipe
6 five-speed gearbox
7 swinging-arm rear fork
8 number plate (*Am.* license plate)
9 stop and tail light (rear light)
10 headlight (headlamp)
11 front drum brake
12 brake cable (brake line), a Bowden cable
13 rear drum brake
14 racing-style twin seat
15 upswept exhaust
16 scrambling motorcycle (cross-country motorcycle) [125 cc], a light motorcycle
17 lightweight cradle frame
18 number disc (disk)
19 solo seat
20 cooling ribs
21 motorcycle stand
22 motorcycle chain
23 telescopic shock absorber
24 spokes
25 rim (wheel rim)
26 motorcycle tyre (*Am.* tire)
27 tyre (*Am.* tire) tread
28 gear-change lever (gearshift lever)
29 twist grip throttle control (throttle twist grip)
30 rear-view mirror (mirror)
31-58 heavy (heavyweight, large-capacity) motorcycles
31 heavyweight motorcycle with water-cooled engine
32 front disc (disk) brake
33 disc (disk) brake calliper (caliper)
34 floating axle
35 water cooler
36 fuel tank (petrol tank, *Am.* gasoline tank)
37 indicator (indicator light, turn indicator light)
38 kickstarter
39 water-cooled engine
40 speedometer
41 rev counter (revolution counter)
42 rear indicator (indicator light)
43 heavy (heavyweight, high-performance) machine with fairing [1000 cc]
44 integrated streamlining, an integrated fairing
45 indicator (indicator light, turn indicator light)
46 anti-mist windscreen (*Am.* windshield)
47 horizontally-opposed twin engine with cardan transmission
48 light alloy wheel
49 four-cylinder machine [400 cc]
50 air-cooled four-cylinder four-stroke engine
51 four-pipe megaphone exhaust pipe
52 electric starter button
53 sidecar machine
54 sidecar body
55 sidecar crash bar
56 sidelight (*Am.* sidemarker lamp)
57 sidecar wheel
58 sidecar windscreen (*Am.* windshield)

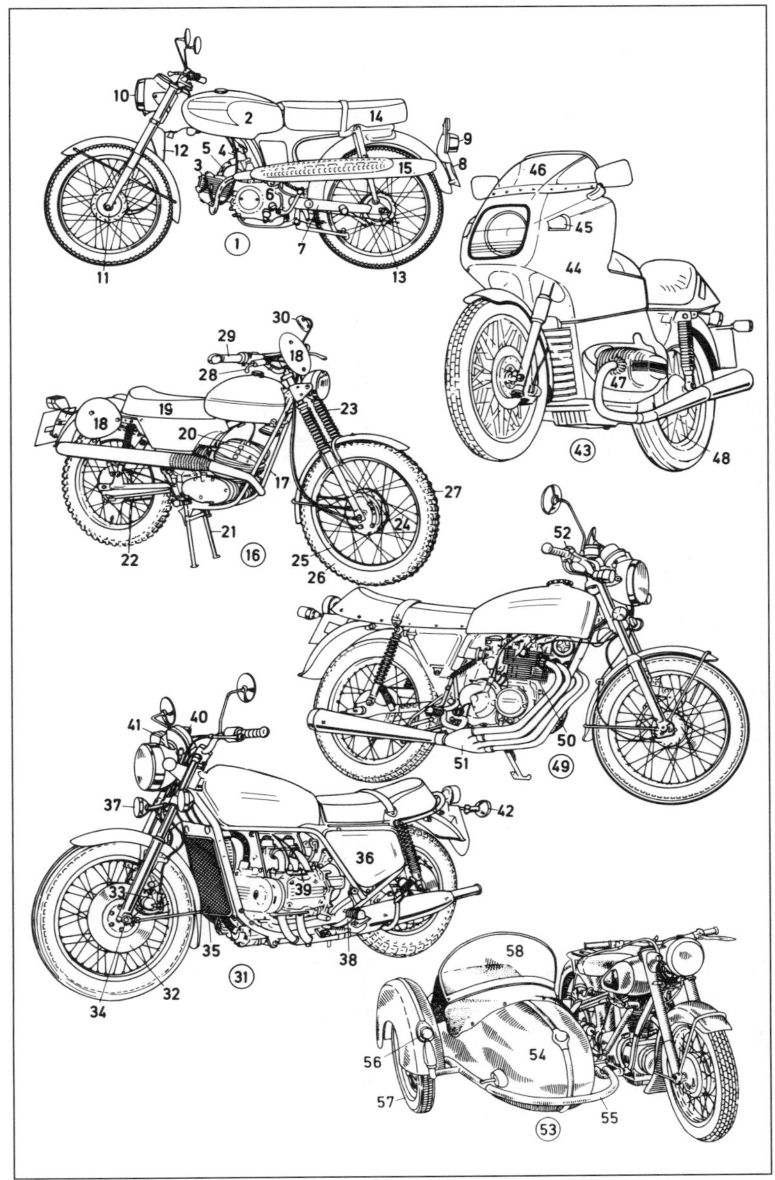

1
2
3
4
5
6
7
8
9
10
11
12
13
14
15
16
17
18
19
20
21
22
23
24
25
26
27
28
29
30
31
32
33
34
35
36
37
38
39
40
41
42
43
44
45
46
47
48
49
50
51
52
53
54
55
56
57
58

1 eight-cylinder V (vee) fuel-injection spark-ignition engine (Otto-cycle engine)
2 cross-section of spark-ignition engine (Otto-cycle internal combustion engine)
3 sectional view of five-cylinder in-line diesel engine
4 cross-section of diesel engine
5 two-rotor Wankel engine (rotary engine)
6 single-cylinder two-stroke internal combustion engine
7 fan
8 fan clutch for viscous drive
9 ignition distributor (distributor) with vacuum timing control
10 double roller chain
11 camshaft bearing
12 air-bleed duct
13 oil pipe for camshaft lubrication
14 camshaft, an overhead camshaft
15 venturi throat
16 intake silencer (absorption silencer, *Am.* absorption muffler)
17 fuel pressure regulator
18 inlet manifold
19 cylinder crankcase
20 flywheel
21 connecting rod (piston rod)
22 cover of crankshaft bearing
23 crankshaft
24 oil bleeder screw (oil drain plug)
25 roller chain of oil pump drive
26 vibration damper
27 distributor shaft for the ignition distributor (distributor)
28 oil filler neck
29 diaphragm spring
30 control linkage
31 fuel supply pipe (*Am.* fuel line)
32 fuel injector (injection nozzle)
33 rocker arm
34 rocker arm mounting
35 spark plug (sparking plug) with suppressor
36 exhaust manifold
37 piston with piston rings and oil scraper ring
38 engine mounting
39 dog flange (dog)
40 crankcase
41 oil sump (sump)
42 oil pump
43 oil filter
44 starter motor (starting motor)
45 cylinder head
46 exhaust valve
47 dipstick
48 cylinder head cover
49 double bushing chain
50 warm-up regulator
51 tapered needle for idling adjustment
52 fuel pressure pipe (fuel pressure line)
53 fuel leak line (drip fuel line)
54 injection nozzle (spray nozzle)
55 heater plug
56 thrust washer
57 intermediate gear shaft for the injection pump drive
58 injection timer unit
59 vacuum pump (low-pressure regulator)
60 cam for vacuum pump
61 water pump (coolant pump)
62 cooling water thermostat
63 thermo time switch
64 fuel hand pump
65 injection pump
66 glow plug
67 oil pressure limiting valve
68 rotor
69 seal
70 torque converter
71 single-plate clutch
72 multi-speed gearing (multi-step gearing)
73 port liners in the exhaust manifold for emission control
74 disc (disk) brake
75 differential gear (differential)
76 generator
77 foot gear-change control (foot gearshift control)
78 dry multi-plate clutch
79 cross-draught (*Am.* cross-draft) carburettor (*Am.* carburetor)
80 cooling ribs
81 V-belt (fan belt)

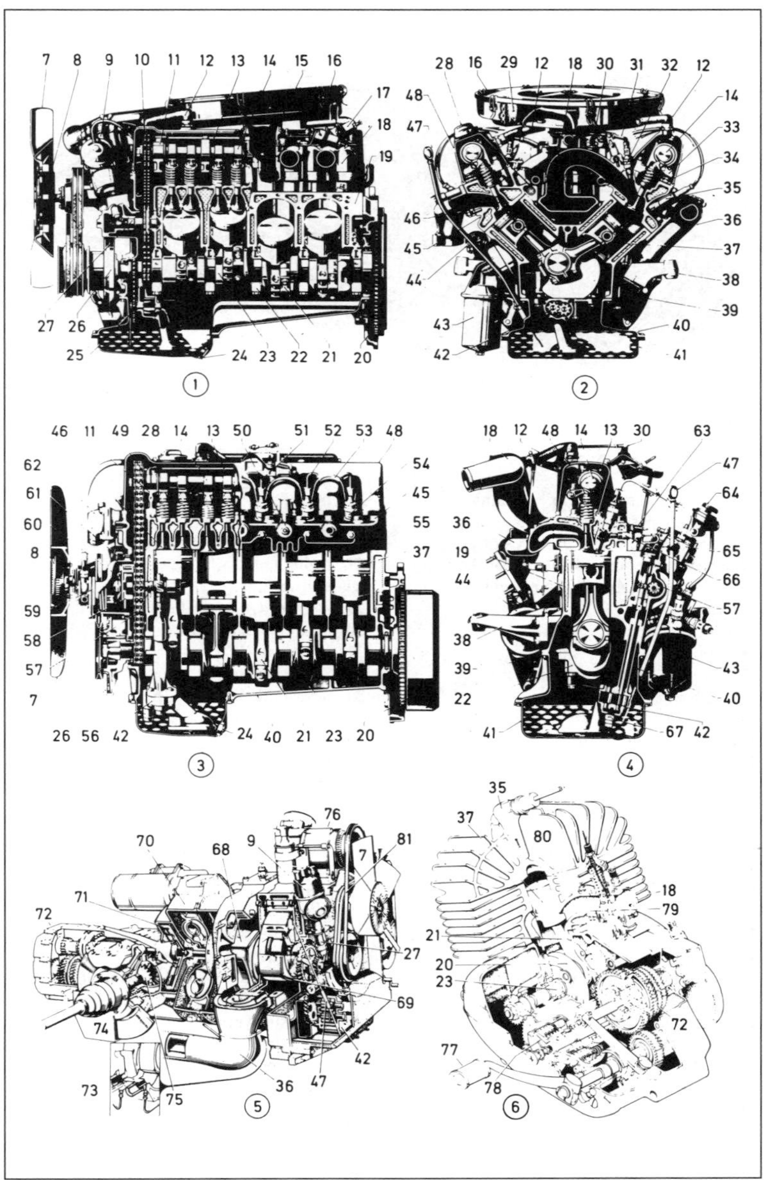
7 8 9 10 11 12 13 14 15 16
17
18
19
27 26
25
24 23 22 21 20
1
28 16 29 12 18 30 31 32 12
48
47
14
33
34
35
46
36
45
37
44
38
39
43
40
42
41
2
46 11 49 28 14 13 50 51 52 53 48
62
54
61
45
60
55
8
37
59
58
57
7
26 56 42
24 40 21 23 20
3
18 12 48 14 13 30 63
47
64
36
19
65
44
66
57
38
43
39
22
40
41
67 42
4
76
70
68 9
81
7
71
72
27
69
74
42
36 47
73
75
5
35
37
80
18
79
21
20
23
72
77
78
6

191 Motor Car (*Am.* Automobile) I

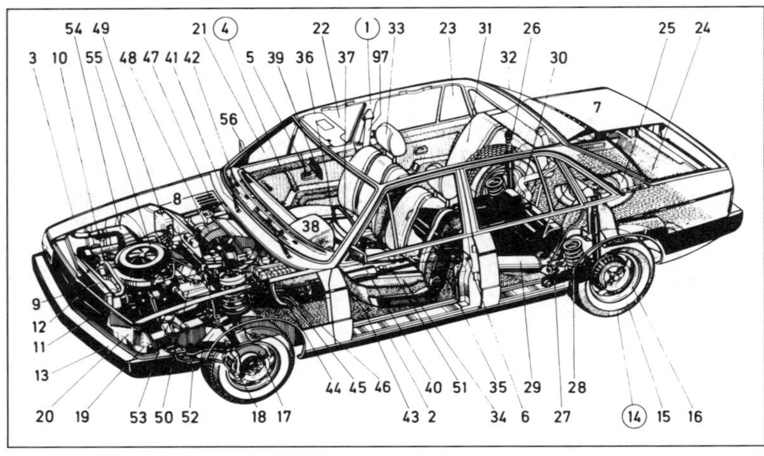

1-56 motor car (car, *Am.* automobile, auto), a passenger vehicle
1 monocoque body (unitary body)
2 chassis, the understructure of the body
3 front wing (*Am.* front fender)
4 car door
5 door handle
6 door lock
7 boot lid (*Am.* trunk lid)
8 bonnet (*Am.* hood)
9 radiator
10 cooling water pipe
11 radiator grill
12 badging
13 rubber-covered front bumper (*Am.* front fender)
14 car wheel, a disc (disk) wheel
15 car tyre (*Am.* automobile tire)
16 rim (wheel rim)
17-18 disc (disk) brake
17 brake disc (disk) (braking disc)
18 calliper (caliper)
19 front indicator light (front turn indicator light)
20 headlight (headlamp) with main beam (high beam), dipped beam (low beam), sidelight (side lamp, *Am.* sidemarker lamp)
21 windscreen (*Am.* windshield), a panoramic windscreen
22 crank-operated car window
23 quarter light (quarter vent)
24 boot (*Am.* trunk)
25 spare wheel
26 damper (shock absorber)
27 trailing arm
28 coil spring
29 silencer (*Am.* muffler)
30 automatic ventilation system
31 rear seats
32 rear window
33 adjustable headrest (head restraint)
34 driver's seat, a reclining seat
35 reclining backrest
36 passenger seat
37 steering wheel
38 centre (*Am.* center) console containing speedometer (*coll.* speedo), revolution counter (rev counter, tachometer), clock, fuel gauge (*Am.* gage), water temperature gauge, oil temperature gauge
39 inside rear-view mirror
40 left-hand wing mirror
41 windscreen wiper (*Am.* windshield wiper)
42 defroster vents
43 carpeting
44 clutch pedal (*coll.* clutch)
45 brake pedal (*coll.* brake)
46 accelerator pedal (*coll.* accelerator)
47 inlet vent
48 blower fan
49 brake fluid reservoir

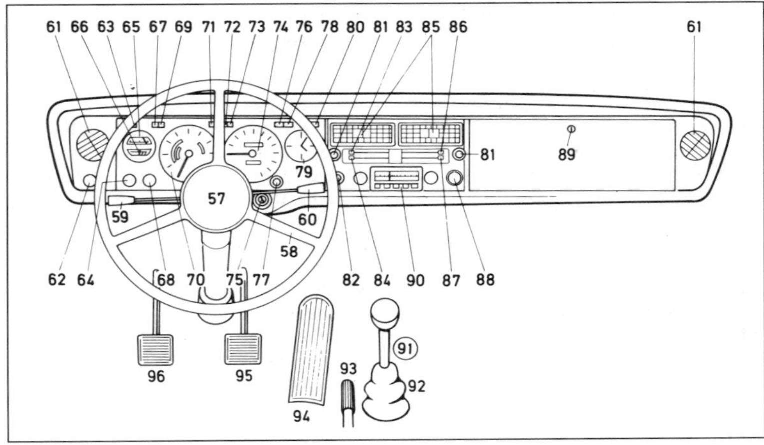

50 battery
51 exhaust pipe
52 front running gear with front wheel drive
53 engine mounting
54 intake silencer (*Am.* intake muffler)
55 air filter (air cleaner)
56 right-hand wing mirror
57-90 dashboard (fascia panel)
57 controlled-collapse steering column
58 steering wheel spoke
59 indicator and dimming switch
60 wiper/washer switch and horn
61 side window blower
62 sidelight, headlight, and parking light switch
63 fog lamp warning light
64 fog headlamp and rear lamp switch
65 fuel gauge (*Am.* gage)
66 water temperature gauge (*Am.* gage)
67 warning light for rear fog lamp
68 hazard flasher switch
69 main beam warning light
70 electric rev counter (revolution counter)
71 fuel warning light
72 warning light for the hand brake and dual-circuit brake system
73 oil pressure warning light
74 speedometer (*coll.* speedo) with trip mileage recorder
75 starter and steering lock
76 warning lights for turn indicators and hazard flashers
77 switch for the courtesy light and reset button for the trip mileage recorder
78 ammeter
79 electric clock
80 warning light for heated rear window
81 switch for the leg space ventilation
82 rear window heating switch
83 ventilation switch
84 temperature regulator
85 fresh-air inlet and control
86 fresh-air regulator
87 warm-air regulator
88 cigar lighter
89 glove compartment (glove box) lock
90 car radio
91 gear lever (gearshift lever), a floor-type gear-change
92 leather gaiter
93 hand brake lever
94 accelerator pedal
95 brake pedal
96 clutch pedal
97 seat belt (safety belt)

1-15 carburettor (*Am.* carburetor), a down-draught (*Am.* down-draft) carburettor
1 idling jet (slow-running jet)
2 idling air jet (idle air bleed)
3 air correction jet
4 compensating airstream
5 main airstream
6 choke flap
7 plunger
8 venturi
9 throttle valve (butterfly valve)
10 emulsion tube
11 idle mixture adjustment screw
12 main jet
13 fuel inlet (*Am.* gasoline inlet) (inlet manifold)
14 float chamber
15 float
16-27 pressure-feed lubricating system
16 oil pump
17 oil sump
18 sump filter
19 oil cooler
20 oil filter
21 main oil gallery (drilled gallery)
22 crankshaft drilling (crankshaft tributary, crankshaft bleed)
23 crankshaft bearing (main bearing)
24 camshaft bearing
25 connecting-rod bearing
26 gudgeon pin (piston pin)
27 bleed
28-47 four-speed synchromesh gearbox
28 clutch pedal
29 crankshaft
30 drive shaft (propeller shaft)
31 starting gear ring
32 sliding sleeve for 3rd and 4th gear
33 synchronizing cone
34 helical gear wheel for 3rd gear
35 sliding sleeve for 1st and 2nd gear
36 helical gear wheel for 1st gear
37 lay shaft
38 speedometer drive
39 helical gear wheel for speedometer drive
40 main shaft
41 gearshift rods
42 selector fork for 1st and 2nd gear
43 helical gear wheel for 2nd gear
44 selector head with reverse gear
45 selector fork for 3rd and 4th gear
46 gear lever (gearshift lever)
47 gear-change pattern (gearshift pattern, shift pattern)
48-55 disc (disk) brake [assembly]
48 brake disc (disk) (braking disc)
49 calliper (caliper), a fixed calliper with friction pads
50 servo cylinder (servo unit)
51 brake shoes
52 brake lining
53 outlet to brake line
54 wheel cylinder
55 return spring
56-59 steering gear (worm-and-nut steering gear)
56 steering column
57 worm gear sector
58 steering drop arm
59 worm
60-64 water-controlled heater
60 air intake
61 heat exchanger (heater box)
62 blower fan
63 flap valve
64 defroster vent
65-71 live axle (rigid axle)
65 propeller shaft
66 trailing arm
67 rubber bush
68 coil spring
69 damper (shock absorber)
70 Panhard rod
71 stabilizer bar
72-84 MacPherson strut unit
72 body-fixing plate
73 upper bearing
74 suspension spring
75 piston rod
76 suspension damper
77 rim (wheel rim)
78 stub axle
79 steering arm
80 track-rod ball-joint
81 trailing link arm
82 bump rubber (rubber bonding)
83 lower bearing
84 lower suspension arm

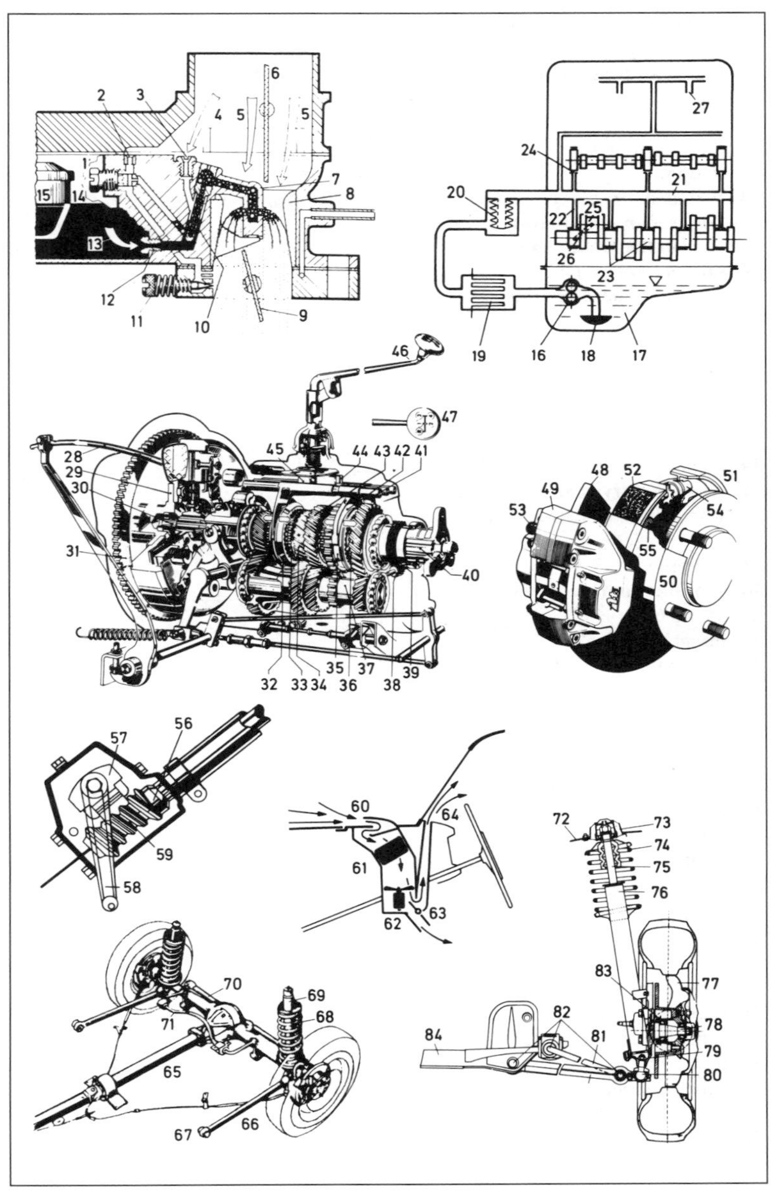
1
2
3
4
5
5
6
7
8
9
10
11
12
13
14
15
16
17
18
19
20
21
22
23
24
25
26
27
28
29
30
31
32
33
34
35
36
37
38
39
40
41
42
43
44
45
46
47
48
49
50
51
52
53
54
55
56
57
58
59
60
61
62
63
64
65
66
67
68
69
70
71
72
73
74
75
76
77
78
79
80
81
82
83
84

193 Motor Car (*Am.* Automobile) III

1-36 car models (*Am.* automobile models)
1 **four-door touring saloon** (*Am.* four-door sedan) in the upper-middle range
2 driver's door
3 rear door
4-10 **four-door saloon** (*Am.* four-door sedan) **and four-door hatchback in the middle range**
4 **saloon** (*Am.* sedan)
5 headrests (head restraints)
6 front seat
7 rear seat (back seat)
8 **fastback saloon** (*Am.* fastback sedan) (stubback saloon, *Am.* stubback sedan)
9 tailgate
10 fastback (stubback)
11 **cross-country vehicle** with all-wheel drive (four-wheel drive)
12 spare wheel
13 roll bar
14 **cabriolet sports coupé** (cabriolet sports car)
15 integral seat
16 automatic hood (*Am.* top) (power-operated hood, *Am.* top)
17 **estate car** (estate, shooting brake, *Am.* station wagon)
18 boot space (luggage compartment)
19 **small three-door car**
20 back (tailgate)
21 sill
22 folding back seat
23 boot (luggage compartment, *Am.* trunk)
24 (sliding) sunroof (steel sliding sunroof)
25 **three-door hatchback**
26 **roadster** (sports cabrio, sports cabriolet), a two-seater
27 hard top
28 **sports coupé,** a two-plus-two (two-seater with occasional seats)
29 fastback
30 occasional seat
31 low-profile tyre (*Am.* tire) (wide wheel)
32 **gran turismo car** (GT car)
33 integral bumper (*Am.* integral fender)
34 rear spoiler
35 back
36 front spoiler

1
2
3
4
5
6
7
8
9
10
11
12
13
14
15
16
17
18
9
19
20
21
22
23
24
25
26
27
28
29
30
31
32
33
34
35
36

1 light cross-country lorry (light truck, pick-up truck) with all-wheel drive (four-wheel drive)
2 cab (driver's cab)
3 loading platform (body)
4 spare tyre (*Am.* spare tire), a cross-country tyre
5 light lorry (light truck, pick-up truck)
6 platform truck
7 medium van
8 sliding side door [for loading and unloading]
9 minibus
10 folding top (sliding roof)
11 rear door
12 hinged side door
13 luggage compartment
14 passenger seat
15 cab (driver's cab)
16 air inlet
17 motor coach (coach, bus)
18 luggage locker
19 hand luggage (suitcase, case)
20 heavy lorry (heavy truck, heavy motor truck)
21 tractive unit (tractor, towing vehicle)
22 trailer (drawbar trailer)
23 swop platform (body)
24 three-way tipper (three-way dump truck)
25 tipping body (dump body)
26 hydraulic cylinder
27 supported container platform
28 articulated vehicle, a vehicle tanker
29 tractive unit (tractor, towing vehicle)
30-33 semi-trailer (skeletal)
30 tank
31 turntable
32 undercarriage
33 spare wheel
34 midi bus [for short-route town operations]
35 outward-opening doors
36 double-deck bus (double-decker bus)
37 lower deck (lower saloon)
38 upper deck (upper saloon)
39 boarding platform
40 trolley bus
41 current collector
42 trolley (trolley shoe)
43 overhead wires
44 trolley bus trailer
45 pneumatically sprung rubber connection

1
2
3
4
5
6
7
8
9
10
11
12
13
14
15
16
17
18
18
18
19
20
21
22
23
24
25
26
27
28
29
30
31
32
33
34
35
36
37
38
39
40
41
42
43
44
45

195 Garage (*Am.* Shop)

1-55 agent's garage (distributor's garage, *Am.* specialty shop)

1-23 diagnostic test bay

1 computer
2 main computer socket
3 computer harness (computer cable)
4 switch from automatic to manual
5 slot for program cards
6 printout machine (printer)
7 condition report (data printout)
8 master selector (hand control)
9 light read-out [green: OK; red: not OK]
10 rack for program cards
11 mains button
12 switch for fast readout
13 firing sequence insert
14 shelf for used cards
15 cable boom
16 oil temperature sensor
17 test equipment for wheel and steering alignment
18 right-hand optic plate
19 actuating transistors
20 projector switch
21 check light for wheel alignment, a row of photocells
22 check light for steering alignment, a row of photocells
23 power screwdriver
24 beam setter
25 hydraulic lift
26 adjustable arm of hydraulic lift
27 hydraulic lift pad
28 excavation
29 pressure gauge (*Am.* gage)
30 grease gun
31 storage box for small parts
32 wall chart [of spare parts]

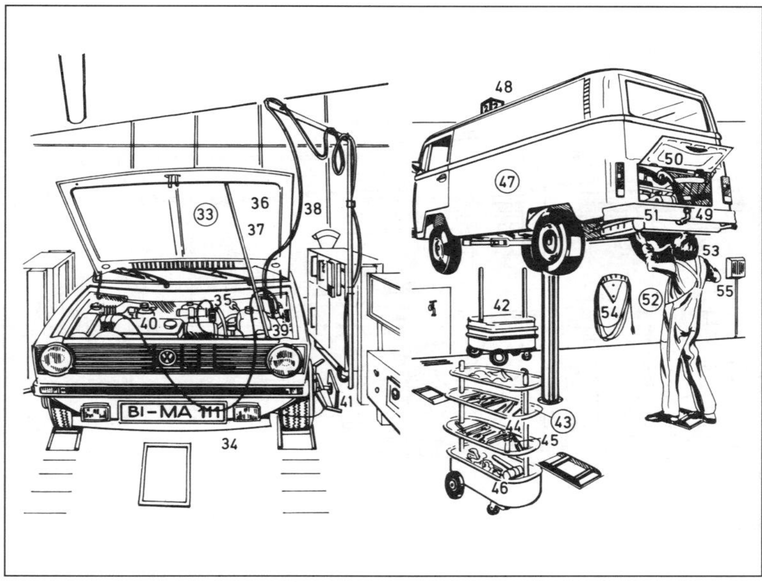

33 automatic computer test
34 motor car (car, *Am.* automobile, auto), a passenger vehicle
35 engine compartment
36 bonnet (*Am.* hood)
37 bonnet support (*Am.* hood support)
38 computer harness (computer cable)
39 main computer socket
40 oil temperature sensor
41 wheel mirror for visual wheel and steering alignment
42 tool trolley
43 tools
44 impact wrench
45 torque wrench
46 body hammer (roughing-out hammer)
47 vehicle under repair, a minibus
48 car location number
49 rear engine
50 tailgate
51 exhaust system
52 exhaust repair
53 motor car mechanic (motor vehicle mechanic, *Am.* automotive mechanic)
54 air hose
55 intercom

1-29 service station (petrol station, filling station, *Am.* gasoline station, gas station), a self-service station
1 petrol (*Am.* gasoline) pump (blending pump) for unleaded (lead-free) premium grade and regular petrol (*Am.* gasoline) (*sim.*: for derv)
2 hose (petrol pump, *Am.* gasoline pump, hose)
3 nozzle
4 cash readout
5 volume readout
6 price display
7 indicator light
8 driver using self-service petrol pump (*Am.* gasoline pump)
9 fire extinguisher
10 paper-towel dispenser
11 paper towel
12 litter receptacle
13 two-stroke blending pump
14 meter
15 engine oil
16 oil can
17 tyre pressure gauge (*Am.* tire pressure gage)
18 air hose
19 static air tank
20 pressure gauge (*Am.* gage) (manometer)
21 air filler neck
22 repair bay (repair shop)
23 car-wash hose, a hose (hosepipe)
24 accessory shop
25 petrol can (*Am.* gasoline can)
26 rain cape
27 car tyres (*Am.* automobile tires)
28 car accessories
29 cash desk (console)

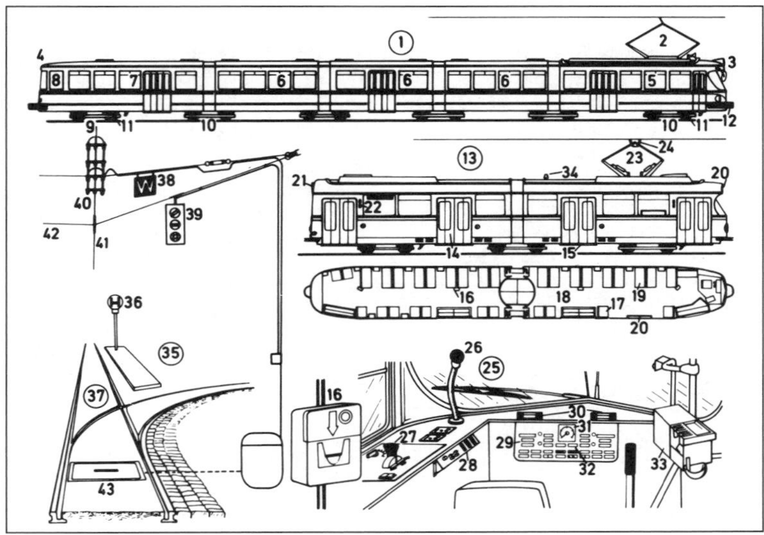

1 twelve-axle articulated railcar for interurban rail service
2 current collector
3 head of the railcar
4 rear of the railcar
5 carriage A containing the motor
6 carriage B (*also:* carriages C and D)
7 carriage E containing the motor
8 rear controller
9 driving bogie
10 carrying bogie
11 wheel guard
12 bumper (*Am.* fender)
13 six-axle articulated railcar ('Mannheim' type) for tram (*Am.* streetcar, trolley) and urban rail services
14 entrance and exit door, a double folding door
15 step
16 ticket-cancelling machine
17 single seat
18 standing room portion
19 double seat
20 route (number) and destination sign
21 route sign (number sign)
22 indicator (indicator light)
23 pantograph (current collector)
24 carbon or aluminium (*Am.* aluminum) alloy trolley shoes
25 driver's position
26 microphone
27 controller
28 radio equipment (radio communication set)
29 dashboard
30 dashboard lighting
31 speedometer
32 buttons controlling doors, windscreen wipers, internal and external lighting
33 ticket counter with change machine
34 radio antenna
35 tram stop (*Am.* streetcar stop, trolley stop)
36 tram stop sign (*Am.* streetcar stop sign, trolley stop sign)
37 electric change points
38 points signal (switch signal)
39 points change indicator
40 trolley wire contact point
41 trolley wire (overhead contact wire)
42 overhead cross wire
43 electric (*also:* electrohydraulic, electromechanical) points mechanism

198 Cross-section of a Street

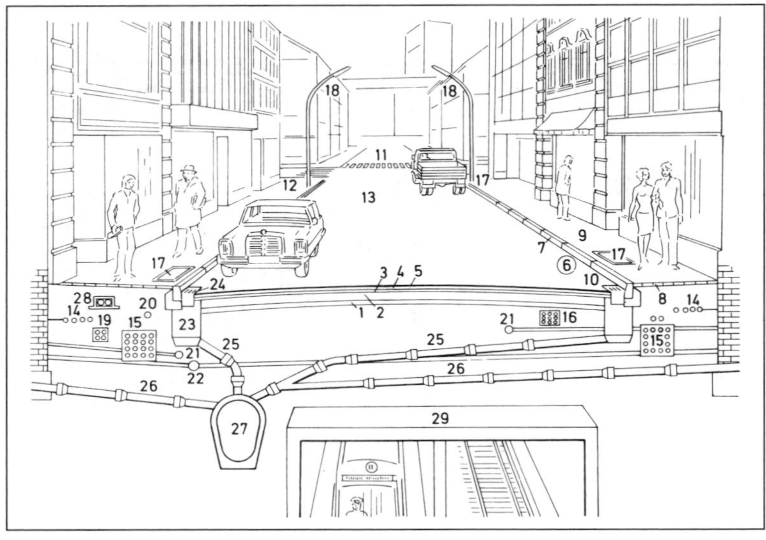

1-5 road layers
1 anti-frost layer
2 bituminous sub-base course
3 base course
4 binder course
5 bituminous surface
6 kerb (curb)
7 kerbstone (curbstone)
8 paving (pavement)
9 pavement (*Am.* sidewalk, walkway)
10 gutter
11 pedestrian crossing (zebra crossing, *Am.* crosswalk)
12 street corner
13 street
14 electricity cables
15 telephone cables
16 telephone cable pipeline
17 cable manhole with cover (with manhole cover)
18 lamp post with lamp
19 electricity cables for technical installations
20 subscribers' (*Am.* customers') telephone lines
21 gas main
22 water main
23 drain
24 drain cover
25 drain pipe
26 waste pipe
27 combined sewer
28 district heating main
29 underground tunnel

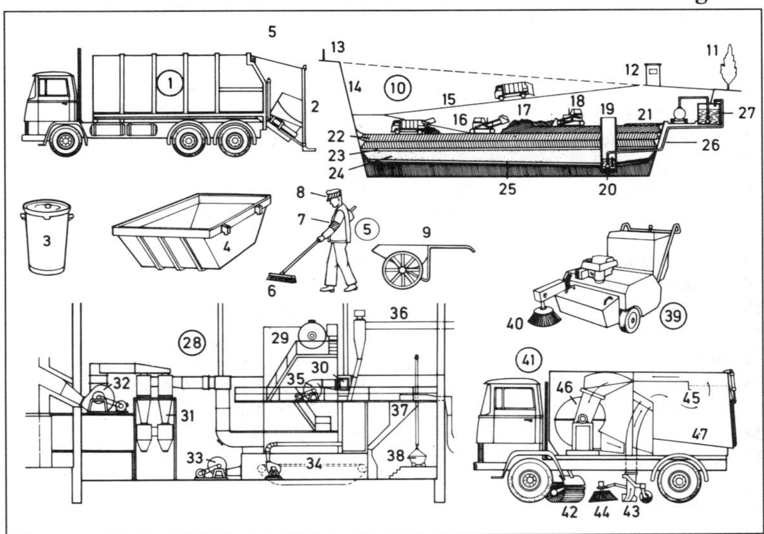

1 refuse collection vehicle (*Am.* garbage truck)
2 dustbin-tipping device (*Am.* garbage can dumping device), a dust-free emptying system
3 dustbin (*Am.* garbage can, trash can)
4 refuse container (*Am.* garbage container)
5 road sweeper (*Am.* street sweeper)
6 broom
7 fluorescent armband
8 cap with fluorescent band
9 road sweeper's (*Am.* street sweeper's) barrow
10 controlled tip (*Am.* sanitary landfill, sanitary fill)
11 screen
12 weigh office
13 fence
14 embankment
15 access ramp
16 bulldozer
17 refuse (*Am.* garbage)
18 bulldozer for dumping and compacting
19 pump shaft
20 waste water pump
21 porous cover
22 compacted and decomposed refuse
23 gravel filter layer
24 morainic filter layer
25 drainage layer
26 drain pipe
27 water tank
28 refuse (*Am.* garbage) incineration unit
29 furnace
30 oil-firing system
31 separation plant
32 extraction fan
33 low-pressure fan for the grate
34 continuous feed grate
35 fan for the oil-firing system
36 conveyor for separately incinerated material
37 coal feed conveyor
38 truck for carrying fuller's earth
39 mechanical sweeper
40 circular broom
41 road-sweeping lorry (street-cleaning lorry, street cleaner)
42 cylinder broom
43 suction port
44 feeder broom
45 air flow
46 fan
47 dust collector

200 Road Construction I (Road Building, Road Making)

1-54 road-building machinery
1 shovel (power shovel, excavator)
2 machine housing
3 caterpillar mounting (*Am.* caterpillar tractor)
4 digging bucket arm (dipper stick)
5 digging bucket (bucket)
6 digging bucket (bucket) teeth
7 tipper (dump truck), a heavy lorry (*Am.* truck)
8 tipping body (*Am.* dump body)
9 reinforcing rib
10 extended front
11 cab (driver's cab)
12 bulk material
13 concrete scraper, an aggregate scraper
14 skip hoist
15 mixing drum (mixer drum), a mixing machine
16 caterpillar hauling scraper
17 scraper blade
18 levelling (*Am.* leveling) blade (smoothing blade)
19 grader (motor grader)
20 scarifier (ripper, road ripper, rooter)
21 grader levelling (*Am.* leveling) blade (grader ploughshare, *Am.* plowshare)
22 blade-slewing gear (slew turntable)
23 light railway (narrow-gauge, *Am.* narrow-gage, railway)
24 light railway (narrow-gauge, *Am.* narrow-gage) diesel locomotive
25 trailer wagon (wagon truck, skip)
26 tamper (rammer) *heavier:* frog
27 guide rods
28 bulldozer
29 bulldozer blade
30 pushing frame
31 road-metal spreading machine (macadam spreader, stone spreader)
32 tamping beam
33 sole-plate
34 side stop
35 side of storage bin
36 three-wheeled roller, a road roller
37 roller
38 all-weather roof
39 mobile diesel-powered air compressor
40 oxygen cylinder
41 self-propelled gritter
42 spreading flap
43 surface finisher
44 side stop
45 bin
46 tar-spraying machine (bituminous distributor) with tar and bitumen heater
47 tar storage tank
48 fully automatic asphalt drying and mixing plant
49 bucket elevator (elevating conveyor)
50 asphalt-mixing drum (asphalt mixer drum)
51 filler hoist
52 filler opening
53 binder injector
54 mixed asphalt outlet
55 typical cross-section of a bituminous road
56 grass verge
57 crossfall
58 asphalt surface (bituminous layer, bituminous coating)
59 base (base course)
60 hardcore sub-base course (Telford base) or gravel sub-base course, an anti-frost layer
61 sub-drainage
62 perforated cement pipe
63 drainage ditch
64 soil covering

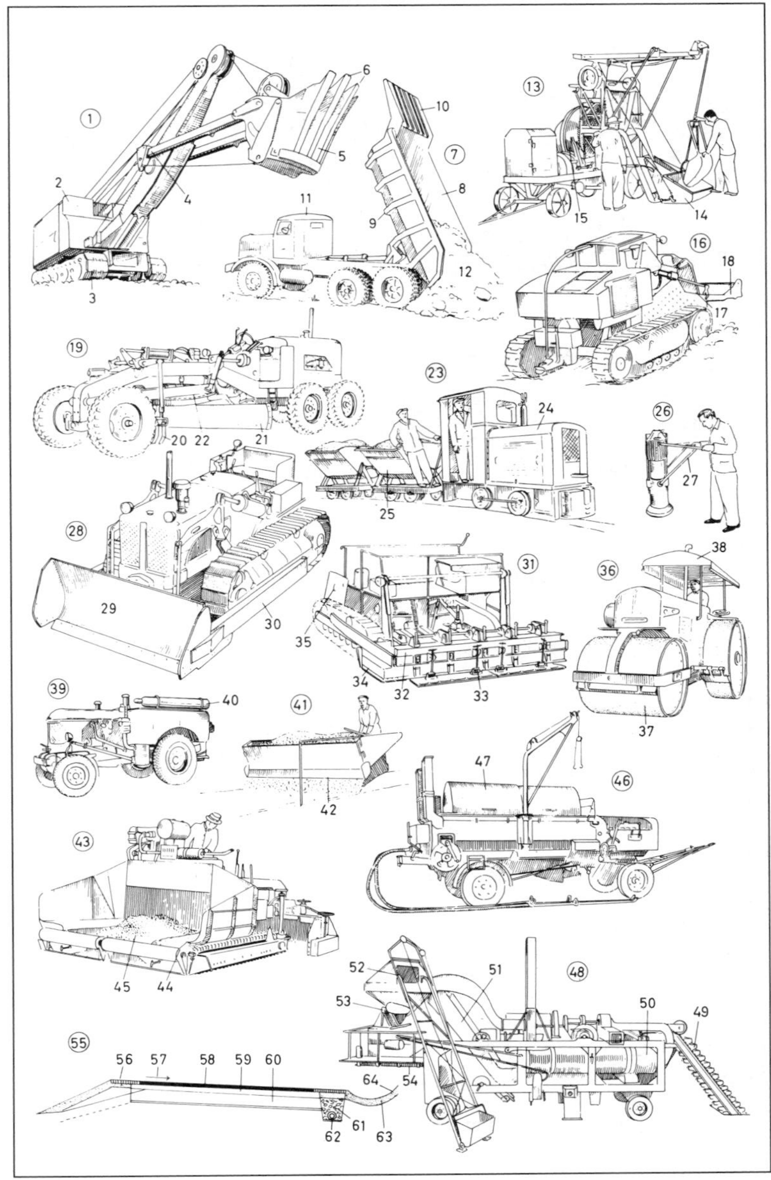
1
2
3
4
5
6
7
8
9
10
11
12
13
14
15
16
17
18
19
20
21
22
23
24
25
26
27
28
29
30
31
32
33
34
35
36
37
38
39
40
41
42
43
44
45
46
47
48
49
50
51
52
53
54
55
56
57
58
59
60
61
62
63
64

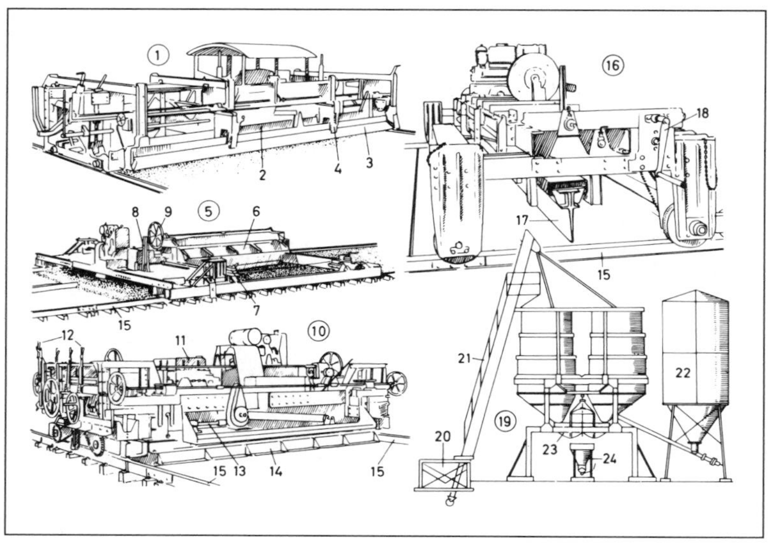

1-24 concrete road construction (highway construction)

1 subgrade grader
2 tamping beam (consolidating beam)
3 levelling (*Am.* leveling) beam
4 roller guides for the levelling (*Am.* leveling) beam
5 concrete spreader
6 concrete spreader box
7 cable guides
8 control levers
9 handwheel for emptying the boxes
10 concrete-vibrating compactor
11 gearing (gears)
12 control levers (operating levers)
13 axle drive shaft to vibrators (tampers) of vibrating beam
14 screeding board (screeding beam)
15 road form
16 joint cutter
17 joint-cutting blade
18 crank for propelling machine
19 concrete-mixing plant, a stationary central mixing plant, an automatic batching and mixing plant
20 collecting bin
21 bucket elevator
22 cement store
23 concrete mixer
24 concrete pump hopper

Railway Line (*Am.* Railroad Track) I 202

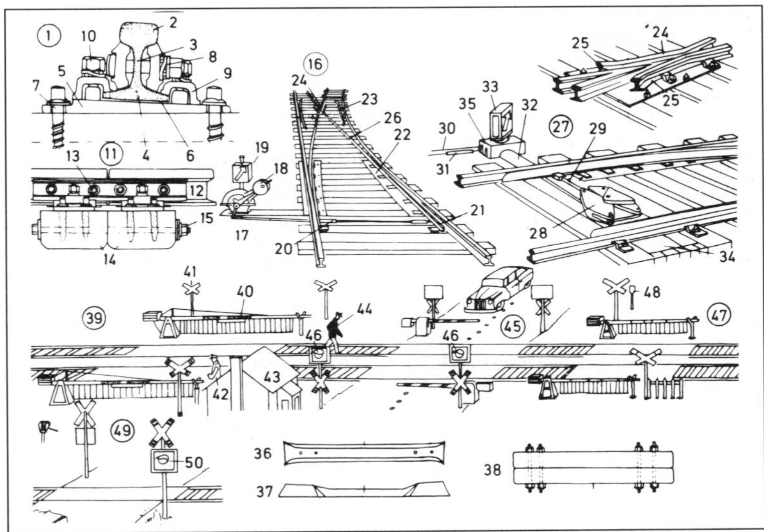

1-38 line (track)
1 rail
2 rail head
3 web (rail web)
4 rail foot (rail bottom)
5 sole-plate (base plate)
6 cushion
7 coach screw (coach bolt)
8 lock washers (spring washers)
9 rail clip (clip)
10 T-head bolt
11 rail joint (joint)
12 fishplate
13 fishbolt
14 coupled sleeper (*Am.* coupled tie, coupled crosstie)
15 coupling bolt
16 manually-operated points (manually-operated switch)
17 switch stand
18 weight
19 points signal (switch signal, points signal lamp, switch signal lamp)
20 pull rod
21 switch blade (switch tongue)
22 slide chair
23 check rail (guard rail)
24 frog
25 wing rail
26 closure rail
27 remote-controlled points (remote-controlled switch)
28 point lock (switch lock)
29 stretcher bar
30 point wire
31 turnbuckle
32 channel
33 electrically illuminated points signal (switch signal)
34 trough
35 points motor with protective casing
36 steel sleeper (*Am.* steel tie, steel crosstie)
37 concrete sleeper (*Am.* concrete tie, concrete crosstie)
38 coupled sleeper (*Am.* coupled tie, coupled crosstie)
39-50 level crossings (*Am.* grade crossings)
39 protected level crossing (*Am.* protected grade crossing)
40 barrier (gate)
41 warning cross (*Am.* crossbuck)
42 crossing keeper (*Am.* gateman)
43 crossing keeper's box (*Am.* gateman's box)
44 linesman (*Am.* trackwalker)
45 half-barrier crossing
46 warning light
47 intercom-controlled crossing; *sim.:* telephone-controlled crossing
48 intercom system
49 unprotected level crossing (*Am.* unprotected grade crossing)
50 warning light

203 Railway Line (*Am.* Railroad Track) II (Signalling Equipment)

1-6 stop signals (main signals)
1 stop signal (main signal), a semaphore signal in 'stop' position
2 signal arm (semaphore arm)
3 electric stop signal (colour light, *Am.* color light, signal) at 'stop'
4 signal position: 'proceed at low speed'
5 signal position: 'proceed'
6 substitute signal
7-24 distant signals
7 semaphore signal at 'be prepared to stop at next signal'
8 supplementary semaphore arm
9 colour light (*Am.* color light) distant signal at 'be prepared to stop at next signal'
10 signal position: 'be prepared to proceed at low speed'
11 signal position: 'proceed main signal ahead'
12 semaphore signal with indicator plate showing a reduction in braking distance of more than 5%
13 triangle (triangle sign)
14 colour light (*Am.* color light) distant signal with indicator light for showing reduced braking distance
15 supplementary white light
16 distant signal indicating 'be prepared to stop at next signal' (yellow light)
17 second distant signal (distant signal with supplementary light, without indicator plate)
18 distant signal with speed indicator
19 distant speed indicator
20 distant signal with route indicator
21 route indicator
22 distant signal without supplementary arm in position: 'be prepared to stop at next signal'
23 distant signal without supplementary arm in 'be prepared to proceed' position
24 distant signal identification plate
25-44 supplementary signals
25 stop board for indicating the stopping point at a control point
26-29 approach signs
26 approach sign 100 m from distant signal
27 approach sign 175 m from distant signal
28 approach sign 250 m from distant signal
29 approach sign at a distance of 5% less than the braking distance on the section
30 chequered sign indicating stop signals (main signals) not positioned immediately to the right of or over the line (track)
31, 32 stop boards to indicate the stopping point of the front of the train
33 stop board indicating 'be prepared to stop'
34, 35 snow plough (*Am.* snowplow) signs
34 'raise snow plough (*Am.* snowplow)' sign
35 'lower snow plough (*Am.* snowplow)' sign
36-44 speed restriction signs
36-38 speed restriction sign [maximum speed $3 \times 10 = 30$ kph]
36 sign for day running
37 speed code number
38 illuminated sign for night running
39 commencement of temporary speed restriction
40 termination of temporary speed restriction
41 speed restriction sign for a section with a permanent speed restriction [maximum speed $5 \times 10 = 50$ kph]
42 commencement of permanent speed restriction
43 speed restriction warning sign [only on main lines]
44 speed restriction sign [only on main lines]
45-52 point signals (switch signals)
45-48 single points (single switches)
45 route straight ahead (main line)
46 [right] branch
47 [left] branch
48 branch [seen from the frog]
49-52 double crossover
49 route straight ahead from left to right
50 route straight ahead from right to left
51 turnout to the left from the left
52 turnout to the right from the right
53 **manually-operated signal box** (*Am.* signal tower, switch tower)
54 lever mechanism
55 points lever (switch lever) [blue], a lock lever
56 signal lever [red]
57 catch
58 route lever
59 block instruments
60 block section panel
61 **electrically-operated signal box** (*Am.* signal tower, switch tower)
62 points (switch) and signal knobs
63 lock indicator panel
64 track and signal indicator
65 **track diagram control layout**
66 track diagram control panel (domino panel)
67 push buttons
68 routes
69 intercom system

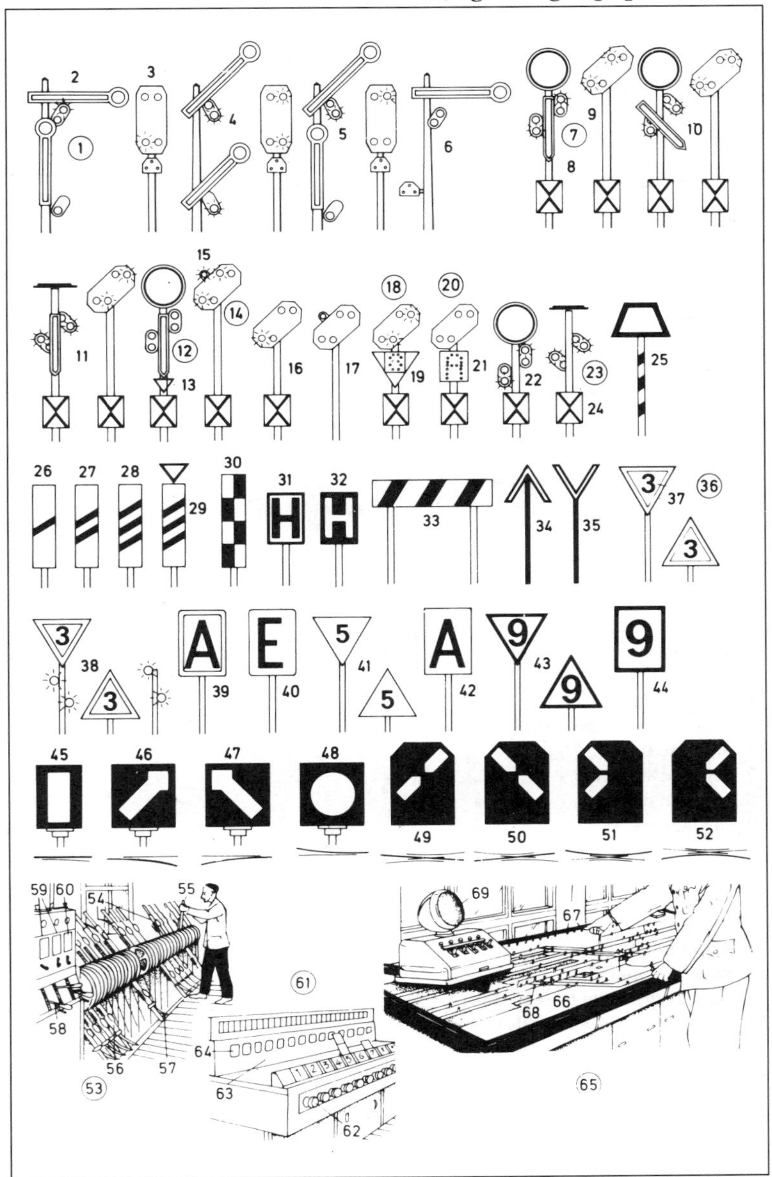
1
2
3
4
5
6
7
8
9
10
11
12
13
14
15
16
17
18
19
20
21
22
23
24
25
26
27
28
29
30
31
32
33
34
35
36
37
38
39
40
41
42
43
44
45
46
47
48
49
50
51
52
53
54
55
56
57
58
59
60
61
62
63
64
65
66
67
68
69
H
H
3
3
3
3
A
E
5
5
A
9
9
9
1 2 3 4 5 6 7

1 parcels office
2 parcels
3 basket [with lock]
4 luggage counter
5 platform scale with dial
6 suitcase (case)
7 luggage sticker
8 luggage receipt
9 luggage clerk
10 poster (advertisement)
11 station post box (*Am.* station mail-box)
12 station guide
13 station restaurant
14 waiting room
15 map of the town (street map)
16 timetable (*Am.* schedule)
17 ticket machine
18 arrivals and departures board (timetable)
19 arrival timetable (*Am.* arrival schedule)
20 departure timetable (*Am.* departure schedule)

21 left luggage lockers
22 change machine
23 tunnel to the platforms
24 passengers
25 steps to the platforms
26 station bookstall (*Am.* station bookstand)
27 left luggage office (left luggage)
28 travel centre (*Am.* center); *also:* accommodation bureau
29 information office (*Am.* information bureau)
30 station clock
31 bank branch with foreign exchange counter
32 indicator board showing exchange rates
33 railway map (*Am.* railroad map)
34 ticket office
35 ticket counter
36 ticket
37 revolving tray
38 grill
39 ticket clerk (*Am.* ticket agent)
40 pane of glass (window)
41 pocket timetable (*Am.* pocket train schedule)
42 luggage rest
43 first aid station
44 Travellers' (*Am.* Travelers') Aid
45 railway (*Am.* railroad) information clerk
46 official timetable (official railway guide, *Am.* train schedule)

205 Station Platform

1 platform
2 steps to the platform
3 bridge
4 platform number
5 platform roofing
6 passengers
7-12 luggage
7 suitcase (case)
8 luggage label
9 hotel sticker
10 travelling (*Am.* traveling) bag
11 hat box
12 umbrella, a walking-stick umbrella
13 offices
14 platform
15 crossing
16 news trolley
17 news vendor (*Am.* news dealer)
18 reading matter for the journey
19 edge of the platform
20 railway policeman (*Am.* railroad policeman)
21 destination board
22 destination indicator
23 departure time indicator
24 delay indicator
25 suburban train, a railcar
26 special compartment
27 platform loudspeaker
28 station sign
29 electric trolley (electric truck)
30 loading foreman
31 porter (*Am.* redcap)
32 barrow
33 drinking fountain
34 electric Eurocity express; *also:* IC express (Intercity express)
35 electric locomotive, an express locomotive
36 collector bow (sliding bow)
37 secretarial compartment
38 destination board
39 wheel tapper
40 wheel-tapping hammer
41 station foreman
42 signal

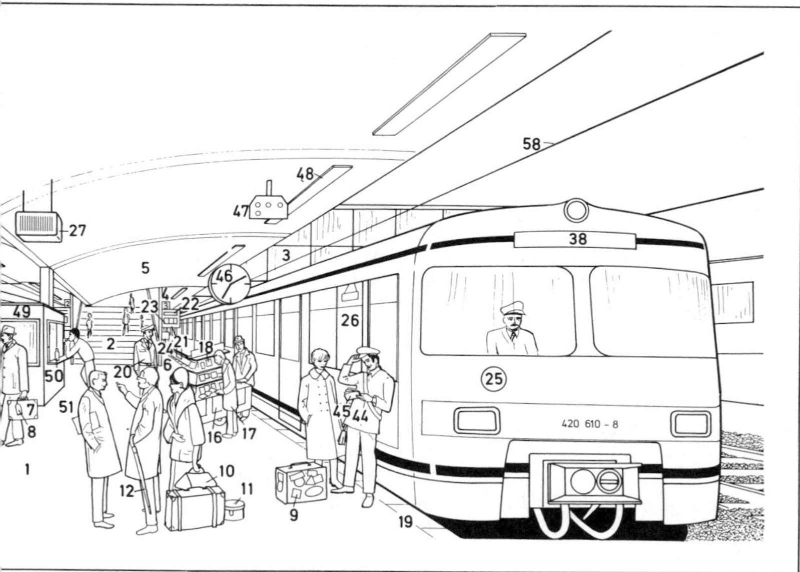

43 red cap
44 inspector
45 pocket timetable (*Am.* pocket train schedule)
46 platform clock
47 starting signal
48 platform lighting
49 refreshment kiosk
50 beer bottle
51 newspaper
52 parting kiss
53 embrace
54 platform seat
55 litter bin (*Am.* trash bin)
56 platform post box (*Am.* platform mailbox)
57 platform telephone
58 trolley wire (overhead contact wire)
59-61 track
59 rail
60 sleeper (*Am.* tie, crosstie)
61 ballast (bed)

206 Goods Station (Freight Depot)

1 ramp (vehicle ramp); *sim.:* livestock ramp
2 electric truck
3 trailer
4 part loads (*Am.* package freight, less-than-carload freight); *in general traffic:* general goods in general consignments (in mixed consignments)
5 crate
6 goods van (*Am.* freight car)
7 goods shed (*Am.* freight house)
8 loading strip
9 loading dock
10 bale of peat
11 bale of linen (of linen cloth)
12 fastening (cord)
13 wicker bottle (wickered bottle, demijohn)
14 trolley
15 goods lorry (*Am.* freight truck)
16 forklift truck (fork truck, forklift)
17 loading siding
18 bulky goods
19 small railway-owned (*Am.* railroad-owned) container
20 showman's caravan (*sim.* circus caravan)
21 flat wagon (*Am.* flat freight car)
22 loading gauge (*Am.* gage)
23 bale of straw
24 flat wagon (*Am.* flatcar) with side stakes
25 fleet of lorries (*Am.* trucks)
26-39 **goods shed** (*Am.* freight house)
26 goods office (forwarding office, *Am.* freight office)
27 part-load goods (*Am.* package freight)
28 forwarding agent (*Am.* freight agent, shipper)
29 loading foreman
30 consignment note (waybill)
31 weighing machine
32 pallet
33 porter
34 electric cart (electric truck)
35 trailer
36 loading supervisor
37 goods shed door (*Am.* freight house door)
38 rail (slide rail)
39 roller
40 weighbridge office
41 weighbridge
42 marshalling yard (*Am.* classification yard, switch yard)
43 shunting engine (shunting locomotive, shunter, *Am.* switch engine, switcher)
44 marshalling yard signal box (*Am.* classification yard switch tower)
45 yardmaster
46 hump
47 sorting siding (classification siding, classification track)
48 rail brake (retarder)
49 slipper brake (slipper)
50 storage siding (siding)
51 buffer (buffers, *Am.* bumper)
52 wagon load (*Am.* carload)·
53 warehouse
54 container station
55 gantry crane
56 lifting gear (hoisting gear)
57 container
58 container wagon (*Am.* container car)
59 semi-trailer

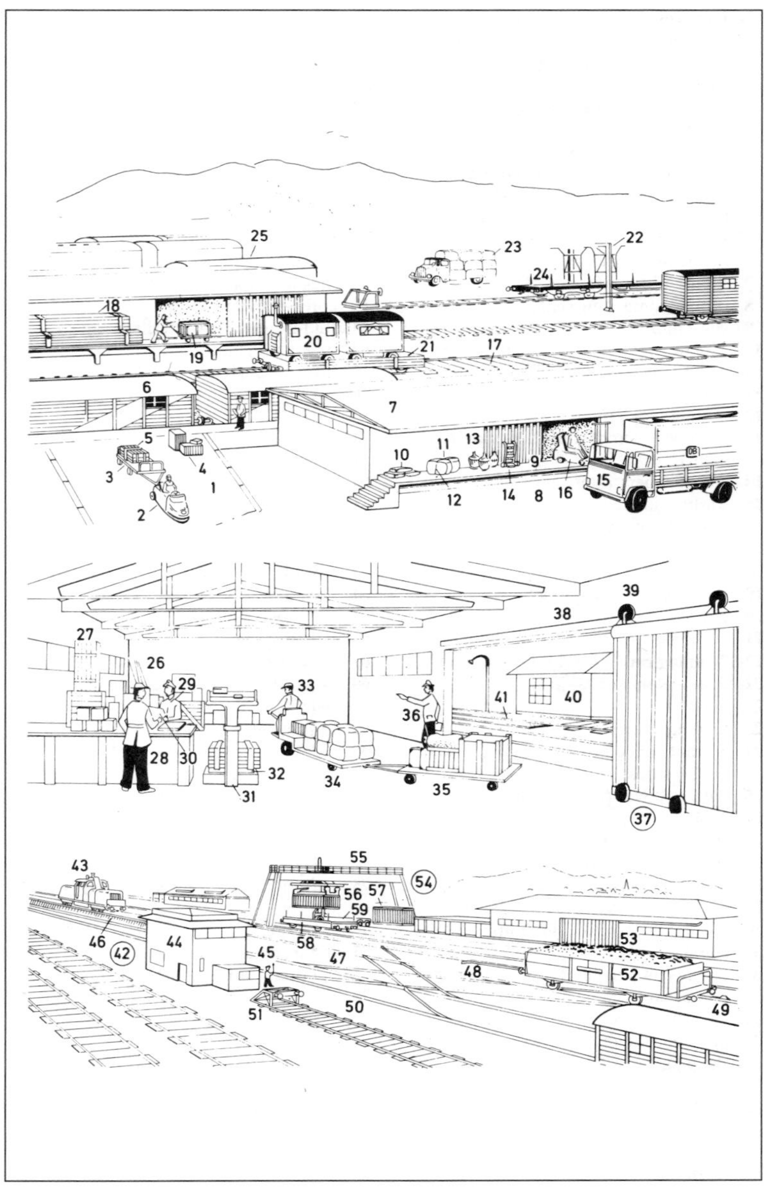
25
23
22
24
18
20
19
21
17
6
7
5
4
3
1
2
10
11
13
9
12
14
8
16
15
DB
39
38
27
26
29
33
41
40
36
28
30
32
31
34
35
37
43
55
54
56
57
59
58
46
42
44
45
47
48
53
52
51
50
49

207 Railway Vehicles (Rolling Stock) I

1-21 express train coach (express train carriage, express train car, corridor compartment coach), a passenger coach
1 side elevation (side view)
2 coach body
3 underframe (frame)
4 bogie (truck) with steel and rubber suspension and shock absorbers
5 battery containers (battery boxes)
6 steam and electric heat exchanger for the heating system
7 sliding window
8 rubber connecting seal
9 ventilator
10-21 plan
10 second-class section
11 corridor
12 folding seat (tip-up seat)
13 passenger compartment (compartment)
14 compartment door
15 washroom
16 toilet (lavatory, WC)
17 first-class section
18 swing door
19 sliding connecting door
20 door
21 vestibule
22-32 dining car (restaurant car, diner)
22-25 side elevation (side view)
22 door
23 loading door
24 current collector for supplying power during stops
25 battery boxes (battery containers)
26-32 plan
26 staff washroom
27 storage cupboard
28 washing-up area
29 kitchen
30 electric oven with eight hotplates
31 counter
32 dining compartment
33 dining car kitchen
34 chef (head cook)
35 kitchen cabinet
36 sleeping car (sleeper)
37 side elevation (side view)
38-42 plan
38 two-seat twin-berth compartment (two-seat two-berth compartment, *Am.* bedroom)
39 folding doors
40 washstand
41 office
42 toilet (lavatory, WC)
43 express train compartment
44 upholstered reclining seat
45 armrest
46 ashtray in the armrest
47 adjustable headrest
48 antimacassar
49 mirror
50 coat hook
51 luggage rack
52 compartment window
53 fold-away table (pull-down table)
54 heating regulator
55 litter receptacle
56 curtain
57 footrest
58 corner seat
59 open car
60 side elevation (side view)
61-72 plan
61 open carriage
62 row of single seats
63 row of double seats
64 reclining seat
65 seat upholstery
66 backrest
67 headrest
68 down-filled headrest cushion with nylon cover
69 armrest with ashtray
70 cloakroom
71 luggage compartment
72 toilet (lavatory, WC)
73 buffet car (quick-service buffet car), a self-service restaurant car
74 side elevation (side view)
75 current collector for supplying power during stops
76 plan
77 dining compartment
78-79 buffet (buffet compartment)
78 customer area
79 serving area
80 kitchen
81 staff compartment
82 staff toilet (staff lavatory, staff WC)
83 food compartments
84 plates
85 cutlery
86 till (cash register)

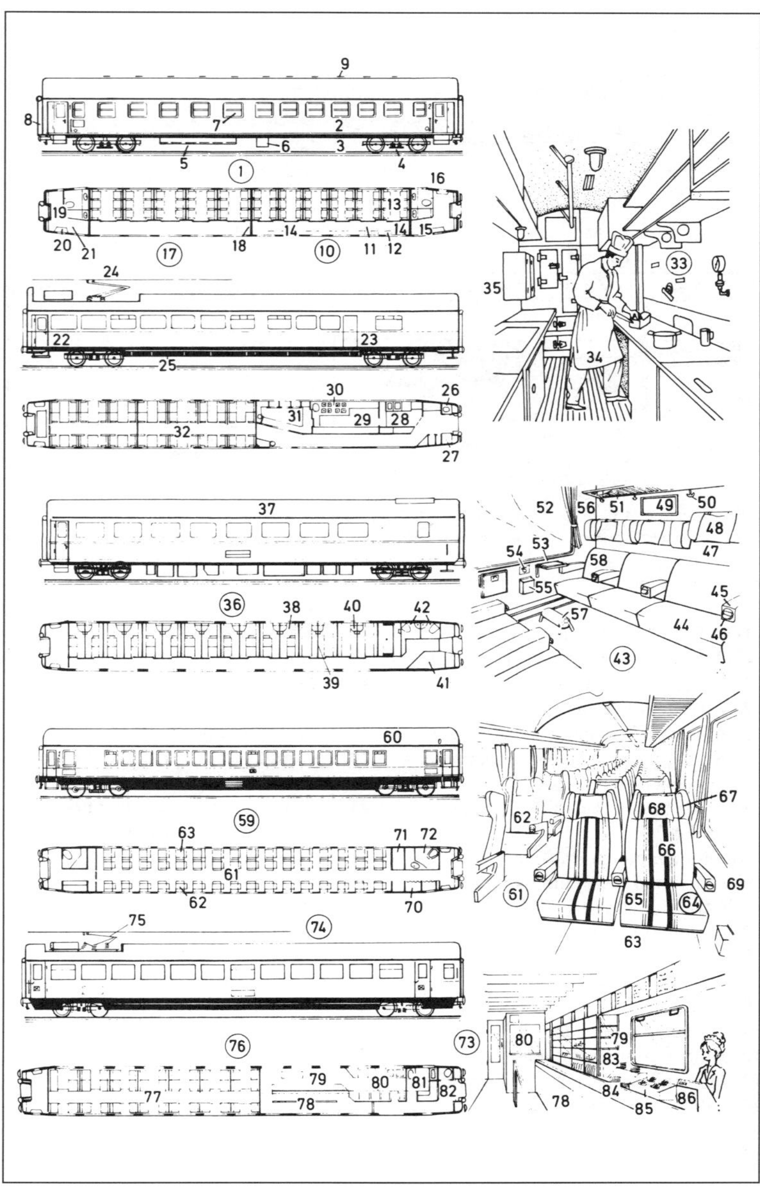
9
8
7
2
6
3
5
1
4
16
19
13
20
21
18
14
14
15
17
10
11
12
24
35
33
22
23
25
34
30
26
31
29
28
32
27
37
52
56
51
49
50
48
54
53
47
58
55
45
36
38
40
42
57
44
46
43
39
41
60
67
68
62
59
63
71
72
66
61
69
61
65
64
62
70
75
74
63
73
80
79
76
83
79
80
81
82
84
77
78
86
78
85

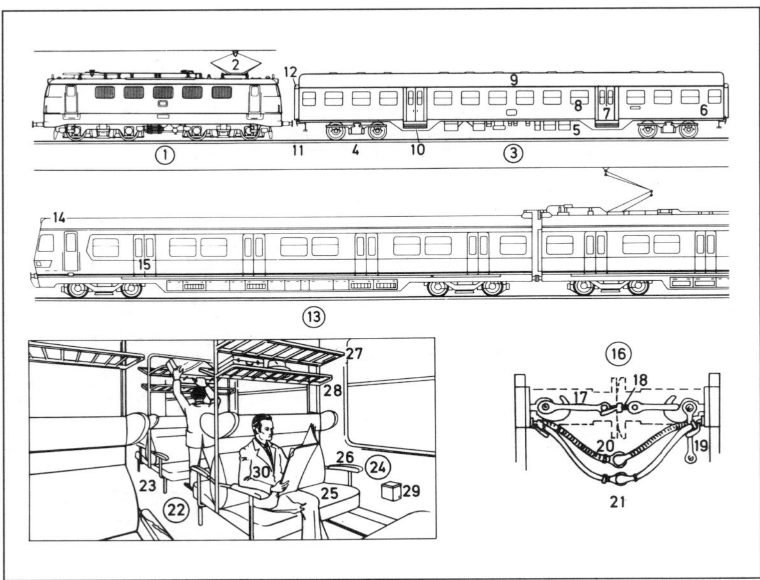

1-30 local train service

1-12 local train (short-distance train)

1 electric locomotive

2 current collector

3 four-axled coach (four-axled car) for short-distance routes, a passenger coach (passenger car)

4 bogie (truck) [with disc (disk) brakes]

5 underframe (frame)

6 coach body with metal panelling (*Am.* paneling)

7 double folding doors

8 compartment window

9 open carriage

10 entrance

11 connecting corridor

12 rubber connecting seal

13 light railcar, a short-distance railcar

14 cab (driver's cab, *Am.* engineer's cab)

15 carriage door

16 connecting hoses and coupling

17 coupling link

18 tensioning device (coupling screw with tensioning lever)

19 unlinked coupling

20 heating coupling hose (steam coupling hose)

21 coupling hose (connecting hose) for the compressed-air braking system

22 second-class section

23 central gangway

24 compartment

25 upholstered seat

26 armrest

27 luggage rack

28 hat and light luggage rack

29 ashtray

30 passenger

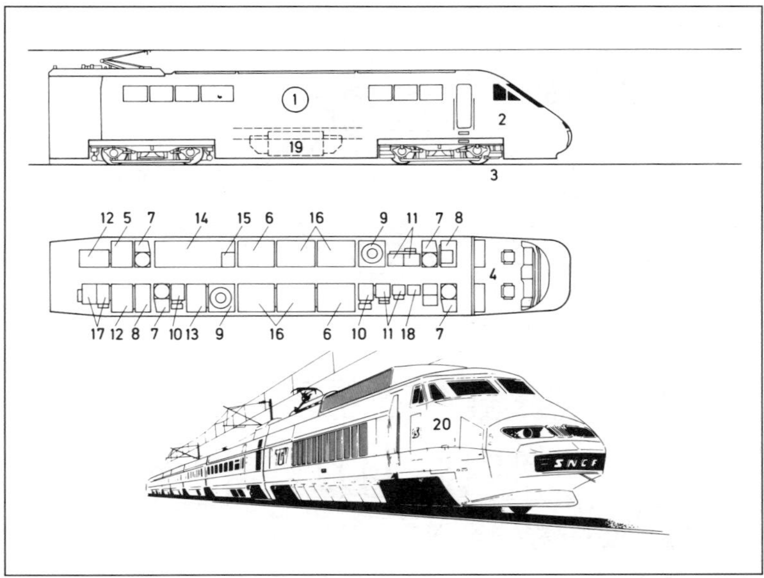

1-19 Intercity Express
1 German Federal Railway trainset
2 driving unit (power car)
3 driving bogie with traction motors
4 cab (driver's cab, *Am.* engineer's cab)
5 power supply (traction current filter)
6 contactors (converters, inductance)
7 traction motor blower
8 inductance protection (converter)
9 oil-cooling plant
10 converter for the auxiliaries
11 electronics
12 control current equipment
13 auxiliaries (switchgear)
14 pneumatic equipment
15 air-conditioning plant
16 main current converters
17 measuring equipment (diagnosis)
18 continuous automatic train-running control
19 transformer

20 **TGV** (Train à Grande Vitesse) of the Société Nationale des Chemins de Fer Français (SNCF)

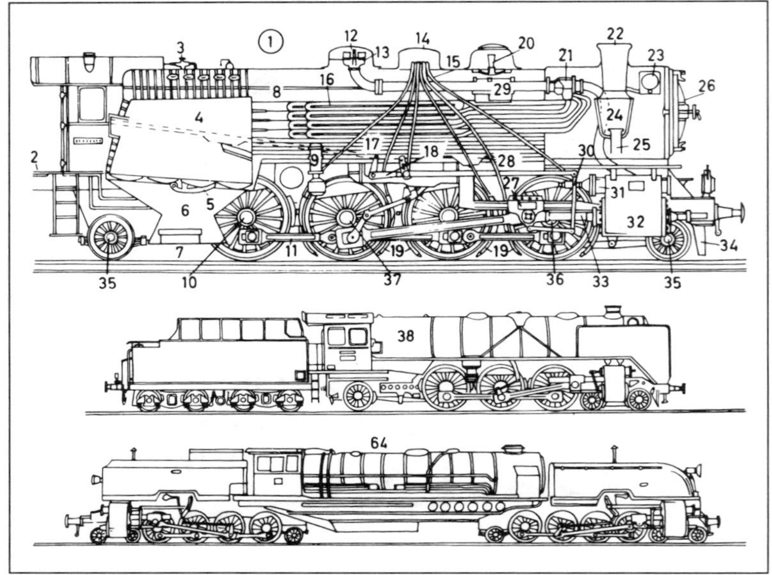

1-69 steam locomotives

2-37 locomotive boiler and driving gear

2 tender platform with coupling
3 safety valve for excess boiler pressure
4 firebox
5 drop grate
6 ashpan with damper doors
7 bottom door of the ashpan
8 smoke tubes (flue tubes)
9 feed pump
10 axle bearing
11 coupling rod
12 steam dome
13 regulator valve (regulator main valve)
14 sand dome
15 sand pipes (sand tubes)
16 boiler (boiler barrel)
17 fire tubes or steam tubes
18 reversing gear (steam reversing gear)
19 sand pipes
20 feed valve
21 steam collector
22 chimney (smokestack, smoke outlet and waste steam exhaust)
23 feedwater preheater (feedwater heater, economizer)
24 spark arrester
25 blast pipe
26 smokebox door
27 cross head
28 mud drum
29 top feedwater tray
30 combination lever
31 steam chest
32 cylinder
33 piston rod with stuffing box (packing box)
34 guard iron (rail guard, *Am.* pilot, cowcatcher)
35 carrying axle (running axle, dead axle)
36 coupled axle
37 driving axle
38 express locomotive with tender

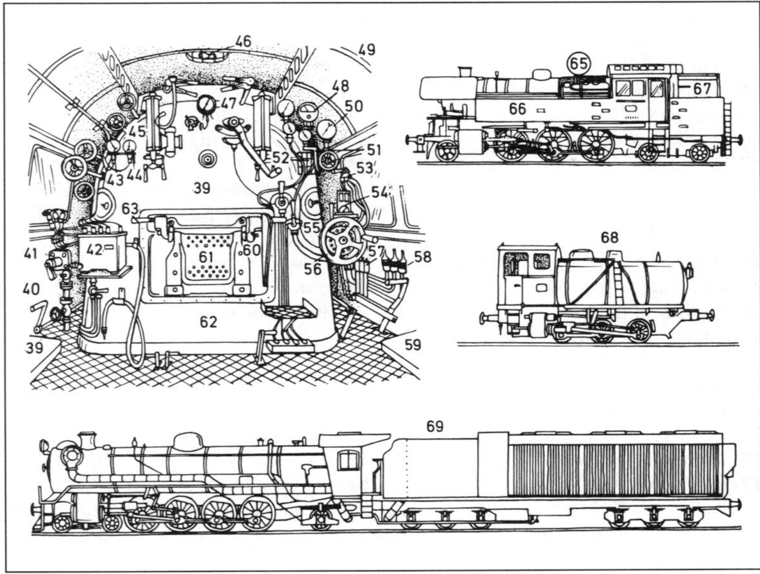

39-63 cab (driver's cab, *Am.* engineer's cab)
39 fireman's seat
40 drop grate lever
41 line steam injector
42 automatic lubricant pump (automatic lubricator)
43 preheater pressure gauge (*Am.* gage)
44 carriage heating pressure gauge (*Am.* gage)
45 water gauge (*Am.* gage)
46 light
47 boiler pressure gauge (*Am.* gage)
48 distant-reading temperature gauge (*Am.* gage)
49 cab (driver's cab, *Am.* engineer's cab)
50 brake pressure gauge (*Am.* gage)
51 whistle valve handle
52 driver's timetable (*Am.* engineer's schedule)
53 driver's brake valve (*Am.* engineer's brake valve)
54 speed recorder (tachograph)
55 sanding valve
56 reversing wheel
57 emergency brake valve
58 release valve
59 driver's seat (*Am.* engineer's seat)
60 firehole shield
61 firehole door
62 vertical boiler
63 firedoor handle handgrip
64 articulated locomotive (Garratt locomotive)
65 tank locomotive
66 water tank
67 fuel tender
68 steam storage locomotive (fireless locomotive)
69 condensing locomotive (locomotive with condensing tender)

211 Railway Vehicles (Rolling Stock) V

1 **electric locomotive**
2 current collector
3 main switch
4 high-tension transformer
5 roof cable
6 traction motor
7 inductive train control system
8 main air reservoir
9 whistle
10-18 **plan of locomotive**
10 transformer with tap changer
11 oil cooler with blower
12 oil-circulating pump
13 tap changer driving mechanism
14 air compressor
15 traction motor blower
16 terminal box
17 capacitors for auxiliary motors
18 commutator cover
19 **cab** (driver's cab, *Am.* engineer's cab)
20 controller handwheel
21 dead man's handle
22 driver's brake valve (*Am.* engineer's brake valve)
23 ancillary brake valve (auxiliary brake valve)
24 pressure gauge (*Am.* gage)
25 bypass switch for the dead man's handle
26 tractive effort indicator
27 train heating voltage indicator
28 contact wire voltage indicator (overhead wire voltage indicator)
29 high-tension voltage indicator
30 on/off switch for the current collector
31 main switch
32 sander switch (sander control)
33 anti-skid brake switch
34 visual display for the ancillary systems
35 speedometer
36 running step indicator
37 clock
38 controls for the inductive train control system
39 cab heating switch
40 whistle lever
41 **contact wire maintenance vehicle** (overhead wire maintenance vehicle), a diesel railcar
42 work platform (working platform)
43 ladder
44-54 **mechanical equipment of the contact wire maintenance vehicle**
44 air compressor
45 blower oil pump
46 generator
47 diesel engine
48 injection pump
49 silencer (*Am.* muffler)
50 change-speed gear
51 cardan shaft
52 wheel flange lubricator
53 reversing gear
54 torque converter bearing
55 **accumulator railcar** (battery railcar)
56 battery box (battery container)
57 cab (driver's cab, *Am.* engineer's cab)
58 second-class seating arrangement
59 toilet (lavatory, WC)
60 **fast electric multiple-unit train**
61 front railcar
62 driving trailer car

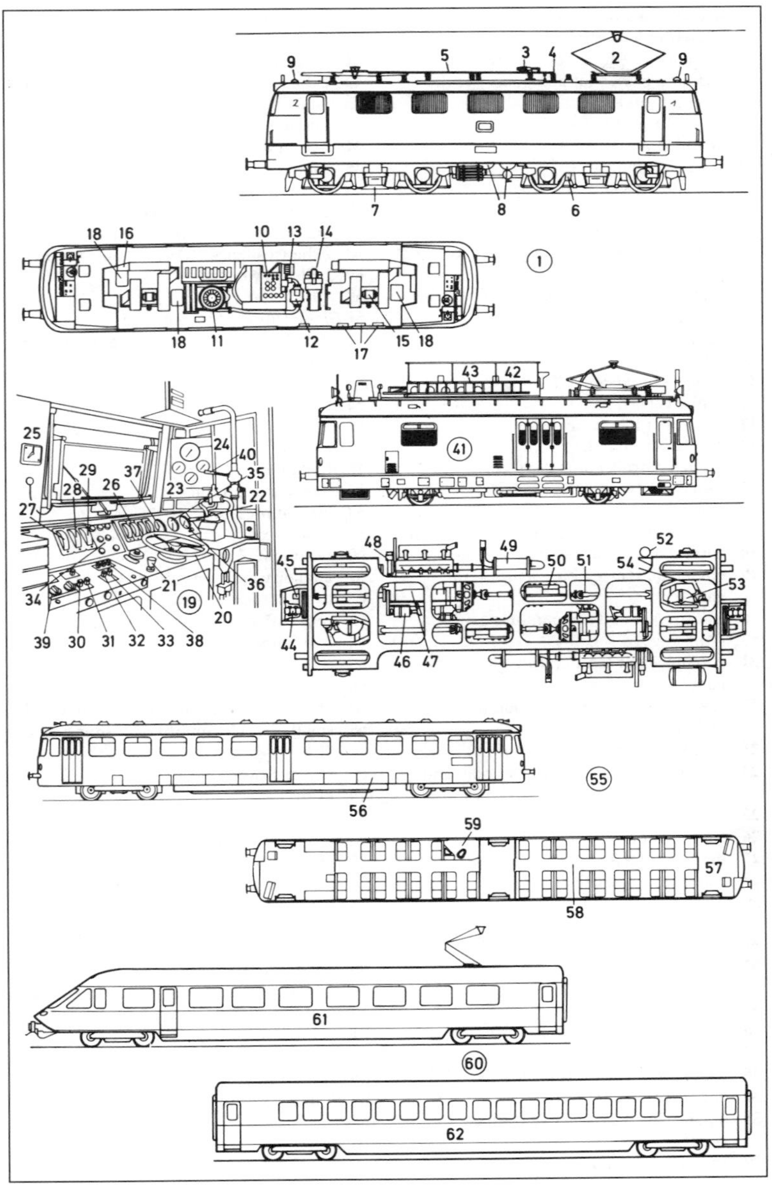
9
5
3
4
2
9
7
8
6
18
16
10
13
14
1
18
11
12
17
15
18
43
42
41
25
24
40
29
37
35
28
26
23
22
27
21
36
34
19
20
39
30
31
32
33
38
48
49
52
45
50
51
54
53
44
46
47
55
56
59
57
58
61
60
62

1-84 diesel locomotives
1 **diesel-hydraulic locomotive,** a mainline locomotive (diesel locomotive) for medium passenger and goods service (freight service)
2 bogie (truck)
3 wheel and axle set
4 main fuel tank
5 cab (driver's cab, *Am.* engineer's cab) of a diesel locomotive
6 main air pressure gauge (*Am.* gage)
7 brake cylinder pressure gauge (*Am.* gage)
8 main air reservoir pressure gauge (*Am.* gage)
9 speedometer
10 auxiliary brake
11 driver's brake valve (*Am.* engineer's brake valve)
12 controller handwheel
13 dead man's handle
14 inductive train control system
15 signal lights
16 clock
17 voltage meter for the train heating system
18 current meter for the train heating system
19 engine oil temperature gauge (*Am.* gage)
20 transmission oil temperature gauge (*Am.* gage)
21 cooling water temperature gauge (*Am.* gage)
22 revolution counter (rev counter, tachometer)
23 radio telephone
24 diesel-hydraulic locomotive [plan and elevation]
25 diesel engine
26 cooling unit
27 fluid transmission
28 wheel and axle drive
29 cardan shaft
30 starter motor
31 instrument panel
32 driver's control desk (*Am.* engineer's control desk)
33 hand brake
34 air compressor with electric motor
35 equipment locker
36 heat exchanger for transmission oil
37 engine room ventilator
38 magnet for the inductive train control system
39 train heating generator
40 casing of the train heating system transformer
41 preheater
42 exhaust silencer (*Am.* exhaust muffler)
43 auxiliary heat exchanger for the transmission oil
44 hydraulic brake
45 tool box
46 starter battery
47 **diesel-hydraulic locomotive** for light and medium shunting service
48 exhaust silencer (*Am.* exhaust muffler)
49 bell and whistle
50 yard radio

51-67 elevation of locomotive
51 diesel engine with supercharged turbine
52 fluid transmission
53 output gear box
54 radiator
55 heat exchanger for the engine lubricating oil
56 fuel tank
57 main air reservoir
58 air compressor
59 sand boxes
60 reserve fuel tank
61 auxiliary air reservoir
62 hydrostatic fan drive
63 seat with clothes compartment
64 hand brake wheel
65 cooling water
66 ballast
67 engine and transmission control wheel
68 **small diesel locomotive** for shunting service
69 exhaust casing
70 horn
71 main air reservoir
72 air compressor
73 eight-cylinder diesel engine
74 Voith transmission with reversing gear
75 heating oil tank (fuel oil tank)
76 sand box
77 cooling unit
78 header tank for the cooling water
79 oil bath air cleaner (oil bath air filter)
80 hand brake wheel
81 control wheel
82 coupling
83 cardan shaft
84 louvred shutter

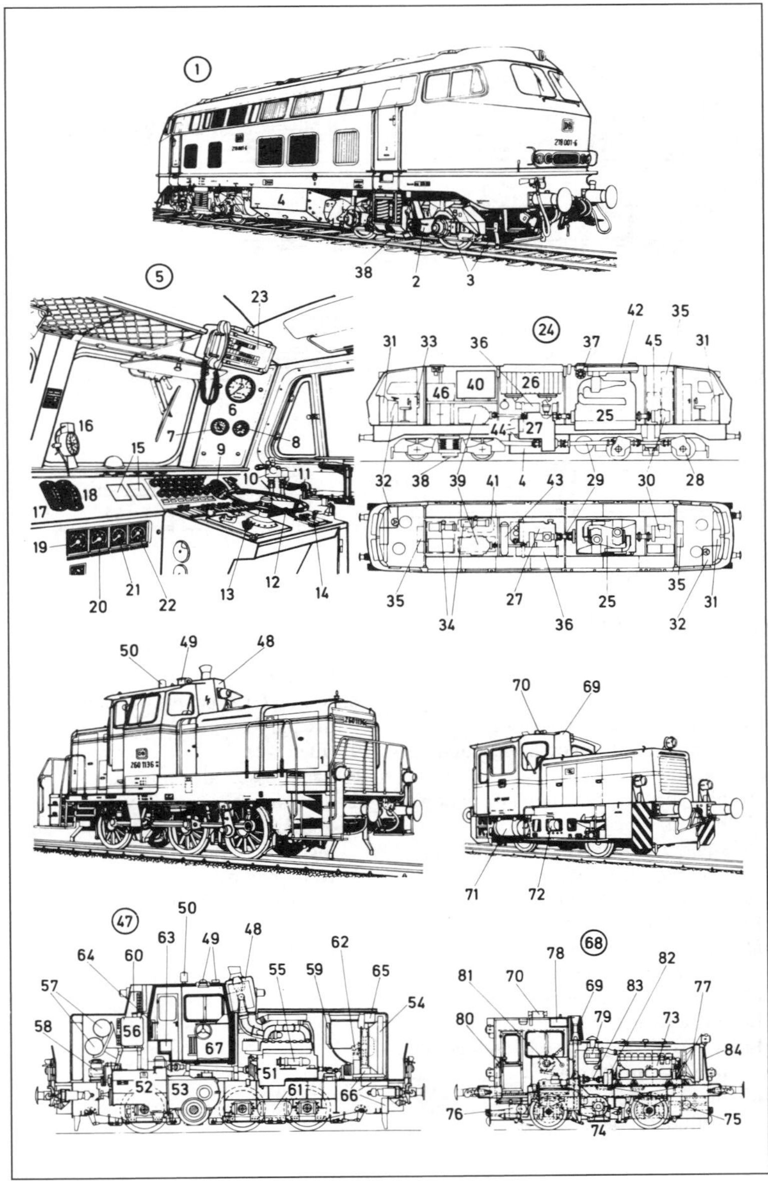
1
4
218 001-6
38
2
3
5
23
16
6
7
8
15
9
10
11
18
17
19
20
21
22
13
12
14
24
42
35
31
33
36
37
45
31
46
40
26
25
44
27
32
38
39
41
4
43
29
30
28
35
34
27
36
25
35
32
31
50
49
48
260 1136
70
69
71
72
47
50
63
49
48
62
64
60
55
59
65
57
54
58
56
67
51
52
53
61
66
68
78
82
81
70
69
83
77
80
79
73
84
76
74
75

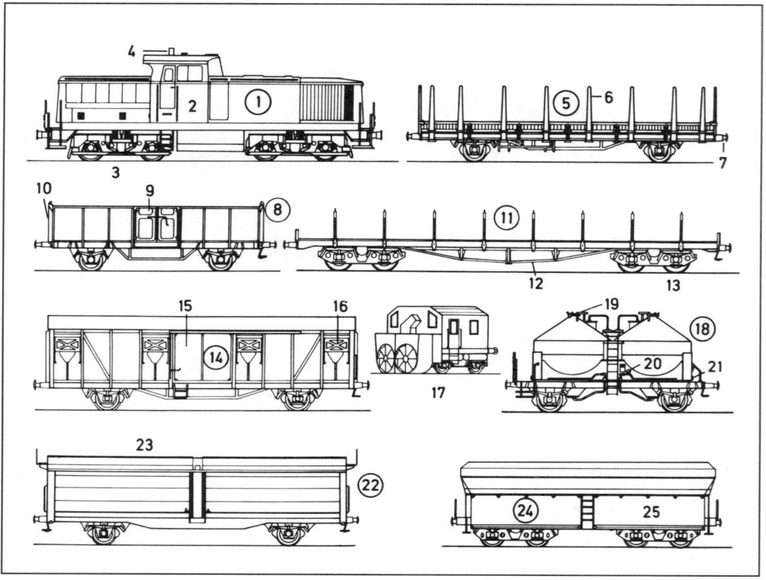

1 diesel-hydraulic locomotive
2 cab (driver's cab, *Am.* engineer's cab)
3 wheel and axle set
4 aerial for the yard radio
5 standard flat wagon (*Am.* standard flatcar)
6 hinged steel stanchion (stanchion)
7 buffers
8 standard open goods wagon (*Am.* standard open freight car)
9 revolving side doors
10 hinged front
11 standard flat wagon (*Am.* standard flatcar) with bogies
12 sole bar reinforcement
13 bogie (truck)
14 covered goods van (covered goods wagon, *Am.* boxcar)
15 sliding door
16 ventilation flap
17 snow blower (rotary snow plough, *Am.* snowplow), a track-clearing vehicle
18 wagon (*Am.* car) with pneumatic discharge
19 filler hole
20 compressed-air supply
21 discharge connection valve
22 goods van (*Am.* boxcar) with sliding roof
23 roof opening
24 bogie open self-discharge wagon (*Am.* bogie open self-discharge freight car)
25 discharge flap (discharge door)

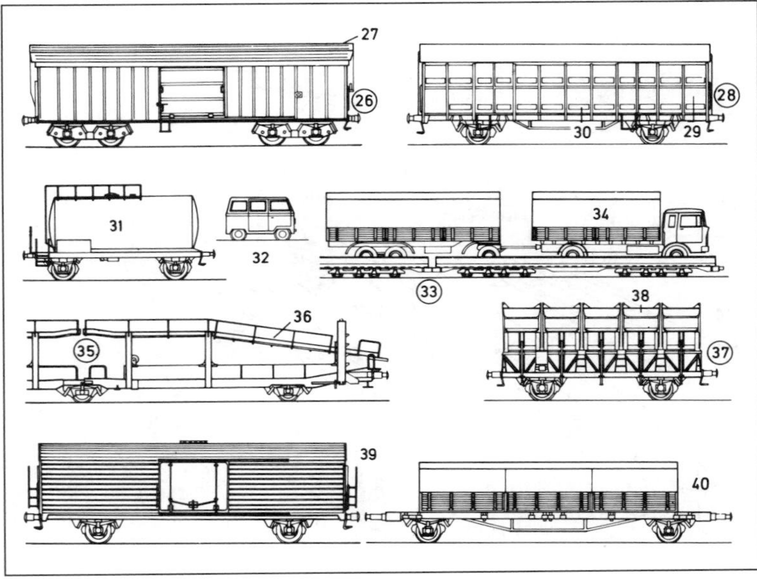

26 bogie wagon with swivelling (*Am.* swiveling) roof
27 swivelling (*Am.* swiveling) roof
28 large-capacity wagon (*Am.* large-capacity car) for small livestock
29 sidewall with ventilation flaps (slatted wall)
30 ventilation flap
31 tank wagon (*Am.* tank car)
32 track inspection railcar
33 open special wagons (*Am.* open special freight cars)
34 lorry (*Am.* truck) with trailer
35 two-tier car carrier (double-deck car carrier)
36 hinged upper deck
37 tipper wagon (*Am.* dump car) with skips
38 skip
39 general-purpose refrigerator wagon (refrigerator van, *Am.* refrigerator car)
40 interchangeable bodies for flat wagons (*Am.* flatcars)

214 Mountain Railways (*Am.* Railroads) and Cableways

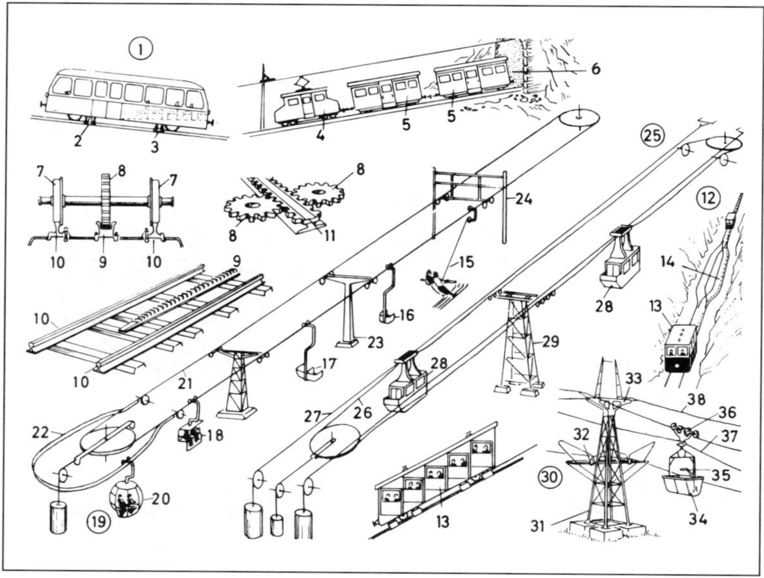

1-14 mountain railways (*Am.* mountain railroads)

1 adhesion railcar

2 drive

3 emergency brake

4, 5 rack mountain railway (rack-and-pinion railway, cog railway, *Am.* cog railroad, rack railroad)

4 electric rack railway locomotive (*Am.* electric rack railroad locomotive)

5 rack railway coach (rack railway trailer, *Am.* rack railroad car)

6 tunnel

7-11 rack railways (rack-and-pinion railways, *Am.* rack railroads) [systems]

7 running wheel (carrying wheel)

8 driving pinion

9 rack [with teeth machined on top edge]

10 rail

11 rack [with teeth on both outer edges]

12 funicular railway (funicular, cable railway)

13 funicular railway car

14 haulage cable

15-38 cableways (ropeways, cable suspension lines)

15-24 single-cable ropeways (single-cable suspension lines), endless cableways, endless ropeways

15 drag lift

16-18 chair lift

16 lift chair, a single chair

17 double lift chair, a two-seater chair

18 double chair (two-seater chair) with coupling

19 gondola cableway, an endless cableway

20 gondola (cabin)

21 endless cable, a suspension (supporting) and haulage cable

22 U-rail

23 single-pylon support

24 gantry support

25 double-cable ropeway (double-cable suspension line), a suspension line with balancing cabins

26 haulage cable

27 suspension cable (supporting cable)

28 cabin

29 intermediate support

30 cableway (ropeway, suspension line), a double-cable ropeway (double-cable suspension line)

31 pylon

32 haulage cable roller

33 cable guide rail (suspension cable bearing)

34 skip, a tipping bucket (*Am.* dumping bucket)

35 stop

36 pulley cradle

37 haulage cable

38 suspension cable (supporting cable)
39 **valley station** (lower station)
40 tension weight shaft
41 tension weight for the suspension cable (supporting cable)
42 tension weight for the haulage cable
43 tension cable pulley
44 suspension cable (supporting cable)
45 haulage cable
46 balance cable (lower cable)
47 auxiliary cable (emergency cable)
48 auxiliary-cable tensioning mechanism (emergency-cable tensioning mechanism)
49 haulage cable rollers
50 spring buffer (*Am.* spring bumper)
51 valley station platform (lower station platform)
52 cabin (cableway gondola, ropeway gondola, suspension line gondola), a large-capacity cabin
53 pulley cradle
54 suspension gear
55 stabilizer
56 guide rail
57 **top station** (upper station)
58 suspension cable guide (supporting cable guide)
59 suspension cable anchorage (supporting cable anchorage)
60 haulage cable rollers
61 haulage cable guide wheel
62 haulage cable driving pulley
63 main drive
64 standby drive
65 control room
66 **cabin pulley cradle**
67 main pulley cradle
68 double cradle
69 two-wheel cradle
70 running wheels
71 suspension cable brake (supporting cable brake), an emergency brake in case of haulage cable failure
72 suspension gear bolt
73 haulage cable sleeve
74 balance cable sleeve (lower cable sleeve)
75 derailment guard
76 **cable supports** (ropeway supports, suspension line supports, intermediate supports)
77 pylon, a framework support
78 tubular steel pylon, a tubular steel support
79 suspension cable guide rail (supporting cable guide rail, support guide rail)
80 support truss, a frame for work on the cable
81 base of the support

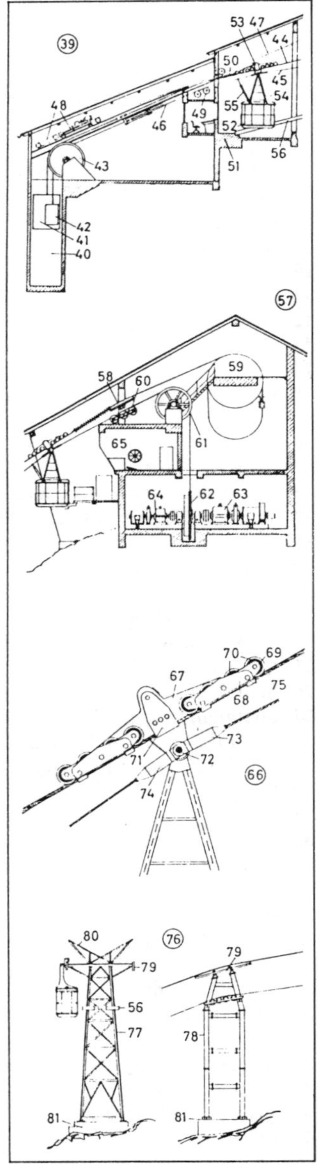

215 Bridges

1 cross-section of a bridge
2 orthotropic roadway (orthotropic deck)
3 truss (bracing)
4 diagonal brace (diagonal strut)
5 hollow tubular section
6 deck slab
7 solid-web girder bridge (beam bridge)
8 road surface
9 top flange
10 bottom flange
11 fixed bearing
12 movable bearing
13 clear span
14 span
15 rope bridge (primitive suspension bridge)
16 carrying rope
17 suspension rope
18 woven deck (woven decking)
19 stone arch bridge, a solid bridge
20 arch
21 pier
22 statue
23 trussed arch bridge
24 truss element
25 trussed arch
26 arch span
27 abutment (end pier)
28 spandrel-braced arch bridge
29 abutment (abutment pier)
30 bridge strut
31 crown
32 covered bridge of the Middle Ages (the *Ponte Vecchio* in Florence)
33 goldsmiths' shops
34 steel lattice bridge
35 counterbrace (crossbrace, diagonal member)
36 vertical member
37 truss joint
38 portal frame
39 suspension bridge
40 suspension cable
41 suspender (hanger)
42 tower
43 suspension cable anchorage
44 tied beam [with roadway]
45 abutment
46 cable-stayed bridge
47 inclined tension cable
48 inclined cable anchorage
49 reinforced concrete bridge
50 reinforced concrete arch
51 inclined cable system (multiple cable system)
52 flat bridge, a plate girder bridge
53 stiffener
54 pier
55 bridge bearing
56 cutwater
57 straits bridge, a bridge built of precast elements
58 precast construction unit
59 viaduct
60 valley bottom
61 reinforced concrete pier
62 scaffolding
63 lattice swing bridge
64 turntable
65 pivot pier
66 pivoting half (pivoting section, pivoting span, movable half) of bridge
67 flat swing bridge
68 middle section
69 pivot
70 parapet (handrailing)

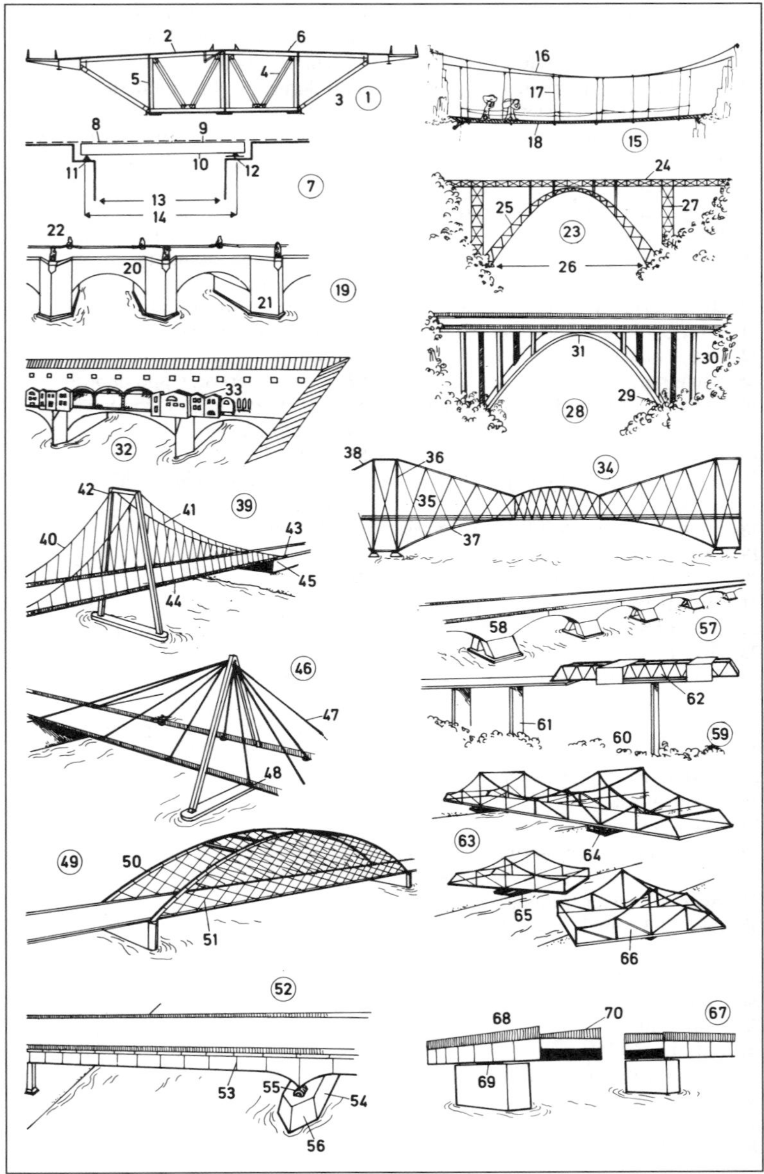
1
2
3
4
5
6
7
8
9
10
11
12
13
14
15
16
17
18
19
20
21
22
23
24
25
26
27
28
29
30
31
32
33
34
35
36
37
38
39
40
41
42
43
44
45
46
47
48
49
50
51
52
53
54
55
56
57
58
59
60
61
62
63
64
65
66
67
68
69
70

1 **cable ferry** (*also:* chain ferry), a passenger ferry
2 ferry rope (ferry cable)
3 river branch (river arm)
4 river island (river islet)
5 collapsed section of riverbank, flood damage
6 **motor ferry**
7 ferry landing stage (motorboat landing stage)
8 pile foundations
9 current (flow, course)
10 **flying ferry** (river ferry), a car ferry
11 ferry boat
12 buoy (float)
13 anchorage
14 harbour (*Am.* harbor) for laying up river craft
15 **ferry boat** (punt)
16 pole (punt pole, quant pole)
17 ferryman
18 blind river branch (blind river arm)
19 groyne (*Am.* groin)
20 groyne (*Am.* groin) head
21 fairway (navigable part of river)
22 **train of barges**
23 river tug
24 tow rope (tow line, towing hawser)
25 barge (freight barge, cargo barge, lighter)
26 bargeman (bargee, lighterman)
27 **towing** (hauling, haulage)
28 towing mast
29 towing engine
30 towing track; *form.:* tow path (towing path)
31 river after river training
32 **dike** (dyke, main dike, flood wall, winter dike)
33 drainage ditch
34 dike (dyke) drainage sluice
35 wing wall
36 outfall
37 drain (infiltration drain)
38 berm (berme)
39 top of dike (dyke)
40 dike (dyke) batter (dike slope)
41 flood bed (inundation area)
42 flood containment area
43 current meter
44 kilometre (*Am.* kilometer) sign
45 dikereeve's (dykereeve's) house (dikereeve's cottage); *also:* ferryman's house (cottage)
46 dikereeve (dykereeve)
47 dike (dyke) ramp
48 summer dike (summer dyke)
49 levee (embankment)
50 sandbags
51-55 **bank protection** (bank stabilization, revetment)
51 riprap
52 alluvial deposit (sand deposit)
53 fascine (bundle of wooden sticks)
54 wicker fences
55 stone pitching
56 **floating dredging machine** (dredger), a multi-bucket ladder dredge
57 bucket elevator chain
58 dredging bucket
59 **suction dredger** (hydraulic dredger) with trailing suction pipe or barge sucker
60 centrifugal pump
61 back scouring valve
62 suction pump, a jet pump with scouring nozzles

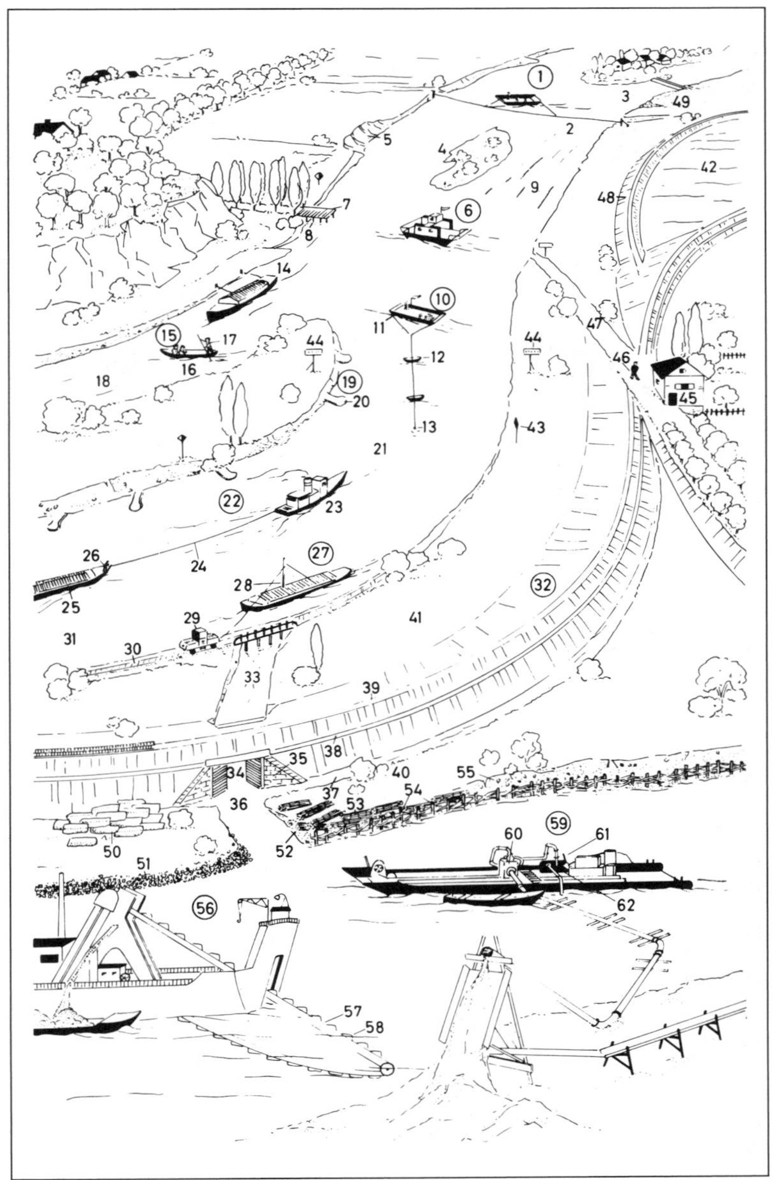
1
2
3
4
5
6
7
8
9
10
11
12
13
14
15
16
17
18
19
20
21
22
23
24
25
26
27
28
29
30
31
32
33
34
35
36
37
38
39
40
41
42
43
44
44
45
46
47
48
49
50
51
52
53
54
55
56
57
58
59
60
61
62

217 Waterway and Hydraulic Engineering

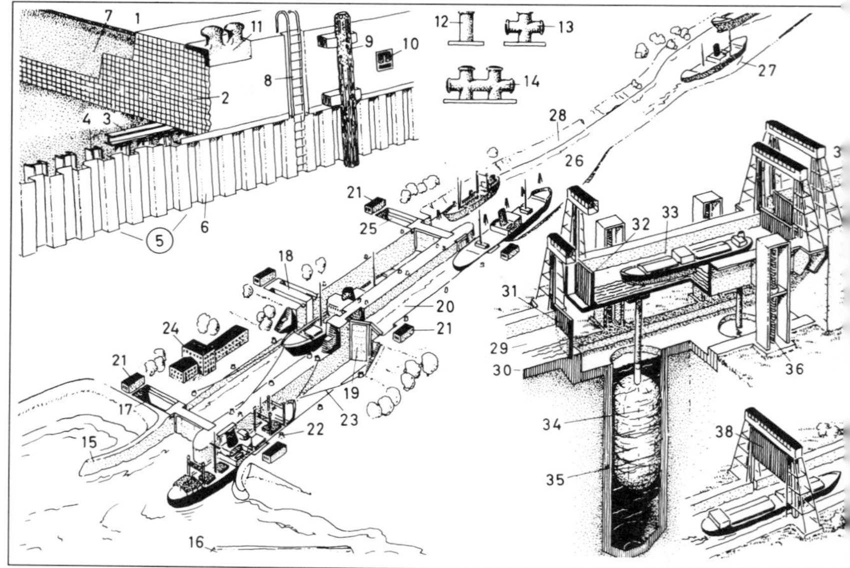

1-14 quay wall
1 road surface
2 body of wall
3 steel sleeper
4 steel pile
5 sheet pile wall (sheet pile bulkhead, sheet piling)
6 box pile
7 backfilling (filling)
8 ladder
9 fender (fender pile)
10 recessed bollard
11 double bollard
12 bollard
13 cross-shaped bollard (cross-shaped mooring bitt)
14 double cross-shaped bollard (double cross-shaped mooring bitt)
15-28 canal
15, 16 canal entrance
15 mole
16 breakwater
17-25 staircase of locks
17 lower level
18 lock gate, a sliding gate
19 mitre (*Am.* miter) gate
20 lock (lock chamber)
21 power house
22 warping capstan (hauling capstan), a capstan
23 warp
24 offices (e.g. canal administration, river police, customs)
25 upper level (head)
26 lock approach
27 lay-by
28 bank slope
29-38 boat lift (*Am.* boat elevator)
29 lower pound (lower reach)
30 canal bed
31 pound lock gate, a vertical gate
32 lock gate
33 boat tank (caisson)
34 float
35 float shaft
36 lifting spindle
37 upper pound (upper reach)
38 vertical gate

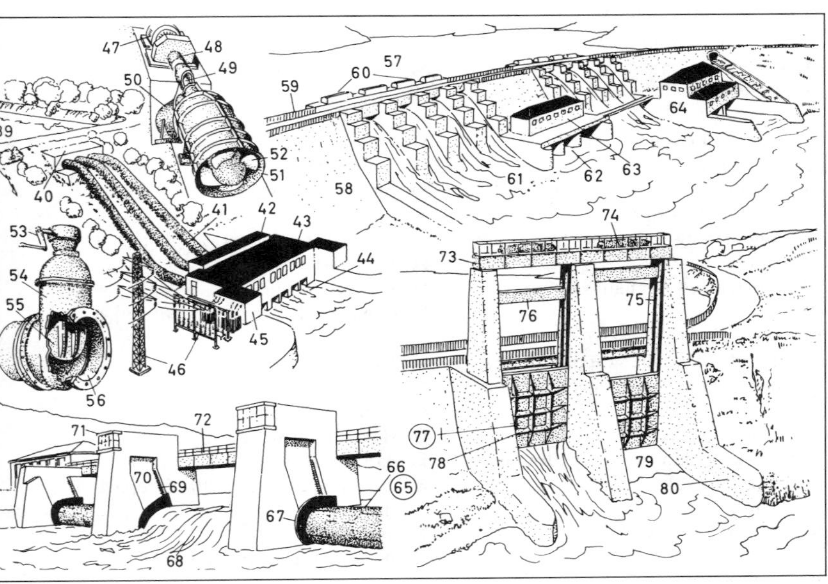

39-46 pumping plant and reservoir
39 forebay
40 surge tank
41 pressure pipeline
42 valve house (valve control house)
43 turbine house (pumping station)
44 discharge structure (outlet structure)
45 control station
46 transformer station
47-52 axial-flow pump (propeller pump)
47 drive motor
48 gear
49 drive shaft
50 pressure pipe
51 suction head
52 impeller wheel
53-56 sluice valve (sluice gate)
53 crank drive
54 valve housing
55 sliding valve (sliding gate)
56 discharge opening
57-64 dam (barrage)
57 reservoir (storage reservoir, impounding reservoir, impounded reservoir)
58 masonry dam
59 crest of dam
60 spillway (overflow spillway)
61 stilling basin (stilling box, stilling pool)
62 scouring tunnel (outlet tunnel, waste water outlet)
63 valve house (valve control house)
64 power station
65-72 rolling dam (weir), a barrage; *other system:* shutter weir
65 roller, a barrier
66 roller top
67 flange
68 submersible roller
69 rack track
70 recess
71 hoisting gear cabin
72 service bridge (walkway)
73-80 sluice dam
73 hoisting gear bridge
74 hoisting gear (winding gear)
75 guide groove
76 counterweight (counterpoise)
77 sluice gate (floodgate)
78 reinforcing rib
79 dam sill (weir sill)
80 wing wall

1-6 Germanic rowing boat [ca. AD 400]; the Nydam boat
1 stern post
2 steersman
3 oarsman
4 stem post (stem)
5 oar, for rowing
6 rudder (steering oar), a side rudder, for steering
7 dugout, a hollowed-out tree trunk
8 paddle
9-12 trireme, a Roman warship
9 ram
10 forecastle (fo'c'sle)
11 grapple (grapnel, grappling iron), for fastening the enemy ship alongside
12 three banks (tiers) of oars
13-17 Viking ship (longship, dragon ship) [Norse]
13 helm (tiller)
14 awning crutch with carved horses' heads
15 awning
16 dragon figurehead
17 shield
18-26 cog (Hansa cog, Hansa ship)
18 anchor cable (anchor rope, anchor hawser)
19 forecastle (fo'c'sle)
20 bowsprit
21 furled (brailed-up) square sail
22 town banner (city banner)
23 aftercastle (sterncastle)
24 rudder, a stem rudder
25 elliptical stern (round stern)
26 wooden fender
27-43 caravel (carvel) ['Santa Maria' 1492]
27 admiral's cabin
28 spanker boom
29 mizzen (mizen, mutton spanker, lateen spanker), a lateen sail
30 lateen yard
31 mizzen (mizen) mast
32 lashing
33 mainsail (main course), a square sail
34 bonnet, a removable strip of canvas
35 bowline
36 bunt line (martinet)
37 main yard
38 main topsail
39 main topsail yard
40 mainmast
41 foresail (fore course)
42 foremast
43 spritsail
44-50 galley [15th to 18th century], a slave galley
44 lantern
45 cabin
46 central gangway
47 slave driver with whip
48 galley slaves
49 covered platform in the forepart of the ship
50 gun
51-60 ship of the line (line-of-battle ship) [18th to 19th century], a three-decker
51 jib boom
52 fore topgallant sail
53 main topgallant sail
54 mizzen (mizen) topgallant sail
55-57 gilded stern
55 upper stern
56 stern gallery
57 quarter gallery, a projecting balcony with ornamental portholes
58 lower stern
59 gunports for broadside fire
60 gunport shutter

1
2
3
4
5
6
7
8
9
10
11
12
13
14
15
16
17
18
19
20
21
22
23
24
25
26
27
28
29
30
31
32
33
34
35
36
37
38
39
40
41
42
43
44
45
46
47
48
49
50
51
52
53
54
55
56
57
58
59
60

219 Sailing Ship I

1-72 rigging (rig, tackle) and sails of a bark (barque)
1-9 masts
1 bowsprit with jib boom
2-4 foremast
2 lower foremast
3 fore topmast
4 fore topgallant mast
5-7 mainmast
5 lower mainmast
6 main topmast
7 main topgallant mast
8, 9 mizzen (mizen) mast
8 lower mizzen (lower mizen)
9 mizzen (mizen) topmast
10-19 standing rigging
10 forestay, mizzen (mizen) stay, mainstay
11 fore topmast stay, main topmast stay, mizzen (mizen) topmast stay
12 fore topgallant stay, mizzen (mizen) topgallant stay, main topgallant stay
13 fore royal stay (main royal stay)
14 jib stay
15 bobstay
16 shrouds
17 fore topmast rigging (main topmast rigging, mizzen (mizen) topmast rigging)
18 fore topgallant rigging (main topgallant rigging)
19 backstays
20-31 fore-and-aft sails
20 fore topmast staysail
21 inner jib
22 outer jib
23 flying jib
24 main topmast staysail
25 main topgallant staysail
26 main royal staysail
27 mizzen (mizen) staysail
28 mizzen (mizen) topmast staysail
29 mizzen (mizen) topgallant staysail
30 mizzen (mizen, spanker, driver)
31 gaff topsail
32-45 spars
32 foreyard
33 lower fore topsail yard
34 upper fore topsail yard
35 lower fore topgallant yard
36 upper fore topgallant yard
37 fore royal yard
38 main yard
39 lower main topsail yard
40 upper main topsail yard
41 lower main topgallant yard
42 upper main topgallant yard
43 main royal yard
44 spanker boom
45 spanker gaff
46 footrope
47 lifts
48 spanker boom topping lift
49 spanker peak halyard
50 foretop
51 fore topmast crosstrees
52 maintop
53 main topmast crosstrees
54 mizzen (mizen) top
55-66 square sails
55 foresail (fore course)
56 lower fore topsail
57 upper fore topsail
58 lower fore topgallant sail
59 upper fore topgallant sail
60 fore royal
61 mainsail (main course)
62 lower main topsail
63 upper main topsail
64 lower main topgallant sail
65 upper main topgallant sail
66 main royal sail
67-71 running rigging
67 braces
68 sheets
69 spanker sheet
70 spanker vangs
71 bunt line
72 reef

1 2 3 4 5 6 7 8 9 10 11 12 13 14 15 16 17 18 19 20 21 22 23 24 25 26 27 28 29 30 31
32 33 34 35 36 37 38 39 40 41 42 43 44 45 46 47 48 49 50 51 52 53 54
55 56 57 58 59 60 61 62 63 64 65 66 67 68 69 70 71 72

220 Sailing Ship II

1-5 sail shapes
1 gaffsail (*small:* trysail, spencer)
2 jib
3 lateen sail
4 lugsail
5 spritsail
6-8 single-masted sailing boats (*Am.* sailboats)
6 tjalk
7 leeboard
8 cutter
9, 10 mizzen (mizen) masted sailing boats (*Am.* sailboats)
9 ketch-rigged sailing barge
10 yawl
11-17 two-masted sailing boats (*Am.* sailboats)
11-13 topsail schooner
11 mainsail
12 boom foresail
13 square foresail
14 brigantine
15 half-rigged mast with fore-and-aft sails
16 full-rigged mast with square sails
17 brig
18-27 three-masted sailing vessels (three-masters)
18 three-masted schooner
19 three-masted topsail schooner
20 bark (barque) schooner
21-23 bark (barque) [cf. illustration of rigging and sails in plate 219]
21 foremast
22 mainmast
23 mizzen (mizen) mast
24-27 full-rigged ship
24 mizzen (mizen) mast
25 crossjack yard (crojack yard)
26 crossjack (crojack)
27 ports
28-31 four-masted sailing ships (four-masters)
28 four-masted schooner
29 four-masted bark (barque)
30 mizzen (mizen) mast
31 four-masted full-rigged ship
32-34 five-masted bark (barque)
32 skysail
33 middle mast
34 mizzen (mizen) mast
35-37 development of sailing ships over 400 years
35 five-masted full-rigged ship 'Preussen' 1902-10
36 English clipper ship 'Spindrift' 1867
37 caravel (carvel) 'Santa Maria' 1492

1
2
3
4
5
6
7
8
9
10
11
12
13
14
15
16
17
18
19
20
21
22
23
24
25
26
27
28
29
30
31
32
33
34
35
36
37

221 Types of Ship

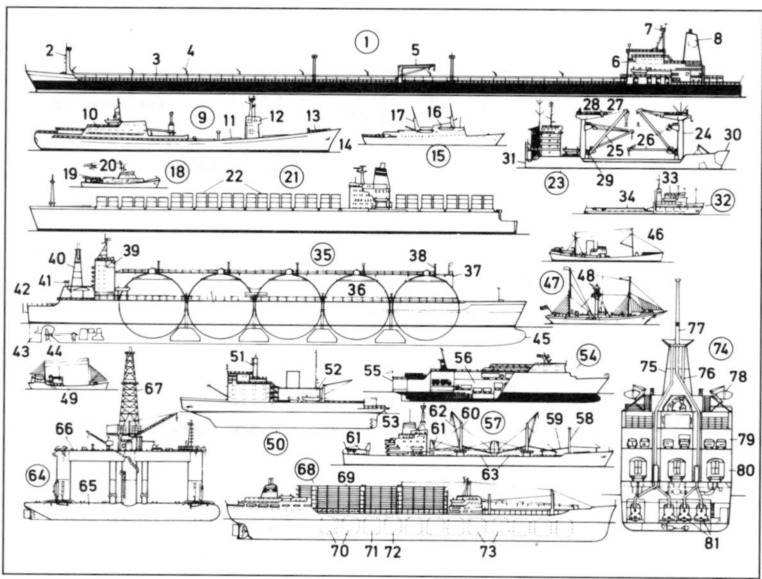

1 **ULCC** (ultra-large crude carrier) of the 'all-aft' type
2 foremast
3 catwalk with pipes
4 fire gun (fire nozzle)
5 deck crane
6 deckhouse with bridge
7 aft signal (signalling) and radar mast
8 funnel
9 **nuclear research ship** 'Otto Hahn', a bulk carrier
10 aft superstructure (engine room)
11 cargo hatchway for bulk goods (bulk cargoes)
12 bridge
13 forecastle (fo'c'sle)
14 stem
15 **seaside pleasure boat**
16 dummy funnel
17 exhaust mast
18 **rescue cruiser**
19 helicopter platform (working deck)
20 rescue helicopter
21 **all-container ship**
22 containers stowed on deck
23 **cargo ship**
24-29 cargo gear (cargo-handling gear)
24 bipod mast
25 jumbo derrick boom (heavy-lift derrick boom)
26 derrick boom (cargo boom)
27 tackle
28 block
29 thrust bearing
30 bow doors
31 stern loading door
32 **offshore drilling rig supply vessel**
33 compact superstructure
34 loading deck (working deck)
35 **liquefied-gas tanker**
36 spherical tank
37 navigational television receiver mast
38 vent mast
39 deckhouse
40 funnel
41 ventilator
42 transom stern (transom)
43 rudder blade (rudder)
44 ship's propeller (ship's screw)
45 bulbous bow
46 steam trawler
47 **lightship** (light vessel)
48 lantern (characteristic light)
49 smack
50 **ice breaker**
51 steaming light mast
52 helicopter hangar
53 stern towing point, for gripping the bow of ships in tow
54 **roll-on-roll-off (ro-ro) trailer ferry**
55 stern port (stern opening) with ramp
56 heavy vehicle lifts (*Am.* heavy vehicle elevators)
57 **multi-purpose freighter**
58 ventilator-type samson (sampson) post (ventilator-type king post)
59 derrick boom (cargo boom, cargo gear, cargo-handling gear)
60 derrick mast
61 deck crane
62 jumbo derrick boom (heavy-lift derrick boom)
63 cargo hatchway
64 **semisubmersible drilling vessel**
65 floating vessel with

machinery
66 drilling platform
67 derrick
68 **cattleship** (cattle vessel)
69 superstructure for transporting livestock
70 fresh water tanks
71 fuel tank
72 dung tank
73 fodder tanks
74 **train ferry** [cross section]
75 funnel
76 exhaust pipes
77 mast
78 ship's lifeboat hanging at the davit
79 car deck
80 main deck (train deck)
81 main engines
82 **passenger liner** (liner, ocean liner)
83 stem
84 funnel with lattice casing
85 flag dressing (rainbow dressing, string of flags extending over mastheads, e.g., on the maiden voyage)
86 **trawler,** a factory ship
87 gallows
88 stern ramp
89 **container ship**
90 loading bridge (loading platform)
91 sea ladder (jacob's ladder, rope ladder)
92 **barge and push tug assembly**
93 push tug
94 tug-pushed dumb barge (tug-pushed lighter)
95 pilot boat
96 **combined cargo and passenger liner**
97 passengers disembarking by boat
98 accommodation ladder
99 coaster (coasting vessel)
100 customs or police launch
101-128 **excursion steamer** (pleasure steamer)
101-106 lifeboat launching gear
101 davit
102 wire rope span
103 lifeline
104 tackle
105 block
106 fall
107 ship's lifeboat (ship's boat) covered with tarpaulin
108 stem
109 passenger
110 steward
111 deck-chair
112 deck hand
113 deck bucket
114 boatswain (bo's'n, bo'sun, bosun)
115 tunic
116 awning
117 stanchion
118 ridge rope (jackstay)
119 lashing
120 bulwark
121 guard rail
122 handrail (top rail)
123 companion ladder (companionway)
124 lifebelt (lifebuoy)
125 lifebuoy light (lifebelt light, signal light)
126 officer of the watch (watchkeeper)
127 reefer (*Am.* pea jacket)
128 binoculars

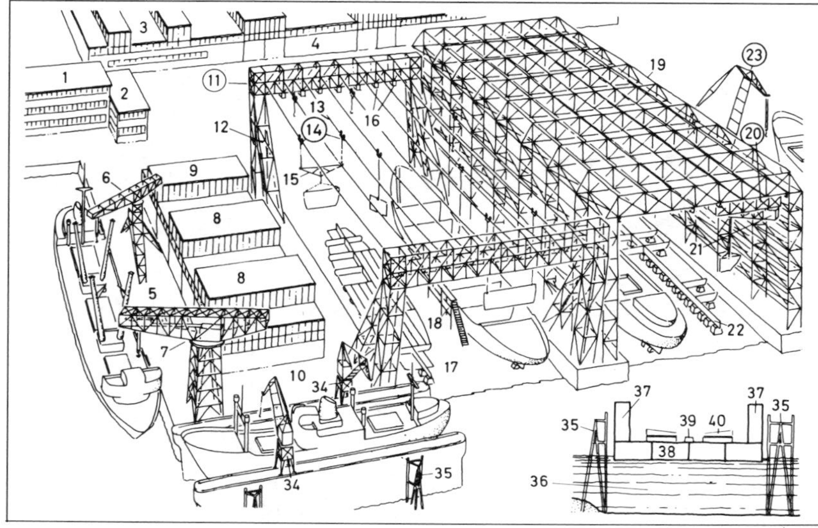

1-43 shipyard (shipbuilding yard, dockyard, *Am.* navy yard)
1 administrative offices
2 ship-drawing office
3, 4 shipbuilding sheds
3 mould (*Am.* mold) loft
4 erection shop
5-9 fitting-out quay
5 quay
6 tripod crane
7 hammer-headed crane
8 engineering workshop
9 boiler shop
10 repair quay
11-26 slipways (slips, building berths, building slips, stocks)
11-18 cable crane berth, a slipway (building berth)
11 slipway portal
12 bridge support
13 crane cable
14 crab (jenny)
15 cross piece
16 crane driver's cabin (crane driver's cage)
17 slipway floor
18 staging, a scaffold
19-21 frame slipway
19 slipway frame
20 overhead travelling (*Am.* traveling) crane (gantry crane)
21 slewing crab
22 keel in position
23 luffing jib crane, a slipway crane
24 crane rails (crane track)
25 gantry crane
26 gantry (bridge)
27 trestles (supports)
28 crab (jenny)
29 hull frames in position
30 ship under construction
31-33 dry dock
31 dock floor (dock bottom)
32 dock gates (caisson)
33 pumping station (power house)
34-43 floating dock (pontoon dock)
34 dock crane (dockside crane), a jib crane
35 fender pile
36-43 working of docks
36 dock basin
37, 38 dock structure
37 side tank (side wall)
38 bottom tank (bottom pontoon)
39 keel block
40 bilge block (bilge shore, side support)

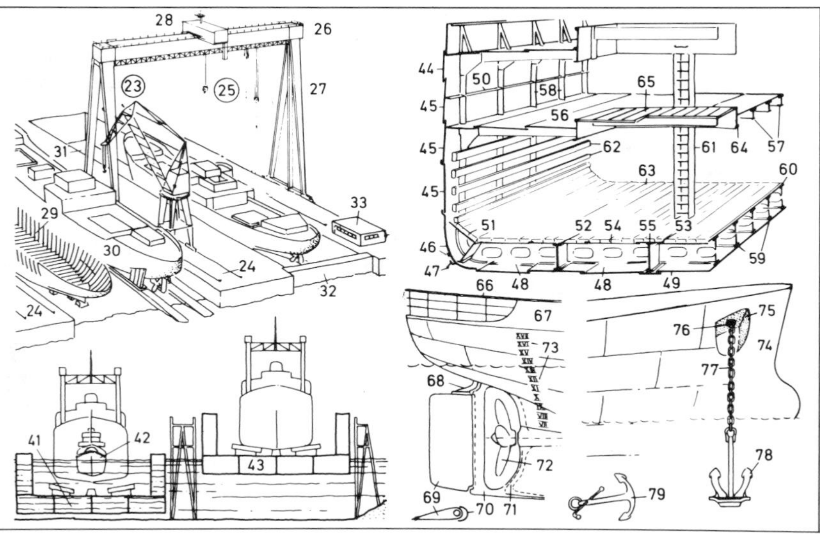

41-43 docking a ship
41 flooded floating dock
42 tug towing the ship
43 emptied (pumped-out) dock
44-61 structural parts of the ship
44-56 longitudinal structure
44-49 shell (shell plating, skin)
44 sheer strake
45 side strake
46 bilge strake
47 bilge keel
48 bottom plating
49 flat plate keel (keel plate)
50 stringer (side stringer)
51 tank margin plate
52 longitudinal side girder
53 centre (*Am.* center) plate girder (centre girder, kelson, keelson, vertical keel)
54 tank top plating (tank top, inner bottom plating)
55 centre (*Am.* center) strake
56 deck plating
57 deck beam
58 frame (rib)
59 floor plate
60 cellular double bottom
61 hold pillar (pillar)
62, 63 dunnage
62 side battens (side ceiling, spar ceiling)
63 ceiling (floor ceiling)
64, 65 hatchway
64 hatch coaming
65 hatch cover (hatchboard)
66-72 stern
66 guard rail
67 bulwark
68 rudder stock
69, 70 Oertz rudder
69 rudder blade (rudder)
70, 71 stern frame
70 rudder post
71 propeller post (screw post)
72 ship's propeller (ship's screw)
73 draught (draft) marks
74-79 bow
74 stem, a bulbous stem (bulbous bow)
75 hawse
76 hawse pipe
77 anchor cable (chain cable)
78 stockless anchor (patent anchor)
79 stocked anchor

223 Motor Ship

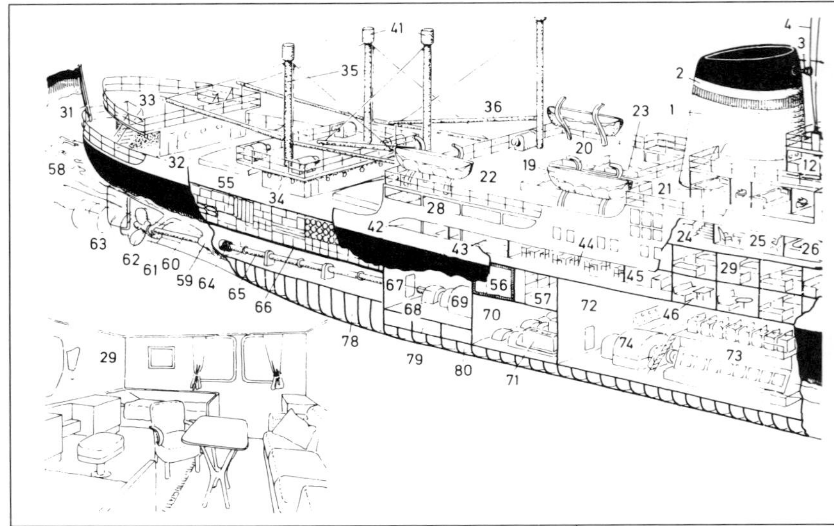

1-71 combined cargo and passenger ship [of the older type]
1 funnel
2 funnel marking
3 siren (fog horn)
4-11 compass platform (compass bridge, compass flat, monkey bridge)
4 antenna lead-in (antenna down-lead)
5 radio direction finder (RDF) antenna (direction finder antenna, rotatable loop antenna, aural null loop antenna)
6 magnetic compass (mariner's compass)
7 morse lamp (signalling, *Am.* signaling, lamp)
8 radar antenna (radar scanner)
9 code flag signal
10 code flag halyards
11 triatic stay (signal stay)
12-18 bridge deck (bridge)
12 radio room
13 captain's cabin
14 navigating bridge
15 starboard sidelight [green; port sidelight red]
16 wing of bridge
17 shelter (weather cloth, dodger)
18 wheelhouse
19-21 boat deck
19 ship's lifeboat
20 davit
21 officer's cabin
22-27 promenade deck
22 sun deck (lido deck)
23 swimming pool
24 companion ladder (companionway)
25 library (ship's library)
26 lounge
27 promenade
28-30 A-deck
28 semi-enclosed deck space
29 double-berth cabin, a cabin
30 de luxe cabin
31 ensign staff
32-47 B-deck (main deck)
32 after deck
33 poop
34 deckhouse
35 samson (sampson) post (king post)
36 derrick boom (cargo boom)
37 crosstrees (spreader)
38 crow's nest
39 topmast
40 forward steaming light

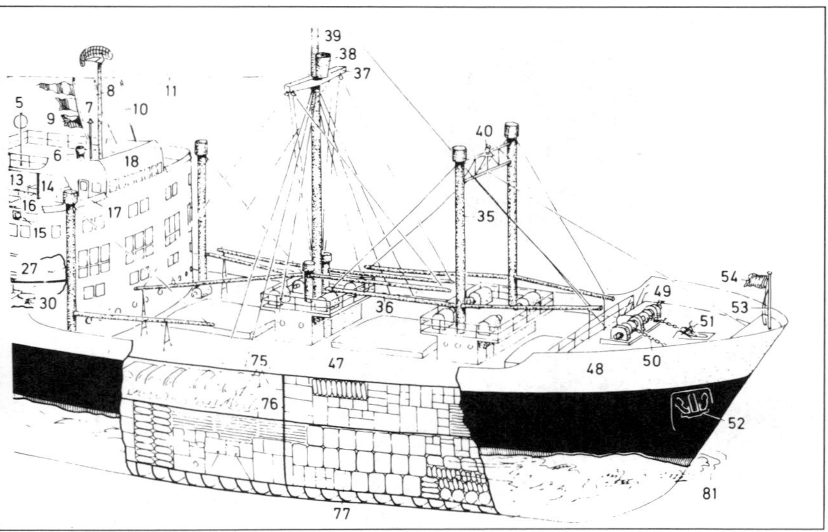

41 ventilator lead
42 galley (caboose, cookroom, ship's kitchen)
43 ship's pantry
44 dining room
45 purser's office
46 single-berth cabin
47 foredeck
48 forecastle (fo'c'sle)
49-51 ground tackle
49 windlass
50 anchor cable (chain cable)
51 compressor (chain compressor)
52 anchor
53 jackstaff
54 jack
55 after holds
56 cold storage room (insulated hold)
57 store room
58 wake
59 shell bossing (shaft bossing)
60 tail shaft (tail end shaft)
61 shaft strut (strut, spectacle frame, propeller strut, propeller bracket)
62 three-blade ship's propeller (ship's screw)
63 rudder blade (rudder)
64 stuffing box
65 propeller shaft
66 shaft alley (shaft tunnel)
67 thrust block
68-74 diesel-electric drive
68 electric engine room
69 electric motor
70 auxiliary engine room
71 auxiliary engines
72 main engine room
73 main engine, a diesel engine
74 generator
75 forward holds
76 tween deck
77 cargo
78 ballast tank (deep tank) for water ballast
79 fresh water tank
80 fuel tank
81 bow wave

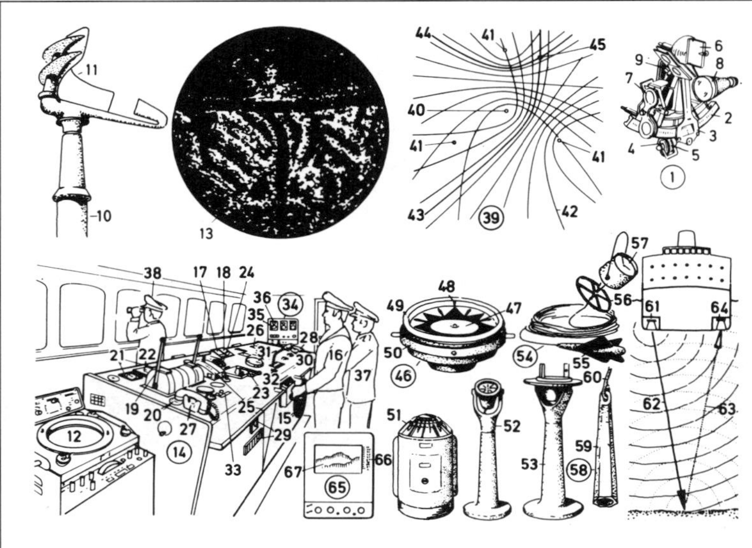

1 **sextant**
2 graduated arc
3 index bar (index arm)
4 decimal micrometer
5 vernier
6 index mirror
7 horizon glass (horizon mirror)
8 telescope
9 grip (handgrip)
10-13 **radar equipment** (radar apparatus)
10 radar pedestal
11 revolving radar reflector
12 radar display unit (radar screen)
13 radar image (radar picture)
14-38 **wheelhouse**
14 steering and control position
15 ship's wheel for controlling the rudder mechanism
16 helmsman (*Am.* wheelsman)
17 rudder angle indicator
18 automatic pilot (autopilot)
19 control lever for the variable-pitch propeller (reversible propeller, feathering propeller, feathering screw)
20 propeller pitch indicator
21 main engine revolution indicator
22 ship's speedometer (log)
23 control switch for bow thruster (bow-manoeuvring, *Am.* maneuvering, propeller)
24 echo recorder (depth recorder, echograph)
25 engine telegraph (engine order telegraph)
26 controls for the anti-rolling system (for the stabilizers)
27 local-battery telephone
28 shipping traffic radio telephone
29 navigation light indicator panel (running light indicator panel)
30 microphone for ship's address system
31 gyro compass (gyroscopic compass), a compass repeater
32 control button for the ship's siren (ship's fog horn)
33 main engine overload indicator
34 Decca position-finder (Decca Navigator)
35 rough focusing indicator
36 fine focusing indicator
37 navigating officer
38 captain
39 **Decca navigation system**
40 master station
41 slave station
42 null hyperbola
43 hyperbolic position line 1
44 hyperbolic position line 2
45 position (fix, ship fix)
46-53 **compasses**
46 liquid compass (fluid compass, spirit compass, wet compass), a magnetic compass
47 compass card
48 lubber's line (lubber's mark, lubber's point)
49 compass bowl
50 gimbal ring
51-53 gyro compass (gyroscopic compass, gyro compass unit)
51 master compass (master gyro compass)
52 compass repeater (gyro repeater)
53 compass repeater with pelorus
54 **patent log** (screw log, mechanical log, towing log, taffrail log, speedometer)
55 rotator
56 governor

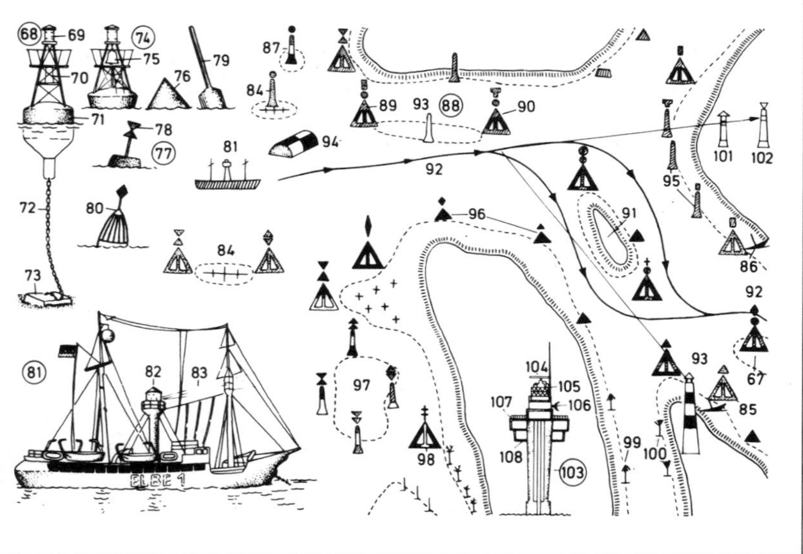

57 log clock
58-67 leads
58 hand lead
59 lead (lead sinker)
60 leadline
61-67 echo sounder (echo sounding machine)
61 sound transmitter
62 sound wave (sound impulse)
63 echo (sound echo, echo signal)
64 echo receiver (hydrophone)
65 echograph (echo sounding machine recorder)
66 depth scale
67 echogram (depth recording, depth reading)
68-108 sea marks (floating navigational marks) for buoyage and lighting systems
68-83 fairway marks (channel marks)
68 light and whistle buoy
69 light (warning light)
70 whistle
71 buoy
72 mooring chain
73 sinker (mooring sinker)
74 light and bell buoy
75 bell
76 conical buoy
77 can buoy
78 topmark
79 spar buoy
80 topmark buoy
81 lightship (light vessel)
82 lantern mast (lantern tower)
83 beam of light
84-102 fairway markings (channel markings)
84 wreck [green buoys]
85 wreck to starboard
86 wreck to port
87 shoals (shallows, shallow water, *Am.* flats)
88 middle ground to port
89 division (bifurcation) [beginning of the middle ground; topmark: red cylinder above red ball]
90 convergence (confluence) [end of the middle ground; topmark: red St. Antony's cross above red ball]
91 middle ground
92 main fairway (main navigable channel)
93 secondary fairway (secondary navigable channel)
94 can buoy
95 port hand buoys (port hand marks) [red]
96 starboard hand buoys (starboard hand marks) [black]
97 shoals (shallows, shallow water, *Am.* flats) outside the fairway
98 middle of the fairway (mid-channel)
99 starboard markers [inverted broom]
100 port markers [upward-pointing broom]
101, 102 range lights (leading lights)
101 lower range light (lower leading light)
102 higher range light (higher leading light)
103 lighthouse
104 radar antenna (radar scanner)
105 lantern (characteristic light)
106 radio direction finder (RDF) antenna
107 machinery and observation platform (machinery and observation deck)
108 living quarters

225 Docks, Port, Harbour (*Am.* Harbor) I

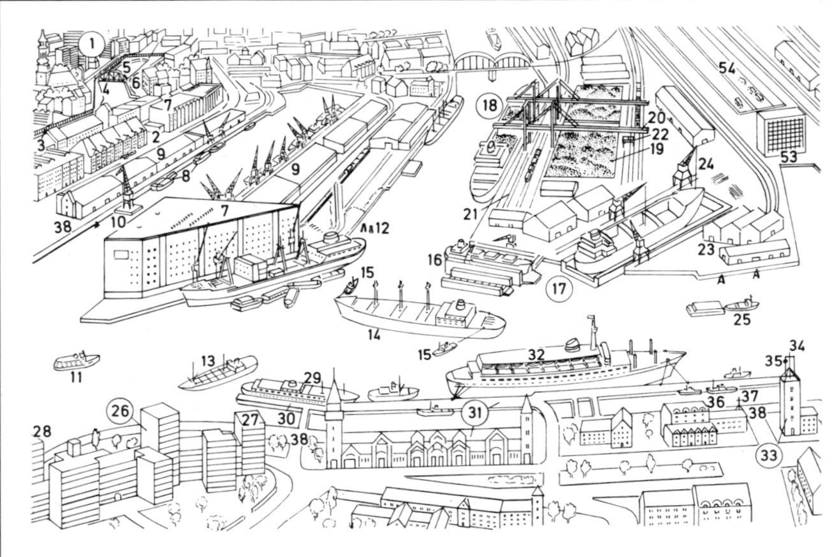

1 dock area
2 free port (foreign trade zone)
3 free zone frontier (free zone enclosure)
4 customs barrier
5 customs entrance
6 port custom house
7 entrepôt
8 barge (dumb barge, lighter)
9 break-bulk cargo transit shed (general cargo transit shed, package cargo transit shed)
10 floating crane
11 harbour (*Am.* harbor) ferry (ferryboat)
12 fender (dolphin)
13 bunkering boat
14 break-bulk carrier (general cargo ship)
15 tug
16 floating dock (pontoon dock)
17 dry dock
18 coal wharf
19 coal bunker
20 transporter loading bridge
21 quayside railway
22 weighing bunker
23 warehouse
24 quayside crane
25 launch and lighter
26 port hospital
27 quarantine wing
28 Institute of Tropical Medicine
29 excursion steamer (pleasure steamer)
30 jetty
31 passenger terminal
32 liner (passenger liner, ocean liner)
33 meteorological office, a weather station
34 signal mast (signalling mast)
35 storm signal
36 port administration offices
37 tide level indicator
38 quayside road (quayside roadway)

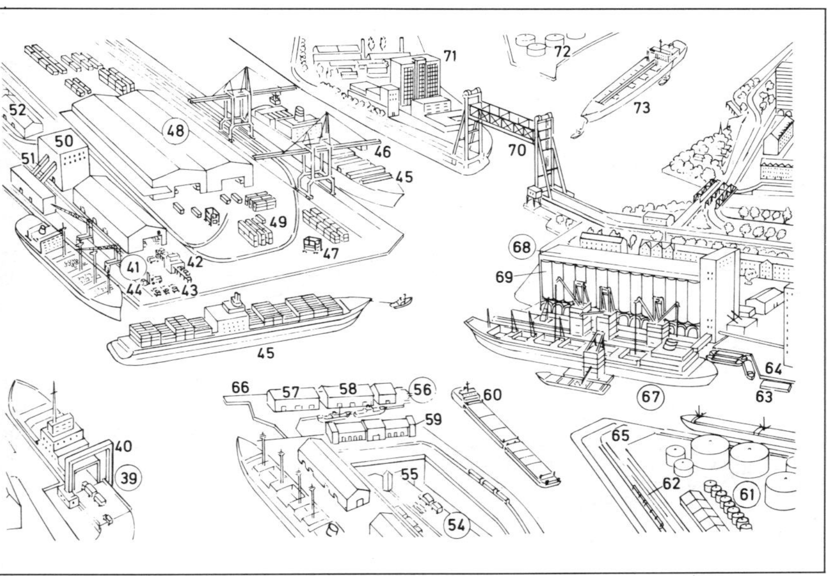

39 roll-on roll-off (ro-ro) system (roll-on roll-off operation)
40 gantry
41 truck-to-truck system (truck-to-truck operation)
42 foil-wrapped unit loads
43 pallets
44 forklift truck (fork truck, forklift)
45 container ship
46 transporter container-loading bridge
47 container carrier truck
48 container terminal (container berth)
49 unit load
50 cold store
51 conveyor belt (conveyor)
52 fruit storage shed (fruit warehouse)
53 office building
54 urban motorway (*Am.* freeway)
55 harbour (*Am.* harbor) tunnels
56 fish dock
57 fish market
58 auction room
59 fish-canning factory
60 push tow
61 tank farm
62 railway siding
63 landing pontoon (landing stage)
64 quay
65 breakwater (mole)
66 pier (jetty), a quay extension
67 bulk carrier
68 silo
69 silo cylinder
70 lift bridge
71 industrial plant
72 storage tanks
73 tanker

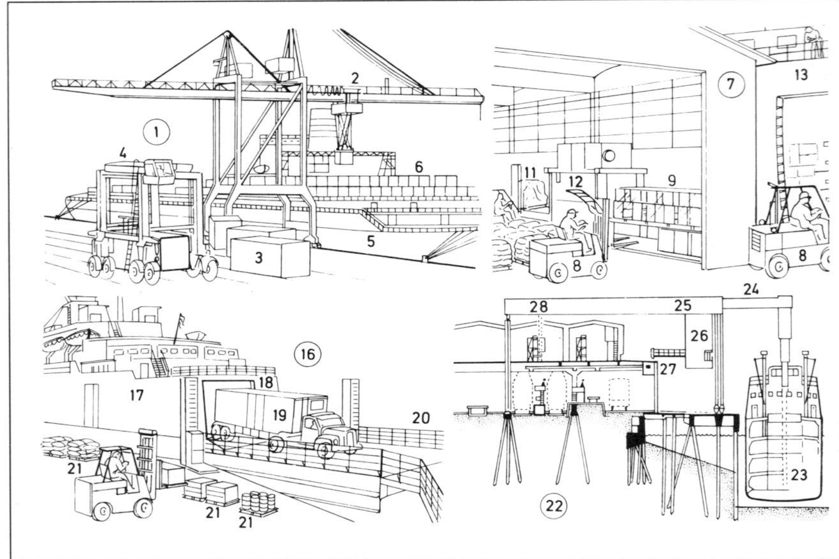

1 container terminal (container berth), a modern cargo-handling berth
2 transporter container-loading bridge (loading bridge); *sim.:* transtainer crane (transtainer)
3 container
4 truck (carrier)
5 all-container ship
6 containers stowed on deck
7 truck-to-truck handling (horizontal cargo handling with pallets)
8 forklift truck (fork truck, forklift)
9 unitized foil-wrapped load (unit load)
10 flat pallet, a standard pallet
11 unitized break-bulk cargo
12 heat sealing machine
13 break-bulk carrier (general cargo ship)
14 cargo hatchway
15 receiving truck on board ship
16 multi-purpose terminal
17 roll-on roll-off ship (ro-ro-ship)
18 stern port (stern opening)
19 driven load, a lorry (*Am.* truck)
20 ro-ro depot
21 unitized load (unitized package)
22 banana-handling terminal [section]
23 seaward tumbler
24 jib
25 elevator bridge
26 chain sling
27 lighting station
28 shore-side tumbler for loading trains and lorries (*Am.* trucks)

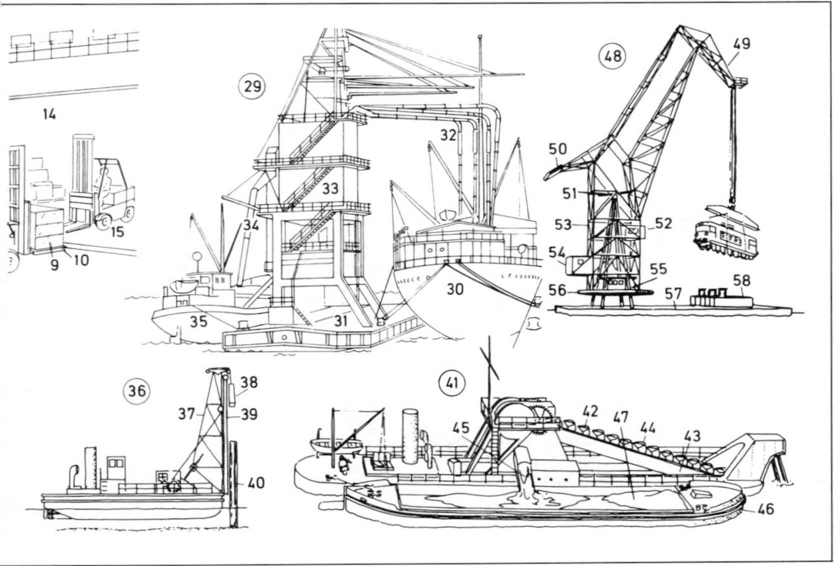

29 bulk cargo handling
30 bulk carrier
31 floating bulk-cargo elevator
32 suction pipes
33 receiver
34 delivery pipe
35 bulk transporter barge
36 floating pile driver
37 pile driver frame
38 pile hammer
39 driving guide rail
40 pile
41 bucket dredger, a dredger
42 bucket chain
43 bucket ladder
44 dredger bucket
45 chute
46 hopper barge
47 spoil
48 floating crane
49 jib (boom)
50 counterweight (counterpoise)
51 adjusting spindle
52 crane driver's cabin (crane driver's cage)
53 crane framework
54 winch house
55 control platform
56 turntable
57 pontoon, a pram
58 engine superstructure (engine mounting)

227 Salvage (Salving) and Towage

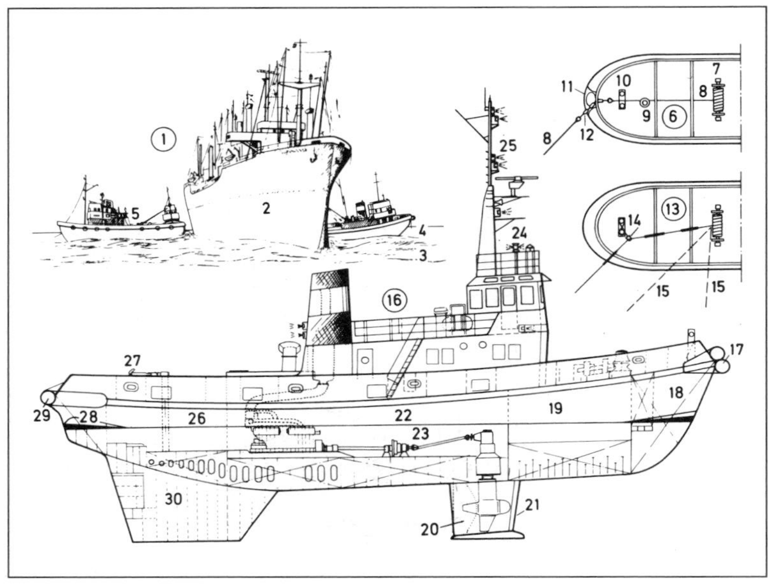

1 salvaging (salving) of a ship run aground
2 ship run aground (damaged vessel)
3 sandbank; *also:* quicksand
4 open sea
5 tug (salvage tug)
6-15 towing gear
6 towing gear for towing at sea
7 towing winch (towing machine, towing engine)
8 tow rope (tow line, towing hawser)
9 tow rope guide
10 cross-shaped bollard
11 hawse hole
12 anchor cable (chain cable)
13 towing gear for work in harbours (*Am.* harbors)
14 guest rope
15 position of the tow rope (tow line, towing hawser)
16 tug (salvage tug) [vertical elevation]
17 bow fender (pudding fender)
18 forepeak
19 living quarters
20 Schottel propeller
21 Kort vent
22 engine and propeller room
23 clutch coupling
24 compass platform (compass bridge, compass flat, monkey bridge)
25 fire-fighting equipment
26 stowage
27 tow hook
28 afterpeak
29 stern fender
30 main manoeuvring (*Am.* maneuvering) keel

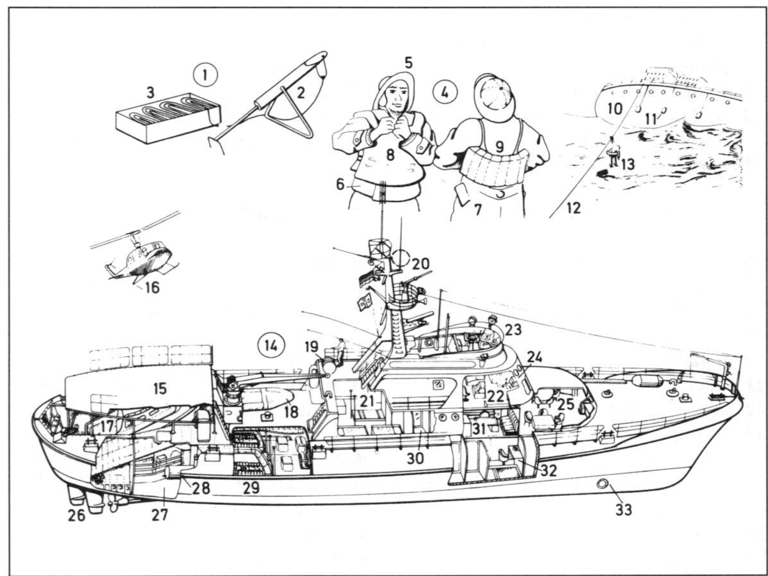

1 rocket apparatus (rocket gun, line-throwing gun)
2 life rocket (rocket)
3 rocket line (whip line)
4 oilskins
5 sou'wester (southwester)
6 oilskin jacket
7 oilskin coat
8 inflatable life jacket
9 cork life jacket (cork life preserver)
10 stranded ship (damaged vessel)
11 oil bag, for trickling oil on the water surface
12 lifeline
13 breeches buoy
14 rescue cruiser
15 helicopter landing deck
16 rescue helicopter
17 daughter boat
18 inflatable boat (inflatable dinghy)
19 life raft
20 fire-fighting equipment for fires at sea
21 hospital unit with operating cabin and exposure bath
22 navigating bridge
23 upper tier of navigating bridge
24 lower tier of navigating bridge
25 messroom
26 rudders and propeller (screw)
27 stowage
28 foam can
29 side engines
30 shower
31 coxswain's cabin
32 crew member's single-berth cabin
33 bow propeller

229 Aircraft I

1-14 wing configurations
1 high-wing monoplane (high-wing plane)
2 span (wing span)
3 shoulder-wing monoplane (shoulder-wing plane)
4 midwing monoplane (midwing plane)
5 low-wing monoplane (low-wing plane)
6 triplane
7 upper wing
8 middle wing (central wing)
9 lower wing
10 biplane
11 strut
12 cross bracing wires
13 sesquiplane
14 low-wing monoplane (low-wing plane) with cranked wings (inverted gull wings)
15-22 wing shapes
15 elliptical wing
16 rectangular wing
17 tapered wing
18 crescent wing
19 delta wing
20 swept-back wing with semi-positive sweepback
21 swept-back wing with positive sweepback
22 ogival wing (ogee wing)
23-36 tail shapes (tail unit shapes, empennage shapes)
23 normal tail (normal tail unit)
24, 25 vertical tail (vertical stabilizer and rudder)
24 vertical stabilizer (vertical fin, tail fin)
25 rudder
26, 27 horizontal tail
26 tailplane (horizontal stabilizer)
27 elevator
28 cruciform tail (cruciform tail unit)
29 T-tail (T-tail unit)
30 lobe
31 V-tail (vee-tail, butterfly tail)
32 double tail unit (twin tail unit)
33 end plate
34 double tail unit (twin tail unit) of a twin-boom aircraft
35 raised horizontal tail with double booms
36 triple tail unit
37 **system of flaps**
38 extensible slat
39 spoiler
40 double-slotted Fowler flap
41 outer aileron (low-speed aileron)
42 inner spoiler (landing flap, lift dump)
43 inner aileron (all-speed aileron)
44 brake flap (air brake)
45 basic profile
46-48 plain flaps (simple flaps)
46 normal flap
47 slotted flap
48 double-slotted flap
49, 50 split flaps
49 plain split flap (simple split flap)
50 zap flap
51 extending flap
52 Fowler flap
53 slat
54 profiled leading-edge flap (droop flap)
55 Krüger flap

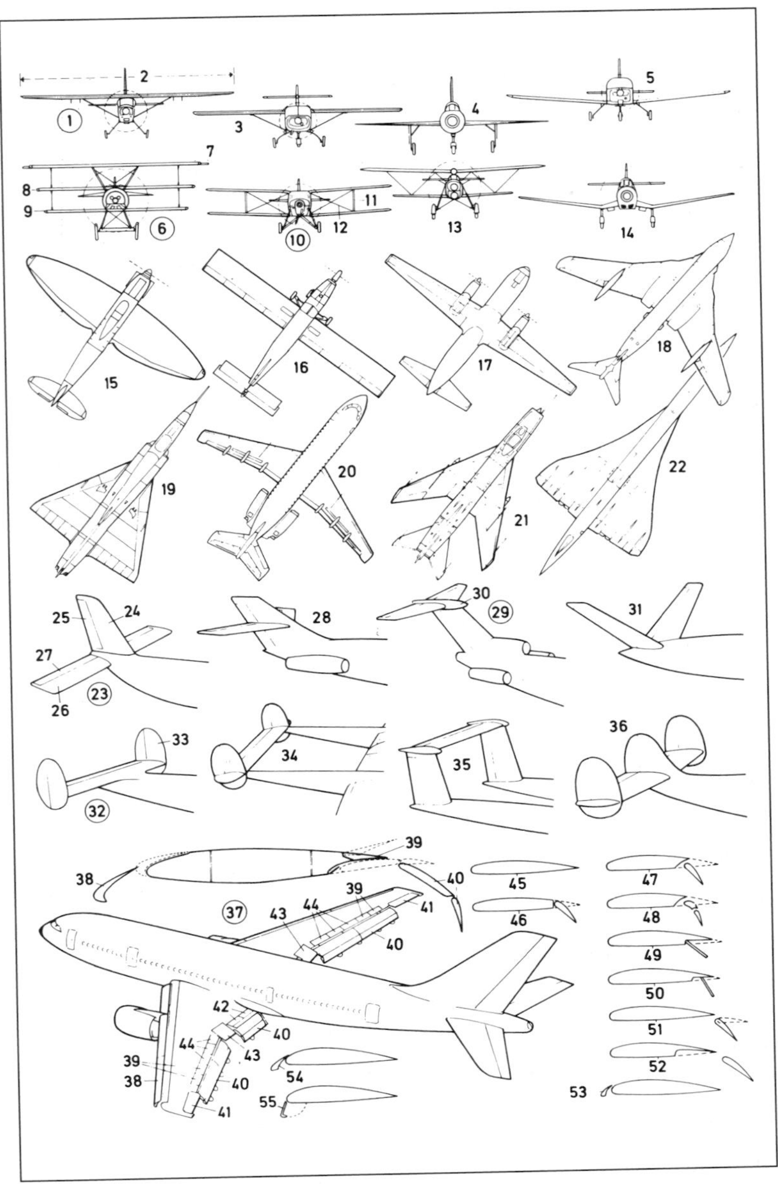
1
2
3
4
5
6
7
8
9
10
11
12
13
14
15
16
17
18
19
20
21
22
23
24
25
26
27
28
29
30
31
32
33
34
35
36
37
38
39
40
41
42
43
44
45
46
47
48
49
50
51
52
53
54
55

1-31 cockpit of a single-engine (single-engined) racing and passenger aircraft (racing and passenger plane)
1 instrument panel
2 air-speed (*Am.* airspeed) indicator
3 artificial horizon (gyro horizon)
4 altimeter
5 radio compass (automatic direction finder)
6 magnetic compass
7 boost gauge (*Am.* gage)
8 tachometer (rev counter, revolution counter)
9 cylinder temperature gauge (*Am.* gage)
10 accelerometer
11 chronometer
12 turn indicator with ball
13 directional gyro
14 vertical speed indicator (rate-of-climb indicator, variometer)
15 VOR radio direction finder [*VOR: very high frequency omnidirectional range*]
16 left tank fuel gauge (*Am.* gage)
17 right tank fuel gauge (*Am.* gage)
18 ammeter
19 fuel pressure gauge (*Am.* gage)
20 oil pressure gauge (*Am.* gage)
21 oil temperature gauge (*Am.* gage)
22 radio and radio navigation equipment
23 map light
24 wheel (control column, control stick) for operating the ailerons and elevators
25 co-pilot's wheel
26 switches
27 rudder pedals
28 co-pilot's rudder pedals
29 microphone for the radio
30 throttle lever (throttle control)
31 mixture control
32-66 single-engine (single-engined) racing and passenger aircraft (racing and passenger plane)
32 propeller (airscrew)
33 spinner
34 flat four engine
35 cockpit
36 pilot's seat
37 co-pilot's seat
38 passenger seats
39 hood (canopy, cockpit hood, cockpit canopy)
40 steerable nose wheel
41 main undercarriage unit (main landing gear unit)
42 step
43 wing
44 right navigation light (right position light)
45 spar
46 rib
47 stringer (longitudinal reinforcing member)
48 fuel tank
49 landing light
50 left navigation light (left position light)
51 electrostatic conductor
52 aileron
53 landing flap
54 fuselage (body)
55 frame (former)
56 chord
57 stringer (longitudinal reinforcing member)
58 vertical tail (vertical stabilizer and rudder)
59 vertical stabilizer (vertical fin, tail fin)
60 rudder
61 horizontal tail
62 tailplane (horizontal stabilizer)
63 elevator
64 warning light (anticollision light)
65 dipole antenna
66 long-wire antenna (long-conductor antenna)
67-72 principal manoeuvres (*Am.* maneuvers) of the aircraft (aeroplane, plane, *Am.* airplane)
67 pitching
68 lateral axis
69 yawing
70 vertical axis (normal axis)
71 rolling
72 longitudinal axis

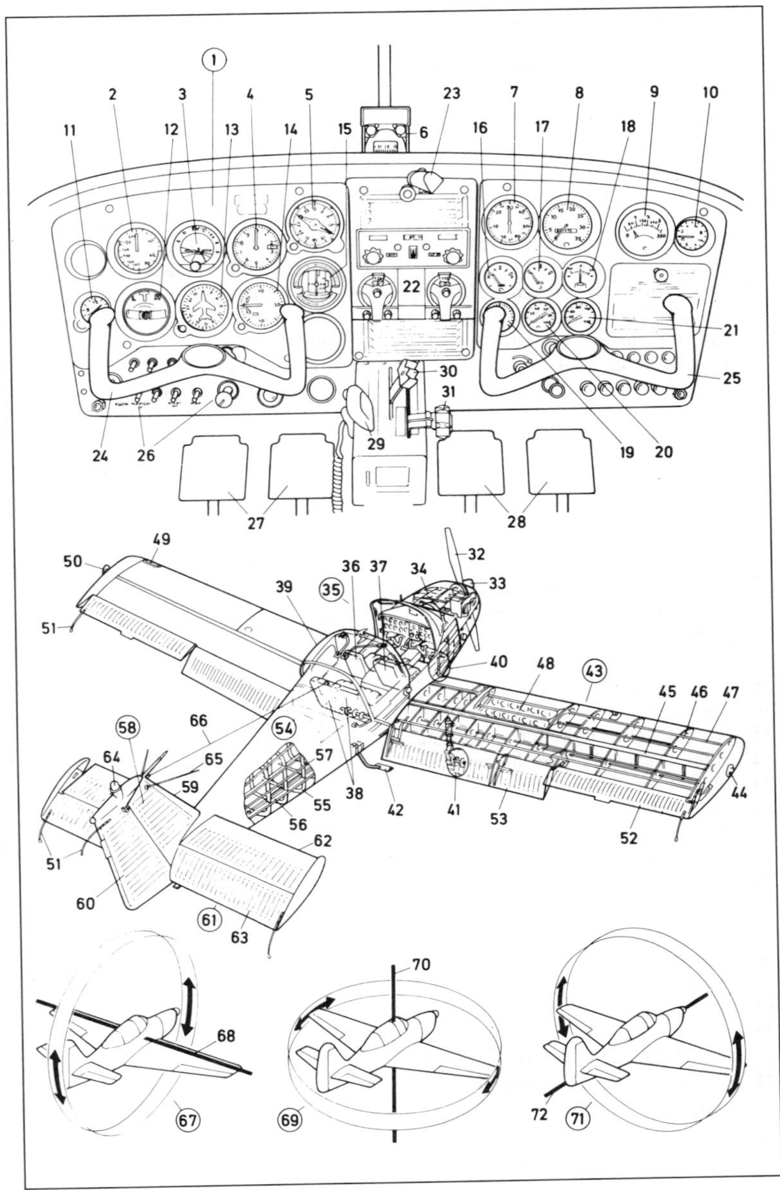
1
2
3
4
5
23
7
8
9
10
11
12
13
14
15
6
16
17
18
22
21
30
25
31
24
26
29
19
20
27
28
49
50
32
36
37
34
33
39
35
51
40
48
43
45
46
47
58
66
54
64
65
57
59
38
55
42
41
53
44
56
62
52
51
60
61
63
70
68
67
69
72
71

1-33 types of aircraft (aeroplanes, planes, *Am.* airplanes)

1-6 propeller-driven aircraft (aeroplanes, planes, *Am.* airplanes)

1 single-engine (single-engined) racing and passenger aircraft (racing and passenger plane), a low-wing monoplane (low-wing plane)

2 single-engine (single-engined) passenger aircraft, a high-wing monoplane (high-wing plane)

3 twin-engine (twin-engined) business and passenger aircraft (business and passenger plane)

4 short/medium haul airliner, a turboprop plane (turbopropeller plane, propeller-turbine plane)

5 turboprop engine (turbopropeller engine)

6 vertical stabilizer (vertical fin, tail fin)

7-33 jet planes (jet aeroplanes, jets, *Am.* jet airplanes)

7 twin-jet business and passenger aircraft (business and passenger plane)

8 fence

9 wing-tip tank (tip tank)

10 rear engine

11 twin-jet short/medium haul airliner

12 tri-jet medium haul airliner

13 four-jet long haul airliner

14 wide-body long haul airliner (jumbo jet)

15 supersonic airliner *[Concorde]*

16 droop nose

17 **twin-jet wide-body airliner** for short/medium haul routes (airbus)

18 radar nose (radome, radar dome) with weather radar antenna

19 cockpit

20 galley

21 cargo hold (hold, underfloor hold)

22 passenger cabin with passenger seats

23 retractable nose undercarriage unit (retractable nose landing gear unit)

24 nose undercarriage flap (nose gear flap)

25 centre (*Am.* center) passenger door

26 engine pod with engine (turbojet engine, jet turbine engine, jet engine, jet turbine)

27 electrostatic conductors

28 retractable main undercarriage unit (retractable main landing gear unit)

29 side window

30 rear passenger door

31 toilet (lavatory, WC)

32 pressure bulkhead

33 auxiliary engine (auxiliary gas turbine) for the generator unit

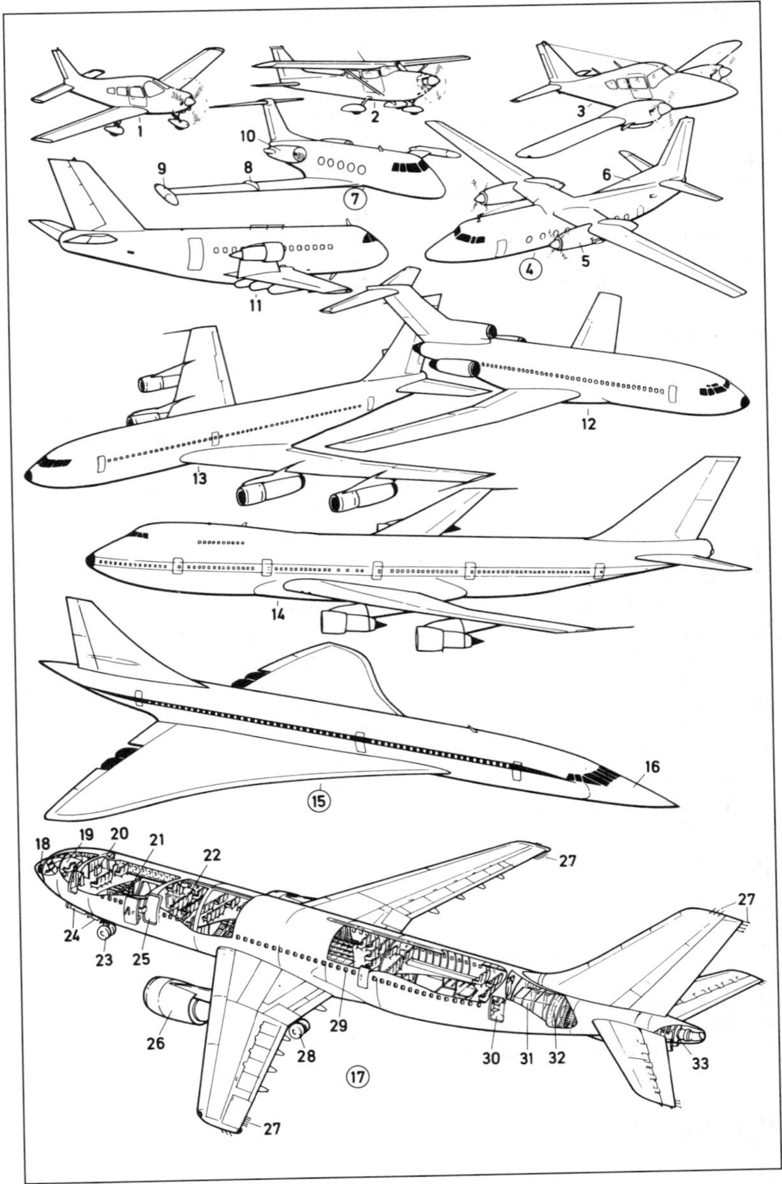
1
2
3
4
5
6
7
8
9
10
11
12
13
14
15
16
17
18
19
20
21
22
23
24
25
26
27
28
29
30
31
32
33

1 **flying boat,** a seaplane
2 hull
3 stub wing (sea wing)
4 tail bracing wires
5 floatplane (float seaplane), a seaplane
6 float
7 vertical stabilizer (vertical fin, tail fin)
8 **amphibian** (amphibian flying boat)
9 hull
10 retractable undercarriage (retractable landing gear)
11-25 **helicopters**
11 light multirole helicopter
12, 13 main rotor
12 rotary wing (rotor blade)
13 rotor head
14 tail rotor (anti-torque rotor)
15 landing skids
16 flying crane
17 turbine engines
18 lifting undercarriage
19 lifting platform
20 reserve tank
21 transport helicopter
22 rotors in tandem
23 rotor pylon
24 turbine engine
25 tail loading gate
26-32 **V/STOL aircraft** (vertical/short take-off and landing aircraft)
26 tilt-wing aircraft, a VTOL aircraft (vertical take-off and landing aircraft)
27 tilt wing in vertical position
28 contrarotating tail propellers
29 gyrodyne
30 turboprop engine (turbopropeller engine)
31 convertiplane
32 tilting rotor in vertical position
33-60 **aircraft engines** (aero engines)
33-50 jet engines (turbojet engines, jet turbine engines, jet turbines)
33 front fan-jet
34 fan
35 low-pressure compressor
36 high-pressure compressor
37 combustion chamber
38 fan-jet turbine
39 nozzle (propelling nozzle, propulsion nozzle)
40 turbines
41 bypass duct
42 aft fan-jet
43 fan
44 bypass duct
45 nozzle (propelling nozzle, propulsion nozzle)
46 bypass engine
47 turbines
48 mixer
49 nozzle (propelling nozzle, propulsion nozzle)
50 secondary air flow (bypass air flow)
51 turboprop engine (turbopropeller engine), a twin-shaft engine
52 annular air intake
53 high-pressure turbine
54 low-pressure turbine
55 nozzle (propelling nozzle, propulsion nozzle)
56 shaft
57 intermediate shaft
58 gear shaft
59 reduction gear
60 propeller shaft

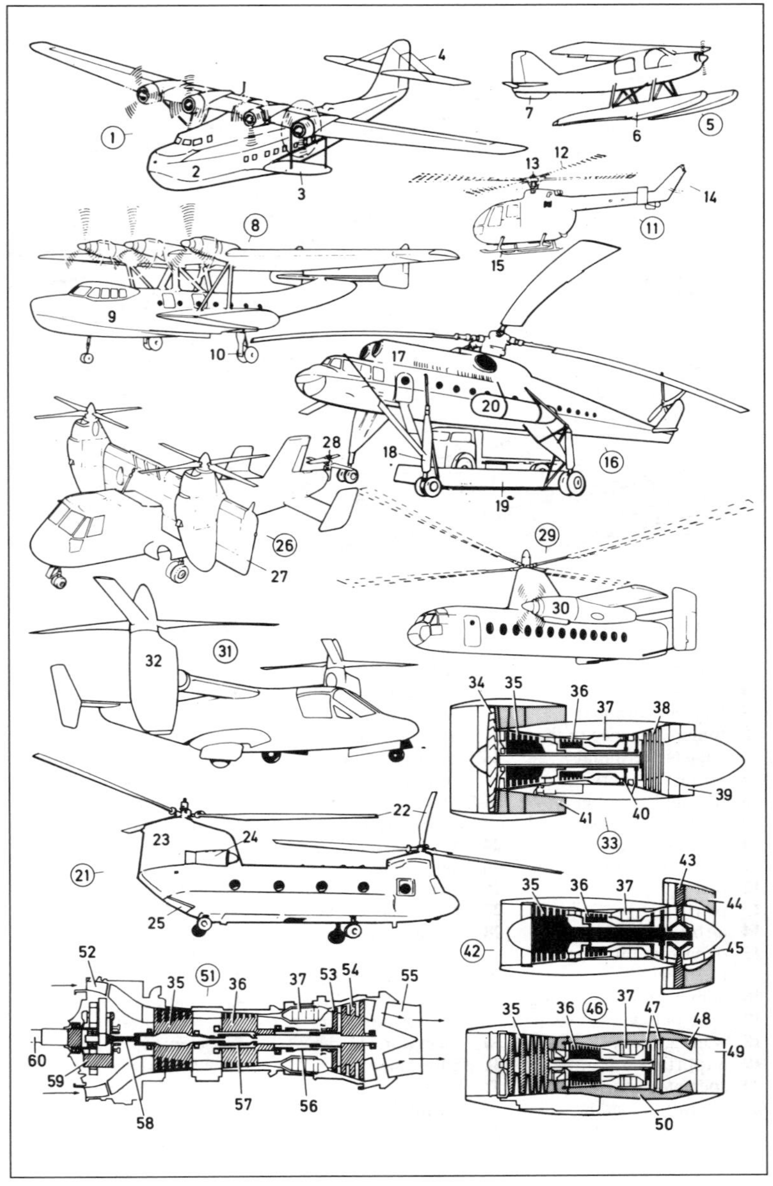
1
2
3
4
5
6
7
8
9
10
11
12
13
14
15
16
17
18
19
20
21
22
23
24
25
26
27
28
29
30
31
32
33
34
35
36
37
38
39
40
41
42
35
36
37
43
44
45
46
35
36
37
47
48
49
50
51
52
35
36
37
53
54
55
56
57
58
59
60

233 Airport

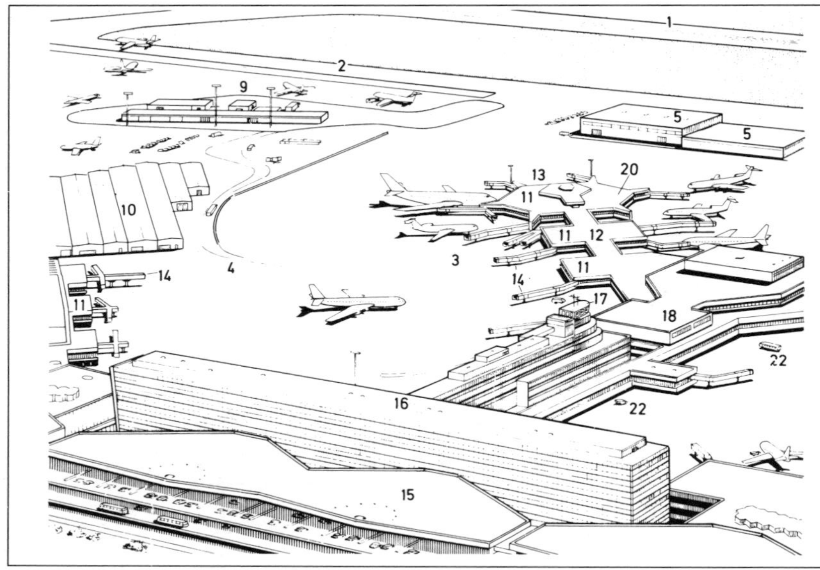

1 runway
2 taxiway
3 apron
4 apron taxiway
5 baggage terminal
6 tunnel entrance to the baggage terminal
7 airport fire service
8 fire appliance building
9 mail and cargo terminal
10 cargo warehouse
11 assembly point
12 pier
13 pierhead
14 airbridge
15 departure building (terminal)
16 administration building
17 control tower (tower)
18 waiting room (lounge)
19 airport restaurant
20 spectators' terrace
21 aircraft in loading position (nosed in)
22 service vehicles, e.g. baggage loaders, water tankers, galley loaders, toilet-cleaning vehicles, ground power units, tankers
23 aircraft tractor (aircraft tug)
24-53 airport information symbols (pictographs)
24 'airport'
25 'departures'
26 'arrivals'
27 'transit passengers'
28 'waiting room' ('lounge')
29 'assembly point' ('meeting point', 'rendezvous point')
30 'spectators' terrace'
31 'information'
32 'taxis'
33 'car hire'
34 'trains'
35 'buses'
36 'entrance'
37 'exit'
38 'baggage reclaim'
39 'luggage lockers'
40 'telephone – emergency calls only'
41 'emergency exit'
42 'passport check'
43 'press facilities'
44 'doctor'
45 'chemist' (*Am.* 'druggist')
46 'showers'
47 'gentlemen's toilet' ('gentlemen')
48 'ladies' toilet' ('ladies')
49 'chapel'
50 'restaurant'
51 'change'
52 'duty free shop'
53 'hairdresser'

2
2
4
6
7
8
3
19
20
14
4
11
13
14
21
22
23
3
22
12
11
11

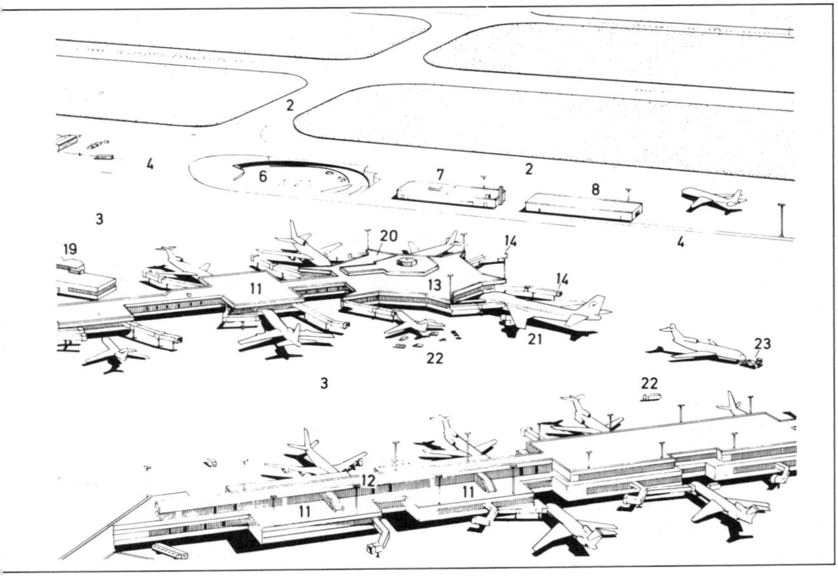

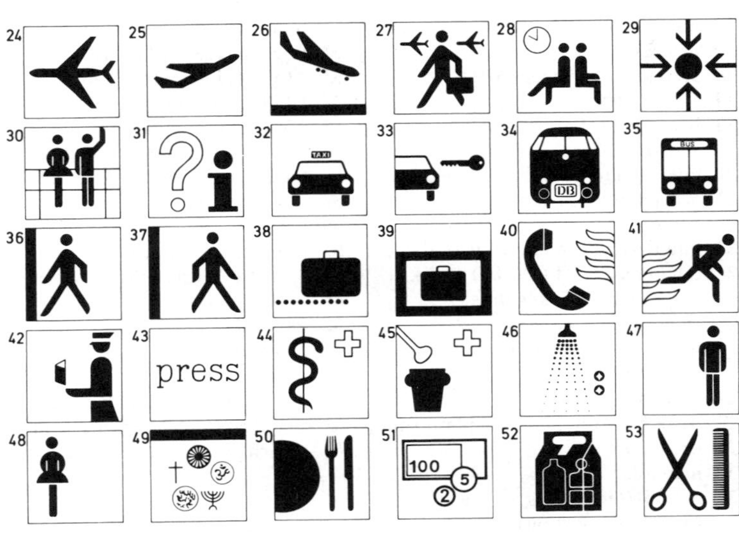

24
25
26
27
28
29
30
31
32
TAXI
33
34
DB
35
BUS
36
37
38
39
40
41
42
43
press
44
45
46
47
48
49
50
51
100
5
2
52
53

1 **Saturn V 'Apollo' booster** (booster rocket) [overall view]
2 Saturn V 'Apollo' booster (booster rocket) [overall sectional view]
3 first rocket stage (S-IC)
4 F-1 engines
5 heat shield (thermal protection shield)
6 aerodynamic engine fairings
7 aerodynamic stabilizing fins
8 stage separation retro-rockets, 8 rockets arranged in 4 pairs
9 kerosene (RP-1) tank [capacity: 811,000 litres]
10 liquid oxygen (LOX, LO_2) supply lines, total of 5
11 anti-vortex system (device for preventing the formation of vortices in the fuel)
12 liquid oxygen (LOX, LO_2) tank [capacity: 1,315,000 litres]
13 anti-slosh baffles
14 compressed-helium bottles (helium pressure bottles)
15 diffuser for gaseous oxygen
16 inter-tank connector (inter-tank section)
17 instruments and system-monitoring devices
18 second rocket stage (S-II)
19 J-2 engines
20 heat shield (thermal protection shield)
21 engine mounts and thrust structure
22 acceleration rockets for fuel acquisition
23 liquid hydrogen (LH_2) suction line
24 liquid oxygen (LOX, LO_2) tank [capacity: 1,315,000 litres]
25 standpipe
26 liquid hydrogen (LH_2) tank [capacity: 1,020,000 litres]
27 fuel level sensor
28 work platform (working platform)
29 cable duct
30 manhole
31 *S-IC/S-II* inter-stage connector (inter-stage section)
32 compressed-gas container (gas pressure vessel)
33 third rocket stage *(S-IVB)*
34 J-2 engine
35 nozzle (thrust nozzle)
36 *S-II/S-IVB* inter-stage connector (inter-stage section)
37 four second-stage *(S-II)* separation retro-rockets
38 attitude control rockets
39 liquid oxygen (LOX, LO_2) tank [capacity: 77,200 litres]
40 fuel line duct
41 liquid hydrogen (LH_2) tank [capacity: 253,000 litres]
42 measuring probes
43 compressed-helium tanks (helium pressure vessels)
44 tank vent
45 forward frame section
46 work platform (working platform)
47 cable duct
48 acceleration rockets for fuel acquisition
49 aft frame section
50 compressed-helium tanks (helium pressure vessels)
51 liquid hydrogen (LH_2) line
52 liquid oxygen (LOX, LO_2) line
53 24-panel instrument unit
54 LM hangar (lunar module hangar)
55 LM (lunar module)
56 Apollo SM (service module), containing supplies and equipment
57 SM (service module) main engine
58 fuel tank
59 nitrogen tetroxide tank
60 pressurized gas delivery system
61 oxygen tanks
62 fuel cells
63 manoeuvring (*Am.* maneuvering) rocket assembly
64 directional antenna assembly
65 space capsule (command section)
66 launch phase escape tower

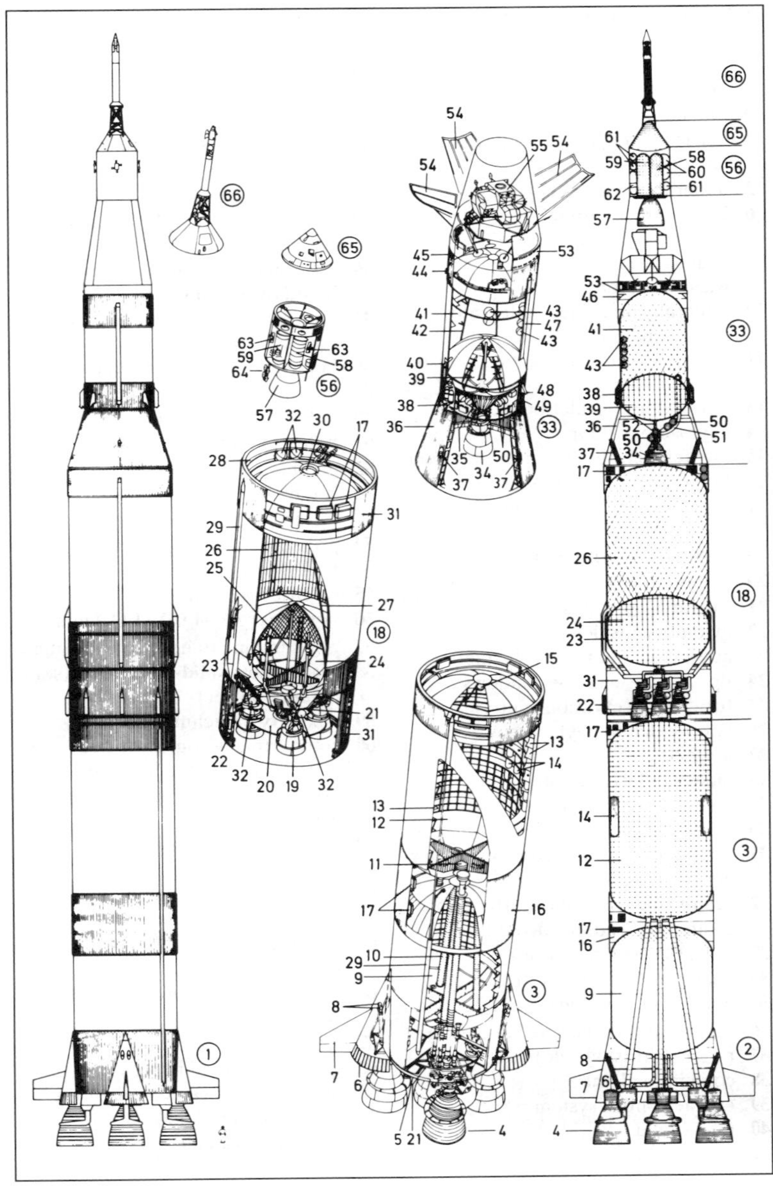

1-45 Space Shuttle-Orbiter

1 twin-spar (two-spar, double-spar) vertical fin
2 engine compartment structure
3 fin post
4 fuselage attachment [of payload bay doors]
5 upper thrust mount
6 lower thrust mount
7 keel
8 heat shield
9 waist longeron
10 integrally machined (integrally milled) main rib
11 integrally stiffened light alloy skin
12 lattice girder
13 payload bay insulation
14 payload bay door
15 low-temperature surface insulation
16 flight deck (crew compartment)
17 captain's seat (commander's seat)
18 pilot's seat (co-pilot's seat)
19 forward pressure bulkhead
20 carbon fibre reinforced nose cone
21 forward fuel tanks
22 avionics consoles
23 automatic flight control panel
24 upward observation windows
25 forward observation windows
26 entry hatch to payload bay
27 air lock
28 ladder to lower deck
29 payload manipulator arm
30 hydraulically steerable nose wheel
31 hydraulically operated main landing gear
32 removable (reusable) carbon fibre reinforced leading edge [of wing]
33 movable elevon sections
34 heat-resistant elevon structure
35 main liquid hydrogen (LH_2) supply
36 main liquid-fuelled rocket engine
37 nozzle (thrust nozzle)
38 coolant feed line
39 engine control system
40 heat shield
41 high-pressure liquid hydrogen (LH_2) pump
42 high-pressure liquid oxygen (LOX, LO_2) pump
43 thrust vector control system
44 electromechanically controlled orbital manoeuvring (*Am.* maneuvering) main engine
45 nozzle fuel tanks (thrust nozzle fuel tanks)
46 **jettisonable liquid hydrogen and liquid oxygen tank** (fuel tank)
47 integrally stiffened annular rib (annular frame)
48 hemispherical end rib (end frame)
49 aft attachment to Orbiter
50 liquid hydrogen (LH_2) line
51 liquid oxygen (LOX, LO_2) line
52 manhole
53 surgebaffle system (slosh baffle system)
54 pressure line to liquid hydrogen tank
55 electrical system bus
56 liquid oxygen (LOX, LO_2) line
57 pressure line to liquid oxygen tank
58 **recoverable solid-fuel rocket** (solid rocket booster)
59 auxiliary parachute bay
60 compartment housing the recovery parachutes and the forward separation rocket motors
61 cable duct
62 aft separation rocket motors
63 aft skirt
64 swivel nozzle (swivelling, *Am.* swiveling, nozzle)
65 **Spacelab** (space laboratory, space station)
66 multi-purpose laboratory (orbital workshop)
67 astronaut
68 gimbal-mounted telescope
69 measuring instrument platform
70 spaceflight module
71 crew entry tunnel

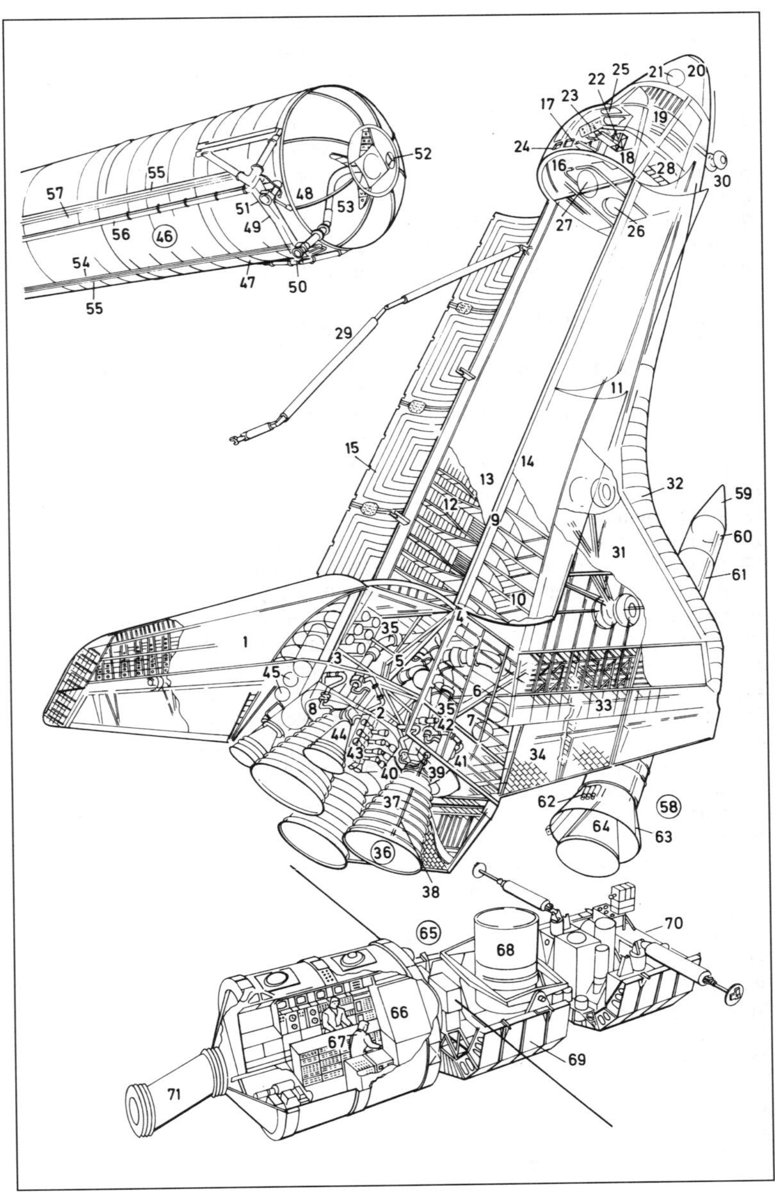
25
21
20
22
23
17
19
24
18
52
16
28
30
55
57
48
51
53
27
26
49
56
46
54
47
50
55
29
11
15
14
13
32
59
12
9
60
31
61
10
4
35
1
3
5
45
6
8
2
35
33
42
7
44
43
34
41
40
39
62
58
37
64
63
36
38
65
70
68
66
67
69
71

1-30 main hall
1 parcels counter
2 parcels scales
3 parcel
4 stick-on address label with parcel registration slip
5 glue pot
6 small parcel
7 franking machine (*Am.* postage meter) for parcel registration cards
8 telephone box (telephone booth, telephone kiosk, call box)
9 coin-box telephone (pay phone, public telephone)
10 telephone directory rack
11 directory holder
12 telephone directory (telephone book)
13 post office boxes
14 post office box
15 stamp counter
16 counter clerk (counter officer)
17 company messenger
18 record of posting book
19 counter stamp machine
20 stamp book
21 sheet of stamps
22 security drawer
23 change rack
24 letter scales
25 paying-in (*Am.* deposit), post office savings, and pensions counter
26 accounting machine
27 franking machine for money orders and paying-in slips (*Am.* deposit slips)
28 change machine (*Am.* changemaker)
29 receipt stamp
30 hatch
31-44 letter-sorting installation
31 letter feed
32 stacked letter containers
33 feed conveyor
34 intermediate stacker
35 coding station
36 pre-distributor channel
37 process control computer
38 distributing machine
39 video coding station
40 screen
41 address display
42 address
43 post code (postal code, *Am.* zip code)
44 keyboard
45 handstamp
46 roller stamp
47 franking machine
48 feed mechanism
49 delivery mechanism
50-55 postal collection and delivery
50 postbox (*Am.* mailbox)
51 collection bag
52 post office van (mail van)
53 postman (*Am.* mail carrier, letter carrier, mailman)
54 delivery pouch (postman's bag, mailbag)
55 letter-rate item
56-60 postmarks
56 postmark advertisement
57 date stamp postmark
58 charge postmark
59 special postmark
60 roller postmark
61 stamp (postage stamp)
62 perforations

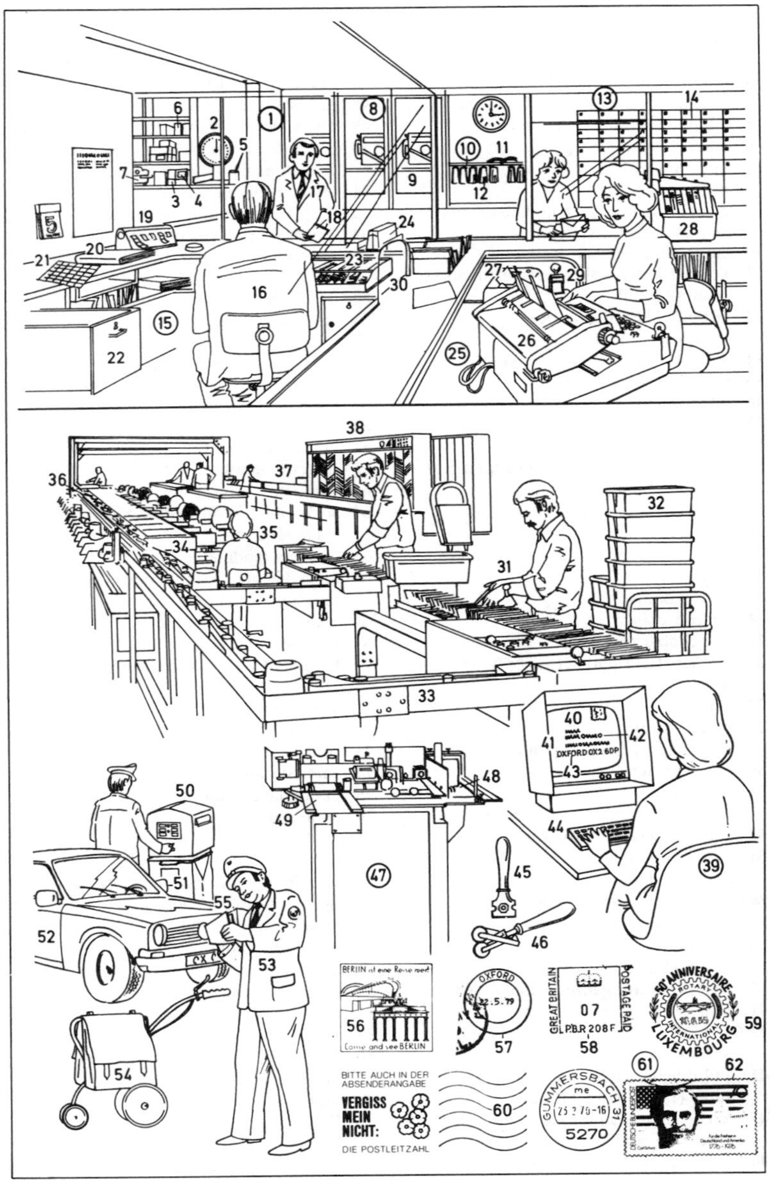

OXFORD OX2 6DP
BERLIN ist eine Reise wert
Come and see BERLIN
OXFORD
22.5.79
GREAT BRITAIN
POSTAGE PAID
07
P.B.R 208 F
50e ANNIVERSAIRE
ROTARY
INTERNATIONAL
LUXEMBOURG
BITTE AUCH IN DER
ABSENDERANGABE
VERGISS
MEIN
NICHT:
DIE POSTLEITZAHL
GUMMERSBACH 31
me
25.2.76-16
5270
DEUTSCHE BUNDESPOST

237 Post Office II (Telecommunications)

1-41 telephone
1 dial telephone
2 handset (telephone receiver)
3 receiver cord (handset cord)
4 telephone cable (telephone cord)
5 telephone casing (telephone cover)
6 emergency numbers
7 line number
8 dial
9 compact telephone (slimline telephone), an added-feature telephone
10 earpiece (receiver)
11 keypad with number and function keys (feature keys)
12 last number redial button
13 abbreviated dialling key
14 speaker key (loudspeaker key)
15 mouthpiece
16 line reset button
17 speaker (loudspeaker)
18 call indicator
19 push-button telephone, an added-feature telephone
20 display
21 lock
22 novelty telephone, an added-feature telephone
23 (telephone) cradle
24 dummy crank
25 detachable keypad
26 cordless (tele)phone (radiophone, mobile phone)
27 aerial
28 battery strength light
29 out of signal-range indicator
30 power switch
31 cardphone
32 split display showing call charges
33 language select button for the display
34 follow-on call button
35 phonecard slot
36 phonecard (*here:* telephone credit card)
37 phonecard symbol
38 cardholder's name
39 card number
40 arrow indicating direction of insertion
41 chips
42-62 ISDN (Integrated Services Digital Network)
42 multifunction telecommunications terminal (ISDN workstation)
43 screen (monitor) for viewdata, video telephone, and Teletex
44 central processing and memory unit
45 fax unit (fax)
46 input device (keyboard)
47 telephone receiver (link to the telephone network)
48 acoustic coupler (modem)
49 telecontrol network (TEMEX network)
50 public telephone network (switched telephone network)
51 telecontrol centres
52 TEMEX main control centre
53 TEMEX transmission equipment
54 telecommunications line (telephone line)
55 TEMEX network termination
56 slave station
57 telecontrol terminal equipment
58 telecontrol terminal equipment (detector, sensor, *or* control equipment)
59 glass-break detector
60 temperature controller
61 emergency call
62 meter (electricity meter)
63 communications satellite
64 solar panel (solar paddle, solar array, solar generator)
65 antenna module
66 receiving antenna for control commands
67 parabolic antennas
68 communications module
69 propulsion module
70 broadcasting satellite (television satellite)
71 service module
72 fuel tanks
73 control jets
74 earth station
75 parabolic antenna
76 main reflector
77 feed antenna
78 radio beams
79 satellite broadcasting, satellite television, and cable television
80 broadcasting satellite
81 television studio
82 television tower
83 cablehead station
84 terrestrial broadcasting
85 satellite broadcasting
86 line-of-sight link (microwave link)
87 cable network
88 cable connections

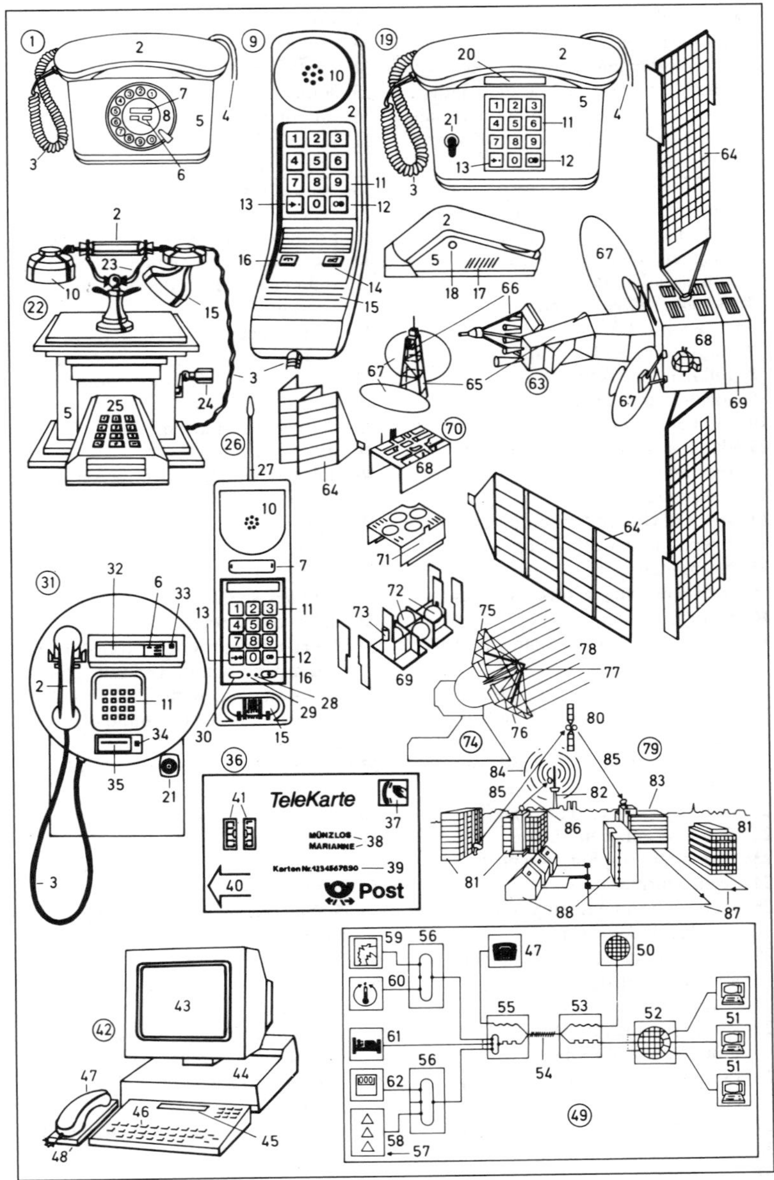
TeleKarte
MÜNZLOS
MARIANNE
Karten Nr. 1234567890
Post

1-6 central recording channel of a radio station
1 monitoring and control panel
2 data display terminal (video data terminal, video monitor) for visual display of computer-controlled programmes (*Am.* programs)
3 amplifier and mains power unit
4 magnetic sound recording and playback deck for 1/4" magnetic tape
5 magnetic tape, a 1/4" tape
6 film spool holder
7-15 radio switching centre (*Am.* center) control room
7 monitoring and control panel
8 talkback speaker
9 local-battery telephone
10 talkback microphone
11 data display terminal (video data terminal)
12 teleprinter
13 input keyboard for computer data
14 telephone switchboard panel
15 monitoring speaker (control speaker)
16-26 broadcasting centre (*Am.* center)
16 recording room
17 production control room (control room)
18 studio
19 sound engineer (sound control engineer)
20 sound control desk (sound control console)
21 newsreader (newscaster)
22 duty presentation officer
23 telephone for phoned reports
24 record turntable
25 recording room mixing console (mixing desk, mixer)
26 sound technician (sound mixer, sound recordist)
27-53 television post-sync studio
27 sound production control room (sound control room)
28 dubbing studio (dubbing theatre, *Am.* theater)
29 studio table
30 visual signal
31 electronic stopclock
32 projection screen
33 monitor
34 studio microphone
35 sound effects box
36 microphone socket panel
37 recording speaker (recording loudspeaker)
38 control room window (studio window)
39 producer's talkback microphone
40 local-battery telephone
41 sound control desk (sound control console)
42 group selector switch
43 visual display
44 limiter display (clipper display)
45 control modules
46 pre-listening buttons
47 slide control
48 universal equalizer (universal corrector)
49 input selector switches
50 pre-listening speaker
51 tone generator
52 talkback speaker
53 talkback microphone
54-59 pre-mixing room for transferring and mixing 16 mm, 17.5 mm, 35 mm perforated magnetic film
54 sound control desk (sound control console)
55 compact magnetic tape recording and playback equipment
56 single playback deck
57 central drive unit
58 single recording and playback deck
59 rewind bench
60-65 final picture quality checking room
60 preview monitor
61 programme (*Am.* program) monitor
62 stopclock
63 vision mixer (vision-mixing console, vision-mixing desk)
64 talkback system (talkback equipment)
65 camera monitor (picture monitor)

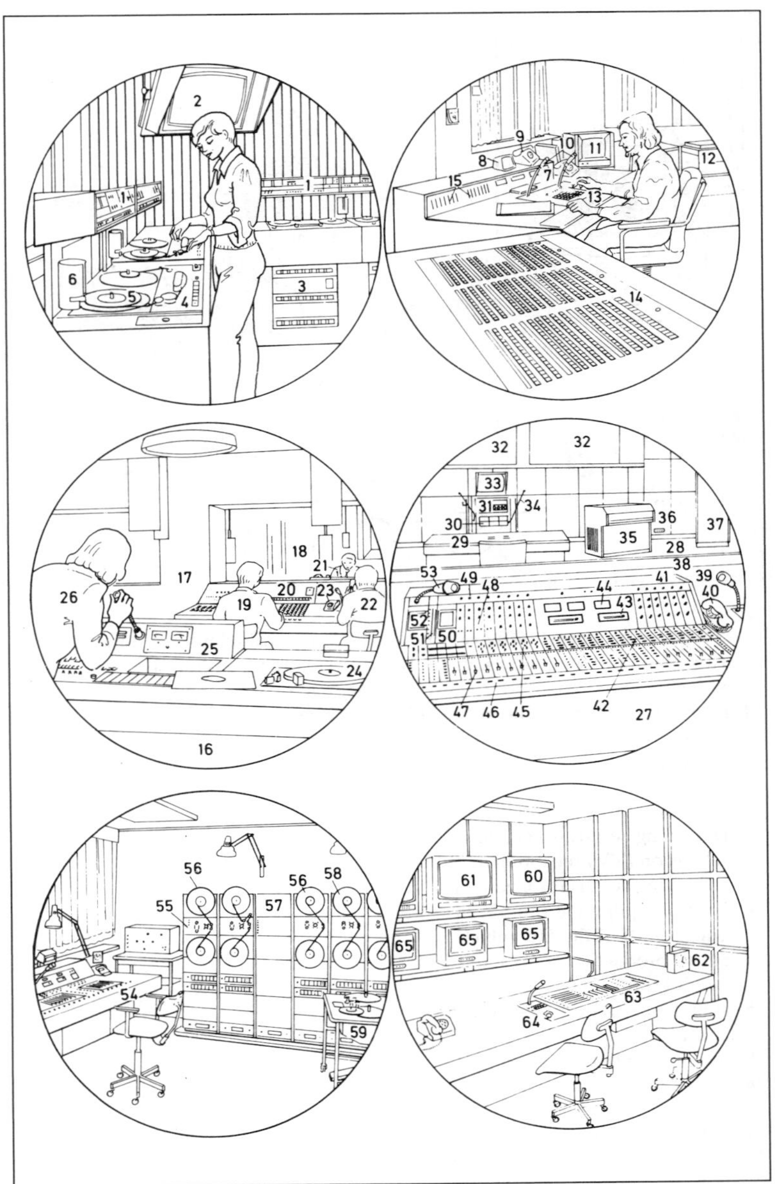
1
2
3
4
5
6
7
8
9
10
11
12
13
14
15
16
17
18
19
20
21
22
23
24
25
26
27
28
29
30
31
32
33
34
35
36
37
38
39
40
41
42
43
44
45
46
47
48
49
50
51
52
53
54
55
56
57
58
59
60
61
62
63
64
65

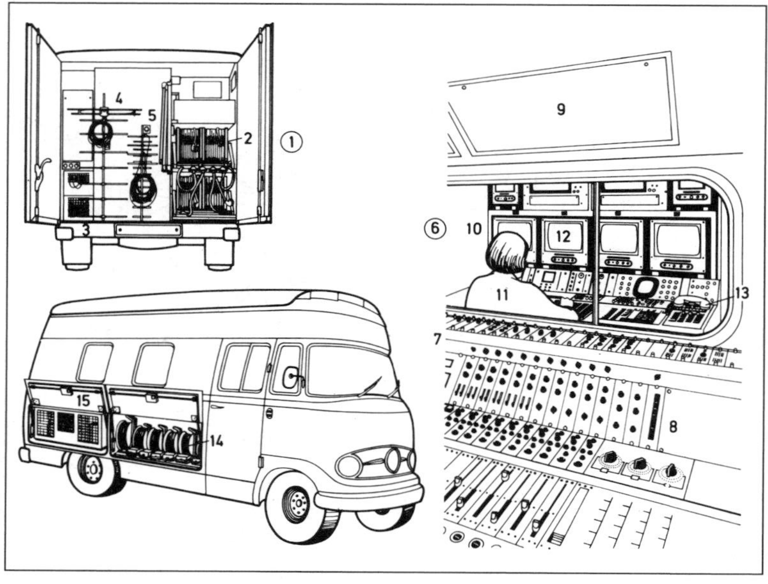

1-15 outside broadcast (OB) vehicle (television OB van; *also:* sound OB van, radio OB van)

1-4 rear equipment section of the OB vehicle

2 camera cable

3 cable connection panel

4 television (TV) reception aerial (receiving aerial) for Channel I

5 television (TV) reception aerial (receiving aerial) for Channel II

6 interior equipment (on-board equipment) of the OB vehicle

7 sound production control room (sound control room)

8 sound control desk (sound control console)

9 monitoring loudspeaker

10 vision control room (video control room)

11 video controller (vision controller)

12 camera monitor (picture monitor)

13 on-board telephone (intercommunication telephone)

14 microphone cables

15 air-conditioning plant

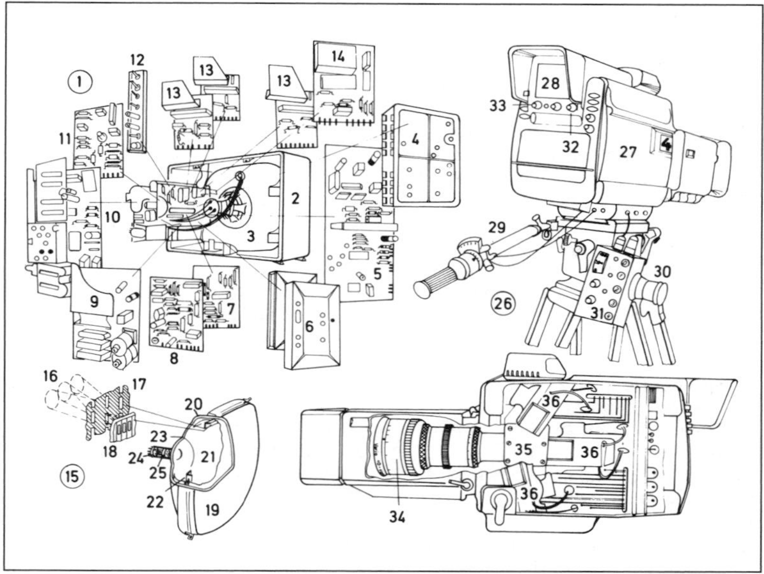

1 **colour** (*Am.* color) **television** (TV) **receiver** (colour television set) of modular design
2 television cabinet
3 television tube (picture tube)
4 IF (intermediate frequency) amplifier module
5 colour (*Am.* color) decoder module
6 VHF and UHF tuner
7 horizontal synchronizing module
8 vertical deflection module
9 horizontal linearity control module
10 horizontal deflection module
11 control module
12 convergence module
13 colour (*Am.* color) output stage module
14 sound module
15 colour (*Am.* color) picture tube
16 electron beams
17 shadow mask with elongated holes
18 strip of fluorescent (luminescent, phosphorescent) material
19 coating (film) of fluorescent material
20 inner magnetic screen (screening)
21 vacuum
22 temperature-compensated shadow mask mount
23 centring (*Am.* centering) ring for the deflection system
24 electron gun assembly
25 rapid heat-up cathode
26 **television (TV) camera**
27 camera head
28 camera monitor
29 control arm (control lever)
30 focusing adjustment
31 control panel
32 contrast control
33 brightness control
34 zoom lens
35 beam-splitting prism (beam splitter)
36 pick-up unit (colour, *Am.* color, pick-up tube)

241 Music Systems (Audio Systems) I

1-17 stereo system (hi-fi system), a midi system
1 hi-fi stack
2 rack lid (rack dust cover, [housing] lid)
3 rack (housing) with glass door
4 record player (record deck, analogue [*Am.* analog] record player)
5 tuner (receiver, radio tuner)
6 amplifier (power amplifier)
7 double cassette deck (double cassette recorder)
8 CD player (compact disc player)
9 cassette rack
10 record and compact disc rack
11 castor
12 speaker (loudspeaker), a three-way bass reflex speaker
13 tweeter, a dome tweeter or piezo tweeter
14 mid-range speaker (squawker)
15 bass speaker (woofer)
16 port
17 infrared remote control [unit] (IR remote control [unit])
18 record player (record deck, analogue [*Am.* analog] record player)
19 turntable with direct drive or belt drive
20 strobe light (strobe speed control)
21 pitch control
22 rpm display
23 stop button
24 auto-return button
25 rpm selector (speed selector)
26 cue button (down)
27 cue button (up)
28 stylus (needle)
29 pick-up
30 size selector (record size selector)
31 tone arm (pick-up arm)
32 tone arm support (pick-up arm support)
33 stylus pressure control
34 anti-skate control
35 tone arm counterweight (pick-up arm counterweight)
36 lid (dust cover)
37 tuner (receiver, radio tuner)
38 power switch
39 tuning button (tuning control)
40 manual and automatic tuning selection button with muting
41 stereo/mono selection button
42 strength-of-signal display button
43 memory button
44 station selection buttons
45 frequency selection buttons ([wave] band selection buttons)
46 station select display
47 fluorescent digital display indicating wave band, frequency, and strength of signal
48 LED indicator for stereo and mono mode and automatic tuning
49 amplifier (power amplifier)
50 function select buttons for the turntable, tuner, cassette deck (tape deck), CD player, and monitor (tape monitor)
51 filter buttons (high and low filter buttons)
52 bass control
53 treble control
54 balance control
55 loudness button
56 volume control
57 headphone socket
58 speaker select buttons
59 LED display, a multifunction display
60 function display
61 receiver, a combined tuner-amp[lifier]
62 display select button
63 liquid crystal display (LCD), a multifunction display
64 [graphic] equalizer, a 2 × 7 band [graphic] equalizer
65 equalizer slide controls
66 LED-display spectrum analyser
67 headphones (stereo headphones)
68 ear pads (ear cushions)
69, 70 microphones
69 directional microphone (stereo directional microphone)
70 electret condenser microphone with omnidirectional pick-up characteristic

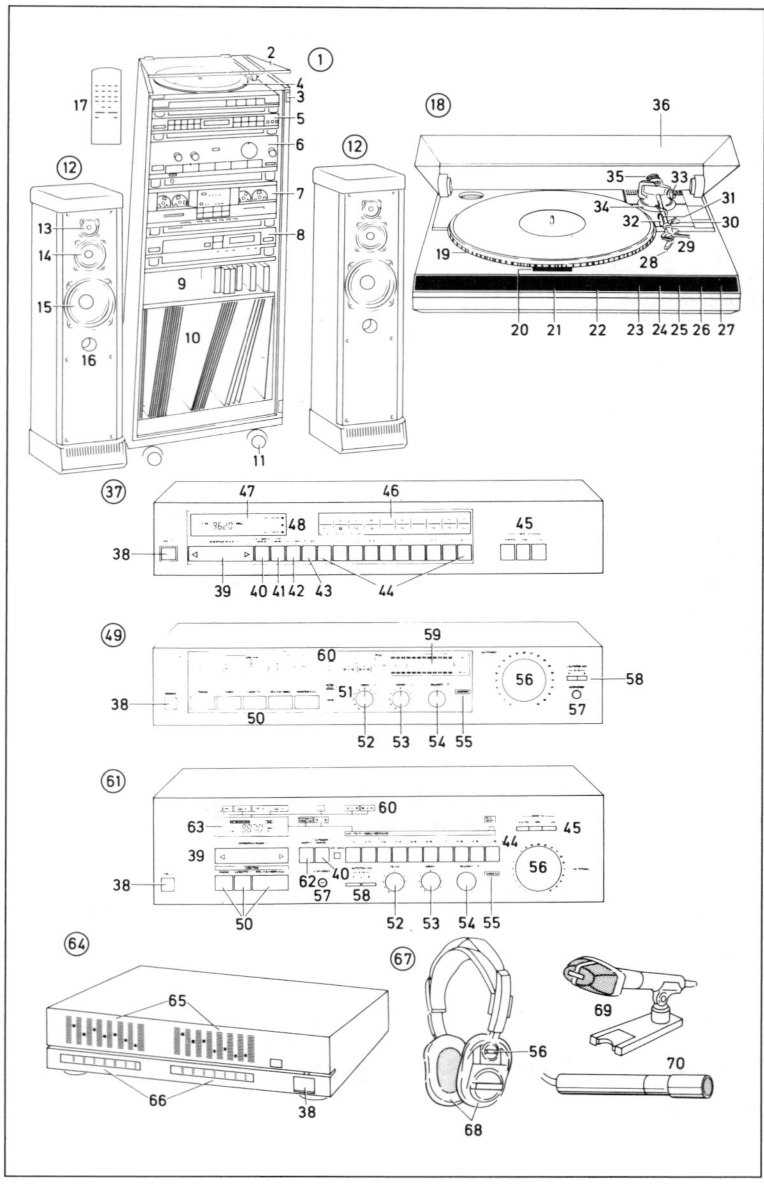
1
2 3 4 5 6 7 8 9 10 11
12
13 14 15 16 17
18
19 20 21 22 23 24 25 26 27 28 29 30 31 32 33 34 35 36
37
38 39 40 41 42 43 44 45 46 47 48
49
50 51 52 53 54 55 56 57 58 59 60
61
62 63
64
65 66
67
68 69 70

242 Music Systems (Audio Systems) II

1 **cassette deck** (cassette recorder)
2 power switch
3 [stop and] eject button
4 cassette holder (cassette drive, cassette transport)
5 dust cover
6 counter (tape counter)
7-12 transport buttons
7 stop button
8 rewind button
9 play buttons for both directions (bidirectional play buttons)
10 fast forward button
11 record button
12 pause button
13 counter reset button
14 noise reduction buttons (Dolby select buttons)
15 auto-reverse buttons
16 recording level control
17 microphone sockets
18 headphone socket
19 level indicator display (VU meter), an LED display
20 tape type indicator (tape-bias indicator), an LED display
21 **double cassette deck** (double cassette recorder)
22 play button
23 [stop and] eject button
24 high-speed dubbing button
25 function select button
26 recording indicator light
27 on-off light (power indicator light)
28 **CD player** (compact disc player, digital compact disc player)
29 CD drawer
30 open/close button for the CD drawer
31 search button and index search button
32 skip buttons (skip-track buttons)
33 headphone volume control
34 function select buttons
35 programming, track and disc repeat, and pause indicators
36 LED display
37 remaining time and track-index indicators
38 **portable radio recorder** with integral CD player
39 handle
40 [radio] receiver (receiver and amplifier)
41 CD player
42 quartz clock with digital display and timer
43 double cassette recorder
44 loudspeaker
45-49 audio-cassette (cassette)
45-47 types of tape
45 ferric cassette (iron oxide cassette, normal cassette)
46 chrome dioxide cassette (chrome cassette)
47 metal cassette (metal oxide cassette)
48 tape type indication (indicating hole)
49 record-protected cassettes
50 **world receiver** for receiving ultra-short wave (USW), medium wave (MW), long wave (LW), and short wave (SW)
51 aerial (rod aerial), a telescopic aerial
52 function buttons
53 station select buttons
54 manual tuning knob
55 liquid crystal display (LCD) showing waveband, frequency, and memory number
56 (sliding) volume control
57 **cassette player** (Walkman® with radio)
58 headphones
59 equalizer, a 3-band equalizer
60 **portable CD player** (Discman®)
61 compact disc (CD)
62 lid
63 casing with transport, amplifier, display, and function buttons
64 **compact hi-fi system** (compact stereo system)
65 amplifier section
66 **DAT recorder** (digital cassette recorder) (DAT = Digital Audio Tape)
67 infrared sensor (IR sensor) for the remote control
68 input selection buttons for mono, analogue (*Am.* analog), and digital signals
69 index and program selection buttons
70 index number display
71 auto-scan button
72 end-record search button

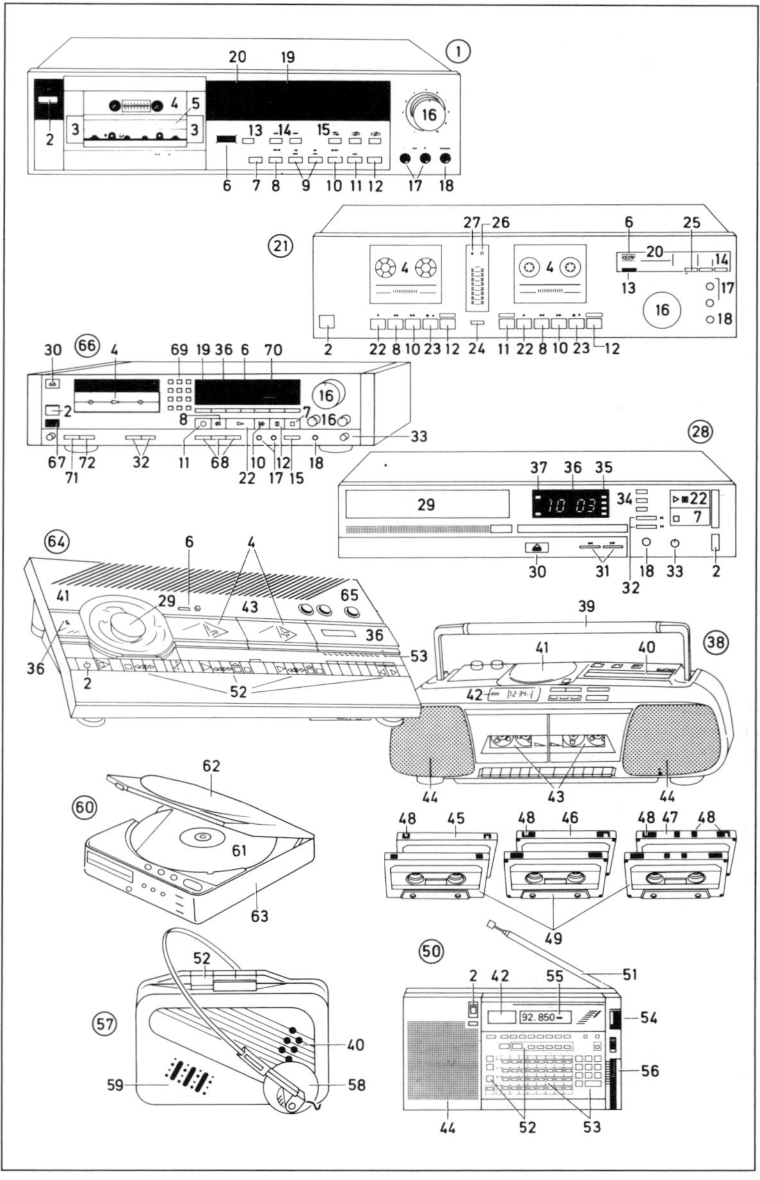

243 Video Equipment

1 camcorder (camera recorder), *form:* two-component system (separate camera and recorder)
2 pocket camcorder, a video-8 camcorder
3 lens, a x6 zoom lens (11-66 mm)
4 viewfinder (ocular)
5 CCD image converter (image sensor) and high-speed shutter, a half-inch chip with shutter functions
6 video cassette
7 videotape
8 head drum
9 autofocus motor
10 built-in microphone (integral microphone)
11 VHS head drum (VHS: Video Home System)
12 erase head
13 guide pin
14 tape guide
15 capstan
16 audio sync head
17 pinch roller
18 video head
19 grooves in the wall of the head drum to promote air cushion formation
20 VHS track format
21 direction of tape movement
22 direction of recording
23 video track, a slant track (only a few tracks shown)
24 sound track (audio track)
25 sync track
26 sync head
27 sound head (audio head)
28 video head
29 video recorder
30 infrared remote control
31 program scale (program dial), a multidisplay
32 cassette compartment
33 jog shuttle knob for forward or reverse movement of the [video] picture
34 multidisc player
35 infrared remote control
36 disc drawer
37-41 disc formats
37 single compact disc (single CD)
38 audio CD
39 video CD
40 small laser disc (20 cm)
41 large laser disc (30 cm)
42 laser scanning system
43 [disc] spindle
44 laser-head tracing spindle
45 laser head (laser unit)

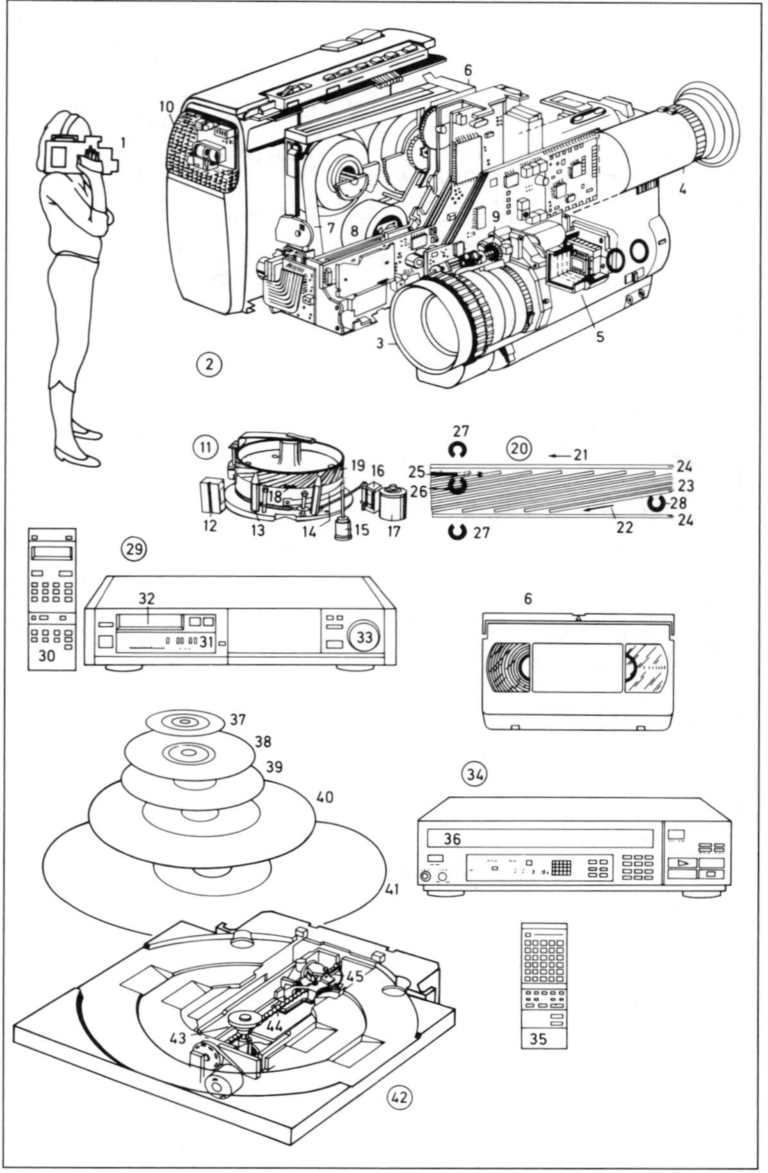
1
2
3
4
5
6
7
8
9
10
11
12
13
14
15
16
17
18
19
20
21
22
23
24
25
26
27
28
29
30
31
32
33
34
35
36
37
38
39
40
41
42
43
44
45

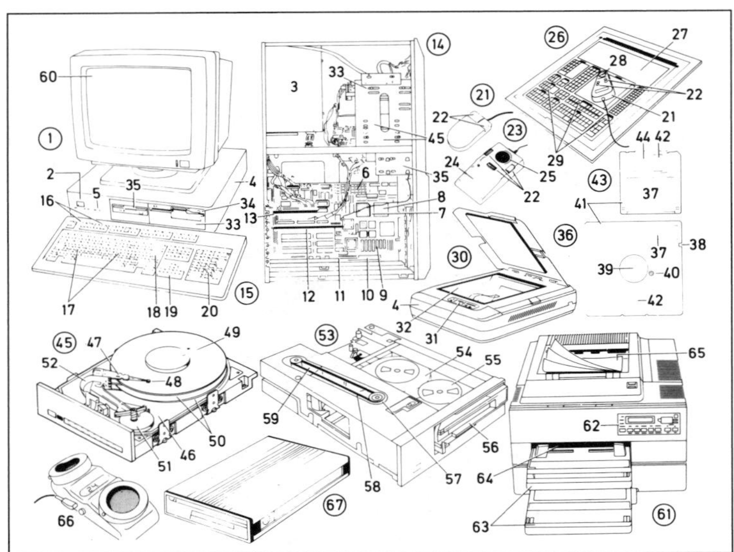

1 **personal computer** (PC; *sim.:* laptop)
2 power switch
3 power supply (power pack)
4 housing
5 fixed-disk access light
6 main memory
7 coprocessor socket
8 central processing unit (CPU), a microprocessor
9 cache memory (cache controller)
10 expansion memory slot
11 graphics card slot
12 combined fixed and floppy disk controller
13 serial and parallel communication card
14 **PC tower** *interior view*
15-67 peripherals
15-32 built-in devices
15 **keyboard**
16 function keys
17 letter keys and number keys (numeric keys)
18 enter key (return key)
19 cursor keys
20 number [key]pad (numeric [key]pad)
21 **mouse**
22 mouse buttons
23 **trackerball** (trackball)
24 handrest
25 roller ball
26 **digitizing tablet** (digitizer, *also:* graphics tablet)
27 graphics area
28 cross hairs
29 receiving grids
30 **scanner**
31 control panel with function keys
32 scanning surface
33-59 mass storage devices (magnetic stores, magnetic memories)
33-44 disk drives (drives, floppy disk drives)
33 minifloppy disk drive (5 1/4 inch [floppy] disk drive)
34 latch
35 microfloppy disk drive (3 1/2 inch [floppy] disk drive)
36-44 diskettes (disks, floppy disks, floppies)
36 minifloppy (minifloppy disk, 5 1/4 inch disk, flexible disk)
37 label
38 write-protect notch
39 hole for engaging the drive hub
40 registration hole
41 disk cover (envelope)
42 access slot for the read-write head
43 microfloppy (3 1/2 inch [floppy] disk)
44 sliding shutter
45 **fixed-disk drive** (fixed disk, hard disk)
46 base plate
47 access arm (actuator)
48 read-write head
49 drive motor for the aluminium (*Am.* aluminum) platters, a spindle drive motor
50 magnetic-coated aluminium (*Am.* aluminum) platters
51 read-write head drive motor, a linear motor or stepping motor (stepper motor)
52 data, address, and control bus
53 **magnetic tape unit** (magnetic tape drive, streamer)
54 magnetic tape
55 magnetic tape reel
56 magnetic tape cassette (magnetic tape cartridge)
57 drive post
58 drive band
59 drive motor
60-65 output devices
60 **screen** (monitor, display) a high-resolution colour (*Am.* color) monitor
61 **printer,** a dot-matrix printer (*here:* laser printer; *also:* inkjet printer, needle printer)
62 control panel with function keys and display
63 paper tray (paper cassette)
64 paper feed path
65 paper output tray
66, 67 devices for long-distance data transmission
66 acoustic coupler
67 modem

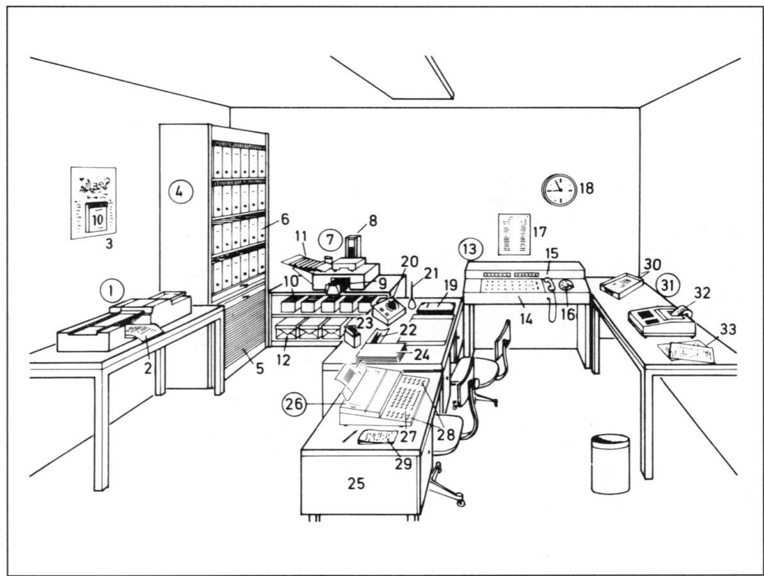

1-33 receptionists office (secretary's office)
1 fax machine
2 transmitted or received copy
3 wall calendar
4 filing cabinet
5 tambour door (roll-up door)
6 file (document file)
7 transfer-type addressing machine
8 vertical stencil magazine
9 stencil ejection
10 stencil storage drawer
11 paper feed
12 stock of notepaper
13 switchboard (internal telephone exchange)
14 push-button keyboard for internal connections
15 handset
16 dial
17 internal telephone list
18 master clock (main clock)
19 folder containing documents, correspondence, etc. for signing (to be signed)
20 intercom (office intercom)
21 pen
22 pen and pencil tray
23 card index
24 stack (set) of forms
25 typing desk
26 electronic memory typewriter
27 keyboard
28 function keys
29 shorthand pad (*Am.* steno pad)
30 letter tray
31 office calculator
32 printer
33 business letter

246 Office II

1-36 executive's office

1 swivel chair
2 desk
3 desk top
4 desk drawer
5 cupboard (storage area) with door
6 desk mat (blotter)
7 business letter
8 appointments diary
9 desk set
10 intercom (office intercom)
11 desk lamp
12 pocket calculator (electronic calculator)
13 telephone, an executive-secretary system
14 dial; *also:* push-button keyboard
15 call buttons
16 receiver (telephone receiver)
17 dictating machine
18 position indicator
19 control buttons (operating keys)
20 cabinet
21 visitor's chair
22 safe
23 bolts
24 armour-plated (*Am.* armor-plated) lock area
25 confidential documents
26 patent
27 petty cash
28 picture
29 bar (drinks cabinet)
30 bar set

31-36 conference grouping

31 conference table
32 pocket-sized dictating machine, a micro-cassette recorder
33 ashtray
34 corner table
35 table lamp
36 two-seater sofa [part of the conference grouping]

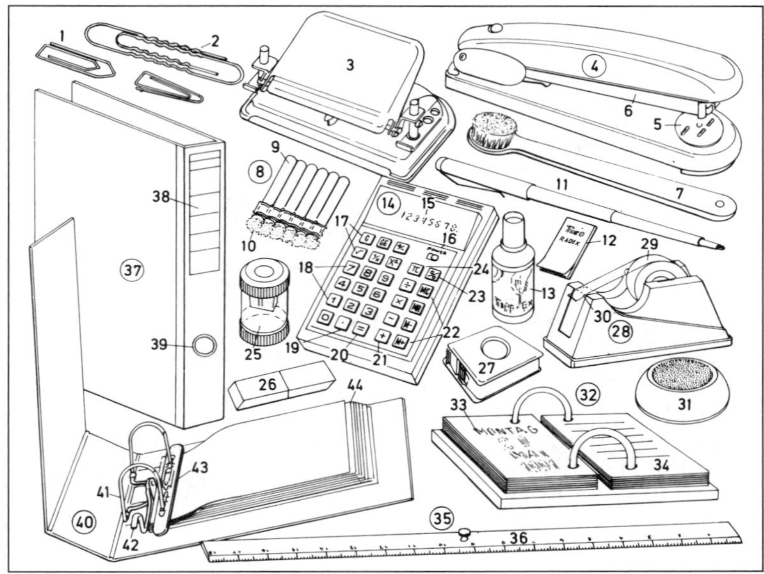

1-44 office equipment (office supplies, office materials)
1, 2 paper clips
3 punch
4 stapler (stapling machine)
5 anvil
6 spring-loaded magazine
7 type-cleaning brush
8 type cleaner (type-cleaning kit)
9 fluid container (fluid reservoir)
10 cleaning brush
11 felt tip pen
12 correcting paper [for typing errors]
13 correcting fluid [for typing errors]
14 electronic pocket calculator
15 eight-digit fluorescent display
16 on/off switch
17 function keys
18 number keys
19 decimal key
20 'equals' key
21 instruction keys (command keys)
22 memory keys
23 percent key (percentage key)
24 π-key (pi-key) for mensuration of circles
25 pencil sharpener
26 typewriter rubber
27 adhesive tape dispenser
28 adhesive tape holder (roller-type adhesive tape dispenser)
29 roll of adhesive tape
30 tear-off edge
31 moistener
32 desk diary
33 date sheet (calendar sheet)
34 memo sheet
35 ruler
36 centimetre and millimetre (*Am.* centimeter and millimeter) graduations
37 file (document file)
38 spine label (spine tag)
39 finger hole
40 arch board file
41 arch unit
42 release lever (locking lever, release/lock lever)
43 compressor
44 bank statement (statement of account)

248 Office IV

1-48 open plan office

1 partition wall (partition screen)
2 filing drawer with suspension file system
3 suspension file
4 file tab
5 file (document file)
6 filing clerk
7 clerical assistant
8 note for the files
9 telephone
10 filing shelves
11 clerical assistant's desk
12 office cupboard
13 plant stand (planter)
14 indoor plants (houseplants)
15 programmer
16 data display terminal (visual display unit)
17 customer service representative
18 customer
19 computer-generated design
20 sound-absorbing partition
21 typist
22 typewriter
23 filing drawer
24 customer card index
25 office chair, a swivel chair
26 typing desk
27 card index box
28 multi-purpose shelving
29 proprietor
30 business letter
31 proprietor's secretary
32 shorthand pad (*Am.* steno pad)
33 audio typist
34 dictating machine
35 earphone
36 statistics chart
37 pedestal containing a cupboard or drawers
38 sliding-door cupboard
39 office furniture arranged in an angular configuration
40 wall-mounted shelf
41 letter tray

42 wall calendar
43 data centre (*Am.* center)
44 calling up information on the data display terminal (visual display unit)
45 waste paper basket
46 sales statistics
47 EDP print-out, a continuous fan-fold sheet
48 connecting element

1 **electric typewriter,** a golf ball typewriter
2-6 keyboard
2 space bar
3 shift key
4 line space and carrier return key
5 shift lock
6 margin release key
7 tabulator key
8 tabulator clear key
9 on/off switch
10 striking force control (impression control)
11 ribbon selector
12 margin scale
13 left margin stop
14 right margin stop
15 golf ball (spherical typing element) bearing the types
16 ribbon cassette
17 paper bail with rollers
18 platen
19 typing opening (typing window)
20 paper release lever
21 carrier return lever
22 platen knob
23 line space adjuster
24 variable platen action lever
25 push-in platen variable
26 erasing table
27 transparent cover
28 exchange golf ball (exchange typing element)
29 type
30 golf ball cap (cap of typing element)
31 teeth
32 **photocopier** (copier, photocopying machine)
33 copyboard cover with single-copy (single-sheet) delivery tray
34 universal paper cassette
35 adjustable paper cassettes
36 front door
37 dual vertical transport unit
38 sorter
39 copy delivery bins
40-43 control panel displays and control keys
40 enlargement, reduction, and program selection keys
41 sort mode and two-sided copy keys
42 display with colour, exposure, format, and copy number selection keys
43 start key (copy start key)
44 **letter-folding machine**
45 paper feed
46 folding mechanism
47 receiving tray
48 **small offset press**
49 paper feed
50 lever for inking the plate cylinder
51, 52 inking unit (inker unit)
51 distributing roller (distributor)
52 ink roller (inking roller, fountain roller)
53 pressure adjustment
54 sheet delivery (receiving table)
55 printing speed adjustment
56 jogger for aligning the piles of sheets
57 pile of paper (pile of sheets)
58 folding machine
59 gathering machine (collating machine, assembling machine) for short runs
60 gathering station (collating station, assembling station)
61 adhesive binder (perfect binder) for hot adhesives
62 **magnetic tape dictating machine**
63 headphones (headset, earphones)
64 on/off switch
65 microphone cradle
66 foot control socket
67 telephone adapter socket
68 headphone socket (earphone socket, headset socket)
69 microphone socket
70 built-in loudspeaker
71 indicator lamp (indicator light)
72 cassette compartment
73 forward wind, rewind, and stop buttons
74 time scale with indexing marks
75 time scale stop

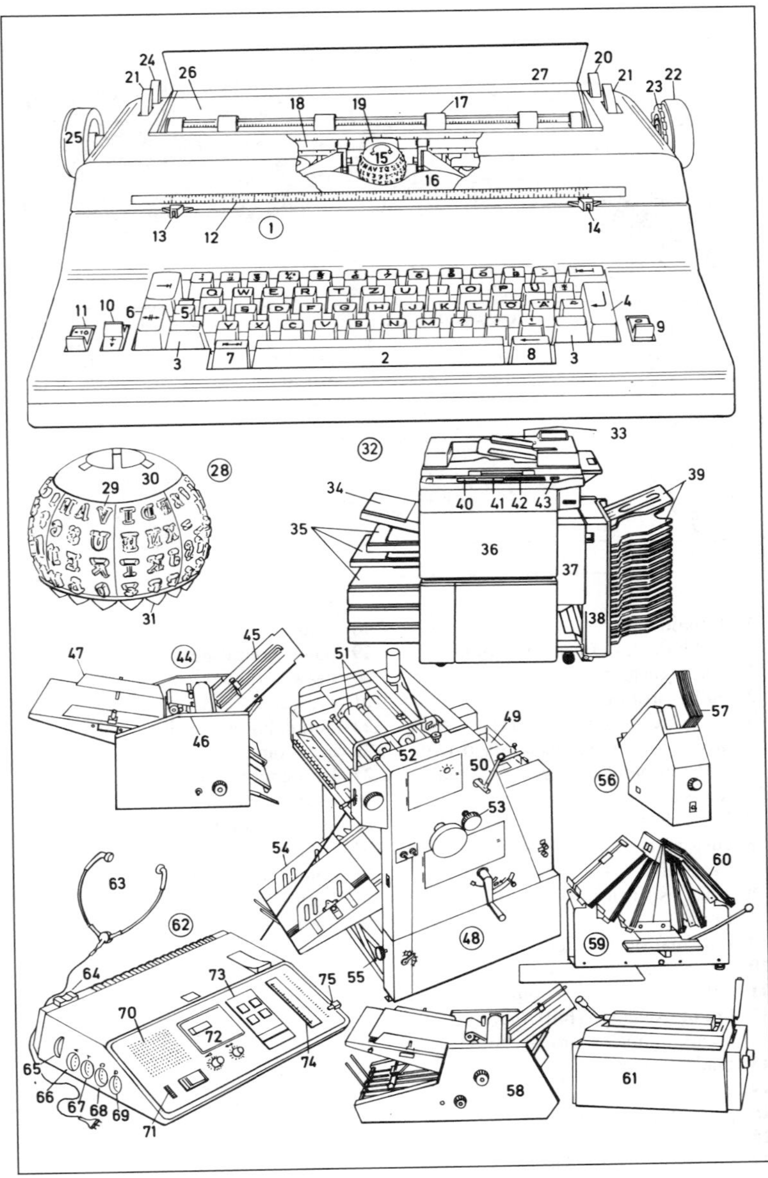
24
21
26
27
20
21
22
23
25
18
19
17
15
16
13
12
1
14
11
10
6
5
4
9
3
7
2
8
3
28
29
30
31
32
33
34
35
36
37
38
39
40
41
42
43
44
45
46
47
48
49
50
51
52
53
54
55
56
57
58
59
60
61
62
63
64
65
66
67
68
69
70
71
72
73
74
75

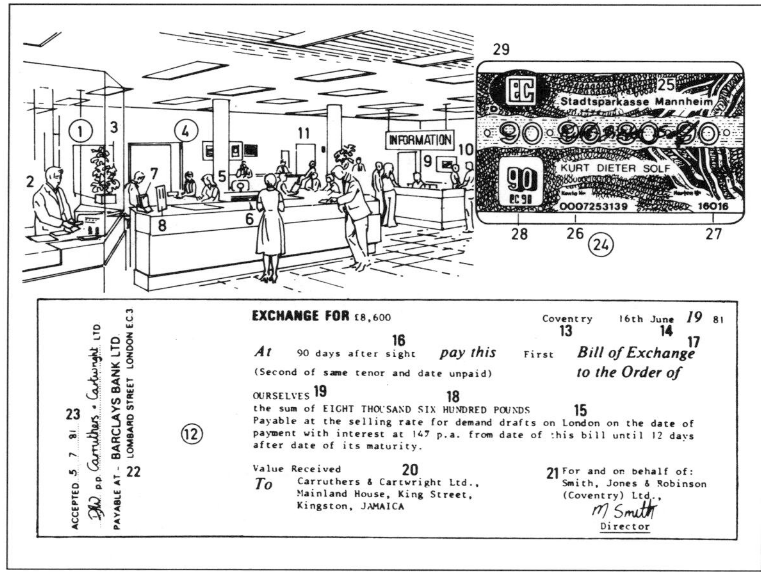

1-11 main hall

1 cashier's desk (cashier's counter)
2 teller (cashier)
3 bullet-proof glass
4 service counters (for service and advice on savings accounts, private and company accounts, personal loans)
5 bank clerk
6 customer
7 brochures
8 stock list (price list, list of quotations)
9 information counter
10 foreign exchange counter
11 entrance to strong room
12 **bill of exchange** (bill); *here:* a draft, an acceptance (bank acceptance)
13 place of issue
14 date of issue
15 place of payment
16 date of maturity (due date)
17 bill clause (draft clause)
18 value
19 payee (remittee)
20 drawee (payer)
21 drawer
22 domicilation (paying agent)
23 acceptance
24 Eurocheque card
25 issuing bank (drawee bank)
26 account number
27 card number
28 hologram, a white light hologram (rainbow hologram)
29 *(on the back:)* magnetic strip

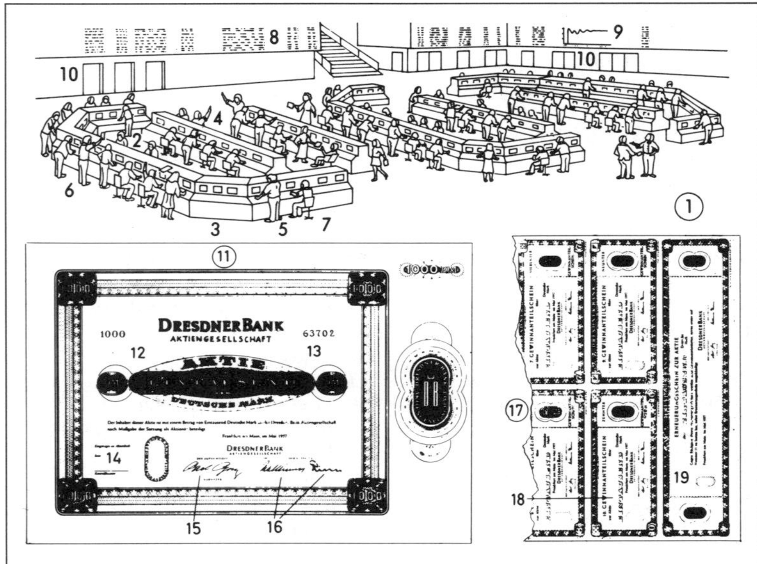

1-10 stock exchange

1 exchange hall (exchange floor)

2 market for securities

3 broker's post

4 sworn stockbroker (exchange broker, stockbroker, *Am.* specialist), an inside broker

5 kerbstone broker (kerbstoner, curbstone broker, curbstoner, outside broker), a commercial broker dealing in unlisted securities

6 member of the stock exchange (stockjobber, *Am.* floor trader, room trader)

7 stock exchange agent (boardman), a bank employee

8 quotation board

9 index curve

10 telephone box (telephone booth, telephone kiosk, call box)

11-19 securities; *kinds:* share (*Am.* stock), fixed-income security, annuity, bond, debenture bond, municipal bond (corporation stock), industrial bond, convertible bond

11 share certificate (*Am.* stock certificate); *here:* bearer share (share warrant)

12 par (par value, nominal par, face par) of the share

13 serial number

14 page number of entry in bank's share register (bank's stock ledger)

15 signature of the chairman of the board of governors

16 signature of the chairman of the board of directors

17 sheet of coupons (coupon sheet, dividend coupon sheet)

18 dividend warrant (dividend coupon)

19 talon

1-29 coins (coin, coinage, metal money, specie, *Am.* hard money); *kinds:* gold, silver, nickel, copper, or aluminium, *Am.* aluminum, coins
1 Athens: tetradrachm (tetradrachmon, tetradrachma)
2 the owl [emblem of the city of Athens]
3 aureus of Constantine the Great
4 bracteate of Emperor Frederick I Barbarossa
5 Louis XIV louis-d'or
6 Prussia: I reichstaler (speciestaler) of Frederick the Great
7 Federal Republic of Germany: 5 Deutschmarks (DM); 1 DM = 100 pfennigs
8 obverse
9 reverse (subordinate side)
10 mint mark (mintage, exergue)
11 legend (inscription on the edge of a coin)
12 device (type), a provincial coat of arms
13 Austria: 25 schillings; 1 sch = 100 groschen
14 provincial coats of arms
15 Switzerland: 5 francs; 1 franc = 100 centimes
16 France: 1 franc = 100 centimes
17 Belgium: 100 francs
18 Luxembourg (Luxemburg): 1 franc
19 Netherlands: 2 1/2 guilders; 1 guilder (florin, gulden) = 100 cents
20 Italy: 200 lire (*sg.* lira)
21 Vatican City: 100 lire (*sg.* lira)
22 Spain: 1 peseta = 100 céntimos
23 Portugal: 1 escudo = 100 centavos
24 Denmark: 1 krone = 100 öre
25 Sweden: 1 krona = 100 öre
26 Norway: 1 krone = 100 öre
27 Czechoslovakia: 1 koruna = 100 heller
28 Yugoslavia: 1 dinar = 100 paras
29 United Kingdom of Great Britain and Northern Ireland: 1 pound sterling (£1) = 100 new pence (100 p) (*sg.* new penny, new p)
30-39 banknotes (*Am.* bills) (paper money, notes, treasury notes)
30 Federal Republic of Germany: 100 DM
31 bank of issue (bank of circulation)
32 watermark [a portrait]
33 denomination
34 USA: 1 dollar ($1) = 100 cents
35 facsimile signatures
36 impressed stamp
37 serial number
38 Greece: 1,000 drachmas (drachmae); 1 drachma = 100 lepta (*sg.* lepton)
39 portrait
40-44 striking of coins (coinage, mintage)
40, 41 coining dies (minting dies)
40 upper die
41 lower die
42 collar
43 coin disc (flan, planchet, blank)
44 coining press (minting press)

1
2
3
4
5
EIN REICHSTHALER
1785
6
7
BUNDESREPUBLIK DEUTSCHLAND
5
DEUTSCHE MARK
8
9
1975
10
11
12
13
REPUBLIK ÖSTERREICH
25
SCHILLING
14
5FR
1968
15
LIBERTÉ · EGALITÉ · FRATERNITÉ
1
FRANC
1960
16
BELGIË
17
18
1970
$2\frac{1}{2}$ G
NEDERLAND
19
200
LIRE
1977
20
CITTA DEL VATICANO
21
1
PESETA
22
1
ESCUDO
23
1975
1 KRONE
24
1975
1 KR
FRAMFÖR · ALLT
25
NORGE
1954
1 KRONE
26
100
ČESKOSLOVENSKA REPUBLIKA
27
1
DINAR
1969
28
29
AD0366403D3
DEUTSCHE BUNDESBANK
100
HUNDERT DEUTSCHE MARK
30
31
32
33
UNITED STATES OF AMERICA
A 37400134 B
ONE DOLLAR
WASHINGTON DC
34
35
36
37
ΤΡΑΠΕΖΑ ΤΗΣ ΕΛΛΑΔΟΣ
ΔΡΑΧΜΕΣ
ΧΙΛΙΕΣ
1000
05M 044520
38
39
40
41
42
43
44

253 Flags

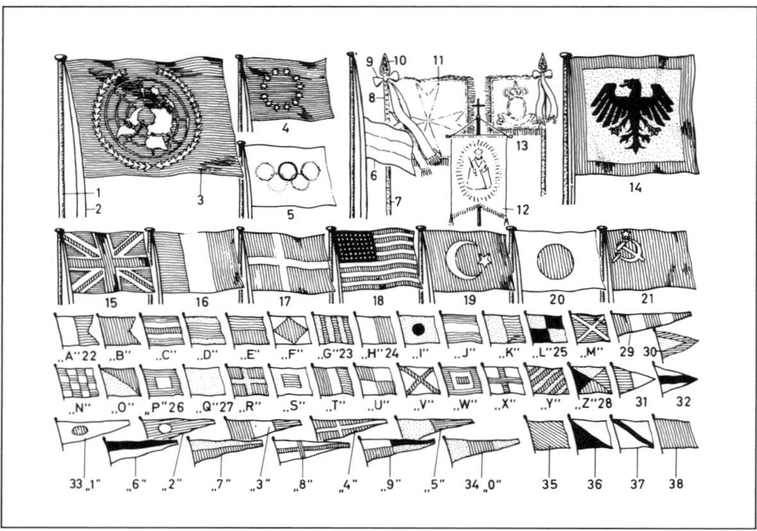

1-3 flag of the United Nations
1 flagpole (flagstaff) with truck
2 halyard (halliard, haulyard)
3 bunting
4 flag of the Council of Europe
5 Olympic flag
6 flag at half-mast (*Am.* at half-staff) [as a token of mourning]
7-11 flag
7 flagpole (flagstaff)
8 ornamental stud
9 streamer
10 pointed tip of the flagpole
11 bunting
12 banner (gonfalon)
13 cavalry standard (flag of the cavalry)
14 standard of the German Federal President [ensign of head of state]
15-21 national flags
15 the Union Jack (Great Britain)
16 the Tricolour (*Am.* Tricolor) (France)
17 the Danebrog (Dannebrog) (Denmark)
18 the Stars and Stripes (Star-Spangled Banner) (USA)
19 the Crescent (Turkey)
20 the Rising Sun (Japan)
21 the Hammer and Sickle (USSR)
22-34 signal flags, a hoist
22-28 letter flags
22 letter A, a burgee (swallow-tailed flag)
23 G, pilot flag
24 H ('pilot on board')
25 L ('you should stop, I have something important to communicate')
26 P, the Blue Peter ('about to set sail')
27 W ('I require medical assistance')
28 Z, an oblong pennant (oblong pendant)
29 code pennant (code pendant), used in the International Signals Code
30-32 substitute flags (repeaters), triangular flags (pennants, pendants)
33, 34 numeral pennants (numeral pendants)
33 number 1
34 number 0
35-38 customs flags
35 customs boat pennant (customs boat pendant)
36 'ship cleared through customs'
37 customs signal flag
38 powder flag ['inflammable (flammable) cargo']

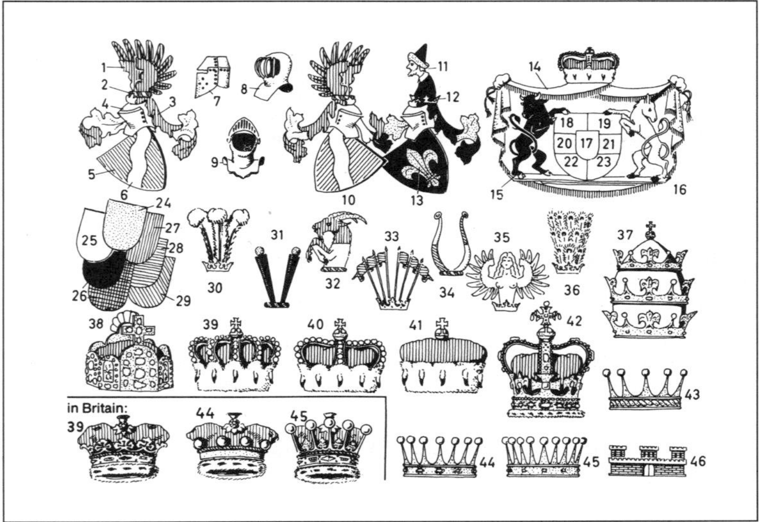

1-36 heraldry (blazonry)
1, 11, 30-36 crests
1-6 coat-of-arms (achievement of arms, hatchment, achievement)
1 crest
2 wreath of the colours (*Am.* colors)
3 mantle (mantling)
4, 7-9 helmets (helms)
4 tilting helmet (jousting helmet)
5 shield
6 bend sinister wavy
7 pot-helmet (pot-helm, heaume)
8 barred helmet (grilled helmet)
9 helmet affronty with visor open
10-13 marital achievement (marshalled, *Am.* marshaled, coat-of-arms)
10 arms of the baron (of the husband)
11-13 arms of the family of the femme (of the wife)
11 demi-man; *also:* demi-woman
12 crest coronet
13 fleur-de-lis
14 heraldic tent (mantling)
15, 16 supporters (heraldic beasts)
15 bull
16 unicorn
17-23 blazon
17 inescutcheon (heart-shield)
18-23 quarterings one to six
18, 20, 22 dexter (right)
18, 19 chief
19, 21, 23 sinister (left)
22, 23 base
24-29 tinctures
24, 25 metals
24 or (gold) [yellow]
25 argent (silver) [white]
26 sable
27 gules
28 azure
29 vert
30 ostrich feathers (treble plume)
31 truncheon
32 demi-goat
33 tournament pennons
34 buffalo horns
35 harpy
36 plume of peacock's feathers
37, 38, 42-46 crowns and coronets [continental type]
37 tiara (papal tiara)
38 Imperial Crown [German, until 1806]
39 ducal coronet (duke's coronet)
40 prince's coronet
41 elector's coronet
42 English Royal Crown
43-45 coronets of rank
43 baronet's coronet
44 baron's coronet (baronial coronet)
45 count's coronet
46 mauerkrone (mural crown) of a city crest

255 Armed Forces I (Army)

1-96 army **armament** (army weaponry)
1-28 **hand weapons**
1 P1 **pistol**
2 barrel
3 front sight (foresight)
4 hammer
5 trigger
6 pistol grip
7 magazine holder
8 MP2 **submachine gun**
9 shoulder rest (butt)
10 casing (mechanism casing)
11 barrel clamp (barrel-clamping nut)
12 cocking lever (cocking handle)
13 palm rest
14 safety catch
15 magazine
16 G3-A3 **self-loading rifle**
17 flash hider (flash eliminator)
18 trigger mechanism
19 notch (sighting notch, rear sight)
20 front sight block (foresight block) with front sight (foresight)
21 rifle butt (butt)
22 44 2A1 **light anti-tank rocket launcher**
23 rocket (projectile)
24 telescopic sight (telescope sight)
25 cheek rest
26 MG3 **machine gun** (Spandau)
27 recoil booster
28 belt-changing flap
29-61 **artillery weapons** mounted on self-propelled gun carriages
29 SFM 110 A2 **self-propelled howitzer**
30-32 gun carriage
30 drive wheel
31 track
32 road wheel
33 hull
34 spade
35 spade piston
36 hydraulic system
37 elevating piston
38 breech ring
39 barrel
40 muzzle
41 buffer (buffer recuperator)
42 M 109 A3 G **self-propelled howitzer**
43 armoured (*Am.* armored) turret
44 fighting compartment
45 barrel clamp
46 fume extractor
47 barrel recuperator
48 light anti-aircraft (AA) machine gun
49 SF Lance **missile launch system** (missile launcher)
50 skirt
51 tracked vehicle
52 missile (guided missile)
53 elevating gear
54 launching ramp
55 110 SF 2 **rocket launcher**
56 fire control system
57 launching tubes
58 tube bins
59 turntable
60 jack
61 driver's cab
62-87 **armoured** (*Am.* armored) **vehicles**
62 Leopard 2 **tank**
63 smooth-barrelled gun
64 driver's hatch
65 commander's periscope
66 smoke canister (smoke dispenser)
67 Luchs **armoured** (*Am.* armored) **reconnaissance vehicle,** an amphibious vehicle
68 cannon
69 hatch
70 antenna
71 propeller (for propulsion in water)
72 **Jagdpanzer** Jaguar 1 **ATGW vehicle** (HOT)
73 guidance system (upper part) with guidance unit
74 HOT guided-missile launcher
75 firing mechanism (upper part)
76 commander's cupola
77 Marder **armoured** (*Am.* armored) **personnel carrier**
78 searchlight
79 MILAN anti-tank guided-missile system
80 Fuchs **armoured** (*Am.* armored) **personnel and load carrier,** an amphibious vehicle
81 rear door
82 Gepard **anti-aircraft tank**
83 surveillance radar
84 tracking radar for fire control
85 twin 35 mm cannon
86 M113 A1 G **armoured** (*Am.* armored) **personnel carrier**
87 machine gun on a traversing mount
88-96 **helicopters**
88 CH-53 G **transport helicopter**
89 single rotor
90 turbine
91 stabilizing tail rotor
92 fuselage
93 cockpit
94 BO-105P **anti-tank helicopter**
95 skid
96 HOT anti-tank guided-missile launcher

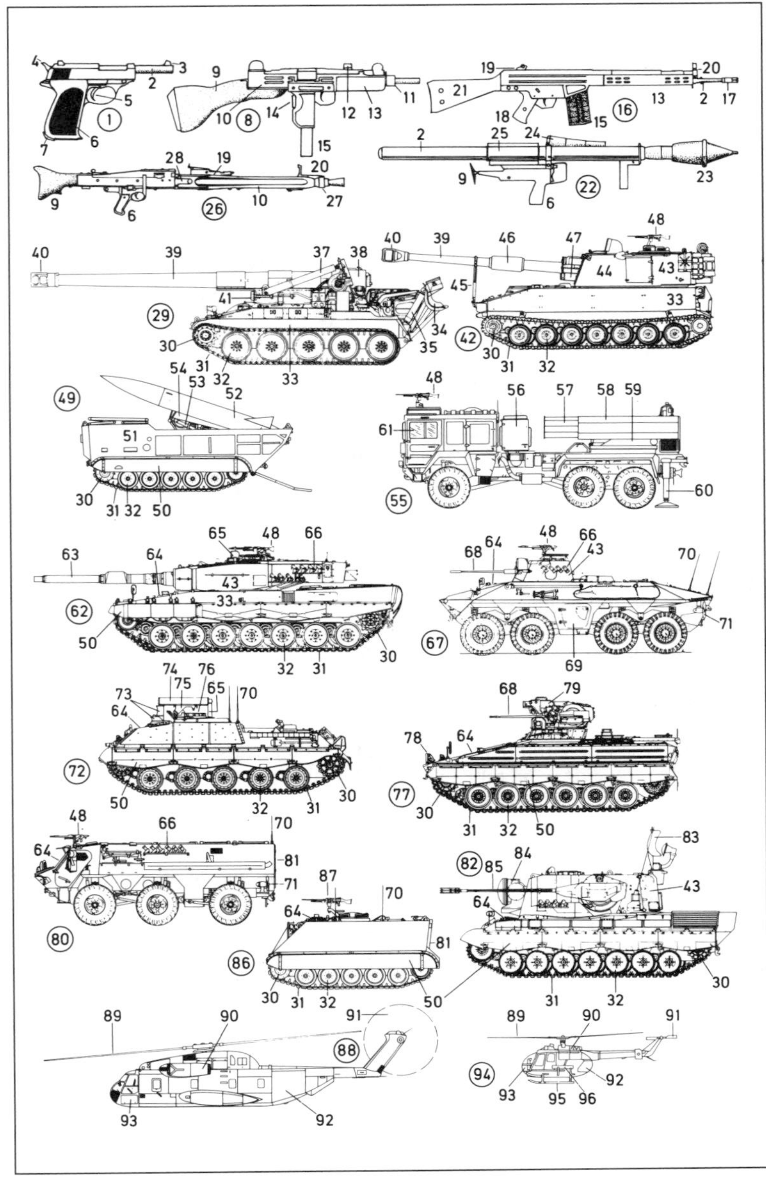
4 3 2 5 1 6 7
9 10 8 14 12 13 11 15
19 20 21 13 2 17 18 15 16
2 25 24 9 6 22 23
28 19 20 9 6 26 10 27
40 39 37 38 41 29 30 31 32 33 34 35
40 39 46 47 48 45 44 43 33 42 30 31 32
54 53 52 49 51 30 31 32 50
48 56 57 58 59 61 55 60
65 48 66 63 64 43 33 62 50 32 31 30
68 64 48 66 43 70 71 67 69
74 76 75 65 70 73 64 72 50 32 31 30
68 79 78 64 77 30 31 32 50
48 66 70 64 81 71 80
87 70 64 81 86 30 31 32 50
83 84 82 85 43 64 31 32 30
89 90 91 88 93 92
89 90 91 94 92 93 95 96

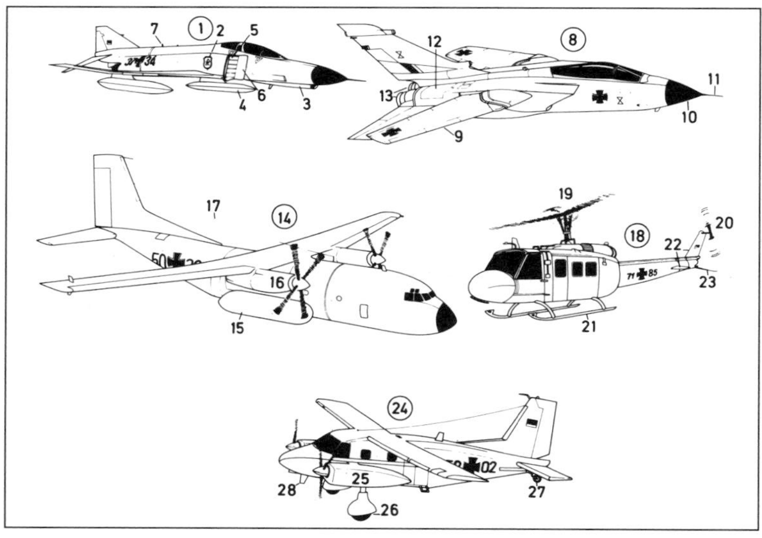

1 *McDonnell-Douglas F-4F Phantom II* **interceptor and fighter-bomber**
2 squadron marking
3 aircraft cannon
4 wing tank (underwing tank)
5 air intake
6 boundary layer control flap
7 in-flight refuelling (*Am.* refueling) probe (flight refuelling probe, air refuelling probe)
8 *Panavia 2000 Tornado* **multirole combat aircraft** (MRCA)
9 swing wing
10 radar nose (radome, radar dome)
11 pitot-static tube (pitot tube)
12 brake flap (air brake)
13 afterburner exhaust nozzles of the engines
14 *C160 Transall* **medium-range transport aircraft**
15 undercarriage housing (landing gear housing)
16 propeller-turbine engine (turboprop engine)
17 antenna
18 *Bell UH-ID Iroquois* **light transport and rescue helicopter**
19 main rotor
20 tail rotor
21 landing skids
22 stabilizing fins (stabilizing surfaces, stabilizers)
23 tail skid
24 *Dornier DO 28 D-2 Skyservant* **transport and communications aircraft**
25 engine pod
26 main undercarriage unit (main landing gear unit)
27 tail wheel
28 sword antenna

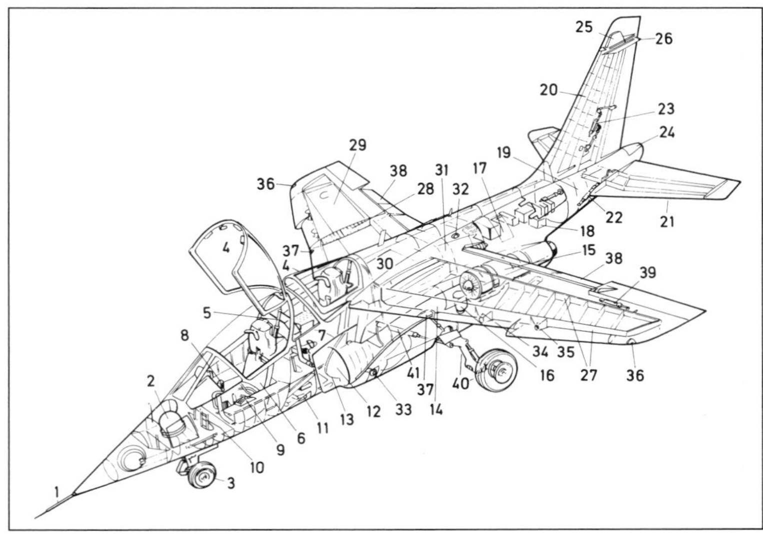

1-41 *Dornier-Dassault-Breguet Alpha Jet* Franco-German jet trainer
1 pitot-static tube (pitot tube)
2 oxygen tank
3 forward-retracting nose wheel
4 cockpit canopy (cockpit hood)
5 canopy jack
6 pilot's seat (student pilot's seat), an ejector seat (ejection seat)
7 observer's seat (instructor's seat), an ejector seat (ejection seat)
8 control column (control stick)
9 thrust lever
10 rudder pedals with brakes
11 front avionics bay
12 air intake to the engine
13 boundary layer control flap
14 air intake duct
15 turbine engine
16 reservoir for the hydraulic system
17 battery housing
18 rear avionics bay
19 baggage compartment
20 triple-spar tail construction
21 horizontal tail
22 servo-actuating mechanism for the elevator
23 servo-actuating mechanism for the rudder
24 brake chute housing (drag chute housing)
25 VHF (very high frequency) antenna (UHF antenna)
26 VOR (very high frequency omnidirectional range) antenna
27 twin-spar wing construction
28 former with integral spars
29 integral wing tanks
30 centre-section (*Am.* center-section) fuel tank
31 fuselage tanks
32 gravity fuelling (*Am.* fueling) point
33 pressure fuelling (*Am.* fueling) point
34 inner wing suspension
35 outer wing suspension
36 navigation lights (position lights)
37 landing lights
38 landing flap
39 aileron actuator
40 forward-retracting main undercarriage unit (main landing gear unit)
41 undercarriage hydraulic cylinder (landing gear hydraulic cylinder)

1 Hamburg class **guided-missile destroyer**
2 hull of flush-deck vessel
3 bow (stem)
4 flagstaff (jackstaff)
5 anchor, a stockless anchor (patent anchor)
6 anchor capstan (windlass)
7 breakwater (*Am.* manger board)
8 chine strake
9 main deck
10-28 superstructures
10 superstructure deck
11 life rafts
12 cutter (ship's boat)
13 davit (boat-launching crane)
14 bridge (bridge superstructure)
15 side navigation light (side running light)
16 antenna
17 radio direction finder (RDF) frame
18 lattice mast
19 forward funnel
20 aft funnel
21 cowl
22 aft superstructure (poop)
23 capstan
24 companion ladder (companionway, companion hatch)
25 ensign staff
26 stern, a transom stern
27 waterline
28 searchlight
29-37 armament
29 100 mm gun turret
30 four-barrel anti-submarine rocket launcher (missile launcher)
31 40 mm twin anti-aircraft (AA) gun
32 MM 38 anti-aircraft (AA) rocket launcher (missile launcher) in launching container
33 anti-submarine torpedo tube
34 depth-charge thrower
35 weapon system radar
36 radar antenna (radar scanner)
37 optical rangefinder
38 Lütjens class **guided-missile destroyer**
39 bower anchor
40 propeller guard
41 tripod lattice mast
42 pole mast
43 ventilator openings (ventilator grill)
44 exhaust pipe
45 ship's boat
46 antenna
47 radar-controlled 127 mm all-purpose gun in turret
48 127 mm all-purpose gun
49 launcher for Tartar missiles
50 anti-submarine rocket (ASROC) launcher (missile launcher)
51 fire control radar antennas
52 radome (radar dome)
53 Bremen class **frigate**
54 radar-controlled 76 mm rapid-fire gun
55 Sea Sparrow surface-to-air missiles
56 radar and fire control system
57 Harpoon surface-to-surface missiles
58 funnel
59 cowl
60 air/surface search radar
61 cutter
62 close-range surface-to-air missiles
63 helicopter deck
64 type 206 **submarine**
65 flooded foredeck
66 pressure hull
67 turret
68 retractable instruments
69 type 148 **missile-firing fast attack craft**
70 76 mm all-purpose gun with turret
71 missile-launching housing
72 deckhouse
73 40 mm anti-aircraft (AA) gun
74 propeller guard moulding (*Am.* molding)
75 type 143 **missile-firing fast attack craft**
76 breakwater (*Am.* manger board)
77 radome (radar dome)
78 torpedo tube
79 exhaust escape flue
80 type 331 **mine hunter**
81 reinforced rubbing strake
82 inflatable boat (inflatable dinghy)
83 davit
84 type 341 **minesweeper**
85 cable winch
86 towing winch (towing machine, towing engine)
87 mine-sweeping gear (paravanes)
88 crane (davit)
89 Barbe class **landing craft**
90 bow ramp
91 stern ramp
92 Rhein class **tender**
93 Lüneburg class **support ship**
94 Sachsenwald class **mine transport**
95 Helgoland class **salvage tug**
96 **replenishment tanker** 'Eifel'

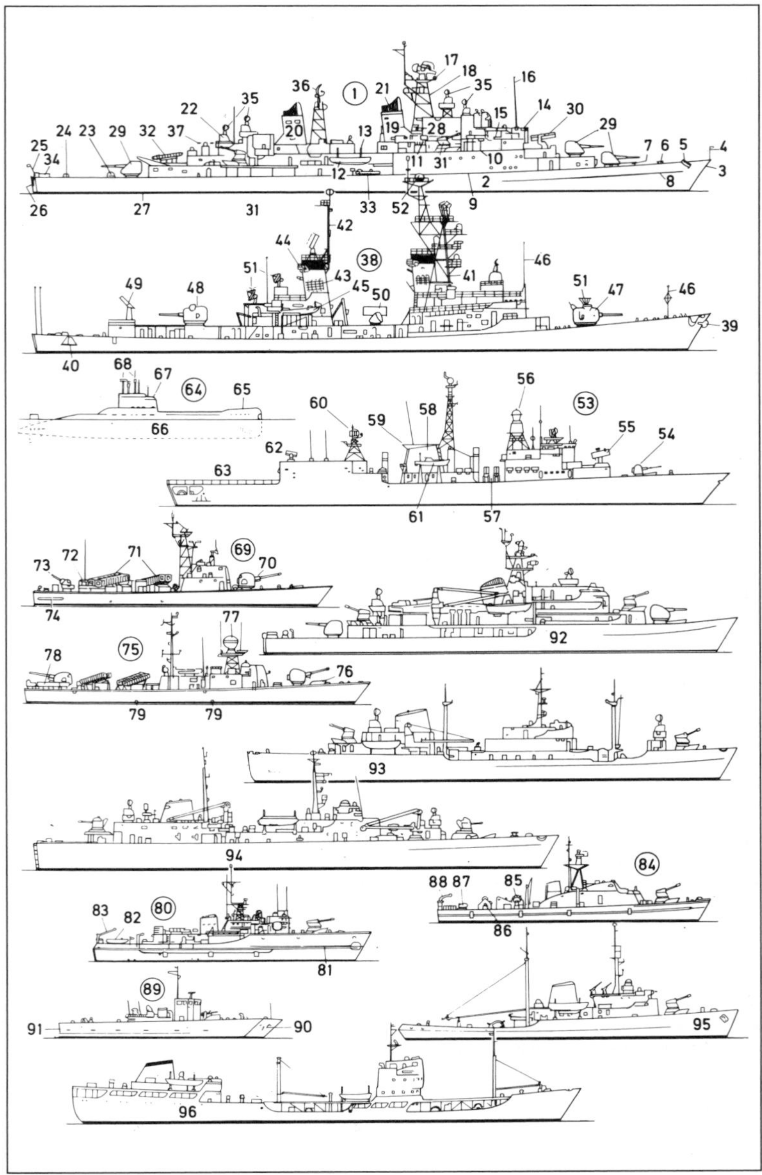

17 18 16 35
36 (1) 21 35 14 30
22 15 29
24 23 29 32 37 20 13 19 28
25 7 6 5 4
34 11 31 10
12 2 3
8
26 27 31 33 52 9
42
44 46
51 (38) 43
49 48 45 41 51 47 46
50
39
40
68 67
(64) 65 56
66 60 58 (53)
59 55 54
62
63
61 57
(69)
72 71 70
73
74
92
77
78 (75) 76
79 79
93
94
(84)
88 87 85
83 82 (80)
86
81
(89)
91 90 95
96

259 Warships II (Modern Fighting Ships)

1 **nuclear-powered aircraft carrier** *Nimitz ICVN68* (USA)
2-11 body plan
2 flight deck
3 island (bridge)
4 aircraft lift (*Am.* aircraft elevator)
5 eight-barrel anti-aircraft (AA) rocket launcher (missile launcher)
6 pole mast (antenna mast)
7 antenna
8 radar antenna (radar scanner)
9 fully enclosed bow
10 deck crane
11 transom stern
12-20 deck plan
12 angle deck (flight deck)
13 aircraft lift (*Am.* aircraft elevator)
14 twin launching catapult
15 hinged (movable) baffle board
16 arrester wire
17 emergency crash barrier
18 safety net
19 caisson (cofferdam)
20 eight-barrel anti-aircraft (AA) rocket launcher (missile launcher)
21 *Kara class* **rocket cruiser** (missile cruiser) (USSR)
22 hull of flush-deck vessel
23 sheer
24 twelve-barrel underwater salvo rocket launcher (missile launcher)
25 twin anti-aircraft (AA) rocket launcher (missile launcher)
26 launching housing for 4 short-range rockets (missiles)
27 baffle board
28 bridge
29 radar antenna (radar scanner)
30 twin 76 mm anti-aircraft (AA) gun turret
31 turret
32 funnel
33 twin anti-aircraft (AA) rocket launcher (missile launcher)
34 automatic anti-aircraft (AA) gun
35 ship's boat
36 underwater 5-torpedo housing
37 underwater 6-salvo rocket launcher (missile launcher)
38 helicopter hangar
39 helicopter landing platform
40 variable depth sonar (VDS)
41 *California class* **rocket cruiser** (missile cruiser) (USA)
42 hull
43 forward turret
44 aft turret
45 forward superstructure
46 landing craft
47 antenna
48 radar antenna (radar scanner)
49 radome (radar dome)
50 surface-to-air rocket launcher (missile launcher)
51 underwater rocket launcher (missile launcher)
52 127 mm gun with turret
53 helicopter landing platform
54 **nuclear-powered fleet submarine**
55-74 middle section [diagram]
55 pressure hull
56 auxiliary engine room
57 rotary turbine pump
58 steam turbine generator
59 propeller shaft
60 thrust block
61 reduction gear
62 high and low pressure turbine
63 high-pressure steam pipe for the secondary water circuit (auxiliary water circuit)
64 condenser
65 primary water circuit
66 heat exchanger
67 nuclear reactor casing (atomic pile casing)
68 reactor core
69 control rods
70 lead screen
71 turret
72 snorkel (schnorkel)
73 air inlet
74 retractable instruments
75 **patrol submarine** with conventional (diesel-electric) drive
76 pressure hull
77 flooded foredeck
78 outer flap (outer doors) [for torpedoes]
79 torpedo tube
80 bow bilge
81 anchor
82 anchor winch
83 battery
84 living quarters with folding bunks
85 commanding officer's cabin
86 main hatchway
87 flagstaff
88-91 retractable instruments
88 attack periscope
89 antenna
90 snorkel (schnorkel)
91 radar antenna (radar scanner)
92 exhaust outlet
93 heat space (hot-pipe space)
94 diesel generators
95 aft diving plane and vertical rudder
96 forward vertical rudder

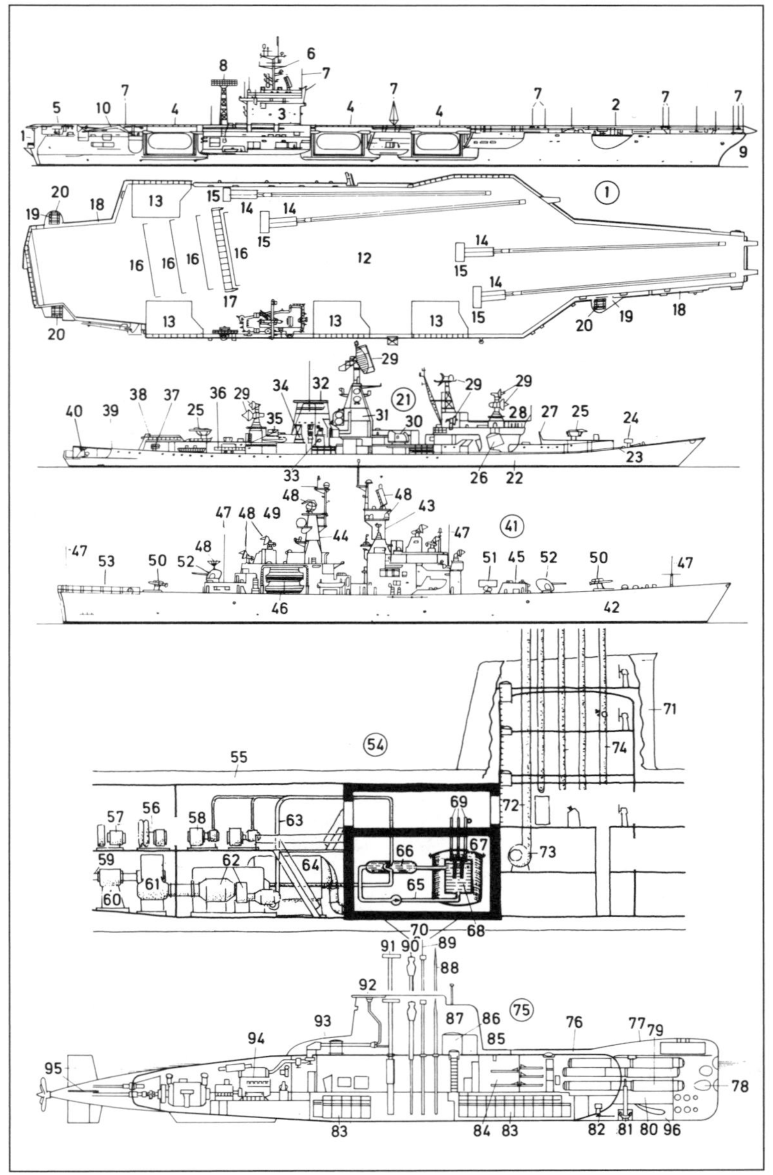

5 10 7 4 8 6 7 3 4 7 4 7 2 7 7
1 9
①
20 19 18 13 15 14 14 15 16 16 16 16 12 17 13 13 13 15 14 15 14 15 20 19 18 20
㉑
40 39 38 37 25 36 29 34 32 35 33 29 31 30 29 29 28 27 25 24 23 26 22
㊶
47 53 50 52 48 47 48 49 48 44 48 43 47 46 51 45 52 50 47 42
54
55 57 56 58 63 59 61 60 62 64 66 65 69 67 68 70 72 73 74 71
75
91 90 89 88 92 93 94 95 87 86 85 76 77 79 78 83 84 83 82 81 80 96

1-85 primary school
1-45 classroom
1 arrangement of desks in a horseshoe
2 double desk
3 pupils (children) in a group (sitting in a group)
4 exercise book
5 pencil
6 wax crayon
7 school bag
8 handle
9 school satchel (satchel)
10 front pocket
11 strap (shoulder strap)
12 pen and pencil case
13 zip (*Am.* zipper)
14 fountain pen (pen)
15 loose-leaf file (ring file)
16 reader
17 spelling book
18 exercise book (notebook)
19 felt tip pen
20 pupil raising her hand
21 teacher
22 teacher's desk
23 register
24 pen and pencil tray
25 desk mat (blotter)
26 window painting with finger paints (finger painting)
27 pupils' (children's) paintings (watercolours, *Am.* watercolors)
28 cross
29 three-part blackboard
30 bracket for holding charts
31 chalk ledge
32 chalk
33 blackboard drawing
34 diagram
35 reversible side blackboard
36 projection screen
37 triangle
38 protractor
39 divisions
40 blackboard compass
41 sponge tray
42 blackboard sponge (sponge)
43 classroom cupboard
44 map (wall map)
45 brick wall
46-85 craft room
46 workbench
47 vice (*Am.* vise)
48 vice (*Am.* vise) bar
49 scissors
50-52 working with glue (sticking paper, cardboard, etc.)
50 surface to be glued
51 tube of glue
52 tube cap
53 fretsaw
54 fretsaw blade (saw blade)
55 wood rasp (rasp)
56 piece of wood held in the vice (*Am.* vise)
57 glue pot
58 stool
59 brush
60 pan (dustpan)
61 broken china
62 enamelling (*Am.* enameling)
63 electric enamelling (*Am.* enameling) stove
64 unworked copper
65 enamel powder
66 hair sieve
67-80 pupils' (children's) work
67 clay models (models)
68 window decoration of coloured (*Am.* colored) glass
69 glass mosaic picture (glass mosaic)
70 mobile
71 paper kite (kite)
72 wooden construction
73 polyhedron
74 hand puppets
75 clay masks
76 cast candles (wax candles)
77 wood carving
78 clay jug
79 geometrical shapes made of clay
80 wooden toys
81 materials
82 stock of wood
83 inks for wood cuts
84 paintbrushes
85 bag of plaster of Paris

water cycle.
condensation
beaker
icecubes
drops of water
steam
water
READER
DUDEN
GYPSUM POWDER
GLUE

261 School II (Secondary School, High School)

1-45 grammar school; *also:* upper band of a comprehensive school (*Am.* alternative school)

1-13 chemistry

1 chemistry lab (chemistry laboratory) with tiered rows of seats
2 chemistry teacher
3 demonstration bench (teacher's bench)
4 water pipe
5 tiled working surface
6 sink
7 television monitor, a screen for educational programmes (*Am.* programs)
8 overhead projector
9 projector top for skins
10 projection lens with right-angle mirror
11 pupils' (*Am.* students') bench with experimental apparatus
12 electrical point (socket)
13 projection table

14-34 biology preparation room (biology prep room)

14 skeleton
15 casts of skulls
16 calvarium of Pithecanthropus erectus
17 skull of Steinheim man
18 calvarium of Peking man (of Sinanthropus)
19 skull of Neanderthal man, a skull of primitive man
20 Australopithecine skull (skull of Australopithecus)
21 skull of present-day man
22 dissecting bench
23 chemical bottles
24 gas tap
25 petri dish
26 measuring cylinder
27 work folder containing teaching material
28 textbook
29 bacteriological cultures
30 incubator
31 test tube rack
32 washing bottle
33 water tank
34 sink

35 language laboratory

36 blackboard
37 console
38 headphones (headset)
39 microphone
40 earcup
41 padded headband (padded headpiece)
42 programme (*Am.* program) recorder, a cassette recorder
43 pupil's (*Am.* student's) volume control
44 master volume control
45 control buttons (operating keys)

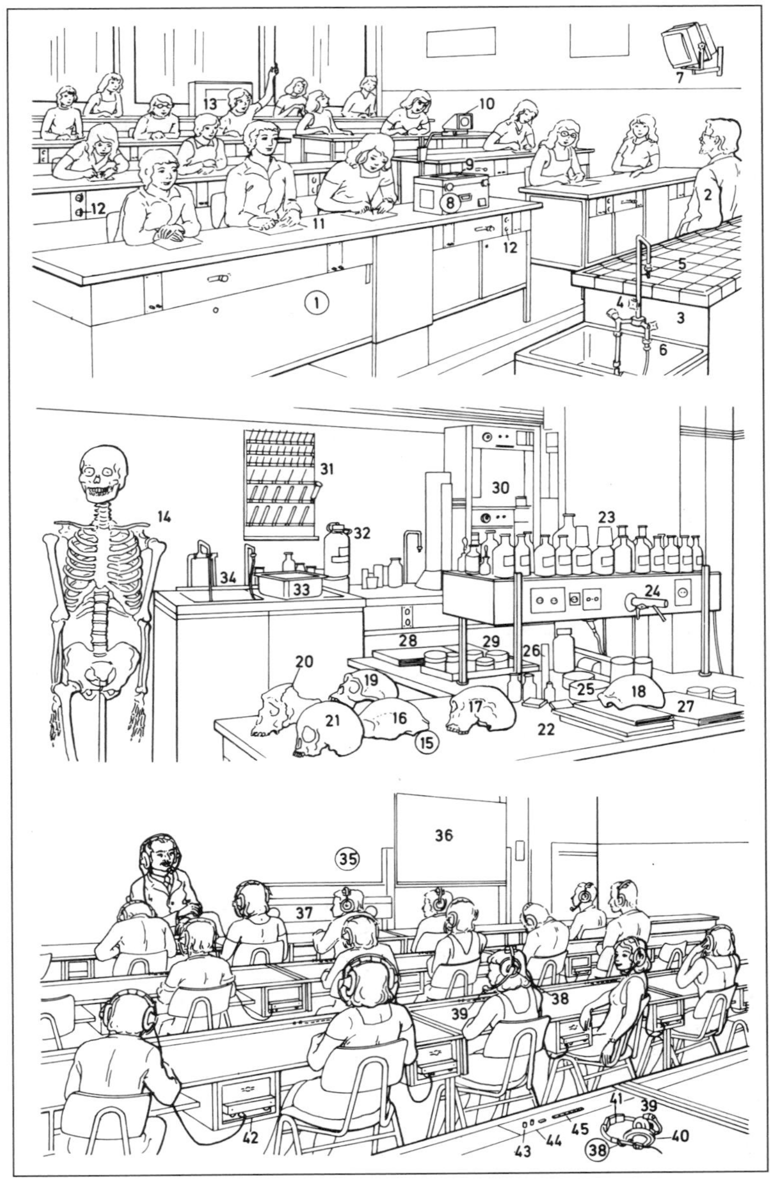
7
13
10
9
2
8
12
11
12
5
1
4
3
6
31
30
14
32
23
34
33
24
28
29
26
20
19
25
18
17
27
21
16
22
15
36
35
37
38
39
41
39
42
45
40
44
43
38

1-28 university (college)
1 lecture
2 lecture room (lecture theatre, *Am.* theater)
3 university lecturer (lecturer, college lecturer, *Am.* assistant professor)
4 lectern
5 microphone
6 remote-controlled blackboard
7 overhead projector
8 projection screen for projecting pictures by means of a film projector, slide projector, or an epidiascope
9, 10 students
11-28 university library; *sim.:* national library, regional or municipal scientific library
11 stack (book stack) with the stock of books
12 bookshelf, a steel shelf
13 reading room
14 member of the reading room staff, a librarian
15 periodicals rack with periodicals
16 newspaper shelf
17 reference library with reference books (handbooks, encyclopedias, dictionaries)
18 lending library and catalogue (*Am.* catalog) room
19 librarian
20 issue desk
21 main catalogue (*Am.* catalog)
22 card catalogue (*Am.* catalog)
23 card catalogue (*Am.* catalog) drawer
24 library user
25 borrower's ticket (library ticket)
26 issue terminal
27 microfiche (fiche)
28 microfiche reader

1-15 election meeting, a public meeting
1, 2 committee
1 chairman
2 committee member
3 committee table
4 pamphlet
5 election speaker (speaker)
6 rostrum
7 microphone
8 meeting (audience)
9 man distributing leaflets
10 stewards
11 armband (armlet)
12 banner
13 placard
14 proclamation
15 heckler
16-29 election
16 polling station (polling place)
17 polling officers
18 electoral list
19 polling card with registration number (polling number)
20 ballot paper with the names of the parties and candidates
21 ballot envelope
22 voter
23 polling booth
24 elector (qualified voter)
25 election regulations
26 electoral register
27 election supervisor
28 ballot box
29 slot

264 Police

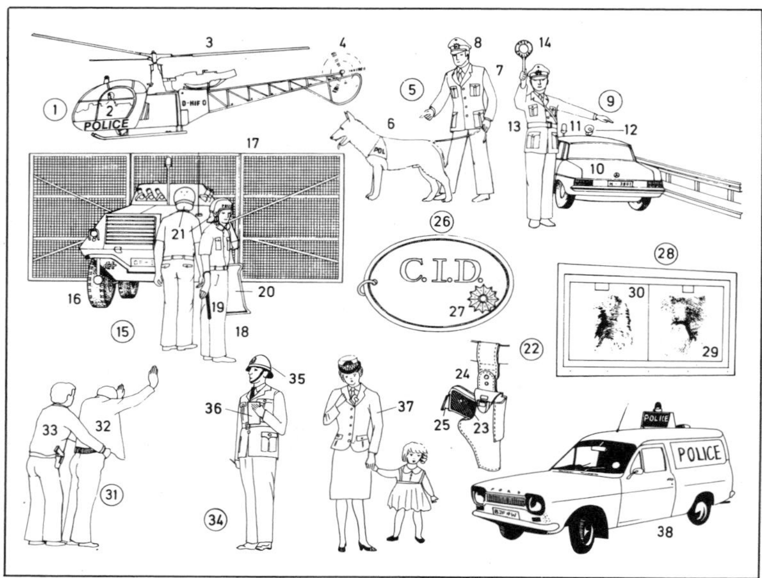

1-33 police duties

1 **police helicopter** (traffic helicopter) for controlling traffic from the air

2 cockpit

3 rotor (main rotor)

4 tail rotor

5 **use of police dogs**

6 police dog

7 uniform

8 uniform cap, a peaked cap with cockade

9 **traffic control** by a mobile traffic patrol

10 patrol car

11 blue light

12 loud hailer (loudspeaker)

13 patrolman (police patrolman)

14 police signalling (*Am.* signaling) disc (disk)

15 **riot duty**

16 special armoured (*Am.* armored) car

17 barricade

18 policeman (police officer) in riot gear

19 truncheon (baton)

20 riot shield

21 protective helmet (helmet)

22 **service pistol**

23 pistol grip

24 quick-draw holster

25 magazine

26 **police identification disc (disk)**

27 police badge

28 **fingerprint identification** (dactyloscopy)

29 fingerprint

30 illuminated screen

31 **search**

32 suspect

33 detective (plainclothes policeman)

34 English policeman

35 helmet

36 pocket book

37 policewoman

38 police van

1-31 café; *sim.:* espresso bar, tea room, ice-cream parlour (*Am.* parlor)

1 counter (cake counter)

2 coffee urn

3 tray for the money

4 gateau

5 meringue with whipped cream

6 trainee pastry cook

7 counter assistant

8 newspaper shelves (newspaper rack)

9 wall lamp

10 corner seat, an upholstered seat

11 café table

12 marble top

13 waitress

14 tray

15 bottle of lemonade

16 lemonade glass

17 chess players playing a game of chess

18 coffee set

19 cup of coffee

20 small sugar bowl

21 cream jug (*Am.* creamer)

22-24 café customers

22 gentleman

23 lady

24 man reading a newspaper

25 newspaper

26 newspaper holder

27 espresso

28 ice cream in assorted flavours (*Am.* flavors)

29 ice-cream dish (sundae dish)

30 iced coffee

31 (drinking) straw

1-27 restaurant
1-11 bar (counter)
1 beer pump (beerpull)
2 drip tray
3 beer glass
4 froth (head)
5 spherical ashtray for cigarette and cigar ash
6 beer glass (beer mug)
7 beer warmer
8 bartender (barman, *Am.* barkeeper, barkeep)
9 shelf for glasses
10 shelf for bottles
11 stack of plates
12 coat stand
13 hat peg
14 coat hook
15 wall ventilator
16 bottle
17 complete meal
18 waitress
19 tray
20 dessert, a slice of cake
21 menu (menu card)
22 cruet stand
23 toothpick holder
24 matchbox holder
25 customer
26 beer mat
27 meal of the day
28-44 wine restaurant (wine bar)
28 tablecloth
29 glass of water
30 wine waiter, a head waiter
31 wine list
32 wine carafe
33 wineglass
34 tiled stove
35 stove tile
36 stove bench
37 wooden panelling (*Am.* paneling)
38 corner seat
39 table reserved for regular customers
40 regular customer

41 cutlery chest
42 wine cooler
43 bottle of wine
44 ice cubes (ice, lumps of ice)
45-78 self-service restaurant
45 stack of trays
46 drinking straws (straws)
47 serviettes (napkins)
48 cutlery holders
49 cool shelf
50 slice of honeydew melon
51 plate of salad
52 plate of cheeses
53 fish dish
54 filled roll
55 meat dish with trimmings
56 half chicken
57 basket of fruit
58 fruit juice
59 drinks shelf
60 bottle of milk
61 bottle of mineral water
62 vegetarian meal (diet meal)
63 tray
64 tray counter
65 food price list
66 serving hatch
67 hot meal
68 beer pump (beerpull)
69 cash desk
70 cashier
71 proprietor
72 rail
73 dining area
74 table
75 open sandwich
76 ice-cream sundae
77 salt cellar and pepper pot
78 table decoration (flower arrangement)

1-26 vestibule (foyer, reception hall)
1 doorman (commissionaire)
2 letter rack with pigeon holes
3 key rack
4 globe lamp, a frosted glass globe
5 indicator board
6 indicator light
7 chief receptionist
8 register (hotel register)
9 room key
10 number tag (number tab) showing room number
11 hotel bill
12 block of registration forms
13 passport
14 hotel guest
15 lightweight suitcase [for air travel]
16 wall desk
17 porter (*Am.* baggage man)
18-26 lobby (hotel lobby)
18 page (pageboy, *Am.* bell boy)
19 hotel manager
20 dining room (hotel restaurant)
21 chandelier
22 fireside
23 fireplace
24 mantelpiece (mantelshelf)
25 fire
26 armchair
27-38 hotel room, a double room with bath
27 double door
28 service bell panel
29 wardrobe (*Am.* clothes closet)
30 clothes compartment
31 linen compartment
32 double washbasin
33 room waiter
34 room telephone
35 velour (velours) carpet
36 flower stand
37 flower arrangement
38 double bed
39 function room (banqueting hall)
40-43 private party

40 speaker proposing a toast
41 42's neighbour (*Am.* neighbor)
42 43's partner
43 42's partner
44 bar trio
45 violinist
46 couple dancing (dancing couple)
47 waiter
48 napkin
49 cigarette
50 ashtray
51 **hotel bar**
52 foot rail
53 bar stool
54 bar
55 bar customer
56 cocktail glass (*Am.* highball glass)
57 whisky (whiskey) glass
58 champagne cork
59 champagne bucket (champagne cooler)
60 measuring beaker (measure)
61 cocktail shaker
62 bartender (barman, *Am.* barkeeper, barkeep)
63 barmaid
64 shelf for bottles
65 shelf for glasses
66 mirrored panel
67 ice bucket
68 hotel foyer

268 Town (Town Centre, *Am.* Downtown)

1 parking meter
2 map of the town (street map)
3 illuminated board
4 key
5 litter bin (*Am.* trash bin)
6 street lamp (street light)
7 street sign showing the name of the street
8 drain
9 clothes shop (fashion house)
10 shop window
11 window display (shop window display)
12 window decoration (shop window decoration)
13 entrance
14 window
15 window box
16 neon sign
17 tailor's workroom
18 pedestrian
19 shopping bag
20 road sweeper (*Am.* street sweeper)
21 broom
22 rubbish (litter)
23 tramlines (*Am.* streetcar tracks)
24 pedestrian crossing (zebra crossing, *Am.* crosswalk)
25 tram stop (*Am.* streetcar stop, trolley stop)
26 tram stop sign (*Am.* streetcar stop sign, trolley stop sign)
27 tram timetable (*Am.* streetcar schedule, trolley schedule)
28 ticket machine
29 'pedestrian crossing' sign
30 traffic policeman on traffic duty (point duty)
31 traffic control cuff
32 white cap
33 hand signal
34 motorcyclist
35 motorcycle
36 pillion passenger (pillion rider)
37 bookshop

38 hat shop (hatter's shop); *for ladies' hats:* milliner's shop
39 shop sign
40 insurance company office
41 department store
42 shop front
43 advertisement
44 flags
45 illuminated letters
46 tram (*Am.* streetcar, trolley)
47 furniture lorry (*Am.* furniture truck)
48 flyover
49 suspended street lamp
50 stop line
51 pedestrian crossing (*Am.* crosswalk)
52 traffic lights
53 traffic light post
54 set of lights
55 pedestrian lights
56 telephone box (telephone booth, telephone kiosk, call box)
57 cinema (*Am.* movie) advertisement (film poster, *Am.* movie poster)
58 pedestrian precinct (paved zone)
59 street café
60 group seated (sitting) at a table
61 sunshade
62 steps to the public lavatories (public conveniences)
63 taxi rank (taxi stand)
64 taxi (taxicab, cab)
65 taxi sign
66 'taxi rank' ('taxi stand') sign
67 taxi telephone
68 post office
69 cigarette machine
70 advertising pillar
71 poster (advertisement)
72 white line
73 lane arrow for turning left
74 lane arrow for going straight ahead
75 news vendor (*Am.* news dealer)

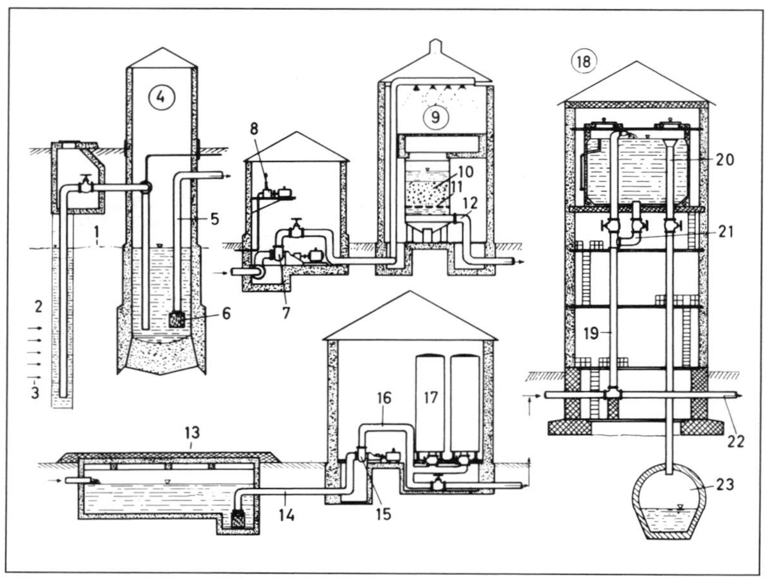

1-66 drinking water supply
1 water table (groundwater level)
2 water-bearing stratum (aquifer, aquafer)
3 groundwater stream (underground stream)
4 collector well for raw water
5 suction pipe
6 pump strainer with foot valve
7 bucket pump with motor
8 vacuum pump with motor
9 rapid-filter plant
10 filter gravel (filter bed)
11 filter bottom, a grid
12 filtered water outlet
13 purified water tank
14 suction pipe with pump strainer and foot valve
15 main pump with motor
16 delivery pipe
17 compressed-air vessel (air vessel, air receiver)
18 water tower
19 riser pipe (riser)
20 overflow pipe
21 outlet
22 distribution main
23 excess water conduit

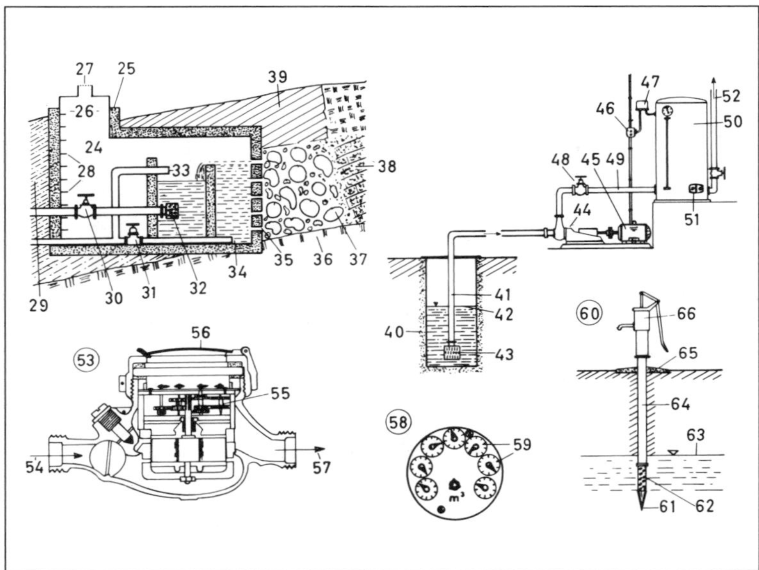

24-39 tapping a spring
24 chamber
25 chamber wall
26 manhole
27 ventilator
28 step irons
29 filling (backing)
30 outlet control valve
31 outlet valve
32 strainer
33 overflow pipe (overflow)
34 bottom outlet
35 earthenware pipes
36 impervious stratum (impermeable stratum)
37 rough rubble
38 water-bearing stratum (aquifer, aquafer)
39 loam seal (clay seal)
40-52 individual water supply
40 well
41 suction pipe
42 water table (groundwater level)
43 pump strainer with foot valve
44 centrifugal pump
45 motor
46 motor safety switch
47 manostat, a switching device
48 stop valve
49 delivery pipe
50 compressed-air vessel (air vessel, air receiver)
51 manhole
52 delivery pipe
53 water meter, a rotary meter
54 water inlet
55 counter gear assembly
56 cover with glass lid
57 water outlet
58 water-meter dial
59 counters
60 driven well (tube well, drive well)
61 pile shoe
62 filter
63 water table (groundwater level)
64 well casing
65 well head
66 hand pump

270 Fire Service (*Am.* Fire Department)

1-46 fire service drill (extinguishing, climbing, ladder, and rescue work)
1-3 fire station
1 engine and appliance room
2 firemen's (*Am.* firefighters') quarters
3 drill tower
4 fire alarm (fire alarm siren, fire siren)
5 fire engine
6 blue light (warning light), a flashing light (*Am.* flashlight)
7 horn (hooter)
8 motor pump, a centrifugal pump
9 motor turntable ladder (*Am.* aerial ladder)
10 ladder, a steel ladder (automatic extending ladder)
11 ladder mechanism
12 jack
13 ladder operator
14 extension ladder
15 ceiling hook (*Am.* preventer)
16 hook ladder (*Am.* pompier ladder)
17 holding squad
18 jumping sheet (sheet)
19 ambulance car (ambulance)
20 resuscitator (resuscitation equipment), oxygen apparatus
21 ambulance attendant (ambulance man)
22 armband (armlet, brassard)
23 stretcher
24 unconscious man
25 pit hydrant
26 standpipe (riser, vertical pipe)
27 hydrant key
28 hose reel (*Am.* hose cart, hose wagon, hose truck, hose carriage)
29 hose coupling
30 soft suction hose
31 delivery hose
32 dividing breeching
33 branch
34 branchmen
35 surface hydrant (fire plug)

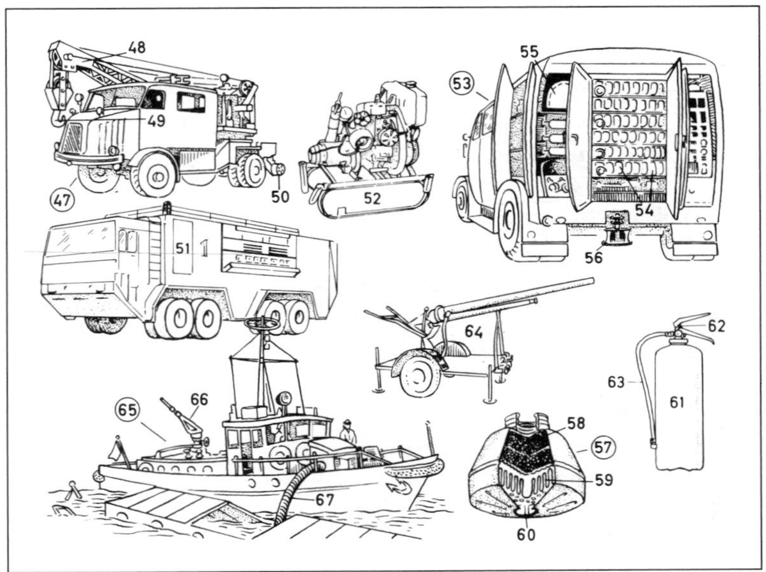

36 officer in charge
37 fireman (*Am.* firefighter)
38 helmet (fireman's helmet, *Am.* fire hat) with neck guard (neck flap)
39 breathing apparatus
40 face mask
41 walkie-talkie set
42 hand lamp
43 small axe (*Am.* ax, pompier hatchet)
44 hoot belt
45 beltline
46 protective clothing of asbestos (asbestos suit) or of metallic fabric
47 breakdown lorry (*Am.* crane truck, wrecking crane)
48 lifting crane
49 load hook (draw hook, *Am.* drag hook)
50 support roll
51 water tender
52 portable pump
53 hose layer
54 flaked lengths of hose
55 cable drum
56 winch
57 face mask filter
58 active carbon (activated carbon, activated charcoal)
59 dust filter
60 air inlet
61 portable fire extinguisher
62 operating valve
63 hose with spray nozzle
64 foam-making branch (*Am.* foam gun)
65 fireboat
66 monitor (water cannon)
67 suction hose

271 Department Store

1 cashier
2 electronic cash register (till) (scanner till)
3 number keys
4 scanner (light pen)
5 cash drawer (till)
6 compartments (money compartments) for coins and notes (*Am.* bills)
7 receipt (sales check)
8 amount [to be paid]
9 function keys
10 goods
11 glass-roofed well
12 men's wear department
13 showcase (display case, indoor display window)
14 wrapping counter
15 tray for purchases
16 customer
17 hosiery department
18 shop assistant (*Am.* salesgirl, saleslady)
19 price card
20 glove stand
21 duffle coat, a three-quarter length coat
22 escalator
23 fluorescent light (fluorescent lamp)
24 office (*e.g.* customer accounts office, travel agency, manager's office)
25 poster (advertisement)
26 theatre (*Am.* theater) and concert booking office (advance booking office)
27 shelves
28 ladies' wear department
29 ready-made dress (ready-to-wear dress, *coll.* off-the-peg dress)
30 dust cover
31 clothes rack
32 changing booth (fitting booth)
33 mirror
34 dummy
35 seat (chair)

36 fashion journal (fashion magazine)
37 tailor marking a hemline
38 measuring tape (tape measure)
39 tailor's chalk (French chalk)
40 hemline marker
41 loose-fitting coat
42 sales counter
43 warm-air curtain
44 stairs
45 lift (*Am.* elevator)
46 lift cage (lift car, *Am.* elevator car)
47 direction indicators
48 controls (lift controls, *Am.* elevator controls)
49 floor indicator
50 sliding door
51 lift shaft (*Am.* elevator shaft)
52 bearer cable
53 control cable
54 guide rail
55 customer
56 hosiery
57 linen goods (table linen and bed linen)
58 fabric department
59 roll of fabric (roll of material, roll of cloth)
60 head of department (department manager)
61 sales counter
62 jewellery (*Am.* jewelry) department
63 customer assistant
64 special counter (extra counter)
65 placard advertising special offers
66 curtain department
67 display on top of the shelves

272 Park

1-40 formal garden (French Baroque garden), palace gardens
1 grotto (cavern)
2 stone statue, a river nymph
3 orangery (orangerie)
4 boscage (boskage)
5 maze (labyrinth of paths and hedges)
6 open-air theatre (*Am.* theater)
7 Baroque palace
8 fountains
9 cascade (broken artificial waterfall, artificial falls)
10 statue, a monument
11 pedestal
12 globe-shaped tree
13 conical tree
14 ornamental shrub
15 wall fountain
16 park bench
17 pergola (bower, arbour, *Am.* arbor)
18 gravel path (gravel walk)
19 pyramid tree (pyramidal tree)
20 cupid (cherub, amoretto, amorino)
21 fountain
22 fountain
23 overflow basin
24 basin
25 kerb (curb)
26 man out for a walk
27 tourist guide
28 group of tourists
29 park by-laws (bye-laws)
30 park keeper
31 garden gates made of wrought iron
32 park entrance
33 park railings
34 railing (bar)
35 stone vase
36 lawn
37 border, a trimmed (clipped) hedge
38 park path
39 parterre
40 birch (birch tree)

41-72 landscaped park (jardin anglais)
41 flower bed
42 park bench (garden seat)
43 litter bin (*Am.* trash bin)
44 play area
45 stream
46 jetty
47 bridge
48 park chair
49 animal enclosure
50 pond
51-54 waterfowl
51 wild duck with young
52 goose
53 flamingo
54 swan
55 island
56 water lily
57 open-air café
58 sunshade
59 park tree (tree)
60 treetop (crown)
61 group of trees
62 fountain
63 weeping willow
64 modern sculpture
65 hothouse
66 park gardener
67 broom
68 minigolf course
69 minigolf player
70 minigolf hole
71 mother with pram (baby carriage)
72 courting couple (young couple)

273 Children's Playground

1 table tennis
2 table
3 table tennis net
4 table tennis racket (raquet) (table tennis bat)
5 table tennis ball
6 badminton game (shuttlecock game)
7 shuttlecock
8 maypole swing
9 child's bicycle
10 football (soccer)
11 goal (goalposts)
12 football
13 goal scorer
14 goalkeeper
15 skipping (*Am.* jumping rope)
16 skipping rope (*Am.* skip rope, jump rope, jumping rope)
17 climbing tower
18 rubber tyre (*Am.* tire) swing
19 lorry tyre (*Am.* truck tire)
20 bouncing ball
21 adventure playground
22 log ladder
23 lookout platform
24 slide
25 litter bin (*Am.* trash bin)
26 teddy bear
27 wooden train set
28 paddling pool
29 sailing boat (yacht, *Am.* sailboat)
30 toy duck
31 pram (baby carriage)
32 high bar (bar)
33 go-cart (soap box)
34 starter's flag
35 seesaw
36 robot

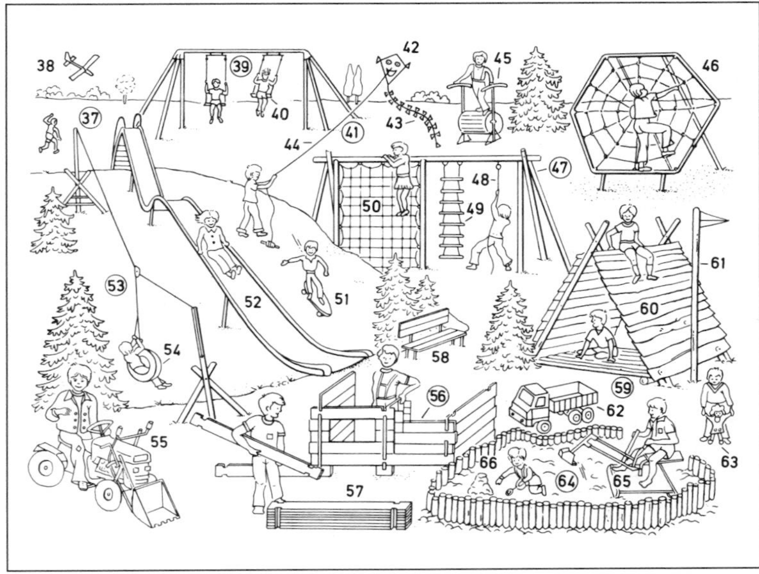

37 flying model aeroplanes (*Am.* airplanes)
38 model aeroplane (*Am.* airplane)
39 double swing
40 swing seat
41 flying kites
42 kite
43 tail of the kite
44 kite string
45 revolving drum
46 spider's web
47 climbing frame
48 climbing rope
49 rope ladder
50 climbing net
51 skateboard
52 up-and-down slide
53 rubber tyre (*Am.* tire) cable car
54 rubber tyre (*Am.* tire)
55 tractor, a pedal car
56 den
57 presawn boards
58 seat (bench)
59 Indian hut
60 climbing roof
61 flagpole (flagstaff)
62 toy lorry (*Am.* toy truck)
63 walking doll
64 sandpit (*Am.* sandbox)
65 toy excavator (toy digger)
66 sandhill

1-21 spa gardens
1-7 salina (salt works)
1 thorn house (graduation house)
2 thorns (brushwood)
3 brine channels
4 brine pipe from the pumping station
5 salt works attendant
6, 7 inhalational therapy
6 open-air inhalatorium (outdoor inhalatorium)
7 patient inhaling (taking an inhalation)
8 hydropathic (pump room) with kursaal (casino)
9 colonnade
10 spa promenade
11 avenue leading to the mineral spring
12-14 rest cure
12 sunbathing area (lawn)
13 deck-chair
14 sun canopy
15 pump room
16 rack for glasses
17 tap
18 patient taking the waters
19 bandstand
20 spa orchestra giving a concert
21 conductor

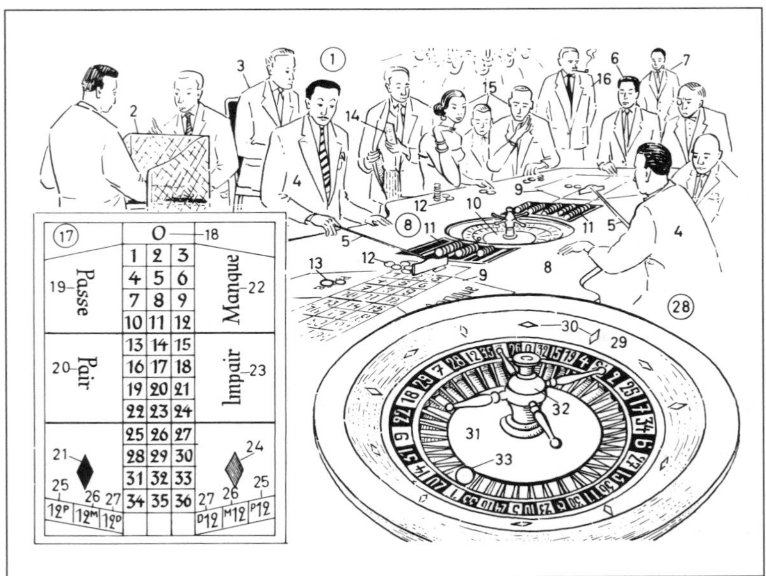

1-33 roulette, a game of chance (gambling game)

1 gaming room in the casino (in the gambling casino)

2 cash desk

3 tourneur (dealer)

4 croupier

5 rake

6 head croupier

7 hall manager

8 roulette table (gaming table, gambling table)

9 roulette layout

10 roulette wheel

11 bank

12 chip (check, plaque)

13 stake

14 membership card

15 roulette player

16 private detective (house detective)

17 roulette layout

18 zero (nought, 0)

19 passe (high) [numbers 19 to 36]

20 pair (even numbers)

21 noir (black)

22 manque (low) [numbers 1 to 18]

23 impair [odd numbers]

24 rouge (red)

25 douze premier (first dozen) [numbers 1 to 12]

26 douze milieu (second dozen) [numbers 13 to 24]

27 douze dernier (third dozen) [numbers 25 to 36]

28 roulette wheel (roulette)

29 roulette bowl

30 fret (separator)

31 revolving disc (disk) showing numbers 0 to 36

32 spin

33 roulette ball

276 Board Games and Party Games

1-16 chess, a game involving combinations of moves, a positional game
1 chessboard (board) with the men (chessmen) in position
2 white square (chessboard square)
3 black square
4 white chessmen (white pieces) [white = W]
5 black chessmen (black pieces) [black = B]
6 letters and numbers for designating chess squares in the notation of chess moves and chess problems
7 individual chessmen (individual pieces)
8 king
9 queen
10 bishop
11 knight
12 rook (castle)
13 pawn
14 moves of the individual pieces
15 mate (checkmate), a mate by knight
16 chess clock, a double clock for chess matches (chess championships)
17-19 draughts (*Am.* checkers)
17 draughtboard (*Am.* checkerboard)
18 white draughtsman (*Am.* checker, checkerman); *also:* piece for backgammon and nine men's morris
19 black draughtsman (*Am.* checker, checkerman)
20 salta
21 salta piece
22 backgammon board
23-25 nine men's morris
23 nine men's morris board
24 mill
25 double mill
26-28 halma
26 halma board
27 yard (camp, corner)
28 halma pieces (halma men) of various colours (*Am.* colors)
29 dice (dicing)
30 dice cup
31 dice
32 spots (pips)
33 dominoes
34 domino (tile)
35 double
36 playing cards
37 playing card (card)
38-45 suits
38 clubs
39 spades
40 hearts
41 diamonds
42-45 German suits
42 acorns
43 leaves
44 hearts
45 bells (hawkbells)

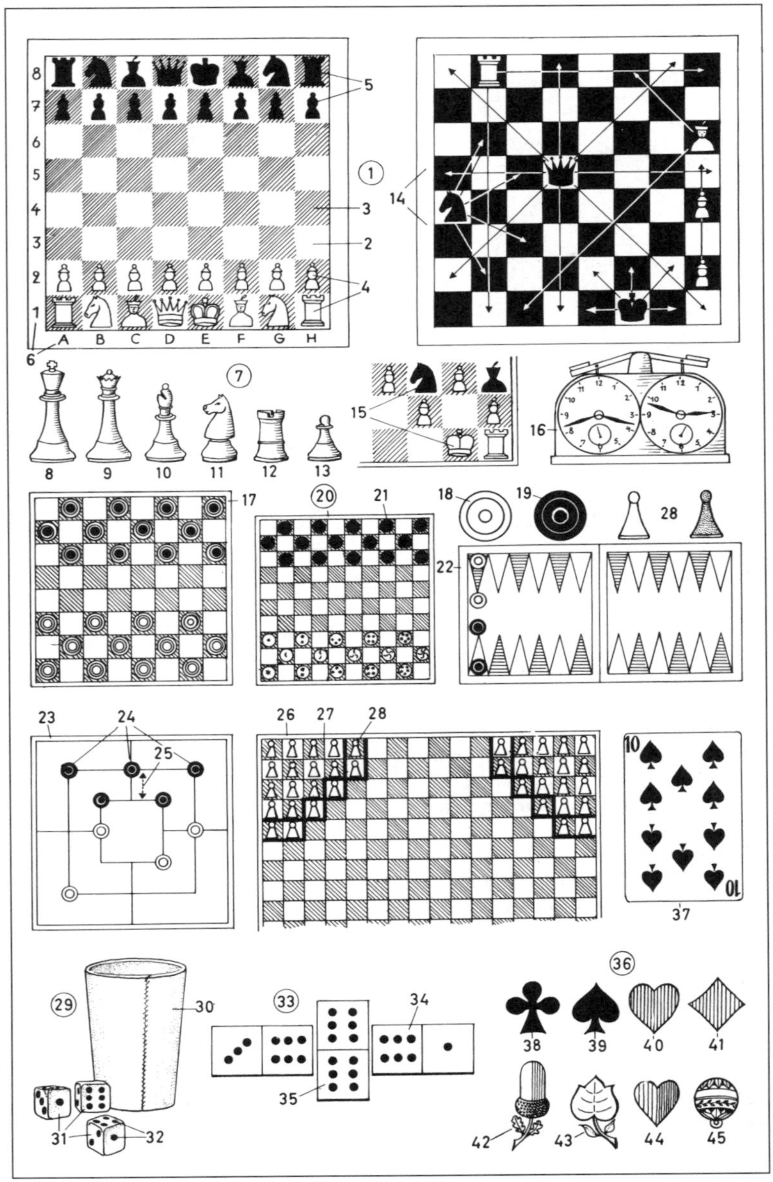
8
7
6
5
4
3
2
1
A
B
C
D
E
F
G
H
1
2
3
4
5
6
7
8
9
10
11
12
13
14
15
16
17
18
19
20
21
22
23
24
25
26
27
28
29
30
31
32
33
34
35
36
37
38
39
40
41
42
43
44
45

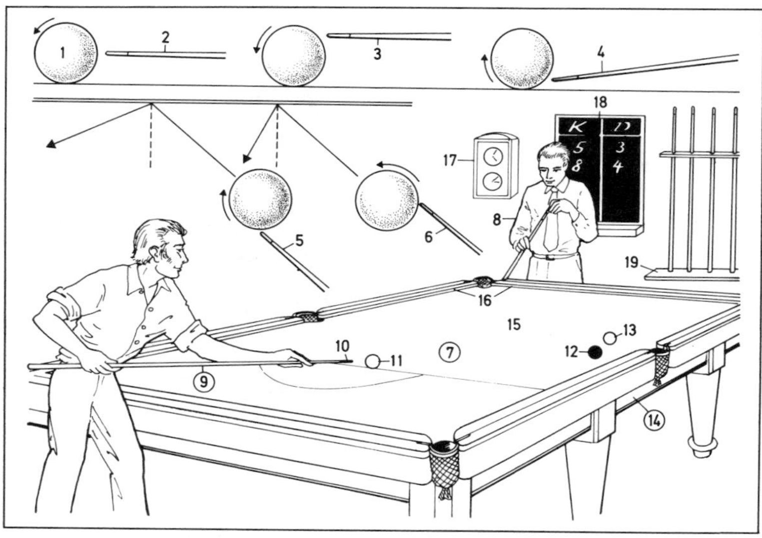

1-19 billiards
1 billiard ball, an ivory or plastic ball
2-6 billiard strokes
2 plain stroke (hitting the cue ball dead centre, *Am.* center)
3 top stroke [promotes extra forward rotation]
4 screw-back [imparts a direct recoil or backward motion]
5 side (running side, *Am.* English)
6 check side
7-19 billiard room (*Am.* billiard parlor, billiard saloon, poolroom)
7 billiards (English billiards); *sim.:* pool, carrom (carrom billiards)
8 billiard player
9 cue (billiard cue)
10 leather cue tip
11 white cue ball
12 red object ball
13 white spot ball (white dot ball)
14 billiard table
15 table bed with green cloth (billiard cloth, green baize covering)
16 cushions (rubber cushions, cushioned ledge)
17 billiard clock, a timer
18 billiard marker
19 cue rack

1-59 camp site (camping site, *Am.* campground)
1 reception (office)
2 site warden
3 folding trailer (collapsible caravan, collapsible trailer)
4 hammock
5, 6 washing and toilet facilities
5 toilets and washrooms (*Am.* lavatories)
6 washbasins and sinks
7 bungalow (chalet)
8-11 scout camp
8 bell tent
9 pennon
10 camp fire
11 boy scout (scout)
12 sailing boat (yacht, *Am.* sailboat)
13 landing stage (jetty)
14 inflatable boat (inflatable dinghy)
15 outboard motor (outboard)
16 trimaran
17 thwart (oarsman's bench)
18 rowlock (oarlock)
19 oar
20 boat trailer (boat carriage)
21 ridge tent
22 flysheet
23 guy line (guy)
24 tent peg (peg)
25 mallet
26 groundsheet ring
27 bell end
28 erected awning
29 storm lantern, a paraffin lamp
30 sleeping bag
31 air mattress (inflatable air-bed)
32 water carrier (drinking water carrier)
33 double-burner gas cooker for propane gas or butane gas
34 propane or butane gas bottle
35 pressure cooker
36 frame tent
37 awning
38 tent pole
39 wheelarch doorway
40 mesh ventilator
41 transparent window
42 pitch number
43 folding camp chair
44 folding camp table
45 camping eating utensils
46 camper
47 charcoal grill (barbecue)
48 charcoal
49 bellows
50 roof rack
51 roof lashing
52 caravan (*Am.* trailer)
53 box for gas bottle
54 jockey wheel
55 drawbar coupling
56 roof ventilator
57 caravan awning
58 inflatable igloo tent
59 camp bed (*Am.* camp cot)

279 Surf Riding (Surfing), Skin Diving

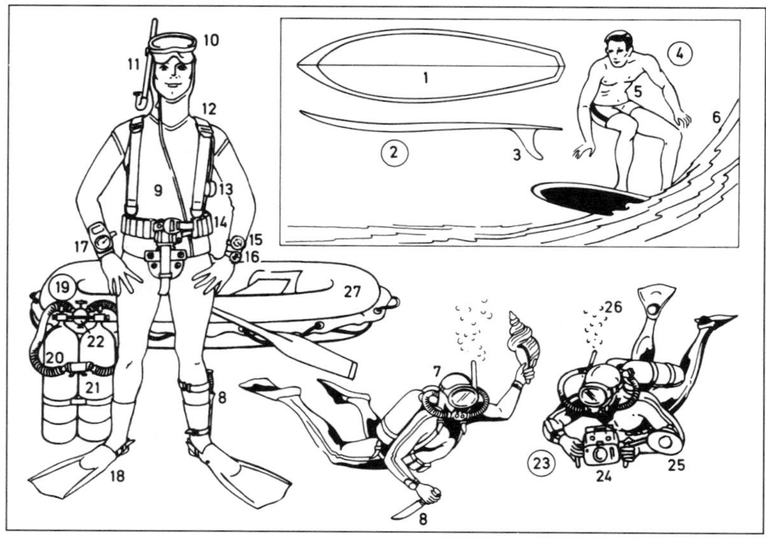

1-6 surf riding (surfing)
1 plan view of surfboard
2 section of surfboard
3 skeg (stabilizing fin)
4 big wave riding
5 surfboarder (surfer)
6 breaker
7-27 skin diving (underwater swimming)
7 skin diver (underwater swimmer)
8-22 underwater swimming set
8 knife
9 neoprene wetsuit
10 diving mask (face mask, mask), a pressure-equalizing mask
11 snorkel (schnorkel)
12 harness of diving apparatus
13 compressed-air pressure gauge (*Am.* gage)
14 weight belt
15 depth gauge (*Am.* gage)
16 waterproof watch for checking duration of dive
17 decometer for measuring stages of ascent
18 fin (flipper)
19 diving apparatus (aqualung, scuba) with two cylinders (bottles)
20 two-tube demand regulator
21 compressed-air cylinder (compressed-air bottle)
22 on/off valve
23 underwater photography
24 underwater camera
25 underwater flashlight
26 exhaust bubbles
27 inflatable boat (inflatable dinghy)

1 lifesaver (lifeguard)
2 lifeline
3 lifebelt (lifebuoy)
4 storm signal
5 time ball
6 warning sign
7 tide table, a notice board showing times of low tide and high tide
8 board showing water and air temperature
9 bathing platform
10 pennon staff
11 pennon
12 paddle boat (pedal boat)
13 surf riding (surfing) behind motorboat
14 surfboarder (surfer)
15 surfboard
16 water ski
17 inflatable beach mattress
18 beach ball
19-23 beachwear
19 beach suit
20 beach hat
21 beach jacket
22 beach trousers
23 beach shoe (bathing shoe)
24 beach bag
25 bathing gown (bathing wrap)
26 bikini (ladies' two-piece bathing suit)
27 bikini bottom
28 bikini top
29 bathing cap (swimming cap)
30 bather
31 deck tennis (quoits)
32 rubber ring (quoit)
33 inflatable rubber animal
34 beach attendant
35 sandcastle
36 roofed wicker beach chair
37 underwater swimmer
38 diving goggles
39 snorkel (schnorkel)
40 hand harpoon (fish spear, fish lance)
41 fin (flipper) for diving (for underwater swimming)
42 bathing suit (swimsuit)
43 bathing trunks (swimming trunks)
44 bathing cap (swimming cap)
45 beach tent, a ridge tent
46 lifeguard station

281 Swimming Bath (Leisure Centre, *Am.* Center)

1-9 wave pool, an indoor pool
1 artificial waves
2 beach area
3 edge of the pool
4 swimming pool attendant (pool attendant, swimming bath attendant)
5 sun bed
6 lifebelt
7 water wings
8 bathing cap
9 channel to outdoor mineral bath
10 solarium
11 sunbathing area
12 sunbather
13 sun ray lamp
14 bathing towel
15 nudist sunbathing area
16 nudist (naturist)
17 screen (fence)
18 mixed sauna
19 wood panelling (*Am.* paneling)
20 tiered benches
21 sauna stove
22 stones
23 hygrometer
24 thermometer
25 towel
26 water tub for moistening the stones in the stove
27 birch rods (birches) for beating the skin
28 cooling room for cooling off (cooling down) after the sauna
29 lukewarm shower
30 cold bath
31 hot whirlpool (underwater massage bath)
32 step into the bath
33 massage bath
34 jet blower
35 hot whirlpool [diagram]
36 section of the bath
37 step
38 circular seat
39 water extractor
40 water jet pipe
41 air jet pipe

1
2
3
4
5
6
7
8
9
10
11
12
13
14
15
16
17
18
19
20
21
22
23
24
25
26
27
28
29
30
31
32
33
34
35
36
37
38
39
40
41

1-32 swimming pool, an open-air swimming pool
1 changing cubicle
2 shower (shower bath)
3 changing room
4 sunbathing area
5-10 diving boards (diving apparatus)
5 diver (highboard diver)
6 diving platform
7 ten-metre (*Am.* ten-meter) platform
8 five-metre (*Am.* five-meter) platform
9 three-metre (*Am.* three-meter) springboard (diving board)
10 one-metre (*Am.* one-meter) springboard
11 diving pool
12 straight header
13 feet-first jump
14 tuck jump (haunch jump)
15 swimming pool attendant (pool attendant, swimming bath attendant)
16-20 swimming instruction
16 swimming instructor (swimming teacher)
17 learner-swimmer
18 float; *sim.:* water wings
19 swimming belt (cork jacket)
20 land drill
21 non-swimmers' pool
22 footbath
23 swimmers' pool
24-32 freestyle relay race
24 timekeeper (lane timekeeper)
25 placing judge
26 turning judge
27 starting block (starting place)
28 competitor touching the finishing line
29 starting dive (racing dive)
30 starter
31 swimming lane
32 rope with cork floats
33-39 swimming strokes
33 breaststroke
34 butterfly stroke
35 dolphin butterfly stroke
36 side stroke
37 crawl stroke (crawl); *sim.:* trudgen stroke (trudgen, double overarm stroke)
38 diving (underwater swimming)
39 treading water
40-45 diving (acrobatic diving, fancy diving, competitive diving, highboard diving)
40 standing take-off pike dive
41 one-half twist isander (reverse dive)
42 backward somersault (double backward somersault)
43 running take-off twist dive
44 screw dive
45 armstand dive (handstand dive)
46-50 water polo
46 goal
47 goalkeeper
48 water polo ball
49 back
50 forward

1
2
3
4
5
6
7
8
9
10
11
12
13
14
15
16
17
18
19
20
21
22
23
24
25
26
27
28
29
30
31
32
33
34
35
36
37
38
39
40
41
42
43
44
45
46
47
48
49
50

283 Rowing and Canoeing

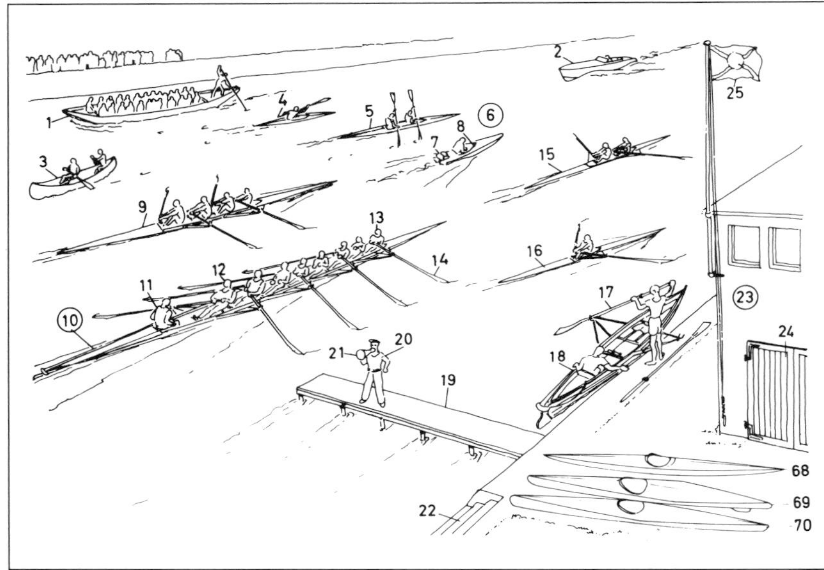

1-18 taking up positions for the regatta
1 punt, a pleasure boat
2 motorboat
3 Canadian canoe
4 kayak (Alaskan canoe, slalom canoe), a canoe
5 tandem kayak
6 outboard motorboat (outboard speedboat, outboard)
7 outboard motor (outboard)
8 cockpit
9-16 racing boats (sportsboats)
9-15 shells (rowing boats, *Am.* rowboats)
9 coxless four, a carvel-built boat
10 eight (eight-oared racing shell)
11 cox
12 stroke, an oarsman
13 bow ('number one')
14 oar
15 coxless pair
16 single sculler (single skuller, racing sculler, racing skuller, skiff)
17 scull (skull)
18 coxed single, a clinker-built single
19 jetty (landing stage)
20 rowing coach
21 megaphone
22 quayside steps
23 clubhouse (club)
24 boathouse
25 club's flag
26-33 four-oared gig, a touring boat
26 oar
27 cox's seat
28 thwart (seat)
29 rowlock (oarlock)
30 gunwale (gunnel)
31 rising
32 keel
33 skin (shell, outer skin) [clinker-built]
34 single-bladed paddle (paddle)
35-38 oar (scull, skull)

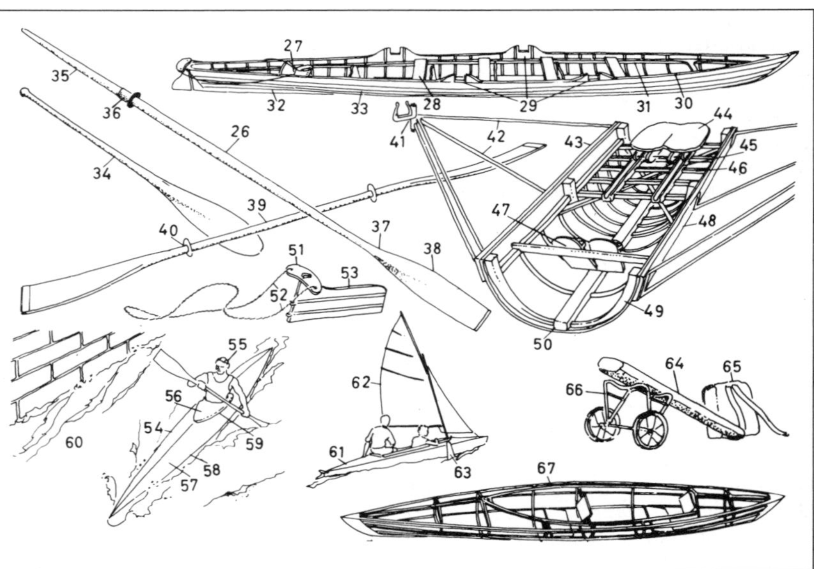

35 grip
36 leather sheath
37 shaft (neck)
38 blade
39 double-bladed paddle (double-ended paddle)
40 drip ring
41-50 sliding seat
41 rowlock (oarlock)
42 outrigger
43 saxboard
44 sliding seat
45 runner
46 strut
47 stretcher
48 skin (shell, outer skin)
49 frame (rib)
50 kelson (keelson)
51-53 rudder (steering rudder)
51 yoke
52 lines (steering lines)
53 blade (rudder blade, rudder)
54-66 folding boats (foldboats, canoes)
54 one-man kayak
55 canoeist
56 spraydeck
57 deck
58 rubber-covered canvas hull
59 cockpit coaming (coaming)
60 channel for rafts alongside weir
61 two-seater folding kayak, a touring kayak
62 sail of folding kayak
63 leeboard
64 bag for the rods
65 rucksack
66 boat trailer (boat carriage)
67 frame of folding kayak
68-70 kayaks
68 Eskimo kayak
69 wild-water racing kayak
70 touring kayak

1-9 windsurfing
1 windsurfer
2 sail
3 transparent window (window)
4 mast
5 surfboard
6 universal joint (movable bearing) for adjusting the angle of the mast and for steering
7 wishbone
8 retractable centreboard (*Am.* centerboard)
9 rudder
10-48 yacht (sailing boat, *Am.* sailboat)
10 foredeck
11 mast
12 trapeze
13 crosstrees (spreader)
14 hound
15 forestay
16 jib (Genoa jib)
17 jib downhaul
18 side stay (shroud)
19 lanyard (*also:* turnbuckle)
20 foot of the mast
21 kicking strap (vang)
22 jam cleat
23 foresheet (jib sheet)
24 centreboard (*Am.* centerboard) case
25 bitt
26 centreboard (*Am.* centerboard)
27 traveller (*Am.* traveler)
28 mainsheet
29 foresheet fairlead (jib fairlead)
30 toestraps (hiking straps)
31 tiller extension (hiking stick)
32 tiller
33 rudderhead (rudder stock)
34 rudder blade (rudder)
35 transom
36 drain plug
37 gooseneck
38 window
39 boom
40 foot
41 clew
42 luff (leading edge)
43 leech pocket (batten cleat, batten pocket)
44 batten
45 leech (trailing edge)
46 mainsail
47 headboard
48 racing flag (burgee)
49-65 yacht classes
49 Flying Dutchman
50 O-Joller
51 Finn dinghy (Finn)
52 pirate
53 12.00 m^2 sharpie
54 tempest
55 star
56 soling
57 dragon
58 5.5-metre (*Am.* 5.5-meter) class
59 6-metre (*Am.* 6-meter) R-class
60 30.00 m^2 cruising yacht (coastal cruiser)
61 30.00 m^2 dinghy cruiser
62 25.00 m^2 one-design keelboat
63 KR-class
64 catamaran
65 twin hull

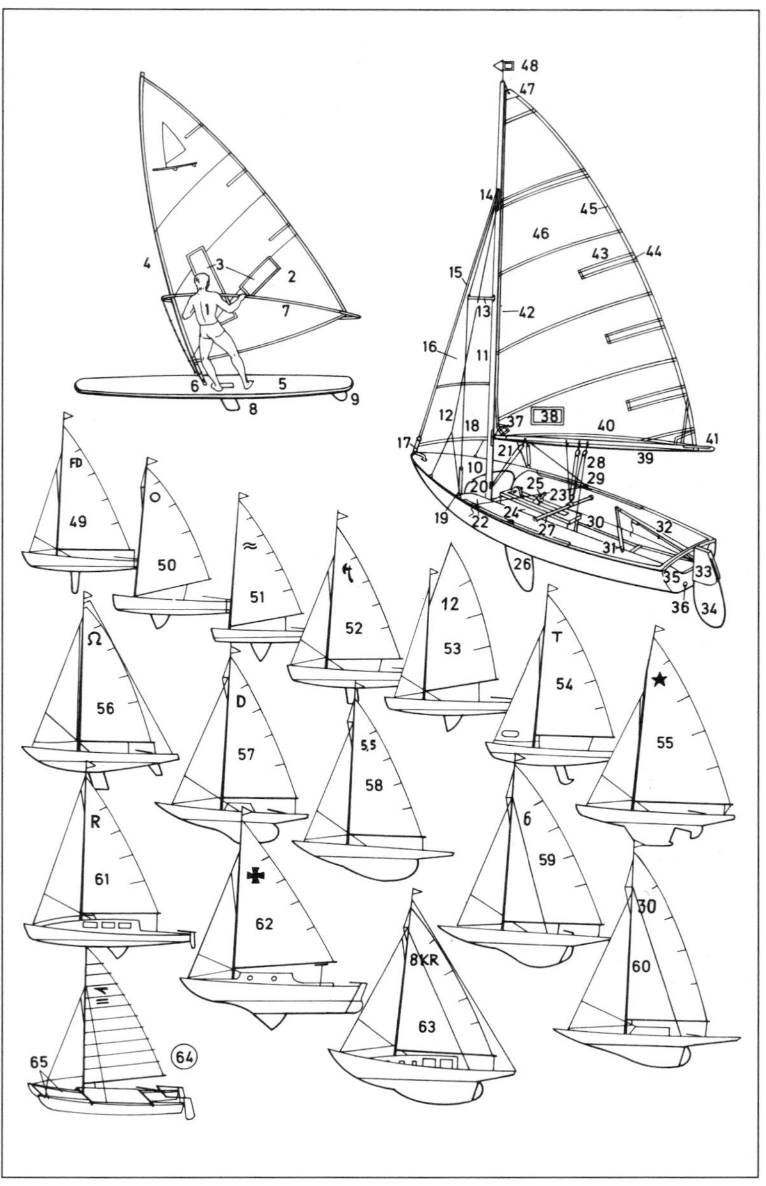

1
2
3
4
5
6
7
8
9
10
11
12
13
14
15
16
17
18
19
20
21
22
23
24
25
26
27
28
29
30
31
32
33
34
35
36
37
38
39
40
41
42
43
44
45
46
47
48
FD
49
O
50
51
52
12
53
T
54
55
Ω
56
D
57
5,5
58
6
59
30
60
R
61
62
8KR
63
64
65

285 Sailing II

1-13 points of sailing and wind directions
1 sailing downwind (running)
2 mainsail
3 jib
4 sails set goose-winged
5 centre (*Am.* center) line
6 wind direction
7 yacht stopped head to wind
8 sail, shivering
9 luffing
10 sailing close-hauled
11 sailing with wind abeam
12 sailing with free wind
13 quartering wind (quarter wind)
14-24 regatta course
14 starting and finishing buoy
15 committee boat
16 triangular course (regatta course)
17 buoy (mark) to be rounded
18 buoy to be passed
19 first leg
20 second leg
21 third leg
22 windward leg
23 downwind leg
24 reaching leg
25-28 tacking
25 tack
26 gybing (jibing)
27 going about
28 loss of distance during the gybe (jibe)
29-41 types of yacht hull
29-34 cruiser keelboat
29 stern
30 spoon bow
31 waterline
32 keel (ballast keel)
33 ballast
34 rudder
35 racing keelboat
36 lead keel
37-41 keel-centreboard (*Am.* centerboard) yawl
37 retractable rudder
38 cockpit
39 cabin superstructure (cabin)
40 straight stem
41 retractable centreboard (*Am.* centerboard)
42-49 types of yacht stern
42 yacht stern
43 square stern
44 canoe stern
45 cruiser stern
46 name plate
47 deadwood
48 transom stern
49 transom
50-57 timber planking
50-52 clinker planking (clench planking)
50 outside strake
51 frame (rib)
52 clenched nail (riveted nail)
53 carvel planking
54 ribband-carvel construction
55 ribband, a stringer
56 diagonal carvel planking
57 inner planking

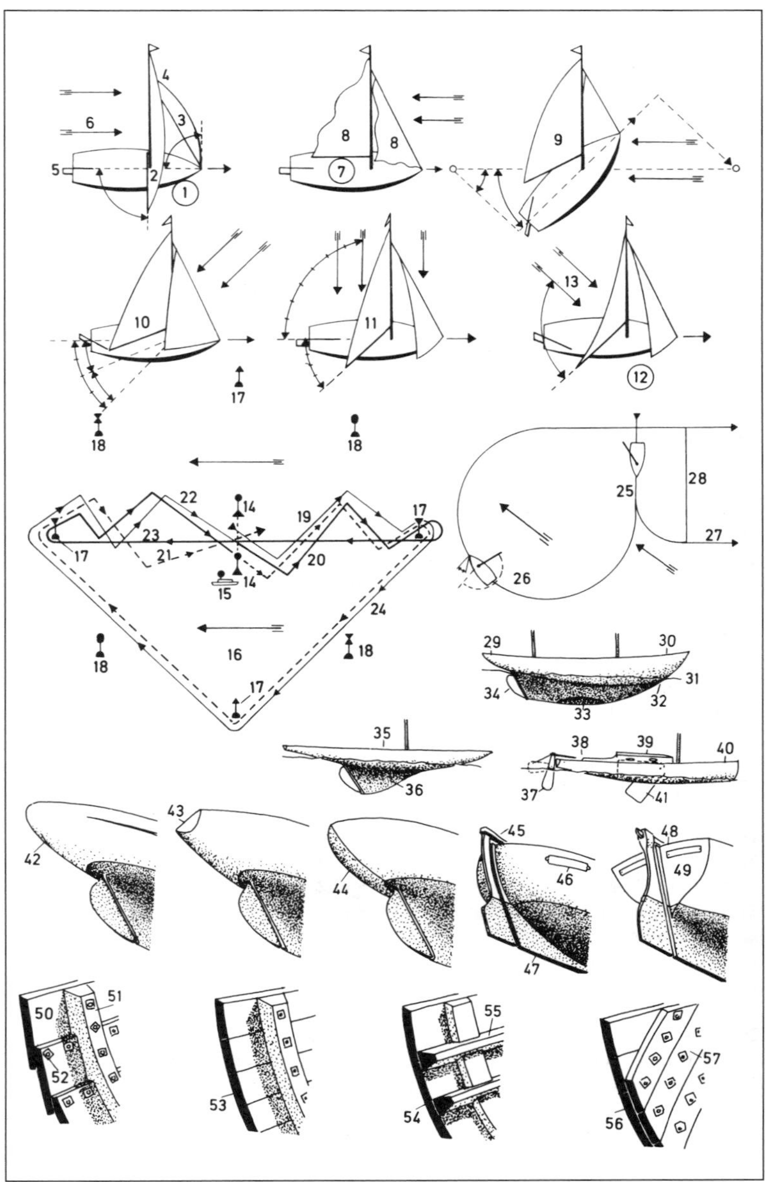
1
2
3
4
5
6
7
8
8
9
10
11
12
13
14
14
14
15
16
17
17
17
17
17
18
18
18
18
19
20
21
22
23
24
25
26
27
28
29
30
31
32
33
34
35
36
37
38
39
40
41
42
43
44
45
46
47
48
49
50
51
52
53
54
55
56
57

1-5 motorboats (powerboats, sportsboats)
1 inflatable sportsboat with outboard motor (outboard inflatable)
2 Z-drive motorboat (outdrive motorboat)
3 cabin cruiser
4 motor cruiser
5 30-metre (*Am.* 30-meter) ocean-going cruiser
6 association flag
7 name of craft (*or:* registration number)
8 club membership and port of registry (*Am.* home port)
9 association flag on the starboard crosstrees
10-14 navigation lights of sportsboats in coastal and inshore waters
10 white top light
11 green starboard sidelight
12 red port sidelight
13 green and red bow light (combined lantern)
14 white stern light
15-18 anchors
15 stocked anchor (Admiralty anchor), a bower anchor
16-18 lightweight anchor
16 CQR anchor (plough, *Am.* plow, anchor)
17 stockless anchor (patent anchor)
18 Danforth anchor
19 life raft
20 life jacket
21-44 powerboat racing
21 catamaran with outboard motor
22 hydroplane
23 racing outboard motor
24 tiller
25 fuel pipe
26 transom
27 buoyancy tube
28 start and finish
29 start
30 starting and finishing line
31 buoy to be rounded
32-37 displacement boats
32-34 round-bilge boat
32 view of hull bottom
33 section of fore ship
34 section of aft ship
35-37 V-bottom boat (vee-bottom boat)
35 view of hull bottom
36 section of fore ship
37 section of aft ship
38-44 planing boats (surface skimmers, skimmers)
38-41 stepped hydroplane (stepped skimmer)
38 side view
39 view of hull bottom
40 section of fore ship
41 section of aft ship
42 three-point hydroplane
43 fin
44 float
45-62 water skiing
45 water skier
46 deep-water start
47 tow line (towing line)
48 handle
49-55 water-ski signalling (code of hand signals from skier to boat driver)
49 signal for 'faster'
50 signal for 'slower' ('slow down')
51 signal for 'speed OK'
52 signal for 'turn'
53 signal for 'stop'
54 signal for 'cut motor'
55 signal for 'return to jetty' ('back to dock')
56-62 types of water ski
56 trick ski (figure ski), a monoski
57, 58 rubber binding
57 front foot binding
58 heel flap
59 strap support for second foot
60 slalom ski
61 skeg (fixed fin, fin)
62 jump ski
63 hovercraft (air-cushion vehicle)
64 propeller
65 rudder
66 skirt enclosing air cushion

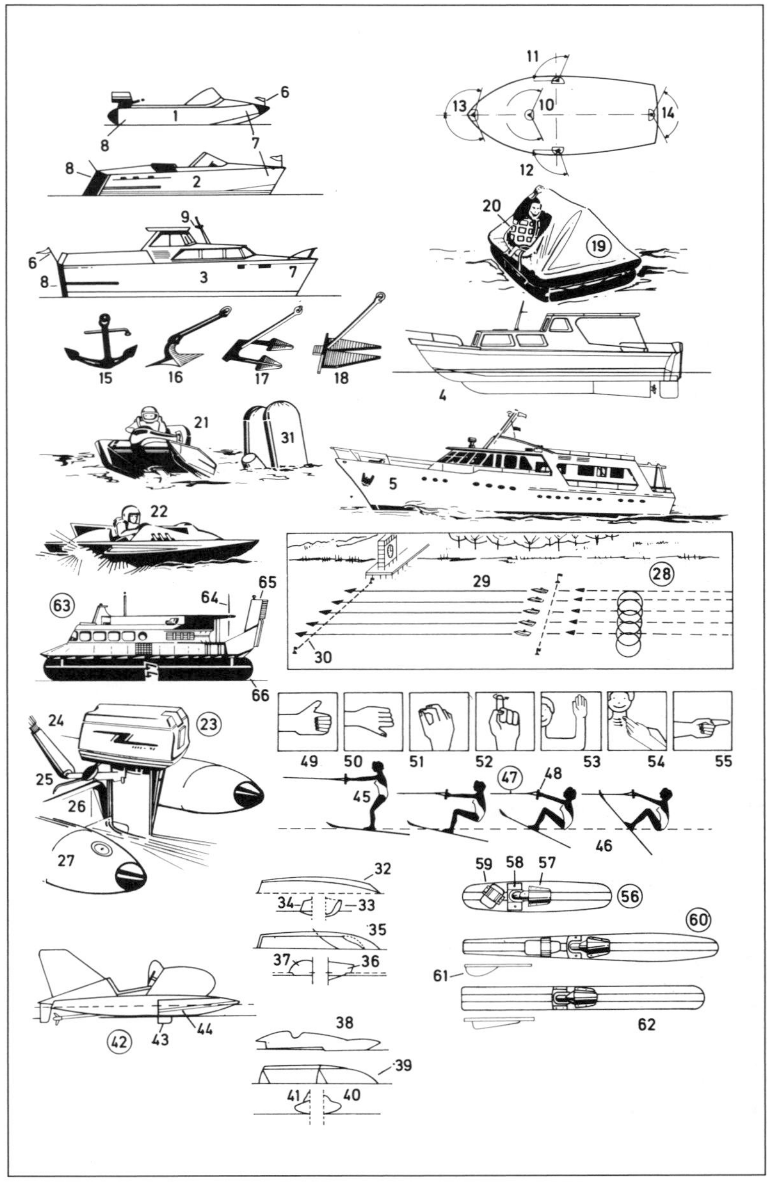
1 2 3 4 5 6 7 8 9
10 11 12 13 14
15 16 17 18
19 20
21 22
23 24 25 26 27
28 29 30 31
32 33 34 35 36 37
38 39 40 41
42 43 44
45 46 47 48
49 50 51 52 53 54 55
56 57 58 59
60 61 62
63 64 65 66

287 Gliding (Soaring)

1 aeroplane (*Am.* airplane) tow launch (aerotowing)
2 tug (towing plane)
3 towed glider (towed sailplane)
4 tow rope
5 winched launch
6 motor winch
7 cable parachute
8 motorized glider (powered glider)
9 high-performance glider (high-performance sailplane)
10 T-tail (T-tail unit)
11 wind sock (wind cone)
12 control tower (tower)
13 glider field
14 hangar
15 runway for aeroplanes (*Am.* airplanes)
16 wave soaring
17 lee waves (waves, wave system)
18 rotor
19 lenticular clouds (lenticulars)
20 thermal soaring
21 thermal
22 cumulus cloud (heap cloud, cumulus, woolpack cloud)
23 storm-front soaring
24 storm front
25 frontal upcurrent
26 cumulonimbus cloud (cumulonimbus)
27 slope soaring
28 hill upcurrent (orographic lift)
29 multispar wing
30 main spar, a box spar
31 connector fitting
32 anchor rib
33 diagonal spar
34 leading edge
35 main rib
36 nose rib (false rib)
37 trailing edge
38 brake flap (spoiler)
39 torsional clamp
40 covering (skin)
41 aileron
42 wing tip
43 hang gliding
44 hang glider
45 hang glider pilot
46 control frame

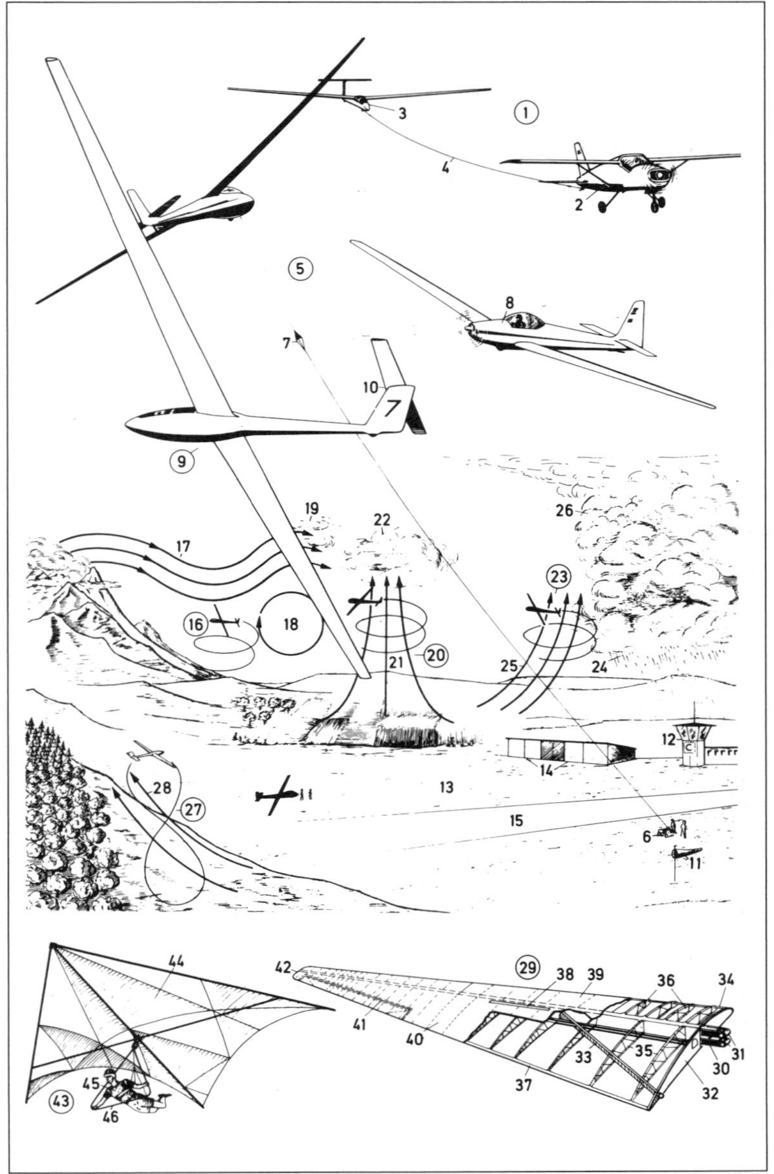
1
2
3
4
5
6
7
8
9
10
11
12
13
14
15
16
17
18
19
20
21
22
23
24
25
26
27
28
29
30
31
32
33
34
35
36
37
38
39
40
41
42
43
44
45
46

1-9 **aerobatics** (aerobatic manoeuvres, *Am.* maneuvers)
1 loop
2 horizontal eight
3 rolling circle
4 stall turn (hammer head)
5 tail slide (whip stall)
6 vertical flick spin
7 spin
8 horizontal slow roll
9 inverted flight (negative flight)
10 **cockpit**
11 instrument panel
12 compass
13 radio and navigation equipment
14 control column (control stick)
15 throttle lever (throttle control)
16 mixture control
17 radio equipment
18 **two-seater plane for racing and aerobatics**
19 cabin
20 antenna
21 vertical stabilizer (vertical fin, tail fin)
22 rudder
23 tailplane (horizontal stabilizer)
24 elevator
25 trim tab (trimming tab)
26 fuselage (body)
27 wing
28 aileron
29 landing flap
30 trim tab (trimming tab)
31 navigation light (position light) [red]
32 landing light
33 main undercarriage unit (main landing gear unit)
34 nose wheel
35 engine
36 propeller (airscrew)
37-62 **parachuting** (sport parachuting)
37 parachute
38 canopy
39 pilot chute
40 suspension lines
41 steering line
42 riser
43 harness
44 pack
45 system of slots of the sports parachute
46 turn slots
47 apex
48 skirt
49 stabilizing panel
50, 51 style jump
50 back loop
51 spiral
52-54 ground signals
52 signal for 'permission to jump' ('conditions are safe') (target cross)
53 signal for 'parachuting suspended–repeat flight'
54 signal for 'parachuting suspended–aircraft must land'
55 accuracy jump
56 target cross
57 inner circle [radius 25 m]
58 middle circle [radius 50 m]
59 outer circle [radius 100 m]
60-62 free-fall positions
60 full spread position
61 frog position
62 T position
63-84 **ballooning**
63 gas balloon
64 gondola (balloon basket)
65 ballast (sandbags)
66 mooring line
67 hoop
68 flight instruments (instruments)
69 trail rope
70 mouth (neck)
71 neck line
72 emergency rip panel
73 emergency ripping line
74 network (net)
75 rip panel
76 ripping line
77 valve
78 valve line
79 hot-air balloon
80 burner platform
81 mouth
82 vent
83 rip panel
84 balloon take-off
85-91 **flying model aeroplanes** (*Am.* airplanes)
85 radio-controlled model flight
86 remote-controlled free flight model
87 remote control radio
88 antenna (transmitting antenna)
89 control line model
90 mono-line control system
91 flying kennel, a K9-class model

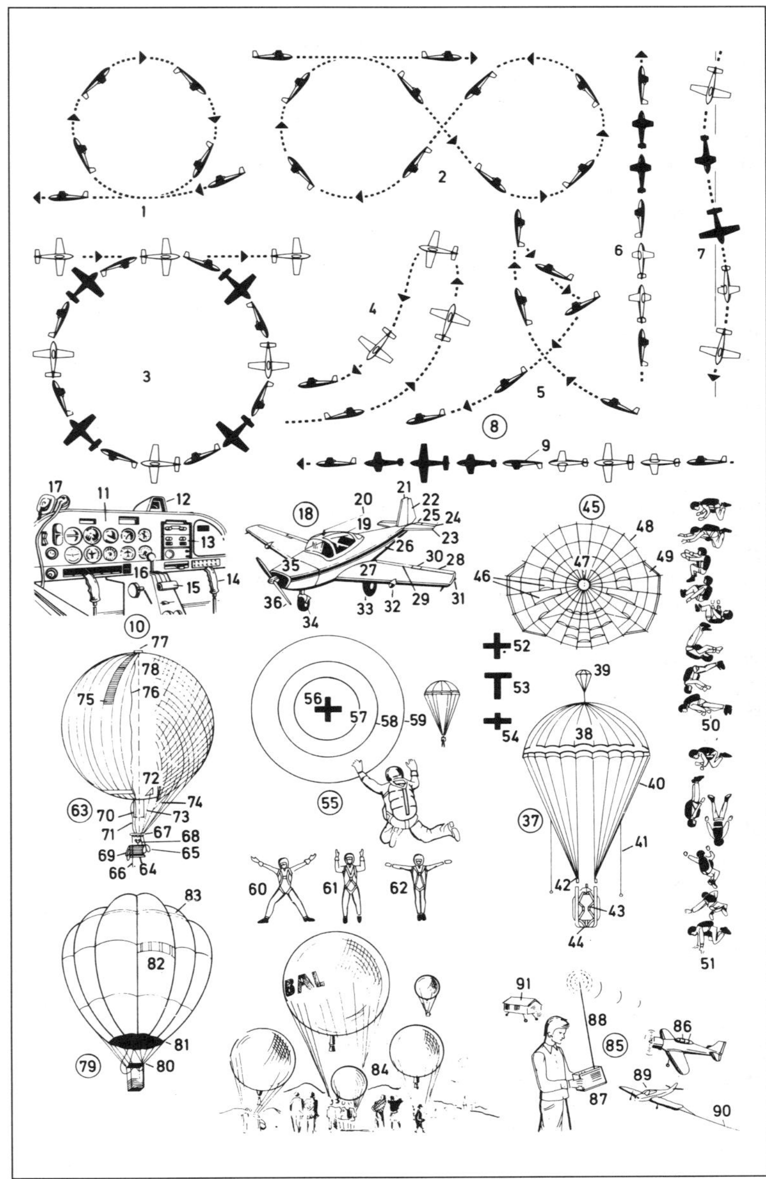
1
2
3
4
5
6
7
8
9
10
11
12
13
14
15
16
17
18
19
20
21
22
23
24
25
26
27
28
29
30
31
32
33
34
35
36
37
38
39
40
41
42
43
44
45
46
47
48
49
50
51
52
53
54
55
56
57
58
59
60
61
62
63
64
65
66
67
68
69
70
71
72
73
74
75
76
77
78
79
80
81
82
83
84
BAL
85
86
87
88
89
90
91

289 Horsemanship, Equestrian Sport

1-7 dressage
1 arena (dressage arena)
2 rail
3 school horse
4 dark coat (black coat)
5 white breeches
6 top hat
7 gait (*also:* school figure)
8-14 show jumping
8 obstacle (fence), an almost-fixed obstacle; *sim.:* gate, gate and rails, palisade, oxer, mound, wall
9 jumper
10 jumping saddle
11 girth
12 snaffle
13 red coat (hunting pink, pink; *also:* dark coat)
14 hunting cap (riding cap)
15 bandage
16-19 three-day event
16 endurance competition
17 cross-country
18 helmet (*also:* hard hat, hard hunting cap)
19 course markings
20-22 steeplechase
20 water jump, a fixed obstacle
21 jump
22 riding switch
23-40 harness racing (harness horse racing)
23 harness racing track (track)
24 sulky
25 spoke wheel (spoked wheel) with plastic wheel disc (disk)
26 driver in trotting silks
27 rein
28 trotter
29 piebald horse
30 shadow roll
31 elbow boot
32 rubber boot
33 number
34 glass-covered grandstand with totalizator windows (tote windows) inside
35 totalizator (tote)
36 number
37 odds (price, starting price, price offered)
38 winners' table
39 winner's price
40 time indicator
41-49 hunt, a drag hunt; *sim.:* fox hunt, paper chase (paper hunt, hare-and-hounds)
41 field
42 hunting pink
43 whipper-in (whip)
44 hunting horn
45 Master (Master of foxhounds, MFH)
46 pack of hounds (pack)
47 staghound
48 drag
49 scented trail (artificial scent)
50 **horse racing** (racing)
51 field (racehorses)
52 favourite (*Am.* favorite)
53 outsider

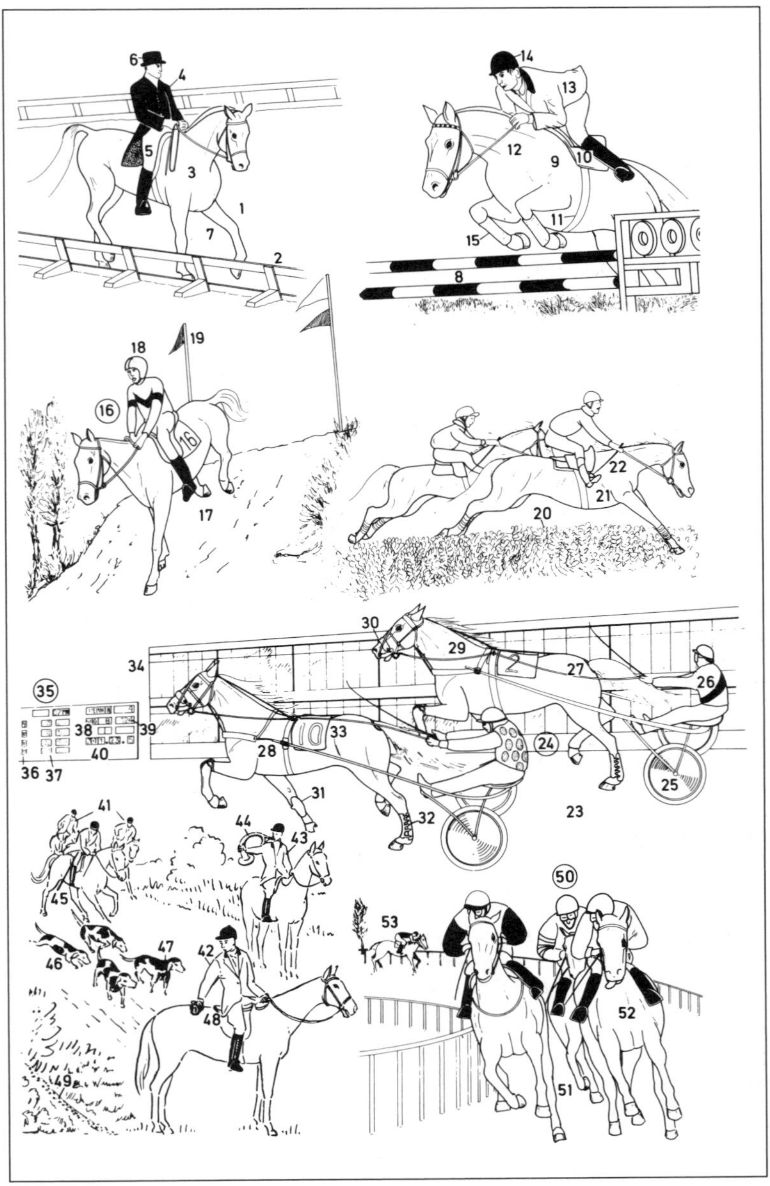
1
2
3
4
5
6
7
8
9
10
11
12
13
14
15
16
17
18
19
20
21
22
23
24
25
26
27
28
29
30
31
32
33
34
35
36
37
38
39
40
41
42
43
44
45
46
47
48
49
50
51
52
53

1-23 cycle racing
1 cycling track (cycle track); *here:* indoor track
2-7 six-day race
2 six-day racer, a track racer (track rider) on the track
3 crash hat
4 stewards
5 judge
6 lap scorer
7 rider's box (racer's box)
8-10 road race
8 road racer, a racing cyclist
9 racing jersey
10 water bottle
11-15 motor-paced racing (long-distance racing)
11 pacer, a motorcyclist
12 pacer's motorcycle
13 roller, a safety device
14 stayer (motor-paced track rider)
15 motor-paced cycle, a racing cycle
16 racing cycle (racing bicycle) for road racing (road race bicycle)
17 racing saddle, an unsprung saddle
18 racing handlebars (racing handlebar)
19 tubular tyre (*Am.* tire) (racing tyre)
20 chain
21 toe clip (racing toe clip)
22 strap
23 spare tubular tyre (*Am.* tire)
24-38 motorsports
24-28 motorcycle racing; *disciplines:* grasstrack racing, road racing, sand track racing, cement track racing, speedway [on ash or shale tracks], mountain racing, ice racing (ice speedway), scramble racing, trial, moto cross
24 sand track
25 racing motorcyclist (rider)
26 leather overalls (leathers)
27 racing motorcycle, a solo machine
28 number (number plate)
29 sidecar combination on the bend
30 sidecar
31 streamlined racing motorcycle [500 cc.]
32 gymkhana, a competition of skill; *here:* motorcyclist performing a jump
33 cross-country race, a test in performance
34-38 racing cars
34 Formula One racing car (a mono posto)
35 rear spoiler (aerofoil, *Am.* airfoil)
36 Formula Two racing car
37 Super-Vee racing car
38 prototype, a racing car

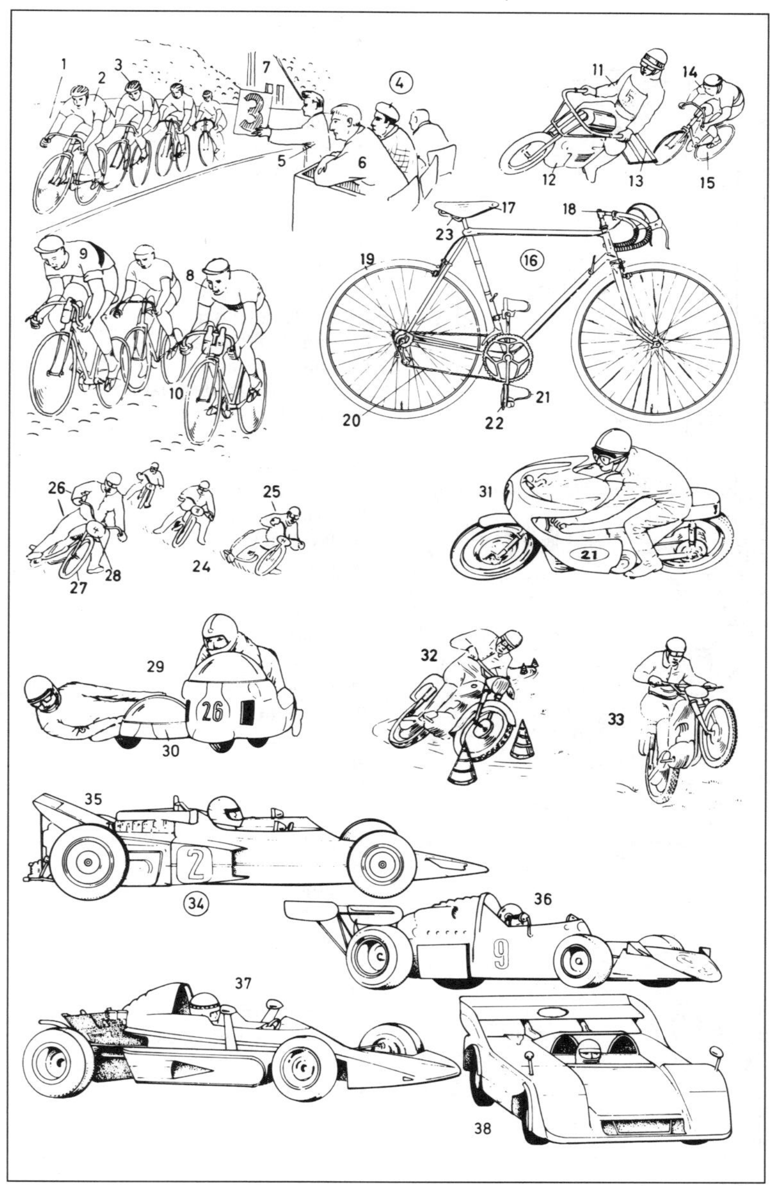
1
2
3
4
5
6
7
8
9
10
11
12
13
14
15
16
17
18
19
20
21
22
23
24
25
26
27
28
29
30
31
32
33
34
35
36
37
38

291 Ball Games I (Football, Association Football, Soccer)

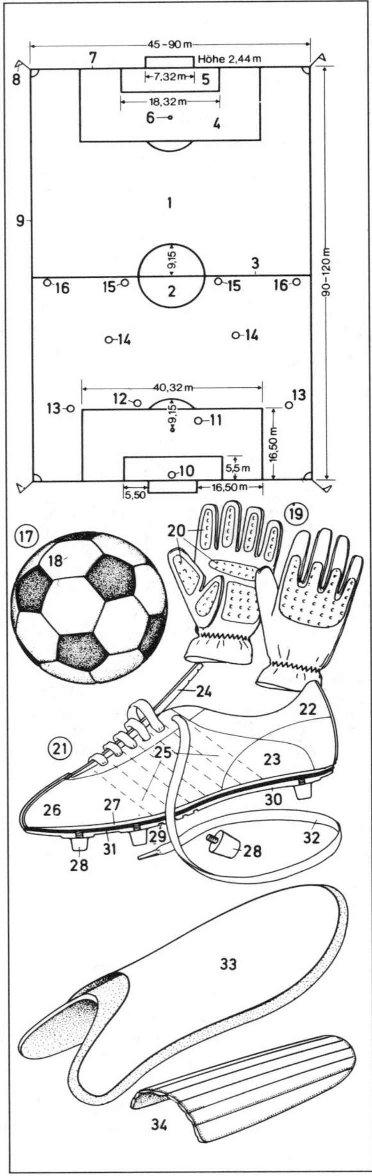

1-16 football pitch
1 field (park)
2 centre (*Am.* center) circle
3 half-way line
4 penalty area
5 goal area
6 penalty spot
7 goal line (by-line)
8 corner flag
9 touch line
10 goalkeeper
11 sweeper (libero)
12 inside defender
13 outside defender
14 midfield players
15 inside forward (striker)
16 outside forward (winger)
17 football
18 valve
19 goalkeeper's gloves
20 foam rubber padding
21 football boot
22 leather lining
23 counter
24 foam rubber tongue
25 bands
26 shaft
27 insole
28 screw-in stud
29 groove
30 nylon sole
31 inner sole
32 lace (bootlace)
33 football pad with ankle guard
34 shin guard
35 goal
36 crossbar
37 post (goalpost)
38 goal kick
39 save with the fists
40 penalty (penalty kick)
41 corner (corner kick)
42 offside
43 free kick
44 wall
45 bicycle kick (overhead bicycle kick)

46 header
47 pass (passing the ball)
48 receiving the ball (taking a pass)
49 short pass (one-two)
50 foul (infringement)
51 obstruction
52 dribble
53 throw-in
54 substitute
55 coach
56 shirt (jersey)
57 shorts
58 sock (football sock)
59 linesman
60 linesman's flag
61 sending-off
62 referee
63 red card; *also:* yellow card
64 centre (*Am.* center) flag

1 **handball** (indoor handball)
2 handball player, a field player
3 attacker, making a jump throw
4 defender
5 penalty line
6 **hockey**
7 goal
8 goalkeeper
9 pad (shin pad, knee pad)
10 kicker
11 face guard
12 glove
13 hockey stick
14 hockey ball
15 hockey player
16 striking circle
17 sideline
18 corner
19 **rugby** (rugby football)
20 scrum (scrummage)
21 rugby ball
22 **American football** (*Am.* football)
23 player (football player) carrying the ball
24 helmet
25 face guard
26 padded jersey
27 ball (pigskin)
28 **basketball**
29 basketball
30 backboard
31 backboard support
32 basket
33 basket ring
34 target rectangle
35 basketball player shooting
36 end line
37 restricted area
38 free-throw line
39 substitute
40-69 **baseball**
40-58 field (park)
40 spectator barrier
41 outfielder
42 short stop
43 second base
44 baseman
45 runner
46 first base
47 third base
48 foul line (base line)
49 pitcher's mound
50 pitcher
51 batter's position
52 batter
53 home base (home plate)
54 catcher
55 umpire
56 coach's box
57 coach
58 batting order
59, 60 baseball gloves (baseball mitts)
59 fielder's glove (fielder's mitt)
60 catcher's glove (catcher's mitt)
61 baseball
62 bat
63 batter at bat
64 catcher
65 umpire
66 runner
67 base plate
68 pitcher
69 pitcher's mound
70-76 **cricket**
70 wicket with bails
71 bowling crease
72 popping crease
73 wicket keeper of the fielding side
74 batsman
75 bat (cricket bat)
76 fielder (bowler)
77-82 **croquet**
77 winning peg
78 hoop
79 corner peg
80 croquet player
81 croquet mallet
82 croquet ball

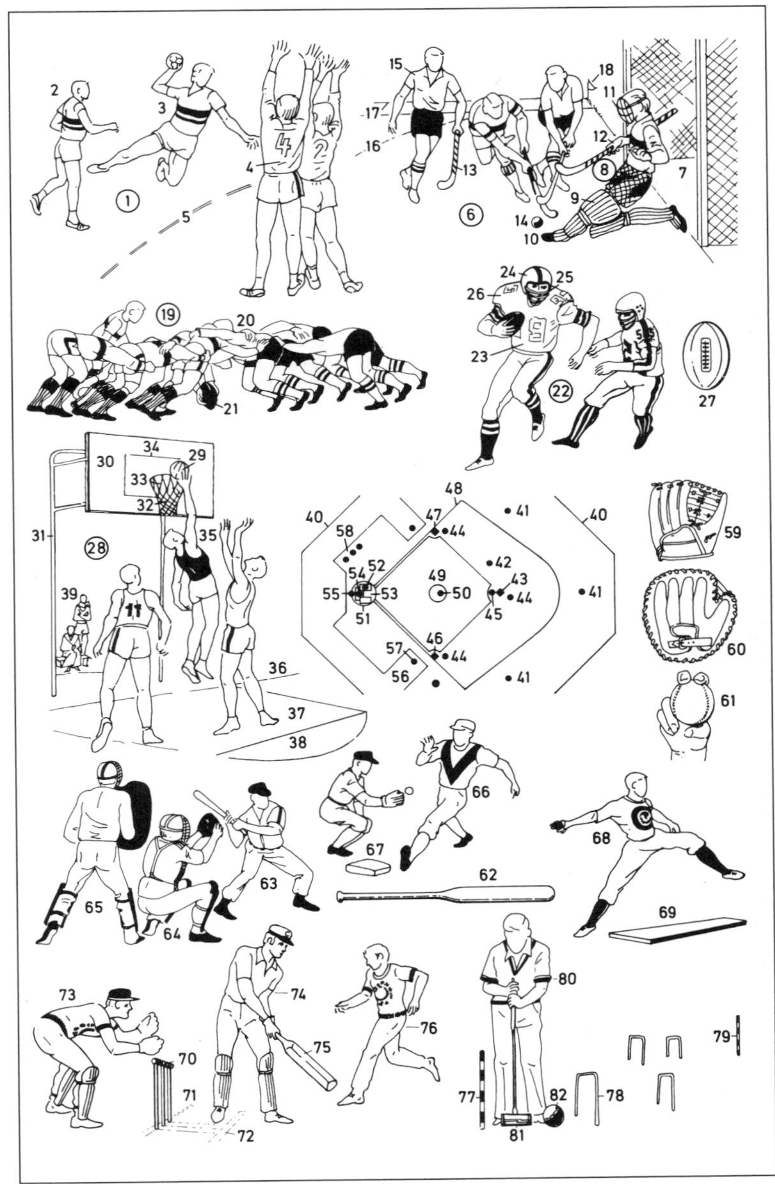
1
2
3
4
5
6
7
8
9
10
11
12
13
14
15
16
17
18
19
20
21
22
23
24
25
26
27
28
29
30
31
32
33
34
35
36
37
38
39
40
41
42
43
44
45
46
47
48
49
50
51
52
53
54
55
56
57
58
59
60
61
62
63
64
65
66
67
68
69
70
71
72
73
74
75
76
77
78
79
80
81
82

293 Ball Games III

1-42 tennis
1 tennis court
2-3 doubles sideline (sideline for doubles matches); *kinds of doubles:* men's doubles, women's doubles, mixed doubles
3-10 base line
4-5 singles sideline (sideline for singles matches); *kinds of singles:* men's singles, women's singles
6-7 service line
8-9 centre (*Am.* center) line
11 centre (*Am.* center) mark
12 service court
13 net (tennis net)
14 net strap
15 net post
16 tennis player
17 smash
18 opponent
19 umpire
20 umpire's chair
21 umpire's microphone
22 ball boy
23 net-cord judge
24 foot-fault judge
25 centre (*Am.* center) line judge
26 base line judge
27 service line judge
28 tennis ball
29 tennis racket (tennis racquet, racket, racquet)
30 racket handle (racquet handle)
31 strings (striking surface)
32 press (racket press, racquet press)
33 tightening screw
34 scoreboard
35 results of sets
36 player's name
37 number of sets
38 state of play
39 backhand stroke
40 forehand stroke
41 volley (forehand volley at normal height)
42 service
43, 44 badminton
43 badminton racket (badminton racquet)
44 shuttle (shuttlecock)
45-55 table tennis
45 table tennis racket (racquet) (table tennis bat)
46 racket (racquet) handle (bat handle)
47 blade covering
48 table tennis ball
49 table tennis players; *here:* mixed doubles
50 receiver
51 server
52 table tennis table
53 table tennis net
54 centre (*Am.* center) line
55 sideline
56-71 volleyball
56, 57 correct placing of the hands
58 volleyball
59 serving the volleyball
60 blocker
61 service area
62 server
63 front-line player
64 attack area
65 attack line
66 defence (*Am.* defense) area
67 referee
68 umpire
69 linesman
70 scoreboard
71 scorer
72-78 faustball
72 base line
73 tape
74 faustball
75 forward
76 centre (*Am.* center)
77 back
78 hammer blow
79-93 golf
79-82 course (holes)
79 teeing ground
80 rough
81 bunker (*Am.* sand trap)
82 green (putting green)
83 golfer, driving
84 follow-through
85 golf trolley
86 putting (holing out)
87 hole
88 pin (flagstick)
89 golf ball
90 tee
91 wood, a driver; *sim.:* brassie (brassy, brassey)
92 iron
93 putter

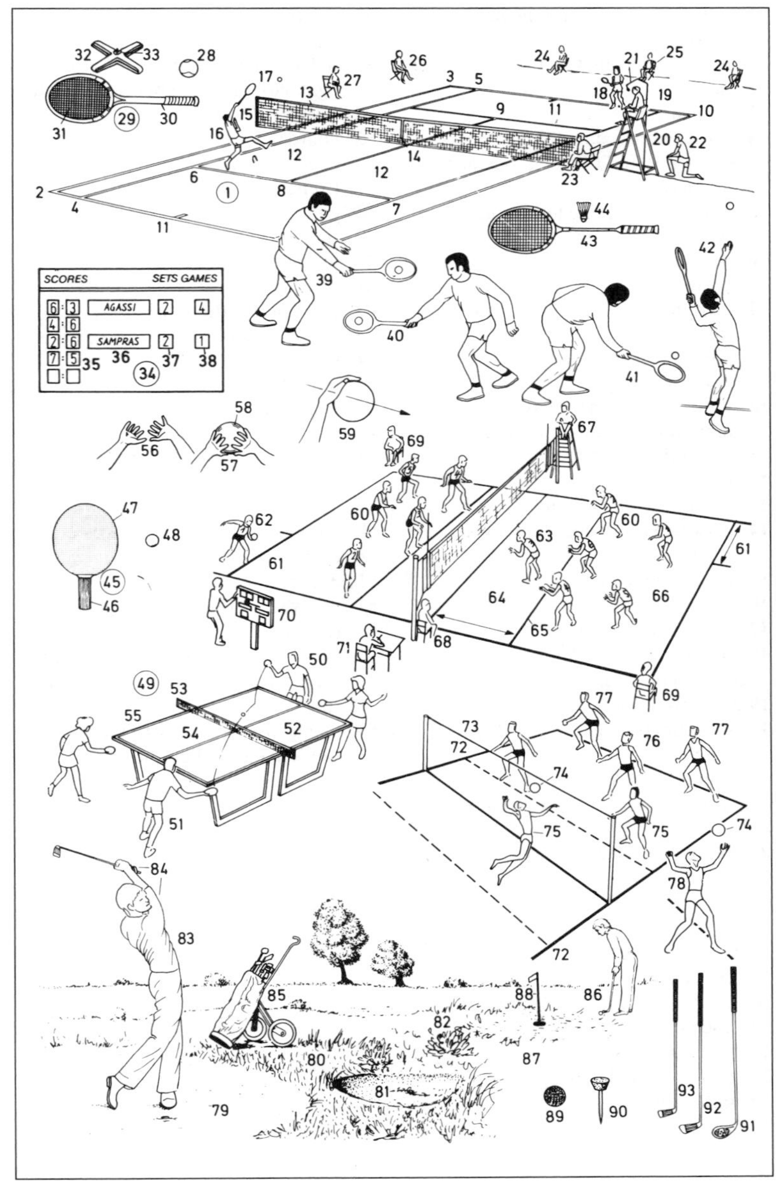
SCORES
SETS GAMES
AGASSI
SAMPRAS

1-33 fencing (modern fencing)
1-18 foil
1 fencing master (fencing instructor)
2 piste
3 on guard line
4 centre (*Am.* center) line
5, 6 fencers (foil fencers, foilsmen, foilists) in a bout
5 attacker (attacking fencer) in lunging position (lunging)
6 defender (defending fencer), parrying
7 straight thrust, a fencing movement
8 parry of the tierce
9 line of fencing
10 the three fencing measures (short, medium, and long measure)
11 foil, a thrust weapon
12 fencing glove
13 fencing mask (foil mask)
14 neck flap (neck guard) on the fencing mask
15 metallic jacket
16 fencing jacket
17 heelless fencing shoes
18 first position for fencer's salute (initial position, on guard position)
19-24 sabre (*Am.* saber) fencing
19 sabreurs (sabre fencers, *Am.* saber fencers)
20 (light) sabre (*Am.* saber)
21 sabre (*Am.* saber) glove (sabre gauntlet)
22 sabre (*Am.* saber) mask
23 cut at head
24 parry of the fifth (quinte)
25-33 épée, with electrical scoring equipment
25 épéeist
26 electric épée; *also:* electric foil
27 épée point
28 scoring lights
29 spring-loaded wire spool
30 indicator light
31 wire
32 electronic scoring equipment
33 on guard position
34-45 fencing weapons
34 light sabre (*Am.* saber), a cut and thrust weapon
35 guard
36 épée, a thrust weapon
37 French foil, a thrust weapon
38 guard (coquille)
39 Italian foil
40 foil pommel
41 handle
42 cross piece (quillons)
43 guard (coquille)
44 blade
45 button
46 engagements
47 quarte (carte) engagement
48 tierce engagement (*also:* sixte engagement)
49 circling engagement
50 seconde engagement (*also:* octave engagement)
51-53 target areas
51 the whole body in épée fencing (men)
52 head and upper body down to the groin in sabre (*Am.* saber) fencing (men)
53 trunk from the neck to the groin in foil fencing (ladies and men)

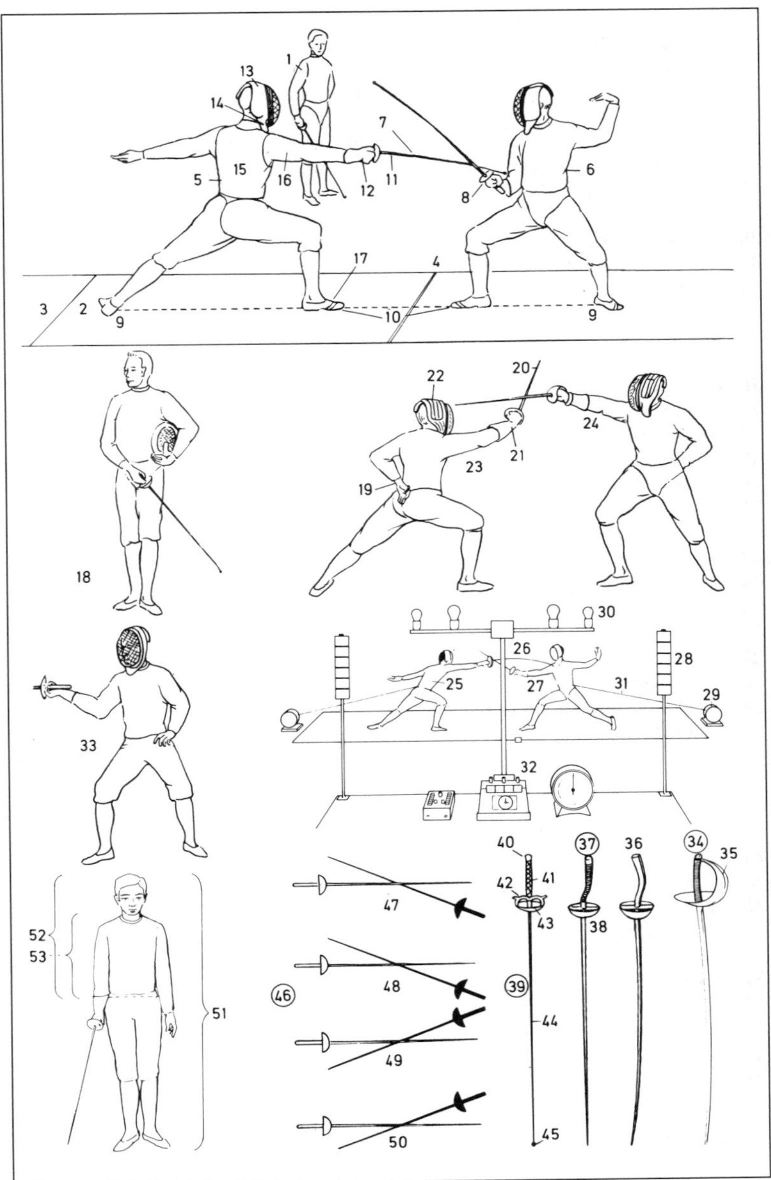
1
2
3
4
5
6
7
8
9
10
11
12
13
14
15
16
17
18
19
20
21
22
23
24
25
26
27
28
29
30
31
32
33
34
35
36
37
38
39
40
41
42
43
44
45
46
47
48
49
50
51
52
53

295 Free Exercise

1 basic position (starting position)
2 running posture
3 side straddle
4 straddle (forward straddle)
5 toe stand
6 crouch
7 upright kneeling position
8 kneeling position, seat on heels
9 squat
10 L seat (long sitting)
11 tailor seat (sitting tailor-style)
12 hurdle (hurdle position)
13 V-seat
14 side split
15 forward split
16 L-support
17 V-support
18 straddle seat
19 bridge
20 kneeling front support
21 front support
22 back support
23 crouch with front support
24 arched front support
25 side support
26 forearm stand (forearm balance)
27 handstand
28 headstand
29 shoulder stand (shoulder balance)
30 forward horizontal stand (arabesque)
31 rearward horizontal stand
32 trunk-bending sideways
33 trunk-bending forwards
34 arch
35 astride jump (butterfly)
36 tuck jump
37 astride jump
38 pike
39 scissor jump
40 stag jump (stag leap)
41 running step
42 lunge
43 forward pace
44 lying on back
45 prone position
46 lying on side
47 holding arms downwards
48 holding (extending) arms sideways
49 holding arms raised upward
50 holding (extending) arms forward
51 arms held (extended) backward
52 hands clasped behind the head

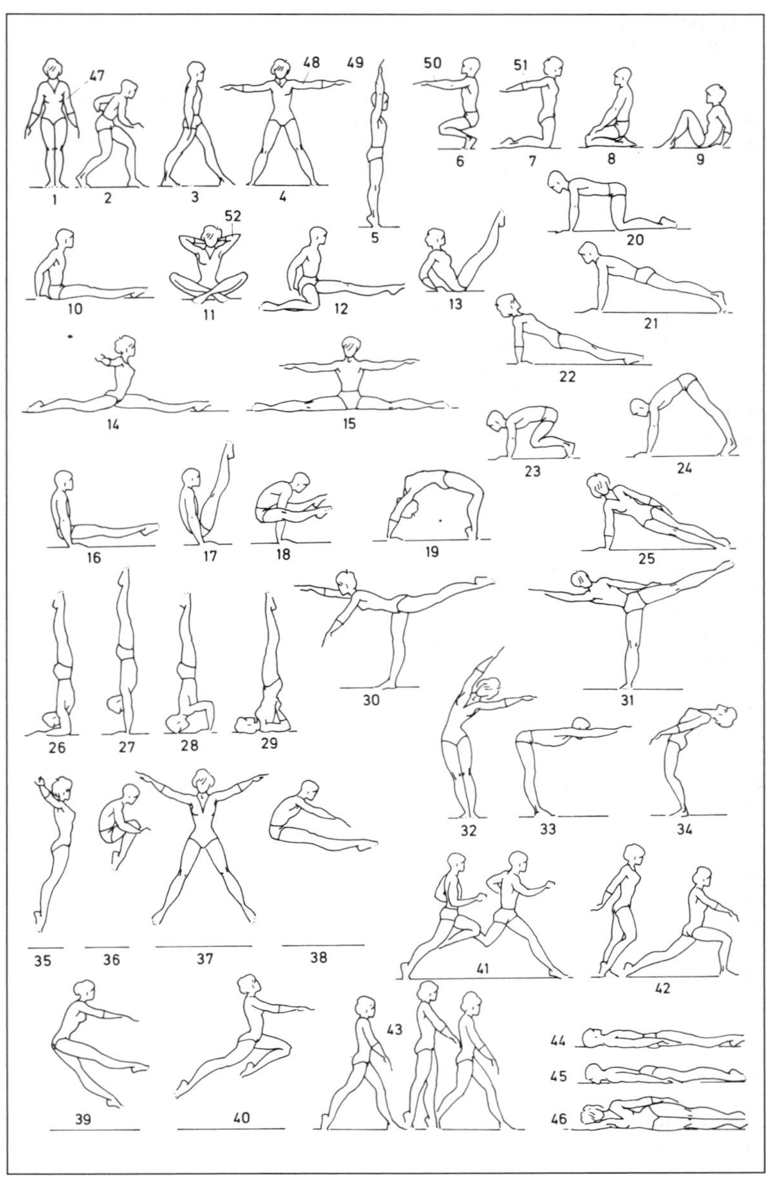
47
48
49
50
51
52
1
2
3
4
5
6
7
8
9
10
11
12
13
14
15
16
17
18
19
20
21
22
23
24
25
26
27
28
29
30
31
32
33
34
35
36
37
38
39
40
41
42
43
44
45
46

1-11 gymnastics apparatus in men's Olympic gymnastics
1 long horse (horse, vaulting horse)
2 parallel bars
3 bar
4 rings (stationary rings)
5 pommel horse (side horse)
6 pommel
7 horizontal bar (high bar)
8 bar
9 upright
10 stay wires
11 floor (12 m × 12 m floor area)
12-21 auxiliary apparatus and apparatus for school and club gymnastics
12 springboard (Reuther board)
13 landing mat
14 bench
15 box
16 small box
17 buck
18 mattress
19 climbing rope (rope)
20 wall bars
21 window ladder
22-39 positions in relation to the apparatus
22 side, facing
23 side, facing away
24 end, facing
25 end, facing away
26 outside, facing
27 inside, facing
28 front support
29 back support
30 straddle position
31 seated position outside
32 riding seat outside
33 hang
34 reverse hang
35 hang with elbows bent
36 piked reverse hang
37 straight inverted hang
38 straight hang
39 bent hang
40-46 grasps (kinds of grasp)
40 overgrasp on the horizontal bar
41 undergrasp on the horizontal bar
42 combined grasp on the horizontal bar
43 cross grasp on the horizontal bar
44 rotated grasp on the horizontal bar
45 outside grip on the parallel bars
46 rotated grasp on the parallel bars
47 leather handstrap
48-60 apparatus exercises
48 long-fly on the horse
49 rise to straddle on the parallel bars
50 crucifix on the rings
51 scissors (scissors movement) on the pommel horse
52 legs raising into a handstand on the floor
53 squat vault on the horse
54 double leg circle on the pommel horse
55 hip circle backwards on the rings
56 lever hang on the rings
57 rearward swing on the parallel bars
58 forward kip into upper arm hang on the parallel bars
59 backward underswing on the horizontal bar
60 backward grand circle on the horizontal bar
61-63 gymnastics kit
61 singlet (vest, *Am.* undershirt)
62 gym trousers
63 gym shoes
64 wristband

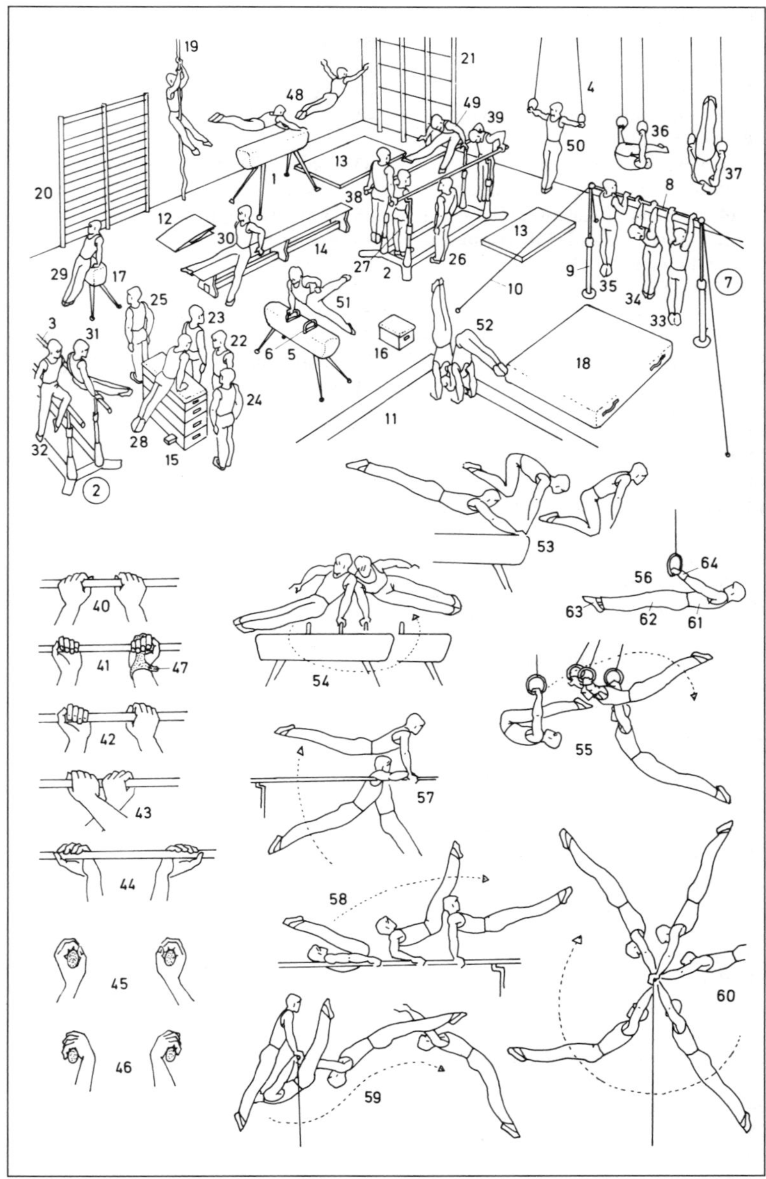
19
21
48
4
49
39
36
13
50
1
37
20
38
8
12
30
13
14
29
17
27
2
26
9
10
35
34
7
25
51
23
52
33
3
31
22
6
5
16
18
24
11
28
32
15
2
53
64
56
40
63
62
61
41
47
54
42
55
57
43
44
58
45
60
46
59

297 Apparatus Gymnastics II (Women's Gymnastics)

1-6 gymnastics apparatus in women's Olympic gymnastics
1 horse (vaulting horse)
2 beam
3 asymmetric bars (uneven bars)
4 bar
5 stay wires
6 floor (12 m × 12 m floor area)
7-14 auxiliary apparatus and apparatus for school and club gymnastics
7 landing mat
8 springboard (Reuther board)
9 small box
10 trampoline
11 sheet (web)
12 frame
13 rubber springs
14 springboard trampoline
15-32 apparatus exercises
15 backward somersault
16 spotting position (standing-in position)
17 vertical backward somersault on the trampoline
18 forward somersault on the springboard trampoline
19 forward roll on the floor
20 long-fly to forward roll on the floor
21 cartwheel on the beam
22 handspring on the horse
23 backward walkover
24 back flip (flik-flak) on the floor
25 free walkover forward on the floor
26 forward walkover on the floor
27 headspring on the floor
28 upstart on the asymmetric bars
29 free backward circle on the asymmetric bars
30 face vault over the horse
31 flank vault over the horse
32 back vault (rear vault) over the horse
33-50 gymnastics with hand apparatus
33 hand-to-hand throw
34 gymnastic ball
35 high toss
36 bounce
37 hand circling with two clubs
38 gymnastic club
39 swing
40 tuck jump
41 bar
42 skip
43 rope (skipping rope)
44 criss-cross skip
45 skip through the hoop
46 gymnastic hoop
47 hand circle
48 serpent
49 gymnastic ribbon
50 spiral
51, 52 gymnastics kit
51 leotard
52 gym shoes

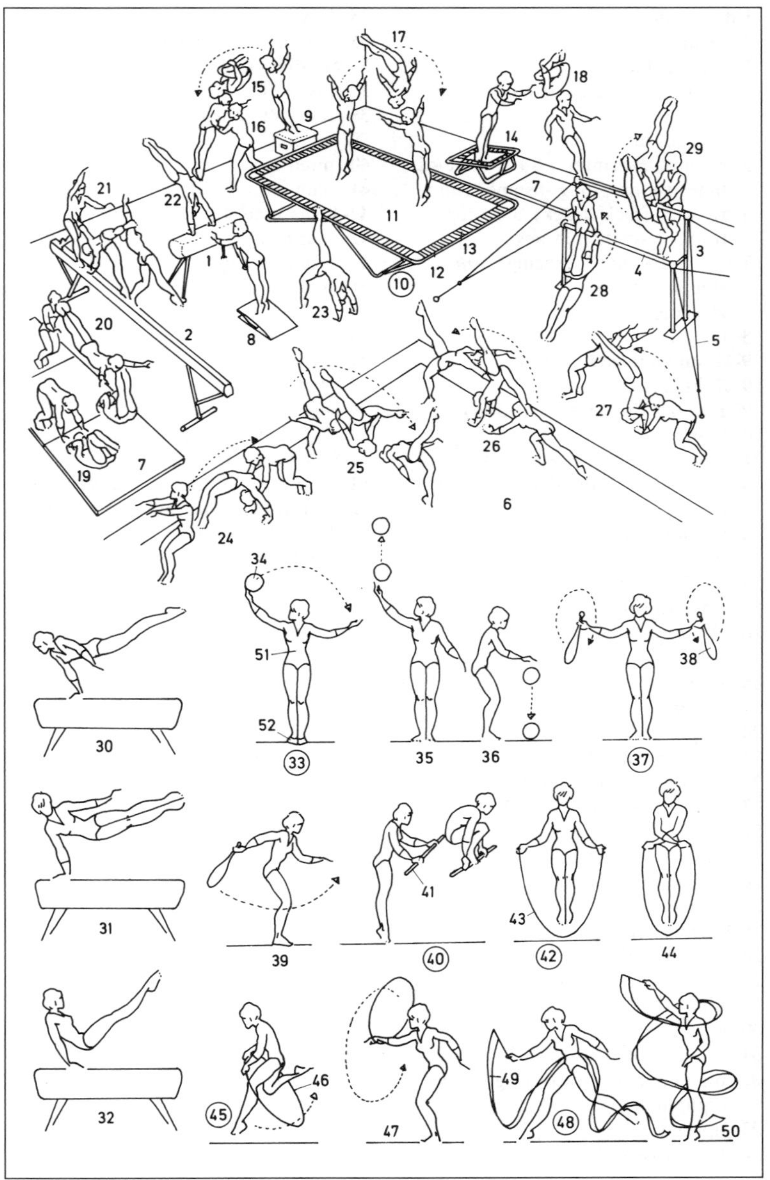
17
15
18
9
16
14
29
21
22
7
11
1
13
3
12
4
10
28
23
8
20
2
5
27
26
25
7
19
6
24
34
51
38
52
30
33
35
36
37
31
39
41
43
40
42
44
46
49
45
47
48
50

1-8 running
1-6 start
1 starting block
2 adjustable block (pedal)
3 start
4 crouch start
5 runner, a sprinter; *also:* middle-distance runner, long-distance runner
6 running track (track), a cinder track or synthetic track
7, 8 hurdles (hurdle racing); *sim.:* steeplechase
7 clearing the hurdle
8 hurdle
9-41 jumping and vaulting
9-27 high jump
9 Fosbury flop (Fosbury, flop)
10 high jumper
11 body rotation (rotation on the body's longitudinal and latitudinal axes)
12 shoulder landing
13 upright
14 bar (crossbar)
15 Eastern roll
16 Western roll
17 roll
18 rotation
19 landing
20 height scale
21 Eastern cut-off
22 scissors (scissor jump)
23 straddle (straddle jump)
24 turn
25 vertical free leg
26 take-off
27 free leg
28-36 pole vault
28 pole (vaulting pole)
29 pole vaulter (vaulter) in the pull-up phase
30 swing
31 crossing the bar
32 high jump apparatus (high jump equipment)
33 upright
34 bar (crossbar)
35 box
36 landing area (landing pad)
37-41 long jump
37 take-off
38 take-off board
39 landing area
40 hitch-kick
41 hang
42-47 hammer throw
42 hammer
43 hammer head
44 handle
45 grip
46 holding the grip
47 glove
48 shot put
49 shot (weight)
50 O'Brien technique
51-53 javelin throw
51 grip with thumb and index finger
52 grip with thumb and middle finger
53 horseshoe grip
54 binding

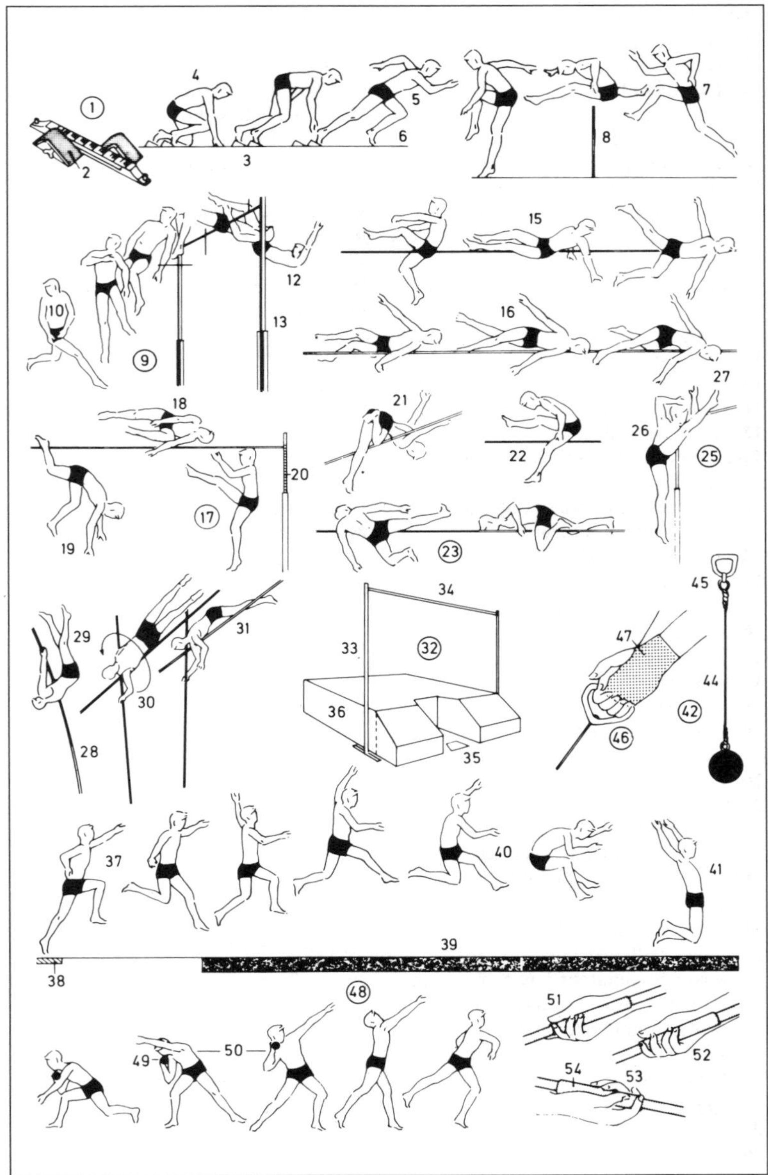
1
2
3
4
5
6
7
8
9
10
12
13
15
16
17
18
19
20
21
22
23
25
26
27
28
29
30
31
32
33
34
35
36
37
38
39
40
41
42
44
45
46
47
48
49
50
51
52
53
54

299 Weightlifting and Combat Sports

1-5 weightlifting
1 squat-style snatch
2 weightlifter
3 disc (disk) barbell
4 jerk with split
5 maintained lift
6-12 wrestling
6-9 Greco-Roman wrestling
6 standing wrestling (wrestling in standing position)
7 wrestler
8 on-the-ground wrestling (*here:* the referee's position)
9 bridge
10-12 freestyle wrestling
10 bar arm (arm bar) with grapevine
11 double leg lock
12 wrestling mat (mat)
13-17 judo (*sim.:* ju-jitsu, jiu-jitsu, ju-jutsu)
13 drawing the opponent off balance to the right and forward
14 judoka (judoist)
15 coloured (*Am.* colored) belt, as a symbol of Dan grade
16 referee
17 judo throw
18, 19 karate
18 karateka
19 side thrust kick, a kicking technique
20-50 boxing (boxing match)
20-24 training apparatus (training equipment)
20 spring-supported punch ball
21 punch bag (*Am.* punching bag)
22 speed ball
23 suspended punch ball
24 punch ball
25 boxer, an amateur boxer (boxes in a singlet, vest, *Am.* undershirt) or a professional boxer (boxes without singlet)
26 boxing glove
27 sparring partner
28 straight punch (straight blow)
29 ducking and sidestepping
30 headguard
31 infighting; *here:* clinch
32 uppercut
33 hook to the head; *here:* right hook
34 punch below the belt, a foul punch (illegal punch, foul)
35-50 boxing match (boxing contest), a title fight (title bout)
35 boxing ring (ring)
36 ropes
37 stay wire (stay rope)
38 neutral corner
39 winner
40 loser by a knockout
41 referee
42 counting out
43 judge
44 second
45 manager
46 gong
47 timekeeper
48 record keeper
49 press photographer
50 sports reporter (reporter)

1
2
3
4
5
6
7
8
9
10
11
12
13
14
15
16
17
18
19
20
21
22
23
24
25
26
27
28
29
30
31
32
33
34
35
36
37
38
39
40
41
42
43
44
45
46
47
48
49
50

300 Mountaineering

1-57 mountaineering (mountain climbing, Alpinism)
1 hut (Alpine Club hut, mountain hut, base)
2-13 climbing (rock climbing) [rock climbing technique]
2 rock face (rock wall)
3 fissure (vertical, horizontal, or diagonal fissure)
4 ledge (rock ledge, grass ledge, scree ledge, snow ledge, ice ledge)
5 mountaineer (climber, mountain climber, Alpinist)
6 anorak (high-altitude anorak, snowshirt, padded jacket)
7 breeches (climbing breeches)
8 chimney
9 belay (spike, rock spike)
10 belay
11 rope sling (sling)
12 rope
13 spur
14-21 snow and ice climbing [snow and ice climbing technique]
14 ice slope (firn slope)
15 snow and ice climber
16 ice axe (*Am.* ax)
17 step (ice step)
18 snow goggles
19 hood (anorak hood)
20 cornice (snow cornice)
21 ridge (ice ridge)
22-27 rope (roped party)
22 glacier
23 crevasse
24 snow bridge
25 leader
26 second man (belayer)
27 third man (non-belayer)
28-30 roping down (abseiling, rapelling)
28 abseil sling
29 sling seat
30 Dülfer seat
31-57 mountaineering equipment (climbing equipment, snow and ice climbing equipment)
31 ice axe (*Am.* ax)
32 wrist sling
33 pick
34 adze (*Am.* adz)
35 karabiner hole
36 short-shafted ice axe (*Am.* ax)
37 hammer axe (*Am.* ax)
38 general-purpose piton
39 abseil piton (ringed piton)
40 ice piton (semi-tubular screw ice piton, corkscrew piton)
41 drive-in ice piton
42 mountaineering boot
43 corrugated sole
44 climbing boot
45 roughened stiff rubber upper
46 karabiner
47 screwgate
48 crampons (lightweight crampons, twelve-point crampons, ten-point crampons)
49 front points
50 point guards
51 crampon strap
52 crampon cable fastener
53 safety helmet (protective helmet)
54 helmet lamp
55 snow gaiters
56 climbing harness
57 sit harness

20
21
12
8
9
10
11
13
28
30
6
19
18
14
5
7
2
2
4
15
16
3
29
17
1
27
22
26
25
24
56
53
54
49
57
23
48
40
46
51
33
35
34
38
47
50
55
32
42
43
36
31
39
41
31
52
44
37
45

301 Winter Sports I (Skiing)

1-72 skiing
1 compact ski
2 safety binding (release binding)
3 strap
4 steel edge
5 ski stick (ski pole)
6 grip
7 loop
8 basket
9 ladies' one-piece ski suit
10 skiing cap (ski cap)
11 skiing goggles
12 cemented sole skiing boot
13 crash helmet
14-20 cross-country equipment
14 cross-country ski
15 cross-country rat trap binding
16 cross-country boot
17 cross-country gear
18 peaked cap
19 sunglasses
20 cross-country poles made of bamboo
21-24 ski-waxing equipment
21 ski wax
22 waxing iron (blowlamp, blowtorch)
23 waxing cork
24 wax scraper
25 downhill racing pole
26 herringbone, for climbing a slope
27 sidestep, for climbing a slope
28 ski bag
29 slalom
30 gate pole
31 racing suit
32 downhill racing
33 'egg' position, the ideal downhill racing position
34 downhill ski
35 ski jumping
36 lean forward
37 number
38 ski jumping ski
39 grooves (3 to 5 grooves)
40 cable binding
41 ski jumping boots
42 cross-country
43 cross-country stretch-suit
44 course
45 course-marking flag
46 layers of a modern ski
47 special core
48 laminates
49 stabilizing layer (stabilizer)
50 steel edge
51 aluminium (*Am.* aluminum) upper edge
52 synthetic bottom (artificial bottom)
53 safety jet
54-56 parts of the binding
54 automatic heel unit
55 toe unit
56 ski stop
57-63 ski lift
57 double chair lift
58 safety bar with footrest
59 ski lift
60 track
61 hook
62 automatic cable pulley
63 haulage cable
64 slalom
65 open gate
66 closed vertical gate
67 open vertical gate
68 transversal chicane
69 hairpin
70 elbow
71 corridor
72 Allais chicane

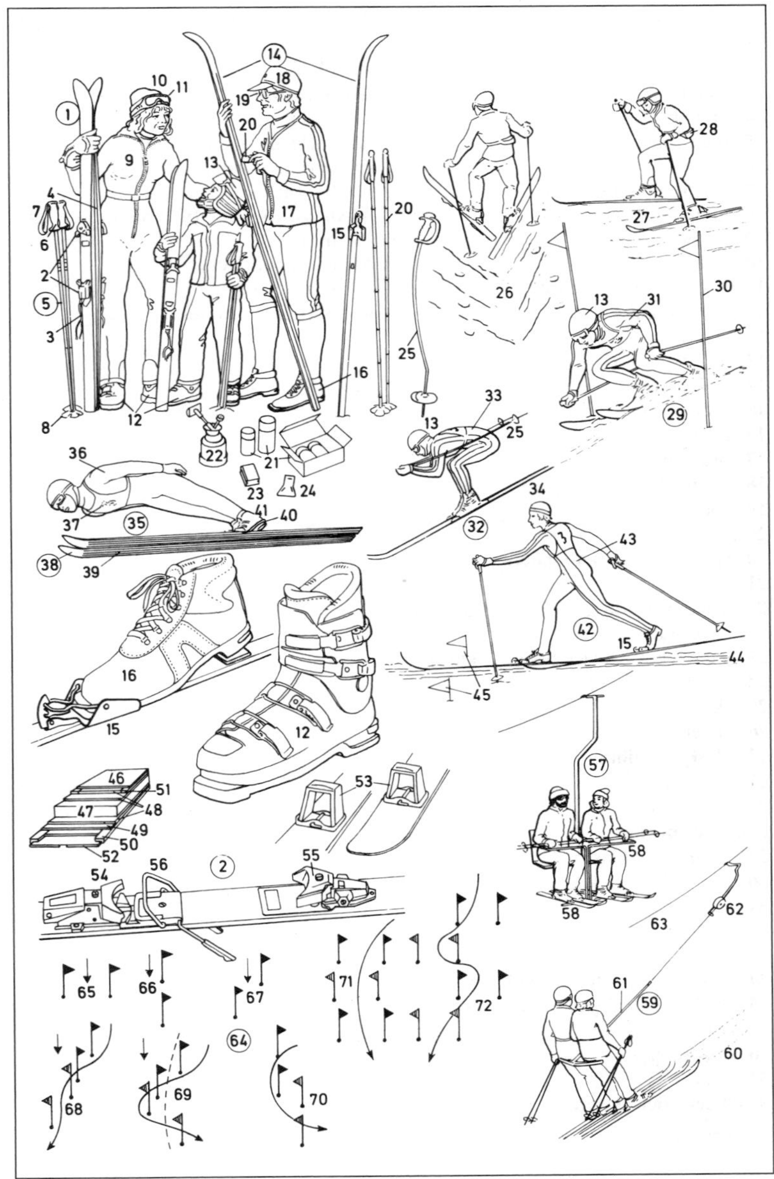

1-26 ice skating
1 ice skater, a solo skater
2 tracing leg
3 free leg
4 pair skaters
5 death spiral
6 pivot
7 stag jump (stag leap)
8 jump-sit-spin
9 upright spin
10 holding the foot
11-19 compulsory figures
11 curve eight
12 change
13 three
14 double-three
15 loop
16 change loop
17 bracket
18 counter
19 rocker
20-25 ice skates
20 speed skating set (speed skate)
21 edge
22 hollow grinding (hollow ridge, concave ridge)
23 ice hockey set (ice hockey skate)
24 ice skating boot
25 skate guard
26 speed skater
27, 28 skate sailing
27 skate sailor
28 hand sail
29-37 ice hockey
29 ice hockey player
30 ice hockey stick
31 stick handle
32 stick blade
33 shin pad
34 headgear (protective helmet)
35 puck, a vulcanized rubber disc (disk)
36 goalkeeper
37 goal
38-40 ice-stick shooting (Bavarian curling)
38 ice-stick shooter (Bavarian curler)
39 ice stick
40 block
41-43 curling
41 curler
42 curling stone (granite)
43 curling brush (curling broom, besom)
44-46 ice yachting (iceboating, ice sailing)
44 ice yacht (iceboat)
45 steering runner
46 outrigged runner

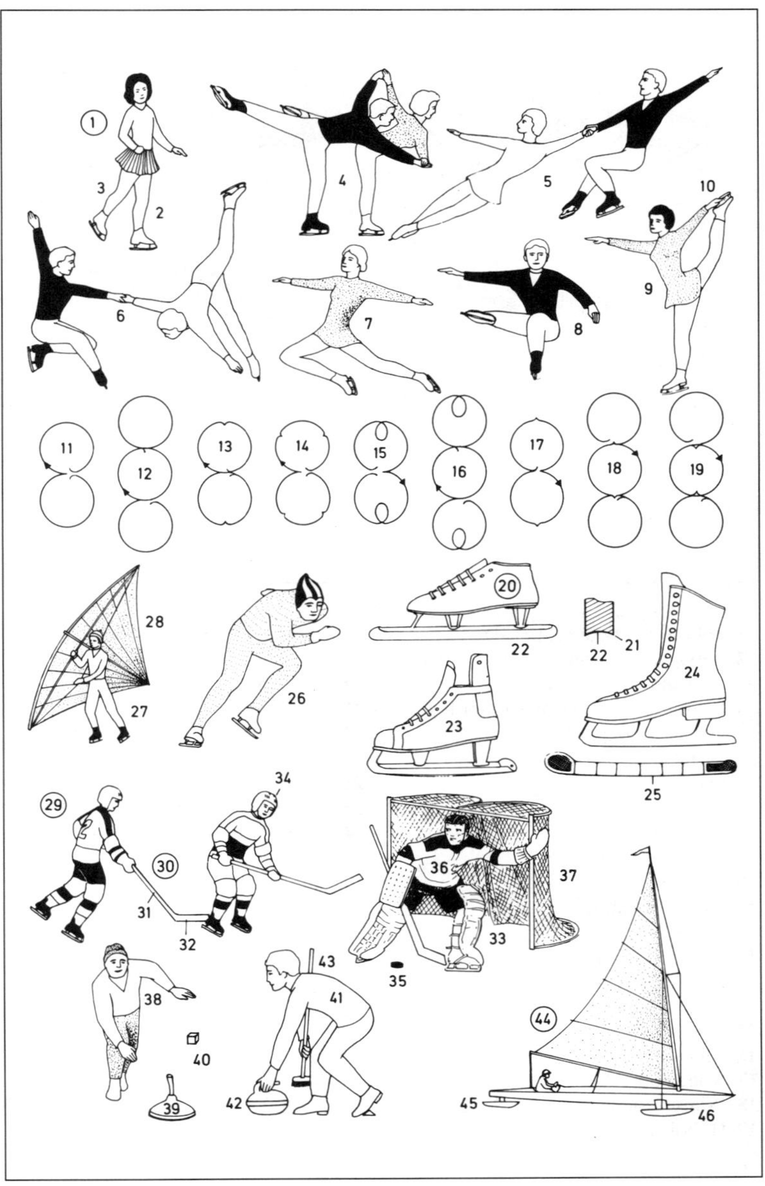
1
2
3
4
5
6
7
8
9
10
11
12
13
14
15
16
17
18
19
20
21
22
23
24
25
26
27
28
29
30
31
32
33
34
35
36
37
38
39
40
41
42
43
44
45
46

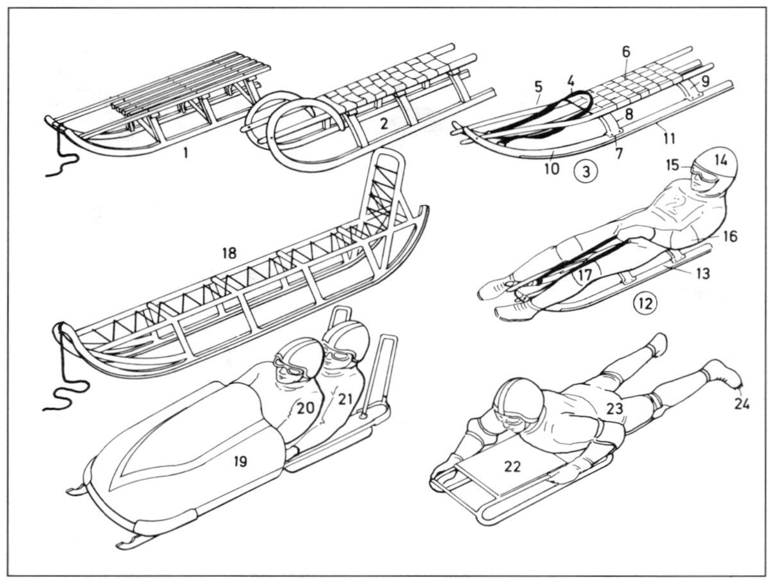

1 toboggan (sledge, *Am.* sled)
2 toboggan (sledge, *Am.* sled) with seat of plaid straps
3 junior luge toboggan (junior luge, junior toboggan)
4 rein
5 bar (strut)
6 seat
7 bracket
8 front prop
9 rear prop
10 movable runner
11 metal face
12 luge tobogganer
13 luge toboggan (luge, toboggan)
14 crash helmet
15 goggles
16 elbow pad
17 knee pad
18 Nansen sledge, a polar sledge
19-21 bobsleigh (bobsledding)
19 bobsleigh (bobsled), a two-man bobsleigh (a boblet)
20 steersman
21 brakeman
22-24 skeleton tobogganing (Cresta tobogganing)
22 skeleton (skeleton toboggan)
23 skeleton rider
24 rake, for braking and steering

1 avalanche (snow avalanche, *Am.* snowslide); *kinds:* wind avalanche, ground avalanche
2 avalanche wall, a deflecting wall (diverting wall); *sim.:* avalanche wedge
3 avalanche gallery
4 snowfall
5 snowdrift
6 snow fence
7 avalanche forest [planted as protection against avalanches]
8 street-cleaning lorry (street cleaner)
9 snow plough (*Am.* snowplow) attachment
10 snow chain (skid chain, tyre chain, *Am.* tire chain)
11 radiator bonnet (*Am.* radiator hood)
12 radiator shutter and shutter opening (louvre shutter)
13 snowman
14 snowball fight
15 snowball
16 ski bob
17 slide
18 boy, sliding
19 icy surface (icy ground)
20 covering of snow (on the roof)
21 icicle
22 man clearing snow
23 snow push (snow shovel)
24 heap of snow
25 horse-drawn sleigh (horse sleigh)
26 sleigh bells (bells, set of bells)
27 foot muff (*Am.* foot bag)
28 earmuff
29 handsledge (tread sledge); *sim.:* push sledge
30 slush

1-13 skittles
1-11 skittle frame
1 front pin (front)
2 left front second pin (left front second)
3 running three [left]
4 right front second pin (right front second)
5 running three [right]
6 left corner pin (left corner), a corner (copper)
7 landlord
8 right corner pin (right corner), a corner (copper)
9 back left second pin (back left second)
10 back right second pin (back right second)
11 back pin (back)
12 pin
13 landlord
14-20 tenpin bowling
14 frame
15 bowling ball (ball with finger holes)
16 finger hole
17-20 deliveries
17 straight ball
18 hook ball (hook)
19 curve
20 back-up ball (back-up)
21 **boules;** *sim.:* Italian game of boccie, green bowls (bowls)
22 boules player
23 jack (target jack)
24 grooved boule
25 group of players
26 **rifle shooting**
27-29 shooting positions
27 standing position
28 kneeling position
29 prone position
30-33 targets
30 target for 50 m events (50 m target)
31 circle
32 target for 100 m events (100 m target)
33 bobbing target (turning target, running-boar target)
34-39 ammunition
34 air rifle cartridge
35 rimfire cartridge for zimmerstutzen (indoor target rifle), a smallbore German single-shot rifle
36 case head
37 caseless round
38 .22 long rifle cartridge
39 .222 Remington cartridge
40-49 sporting rifles
40 air rifle
41 optical sight
42 front sight (foresight)
43 smallbore standard rifle
44 international smallbore free rifle
45 palm rest for standing position
46 butt plate with hook
47 butt with thumb hole
48 smallbore rifle for bobbing target (turning target)
49 telescopic sight (riflescope, telescope sight)
50 optical ring sight
51 optical ring and bead sight
52-66 archery (target archery)
52 shot
53 archer
54 competition bow
55 riser
56 point-of-aim mark
57 grip (handle)
58 stabilizer
59 bow string (string)
60 arrow
61 pile (point) of the arrow
62 fletching
63 nock
64 shaft
65 cresting
66 target
67 Basque game of **pelota** *(jai alai)*
68 pelota player
69 wicker basket (cesta)
70-78 skeet (skeet shooting), a kind of clay pigeon shooting
70 skeet over-and-under shotgun
71 muzzle with skeet choke
72 ready position on call
73 firing position
74 shooting range
75 high house
76 low house
77 target's path
78 shooting station (shooting box)
79 **aero wheel**
80 handle
81 footrest
82 **go-karting** (karting)
83 go-kart (kart)
84 number plate (number)
85 pedals
86 pneumatic tyre (*Am.* tire)
87 petrol tank (*Am.* gasoline tank)
88 frame
89 steering wheel
90 bucket seat
91 protective bulkhead
92 two-stroke engine
93 silencer (*Am.* muffler)

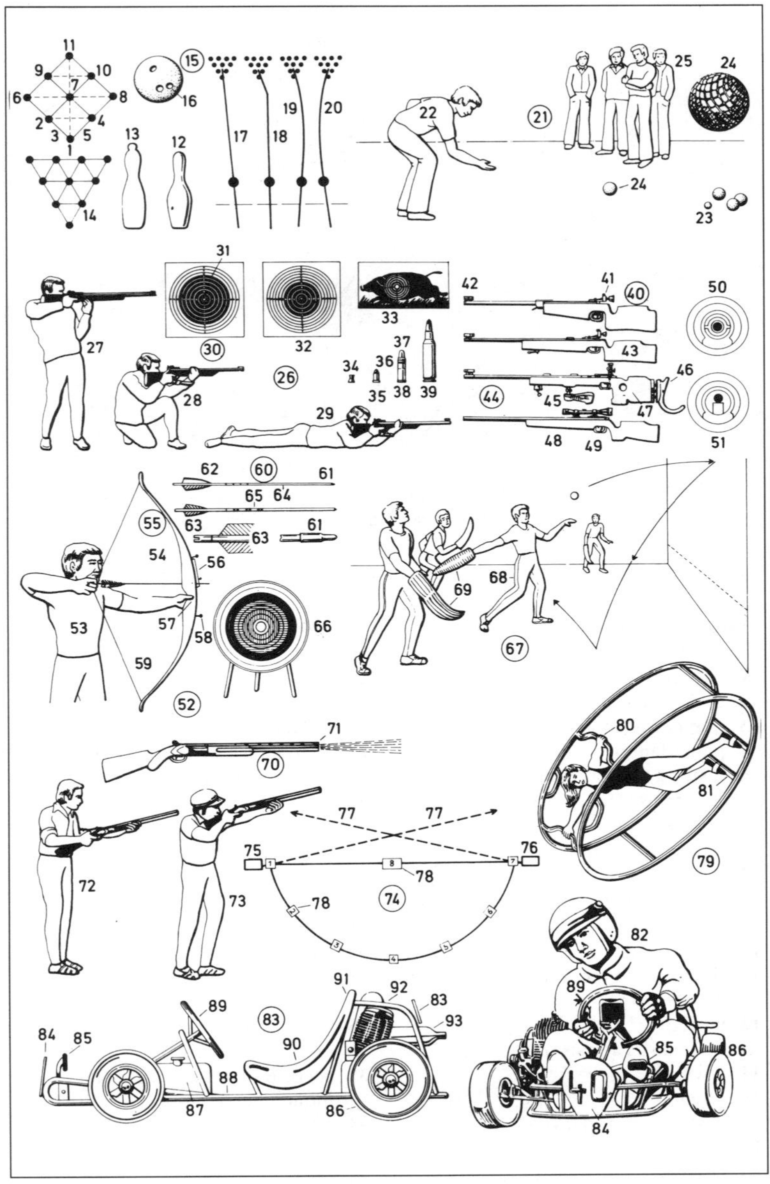

1-48 masked ball (masquerade, fancy-dress ball)
1 ballroom
2 dance band
3 pop musician
4 paper lantern
5 festoon (string of decorations)
6-48 disguise (fancy dress) at the masquerade
6 witch
7 mask
8 fur trapper (trapper)
9 Apache girl
10 net stocking
11 first prize in the tombola (raffle), a hamper
12 pierette
13 half mask (domino)
14 devil
15 domino
16 hula-hula girl (Hawaii girl)
17 garland
18 grass skirt (hula skirt)
19 pierrot
20 ruff
21 midinette
22 Biedermeier dress
23 poke bonnet
24 décolletage with beauty spot
25 bayadère (Hindu dancing girl)
26 grandee
27 Columbine
28 maharaja (maharajah)
29 mandarin, a Chinese dignitary
30 exotic girl (exotic)
31 cowboy; *sim.:* gaucho (vaquero)
32 vamp, in fancy dress
33 dandy (fop, beau)
34 rosette
35 harlequin
36 gipsy (gypsy) girl
37 cocotte (demi-monde, demi-mondaine, demi-rep)
38 owl-glass, a fool (jester, buffoon)
39 foolscap (jester's cap and bells)
40 rattle

41 odalisque, Eastern female slave in Sultan's seraglio
42 chalwar (pantaloons)
43 pirate (buccaneer)
44 tattoo
45 paper hat
46 false nose
47 clapper (rattle)
48 slapstick
49-54 fireworks
49 percussion cap
50 cracker
51 banger
52 jumping jack
53 cannon cracker (maroon, marroon)
54 rocket
55 paper ball
56 jack-in-the-box
57-70 carnival procession
57 carnival float (carnival truck)
58 King Carnival
59 bauble (fool's sceptre, *Am.* scepter)
60 fool's badge
61 Queen Carnival
62 confetti
63 giant
64 beauty queen
65 fairy-tale figure
66 paper streamer
67 majorette
68 king's guard
69 buffoon, a clown
70 lansquenet's drum

307 Circus

1-63 travelling (*Am.* traveling) circus
1 circus tent (big top), a four-pole tent
2 tent pole
3 spotlight
4 lighting technician
5 trapeze platform
6 trapeze
7 trapeze artist
8 rope ladder
9 bandstand
10 circus band
11 ring entrance (arena entrance)
12 wings
13 tent prop (prop)
14 safety net
15 seats for the spectators
16 circus box
17 circus manager
18 agent
19 entrance and exit
20 steps
21 ring (arena)
22 ring fence
23 musical clown (clown)
24 clown
25 comic turn (clown act), a circus act
26 circus riders (bareback riders)
27 ring attendant, a circus attendant
28 pyramid
29 support
30, 31 performance by liberty horses
30 circus horse, performing the levade (pesade)
31 ringmaster
32 vaulter

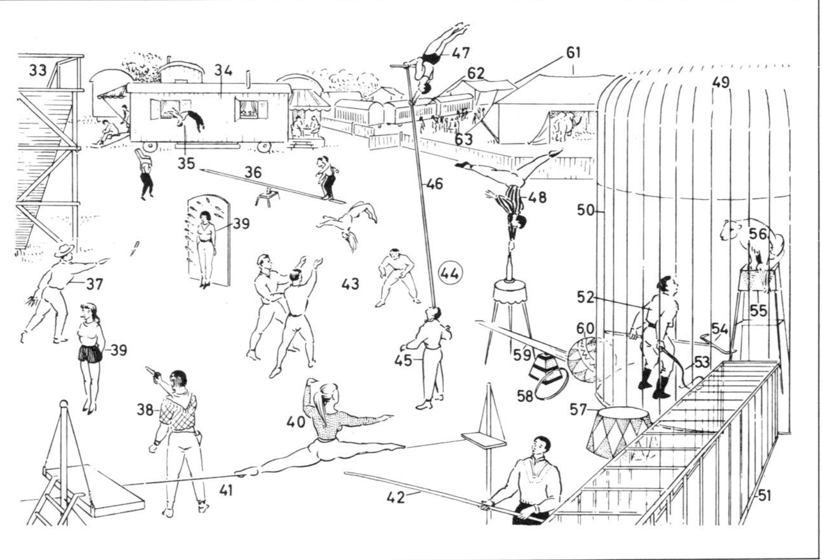

33 emergency exit
34 caravan (circus caravan, *Am.* trailer)
35 springboard acrobat (springboard artist)
36 springboard
37 knife thrower
38 circus marksman
39 assistant
40 tightrope dancer
41 tightrope
42 balancing pole
43 throwing act
44 balancing act
45 support
46 pole (bamboo pole)
47 acrobat
48 equilibrist (balancer)
49 wild animal cage, a round cage
50 bars of the cage
51 passage (barred passage, passage for the wild animals)
52 tamer (wild animal tamer)
53 whip
54 fork
55 pedestal
56 wild animal (tiger, lion)
57 stand
58 hoop (jumping hoop)
59 seesaw
60 ball
61 camp
62 cage caravan
63 menagerie

308 Fair, Fairground

1-69 fair (annual fair)
1 fairground
2 children's merry-go-round (whirligig), a roundabout (*Am.* carousel)
3 refreshment stall (drinks stall)
4 chairoplane
5 up-and-down roundabout
6 show booth (booth)
7 box (box office)
8 barker
9 medium
10 showman
11 try-your-strength machine
12 hawker
13 balloon
14 paper serpent
15 windmill
16 pickpocket (thief)
17 vendor
18 nougat
19 ghost train
20 monster
21 dragon
22 monster
23 beer marquee
24 sideshow
25-28 travelling (*Am.* traveling) artistes (travelling show people)
25 fire eater
26 sword swallower
27 strong man
28 escapologist
29 spectators
30 ice-cream vendor (ice-cream man)
31 ice-cream cornet, with ice cream
32 sausage stand
33 grill (*Am.* broiler)
34 bratwurst (grilled sausage, *Am.* broiled sausage)
35 sausage tongs
36 fortune teller
37 big wheel (Ferris wheel)
38 orchestrion (automatic organ), an automatic musical instrument
39 scenic railway (switchback)

40 toboggan slide (chute)
41 swing boats
42 swing boat, turning full circle
43 full circle
44 lottery booth (tombola booth)
45 wheel of fortune
46 devil's wheel (typhoon wheel)
47 throwing ring (quoit)
48 prizes
49 sandwich man on stilts
50 sandwich board (placard)
51 cigarette seller, an itinerant trader (a hawker)
52 tray
53 fruit stall
54 wall-of-death rider
55 hall of mirrors
56 concave mirror
57 convex mirror
58 shooting gallery
59 giant swing boat
60 junk stalls (second-hand stalls)
61 first aid tent (first aid post)
62 dodgems (bumper cars)
63 dodgem (bumper car)
64-66 pottery stand
64 barker
65 market woman
66 pottery
67 visitors to the fair
68 waxworks
69 wax figure

309 Flea Market

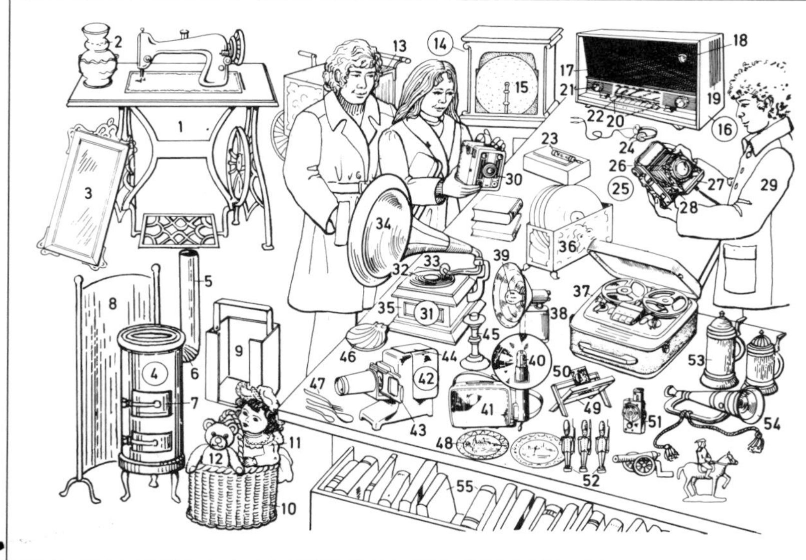

1 treadle sewing machine
2 flower vase
3 wall mirror
4 cylindrical stove
5 stovepipe
6 stovepipe elbow
7 stove door
8 stove screen
9 coal scuttle
10 firewood basket
11 doll
12 teddy bear
13 barrel organ
14 orchestrion
15 metal disc (disk)
16 radio (radio set, *joc.:* 'steam radio'), a superheterodyne (superhet)
17 baffle board
18 'magic eye', a tuning indicator valve
19 loudspeaker aperture
20 station selector buttons (station preset buttons)
21 tuning knob
22 frequency bands
23 crystal detector (crystal set)
24 headphones (headset)
25 folding camera
26 bellows
27 hinged cover
28 spring extension
29 salesman
30 box camera
31 gramophone
32 record (gramophone record)
33 needle head with gramophone needle
34 horn
35 gramophone box
36 record rack
37 portable tape recorder
38 flashgun
39 flash bulb
40, 41 electronic flash (electronic flash-gun)
40 flash head
41 accumulator
42 slide projector
43 slide holder
44 lamphouse

45 candlestick
46 scallop shell
47 cutlery
48 souvenir plate
49 drying rack for photographic plates
50 photographic plate
51 delayed-action release
52 tin soldiers (*sim.:* lead soldiers)
53 beer mug (stein)
54 bugle
55 second-hand books
56 grandfather clock
57 clock case
58 pendulum
59 time weight
60 striking weight
61 rocking chair
62 sailor suit
63 sailor's hat
64 washing set
65 washing basin
66 water jug
67 washstand
68 dolly
69 washtub
70 washboard
71 humming top
72 slate
73 pencil box
74 adding machine
75 paper roll
76 number keys
77 abacus
78 inkwell, with lid
79 typewriter
80 [hand-operated] calculating machine (calculator)
81 operating handle
82 result register (product register)
83 rotary counting mechanism (rotary counter)
84 kitchen scales
85 waist slip (underskirt)
86 wooden handcart
87 wall clock
88 bed warmer
89 milk churn

1-13 film studios (studio complex, *Am.* movie studios)
1 lot (studio lot)
2 processing laboratories (film laboratories, motion picture laboratories)
3 cutting rooms
4 administration building (office building, offices)
5 film (motion picture) storage vault (film library, motion picture library)
6 workshop
7 film set (*Am.* movie set)
8 power house
9 technical and research laboratories
10 groups of stages
11 concrete tank for marine sequences
12 cyclorama
13 hill
14-60 shooting (filming)
14 music recording studio (music recording theatre, *Am.* theater)
15 'acoustic' wall lining
16 screen (projection screen)
17 film orchestra
18 exterior shooting (outdoor shooting, exterior filming, outdoor filming)
19 camera with crystal-controlled drive
20 cameraman
21 assistant director
22 boom operator (boom swinger)
23 recording engineer (sound recordist)
24 portable sound recorder with crystal-controlled drive
25 microphone boom
26-60 shooting (filming) in the studio (on the sound stage, on the stage, in the filming hall)
26 production manager
27 leading lady (film actress, film star, star)
28 leading man (film actor, film star, star)
29 film extra (extra)
30 arrangement of microphones for stereo and sound effects

31 studio microphone
32 microphone cable
33 side flats and background
34 clapper boy
35 clapper board (clapper) with slates (boards) for the film title, shot number (scene number), and take number
36 make-up artist (hairstylist)
37 lighting electrician (studio electrician, lighting man, *Am.* gaffer)
38 diffusing screen
39 continuity girl (script girl)
40 film director (director)
41 cameraman (first cameraman)
42 camera operator, an assistant cameraman (camera assistant)
43 set designer (art director)
44 director of photography
45 filmscript (script, shooting script, *Am.* movie script)
46 assistant director
47 soundproof film camera (soundproof motion picture camera), a wide screen camera (cinemascope camera)
48 soundproof housing (soundproof cover, blimp)
49 camera crane (dolly)
50 hydraulic stand
51 mask (screen) for protection from spill light (gobo)
52 tripod spotlight (fill-in light, filler light, fill light, filler)
53 spotlight catwalk
54 recording room
55 recording engineer (sound recordist)
56 mixing console (mixing desk)
57 sound assistant (assistant sound engineer)
58 magnetic sound recording equipment (magnetic sound recorder)
59 amplifier and special effects equipment, e.g. for echo and sound effects
60 sound recording camera (optical sound recorder)

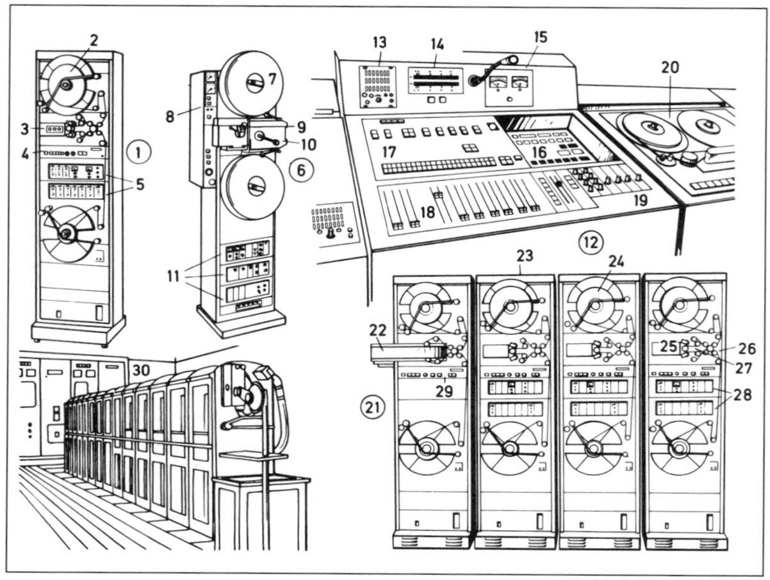

1-46 sound recording and re-recording (dubbing)

1 magnetic sound recording equipment (magnetic sound recorder)

2 magnetic film spool

3 magnetic head support assembly

4 control panel

5 magnetic sound recording and playback amplifier

6 optical sound recorder (sound recording camera, optical sound recording equipment)

7 daylight film magazine

8 control and monitoring panel

9 eyepiece for visual control of optical sound recording

10 deck

11 recording amplifier and mains power unit

12 control desk (control console)

13 monitoring loudspeaker (control loudspeaker)

14 recording level indicators

15 monitoring instruments

16 jack panel

17 control panel

18 sliding control

19 equalizer

20 magnetic sound deck

21 mixer for magnetic film

22 film projector

23 recording and playback equipment

24 film reel (film spool)

25 head support assembly for the recording head, playback head, and erase head

26 film transport mechanism

27 synchronizing filter

28 magnetic sound amplifier

29 control panel

30 film-processing machines (film-developing machines) in the processing laboratory (film laboratory, motion picture laboratory)

31 echo chamber
32 echo chamber loudspeaker
33 echo chamber microphone
34-36 sound mixing (sound dubbing, mixing of several sound tracks)
34 mixing room (dubbing room)
35 mixing console (mixing desk) for mono or stereo sound
36 dubbing mixers (recording engineers, sound recordists) dubbing (mixing)
37-41 synchronization (syncing, dubbing, post-synchronization, post-syncing)
37 dubbing studio (dubbing theatre, *Am.* theater)
38 dubbing director
39 dubbing speaker (dubbing actress)
40 boom microphone
41 microphone cable
42-46 cutting (editing)
42 cutting table (editing table, cutting bench)
43 film editor (cutter)
44 film turntables for picture and sound tracks
45 projection of the picture
46 loudspeaker

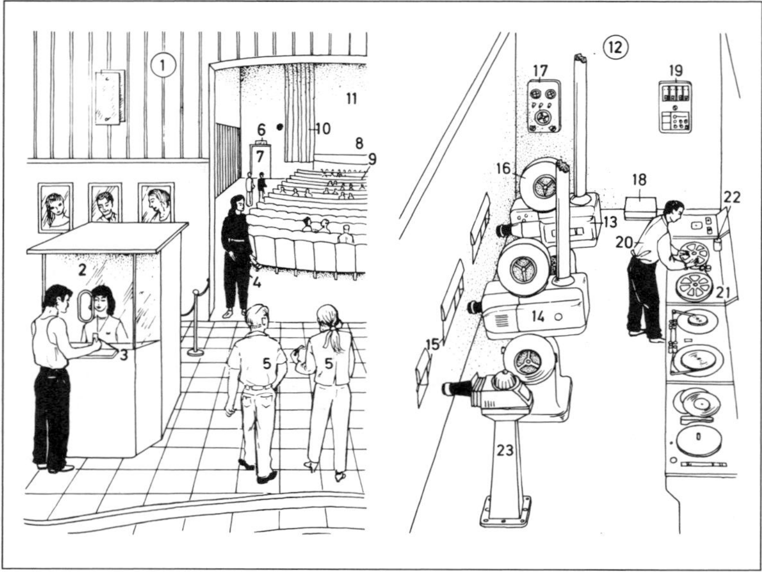

1-23 film projection (motion picture projection)
1 cinema (picture house, *Am.* movie theater, movie house)
2 cinema box office (*Am.* movie theater box office)
3 cinema ticket (*Am.* movie theater ticket)
4 usherette
5 cinemagoers (filmgoers, cinema audience, *Am.* moviegoers, movie audience)
6 safety lighting (emergency lighting)
7 emergency exit
8 stage
9 rows of seats (rows)
10 stage curtain (screen curtain)
11 screen (projection screen)
12 projection room (projection booth)
13 lefthand projector
14 righthand projector
15 projection room window with projection window and observation port
16 reel drum (spool box)
17 house light dimmers (auditorium lighting control)
18 rectifier, a selenium or mercury vapour rectifier for the projection lamps
19 amplifier
20 projectionist
21 rewind bench for rewinding the film
22 film cement (splicing cement)
23 slide projector for advertisements
24-52 film projectors
24 sound projector (film projector, cinema projector, theatre projector, *Am.* movie projector)
25-38 projector mechanism
25 fireproof reel drums (spool boxes) with circulating oil cooling system
26 feed sprocket (supply sprocket)
27 take-up sprocket
28 magnetic head cluster
29 guide roller (guiding roller) with framing control

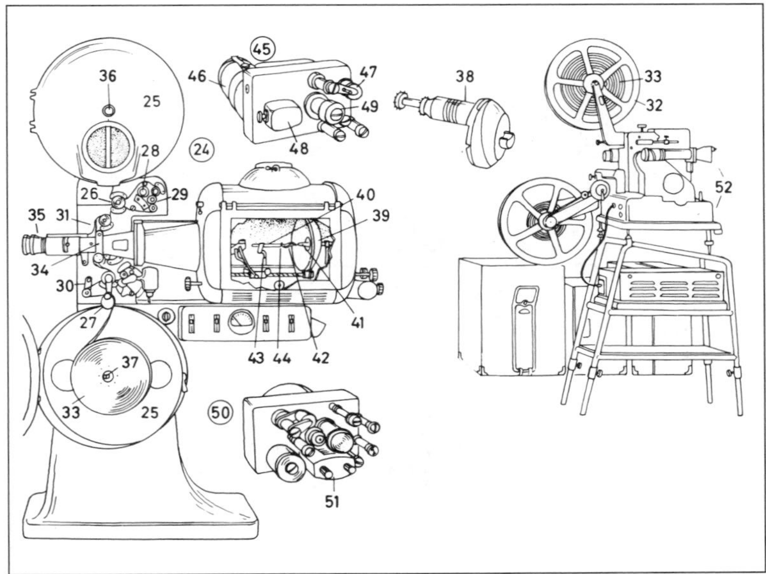

30 loop former for smoothing out the intermittent movement; *also:* film break detector
31 film path
32 film reel (film spool)
33 reel of film
34 film gate (picture gate, projector gate) with cooling fan
35 projection lens (projector lens)
36 feed spindle
37 take-up spindle with friction drive
38 maltese cross mechanism (maltese cross movement, Geneva movement)
39-44 lamphouse
39 mirror arc lamp, with aspherical (non-spherical) concave mirror and blowout magnet for stabilizing the arc (*also:* high-pressure xenon arc lamp)
40 positive carbon (positive carbon rod)
41 negative carbon (negative carbon rod)
42 arc
43 carbon rod holder
44 crater (carbon crater)
45 optical sound unit [also designed for multi-channel optical stereophonic sound and for push-pull sound tracks]
46 sound optics
47 sound head
48 exciter lamp in housing
49 photocell in hollow drum
50 attachable four-track magnetic sound unit (penthouse head, magnetic sound head)
51 four-track magnetic head
52 narrow-gauge (*Am.* narrow-gage) cinema projector for mobile cinema

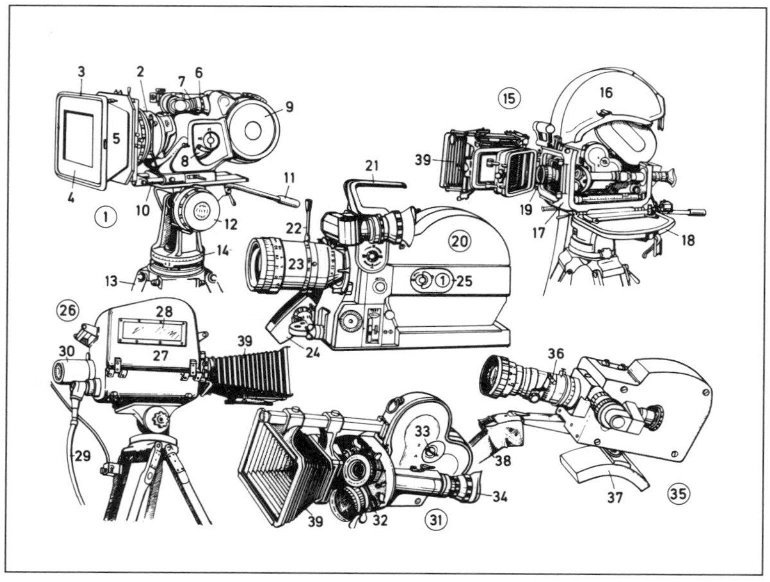

1-39 motion picture cameras (film cameras)
1 standard-gauge (*Am.* standard-gage) motion picture camera (standard-gauge, *Am.* standard-gage, 35 mm camera)
2 lens (object lens, taking lens)
3 lens hood (sunshade) with matte box
4 matte (mask)
5 lens hood barrel
6 viewfinder eyepiece
7 eyepiece control ring
8 opening control for the segment disc (disk) shutter
9 magazine housing
10 slide bar for the lens hood
11 control arm (control lever)
12 pan and tilt head
13 wooden tripod
14 degree scale
15 soundproof (blimped) motion picture camera (film camera)
16-18 soundproof housing (blimp)
16 upper section of the soundproof housing
17 lower section of the soundproof housing
18 open sidewall of the soundproof housing
19 camera lens
20 lightweight professional motion picture camera
21 grip (handgrip)
22 zooming lever
23 zoom lens (variable focus lens, varifocal lens) with infinitely variable focus
24 handgrip with shutter release
25 camera door
26 sound camera (newsreel camera) for recording sound and picture
27 soundproof housing (blimp)
28 window for the frame counters and indicator scales
29 pilot tone cable (sync pulse cable)
30 pilot tone generator (signal generator, pulse generator)
31 professional narrow-gauge (*Am.* narrow-gage) motion picture camera, a 16 mm camera
32 lens turret (turret head)
33 housing lock
34 eyecup
35 high-speed camera, a special narrow-gauge (*Am.* narrow-gage) camera
36 zooming lever
37 rifle grip
38 handgrip with shutter release
39 lens hood bellows

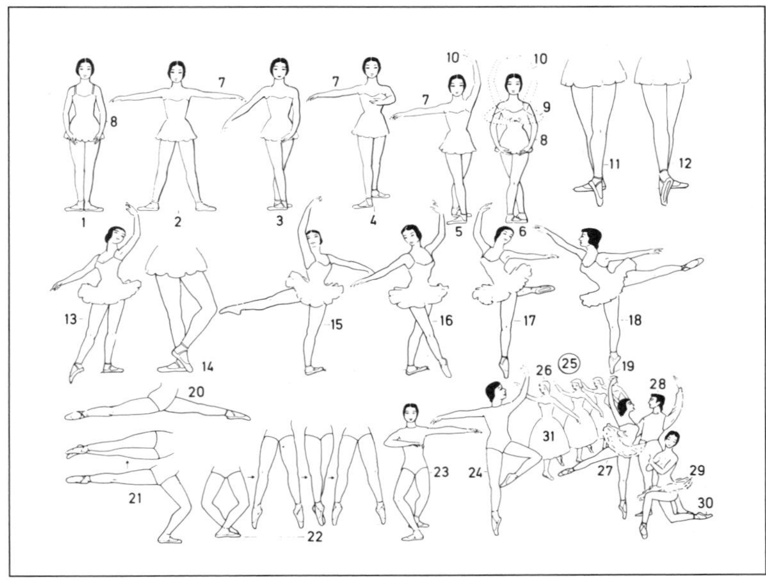

1-6 the five positions (ballet positions)
1 first position
2 second position
3 third position
4 fourth position [open]
5 fourth position [crossed; extended fifth position]
6 fifth position
7-10 ports de bras (arm positions)
7 port de bras à coté
8 port de bras en bas
9 port de bras en avant
10 port de bras en haut
11 dégagé à la quatrième devant
12 dégagé à la quatrième derrière
13 effacé
14 sur le cou-de-pied
15 écarté
16 croisé
17 attitude
18 arabesque
19 à pointe (on full point)
20 splits
21 cabriole (capriole)
22 entrechat (entrechat quatre)
23 préparation [e.g. for a pirouette]
24 pirouette
25 corps de ballet
26 ballet dancer (ballerina)
27, 28 pas de trois
27 prima ballerina
28 principal male dancer (leading soloist)
29 tutu
30 point shoe, a ballet shoe (ballet slipper)
31 ballet skirt

315 Theatre (*Am.* Theater) I

1-4 types of curtain operation
1 draw curtain (side parting)
2 tableau curtain (bunching up sideways)
3 fly curtain (vertical ascent)
4 combined fly and draw curtain
5-11 cloakroom hall (*Am.* checkroom hall)
5 cloakroom (*Am.* checkroom)
6 cloakroom attendant (*Am.* checkroom attendant)
7 cloakroom ticket (*Am.* check)
8 playgoer (theatregoer, *Am.* theatergoer)
9 opera glass (opera glasses)
10 commissionaire
11 theatre (*Am.* theater) ticket, an admission ticket
12, 13 foyer (lobby, crush room)
12 usher; *form.:* box attendant
13 programme (*Am.* program)
14-27 auditorium and stage
14 stage
15 proscenium
16-20 auditorium
16 gallery (balcony)
17 upper circle
18 dress circle (*Am.* balcony, mezzanine)
19 front stalls
20 seat (theatre seat, *Am.* theater seat)
21-27 rehearsal (stage rehearsal)
21 chorus
22, 23 singer
24 orchestra pit
25 orchestra
26 conductor
27 baton (conductor's baton)
28-42 paint room, a workshop
28 stagehand (scene shifter)
29 catwalk (bridge)
30 set piece
31 reinforcing struts
32 built piece (built unit)
33 backcloth (backdrop)
34 portable box for paint containers
35 scene painter
36 paint trolley
37 stage designer (set designer)
38 costume designer
39 design for a costume
40 sketch for a costume
41 model stage
42 model of the set
43-52 dressing room
43 dressing room mirror
44 make-up gown
45 make-up table
46 greasepaint stick
47 chief make-up artist (chief make-up man)
48 make-up artist (hairstylist)
49 wig
50 props (properties)
51 theatrical costume
52 call light

1
2
3
4
5
6
7
8
9
10
11
12
13
14
15
16
17
18
19
20
21
22
23
24
25
26
27
28
29
30
31
32
33
34
35
36
37
38
39
40
41
42
43
44
45
46
47
48
49
50
51
52

1-60 stagehouse with machinery (machinery in the flies and below stage)
1 control room
2 control console (lighting console, lighting control console) with preset control for presetting lighting effects
3 lighting plot (light plot)
4 grid (gridiron)
5 fly floor (fly gallery)
6 sprinkler system for fire prevention (for fire protection)
7 fly man
8 fly lines (lines)
9 cyclorama
10 backcloth (backdrop, background)
11 arch, a drop cloth
12 border
13 compartment (compartment-type, compartmentalized) batten (*Am.* border light)
14 stage lighting units (stage lights)
15 horizon lights (backdrop lights)
16 adjustable acting area lights (acting area spotlights)
17 scenery projectors (projectors)
18 monitor (water cannon) (piece of safety equipment)
19 travelling (*Am.* traveling) lighting bridge (travelling lighting gallery)
20 lighting operator (lighting man)
21 portal spotlight (tower spotlight)
22 adjustable proscenium
23 curtain (theatrical curtain)
24 iron curtain (safety curtain, fire curtain)
25 forestage (apron)
26 footlight (footlights, floats)
27 prompt box
28 prompter
29 stage manager's desk
30 stage director (stage manager)
31 revolving stage
32 trap opening
33 lift (*Am.* elevator)
34 bridge (*Am.* elevator), a rostrum
35 pieces of scenery
36 scene
37 actor
38 actress
39 extras (supers, supernumeraries)
40 director (producer)
41 prompt book (prompt script)
42 director's table (producer's table)
43 assistant director (assistant producer)
44 director's script (producer's script)
45 stage carpenter
46 stagehand (scene shifter)
47 set piece
48 mirror spot (mirror spotlight)
49 automatic filter change (with colour filters, colour mediums, gelatines)
50 hydraulic plant room
51 water tank
52 suction pipe
53 hydraulic pump
54 pressure pipe
55 pressure tank (accumulator)
56 pressure gauge (*Am.* gage)
57 level indicator (liquid level indicator)
58 control lever
59 operator
60 rams

4
8
6
5
3
2
1
7
9
10
11
12
13
15
16
17
18
13
20
19
14
24
17
8
21
22
23
17
36
39
37
35
30
29
25
31
27
28
26
38
33
34
32
44
43
47
40
41
47
42
45
46
50
55
33
51
56
60
58
52
57
17
53
59
48
49
54

317 Discotheque

1 bar
2 barmaid
3 bar stool
4 shelf for bottles
5 shelf for glasses
6 beer glass
7 wine and liqueur glasses
8 beer tap (tap)
9 bar
10 refrigerator (fridge, *Am.* icebox)
11 bar lamps
12 indirect lighting
13 colour (*Am.* color) organ (clavilux)
14 dance floor lighting
15 speaker (loudspeaker)
16 dance floor
17, 18 dancing couple (dancers)
19 record player
20 microphone
21 tape recorder
22, 23 stereo system (stereo equipment)
22 tuner
23 amplifier
24 records (discs)
25 disc jockey
26 mixing console (mixing desk, mixer)
27 tambourine
28 mirrored wall
29 ceiling tiles
30 ventilators
31 toilets (lavatories, WC)
32 long drink
33 cocktail (*Am.* highball)

1-33 nightclub (night spot)
1 cloakroom (*Am.* checkroom)
2 cloakroom attendant (*Am.* checkroom attendant)
3 band
4 clarinet
5 clarinettist (*Am.* clarinetist)
6 trumpet
7 trumpeter
8 guitar
9 guitarist (guitar player)
10 drums
11 drummer
12 speaker (loudspeaker)
13 bar
14 barmaid
15 bar
16 bar stool
17 tape recorder
18 receiver
19 spirits
20 cine projector for porno films (sex films, blue movies)
21 box containing screen
22 stage
23 stage lighting
24 spotlight
25 festoon lighting
26 festoon lamp (lamp, light bulb)
27-32 striptease act (striptease number)
27 striptease artist (stripper)
28 suspender (*Am.* garter)
29 brassière (bra)
30 fur stole
31 gloves
32 stocking
33 hostess

319 Bullfighting, Rodeo

1-33 **bullfight** (corrida, corrida de toros)
1 mock bullfight
2 novice (aspirant matador, novillero)
3 mock bull (dummy bull)
4 novice banderillero (apprentice banderillero)
5 bullring (plaza de toros) [diagram]
6 main entrance
7 boxes
8 stands
9 arena (ring)
10 bullfighters' entrance
11 torril door
12 exit gate for killed bulls
13 slaughterhouse
14 bull pens (corrals)
15 paddock
16 lancer on horseback (picador)
17 lance (pike pole, javelin)
18 armoured (*Am.* armored) horse
19 leg armour (*Am.* armor)
20 picador's round hat
21 banderillero, a torero
22 banderillas (barbed darts)
23 shirtwaist
24 bullfight
25 matador (swordsman), a torero
26 queue, a distinguishing mark of the matador
27 red cloak (capa)
28 fighting bull
29 montera [hat made of tiny black silk chenille balls]
30 killing the bull (kill, estocada)
31 matador in charity performances [without professional uniform]
32 estoque (sword)
33 muleta
34 **rodeo**
35 young bull
36 cowboy
37 stetson (stetson hat)
38 scarf (necktie)
39 rodeo rider
40 lasso

1
2
3
4
5
6
7
8
9
10
11
12
13
14
15
16
17
18
19
20
21
22
23
24
25
26
27
28
29
30
31
32
33
34
35
36
37
38
39
40

1, 2 medieval (mediaeval) notes
1 plainsong notation (neumes, neums, pneumes, square notation)
2 mensural notation
3-7 musical note (note)
3 note head
4 note stem (note tail)
5 hook
6 stroke
7 dot indicating augmentation of note's value
8-11 clefs
8 treble clef (G-clef, violin clef)
9 bass clef (F-clef)
10 alto clef (C-clef)
11 tenor clef
12-19 note values
12 breve (brevis, *Am.* double-whole note)
13 semibreve (*Am.* whole note)
14 minim (*Am.* half note)
15 crotchet (*Am.* quarter note)
16 quaver (*Am.* eighth note)
17 semiquaver (*Am.* sixteenth note)
18 demisemiquaver (*Am.* thirty-second note)
19 hemidemisemiquaver (*Am.* sixty-fourth note)
20-27 rests
20 breve rest
21 semibreve rest (*Am.* whole rest)
22 minim rest (*Am.* half rest)
23 crotchet rest (*Am.* quarter rest)
24 quaver rest (*Am.* eighth rest)
25 semiquaver rest (*Am.* sixteenth rest)
26 demisemiquaver rest (*Am.* thirty-second rest)
27 hemidemisemiquaver rest (*Am.* sixty-fourth rest)
28-42 time (time signatures, measure, *Am.* meter)
28 two-eight time
29 two-four time
30 two-two time
31 four-eight time
32 four-four time (common time)
33 four-two time
34 six-eight time
35 six-four time
36 three-eight time
37 three-four time
38 three-two time
39 nine-eight time
40 nine-four time
41 five-four time
42 bar (bar line, measure line)
43, 44 staff (stave)
43 line of the staff
44 space
45-49 scales
45 C major scale naturals: c, d, e, f, g, a, b, c
46 A minor scale [natural] naturals: a, b, c, d, e, f, g, a
47 A minor scale [harmonic]
48 A minor scale [melodic]
49 chromatic scale
50-54 accidentals (inflections, key signatures)
50, 51 signs indicating the raising of a note
50 sharp (raising the note a semitone or half-step)
51 double sharp (raising the note a tone or full-step)
52, 53 signs indicating the lowering of a note
52 flat (lowering the note a semitone or half-step)
53 double flat (lowering the note a tone or full-step)
54 natural
55-68 keys (major keys and the related minor keys having the same signature)
55 C major (A minor)
56 G major (E minor)
57 D major (B minor)
58 A major (F sharp minor)
59 E major (C sharp minor)
60 B major (G sharp minor)
61 F sharp major (D sharp minor)
62 C major (A minor)
63 F major (D minor)
64 B flat major (G minor)
65 E flat major (C minor)
66 A flat major (F minor)
67 D flat major (B flat minor)
68 G flat major (E flat minor)

1
Magni - fi-cat
2
Nu kom der heidē Heiland,
3
4
5
6
7
8 9 10 11 12 13 14 15 16 17 18 19 20 21 22 23 24 25 26 27
28 29 30 31 32 33 34 35 36 37 38 39 40 41 42 43 44
45
46
47
48
49
50 51 52 53 54
55 56 57 58 59 60 61
62 63 64 65 66 67 68

321 Musical Notation II

1-5 chord
1-4 triad
1 major triad
2 minor triad
3 diminished triad
4 augmented triad
5 chord of four notes, a chord of the seventh (seventh chord, dominant seventh chord)
6-13 intervals
6 unison (unison interval)
7 major second
8 major third
9 perfect fourth
10 perfect fifth
11 major sixth
12 major seventh
13 perfect octave
14-22 ornaments (graces, grace notes)
14 long appoggiatura
15 acciaccatura (short appoggiatura)
16 slide
17 trill (shake) without turn
18 trill (shake) with turn
19 upper mordent (inverted mordent, pralltriller)
20 lower mordent (mordent)
21 turn
22 arpeggio
23-26 other signs in musical notation
23 triplet; *corresponding groupings:* duplet (couplet), quadruplet, quintuplet, sextolet (sextuplet), septolet (septuplet, septimole)
24 tie (bind)
25 pause (pause sign)
26 repeat mark
27-41 expression marks (signs of relative intensity)
27 marcato (marcando, markiert, attack, strong accent)
28 presto (quick, fast)
29 portato (lourer, mezzo staccato, carried)
30 tenuto (held)
31 crescendo (increasing gradually in power)
32 decrescendo (diminuendo, decreasing or diminishing gradually in power)
33 legato (bound)
34 staccato (detached)
35 piano (soft)
36 pianissimo (very soft)
37 pianissimo piano (as soft as possible)
38 forte (loud)
39 fortissimo (very loud)
40 forte fortissimo (double fortissimo, as loud as possible)
41 forte piano (loud and immediately soft again)
42-50 divisions of the compass
42 subcontra octave (double contra octave)
43 contra octave
44 great octave
45 small octave
46 one-line octave
47 two-line octave
48 three-line octave
49 four-line octave
50 five-line octave

1 2 3 4 5 6 7 8 9 10 11 12 13
tr tr
14 15 16 17 18 19 20 21
3
27 24 25 26
22 23
28 Presto
29
30 ten.
33
cresc.
decresc.
cresc. 31
decresc. 32
34
p *pp* *ppp* *f* *ff* *fff* *fp*
35 36 37 38 39 40 41
8va sopra
42 43 44 45 46 47 48 49 50
8va bassa
$_2A$ $_2B$ $_2H$ $_1C$ usw
in Britain:
A_2 $B\flat_2 B_2 C_1$ etc.
$_1H$ C H c h c^1 $h^1 c^2 h^2 c^3 h^3 c^4 h^4 c^5$
B_1 C B c b c′ b′c″b″c‴b‴c⁗b⁗c⁗′

1 lur, a bronze trumpet
2 panpipes (Pandean pipes, syrinx)
3 aulos, a double shawm
4 aulos pipe
5 phorbeia (peristomion, capistrum, mouth band)
6 crumhorn (crummhorn, cromorne, krumbhorn, krummhorn)
7 recorder (fipple flute)
8 bagpipe; *sim.:* musette
9 bag
10 chanter (melody pipe)
11 drone (drone pipe)
12 curved cornett (zink)
13 serpent
14 shawm (schalmeyes); *larger:* bombard (bombarde, pommer)
15 cythara (cithara); *sim. and smaller:* lyre
16 arm
17 bridge
18 sound box (resonating chamber, resonator)
19 plectrum, a plucking device
20 kit (pochette), a miniature violin
21 cittern (cithern, cither, cister, citole), a plucked instrument; *sim.:* pandora (bandora, bandore)
22 sound hole
23 viol (descant viol, treble viol, a viola da gamba); *larger:* tenor viol, bass viol (viola da gamba, gamba), violone (double bass viol)
24 viol bow
25 hurdy-gurdy (vielle à roue, symphonia, armonie, organistrum)
26 friction wheel
27 wheel cover (wheel guard)
28 keyboard (keys)
29 resonating body (resonator, sound box)
30 melody strings
31 drone strings (drones, bourdons)
32 dulcimer
33 rib (resonator wall)
34 beater for the Valasian dulcimer
35 hammer (stick) for the Appenzell dulcimer
36 clavichord; *kinds:* fretted or unfretted clavichord
37 clavichord mechanism
38 key (key lever)
39 balance rail
40 guiding blade
41 guiding slot
42 resting rail
43 tangent
44 string
45 harpsichord (clavicembalo, cembalo), a wing-shaped stringed keyboard instrument; *sim.:* spinet (virginal)
46 upper keyboard (upper manual)
47 lower keyboard (lower manual)
48 harpsichord mechanism
49 key (key lever)
50 jack
51 slide (register)
52 tongue
53 quill plectrum
54 damper
55 string
56 portative organ, a portable organ; *larger:* positive organ (positive)
57 pipe (flue pipe)
58 bellows

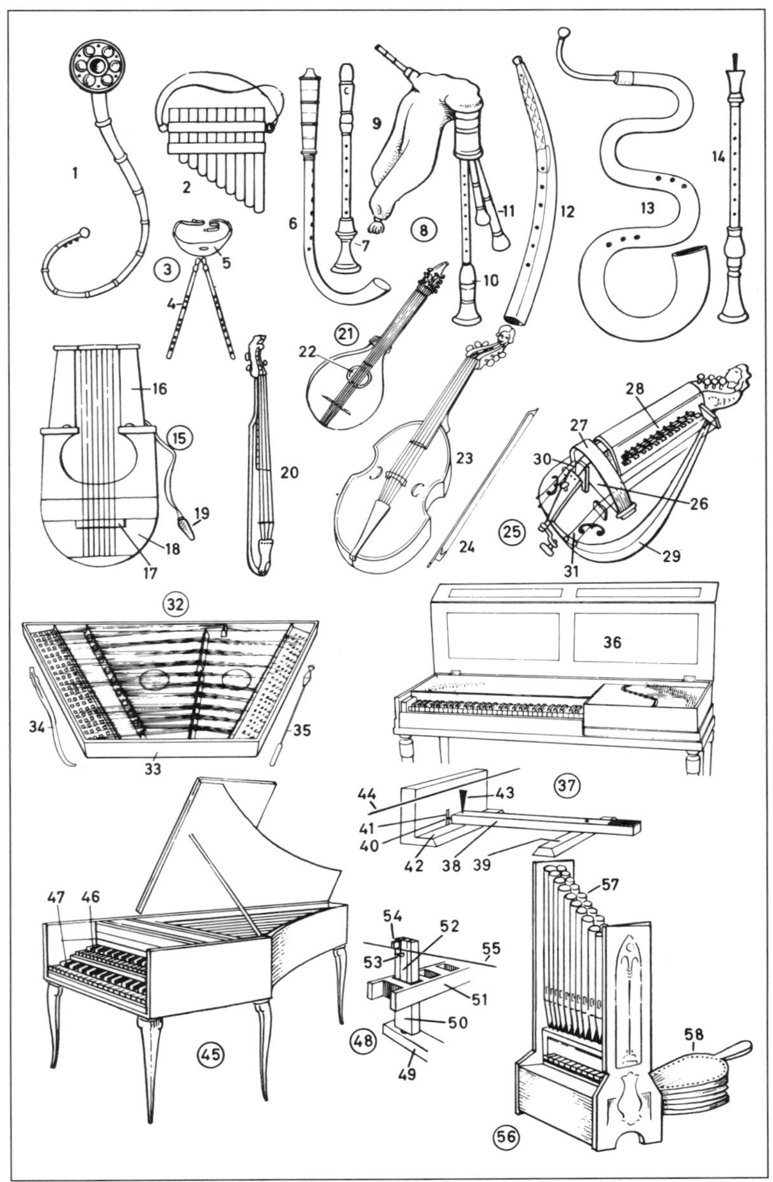
1
2
3
4
5
6
7
8
9
10
11
12
13
14
15
16
17
18
19
20
21
22
23
24
25
26
27
28
29
30
31
32
33
34
35
36
37
38
39
40
41
42
43
44
45
46
47
48
49
50
51
52
53
54
55
56
57
58

323 Musical Instruments II

1-62 orchestral instruments
1-27 stringed instruments, bowed instruments
1 violin
2 neck of the violin
3 resonating body (violin body, sound box of the violin)
4 rib (side wall)
5 violin bridge
6 F-hole, a sound hole
7 tailpiece
8 chin rest
9 strings (violin strings, fiddle strings): G-string, D-string, A-string, E-string
10 mute (sordino)
11 resin (rosin, colophony)
12 violin bow (bow)
13 nut (frog)
14 stick (bow stick)
15 hair of the violin bow (horsehair)
16 violoncello (cello), a member of the da gamba violin family
17 scroll
18 tuning peg (peg)
19 pegbox
20 nut
21 fingerboard
22 spike (tailpin)
23 double bass (contrabass, violone, double bass viol, *Am.* bass)
24 belly (top, soundboard)
25 rib (side wall)
26 purfling (inlay)
27 viola
28-38 woodwind instruments (woodwinds)
28 bassoon; *larger:* double bassoon (contrabassoon)
29 tube with double reed
30 piccolo (small flute, piccolo flute, flauto piccolo)
31 flute (German flute), a cross flute (transverse flute, side-blown flute)
32 key
33 fingerhole
34 clarinet; *larger:* bass clarinet
35 key (brille)
36 mouthpiece
37 bell
38 oboe (hautboy); *kinds:* oboe d'amore; tenor oboes: oboe da caccia, cor anglais; heckelphone (baritone oboe)
39-48 brass instruments (brass)
39 tenor horn
40 valve
41 French horn (horn, waldhorn), a valve horn
42 bell
43 trumpet; *larger:* Bb cornet; *smaller:* cornet
44 bass tuba (tuba, bombardon); *sim.:* helicon (pellitone), contrabass tuba
45 thumb hold
46 trombone; *kinds:* alto trombone, tenor trombone, bass trombone
47 trombone slide (slide)
48 bell
49-59 percussion instruments
49 triangle
50 cymbals
51-59 membranophones
51 side drum (snare drum)
52 drum head (head, upper head, batter head, vellum)
53 tensioning screw
54 drumstick
55 bass drum (Turkish drum)
56 stick (padded stick)
57 kettledrum (timpano), a screw-tensioned drum; *sim.:* machine drum (mechanically tuned drum)
58 kettledrum skin (kettledrum vellum)
59 tuning screw
60 harp, a pedal harp
61 strings
62 pedal

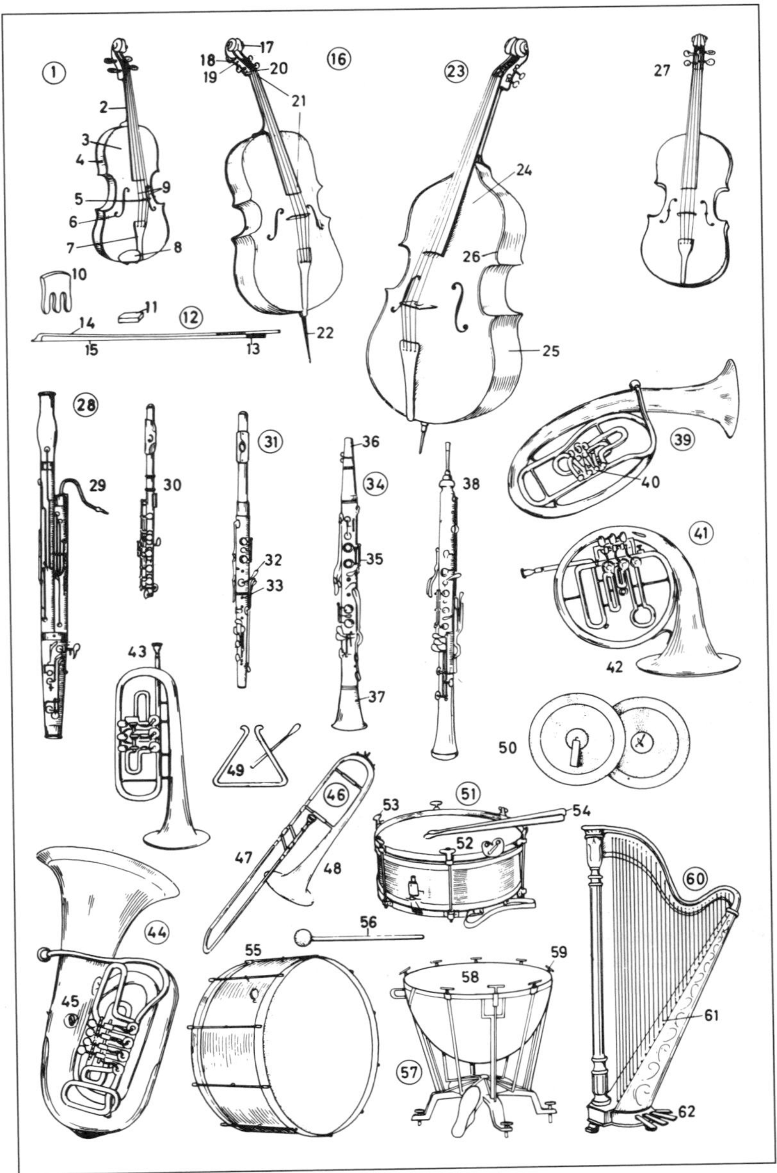
1
2
3
4
5
6
7
8
9
10
11
12
13
14
15
16
17
18
19
20
21
22
23
24
25
26
27
28
29
30
31
32
33
34
35
36
37
38
39
40
41
42
43
44
45
46
47
48
49
50
51
52
53
54
55
56
57
58
59
60
61
62

1-46 popular musical instruments (folk instruments)
1-31 stringed instruments
1 lute; *larger:* theorbo, chitarrone
2 resonating body (resonator)
3 soundboard (belly, table)
4 string fastener (string holder)
5 sound hole (rose)
6 string, a gut (catgut) string
7 neck
8 fingerboard
9 fret
10 head (bent-back pegbox, swan-head pegbox, pegbox)
11 tuning peg (peg, lute pin)
12 guitar
13 string holder
14 string, a gut (catgut) or nylon string
15 resonating body (resonating chamber, resonator, sound box)
16 mandolin (mandoline)
17 sleeve protector (cuff protector)
18 neck
19 pegdisc
20 plectrum
21 zither (plucked zither)
22 pin block (wrest pin block, wrest plank)
23 tuning pin (wrest pin)
24 accompaniment strings (bass strings, unfretted strings, open strings)
25 melody strings (fretted strings, stopped strings)
26 semicircular projection of the resonating sound box (resonating body)
27 ring plectrum
28 balalaika
29 banjo
30 tambourine-like body
31 parchment membrane
32 ocarina, a globular flute
33 mouthpiece
34 fingerhole
35 mouth organ (harmonica)
36 accordion; *sim.:* piano accordion, concertina, bandoneon
37 bellows
38 bellows strap
39 melody side (keyboard side, melody keys)
40 keyboard (keys)
41 treble stop (treble coupler, treble register)
42 stop lever
43 bass side (accompaniment side, bass studs, bass press-studs, bass buttons)
44 bass stop (bass coupler, bass register)
45 tambourine
46 castanets
47-78 jazz band instruments (dance band instruments)
47-58 percussion instruments
47-54 drum kit (drum set, drums)
47 bass drum
48 small tom-tom
49 large tom-tom
50 high-hat cymbals (choke cymbals, Charleston cymbals, cup cymbals)
51 cymbal
52 cymbal stand (cymbal holder)
53 wire brush
54 pedal mechanism
55 conga drum (conga)
56 tension hoop
57 timbales
58 bongo drums (bongos)
59 maracas; *sim.:* shakers
60 guiro
61 xylophone; *form.:* straw fiddle; *sim.:* marimbaphone (steel marimba), tubaphone
62 wooden slab
63 resonating chamber (sound box)
64 beater
65 jazz trumpet
66 valve
67 finger hook
68 mute (sordino)
69 saxophone
70 bell
71 crook
72 mouthpiece
73 struck guitar (jazz guitar)
74 hollow to facilitate fingering
75 vibraphone (*Am.* vibraharp)
76 metal frame
77 metal bar
78 tubular metal resonator

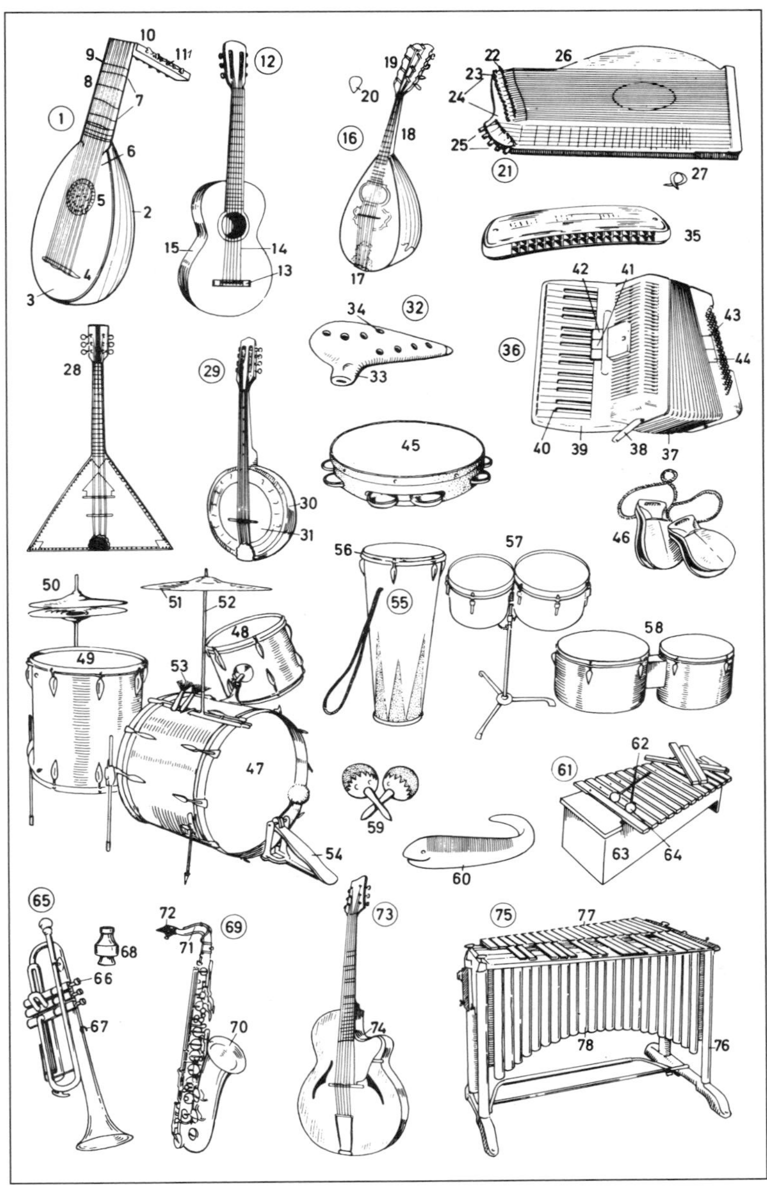
1
2
3
4
5
6
7
8
9
10
11
12
13
14
15
16
17
18
19
20
21
22
23
24
25
26
27
28
29
30
31
32
33
34
35
36
37
38
39
40
41
42
43
44
45
46
47
48
49
50
51
52
53
54
55
56
57
58
59
60
61
62
63
64
65
66
67
68
69
70
71
72
73
74
75
76
77
78

325 Musical Instruments IV

1 **piano** (pianoforte, upright piano, upright, vertical piano, spinet piano, console piano), a keyboard instrument (keyed instrument); *smaller form:* cottage piano (pianino); *earlier forms:* pantaleon; celesta, with steel bars instead of strings
2-18 piano action (piano mechanism)
2 iron frame
3 hammer; *collectively:* striking mechanism
4, 5 keyboard (piano keys)
4 white key (ivory key)
5 black key (ebony key)
6 piano case
7 strings (piano strings)
8, 9 piano pedals
8 right pedal (sustaining pedal, damper pedal; *loosely:* forte pedal, loud pedal) for raising the dampers
9 left pedal (soft pedal; *loosely:* piano pedal) for reducing the striking distance of the hammers on the strings
10 treble strings
11 treble bridge (treble belly bridge)
12 bass strings
13 bass bridge (bass belly bridge)
14 hitch pin
15 hammer rail
16 brace
17 tuning pin (wrest pin, tuning peg)
18 pin block (wrest pin block, wrest plank)
19 metronome
20 tuning hammer (tuning key, wrest)
21 tuning wedge
22-39 key action (key mechanism)
22 beam
23 damper-lifting lever
24 felt-covered hammer head
25 hammer shank
26 hammer rail
27 check (back check)
28 check felt (back check felt)
29 wire stem of the check (wire stem of the back check)
30 sticker (hopper, hammer jack, hammer lever)
31 button
32 action lever
33 pilot
34 pilot wire
35 tape wire
36 tape
37 damper (damper block)
38 damper lifter
39 damper rest rail
40 **grand piano** (horizontal piano, grand, concert grand; *smaller:* baby grand piano, boudoir piano; *sim.:* square piano, table piano)
41 grand piano pedals; right pedal for raising the dampers; left pedal for softening the tone (shifting the keyboard so that only one string is struck 'una corda')
42 pedal bracket
43 **harmonium** (reed organ, melodium)
44 draw stop (stop, stop knob)
45 knee lever (knee swell, swell)
46 pedal (bellows pedal)
47 harmonium case
48 harmonium keyboard (manual)

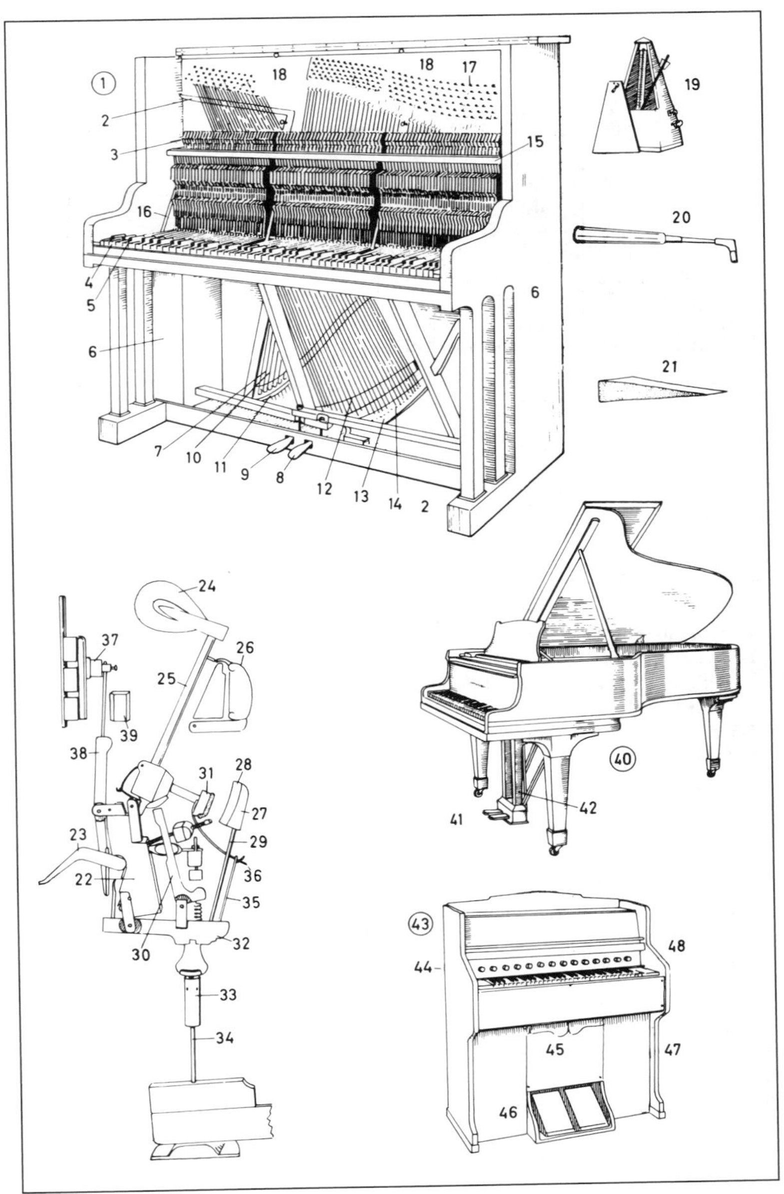
1
2
3
4
5
6
7
8
9
10
11
12
13
14
15
16
17
18
19
20
21
22
23
24
25
26
27
28
29
30
31
32
33
34
35
36
37
38
39
40
41
42
43
44
45
46
47
48

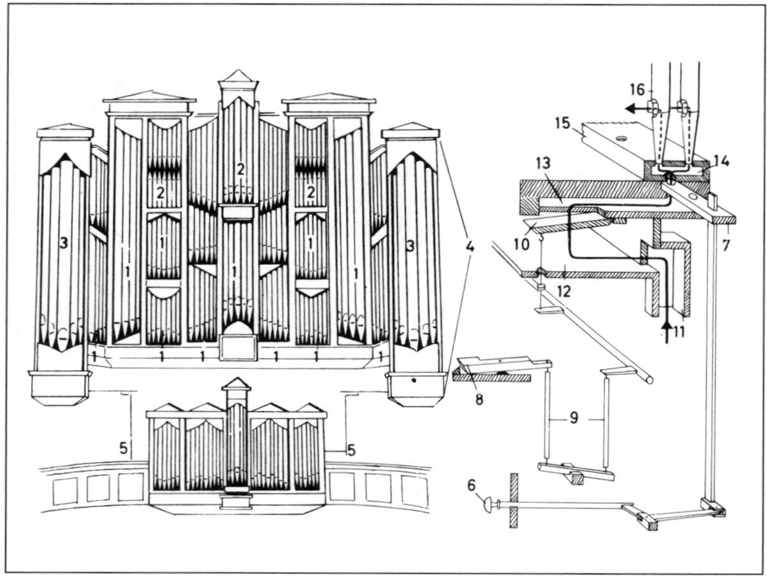

1-52 organ (church organ)
1-5 front view of organ (organ case) [built according to classical principles]
1-3 display pipes (face pipes)
1 Hauptwerk
2 Oberwerk
3 pedal pipes
4 pedal tower
5 Rückpositiv
6-16 tracker action (mechanical action); *other systems:* pneumatic action, electric action
6 draw stop (stop, stop knob)
7 slider (slide)
8 key (key lever)
9 sticker
10 pallet
11 wind trunk
12-14 wind chest, a slider wind chest; *other types:* sliderless wind chest (unit wind chest), spring chest, kegellade chest (cone chest), diaphragm chest
12 wind chest (wind chest box)
13 groove
14 upper board groove
15 upper board
16 pipe of a particular stop
17-35 organ pipes (pipes)
17-22 metal reed pipe (*set of pipes:* reed stop), a posaune stop
17 boot
18 shallot
19 tongue
20 block
21 tuning wire (tuning crook)
22 tube
23-30 open metal flue pipe, a salicional
23 foot

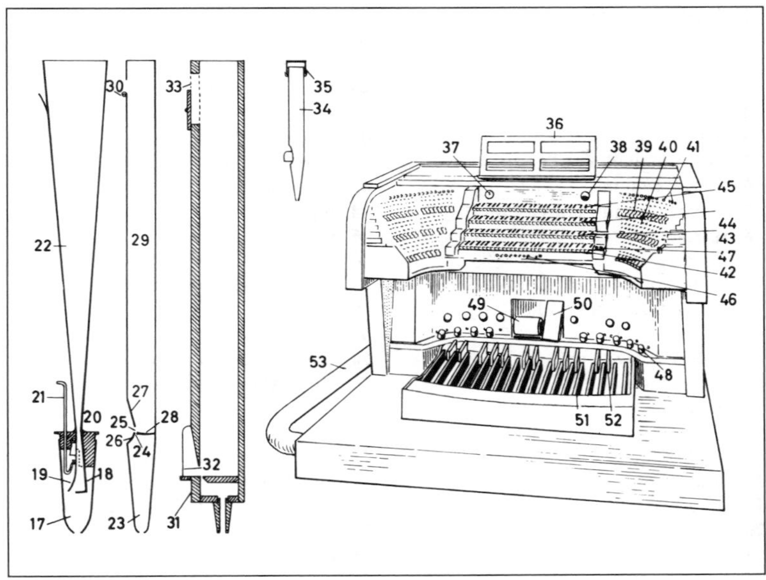

24 flue pipe windway (flue pipe duct)
25 mouth (cutup)
26 lower lip
27 upper lip
28 languid
29 body of the pipe (pipe)
30 tuning flap (tuning tongue), a tuning device
31-33 open wooden flue pipe (open wood), principal (diapason)
31 cap
32 ear
33 tuning hole (tuning slot), with slide
34 stopped flue pipe
35 stopper
36-52 organ console (console) of an electric action organ
36 music rest (music stand)
37 crescendo roller indicator
38 voltmeter
39 stop tab (rocker)
40 free combination stud (free combination knob)
41 cancel buttons for reeds, couplers etc.
42 manual I, for the Rückpositiv
43 manual II, for the Hauptwerk
44 manual III, for the Oberwerk
45 manual IV, for the Schwellwerk
46 thumb pistons controlling the manual stops (free or fixed combinations) and buttons for setting the combinations
47 switches for current to blower and action
48 toe piston, for the coupler
49 crescendo roller (general crescendo roller)
50 balanced swell pedal
51 pedal key [natural]
52 pedal key [sharp or flat]
53 cable (transmission cable)

327 Fabulous Creatures (Fabled Beings)

1-61 fabulous creatures (fabulous animals), mythical creatures
1 dragon
2 serpent's body
3 claws (claw)
4 bat's wing
5 fork-tongued mouth
6 forked tongue
7 unicorn [symbol of virginity]
8 spirally twisted horn
9 Phoenix
10 flames or ashes of resurrection
11 griffin (griffon, gryphon)
12 eagle's head
13 griffin's claws
14 lion's body
15 wing
16 chimera (chimaera), a monster
17 lion's head
18 goat's head
19 dragon's body
20 sphinx, a symbolic figure
21 human head
22 lion's body
23 mermaid (nix, nixie, water nixie, sea maid, sea maiden, naiad, water nymph, water elf, ocean nymph, sea nymph, river nymph); *sim.:* Nereids, Oceanids (sea divinities, sea deities, sea goddesses); *male:* nix (merman, seaman)
24 woman's trunk
25 fish's tail (dolphin's tail)
26 Pegasus (favourite, *Am.* favorite, steed of the Muses, winged horse); *sim.:* hippogryph
27 horse's body
28 wings
29 Cerberus (hellhound)
30 three-headed dog's body
31 serpent's tail
32 Lernaean (Lernean) Hydra
33 nine-headed serpent's body
34 basilisk (cockatrice)
35 cock's head
36 dragon's body
37 giant (titan)
38 rock
39 serpent's foot
40 triton, a merman (demigod of the sea)
41 conch shell trumpet
42 horse's hoof
43 fish's tail
44 hippocampus
45 horse's trunk
46 fish's tail
47 sea ox, a sea monster
48 monster's body
49 fish's tail
50 seven-headed dragon of St. John's Revelation (Revelations, Apocalypse)
51 wing
52 centaur (hippocentaur), half man and half beast
53 man's body with bow and arrow
54 horse's body
55 harpy, a winged monster
56 woman's head
57 bird's body
58 siren, a daemon
59 woman's body
60 wing
61 bird's claw

1
2
3
4
5
6
7
8
9
10
11
12
13
14
15
16
17
18
19
20
21
22
23
24
25
26
27
28
29
30
31
32
33
34
35
36
37
38
39
40
41
42
43
44
45
46
47
48
49
50
51
52
53
54
55
56
57
58
59
60
61

1-40 prehistoric finds
1-9 **Old Stone Age** (Palaeolithic, Paleolithic, period) and **Mesolithic period**
1 hand axe (*Am.* ax) (fist hatchet), a stone tool
2 head of throwing spear, made of bone
3 bone harpoon
4 head
5 harpoon thrower, made of reindeer antler
6 painted pebble
7 head of a wild horse, a carving
8 Stone Age idol, an ivory statuette
9 bison, a cave painting (rock painting) [cave art, cave painting]
10-20 **New Stone Age** (Neolithic period)
10 amphora [corded ware]
11 bowl [menhir group]
12 collared flask [Funnel-Beaker culture]
13 vessel with spiral pattern [spiral design pottery]
14 bell beaker [bell beaker culture]
15 pile dwelling (lake dwelling, lacustrine dwelling)
16 dolmen (cromlech), a megalithic tomb (*coll.:* giant's tomb); *other kinds:* passage grave, gallery grave (long cist); *when covered with earth:* tumulus (barrow, mound)
17 stone cist, a contracted burial
18 menhir (standing stone), a monolith
19 boat axe (*Am.* ax), a stone battle axe
20 clay figurine, an idol
21-40 **Bronze Age** and **Iron Age;** *epochs:* Hallstatt period, La Tène period
21 bronze spear head
22 hafted bronze dagger
23 socketed axe (*Am.* ax), a bronze axe with haft fastened to rings
24 girdle clasp
25 necklace (lunula)
26 gold neck ring
27 violin-bow fibula (safety pin)
28 serpentine fibula; *other kinds:* boat fibula, arc fibula
29 bulb-head pin, a bronze pin
30 two-piece spiral fibula; *sim.:* disc (disk) fibula
31 hafted bronze knife
32 iron key
33 ploughshare (*Am.* plowshare)
34 sheet-bronze situla, a funerary vessel
35 pitcher [chip-carved pottery]
36 miniature ritual cart (miniature ritual chariot)
37 Celtic silver coin
38 face urn, a cinerary urn; *other kinds:* domestic urn, embossed urn
39 urn grave in stone chamber
40 urn with cylindrical neck

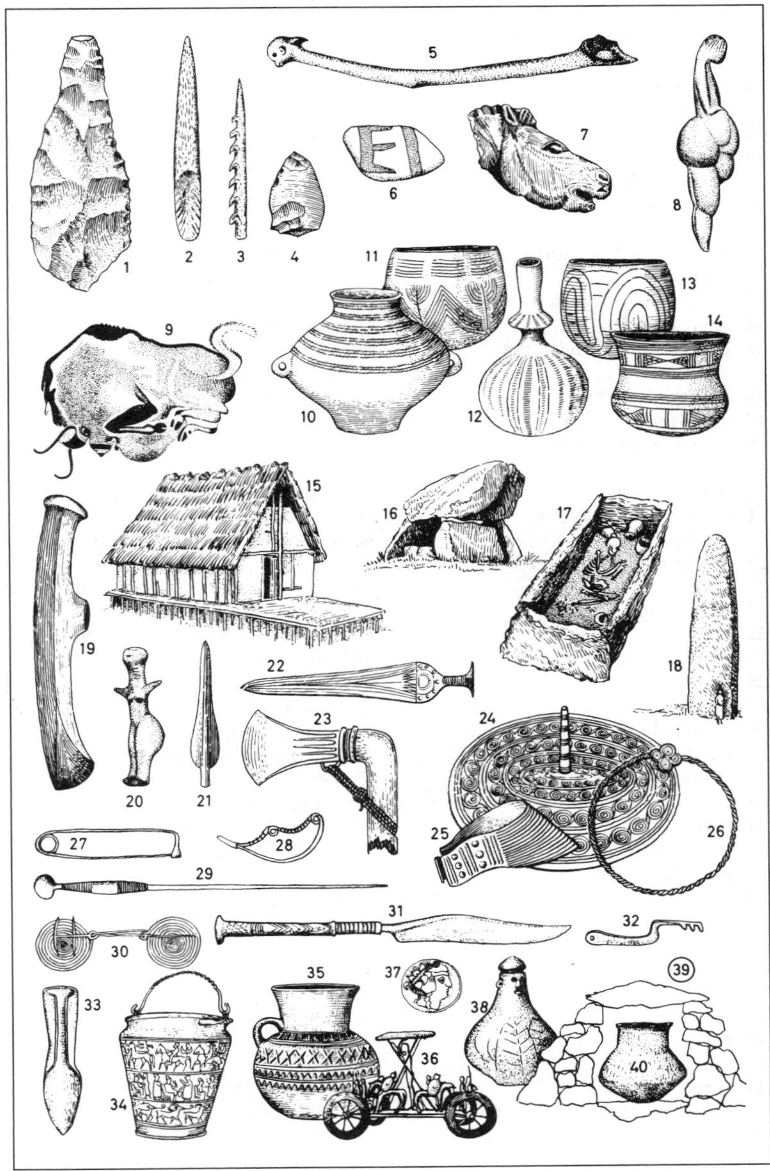
1
2
3
4
5
6
7
8
9
10
11
12
13
14
15
16
17
18
19
20
21
22
23
24
25
26
27
28
29
30
31
32
33
34
35
36
37
38
39
40

329 Chivalry

1 **knight's castle** (castle)
2 inner ward (inner bailey)
3 draw well
4 keep (donjon)
5 dungeon
6 battlements (crenellation)
7 merlon
8 tower platform
9 watchman
10 ladies' apartments (bowers)
11 dormer window (dormer)
12 balcony
13 storehouse (magazine)
14 angle tower
15 curtain wall (curtains, enclosure wall)
16 bastion
17 angle tower
18 crenel (embrasure)
19 inner wall
20 battlemented parapet
21 parapet (breastwork)
22 gatehouse
23 machicolation (machicoulis)
24 portcullis
25 drawbridge
26 buttress
27 offices and service rooms
28 turret
29 chapel
30 great hall
31 outer ward (outer bailey)
32 castle gate
33 moat (ditch)
34 approach
35 watchtower (turret)
36 palisade (pallisade, palisading)
37 moat (ditch, fosse)
38-65 **knight's armour** (*Am.* armor)
38 suit of armour (*Am.* armor)
39-42 helmet
39 skull
40 visor (vizor)
41 beaver
42 throat piece
43 gorget
44 épaulière
45 pallette (pauldron, besageur)
46 breastplate (cuirass)
47 brassard (rear brace and vambrace)
48 cubitière (coudière, couter)
49 tasse (tasset)
50 gauntlet
51 habergeon (haubergeon)
52 cuisse (cuish, cuissard, cuissart)
53 knee cap (knee piece, genouillère, poleyn)
54 jambeau (greave)
55 solleret (sabaton, sabbaton)
56 pavis (pavise, pavais)
57 buckler (round shield)
58 boss (umbo)
59 iron hat
60 morion
61 light casque
62 types of mail and armour (*Am.* armor)
63 mail (chain mail, chain armour, *Am.* armor)
64 scale armour (*Am.* armor)
65 plate armour (*Am.* armor)
66 **accolade** (dubbing, knighting)
67 liege lord, a knight
68 esquire
69 cup bearer
70 minstrel (minnesinger, troubadour)
71 **tournament** (tourney, joust, just, tilt)
72 crusader
73 Knight Templar
74 caparison (trappings)
75 herald (marshal at tournament)
76 tilting armour (*Am.* armor)
77 tilting helmet (jousting helmet)
78 panache (plume of feathers)
79 tilting target (tilting shield)
80 lance rest
81 tilting lance (lance)
82 vamplate
83-88 horse armour (*Am.* armor)
83 neck guard (neck piece)
84 chamfron (chaffron, chafron, chamfrain, chanfron)
85 poitrel
86 flanchard (flancard)
87 tournament saddle
88 rump piece (quarter piece)

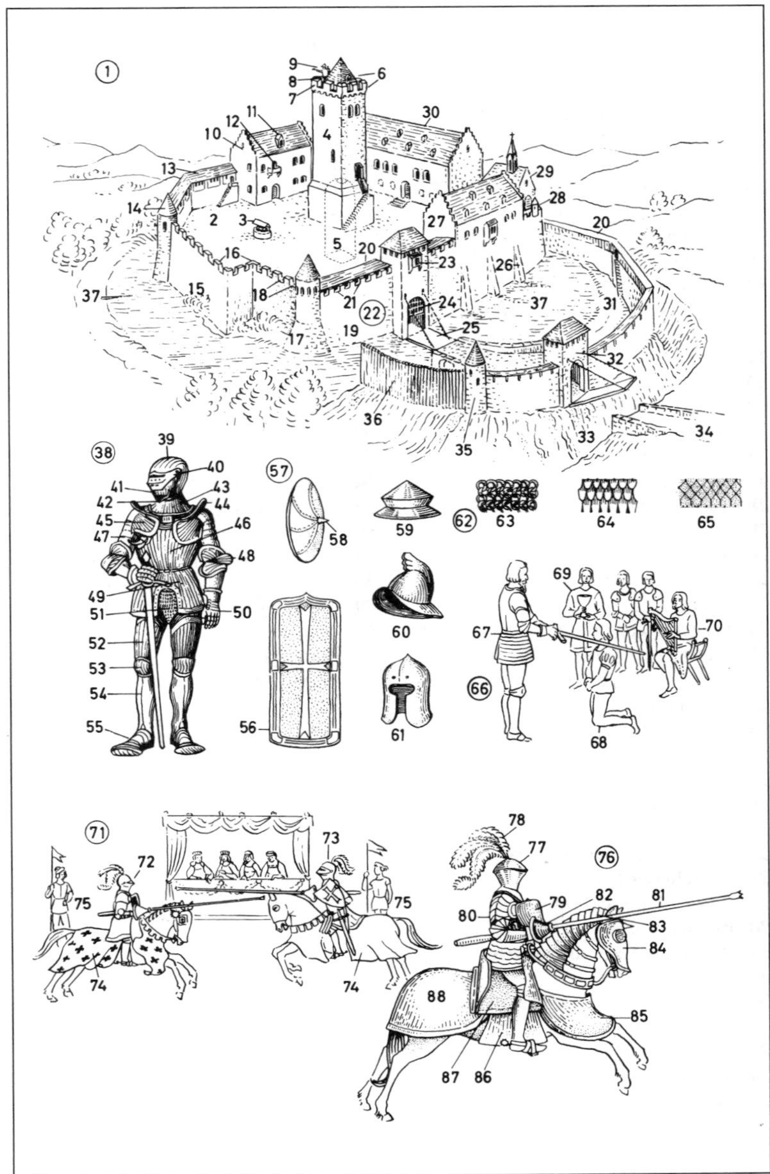
1
2
3
4
5
6
7
8
9
10
11
12
13
14
15
16
17
18
19
20
21
22
23
24
25
26
27
28
29
30
31
32
33
34
35
36
37
38
39
40
41
42
43
44
45
46
47
48
49
50
51
52
53
54
55
56
57
58
59
60
61
62
63
64
65
66
67
68
69
70
71
72
73
74
75
76
77
78
79
80
81
82
83
84
85
86
87
88

1-30 Protestant church
1 chancel
2 lectern
3 altar carpet
4 altar (communion table, Lord's table, holy table)
5 altar steps
6 altar cloth
7 altar candle
8 pyx (pix)
9 paten (patin, patine)
10 chalice (communion cup)
11 Bible (Holy Bible, Scriptures, Holy Scripture)
12 altar crucifix
13 altarpiece
14 church window
15 stained glass
16 wall candelabrum
17 vestry door (sacristy door)
18 pulpit steps
19 pulpit
20 antependium
21 canopy (soundboard, sounding board)
22 preacher (pastor, vicar, clergyman, rector) in his robes (vestments, canonicals)
23 pulpit balustrade
24 hymn board showing hymn numbers
25 gallery
26 verger (sexton, sacristan)
27 aisle
28 pew; *collectively:* pews (seating)
29 churchgoer (worshipper); *collectively:* congregation
30 hymn book

31-62 Roman Catholic church
31 altar steps
32 presbytery (choir, chancel, sacrarium, sanctuary)
33 altar
34 altar candles
35 altar cross
36 altar cloth
37 lectern
38 missal (mass book)
39 priest
40 server
41 sedilia
42 tabernacle
43 stele (stela)
44 paschal candle (Easter candle)
45 paschal candlestick (Easter candlestick)
46 sanctus bell
47 processional cross
48 altar decoration (foliage, flower arrangement)
49 sanctuary lamp
50 altarpiece, a picture of Christ
51 Madonna (statue of the Virgin Mary)
52 pricket
53 votive candles
54 station of the Cross
55 offertory box
56 literature stand
57 literature (pamphlets, tracts)
58 verger (sexton, sacristan)
59 offertory bag
60 offering
61 man praying
62 prayer book

1
2
3
4
5
6
7
8
9
10
11
12
13
14
15
16
17
18
19
20
21
22
23
24
25
26
27
28
29
30
31
32
33
34
35
36
37
38
39
40
41
42
43
44
45
46
47
48
49
50
51
52
53
54
55
56
57
58
59
60
61
62
123
1-4
26

331 Church II

1 **church**
2 steeple
3 weathercock
4 weather vane (wind vane)
5 spire ball
6 church spire (spire)
7 church clock (tower clock)
8 belfry window
9 electrically operated bell
10 ridge cross
11 church roof
12 memorial chapel
13 vestry (sacristy), an annexe (annex)
14 memorial tablet (memorial plate, wall memorial, wall stone)
15 side entrance
16 church door (main door, portal)
17 churchgoer
18 graveyard wall (churchyard wall)
19 graveyard gate (churchyard gate, lichgate, lychgate)
20 vicarage (parsonage, rectory)
21-41 **graveyard** (churchyard, God's acre, *Am.* burying ground)
21 mortuary
22 grave digger
23 grave (tomb)
24 grave mound
25 cross
26 gravestone (headstone, tombstone)
27 family grave (family tomb)
28 graveyard chapel
29 child's grave
30 urn grave
31 urn
32 soldier's grave
33-41 funeral (burial)
33 mourners
34 grave
35 coffin (*Am.* casket)
36 spade
37 clergyman
38 the bereaved
39 widow's veil, a mourning veil
40 pallbearers
41 bier
42-50 **procession** (religious procession)
42 processional crucifix
43 cross bearer (crucifer)
44 processional banner, a church banner
45 acolyte
46 canopy bearer
47 priest
48 monstrance with the Blessed Sacrament (consecrated Host)
49 canopy (baldachin, baldaquin)
50 nuns
51 participants in the procession
52-58 **monastery**
52 cloister
53 monastery garden
54 monk, a Benedictine monk
55 habit (monk's habit)
56 cowl (hood)
57 tonsure
58 breviary
59 **catacomb,** an early Christian underground burial place
60 niche (tomb recess, arcosolium)
61 stone slab

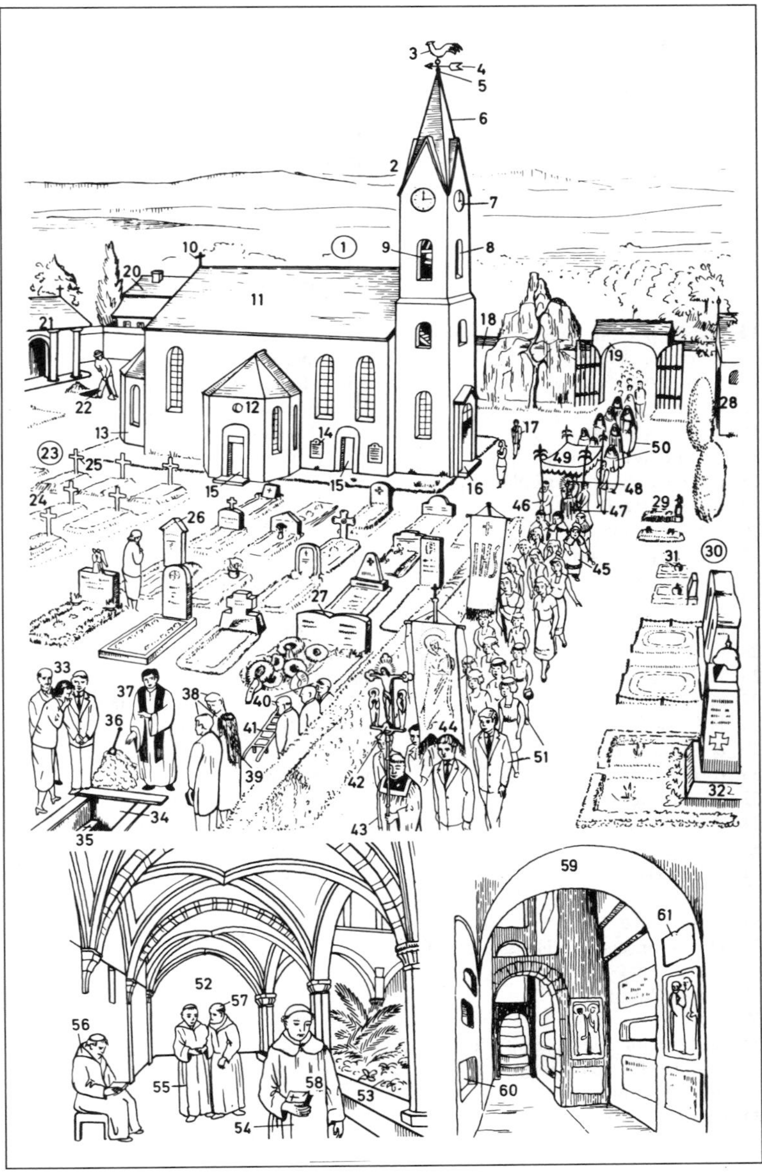
1
2
3
4
5
6
7
8
9
10
11
12
13
14
15
15
16
17
18
19
20
21
22
23
24
25
26
27
28
29
30
31
32
33
34
35
36
37
38
39
40
41
42
43
44
45
46
47
48
49
50
51
52
53
54
55
56
57
58
59
60
61

1 Christian baptism (christening)
2 baptistery (baptistry)
3 Protestant clergyman
4 robes (vestments, canonicals)
5 bands
6 collar
7 child to be baptized (christened)
8 christening robe (christening dress)
9 christening shawl
10 font
11 font basin
12 baptismal water
13 godparents
14 church wedding (wedding ceremony, marriage ceremony)
15, 16 bridal couple
15 bride
16 bridegroom (groom)
17 ring (wedding ring)
18 bride's bouquet (bridal bouquet)
19 bridal wreath
20 veil (bridal veil)
21 [myrtle] buttonhole
22 clergyman
23 witnesses [to the marriage]
24 bridesmaid
25 kneeler
26 Holy Communion
27 communicants
28 Host (wafer)
29 communion cup
30 rosary
31 paternoster
32 Ave Maria; *set of 10:* decade
33 crucifix
34-54 liturgical vessels (ecclesiastical vessels)
34 monstrance
35 Host (consecrated Host, Blessed Sacrament)
36 lunula (lunule)
37 rays
38 censer (thurible), for offering incense (for incensing)
39 thurible chain
40 thurible cover
41 thurible bowl
42 incense boat
43 incense spoon
44 cruet set
45 water cruet
46 wine cruet
47 holy water basin
48 ciborium containing the sacred wafers
49 chalice
50 dish for communion wafers
51 paten (patin, patine)
52 altar bells
53 pyx (pix)
54 aspergillum
55-72 forms of Christian crosses
55 Latin cross (cross of the Passion)
56 Greek cross
57 Russian cross
58 St. Peter's cross
59 St. Anthony's cross (tau cross)
60 St. Andrew's cross (saltire cross)
61 Y-cross
62 cross of Lorraine
63 ansate cross
64 patriarchal cross
65 cardinal's cross
66 papal cross
67 Constantinian cross, a monogram of Christ (CHR)
68 crosslet
69 cross moline
70 cross of Jerusalem
71 cross botonnée (cross treflée)
72 fivefold cross (quintuple cross)
73 Celtic cross

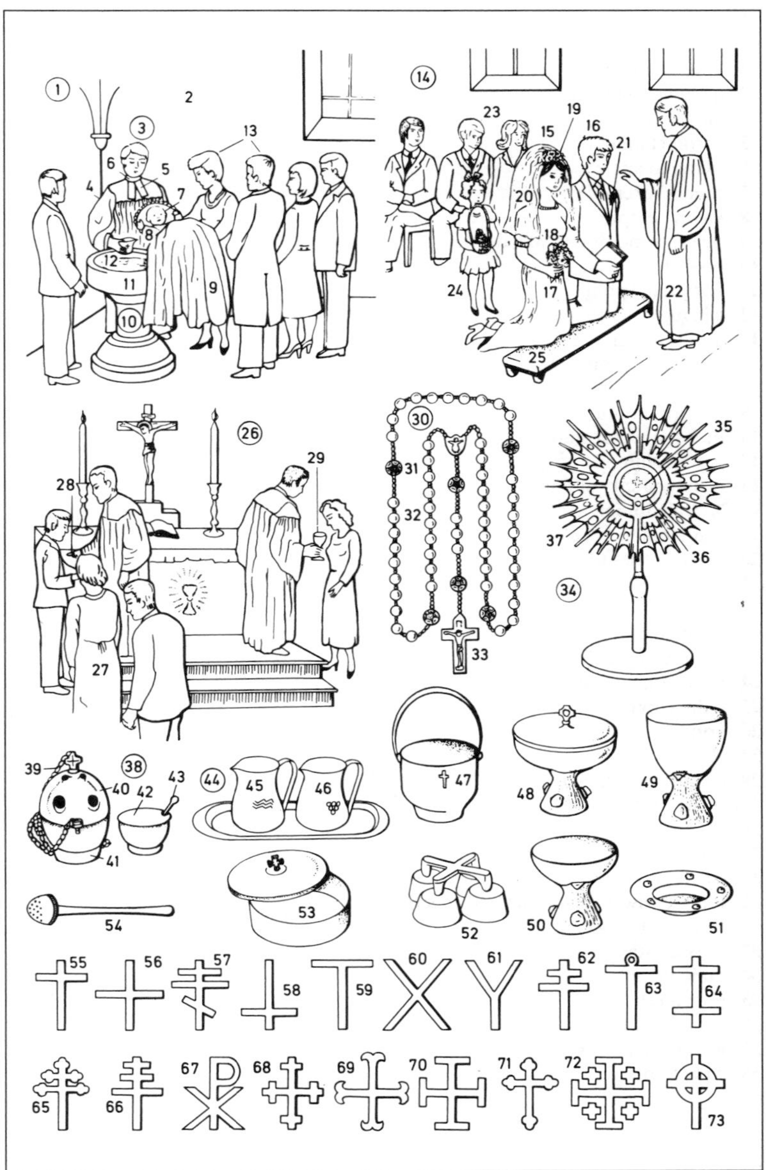
1
2
3
4
5
6
7
8
9
10
11
12
13
14
15
16
17
18
19
20
21
22
23
24
25
26
27
28
29
30
31
32
33
34
35
36
37
38
39
40
41
42
43
44
45
46
47
48
49
50
51
52
53
54
55
56
57
58
59
60
61
62
63
64
65
66
67
68
69
70
71
72
73

333 Art I

1-18 Egyptian art
1 pyramid, a royal tomb
2 king's chamber
3 queen's chamber
4 air passage
5 coffin chamber
6 pyramid site
7 funerary temple
8 valley temple
9 pylon, a monumental gateway
10 obelisks
11 Egyptian sphinx
12 winged sun disc (sun disk)
13 lotus column
14 knob-leaf capital (bud-shaped capital)
15 papyrus column
16 bell-shaped capital
17 palm column
18 ornamented column
19, 20 Babylonian art
19 Babylonian frieze
20 glazed relief tile
21-28 art of the Persians
21 tower tomb
22 stepped pyramid
23 double bull column
24 projecting leaves
25 palm capital
26 volute (scroll)
27 shaft
28 double bull capital
29-36 art of the Assyrians
29 Sargon's Palace, palace buildings
30 city wall
31 castle wall
32 temple tower (ziggurat), a stepped (terraced) tower
33 outside staircase
34 main portal
35 portal relief
36 portal figure
37 art of Asia Minor
38 rock tomb

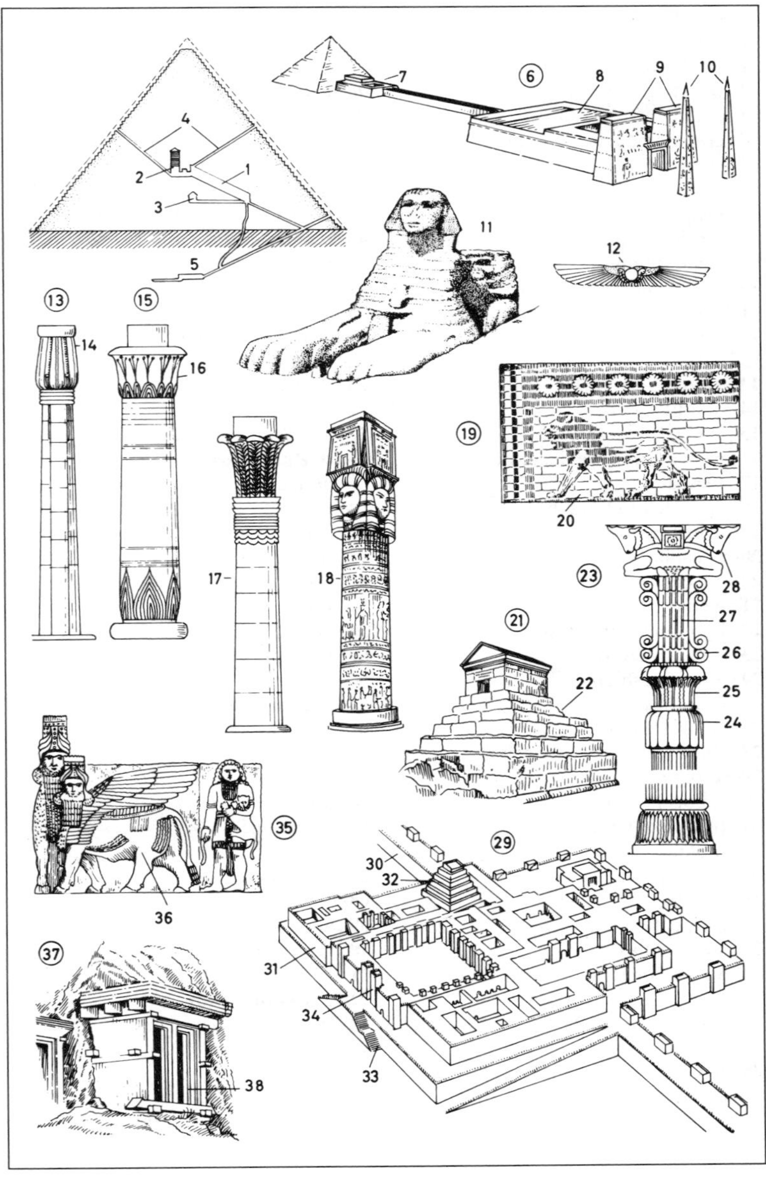
1
2
3
4
5
6
7
8
9
10
11
12
13
14
15
16
17
18
19
20
21
22
23
24
25
26
27
28
29
30
31
32
33
34
35
36
37
38

1-48 Greek art
1-7 the Acropolis
1 the Parthenon, a Doric temple
2 peristyle
3 pediment
4 crepidoma (stereobate)
5 statue
6 temple wall
7 propylaea
8 Doric column
9 Ionic column
10 Corinthian column
11-14 cornice
11 cyma
12 corona
13 mutule
14 dentils
15 triglyph
16 metope, a frieze decoration
17 regula
18 epistyle (architrave)
19 cyma (cymatium, kymation)
20-25 capital
20 abacus
21 echinus
22 hypotrachelium (gorgerin)
23 volute (scroll)
24 volute cushion
25 acanthus
26 column shaft
27 flutes (grooves, channels)
28-31 base
28 [upper] torus
29 trochilus (concave moulding, *Am.* molding)
30 [lower] torus
31 plinth
32 stylobate
33 stele (stela)
34 acroterion (acroterium, acroter)
35 herm (herma, hermes)
36 caryatid; *male:* Atlas
37 Greek vase
38-43 Greek ornamentation (Greek decoration, Greek decorative designs)
38 bead-and-dart moulding (*Am.* molding), an ornamental band
39 running dog (Vitruvian scroll)
40 leaf ornament
41 palmette
42 egg and dart (egg and tongue, egg and anchor) cyma
43 meander
44 Greek theatre (*Am.* theater)
45 scene
46 proscenium
47 orchestra
48 thymele (altar)
49-52 Etruscan art
49 Etruscan temple
50 portico
51 cella
52 entablature
53-60 Roman art
53 aqueduct
54 conduit (water channel)
55 centrally-planned building (centralized building)
56 portico
57 reglet
58 cupola
59 triumphal arch
60 attic
61-71 Early Christian art
61 basilica
62 nave
63 aisle
64 apse
65 campanile
66 atrium
67 colonnade
68 fountain
69 altar
70 clerestory (clearstory)
71 triumphal arch
72-75 Byzantine art
72, 73 dome system
72 main dome
73 semidome
74 pendentive
75 eye, a lighting aperture

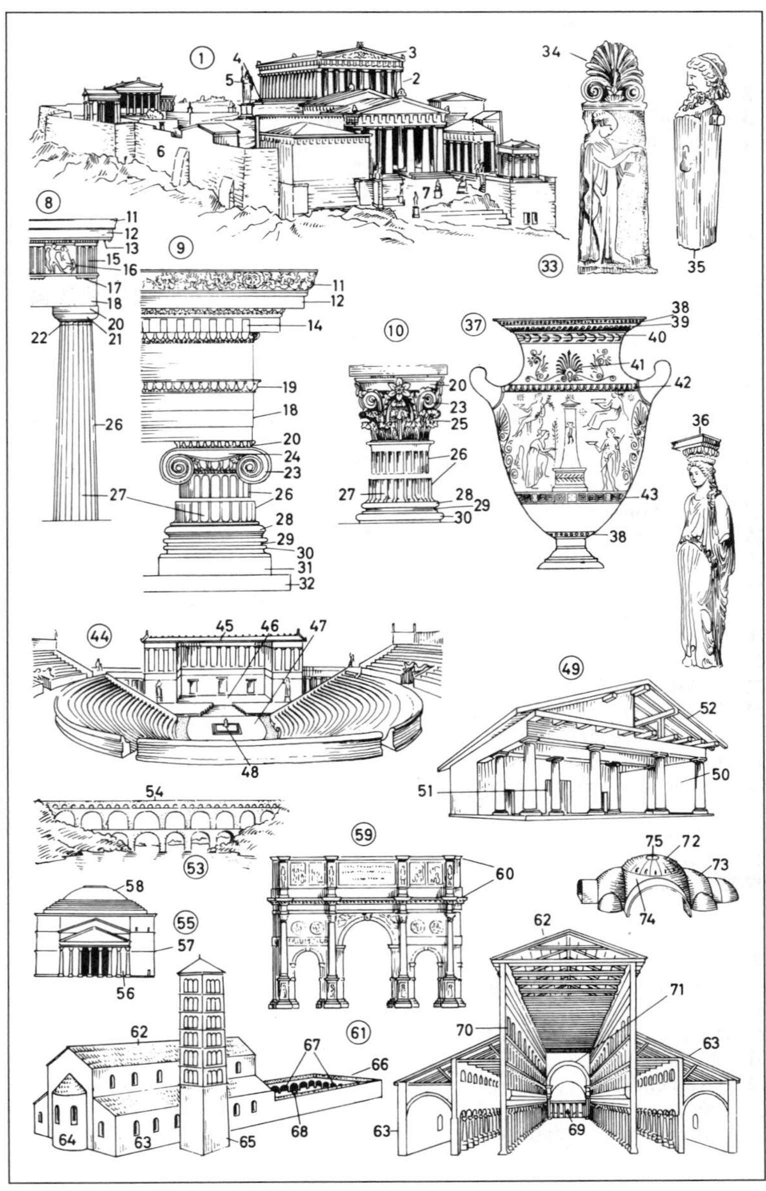
1
2
3
4
5
6
7
8
9
10
11
12
13
14
15
16
17
18
19
20
21
22
23
24
25
26
27
28
29
30
31
32
33
34
35
36
37
38
39
40
41
42
43
44
45
46
47
48
49
50
51
52
53
54
55
56
57
58
59
60
61
62
63
64
65
66
67
68
69
70
71
72
73
74
75

335 Art III

1-21 Romanesque art
1-13 Romanesque church, a cathedral
1 nave
2 aisle
3 transept
4 choir (chancel)
5 apse
6 central tower (*Am.* center tower)
7 pyramidal tower roof
8 arcading
9 frieze of round arcading
10 blind arcade (blind arcading)
11 lesene, a pilaster strip
12 circular window
13 side entrance
14-16 Romanesque ornamentation (Romanesque decoration, Romanesque decorative designs)
14 chequered (*Am.* checkered) pattern (chequered design)
15 imbrication (imbricated design)
16 chevron design
17 Romanesque system of vaulting
18 transverse arch
19 barrel vault (tunnel vault)
20 pillar
21 cushion capital
22-41 Gothic art
22 Gothic church [westwork, west end, west façade], a cathedral
23 rose window
24 church door (main door, portal), a recessed portal
25 archivolt
26 tympanum
27-35 Gothic structural system
27, 28 buttresses
27 buttress
28 flying buttress
29 pinnacle
30 gargoyle
31, 32 cross vault (groin vault)
31 ribs (cross ribs)
32 boss (pendant)
33 triforium
34 clustered pier (compound pier)
35 respond (engaged pillar)
36 pediment
37 finial
38 crocket
39-41 tracery window, a lancet window
39, 40 tracery
39 quatrefoil
40 cinquefoil
41 mullions
42-54 Renaissance art
42 Renaissance church
43 projection, a projecting part of the building
44 drum
45 lantern
46 pilaster (engaged pillar)
47 Renaissance palace
48 cornice
49 pedimental window
50 pedimental window with round gable
51 rustication (rustic work)
52 string course
53 sarcophagus
54 festoon (garland)

14
15
16
6
7
1
8
9
2
12
13
10
11
4
3
5
17
18
19
20
21
22
23
25
24
26
36
37
38
39
40
41
32
31
28
29
27
35
33
30
34
53
54
42
45
44
46
43
48
47
51
49
50
52

1-8 Baroque art
1 Baroque church
2 bull's eye
3 bulbous cupola
4 dormer window (dormer)
5 curved gable
6 twin columns
7 cartouche
8 scrollwork
9-13 Rococo art
9 Rococo wall
10 coving, a hollow moulding (*Am.* molding)
11 framing
12 ornamental moulding (*Am.* molding)
13 rocaille, a Rococo ornament
14 table in Louis Seize style (Louis Seize table)
15 neoclassical building (building in neoclassical style), a gateway
16 Empire table (table in the Empire style)
17 Biedermeier sofa (sofa in the Biedermeier style)
18 Art Nouveau easy chair (easy chair in the Art Nouveau style)
19-37 types of arch
19 arch
20 abutment
21 impost
22 springer, a voussoir (wedge stone)
23 keystone
24 face
25 intrados
26 extrados
27 round arch
28 segmental arch (basket handle)
29 parabolic arch
30 horseshoe arch
31 lancet arch
32 trefoil arch
33 shouldered arch
34 convex arch
35 tented arch
36 ogee arch (keel arch)
37 Tudor arch
38-50 types of vault
38 barrel vault (tunnel vault)
39 crown
40 side
41 cloister vault (cloistered vault)
42 groin vault (groined vault)
43 rib vault (ribbed vault)
44 stellar vault
45 net vault
46 fan vault
47 trough vault
48 trough
49 cavetto vault
50 cavetto

1
3
2
4
5
6
10
11
9
12
13
14
16
7
8
17
18
15
19
26 23
25
22
21
20
24
27
28
29
30
31
32
33
34
35
36
37
39 40
38
40
40
41
42
43
44
45
46
40
47
48
49
50

1-6 Chinese art
1 pagoda (multi-storey, multistory, pagoda), a temple tower
2 storey (story) roof (roof of storey)
3 pailou (pailoo), a memorial archway
4 archway
5 porcelain vase
6 incised lacquered work
7-11 Japanese art
7 temple
8 bell tower
9 supporting structure
10 bodhisattva (boddhisattva), a Buddhist saint
11 torii, a gateway
12-18 Islamic art
12 mosque
13 minaret, a prayer tower
14 mihrab
15 minbar (mimbar, pulpit)
16 mausoleum, a tomb
17 stalactite vault (stalactitic vault)
18 Arabian capital
19-28 Indian art
19 dancing Siva (Shiva), an Indian god
20 statue of Buddha
21 stupa (Indian pagoda), a mound (dome), a Buddhist shrine
22 umbrella
23 stone wall (*Am.* stone fence)
24 gate
25 temple buildings
26 shikara (sikar, sikhara, temple tower)
27 chaitya hall
28 chaitya, a small stupa

1
2
3
4
5
6
7
8
9
10
11
12
13
13
14
15
16
17
18
19
20
27
22
21
22
24
23
25
26
28

338 Artist's Studio

1-43 studio
1 studio skylight
2 painter, an artist
3 studio easel
4 chalk sketch, a rough draft
5 crayon (piece of chalk)
6-19 painting materials
6 flat brush
7 camel hair brush
8 round brush
9 priming brush
10 box of paints (paintbox)
11 tube of oil paint
12 varnish
13 thinner
14 palette knife
15 spatula
16 charcoal pencil (charcoal, piece of charcoal)
17 tempera (gouache)
18 watercolour (*Am.* watercolor)
19 pastel crayon
20 wedged stretcher (canvas stretcher)
21 canvas
22 piece of hardboard, with painting surface
23 wooden board
24 fibreboard (*Am.* fiberboard)
25 painting table
26 folding easel
27 still life group, a motif
28 palette
29 palette dipper
30 platform
31 lay figure (mannequin, manikin)
32 nude model (model, nude)
33 drapery
34 drawing easel
35 sketch pad
36 study in oils
37 mosaic (tessellation)
38 mosaic figure
39 tesserae
40 fresco (mural)
41 sgraffito
42 plaster
43 cartoon

1 sculptor
2 proportional dividers
3 calliper (caliper)
4 plaster model, a plaster cast
5 block of stone (stone block)
6 modeller (*Am.* modeler)
7 clay figure, a torso
8 roll of clay, a modelling (*Am.* modeling) substance
9 modelling (*Am.* modeling) stand
10 wooden modelling (*Am.* modeling) tool
11 wire modelling (*Am.* modeling) tool
12 beating wood
13 claw chisel (toothed chisel, tooth chisel)
14 flat chisel
15 point (punch)
16 iron-headed hammer
17 gouge (hollow chisel)
18 spoon chisel
19 wood chisel, a bevelled-edge chisel
20 V-shaped gouge
21 mallet
22 framework
23 baseboard
24 armature support (metal rod)
25 armature
26 wax model
27 block of wood
28 wood carver (wood sculptor)
29 sack of gypsum powder (gypsum)
30 clay box
31 modelling (*Am.* modeling) clay
32 statue, a sculpture
33 low relief (bas-relief)
34 modelling (*Am.* modeling) board
35 wire frame, wire netting
36 circular medallion (tondo)
37 mask
38 plaque

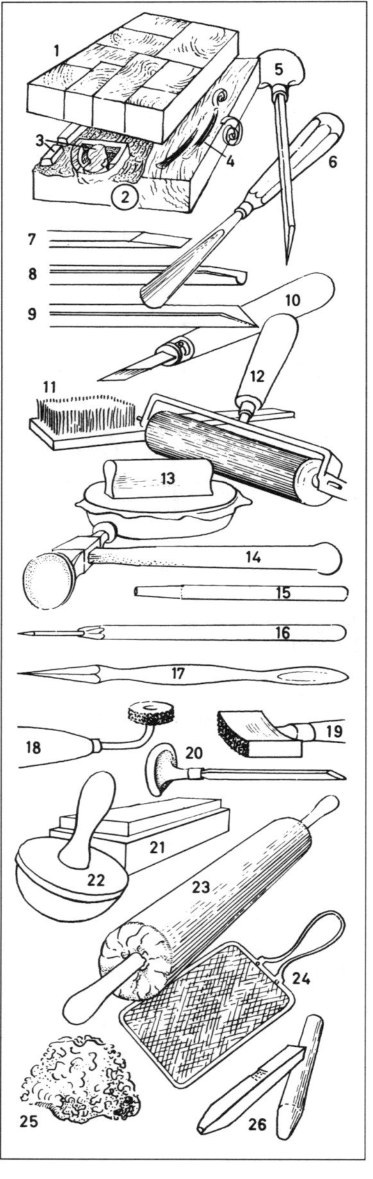

1-13 wood engraving (xylography), a relief printing method (a letter-press printing method)

1 end-grain block for wood engravings, a wooden block

2 wooden plank for woodcutting, a relief image carrier

3 positive cut

4 plank cut

5 burin (graver)

6 U-shaped gouge

7 scorper (scauper, scalper)

8 scoop

9 V-shaped gouge

10 contour knife

11 brush

12 roller (brayer)

13 pad (wiper)

14-24 copperplate engraving (chalcography), an intaglio process; *kinds:* etching, mezzotint, aquatint, crayon engraving

14 hammer

15 burin

16 etching needle (engraver)

17 scraper and burnisher

18 roulette

19 rocking tool (rocker)

20 round-headed graver, a graver (burin)

21 oilstone

22 dabber (inking ball, ink ball)

23 leather roller

24 sieve

25, 26 lithography (stone lithography), a planographic printing method

25 sponge for moistening the lithographic stone

26 lithographic crayons (greasy chalk)

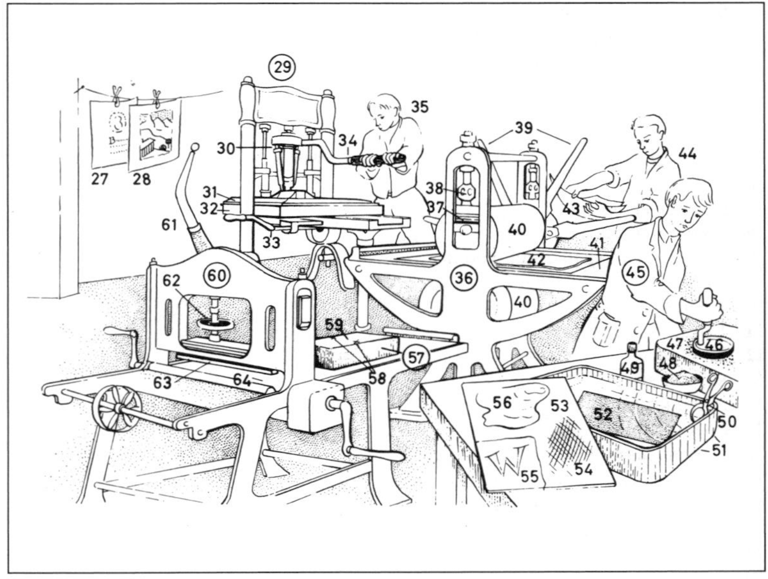

27-64 graphic art studio, a printing office (*Am.* printery)

27 broadside (broadsheet, single sheet)

28 full-colour (*Am.* full-color) print (colour print, chromolithograph)

29 platen press, a hand press

30 toggle

31 platen

32 type forme (*Am.* form)

33 feed mechanism

34 bar (devil's tail)

35 pressman

36 copperplate press

37 tympan

38 pressure regulator

39 star wheel

40 cylinder

41 bed

42 felt cloth

43 proof (pull)

44 copperplate engraver

45 lithographer (litho artist), grinding the stone

46 grinding disc (disk)

47 grain (granular texture)

48 pulverized glass

49 rubber solution

50 tongs

51 etching bath for etching

52 zinc plate

53 polished copperplate

54 cross hatch

55 etching ground

56 non-printing area

57 lithographic stone

58 register marks

59 printing surface (printing image carrier)

60 lithographic press

61 lever

62 scraper adjustment

63 scraper

64 bed

341 Script I

1-20 scripts of various peoples
1 ancient Egyptian hieroglyphics, a pictorial system of writing
2 Arabic
3 Armenian
4 Georgian
5 Chinese
6 Japanese
7 Hebrew (Hebraic)
8 cuneiform script
9 Devanagari, script employed in Sanskrit
10 Siamese
11 Tamil
12 Tibetan
13 Sinaitic script
14 Phoenician
15 Greek
16 Roman capitals
17 uncial (uncials, uncial script)
18 Carolingian (Carlovingian, Caroline) minuscule
19 runes
20 Cyrillic
21-26 ancient **writing implements**
21 Indian steel stylus for writing on palm leaves
22 ancient Egyptian reed pen
23 writing cane
24 brush
25 Roman metal pen (stylus)
26 quill (quill pen)
27 Korean

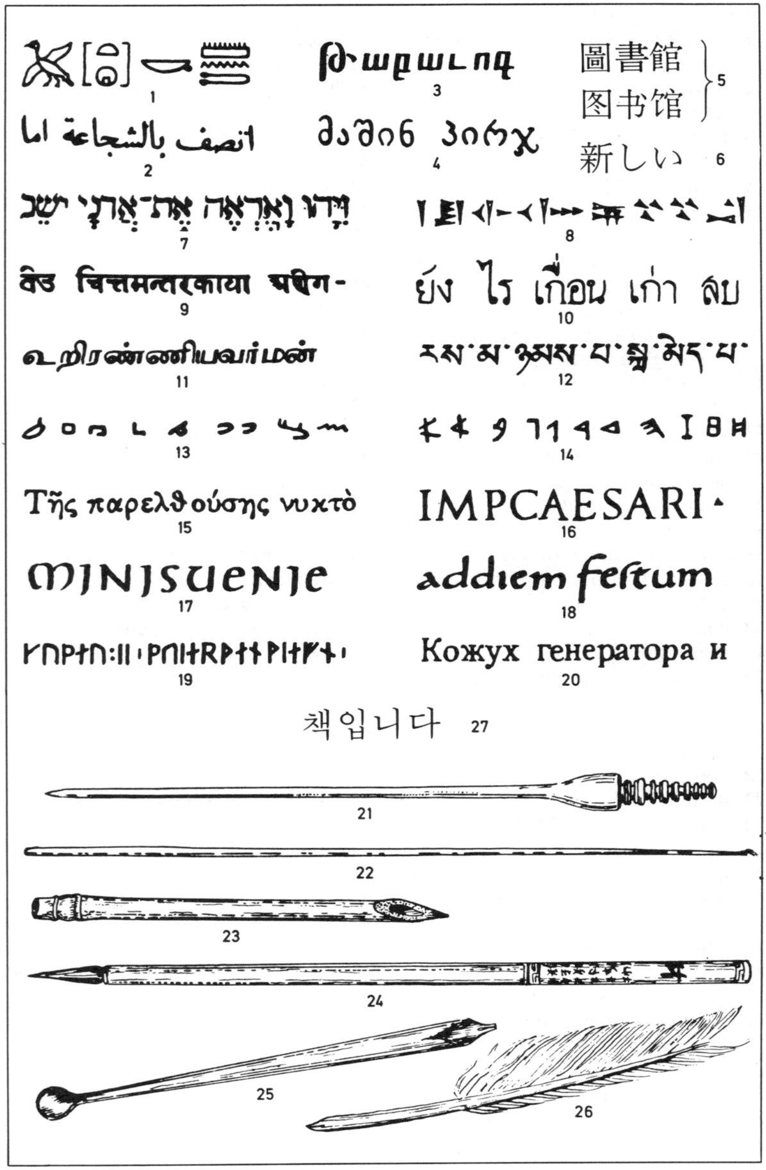

1

Թ·ագաւոր

3

圖書館
图书馆 } 5

انصف بالشجاعة اما

2

4

新しい 6

7

8

9

ยัง ไร เกื่อน เก่า ลบ

10

11

12

13

14

Τῆς παρελθούσης νυκτὸ

15

IMPCAESARI·

16

MINISUENIE

17

addiem feſtum

18

19

Кожух генератора и

20

책입니다 27

21

22

23

24

25

26

1-15 types (type faces)
1 Gothic type (German black-letter type)
2 Schwabacher type (German black-letter type)
3 Fraktur (German black-letter type)
4 Humanist (Mediaeval)
5 Transitional
6 Didone
7 Sanserif (Sanserif type, Grotesque)
8 Egyptian
9 typescript (typewriting)
10 English hand (English handwriting, English writing)
11 German hand (German handwriting, German writing)
12 Latin script
13 shorthand (shorthand writing, stenography)
14 phonetics (phonetic transcription)
15 Braille
16-29 punctuation marks (stops)
16 full stop (period, full point)
17 colon
18 comma
19 semicolon
20 question mark (interrogation point, interrogation mark)
21 exclamation mark (*Am.* exclamation point)
22 apostrophe
23 dash (em rule)
24 parentheses (round brackets)
25 square brackets
26 quotation mark (double quotation marks, paired quotation marks, inverted commas)
27 guillemet (French quotation mark)
28 hyphen
29 marks of omission (ellipsis)
30-35 accents and diacritical marks (diacritics)
30 acute accent (acute)
31 grave accent (grave)
32 circumflex accent (circumflex)
33 cedilla [under c]
34 diaeresis (*Am.* dieresis) [over e]
35 tilde [over n]
36 section mark
37-70 newspaper, a national daily newspaper
37 newspaper page
38 front page
39 newspaper heading
40 contents
41 price
42 date of publication
43 place of publication
44 headline
45 column
46 column heading
47 column rule
48 leading article (leader, editorial)
49 reference to related article
50 brief news item
51 political section
52 page heading
53 cartoon
54 report by newspaper's own correspondent
55 news agency's sign
56 advertisement (*coll.* ad)
57 sports section
58 press photo
59 caption
60 sports report
61 sports news item
62 home and overseas news section
63 news in brief (miscellaneous news)
64 television programmes (*Am.* programs)
65 weather report
66 weather chart (weather map)
67 arts section (feuilleton)
68 death notice
69 advertisements (classified advertising)
70 job advertisement, a vacancy (a situation offered)

Oxford 1
Oxford 2
Oxford 3
Oxford 4
Oxford 5
Oxford 6
Oxford 7
Oxford 8
Oxford 9
Oxford 10
Oxford 11
Oxford 12
13
ˈɔksfəd 14
15
. 16
: 17
, 18
; 19
? 20
! 21
’ 22
— 23
() 24
[] 25
„ “ 26
» « 27
- 28
... 29
é 30
è 31
ê 32
ç 33
ë 34
ñ 35
§ 36
37
69
GUARDIAN PERSONAL
68
THE GUARDIAN
48
PARLIAMENT 52
51
Unions will have to pay to strike soon, says PM
Walker plan to cut
54
ARTS GUARDIAN 67
OVERSEAS NEWS 62
HOMEFINDER
A houseproud nation?
APPOINTMENTS
70
SPORTS GUARDIAN
57
McKenzie—just one of the lads
60
Fulham win a round in pay inquiry
TELEVISION/RAD
64
46
45
ENTERTAINMENTS
39 THE GUARDIAN
43
Printed in London and Manchester
42
Friday February 15 1980
41
A belligerent premier condemns 'intimidating' picket as Hadfields closes
Steelmen cheer rejection of 14pc offer
44
Thatcher will cut strikers' benefit
NEWS IN BRIEF
GEC 63 loses takeover battle
Mugabe banned from campaign in two areas
NEWS IN BRIEF
Kidnap shooting widow's despair
of its own
58
61
59
47
Anxiety over Tito
49
50
Plan to dock state pay revived
38
53
Colin will be 8 years old for the rest of his life.
INSIDE
40
Iran 'hostage solution' on Carter's desk
55
56
66
65
FAKENHAM

343 Colour (*Am.* Color)

1 red
2 yellow
3 blue
4 pink
5 brown
6 azure (sky blue)
7 orange
8 green
9 violet
10 additive mixture of colours (*Am.* colors)
11 white
12 subtractive mixture of colours (*Am.* colors)
13 black
14 solar spectrum (colours, *Am.* colors, of the rainbow)
15 grey (*Am.* gray) scale
16 heat colours (*Am.* colors)

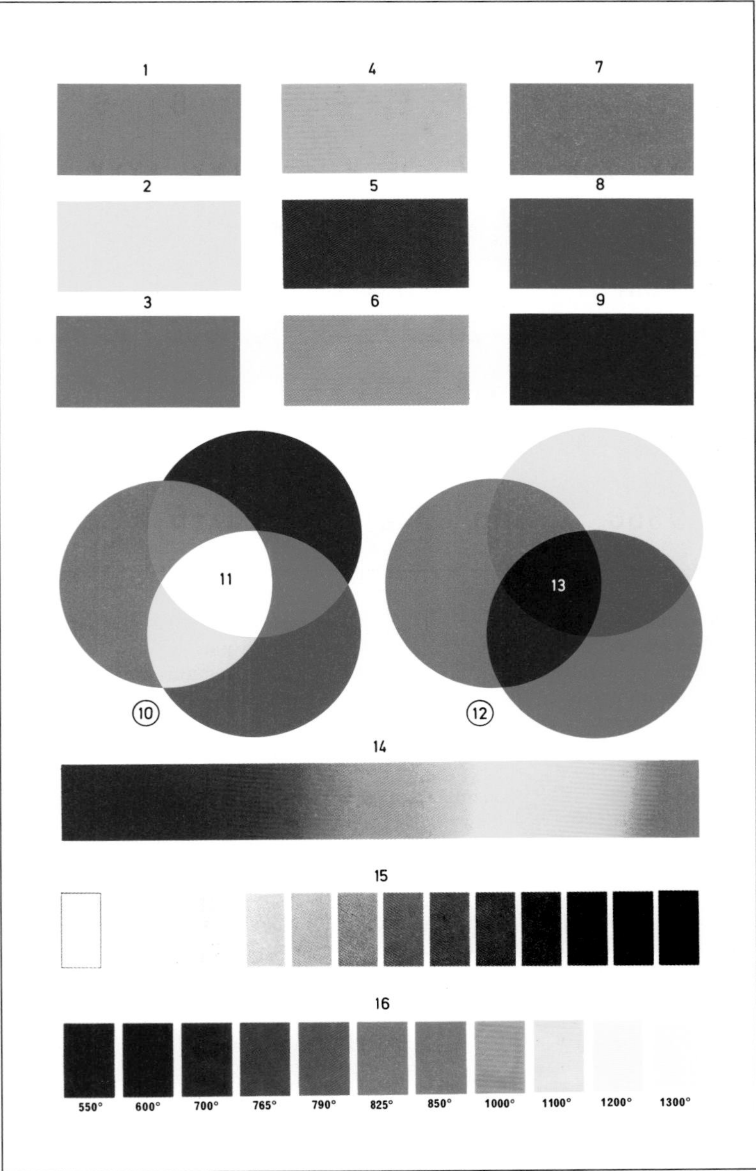
1
4
7
2
5
8
3
6
9
11
13
10
12
14
15
16
550°
600°
700°
765°
790°
825°
850°
1000°
1100°
1200°
1300°

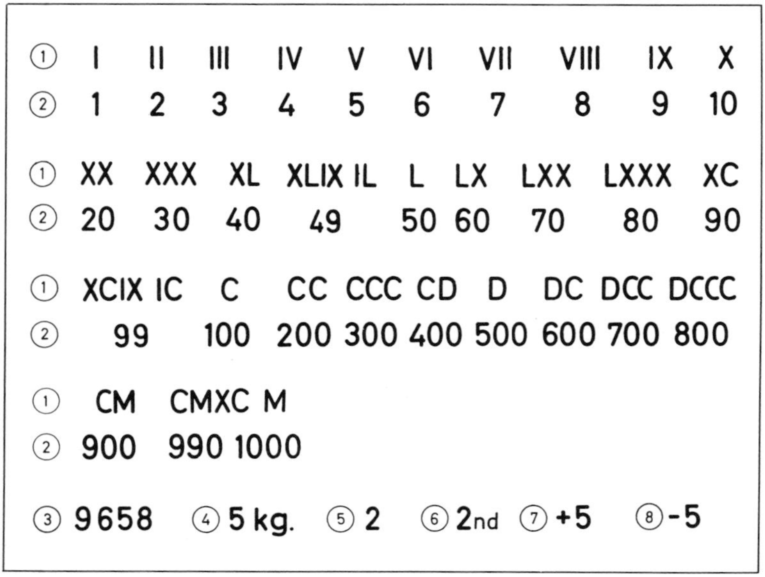

① I II III IV V VI VII VIII IX X
② 1 2 3 4 5 6 7 8 9 10

① XX XXX XL XLIX IL L LX LXX LXXX XC
② 20 30 40 49 50 60 70 80 90

① XCIX IC C CC CCC CD D DC DCC DCCC
② 99 100 200 300 400 500 600 700 800

① CM CMXC M
② 900 990 1000

③ 9658 ④ 5 kg. ⑤ 2 ⑥ 2nd ⑦ +5 ⑧ -5

1-26 arithmetic
1-22 numbers
1 Roman numerals
2 Arabic numerals
3 abstract number, a four-figure number [8: units; 5: tens; 6: hundreds; 9: thousands]
4 concrete number (physical quantity consisting of the numerical value and the unit or unit symbol)
5 cardinal number (cardinal)
6 ordinal number (ordinal)
7 positive number [with plus sign]
8 negative number [with minus sign]
9 algebraic symbols
10 mixed number [3: whole number (integer); $^1/_3$: fraction]
11 even numbers
12 odd numbers
13 prime numbers
14 complex number [3: real part; $2\sqrt{-1}$: imaginary part]
15, 16 vulgar fractions
15 proper fraction [2: numerator, horizontal line; 3: denominator]
16 improper fraction, also the reciprocal of item 15
17 compound fraction (complex fraction)
18 improper fraction [when cancelled down produces a whole number]
19 fractions of different denominations [35: common denominator]
20 proper decimal fraction with decimal point and decimal places [3: tenths; 5: hundredths; 7: thousandths]
21, 22 recurring decimal

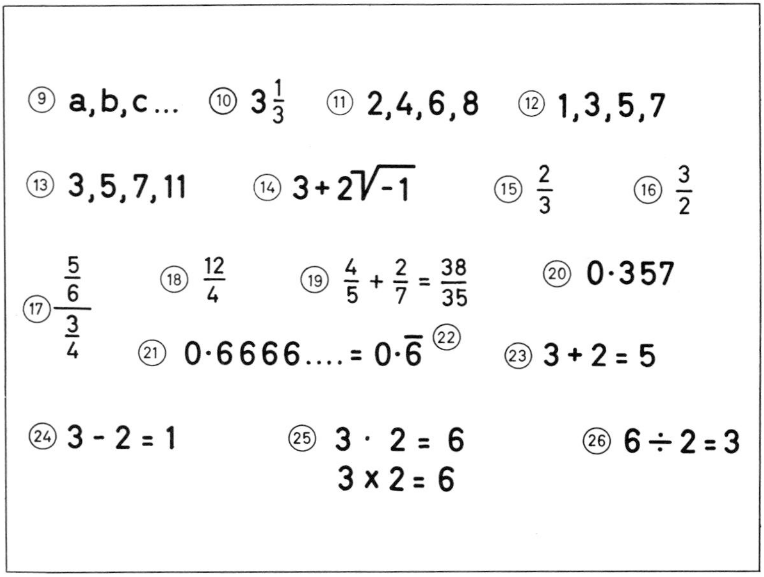

(9) a, b, c... (10) $3\frac{1}{3}$ (11) 2, 4, 6, 8 (12) 1, 3, 5, 7

(13) 3, 5, 7, 11 (14) $3+2\sqrt{-1}$ (15) $\frac{2}{3}$ (16) $\frac{3}{2}$

(17) $\frac{\frac{5}{6}}{\frac{3}{4}}$ (18) $\frac{12}{4}$ (19) $\frac{4}{5}+\frac{2}{7}=\frac{38}{35}$ (20) 0·357

(21) $0{\cdot}6666.... = 0{\cdot}\overline{6}$ (22) (23) $3+2=5$

(24) $3-2=1$ (25) $3 \cdot 2 = 6$ $3 \times 2 = 6$ (26) $6 \div 2 = 3$

23-26 fundamental arithmetical operations

23 addition (adding) [3 and 2: the terms of the sum; + : plus sign; = : equals sign; 5: the sum]

24 subtraction (subtracting); [3: the minuend; – : minus sign; 2: the subtrahend; 1: the remainder (difference)]

25 multiplication (multiplying); [3: the multiplicand; ×: multiplication sign; 2: the multiplier; 2 and 3: factors; 6: the product]

26 division (dividing); [6: the dividend; ÷: division sign; 2: the divisor; 3: the quotient]

① $3^2 = 9$ ② $\sqrt[3]{8} = 2$ ③ $\sqrt{4} = 2$

④ $3x + 2 = 12$

⑤ $4a + 6ab - 2ac = 2a(2 + 3b - c)$ ⑥ $\log_{10} 3 = 0{\cdot}4771$

⑦ $$\frac{P[£1000] \times R[5\%] \times T[2\,\text{years}]}{100} = I[£100]$$

1-24 arithmetic

1-10 advanced arithmetical operations

1 raising to a power [three squared (3^2): the power; 3: the base; 2: the exponent (index); 9: value of the power]

2 evolution (extracting a root); [cube root of 8: cube root; 8: the radical; 3: the index (degree) of the root; √: radical sign; 2: value of the root]

3 square root

4, 5 algebra

4 simple equation [3, 2: the coefficients; × : the unknown quantity]

5 identical equation; [a, b, c: algebraic symbols]

6 logarithmic calculation (taking the logarithm, log); [log: logarithm sign; 3: number whose logarithm is required; 10: the base; 0: the characteristic; 4771: the mantissa; 0.4771: the logarithm]

7 simple interest formula [P: the principal; R: rate of interest; T: time; I: interest (profit); %: percentage sign]

8-10 rule of three (rule-of-three sum, simple proportion)

8 statement with the unknown quantity ×

9 equation (conditional equation)

10 solution

11-14 higher mathematics

11 arithmetical series with the elements 2, 4, 6, 8

12 geometrical series

13, 14 infinitesimal calculus

13 derivative [dx, dy: the differentials; d: differential sign]

14 integral (integration) [x: the variable; C: constant of integration; ∫: the integral sign; dx: the differential]

(8) 2 years @ £ 50
4 years @ £ x

(9) $2 : 50 = 4 : x$

(10) $x = £100$

(11) $2 + 4 + 6 + 8 \ldots$

(12) $2 + 4 + 8 + 16 + 32 \ldots$

(13) $\frac{dy}{dx}$

(14) $\int axdx = a\int xdx = \frac{ax^2}{2} + C$

(15) ∞ (16) $\equiv$ (17) $\approx$ (18) $\neq$ (19) $>$

(20) $<$ (21) $\parallel$ (22) $\sim$ (23) $\angle$ (24) $\triangle$

15-24 mathematical symbols
15 infinity
16 identically equal to (the sign of identity)
17 approximately equal to
18 unequal to
19 greater than
20 less than
21-24 geometrical symbols
21 parallel (sign of parallelism)
22 similar to (sign of similarity)
23 angle symbol
24 triangle symbol

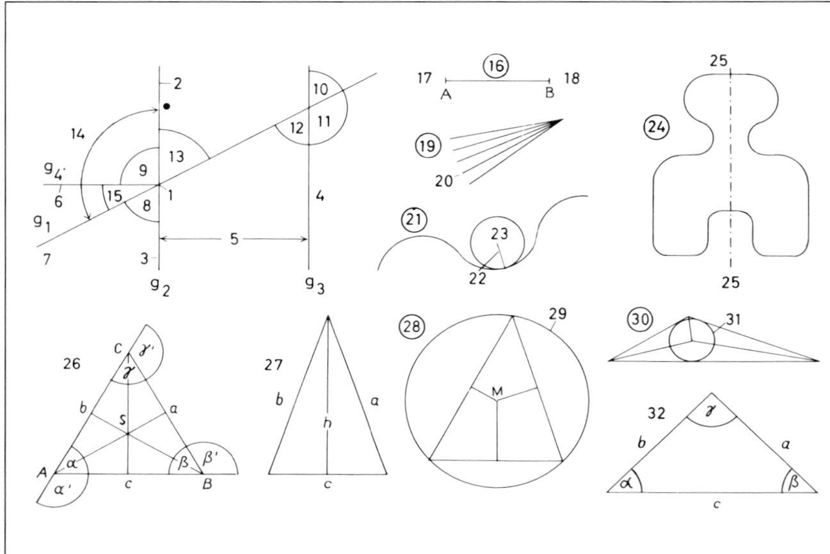

1-58 plane geometry (elementary geometry, Euclidian geometry)

1-23 point, line, angle

1 point [point of intersection of g_1 and g_2], the angular point of **8**

2, 3 straight line g_2

4 the parallel to g_2

5 distance between the straight lines g_2 and g_3

6 perpendicular (g_4) on g_2

7, 3 the arms of **8**

8, 13 vertically opposite angles

8 angle

9 right angle [90°]

10, 11, 12 reflex angle

10 acute angle, also the alternate angle to **8**

11 obtuse angle

12 corresponding angle to **10**

13, 9, 15 straight angle [180°]

14 adjacent angle; *here:* supplementary angle to 13

15 complementary angle to **8**

16 straight line AB

17 end A

18 end B

19 pencil of rays

20 ray

21 curved line

22 radius of curvature

23 centre (*Am.* center) of curvature

24-58 plane surfaces

24 symmetrical figure

25 axis of symmetry

26-32 plane triangles

26 equilateral triangle [A, B, C: the vertices; a, b, c: the sides; α (alpha), β (beta), γ (gamma): the interior angles; α', β', γ': the exterior angles; S: the centre (*Am.* center)]

27 isosceles triangle [a, b: the sides (legs); c: the base; h: the perpendicular, an altitude]

28 acute-angled triangle with perpendicular bisectors of the sides

29 circumcircle (circumscribed circle)

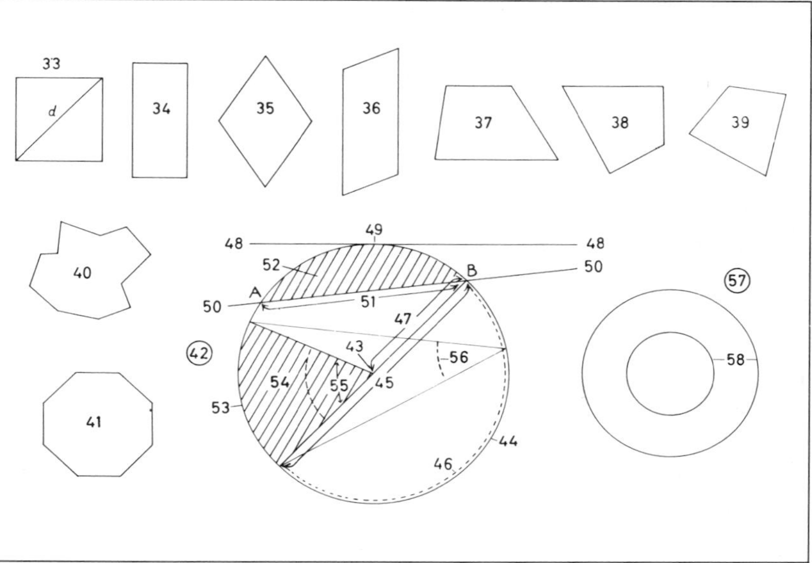

30 obtuse-angled triangle with bisectors of the angles

31 inscribed circle

32 right-angled triangle and the trigonometrical functions of angles [a, b: the catheti; c: the hypotenuse; γ: the right angle; $a/c = \sin\alpha$ (sine); $b/c = \cos\alpha$ (cosine); $a/b = \tan\alpha$ (tangent); $b/a = \cot\alpha$ (cotangent)]

33-39 quadrilaterals

33-36 parallelograms

33 square [d: a diagonal]

34 rectangle

35 rhombus (rhomb, lozenge)

36 rhomboid

37 trapezium

38 deltoid (kite)

39 irregular quadrilateral

40 polygon

41 regular polygon

42 **circle**

43 centre (*Am.* center)

44 circumference (periphery)

45 diameter

46 semicircle

47 radius (r)

48 tangent

49 point of contact (P)

50 secant

51 the chord AB

52 segment

53 arc

54 sector

55 angle subtended by the arc at the centre (*Am.* center) (centre, *Am.* center, angle)

56 circumferential angle

57 ring (annulus)

58 concentric circles

347 Mathematics IV (Geometry II)

1 **system of right-angled coordinates**
2, 3 axes of coordinates (coordinate axes)
2 axis of abscissae (x-axis)
3 axis of ordinates (y-axis)
4 origin of ordinates
5 quadrant [I-IV: 1st to 4th quadrant]
6 positive direction
7 negative direction
8 points [P_1 and P_2] in the system of coordinates; x_1 and y_1 [and x_2 and y_2 respectively] their coordinates
9 values of the abscissae [x_1 and x_2] (the abscissae)
10 values of the ordinates [y_1 and y_2] (the ordinates)
11-29 conic sections
11 **curves** in the system of coordinates
12 plane curves [a: the gradient (slope) of the curve; b: the ordinates' intersection of the curve; c: the root of the curve]
13 inflected curves
14 **parabola,** a curve of the second degree
15 branches of the parabola
16 vertex of the parabola
17 axis of the parabola
18 **a curve of the third degree**
19 maximum of the curve
20 minimum of the curve
21 point of inflexion (of inflection)
22 **ellipse**
23 transverse axis (major axis)
24 conjugate axis (minor axis)
25 foci of the ellipse [F_1 and F_2]
26 **hyperbola**
27 foci [F_1 and F_2]
28 vertices [S_1 and S_2]
29 asymptotes [a and b]
30-46 solids
30 cube
31 square, a plane (plane surface)
32 edge
33 corner
34 quadratic prism
35 base
36 parallelepiped
37 triangular prism
38 cylinder, a right cylinder
39 base, a circular plane
40 curved surface
41 sphere
42 ellipsoid of revolution
43 cone
44 height of the cone (cone height)
45 truncated cone (frustum of a cone)
46 quadrilateral pyramid

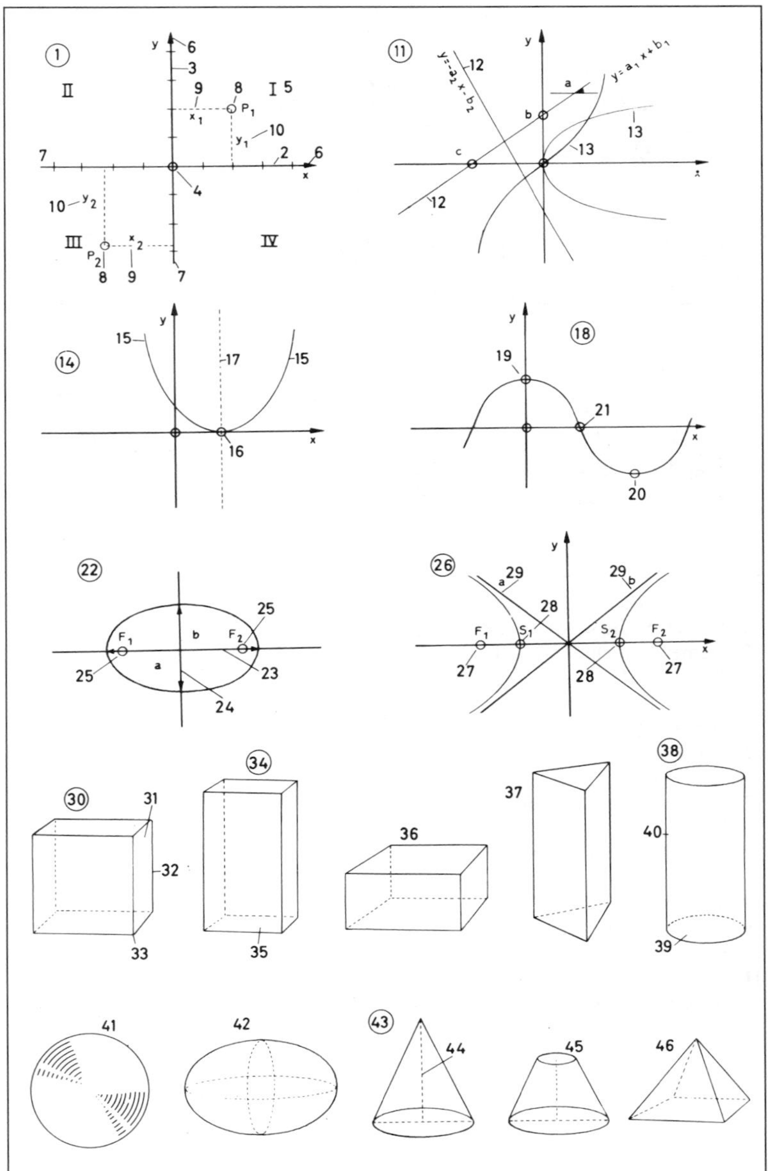

1
2
3
4
5
6
7
8
9
10
I
II
III
IV
P_1
P_2
x_1
x_2
y_1
y_2
x
y
11
12
13
$y=a_1x+b_1$
$y=-a_2x-b_2$
a
b
c
14
15
16
17
18
19
20
21
22
23
24
25
F_1
F_2
26
27
28
29
S_1
S_2
30
31
32
33
34
35
36
37
38
39
40
41
42
43
44
45
46

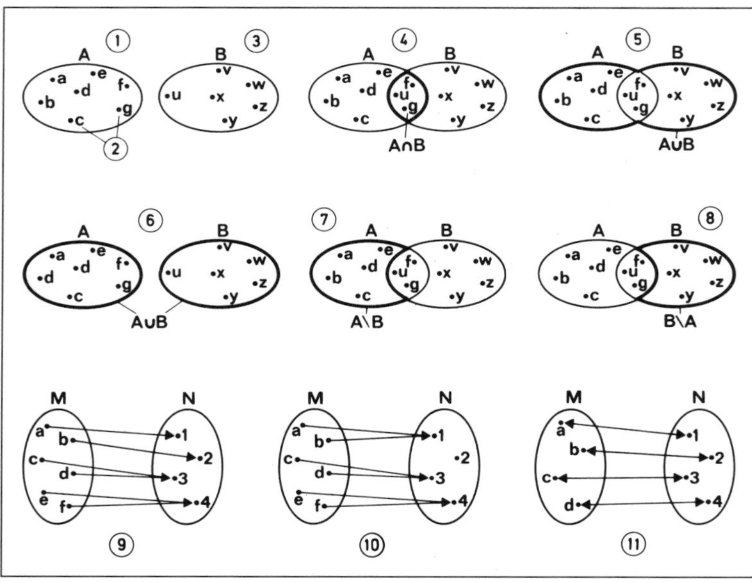

1 the set A, the set {a, b, c, d, e, f, g}
2 elements (members) of the set A
3 the set B, the set {u, v, w, x, y, z}
4 intersection of the sets A and B, $A \cap B = \{f, g, u\}$
5, 6 union of the sets A and B, $A \cup B = \{a, b, c, d, e, f, g, u, v, w, x, y, z\}$
7 complement of the set B, B' = {a, b, c, d, e}
8 complement of the set A, A' = {v, w, x, y, z}
9-11 mappings
9 mapping of the set M *onto* the set N
10 mapping of the set M *into* the set N
11 one-to-one mapping of the set M on to the set N

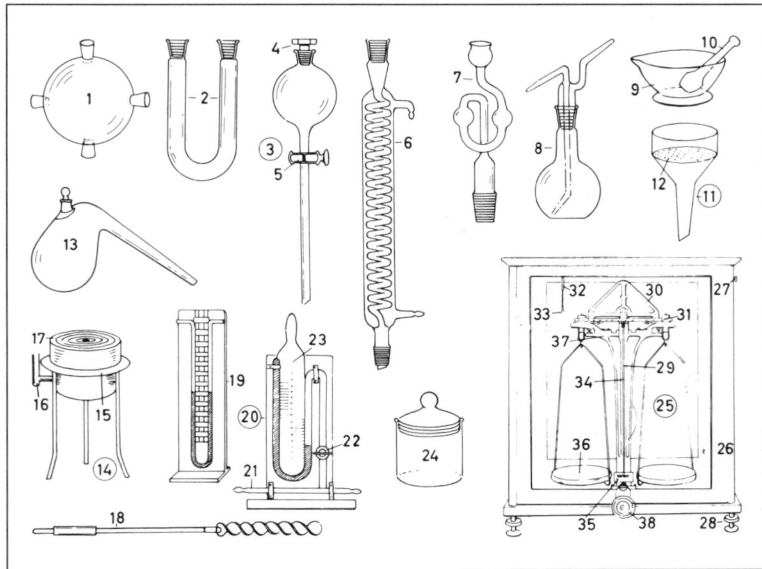

1-38 laboratory apparatus (laboratory equipment)
1 Scheidt globe
2 U-tube
3 separating funnel
4 octagonal ground-glass stopper
5 tap (*Am.* faucet)
6 coiled condenser
7 air lock
8 wash-bottle
9 mortar
10 pestle
11 filter funnel (Büchner funnel)
12 filter (filter plate)
13 retort
14 water bath
15 tripod
16 water gauge (*Am.* gage)
17 insertion rings
18 stirrer
19 manometer for measuring positive and negative pressures
20 mirror manometer for measuring small pressures
21 inlet
22 tap (*Am.* faucet)
23 sliding scale
24 weighing bottle
25 analytical balance
26 case
27 sliding front panel
28 three-point support
29 column (balance column)
30 balance beam (beam)
31 rider bar
32 rider holder
33 rider
34 pointer
35 scale
36 scale pan
37 stop
38 stop knob

350 Chemistry Laboratory II

1-63 laboratory apparatus (laboratory equipment)
1 Bunsen burner
2 gas inlet (gas inlet pipe)
3 air regulator
4 Teclu burner
5 pipe union
6 gas regulator
7 stem
8 air regulator
9 bench torch
10 casing
11 oxygen inlet
12 hydrogen inlet
13 oxygen jet
14 tripod
15 ring (retort ring)
16 funnel
17 pipe clay triangle
18 wire gauze
19 wire gauze with asbestos centre (*Am.* center)
20 beaker
21 burette (for measuring the volume of liquids)
22 burette stand
23 burette clamp
24 graduated pipette
25 pipette
26 measuring cylinder (measuring glass)
27 measuring flask
28 volumetric flask
29 evaporating dish (evaporating basin), made of porcelain
30 tube clamp (tube clip, pinchcock)
31 clay crucible with lid
32 crucible tongs
33 clamp
34 test tube
35 test tube rack
36 flat-bottomed flask
37 ground glass neck
38 long-necked round-bottomed flask
39 Erlenmeyer flask (conical flask)
40 filter flask
41 fluted filter
42 one-way tap
43 calcium chloride tube
44 stopper with tap
45 cylinder
46 distillation apparatus (distilling apparatus)
47 distillation flask (distilling flask)
48 condenser
49 return tap, a two-way tap
50 distillation flask (distilling flask, Claisen flask)
51 desiccator
52 lid with fitted tube
53 tap
54 desiccator insert made of porcelain
55 three-necked flask
56 connecting piece (Y-tube)
57 three-necked bottle
58 gas-washing bottle
59 gas generator (Kipp's apparatus, *Am.* Kipp generator)
60 overflow container
61 container for the solid
62 acid container
63 gas outlet

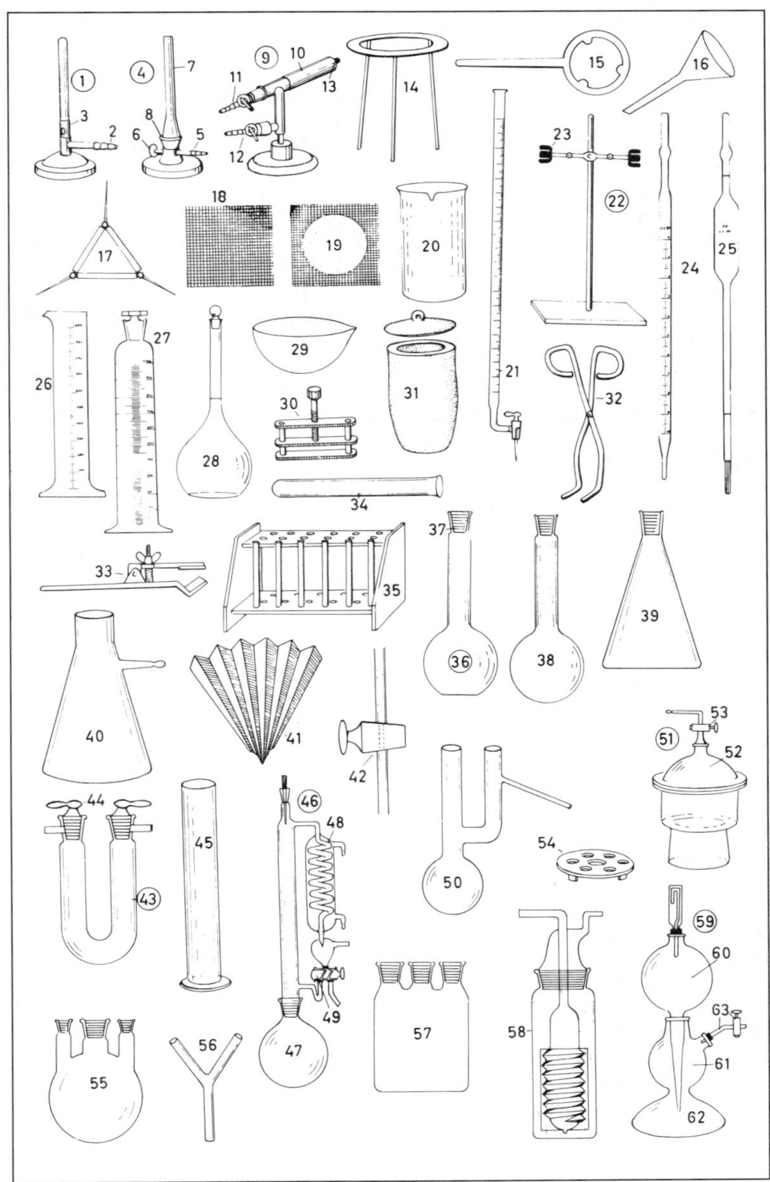
1
2
3
4
5
6
7
8
9
10
11
12
13
14
15
16
17
18
19
20
21
22
23
24
25
26
27
28
29
30
31
32
33
34
35
36
37
38
39
40
41
42
43
44
45
46
47
48
49
50
51
52
53
54
55
56
57
58
59
60
61
62
63

351 Crystals, Crystallography

1-26 basic crystal forms and crystal combinations [structure of crystals]
1-17 regular (cubic, tesseral, isometric) **crystal system**
1 tetrahedron (four-faced polyhedron) [tetrahedrite, fahlerz, fahl ore]
2 hexahedron (cube, six-faced polyhedron), a holohedron [rock salt]
3 centre (*Am.* center) of symmetry (crystal centre)
4 axis of symmetry (rotation axis)
5 plane of symmetry
6 octahedron (eight-faced polyhedron) [gold]
7 rhombic dodecahedron [garnet]
8 pentagonal dodecahedron [pyrite, iron pyrites]
9 pentagon (five-sided polygon)
10 triakis-octahedron [diamond]
11 icosahedron (twenty-faced polyhedron), a regular polyhedron
12 icositetrahedron (twenty-four-faced polyhedron) [leucite]
13 hexakis-octahedron (hexoctahedron, forty-eight-faced polyhedron) [diamond]
14 octahedron with cube [galena]
15 hexagon (six-sided polygon)
16 cube with octahedron [fluorite, fluorspar]
17 octagon (eight-sided polygon)
18, 19 tetragonal crystal system
18 tetragonal dipyramid (tetragonal bipyramid)
19 protoprism with protopyramid [zircon]
20-22 hexagonal crystal system
20 protoprism with protopyramid, deutero-pyramid and basal pinacoid [apatite]
21 hexagonal prism
22 hexagonal (ditrigonal) biprism with rhombohedron [calcite]
23 orthorhombic pyramid (rhombic crystal system) [sulphur, *Am.* sulfur]
24, 25 monoclinic crystal system
24 monoclinic prism with clinoprinacoid and hemipyramid (hemihedron) [gypsum]
25 orthopinacoid (swallowtail twin crystal) [gypsum]
26 triclinic pinacoids (triclinic crystal system) [copper sulphate, *Am.* copper sulfate]
27-33 apparatus for measuring crystals (for crystallometry)
27 contact goniometer
28 reflecting goniometer
29 crystal
30 collimator
31 observation telescope
32 divided circle (graduated circle)
33 lens for reading the angle of rotation

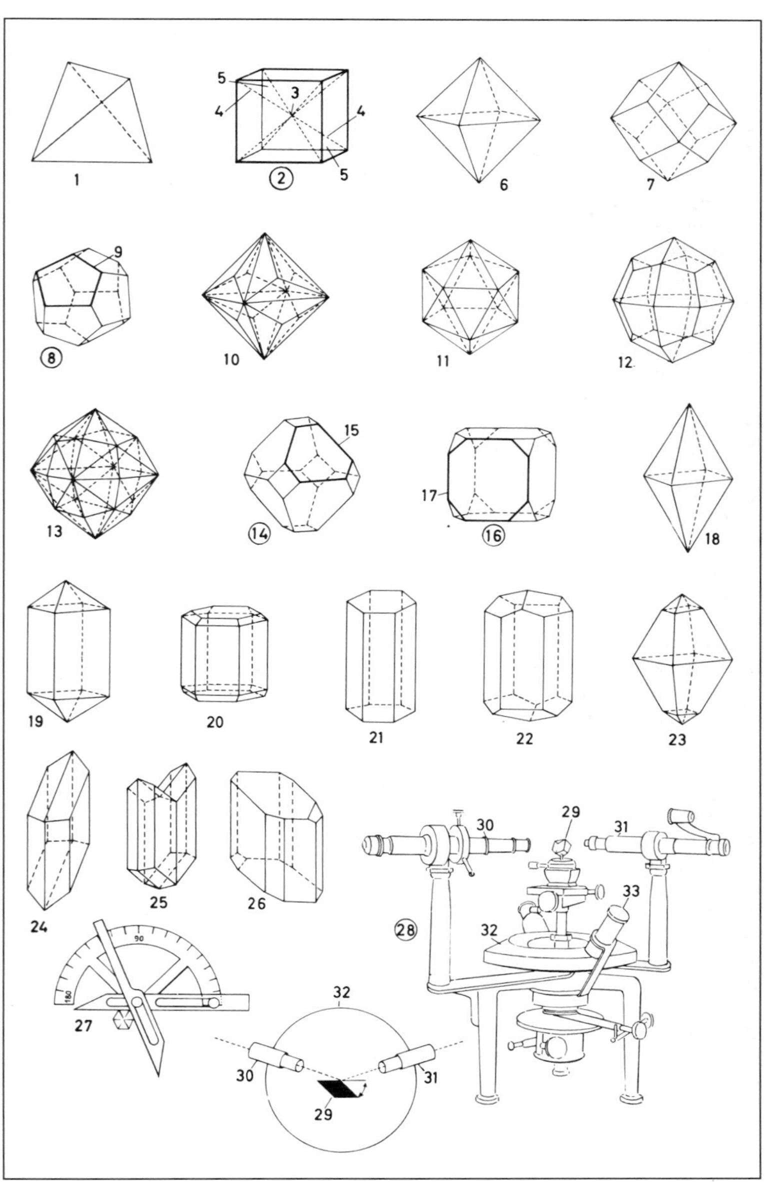
1
2
3
4
5
6
7
8
9
10
11
12
13
14
15
16
17
18
19
20
21
22
23
24
25
26
27
28
29
30
31
32
33
90
180

352 Ethnology I

1 totem pole
2 totem, a carved and painted pictorial or symbolic representation
3 plains Indian
4 mustang, a prairie horse
5 lasso, a long throwing-rope with running noose
6 pipe of peace
7 wigwam (tepee, teepee)
8 tent pole
9 smoke flap
10 squaw, an Indian woman
11 Indian chief
12 headdress, an ornamental feather headdress
13 war paint
14 necklace of bear claws
15 scalp (cut from enemy's head), a trophy
16 tomahawk, a battle axe (*Am.* ax)
17 leggings
18 moccasin, a shoe of leather and bast
19 canoe of the forest Indians
20 Maya temple, a stepped pyramid
21 mummy
22 quipa (knotted threads, knotted code of the Incas)
23 Indio (Indian of Central and South America); *here:* highland Indian
24 poncho, a blanket with a head opening used as an armless cloak-like wrap
25 Indian of the tropical forest
26 blowpipe
27 quiver
28 dart
29 dart point
30 shrunken head, a trophy
31 bola (bolas), a throwing and entangling device
32 leather-covered stone or metal ball
33 pile dwelling
34 duk-duk dancer, a member of a duk-duk (men's secret society)
35 outrigger canoe (canoe with outrigger)
36 outrigger
37 Australian aborigine
38 loincloth of human hair
39 boomerang, a wooden missile
40 throwing stick (spear thrower) with spears

1
2
3
4
5
6
7
8
9
10
11
12
13
14
15
16
17
18
19
20
21
22
23
24
25
26
27
28
29
30
31
32
33
34
35
36
37
38
39
40

353 Ethnology II

1 Eskimo
2 sledge dog (sled dog), a husky
3 dog sledge (dog sled)
4 igloo, a dome-shaped snow hut
5 block of snow
6 entrance tunnel
7 blubber-oil lamp
8 wooden missile
9 lance
10 harpoon
11 skin float
12 kayak, a light one-man canoe
13 skin-covered wooden or bone frame
14 paddle
15 reindeer harness
16 reindeer
17 Ostyak (Ostiak)
18 passenger sledge
19 yurt (yurta), a dwelling tent of the western and central Asiatic nomads
20 felt covering
21 smoke outlet
22 Kirghiz
23 sheepskin cap
24 shaman
25 decorative fringe
26 frame drum
27 Tibetan
28 flintlock with bayonets
29 prayer wheel
30 felt boot
31 houseboat (sampan)
32 junk
33 mat sail
34 rickshaw (ricksha)
35 rickshaw coolie (cooly)
36 Chinese lantern
37 samurai
38 padded armour (*Am.* armor)
39 geisha
40 kimono
41 obi
42 fan
43 coolie (cooly)
44 kris (creese, crease), a Malayan dagger
45 snake charmer
46 turban
47 flute
48 dancing snake

1
2
3
4
5
6
7
8
9
10
11
12
13
14
15
16
17
18
19
20
21
22
23
24
25
26
27
28
29
30
31
32
33
34
35
36
37
38
39
40
41
42
43
44
45
46
47
48

354 Ethnology III

1 camel caravan
2 riding animal
3 pack animal
4 oasis
5 grove of palm trees
6 bedouin (beduin)
7 burnous
8 Masai warrior
9 headdress (hairdress)
10 shield
11 painted ox hide
12 long-bladed spear
13 negro
14 dance drum
15 throwing knife
16 wooden mask
17 figure of an ancestor
18 slit gong
19 drumstick
20 dugout, a boat hollowed out of a tree trunk
21 negro hut
22 negress
23 lip plug (labret)
24 grinding stone
25 Herero woman
26 leather cap
27 calabash (gourd)
28 beehive-shaped hut
29 bushman
30 earplug
31 loincloth
32 bow
33 knobkerry (knobkerrie), a club with round, knobbed end
34 bushman woman making a fire by twirling a stick
35 windbreak
36 Zulu in dance costume
37 dancing stick
38 bangle
39 ivory war horn
40 string of amulets and bones
41 pigmy
42 magic pipe for exorcising evil spirits
43 fetish

2
4
5
3
1
7
6
9
8
13
15
10
17
12
14
16
11
19
18
26
21
25
23
20
22
24
27
28
36
37
39
41
29
30
42
32
31
40
38
34
35
43
33

355 Historical Costumes

1 Greek woman
2 peplos
3 Greek
4 petasus (Thessalonian hat)
5 chiton, a linen gown worn as a basic garment
6 himation, woollen (*Am.* woolen) cloak
7 Roman woman
8 toupee wig (partial wig)
9 stola
10 palla, a coloured (*Am.* colored) wrap
11 Roman
12 tunica (tunic)
13 toga
14 purple border (purple band)
15 Byzantine empress
16 pearl diadem
17 jewels
18 purple cloak
19 long tunic
20 German princess [13th cent.]
21 crown (diadem)
22 chinband
23 tassel
24 cloak cord
25 girt-up gown (girt-up surcoat, girt-up tunic)
26 cloak
27 German dressed in the Spanish style [ca. 1575]
28 wide-brimmed cap
29 short cloak (Spanish cloak, short cape)
30 padded doublet (stuffed doublet, peasecod)
31 stuffed trunk-hose
32 lansquenet (German mercenary soldier) [ca. 1530]
33 slashed doublet (paned doublet)
34 Pluderhose (loose breeches, paned trunk-hose, slops)
35 woman of Basle [ca. 1525]
36 overgown (gown)
37 undergown (petticoat)
38 woman of Nuremberg [ca. 1500]
39 shoulder cape
40 Burgundian [15th cent.]
41 short doublet

42 piked shoes (peaked shoes, copped shoes, crackowes, poulaines)
43 pattens (clogs)
44 young nobleman [ca. 1400]
45 short, padded doublet (short, quilted doublet, jerkin)
46 dagged sleeves (petal-scalloped sleeves)
47 hose
48 Augsburg patrician lady [ca. 1575]
49 puffed sleeve
50 overgown (gown, open gown, sleeveless gown)
51 French lady [ca. 1600]
52 millstone ruff (cartwheel ruff, ruff)
53 corseted waist (wasp waist)
54 gentleman [ca. 1650]
55 wide-brimmed felt hat (cavalier hat)
56 falling collar (wide-falling collar) of linen
57 white lining
58 jack boots (bucket-top boots)
59 lady [ca. 1650]
60 full puffed sleeves (puffed sleeves)
61 gentleman [ca. 1700]
62 three-cornered hat
63 dress sword
64 lady [ca. 1700]
65 lace fontange (high headdress of lace)
66 lace-trimmed loose-hanging gown (loose-fitting housecoat, robe de chambre, negligée, contouche)
67 band of embroidery
68 lady [ca. 1880]
69 bustle
70 lady [ca. 1858]
71 poke bonnet
72 crinoline
73 gentleman of the Biedermeier period
74 high collar (choker collar)
75 embroidered waistcoat (vest)
76 frock coat
77 pigtail wig
78 ribbon (bow)
79 ladies in court dress [ca. 1780]
80 train
81 upswept Rococo coiffure
82 hair decoration
83 panniered overskirt

1 outdoor enclosure
2 rocks
3 moat
4 enclosing wall
5 animals on show; *here:* a pride of lions
6 visitor to the zoo
7 notice
8 aviary
9 elephant enclosure
10 animal house (*e.g.* carnivore house, giraffe house, elephant house, monkey house)
11 outside cage (summer quarters)
12 reptile enclosure
13 Nile crocodile
14 terrarium and aquarium
15 glass case
16 fresh-air inlet
17 ventilator
18 underfloor heating
19 aquarium
20 information plate
21 flora in artificially maintained climate

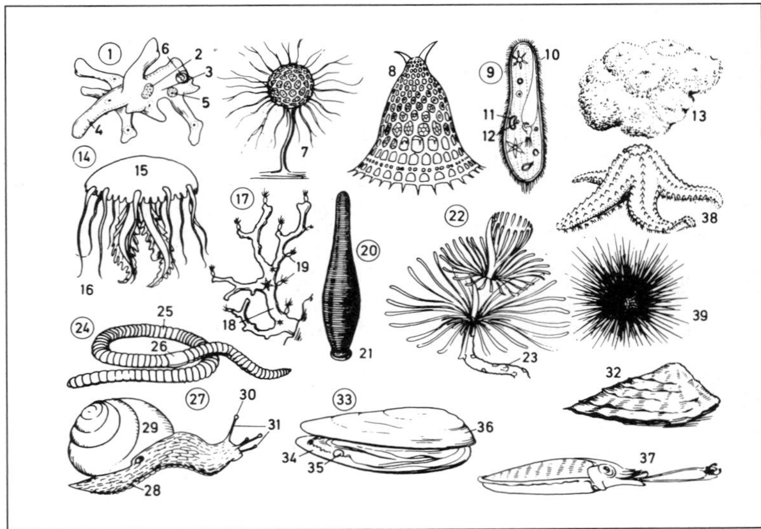

1-12 unicellular (one-celled, single-celled) **animals** (protozoans)
1 amoeba, a rhizopod
2 cell nucleus
3 protoplasm
4 pseudopod
5 excretory vacuole (contractile vacuole, an organelle)
6 food vacuole
7 Actinophrys, a heliozoan
8 radiolarian; *here:* siliceous skeleton
9 slipper animalcule, a Paramecium (ciliate infusorian)
10 cilium
11 macronucleus (meganucleus)
12 micronucleus
13-39 multicellular animals (metazoans)
13 bath sponge, a porifer (sponge)
14 medusa, a discomedusa, a coelenterate
15 umbrella
16 tentacle
17 red coral (precious coral), a coral animal (anthozoan, reef-building animal)
18 coral colony
19 coral polyp
20-26 worms (Vermes)
20 leech, an annelid
21 sucker
22 Spirographis, a bristle worm
23 tube
24 earthworm
25 segment
26 clitellum [accessory reproductive organ]
27-36 molluscs (*Am.* mollusks)
27 edible snail, a snail
28 creeping foot
29 shell (snail shell)
30 stalked eye
31 tentacles (feelers)
32 oyster
33 freshwater pearl mussel
34 mother-of-pearl (nacre)
35 pearl
36 mussel shell
37 cuttlefish, a cephalopod
38, 39 echinoderms
38 starfish (sea star)
39 sea urchin (sea hedgehog)

1, 2 crustaceans
1 mitten crab, a crab
2 water slater
3-39, 48-56 insects
3 water nymph (dragonfly), a homopteran (homopterous insect)
4 water scorpion (water bug), a rhynchophore
5 raptorial leg
6 mayfly (dayfly, ephemerid)
7 compound eye
8 green grasshopper (green locust, meadow grasshopper), an orthopteron (orthopterous insect)
9 larva (grub)
10 adult insect, an imago
11 leaping hind leg
12 caddis fly (spring fly, water moth), a neuropteran
13 aphid (greenfly), a plant louse
14 wingless aphid
15 winged aphid
16-20 dipterous insects (dipterans)
16 gnat (mosquito, midge), a culicid
17 proboscis (sucking organ)
18 bluebottle (blowfly), a fly
19 maggot (larva)
20 chrysalis (pupa)
21-23 Hymenoptera
21, 22 ant
21 winged female
22 worker
23 bumblebee (humblebee)
24-39 beetles (Coleoptera)
24 stag beetle, a lamellicorn beetle
25 mandibles
26 trophi
27 antenna (feeler)
28 head
29, 30 thorax
29 thoracic shield (prothorax)
30 scutellum
31 tergites
32 stigma
33 wing (hind wing)
34 nervure
35 point at which the wing folds
36 elytron (forewing)
37 ladybird (*Am.* ladybug), a coccinellid
38 Ergates faber, a longicorn beetle (longicorn)
39 dung beetle, a lamellicorn beetle
40-47 arachnids
40 Euscorpius flavicandus, a scorpion
41 cheliped with chelicer
42 maxillary antenna (maxillary feeler)
43 tail sting
44-46 spiders
44 wood tick (dog tick)
45 cross spider (garden spider), an orb spinner
46 spinneret
47 spider's web (web)
48-56 Lepidoptera (butterflies and moths)
48 mulberry-feeding moth (silk moth), a bombycid moth
49 eggs
50 silkworm
51 cocoon
52 swallowtail, a butterfly
53 antenna (feeler)
54 eyespot
55 privet hawkmoth, a hawkmoth (sphinx)
56 proboscis

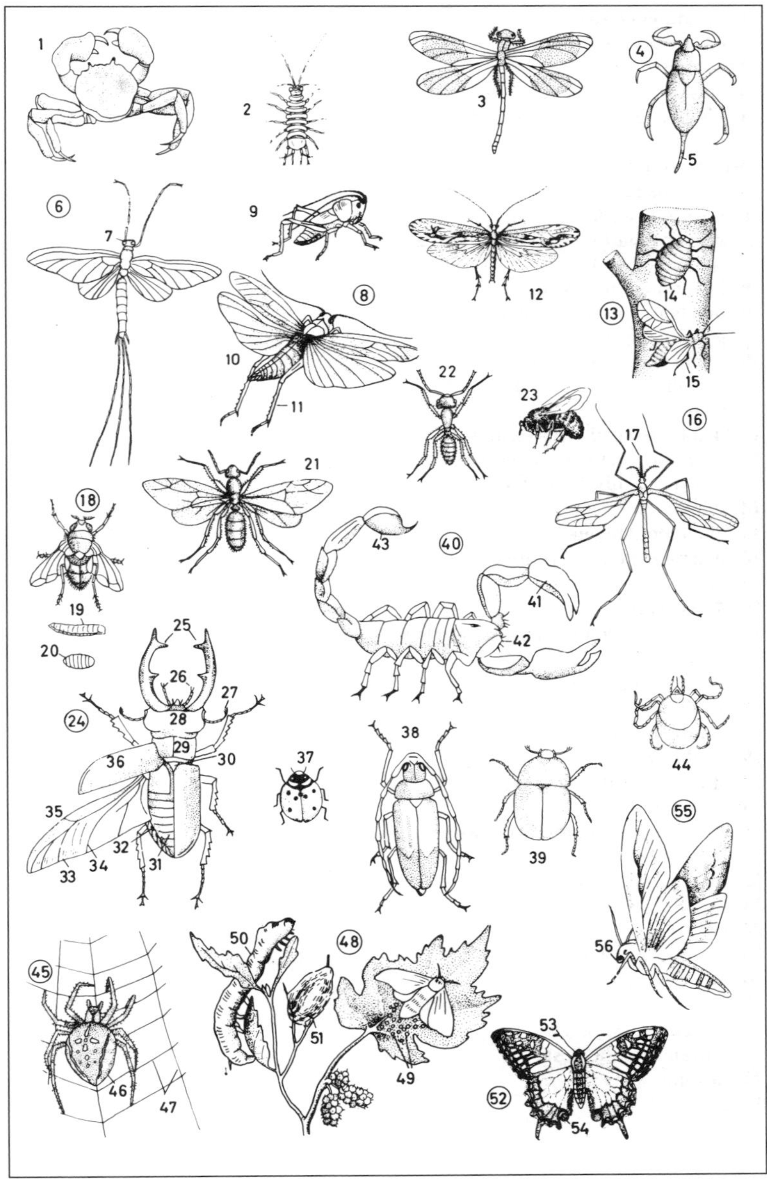
1
2
3
4
5
6
7
8
9
10
11
12
13
14
15
16
17
18
19
20
21
22
23
24
25
26
27
28
29
30
31
32
33
34
35
36
37
38
39
40
41
42
43
44
45
46
47
48
49
50
51
52
53
54
55
56

359 Birds I

1-3 flightless birds
1 cassowary; *sim.:* emu
2 ostrich
3 clutch of ostrich eggs [12 - 14 eggs]
4 king penguin, a penguin, a flightless bird
5-10 web-footed birds
5 white pelican
6 webfoot (webbed foot)
7 web (palmations) of webbed foot (palmate foot)
8 lower mandible with gular pouch
9 northern gannet (gannet, solan goose), a gannet
10 green cormorant (shag), a cormorant displaying with spread wings
11-14 long-winged birds (seabirds)
11 common sea swallow, a sea swallow (tern), diving for food
12 fulmar
13 guillemot, an auk
14 black-headed gull (mire crow), a gull
15-17 Anseres
15 goosander (common merganser), a sawbill
16 mute swan, a swan
17 knob on the bill
18 common heron, a heron
19-21 plovers
19 stilt (stilt bird, stilt plover)
20 coot, a rail
21 lapwing (green plover, peewit, pewit)
22 quail, a gallinaceous bird
23 turtle dove, a pigeon
24 swift
25 hoopoe, a roller
26 erectile crest
27 spotted woodpecker, a woodpecker; *related:* wryneck
28 entrance to the nest
29 nesting cavity
30 cuckoo

1
2
4
3
8
11
12
9
5
13
10
6
7
14
15
17
16
20
21
18
19
22
29
28
24
27
26
23
25
30

360 Birds II (European Birds)

1, 3, 4, 5, 7, 9, 10 songbirds
1 goldfinch, a finch
2 bee eater
3 redstart (star finch), a thrush
4 bluetit, a tit (titmouse), a resident bird (non-migratory bird)
5 bullfinch
6 common roller (roller)
7 golden oriole, a migratory bird
8 kingfisher
9 white wagtail, a wagtail
10 chaffinch

1
2
3
4
5
6
7
8
9
10
S. Vogel

361 Birds III (Passerines)

1-20 songbirds
1-3 Corvidae (corvine birds, crows)
1 jay (nutcracker)
2 rook, a crow
3 magpie
4 starling (pastor, shepherd bird)
5 house sparrow
6-8 finches
6, 7 buntings
6 yellowhammer (yellow bunting)
7 ortolan (ortolan bunting)
8 siskin (aberdevine)
9 great titmouse (great tit, ox eye), a titmouse (tit)
10 golden-crested wren (goldcrest); *sim.:* firecrest, one of the Regulidae
11 nuthatch
12 wren
13-17 thrushes
13 blackbird
14 nightingale (*poet.:* philomel, philomela)
15 robin (redbreast, robin redbreast)
16 song thrush (throstle, mavis)
17 thrush nightingale
18, 19 larks
18 woodlark
19 crested lark (tufted lark)
20 common swallow (barn swallow, chimney swallow), a swallow

1-13 diurnal birds of prey
1-4 falcons
1 merlin
2 peregrine falcon
3 leg feathers
4 tarsus
5-9 eagles
5 white-tailed sea eagle (white-tailed eagle, grey sea eagle, erne)
6 hooked beak
7 claw (talon)
8 tail
9 common buzzard
10-13 accipiters
10 goshawk
11 common European kite (glede, kite)
12 sparrow hawk (spar-hawk)
13 marsh harrier (moor buzzard, moor harrier, moor hawk)
14-19 owls
14 long-eared owl (horned owl)
15 eagle-owl (great horned owl)
16 plumicorn (feathered ear, ear tuft, ear, horn)
17 barn owl (white owl, silver owl, yellow owl, church owl, screech owl)
18 facial disc (disk)
19 little owl (sparrow owl)

363 Birds V (Exotic Birds)

1 sulphur-crested cockatoo, a parrot
2 blue-and-yellow macaw
3 blue bird of paradise
4 sappho
5 cardinal (cardinal bird)
6 toucan (red-billed toucan), one of the Piciformes

1
2
3
4
5
6

1-18 fishes
1 man-eater (blue shark, requin), a shark
2 nose (snout)
3 gill slit (gill cleft)
4 mirror carp
5 gill cover (operculum)
6 dorsal fin
7 pectoral fin
8 pelvic fin (abdominal fin, ventral fin)
9 anal fin
10 caudal fin (tail fin)
11 scale
12 catfish (sheatfish, sheathfish, wels)
13 barbel
14 herring
15 brown trout
16 pike (northern pike)
17 freshwater eel (eel)
18 sea horse (Hippocampus, horse-fish)
19 tufted gills
20-26 **Amphibia** (amphibians)
20-22 salamanders
20 greater water newt (crested newt), a water newt
21 dorsal crest
22 fire salamander, a salamander
23-26 salientians (anurans, batrachians)
23 European toad, a toad
24 tree frog (tree toad)
25 vocal sac (vocal pouch, croaking sac)
26 adhesive disc (disk)
27-41 **reptiles**
27, 30-37 lizards
27 sand lizard
28 hawksbill turtle (hawksbill)
29 carapace (shell)
30 basilisk
31 desert monitor, a monitor lizard (monitor)
32 common iguana, an iguana
33 chameleon, one of the Chamaeleontidae (Rhiptoglossa)
34 prehensile foot
35 prehensile tail
36 wall gecko, a gecko
37 slowworm (blindworm), one of the Anguidae
38-41 **snakes**
38 ringed snake (ring snake, water snake, grass snake), a colubrid
39 collar
40, 41 vipers (adders)
40 common viper, a poisonous (venomous) snake
41 asp (asp viper)

1
2
3
4
5
6
7
8
9
10
11
12
13
14
15
16
17
18
19
20
21
22
23
24
25
26
27
28
29
30
31
32
33
34
35
36
37
38
39
40
41

365 Lepidoptera (Butterflies and Moths)

1-6 butterflies
1 red admiral
2 peacock butterfly
3 orange tip (orange tip butterfly)
4 brimstone (brimstone butterfly)
5 Camberwell beauty (mourning cloak, mourning cloak butterfly)
6 blue (lycaenid butterfly, lycaenid)
7-11 moths (Heterocera)
7 garden tiger
8 red underwing
9 death's-head moth (death's-head hawkmoth), a hawkmoth (sphinx)
10 caterpillar
11 chrysalis (pupa)

1
2
3
4
5
6
7
8
9
10
11

1 platypus (duck-bill, duck-mole), a monotreme (oviparous mammal)
2, 3 **marsupial mammals** (marsupials)
2 New World opossum, a didelphid
3 red kangaroo (red flyer), a kangaroo
4-7 **insectivores** (insect-eating mammals)
4 mole
5 hedgehog
6 spine
7 shrew (shrew mouse), one of the Soricidae
8 nine-banded armadillo (peba)
9 long-eared bat (flitter-mouse), a flying mammal (chiropter, chiropteran)
10 pangolin (scaly ant-eater), a scaly mammal
11 two-toed sloth (unau)
12-19 **rodents**
12 guinea pig (cavy)
13 porcupine
14 beaver
15 jerboa
16 hamster
17 water vole
18 marmot
19 squirrel
20 African elephant, a proboscidean (proboscidian)
21 trunk (proboscis)
22 tusk
23 manatee (manati, lamantin), a sirenian
24 South African dassie (das, coney, hyrax), a procaviid
25-31 **ungulates**
25-27 **odd-toed ungulates**
25 African black rhino, a rhinoceros (nasicorn)
26 Brazilian tapir, a tapir
27 zebra
28-31 **even-toed ungulates**
28-30 **ruminants**
28 llama
29 Bactrian camel (two-humped camel)
30 guanaco
31 hippopotamus

1
2
3
4
5
6
7
8
9
10
11
12
13
14
15
16
17
18
19
20
21
22
23
24
25
26
27
28
29
30
31

367 Mammals II

1-10 ungulates, ruminants
1 elk (moose)
2 wapiti (*Am.* elk)
3 chamois
4 giraffe
5 black buck, an antelope
6 mouflon (moufflon)
7 ibex (rock goat, bouquetin, steinbock)
8 water buffalo (Indian buffalo, water ox)
9 bison
10 musk ox
11-22 carnivores (beasts of prey)
11-13 Canidae
11 black-backed jackal (jackal)
12 red fox
13 wolf
14-17 martens
14 stone marten (beach marten)
15 sable
16 weasel
17 sea otter, an otter
18-22 seals (pinnipeds)
18 fur seal (sea bear, ursine seal)
19 common seal (sea calf, sea dog)
20 walrus (morse)
21 whiskers
22 tusk
23-29 whales
23 bottle-nosed dolphin (bottle-nose dolphin)
24 common dolphin
25 sperm whale (cachalot)
26 blowhole (spout hole)
27 dorsal fin
28 flipper
29 tail flukes (tail)

1
2
3
4
5
6
7
8
9
10
11
12
13
14
15
16
17
18
19
20
21
22
23
24
25
26
27
28
29

1-11 carnivores (beasts of prey)
1 striped hyena, a hyena
2-8 felines (cats)
2 lion
3 mane (lion's mane)
4 paw
5 tiger
6 leopard
7 cheetah (hunting leopard)
8 lynx
9-11 bears
9 raccoon (racoon, *Am.* coon)
10 brown bear
11 polar bear (white bear)
12-16 primates
12, 13 monkeys
12 rhesus monkey (rhesus, rhesus macaque)
13 baboon
14-16 anthropoids (anthropoid apes, great apes)
14 chimpanzee
15 orang-utan (orang-outan)
16 gorilla

1
3
2
4
5
6
7
8
9
10
11
14
12
15
16
13

1
2
3
4
5
6
7
8
9
10
11
12
13
14
15
16
17
18
19
20
S. Vogel

1 Gigantocypris agassizi
2 Eupharynx pelecanoides (pelican eel, pelican fish)
3 Metacrinus (feather star), a sea lily, an echinoderm
4 Lycoteuthis diadema (jewelled squid), a cuttlefish [luminescent]
5 Atolla, a deep-sea medusa, a coelenterate
6 Melanocetes, a pediculate [luminescent]
7 Lophocalyx philippensis, a glass sponge
8 Mopsea, a sea fan [colony]
9 Hydrallmania, a hydroid polyp, a coelenterate [colony]
10 Malacosteus indicus, a stomiatid [luminescent]
11 Brisinga endecacnemos, a sand star (brittle star), an echinoderm [luminescent only when stimulated]
12 Pasiphaea, a shrimp, a crustacean
13 Echiostoma, a stomiatid, a fish [luminescent]
14 Umbellula encrinus, a sea pen (sea feather), a coelenterate [colony, luminescent]
15 Polycheles, a crustacean
16 Lithodes, a crustacean, a crab
17 Archaster, a starfish (sea star), an echinoderm
18 Oneirophanta, a sea cucumber, an echinoderm
19 Palaeopneustes niasicus, a sea urchin (sea hedgehog), an echinoderm
20 Chitonactis, a sea anemone (actinia), a coelenterate

1 tree
2 bole (tree trunk, trunk, stem)
3 crown of tree (crown)
4 top of tree (treetop)
5 bough (limb, branch)
6 twig (branch)
7 bole (tree trunk) [cross section]
8 bark (rind)
9 phloem (bast sieve tissue, inner fibrous bark)
10 cambium (cambium ring)
11 medullary rays (vascular rays, pith rays)
12 sapwood (sap, alburnum)
13 heartwood (duramen)
14 pith
15 **plant**
16-18 root
16 primary root
17 secondary root
18 root hair
19-25 shoot (sprout)
19 leaf
20 stalk
21 side shoot (offshoot)
22 terminal bud
23 flower
24 flower bud
25 leaf axil with axillary bud
26 **leaf**
27 leaf stalk (petiole)
28 leaf blade (blade, lamina)
29 venation (veins, nervures, ribs)
30 midrib (nerve)
31-38 leaf shapes
31 linear
32 lanceolate
33 orbicular (orbiculate)
34 acerose (acerous, acerate, acicular, needle-shaped)
35 cordate
36 ovate
37 sagittate
38 reniform
39-42 compound leaves
39 digitate (digitated, palmate, quinquefoliolate)
40 pinnatifid
41 abruptly pinnate
42 odd-pinnate
43-50 leaf margin shapes
43 entire
44 serrate (serrulate, saw-toothed)
45 doubly toothed
46 crenate
47 dentate
48 sinuate
49 ciliate (ciliated)
50 cilium
51 **flower**
52 flower stalk (flower stem, scape)
53 receptacle (floral axis, thalamus, torus)
54 ovary
55 style
56 stigma
57 stamen
58 sepal
59 petal
60 ovary and stamen [section]
61 ovary wall
62 ovary cavity
63 ovule
64 embryo sac
65 pollen
66 pollen tube
67-77 inflorescences
67 spike (racemose spike)
68 raceme (simple raceme)
69 panicle
70 cyme
71 spadix (fleshy spike)
72 umbel (simple umbel)
73 capitulum
74 composite head (discoid flower head)
75 hollow flower head
76 bostryx (helicoid cyme)
77 cincinnus (scorpioid cyme, curled cyme)
78-82 roots
78 adventitious roots
79 tuber (tuberous root, swollen taproot)
80 adventitious roots (aerial roots)
81 root thorns
82 pneumatophores
83-85 blade of grass
83 leaf sheath
84 ligule (ligula)
85 leaf blade (lamina)
86 embryo (seed, germ)
87 cotyledon (seed leaf, seed lobe)
88 radicle
89 hypocotyl
90 plumule (leaf bud)
91-102 fruits
91-96 dehiscent fruits
91 follicle
92 legume (pod)
93 siliqua (pod)
94 schizocarp
95 pyxidium (circumscissile seed vessel)
96 poricidal capsule (porose capsule)
97-102 indehiscent fruits
97 berry
98 nut
99 drupe (stone fruit) (cherry)
100 aggregate fruit (compound fruit) (rose hip)
101 aggregate fruit (compound fruit) (raspberry)
102 pome (apple)

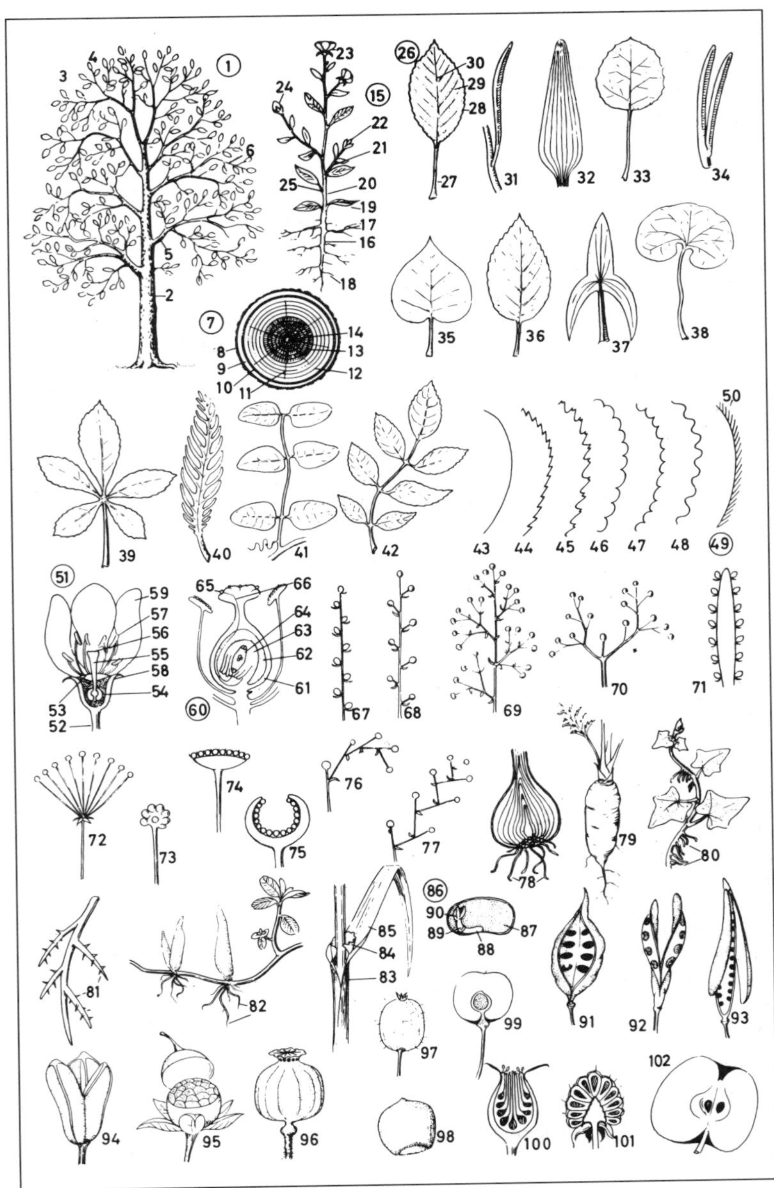
1
2
3
4
5
6
7
8
9
10
11
12
13
14
15
16
17
18
19
20
21
22
23
24
25
26
27
28
29
30
31
32
33
34
35
36
37
38
39
40
41
42
43
44
45
46
47
48
49
50
51
52
53
54
55
56
57
58
59
60
61
62
63
64
65
66
67
68
69
70
71
72
73
74
75
76
77
78
79
80
81
82
83
84
85
86
87
88
89
90
91
92
93
94
95
96
97
98
99
100
101
102

371 Deciduous Trees

1-73 deciduous trees
1 oak (oak tree)
2 flowering branch
3 fruiting branch
4 fruit (acorn)
5 cupule (cup)
6 female flower
7 bract
8 male inflorescence
9 birch (birch tree)
10 branch with catkins, a flowering branch
11 fruiting branch
12 scale (catkin scale)
13 female flower
14 male flower
15 poplar
16 flowering branch
17 flower
18 fruiting branch
19 fruit
20 seed
21 leaf of the aspen (trembling poplar)
22 infructescence
23 leaf of the white poplar (silver poplar, silverleaf)
24 sallow (goat willow)
25 branch with flower buds
26 catkin with single flower
27 branch with leaves
28 fruit
29 osier branch with leaves
30 alder
31 fruiting branch
32 branch with previous year's cone
33 beech (beech tree)
34 flowering branch
35 flower
36 fruiting branch
37 beech nut
38 ash (ash tree)
39 flowering branch
40 flower
41 fruiting branch
42 mountain ash (rowan, quickbeam)
43 inflorescence
44 infructescence
45 fruit [longitudinal section]
46 lime (lime tree, linden, linden tree)
47 fruiting branch
48 inflorescence
49 elm (elm tree)
50 fruiting branch
51 flowering branch
52 flower
53 maple (maple tree)
54 flowering branch
55 flower
56 fruiting branch
57 maple seed with wings (winged maple seed)
58 horse chestnut (horse chestnut tree, chestnut, chestnut tree, buck-eye)
59 branch with young fruits
60 chestnut (horse chestnut)
61 mature (ripe) fruit
62 flower [longitudinal section]
63 hornbeam (yoke elm)
64 fruiting branch
65 seed
66 flowering branch
67 plane (plane tree)
68 leaf
69 infructescence and fruit
70 false acacia (locust tree)
71 flowering branch
72 part of the infructescence
73 base of the leaf stalk with stipules

1
4
♀
2
5
♂
4
3
6
7
8
♀
9
12
11
10 ♂
13
14
15
♀
19
17
18
♂
16
20
19
♀
30
26
24
21
25
31
♂
23
22
27
33
37
37
26
♀
32
29
♀
28
♂
36
40
35
♂
34
35
38
41
42
46 ♂
45
♀
47
49
39
44
48
50
52
43
55
51
53
63
70
65
54
64
66
♀
71
58
59
56
♂
57
67
60
61
62
69
68
72
73

1-71 coniferous trees (conifers)
1 silver fir (European silver fir, common silver fir)
2 fir cone, a fruit cone
3 cone axis
4 female flower cone
5 bract scale (bract)
6 male flower shoot
7 stamen
8 cone scale
9 seed with wing (winged seed)
10 seed [longitudinal section]
11 fir needle (needle)
12 spruce (spruce fir)
13 spruce cone
14 cone scale
15 seed
16 female flower cone
17 male inflorescence
18 stamen
19 spruce needle
20 pine (Scots pine)
21 dwarf pine
22 female flower cone
23 short shoot with bundle of two leaves
24 male inflorescences
25 annual growth
26 pine cone
27 cone scale
28 seed
29 fruit cone of the arolla pine (Swiss stone pine)
30 fruit cone of the Weymouth pine (white pine)
31 short shoot [cross section]
32 larch
33 flowering branch
34 scale of the female flower cone
35 anther
36 branch with larch cones (fruit cones)
37 seed
38 cone scale
39 arbor vitae (tree of life, thuja)
40 fruiting branch
41 fruit cone
42 scale
43 branch with male and female flowers
44 male shoot
45 scale with pollen sacs
46 female shoot
47 juniper (juniper tree)
48 female shoot [longitudinal section]
49 male shoot
50 scale with pollen sacs
51 fruiting branch
52 juniper berry
53 fruit [cross section]
54 seed
55 stone pine
56 male shoot
57 fruit cone with seeds [longitudinal section]
58 cypress
59 fruiting branch
60 seed
61 yew (yew tree)
62 male flower shoot and female flower cone
63 fruiting branch
64 fruit
65 cedar (cedar tree)
66 fruiting branch
67 fruit scale
68 male flower shoot and female flower cone
69 mammoth tree (Wellingtonia, sequoia)
70 fruiting branch
71 seed

1
2
3
4
5
6
7
8
9
10
11
12
13
14
15
16
17
18
19
20
21
22
23
24
25
26
27
28
29
30
31
32
33
34
35
36
37
38
39
40
41
42
43
44
45
46
47
48
49
50
51
52
53
54
55
56
57
58
59
60
61
62
63
64
65
66
67
68
69
70
71
♀
♂

373 Ornamental Shrubs and Trees I

1 forsythia
2 ovary and stamen
3 leaf
4 yellow-flowered jasmine (jasmin, jessamine)
5 flower [longitudinal section] with styles, ovaries, and stamens
6 privet (common privet)
7 flower
8 infructescence
9 mock orange (sweet syringa)
10 snowball (snowball bush, guelder rose)
11 flower
12 fruits
13 oleander (rosebay, rose laurel)
14 flower [longitudinal section]
15 red magnolia
16 leaf
17 japonica (japanese quince)
18 fruit
19 common box (box, box tree)
20 female flower
21 male flower
22 fruit [longitudinal section]
23 weigela (weigelia)
24 yucca [part of the inflorescence]
25 leaf
26 dog rose (briar rose, wild briar)
27 fruit
28 kerria
29 fruit
30 cornelian cherry
31 flower
32 fruit (cornelian cherry)
33 sweet gale (gale)

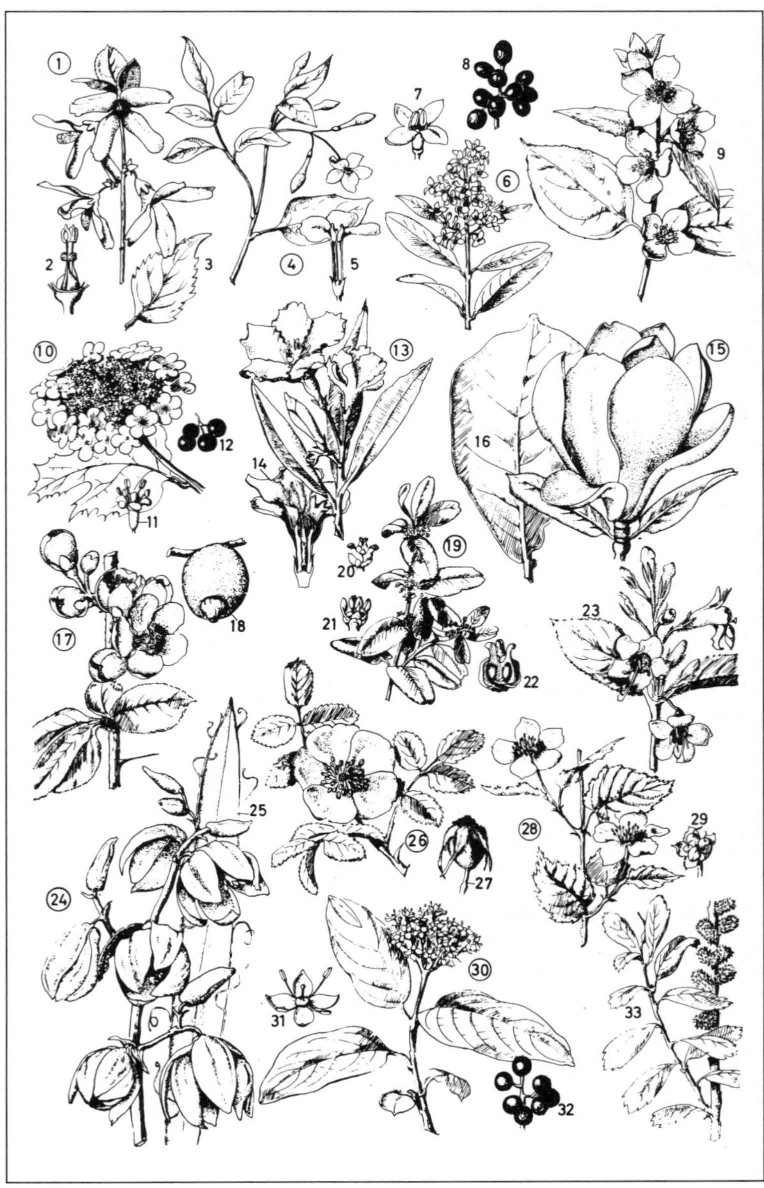
1
2
3
4
5
6
7
8
9
10
11
12
13
14
15
16
17
18
19
20
21
22
23
24
25
26
27
28
29
30
31
32
33

374 Ornamental Shrubs and Trees II

1 tulip tree (tulip poplar, saddle tree, whitewood)
2 carpels
3 stamen
4 fruit
5 hyssop
6 flower [front view]
7 flower
8 calyx with fruit
9 holly
10 androgynous (hermaphroditic, hermaphrodite) flower
11 male flower
12 fruit with stones exposed
13 honeysuckle (woodbine, woodbind)
14 flower buds
15 flower [cut open]
16 Virginia creeper (American ivy, woodbine)
17 open flower
18 infructescence
19 fruit [longitudinal section]
20 broom
21 flower with the petals removed
22 immature (unripe) legume (pod)
23 spiraea
24 flower [longitudinal section]
25 fruit
26 carpel
27 blackthorn (sloe)
28 leaves
29 fruits
30 single-pistilled hawthorn (thorn, may)
31 fruit
32 laburnum (golden chain, golden rain)
33 raceme
34 fruits
35 black elder (elder)
36 elder flowers
37 elderberries

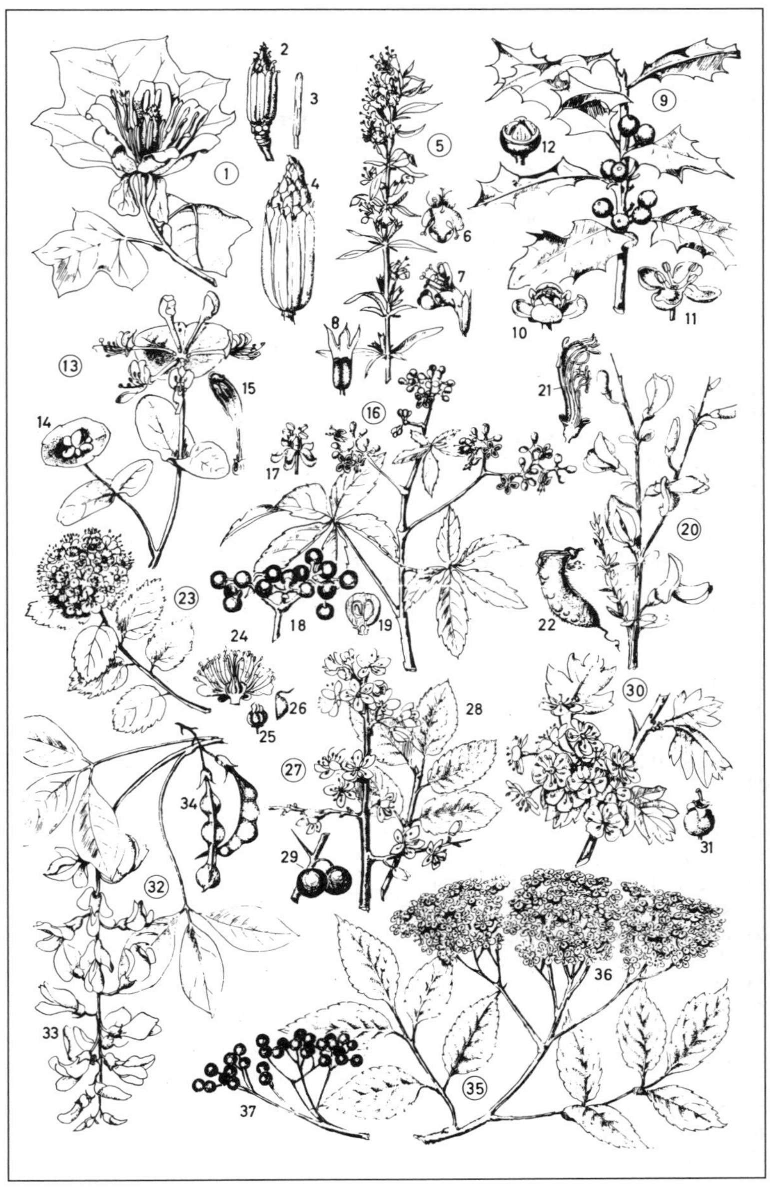
1
2
3
4
5
6
7
8
9
10
11
12
13
14
15
16
17
18
19
20
21
22
23
24
25
26
27
28
29
30
31
32
33
34
35
36
37

375 Meadow Flowers and Wayside Flowers (Wild Flowers) I

1 rotundifoliate (rotundifolious) saxifrage (rotundifoliate breakstone)
2 leaf
3 flower
4 fruit
5 anemone (windflower)
6 flower [longitudinal section]
7 fruit
8 buttercup (meadow buttercup, butterflower, goldcup, king cup, crowfoot)
9 basal leaf
10 fruit
11 lady's smock (ladysmock, cuckoo flower)
12 basal leaf
13 fruit
14 harebell (hairbell, bluebell)
15 basal leaf
16 flower [longitudinal section]
17 fruit
18 ground ivy (ale hoof)
19 flower [longitudinal section]
20 flower [front view]
21 stonecrop
22 speedwell
23 flower
24 fruit
25 seed
26 moneywort
27 dehisced fruit
28 seed
29 small scabious
30 basal leaf
31 ray floret (flower of outer series)
32 disc (disk) floret (flower of inner series)
33 involucral calyx with pappus bristles
34 ovary with pappus
35 fruit
36 lesser celandine
37 fruit
38 leaf axil with bulbil
39 annual meadow grass
40 flower
41 spikelet [side view]
42 spikelet [front view]
43 caryopsis, an indehiscent fruit
44 tuft of grass (clump of grass)
45 comfrey
46 flower [longitudinal section]
47 fruit

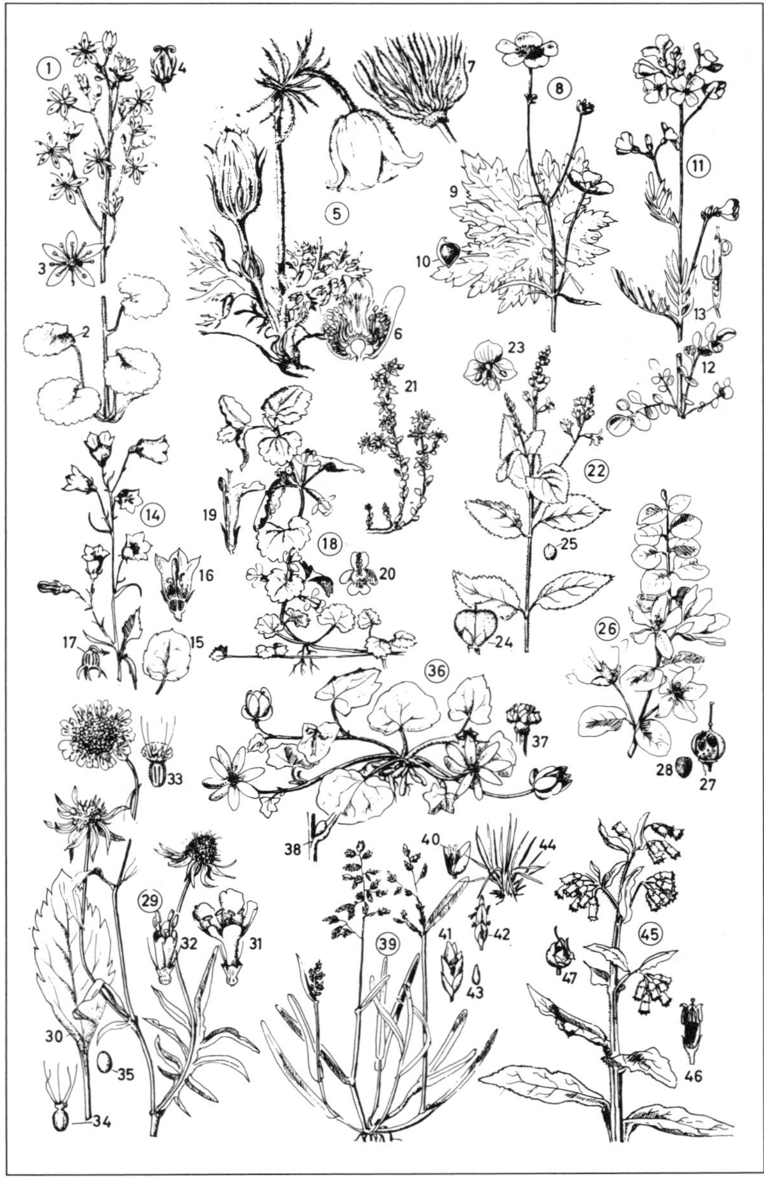
1
4
7
8
11
9
5
10
3
13
2
6
23
21
12
22
14
19
18
25
16
20
17
24
15
26
36
37
33
28
27
38
40
44
29
32
31
41
42
45
39
43
47
30
35
46
34

376 Meadow Flowers and Wayside Flowers (Wild Flowers) II

1 daisy (*Am.* English daisy)
2 flower
3 fruit
4 oxeye daisy (white oxeye daisy, marguerite)
5 flower
6 fruit
7 masterwort
8 cowslip
9 great mullein (Aaron's rod, shepherd's club)
10 bistort (snakeweed)
11 flower
12 knapweed
13 common mallow
14 fruit
15 yarrow
16 self-heal
17 bird's foot trefoil (bird's foot clover)
18 horsetail (equisetum) [a shoot]
19 flower (strobile)
20 campion (catchfly)
21 ragged robin (cuckoo flower)
22 birthwort
23 flower
24 crane's bill
25 wild chicory (witloof, succory, wild endive)
26 common toadflax (butter-and-eggs)
27 lady's slipper (Venus's slipper, *Am.* moccasin flower)
28 orchis (wild orchid), an orchid

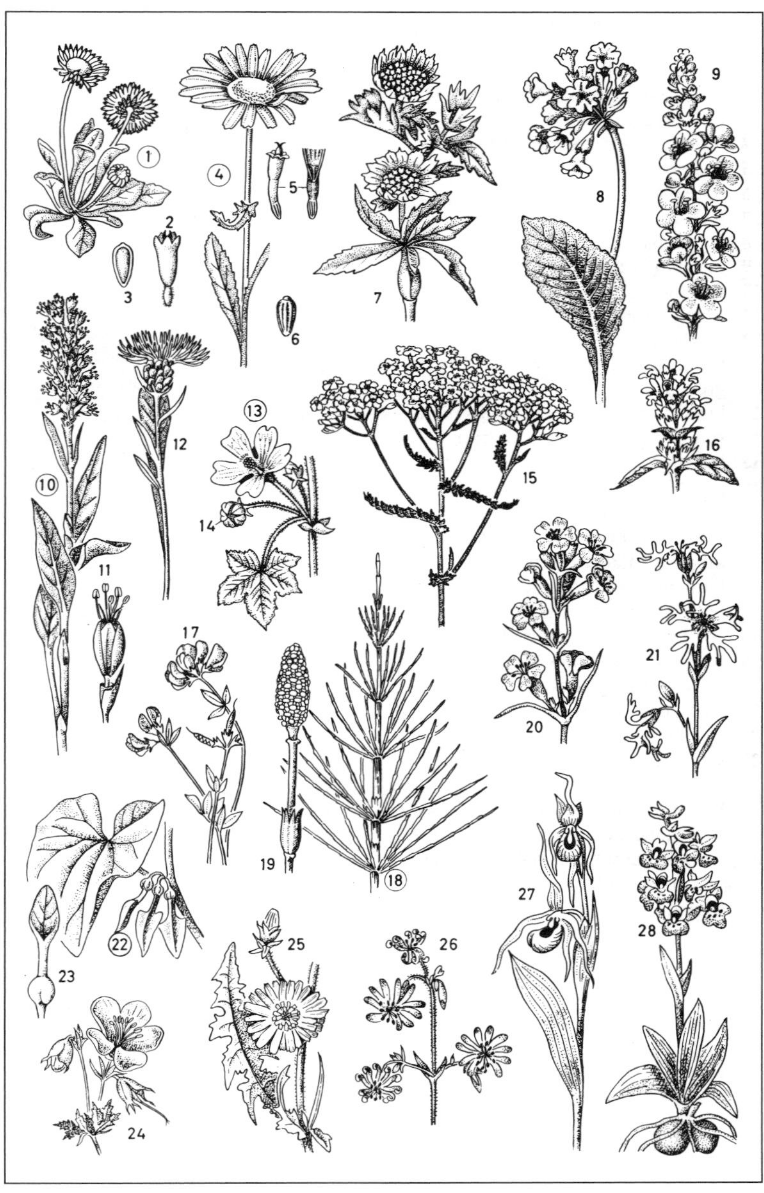
1
2
3
4
5
6
7
8
9
10
11
12
13
14
15
16
17
18
19
20
21
22
23
24
25
26
27
28

377 Plants of Forest, Marsh, and Heathland

1 wood anemone (anemone, windflower)
2 lily of the valley
3 cat's foot (milkwort); *sim.*: sandflower (everlasting)
4 turk's cap (turk's cap lily)
5 goatsbeard (goat's beard)
6 ramson
7 lungwort
8 corydalis
9 orpine (livelong)
10 daphne
11 touch-me-not
12 staghorn (stag horn moss, stag's horn, stag's horn moss, coral evergreen)
13 butterwort, an insectivorous plant
14 sundew; *sim.*: Venus's flytrap
15 bearberry
16 polypody (polypod), a fern; *sim.*: male fern, brake (bracken, eagle fern), royal fern (royal osmund, king's fern, ditch fern)
17 haircap moss (hair moss, golden maidenhair), a moss
18 cotton grass (cotton rush)
19 heather (heath, ling); *sim.*: bell heather (cross-leaved heather)
20 rock rose (sun rose)
21 marsh tea
22 sweet flag (sweet calamus, sweet sedge)
23 bilberry (whortleberry, huckleberry, blueberry); *sim.*: cowberry (red whortleberry), bog bilberry (bog whortleberry), crowberry (crakeberry)

1
2
3
4
5
6
7
8
9
10
11
12
13
14
15
16
17
18
19
20
21
22
23

378 Alpine Plants, Aquatic Plants (Water Plants), and Marsh Plants

1-13 alpine plants
1 alpine rose (alpine rhododendron)
2 flowering shoot
3 alpine soldanella (soldanella)
4 corolla opened out
5 seed vessel with the style
6 alpine wormwood
7 inflorescence
8 auricula
9 edelweiss
10 flower shapes
11 fruit with pappus tuft
12 part of flower head (of capitulum)
13 stemless alpine gentian
14-57 aquatic plants (water plants) **and marsh plants**
14 white water lily
15 leaf
16 flower
17 Queen Victoria water lily (Victoria regia water lily, royal water lily, Amazon water lily)
18 leaf
19 underside of the leaf
20 flower
21 reed mace bulrush (cattail, cat's tail, cattail flag, club rush)
22 male part of the spadix
23 male flower
24 female part
25 female flower
26 forget-me-not
27 flowering shoot
28 flower [section]
29 frog's bit
30 watercress
31 stalk with flowers and immature (unripe) fruits
32 flower
33 siliqua (pod) with seeds
34 two seeds
35 duckweed (duck's meat)
36 plant in flower
37 flower
38 fruit
39 flowering rush
40 flower umbel
41 leaves
42 fruit
43 green alga
44 water plantain
45 leaf
46 panicle
47 flower
48 honey wrack, a brown alga
49 thallus (plant body, frond)
50 holdfast
51 arrow head
52 leaf shapes
53 inflorescence with male flowers [above] and female flowers [below]
54 sea grass
55 inflorescence
56 Canadian waterweed (Canadian pondweed)
57 flower

1
2
3
4
5
6
7
8
9
10
11
12
13
14
15
16
17
18
19
20
21
22
23
24
25
26
27
28
29
30
31
32
33
34
35
36
37
38
39
40
41
42
43
44
45
46
47
48
49
50
51
52
53
54
55
56
57

379 Poisonous Plants

1 aconite (monkshood, wolfsbane, helmet flower)
2 foxglove (Digitalis)
3 meadow saffron (naked lady, naked boys)
4 hemlock (Conium)
5 black nightshade (common nightshade, petty morel)
6 henbane
7 deadly nightshade (belladonna, banewort, dwale), a solanaceous herb
8 thorn apple (stramonium, stramony, *Am.* jimson weed, jimpson weed, Jamestown weed, stinkweed)
9 cuckoo pint (lords-and-ladies, wild arum, wake-robin)
10-13 poisonous fungi (poisonous mushrooms, toadstools)
10 fly agaric (fly amanita, fly fungus), an agaric
11 amanita
12 Satan's mushroom
13 woolly milk cap

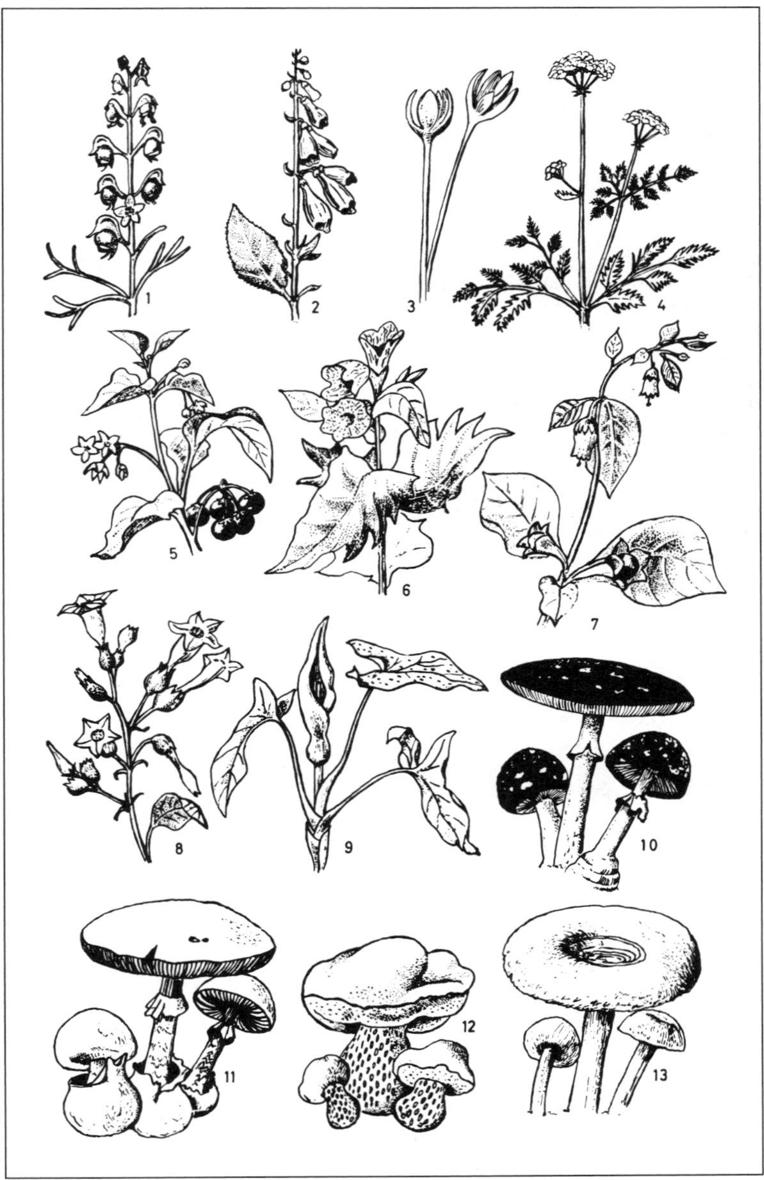
1
2
3
4
5
6
7
8
9
10
11
12
13

380 Medicinal Plants

1 camomile (chamomile, wild camomile)
2 arnica
3 peppermint
4 wormwood (absinth)
5 valerian (allheal)
6 fennel
7 lavender
8 coltsfoot
9 tansy
10 centaury
11 ribwort (ribwort plantain, ribgrass)
12 marshmallow
13 alder buckthorn (alder dogwood)
14 castor-oil plant (Palma Christi)
15 opium poppy
16 senna (cassia); *the dried leaflets:* senna leaves
17 cinchona (chinchona)
18 camphor tree (camphor laurel)
19 betel palm (areca, areca palm)
20 betel nut (areca nut)

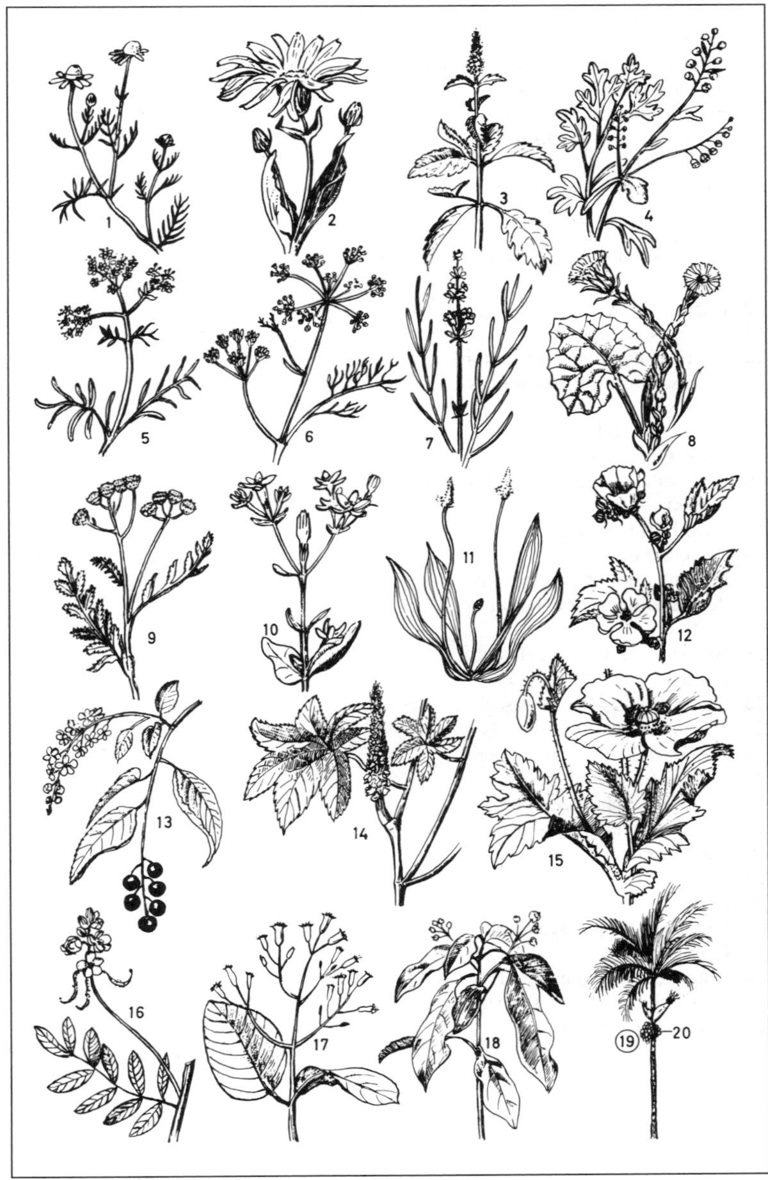
1
2
3
4
5
6
7
8
9
10
11
12
13
14
15
16
17
18
19
20

381 Edible Fungi (Esculent Fungi)

1 meadow mushroom (field mushroom)
2 mycelial threads (hyphae, mycelium) with fruiting bodies
3 mushroom [longitudinal section]
4 cap (pileus) with gills
5 veil (velum)
6 gill [section]
7 basidia [on the gill with basidiospores]
8 germinating basidiospores (spores)
9 truffle
10 truffle [external view]
11 truffle [section]
12 interior showing asci [section]
13 two asci with the ascospores (spores)
14 chanterelle (chantarelle)
15 Chestnut Boletus
16 cep (cepe, squirrel's bread, Boletus edulis)
17 layer of tubes (hymenium)
18 stem (stipe)
19 puffball (Bovista nigrescens)
20 devil's tobacco pouch (common puffball)
21 Brown Ring Boletus (Boletus luteus)
22 Birch Boletus (Boletus scaber)
23 Russula vesca
24 scaled prickle fungus
25 slender funnel fungus
26 morel (Morchella esculenta)
27 morel (Morchella conica)
28 honey fungus
29 saffron milk cap
30 parasol mushroom
31 hedgehog fungus (yellow prickle fungus)
32 yellow coral fungus (goatsbeard, goat's beard, coral Clavaria)
33 little cluster fungus

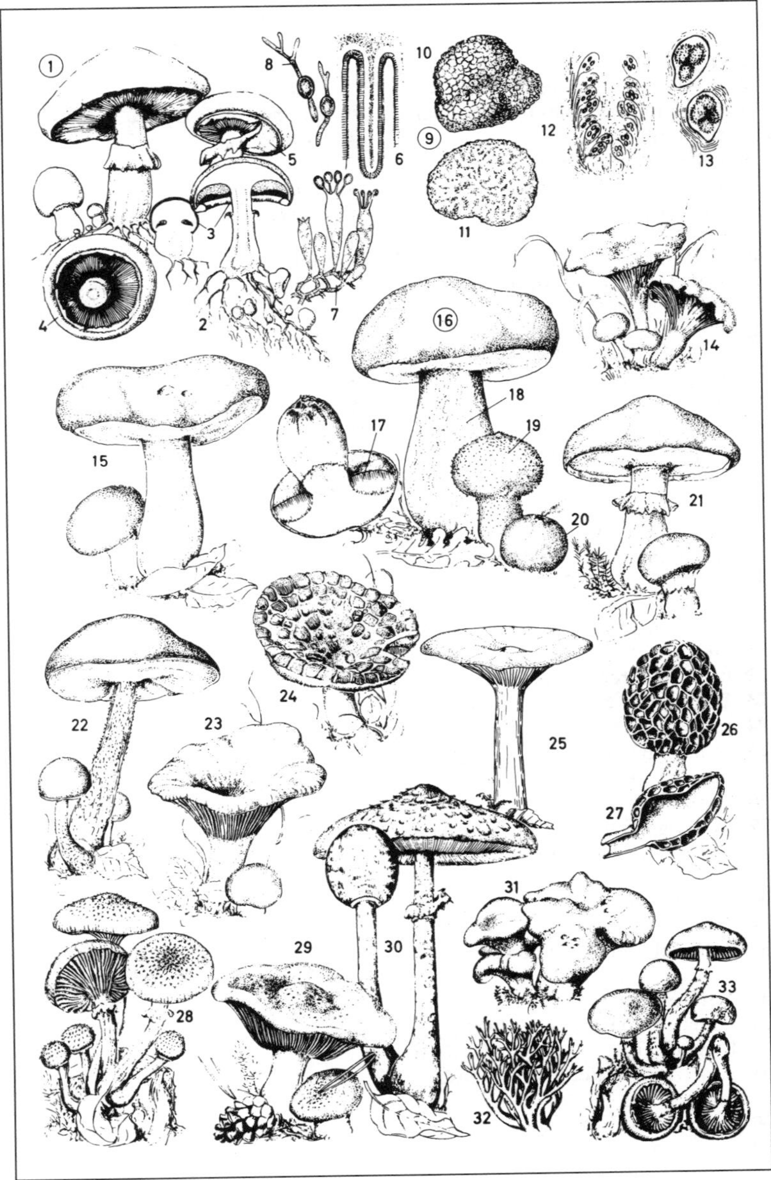
1
8
10
12
5
6
9
13
4
3
7
11
2
16
14
18
17
19
15
21
20
24
22
23
25
26
27
31
29
30
33
28
32

382 Tropical Plants used as Stimulants, Spices, and Flavourings (*Am.* Flavorings)

1 coffee tree (coffee plant)
2 fruiting branch
3 flowering branch
4 flower
5 fruit with two beans [longitudinal section]
6 coffee bean; *when processed:* coffee
7 tea plant (tea tree)
8 flowering branch
9 tea leaf; *when processed:* tea
10 fruit
11 maté shrub (maté, yerba maté, Paraguay tea)
12 flowering branch with androgynous (hermaphroditic, hermaphrodite) flowers
13 male flower
14 androgynous (hermaphroditic, hermaphrodite) flower
15 fruit
16 cacao tree (cacao)
17 branch with flowers and fruits
18 flower [longitudinal section]
19 cacao beans (cocoa beans); *when processed:* cocoa, cocoa powder
20 seed [longitudinal section]
21 embryo
22 cinnamon tree (cinnamon)
23 flowering branch
24 fruit
25 cinnamon bark; *when crushed:* cinnamon
26 clove tree
27 flowering branch
28 flower bud; *when dried:* clove
29 flower
30 nutmeg tree
31 flowering branch
32 female flower [longitudinal section]
33 mature (ripe) fruit
34 nutmeg with mace, a seed with laciniate aril
35 seed [cross section]; *when dried:* nutmeg
36 pepper plant
37 fruiting branch
38 inflorescence
39 fruit [longitudinal section] with seed (peppercorn); *when ground:* pepper
40 Virginia tobacco plant
41 flowering shoot
42 flower
43 tobacco leaf; *when cured:* tobacco
44 mature (ripe) fruit capsule
45 seed
46 vanilla plant
47 flowering shoot
48 vanilla pod; *when cured:* stick of vanilla
49 pistachio tree
50 flowering branch with female flowers
51 drupe (pistachio, pistachio nut)
52 sugar cane
53 plant in bloom
54 panicle
55 flower

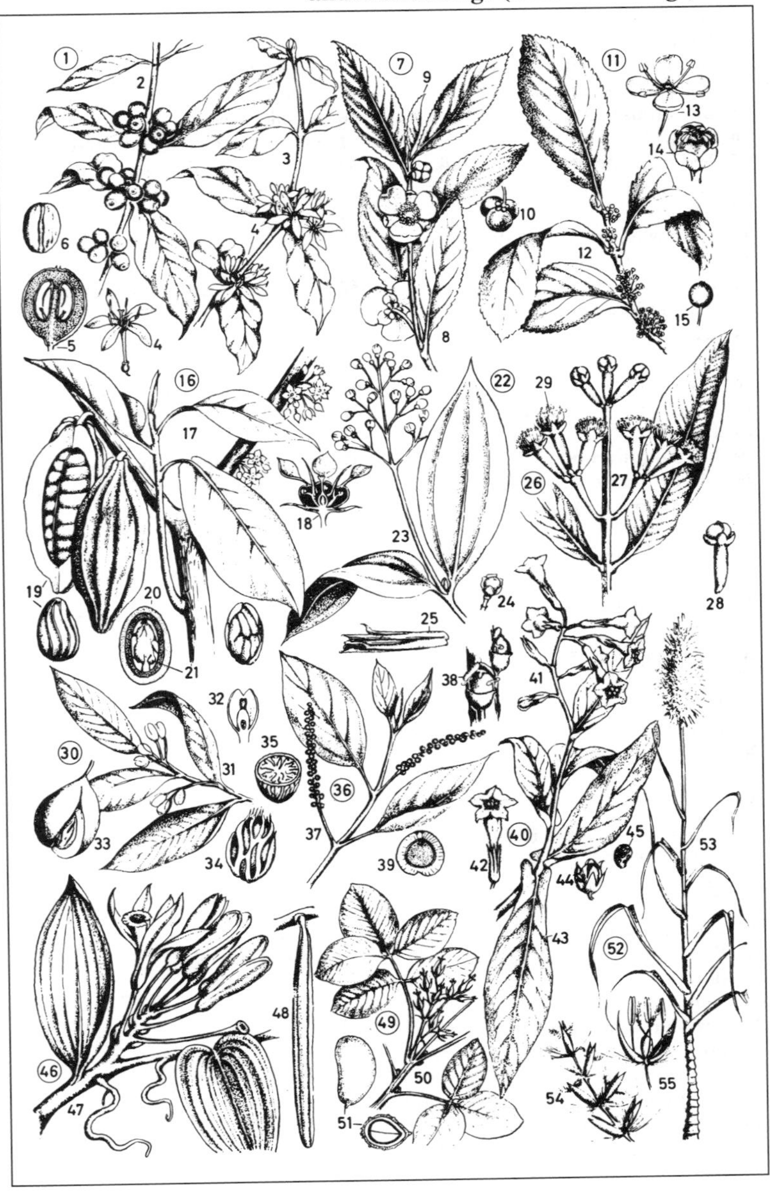
1
2
3
4
5
6
7
8
9
10
11
12
13
14
15
16
17
18
19
20
21
22
23
24
25
26
27
28
29
30
31
32
33
34
35
36
37
38
39
40
41
42
43
44
45
46
47
48
49
50
51
52
53
54
55

383 Plants used in Industry

1 rape (cole, coleseed)
2 basal leaf
3 flower [longitudinal section]
4 mature (ripe) siliqua (pod)
5 oleiferous seed
6 flax
7 peduncle (pedicel, flower stalk)
8 seed vessel (boll)
9 hemp
10 fruiting female (pistillate) plant
11 female inflorescence
12 flower
13 male inflorescence
14 fruit
15 seed
16 cotton
17 flower
18 fruit
19 lint [cotton wool]
20 silk-cotton tree (kapok tree, capoc tree, ceiba tree)
21 fruit
22 flowering branch
23 seed
24 seed [longitudinal section]
25 jute
26 flowering branch
27 flower
28 fruit
29 olive tree (olive)
30 flowering branch
31 flower
32 fruit
33 rubber tree (rubber plant)
34 fruiting branch
35 fig
36 flower
37 gutta-percha tree
38 flowering branch
39 flower
40 fruit
41 peanut (ground nut, monkey nut)
42 flowering shoot
43 root with fruits
44 nut (kernel) [longitudinal section]
45 sesame plant (simsim, benniseed)
46 flowers and fruiting branch
47 flower [longitudinal section]
48 coconut palm (coconut tree, coco palm, cocoa palm)
49 inflorescence
50 female flower
51 male flower [longitudinal section]
52 fruit [longitudinal section]
53 coconut (cokernut)
54 oil palm
55 male spadix
56 infructescence with fruit
57 seed with micropyles (foramina) (foraminate seed)
58 sago palm
59 fruit
60 bamboo stem (bamboo culm)
61 branch with leaves
62 spike
63 part of bamboo stem with joints
64 papyrus plant (paper reed, paper rush)
65 umbel
66 spike

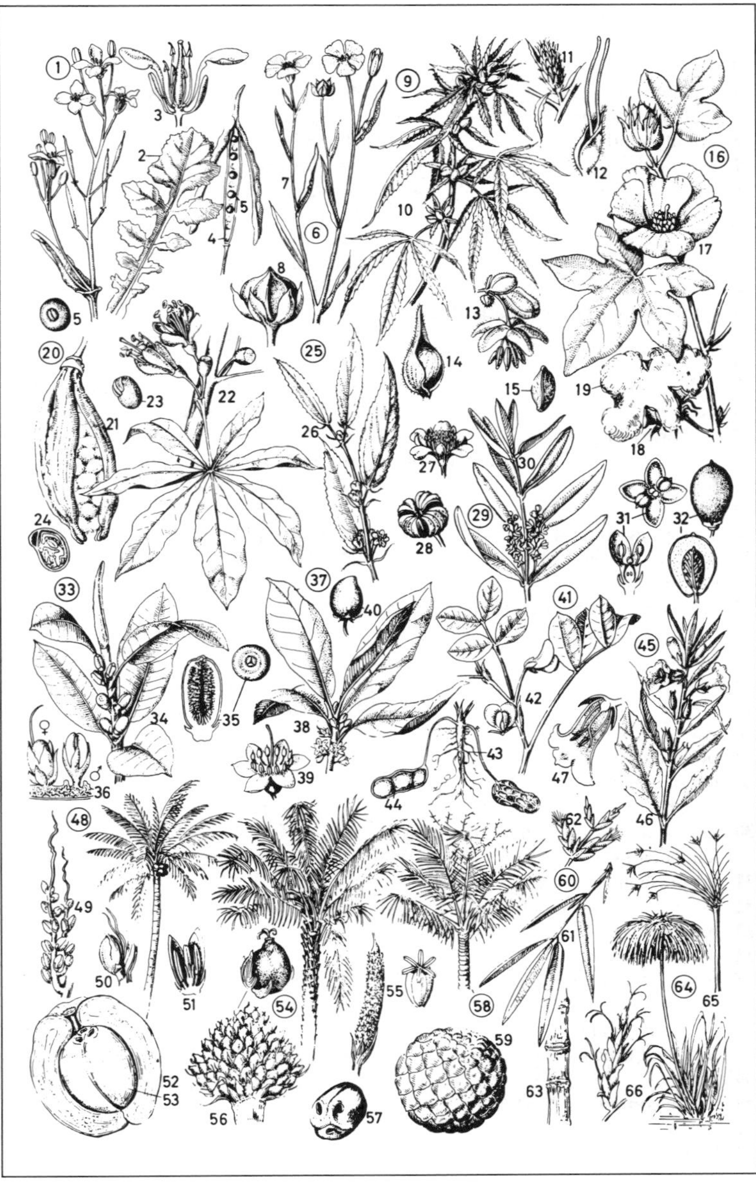
1
3
2
4
5
7
6
8
9
11
12
10
16
17
13
14
5
20
23
22
25
26
15
19
18
21
27
30
28
29
31
32
24
33
37
40
41
45
34
35
38
42
43
47
46
36
39
44
♀
♂
48
62
60
49
50
51
54
55
61
58
64
65
59
52
53
56
57
63
66

384 Southern Fruits (Tropical, Subtropical, and Mediterranean Fruits)

1 date palm (date)
2 fruiting palm
3 palm frond
4 male spadix
5 male flower
6 female spadix
7 female flower
8 stand of fruit
9 date
10 date kernel
11 fig
12 branch with pseudocarps
13 fig with flowers [longitudinal section]
14 female flower
15 male flower
16 pomegranate
17 flowering branch
18 flower [longitudinal section, corolla removed]
19 fruit
20 seed [longitudinal section]
21 seed [cross section]
22 embryo
23 lemon; *sim.:* tangerine (mandarin), orange, grapefruit
24 flowering branch
25 orange flower [longitudinal section]
26 fruit
27 orange [cross section]
28 banana plant (banana tree)
29 crown
30 herbaceous stalk with overlapping leaf sheaths
31 inflorescence with young fruits
32 infructescence (bunch of fruit)
33 banana
34 banana flower
35 banana leaf [diagram]
36 almond
37 flowering branch
38 fruiting branch
39 fruit
40 drupe containing seed [almond]
41 carob
42 branch with female flowers
43 female flower
44 male flower
45 fruit
46 siliqua (pod) [cross section]
47 seed
48 sweet chestnut (Spanish chestnut)
49 flowering branch
50 female inflorescence
51 male flower
52 cupule containing seeds
53 Brazil nut
54 flowering branch
55 leaf
56 flower [from above]
57 flower [longitudinal section]
58 opened capsule containing seeds
59 Brazil nut [cross section]
60 nut [longitudinal section]
61 pineapple plant (pineapple)
62 pseudocarp with crown of leaves
63 syncarp
64 pineapple flower
65 flower [longitudinal section]

1
2
3
4
5
6
7
8
9
10
11
12
13
14
15
16
17
18
19
20
21
22
23
24
25
26
27
28
29
30
31
32
33
34
35
36
37
38
39
40
41
42
43
44
45
46
47
48
49
50
51
52
53
54
55
56
57
58
59
60
61
62
63
64
65

Index

10 film غشاء رقيق
11 film-ring dosimeter مِقْيَاس جُرْعات إشْعاعِيَّة غِشائي حَلَقِي
12 filter مُرَشِّح، فلتر
13 film غِشاء رقيق
14 cover with filter غطاء مُزَوَّد بمُرَشِّح
15 pocket meter (pen meter, pocket chamber) مِقْيَاس جيب
16 window حُجْرَة
17 ionization chamber (ion chamber) غُرْفَة التأيُن
18 clip (pen clip) مشْبك
19 Geiger counter (Geiger-Müller counter) عَدَّاد "جايْجَر"
20 counter tube casing غلاف أنْبُوب العَدَّاد
21 counter tube أنْبُوب العَدَّاد
22 instrument housing مَبيت الآلة
23 measurement range selector مِفْتَاح انْتِقَاء مَدَى القِيَاس
24 Wilson cloud chamber (Wilson chamber) حُجْرَة "وِلْسُن" الغَيْمِيَّة
25 compression plate لَوْح ضَغْط
26 cloud chamber photograph صُورَة الحُجْرَة الغَيْمِيَّة
27 cloud chamber track of an alpha particle مَسَار جُسَيْم ألفا في الحُجْرَة الغَيْمِيَّة
28 telecobalt unit (*coll.* cobalt bomb) وَحْدَة تليكوبلت (قُنْبلَة الكوبلت)
29 pillar stand دِعَامَة عَمُودِيَّة
30 support cables كيبلات إسْنَاد
31 radiation shield (radiation shielding) دِرْعُ الإشْعَاع
32 sliding shield دِرْعُ انزلاقيّ
33 bladed diaphragm رَقٌ مُنَصَّل
34 light-beam positioning device جِهَاز تَوْضِيع الحزْمَة الضَّوْئِيَّة
35 pendulum device (pendulum) جِهَاز بندوليّ (بندول)
36 irradiation table طاولة التَّشَعُّع
37 rail (track) مَسَار
38 manipulator with sphere unit جِهَاز مُعَالَجَة مُزَوَّد بوَحْدَة كرَوِيَّة
39 handle مِقْبَض
40 safety catch (locking lever) زِرّ الأمان (ذراع قَفْل)
41 wrist joint وَصْلَة رُسْغِيَّة
42 master arm الذرَاع الرئيسي
43 clamping device (clamp) جِهَاز تَثْبِيت (قامطة)
44 tongs كُلابَتَان
45 slotted board لَوْح مُثَقَّب
46 radiation shield (protective shield, protective shielding), a lead shielding wall [section] دِرْعُ الإشْعَاع (دِرْع واقٍ من الإشْعَاع، جِدَار مُدَرَّع بالرصاص) [مَقْطَع]
47 grasping arm of a pair of manipulators (of a master/slave manipulator) ذِرَاع الإمْسَاك الخاصة بزَوْج من أجْهِزَة المُعَالَجَة (لجِهَاز مُعَالَجَة رئيسى/تابع)
48 dust shield وِقَاء التُّراب
49 synchrotron السِّينكرتْرُون
50 danger zone مِنْطَقَة الخطر
51 magnet مغناطيس
52 pumps for emptying the vacuum chamber مِضَخات تَفْرِيغ الحُجْرَة الخَوَائِيَّة

3 Astronomy I الفَلَك (1)

1-35 star map of the northern sky (northern hemisphere) **خَرِيطَة النُّجُوم الخاصة بالسَّمَاء الشَّمَالِيَّة** (نِصْف الكُرَة الشَّمَالِي)
1-8 divisions of the sky أقْسَام السَّمَاء
1 celestial pole with the Pole Star (Polaris, the North Star) القُطْب السَّمَاوِي مع النَّجْم القُطْبِي (النَّجْمُ الشَّمَالِي)
2 ecliptic (apparent annual path of the sun) فَلَك البُرُوج (مَدَار الشَّمْس السَّنَوِيّ الظَّاهِرِي بَيْن البُرُوج)
3 celestial equator (equinoctial line) خط الاسْتِوَاء السَّمَاوِي
4 tropic of Cancer مَدَار السَّرَطَان
5 circle enclosing circumpolar stars الدائرة المحيطة بالنُّجُوم الكائنة حَوْل القُطْب
6-7 equinoctial points (equinoxes) **نُقْطَتَا الاعْتِدَال الرَّبِيعِي و الخَرِيفِي**
6 vernal equinoctial point (first point of Aries) نُقْطَة الاعْتِدَال الرَّبِيعِي
7 autumnal equinoctial point نُقْطَة الاعْتِدَال الخَرِيفي
8 summer solstice الانْقِلاب الصَّيْفِي
9-48 constellations (grouping of fixed stars into figures) **and names of stars الكَوْكَبَات وأسْمَاء النُّجُوم**
9 Aquila (the Eagle) with Altair the principal star (the brightest star) العُقَاب مع النّسر الطائر (أكثر النُّجُوم سُطُوعاً)
10 Pegasus (the Winged Horse) الفَرَس الأعْظَم (الفَرَس المُجَنَّح)
11 Cetus (the Whale) with Mira, a variable star قَيْطُس (الحُوت) مع ميرا
12 Eridamus (the Celestial River) النَّهْر
13 Orion (the Hunter) with Rigel, Betelgeuse and Bellatrix الجَوْزَاء مع رِجْل الجَوْزَاء اليُسْرَى
14 Canis Major (the Great Dog, the Greater Dog) with Sirius (the Dog Star), a star of the first magnitude الكَلْب الأكْبَر مع الشِّعْرَى اليَمَانِيَّة
15 Canis Minor (the Little Dog, the Lesser Dog) with Procyon الكَلْب الأصْغَر مع الشِّعْرَى الشَّامِيَّة
16 Hydra (the Water Snake, the Sea Serpent) الشُّجاع (ثُعْبَان الماء)
17 Leo (the Lion) with Regulus الأسَد مع قَلْب الأسَد

18 Virgo (the Virgin) with Spica — العَذْرَاء مع السُّنْبُلَة
19 Libra (the Balance, the Scales) — المِيزان
20 Serpens (the Serpent) — الثُّعْبَان
21 Hercules — هِرَقْل، الجاثي
22 Lyra (the Lyre) with Vega — القِيثَارة مع النَّسر الوَاقع
23 Cygnus (the Swan, the Northern Cross) with Deneb — الدَّجَاجَة مع ذَنَب الدَّجَاجَة
24 Andromeda — اندروميدا: المَرْأة المُسَلْسَلَة
25 Taurus (the Bull) with Aldebaran — الثَّوْر مع الدَّبَرَان
26 The Pleiades (Pleiads, the Seven Sisters) an open cluster of stars — الثرَيَّا
27 Auriga (the Wagoner, the Charioteer) with Capella — العَنَّاز مع العَيُّوق
28 Gemini (the Twins) with Castor and Pollux — الجَوْزَاء مع نيِّر التَّوْأمَيْن ورَأس التَّوْأم المُوَخَّر
29 Ursa Major (the Great Bear, the Greater Bear, the Plough, Charles's Wain, *Am.* the Big Dipper) with the double star (binary star) Mizar and Alcor — الدُّبّ الأكْبَر مع الإزَار والْكُور
30 Boötes (the Herdsman) with Arcturus — راعِي الشَّاء/العَوَّاء مع السِّمَاك الرامح
31 Corona Borealis (the Northern Crown) — الإكْلِيل الشَّمَالِي
32 Draco (the Dragon) — التِّنِّين
33 Cassiopeia — ذات الكرسيّ
34 Ursa Minor (the Little Bear, Lesser Bear, *Am.* Little Dipper) with the Pole Star (Polaris, the North Star) — الدُّبّ الأصْغر مع النَّجْم القُطْبي
35 the Milky Way (the Galaxy) — دَرْب التَّبَّانَة (المَجَرَّة)

36-48 the southern sky — **السَّمَاء الجنوبية**

36 Capricorn (the Goat, the Sea Goat) — الجَدْي
37 Sagittarius (the Archer) — القَوْس
38 Scorpio (the Scorpion) — العَقْرَب
39 Centaurus (the Centaur) — قَنْطُورس، الظُّلْمان
40 Triangulum Australe (the Southern Triangle) — المُثَلَّث الجَنُوبي
41 Pavo (the Peacock) — الطَّاوُوس
42 Grus (the Crane) — الكَرْكِي
43 Octans (the Octant) — الثُّمن
44 Crux (the Southern Cross, the Cross) — الصَّلِيب الجَنُوبي
45 Argo (the Celestial Ship) — بُرْج السَّفِينَة
46 Carina (the Keel) — الجُؤْجُؤ
47 Pictor (the Painter) — كُرسي المُصَوِّر
48 Reticulum (the Net) — الشبكة

4 Astronomy II — الفَلَك (2)

1-9 the moon — **القَمَر**

1 moon's path (moon's orbit round the earth) — مَدَار القَمَر حَوْل الأَرْض

2-7 lunar phases (moon's phases) (lunation) — **مَنَازل القَمَر**

2 new moon — قَمَر أوَّل الشَّهر
3 crescent (crescent moon, waxing moon) — هِلال
4 half-moon (first quarter) — التَّرْبِيع الأوَّل
5 full moon — بَدْر
6 half-moon (last quarter, third quarter) — التَّرْبِيع الأخير
7 crescent (crescent moon, waning moon) — مُحَاق (هِلال)
8 the earth (terrestrial globe) — الأَرْض (الكُرَة الأرْضيَّة)
9 direction of the sun's rays — اتجاه أشِعَّة الشَّمْس

10-21 apparent path of the sun at the beginning of the seasons — **المَسَار الظاهِري للشَّمْس في بداية الفصول**

10 celestial axis — المِحْوَر الفلَكي/السَّمَاوِي
11 zenith — سَمْت الرَّأس
12 horizonal plane — مُسْتَوَى أُفقِي
13 nadir — نَظِير السَّمْت
14 east point — نُقْطَة الشَّرْق
15 west point — نُقْطَة الغَرْب
16 north point — نُقْطَة الشَّمَال
17 south point — نُقْطَة الجَنُوب
18 apparent path of the sun on 21 December — المَسَار الظَاهِري للشمس يوم 21 دِيسمبر
19 apparent path of the sun on 21 March and 23 September — المَسَار الظَاهِري للشمس يوم 21 مارس ويوم 23 سبتمبر
20 apparent path of the sun on 21 June — المَسَار الظَّاهِري للشمس يوم 21 يونيو
21 border of the twilight area — حَدُّ مِنْطَقة الشَّفَق/السَّحَر

22-28 rotary motions of the earth's axis — **الحَرَكَات الدَّوَرَانيَّة لمحْوَر الأرْض**

22 axis of the ecliptic — مِحْوَر مَدَار الشَّمْس الظَّاهِري بَيْن البروج
23 celestial sphere — القُبَّة السَّمَاوِيَّة
24 path of the celestial pole [precession and nutation] — مَسَار القُطْب السَّمَاوِي
25 instantaneous axis of rotation — المِحْوَر اللَّحْظِي للدوَرَان
26 celestial pole — القُطْب السَّمَاوِي
27 mean axis of rotation — المِحْوَر المُتَوَسِّط للدوَرَان
28 polhode — منحى دوران محوري

29-35 solar and lunar eclipse (not to scale) — **كُسُوف الشَّمْس وخُسُوف القَمَر**

29 the sun — الشَّمْس

30 the earth الأَرْض
31 the moon القَمَر
32 solar eclipse كُسُوف شَمْسِي
33 area of the earth in which the eclipse appears total مِنْطَقَة الأَرْض التي يظهر فيها الكُسُوف كامِلا
34-35 lunar eclipse **خُسُوف قَمَرِي**
34 penumbra (partial shadow) الشَعْشَاع ، الظِّل النَّاقِص
35 umbra (total shadow) سُوَيْدَاء الظِّل
36-41 the sun **الشَّمْس**
36 solar disc (disk) (solar globe, solar sphere) قُرْص الشَّمْس
37 sunspots كَلَف الشَّمْس
38 cyclones in the area of sunspots أعاصير في مِنْطَقَة كَلَف الشَّمْس
39 corona (solar corona), observable during total solar eclipse or by means of special instruments هَالَة ، إِكْلِيل
40 prominences (solar prominences) شُوَاظ شَمْسِي
41 moon's limb during a total solar eclipse حافَة قُرْص القَمَر أَثْناء كُسُوف كُلِّي للشمس
42-52 planets (planetary system, solar system) [not to scale] **and planet symbols** **الكَوَاكِب ورموز الكَوَاكِب**
42 the sun الشَّمْس
43 Mercury عُطَارِد
44 Venus الزُّهَرَة
45 Earth, with the moon, a satellite الأَرْض والقَمَر
46 Mars, with two moons المَرِّيخ ويتبعه قَمَرَان
47 asteroids (minor planets) كُوَيْكِبَات سَيَّارة
48 Jupiter المُشْتَرَى
49 Saturn زُحَل
50 Uranus أُورَانُوس
51 Neptune نِبْتُون
52 Pluto, with the moon Charon بلُوتو مع القَمَر شَارُون
53-64 signs of the zodiac (zodiacal signs) **رموز دائرة البروج**
53 Aries (the Ram) الحَمَل
54 Taurus (the Bull) الثَّوْر
55 Gemini (the Twins) الجَوْزاء
56 Cancer (the Crab) السَّرَطَان
57 Leo (the Lion) الأَسَد
58 Virgo (the Virgin) العَذْرَاء
59 Libra (the Balance, the Scales) الميزَان
60 Scorpio (the Scorpion) العَقْرَب
61 Sagittarius (the Archer) القَوْس
62 Capricorn (the Goat, the Sea Goat) الجَدْي
63 Aquarius (the Water Carrier, the Water Bearer) الدَّلْو
64 Pisces (the Fish) الحُوت

5 Astronomy III الفَلَك (3)

1-16 the European Southern Observatory (ESO) on *Cerro la Silla, Chile*, an observatory [section] المَرْصَد الأوروبي الجنوبيّ المُطِلّ على "سيرو لا سيلا"، شيلي [مقطع]
1 primary mirror (main mirror) with a diameter of 3.6 m (144 inches) المِرْآة الرئيسيَّة وقُطْرها 3,6 م (144 بُوصَة)
2 prime focus cage with mounting for secondary mirrors هَيْكَل التركيز البُؤَرِي الرئيسي مزود بحامِل المَرَايا الثانوية
3 flat mirror for the coudé ray path مِرْآة مُسَطَّحَة لمَسَار أشِعَّة "كُودِيه"
4 Cassegrain cage قَفَص "كاسْجِرين"
5 grating spectrograph سبكتروجراف شَبَكِي
6 spectrographic camera كاميرا سبكتروجرافية
7 hour axis drive ذِرَاع تَدْوِير المِحْوَر السَّاعِي
8 hour axis المِحْوَر السَّاعِي
9 horseshoe mounting حامِل على شكل حدْوَة فَرَس
10 hydrostatic bearing سَطْح ارْتِكَاز هيدروستاتي
11 primary and secondary focusing devices أجْهِزَة التَّرْكِيز البُؤَرِي الرئيسيَّة والثانويَّة
12 observatory dome, a revolving dome قُبَّة المَرْصَد ، قُبَّة دَوَّارَة
13 observation opening فَتْحَة المَرْصَد
14 vertically movable dome shutter غِطاء قُبَّة يتحرك رأسِيًّا
15 wind screen حاجِب الريح
16 siderostat عاكسة نجمية ثابتة التوجيه (سيدروستات)
17-28 the *Stuttgart* Planetarium [section] قُبَّة "شتوتجارت" الفلكية ، مِفْلاك "شتوتجارت" [مَقْطَع]
17 administration, workshop, and store area مِنْطَقَة الإدارة والوَرْشة والمَخْزَن
18 steel scaffold سقَالة حَدِيدِيَّة
19 glass pyramid هَرَم زُجَاجِي
20 revolving arched ladder سُلَّم مُقَوَّس دَوَّار
21 projection dome قُبَّة الإِسْقَاط
22 light stop حاجِز الضَّوْء
23 planetarium projector بروجكتور المِفْلاك
24 well بِئْـر
25 foyer دِهْلِيز
26 theatre (*Am.* theater) مَسْرَح
27 projection booth حُجَيْرَة الإِسْقَاط
28 foundation pile خازوق الأَسَاس
29-33 the *Kitt Peak* solar observatory near *Tucson, Ariz.* [section] مَرْصَد "كيت بيك" الشَّمْسي بالقُرْب من "تاكسون"، "أريز" [قِطاع]
29 heliostat هليوستات
30 sunken observation shaft عَمُود رَصْد غاطِس
31 water-cooled windshield حاجِب ريح مُبَرَّد بالماء
32 concave mirror مِرْآة مُقَعَّرَة

33 observation room housing the spectrograph — حُجْرَة الرَّصْد وبها سبكتروجراف

6 Moon Landing — الهبُوط علَى سَطْح القَمَر

1 Apollo spacecraft — سَفِينَة الفَضَاء "أبوللو"
2 service module (SM) — مُودْيُول (حُجْرَة انْفِصَاليَّة) خدمَة
3 nozzle of the main rocket engine — مَنْفَث المُحَرِّك الرئيسي للصارُوخ
4 directional antenna — هَوَائي اتجاهي
5 manoeuvering (*Am.* maneuvering) rockets — صواريخ المُنَاوَرَة
6 oxygen and hydrogen tanks for the spacecraft's energy system — خَزَّانات الأكسجين والهيدروجين الخاصة بنظام طاقَة السَّفينة
7 fuel tank — خَزَّان وَقُود
8 radiators of the spacecraft's energy system — مُشِعَّات نِظام طاقَة سفينة الفضاء
9 command module (Apollo space capsule) — مُودْيُول القِيَادة
10 entry hatch of the space capsule — فتحة دخول الكَبْسُولَة الفضائية
11 astronaut — رائِد فَضَاء
12 lunar module (LM) — مُودْيُول قَمَري
13 moon's surface (lunar surface), a dust-covered surface — سَطْح القَمَر
14 lunar dust — تُرَاب قَمَري
15 piece of rock — قِطْعَة صَخْرِيَّة
16 meteorite crater — حُفْرَة نَيْزَكيَّة
17 the earth — الأَرْض (الكُرَة الأَرْضيَّة)
18-27 space suit (extra-vehicular suit) — **بَدْلَة الفَضَاء**
18 emergency oxygen apparatus — جِهَاز الأكسجين الخاص بالطوارئ
19 sunglass pocket [with sunglasses for use on board] — جيب للنَّظَّارة الشَّمْسِيَّة [به نَظَارَة شَمْسِيَّة للاستخدام على مَتْن السفينة]
20 life support system (life support pack), a backpack unit — نظام دَعْم الحَيَاة
21 access flap — قَلاَّبَة
22 space suit helmet with sun filters — خُوذَة البَدْلَة الفضائية مُزودة بمُرَشِّحات شمسيَّة
23 control box of the life support pack — صُنْدُوق التحكم الخاص بنظام دَعْم الحَيَاة
24 penlight pocket — جيب لِكَشَّاف في حَجْم القَلَم
25 access flap for the purge valve — قلابة صِمَام التنظيف
26 tube and cable connections for the radio, ventilation, and water-cooling systems — تَوْصِيلة الأُنْبُوب والكيبل الخاصة بأنظمة الرَّادْيُو والتَّهْوِيَة وتَبْرِيد الماء
27 pocket for pens, tools, etc. — جيب للأقلام و الأدوات، إلخ.
28-36 descent stage — **مَرْحَلَة الهبوط**
28 connector — آليَّة تَوْصيل
29 fuel tank — خَزَّان وَقُود
30 engine — مُحَرِّك
31 mechanism for unfolding the legs — آليَّة فَرْد أَرْجُل السفينة
32 main shock absorber — مُخَفِّف الصَّدْمَة الرئيسي
33 landing pad — مِسْنَد الهبوط
34 ingress/egress platform (hatch platform) — مِنَصَّة دخول/خروج
35 ladder to platform and hatch — سُلَّم مُؤدي إلى المِنَصَّة والفَتْحَة
36 cardan mount for engine — حامِل كرداني للمُحَرِّك
37-47 ascent stage — **مَرْحَلَة الصعود**
37 fuel tank — خَزَّان وَقُود
38 ingress/egress hatch (entry/exit hatch) — فَتْحَة الدخول والخروج
39 LM manoeuvering (*Am.* maneuvering) rockets — صَوَاريخ المُنَاوَرَة الخاصة بالموديولات القَمَريَّة
40 window — شُبَّاك
41 crew compartment — حُجَيْرَة الطَّاقم/المَلاحين
42 rendezvous radar antenna — هَوَائي رادار من أجْل الالْتِقاء
43 inertial measurement unit — وَحْدَة قِيَاس القُصُور الذَّاتي
44 directional antenna for ground control — هَوَائي اتجاهي للتحكم الأَرْضي
45 upper hatch (docking hatch) — فَتْحَة علوية
46 inflight antenna — هَوَائي طيران
47 docking target recess — تجويف الالتحام بمركبة أخرى في الفضاء

7 Atmosphere — الغلاف الجَوِّي

1 the troposphere — التروبوسفير
2 thunderclouds — سُحُب رَعْدِيَّة
3 the highest mountain, Mount Everest [8,882 m] — أعلى جَبَل، جَبَل افرست [8882 م]
4 rainbow — قَوس قُزَح
5 jet stream level — مُسْتَوَى التيار المُتَدَفِّق
6 zero level [inversion of vertical air movement] — مُسْتَوَى صِفْر [انعكاس حركة الهواء الرأسية]
7 ground layer (surface boundary layer) — الطَّبَقَة الأَرْضيَّة
8 the stratosphere — الاستراتوسفير
9 tropopause — مِنْطَقَة الرُّكُود (تروبوبوز)
10 separating layer (layer of weaker air movement) — طَبَقَة فاصلة(طبقة حركة تيار هوائي أضعف)
11 atomic explosion — انْفِجَار ذَرِّي
12 hydrogen bomb explosion — انْفِجَار قنبلة هيدروجينية
13 ozone layer — طَبَقَة الأوزون
14 range of sound wave propagation — مَدَى انتشار المَوْجَات الصَّوْتِيَّة
15 stratosphere aircraft — طائرة استراتوسفيرية
16 manned balloon — مِنْطَاد مُزَوَّد بأفْرَاد
17 sounding balloon — مِنْطَاد/بالون رَصْد جَوِّي

18 meteor — نَيْزَك، شهاب
19 upper limit of ozone layer — الحَدُّ العلويّ لطَبَقَة الأوزون
20 zero level — مُسْتَوَى صفر
21 eruption of Krakatoa — انفجار بُرْكَان "كراكاتوا"
22 luminous clouds (noctilucent clouds) — سُحُب (لَيْلِيَّة) مُضِيئة
23 the ionosphere — الأيونوسفير
24 range of research rockets — مَدَى صواريخ البحوث
25 shooting star — شِهَاب، نَيْزَك
26 short wave (high frequency) — مَوْجَة قَصِيرَة (تَرَدُّد عالٍ)
27 E-layer (Heaviside-Kennelly Layer) — طَبَقَة "كِنِلِّي" و"هِيفِيسَايد"
28 F1-layer — طبقة أبلِتون – 1
29 F2-layer — طبقة أبلِتون – 2
30 aurora (polar light) — الشَّفَق (ضَوْء قُطْبيّ)
31 the exosphere — الإكسوسفير
32 atom layer — طَبَقَة ذَرِّيَّة
33 range of satellite sounding — مَدَى السَّبْر بالقَمَر الصناعي
34 fringe region — منْطَقَة حافيَّة
35 altitude scale — مِقْيَاس الارتفاع
36 temperature scale (thermometric scale) — مقياس الحرارة
37 temperature graph — الرَّسْم البياني للحرارة

8 Meteorology I — الأَرْصَاد الجَوِّيَّة (1)

1-19 clouds and weather — **السُّحُب والطَّقْس**

1-4 clouds found in homogeneous air masses — **السُّحُب الموجودة في كُتَل الهواء المُتَجَانِسَة**

1 cumulus (woolpack cloud), a heap cloud; here: cumulus humilis (fair-weather cumulus), a flat-based heap cloud — رُكام، سِحَاب كَنَهْوَري
2 cumulus congestus, a heap cloud with more marked vertical development — رُكام كَوْمِيّ
3 stratocumulus, a layer cloud (sheet cloud) arranged in heavy masses — رُكاميّ طَبَقِيّ
4 stratus (high fog), a thick, uniform layer cloud (sheet cloud) — رَهَل : سحاب طبقيّ كَثِيف مُنْبَسِط

5-12 clouds found at warm fronts — **السُّحُب في الجَبَهات الدافئة**

5 warm front — جَبْهة دافئة
6 cirrus, a high to very high ice-crystal cloud, thin and assuming a wide variety of forms — قَزَع، طَخَاء:سحاب رقيق سِمْحَاقيّ
7 cirrostratus, an ice-crystal cloud veil — سِمْحَاقيّ طَبَقِي
8 altostratus, a layer cloud (sheet cloud) of medium height — سحاب طَبَقِيّ متوسط، رَبَاب
9 altostratus praecipitans, a layer cloud (sheet cloud) with precipitation in its upper parts — سحاب طَبَقِيّ متوسط يَحْمِل أمطاراً/ثلوجاً في أجْزَائِه العلْوِيَّة
10 nimbostratus, a rain cloud, a layer cloud (sheet cloud) of very large vertical extent which produces precipitation (rain or snow) — مُزْن طَبَقِيّ مَطِير، الخَسِيف
11 fractostratus, a ragged cloud occurring beneath nimbostratus — مُزْن جُزْئيّ يظهر أسفل الخَسِيف
12 fractocumulus, a ragged cloud like **11** but with billowing shapes — رُكاميّ جُزْئيّ

13-17 clouds at cold fronts — **السُّحُب في الجَبَهات البارِدة**

13 cold front — جَبْهة باردة
14 cirrocumulus, thin fleecy cloud in the form of globular masses; covering the sky: mackerel sky — سِمْحَاقي رُكاميّ؛ عنْدَما يُغَطِّي السَّماء يُطْلَق عليْها السَّماء الإسْقُمْرِيَّة
15 altocumulus, a cloud in the form of large globular masses — سحاب رُكاميّ متوسط
16 altocumulus castellanus and altocumulus floccus, species of **15** — سحاب صَيْفِي قلاعيّ وندفة سحاب طبقيّ متوسط (نوع من السحاب الرُّكاميّ المتوسط)
17 cumulonimbus, a heap cloud of very large vertical extent, to be classified under **1-4** in the case of tropical storms — رُكاميّ مُمْطِر، يُصَنَّف تحت الأنْوَاع من 1–4 في حالَة العَوَاصِف المَدَارِيَّة

18-19 types of precipitation — **نَوْعَا التَّسَاقُط**

18 steady rain or snow covering a large area, precipitation of uniform intensity — تَسَاقُط ذو كَثَافَة مُنْتَظِمَة، أمْطار أو ثُلوج مُتَوَاصِلَة تُغَطِّي مِنْطَقَة وَاسِعَة
19 shower, scattered precipitation — وابِل، هَمْرَة

9 Meteorology II and Climatology — الأَرْصَاد الجَوِّيَّة (2) وعلم المناخ

1-39 weather chart (weather map, surface chart, surface synoptic chart) — **خَرِيطة الطَّقس الجَوِّي**

1 isobar (line of equal or constant atmospheric or barometric pressure at sea level) — أيْسُوبار : خط تساوي الضغط الجَوِّي
2 pleiobar (isobar of over — بلايوبار (أيْسُوبار يزيد عن

1,000 mb) | 1000 مليبار)
3 meiobar (isobar of under 1,000 mb) | مايوبار(أيْسُوبار يقل عن 1000 مليبار)
4 atmospheric (barometric) pressure given in millibars | الضغط الجوِّي مُقَاساً بالمليبار
5 low-pressure area (low, cyclone, depression) | مِنْطَقَة ضَغْط مُنْخَفِض
6 high-pressure area (high, anticyclone) | مِنْطَقَة ضَغْط مُرْتَفِع
7 observatory (meteorological watch office, weather station) or ocean station vessel (weather ship) | مَرْصَد (محطَّة أرصاد جوية) أو سفينة أرْصَاد جَوِّيَّة
8 temperature | دَرَجَة الحرارة
9-19 means of representing wind direction (wind-direction symbols) | **طُرُق/رموز تمثيل اتجاه الرِّيح**
9 wind-direction shaft (wind arrow) | سَهْم تحديد اتجاه الرِّيح
10 wind-speed barb (wind-speed feather) indicating wind speed | ريشة تحديد سُرْعَة الرِّيح
11 calm | هادئة
12 1-2 knots (1 knot = 1.852 kph) | 1–2 عُقْدَة (العُقْدَة = 1,852 كم/س)
13 3-7 knots | 3–7 عُقَد
14 8-12 knots | 8–12 عُقْدَة
15 13-17 knots | 13–17 عُقْدَة
16 18-22 knots | 18–22 عُقْدَة
17 23-27 knots | 23–27 عُقْدَة
18 28-32 knots | 28–32 عُقْدَة
19 58-62 knots | 58–62 عُقْدَة
20-24 state of the sky (distribution of the cloud cover) | **حالَة السَّماء** (تَوْزيع السُّحُب)
20 clear (cloudless) | صافِيَة (خالية من الغُيوم)
21 fair | سُحُب قليلة
22 partly cloudy | غائِمَة جُزْئيّاً
23 cloudy | غائِمَة
24 overcast (sky mostly or completely covered) | ملبدة بالغيوم
25-29 fronts and air currents | **الجبهات والتيارات الهوائية**
25 occlusion (occluded front) | جَبْهَة مُقْفَلَة
26 warm front | جَبْهَة دافِئة
27 cold front | جَبْهَة بارِدة
28 warm airstream (warm current) | تيَّار (هواء) دافِئ
29 cold airstream (cold current) | تيَّار (هواء) بارِد
30-39 meteorological phenomena | **الظَّواهِر المناخيَّة**
30 precipitation area | مِنْطَقَة تَسَاقُط (مَطَر أو ثَلْج أو نَدَى)
31 fog | ضَبَاب
32 rain | مَطَر
33 drizzle | رَذَاذ
34 snow | ثَلْج
35 ice pellets (graupel, soft hail) | بَرَد رَخْو
36 hail | بَرَد
37 shower | وَابِل
38 thunderstorm | عاصِفَة رَعْدِيَّة
39 lightning | بَرْق
40-58 climatic map | **الخريطة المناخيَّة**
40 isotherm (line connecting points having equal mean temperature) | خَط تَسَاوِي دَرَجَة الحرارة الأَرْضِيَّة، خط التَّحَارُر
41 0°C (zero) isotherm (line connecting points having a mean annual temperature of 0°C) | خط التَّحَارُر الصِّفْري (خط يربط نقاطاً لها متوسط درجة حرارة سَنَوِيّ يبلغ صِفْراً مئويّاً)
42 isocheim (line connecting points having equal mean winter temperature) | خط تَسَاوِي القرّ (خط يربط نقاطاً لها متوسط حرارة متساوٍ في الشِّتاء)
43 isothere (line connecting points having equal mean summer temperature) | خط تَسَاوِي القَيْظ (خط يربط نقاطاً لها متوسط حرارة متساوٍ في الصَّيْف)
44 isohel (line connecting points having equal duration of sunshine) | خط تَسَاوِي السُّطُوع الشَّمْسِيّ
45 isohyet (line connecting points having equal amounts of precipitation) | خط تَسَاوِي المطر (خط يربط نقاطاً لها كمية مُتَسَاوِيَة من التَّساقُط)
46-52 atmospheric circulation (wind systems) | **الدَّوْرَة الجويَّة** (أنْظِمَة الرِّياح)
46-47 calm belts | **حزَامان ساكنان**
46 equatorial trough (equatorial calms, doldrums) | نِطَاق الرَّهْو الاستوائي
47 subtropical high-pressure belts (horse latitudes) | عروض الخيل(منطقتان مستقرتا الطَّقْس بيْن القُطْبَيْن)
48 north-east trade winds (north-east trades, tropical easterlies) | رياح تجارية شماليَّة شرقيَّة
49 south-east trade winds (south-east trades, tropical easterlies) | رياح تجارية جنوبيَّة شرقيَّة
50 zones of the variable westerlies | مناطق الرِّياح الغربيَّة المتغيِّرَة
51 polar wind zones | مناطق الرِّياح القطبيَّة
52 summer monsoon | رياح موسميَّة صيفيَّة
53-58 earth's climates | **الأقاليم المناخيَّة الأرْضيَّة**
53 equatorial climate: tropical zone (tropical rain zone) | المناخ الاسْتِوَائِيّ: المنْطَقَة المداريَّة (مِنْطَقَة الأمطار الاستوائيَّة)
54 the two arid zones (equatorial dry zones): desert and steppe zones | المنطقتان القاحلتان: منطقتا الصحراء والسَّهْب

55 the two temperate rain zones — منطقتا الأمطار المعتدلة
56 boreal climate (snow forest climate) — مناخ شماليّ (مناخ الغابة الجليديَّة)
57-58 polar climates — **نوعا المناخ القطبيّ**
57 tundra climate — مناخ تندرا (القطب الشمالي)
58 perpetual frost climate — مناخ الصَّقيع المستمر

10 Meteorological Instruments — أجْهِزَة الأرْصَاد الجوِّيَّة

1 mercury barometer, a siphon barometer, a liquid-column barometer — بارومتر زئْبَقي، بارومتر بعمود سائِل
2 mercury column — عمود الزِّئْبَق
3 millibar scale, a millimetre (*Am.* millimeter) scale — مِقْيَاس المليبار
4 barograph, a self-registering aneroid barometer — بَارُوجْرَاف (مِرْسَمَة الضغط الجوِّي)
5 drum (recording drum) — طَبْلَة/أسْطُوَانَة التَّسْجيل
6 bank of aneroid capsules (aneroid boxes) — مَجْمُوعَة كَبْسُولات لاسائليَّة
7 recording arm — ذِرَاع التَّسْجيل
8 hygrograph — مِرْسَمَة الرِّطُوبَة النِّسْبيَّة
9 hygrometer element (hair element) — هيجروميتر شَعْري (مِقْيَاس الرِّطُوبَة النِّسْبيَّة في الجوّ)
10 reading adjustment — مُعايَرَة القراءة
11 amplitude adjustment — مُعايَرَة / ضَبْط السِّعَة
12 recording arm — ذِرَاع التَّسْجيل
13 recording pen — قَلَم التَّسْجيل
14 change gears for the clockwork drive — تُروس التغيير الخاصة بحَرَكَة آليَّة السَّاعَة
15 off switch for the recording arm — زرّ الإيقاف الخاص بذِرَاع التَّسْجيل
16 drum (recording drum) — طَبْلَة/أسْطُوَانَة التَّسْجيل
17 time scale — مِقْيَاس زَمَنِيّ
18 case (housing) — غلاف/إطار تثبيت
19 thermograph — ثِرْمُوجِرَاف
20 drum (recording drum) — طَبْلَة/أسْطُوَانَة التَّسْجيل
21 recording arm — ذراع التَّسْجيل
22 sensing element — عُنْصُر الاسْتِشْعَار
23 silver-disc (silver-disk) pyrheliometer, an instrument for measuring the sun's radiant energy — برليوميتر ذو قُرْص فضِّي (مقْيَاس حرارة الإشْعَاع الشَّمْسيّ)
24 silver disc (disk) — قُرْص فضِّي
25 thermometer — ترمومتر
26 wooden insulating casing — غِلاف خشبي عازِل
27 tube with diaphragm (diaphragmed tube) — أُنْبُوب رقّي
28 wind gauge (*Am.* gage) (anemometer) — مِقْيَاس سُرْعَة الرِّيَاح
29 wind-speed indicator (wind-speed meter) — مؤشر سُرْعَة الرِّيَاح (مِقْيَاس سُرْعَة الرِّيَاح)
30 cross arms with hemispherical cups — أذْرُع متعامِدَة مُزَوَّدَة بوَصَلات نِصْف كُرَويَّة
31 wind-direction indicator — مُؤشِّر اتجاه الرِّيَاح
32 wind vane — دوَّارة الرِّيح
33 aspiration psychrometer — مِقْيَاس رطوبة الجوّ السافط
34 dry bulb thermometer — ترمومتر ذو بُصَيْلَة جافَة
35 wet bulb thermometer — ترمومتر ذو بُصَيْلَة مُخَضَّلَة
36 solar radiation shielding — وقاء/حاجِب الإشْعَاع الشَّمْسيّ
37 suction tube — أُنْبُوب ماص
38 recording rain gauge (*Am.* gage) — مِقْيَاس تسجيل كمية المطر
39 protective housing (protective casing) — غِلاف واقٍ
40 collecting vessel — وعاء تَجْميع
41 rain cover — غِطاء واقٍ من المطر
42 recording mechanism — آليَّة التَّسْجيل
43 siphon tube — مَمَص أنْبُوبي مُنْحَني
44 precipitation gauge (*Am.* gage) (rain gauge) — مِقْيَاس التَّساقُط
45 collecting vessel — وعاء تَجْميع
46 storage vessel — وعاء تَخْزين
47 measuring glass — مَخْبار قياس
48 insert for measuring snowfall — وَلِيجَة لقياس كمية سقوط الجليد
49 thermometer screen (thermometer shelter) — وقاء الترمومتر
50 hygrograph — مِرْسَمَة الرِّطُوبَة النِّسْبيَّة (هيجروجراف)
51 thermograph — ثرموجراف
52 psychrometer (wet and dry bulb thermometer) — مِقْيَاس رطوبة الجوّ
53-54 thermometers for measuring extremes of temperature — **ترمومترات لقياس دَرجَات الحرارة القُصْوَى والدُّنْيَا**
53 maximum thermometer — ترمومتر دَرَجَة الحرارة القُصْوَى
54 minimum thermometer — ترمومتر دَرَجَة الحرارة الدُّنْيَا
55 radiosonde assembly — مجموعة مَسَار لاسلكي
56 hydrogen balloon — منْطاد/بالون هيدروجين
57 parachute — مَظَلَّة، براشوت
58 radar reflector with spacing lines — عاكِس راداري ذو خطوط مباعدة
59 instrument housing with radiosonde [a short-wave transmitter] and antenna — مقر/غلاف الآلة مُزَوَّد بمَسَار لاسلكي (جهاز إرسال مَوْجَات قصيرة) وهوائي
60 transmissometer, an instrument for measuring visibility — مِقْيَاس إنْفَاذيَّة الجوّ
61 recording instrument (recorder) — آلة تسجيل
62 transmitter — جِهَاز إرْسَال
63 receiver — جِهَاز اسْتِقْبَال
64 weather satellite (ITOS satellite) — قَمَر صناعي للرصْد الجوِّي
65 temperature regulation flaps — قلابات تَنْظيم دَرَجَة الحرارة

66 solar panel تَصْفيحَة شمسية
67 television camera آلة تَصْوير تليفزيوني
68 antenna هوائي
69 solar sensor (sun sensor) جهاز اسْتِشْعَار شمسي
70 telemetry antenna هوائي اسْتِشْعَار عن بُعْد
71 radiometer راديومتر (جهاز قياس الإشْعَاع)

11 Physical Geography I الجُغْرَافية الطَّبيعيَّة (1)

1-5 layered structure of the earth **الهَيْكَل الطِّباقي للأرْض**
1 earth's crust (outer crust of the earth, lithosphere, oxysphere) القِشْرَة الأرْضيَّة
2 hydrosphere غلاف الأرْض المائي
3 mantle الغلاف الصَّخْري، الدِّثَار، وشَاح الأرْض
4 sima (intermediate layer) سِيما: القِشْرة العميقة (طبقة متوسطة)
5 core (earth core, centrosphere, barysphere) اللُب، جَوْف الأرْض (الكُرَة الباطنيَّة الثَّقيلة)
6-12 hypsographic curve of the earth's surface **مُنْحَنى هِبْسُوجرافي لسَطْح الأرْض**
6 peak قمَّة، ذِرْوَة
7 continental mass كُتْلة قارِّيَّة
8 continental shelf (continental platform, shelf) رَصِيف قاريّ
9 continental slope مُنْحَدَر قاريّ
10 **deep-sea floor** (abyssal plane) **قاع البَحْر** (سَطْح مُسْتَوٍ غَوْري)
11 sea level مُسْتَوَى سَطْح البحر
12 deep-sea trench وَهْد تحت البحر
13-28 volcanism (vulcanicity) **البُرْكانيَّة**
13 shield volcano بُرْكان قِبَابي
14 lava plateau هَضَبَة لابيَّة
15 active volcano, a stratovolcano (composite volcano) بُرْكان نَشِط
16 volcanic crater (crater) فُوَّهَة بُرْكانيَّة
17 volcanic vent فَتْحَة البُرْكان
18 lava stream مَجْرَى اللابَة
19 tuff (fragmented volcanic material) طُفَّة
20 subterranean volcano بُرْكان باطنيّ
21 geyser حَمَّة فَوَّارة
22 jet of hot water and steam نَفْث من الماء الساخِن والبُخار
23 sinter terraces (siliceous sinter terraces, fiorite terraces, pearl sinter terraces) شَرُفات لَبِيْدة
24 cone مَخْرُوط
25 maar (extinct volcano) فُوَّهَة بُرْكانيَّة (بُرْكان خامِد)
26 tuff deposit رَوَاسِب طُفِّيَّة
27 breccia بَرِيْشَة
28 vent of extinct volcano فَتْحَة بُرْكان خامِد
29-31 plutonic magmatism **المغناطيسية البلُوتونيَّة**
29 batholite (massive protrusion) باثُوليت
30 lacolith, an intrusion لاكوليت، تَدَاخُل
31 sill, an ore deposit سَدّ ناريّ
32-38 earthquake (*kinds:* tectonic quake, volcanic quake) and seismology **الزِّلْزَال** (نوْعاه: تكتوني، بُرْكاني) **وعِلْم الزَّلازِل**
32 earthquake focus (seismic focus, hypocentre, *Am.* hypocenter) مركز الزِّلْزَال الجَوْفيّ
33 epicentre (*Am.* epicenter), point on the earth's surface directly above the focus مركز الزِّلْزَال السَطْحي
34 depth of focus عُمْق مركز الزِّلْزَال
35 shock wave مَوْجَة صَدْميَّة
36 surface waves (seismic waves) مَوْجَات زِلْزَاليَّة سَطْحيَّة
37 isoseismal (line connecting points of equal intensity of earthquake shock) خَطّ تَسَاوي شِدَّة الزَّلْزَلَة
38 epicentral area, an area of macroseismic vibration مِنْطَقَة مركز الزِّلْزَال السَطْحي
39 horizontal seismograph (seismometer) سزموجراف أفقي
40 electromagnetic damper مُضَائِل كهرومغناطيسي
41 adjustment knob for the period of free oscillation of the pendulum مِقْبَض التعديل الخاص بفترة التَذَبْذُب الحُر للبندول
42 spring attachment for the suspension of the pendulum وَصْلَة النَّابِض الخاصة بتعليق البندول
43 mass كُتْلَة
44 induction coils for recording the voltage of the galvanometer ملفات الحَثّ الخاصة بتسجيل فُولْطيَّة الجلفانومتر
45-54 effects of earthquakes **آثار الزَّلازِل**
45 waterfall (cataract, falls) شلال
46 landslide (rockslide, landslip, *Am.* rock slip) انْزِلاق أرْضي، انْهِيَار
47 talus (rubble, scree) رُكَام
48 scar (scaur, scaw) صَخْرَة خَفِيضَة
49 sink (sinkhole, swallowhole) حُفْرَة بالوعيَّة، دَحْل
50 dislocation (displacement) انْفِصَام، زَحْزَحَة، انْخِلاع
51 solifluction lobe (solifluction tongue) وَقْبَة زَحْف التُّرْبَة
52 fissure شَقّ، فاصِل
53 tsunami (seismic sea مَوْجَة سِنَامِيَّة ناتجة عن

wave) produced by seaquake (submarine earthquake) — زِلْزَال تحت البحر

54 raised beach — قَضّة مُرْتَفِعَة

12 Physical Geography II — الجُغْرَافِيَة الطَّبِيعِيَّة (2)

1-33 geology — **الجيولوجيا**

1 stratification of sedimentary rock — تَكَوُّن طَبَقَات الصخور الرُّسُوبِيَّة

2 strike — مُتَّجَه الطَّبَقَة

3 dip (angle of dip, true dip) — مَيْل الطَّبَقَة الأَرْضية بالنِّسْبَة إلى الأُفُق

4-20 orogeny (orogenis, tectogenis, deformation of rocks by folding and faulting) — **نُشُوء الجِبَال**

4-11 fault-block mountain (block mountain) — **الجِبَال الإِنْكِسَارِيَّة** (الجِبَال الكُتَلِيَّة)

4 fault — صَدْع ، فالِق

5 fault line (fault trace) — خَطّ الصَّدْع

6 fault throw — رَمْيَة الصَّدْع

7 normal fault (gravity fault, normal slip fault, slump fault) — صَدْع عادي

8-11 complex faults — **صُدُوع مُرَكَّبَة/مُعَقَّدَة**

8 step fault (distributive fault, multiple fault) — صُدُوع دَرَجِيَّة/مُدَرَّجَة

9 tilt block — كُتَل مائِلَة

10 horst — هَضَبَة انْدِفاعِيَّة ، ظَهْر

11 graben — خَسْف ، غَوْر ، أُخْدُود

12-20 range of fold mountains (folded mountains) — **سِلْسِلة جبال إلتوائِيَّة**

12 symmetrical fold (normal fold) — طَيَّة مُتَمَاثِلَة

13 asymmetrical fold — طَيَّة غير مُتَمَاثِلَة

14 overfold — طَيَّة مُنْكَفِئَة

15 recumbent fold (reclined fold) — طَيَّة مُضْطَجِعَة

16 saddle (anticline) — طَيَّة سَرْجِيَّة

17 anticlinal axis — مِحْوَر الطَّيَّة المُحَدَّبَة

18 trough (syncline) — طَيَّة مُقَعَّرَة

19 trough surface (trough plane, synclinal axis) — مِحْوَر الطَّيَّة المُقَعَّرَة

20 anticlinorium — طَيَّة مُحَدَّبَة مُرَكَّبَة

21 groundwater under pressure (artesian water) — مياه جَوْفِيَّة ارتوازية

22 water-bearing stratum (aquifer, aquafer) — طَبَقَة خازِنَة للماء

23 impervious rock (impermeable rock) — صَخْر غير مُنْفِذ

24 drainage basin (catchment area) — حَوْض الصَّرْف

25 artesian well — بِئْر ارتوازِيَّة

26 rising water, an artesian spring — نَبْع/عَيْن ارتوازِيَّة

27 petroleum reservoir in an anticline — مَكْمَن بترول في طَيَّة مُحَدَّبَة

28 impervious stratum (impermeable stratum) — طَبَقَة غير مُنْفِذة

29 porous stratum acting as reservoir rock — طَبَقَة مَسَامِيَّة تقوم بِدَوْر صخر المَكْمَن

30 natural gas, a gas cap — غازٌ طبيعي (قَلَنْسُوَة غازِيَّة)

31 petroleum (crude oil) — بترول (زَيْت خام)

32 underlying water — مِيَاه تَحْتِيَّة

33 derrick — بُرْج الحَفْر

34 mountainous area — مِنْطَقَة جَبَلِيَّة

35 rounded mountain top — قِمَّة جَبَلِيَّة مُسْتَدِيرَة

36 mountain ridge (ridge) — نُتوء جَبَلِيّ

37 mountain slope — مُنْحَدَر جَبَلِيّ

38 hillside spring — نَبْع جانِب المُنْحَدَر

39-47 high-mountain region — **إقليم جبلي مرتفع**

39 mountain range, a massif — سِلْسِلة جَبَلِيَّة ، كُتْلَة جَبَلِيَّة

40 summit (peak, top of the mountain) — قِمَّة الجَبَل

41 shoulder — كتف

42 saddle — سَرْج

43 rock face (steep face) — واجِهَة صَخْرِيَّة

44 gully — شِعْب

45 talus (scree, detritus) — رُكام المُنْحَدَرَات (هَشِيم)

46 bridle path — مَمَرّ بَرِّي

47 pass (col) — مَمَرّ

48-56 glacial ice — **الثَّلْج الجَلِيدِيّ**

48 firn field (firn basin, nevé) — حَوْض الثلج الجَلِيدِيّ

49 valley glacier — مُثَلَّجَة الوَادي

50 crevasse — شَقّ جَلِيدِيّ

51 glacier snout — خُرْطُوم المُثَلَّجَة

52 subglacial stream — مَجْرَى مائِيّ أسفل المُثَلَّجَة

53 lateral moraine — رُكام الجَلِيد الجانبِيّ

54 medial moraine — رُكام الجَلِيد الوَسَطِيّ

55 end moraine — رُكام الجَلِيد النهائِيّ

56 glacier table — مائدة جليدِيَّة

13 Physical Geography III — الجُغْرَافِيَة الطَّبِيعِيَّة (3)

1-13 fluvial topography — **طبوغرافيا نَهْرِيَّة**

1 river mouth, a delta — مَصَبُّ النَّهْر

2 distributary (distributary channel), a river branch (river arm) — رافِد (من نَهْر)

3 lake — بُحَيْرَة

4 bank — ضفة

5 peninsula (spit) — شِبْه جَزِيرَة (لِسَان ساحلِيّ)

6 island — جَزِيرَة

7 bay (cove) — خَلِيج

8 stream (brook, rivulet, creek) — مَجْرَى مائِيّ

9 levee — شَطّ ، شاطِئ

10 alluvial plain — سَهْل غَرِيني

11 meander (river bend) — ميندر ، مُنْعَطَف

12 meander core (rock island) — قلب المُنْعَطَف

13 meadow — أَرْض مُعَشَّبَة

14-24 bog (marsh)	**مُسْتَنْقَع** (مُسْتَنْقَع ملح، هَوْر)
14 low-moor bog	مُسْتَنْقَع سَبِخ مُنْخَفِض
15 layers of decayed vegetable matter	طبقات مَوَاد نباتيَّة مُتَعَفِّنَة
16 entrapped water	مياه مَحْصُورَة
17 fen peat [consisting of rush and sedge]	خَثٌّ هَوْرِيّ
18 alder-swamp peat	خَثٌّ مُسْتَنْقَع جار الماء
19 high-moor bog	مُسْتَنْقَع سَبِخ مُرْتَفِع
20 layer of recent sphagnum mosses	طَبَقَة من طَحَالِب الإسْفَغْنُوم حَدِيثَة التكوين
21 boundary between layers (horizons)	الحدود الفاصِلَة بين الطَّبَقَات
22 layer of older sphagnum mosses	طَبَقَة من طَحَالِب الإسْفَغْنُوم أقدم في التكوين
23 bog pool	بِرْكَة المُسْتَنْقَع
24 swamp	مُسْتَنْقَع
25-31 cliffline (cliffs)	**المُرْتَفَعات الصَّخْرِيَّة**
25 rock	صَخْرَة
26 sea (ocean)	بَحْرٌ (مُحِيط)
27 surf	زَبَد
28 cliff (cliff face, steep rock face)	مُنْحَدَر صَخْرِي، جُرْف
29 scree	رُكَام صَخْرِي انهيارِيّ
30 [wave-cut] notch	ثُلْمَة
31 abrasion platform (wave-cut platform)	سَطْح/رصيف السَّحْج
32 atoll, a ring-shaped coral reef	شُعْب حلقيّ مَرْجَانِيّ
33 lagoon	بُحَيْرَة شاطئيَّة ضَحِلَة
34 breach (hole)	فَتْحَة، ثغرة
35-44 beach	**شاطئ**
35 high-water line (high-water mark, tidemark)	علامَة المَدّ
36 waves breaking on the shore	أمْوَاج تَتَكَسَّر على الشاطئ
37 groyne (*Am.* groin)	حاجِز أمْوَاج (لمَنْع تآكل الشاطئ)
38 groyne (*Am.* groin) head	رأس حاجِز الأمْوَاج
39 wandering dune (migratory dune, travelling, *Am.*traveling, dune), a dune	كُثَيْب رَمْلِيّ مُتَنَقِّل
40 barchan (barchane, barkhan, crescentic dune)	بَرْخَان، كُثَيْب هِلالِيّ
41 ripple marks	عَلامَات النَّيم
42 hummock	رَبْوَة، رابِيَة
43 wind cripple	حاجِز ريح
44 coastal lake	بُحَيْرَة ساحِلِيَّة
45 canyon (cañon, coulee)	وادٍ سحيق، هُوَّة
46 plateau (tableland)	هَضَبَة
47 rock terrace	شَرْفَة صَخْرِيَّة
48 sedimentary rock stratified rock)	صَخْرَة رسُوبِيَّة
49 river terrace (bed)	شَرْفَة نَهْرِيَّة
50 joint	فَلْق، فِلْقَة
51 canyon river	نهر أخْدُودِيّ
52-56 types of valley [cross section]	**أنْوَاع الوِدْيَان** [قِطَاع عَرْضِي]
52 gorge (ravine)	وادٍ عَمِيق ضَيِّق
53 V-shaped valley (V-valley)	وادٍ مُنْفَرِج
54 widened V-shaped valley	وادٍ مُنْفَرِج مُتَّسِع
55 U-shaped valley (U-valley, trough valley)	وادٍ غَوْرِيّ
56 synclinal valley	وادٍ قَعِيري/إلتوائيّ
57-70 river valley	**وادي النهر**
57 scarp (escarpment)	جُرْف، مُنْحَدَر شديد
58 slip-off slope	مُنْحَدَر انزلاقي
59 mesa	الميسا: هضبة صغيرة مُسَطَّحة ذات سفوح شديدة الانْحدار
60 ridge	مرْتَفَع صَخْرِيّ
61 river	نَهْر
62 flood plain	سَهْل فَيْضِي
63 river terrace	شَرْفَة نهريَّة
64 terracette	شُرَيْفَة، شَرْفَة صغيرة
65 pediment	رصيف صخري تَحَاتي خفيف الانْحِدار، رَاحَة، سَنَد
66 hill	تَلّ
67 valley floor (valley bottom)	قاع الوادي
68 riverbed	قاع النَّهْر
69 sediment	رَوَاسِب
70 bedrock	صَخْر القاعدة
71-83 karst formation in limestone	**تكوين الكارست في الحَجَر الجيري**
71 dolina, a sink (sinkhole, swallowhole)	دَحل، دولينا
72 polje	البُولْج: مُنْخَفَض مُمْتَد له أرْضِيَّة مسَطَّحة وجدران شديدة الانْحِدار وليس به مجرى مائي أرْضي
73 percolation of a river	تَخَلُّل/رَشْحُ نَهْر
74 karst spring	نبع/عين الكارست
75 dry valley	وادٍ جاف
76 system of caverns (system of caves)	نِظَام الكهوف
77 water level (water table) in a karst formation	مُسْتَوَى الماء في تَكْوين الكارست
78 impervious rock (impermeable rock)	صَخْر غير مُنْفِذ
79 limestone cave (dripstone cave)	كَهْف من الحَجَر الجيري
80-81 speleothems (cave formations)	**رَوَاسب معدنيَّة ثانويَّة تتكوَّن في الكهوف**
80 stalactite (dripstone)	هابِطَة
81 stalagmite	صاعِدَة
82 linked-up stalagmite and stalactite	صاعِدَة وهابِطَة متصلتان
83 subterranean river	نَهْر باطنيّ

14 Map I	**الخَرِيطَة (1)**
1-7 graticule of the earth (network of meridians and parallels on the earth's surface)	**شَبكَة خُطوط الطُول والعَرْض على الخَرِيطَة**
1 equator	خَطّ الاسْتِوَاء
2 line of latitude (parallel of latitude, parallel)	خَطّ عَرْض
3 pole (North Pole or South Pole), a terrestrial pole (geographical pole)	قُطْب (القُطْب الشَّمالِيّ أو القُطْب الجَنُوبِيّ)، قُطْب أرْضِيّ
4 line of longitude (meridian of longitude, meridian, terrestrial meridian)	خَطّ طُول
5 Standard meridian (Prime meridian, Greenwich meridian, meridian of Greenwich)	خَطّ الزَّوَال الرئيسي
6 latitude	ارْتِفَاع
7 longitude	طُول
8-9 map projections	**مَسَاقِط الخَرِيطَة**
8 conical (conic) projection	مَسْقَط مخروطي
9 cylindrical projection (Mercator projection, Mercator's projection)	مَسْقَط أُسْطُوَانِيّ (مركاتوري)
10-45 map of the world	**خَرِيطَة العَالَم**
10 tropics	المَدَارَان
11 polar circles	الدَّائرَتان القُطْبِيَّتان
12-18 continents	**القارات**
12-13 America	**أمريكا**
12 North America	أمريكا الشماليَّة
13 South America	أمريكا الجنوبيَّة
14 Africa	أفريقيا
15-16 Europe and Asia	**أوروبا وآسيا**
15 Europe	أوروبا
16 Asia	آسيا
17 Australia	**استراليا**
18 Antarctica (Antarctic Continent)	أنتاركتيكا (القارة القطبيَّة)
19-26 ocean (sea)	**المُحِيطَات**
19 Pacific Ocean	المُحِيط الباسيفيكي
20 Atlantic Ocean	المُحِيط الأَطْلَسِي (الأَطْلَنْطِي)
21 Arctic Ocean	المُحِيط القُطْبِيّ الشمالِيّ
22 Antarctic Ocean (Southern Ocean)	المُحِيط القُطْبِيّ الجنوبِيّ
23 Indian Ocean	المُحِيط الهِنْدِي
24 Strait of Gibraltar, a sea strait	مَضِيق جَبَل طَارِق
25 Mediterranean (Mediterranean Sea, European Mediterranean)	البَحْر الأَبْيَض المُتَوَسِّط
26 North Sea, a marginal sea (epeiric sea, epicontinental sea)	بَحْر الشَّمال
27-29 key (explanation of map symbols)	**مِفْتَاح الخَرِيطَة**
27 cold ocean current	تَيَّار مُحِيطِيّ بارِد
28 warm ocean current	تَيَّار مُحِيطِيّ ساخِن
29 scale	مِقْيَاس الرَّسْم
30-45 ocean (oceanic) **currents** (ocean drifts)	**التَيَّارات المُحِيطِيَّة البحريَّة**
30 Gulf Stream (North Atlantic Drift)	جَرْف شمال الأَطْلَنْطِي
31 Kuroshio (Kuro Siwo, Japan Current)	كُورُشِيُو (تيَّار اليابان)
32 North Equatorial Current	التَّيَّار الاسْتِوَائيّ الشماليّ
33 Equatorial Countercurrent	التَّيَّار الاسْتِوَائيّ المُعَاكِس
34 South Equatorial Current	التَّيَّار الاسْتِوَائيّ الجنوبيّ
35 Brazil Current	التَّيَّار البرازيليّ
36 Somali Current	التَّيَّار الصوماليّ
37 Agulhas Current	تَيَّار أجُولاس
38 East Australian Current	تَيَّار شَرْق استراليا
39 California Current	تَيَّار كاليفورنيا
40 Labrador Current	تَيَّار لا برادور
41 Canary Current	تَيَّار الكناري
42 Peru Current	تَيَّار بيرو
43 Benguela (Benguella) Current	تَيَّار بنجويلا
44 West Wind Drift (Antarctic Circumpolar Drift)	جَرْف الرياح الغربيَّة
45 West Australian Current	تَيَّار غَرْب استراليا
46-62 surveying (land surveying, geodetic surveying, geodesy)	**عمليات المَسْح الجُغْرَافي**
46 levelling (*Am.* leveling) (geometrical measurement of height)	قياس المَنَاسِيب
47 graduated measuring rod (levelling, *Am.* leveling, staff)	قضيب قياس مُدَرَّج
48 level (surveying level, surveyor's level), a surveyor's telescope	تليسكوب المَسَّاح
49 triangulation station (triangulation point)	نقطة التثليث
50 supporting scaffold	سقَالة داعمة/إسناد
51 signal tower (signal mast)	بُرْج الإشارة
52-62 theodolite, an instrument for measuring angles	**المِزْوَاة، ثيودوليت**
52 micrometer head	رأس ميكرومتري
53 micrometer eyepiece	عَيْنِيَّة ميكرومتريَّة
54 vertical tangent screw	قلاووظ المَمَاس الرَّأْسي
55 vertical clamp	قامِطَة/مِلْزَمَة رأسيَّة
56 tangent screw	قلاووظ المَمَاس
57 horizontal clamp	قامِطَة/مِلْزَمَة أفقيَّة
58 adjustment for the illuminating mirror	مُعايَرَة المِرْآة المُضِيئة

59 illuminating mirror	مِرْآة مُضيئة
60 telescope	تليسكوب
61 spirit level	ميزان تَسْوِيَة
62 circular adjustment	مُعايَرَة دائريَّة
63-66 photogrammetry (phototopography)	**المَسْح التصْويري**
63 air survey camera for producing overlapping series of pictures	كاميرا مَسْح جَوِّي لإلتقاط مجموعات مُتَراكِبة من الصُّوَر
64 stereoscope	ستريوسكوب ، مجْسَام
65 pantograph	بانتوجراف ، مِنْسَاخ
66 stereoplanigraph	ستريوبلانيجراف

15 Map II — الخَريطَة (2)

1-114 map signs (map symbols, conventional signs) on a 1:25 000 map	**رموز الخَريطَة على خَريطَة بمقْيَاس** 25000:1
1 coniferous wood (coniferous trees)	أشْجَار صَنُوبَرِيَّة
2 clearing	منْطقَة خاليَّة من الأشْجَار
3 forestry office	مكْتَب شؤون الغَابَة
4 deciduous wood (non-coniferous trees)	أشْجَار نَفْضِيَّة
5 heath (rough grassland, rough pasture, heath and moor, bracken)	أرْض عُشْبِيَّة وَعِرَة
6 sand or sand hills	رمال أو تِلال رَمْلِيَّة
7 beach grass	حَشَائش شاطِئِيَّة
8 lighthouse	مَنَارَة
9 mean low water	مياه مُنْخَفِضَة
10 beacon	فنَار (للمياه الضَّحِلَة)
11 submarine contours	مَنَاسيب تحت الماء
12 train ferry	مِعَدِّيَّة
13 lightship	مَنَارَة عائمة
14 mixed wood (mixed trees)	أشْجَار مُتَنَوِّعَة
15 brushwood	دَغَلٌ
16 motorway with slip road (*Am.* freeway with on-ramp, freeway with acceleration lane)	طَريق للعَرَبَات وبه حارة للعَرَبَات المسرعة
17 trunk road	طَريق رئيسي
18 grassland	أرْض عُشْبِيَّة
19 marshy grassland	أرْض عُشْبِيَّة سَبِخَة
20 marsh	مُسْتَنْقَع
21 main line railway (*Am.* trunk line)	خَطّ سِكَّة حديديَّة رئيسيّ
22 road over railway	طَريق يَمُر فَوْق سِكَّة حديديَّة
23 branch line	خَطّ فَرْعِيّ
24 signal box (*Am.* switch tower)	صندوق الإشارة
25 local line	خَطّ مَحَلِّيّ
26 level crossing	مَزْلَقَان ، تقاطع مستو
27 halt	مَوْقف اخْتِيارِيّ
28 residential area	منْطقَة سَكَنِيَّة
29 water gauge (*Am.* gage)	مِقْيَاس الماء
30 good, metalled road	طَريق مَرْصُوف بالحِجَارَة
31 windmill	طاحُونة هوائيَّة
32 thorn house (graduation house, salina, salt-works)	بَيْت الزَّعْرُور (بُحَيْرَة مِلْحِيَّة ، مَلاَّحَة)
33 broadcasting station (wireless or television mast)	مَحَطَّة إذاعة (بُرْج بَث لاسلكي أو تليفزيوني)
34 mine	مَنْجَم
35 disused mine	مَنْجَم مَهْجُور
36 secondary road (B road)	طَريق ثانوي
37 works	مَصْنَع
38 chimney	مِدْخَنَة
39 wire fence	سِيَاج سِلْكِيّ
40 bridge over railway	جِسْر فَوْق سِكَّة حديديَّة
41 railway station (*Am.* railroad station)	مَحَطَّة سِكَّة حديديَّة
42 bridge under railway	جِسْر أسفل سِكَّة حديديَّة
43 footpath	مَمَر المُشَاة
44 bridge for footpath under railway	جِسْر مُشَاة أسفل سِكَّة حديديَّة
45 navigable river	نَهْر ملاحيّ
46 pontoon bridge	جِسْر عائم (على أطْوَاف)
47 vehicle ferry	مِعَدِّيَّة
48 mole	حاجِز أمْوَاج
49 beacon	فنَار (للمياه الضَّحِلَة)
50 stone bridge	جِسْر حَجَرِيّ
51 town or city	بَلْدَة أو مدينة
52 market place (market square)	مِنْطَقَة السُّوق
53 large church with two towers	كَنِيسَة ضخمة ذات بُرْجَيْن
54 public building	مبنى حكومي
55 road bridge	جِسْر عبور الطَريق
56 iron bridge	جِسْر حديديّ
57 canal	قناة
58 lock	هَوِيس
59 jetty	رصيف بحريّ
60 foot ferry (foot passenger ferry)	مِعَدِّيَّة رُكَّاب
61 chapel (church) without tower or spire	أبْرَشِيَّة بدون بُرْج أو قمة هرميَّة
62 contours	خُطُوط كنتوريَّة ، مناسيب
63 monastery or convent	دَيْر
64 church landmark	مَعْلَم كَنِيسَة
65 vineyard	كَرْم
66 weir	سَدّ صغير
67 aerial ropeway	طَريق حَبْلِيّ هوائيّ
68 view point	بُرْج الرؤيَة
69 dam	سَدّ
70 tunnel	نَفَق
71 triangulation station (triangulation point)	نقطة التثليث
72 remains of a building	أنْقَاض مَبْنَى
73 wind pump	مِضَخَّة تُدَار بالرِّيَاح
74 fortress	قَلْعَة ، حِصْن
75 ox-bow lake	بُحَيْرَة قَوْسِيَّة الشكل
76 river	نَهْر
77 watermill	طاحونة مائيَّة

78 footbridge	جِسْر عبور المُشَاة
79 pond	بِرْكَة
80 stream (brook, rivulet, creek)	نُهَيْر، مَجْرَى مائيّ
81 water tower	بُرج خزانات الماء
82 spring	جَدْوَل مياه، عَيْن مياه
83 main road (A road)	طَرِيق رئيسيّ
84 cutting	نَفَق غير مَسْقوف
85 cave	كَهْفٌ
86 lime kiln	قَمِين جير
87 quarry	مَحْجَر
88 clay pit	حُفْرَة طين
89 brickworks	مَصْنَع طُوب
90 narrow-gauge (*Am.* narrow gage) railway	سِكَّة حديديَّة ضَيِّقَة
91 goods depot (freight depot)	مُسْتَوْدَع بضائع
92 monument	نُصُب تذكاريّ
93 site of battle	مَوْقع معركة
94 country estate, a demesne	ضَيْعَة أو عِزْبَة
95 wall	جِدار، سُور
96 stately home	مَنْزِل فاخر
97 park	مُنْتَزَه
98 hedge	سِياج
99 poor or unmetalled road	طَرِيق غير مُعَبَّد
100 well	بِئْر
101 farm	مَزْرَعَة
102 unfenced path (unfenced track)	مَمَر غير مُسَيَّج
103 district boundary	حدود الضاحية
104 embankment	سَدٌّ
105 village	قَرْيَة
106 cemetery	مَدَافِن، جَبَّانَة
107 church or chapel with spire	كَنِيسَة قِمَّتُها هَرَمِيَّة
108 orchard	بُسْتَان
109 milestone	مَعْلَم الطَرِيق
110 guide post	لافتة الطَرِيق
111 tree nursery	مَشْتَل أشْجَار
112 ride (aisle, lane, section line)	مَمَر، دَرْب
113 electricity transmission line	خَطّ نَقْل الكهرباء
114 hop garden	حَدِيقَة حَشِيشَة الدِّينَار

16 Man I — الإنْسَان (1)

1-54 the human body	**جِسْم الإنْسَان**
1-18 head	**الرَّأس**
1 vertex (crown of the head, top of the head)	قمة الرَّأس
2 occiput (back of the head)	القَذَال، القفا، مُؤَخِرَة الرَّأس
3 hair	شَعْر
4-17 face	**الوَجْه**
4-5 forehead	**الجَبْهَة**
4 frontal eminence (frontal protuberance)	بروز الجَبْهَة
5 superciliary arch	القَوْس فَوْقَ الهَدَبي
6 temple	صَدْغ
7 eye	عَيْن
8 zygomatic bone (malar bone, jugal bone, cheekbone)	العَظْم الوَجْني
9 cheek	وَجْنَة
10 nose	أنْف
11 nasolabial fold	ثنية أنْف–شَفَوِيَّة
12 philtrum	ثَرْمَلَة، النثرة
13 mouth	فَمٌ
14 angle of the mouth (labial commissure)	زَاوِيَة الفَم
15 chin	ذَقْن
16 dimple (fossette) in the chin	غمَّازَة، نَقْرَة في الذَّقْن
17 jaw	فَكٌّ
18 ear	أُذُن
19-21 neck	**الرَّقَبَة/العُنُق**
19 throat	الزَوْر
20 hollow of the throat	وَقْرَة الزَوْر
21 nape of the neck	قَفَا الرَّقَبَة
22-41 trunk	**الجِذْع**
22-25 back	**الظَّهْر**
22 shoulder	كَتِف
23 shoulderblade (scapula)	لَوْح الكَتِف
24 loins	خاصِرة
25 small of the back	القَطَن
26 armpit	إبط
27 armpit hair	شَعْر الإبط
28-30 thorax (chest)	**الصَّدْر**
28-29 breasts (breast, mamma)	**الثَّدْيَان**
28 nipple	حَلَمَة
29 areola	لُعْوَة، هالة
30 bosom	مُنْتَصَف الصَّدْر
31 waist	خَصْر
32 flank (side)	جَنْب
33 hip	وِرْك
34 navel	سُرَّة
35-37 abdomen (stomach)	**البَطْن**
35 upper abdomen	الجزء العلوي من البَطْن، فَم المَعِدَة
36 abdomen	بَطْن
37 lower abdomen	الجُزْء السفليّ من البَطْن
38 groin	الأُرْبِيَّة، المَغْبَن
39 pudenda (vulva)	أعضاء التناسُل الخارجيَّة
40 seat (backside, *coll.* bottom)	مِقْعَدَة
41 anal groove (anal cleft)	الحَزُّ الإسْتي
42 gluteal fold (gluteal furrow)	الثَّنْيَة الألْيَوِيَّة
43-54 limbs	**الأطْرَاف**
43-48 arm	**الذِّرَاع**
43 upper arm	عَضُد
44 crook of the arm	ثَنْيَة الذِّرَاع
45 elbow	مِرْفَق
46 forearm	ساعِد
47 hand	يَدٌ

48 fist (clenched fist, clenched hand) قَبْضَة
49-54 leg **السَّاق**
49 thigh فَخْذ
50 knee رُكْبَة
51 popliteal space باطِن الرُّكْبَة
52 shank الرِّجْل
53 calf بطن السَّاق، السِّمَّانَة
54 foot قَدَم

17 Man II الإِنْسَان (2)

1-29 skeleton (bones) **الهَيْكَل العَظْمِي** (العِظَام)
1 skull الجُمْجُمَة
2-5 vertebral column (spinal column, spine, backbone) **العمود الفقَّارِيّ**
2 cervical vertebra فَقْرَة عُنُقِيَّة
3 dorsal vertebra (thoracic vertebra) فَقْرَة ظَهْرِيَّة
4 lumbar vertebra فَقْرَة قَطَنِيَّة
5 coccyx (coccygeal vertebra) العُصْعُص
6-7 shoulder girdle **الحِزَام الكتفيّ**
6 collarbone (clavicle) عَظْم التَّرْقُوَة (التُّرْقُوَة)
7 shoulderblade (scapula) لَوْح الكَتِف
8-11 thorax (chest) **الصَّدر**
8 breastbone (sternum) عَظْم القَصّ
9 true ribs ضلوع حقيقية
10 false ribs ضلوع كاذبة
11 costal cartilage غُضْرُوف ضِلْعِيّ
12-14 arm **الذِّرَاع**
12 humerus العَضُد
13 radius الكُعْبُرَة
14 ulna الزَّنْد
15-17 hand **اليَد**
15 carpus الرُّسْغ
16 metacarpal bone (metacarpal) العِظَام السِّنْعِيَّة
17 phalanx (phalange) سُلامِيَّات
18-21 pelvis **الحَوْض**
18 ilium (hip bone) الحَرْقَفَة
19 ischium الوِرْك
20 pubis العَانَة
21 sacrum العُجُز
22-25 leg **السَّاق**
22 femur (thigh bone, thigh) عَظْم الفَخْذ
23 patella (kneecap) الرَّضَفَة (صابُونَة الرُّكْبَة)
24 fibula (splint bone) الشَّظِيَّة
25 tibia (shinbone) الظُّنْبُوب
26-29 foot **القَدَم**
26 tarsal bones (tarsus) عَظْم رُصْغ (رُسْغ) القَدَم
27 calcaneum (heelbone) العَقِب
28 metatarsus العِظَام المِشْطِيَّة
29 phalanges السُّلامِيَّات
30-41 skull **الجُمْجُمَة**
30 frontal bone العَظْم الجَبْهِيّ
31 left parietal bone العَظْم الجداري الأيسر
32 occipital bone العَظْم القَذَالِيّ
33 temporal bone العَظْم الصَّدْغِيّ
34 external auditory canal قناة السَّمَع الخارجيَّة
35 lower jawbone (lower jaw, mandible) الفَكُّ السفلي
36 upper jawbone (upper jaw, maxilla) الفَكُّ العلوي
37 zygomatic bone (cheekbone) العَظْم الوَجْنِي
38 sphenoid bone (sphenoid) العَظْم الوَتَدي
39 ethmoid bone (ethmoid) العَظْم المِصْفَوي
40 lachrimal (lacrimal) bone العظم الدَّمْعي
41 nasal bone العظم الأنفيّ
42-55 head [section] **الرأس** [مقطع]
42 cerebrum (great brain) المُخ
43 pituitary gland (pituitary body, hypophysis cerebri) الغُدَّة النخاميَّة
44 corpus callosum الجِسْم الثَّفَني
45 cerebellum (little brain) المُخَيخ
46 pons (pons cerebri, pons cerebelli) جِسْر المُخَيخ
47 medulla oblongata (brain stem) النُّخَاع الشَّوْكي
48 spinal cord الحَبْل الشوكي
49 oesophagus (esophagus, gullet) المَرِيء
50 trachea (windpipe) القَصَبَة الهوائيَّة
51 epiglottis لِسان المِزْمَار
52 tongue اللسان
53 nasal cavity التَّجْوِيف الأنفي
54 sphenoidal sinus الجيب الوَتَدي
55 frontal sinus الجيب الجَبْهي
56-65 organ of equilibrium and hearing **عضو التَّوازُن والسَّمَع**
56-58 external ear **الأُذُن الخارجيَّة**
56 auricle صيوَان الأُذُن
57 ear lobe فُصَيْص الأُذُن
58 external auditory canal قناة السَّمَع الخارجيَّة
59-61 middle ear **الأُذُن الوُسْطى**
59 tympanic membrane طَبْلَة الأُذُن، الغشاء الطَّبْلي
60 tympanic cavity التجْوِيف الطَّبْلي
61 auditory ossicles: hammer, anvil, and stirrup (malleus, incus, and stapes) عُظَيْمَات السَّمْع: المِطْرَقَة والسِّنْدَان والرِّكَاب
62-64 inner ear (internal ear) **الأُذُن الداخليَّة**
62 labyrinth التِّيه
63 cochlea القَوْقَعَة
64 auditory nerve العَصَب السَّمْعي
65 eustachian tube قناة استاكيوس

18 Man III الإِنْسَان (3)

1-21 blood circulation (circulatory system) **الدَّوْرَة الدَّمَوِيَّة** (الجِهَاز الدَّوْرِيّ)
1 common carotid artery, شُرْيَان سُبَاتيّ عادي

an artery
2 jugular vein, a vein وَريد وَدَجيّ
3 temporal artery شُرْيان صَدْغيّ
4 temporal vein وَريد صَدْغيّ
5 frontal artery شُرْيان جَبْهيّ
6 frontal vein وَريد جَبْهي
7 subclavian artery الشُّرْيان تحت التَّرْقُويّ
8 suvclavian vein الوَريد تحت التَّرْقُويّ
9 superior vena cava الوَريد الأجْوَف العلوي
10 arch of the aorta (aorta) الأورطي، الأبْهَر
11 pulmonary artery [with venous blood] الشُّرْيان الرِّئَوي [وبه دَمٌ وَريديّ]
12 pulmonary vein [with arterial blood] الوَريد الرِّئَوي [وبه دَمٌ شرْيَانيّ]
13 lungs الرئتان
14 heart القلب
15 inferior vena cava الوَريد الأجْوَف السفلي
16 abdominal aorta (descending portion of the aorta) الأورطي البطني
17 iliac artery الشُّرْيان الحَرْقَفي
18 iliac vein الوَريد الحَرْقَفي
19 femoral artery الشُّرْيان الفَخْذي
20 tibial artery الشُّرْيان الظُّنْبوبي
21 radial artery الشُّرْيان الكُعْبُري
22-33 nervous system **الجهاز العصبي**
22 cerebrum (great brain) المُخ
23 cerebellum (little brain) المُخَيخ
24 medulla oblongata (brain stem) النُّخاع الشَّوْكي
25 spinal cord الحَبْل الشَّوْكي
26 thoracic nerves الأعْصاب الصَّدْريَّة
27 brachial plexus الضَّفيرَة العَضُديَّة
28 radial nerve العَصَب الكُعْبُري
29 ulnar nerve العَصَب الزَّنْدي
30 great sciatic nerve (lying posteriorly) العَصَب الوِرْكي
31 femoral nerve (anterior crural nerve) العَصَب الفَخْذيّ
32 tibial nerve العَصَب الظُّنْبوبيّ
33 peroneal nerve العَصَب الشَّظَويّ
34-64 musculature (muscular system) **الجِهاز العَضَليّ**
34 sternocleidomastoid muscle(sternomastoid muscle) العَضَلَة القَصِّيَّة التُّرْقُويَّة الحلَميَّة
35 deltoid muscle العَضَلَة الدَّاليَّة
36 pectoralis major (greater pectoralis muscle, greater pectoralis) العَضَلَة الصَّدْريَّة الكُبْرَى
37 biceps brachii (biceps of the arm) العَضَلَة ذات الرأسَيْن العَضُديَّة
38 triceps brachii (triceps of the arm) العَضَلَة ذات الثلاثة رؤوس العَضُديَّة
39 brachioradialis العَضَلَة العَضُديَّة الكُعْبُريَّة
40 flexor carpi radialis (radial flexor of the wrist) العَضَلَة مُثْنِيَة الرُسْغ الكُعْبُريَّة
41 thenar muscle العَضَلَة الرَّاحيَّة
42 serratus anterior العَضَلَة المُسَنَّنَة الأمامية
43 obliquus externus abdominis (external oblique) العَضَلَة الخارجيَّة المائِلة
44 rectus abdominis العَضَلَة المستقيمة البَطْنيَّة
45 sartorius العَضَلَة الخِياطيَّة
46 vastus lateralis and vastus medialis العَضَلَة المُتَّسِعَة الوحشيَّة والعَضَلَة المُتَّسعَة الإنْسيَّة
47 tibialis anterior العَضَلَة الظُنْبوبِيَّة الأمامية
48 tendo calcanaeus (Achilles' tendon) الوَتَر العَقِبي
49 abductor hallucis (abductor of the hallux), a foot muscle العَضَلَة مُبْعِدَة إبْهام القَدَم
50 occipitalis العَضَلَة القذاليَّة
51 splenius of the neck العَضَلَة اللفاحيَّة العُنُقيَّة
52 trapezius العَضَلَة شِبْه المُنْحَرِفَة
53 infraspinatus العَضَلَة تحت الشَّوْكيَّة
54 teres minor (lesser teres) العَضَلَة المُدَوَّرَة الصُّغْرَى
55 teres major (greater teres) العَضَلَة المُدَوَّرَة الكُبْرَى
56 extensor carpi radialis longus (long radial extensor of the wrist) العَضَلَة باسِطَة الرُسْغ الكُعْبُريَّة الطويلة
57 extensor communis digitorum (common extensor of the digits) العَضَلَة الباسِطَة المُوَصِّلَة للأصابِع
58 flexor carpi ulnaris (ulnar flexor of the wrist) العَضَلَة مُثْنِيَة الرُسْغ الكعبرية
59 latissimus dorsi العَضَلَة العريضة الظَّهْريَّة
60 gluteus maximus العَضَلَة الألْيَويَّة الكُبْرَى
61 biceps femoris (biceps of the thigh) العَضَلَة ذات الرأسين الفَخْذيَّة
62 gastrocnemius, medial and lateral heads العَضَلَة التَّوْأميَّة للساق
63 extensor communis digitorum (common extensor of the digits) العَضَلَة الباسِطَة المُوَصِّلَة لأصابِع القَدَم
64 peroneus longus (long peroneus) العَضَلَة الشَّظَويَّة الطَّويلة

19 Man IV الإنْسَان (4)

1-13 head and neck **الرَّأس والعُنُق**
1 sternocleidomastoid muscle (sternomastoid muscle) العَضَلَة القَصِّيَّة التُّرْقُويَّة الحلَميَّة
2 occipitalis العَضَلَة القَذَاليَّة
3 temporalis (temporal, temporal muscle) العَضَلَة الصَّدْغيَّة
4 occipito frontalis (frontalis) العَضَلَة القَذَاليَّة الجَبْهيَّة
5 orbicularis oculi العَضَلَة الدُّوَيْريَّة العَيْنيَّة
6 muscles of facial expression عَضَلات الوَجْه
7 masseter العَضَلَة الماضِغَة
8 orbicularis oris العَضَلَة الدُّوَيْريَّة الفَمَويَّة
9 parotid gland الغُدَّة النَّكَفيَّة

10 lymph node (submandibular lymph gland) العُقدَة الليمْفيَّة
11 submandibular gland (submaxillary gland) الغُدَّة تحت الفَكِّيَّة السفلية
12 muscles of the neck عَضَلات الرَّقَبَة
13 Adam's apple (laryngeal prominence) [in men only] تفاحة آدَم [في الرِّجال فقط]
14-37 mouth and pharynx **الفَم والزَّوْر**
14 upper lip الشَّفَة العليا
15 gum اللِّثَة
16-18 teeth (set of teeth) **الأسْنَان**
16 incisors القَوَاطع
17 canine tooth (canine) ناب
18 premolar (bicuspid) and molar teeth (premolars and molars) الطَّوَاحين والضَّوَاحِك
19 angle of the mouth (labial commissure) زاوِيَة الفَم
20 hard palate الحَنَك الصُّلْب
21 soft palate (velum palati, velum) الحَنَك الرَّخْو
22 uvula عَضَلَة اللهاة
23 palatine tonsil (tonsil) لَوْزَة
24 pharyngeal opening (pharynx) فَتْحَة البِلْعَوْم
25 tongue اللسان
26 lower lip الشَّفَة السفلى
27 upper jaw (maxilla) الفك العلوي
28-37 tooth **سِنّ**
28 periodontal membrane (periodontium, pericementum) الغِشاء حَوْل السِّنِّي
29 cement (dental cementum, crusta petrosa) المِلاط
30 enamel المينا
31 dentine (dentin) العَاج
32 dental pulp (tooth pulp, pulp) اللُّب السِّنِّي
33 nerves and blood vessels الأعْصَاب والأوْعِيَة الدَّمَوِيَّة
34 incisor قاطع
35 molar tooth (molar) ضِرْس، طاحِن
36 root (fang) جَذْر، جُذْمُور
37 crown تاج
38-51 eye **العَيْن**
38 eyebrow (supercilium) حاجِب
39 upper eyelid (upper palpebra) جِفْن علوي
40 lower eyelid (lower palpebra) جِفْن سفلي
41 eyelash (cilium) رِمْش، هَدَب
42 iris القَزَحِيَّة
43 pupil الحدَقَة
44 eye muscles (ocular muscles) عَضَلات العَيْن
45 eyeball المُقْلَة
46 vitreous body الجِسْم الزُّجَاجي
47 cornea القَرَنِيَّة
48 lens العَدَسَة
49 retina الشبكيَّة
50 blind spot البُقْعَة العَمْيَاء
51 optic nerve عَصَب بَصَري
52-63 foot **القدَم**
52 big toe (great toe, first toe, hallux, digitus I) إبْهَام القَدَم
53 second toe (digitus II) الإصْبَع الثاني
54 third toe (digitus III) الإصْبَع الثالث
55 fourth toe (digitus IV) الإصْبَع الرابع
56 little toe (digitus minimus, digitus V) الإصْبَع الصغير
57 toenail ظفر إصْبَع القَدَم
58 ball of the foot الضَّرَّة
59 lateral malleolus (external malleolus, outer malleolus, malleolus fibulae) النتْوء الكَعْبي الوحشي
60 medial malleolus (internal malleolus, inner malleolus, malleolus tibulae, malleolus medialis) النتوء الكَعْبي الوحشي الأنْسِي
61 instep (medial longitudinal arch, dorsum of the foot, dorsum pedis) وَجْه القدَم
62 sole of the foot إخْمَص القَدَم
63 heel عقِب، كَعْب
64-83 hand **اليَد**
64 thumb (pollex, digitus I) الإبْهَام
65 index finger (forefinger, second finger, digitus II) السَّبَّابَة
66 middle finger (third finger, digitus medius, digitus III) الوُسْطَى
67 ring finger (fourth finger, digitus anularis, digitus IV) البِنْصَر
68 little finger (fifth finger, digitus minimus, digitus V) الخِنْصَر
69 radial side of the hand الجانِب الكُعْبُري لليَد
70 ulnar side of the hand الجانِب الزَّنْدي لليَد
71 palm of the hand (palma manus) راحَة اليَد
72-74 lines of the hand **خطُوط الكَفّ**
72 life line (line of life) خَطّ العُمْر
73 head line (line of the head) خَطّ الرَّأس
74 heart line (line of the heart) خَطّ القَلْب
75 ball of the thumb (thenar eminence) كُوَّة اليَد
76 wrist (carpus) رُسْغ
77 phalanx (phalange) سُلاميَّات
78 finger pad لينة الأصابع

79 fingertip طَرَف الإصْبع
80 fingernail (nail) ظُفْر الإصْبع
81 lunule (lunula) of the nail هَيْكَل الظُّفْر
82 knuckle عُقْلَة
83 back of the hand (dorsum of the hand, dorsum manus) ظَهْر اليَد

20 Man V الإنْسَان (5)

1-57 internal organs [front view] **الأعْضَاء الدَّاخليَّة** [مَنْظَر أمَامي]
1 thyroid gland الغُدَّة الدَّرَقيَّة
2-3 larynx **الحَنْجَرَة**
2 hyoid bone (hyoid) العَظْم اللامي
3 thyroid cartilage غُضْرُوف دَرَقي
4 trachea (windpipe) القَصَبَة الهوائيَّة
5 brochus شُعْبَة هوائيَّة
6 right lung الرِّئَة اليُمْنَى
7 upper pulmonary lobe (upper lobe of the lung) [section] الفَص الصَّدْري/الرِّئَويّ العلْوي [مقطع]
8 heart القَلْب
9 diaphragm الحِجَاب الحاجِز
10 liver الكَبد
11 gall bladder الحَوْصَلَة الصَّفْرَاويَّة
12 spleen الطِّحَال
13 stomach المَعدَة
14-22 intestines (bowel) **الأمْعَاء**
14-16 small intestine (intestinum tenue) **الأمْعَاء الرفيعة**
14 duodenum الإثنا عَشْري
15 jejunum الصَّائم
16 ileum اللفائفي
17-22 large intestine (intestinum crassum) **الأمْعَاء الغليظة**
17 caecum (cecum) الأعْوَر
18 appendix (vermiform appendix) الزَّائدة الدُّوديَّة
19 ascending colon القَوْلُون الصَّاعد
20 transverse colon القَوْلُون المُسْتَعْرَض
21 descending colon القَوْلُون النَّازل
22 rectum المُسْتَقيم
23 oesophagus (esophagus, gullet) المَرِيء
24, 25 heart القلب
24 auricle صيوَان
25 anterior longitudinal cardiac sulcus تَلَم أمامي طُولي
26 diaphragm الحِجَاب الحاجِز
27 spleen الطِّحَال
28 right kidney الكلْيَة اليُمْنَى
29 suprarenal gland الغُدَّة فَوْق الكَظَريَّة
30-31 left kidney [longitudinal section] **الكلْيَة اليُسْرَى** [مقطع طولي]
30 calyx (renal calyx) كَأْس
31 renal pelvis حَوْض الكِلْيَتَيْن
32 ureter حالِب
33 bladder المثانة
34-35 liver [from behind] **الكَبد** [من الخلف]
34 falciform ligament of the liver الرِّبَاط المنجلي للكَبِد
35 lobe of the liver فص الكَبد
36 gall bladder الحَوْصَلَة الصَّفْرَاويَّة
37-38 common bile duct **القناة الصَّفْرَاويَّة**
37 hepatic duct (common hepatic duct) القناة الكَبِديَّة
38 cystic duct القناة الحَوْصَليَّة
39 portal vein (hepatic portal vein) الوَريد (الكَبِديّ) البابي
40 oesophagus (esophagus, gullet) المَرِيء
41-42 stomach **المَعدَة**
41 cardiac orifice فَتْحَة الفُؤاد
42 pylorus البَوَّاب
43 duodenum الإثنا عَشْري
44 pancreas البَنكِرْيَاس
45-57 heart (longitudinal section) **القَلْب** (مقطع طولي)
45 atrium أُذَيْن القَلْب
46-47 valves of the heart **صِمَامات القَلْب**
46 tricuspid valve (right atrioventricular valve) الصِمَام ثلاثي الشُرَف
47 bicuspid valve (mitral valve, left atrioventricular valve) الصِمَام ثنائي الشُرَف (الميترالي)
48 cusp شُرْفَة
49 aortic valve صِمام الأَبْهر
50 pulmonary valve صِمام رِئَوِي
51 ventricle بُطَيْن
52 ventricular septum (interventricular septum) حاجِز بُطَيْني
53 superior vena cava الوَريد الأجْوَف العلوي
54 aorta الأبْهَر، الأورطي
55 pulmonary artery الشُرْيَان الرِّئَوي
56 pulmonary vein وَريد رئَوي
57 inferior vena cava الوَريد الأجْوَف السفلي
58 peritoneum البريتون، الغشاء البريتوني
59 sacrum العُجُز
60 coccyx (coccygeal vertebra) العُصْعُص
61 rectum المُسْتَقيم
62 anus الشَّرَج
63 anal sphincter العَضَلَة المُصِرَّة الشَّرَجيَّة
64 perineum العِجَان
65 pubic symphisis (symphisis pubis) الارْتفَاق العانيّ
66-77 male sex organ [longitudinal section] **الأعضاء التناسليَّة للذَّكَر** [مقطع طولي]
66 penis القضيب
67 corpus cavernosum and spongiosum of the penis (erectile tissue of the penis) تَرَابيق الأجْسَام الكَهْفيَّة والإسْفَنْجيَّة للقَضيب
68 urethra المَبَال
69 glans penis حَشَفَة القضيب
70 prepuce (foreskin) القُلْفَة

71 scrotum — الصَّفَن
72 right testicle (testis) — الخصْيَة اليُمْنَى
73 epididymis — البَرْبَخ
74 spermatic duct (vas deferens) — القناة المَنَوِيَّة
75 Cowper's gland (bulbourethral gland) — غُدَّة كُوبَر
76 prostate (prostate gland) — البروسْتاتا
77 seminal vesicle — الحُوَيْصَلات المَنَوِيَّة
78 bladder — المَثَانة
79-88 female sex organs [longitudinal section] — **الأعضاء التناسليَّة للأُنْثَى** [مقطع طولي]
79 uterus (matrix, womb) — الرَّحِم
80 cavity of the uterus — تجويف الرَّحِم
81 fallopian tube (uterine tube, oviduct) — قناة فالوب
82 fimbria (fimbriated extremity) — هَدَب
83 ovary — مِبْيَض
84 follicle with ovum (egg) — جُرَيْب وبه بييْضَة (بُوَيْضَة)
85 os uteri externum — فُوهَة عُنُق الرَّحِم الظَّاهِرة
86 vagina — المِهْبَل
87 lip of the pudendum (lip of the vulva) — شفة الفَرْج
88 clitoris — البَظْر

21 First Aid — الإسْعافَات الأوَلِيَّة

1-13 emergency bandages — **عصَابات الطَّوارِئ**
1 arm bandage — عِصَابة الذِّرَاع
2 triangular cloth used as a sling (an arm sling) — عَلَّاقَة الذِّرَاع (قطْعَة قماش مُثَلَّثة تُسْتَخْدَم كعَلاَّقَة للذِّرَاع)
3 head bandage (capeline) — ضِمَادَة رَأس
4 first aid kit — حَقيبَة الإسْعافات الأوَّلِيَّة
5 first aid dressing — ضِمادات الإسْعافات الأوَّلِيَّة
6 sterile gauze dressing — ضِمَادات شَاش مُعَقَّمَة
7 adhesive plaster (sticking plaster) — بلاستر ، شريط لاصق
8 wound — جَرْح
9 bandage — ضِمَادة، رباط ، عِصَابة
10 emergency splint for a broken limb (fractured limb) — جَبِيرَة طَوارِئ لِطَرَف مكْسُور
11 fractured leg (broken leg) — ساق مكْسُورَة
12 splint — جَبِيرَة
13 headrest — مِسْنَد للرأس
14-17 measures for stanching the blood flow (tying up (ligature) of a blood vessel) — **إجراءات وَقْف النَّزيف الدَّمَوي** (ربْط وِعاء دَمَوِيّ)
14 pressure points of the arteries — نِقاط الضَّغْط على الشَّرايين لإيقاف تَدَفُّق الدَّم
15 emergency tourniquet on the thigh — عاصِبة طَوارِئ لإيقاف النَّزيف في إصابات الفَخْذ
16 walking stick used as a screw — عَصًا تُسْتَخْدَم في إحكَام الجَبِيرَة
17 compression bandage — ضِمَادَة ضَغْط
18-23 rescue and transport of an injured person — **إنْقَاذ ونَقْل الشَّخْص المُصَاب**
18 Rautek grip (for rescue of a car accident victim) — مَسْكَة "راوْتِك" (لإنقاذ ضَحِيَّة في حَادِث سَيَّارَة)
19 helper — مُسَاعِد
20 injured person (casualty) — شَخْص مُصَاب
21 chair grip — مَسْكَة المَقْعَد
22 carrying grip — مَسْكَة الحَمْل
23 emergency stretcher of sticks and a jacket — نَقَّالَة طَوارِئ مصنوعة من عِصي وسُتْرَة
24-27 positioning of an unconscious person and artificial respiration (resuscitation) — **الوَضْع الصَّحيح لِشخص فاقد الوَعْي والتَّنَفُّس الصِّناعيّ** (إنْعَاش القَلْب والرِّئَتَيْن)
24 coma position — وَضْع الغَيْبُوبَة
25 unconscious person — شَخْص فاقد الوَعْيّ
26 mouth-to-mouth resuscitation (*variation:* mouth-to-nose resuscitation) — **إنْعَاش القَلْب والرِّئتَيْن عن طَريق الفَم** (قُبْلَة الحَيَاة)
27 resuscitator (respiratory apparatus, resuscitation apparatus), a respirator (artificial breathing device) — جِهَاز إنْعَاش القَلْب والرِّئَتَيْن، جِهَاز تنفُّس صناعي
28-33 methods of rescue in ice accidents — **طَريقة الإنْقَاذ في حَوَادِث الجَلِيد**
28 person who has fallen through the ice — الشَّخْص الذي سَقَط في انهيار الجَلِيد
29 rescuer — المُنْقِذ
30 rope — حَبْل
31 table (or similar device) — طاوِلَة (أو ما شَابَه ذلك)
32 ladder — سُلَّم
33 self-rescue — إنْقاذ ذاتي
34-38 rescue of a drowning person — **إنْقَاذ غَرِيق**
34 method of release (release grip, release) to free rescuer from the clutch of a drowning person — طَرِيقة تَحَرُّر المُنْقِذ من الغَرِيق
35 drowning person — الغَرِيق
36 lifesaver — المُنْقِذ
37, 38 towing (tows) — القَطْر
37 double shoulder tow — مَسْكَة القَطْر المُزْدَوَجة من الكَتِفَيْن
38 head tow — مَسْكَة القَطْر من الرَّأس

22 Doctor I — الطَّبيب (1)

1-74 general practice (*Am.* physician's office) — **عِيادَة الطَّبِيب**
1 waiting room — غُرْفَة الانْتِظَار
2 patient — مَرِيض

3 patients with appointments (for a routine check-up or renewal of prescription) — مَرْضَى بمَوَاعيد مُسْبَقَة (لفَحْص دَوْريّ أو اسْتِشَارَة)
4 magazines [for waiting patients] — مجلات
5 reception — الاسْتِقْبَال
6 patients file — مَلَف المَرْضَى
7 eliminated index cards — بطَاقَات مُفَهْرَسَة مَطْرُوحَة جَانِباً
8 medical record (medical card) — سِجِل طِبِّي
9 health insurance certificate — شهادة تأمين صِحِّي
10 advertising calendar (publicity calendar) — رُوزْنَامَة تِجَارِيَّة للدعَايَة
11 appointments book — دَفْتَر حَجْز المَوَاعِيد
12 correspondence file — مَلَف المُرَاسَلات
13 automatic telephone answering and recording set (telephone answering device) — جِهَاز للرَّد على المكالَمات الهاتِفِيَّة و تَسْجِيلِها آلِيّاً
14 radiophone — سَمَّاعَة داخليَّة
15 microphone — مُكَبِّر الصوت
16 illustrated chart — رَسْم تخطيطي مُصَوَّر
17 wall calendar — رُوزْنَامَة حائِط
18 telephone — هاتِف، تليفون
19 [doctor's] assistant — مساعد/مساعدة [الطبيب]
20 prescription — رُوشِتَّة، تَذْكَرَة طبيَّة
21 telephone index — فهرس التليفون
22 medical dictionary — قامُوس طِبِّي
23 pharmacopoeia (list of registered medicines) — قائمة العَقَاقِير والأدْوِيَة المُسَجَّلَة
24 franking machine (*Am.* postage meter) — ماكينة دَمْغ الرَّسَائِل
25 stapler — دَبَّاسَة
26 diabetics file — ملفّ السُكَّرِي
27 dictating machine — المِمْلاة
28 paper punch — خَرَّامَة وَرَق
29 doctor's stamp — خاتَم الطبيب
30 ink pad — حَبَّارَة الخاتم
31 pencil holder — حَامِل أقْلام
32-74 surgery — **الجِرَاحَة**
32 chart of eyegrounds — رَسْم تخطيطي لِقَاع العَيْن
33 doctor's bag (doctor's case) — حَقِيبَة الطَّبِيب
34 intercom — جِهَاز اتِّصَال داخِلي (انتركوم)
35 medicine cupboard — صَيْدَلِيَّة مَنْزِليَّة
36 swab dispenser — وعَاء رَمْي القَطِيلَة
37 inflator (Politzer bag) — حَقِيبَة البَلْزَرَة
38 electrotome — مِقْطَع كهربائي
39 steam sterilizer — جِهَاز تَعْقِيم بالبُخَار
40 cabinet — خِزَانَة ، صوان
41 medicine samples (from the pharmaceutical industry) — عَيِّنَات أدْوِيَة
42 baby scales — مِيزَان أطْفَال رُضَّع
43 examination couch — سَرِير الفَحْص
44 directional lamp — مِصْبَاح مُتَحَرِّك
45 instrument table — طاولَة الأدوَات
46 tube holder — حَامِل أنَابِيب
47 tube of ointment — أنْبُوب مَرْهَم
48-50 instruments for minor surgery — **أدوَات الجِرَاحَة البَسِيطَة**
48 mouth gag — أدَاة فَتْح الفَم
49 Kocher's forceps — جِفْت "كوتشر"
50 scoop (curette) — مِجْرَفَة
51 angled scissors — مِقَصّ طَرَفُه مائل بزاوية
52 forceps — جِفْت، مِلْقَاط
53 olive-pointed (bulb-headed) probe — مِجَسّ ذو رأس مُنْتَفِخ
54 syringe for irrigations of the ear or bladder — مِحْقَن غَسِيل الأذُن أو المَثَانَة
55 adhesive plaster (sticking plaster) — شَرِيط لاصِق، بِلاسْتَر
56 surgical suture material — خَيْط جِرَاحة
57 curved surgical needle — إبْرَة طِبِّيَّة مُنْحَنِيَة
58 sterile gauze — شَاش مُعَقَّم
59 needle holder — حَامِل الإبَر
60 spray for disinfecting the skin — رشَّاش لتطهير الجِلْد
61 thread container — حاوِيَة الخَيْط
62 ophthalmoscope — مِنْظَار الكَشْف على العَيْن
63 freezer for cryosurgery — فريزر لجِرَاحات القَرَنِيَّة
64 dispenser for plasters and small pieces of equipment — سَلَّة مُهْمَلات للأشْرِطَة اللاصِقة والمُخَلَّفَات الصغيرة
65 disposable hypodermic needles and syringes — سَلَّة مُهْمَلات للحُقَن والإبَر تحت الجِلْدِيَّة
66 scales, sliding-weight scales — مِيزَان (مِيزَان ذو ثِقْل مُنْزَلِق)
67 weighing platform — منصة الوَزْن
68 sliding weight (jockey) — ثِقْل انزلاقي/مُتَحَرِّك
69 height gauge (*Am.* gage) — مِقْيَاس الطُول
70 waste bin (*Am.* trash bin) — سَلَّة مُهْمَلات
71 hot-air sterilizer — جِهَاز تَعْقِيم بالهَوَاء الساخِن
72 pipette — مَمَص
73 percussor — مِطْرَقَة
74 aural speculum (auriscope, aural syringe) — مِنْظَار جَوْفي للأذُن (مِنْظَار الأذُن، مِحْقَن الأذُن)

23 Doctor II — الطَّبِيب (2)

1 consulting room — غُرْفَة الفَحْص
2 general practitioner — مُمَارِس عام
3-21 instruments for gynaecological and proctological examinations — **أدوَات فَحْص أمراض النِّسَاء والمُسْتَقِيم**
3 warming the instruments up to body temperature — تَدْفِئة الأدوَات إلى دَرَجَة حرارة الجِسْم
4 examination couch — سَرِير الفَحْص
5 colposcope — مِنْظَار المِهْبَل
6 binocular eyepiece — عَيْنِيَّة المِنْظَار

7	miniature camera	كاميرا صغيرة
8	cold light source	مصدر ضَوْء بارد
9	cable release	زرّ تحرير الكيبل
10	bracket for the leg support	كُتيفَة تثبيت الساقَيْن
11	leg support (leg holder)	حَامِل السَّاق
12	holding forceps (sponge holder)	جِفْت إمْسَاك الإسْفِنْج
13	vaginal speculum	مِنْظَار جَوْفي مِهْبَلي
14	lower blade of the vaginal speculum	اللَوْح السفلي للمِنْظَار الجَوْفي المِهْبَلي
15	platinum loop (for smears)	لَوْلَب بلاتيني
16	rectoscope	مِنْظَار المُسْتَقِيم
17	biopsy forceps used with the rectoscope (proctoscope)	جِفْت أخْذ العَيِّنَة المُسْتَخْدَم مع مِنْظَار المُسْتَقِيم
18	insufflator for proctoscopy (rectoscopy)	مِنْفَاخ تَنْظِير المُسْتَقِيم
19	proctoscope (rectal speculum)	مِنْظَار جَوْفي للمُسْتَقِيم
20	urethroscope	مِنْظَار الإحليل
21	guide for inserting the proctoscope	دليل إدخال المِنْظَار الجَوْفي للمُسْتَقِيم
22	diathermy unit (short-wave therapy apparatus)	وَحْدَة إنْفَاذ الحرارة
23	radiator	جِهَاز الإشْعَاع
24	inhaling apparatus (inhalator)	جِهَاز الاسْتِنْشَاق
25	basin (for sputum)	حَوْض (للبصاق)
26-31	**ergometry**	**القياسات**
26	bicycle ergometer	عَجَلَة لقياس النَّبْض والتَّنَفُّس ورَسْم القلب
27	monitor (for visual display of the ECG and of pulse and respiratory rates when performing work)	شاشَة للعَرْض البَصَري لرَسَّام القَلْب الكَهْرَبائي ومُعَدَّل النَّبْض والتَّنَفُّس عِنْد القيام بمَجْهود
28	ECG (electrocardiograph)	رَسَّام القَلْب الكَهْرَبائي
29	suction electrodes	الكترودات ماصة
30	strap-on electrodes for the limbs	الكترودات شِريطيَّة للأطْرَاف
31	spirometer (for measuring respiratory functions)	مِقْيَاس النَّفَس
32	measuring blood pressure	قِيَاس ضَغْط الدَّم
33	sphygmomanometer	جِهَاز قِيَاس ضَغْط الدَّم
34	inflatable cuff	كُفَّة نَفَّاخِيَّة
35	stethoscope	سَمَّاعَة طِبِّيَّة
36	microwave treatment unit	وَحْدَة مُعَالَجَة بالميكرويف
37	faradization unit (for applying low-frequency currents with different pulse shapes)	وَحْدَة المُعَالَجَة الفارادية
38	automatic tuner	زِرّ الضَّبْط الدقيق آلياً
39	short-wave therapy apparatus	جِهَاز العِلاج بالمَوْجَات القصيرة
40	timer	جِهَاز توقيت
41-59	**laboratory**	**المَعْمَل ، المُخْتَبَر**
41	medical laboratory technician	فَنِّي المَعْمَل الطِّبِّيّ
42	capillary tube stand for blood sedimentation	حَامِل أنابيب شعريَّة لترسيب الدَّم
43	measuring cylinder	أسْطُوَانَة قياس
44	automatic pipette	جِهَاز شفط آلي
45	kidney dish	طبق مَعْمَل
46	portable ECG machine for emergency use	رَسَّام قَلْب كَهْرَبائي نقَّالي للاستخدام في الطَّوَارِئ
47	automatic pipetting device	جِهَاز الشفط الآلي
48	constant temperature water bath	حَمَّام ماء ثابِت الحرارة
49	tap with water jet pump	حنفيَّة/صنبور ذو مِضَخَّة نفَّاثة
50	staining dish (for staining blood smears, sediments, and other smears)	طَبَق تلوين ، طَبَق صَبْغ
51	binocular research microscope	ميكروسكوب فَحْص ذو عَيْنِيَتَيْن
52	pipette stand for photometry	حَامِل ممصات للقياس الضَّوْئي
53	computer and analyser for photometry	حاسِب آلي وجِهَاز تحليل للقياس الضَّوْئي
54	photometer	جِهَاز القياس الضَّوْئي
55	potentiometric recorder	مُسَجِّل قياس فَرْق الجُهْد
56	transforming section	قِسْم التحويل
57	laboratory apparatus (laboratory equipment)	معدات مَعْمَلِيَّة
58	urine sediment chart	رَسْم تخطيطي لترسيب البول
59	centrifuge	مِمْخَضَة ، فَرَّازة بالطرد المركزي

24 Dentist — طَبيب الأسْنَان

1	dentist (dental surgeon)	طَبِيب الأسْنَان (جَرَّاح الأسْنَان)
2	patient	مريض
3	dentist's chair	مقعد طَبيب الأسْنَان
4	dental instruments	أدوات طِبّ الأسْنَان
5	instrument tray	صينيَّة أدوات
6	drills with different handpieces	مَثَاقِب/مَحَافِر ذات مَقابض مختلفة
7	medicine case	حقيبة طِبِّيَّة
8	storage unit (for dental instruments)	وَحْدَة تخزين أدوات طِبّ الأسْنَان
9	assistant's unit	وَحْدَة المُساعِد/المُساعِدة
10	multi-purpose syringe (for cold and warm water, spray, or air)	مِحْقَن مُتَعَدِّد الأغراض
11	suction apparatus	جِهَاز ماص
12	basin	حَوْض
13	water glass, filled automatically	كوب ماء يُمْلأ آلياً
14	stool	مقعد صغير

15 washbasin حَوْض غسيل
16 instrument cabinet خزانة/صوان الأدوات
17 drawer for drills دُرْج المَثَاقِب
18 dentist's assistant مُسَاعدة طبيب الأسْنَان
19 dentist's lamp مِصْباح وَحْدَة الأسْنَان
20 ceiling light ضَوْء مُعلَّق بالسقف
21 X-ray apparatus for panoramic pictures جِهَاز الأشعَّة السِّينيَّة لالْتِقاط صُوَر بانُورَاميَّة
22 X-ray generator مُوَلِّد الأشعَّة السِّينيَّة
23 microwave treatment unit, a radiation unit وَحْدَة المعالجة بالميكرويف، وَحْدَة إشْعَاع
24 seat مقعد
25 denture (set of false teeth) طاقَم أسْنَان
26 bridge (dental bridge) كوبري، جسر
27 prepared stump of the tooth جَذْر مُعَدّ لتركيب كُوبْرِي
28 crown (kinds: gold crown, jacket crown) تاج (نَوْعان: تاج ذَهَب، طَرْبُوش)
29 porcelain tooth (porcelain pontic) سن من مادة البورْسَلين
30 filling حَشْوَة
31 post crown تاج ذو وَتَد
32 facing سطح، واجِهة
33 diaphragm حاجِز
34 post وَتَد تثبيت التَّاج
35 carborundum disc (disk) قُرْص من الكربورندوم
36 grinding wheel عَجَلَة السَّحْل
37 burs سَنَابل (جمع سنبلة)
38 flame-shaped finishing bur سنبلة إنهاء على شكل لهب
39 fissure burs سنابل شاقَّة
40 diamond point طَرَف ماسِيّ
41 mouth mirror مِرْآة الفم
42 mouth lamp مصباح الفَم
43 cautery مِحْسَمَة الكَيّ
44 platinum-iridium electrode الكترود بلاتيني
45 tooth scalers مَقَاشِط، مَقَالِح، أدوات تنظيف الأسْنَان
46 probe مِسْبَار، مِجَسّ
47 extraction forceps كَمَّاشَة خَلْع الأسنان
48 tooth-root elevator مِرْفَع جَذْر السِّن
49 bone chisel مِنْحَت/إزْميل العَظْم
50 spatula مِلْوَقة (أداة المَزْج)
51 mixer for filling material خلاط مادَة الحَشْو
52 synchronous timer جِهَاز توقيت تزامُني
53 hypodermic syringe for injection of local anaesthetic مِحْقَن المُخَدِّر المَوْضِعي
54 hypodermic needle إبْرَة للحقْن تحت الجِلْد
55 matrix holder حَامِل المِسْنَدة
56 impression tray طابعة (وعاء الطابع)
57 spirit lamp لَمْبَة كحوليَّة

25 Hospital 1 المُسْتَشْفَى (1)

1-30 intensive care unit **وَحْدَة العِنَايَة المُرَكَّزَة**

1-9 control room **غُرْفَة التحكُّم**

1 central control unit for monitoring heart rhythm (cardiac rhythm) and blood pressure وَحْدَة التحكُّم المركزيَّة لتنظيم ضَرَبَات القَلْب وضغط الدَّم
2 electrocardiogram monitor (ECG monitor) شَاشَة رَسَّام القَلْب الكهربائي
3 recorder مُسَجِّل
4 recording paper وَرَق تسجيل
5 patient's card بِطَاقة مَرِيض
6 indicator lights (with call buttons for each patient) أَضْوَاء إرْشاديَّة لاسْتِدْعَاء المَرْضَى
7 spatula مِلْوَقَة (أداة لمَزْج البُودْرَة والمحاليل)
8 window (observation window, glass partition) نافِذة زجاجيَّة للمُلاحَظَة
9 blind سِتارَة حاجِبة للضوء
10 bed (hospital bed) سَرِير مُسْتَشْفَي
11 stand for infusion apparatus حَامِل جِهَاز المحاليل
12 infusion bottle زُجَاجَة/قنينة محاليل
13 tube for intravenous drips خرطوم تَنْقِيط المحاليل الوَرِيديَّة
14 infusion device for water-soluble medicaments جِهَاز محاليل الأدوية القابلة للذوبان في الماء
15 sphygmomanometer جِهَاز قياس ضغط الدَّم
16 cuff كُفَّة
17 inflating bulb مِنْفَاخ كفَّة جِهَاز الضغط
18 mercury manometer مانومتر زئبقيّ
19 bed monitor شَاشَة سَرِير المستشفي
20 connecting lead to the central control unit كيبل التوصيل بوَحْدَة التَّحكُّم المركزيَّة
21 electrocardiogram monitor (ECG monitor) شاشة رَسَّام القَلْب الكهربائيّ
22 manometer for the oxygen supply مِقْيَاس إمْدَاد الأكسجين
23 wall connection for oxygen treatment وَصْلَة في الحائط لتمديد جِهَاز الأكسجين
24 mobile monitoring unit وَحْدَة شَاشَة عَرْض مُتَنَقِّلَة
25 electrode lead to the short-term pacemaker كيبل تَوْصِيل الالكترود بمُنَظِّم ضَرَبَات القَلْب قصير الأجل
26 electrodes for shock treatment الكترودات للمُعَالَجَة الصَّدْميَّة
27 ECG recording unit وَحْدَة تسجيل رَسَّام القَلْب الكهربائي
28 electrocardiogram monitor (ECG monitor) شَاشَة رَسَّام القَلْب الكهربائي
29 control switches and knobs (controls) for adjusting the monitor مفاتيح التَّحكُّم لضبط وتعديل الشَّاشَة
30 control buttons for the pacemaker unit مفاتيح التحكم في وَحْدَة مُنَظِّم ضَرَبَات القَلْب
31 pacemaker (cardiac pacemaker) مُنَظِّم ضَرَبَات القَلْب

32 mercury battery	بطارية زِئْبَقِيَّة
33 programmed impulse generator	مُوَلِّد نَبَضَات مُبَرْمَج
34 electrode exit point	مَوْضِع خروج كيبل الالكترود
35 electrode	الكترود
36 implantation of the pacemaker	زَرْع مُنَظِّم ضَرَبَات القَلْب
37 internal cardiac pacemaker (internal pacemaker, pacemaker)	مُنَظِّم ضَرَبَات قَلْب داخلي
38 electrode inserted through the vein	الكترود داخِل الوَرِيد
39 cardiac silhouette on the X-ray	صُورَة القَلْب على فيلم الأشعة السِّينِيَّة
40 pacemaker control unit	وَحْدَة التحكم في مُنَظِّم ضَرَبَات القَلْب
41 electrocardiograph (ECG recorder)	رَسَّام قَلْب كهربائي
42 automatic impulse meter	مِقْيَاس نَبْض آليّ
43 ECG lead to the patient	كيبل توصيل رَسَّام القَلْب الكهربائي بالمريض
44 monitor unit for visual monitoring of the pacemaker impulses	وَحْدَة الشَّاشَة الخاصة بالمراقبة البَصَرِيَّة لنبضات مُنَظِّم ضَرَبَات القَلْب
45 long-term ECG analyser	مُحَلِّل رَسْم القَلْب الكهربائي المُمْتَد
46 magnetic tape for recording the ECG impulses during analysis	شَرِيط مغناطيسي لتسجيل نبضات رَسَّام القَلْب أثناء التحليل
47 ECG monitor	شَاشَة رَسَّام القَلْب الكهربائي
48 automatic analysis on paper of the ECG rhythm	تحليل آليّ على الوَرَق لنَظْم رَسَّام القَلْب الكهربائي
49 control knob for the ECG amplitude	ذراع التَّحَكُّم في سِعَة رَسَّام القَلْب الكهربائي
50 program selector switches for the ECG analysis	مفاتيح اختيار برامج تَحْلِيل رَسَّام القَلْب الكهربائي
51 charger for the pacemaker batteries	جِهَاز شحن بطاريات مُنَظِّم ضَرَبَات القَلْب
52 battery tester	جِهَاز اختبار البطاريات
53 pressure gauge (*Am.* gage) for the right cardiac catheter	مقياس الضغط الخاص بقَثْطَرَة القَلْب
54 trace monitor	شَاشَة المتابعة
55 pressure indicator	مُؤَشِّر الضغط
56 connecting lead to the paper recorder	كيبل تَوْصِيل إلى جِهَاز التسجيل على الوَرَق
57 paper recorder for pressure traces	جِهَاز التسجيل على الوَرَق الخاص بتتبع الضغط

26 Hospital II — المُسْتَشْفَى (2)

1-54 surgical unit — **وَحْدَة الجِرَاحَة**

1-33 operating theatre (*Am.* theater) — **غُرْفَة العمليَّات**

1 anaesthesia and breathing apparatus (respiratory machine)	جِهَاز التَّخْدِير والتَّنَفُّس
2 inhalers (inhaling tubes)	خَرَاطِيم الاسْتِنْشَاق
3 flowmeter for nitrous oxide	مِقْيَاس تَدَفُّق أكسيد النيتروجين
4 oxygen flow meter	مِقْيَاس تَدَفُّق الأكسجين
5 pedestal operating table	سَرِير عمليات يتم خَفْضُه ورَفْعُه ببَدَّالَة سفليَّة
6 table pedestal	بَدَّالَة السَّرِير
7 control device (control unit)	وَحْدَة التَّحَكُّم
8 adjustable top of the operating table	سَطْح سَرِير العمليَّات القابل للتعديل
9 stand for intravenous drips	حَامِل المحاليل الوَرِيدِيَّة
10 swivel-mounted shadow-free operating lamp	نِظَام إنارَة للعمليات الجراحيَّة عديم الظِّلال مُعَلَّق على مِحْوَر دَوَّار
11 individual lamp	مِصْبَاح مُفْرَد
12 handle	ذراع، مقبض
13 swivel arm	ذِرَاع تدوير/ دَوَّار
14 mobile fluoroscope	مِنْظَار فلُورِيَّة نقَّالي
15 monitor of the image converter	شَاشَة عَرْض مُحَوِّل الصورة
16 monitor [back]	شَاشَة عَرْض [من الخَلْف]
17 tube	خُرْطُوم، أُنْبُوب
18 image converter	مُحَوِّل الصورة
19 C-shaped frame	إطار قَوْسِيّ
20 control panel for the air-conditioning	وَحْدَة التحكم في مكَيِّف الهواء
21 surgical suture material	خَيْط جِرَاحَة
22 mobile waste tray	سَلَّة مُهْمَلات مُتَحَرِّكَة
23 containers for unsterile (unsterilized) pads	حاوِية للحَشِيَّات غير المُعَقَّمَة
24 anaesthesia and respiratory apparatus	جِهَاز التَّخْدِير والتَّنَفُّس
25 respirator	جِهَاز تَنَفُّس صناعي
26 fluothane container (halothane container)	أُسْطُوَانَة الهالوثان
27 ventilation control knob	مِقْبَض التَّحَكُّم في التَّهْوِيَة
28 indicator with pointer for respiratory volume	شَاشَة ومُؤَشِّر حَجْم التَّنَفُّس
29 stand with inhalers (inhaling tubes) and pressure gauges (*Am.* gages)	حَامِل مقاييس خَرَاطِيم الإسْتِنْشَاق والضغط
30 catheter holder	حَامِل القَثْطَرَة
31 catheter in sterile packing	قَثْطَرَة في غِلاف مُعَقَّم
32 sphygmograph	مُخَطِّط النَّبْض
33 monitor	شَاشَة عَرْض
34-54 preparation and sterilization room	**غُرْفَة الإعْداد والتَّعْقِيم**
34 dressing material	ضمادات
35 small sterilizer	جِهَاز تَعْقِيم صغير
36 carriage of the	عَرَبَة سَرِير العمليَّات

operating table
37 mobile instrument table — طاولَة أدوات نقالة
38 sterile cloth — نَسيج مُعَقَّم
39 instrument tray — صينية الأدَوَات
40-53 surgical instruments — **الأدوات الجِراحيَّة**
40 olive-pointed (bulb-headed) probe — مِجَسّ ذو رأس مُنْتَفِخ
41 hollow probe — مِجَسّ أجوف
42 curved scissors — مقصّ مُنْحَنِي الطرف
43 scalpel (surgical knife) — مِشْرَط
44 ligature-holding forceps — جِفْت مَسْك الأربطة
45 sequestrum forceps — جِفْت الوَشِيظ
46 jaw — فَكّ
47 drainage tube — أنْبُوب تصريف
48 surgeon's tourniquet — عاصِبة الجَرَّاح
49 artery forceps — جِفْت شرايين
50 blunt hook — خُطَّاف
51 bone nippers (bone-cutting forceps) — جِفْت العِظَام
52 scoop (curette) for erasion (curettage) — مِكْشَطَة ، مِكْحَتَة
53 obstetrical forceps — جِفْت توليد
54 roll of plaster — بكَرَة شَريط لاصِق/ بلاستر

27 Hospital III — المُسْتَشْفَى (3)

1-35 X-ray unit — **وَحْدَة الأشعَّة السِّينيَّة**
1 X-ray examination table — طاولة الفحص بالأشِعَّة السِّينِيَّة
2 support for X-ray cassettes — حَامِل كاسيتات أفلام الأشِعَّة السِّينيَّة
3 height adjustment of the central beam for lateral views — ضَبْط ارتفاع العمود المركزيّ من أجْل الرؤيَّة العَرْضيَّة
4 compress for pyelography and cholecystography — مِضْغَط تصوير حَوْض الكِلَى والحالِب وتصوير المَرَارة
5 instrument basin — جِفْنَة الأدوات
6 X-ray apparatus for pyelograms — جِهَاز الأشِعَّة السِّينيَّة الخاص بتصوير حَوْض الكِلَى والحالب
7 X-ray tube — أنْبُوب الأشعَّة السِّينيَّة
8 telescopic X-ray support — حَامِل أشِعَّة سِينيَّة تليسكوبي
9 central X-ray control unit — وَحْدَة التحكم المركزية للأشعَّة السِّينيَّة
10 control panel (control desk) — لَوْحَة التَّحكُّم
11 radiographer (X-ray technician) — فَنِّي أشِعَّة
12 window to the angiography room — نافذة تطل على غُرْفَة التصوير الوعائي
13 oxymeter — مِقْيَاس الأكسجين
14 pyelogram cassettes — كاسيتات تصوير حَوْض الكِلَى والحالِب
15 contrast medium injector — حاقِن وسط التباين
16 X-ray image intensifier — مُكَثِّف صورة الأشِعَّة السِّينيَّة
17 C-shaped frame — إطار قَوْسيّ
18 X-ray head with X-ray tube — رأس توليد الأشعَّة السِّينيَّة المُزَوَّد بأنْبُوب الأشعَّة
19 image converter with converter tube — مُحَوِّل الصورة المُزَوَّد بصمام المُحَوِّل
20 film camera — آلَة تصوير أفلام الأشِعَّة
21 foot switch — مِفْتَاح سفلي
22 mobile mounting — حَامِل مُتَحَرِّك
23 monitor — شَاشَة
24 swivel-mounted monitor support — حَامِل شَاشَة مُثَبَّت على مِحْوَر دَوَراني
25 operating lamp — مِصْبَاح
26 angiographic examination table — سَرِير التصوير الوِعَائي
27 pillow — وِسَادَة
28 eight-channel recorder — مُسَجِّل ذو ثُماني قَنَوَات
29 recording paper — وَرَق تسجيل
30 catheter gauge (*Am.* gage) unit for catheterization of the heart — وَحْدَة جِهَاز القَثْطَرَة الخاصة بقثطرة القَلْب
31 six-channel monitor for pressure graphs and ECG — شَاشَة ذات ست قَنَوَات لمُخَطَّط الضَّغْط ورَسَّام القَلْب الكهربائي
32 slide-in units of the pressure transducer — وَحَدَات مُحَوِّل طاقة الضَّغْط
33 paper recorder unit with developer for photographic recording — وَحْدَة التسجيل على الوَرَق الخاصة بالتسجيل الفوتوغرافي وبها وحدة تحميض
34 recording paper — وَرَق تسجيل
35 timer — جِهَاز تَوْقيت
36-50 spirometry — **قياس التَّنَفُّس**
36 spirograph for pulmonary function tests — تخطيط التَّنَفُّس لاختبارات كفاءة وظيفة الرئتين
37 breathing tube — أنْبُوب التَّنَفُّس
38 mouthpiece — مِبْسَم (الجزء الذي يوضع بالفم)
39 soda-lime absorber — مادة ماصَة من جير الصودا
40 recording paper — وَرَق تسجيل
41 control knobs for gas supply — مفاتيح التحكم في مُعَدَّل إمداد الغاز
42 O_2 stabilizer — مُوَازِن الأكسجين
43 throttle valve — صِمَام خانِق
44 absorber attachment — وَصْلَة جِهَاز الامتصاص
45 oxygen cylinder — أسْطُوَانَة الأكسجين
46 water supply — مَصْدَر إمداد الماء
47 tube support — حَامِل الأنْبُوب
48 mask — قِنَاع ، كَمَّامَة
49 CO_2 consumption meter — مقياس استهلاك ك أ2 (ثاني أكسيد الكربون)
50 stool for the patient — مقعد المريض

28 Infant Care and Layette — العِنَايَة بالطِّفْل ولَوَازِم الأطْفَال

1 collapsible cot — سَرير طَفْل قابل للطي
2 bouncing cradle — مَهْد هَزَّاز
3 baby bath — حَمَّام أطْفال ، بانيو أطْفال
4 changing top — طاولة تغيير الملابس
5 baby (new-born baby) — طِفْل (رَضِيع)
6 mother — أُمّ

7 hairbrush — فُرْشَاة شَعْر
8 comb — مُشْط
9 hand towel — مِنْشَفَة يد ، فوطة
10 toy duck — لُعْبَة على شكل بَطَّة
11 changing unit — صوان الغِيَارَات
12 teething ring — عَضَّاضَة ، حَلَقَة التسنين
13 cream jar — وعاء/قنينة كريم
14 box of baby powder — عُلْبَة بُودْرَة أطفال
15 dummy — دُمْيَة
16 ball — كُرَة
17 sleeping bag — كِيس نَوْم
18 layette box — صُنْدُوق لَوَازِم الطفل المَوْلُود
19 feeding bottle — رَضَّاعَة ، زُجَاجَة الإِرْضَاع
20 teat — حَلَمَة
21 bottle warmer — صُنْدُوق تَدْفِئَة الرَّضَّاعَة
22 rubber baby pants for disposable nappies (*Am.* diapers) — حفاضات للطفل تستعمل مرة واحدة فقط
23 vest — صَدْرِيَّة
24 leggings — الطِّمَاق
25 baby's jacket — سُتْرَة طفل
26 hood — قلنسوة: غطاء للرأس والعُنُق معاً
27 baby's cup — كُوب أَطْفَال
28 baby's plate, a stay-warm plate — طَبَق أَطْفَال ، طبق يحفظ الطعام دافئاً
29 thermometer — ترمومتر
30 bassinet, a wicker pram — مَهْد شَبِيه بالسَّلَّة
31 set of bassinet covers — طاقم أَغْطِية المَهْد
32 canopy — ظُلَّة ، غطاء شفَّاف
33 baby's high chair, a folding chair — كُرْسِيّ أَطْفَال مُرْتَفِع ، كُرْسِيّ قابل للطي
34 pram (baby-carriage) [with windows] — عَرَبَة أَطْفَال [ذات نوافذ]
35 folding hood — غطاء قابل للطي
36 window — نافذة
37 pushchair (*Am.* stroller) — عَرَبَة أَطْفَال ، كُرْسِيّ مُتَحَرِّك للأَطْفَال
38 foot-muff (*Am.* foot-bag) — مُوفَة (تدفئة) القَدَمَيْن
39 play pen — حُجَيْرَة اللعِب
40 floor of the play pen — أرضيَّة حُجَيْرَة اللعِب
41 building blocks (building bricks) — مكعَّبَات بِنَاء
42 small child — طفل صغير
43 bib — صَدْرِيَّة الطِّفْل (توضع تحت ذَقَنِه أثناء الطَّعام)
44 rattle (baby's rattle) — خُشْخِيشَة
45 bootees — حِذَاء قصير ، جَوْرَب صوف للأطفال
46 teddy bear — دُبّ لُعْبَة
47 potty (baby's pot) — نُونِيَّة للأطفال
48 carrycot — مَهْد يُحْمَل يدوياً
49 window — نافذة
50 handles — مقبضان

29 Children's Clothes — مَلَابِس الأَطْفَال

1-12 baby clothes — **ملابِس الطفل الرَّضِيع**

1 pram suit — بَدْلَة خُروج
2 hood — قَلَنْسُوَة (تغطي الرأس والعُنُق معاً)
3 pram jacket (matinée coat) — سُتْرَة ماتينيه (مِعْطَف صُوفِيّ)
4 pompon (bobble) — بُمْبُونَة ، شُرَّابة
5 bootees — حذاء صُوفِيّ للطفل
6 sleeveless vest — صَدْرِيَّة بدون أكْمَام
7 envelope-neck vest — صَدْرِيَّة ذات فتحة رقبة ظرفية
8 wrapover vest — صَدْرِيَّة تدثير خارجيَّة
9 baby's jacket — سُتْرَة طفل
10 rubber baby pants — حفاض
11 playsuit — لِبَاس اللعِب
12 two-piece suit — بَدْلَة مكونة من قطعتين
13-30 infants' wear — **ملابس أطفال**
13 child's sundress, a pinafore dress — مِئْزَر للأطفال من غير أكْمَام
14 frilled shoulder strap — حَمَّالَة كتف مُكَشْكَشَة
15 shirred top — جزء علوي مُدَرَّز
16 sun hat — قبعة واقيَّة من الشمس
17 one-piece jersey suit — جُرْس صُوفِي قطعة واحدة
18 front zip (*Am.* zipper) — سوستة أماميَّة
19 catsuit (playsuit) — لِبَاس اللعِب
20 motif (appliqué) — زَخَارِف أَبْلِكَة
21 romper — سِروال قصير للَّعِب
22 playsuit (romper suit) — لِبَاس للَّعِب
23 coverall (sleeper and strampler) — مِئْزَر ، كفرول
24 dressing gown (bath robe) — رُوب حَمَّام (بُرْنُس)
25 children's shorts — بنطلون قصير للأطفال (شورت)
26 braces (*Am.* suspenders) — حَمَّالتان
27 children's T-shirt — تي شيرت للأطفال ، كِنْزَة تائيَّة
28 jersey dress (knitted dress) — فُسْتَان جرسيه (فستان تريكو)
29 embroidery — تطريز
30 children's ankle socks — جَوْرَب قصير للأطفال
31-47 school children's wear — **ملابس المَدْرَسَة للأطفال**
31 raincoat — معْطَف واقٍ من المَطَر
32 leather shorts (lederhosen) — بَنْطَلُون جِلْدِيّ قصير
33 staghorn button — زِرّ
34 braces (*Am.* suspenders) — حَمَّالتان
35 flap — قلابَة
36 girl's dirndl — درندل بناتي
37 cross lacing — رباط (شَرِيط) متقاطع
38 snow suit (quilted suit) — بَدْلَة مُبَطَّنَة
39 quilt stitching (quilting) — غُرْزَة تضريبية
40 dungarees (bib and brace) — دنغري: سِرْوَال من قماش خَشِن
41 bib skirt (bib top pinafore) — تَنُّورَة بصَدْرِيَّة
42 tights — جَوْرَب طويل ضيق يغطي

نصف الجسم

43 sweater (jumper) سويتر، كَنْزَة

44 pile jacket سُتْرَة مَخْمَلِيَّة

45 leggings طمَاق

46 girl's skirt تنُّورة (جوب، جونيلة)

47 child's jumper بلوزة تريكو للأطفال

48-68 teenagers' clothes **ملابس المراهقين**

48 girl's overblouse (over-top) بُلوزة خارجيَّة

49 slacks بنطلون

50 girl's skirt suit بدلة (للفتيات) مكونة من سُتْرَة وتنُّورة

51 jacket سُتْرَة، جاكت

52 skirt تنُّورة (جوب، جونلة)

53 knee-length socks جَوْرَب يصل إلى الرُّكْبَة

54 girl's coat مِعْطَف بناتي

55 tie belt حزام يُرْبَط في شكل عُقْدَة

56 girl's bag حقيبة يد بناتي

57 woollen (*Am.* woolen) hat قبعة صوفيَّة

58 girl's blouse بلُوزة بناتي

59 culottes كُولُوت (تنُّورَة مَخيطة في شكل بنطلون)

60 boy's trousers بنطلون أولادي

61 boy's shirt قميص أولادي

62 anorak معْطَف قصير ذو قَلَنْسُوَة

63 inset pockets جيب داخلي (مُثَبَّت بالخياطَة داخل الثوب)

64 hood drawstring (draw-string) رباط إحكام القَلَنْسُوَة

65 knitted welt أسْورة كم مَخيطة/مشغولة

66 parka coat (parka) معْطَف قصير مزود بقَلَنْسُوَة

67 drawstring (draw cord) رباط إحكَام المِعْطَف عند الخَصْر

68 patch pockets جيب خارجي (مُثَبَّت بالخياطة فوق الثوب)

30 Ladies' Wear I (Winter Wear) ملابس السَّيِّدات (1) (الملَابس الشِّتْويَّة)

1 mink jacket جاكِت/سُتْرَة من فرْو المِنك

2 cowl neck jumper بلُوزة تريكو فَضْفَاضَة مُزَوَّدَة بقَلَنْسُوَة

3 cowl collar ياقَة كُول (مقلنسة الشكل)

4 knitted overtop قَميص خارجي مَخِيط/مَشْغُول

5 turndown collar ياقَة (قلابَة)

6 turn-up (turnover) sleeve كُمّ يَطْوَى لأعلى

7 polo neck jumper بلوزة تريكو برَقَبَة عاليَة ضَيِّقَة

8 pinafore dress فستان بدون أكْمام

9 blouse (with reverse collar) بلوزة (بياقَة قلاَّبة)

10 shirt-waister dress, a button-through dress ثَوْب/فستان بأزْرَار من الأمام حتى نهايته

11 belt حزام

12 winter dress ثَوْب/فستان شِتْويّ

13 piping حاشيَة أو شَريط تَزْيين

14 cuff أسْورة كُمّ الثَّوْب

15 long sleeve كُمّ طويل

16 quilted waistcoat صَدْريَّة مُبَطَّنَة

17 quilt stitching (quilting) غُرْزَة تضريبيَّة

18 leather trimming قَلامَة جِلْديَّة

19 winter slacks بنطلون حريمي شتويّ

20 striped polo jumper كَنْزَة مُخَطَّطَة ذات رقبة عالية ضيقة

21 boiler suit (dungarees, bib and brace) بدلة دنغري

22 patch pocket جيب خارجي (مُثَبَّت بالخياطة فوق الثوب)

23 front pocket جيب أمامي

24 bib صدريَّة التنُّورَة

25 wrapover dress (wrap-around dress) ثوب شَبيه بالعَبَاءة

26 shirt قميص

27 peasant-style dress فستان/ ثوب (شبيه بلباس الفلاحين)

28 floral braid زَرْكَشَة بالوَرْد

29 tunic (tunic top) التنك: بلوزة أو سُتْرَة طويلة

30 ribbed cuff كُفَّة/أسْورة كُمّ مُضَلَّعَة

31 quilted design تصميم تضريبي

32 pleated skirt تَنُّورَة مكَسَّرَة

33 two-piece knitted dress ثَوْب/فستان تريكو من قطعتين

34 boat neck, a neckline خط الرقبة

35 turn-up طيَّة (في الكُم) لأعلى

36 kimono sleeve كُمّ كيمونو (بدون كتف)

37 knitted design تصميم دَرْزيّ

38 lumber-jacket سُتْرَة متينة للعمل

39 cable pattern زَرْكَشَة كبلية

40 shirt-blouse بلوزة

41 loop fastening عُرْوَة زر أنشوطية

42 embroidery تَطْريز

43 stand-up collar ياقَة عالية

44 cossack trousers بنطلون قوقازي (موديل)

45 two-piece combination (shirt top and long skirt) ثوب من قطعتين (قميص وتنورة طويلة)

46 tie (bow) عُقْدَة أنشوطية

47 decorative facing تخريج: قماش يُخَاط على الثّوب للتزيين

48 cuff slit فتحة أسْورة الكُمّ

49 side slit فتحة جانبيَّة

50 tabard بلوزة فضفاضة (طَبَرْد) غير مُحَاكة من الجانبين

51 inverted pleat skirt تَنُّورَة ذات طيَّة مقلوبة

52 godet جُوديه، طيَّة/كَسْرَة إلى الداخل

53 evening gown فستان مسائي

54 pleated bell sleeve كُمّ بليسيه جَرَسيّ الشكل

55 party blouse بلوزة سَهْرَة

56 party skirt تَنُّورَة سَهْرَة

57 trouser suit (slack suit) بدلة حريمي فضفاضة

58 suede jacket جاكت شمواه

59 fur trimming قَلامَة من الفَرْو

60 fur coat (kinds: Persian lamb, broadtail, mink, مِعْطَف من الفَرْو (الأنواع: الحَمَل الفارسيّ، القَرَكول،

sable)	المنك، السَّمُّور)
61 winter coat (cloth coat)	معْطَف شتويّ
62 fur cuff (fur-trimmed cuff)	كُفَّة من الفَرْو
63 fur collar (fur-trimmed collar)	ياقَة من الفَرْو
64 loden coat	معطَف شَبيه بالكاب
65 cape	كاب
66 toggle fastenings	زِرّ عُقَدِيّ
67 loden skirt	تَنُّورَة فضفاضة
68 poncho-style coat	معْطَف شَبيه بالعَبَاءة
69 hood	قلنسوة

31 Ladies' Wear II (Summer Wear) — مَلابس السَّيِّدات (2) (المَلابس الصَّيْفِيَّة)

1 skirt suit	تايير
2 jacket	جَاكت
3 skirt	تَنُّورَة
4 inset pocket	جيب داخلي
5 decorative stitching	غرَز تَطْريزيَّة
6 dress and jacket combination	طاقم من فُسْتَان وجَاكت
7 piping	شَريط تَزْيين
8 pinafore dress	فُسْتَان بدُون أكْمام
9 summer dress	فُسْتَان صَيْفي
10 belt	حزام
11 two-piece dress	فُسْتَان من قطعتَيْن
12 belt buckle	إبْزيم الحِزام
13 wrapover (wrap-around) skirt	تنورة تلتف حول الجسم
14 pencil silhouette	سلويت رَفيع
15 shoulder buttons	أزْرار فَوْق الكتف
16 batwing sleeve	كُمّ خُفَّاش
17 overdress	ثَوْب فَوْقي
18 kimono yoke	كتف كيمونو
19 tie belt	حزام يُربط في شكل عُقْدَة
20 summer coat	معْطَف صيفيّ
21 detachable hood	قَلَنْسُوَة قابلة للفَصْل من الثَّوْب
22 summer blouse	بلوزة صيفيَّة
23 lapel	طَيَّة صَدْر البلوزة
24 skirt	تَنُّورَة
25 front pleat	طَيَّة أماميَّة
26 dirndl (dirndl dress)	درندل (فُسْتَان الدرندل)
27 puffed sleeve	كُمّ مَنْفُوش
28 dirndl necklace	عقْد الدرندل
29 dirndl blouse	بلوزة الدرندل
30 bodice	صَدْر الثَّوْب
31 dirndl apron	مَرْيلَة الدرندل
32 lace trimming (lace), cotton lace	دانتيلا قُطْنيَّة (تدْريز)
33 frilled apron	مَرْيلَة مكَشْكَشَة
34 frill	كَشْكَشَة
35 smock overall	أوفَرُول "سموك"
36 house frock (house dress)	فُسْتَان بيت
37 poplin jacket	جَاكت بُوبلين
38 T-shirt	تي شيرت
39 ladies' shorts	بنْطَال قَصير للسَّيِّدات
	(شورت حريمي)
40 trouser turn-up	ثنية الشورت
41 waistband	كَمَر الخَصْر
42 bomber jacket	جَاكت مُنتفخ للسيدات
43 stretch welt	حاشِيَة/سَيْر مطَّاطي للتزيين
44 Bermuda shorts	بنْطَال برمودا قصير
45 saddle stitching	غُرَز سَرْجِيَّة، سِراجَة
46 frill collar	ياقَة مُكَشْكَشَة
47 knot	عُقْدَة
48 culotte	كولوت
49 twin set	طَاقم توينز
50 cardigan	سُتْرَة ضَيِّقَة
51 sweater	صَدْريَّة، سويتر
52 summer (lightweight) slacks	بنْطَال صيفيّ (خَفيف)
53 jumpsuit	بَدْلَة قطعة واحِدة بسُوسْتَة أماميَّة
54 turn-up	طَيَّة كُمّ لأعْلَى
55 zip (*Am.* zipper)	سُوسْتَة، سَحَّاب
56 patch pocket	جيب خارجي
57 scarf (neckerchief)	إيشارب، وشَاح
58 denim suit	بذلة من الدنيم (بَدْلَة جينز)
59 denim waistcoat	جَاكت البذلة الدنيم
60 jeans (denims)	بنْطَال جينز
61 overblouse	بلوزة خارجيَّة
62 turned-up sleeve	كُمّ مَثْني لأعْلَى
63 stretch belt	حزام مطَّاط (سترتش)
64 halter top	صَدْريَّة مكْشُوفة الظَّهْر
65 knitted overtop	صَدْريَّة تريكو تُرْتَدَى فوق الملابس
66 drawstring waist	وسط يُحكَم بشَدّ الرباط
67 short-sleeved jumper	بلوزة تريكو ذات كُمّ قصير
68 V-neck (vee-neck)	رَقَبَة على شكل V
69 turndown collar	ياقَة قلابة
70 knitted welt	حاشية/سَيْر مشغول بالصنارة (تريكو)
71 shawl	شَال

32 Underwear, Nightwear — المَلابس الدَّاخليَّة، مَلابس النَّوْم

1-15 ladies' underwear (ladies' underclothes, lingerie)	**المَلاَبس الداخليَّة النِّسائيَّة**
1 brassière (bra)	صَدْريَّة للثَّدْيَيْن (سوتيان)
2 pantie-girdle	سِرْوَال داخلي بمِشَدّ
3 pantie-corselette	كورسيه بسروال داخلي
4 longline brassière (longline bra)	سوتيان كاش
5 stretch girdle	مشَدّ، إزَار مطَّاطي
6 suspender	مِشَدّ الجَوَارب
7 vest	قَميص داخلي قصير
8 pantie briefs	سِرْوَال حريمي داخلي قصير
9 ladies' knee-high stocking	جَوْرَب حريمي طَويل حتى الرُّكْبَة
10 long-legged (long leg) panties	سِرْوَال داخلي طَويل
11 long pants	سِرْوَال طَويل
12 tights (pantie-hose)	جَوْرَب طَويل ضيق يغطي

نصف الجسم السفلي

13 slip — قميص داخلي طَويل
14 waist slip — جيبُونَة
15 bikini briefs — سِرْوَال بكيني
16-21 ladies' nightwear — **ملابس النَّوْم النسائيَّة**
16 nightdress (nightgown, nightie) — قميص نَوْم
17 pyjamas (*Am.* pajamas) — بيجاما
18 pyjama top — جَاكت البيجاما
19 pyjama trousers — بنْطَال البيجاما
20 housecoat — رُوب منْزلي
21 vest and shorts set [for leisure wear and as nightwear] — طاقم فانلة وشورت [للتنزه ولِبَاس لَيْلي]
22-29 men's underwear (men's underclothes) — **الملابس الداخليَّة الرجاليَّة**
22 string vest — فانلة غرْبَاليَّة
23 string briefs — سِرْوَال غرْبالي
24 front panel — بِطَانة السِّرْوَال الأماميَّة
25 sleeveless vest — فانلَّة بحمَّالات (بدون أكْمَام)
26 briefs — سِرْوَال داخلي قصير
27 trunks — سِرْوَال شورت
28 short-sleeved vest — فانلة داخليَّة بأكْمَام قصيرة
29 long johns — سِرْوَال طويل
30 braces (*Am.* suspenders) — حمَّالَة
31 braces clip — مشبك حمَّالَة
32-34 men's socks — **الجَوَارِب الرجالي**
32 knee-length sock — جَوْرَب طَويل حتى الرُكْبَة
33 elasticated top — أَسْتِك (الطرف المطاطي) الجَوْرَب
34 long sock — جَوْرَب طَويل
35-37 men's nightwear — **ملابس النَّوْم الرجاليَّة**
35 dressing gown — رُوب نَوْم قصير
36 pyjamas (*Am.* pajamas) — بيجاما
37 nightshirt — قميص للنوم
38-47 men's shirts — **قمصان رجالي**
38 casual shirt — قميص خارجي (كاجوال)
39 belt — حِزَام
40 cravat — كَرَافت
41 tie — رِباط العُنُق
42 knot — عُقْدَة
43 dress shirt — قميص بَدْلَة
44 frill (frill front) — كَشْكَشَة
45 cuff — أَسْوِرَة القميص
46 cuff link — زِرّ معدني لِكُمّ القميص
47 bow-tie — بَابيون، رابطة عُنُق أنشوطيَّة

33 Men's Wear — ملابس الرِّجَال

1-67 men's fashion — **الأزْيَاء الرِّجَالي**
1 single-breasted suit, a men's suit — بَدْلَة رِجَالي
2 jacket — جَاكت، سُتْرَة
3 suit trousers — بنْطَال البَدْلَة
4 waistcoat (vest) — صُدَيْري
5 lapel — يَاقَة/طَيَّة صَدْر الجَاكت
6 trouser leg with crease — رِجْل بِنْطَال ذات ثَنْيَة أماميَّة
7 dinner dress, an evening suit — بَدْلَة سَهْرَة
8 silk lapel — يَاقَة حَرِير، صَدْر حَرِير
9 breast pocket — جَيْب الصَّدْر
10 dress handkerchief — مِنْديل بَدْلَة
11 bow-tie — بَابيون
12 side pocket — جَيْب جانبي
13 tailcoat (tails), evening dress — بَدْلَة رِدِنْجُوت، بَدْلَة سَهْرَة
14 coat-tail — ذَيْل الجَاكت
15 white waistcoat (vest) — صُدَيْري أَبْيَض
16 white bow-tie — بابيون أَبْيَض
17 casual suit — بَدْلَة كاجْوَال
18 pocket flap — قلابة/غطاء الجَيْب
19 front yoke — سُفْرَة أماميَّة، كَمَر
20 denim suit — بَدْلَة دنيم (بَدْلَة جينز)
21 denim jacket — جَاكت دنيم
22 jeans (denims) — بنْطَال جينز (دنيم)
23 waistband — كَمَر الخَصْر
24 beach suit — لِبَاس البحر
25 shorts — شورت (بِنْطَال قصير)
26 short-sleeved jacket — جَاكت بِكُمّ قصير
27 tracksuit — بَدْلَة/لِبَاس التدريب
28 tracksuit top with zip — سُتْرَة لِبَاس تدريب مزودة بسُوسْتَة
29 tracksuit bottoms — بنْطَال لِبَاس التدريب
30 cardigan — جَاكت/سُتْرَة صُوف
31 knitted collar — يَاقَة مَشْغُولَة بالصِّنَّارَة
32 men's short-sleeved pullover (men's short-sleeved sweater) — بلوفر بأكْمَام قصيرة
33 short-sleeved shirt — قَمِيص بِكُمّ قصير
34 shirt button — زِرّ قَمِيص
35 turn-up — طَيَّة خارجيَّة
36 knitted shirt — فانلة خارجيَّة مَشْغُولَة بالصِّنَّارَة
37 casual shirt — قَمِيص كاجْوَال
38 patch pocket — جَيْب خارجي (مُحاك على القَمِيص من الخارج)
39 casual jacket — جَاكت كاجْوَال
40 knee-breeches — بنْطَال قصير (لركوب الخيل)
41 knee strap — شَريط/رباط الرُكْبَة
42 knee-length sock — جَوْرَب طويل حتى الرُكْبَة
43 leather jacket — جَاكت جِلْدِي
44 bib and brace overalls — أوفرول مفتوح
45 adjustable braces (*Am.* suspenders) — حمَّالتان
46 front pocket — جَيْب أمامي
47 trouser pocket — جَيْب بِنْطَال
48 fly — لسان تَغطية السُوسْتَة
49 rule pocket — جَيْب جانبي صغير لِوَضْع المسطرة وخلافه
50 check shirt — قَمِيص كارُوه (مربعات)
51 men's pullover — بلوفر رجالي
52 heavy pullover — بلوفر ثقيل
53 knitted waistcoat (vest) — صُدَيْري مَشْغُول بالصِّنَّارَة
54 blazer — جَاكت بليزر (ذو صَفَّيْن من الأزْرَار)
55 jacket button — زِرّ جَاكت

56 overall	أوفرول (بالطو)
57 trenchcoat	معْطَف واقٍ من المَطَر
58 coat collar	ياقَة المعْطَف
59 coat belt	حِزام المعْطَف
60 poplin coat	معْطَف بوبْلين
61 coat pocket	جَيْب المعْطَف
62 fly front	لسان تغطية الأزرار (أو السوستة)
63 car coat	معْطَف قصير
64 coat button	زِرّ المعْطَف
65 scarf	وِشاح
66 cloth coat	معْطَف طويل
67 glove	قُفّاز

34 Hairstyles and Beards — قَصّات الشَّعْر وأشْكَال اللِّحْيَة

1-25 men's beards and hairstyles (haircuts)	**اللِّحْيَات وقَصّات الشَّعْر الرِّجاليَّة**
1 long hair worn loose	شَعْر طَويل مُسْتَرْسِل
2 allonge periwig (full-bottomed wig), a wig; *shorter and smoother:* bob wig, toupet	شَعْر مُسْتَعَار (بارُوكة) في شَكْل عَقْصَات
3 curls	عَقْصَة ، جَعْدَة
4 bag wig (purse wig)	شَعْر مُسْتَعَار (بارُوكة) على شَكْل كِيس
5 pigtail wig	شَعْر مُسْتَعَار (بارُوكة) على شَكْل ضفيرة في مُؤَخِرَة الرأس
6 queue (pigtail)	ضَفِيرَة صغيرة تَتَدَلَّى من مُؤَخِّرَة الرأس
7 bow (ribbon)	شَريط
8 handlebars (handlebar moustache, *Am.* mustache)	شارِب مُسْتَقيم
9 centre (*Am.* center) parting	فَرْق الشَّعْر بمنتصف الرأس
10 goatee (goatee beard), chintuft	العُثْنُون: لِحْيَة صغيرة مُشَذَّبَة
11 closely-cropped head of hair (crew cut)	تَسْريحَة الشَّعْر القصير
12 whiskers	سَبَلَة
13 Vandyke beard (stiletto beard, bodkin beard), with waxed moustache (*Am.* mustache)	لِحْيَة "فانْدايك" (لِحْيَة مُدَبَّبَة الطرف) مع شارِب مُشَمَّع
14 side parting	فَرْق جانِب الرأس
15 full beard (circular beard, round beard)	لِحْيَة كامِلة/مُسْتَديرة
16 tile beard	لِحْيَة مُسْتَطيلة
17 shadow	شارِب صغير مُدَبَّب الطرفيْن
18 head of curly hair	شَعْر مُجَعَّد
19 military moustache (*Am.* mustache) (English-style moustache)	شارب عسكريّ (موديل إنجليزيّ)
20 partly bald head	رَأْس صَلْعَاء جُزْئياً
21 bald patch	مِنْطَقَة صَلْعَاء
22 bald head	رَأْس صَلْعَاء
23 stubble beard (stubble, short beard bristles)	لِحْيَة مُنَبَّتَة
24 side-whiskers (sideboards, sideburns)	سَوَالِف ، سَبَلات
25 clean shave	حلاقة ناعمة
26 Afro look (for men and women)	تَسْريحَة أفْريقي(كَنيش) للرجال والنساء
27-38 ladies' hairstyles (coiffures, women's and girls' hairstyles)	**تَسْرِيحات الشَّعْر النسائيَّة**
27 ponytail	ذَيْل حصان (كودو شقال)
28 swept-back hair (swept-up hair, pinned-up hair)	شَعْر مَمْشُوط للخلف
29 bun (chignon)	كَعْكَة (شِينْيُون)
30 plaits (punches)	ضَفيرَتان
31 chaplet hairstyle (Gretchen style)	تَسْرِيحَة الإكْلِيل
32 chaplet (coiled plaits)	إكْلِيل ملْفُوف
33 curled hair	شَعْر مَعْقُوص/مُجَعَّد
34 shingle (shingled hair, bobbed hair)	قَصَّة الشَّعْر القصير
35 pageboy style	تَسْرِيحَة شعْر نسائيَّة يُرْسَل فيها الشعر حتى الكتفين ويلْتَفّ إلى الداخل
36 fringe (*Am.* bangs)	شَعْر مُصَفَّف فَوْق الجبين
37 earphones	تَسْرِيحَة الكَعْكَتَيْن
38 earphone (coiled plait)	ضَفيرة ملْفُوفة

35 Headgear — أغْطِيَة الرَّأس

1-21 ladies' hats and caps	**القُبَّعَات والقَلَنْسُوات النسائية**
1 milliner making a hat	مُصَمِّمَة قُبَّعات نسائيَّة تَصْنَع قُبَّعَة
2 hood	قَلَنْسُوَة
3 block	قالَب
4 decorative pieces	قِطَع للزينة
5 sombrero	صُومْبريرَة (موديل مكسيكيّ)
6 mohair hat with feathers	قُبَّعَة من المُهير والرِّيش
7 model hat with fancy appliqué	قُبَّعَة ذات أبْليك مُزَخْرَف
8 linen cap (jockey cap)	كاب من الكتَّان (كاب الفروسية)
9 hat made of thick candlewick yarn	قُبَّعَة مصنوعة من غَزْل قطنيّ ثقيل
10 woollen (*Am.* woolen) hat (knitted hat)	قُبَّعَة صوفيَّة
11 mohair hat	قُبَّعَة من المُهير
12 cloche with feathers	قُبَّعَة جَرَسِيَّة الشكْل مُزَخْرَفَة بريش
13 large men's hat made of sisal with corded ribbon	قُبَّعَة رجاليَّة كبيرة مصنوعة من السيزال وشريط مُضَلَّع
14 trilby-style hat with fancy ribbon	قُبَّعَة إفرنجية من الجُوخ الناعِم ذات شَريط زخرفيّ
15 soft felt hat	قُبَّعَة من اللباد الناعِم
16 Panama hat with scarf	قُبَّعَة بنما مُزَيَّنَة بوشاح
17 peaked mink cap	قُبَّعَة من فِراء المِنْك ذات

قمَّة مستديرة

18 mink hat — قُبَّعَة من فرَاء المنك

19 fox hat with leather top — قُبَّعَة من فرَاء الثَّعلَب ذات قمة جِلْدِيَّة

20 mink cap — كاب من فرَاء المنك

21 slouch hat trimmed with flowers — قُبَّعَة من الجُوخ ذات حافة عَرِيضة من الزهور

22-40 men's hats and caps — **القُبَّعات والقَلَنْسُوَات الرِّجاليَّة**

22 trilby hat (trilby) — قُبَّعَة إفرنجية من الجُوخ الناعم

23 loden hat (Alpine hat) — قُبَّعَة أَلْبينيَّة

24 felt hat with tassels (Tyrolean hat, Tyrolese hat) — قُبَّعَة من اللباد ذات شُرَّابَة من الخَلْف

25 corduroy cap — كاب من القطيفة المُضَلَّعَة

26 woollen (*Am.* woolen) hat — قُبَّعَة صُوفيَّة

27 beret — بيريه

28 German sailor's cap ('Prinz Heinrich' cap) — كاب البَحَّار الألْمانيّ

29 peaked cap (yachting cap) — كاب كابْتِن بَحَّار

30 sou'wester (south-wester) — قُبَّعَة من المشَمَّع لها حافة خلفية عريضة

31 fox cap with earflaps — قُبَّعَة من فرَاء الثعلب مُزَوَّدة بغطاءَيْن للأذُنَيْن

32 leather cap with fur flaps — قُبَّعَة جِلْدِيَّة ذات قلابات من الفرَاء

33 musquash cap — قُبَّعَة من فراء فَأْر المِسْك

34 astrakhan cap, a real or imitation astrakhan cap — كاب من صُوف الأَسْتراخان

35 boater — قُبَّعَة قش عريضة الحافة

36 (grey, *Am.* gray, or black) top hat made of silk taffeta; *collapsible:* crush hat (opera hat, claque) — قُبَّعَة رَسْميَّة من تَفْتَاه الحرير، قبعة سوداء حريرية عالية قابلة للطي

37 sun hat (lightweight hat (made of cloth with small patch pocket — قُبَّعَة شمس (من القماش وبها جَيْب خارجي صغير)

38 wide-brimmed hat — قُبَّعَة ذات إفريز مُتَّسِع

39 toboggan cap (skiing cap, ski cap) — قُبَّعَة التزحلق على الجليد

40 workman's cap — قُبَّعَة العُمَّال (للمُزارعين وعُمَّال الغَابات والحِرَفيين)

36 Jewellery (*Am.* Jewelry) — المُجَوْهَرَات

1 set of jewellery (*Am.* jewelry) — طاقم المُجَوْهَرَات

2 necklace — عِقْد، قِلادَة

3 bracelet — سِوَار، أُسْوِرَة

4 ring — خَاتَم

5 wedding rings — دبلتا/خَاتَما الزَّوَاج

6 wedding ring box — عُلْبَة خَاتَمي الزَّوَاج

7 brooch, a pearl brooch — بُرُوش، بروش لُؤْلُؤ

8 pearl — لُؤْلُؤَة

9 cultured pearl bracelet — سِوَار/أُسْوِرَة من اللُؤْلُؤ الصناعي

10 clasp, a white gold clasp — إبزيم، مِشْبَك من الذَّهَب الأَبْيَض

11 pendant earrings (drop earrings) — حلَق دَلايَة

12 cultured pearl necklace — عِقْد من اللُؤْلُؤ الصناعي

13 earrings — حلَق

14 gemstone pendant — حلْيَة مُرَصَّعَة بالأحْجَار الكريمة

15 gemstone ring — خَاتَم به حجر كريم

16 choker (collar, neck-band) — عِقْد ضَيِّق، كُوليه

17 bangle — سِوَار للمِعْصَم أو خلخال للقَدَم

18 diamond pin — دَبُّوس أَلْماس

19 modern-style brooches — بروش (موديل حديث)

20 man's ring — خَاتَم رِجالي

21 cuff links — دَبُّوسَان لأُسْوِرَة القَمِيص

22 tiepin — دَبُّوس رباط العنق

23 diamond ring with pearl — خَاتَم أَلْماس بلُؤْلُؤَة

24 modern-style diamond ring — خَاتَم أَلْماس (موديل حديث)

25 gemstone bracelet — سِوَار مُرَصَّع بالأحْجَار الكريمة

26 asymmetrical bangle — سِوَار/أُسْوِرَة مِعْصَم، خلخال قَدَم لامُتَمَاثِل

27 asymmetrical ring — خَاتَم لامُتَمَاثِل

28 ivory necklace — عِقْد عاج

29 ivory rose — وَرْدَة عاج

30 ivory brooch — بروش عاج

31 jewel box (jewel case) — صندوق مُجَوْهَرَات

32 pearl necklace — عِقْد لُؤْلُؤ

33 bracelet watch — ساعَة سِوَار/أُسْوِرَة

34 coral necklace — عِقْد مَرْجَان

35 charms — حلْيَات صغيرة

36 coin bracelet — سِوَار/أُسْوِرَة مُزَوَّدة بعُمْلَة ذهبيَّة

37 gold coin — عُمْلَة ذَهَبيَّة

38 coin setting — إطار تثْبيت العُمْلَة

39 link — وَصْلَة

40 signet ring — خَاتَم يُحْفَر عليه الاسم

41 engraving (monogram) — حَفْر (مونوجرام)

42-86 cuts and forms — **أنْماط القَطْعيَّات والأشكال**

42-71 faceted stones — **الأحْجَار ذات الأَوْجُه**

42-43 standard round cut — **القَطْع الدائريّ العادي**

44 brilliant cut — القَطْع الماسي

45 rose cut — قَطْع وَرْدِي/نَجْميّ الشَكْل

46 flat table — قَطْع مُسْتو

47 table en cabochon — سَطْح قِبابيّ

48 standard cut — قَطْع عادي

49 standard antique cut — قَطْع أنتيكي عادي

50 rectangular step-cut — قَطْع دَرَجيّ مُسْتَطيل

51 square step-cut — قَطْع دَرَجيّ مُرَبَّع

52 octagonal step-cut — قَطْع دَرَجيّ ثُماني

53 octagonal cross-cut — قَطْع صَلِيبي ثُماني

54 standard pear-shape (pendeloque) — قَطْع بندولي عادي

55 marquise (navette)	قَطْع مركيزي
56 standard barrel-shape	شَكْل برميلي عادي
57 trapezium step-cut	قَطْع دَرَجي ترابيزي (شَكْل المُعَيَّن المُنْحَرِف)
58 trapezium cross-cut	قَطْع صَلِيبي تَرابيزي
59 rhombus step-cut	قَطْع شَكْل المُعَيَّن
60-61 triangular step-cut	**القَطْع الدَّرَجي المثلثي**
62 hexagonal step-cut	قَطْع دَرَجي متساوي الساقَيْن
63 oval hexagonal cross-cut	قَطْع صَلِيبي سُداسيّ بيضويّ
64 round hexagonal step-cut	قَطْع دَرَجي سُداسيّ مستدير
65 round hexagonal cross-cut	قَطْع صَلِيبي سُداسيّ مستدير
66 chequer-board cut	قَطْع كاروهات
67 triangle cut	قَطْع مثلثيّ
68-71 fancy cuts	**أنماط القَطْع الزُخْرُفي**
72-77 ring gemstones	**الأحْجَار الكريمة الخاصة بالخواتم**
72 oval flat table	وَجْه مُسَطح بيضوي
73 rectangular flat table	وَجْه مُسَطح مثلثي
74 octagonal flat table	وَجْه مُسَطح ثُماني
75 barrel-shape	شَكْل برميليّ
76 antique table en cabochon	سَطْح أنتيكي قِبَابي
77 rectangular table en cabochon	سَطْح مستطيل قِبَابي
78-81 cabochons	**الأشكال القِبَابية**
78 round cabochon (simple cabochon)	قِبَابي دائري (قِبَابي بسيط)
79 high dome (high cabochon)	قِبَابي مرتفع
80 oval cabochon	قِبَابي بَيْضَوي
81 octagonal cabochon	قِبَابي ثُماني
82-86 spheres and pear-shapes	**الأشكال الكَرَوِيَّة والكُمَثْرِيَّة**
82 plain sphere	كُرَويّ أمْلَس
83 plain pear-shape	كُمَثْريّ أملَس
84 faceted pear-shape	كُمَثْريّ مُتَعَدِّد الأسَطْح/الأوجه
85 plain drop	قَطْرَة مَلْسَاء
86 faceted briolette	كُمَثْريّ بَيْضَويّ مُتَعَدِّد الأسَطْح

37 Types of Dwelling — أنْوَاع المَسَاكِن

1-53 detached house	**مَنْزِل مُنْفَصِل**
1 basement	طابَق تحت الأرض (بدروم)
2 ground floor (*Am.* first floor)	طابَق أرضي
3 upper floor (first floor, *Am.* second floor)	طابَق علوي
4 loft	علية (سَنْدَرَة)
5 roof, a gable roof (saddle roof, saddle-back roof)	سَطْح المَبْنَى ، سَطْح جَمَلُوني
6 gutter	مُزرَاب
7 ridge	حَرْف الجَمَلُون
8 verge with bargeboards	حافة ألْوَاح خشبيَّة
9 eaves, rafter-supported eaves	إفريز ، رَفْرَف السطْح
10 chimney	مِدْخَنَة
11 gutter	مُزراب
12 swan's neck (swan-neck)	عُنُق إوزة
13 rainwater pipe (down-pipe, *Am.* downspout, leader)	مَاسُورَة تصريف ماء المَطَر
14 vertical pipe, a cast-iron pipe	مَاسُورَة من الحديد الزَّهْر
15 gable (gable end)	جَمَلُون (طرف جَمَلُوني)
16 glass wall	جِدَار زجاجي
17 base course (plinth)	مِدْمَاك قاعِدة المَبْنَى
18 balcony	بلكونة ، شرفة
19 parapet	حاجز الشرفة
20 flower box	صندوق وضع الزهور
21 French window (French windows (opening on to the balcony)	شُبَّاك فرنسي يَفْتَح على الشرفة
22 double casement window	شُبَّاك ذو ضَلَفْتَيْن
23 single casement window	شُبَّاك ذو ضَلْفَة واحدة
24 window breast with window sill	صَدْر النَافِذَة وبه عَتَبَة النَافذَة
25 lintel (window head)	رَأْس النَافِذَة
26 reveal	حافة الجِدَار حَوْل النَافذَة (أو الباب)
27 cellar window	نافِذَة البدروم/القَبو
28 rolling shutter	شيش قابل للطيّ
29 rolling shutter frame	إطار الشيش
30 window shutter (folding shutter)	شيش النَافِذَة
31 shutter catch	شَنْكَل الشيش
32 garage with tool shed	كاراج/مِرْآب به عَنْبر الأدوات
33 espalier	تَعْرِيشَة
34 batten door (ledged door)	بابَ مُضَلَّع بألواح خشبيَّة
35 fanlight with mullion and transom	شُرَّاعة مزودة بعمود تقسيم ورافدة مستعرضة
36 terrace	تراس ، شرفة واسعة
37 garden wall with coping stones	جِدَار حديقة مُزَوَّد بأحْجَار افريز
38 garden light	مِصْبَاح الحديقة
39 steps	دَرَجَات سُلَّم
40 rockery (rock garden)	حديقة صَخْرِيَّة
41 outside tap (*Am.* faucet) for the hose	صُنْبُور خارجي لخُرطوم الحديقة
42 garden hose	خُرطوم الحديقة
43 lawn sprinkler	مِرَشَّة العُشْب
44 paddling pool	حَوْض ماء ضَحل للأطفال
45 stepping stones	أحجار للخطو
46 sunbathing area (lawn)	مِنْطَقَة الحَمَّام الشمسيّ
47 deck-chair	كُرْسي قماش
48 sunshade (garden parasol)	شَمَّاسة ، شَمْسِيَّة
49 garden chair	كُرْسي حديقة

50 garden table طاولة الحديقة
51 frame for beating carpets إطار لتنفيض السجاجيد
52 garage driveway مَمَرّ الجَراج
53 fence, a wooden fence سِياج، سور خشبي
54-57 housing estate (housing development) **مِنْطَقَة إسْكان، مِنْطَقَة سَكَنِيَّة**
54 house on a housing estate (on a housing development) مَنْزِل في مِنْطَقَة سكنية
55 pent roof (penthouse roof) سَقْف مَبْنَى جانبي مُلْحَق
56 dormer (dormer window) شُبَّاك جَمَلُون بارِز
57 garden حديقة
58-63 terraced house [one of a row of terraced houses], stepped **مَنْزِل في صَف من المنازل مُلْتَصِق كل منهما بالآخَر**
58 front garden حديقة أماميَّة
59 hedge سِياج
60 pavement (*Am.* sidewalk, walkway) مَمْشَى جانبي، رصيف
61 street (road) شارِع (طريق)
62 street lamp (street light) فانوس الشارِع
63 litter bin (*Am.* trash bin) صفيحة نفايات
64-68 house divided into two flats (*Am.* house divided into two apartments, duplex house) **مَنْزِل مُقَسَّم إلى شَقَّتَيْن** (بَيْت دوبلكس)
64 hip (hipped) roof سقف مُسَنَّم
65 front door باب أمامي
66 front steps دَرَجات سُلَّم أمامي
67 canopy مظلة، تندة
68 flower window (window for house plants) نافذَة لتعليق الزهور
69-71 pair of semi-detached houses divided into four flats (*Am.* apartments) **مَنْزِلان متصلان ببعضهما من جانب واحد فقط مقسمان إلى أربع شقق**
69 balcony بلكونة، شرفة
70 sun lounge (*Am.* sun parlor) استراحة، غرفة جلوس
71 awning (sun blind, sunshade) ظُلَّة، تَنْدَة
72-76 block of flats (*Am.* apartment building, apartment house) with access balconies **مَبْنَى سَكَنِيّ، مجموعة شُقَق سكنيَّة**
72 staircase بَيْت الدَّرَج
73 balcony بلكون، شرفة
74 studio flat (*Am.* studio apartment) شَقَّة ستوديو
75 sun roof, a sun terrace شرفة شمسية
76 open space مِنْطَقَة مفتوحة
77-81 multi-storey block of flats (*Am.* multistory apartment building, multistory apartment house) **مَبْنَى سَكَنِيّ مُتَعَدِّد الطوابِق**
77 flat roof سَطْح مستوٍ
78 pent roof (shed roof, lean-to roof) سقف مَبْنَى جانبي مُلْحَق
79 garage كاراج
80 pergola برغولا، تَعْرِيشَة فَوْق مَمَرّ الحديقة
81 staircase window نافذَة بَيْت الدَّرَج
82 high-rise block of flats (*Am.* high-rise apartment building, high-rise apartment house) مَبْنَى سَكَنِيّ مرتفع
83 penthouse مَبْنَى مُلْحَق
84-86 weekend house, a timber house **بَيْت خشبي للعطلات الأسبوعيَّة**
84 horizontal boarding ألواح أفقيَّة
85 natural stone base course (natural stone plinth) مِدْماك من الحَجَر الطبيعي
86 strip windows (ribbon windows) نافذَة طَويلة ضَيِّقَة مُقَسَّمَة بفواصِل خشبيَّة

38 Roof and Boiler Room السَّطْح وحُجْرَة الغَلايَة

1-29 attic **عِلِيَّة، سَنْدَرة**
1 roof cladding (roof covering) غِطاء السقف
2 skylight كُوَّة السقف، قَمَرِيَّة
3 gangway سِقالة مُؤَقَّتَة
4 cat ladder (roof ladder) سُلَّم السقف
5 chimney مِدْخَنَة
6 roof hook خُطَّاف السقف
7 dormer window (dormer) شُبَّاك جَمَلُوني بارز
8 snow guard (roof guard) وقاء الجليد
9 gutter مِزْراب
10 rainwater pipe (downpipe, *Am.* downspout, leader) مَاسُورَة تصريف مياه الأمطار
11 eaves إفريز، رَفْرَف السقف
12 pitched roof سقف مائل
13 trapdoor باب مَسْحُور
14 hatch كُوَّة
15 ladder سُلَّم نقَّالي
16 stile مَرْقَى دَرَجي
17 rung دَرَجَة (سُلَّم)
18 loft (attic) عِلِيَّة، سَنْدَرة
19 wooden partition حاجِز/فاصِل خشبي
20 lumber room door (boxroom door) باب غُرْفَة من اللوائح الخشبيَّة
21 padlock قُفْل
22 hook [for washing line] خُطَّاف [لحبْل الغسيل]
23 clothes line (washing line) حَبْل غسيل
24 expansion tank for boiler خَزَّان التمدد الخاص بالمِرْجَل
25 wooden steps and دَرَجات خشبيَّة ودرابزين

balustrade
26 string (*Am.* stringer) عارضة جانبيَّة
27 step دَرَجَة سُلَّم
28 handrail (guard rail) مُتَّكأ الدرابزين
29 baluster عمود الدرابزين
30 lightning conductor (lightning rod) واقِيَة الصواعِق
31 chimney sweep (*Am.* chimney sweeper) مُنَظِّف المِدْخَنَة
32 brush with weight فُرْشَاة مُزَوَّدة بثِقْل
33 shoulder iron حديدة الكتف
34 sack for soot كيس للسِّناج
35 flue brush فُرْشَاة مَسْرَب المِدْخَنَة
36 broom (besom) مِكْنَسَة
37 broomstick (broom handle) عصا المِكْنَسَة
38-81 hot-water heating system, full central heating **نظام تسخين الماء، تسخين مركزيّ كامل**
38-43 boiler room **حُجْرَة المِرْجَل/الغلاية**
38 coke-fired central heating system نظام تسخين مركزي يعمل بحرْق الكُوك
39 ash box door (*Am.* cleanout door) باب صندوق الرَّمَاد
40 flueblock كتلة مَسْرَب المدخنة
41 poker مِحْراك (الجَمْر)، مِسْعَار
42 rake مِدَمَّة
43 coal shovel جاروف الفَحْم
44-60 oil-fired central heating system **نظام تسخين مركزي يعمل بحرْق الزيْت**
44 oil tank صهريج الزيْت
45 manhole فتحة الدخول
46 manhole cover غِطاء فتحة الدخول
47 tank inlet مَدْخَل/مَنْفَذ الصهريج
48 dome cover غِطاء قِبابي
49 tank bottom valve صِمام قاع الصهريج
50 fuel oil (heating oil) زَيْت وَقُود (زَيْت تدفئة)
51 air-bleed duct مَاسُورَة التهْوِيَة
52 air vent cap غطاء فتحة التهوية
53 oil level pipe أنْبُوب مُسْتَوَى الزَّيْت
54 oil gauge (*Am.* gage) مِقْيَاس الزَّيْت
55 suction pipe مَاسُورَة ماصة
56 return pipe أنْبُوب إرْجَاع
57 central heating furnace (oil heating furnace) فرن التسخين المركزيّ (فرن التسخين بالزَّيْت)
58-60 oil burner **حارق زَيْتيّ**
58 fan مِرْوَحة
59 electric motor مُحَرِّك كهربي
60 covered pilot light ضَوْء إرْشادي مُغَطَّى
61 charging door بوَّابة الإلْقام
62 inspection window نَافِذَة المُعايَنَة
63 water gauge (*Am.* gage) مِقْيَاس الماء
64 furnace thermometer ترمومتر الفُرْن
65 bleeder مِحْبَس، صِمام صَرْف
66 furnace bed قاعدة الفرن
67 control panel لَوْحَة التَّحكُّم
68 hot water tank (boiler) صهريج الماء الساخِن (الغلايَّة)
69 overflow pipe (overflow) أنْبُوب الفائض
70 safety valve صِمام أمان
71 main distribution pipe أنْبُوب التوزيع الرئيسي
72 lagging مواد عازلة لتغليف الأنابيب
73 valve صِمام
74 flow pipe أنْبُوب الدَّفْق (الماء الصاعِد من الغلاية)
75 regulating valve صِمام تنظيم
76 radiator مُشِعّ
77 radiator rib ضِلع المُشِعّ
78 room thermostat ترموستات الحُجْرَة
79 return pipe (return) أنْبُوب إرْجاع
80 return pipe [in two-pipe system] أنْبُوب إرْجاع [في النظام ثنائي الأنابيب]
81 smoke outlet (smoke extract) فتحة خروج الدُّخان

39 Kitchen المَطْبَخ

1 microwave oven (microwave) فُرْن ميكروويف
2 refrigerator (fridge, *Am.* icebox) ثَلاجَة
3 refrigerator shelf رَفّ الثَّلاَّجَة
4 salad drawer دُرْج الخُضْرَوَات
5 freezing compartment حُجَيْرَة الأطْعِمَة المُجَمَّدَة
6 bottle rack (in storage door) رَفّ القنينات (فى باب الثَّلاجة)
7 upright freezer فريزر رأسيّ
8 wall cupboard, a kitchen cupboard دُولاب مطْبَخ
9 base unit وَحْدَة القاعِدَة
10 cutlery drawer دُرْج لوازِم المائدة (من سكاكين وفِضِّيَّة)
11 work surface (worktop) نَضُد الشُّغْل
12-17 cooker unit **وَحْدَة الطبَّاخ، جِهَاز الطَّبْخ**
12 electric cooker (*also:* gas cooker) طبَّاخ (بوتوجاز) كهربى
13 oven فُرْن
14 oven window نافذة الفُرْن
15 hotplate, an automatic high-speed plate مَوْقِد (عَيْن) البوتوجاز
16 kettle (whistling kettle) غلاَّيَة
17 cooker hood غِطاء جِهَاز الطَّبْخ
18 pot holder حَامِل أواني الطَّبْخ
19 pot holder rack علاَّقة حَامِل أواني الطَّبْخ
20 kitchen clock ساعة المَطْبَخ
21 timer جِهَاز تَوْقِيت
22 hand mixer خلاط يدويّ
23 whisk مِخْفَقَة (للبَيْض، الخ.)
24 electric coffee grinder (with rotating blades) مِطْحَنَة بُنّ كهربائية (ذات مَنَاصِل دَوَّارَة)
25 lead سِلْك تَوْصيل
26 wall socket مَقْبَس جِدَاريّ
27 corner unit وَحْدَة الزَّاوِيَة
28 revolving shelf رَفّ دوَّار
29 pot (cooking pot) وعاء/إناء للطهي
30 jug ابْرِيق

31 spice rack — رف التَّوَابل
32 spice jar — مَرْطَمَان/بَرْطَمَان توابل
33-36 sink unit — **وَحْدَة حَوْض الغسيل**
33 dish drainer — حَامِل تجفيف الأطباق
34 tea plate — طَبَق صغير
35 sink — حَوْض المطبخ
36 water tap (*Am.* faucet); *here:* mixer tap (*Am.* mixing faucet) — حنفيَّة/صنبور الماء؛ هنا: صنبور خلاط
37 pot plant, a foliage plant — نبات زينة فى إصِّيص
38 coffee maker — جِهَاز إعْدَاد القَهْوَة
39 kitchen lamp — مِصْبَاح المَطْبَخ
40 dishwasher (dish-washing machine) — غسَّالة أطْبَاق
41 dish rack — رَفّ أطْبَاق
42 dinner plate — طَبَق واسِع مُفَلْطَح
43 kitchen chair — كُرْسِيّ مَطْبَخ
44 kitchen table — طاوِلَة مَطْبَخ
45 toaster — تُوسْتَر، مِحْمَصَة خُبْز كهربائية

40 Kitchen Utensils and Appliances — أدَوَات وأجْهِزَة المَطْبَخ

1 general-purpose roll holder with kitchen roll (paper towels) — حَامِل مَنَاشِف وَرَقِيَّة مُتَعَدِّد الأغْرَاض
2 set of wooden spoons — طاقم مَلاعِق خَشَبِيَّة
3 mixing spoon — مِلْعَقَة تَقْلِيب (كَبْشَة)
4 frying pan — قَلاَّيَة، إناء القَلْي
5 Thermos jug — تُرْمُس
6 set of bowls — طاقم سُلْطانيَّات/زِبْدِيَّات
7 cheese dish with glass cover — طبق جبن له غطاء زُجاجى
8 three-compartment dish — صينيَّة مُقَسَّمَة إلى ثلاث حُجَيْرَات
9 lemon squeezer — عصَّارة لَيْمُون
10 whistling kettle — غلايَّة مياه (تُصْدِر صفيراً عند الغَلْي)
11 whistle — صفَّارة تحذير
12-16 pan set — **طاقم أواني الطَّهي**
12 pot (cooking pot) — وِعاء/قِدْر طَبْخ
13 lid — غِطاء
14 casserole dish — قِدْر فخَّاري، بِرَام
15 milk pot — لبَّانة، وعاء اللَّبَن
16 saucepan — كَسَرُولة
17 immersion heater — مُسَخِّن كهربي غاطِس
18 corkscrew [with levers] — برِّيمَة نَزْع السَّدَّادَات الفلِّينيَّة [ذات أذْرُع]
19 juice extractor — عَصَّارة
20 tube clamp (tube clip) — ماسك الأنبوب
21 pressure cooker — جِهَاز طَبْخ يَعْمَل بالضغط
22 pressure valve — صِمَام ضغط
23 fruit preserver — آنِيَة حِفْظ الفاكِهة
24 removable rack — حَامِل قابِل للفَصْل
25 preserving jar — إبْرِيق حفظ (مَوَاد غذائيَّة)
26 rubber ring — حَلَقَة مَطَّاطِيَّة
27 spring form — قالِب مُزَوَّد بنابِض
28 cake tin — صينِيَّة كَعْك

29 cake tin — صينيَّة كَعْك
30 microwave oven (microwave) — فُرْن ميكروويف
31 timer — جِهَاز تَوْقِيت
32 rotisserie — مِشْوَاة، شَوَّاية
33 spit — سَفُود، سيخ
34 electric waffle iron — مِحْمَصَة "وفل" كهربائية
35 sliding-weight scales — ميزان مَطْبَخ ذو ثِقْل انزلاقى/مُتَحَرِّك
36 sliding weight — ثِقْل مُنْزَلِق/انزلاقى
37 scale pan — كفَّة الميزان
38 food slicer — مِشْرَحَة الطعام
39 mincer (*Am.* meat chopper) — فرَّامَة اللحوم، مِفْرَمَة
40 blades — رِيَش/أنْصَال المِفْرَمَة
41 chip pan — وِعاء الشرائح
42 basket — سَلَّة
43 potato chipper — ماكينة تقطيع البطاطِس إلى شَرَائح وَرَقائق
44 yoghurt maker — جِهَاز إعداد الزبادى
45 mixer — خلاط
46 blender — المُوَلِّف، جِهَاز المَزْج
47 bag sealer — جِهَاز إحكَام قَفْل الأكياس البلاستيكيَّة

41 Hall — الصَّالَة

1-29 hall (entrance hall) — **الصَّالَة** (رُدْهَة المَدْخَل)
1 coat rack — حمَّالَة، علاَّقة الملابِس
2 coat hook — خُطَّاف تعليق
3 coat hanger — شَمَّاعة ملابس
4 rain cape — رِدَاء خارِجي فضفاض واقٍ من المَطر
5 walking stick — عكَّاز، عصا المَشْي
6 hall mirror — مِرْآة الصَّالة
7 telephone — هاتِف، تليفون
8 chest of drawers for shoes, etc. — خِزانة ذات أدْرَاج لحِفْظ الأحذيَة، الخ.
9 drawer — دُرْج
10 seat — مَقْعَد
11 ladies' hat — قبعة نسائيَّة
12 telescopic umbrella — مِظلَّة مُتَدَاخِلَة الأجْزَاء
13 tennis rackets (tennis racquets) — مَضْرِبَا لعبة التنس الأرضي
14 umbrella stand — حَامِل الشَّمَاسي
15 umbrella — مِظلَّة، شمسيَّة
16 shoes — زَوْج من الأحذيَة
17 briefcase — حقيبة يد
18 fitted carpet — بُسَاط/سجَّادَة تُغَطِّي الأرضيَّة بالكامل
19 fuse box — صُنْدُوق الفيوزات الكهربيَّة
20 miniature circuit breaker — قاطع تيَّار صغير المَدَى
21 tubular steel chair — كُرْسِيّ مَعْدَنِيّ ذو هيكل أنبوبِيّ الشكْل
22 stair light — مِصْبَاح الدَّرَج/السلَّم
23 handrail — مُتَّكَأ الدرابزين
24 step — دَرَجَة سُلَّم
25 front door — باب أمامِيّ
26 door frame — إطار الباب

27 door lock	قُفْل الباب
28 door handle	مِقْبَض الباب
29 spyhole	عَيْن سِحْرِيَّة

42 Living Room — غُرْفَة المَعيشَة

1-20 wall units (shelf units)	**وَحْدات حائطيَّة** (وَحْدَات أَرْفُف)
2 side wall	جِدار جانِبي
3 bookshelf	رَفّ كُتُب
4 row of books	صَفّ من الكُتُب
5 display cabinet unit	دُولاب نِيش
6 cupboard base unit	خِزَانة قاعدة الدُولاب
7 cupboard unit	خِزَانة ، صُوَان
8 television set (TV set)	تِلْفاز
9 stereo system (stereo equipment)	جِهاز ستريو
10 speaker (loudspeaker)	سمَّاعة صَوْت، مكبِّر صَوْت
11 pipe rack	حَامِل الغَلْيُون
12 pipe	غَلْيُون
13 globe	كُرَة أرضيَّة
14 brass kettle	غلاَّية نحاسيَّة
15 telescope	تليسكوب
16 mantle clock	ساعَة رَفّ
17 bust	تمثال نِصْفيّ
18 encyclopaedia [in several volumes]	مَوْسوعَة [فى عِدَّة مُجلَّدات]
19 room divider	حاجِز/فاصِل الغُرْفَة
20 drinks cupboard	خِزَانة/صُوَان المَشْرُوبات (بار)
21-26 upholstered suite (seating group)	**طاقم جلوس مُنَجَّد**
21 armchair	كُرْسِيّ ذو مِسْنَدَيْن
22 arm	ذِرَاع ، مِسْنَد
23 seat cushion (cushion)	وِسَادَة مَقْعَد
24 settee	كَنَبة/أريكة مُنَجَّدة
25 back cushion	مِسْنَد/وِسَادَة الظَّهْر
26 [round] corner section	جزء الزَّاوِيَة [المُسْتَدير]
27 scatter cushion	وِسَادَة صغيرة
28 coffee table	طَاوِلة القهوة/الشاي
29 ashtray	مِنْفَضَة السَّجائر
30 tray	صِينيَّة
31 whisky (whiskey) bottle	زُجَاجَة ويسكي
32 soda water bottle (soda bottle)	زُجَاجَة ماء الصودا
33-34 dining set	**طاقم طاولة الطعام**
33 dining table	طاولة طَعَام
34 chair	كُرْسِيّ
35 net curtain	سِتَارَة شبكيَّة
36 indoor plants (house-plants)	نباتات منزليَّة/داخليَّة

43 Bedroom — غُرْفَة النَّوْم

1 wardrobe (*Am.* clothes closet)	دُولاب/صُوَان المَلابِس
2 linen shelf	رَفّ البَيَاضَات
3 cane chair	كُرْسِيّ من القشّ والخَيْزَران
4-13 double bed (*sim.:* double divan)	**سَرِير مُزْدَوِج/لشَخْصَيْن**
4-6 bedstead	**هَيْكَل السَّرير**
4 foot of the bed	اللَّوْحَة السفليَّة
5 bed frame	مِنْصَب
6 headboard	اللَّوْحَة الرأسيَّة
7 bedspread	مِفْرَش/غِطاء السرير
8 duvet, a quilted duvet	دوفيت، لحاف
9 sheet, a linen sheet	مُلاءة
10 mattress, a foam mattress with drill tick	مَرْتَبَة ، حشيّة (لها كيس من الكتان أو القطن)
11 [wedge-shaped] bolster	مِخَدَّة، وِسَادَة [اسفينية الشكل]
12-13 pillow	**وِسَادَة ، مِخَدَّة**
12 pillowcase (pillowslip)	كِيس مِخَدَّة/وِسَادَة
13 tick	غِلاف الوِسَادَة
14 bookshelf [attached to the headboard]	رَفّ كُتُب (مُلْحَق باللَّوْحَة الرأسيَّة)
15 reading lamp	مِصْبَاح للقراءة
16 electric alarm clock	ساعَة كهربائية مُزَوَّدَة بمُنَبِّه
17 bedside cabinet	خزانة بجانب السَّرِير (كومودينو)
18 drawer	دُرْج
19 bedroom lamp	مِصْباح غُرْفَة النَّوْم
20 picture	صُورة
21 picture frame	إطار/برواز الصُّورة
22 bedside rug	سِجَّادة/بِسَاط صغير
23 fitted carpet	بُسَاط (يُغطى الأرضيَّة بالكامِل)
24 dressing stool	كرسى المزْيَنَة/التسْرِيحَة
25 dressing table	المَزْيَنَة ، التسْرِيحَة
26 perfume spray	مِرَشَّة عِطْر
27 perfume bottle	قنينة عِطْر
28 powder box	عُلْبَة بُودْرَة
29 dressing-table mirror (mirror)	مِرْآة المِزْيَنَة

44 Dining Room — غُرْفَة الطَّعَام

1-11 dining set	**طاقم طاولة الطَّعَام**
1 dining table	مائدة/طاوِلة الطَّعَام
2 table leg	قائمة/رِجْل الطاولة
3 table top	سطح الطاولة
4 place mat	مفرَش صغير(يوضع أمام كل جالِس)
5 place (place setting, cover)	مَوْضِع/مكان (لأحَد الجالسين)
6 soup plate (deep plate)	طَبَق الحَسَاء (طَبَق عميق)
7 dinner plate	طَبَق واسِع مُفَلْطَح
8 soup tureen	سُلْطَانيَّة الحَسَاء
9 wineglass	كَأْس
10 dining chair	كُرْسِيّ طاولة الطعام
11 seat	مَقْعَدة الكُرْسِيّ
12 lamp (pendant lamp)	مِصْبَاح(مُدَلّى من السقف)
13 curtains	ستائر
14 net curtain	سِتارة شبكيَّة
15 curtain rail	قضيب تعليق الستارة
16 carpet	سِجَّادَة، بُسَاط
17 wall unit	وَحْدَة حائطيَّة
18 glass door	باب زُجاجيّ
19 shelf	رَفّ
20 sideboard	بُوفيه، صُوان لوازِم

المائدة

21 cutlery drawer — دُرْج لوازم المائدة

22 linen drawer — دُرْج البَيَاضَات (مَفَارِش وفُوَط المائدة)

23 base — قاعدة

24 round tray — صينِيَّة مُستديرة

25 pot plant — نَبَات (زينَة) في أصِّيص

26 china cabinet (display cabinet) — دُولاب نَيش

27 coffee set (coffee service) — طاقم القَهْوَة

28 coffee pot — دلَّة/رَكْوَة القَهْوَة

29 coffee cup — فِنْجَان القَهْوَة

30 saucer — طَبَق الفِنْجَان

31 milk jug — إبْرِيق اللبن (اللبَّانَة)

32 sugar bowl — سُكَّرِيَّة (وعاء السُّكَّر)

33 dinner set (dinner service) — طاقم صينِي للمائدة

45 Tableware and Cutlery — مَفَارِش ولَوَازِم المَائِدَة

1 dining table — مائدة/طاولة الطَّعَام

2 tablecloth, a damask cloth — مَفْرَش المائدة، مَفْرَش ديباج

3-12 place (place setting, cover) — **مَوْضِع جالِس إلي المائدة**

3 bottom plate — طَبَق سُفْلي

4 dinner plate — طَبَق واسِع مُفَلْطَح

5 deep plate (soup plate) — طَبَق عَمِيق (طَبَق حَسَاء)

6 dessert plate (dessert bowl) — طَبَق الحَلْو (الحَلْوَى أو الفاكِهة)

7 knife and fork — سِكِّين وشَوْكة

8 fish knife and fork — سِكِّين وشَوْكة الأسْماك

9 serviette (napkin, table napkin) — فُوطَة المائدة

10 serviette ring (napkin ring) — حَلَقَة فُوَط المائدة

11 knife rest — مِسْنَد السكاكين

12 wineglasses — كؤوس الخَمْر

13 place card — بطاقَة (تَحْمِل اسْم صاحِب المَوْضِع)

14 soup ladle — مغْرَفَة الحَسَاء

15 soup tureen (tureen) — سلطانية الحَسَاء

16 candelabra — شَمْعدَان

17 sauceboat (gravy boat) — قارِب الصَّلْصَة/المَرَق

18 sauce ladle (gravy ladle) — مِغرفَة الصَّلْصَة/المَرَق

19 table decoration — زِينَة للمائدة

20 bread basket — سَلَّة الخُبْز

21 roll — رَغِيف إفْرَنْجي صغير

22 slice of bread — كِسْرَة/شَرِيحَة خُبْز

23 salad bowl — طَبَق السَّلَطَة

24 salad servers — شَوْكَة ومِلْعَقَة تقديم السَّلَطَة

25 vegetable dish — طَبَق الخُضْرَوَات

26 meat plate (*Am.* meat platter) — طَبَق اللحوم

27 roast meat (roast) — لَحْم مَشْوِي (شواء)

28 fruit dish — طَبَق الفاكِهة

29 fruit bowl — طَبَق فاكِهة(صغير)

30 fruit (stewed fruit) — فاكِهة (فاكِهة مَطْبُوخَة)

31 potato dish — طَبَق البطاطِس

32 serving trolley — ترولِلى تقديم الطَّعَام

33 vegetable plate (*Am.* vegetable platter) — طَبَق الخُضْرَوَات

34 toast — خُبْز مُحَمَّص

35 cheeseboard — قالِب الجُبْن

36 butter dish — طَبَق الزُّبْد

37 open sandwich — شَطِيرَة

38 filling — حَشْو

39 sandwich — سندوتش

40 fruit bowl — طَبَق فاكهة

41 almonds (*also:* potato crisps, peanuts) — لَوْز (أيْضاً: رقائق البطاطِس ، فول سوداني)

42 oil and vinegar bottle — قنينة الزَّيْت والخَل

43 ketchup (catchup, catsup) — كاتشب (صَلْصَة من الطماطِم أو الفطر)

44 sideboard — بوفيه (صُوَان جانبي)

45 electric hotplate — مَوْقِد كهربائى

46 corkscrew — فتَّاحة سدادات فلينية

47 crown cork bottle opener (crown cork opener), a bottle opener — فتَّاحة قنينات ذات سِدَادات فلينيَّة

48 liqueur decanter — دَوْرَق للخَمْر

49 nutcrackers (nut-cracker) — كسَّارة بندق

50 knife — سِكِّين

51 handle — مِقْبَض

52 tang (tongue) — لسان السكِّين

53 ferrule — طُوَيْق معدني

54 blade — نَصْل

55 bolster — سِنَاد

56 back — الطَرف الخلفي للنَّصْل

57 edge (cutting edge) — حافَة (الحافَة القاطِعة)

58 fork — شَوْكَة

59 handle — مِقْبَض

60 prong (tang, tine) — إحدى شُعَب الشَّوْكَة

61 spoon; *here:* dessert spoon, soup spoon — مِلْعَقَة (مِلْعَقَة متوسطة الحَجْم ، مِلْعَقَة شُورْبَة/حساء)

62 handle — مِقْبَض

63 bowl — بطن المِلْعَقَة

64 fish knife — سِكِّين الأسْماك

65 fish fork — شَوْكَة الأسْماك

66 dessert spoon (fruit spoon) — مِلْعَقَة الحَلْوَى أو الفاكِهة

67 salad spoon — مِلْعَقَة السَّلَطَة

68 salad fork — شَوْكَة السَّلَطَة

69-70 carving set (serving cutlery) — **طاقم تقطيع الشواء**

69 carving knife — سِكِّين تقطيع الشواء

70 serving fork — شَوْكَة تقديم الشواء

71 fruit knife — سِكِّين الفاكِهة

72 cheese knife — سِكِّين الجُبْن

73 butter knife — سِكِّين الزُّبْد

74 vegetable spoon, a serving spoon — مِلْعَقَة تقديم الخُضْرَوَات

75 potato server (serving spoon for potatoes) — مِلْعَقَة تقديم البطاطِس

76 cocktail fork — شَوْكَة الكوكتيل
77 asparagus server (asparagus slice) — مِلْعَقَة تقديم الهليون
78 sardine server — شَوْكَة تقديم السردين
79 lobster fork — شَوْكَة تقديم جَرَاد البَحْر
80 oyster fork — شَوْكَة تقديم المَحَّار
81 caviare knife — سِكِين تقديم الكَفْيَار
82 white wine glass — كَأْس نَبِيذ أَبْيَض
83 red wine glass — كَأْس نَبِيذ أَحْمَر
84 sherry glass (madeira glass) — كَأْس نَبِيذ الشَّرِّي
85-86 champagne glasses — **كَأْسَا الشمبانيا**
85 tapered glass — كَأْس مستدقة الطرف
86 champagne glass, a crystal glass — كَأْس شمبانيا كريستال
87 rummer — قَدَح أو كُوب كبير
88 brandy glass — كَأْس البراندى
89 liqueur glass — كَأْس مشروب مُسْكِر
90 spirit glass — كَأْس مشروب كحولي
91 beer glass — كُوب البيرة (الجُعَّة)

46 Flat (Apartment) — الشَّقَّة

1 wall units (shelf units) — وَحْدَات حائطيَّة (أَرْفُف)
2 wardrobe door (*Am.* clothes closet door) — باب صُوان الملابِس
3 body — جِسْم الصوان
4 side wall — جِدار جانبي
5 trim — حافة خشبيَّة زُخْرُفيَّة
6 two-door cupboard unit — خِزَانَة ذات بابَيْن
7 bookshelf unit (book-case unit) [with glass door] — وَحْدَة رَفّ الكُتُب [ذات باب زُجاجيّ]
8 books — كُتُب
9 display cabinet — دُولاب نيش
10 record player — جِهَاز بيك أب، جِهَاز تشغيل الأُسْطُوانات
11 drawer — دُرْج
12 decorative biscuit tin — عُلْبَة بسكويت زُخْرُفيَّة
13 soft toy animal — لُعْبة طريَّة على شكل حيوان
14 television set (TV set) — تِلْفاز
15 records (discs) — تسجيلات
16 bed unit — وَحْدَة السَّرير
17 scatter cushion — وِسَادَة صغيرة
18 bed unit drawer — دُرْج السَّرير
19 bed unit shelf — رَفّ السَّرير
20 magazines — مجلات
21 desk unit (writing unit) — وَحْدَة المكتَب
22 desk — مكْتَب، طاولة الكتابة
23 desk mat (blotter) — نَشَّافَة
24 table lamp — مِصْباح طاولة
25 wastepaper basket — سَلَّة مُهْمَلات
26 desk drawer — دُرْج المكْتَب
27 desk chair — كُرْسِيّ المكْتَب
28 arm — مِسْنَد/ذراع الكُرْسِيّ
29 kitchen unit — وَحْدَة المطبخ
30 wall cupboard — خزانة حائط
31 cooker hood — غطاء الطَّبَّاخ/جِهاز الطَّبْخ
32 electric cooker — جِهَاز طَبْخ كهربائى
33 refrigerator (fridge, *Am.* icebox) — ثلاجَة
34 dining table — طاولة الطعام
35 table runner — مفْرَش مائدة مُزَخْرَف
36 oriental carpet standard lamp — سجَّادة/بساط شَرْقي مِصْباح أعلى حَامِل عمودي

47 Children's Room (Nursery) — غُرْفَة الأطْفَال (حجرة نوم الطفل)

1 children's bed, a bunkbed — سَرِير طِفْل
2 storage box — صُنْدُوق تخزين
3 mattress — حشيَّة، مَرْتَبَة
4 pillow — مِخَدَّة، وِسَادَة
5 ladder — سُلَّم نقَّالي
6 soft toy elephant, a cuddly toy animal — لُعْبَة طَريَّة على شكل فيل
7 soft toy dog — لُعْبَة طَريَّة على شكل كلب
8 cushion — وِسَادَة
9 fashion doll — دُمْيَة أزياء
10 doll's pram — عَرَبَة أطفال للدمية
11 sleeping doll — دُمْيَة نائمة
12 canopy — غطاء، مِظَلَّة
13 blackboard — سَبُّورَة
14 counting beads — خَرَزَات تعليم العَدّ
15 toy horse for rocking and pulling — حصان لُعْبَة هَزَّاز
16 rockers — مِهَزَّات الحصان
17 children's book — كتاب أطفال
18 compendium of games — مجموعة من الألعاب
19 ludo — لُعْبَة اللودو
20 chessboard — رُقْعَة الشطرنج
21 children's cupboard — دُولاب ملابس أطفال
22 linen drawer — دُرْج البياضات
23 drop-flap writing surface — سَطْح كِتَابة قلاب
24 notebook (exercise book) — دَفْتَر (كتاب التمارين)
25 school books — كُتُب مَدْرَسِيَّة
26 pencil (*also:* crayon, felt tip pen, ballpoint pen) — قَلَم رَصَاص(أيضاً: قلم حِبْر سائل ذو طرف لبادي أو طرف كُرَوِيّ)
27 toy shop — مَتْجَر اللُعَب
28 counter — كاونتر (منضدة التاجر)
29 spice rack — حَامِل قنينات التوابل
30 display — مَعْرُوضات
31 assortment of sweets (*Am.* candies) — حلويات مُشَكَّلة (حَلْوَى)
32 bag of sweets (*Am.* candies) — كيس حَلْوَى
33 scales — ميزان
34 cash register — مُسَجِّلَة النقد
35 toy telephone — هاتف لُعبة
36 shop shelves (goods shelves) — أَرْفُف المَتْجَر (أرفف البضائع)
37 wooden train set — طاقم قطار خشبى لُعْبَة
38 dump truck, a toy lorry (toy truck) — شاحِنة قلَّابة لُعْبَة
39 tower crane — ونش/مِرْفاع بُرْجِي
40 concrete mixer — خَلاط خرسانة

41 large soft toy dog	لُعْبَة طرية على شكل كلب كبير
42 dice cup	كَأْس النَّرْد

48 Kindergarten (Day Nursery) رَوْضَة الأطْفَال (الحَضَانة النَّهَارِيَّة)

1-20 pre-school education (nursery education)	**التعليم قبل بلوغ سن المَدْرَسَة** (مرحلة الرَّوْضَة)
1 nursery teacher	مُدَرِّسة الرَّوْضَة
2 nursery child	طفل الرَّوْضَة
3 handicraft	شُغْل يدويّ
4 glue	صَمْغ، غراء
5 watercolour (*Am.* watercolor) painting	رَسْم بألوان مائيَّة
6 paintbox	صُنْدُوق الألْوان
7 paintbrush	فُرْشَاة الألْوان
8 glass of water	كوب ماء
9 jigsaw puzzle (puzzle)	أُحْجِيَة الصُّوَر المقطوعة
10 jigsaw puzzle piece	قطعة من أُحْجِيَة الصُّوَر المقطوعة
11 coloured (*Am.* colored) pencils (wax crayons)	أقلام مُلَوَّنَة
12 modelling (*Am.* modeling) clay (Plasticine)	صلصال
13 clay figures (Plasticine figures)	مُجَسَّمَات/أشكال صلصاليَّة
14 modelling (*Am.* modeling) board	لَوْحَة صنع المُجَسَّمَات الصلصاليَّة
15 chalk (blackboard chalk)	طباشير (طباشير السبورة)
16 blackboard	سبُّورة
17 counting blocks	مكعَّبَات تعليم العَدّ
18 felt pen (felt tip pen)	قَلَم طَرَفه لبادي
19 shapes game	لُعْبَة الأشكال
20 group of players	مجموعة من اللاعبين
21-32 toys	**لُعَب**
21 building and filling cubes	مكَعَّبَات البِنَاء والحَشْو
22 construction set	طاقم تركيب
23 children's books	كُتُب أطفال
24 doll's pram, a wicker pram	عَرَبَة الدُّمْيَة
25 baby doll	دُمْيَة على شكل طفل رضيع
26 canopy	غطاء، مظلة
27 building bricks (building blocks)	مكَعَّبَات البِنَاء
28 wooden model building	نموذج مَبْنَى خَشَبي
29 wooden train set	طاقم قطار خَشَبي
30 rocking teddy bear	دُبّ هَزَّاز
31 doll's pushchair	كُرْسِيّ دُمْيَة يُدْفَع للأمام
32 fashion doll	دُمْيَة أزياء
33 child of nursery school age	طفل فى سن الرَّوْضَة
34 cloakroom	غُرْفَة العَبَاءات والمعاطِف

49 Bathroom and Toilet الحَمَّام ودَوْرَة المِيَاه

1 bath	حَوْض الاسْتِحْمَام (البانيو)
2 mixer tap (*Am.* mixing faucet) for hot and cold water	صُنْبُور خلاط للماء الساخِن والبارِد
3 foam bath (bubble bath)	حمَّام فُقَاعات
4 toy duck	بَطَّة لُعْبَة
5 bath salts	أمْلاح الحَمَّام
6 bath sponge (sponge)	اسْفِنْجَة الحَمَّام
7 bidet	مِشْطَفَة
8 towel rail	حَامِل المنشفة/الفوطة
9 terry towel	منشفة وَبَرِيَّة
10 toilet roll holder (*Am.* bathroom tissue holder)	حَامِل وَرَق الحَمَّام
11 toilet paper (*coll.* loo paper, *Am.* bathroom tissue)	وَرَق حمَّام
12 toilet (lavatory, W.C., *coll.* loo)	دَوْرَة المياه (مِرْحَاض)
13 toilet pan (toilet bowl)	سُلْطَانِيَّة المِرْحَاض
14 toilet lid with terry cover	غطاء مِرْحَاض مُزَوَّد بغِطاء وَبَرِيّ
15 toilet seat	مَقْعَد المِرْحَاض
16 cistern	صندوق الطَّرْد
17 flushing lever	ذراع تشغيل صندوق الطَّرْد
18 pedestal mat	فَرْشَة القاعِدة
19 tile	بلاطة
20 ventilator (extraction vent)	فتحة تهوية
21 soap dish	وعاء الصابونة (صبَّانة)
22 soap	صابونة
23 hand towel	منشفة يد
24 washbasin	حَوْض غسيل الأيْدي
25 overflow	فَتْحَة تَصْريف المِيَاه الفائضة
26 hot and cold water tap	صُنْبُور ماء ساخِن وبارِد
27 washbasin pedestal with trap (anti-syphon trap)	قاعِدة حَوْض الغسيل مزودة بمِحْبَس
28 tooth glass (tooth mug)	كوب غسيل الأسْنان
29 electric toothbrush	فُرْشَاة أسنان كهربائية
30 detachable brush heads	رؤوس فُرْشَاة قابلة للفصل
31 mirrored bathroom cabinet	خزانة حمَّام مُزَوَّدة بمِرْآة
32 fluorescent lamp	لَمْبَة فلورسنت
33 mirror	مِرْآة
34 drawer	دُرْج
35 powder box	علبة البودرة
36 mouthwash	غَسُول للفم
37 electric shaver	ماكينة حلاقة كهربائية
38 aftershave lotion	غَسُول بعد الحلاقة
39 shower cubicle	حُجَيْرَة الدُّش
40 shower curtain	ستارة الدُّش
41 adjustable shower head	رأس دش قابلة للتعديل
42 shower nozzle	فُوَّهة الدُّش
43 shower adjustment rail	قضيب تعديل ارتفاع الدُّش
44 shower base	قاعِدة حُجَيْرَة الدُّش
45 waste pipe	ماسورة تصريف
46 bathroom mule	خُف/شِبْشِب الحَمَّام
47 bathroom scales	ميزان حَمَّام
48 bath mat	فرشة حَمَّام

49 medicine cabinet	خزانة أدْوِيَة
50 Household Appliances and Utensils	**الأَجْهِزَة والأدَوات المَنْزِلِيَّة**
1-20 irons	**المَكَاوِي**
1 electric ironing machine	ماكينة كَيّ كهربائية
2 electric foot switch	مِفْتَاح كَهْرَبي يتم تشغيله بالقَدَم
3 roller covering	غِطَاء الأُسْطُوَانَة
4 ironing head	رَأس الكَيّ
5 sheet	مَلاءَة
6 electric iron (light-weight iron)	مِكْوَاة كهربائية (مِكْوَاة خفيفة)
7 sole-plate	نَعْل المِكْوَاة
8 temperature selector	قُرْص اختيار درجة الحرارة
9 handle (iron handle)	مِقْبَض (مِقْبَض المكواة)
10 pilot light	ضَوْء إرْشَادي
11 steam, spray, and dry iron	مِكْوَاة للكَيّ بالبخار ورَزَاز الماء والكَيّ الجاف
12 filling inlet	فَتْحَة إدخال الماء
13 spray nozzle for damping the washing	فُوَّهة الرَّزَاز لترطيب الغسيل
14 steam hole (steam slit)	فَتْحَة خروج البخار
15 ironing table	طاولة الكَيّ
16 ironing board (ironing surface)	سَطْح الكَيّ
17 ironing-board cover	غِطَاء سَطْح الكَيّ
18 iron well	حَامِل المِكْوَاة، بئر المِكْوَاة
19 aluminium (*Am.* aluminum) frame	إطار من الألومنيوم
20 sleeve board	لَوْحَة كَيّ الأكْمَام
21 linen bin	وِعَاء الغسيل
22 dirty linen	غَسِيل مُتَّسِخ
23-34 washing machines and driers	**الغَسَّالات الكهربائية والمُجَفِّفات**
23 automatic washing machine	غَسَّالة آلِيَّة
24 washing drum	أُسْطُوَانَة الغسَّالة
25 safety latch (safety catch)	مِزْلاج تثبيت للأمان
26 program selector control	قُرْص التحكم في اختيار البرنامج
27 front soap dispenser [with several compartments]	مُوَزِّع صابون أمامي [متعدد الحجيرات]
28 tumble drier	مُجَفِّف دوَّار
29 drum	أُسْطُوَانَة، بِرْميل
30 front door with ventilation slits	باب أمامي ذو فتحات تهوية
31 worktop	سَطْح الشُّغْل
32 airer	مَنْشَر غسيل
33 clothes line (washing line)	حَبْل نَشْر الغسيل
34 extending airer	مَنْشَر غسيل امتدادي
35 stepladder (steps), an aluminium (*Am.* aluminum) ladder	سُلَّم نَقَّالى
36 stile	مَرْقَى دَرَجِي
37 prop	دُعامة، مِسْنَد
38 tread (rung)	مَوْطِئ (دَرَجَة)
39-43 shoe care utensils	**أدوات العِنَايَة بالأحْذِيَة**
39 tin of shoe polish	عُلْبَة وَرْنيش أحْذِية
40 shoe spray, an impregnating spray	وَرْنيش سائِل يُرَش على الأحْذِية
41 shoe brush	فُرْشَاة أحْذِية
42 brush for applying polish	فُرْشَاة دَهْن الوَرْنيش
43 tube of shoe polish	أُنْبُوب وَرْنيش أحْذية
44 clothes brush	فُرْشَاة ملابس
45 carpet brush	فُرْشَاة سجاجيد
46 broom	مِكْنَسة
47 bristles	هُلْب: شَعْر خَشِن
48 broom head	رَأس المِكْنَسة
49 broomstick (broom handle)	عَصَا المِكْنَسة
50 screw thread	أسْنَان اللَوْلَب
51 washing-up brush	فُرْشَاة الكَنْس
52 pan (dustpan)	جَارُوف جَمْع التراب
53-86 floor and carpet cleaning	**تنظيف الأرضيَّة و السِّجَاد**
53 brush	فُرْشَاة
54 bucket (pail)	دَلْو (جَرْدَل)
55 floor cloth (cleaning rag)	مِمْسَحة
56 scrubbing brush	فُرْشَاة البلاط
57 carpet sweeper	مِكْنَسة سجاجيد
58 upright vacuum cleaner	مِكْنَسة كهربائية عمودية
59 changeover switch	مِفْتَاح تَحْوِيل
60 swivel head	رَأس تدور على مِحْوَر
61 bag-full indicator	مؤشِّر امْتِلاء كِيس الأتربَة
62 dust bag container	حاوية كِيس الأتربَة
63 handle	مِقْبَض
64 tubular handle	ذِرَاع أُنْبُوبي
65 flex hook	خُطَّاف مَرِن/قَابِل للإنثناء
66 wound-up flex	كِيبل مَفْرُول مَرِن
67 all-purpose nozzle	مِنْفَث لجميع الأغْرَاض
68 cylinder vacuum cleaner	مِكْنَسة كَهْرَبائيَّة اسطوانيَّة
69 swivel coupling	وَصْلَة تَرَاوحيَّة
70 extension tube	أُنْبُوب تمديد
71 floor nozzle (*sim.:* carpet beater nozzle)	مِنْفَث تنظيف الأرضيَّة
72 suction control	مِفْتَاح التحكم في الشَّفْط
73 bag-full indicator	مُؤَشِّر امْتِلاء كِيس الأتربة
74 sliding fingertip suction control	مِفْتَاح انزلاقي للتحكم في الشفط
75 hose (suction hose)	خُرْطُوم (خُرْطُوم الشفط)
76 combined carpet sweeper and shampooer	ماكينة كَنْس السجاجيد وغسيلها بالشامْبُو
77 electric lead (flex)	كِيبل مَفْرُول مرن
78 plug socket	مَقْبَس
79 carpet beater head (*sim.:* shampooing head, brush head)	رَأس كَنْس السِّجاد وغسيله بالشامبو
80 all-purpose vacuum	مِكْنَسة كَهْرَبائيَّة لجميع

cleaner (wet and dry vacuum cleaner)	الأغراض (مِكْنَسة كَهْرَبائيَّة للكَنْس والمَسْح)
81 castor	دُولاب (عَجلَة) صغير
82 motor unit	وَحْدة المُحَرك(الموتور)
83 lid clip	مشبك الغطاء
84 coarse dirt hose	خُرْطُوم شَفْط القاذورات الخَشِنَة
85 special accessory (special attachment) for coarse dirt	وَصْلَة خاصة للقاذورات الخَشِنَة
86 dust container	حاوية التراب
87 shopper (shopping trolley)	ترولّي مُتَحَرك

51 Flower Garden — حَدِيقَة الأزْهَار

1-35 flower garden	**حَدِيقَة الأزْهَار**
1 pergola	ظُلَّة نفقيَّة، تَعْرِيشة
2 deck-chair	كُرْسِيّ قماش قَابل للطى
3 lawn rake (wire-tooth rake)	مُشْط العُشْب، مِدَمَّة
4 garden rake	مُشْط الحَدِيقَة
5 Virginia creeper (American ivy, woodbine), a climbing plant (climber, creeper)	لَبْلابَة عَذْرَاء، كَرْمَة ، نبات مُتَسَلِّق
6 rockery (rock garden)	حَدِيقَة صَخْرِيَّة
7 rock plants; *varieties:* stonecrop (wall pepper), houseleek, dryas, aubretia	نباتات الرِّدَاة، أنواعها : سِيْدوم (سِيْدوم حَرِّيف) مُخَلَّدة، أُبْرِيَاسِيَّة
8 pampas grass	وَزَيْمِيَّة البمباس
9 garden hedge	سِيَاج الحَدِيقَة
10 blue spruce	راتِنْجِيَّة شائكة
11 hydrangeas	هِدْرَنجيَّات
12 oak (oak tree)	بَلُّوط (شَجَرَة بَلُّوط)
13 birch (birch tree)	بَتولا (شَجرة القضبان)
14 garden path	مَمَر الحَدِيقَة
15 edging	حافَة
16 garden pond	بِرْكَة الحَدِيقَة
17 flagstone (stone slab)	بَلاطة حَجَرِيَّة
18 water lily	زَنْبَق الماء، نيلَوْفَر
19 tuberous begonias	بَغُونِية عُسْقُولِيَّة
20 dahlias	أضاليا
21 watering can (*Am.* sprinkling can)	مِرَشَّة السَّقْي
22 weeding hoe	مِعْزَق تَعْشيب
23 lupin	تُرْمُس
24 marguerites (oxeye daisies, white oxeye daisies)	لُؤلؤية، مَرْغَرِيتا
25 standard rose	وَرْدَة عادِيَّة
26 gerbera	جِرْبَارة
27 iris	سَوْسَن
28 gladioli	سَيْف الغراب، دَلَبُوث
29 chrysanthemums	أُقْحوان
30 poppy	خَشْخَاش
31 blazing star	النجم المتوهج
32 snapdragon (antirrhinum)	أنف العِجل، زَهْرَة الخَطْم
33 lawn	مَرْج
34 dandelion	طَرَخْشَقُون
35 sunflower	عبَّاد/دوَّار الشمس

52 Fruit and Vegetable Garden — بُسْتَان الفَوَاكه والخُضْرَوَات

1-32 allotment (fruit and vegetable garden)	**بُسْتَان الفَوَاكه والخُضْرَوَات**
1, 2, 16, 17, 29 dwarf fruit trees (espaliers, espalier fruit trees)	أشْجَار فَوَاكِه قَزَمِيَّة
1 quadruple cordon, a wall espalier	شَجَرَة مُقَلَّمَة رباعياً
2 vertical cordon	شَجَرَة مُقَلَّمَة عمودياً
3 tool shed (garden shed)	كُشْك الأدوات/الحَدِيقَة
4 water butt (water barrel)	بِرْميل ماء
5 climbing plant (climber, creeper, rambler)	نَبَات مُتَسَلِّق (نَبَات زَاحِف)
6 compost heap	كَوْمَة من السِمَاد العُضْوِيّ
7 sunflower	عبَّاد الشمس
8 garden ladder (ladder)	سُلَّم نقَّالى للحَدِيقَة (سُلَّم)
9 perennial (flowering perennial)	نَبْتَة مُعَمِّرة
10 garden fence (paling fence, paling)	سِيَاج الحَدِيقَة
11 standard berry tree	شَجَرَة عِنَبِيَّة عادية
12 climbing rose (rambling rose) on the trellis arch	وَرْدَة مُتَسَلِّقة على قوس معترش شبكي
13 bush rose (standard rose tree)	شَجَرَة وَرْد عادِيَّة
14 summerhouse (garden house)	استراحة الحَدِيقَة
15 Chinese lantern (paper lantern)	فانوس من الوَرَق
16 pyramid tree (pyramidal tree, pyramid), a free-standing espalier	شَجَرَة هَرَمِيَّة، مِسْنَدة حُرَّة النمو
17 double horizontal cordon	شَجَرَة مزدوجة مُقَلَّمَة أفقيًا
18 flower bed, a border	زَهْرَاء، حدّ
19 berry bush (gooseberry bush, currant bush)	شُجَيْرَة عِنَبِيَّة (كِشْمِش شائك)
20 concrete edging	حافة خَرَسَانِيَّة
21 standard rose (standard rose tree)	وَرْدَة عادية (شَجَرَة وَرْد عادية)
22 border with perennials	حاشية ذات نَبْت مُعَمِّر
23 garden path	مَمَر الحَدِيقَة
24 allotment holder	مالك (أو مُسْتَأجِر) الحَدِيقَة
25 asparagus patch (asparagus bed)	زَهْرَاء/حَوْض الهِلْيُون
26 vegetable patch (vegetable plot)	رُقْعَة زِرَاعَة الخضروات
27 scarecrow	خَيَال المَآتة، نُطَار
28 runner bean (*Am.* scarlet runner), a bean plant on poles (bean poles)	فاصولية إسبانية ، نبات الفاصوليا على أعمدة

29 horizontal cordon — شَجَرَة مُقَلَّمَة أفقيًّا
30 standard fruit tree — شَجَرَة فَوَاكه عاديَّة
31 tree stake — وَتَد تثبيت الشَجَرَة
32 hedge — سِيَاج

53 Indoor Plants (Houseplants) — نَبَاتَات دَاخِلِيَّة (نَبَاتَات المَسَاكِن)

1 pelargonium (crane's bill), a geranium — لَقْلَقي
2 passion flower (Passiflora), a climbing plant (climber, creeper) — زَهْرَة الآلام، نَبَات مُتَسَلِّق (نبات زاحِف)
3 fuchsia, an anagraceous plant — فوْشِيَة
4 nasturtium (Indian cress, tropaeolum) — طَرْطُور الباشا
5 cyclamen, a primulaceous herb — كَفُّ مَرْيَم، عُشْب من الرَّبْعِيَّات
6 petunia, a solanaceous herb — بطونية، تبْغيَّة
7 gloxinia (Sinningia), a gesneriaceous plant — غُلُكْسِيْنة، نبات من الجَسْفِيْرِيَّات
8 Clivia minata, an amaryllis (narcissus) — كلِيْفِية أَرْجَوَانِيَّة
9 African hemp (Sparmannia), a tiliaceous plant, a linden plant — قُنَّب أفريقي، نبات زَيْزَفُوني
10 begonia — بَغُوْنِيَّة
11 myrtle (common myrtle, Myrtus) — آس
12 azalea, an ericaceous plant — أزَالْيَة، صَحْرَاوية، نبات خَلَنْجِي
13 aloe, a liliaceous plant — أَلْوَة، نبات زَنْبَقِي
14 globe thistle (Echinops) — قُنْفُذِيَّة، شَوْك الجِمال
15 stapelia (carrion flower), an asclepiadaceous plant — إِسْتَبِيلة، نبات من الصُقْلابِيَّات
16 Norfolk Island Pine (an araucaria grown as an ornamental) — صنوبر جزيرة نورفولك (أروكارية تُزْرَع كنبات زينة)
17 galingale, a cyperacious plant of the sedge family — خُوْلَنْجَان، نبات من الفصيلة السُعْدِيَّة

54 Propagation of Plants — تَكاثُر النَّبَاتَات

1 seed sowing (sowing) — بَذْر البُذور
2 seed pan — حَوْض البُذور
3 seed — بُذور
4 label — بِطَاقَة تَعْرِيف
5 pricking out (pricking off, transplanting) — نَقل النباتَات
6 seedling (seedling plant) — بَادِرَة، شَتْلَة/غَرْسَة لم تُنْقَل
7 dibber (dibble) — مغْرَس
8 flower pot (pot) — إِصِّيص زهور
9 sheet of glass — لَوْح من الزجَاج
10 propagation by layering — التكاثر بالترقيد مع التجوُّز، التكاثر بالعكْس
11 layer — عكِيس، تَرْقِيدَة
12 layer with roots — تَرْقِيدَة ذات جذور
13 forked stick used for fastening — عصا مُشَعَّبة تُسْتَخْدَم للتثبيت
14 propagation by runners — التكاثُر بالمدَّاد/بالرِّئد
15 parent (parent plant) — النبات الأصل/المصدر
16 runner — رِئْد، مَدَّاد
17 small rooted leaf cluster — عُنْقُود وَرَقة صغير ذو جذور
18 setting in pots — الوَضْع في أصِّيص
19 cutting in water — فَسْل في الماء
20 cutting (slip, set) — فَسْل (قَلَم، وَتَد)
21 root — جَذْر
22 bud cutting on vine tendril — قلم بُرْعُم معلقة في الكَرْم
23 scion bud, a bud — بُرْعُم تَطْعِيم، بُرْعُم
24 sprouting (shooting) cutting — فَسْل رَكْزَة
25 stem cutting (hardwood cutting) — فَسْل بالساق
26 bud — بُرْعُم
27 propagation by bulbils (brood bud bulblets) — التكاثر بالبُصَيْلات
28 old bulb — بَصَلَة كامِلة النمو
29 bulbil (brood bud bulblet) — بُصَيلَة

30-39 grafting (graftage) — **التطعيم**

30 budding; *here:* shield budding) — تطعيم بالبُرْعُم؛ هنا: بَرْعَمَة باستعمال طُعْم يكون جزءا صغيرا من السَّاق
31 budding knife — سكِين التَّطْعِيم
32 T-cut — قَطْع تائى
33 support (stock, rootstock) — ساق سانِدة (فَسِيلَة جذرية)
34 inserted scion bud — بُرْعُم تطعيم مَغْرُوس
35 raffia layer (bast layer) — تَرْقِيدَة رافيَّة
36 side grafting — تَطْعِيم جانبى
37 scion (shoot) — غصْن التَّطْعِيم (رِئْد، فَرْخ)
38 wedge-shaped notch — نَقْرَة اسفينية الشَّكْل
39 splice grafting — تَطْعِيم إنجليزي/تَرَاكُبِي

55 Market Garden (*Am.* Truck Garden, Truck Farm) — مَزْرَعَة الخُضْرَوَات

1-51 market garden (*Am.* truck garden, truck farm) — مَزْرَعَة الخُضْرَوَات

1 tool shed — كُشْك الأدوات
2 water tower (water tank) — بُرْج تَخْزِين المَاء
3 market garden (*Am.* truck garden, truck farm), a tree nursery — مَزْرَعَة الخُضْرَوَات (مَشْتل)
4 hothouse (forcing house, warm house) — دَفِيئَة حارَة (بِنَاء البَوَاكِير)
5 glass roof — سَقْف زُجَاجى
6 [roll of] matting (straw — بُوْرِيَّة (حَصِيرَة من القَصَب

matting, reed matting, shading)	أو سوق السُلْت)
7 boiler room (boiler house)	غُرْفَة المِرْجل
8 heating pipe (pressure pipe)	أنْبوب التسخين (أنبوب الضغط)
9 shading panel (shutter)	لَوْح تظليل
10-11 ventilators (vents)	**فَتَحَات تَهْوِيَة**
10 ventilation window (window vent, hinged ventilator)	نافِذة تَهْوِيَة
11 ridge vent	الفَتْحَة العِلْوِيَّة
12 potting table (potting bench)	نَضَد التأصِيص
13 riddle (sieve, garden sieve, upright sieve)	غُرْبال (غُرْبال الحديقة/قائم)
14 garden shovel (shovel)	مِجْرَفَة الحديقة، جاروف
15 heap of earth (composted earth, prepared earth, garden mould, *Am.* mold)	كَوْمَة تراب (تراب مَمْزُوج بسِمَاد عَضْوي)
16 hotbed (forcing bed, heated frame)	مِدْفأة (دَفيئَة البَوَاكير)
17 hotbed vent (frame vent)	فَتْحَة المدْفأة
18 vent prop	سِنَاد فَتْحَة المـدْفأة
19 sprinkler (sprinkling device)	رَشَّاش (جِهَاز الرَّش)
20 gardener (nursery gardener, grower, commercial grower)	البُسْتَاني، الجَنَائني
21 cultivator (hand cultivator, grubber)	مِسْلفَة، آلة الحِرَاثَة
22 plank	لَوْح خشب ثَخين
23 pricked-out seedlings (pricked-off seedlings)	شَتَلات مَنْقُولة
24 forced flowers [forcing]	زهور مَغْرُوسة [زِرَاعَة البواكير]
25 potted plants (plants in pots, pot plants)	نباتات مُوَصَّصَة
26 watering can (*Am.* sprinkling can)	مِرَشَّة السَّقْي
27 handle	مِقْبَض
28 rose	فُوَّهَة المِرَشَّة
29 water tank	حَوْض ماء
30 water pipe	مَاسُورَة المَاء
31 bale of peat	بالَة طُـرْب
32 warm house (heated greenhouse)	صَوْبَة دَافِئة
33 cold house (unheated greenhouse)	صَوْبَة باردة
34 wind generator	مولِّد يَعْمَل بطَاقَة الرِّيَاح
35 wind wheel	مِرْوَحَة دوَّارة الرياح
36 wind vane	رِيشة المِرْوَحَة
37 shrub bed, a flower bed	زَهْرَاء شُجَيْرَات/زهور
38 hoop edging	حافة طَوْقِيَّة
39 vegetable plot	قِطْعَة أرض لزراعة الخضروات
40 plastic tunnel (polythene greenhouse)	نَفَق بلاستيكي (صَوْبَة من البوليثين)
41 ventilation flap	غطاء تَهْوِيَة
42 central path	مَمَر مَرْكَزِي
43 vegetable crate	صُنْدُوق الخضروات
44 tomato plant	نبات البَنْدُورة/الطَّمَاطِم
45 nursery hand	عامِل المَشْتَل
46 nursery hand	عامِلة المَشْتَل
47 tub plant	نبات مَزْرُوع في برْمِيل
48 tub	برْمِيل
49 orange tree	شَجَرَة بُرْتُقَال
50 wire basket	سَلَّة سِلْكِيَّة
51 seedling box	صُنْدُوق الشتَلات

56 Garden Tools — أدَوَات الحَدِيقَة

1 dibber (dibble)	مِغْرَس
2 spade	جاروف، مِجْراف
3 lawn rake (wire-tooth rake)	مُشْط العُشْب
4 rake	مُشْط الحدائق، قشَّاشة
5 ridging hoe	مِعْزَق، مِعْوَل حَرْث الجديرات
6 trowel	مِسْطَرين
7 combined hoe and fork	مِعْزَق وشوكة
8 sickle	مِنْجلة، شَرْشَرَة
9 gardener's knife (pruning knife, billhook)	سِكِّين البُسْتَاني (مِقْضَب، مِحْطَب)
10 asparagus cutter (asparagus knife)	سِكِّين الهِلْيَوْن
11 tree pruner (long-handled pruner)	مِقَصّ تَقْلِيم/تَشْذِيب الشَّجَر
12 semi-automatic spade	جاروف شِبْه آلي
13 three-pronged cultivator	مِسْلَفَة ثلاثية الشُّعَب
14 tree scraper (bark scraper)	مِكْشَطَة لحاء الشَّجَر
15 lawn aerator (aerator)	أداة تَهْوِيَة العُشْب
16 pruning saw (saw for cutting branches)	منشار تَشْذِيب
17 battery-operated hedge trimmer	مِقَصّ لتَشْذيب السِّيَاج يَعْمَل بالبطارية
18 motor cultivator	مِسْلَفَة بمحرك
19 electric drill	بَذَّارَة كهربائية
20 gear	صُنْدُوق التُرُوس
21 cultivator attachment	مُلْحَق المِسْلَفَة
22 fruit picker	أداة قَطْف الفاكِهة
23 tree brush (bark brush)	فُرْشَاة اللحاء
24 sprayer for pest control	رشَّاش مُكَافَحَة الآفات
25 lance	مِزْرَاق
26 hose reel (reel and carrying cart)	بَكَرَة الخُرْطُوم (بكَرَة و عَرَبَة الحَمْل)
27 garden hose	خُرْطُوم الحديقة
28 motor lawn mower (motor mower)	جَزَّازة مروج بمحرك
29 grassbox	صندوق تَجْمِيع العُشْب
30 two-stroke motor	مُحَرك ثنائي الأشْوَاط
31 electric lawn mower (electric mower)	جَزَّازَة مروج كهربائية
32 electric lead (electric cable)	سِلْك تَوْصِيل كهربائي (كيبل كهربائي)

33 cutting unit — وَحْدَة القَطْع
34 hand mower — جَزَّازة يَدَوِيَّة
35 cutting cylinder — أسطوانة القَطْع
36 blade — سِلاح الجَزَّازة
37 riding mower — جَزَّازة مَرْكَبِيَّة
38 brake lock — مِزْلاج الفَرْمَلَة
39 electric starter — آلِيَّة بِدْء التشغيل الكهربائية
40 brake pedal — دَوَّاسَة الفَرْمَلَة
41 cutting unit — وَحْدَة القَطْع
42 tip-up trailer — مَقْطُورَة بِحافة مرتفعة
43 revolving sprinkler, a lawn sprinkler — آلة رش دَوَّارة ، رشَّاشة العُشْب
44 revolving nozzle — فُوَّهَة دوَّارة
45 hose connector — وَصْلَة الخُرْطُوم
46 oscillating sprinkler — آلة رش مُتَرَجِّحَة
47 wheelbarrow — عَرَبَة يدويَّة بدولابين
48 grass shears — مقصّ العُشْب
49 hedge shears — مقصّ السِّياج
50 secateurs (pruning shears) — مِقَصّ تَقْلِيم وتَشْذِيب

57 Vegetables (Vegetable Plants) — الخُضْرَوَات (نَبَاتَات الخُضَر)

1-11 leguminous plants (Leguminosae) — **القَرْنِيَّات ، القَطانِيَّات**
1 pea, a plant with a papilionaceous corola — بسلَّة ، نبات ذو تُوَيْج فراشي
2 pea flower — زَهْرَة البسلَّة
3 pinnate leaf — وَرَقَة رِيْشِيَّة
4 pea tendril, a leaf tendril — حالق/ عَطْفَة بسلِّيَّة
5 stipule — أُذَنَة ، زَنَمَة
6 legume (pod), a seed vessel (pericarp, legume) — قَرْن (غلاف الثَمَرَة)
7 pea [seed] — [حَبَّة] البسلَّة
8 bean plant (bean), a climbing plant (climber, creeper); *varieties:* broad bean (runner bean, *Am.* scarlet runner), climbing bean (climber, pole bean), scarlet runner bean; smaller: dwarf French bean (bush bean) — نبات الفول/الفاصوليا (نبات مُتَسَلِّق/زاحِف) باقلاء ، باقلاء مُتَسَلِّقة ، أنواعها: فاصوليا اسبانية؛ الأصغر حجما: فاصوليا قَزَمِيَّة
9 bean flower — زَهْرَة الفُول
10 twining beanstalk — ساق فُول مُلْتَفَّة
11 bean [pod with seeds] — نبات الفاصوليا [قَرْن به الحبوب]
12 tomato — الطَّماطِم ، البَنْدُورَة
13 cucumber — الخِيَار
14 asparagus — هِلْيَوْن ، هِلْيُون
15 radish — الفُجْل
16 white radish — الفُجْل الأبْيَض
17 carrot — الجَزَر
18 stump-rooted carrot — جَزَر الأرومة
19 parsley — المَقْدُونس
20 horse-radish — الفُجْل البَرِّي
21 leeks — الكُرَّاث
22 chives — الثُّوم المُعَمَّر
23 pumpkin (*Am.* squash); *sim.:* melon — الكوسي ، القَرْع
24 onion — البَصَل
25 onion skin — قشرة البَصَلَة
26 kohlrabi — الكُرُنْب السَّاقي ، أبو رُكْبَة
27 celeriac — كَرَفس لِفتِي
28-34 brassicas (leaf vegetables) — **الوَرَقِيَّات**
28 chard (Swiss chard, seakale beet) — سِلْق
29 spinach — اسْفَاناخ
30 Brussels sprouts (sprouts) — كُرُنْب بروكسل
31 cauliflower — قَنَّبِيط
32 cabbage (round cabbage, head of cabbage), a brassica; *cultivated races (cultivars):* green cabbage, red cabbage — كُرُنْب ، ملفوف (كُرُنْب مستدير ، رأس من الكُرُنْب) ؛ أنواعه المزروعة: كُرُنْب أخضر ، كُرُنْب أحمر
33 savoy (savoy cabbage) — كُرُنْب سافوي
34 kale (curly kale, kail), a winter green — كُرُنْب لاروِيسي
35 scorzonera (black salsify) — فُومي أسود ، قَعْبَارُون
36-40 salad plants — **نَبَاتات السَّلَطَة**
36 lettuce (cabbage lettuce, head of lettuce) — الخَسّ (رأس من الخَسّ)
37 lettuce leaf — وَرَقَة الخَسّ
38 corn salad (lamb's lettuce) — خَسّ النَّعْجَة
39 endive (endive leaves) — هِنْدبا ، لُعاعة
40 chicory (succory, salad chicory) — هِنْدبا بَرِّيَّة
41 globe artichoke — حَرْشَف ، كَنْكَر
42 sweet pepper (Spanish paprika) — فُلْفُل حلو(فليفلة دَغْلِيَّة)

58 Soft Fruit and Pomes — الفَاكِهَة الطَّرِيَّة والتُّفَّاحِيَّات

1-30 soft fruit (berry bushes) — **الفاكِهَة الطَّرِيَّة**
1-15 Ribes — **الكِشْمِش**
1 gooseberry bush — الكِشْمِش الشائك
2 flowering gooseberry cane — فَرْع كِشْمِش مُزَهَّر
3 leaf — وَرَقَة
4 flower — زَهْرَة
5 magpie moth larva — يَرَقَانَة أَرْفِيَة الكِشْمِش
6 gooseberry flower — زَهْرَة الكِشْمِش
7 epigynous ovary — مِبْيَض علوي
8 calyx (sepals) — الكَأْس (كَأْسِيات)
9 gooseberry, a berry — ثَمَرَة الكِشْمِش
10 currant bush — كِشْمِش
11 cluster of berries — عنقود عِنَبي
12 currant — كِشْمِش
13 stalk — ساق
14 flowering cane of the currant — فَرْع مُزَهَّر من الكِشْمِش

15 raceme	عنقود
16 strawberry plant; *varieties:* wild strawberry (woodland strawberry), garden strawberry, alpine strawberry	نبات الفراولة؛ أنواعه: الفراولة البرِّيَّة، فراولة البساتين، فراولة أُلْبِيَّة
17 flowering and fruit-bearing plant	نبات مُزَهِّر ومُثْمر
18 rhizome	جُذْمُور، جُذْمار
19 ternate leaf (trifoliate leaf)	وَرَقَة ثلاثية
20 runner (prostrate stem)	رِئْد، مَدَّاد
21 strawberry, a pseudocarp	ثَمَرَة الفراولة، ثَمَرَة كاذِبَة
22 epicalyx	كَأْس الزهْرَة الخارجي، كُؤَيْس فَوْقِي
23 achene (seed)	فقيرة
24 flesh (pulp)	لَحْم الثمَرَة
25 raspberry bush	توت العُلَّيق
26 raspberry flower	زَهْرَة توت العُلَّيق
27 flower bud (bud)	بُرْعُم زَهْرَة (بُرْعُم)
28 fruit (raspberry), an aggregate fruit (compound fruit)	ثَمَرَة توت العُلَّيق، ثَمَرَة عُلَّيْقِيَة
29 blackberry	توت شَوْكِي
30 thorny tendril	حالق شَوْكِي
31-61 pomiferous plants	**التُفَّاحِيَّات**
31 pear tree; *wild*: wild pear tree	شَجَرَة الكمثرى، شَجَرَة الكمثرى البَرِّية
32 flowering branch of the pear tree	فَرْع مُزَهِّر من شجرة الكمثرى
33 pear [longitudinal section]	ثَمَرَة الكمثرى [مَقْطَع طُولي]
34 pear stalk (stalk)	ساق الكمثرى (ساق)
35 flesh (pulp)	لَحْم الثمَرَة (لُبّ)
36 core (carpels)	اللُب (أَخْبِيَة)
37 pear pip (seed), a fruit pip	حَبَّة الكمثرى (بِذْرَة فاكهة)
38 pear blossom	نَوْرَة الكمثرى
39 ovules	بذيْرِيَّات
40 ovary	مِبْيَض
41 stigma	مِيْسَم
42 style	حامِل المِيْسَم
43 petal	بَتَلَة، تُوَيْجِيَّة
44 sepal	فِصْلَة، كَأْسِيَّة
45 stamen	سَدَاة
46 quince tree	شجرة السَّفَرْجَل
47 quince leaf	وَرَقَة السَّفَرْجَل
48 stipule	أُذَيْنَة، زَنَمَة
49 apple-shaped quince [longitudinal section]	سفَرْجَلة على شكل تفاحة [مَقْطَع طُولي]
50 pear-shaped quince [longitudinal section]	سَفَرْجَلة على شكل كمثري [مقطع طولي]
51 apple tree; *wild:* crab apple tree	شجرة التُفَّاح؛ البَرِّيَّة: شجرة التُفَّاح البَرِّي
52 flowering branch of the apple tree	فرع مزهِّر من شجرة التفاح
53 leaf	وَرَقَة
54 apple blossom	نَوْرَة التُفَّاح

55 withered flower	زَهْرَة ذابِلَة
56 apple [longitudinal section]	ثَمَرَة التُفَّاح [مَقْطَع طُولى]
57 apple skin	قشْرَة الثمَرَة
58 flesh (pulp)	لَحْم الثمَرَة
59 core (apple core, carpels)	لُبَاب (أَخْبِيَة)
60 apple pip, a fruit pip	حَبَّة التفاح
61 apple stalk (stalk)	ساق ثَمَرَة التُفَّاح (ساق)
62 codling moth (codlin moth)	دودة التُفَّاح
63 burrow (tunnel)	جُـحْر
64 larva (grub, caterpillar) of a small moth	يرقانة دودة صغيرة
65 wormhole	ثُقْب دودة، نُخْرُوب

59 Drupes and Nuts — الجَوْز والنوَاوِيَّات

1-36 drupes (drupaceous plants)	**النوَاوِيَّات**
1-18 cherry tree	**شجرة الكَرَز/القَرَاصيا**
1 flowering branch of the cherry tree (branch of the cherry tree in blossom)	فَرْع مُزَهِّر من شجرة الكَرَز
2 cherry leaf	وَرَقَة الكَرَز
3 cherry flower (cherry blossom)	زَهْرَة الكَرَز
4 peduncle (pedicel, flower stalk)	عُنُق، زَنْد
5 cherry; *varieties:* sweet cherry (heart cherry), wild cherry (bird cherry), sour cherry, morello cherry (morello)	ثَمَرَة الكَرَز؛ أنواعها: الكَرَز الحلو (قراصيا)، الكَرَز البَرِّي، الكَرَز الحامض
6-8 cherry (cherry fruit) [cross section]	**ثَمَرَة الكَرَز** [مَقْطَع عَرْضِي]
6 flesh (pulp)	لحم الثمَرَة (لُبّ)
7 cherry stone	نَوَاة الكَرَز
8 seed	حَبَّة الثمَرَة
9 flower (blossom) [cross section]	زَهْرَة (نَوْرَة) [مَقْطَع عَرْضِي]
10 stamen	سَدَاة
11 petal	بَتَلَة
12 sepal	فِصْلَة، كَأْسِيَّة
13 pistil	مدقَّة
14 ovule enclosed in perigynous ovary	بُذَيْرَة داخل مِبْيَض مُحِيطي
15 style	مِيْسَم
16 stigma	قَلَم المِيْسَم
17 leaf	وَرَقَة
18 nectary (honey gland)	غُدَّة مغْثَر الزَهْرَة (غدَّة عَسَل الزَهْرَة)
19-23 plum tree	**الأجَّاص**
19 fruit-bearing branch	فَرْع مُثْمر
20 oval, black-skinned plum	أجَّاص أسود القشرة
21 plum leaf	وَرَقَة الأجَّاص
22 bud	بُرْعُم

23 plum stone — نواة الأجّاص
24 greengage — بَرْقوق أخضر
25 mirabelle (transparent gage), a plum — مِيْرابلّة
26-32 peach tree — **شجرة الخوخ**
26 flowering branch (branch in blossom) — فَرْع مُزَهَّر
27 peach flower (peach blossom) — زَهْرَة الخوخ (نَوْرة)
28 flower shoot — نَبْتَة الزهْرَة
29 young leaf (sprouting leaf) — وُرَيْقَة نابِتة
30 fruiting branch — فَرْع مُثْمِر
31 peach — ثَمَرَة الخوخ
32 peach leaf — وَرَقَة الخوخ
33-36 apricot tree — **شجرة المشمش**
33 flowering apricot branch (apricot branch in blossom) — فَرْع مشمش مُزَهَّر
34 apricot flower (apricot blossom) — زَهْرَة المشمش
35 apricot — ثَمَرَة المشمش
36 apricot leaf — وَرَقَة المشمش
37-51 nuts — **الجَـوْز**
37-43 walnut tree — **شجرة الجَوْز**
37 flowering branch of the walnut tree — فَرْع مُزَهَّر من شجرة الجَوْز
38 female flower — زَهْرَة أُنْثَى
39 male inflorescence (male flowers, catkins with stamens) — شَكْل ازْهِرار ذَكَري (زهور ذكرية، قدَّة ذات أَسْدِيَة)
40 alternate pinnate leaf — وَرَقَة رِيْشِيَّة متعاقبة
41 walnut, a drupe (stone fruit) — ثَمَرَة الجَوْز (نَوَوِيَّة)
42 soft shell (cupule) — غلاف طَري (قِمْع)
43 walnut, a drupe (stone fruit) — ثَمَرَة الجَوْز (نَوَوِيَّة)
44-51 hazel tree (hazel bush), an anemophilous shrub (a wind-pollinating shrub) — **شجرة البُنْدُق، نبات رِيحيّ الإلْقَاح**
44 flowering hazel branch — فَرْع بندق مُزَهَّر
45 male catkin — قدَّة ذكر
46 female inflorescence — شكل ازْهِرَار أنثى
47 leaf bud — بُرْعُم الوَرَقَة
48 fruit-bearing branch — فَرْع مُثْمِر
49 hazelnut (hazel, cob-nut, cob), a drupe (stone fruit) — ثَمَرَة البُنْدُق (نَوَوِيَّة)
50 involucre (husk) — قُنَاب (قِشْرَة)
51 hazel leaf — وَرَقَة البُنْدُق

60 Garden Flowers — أَزْهار الحَدائِق

1 snowdrop (spring snowflake) — زَهْرَة اللَّبَن الثَّلْجِيَّة (البَصَلَة البَيْضاء الرَّبيعيَّة)
2 garden pansy (heart-sease pansy), a pansy — بَنَفْسج مُثلَّث الألوان
3 trumpet narcissus (trumpet daffodil, Lent lily), a narcissus — نَرْجِس كاذب، نَرْجِس بُوقيّ (نَرْجِس)
4 poet's narcissus (pheasant's eye, poet's daffodil); *sim.*: poly-anthus narcissus — نَرْجِس الشُّعَرَاء
5 bleeding heart (lyre flower), a fumariaceous flower — مِهْمَازِيَّة رَائِقَة، زَهْرَة من الشَّاهْتَرجِيَّات
6 sweet william (bunch pink), a carnation — قَرَنْفُل مُلْتَح، قَرَنْفُل شائع
7 gillyflower (gilliflower, clove pink, clove carnation) — مَنْثُور شِتْوِي (قَرَنْفُل شائع)
8 yellow flag (yellow water flag, yellow iris), an iris — سَوْسَن أصفر، سَوْسَن
9 tuberose — مِسْك الرُّوْم
10 columbine (aquilegia) — أَنْقُولِيَّة (حَوْضِية)
11 gladiolus (sword lily) — دَلَبُوث، سَيْف الغراب
12 Madonna lily (Annunciation lily, Lent lily), a lily — زَنْبَق أَبْيَض (سَوْسَن أَبْيَض)
13 larkspur (delphinium), a ranunculaceous plant — دَلْفِينْيُون، نبات من الفصيلة الحوذانية
14 moss pink (moss phlox), a phlox — قَبَس مِخْرَزي، فَلُوْكس
15 garden rose (China rose) — وَرْدَة الحدائق (وَرْدَة الصين)
16 rosebud, a bud — بُرْعُم الوَرْدَة
17 double rose — وَرْدَة مُفَتَّحَة
18 rose thorn, a thorn — شَوْكَة
19 gaillardia — غَيَّرْدِيَّة
20 African marigold (tagetes) — وَرْدَة الهِنْد (مُخْمَلِيَّة)
21 love-lies-bleeding, an amaranthine flower — ذَيْل الثعلب، زَهْرَة قَطِيفِيَّة
22 zinnia — زَنِّيَّة، زَيْنِيَّة
23 pompon dahlia, a dahlia — أضاليا، دَهْلِيَّة

61 Weeds — نباتات شَيْطَانيَّة، أَعْشَاب ضَارَة

1 corn flower (blue-bottle), a centaury — زَهْرَة الحقول (قَنْطَرْيُون عَنْبَري)
2 corn poppy (field poppy), a poppy — خَشْخَاش مَنْثُور
3 bud — بَرْعَم
4 poppy flower — زَهْرَة الخَشْخَاش المَنْثُور
5 seed capsule containing poppy seeds — عُلَيْبَة الحَبَّة وتحتوي على بذور الخَشْخَاش
6 corn cockle (corn campion, crown-of-the-field) — خُرَّم الحِنْطَة
7 corn marigold (field marigold), a chrysanthemum — أُقْحُوَان الزُّرُوع
8 corn camomile (field camomile, camomile, chamomile) — بَهَار حَقْلي

9 shepherd's purse	كِيس الرَّاعي
10 flower	زَهْرَة
11 fruit (pouch-shaped pod)	ثمرة
12 common groundsel	زَهْرَة الشيخ، شيخة شائعة
13 dandelion	طَرَخْشَقُون
14 flower head (capitulum)	رُؤَيْس الزهْرَة
15 infructescence	عُنْقُود ثَمَر
16 hedge mustard, a mustard	جَرْجِير، كَثَاة، خَرْدَل
17 stonecrop	سِيْدُوم
18 wild mustard (charlock, runch)	خَرْدَل بَري (خَرْدَل الحقول)
19 flower	زَهْرَة
20 fruit, a siliqua (pod)	ثمرة خَرْدَلِيَّة
21 wild radish (jointed charlock)	فُجْل بَرِّي
22 flower	زَهْرَة
23 fruit (siliqua, pod)	ثمرة (خَرْدَلِيَّة)
24 common orache (common orach)	سَرْمَق، قَطَف، إسفاناخ رومي
25 goosefoot	رِجْل الإوَز
26 field bindweed (wild morning glory), a bindweed	لَبْلاب الحَقْل
27 scarlet pimpernel (shepherd's weatherglass, poor man's weatherglass, eyebright)	حَشِيشَة الحلَمَة، عُشْبَة العَلَق، أناغالِس حَقْلِيَّة
28 wild barley (wall barley)	شَعِير بَرِّي
29 wild oat	شُوفان/خَرْطَال بَرِّي
30 common couch grass (couch, quack grass, quick grass, quitch grass, scutch grass, twitch grass, witchgrass); *sim.*: bearded couch grass, sea couch grass	نجيل شائع (نجيل، إبريزة، عِكْرِش)
31 gallant soldier	الجُنْدي النبيل
32 field eryngo (Watling Street thistle), a thistle	قِرْصَعْنَة الحقول، شَوْك
33 stinging nettle, a nettle	قُرَّاص مُحْرِق

62 Farm Buildings (*Am.* Farmstead) مَباني المَزْرَعَة

1 house	مَنْزِل، دار
2 stable	إسْطَبْل
3 house cat (cat)	قِطَّة مَنْزِلِيَّة
4 farmer's wife	زَوْجَة المُزَارِع
5 broom	مِقَشَّة، مِكْنَسة
6 farmer	مُزَارِع
7 cowshed	حَظِيرَة الماشِيَة
8 pigsty (sty, *Am.* pigpen, hogpen)	زريبة الخنازير
9 outdoor trough	مِعْلَف خارجي
10 pig	خِنْزِير
11 above-ground silo (fodder silo)	صَوْمَعَة عَلَف مرتفعة (صَوْمَعَة عَلَف)
12 silo pipe (standpipe for filling the silo)	ماسورة الصَوْمَعَة (ماسورة قائمة لملء الصَوْمَعَة)
13 liquid manure silo	صَوْمَعَة السماد السائل
14 outhouse	بناء إضافي ملْحَق يُسْتعمل كمُلْحق أو إسْطَبْل
15 machinery shed	عَنْبَر المكَن والآلات
16 sliding door	باب مُنْزَلِق
17 door to the workshop	باب يؤدي إلى الوَرْشَة
18 three-way tip-cart, a transport vehicle	عربة نَقْل قلابة
19 tipping cylinder	أَسْطُوَانَة القَلْب
20 shafts	أَعْمِدَة
21 manure spreader (fertilizer spreader, manure distributor)	جِهَاز نَثْر الأسمِدة
22 spreader unit (distributor unit)	وَحْدَة النَّثْر
23 spreader cylinder (distributor cylinder)	أَسْطُوَانَة النَّثْر
24 movable scraper floor	أَرْضِيَّة مِكْشَطة متحركة
25 side planking (side board)	لَوْح جانبي
26 wire mesh front	مُقَدِّمَة شَبكَة سِلْكِيَّة
27 sprinkler cart	عَرَبَة رَشّ
28 sprinkler stand	حَامِل جِهَاز الرَّش (حَامِل المِرَشَّة)
29 sprinkler, a revolving sprinkler	مِرَشَّة، مِرَشَّة دوَّارة
30 sprinkler hoses	خراطيم المِرَشَّة
31 farmyard	ساحة المَزْرَعَة
32 watchdog	كَلْب حِرَاسة
33 calf	عِجْل
34 dairy cow (milch-cow, milker)	بَقَرَة حَلُوب
35 farmyard hedge	سِيَاج ساحَة المَزْرَعَة
36 chicken	دَجَاجَة
37 cock (*Am.* rooster)	ديك
38 tractor	جَرَّار
39 tractor driver	سائق الجَرَّار
40 all-purpose trailer	مَقْطُورَة لجميع الأغراض
41 [folded] pick-up attachment	وَصْلَة بيك أب [مطْوِيَّة]
42 unloading unit	وَحْدَة التفريغ
43 polythene silo, a fodder silo	صوْمَعة مصنوعة من مادة البوليثين، صَوْمَعَة عَلَف
44 meadow	مَرْعَى
45 grazing cattle	ماشِيَة تَرْعَى
46 electrified fence	سُور مكهرب

63 Agriculture (Farming) الزِّرَاعَة

1-41 work in the fields	**العَمَل في الحقول**
1 fallow (fallow field, fallow ground)	أرض مُسْتَرِيحَة، أَرْض السَّبَات
2 boundary stone	حَجَر تعليم الحدود
3 boundary ridge, a balk (baulk)	مَعْلَم الحدود (شَقَّة أرض مستطيلة غير مَحْرُوثَة)

4 field — حَقْل
5 swingletree (*Am.* whiffletree, whippletree) — مَيْزان
6 plough (*Am.* plow) — مِحْرَاث
7 clod — مَدَرَة، طُوبَارَة
8 furrow — تَلَم (شق المِحْرَاث)
9 stone — حَجَر الحَدّ
10-12 sowing — **البَــذْر**
10 sower — عامِل نَثْر البذور
11 seedlip — بَذْر البذور
12 seed corn (seed) — كِيس البذور
13 field guard — حارس الحقول (الخَفير)
14 chemical fertilizer (artificial fertilizer); *kinds:* potash fertilizer, phosphoric acid fertilizer, lime fertilizer, nitrogen fertilizer — سِماد كيماوي (سِماد صِناعي) أنواعه: البُوطاس، وحمض الفوسفوريك والكالسيوم والأزوت
15 cartload of manure (farmyard manure, dung) — حمولة عربة من السماد العضْوي
16 oxteam (team of oxen, *Am.* span of oxen) — ثيران جَرّ (زَوْج من الثيران)
17 fields (farmland) — حقول (أرض المزرعة)
18 farm track (farm road) — طريق المزرعة
19-30 hay harvest (haymaking) — **تَيْبِيس الكَلأ**
19 rotary mower with swather (swath reaper) — محْصَدَة دَوَّارة ذات آلة حَش وتَكْوِيم
20 connecting shaft (connecting rod) — عمود توصيل
21 power take-off (power take-off shaft) — عمود نقل الحركة (مَأْخَذ القُدْرَة)
22 meadow — مَرْعَى
23 swath (swathe) — كَوْمَة
24 tedder (rotary tedder) — مُيَبِّسَة الكَلأ (مِقْلَب كَلأ دوَّار)
25 tedded hay — كَلأ مُيَبَّس
26 rotary swather — آلة حَش وتَكْوِيم دَوَّارة
27 trailer with pick-up attachment — مقطورة لها مَلْحق لربط شاحنة خفيفة
28 fence rack (rickstand), a drying rack for hay — معْلَف القَش
29 rickstand, a drying rack for hay — رف تجفيف الكَلأ
30 hay tripod — حَامِل كلأ ثلاثي
31-41 grain harvest and seedbed preparation — **حصاد الحبوب وتجهيز مُنْتَثَر البذور**
31 combine harvester — الحَصَّادة الدَّرَّاسَة
32 cornfield — حَقْل القمح/الذرة
33 stubble field — حَقْل الجذامات
34 bale of straw — بالَة قَش
35 straw baler (straw press), a high-pressure baler — مِحْزَمة البالات
36 swath (swathe) of straw (windrow of straw) — صَف/كَوْمَة قش
37 hydraulic bale loader — آلة تحميل بالات آليَّة
38 trailer — مقطورة
39 manure spreader — ماكينة نثر السماد
40 four-furrow plough (*Am.* plow) — مِحْرَاث رباعي الشقوق
41 combination seed-harrow — مُشْط التَّسْطِير

64 Agricultural Machinery I — الآلات الزِّرَاعيَّة (1)

1-33 combine harvester (combine) — **الحَصَّادَة الدَّرَّاسة**
1 divider — المُقَسِّم
2 grain lifter — رَافِعة الحبوب
3 cutter bar — قضيب الحَصْد
4 pick-up reel, a spring-tine reel — مِضْرَب الضَّم
5 reel gearing — تروس المِضْرَب
6 auger — حَلَزُون تَغْذِيَة ناقِل
7 chain and slat elevator — سَيْر رافع سلسلي
8 hydraulic cylinder for adjusting the cutting unit — أُسْطُوَانَة هيدرولية لضَبْط وَحْدَة الحَصْد
9 stone catcher (stone trap) — مِصْيَدَة الحَصَى
10 awner — مِنْزَع السفا، مِسْفَاة
11 concave — سَطْح مُقَعَّر
12 threshing drum (drum) — بِرْمِيل الدَّرْس (وعاء)
13 revolving beater [for freeing straw from the drum and preparing it for the shakers] — دَارَة التَّذْرِيَة (المِضْرَب) [لفَصْل القَش من البِرْميل وإمداده للهَزَّازَات]
14 straw shaker (strawwalker) — غِرْبَال هزَّاز (رَدَّاخ)
15 fan for compressed-air winnowing — مروحة التَّذْرِيَة
16 preparation level — سَطْح التجهيز
17 louvred-type sieve — غِرْبَال مزدوج
18 sieve extension — امتداد الغِرْبَال
19 shoe sieve (reciprocating sieve) — غِرْبَال سفلي
20 grain auger — بَرِيمة حَلَزُون الحبوب
21 tailings auger — حَصِيرة نقل القش
22 tailings outlet — فتحة تصريف
23 grain tank — قادوس الحبوب
24 grain tank auger — حَلَزُون قادوس الحبوب
25 augers feeding to the grain tank unloader — حَلَزُونات تغذية آليَّة تفريغ قادوس الحبوب
26 grain unloader spout — مزراب آليَّة تَفْرِيغ القادوس
27 observation ports for checking tank contents — فتحات ملاحظة لمتابعة محتويات القادوس
28 six-cylinder diesel engine — مُحَرِّك ديزل ذو سِت أُسْطُوَانَات
29 hydraulic pump with oil reservoir — مِضَخَّة هيدرولية مع خَزَّان زيت
30 driving axle gearing — تروس مِحْوَر الإدارة
31 driving wheel tyre (*Am.* tire) — إطار عَجَلَة الإدارة
32 rubber-tyred (*Am.* — عَجَلَة ذات إطار مطَّاطي

rubber-tired) wheel on the steering axle	على مِحْوَر التَّوْجِيه
33 driver's position	مَوْضِع السائق
34-39 self-propelled forage harvester (self-propelled field chopper)	**حصَّادة عَلَف متحركة**
34 cutting drum (chopper drum)	بِرْمِيل الحَصْد
35 corn head	رأس حَصْد الذرة
36 cab (driver's cab)	كابينة السائق
37 swivel-mounted spout (discharge pipe)	ماسورة تَصْرِيف مُرَكَّبَة على مِحْوَر دَوَرَاني
38 exhaust	ماسُورة العادم
39 rear-wheel steering system	نظام تَوْجِيه الدولاب الخلفي
40-45 rotary swather	**آلة حَش وتَكْوِيم دَوَّارة**
40 cardan shaft	عمود كردان
41 running wheel	دولاب متحرك
42 double spring tine	شَوْكَة ذات نابضين
43 crank	ذِرَاع التَّدْوِير
44 swath rake	مُشْط الحش
45 three-point linkage	وَصْلَة ثلاثية
46-58 rotary tedder	**ناشِرَة الدَّرِيس الدَّوَّارة**
46 tractor	جَرَّار
47 draw bar	قضيب الجر
48 cardan shaft	عمود كردان (عمود نقل الحركة)
49 power take-off (power take-off shaft)	مَأخَذ القُدْرَة
50 gearing (gears)	تروس السرعة
51 frame bar	قضيب الهيكل
52 rotating head	رأس دَوَّار
53 tine bar	قضيب حَمْل الشوْكَة
54 double spring tine	شَوْكَة ذات نابضين
55 guard rail	قضيب واق
56 running wheel	دولاب متحرك
57 height adjustment crank	ذِراع ضَبْط الارتفاع
58 wheel adjustment	ضَبْط اتجاه الدولاب
59-84 potato harvester	**حصَّادة البطاطس**
59 control levers for the lifters of the digger and the hopper and for adjusting the shaft	أذْرُع التحكم الخاصة بروافع أدوات اقْتِلاع البطاطس والقواديس وضَبْط عمود الكردان
60 adjustable hitch	وَصْلَة رَبْط قابلة للتعديل
61 drawbar	قضيب الجر
62 drawbar support	حَامِل قضيب الجر
63 cardan shaft connection	وَصْلَة عمود الكردان
64 press roller	أسْطُوَانَة المِكْبَس
65 gearing (gears) for the hydraulic system	تروس النظام الهيدرولي
66 disc (disk) coulter (*Am.* colter) (rolling coulter)	سِكِّين قُرْصِيّ
67 three-bladed share	سِلاح ذو ثلاثة أنْصَال
68 disc (disk) coulter (*Am.* colter) drive	إدارة السِكِّين القُرْصِيّ
69 open-web elevator	سَيْر ناقل مكشوف
70 agitator	مِحْرَاك
71 multi-step reduction gearing	تروس خفض السرعة متعددة الخطوات
72 feeder	آليَّة التغذِيَة
73 haulm stripper (flail rotor)	جِهَاز إزالة الأعْشاب
74 rotary elevating drum	بِرْمِيل رَفْع دَوَّار
75 mechanical tumbling separator	فَرَّازة حبوب آلية
76 haulm conveyor with flexible haulm strippers	ناقِل الأعشاب ذو جِهَاز إزالة الأعْشَاب
77 haulm conveyor agitator	مِحْرَاك ناقِل الأعْشَاب
78 haulm conveyor drive with V-belt	إدارة ناقِل الأعْشَاب ذات سَيْر حرف V
79 studded rubber belt for sorting vines, clods and stones	سَيْر مطَّاطي بارز لفَرْز الكروم والمُدَر والحِجَارة
80 trash conveyor	ناقِل الفضلات
81 sorting table	نَضَد الفَرْز
82 rubber-disc (rubber-disk) rollers for pre-sorting	أسْطُوَانَات قُرْصِيَّة مطَّاطيَّة للفَرْز الأوَّلِي
83 discharge conveyor	ناقِل التصريف
84 endless-floor hopper	قادوس الجَمْع
85-96 beet harvester	**حصَّادة الشَّمَنْدَر**
85 topper	آليَّة الشَّرْنَفَة
86 feeler	الحسَّاس
87 topping knife	سِكِّين الشَّرْنَفَة
88 feeler support wheel with depth adjustment	دولاب حَامِل الحسَّاس
89 beet cleaner	أداة تنظيف الشَّمَنْدَر
90 haulm elevator	مصعد الأعْشَاب
91 hydraulic pump	مِضَخَّة هيدرولية
92 compressed-air reservoir	أسْطُوَانَة هواء مضغوط
93 oil tank (oil reservoir)	خزَّان الزَّيْت
94 tensioning device for the beet elevator	جِهَاز الشَّد الخاص بمصعد الشَّمَنْدَر
95 beet elevator belt	سَيْر مصعد الشَّمَنْدَر
96 beet hopper	قادوس جمع الشَّمَنْدَر

65 Agricultural Machinery II — الآلات الزِّرَاعيَّة (2)

1 wheel plough (*Am.* plow), a single-bottom plough [*form.*]	مِحْرَاث بعَجَل، مِحْرَاث ذو بَدَن واحد
2 handle	مِقْبَض، مِقْوَد
3 plough (*Am.* plow) stilt (plough handle)	مِقْبَض المِحْرَاث
4-8 plough (*Am.* plow) **bottom**	**بَدَن المِحْرَاث**
4 mouldboard (*Am.* moldboard)	القلابة، المِقْلَب، المِطْرحة
5 landside	المِسْنَد
6 sole (slade)	المِزْحف
7 ploughshare (share, *Am.* plowshare)	مِقْطَع، سِلاح المِحْرَاث
8 frog (frame)	النِّسْر (إطار)
9 beam (plough beam, *Am.* plowbeam)	قَصَبة المِحْرَاث

10 knife coulter (*Am.* colter), a coulter سِكِّين قَطْع
11 skim coulter (*Am.* colter) مِكْشَط
12 guide-chain crossbar قضيب السِلْسِلة الدليلية
13 guide chain سِلْسِلة دليلية
14-19 forecarriage **العربة الأمامية**
14 adjustable yoke مِقْرن انضباطي
15 land wheel دولاب، عَجَلَة
16 furrow wheel عَجَلَة الفَجّ
17 hake chain سِلْسِلة وَصْلة الجر
18 draught beam (drawbar) قضيب الجر
19 hake وَصْلة الجر
20 tractor (general-purpose tractor) جَرّار للأغراض العامة
21 cab frame (roll bar) إطار كابينة السائق
22 seat مَقْعَد
23 power take-off gear-change (gearshift) مجموعة مَأخذ القُدْرَة
24-29 power lift **مِرْفاع كهربائي**
24 ram piston كَبّاس تضاغطي
25 lifting rod adjustment مضْبَط الرَّفْع
26 drawbar frame هَيْكل قضيب الجر
27 top link وَصْلَة علوية
28 lower link وَصْلَة سفلية
29 lifting rod قضيب الرَّفْع
30 drawbar coupling مِقْرن قضيب الجر
31 live power take-off (live power take-off shaft, take-off shaft) عمود نقل الحركة/ مَأخذ القُدْرَة
32 differential gear (differential) تروس فَرْقِيَّة
33 floating axle مِحْوَر طاف
34 torque converter lever ذِراع محوِّل عَزْم الدَّوَران
35 gear-change (gearshift) نَقْل السرعة، نَقْل التروس
36 multi-speed transmission نَقْل حركة متعدد السرعات
37 fluid clutch (fluid drive) إدارة مائِعِيَّة
38 power take-off gear ترس مَأخذ القُدْرَة
39 main clutch القابض الرئيسي
40 power take-off gear-change (gearshift) with power take-off clutch نَقْل تروس مَأخذ القُدْرَة مع قابض مأخذ القدرة
41 hydraulic power steering and reversing gears توجيه هيدرولي وتروس السرعة الخلفية
42 fuel tank خَزّان الوقود
43 float lever ذراع العَوَّامة
44 four-cylinder diesel engine محرك ديزل رباعي الاسطوانات
45 oil sump and pump for the pressure-feed lubrication system حَوْض ومِضَخَّة الزيْت لنظام التزليق تحت الضغط
46 fresh oil tank خَزّان الزيْت الجديد
47 track rod (*Am.* tie rod) عمود ربط
48 front axle pivot pin بِنْز ارتكاز المِحْوَر الأمامي
49 front axle suspension تَعليق المِحْوَر الأمامي
50 front coupling (front hitch) وَصْلَة جر أمامية
51 radiator الراديايتر، المُشِعّ
52 fan مِرْوَحة
53 battery البطارية
54 oil bath air cleaner (oil bath air filter) مُرَشِّح هواء ذو حمام زيتي
55 cultivator (grubber) عَزّاقة، مِعْزَقة
56 sectional frame إطار مقطعي
57 spring tine أسنان مَرِنَة
58 share, a diamond-shaped share (*sim.:* chisel-shaped share) مِقْطع، سِلاح
59 depth wheel عَجَلَة تحديد الأعماق
60 depth adjustment تعديل العمق
61 coupling (hitch) وَصْلَة الجر
62 reversible plough (*Am.* plow), a mounted plough مِحْرَاث انعكاسي
63 depth wheel عَجَلَة تحديد الأعماق
64-67 plough (*Am.* plow) **bottom**, a general-purpose plough bottom **بدن المِحْرَاث**، بدن مِحْرَاث للأغراض العامة
64 mouldboard (*Am.* moldboard) القلابة، المِقْلَب، المِطْرَحة
65 ploughshare (share, *Am.* plowshare), a pointed share المِقْطع
66 sole (slade) المِزْحَف
67 landside المِسْنَد
68 skim coulter (*Am.* colter) المِكْشَط
69 disc (disk) coulter (*Am.* colter) (rolling coulter) مِكْشَط قرصي
70 plough (*Am.* plow) frame إطار المِحْرَاث
71 beam (plough beam, *Am.* plowbeam) قصبة المِحْرَاث
72 three-point linkage وَصْلَة ثلاثية
73 swivel mechanism آلية مِحْوَر الدوران
74 drill جِهَاز تَسْطير البذور
75 seed hopper صندوق البذور
76 drill coulter (*Am.* colter) مِكْشَط جِهَاز التَّسْطير
77 delivery tube, a telescopic tube أنبوب البذور، أنبوب تليسكوبي
78 feed mechanism آليَّة التلقيم
79 gearbox صندوق التروس
80 drive wheel عَجَلَة الإدارة
81 track indicator مُؤَشِّر الأخاديد
82 disc (disk) harrow, a semimounted implement مُشْط قرصي
83 discs (disks) in X-configuration أقراص في تشكيل متصالب
84 plain disc (disk) قُرْص مستو
85 serrated-edge disc (disk) قُرْص مموَّج
86 quick hitch وَصْلَة الجر
87 combination seed- مُشْط تَسْطير

harrow

88 three-section spike-tooth harrow — مُشْط بأسنان جَسِيئة ثلاثي المقاطع

89 three-section rotary harrow — مُشْط دوراني ثلاثي المقاطع

90 frame — إطار

66 Agricultural Implements — الأدَوَات الزِّرَاعِيَّة

1 draw hoe (garden hoe) — معْزَق يدوي

2 hoe handle — عصا المعْزَق

3 three-pronged (three-tined) hay fork (fork) — شَوْكَة قش ذات ثلاث شُعَب

4 prong (tine) — شُعْبة الشَوْكة

5 potato fork — شَوْكة بطاطس

6 potato hook — شَوْكة بطاطس

7 four-pronged (four-tined) manure fork (fork) — شَوْكة سِماد رباعية الشُعَب

8 manure hoe — معْزَق السِّماد

9 whetting hammer [for scythes] — مطْرَقة شَحْذ [للحاصِدة]

10 peen (pane) — حَدُّ المطْرقة

11 whetting anvil [for scythes] — سِنْدان شَحْذ [للحاصِدة]

12 scythe — حاصِدة، مِحَش، مِنْجل

13 scythe blade — سِلاح الحاصِدة

14 cutting edge — حافة قاطعة

15 heel — كَعْب سلاح الحاصِدة

16 snath (snathe, snead, sneath) — مقْبَض الحاصِدة

17 handle — مقْبَض

18 scythe sheath — غِمْدَ الحاصدة

19 whetstone (scythe-stone) — حَجَر المِسَن

20 potato rake — قشّاشة البطاطس

21 potato planter — زَرّاعة البطاطس

22 digging fork (fork) — شَوْكة حفر (شَوْكة)

23 wooden rake (rake, hayrake) — مُشْط خشبي (مُشْط، مُشْط القش)

24 hoe (potato hoe) — معْزَق (معْزَق البطاطس)

25 potato basket, a wire basket — سَلَّة جمع البطاطس، سَلّة سلكِيَّة

26 clover broadcaster — آلة نَثْر حبوب البرسيم

67 Overhead Irrigation — الرَّيّ بالرَّش

1 oscillating spray line — خَطُّ رَشٍّ تأرْجُحي

2 stand (steel chair) — حَامِل صلب

3 portable irrigation system — نظام رَيّ قابل للحمل

4 revolving sprinkler — مِرَشَّة دَوَّارة

5 standpipe coupler — مقْرِن المواسير القائمة

6 elbow with cardan joint (cardan coupling) — مِرْفَق ذو وَصْلَة كردانية

7 pipe support (trestle) — حَامِل الماسورة (مِنْصَب)

8 pump connection — وَصْلَة المضَخَّة

9 delivery valve — صِمام الطرد

10 pressure gauge (*Am.* gage) (manometer) — مقياس الضغط (مانومتر)

11 centrifugal evacuating pump — مِضَخَّة تفريغ نابذة

12 basket strainer — مِصْفاة سَلِّيَّة

13 channel — قناة

14 chassis of the p.t.o.-driven pump (power take-off-driven pump) — شاسيه مِضَخَّة تعمل بعمود لنقل الحركة

15 p.t.o.-driven (power take-off-driven) pump — مِضَخَّة تعمل بعمود نقل للحركة

16 cardan shaft — عمود كردان

17 tractor — جَرَّار

18 long-range irrigation unit — وَحْدَة رَيّ بعيدة المدى

19 drive connection — وَصْلَة الإدارة

20 turbine — توربين

21 gearing (gears) — التروس

22 adjustable support — حَامِل قابل للضبط

23 centrifugal evacuating pump — مِضَخَّة تفريغ نابذة

24 wheel — عَجَلَة

25 pipe support — حَامِل الماسورة

26 polyester pipe — ماسورة من البوليستر

27 sprinkler nozzle — فُوَّهَة المِرشَّة

28 quick-fitting pipe connection with cardan joint — وَصْلة ماسورة سريعة التركيب ذات وصْلة كردان

29 M-cardan — وَصْلَة كردانية–إم

30 clamp — قَامِطَة تثبيت

31 V-cardan — كردان إسفيني

32 revolving sprinkler, a field sprinkler — مِرَشَّة دَوَّارة

33 nozzle — فُوَّهَة

34 breaker — ذراع قَطْع الرَّش

35 breaker spring — نابِض ذراع إيقاف الرَّش

36 stopper — سِدَادة

37 counterweight — ثِقْل موازن

38 thread — حزوز، لَوْلَبة

68 Arable Crops — المَحَاصِيل الزِّرَاعِيَّة

1-47 arable crops (agricultural produce, farm produce) — **المحاصيل الزِّرَاعِيَّة**

1-37 varieties of grain (grain, cereals, farinaceous plants, bread-corn) — **أنواع من الحبوب** (حَبٌّ، غلال، نباتات طَحِينِيَّة، القمح)

1 rye (*also:* corn, 'corn' often meaning the main cereal of a country or region; in Northern Germany: rye; in Southern Germany and Italy: wheat; in Sweden: barley; in Scotland: oats; in North America: maize; in China: rice) — سُلْت، شَيْلَم (ويعني الغلال الرئيسية في بلد أو إقليم؛ في شمال ألمانيا: شَيْلَم؛ جنوب ألمانيا وإيطاليا: القمح؛ السويد: الشعير؛ اسكوتلندا: الشوفان؛ أمريكا الشمالية: الذرة؛ الصين: الأرز)

2 ear of rye, a spike — سُنْبلة

(head)

3 spikelet سُنَيْبِلَة

4 ergot, a grain deformed by fungus [shown with mycelium] حَبَّة مُصابة بمرض الدَّابْرَة [موضحة بالغَزْل الفِطْري]

5 corn stem after tillering ساق الذرة بعد التفريخ

6 culm (stalk) ساق

7 node of the culm عُقْدة الساق

8 leaf (grain leaf) وَرَقَة (وَرَقَة الحَبَّة)

9 leaf sheath (sheath) غِمْد الوَرَقَة

10 spikelet سُنَيْبِلة

11 glume عَصْفة

12 awn (beard, arista) سَفاة

13 seed (grain, kernel, farinaceous grain) بذرة (حَبَّة، نواة حَبَّة طَحينِيَّة)

14 embryo plant نبات جنيني

15 seed حَبَّة، بذرة

16 embryo جنين

17 root جَذْر

18 root hair شُعَيْرَة جَذْرية

19 grain leaf وَرَقَة الحبوب

20 leaf blade (blade, lamina) نَصْل الوَرَقَة

21 leaf sheath غِمْد الوَرَقَة

22 ligule (ligula) لُسَيْن

23 wheat الحنطة، القمح

24 spelt حنطة مُكْتسية أصلية

25 seed; *unripe:* green spelt, a soup vegetable حبَّة؛ غير ناضجة: حبة خضراء

26 barley الشَّعير

27 oat panicle, a panicle عُثْكُول

28 millet ثُمام، دُخن

29 rice الأرز

30 rice grain حبَّة أرز

31 maize (Indian corn, *Am.* corn); *varieties:* popcorn, dent corn, flint corn (flint maize, *Am.* Yankee corn), pod corn (*Am.* cow corn, husk corn), soft corn (*Am.* flour corn, squaw corn), sweet corn الذرة؛ أنواعها: ذرة مُفَتَّقة، ذرة صفراء، ذرة شامِيَّة مُضَرَّسة، ذرة شامِيَّة، ذرة شامِيَّة حلوة

32 female inflorescence إزْهرار (تنوير) أنثوي

33 husk (shuck) قشرة

34 style حامِل السِّمَة

35 male inflorescence (tassel) إزهرار ذكري (شُرَّابة الذرة)

36 maize cob (*Am.* corn cob) كوز الذرة

37 maize kernel (grain of maize) حَبَّة الذرة

38-45 root crops **المحاصيل الجذرية**

38 potato plant (potato), a tuberous plant; *varieties:* round, round-oval (pear-shaped), flat-oval , long, kidney-shaped potato; *according to colour:* white (*Am.* Irish), yellow, red, purple potato نبات البطاطا/البطاطس أنواعه: مستديرة، أجَّاصية، مستوية أجَّاصية، طويلة، شبيهة بالكلْيَة؛ من حيث اللون: أبيض، أصفر، أحمر، قرمزي

39 seed potato (seed tuber) دَرَنَة بِذْرية

40 potato tuber (potato, tuber) دَرَنَة البطاطس

41 potato top (potato haulm) وَرَقَة البطاطس (قصبة البطاطس)

42 flower زَهْرَة

43 poisonous potato berry (potato apple) سُمّ البطاطس

44 sugar beet, a beet بَنْجَر أو شَمَنْدَر سكري

45 root (beet) جذر

46 beet top رأس ثمرة البَنْجَر

47 beet leaf وَرَقَة البَنْجَر

69 Fodder Plants (Forage Plants) مَحَاصيل العَلَف (نَبَاتَات الكَلأ)

1-28 fodder plants (forage plants) for tillage **نَبَاتَات الكَلأ للفلاحة**

1 red clover (purple clover) نَفَل بنفسجي، نَفَل المروج

2 white clover (Dutch clover) بَرْسِيم هولندي، نَفَل أبيض

3 alsike clover (alsike) بَرْسِيم السويد، نَفَل هجين

4 crimson clover نَفَل مُدمَّى

5 four-leaf (four-leaved) clover بَرْسِيم رباعي الورقات

6 kidney vetch (lady's finger, lady-finger) نَفَل الرمال الأصفر

7 flower زَهْرَة

8 pod سِنْفَة، غُلْفَة، قَرْن

9 lucerne (lucern, purple medick) فِصْفِصة (رطبة)

10 sainfoin (cock's head, cockshead) إيْدُوسارون، رأس الديك

11 bird's foot (bird-foot, bird's foot trefoil) قَرْن الغزال (لوْطَس قُرَيْني)

12 corn spurrey (spurrey, spurry), a spurrey (spurry) إسْبِرْغولة

13 common comfrey, one of the borage family (Boraginaceae) سَنْفِيْتون مَخْزَني، نبات من الحمْحميات

14 flower (blossom) زَهْرَة

15 field bean (broad bean, tick bean, horse bean) فول الحقل

16 pod سِنْفة، غُلْفة، قرْن

17 yellow lupin تُرْمُس أصفر عطر

18 common vetch بِيقِيَّة شائعة

19 chick-pea حِمَّص، المَلانة

20 sunflower عبَّاد/دَوَّار الشمس

21 mangold (mangel-wurzel, mangold-wurzel, field mangel) شَمَنْدَر، بَنْجَر، سِلْق

22 false oat (oat-grass) خرْطال عادي

23 spikelet سُنَيْبِلة

24 meadow fescue grass, a فَسْتوكة

fescue	
25 cock's foot (cocksfoot)	نجيل الإصْبع (إصْبَعيَّة مُجْتَمِعة)
26 Italian ryegrass; *sim.:* perennial ryegrass (English ryegrass)	زُوان إيطالي؛ و مثله : زُوان مُعَمَّر
27 meadow foxtail, a paniculate grass	ثعلبيَّة المروج
28 greater burnet saxifrage	كاسِر الحَجَر

70 Breeds of Dog — فَصَائل الكلاب

1-14 mastiffs	**سلالات الدِّرْواس**
1 bulldog	البُلْدُغ
2 ear, a rose-ear	أُذُن
3 muzzle	الخَطْم
4 nose	أنْف
5 foreleg	الرِّجْل الأمامية
6 forepaw	مِخْلَب أمامي
7 hind leg	الرِّجْل الخلفية
8 hind paw	مِخْلَب خلفي
9 pug (pug dog)	البجّ: جنس من الكلاب الصغيرة يشبه البُلْدُغ وله أنْف أفْطَس
10 boxer	البكْسَر
11 withers	الحَارك، الغارب
12 tail, a docked tail	ذَيْل، ذَيْل مَبْتُور
13 collar	طَوْق
14 Great Dane	الدَّاني: فصيلة من الكلاب الضخمة قصيرة الشعر
15-18 terriers	**سُلالات التَّرْيَر**
15 wire-haired fox terrier	التَّرْيَر ذو الفروة الشائكة (فصيلة من كلاب الصيْد)
16 bull terrier	التَّرْيَر الضخم
17 Scotch terrier (Scottish terrier)	التَّرْيَر الاسكتلندي
18 Bedlington terrier	ترْيَر بدلنجتون
19 Pekinese (Pekingese, Pekinese dog, Pekingese dog)	كَلْب بِكين: جنس من الكلاب الصغيرة
20-22 spitzes	**فصائل الإسْبِتْز**
20 spitz (Pomeranian)	الإسْبِتْز
21 chow (chow-chow)	التْشَاو: كلب صيني
22 husky	كَلْب الإسكيمو
23-24 greyhounds (*Am.* grayhounds)	**سلالات السَّلوقي**
23 Afghan (Afghan hound)	الكلب الأفغاني: كلب سريع من فصيلة السَّلوقي يُستخدم في الصيْد
24 greyhound (*Am.* grayhound), a courser	السَّلوقي
25 Alsatian (German sheepdog, *Am.* German shepherd), a police dog, watch dog, and guide dog	كلب حراسة (الراعي الألماني)، كلب بوليسي
26 flews (chaps)	الجزء المتدلي من شفة الكلب العليا
27 Dobermann terrier	الدوبرمان
28 dog brush	فُرْشَاة الكلاب
29 dog comb	مُشْط الكلاب
30 lead (dog lead, leash); *for hunting:* leash	مِقْوَد الكلب (السلْسلة)
31 muzzle	كِمَامَة الخَطْم
32 feeding bowl (dog bowl)	وِعَاء الطعام
33 bone	عَظْمَة
34 Newfoundland dog	كَلْب نيوفوندلاند
35 schnauzer	الشْنَوْزر
36 poodle; *sim. and smaller:* pygmy (pigmy) poodle	البوْدِل؛ القزم
37 St. Bernard (St. Bernard dog)	السَّنْبِرْنار
37-43 hunting dogs	**كلاب الصَّيْد**
38 cocker spaniel	الكُوكَر: كلب صغير مسترخي الأذنين حريري الشعر يُستخدم في الصَّيْد
39 dachshund, a terrier	الدَّشْهَنْد
40 German pointer	كَلْب صيْد ذو ذَيْل صغير مدبب
41 English setter	السَّاطِر الإنجليزي: كلب صيد تدرب على الوقوف حالما يشْتَم القنص
42 trackhound	قَصَّاص الأثَر (كلب صيد)
43 pointer, a trackhound	قَصَّاص الأثَر (كلب صيد)

71 Horse I — الحصَان/الفَرَس (1)

1-6 equitation (high school riding, haute école)	**ركوب الخيْل، الفروسية**
1 piaffe	هَمْر: ضَرْب الأرض بالحوافر
2 walk	المشي العادي
3 passage	خبب بطئ
4 levade (pesade)	تَوَثُّب: الوقوف على القائمتين الخَلْفِيَّتَيْن
5 capriole	قفْز، وثْب
6 courbette (curvet)	قعْاء
7-25 harness	**طَقْم الفرَس (عُدَّة لِجامِه)**
7-13, 25 bridle	**اللجام**
7-11 headstall (headpiece, halter)	**العِذار**
7 noseband	المَخْطَمة، خِطَام
8 cheek piece (cheek strap)	العِذار
9 browband (front band)	شَريط الجَبْهة
10 crownpiece	الشَّريط العلوي (التاجي)
11 throatlatch (throatlash)	رِبَاط الحلق
12 curb chain	سِلْسلة الشكيمة
13 curb bit	الشَّكِيمة
14 hasp (hook) of the hame (*Am.* drag hook)	مِشْبك السِّمط
15 pointed collar, a collar	طَوْق مدبب الطرَف
16 trappings (side trappings)	الجُلّ
17 saddle-pad	حَشِيَّة السَّرْج
18 girth	حِزَام السَّرْج
19 backband	حِزَام الظَّهْر

20 shaft chain (pole chain)	سِلْسلة عَرِيش العربة
21 pole	عَرِيش، قَضيب
22 trace	سَيْر الجَرّ
23 second girth (emergency girth)	حِزَام احتياطي للسَّرْج
24 trace	سَيْر الجَرّ
25 reins (*Am.* lines)	العنان، السُّرُع
26-36 breast harness	**عُدَّة الصَّدْر**
26 blinker (*Am.* blinder, winker)	غِمامة الفرس
27 breast collar ring	حَلْقَة طَوْق الصَّدْر
28 breast collar (Dutch collar)	طَوْق الصَّدر
29 fork	شَريط مشعَّب
30 neck strap	شَرِيط العنق
31 saddle-pad	حشيَّة السَّرْج
32 loin strap	حِزَام الخاصرة
33 reins (rein, *Am.* line)	العِنان، السُّرُع
34 crupper (crupper-strap)	المذَيْلة (حِزَام كَفَل الحصان)
35 trace	سَيْر الجَرّ
36 girth (belly-band)	حِزَام السَّرْج
37-49 saddles	**أنواع السَّرْج**
37-44 stock saddle (*Am.* western saddle)	**السَّرج الغربي**
37 saddle seat	مَقْعَد السَّرْج
38 pommel horn (horn)	الحِنْو
39 cantle	قَرَبُوس السَّرْج الخلفي
40 flap (*Am.* fender)	قلاَّبة
41 bar	قضيب
42 stirrup leather	معْلاق الرِّكاب
43 stirrup (stirrup iron)	الرِّكاب
44 blanket	فَرْشة
45-49 English saddle (cavalry saddle)	**السَّرْج الإنجليزي** (سَرْج الخيالة)
45 seat	مَقْعَد السَّرْج
46 cantle	قَرَبُوس السَّرْج الخلفي
47 flap	قلاَّبة
48 roll (knee roll)	لفافة
49 pad	حشيَّة
50-51 spurs	**أشكال المِهْماز**
50 box spur (screwed jack spur)	مِهْماز صُنْدُوقي
51 strapped jack spur	مِهْماز شَرِيطي
52 curb bit	الشكيمة
53 gag bit (gag)	الكمامة
54 currycomb	المِحَسَّة، فرْجون
55 horse brush (body brush, dandy brush)	فُرْشَاة الفرس

72 Horse II — الحِصَان/الفَرَس (2)

1-38 points of the horse	**أعْضَاء الحصان**
1-11 head (horse's head)	**الرَّأس** (رأس الحصان)
1 ear	أُذُن
2 forelock	خُصْلَة جَبْهيَّة، الناصية
3 forehead	الجَبْهَة
4 eye	عَيْن
5 face	وَجْه
6 nose	الأنْف، المِنْخَر
7 nostril	فتحة الأنْف
8 upper lip	الشفة العليا
9 mouth	الخَطْم
10 underlip (lower lip)	الشفَة السفلي
11 lower jaw	الفكُّ السفلي
12 crest (neck)	عُرفُ الحصان
13 mane (horse's mane)	شَعْر عنق الحصان
14 crest (horse's crest)	عُرفُ الحصان
15 neck	الرقبة، العنق
16 throat (*Am.* throatlatch, throatlash)	الحَلْق، الزور
17 withers	الحارك، الكاثبة
18-27 forehand	**مُقَدَّم الحصان**
18 shoulder	كتف
19 breast	صَدْر
20 elbow	مِرفَق
21 forearm	ساعد
22-26 forefoot	**القائمة الأمامية**
22 knee (carpus, wrist)	رُكْبَة
23 cannon	الوظيف
24 fetlock	ثُنَّة
25 pastern	مِفْصَل الرَّسْغ
26 hoof	حافر
27 chestnut (castor), a callosity	جَسَأة، الكستانة
28 spur vein	وَرِيد مِهْمَازي
29 back	الظهر، الصهْوَة
30 loins (lumbar region)	الخاصِرة
31 croup (rump, crupper)	كَفَل/ردف الحصان
32 hip	وِرْك
33-37 hind leg	**القائمة الخلفية**
33 stifle (stifle joint)	حَجَبَة (مفصل الحَجَبَة)
34 root (dock) of the tail	العَسِيب (الجزء القاسي من الذَّيْل)
35 haunch	إلْيَة الحصان
36 gaskin	الفَخْذ
37 hock	عرقوب
38 tail	ذَيْل
39-44 gaits of the horse	**أَوْضاع المَشْي والجَرْي عند الحصان**
39 walk	السَيْر العادي
40 pace	الخَبَبَ البطيء
41 trot	الخَبَبَ السريع
42 canter (hand gallop)	العَدْو المتوسط، الركض
43-44 full gallop	**العَدْو السريع، الرمح**
43 full gallop at the moment of descent on to the two forefeet	العَدْو السريع: لحظة الهبوط على القائمتين الأماميتين
44 full gallop at the moment when all four feet are off the ground	العَدْو السريع : لحظة عدم ملامسة الأرْجُل الأربع للأرض

73 Domestic Animals — الحَيَوَانَات الأليفَة

1-8 cattle and horses	**البَقَر و الخَيْل**
1 cow , *a* ruminant; *m.* bull; *c.* ox; *f.* cow; *y.* calf	البَقَر، حيوان ذو قرون (ذكَر: ثَوْر؛أنثى: بقرة؛ صغير: عِجْل)
2 horse; *m.* stallion; *c.* gelding; *f.* mare; *y.* foal	الحصان؛ (ذكَر: فَحْل؛ حصان مخصي؛ أنثى:

	فَرَسَة؛ صغير: مُهْر)
3 donkey	حمار
4 pack saddle (carrying saddle)	سَرْج الحِمْل (بَرْذعة)
5 pack (load)	حمْل
6 tufted tail	ذَيْل ينتهي بخُصْلَة
7 tuft	خُصْلَة
8 mule, a cross between a male donkey and a mare	بَغْل: هجين من ذَكَر الحمار وأنثى الحصان
9 pig, *a* cloven-hoofed animal; *m.* boar; *f.* sow; *y.* piglet	الخنزير، حيوان مَشْقُوق الحافر(ذَكَر: خنزير؛ أنثى: خنزيرة؛ صغير: خَنّوص)
10 pig's snout (snout)	فنطيسة الخنزير
11 pig's ear	أذن الخنزير
12 curly tail	ذَيْل معقوص
13 sheep; *m.* ram; *c.* wether; *f.* ewe; *y.* lamb	شاة؛ (ذَكَر: كَبْش؛ خروف مخصي؛ أنثى: نَعْجَة؛ صغير: حَمَل)
14 goat	مِعْزاة، ماعز
15 goat's beard	لِحْيَة المِعْزاة
16 dog, *a* Leonberger; *m.* dog; *f.* bitch; *y.* pup (puppy, whelp)	الكلب؛ (ذَكَر: كلب ؛أنثى: كلبة؛ صغير: جَرْو)
17 cat, an Angora cat (Persian cat); *m.* tom (tom cat)	القِطُّ (قط سيامي)؛ ذَكَر: قط/هِرّ
18-36 small domestic animals	**حيوانات منزلية صغيرة**
18 rabbit; *m.* buck; *f.* doe	الأرْنَب؛ (ذَكَر: أرنب؛ أنثى: أرنبة)
19-36 poultry (domestic fowl)	**الطيور الداجنة**
19-26 chicken	**فرُّوج**
19 hen	دَجَاجَة
20 crop (craw)	حَوْصَلة
21 cock (*Am.* rooster); *c.* capon	ديك
22 cockscomb (comb, crest)	عُرْفُ الديك
23 lap	طيَّة
24 wattle (gill, dewlap)	غَبَب
25 falcate (falcated) tail	ذَيْل مَعْقُوف
26 spur	شَوْكَة في رِجْل الديك
27 guinea fowl	الغرغر (دجاج حَبَشي)
28 turkey; *m.* turkey cock (gobbler); *f.* turkey hen	ديك رومي، دَجَاجَة روميَّة
29 fan tail	ذَيْل مرْوَحي
30 peacock	طاووس
31 peacock's feather	ريش الطاووس
32 eye (ocellus)	بُقْعَة، عَيْن
33 pigeon; *m.* cock pigeon	الحمام؛ ذكر الحمام
34 goose; *m.* gander; *y.* gosling	الإوزّ؛ ذكر: ذكر الإوز؛ صغير: فرخ الإوز
35 duck; *m.* drake; *y.* duckling	البَطّ؛ ذَكَر: ذَكَر البط؛ صغير: بطيطة، فرخ البط
36 web (palmations) of webbed foot (palmate foot)	وَتَرَة قدم ذات وترات

74 Poultry Farming (Poultry Keeping), Egg Production — مَزْرَعَة/تَرْبِيَة الدَّواجِن، إنْتاج البَيْض

1-27 poultry farming (intensive poultry management)	**مَزْرَعَة الدَّواجِن**
1-17 straw yard (strawed yard) system	**نِظَام ساحَة التبْن**
1 fold unit for growing stock (chick unit)	وَحْدَة تربية الكتاكيت
2 chick	كتكوت، صُوص
3 brooder (hover)	مِفْقَسة
4 adjustable feeding trough	وِعَاء علفة قابل لتعديل حجمه
5 pullet fold unit	وَحْدَة تربية الدجاج الصغير
6 drinking trough	وِعَاء الشرب
7 water pipe	مَاسورة مياه
8 litter	فَضَلات مُبَعْثَرَة، مِهَاد من القش
9 pullet	دَجَاجَة صغيرة
10 ventilator	مَنْفَذ تهوية
11-17 broiler rearing (rearing of broiler chickens)	**تربية الدجاج**
11 chicken run (*Am.* fowl run)	عُشَّة الدجاج
12 broiler chicken (broiler)	دَجَاجَة، فَرُّوج
13 mechanical feeder (self-feeder, feed dispenser)	جِهَاز توزيع علفة آلي
14 chain	سِلْسلة
15 feed supply pipe	أنْبُوب إمداد العلفة
16 mechanical drinking bowl (mechanical drinker)	إناء شرب يمتلئ آليا
17 ventilator	مَنْفَذ تهوية (نِظَام الأقفاص)
18 battery system (cage system)	نِظَام البطارية
19 battery (laying battery)	بطارية وضع البَيْض
20 tiered cage (battery cage, stepped cage)	قَفَص مُتَعَدِّد الأدوار (قَفَص يعمل بالبطارية ، قَفَص مُدَرَّج)
21 feeding trough	وِعَاء العلفة
22 egg collection by conveyor	جَمع البَيْض بواسطة سَيْر ناقل
23-27 mechanical feeding and dunging (manure removal, droppings removal)	**تقديم العلفة والتخلص من الرَوْث آلياً**
23 rapid feeding system for battery feeding (mechanical feeder)	نِظَام تقديم العلفة السريع لتغذية البطاريات
24 feed hopper	قادوس العلفة
25 endless-chain feed conveyor (chain feeder)	جِهَاز تقديم علفة مزود بسِلْسلة مقفلة
26 water pipe (liquid feed pipe)	أنْبُوب الماء (أنْبُوب السوائل)
27 dunging chain	سِلْسلة التخلص من الروث

(dunging conveyor)

28 setting and hatching machine — مَاكِينَة حَضْن وفقس البَيْض

29 ventilation drum [for the setting compartment] — أُسْطُوَانَة/بِرْميل تهوية [لحجيرة الحَضْن]

30 hatching compartment (hatcher) — حُجَيْرَة الفَقْس

31 metal trolley for hatching trays — ترولِّي معدني لِصَوَاني الفَقْس

32 hatching tray — صينية فَقْس

33 ventilation drum motor — محرك/موتور أُسْطُوَانَة التهوية

34-53 egg productions — إنتاج البَيْض

34 egg collection system (egg collection) — نِظَام جمع البَيْض

35 multi-tier transport — نِظَام نقل متعدد الطبقات

36 collection by pivoted fingers — الجمع بواسطة أصابع تدور على مِحْوَر

37 drive motor — موتور الإدارة

38 sorting machine — مَاكِينَة فَرْز

39 conveyor trolley — ترولِّي نَاقِل

40 fluorescent screen — سِتَار فلُوري

41 suction apparatus (suction box) for transporting eggs — جِهَاز شافط لنقل البَيْض

42 shelf for empty and full egg boxes — رَفّ لصناديق البَيْض الفارغة والمملوءة

43 egg weighers — موازين البَيْض

44 grading — وَحْدَة تصنيف

45 egg box — صُنْدُوق بَيْض

46 fully automatic egg-packing machine — مَاكِينَة تعبئة البَيْض آليا بالكامل

47 radioscope box — صُنْدُوق الراديوسكوب

48 radioscope table — طاولة الراديوسكوب

49-51 feeder — جهاز تَلْقِيم العلفة

49 suction transporter — جِهَاز نقل شفَّاط

50 vacuum line — خَطّ تفريغ

51 supply table — طاولة التموين/الإمداد

52 automatic counting and grading — جِهَاز العَدّ والتصنيف الآلي

53 packing box dispenser — مُوَزِّع صناديق التعبئة

54 leg ring — حلقة الساق

55 wing tally (identification tally) — بِطَاقة تعريف (تُثَبَّت فى الجِنَاح)

56 bantam — البَنْطَم (دجاج صغير الحجم)

57 laying hen — دَجَاجَة بيَّاضة

58 hen's egg (egg) — بَيْضَة دَجَاجَة (بَيْضَة)

59 eggshell, an egg integument — قشرة البَيْضة

60 shell membrane — غشاء القشرة (الكُفْت)

61 air space — فراغ به هواء

62 white [of the egg] (albumen) — البَيَاض، زُلال البيض

63 chalaza (*Am.* treadle) — كلازا، خيوط الآح

64 vitelline membrane (yolk sac) — غشاء المُح

65 blastodisc (germinal disc, cock's tread, cock's treadle) — القُرْص الجرثومي

66 germinal vesicle — الحُوَيْصَلة الجرثومية

67 white — زُلال البَيْض

68 yolk — المُح

75 Rearing (*Am.* Raising) of Livestock — تَرْبِيَة المَاشِيَة

1 stable — إِسْطبل

2 horse stall (stall, horse box, box) — مَرْبَط الحصان فى الإسطبل

3 feeding passage — قناة العلف/التغذية

4 pony — مُهْر، حصان صغير

5 bars — قضبان

6 litter — فضلات متناثرة، مِهَاد من القَش

7 bale of straw — بالَة قَش

8 ceiling light — مِصْبَاح السقف

9 sheep pen — حظيرة الخِرَاف

10 mother sheep (ewe) — شاة، نَعْجَة

11 lamb — حَمَل

12 double hay rack — رَفّ تِبْن مزدوج

13 hay — تِبْن/حشيش مُجَفَّف كَعَلَف

14 dairy cow shed — حظيرة البقر الحلوب

15-16 tether — الطِّوَل

15 chain — سِلْسلة

16 rail — قضيب

17 dairy cow (milch-cow, milker) — بقرة حلوب

18 udder — ضَرْع

19 teat — حلَمَة

20 manure gutter — أُخْدُود تصريف الروث

21 manure removal by sliding bars — التخلص من الرَوْث عن طريق قضبان انزلاقية

22 short standing — مَرْبَط قصير

23 milking parlour (*Am.* parlor), a herringbone parlour — عَنْبَر حلب البقر

24 working passage — مَمَر/رَدْهَة العمل

25 milker (*Am.* milkman) — الحَلاَب، الحالب

26 teat cup cluster — مجموعة كأس الحلَمَة

27 milk pipe — أُنْبُوب اللبن

28 air line — خَطّ هواء

29 vacuum line — خَطّ تفريغ

30 teat cup — كأس الحلَمَة

31 window — نافذة

32 pulsator — مِضَخَّة نابضة

33 release phase — طَوْر إطلاق اللبن

34 squeeze phase — طَوْر العَصْر

35 pigsty (*Am.* pigpen, hogpen) — زَرِيبَة الخنازير

36 pen for young pigs — حظيرة صغار الخنازير

37 feeding trough — وِعَاء التغذية (العلف)

38 partition — حَاجِز، فاصل

39 pig, a young pig — خنزير، خَنُوص

40 farrowing and store pen — حظيرة الإخناص والتخزين

41 sow — خنزيرة

42 piglets (*Am.* shoats, — خنانيص (خنانيص رضيعة

shotes) (sucking pigs [for first 8 weeks]) — [مدة الثمانية أسابيع الأولى])
43 farrowing rails — حواجز/قضبان الإخناص
44 liquid manure channel — قناة تصريف الروث السائل

76 Dairy — مَعْمَل الألْبَان

1-48 dairy (dairy plant) — **مَعْمَل الألبان** (مصنع الألبان)
1 milk reception — استقبال اللبن
2 milk tanker — صهريج/خزّان اللبن
3 raw milk pump — مِضَخّة اللبن الخام (غير المخلوط بالماء)
4 flowmeter, an oval (elliptical) gear meter — مقياس تدفق اللبن
5 raw milk storage tank — خزّان اللبن الخام
6 gauge (*Am.* gage) — مقياس
7 central control room — غُرْفَة التحكم المركزي
8 chart of the dairy — مُخَطّط منتجات اللبن
9 flow chart (flow diagram) — مُخَطّط العمليات
10 storage tank gauges (*Am.* gages) — مقاييس صهاريج التخزين
11 control panel — لَوْحَة التحكم
12-48 milk processing area — **مَنْطِقة تصنيع اللبن**
12 sterilizer (homogenizer) — جِهَاز تعقيم
13 milk heater; *sim.:* cream heater — جِهَاز تسخين اللبن؛ مثله: جِهَاز تسخين القِشْدَة
14 cream separator — فرّازة القِشْدَة
15 fresh milk tanks — خزّانات اللبن الطازج
16 tank for sterilized milk — خزّان لبن مُعَقّم
17 skim milk (skimmed milk) tank — خزّان لبن مَنْزُوع الدسم
18 buttermilk tank — خزّان المَخِيض
19 cream tank — خزّان القِشْدَة
20 fresh milk filling and packing plant — مَعْمَل تعبئة وتعليب اللبن الطازج
21 filling machine for milk cartons; *sim.:* milk tub filler — مَاكِينَة تعبئة اللبن في علب كرتون
22 milk carton — عُلْبَة لبن من الكرتون
23 conveyor belt (conveyor) — سَيْر ناقل
24 shrink-sealing machine — مَاكِينَة التَّعبِئة وإحكام سَد العبوات بالانْكِماش
25 pack of twelve in shrink foil — عبوّة تحتوى على 12 عُلْبَة في رَقيقة معدنية
26 ten-litre filling machine — مَاكِينَة تعبئة عُبوّات سِعَة 10 لترات
27 heat-sealing machine — مَاكِينَة إحكام سد الأكياس حرارياً
28 plastic sheets — أفرخ بلاستيك
29 heat-sealed bag — كيس مُحكَم السد حرارياً
30 crate — صُنْدُوق
31 cream maturing vat — راقود إنضاج القِشْدَة
32 butter shaping and packing machine — مَاكِينَة تشكيل وتعبئة الزُّبْد
33 butter churn, a creamery butter machine for continuous butter making — مِمْخَضة الزُّبْد، مَاكِينَة صنع الزُّبْد، المِقْشدة
34 butter supply pipe — أنْبُوب امداد الزُّبْد
35 shaping machine — مَاكِينَة تشكيل الزُّبْد
36 packing machine — مَاكِينَة تعبئة
37 branded butter in 250g packets — عبوات زُبْد مُيَسَّمَة بعلامة تجارية وزن 250 جم
38 plant for producing curd cheese (curd cheese machine) — مَاكِينَة إنتاج الجُبْن الخاثر
39 curd cheese pump — مِضَخّة الجُبْن الخاثر
40 cream supply pump — مِضَخّة إمداد القِشْدَة
41 curds separator — فرّازة الخثار
42 sour milk vat — راقود اللبن الرائب
43 stirrer — ذراع التقليب
44 curd cheese packing machine — مَاكِينَة تعبئة الجُبْن الخاثر
45 packeted curd cheese — جُبْن خاثر مُعَبّأ
46 bottle-capping machine (capper) — مَاكِينَة سدادات زجاجات اللبن
47 cheese machine — مَاكِينَة صنع الجُبْن
48 rennet vat — راقود الأنْفحة/المِنْفَحة

77 Bees and Beekeeping (Apiculture) — النَّحْل و تَرْبِيَة النَّحْل (النحالة)

1-25 bee (honey-bee, hive-bee) — **نَحْلَة** (نَحْلَة العسل، نحلة الخليّة)
1, 4, 5 castes (social classes) of bees — طبقات النَّحْل الاجتماعية
1 worker (worker bee) — شَغَّالة
2 three simple eyes (ocelli) — ثلاث أعْيُن بسيطة
3 load of pollen on the hind leg — حِمْل من اللقاح على الساق الخلفية
4 queen (queen bee) — المَلِكَة
5 drone (male bee) — ذَكَر النَّحْل
6-9 left hind leg of a worker — **القَدَم اليسرى الخلفية لإحدى الشغالات**
6 pollen basket — سَلَّة اللقاح/ غُبَار الطَّلْع
7 pollen comb (brush) — مُشْط (فُرْشَاة) اللقاح/غُبَار الطَّلْع
8 double claw — بُرْثُن/مِخْلَب مزدوج
9 suctorial pad — لبيدة ماصة
10-19 abdomen of the worker — **بطن الشغالة**
10-14 stinging organs — **أعضاء اللدغ**
10 barb — شَوْكَة
11 sting — إبْرَة
12 sting sheath — غِمْد الإبْرَة
13 poison sac — كيس يحتوى على مادة سامّة
14 poison gland — غُدَّة إفراز المادة السامة
15-19 stomachic-intestinal canal — **القناة المِعَدِيَّة المِعَوِيَّة**
15 intestine — الأمْعَاء
16 stomach — المَعِدة
17 contractile muscle — عضلة قابضة
18 honey bag (honey sac) — كيس/جيب العَسَل

19 oesophagus (esophagus, gullet) المَرِئ

20-24 compound eye **عين مُرَكَّبَة**

20 facet عَدَسَة قَرَنِيَّة

21 crystal cone مَخْرُوط بلُّوري

22 light-sensitive section قِطاع حسَّاس للضوْء

23 fibre (*Am.* fiber) of the optic nerve ليفة العَصَب البصري

24 optic nerve عَصَب بصري

25 wax scale طبقة شَمْعِيَّة

26-30 cell **خليَّة**

26 egg بَيْضَة ، بيَيْضة

27 cell with the egg in it خَليَّة بها بَيْضة

28 young larva يَرَقَة صغيرة

29 larva (grub) يَرَقَة ، يَرَقَانَة

30 chrysalis (pupa) خَادِرَة

31-43 honeycomb **قُرْص العسل**

31 brood cell خَليَّة حَضْن

32 sealed (capped) cell with chrysalis (pupa) خَليَّة مُحكَمَة السد بداخلها خَادِرَة

33 sealed (capped) cell with honey (honey cell) خَليَّة عسل مُحكَمَة

34 worker cells خلايا الشغالات

35 storage cells, with pollen خلايا التخزين وبها اللقاح

36 drone cells خلايا ذكور النَّحْل

37 queen cell خَليَّة الملكَة

38 queen emerging from her cell الملِكَة وهى تخرج من خَليَّتها

39 cap (capping) غطاء

40 frame إطار

41 distance piece قطعة مباعدة

42 [artificial] honeycomb قُرْص عَسَل [صناعي]

43 septum (foundation, comb foundation) غشاء فاصل/حَاجِز

44 queen's travelling (*Am.* traveling) box صُنْدُوق نقل الملِكَة

45-50 beehive, a frame hive (movable-frame hive, movable-comb hive) **خليَّة النحل، خَليَّة نَحْل متنقلة**

45 super (honey super) with honeycombs جزء علوي قابل للنزع به أقراص العسل

46 brood chamber with breeding combs حُجْرَة الحَضْن مزودة بأقراص تربية النَّحْل

47 queen-excluder حَاجِز فصل الملِكَة

48 entrance مَدْخَل، فتحة الدخول

49 flight board (alighting board) لَوْح الطيران (لَوْح الهبوط)

50 window نافذة

51 old-fashioned bee shed سقيفة تربية نَحْل طراز قديم

52 straw hive (skep), a hive خَليَّة من القش

53 swarm (swarm cluster) of bees خَشْرَم (جماعة من النَّحْل)

54 swarming net (bag net) شبكة الخَشْرَم

55 hooked pole قضيب ذو خُطَّاف

56 apiary (bee house) مَنْحل (بيت النَّحْل)

57 beekeeper (apiarist, *Am.* beeman) عَامِل المَنْحل (النَّحَّال)

58 bee veil حِجاب واق من النَّحْل

59 bee smoker جِهَاز طَرْد النَّحْل بالدخان

60 natural honeycomb قُرْص عسل طبيعي

61 honey extractor (honey separator) فَرَّازة العسل

62-63 strained honey (honey) عسل مُصَفًّى

62 honey pail دَلْو عسل

63 honey jar مرطبان عسل

64 honey in the comb عسل داخل القُرْص

65 wax taper فتيلة مشمَّعة

66 wax candle شَمْعَة

67 beeswax شَمْع العسل

68 bee sting ointment مَرْهَم لمعالجة لدغ النَّحْل

78 Wine Growing (Viniculture, Viticulture) زِرَاعَة الكُرُوم

1-21 vineyard area **منطقة زراعة الكَرْمَة**

1 vineyard using wire trellises for training vines كَرْم يستخدم فيه تعريشات من السلك لتعريش الكروم

2-9 vine (*Am.* grapevine) **كَـرْم**

2 vine shoot فَرْع كَرْمة

3 long shoot نَبْتَة طويلة

4 vine leaf وَرَقَة من أوراق الكَرْمة

5 bunch of grapes (cluster of grapes) عنقود عنب

6 vine stem ساق الكَرْمة

7 post (stake) وتد

8 guy (guy wire) شدَّادة، حبل/سلك تثبيت

9 wire trellis تعريشة سلْكِيَّة

10 tub for grape gathering دَلْو لجَمْع العِنَب

11 grape gatherer جامع العِنَب

12 secateurs for pruning vines مِقَصّ لتقليم الكروم

13 wine grower (viniculturist, viticulturist) زارِع الكروم

14 dosser carrier حَامِل سَلَّة الكروم

15 dosser (pannier) سَلَّة الكروم

16 crushed grape transporter وِعَاء نقل العِنَب المَعْصُور

17 grape crusher عَصَّارة العِنَب

18 hopper قادوس

19 three-sided flap extension امتداد قلاب ذو ثلاثة أبعاد

20 platform مِنصَّة

21 vineyard tractor, a narrow-track tractor جَرَّار الكَرْم، جَرَّار صغير

79 Wine Cellar قَبْو الخَمْر

1-22 wine cellar (wine vault) **قَبْو الخَمْر**

1 vault قَبْو، سِرْداب

2 wine cask بِرْميل الخَمْر

3 wine vat, a concrete vat راقود الخَمْر، راقود خرساني

4 stainless steel vat (*also:* vat made of synthetic راقود مصنوع من صلب لا

material) يصدأ (أيضا وعَاء مصنوع من مادة صناعية)
5 propeller-type high-speed mixer خلاط بمِرْوَحَة عالي السرعة
6 propeller mixer خلاط مُزَوَّد بمِرْوَحَة/برَفَّاص
7 centrifugal pump مضَخَّة نابذة
8 stainless steel sediment filter مرشِّح رواسب مصنوع من صلب لا يصدأ
9 semi-automatic circular bottling machine مَاكِينَة دوَّارة نصف آلية لتعبئة الزجاجات
10 semi-automatic corking machine مَاكِينَة سدادات فلِّينية نصف آليَّة
11 bottle rack رَفّ الزجاجات
12 cellarer's assistant عَامِل القَبْو، مساعِد مسئول القَبْو
13 bottle basket سَلَّة الزجاجات
14 wine bottle زُجَاجَة خَمْر
15 wine jug دَوْرَق الخَمْر
16 wine tasting تذوق جَوْدَة الخَمْر
17 head cellarman رئيس عَامِلي القَبْو
18 cellarman عَامِل القَبْو
19 wineglass كأس خَمْر
20 inspection apparatus [for spot-checking samples] جِهَاز الفحص [لفحص العَيِّنَات الفوري]
21 horizontal wine press عصَّارة خمور أفقية
22 humidifier جِهَاز ضبط الرطوبة في القَبْو

80 Garden and Field Pests آفَات الحَدائِق والحقُول

1-19 fruit pests **آفَات الفاكهة**
1 gipsy (gypsy) moth قَزِّيَّة إسْفِنْجية
2 batch (cluster) of eggs عنقود بَيْض
3 caterpillar سُرفة، أسْروع
4 chrysalis (pupa) خَادِرَة
5 small ermine moth, an ermine moth فَرَاشَة التفاح
6 larva (grub) يرَقَانَة
7 tent خَيْمَة
8 caterpillar skeletonizing a leaf سُرفَة/أسْروع يأتي على وَرَقَة شجر
9 fruit-surface-eating tortrix moth (summer fruit tortrix moth) عقّاصة، فتَّالة
10 appleblossom weevil, a weevil خُنْفسَاء التفاح
11 punctured, withered flower (blossom) زَهْرَة ذابلة
12 hole for laying eggs حُفْرَة لوضع البَيْض
13 lackey moth قزِّيَّة نِصْطِرْيا
14 caterpillar سُرفة، أسْروع
15 eggs بَيْض
16 winter moth, a geometrid أرَفِيَّة شتوية
17 caterpillar سُرفة، أسْروع
18 cherry fruit fly, a borer ذُبَابَة الكَرَز
19 larva (grub, maggot) يرَقَانَة

20-27 vine pests **آفات الكروم**
20 downy mildew, a mildew, a disease causing leaf drop إرْمِدَاد، فُطْر عفونة الكَرْم
21 grape affected with downy mildew عِنَب مُصاب الإرْمِداد
22 grape-berry moth فَرَاشَة العِنَب
23 first-generation larva of the grape-berry moth (*Am.* grape worm) يرَقَانَة الجيل الأول لفَرَاشَة العنب
24 second-generation larva of the grape-berry moth (*Am.* grape worm) يرَقَانَة الجيل الثاني لفرَاشَة العنب
25 chrysalis (pupa) خَادِرَة
26 root louse, a grape phylloxera فلْكْسِرَة الكَرْم
27 root gall (knotty swelling of the root, nodosity, tuberosity) عفْصة الجذور (توَرُّم عُقَدي للساق)
28 brown-tail moth ليْلِيَّة البقول
29 caterpillar سرفة، أسروع
30 batch (cluster) of eggs عنقود بَيْض
31 hibernation cocoon شَرْنَقَة الإسْبات الشتوي
32 woolly apple aphid (American blight), an aphid أرْقة التفاح القطْنية
33 gall caused by the woolly apple aphid عفْصة أحدثتها أرْقة التفاح القطْنية
34 woolly apple aphid colony مُسْتَعْمَرَة أرْقة التفاح القطْنية
35 San-José scale, a scale insect (scale louse) القِرْمزية الفتَّاكة
36 larvae (grubs) [*male* elongated, *female* round] اليرَقَات [المذكَّرة: مستطيلة المؤنثة: مستديرة]

37-55 field pests **آفات الحقل**
37 click beetle, a snapping beetle (*Am.* snapping bug) الخُنْفسَاء النطَّاطة
38 wireworm, larva of the click beetle دودة السلك، يرَقَانَة الخُنْفسَاء النطَّاطة
39 flea beetle برغوث البساتين
40 Hessian fly, a gall midge (gall gnat) ذُبَابَة هيسّ، الذبَابَة المبيدة
41 larva (grub) يرَقَانَة
42 turnip moth, an earth moth فرَاشَة اللفت
43 chrysalis (pupa) خَادِرَة
44 cutworm, a caterpillar دودة قارضة، سُرفة
45 beet carrion beetle خُنْفسَاء الشَوَنْدَر الكامدة، درقة الشَوَنْدَر
46 larva (grub) يرَقَانَة
47 large cabbage white butterfly فرَاشَة الكرنب الكبيرة
48 caterpillar of the small cabbage white butterfly سُرفة فرَاشَة الكرنب الصغيرة
49 brown leaf-eating weevil, a weevil سُوْسَة ورق الشجر
50 feeding site مكَان التغذية

51 sugar beet eelworm, a nematode (a threadworm, hairworm)	أُنَيْقِلِيس البَنْجَر (دودة خَيْطِيَّة، دودة شَعْرِيَّة)
52 Colorado beetle (potato beetle)	خُنْفَسَاء كلورادو (خُنْفَسَاء البطاطس)
53 mature larva (grub)	يَرَقَانَة ناضجة
54 young larva (grub)	يَرَقَانَة صغيرة
55 eggs	بَيْض

81 House Insects, Food Pests, and Parasites — الحَشَرَات المَنْزِلِيَّة وآفَات الطَّعَام والطُفَيْلِيَّات

1-14 house insects	**الحَشَرَات المنزلية**
1 lesser housefly	ذُبَابَة منزلية صغيرة
2 common housefly	الذُبَابَة المنزلية الشائعة
3 chrysalis (pupa, coarctate pupa)	خادِرة (عَذْراء مَسْتُورة)
4 stable fly (biting housefly)	ذُبَابَة الإسْطبل (ذُبَابَة منزلية لادغة)
5 trichotomous antenna	قَرْن استشعار ثلاثي
6 wood louse (slater, *Am.* sow bug)	حِمَار قبان
7 house cricket	الجُدْجُد: صَرَّار الليل المنزلي
8 wing with stridulating apparatus (stridulating mechanism)	جناح ذو آلية إصْدَار الصرير
9 house spider	العنكَبُوت المنزلي
10 spider's web	بَيْت العنكَبُوت
11 earwig	أبو مقص
12 caudal pincers	مقص ذَيْلي/ذَنَبي
13 clothes moth, a moth	عُثَّة الملابس
14 silverfish (*Am.* slicker),a bristletail	لاحِسة السكر
15-30 food pests (pests to stores)	**حشرات الطعام** (حشرات المخازن)
15 cheesefly	ذُبَابَة الجُبْن
16 grain weevil (granary weevil)	سَوْسَة الحنطة، سَوْسَة الحبوب
17 cockroach (black beetle)	صَرْصُور (خُنْفُسَاء سَوْداء)
18 meal beetle (meal worm beetle, flour beetle)	خُنْفَسَاء الدقيق
19 spotted bruchus	سَوْسَة مُنَقَّطَة، خُنْفَسَاء سَوْسِيَّة مُنَقَّطَة
20 larva (grub)	يَرَقَانَة
21 chrysalis (pupa)	خادِرة (عَذْراء)
22 leather beetle (hide beetle)	حَشَرَة الطَّيْثار
23 yellow meal beetle	خُنْفَسَاء الجَرِيش الصفراء
24 chrysalis (pupa)	خادِرة (عَذْراء)
25 cigarette beetle (tobacco beetle)	خُنْفَسَاء التبغ
26 maize billbug (corn weevil)	سَوْسَة الذرة
27 one of the Cryptolestes, a grain pest	آفة حبوب
28 Indian meal moth	فَرَاشَة الدقيق الهندية
29 Angoumois grain moth (Angoumois moth)	فَرَاشَة حبوب الانجوموِيز
30 Angoumois grain moth caterpillar inside a grain kernel	يُسْرُوع الفَرَاشَة داخل نواة حبة من الحبوب
31-42 parasites of man	**طفيليات الإنسان**
31 round worm (maw worm)	الدودة الأسطوانية
32 female	أنثى
33 head	رَأْس
34 male	ذَكَر
35 tapeworm, a flatworm	دودة شَرِيطِيَّة/خَيْطِيَّة
36 head, a suctorial organ	رَأْس، عضو ماص
37 sucker	مَمَاص، عضو المص
38 crown of hooks	تاج من الخُطَّافات
39 bug (bed bug, *Am.* chinch)	البَقّ (بق الفراش)
40 crab louse (a human louse)	قَمْل العانة (قَمْل الإنسان)
41 clothes louse (body louse, a human louse)	قَمْل الملابس (قَمْل الجسم، قَمْل الإنسان)
42 flea (human flea, common flea)	برغوث شائع
43 tsetse fly	ذُبَابَة تسِي تسِي
44 malaria mosquito	بَعُوضَة الملاريا

82 Forest Pests — الآفَات الحِرَاجِيَّة

1 cockchafer (May bug), a lamellicorn	الدودة البيضاء
2 head	رَأْس
3 antenna (feeler)	قَرْن اسْتِشْعَار
4 thoracic shield (prothorax)	دِرْع زَوْرِي
5 scutellum	صفيحة حُرْشُفِيَّة، حَرْشَفَة
6-8 legs	**الأرْجُل**
6 front leg	رِجْل أمامية
7 middle leg	رِجْل وسطية
8 back leg	رِجْل خلفية
9 abdomen	المَعِدَة
10 elytron (wing case)	غِمْد
11 membranous wing	جناح غشائي
12 cockchafer grub, a larva	يَرَقَانَة الدودة البيضاء
13 chrysalis (pupa)	خادِرة (عَذْراء)
14 processionary moth, a nocturnal moth (night-flying moth)	قَزِّيَّة البلوط الجَرَّارة، فَرَاشَة لَيْلِيَّة
15 moth	فَرَاشَة
16 caterpillars in procession	يُسْرُوع جَرَّار
17 nun moth (black arches moth)	قَزِّيَّة الراهبة
18 moth	فَرَاشَة
19 eggs	بَيْض
20 caterpillar	يُسْرُوع
21 chrysalis (pupa) in its cocoon	خادرة بداخل شرنقتها
22 typographer beetle, a bark beetle	خُنْفَسَاء القَلْف/اللحاء
23-24 galleries under the bark	**دهاليز أسفل اللحاء**

23 egg gallery	دهليز البَيْض
24 gallery made by larva	دِهْلِيز صنعته اليَرَقَانَة
25 larva (grub)	يَرَقَانَة
26 beetle	خُنْفسَاء
27 pine hawkmoth, a hawkmoth	أبو الهول الصنوبري
28 pine moth, a geometrid	قَزِّيَّة الصنوبر
29 male moth	فَرَاشَة ذَكَر
30 female moth	فَرَاشَة أنثى
31 caterpillar	يُسْرُوع
32 chrysalis (pupa)	خادرة (عَذْراء)
33 oak-gall wasp, a gall wasp	زُنْبُور عَفْصَة البلوط
34 oak gall (oak apple), a gall	عَفْصَة البلوط
35 wasp	زُنْبُور
36 larva (grub) in its chamber	يَرَقَانَة في حجرتها
37 beech gall	عَفْصَة المُرّان/الزان
38 spruce-gall aphid	أرَقَة عَفْصَة الرَّاتَنْجِيَّات
39 winged aphid	أرَقَة مُجَنَّحَة
40 pineapple gall	عَفْصَة الأناناس
41 pine weevil	سَوْسَة الصنوبر
42 beetle (weevil)	خُنْفسَاء (سَوْسَة)
43 green oak roller moth (green oak tortrix), a leaf roller	فتَّالة، عقَّاصَة
44 caterpillar	يُسْرُوع
45 moth	فَرَاشَة
46 pine beauty	دودة الصنوبر
47 caterpillar	يُسْرُوع
48 moth	فَرَاشَة

83 Pest Control — مُكَافَحَة الآفَات

1 area spraying	الرَّش النطاقي
2 tractor-mounted sprayer	جِهَاز رش مَحْمُول على جَرَّار
3 spray boom	ذِرَاع الرَّش
4 fan nozzle	فُوَّهَة الرَّفَّاص
5 spray fluid tank	خَزَّانة سائل الرَّش
6 foam canister for blob marking	حاوية الرَّغْوَة
7 spring suspension	تعليق نابضي
8 spray	رَذَاذ
9 blob marker	أداة التعليم
10 foam feed pipe	أنْبُوبَة التغذية بالرَّغْوَة
11 vacuum fumigator (vacuum fumigation plant) of a tobacco factory	وَحْدَة التطهير بالتعريض للدخان فى مَصْنَع تَبْغ
12 vacuum chamber	غُرْفَة خوائية
13 bales of raw tobacco	بالات التبغ الخام
14 gas pipe	أنْبُوبَة الغاز
15 mobile fumigation chamber for fumigating nursery saplings, vine layers, seeds, and empty sacks with hydrocyanic (prussic) acid	غُرْفَة تبخير متنقلة لتطهير شُجَيْرَات المَشَاتِل والكروم والبذور والجُوَالات الخالية بحمض الهايدروسيانيك.
16 gas circulation unit	وَحْدَة تدوير الغاز
17 tray	صينية
18 spray gun	مسدس الرَّش
19 twist grip (control grip, handle) for regulating the jet	قبضة لتنظيم النَّفْث
20 finger guard	وقاء الإصبع
21 control lever (operating lever)	ذِرَاع التشغيل
22 spray tube	أنْبُوبَة الرَّش
23 cone nozzle	فُوَّهَة مخروطية
24 hand spray	رشَّاش يدوي
25 plastic container	حاوية من البلاستيك
26 hand pump	مِضَخَّة يدوية
27 pendulum spray for hop growing on slopes	الرَّش البندولي لزراعة حشيشة الدينار على المنحدرات
28 pistol-type nozzle	فُوَّهَة مُسَدَّسِيَّة النوع
29 spraying tube	أنْبُوبَة الرَّش
30 hose connection	وَصْلَة الخرطوم
31 tube for laying poisoned bait	أنْبُوب وَضْع الطُعْم السَّام
32 fly swat	مِذَبَّة
33 soil injector (carbon disulphide, *Am.* carbon disulfide, injector) for killing the vine root louse	مِحْقَن التربة لقتل آفات جذر الكروم
34 foot lever (foot pedal, foot treadle)	دَوَّاسة
35 gas tube	أنْبُوب غاز
36 mousetrap	مِصْيَدَة فئران
37 vole and mole trap	مِصْيَدَة الخَلَد وفَأْر الحقول
38 mobile orchard sprayer, a wheelbarrow sprayer (carriage sprayer)	مَاكِينَة نقالى لِرَش البساتين
39 spray tank	خَزَّان سائل الرَّش
40 screw-on cover	غطاء ملَوْلَب
41 direct-connected motor-driven pump with petrol motor	مِضَخَّة تُدَار بمحرك بنزين
42 pressure gauge (*Am.* gage) (manometer)	مقياس الضغط (مانومتر)
43 plunger-type knapsack sprayer	مَاكِينَة رش ظَهْرِيَّة من الطراز الغاطس
44 spray canister with pressure chamber	وعاء سائل الرَّش مُزَوَّد بغُرْفَة ضغط
45 piston pump lever	ذِرَاع مكبس المِضَخَّة
46 hand lance with nozzle	مِزْرَاق يدوي ذو فُوَّهَة
47 semi-mounted sprayer	آلة رش نصف راكِبَة
48 vineyard tractor	جَرَّار الكَرْم
49 fan	رفَّاص
50 spray fluid tank	خَزَّان سائل الرَّش
51 row of vines	صف من الكروم
52 dressing machine (seed-dressing machine) for dry-seed dressing (seed dusting)	مَاكِينَة إسْفَاء البذور الجافة
53 dedusting fan (dust removal fan) with	رفَّاص طَرْد الأتربة يعمل بمحرك كهربائي

electric motor	
54 bag filter	مُرَشِّح الأكياس
55 bagging nozzle	فُوَّهَة تعبئة الأكياس
56 dedusting screen (dust removal screen)	غِرْبال فَصْل الأتربة
57 water canister [containing water for spraying]	وعاء الماء (يحتوى على ماء الرَّش)
58 spray unit	وَحْدَة الرَّش
59 conveyor unit with mixing screw	وَحْدَة نقالة ذات برغي خَلْط
60 container for disinfectant powder with dosing mechanism	حاوية المسحوق المُطَهِّر ذات آلية رش جرعات محددة
61 castor	دولاب صغير
62 mixing chamber	غُرْفَة خَلْط محلول الرَّش

84 Forestry I — الحِراجَة (1)

1-34 forest, a wood	**غابَة**
1 ride (aisle, lane, section line)	طريق (غير معبدة عادة)
2 compartment [section]	قِطْعَة [قطاع]
3 wood haulage way, a forest track	طريق النقل داخل الغابة
4-14 clear-felling system	**نظام قَطْع الأشْجَار**
4 standing timber	أشْجَار منتصبة
5 underwood (underbrush, undergrowth, brushwood, *Am.* brush)	أجَمَة
6 seedling nursery, a tree nursery	مَشْتَل شجيرات
7 deer fence (fence), a wire netting fence (protective fence for seedlings); *sim.*: rabbit fence	سِيَاج لحماية الشتلات (سِيَاج)
8 guard rail	قضيب واق
9 seedlings	شَتَلات
10-11 young trees	**أشْجَار صغيرة**
10 tree nursery after transplanting	مَشْتَل أشْجَار بعد نقل وغرس الأشْجَار
11 young plantation	نَبْت صغير
12 young plantation after brashing	نَبْت صغير بعد التشنيب
13 clearing	أرض تم إخلاؤها
14 tree stump (stump, stub)	جذل/أرُومة الشَّجَرَة
15-37 wood cutting (timber cutting, tree felling, *Am.* lumbering)	**قَطْع الأشْجَار**
15 timber skidded to the stack (stacked timber, *Am.* yarded timber)	قطع خشب مُكَدَّسَة
16 stack of logs, one cubic metre (*Am.* meter) of wood	رَصَّة من زَنْد الشجر، متر مكعب من الخشب
17 post (stake)	عِرْق خشب
18 forest labourer (woodsman, *Am.* logger, lumberer, lumberjack, lumberman, timberjack) turning (*Am.* canting) timber	الحَطَّاب وهو يَخْرُط الشجر
19 bole (tree trunk, trunk, stem)	جِذْع شَجَرَة
20 feller numbering the logs	قاطع الخشب يُرَقِّم زَنْد الأشْجَار
21 steel tree calliper (caliper)	قَدَمَة خشب معدنية
22 power saw (motor saw) cutting a bole	مِنْشَار كهربائي يقَطَع جِذْع شَجَرَة
23 safety helmet with visor and ear pieces	خَوْذَة أمان مزودة بواقي للعيْنَيْن والأذُنين
24 annual rings	حلقات تَحْدِيد عُمْر الشَّجَرَة
25 hydraulic felling wedge	إسفين قَطْع هيدرولي
26 protective clothing [orange top, green trousers]	لباس واق [قميص برتقالي وسروال أخضر]
27 felling with a power saw (motor saw)	قَطْع الشجر بمِنْشَار كهربائي
28 undercut (notch, throat, gullet, mouth, sink, kerf, birdsmouth)	ثَلْم قَطْع الشَّجَرَة
29 back cut	قَطْع خلفي
30 sheath holding felling wedge	غِمْد إسفين القَطْع
31 log	زَنْد
32 free-cutting saw for removing underwood and weeds	مِنْشَار القَطْع الحر لإزالة الشجيرات النامية أسفل الأشْجَار الكبيرة والنباتات الشيطانية
33 circular saw (or activated blade) attachment	وَصْلَة مِنْشَار دَوَّار
34 power unit (motor)	وَحْدَة الطاقة (موتور)
35 canister of viscous oil for the saw chain	حاوية زيت تزليق سلسلة المِنْشَار
36 petrol canister (*Am.* gasoline canister)	حاوية البنزين
37 felling of small timber (of small-sized thinnings) (thinning)	قَطْع شَجَرَة صغيرة

85 Forestry II — الحِرَاجَة (2)

1 axe (*Am.* ax)	فَأس
2 edge (cutting edge)	حافة قاطعة
3 handle (helve)	ذِرَاع الفَأس
4 felling wedge (falling wedge) with wood insert and ring	إسفين القَطْع
5 riving hammer (cleaving hammer, splitting hammer)	مِطْرَقة فَلْق
6 lifting hook	خُطَّاف رَفْع
7 cant hook	خُطَّاف مائل
8 barking iron (bark spud)	قضيب نَزْع اللحاء
9 peavy	البيفَة
10 slide calliper (caliper) (calliper square)	قَدَمَة منزلقة
11 billhook, a knife for	مِنْجَل

lopping

12 revolving die hammer (marking hammer, marking iron, *Am.* marker) — مِطْرَقَة ترقيم دَوَّارة

13 power saw (motor saw) — مِنْشَار كهربائي (مِنْشَار بموتور)

14 saw chain — سلسلة المِنْشَار

15 safety brake for the saw chain, with finger guard — مِكْبَح أمان سلسلة المِنْشَار له وقاء للإصبع

16 saw guide — دليل المِنْشَار

17 accelerator lock — قُفْل المسَارِع

18 snedding machine (trimming machine, *Am.* knotting machine, limbing machine) — مَاكِينَة تشذيب

19 feed rolls — درافيل الإلقام

20 flexible blade — نَصْل مَرِن

21 hydraulic arm — ذِرَاع هيدرولي

22 trimming blade — نَصْل التشذيب

23 debarking (barking, bark stripping) of boles — نَزْع لحاء جذوع الشجر

24 feed roller — درافيل إلقام

25 cylinder trimmer — أداة تشذيب أسطوانية

26 rotary cutter — قاطع دَوَّار

27 short-haul skidder — عربة نقل للمسافات القصيرة

28 loading crane — ونْش التحميل

29 log grips — مَاسِكَات زَنْد الشجر

30 post — عمود سانِد

31 Ackermann steering system — نظام توجيه أكريمان

32 log dump — مَخْزون خشب

33 number (identification number) — رقم الزَّنْد

34 skidder — عربة إنزلاقية

35 front blade (front plate) — النَّصْل الأمامي

36 crush-proof safety bonnet (*Am.* safety hood) — كبوت أمان ضد الكسر

37 Ackermann steering system — نظام توجيه أكريمان

38 cable winch — ونْش كيبلي

39 cable drum — أسطوانة الكيبل

40 rear blade (rear plate) — النَّصْل الخلفي

41 boles with butt ends held off the ground — جذوع أشْجَار وأطرافها الخلفية مرفوعة عن الأرض

42 haulage of timber by road — نَقْل الخشب بالعربات بَرِّيًّا

43 tractor (tractor unit) — جَرَّار

44 loading crane — ونْش التحميل

45 hydraulic jack — مِرْفَاع هيدرولي

46 cable winch — ونْش كيبلي

47 post — عمود سانِد

48 bolster plate — لَوْحَة استناد

49 rear bed (rear bunk) — مِرْقَد خلفي

86 Hunting — القَنْص

1-52 kinds of hunting — **أنواع الصَّيْد**

1-8 stalking (deer stalking, *Am.* stillhunting) in the game preserve — **اقتفاء الأثر في الأرض المُخَصصَة للصيْد**

1 huntsman (hunter) — صيَّاد

2 hunting clothes — لباس الصَّيْد

3 knapsack — حقيبة ظهرية

4 sporting gun (sporting rifle, hunting rifle) — بندقية صَيْد

5 huntsman's hat — قبعة الصيَّاد

6 field glasses, binoculars — منظار ميداني، ناظور

7 gun dog — كلب صَيْد لِجَلْب القَنَص

8 track (trail, hoofprints) — أثر (آثار حافر)

9-12 hunting in the rutting season and the pairing season — **الصَّيْد أثناء موسم الدَّوْرَة النَّزَوِيَّة والتزاوُج**

9 hunting screen (screen, *Am.* blind) — سِتَار الصَّيْد

10 shooting stick (shooting seat, seat stick) — مَقْعَد الصَّيْد

11 blackcock, displaying — طائر الشحرور

12 rutting stag — أيِّل في الدَّوْرَة النَّزَوِيَّة

13 hind, grazing — أيِّلَة تأكُل الكَلأ

14-17 hunting from a raised hide (raised stand) — **الصَّيْد من مَخْبَأ مرتفع**

14 raised hide (raised stand, high seat) — مَخْبَأ مرتفع (منصة مرتفعة، مَقْعَد مرتفع)

15 herd within range — قطيع في مَرْمَى القنص

16 game path (*Am.* runway) — ممَر الطرائد

17 roebuck, hit in the shoulder and killed by a finishing shot — حيوان الرَّوْ، أصيب بطلقة في الكتف وأجهز عليه بطلقة أخرى

18 phaeton — مركبة الفَيْتُون

19-27 types of trapping — **أنواع الفِخَاخ**

19 trapping of small predators — الإيقاع بالحيوانات المُفْتَرِسَة الصغيرة في الفَخّ

20 box trap (trap for small predators) — فَخ صَنْدوقي

21 bait — طُعْم

22 marten, a small predator — حيوان الدَّلَق أو السَّمُّور

23 ferreting (hunting rabbits out of their warrens) — صَيْد الأرانب بالاستعانة بابن مِقْرَض

24 ferret — ابن مِقْرَض، النِّمْس

25 ferreter — صائد الأرانب بالاستعانة بابن مِقْرَض

26 burrow (rabbit burrow, rabbit hole) — جُحْر، وِجَار

27 net (rabbit net) over the burrow opening — شَبَكَة فوق فتحة الجُحْر

28 feeding place for game (winter feeding place) — مكان إطعام خاص بالصَّيْد

29 poacher — صَيَّاد يصيد في ضَيْعة خاصة بدون إذن صاحبها

30 carbine, a short rifle — القربينة: بندقية قصيرة

31 boar hunt — صَيْد الخنازير البَرِّيَّة

32 wild sow (sow, wild boar) — خنزير بَرِّي

33 boarhound (hound, hunting dog; *collectively:* pack, pack of hounds) — كلب صَيْد الخنازير البَرِّيَّة

34-39 beating (driving, hare hunting) — **إثارة الطرائد من مخابئها** (صَيْد الأرانب البَرِّيَّة)

34 aiming position — وضع التصويب

35 hare, furred game (ground game) — أرنب برِّي، صَيْد فرائي، صَيْد أرضي

36 retrieving — استرجاع الفريسة للصَّيَّاد

37 beater — صيَّاد يَجُول أرْجاء الغابة مثيراً للفرائس من مخابئها

38 bag (kill) — الحيوانات المُصْطَادة

39 cart for carrying game — عربة لحمل الحيوانات المُصْطَادة

40 waterfowling (wild-fowling, duck shooting, *Am.* duck hunting) — صَيْد الطيور المائية (صَيْد البط)

41 flight of wild ducks, winged game — سِرْب من البط البَرِّي، صَيْد من الطيور

42-46 falconry (hawking) — **الصَّيْد بالصقور**

42 falconer — الصَّقَّار

43 reward, a piece of meat — مكافأة، قِطْعَة لَحْم

44 falcon's hood — قلنسوة الصقر

45 jess — قَيْد البازي

46 falcon, a hawk, a male hawk (tiercel) swooping (stooping) on a heron — صَقْر/باز ينقض على طائر مالِك الحزين

47-52 shooting from a butt — **القَنْص من داخل أرومة**

47 tree to which birds are lured — شَجَرَة تُغْوَى بها الطيور كَطُعْم

48 eagle owl, a decoy bird (decoy) — بُومَة صخَّابة، شَرَك على شكل طائر

49 perch — مَجْثَم الطيور

50 decoyed bird, a crow — طائر يقع في الشَّرَك، غراب

51 butt for shooting crows or eagle owls — أرومة لقنص الغربان والبوم الصَّخَّاب

52 gun slit — فتحة إبراز البندقية

87 Hunting Weapons, Hunting Equipment — أسْلِحَة القَنْص، مُعِدَّات القَنْص

1-40 sporting guns (sporting rifles, hunting rifles) — **بنادق الصَّيْد/القَنْص**

1 single-loader (single-loading rifle) — بندقية صَيْد سِعَة طلقة واحدة

2 repeating rifle, a small-arm (fire-arm), a repeater (magazine rifle, magazine repeater) — بندقية متعددة الطلقات، سلاح ناري صغير (بندقية بمَخْزَن ذخيرة)

3, 4, 6, 13 stock — **الكُتْلَة**

3 butt — الدَّبْشك، الإخْمَص

4 cheek [on the left side] — وَجْنَة [على الجانب الأيسر]

5 sling ring — حلَقَة الحمالة

6 pistol grip — قبضة مسدس

7 small of the butt — الجزء المستدق من الدَّبْشك/الإخْمَص

8 safety catch — سُقَّاطة الأمان

9 lock — الترباس

10 trigger guard — واقي الزِّنَاد

11 second set trigger (firing trigger) — زِنَاد الإطلاق

12 hair trigger (set trigger) — زِنَاد شَعْري

13 foregrip — قبضة أمامية

14 butt plate — كتلة الدَّبْشك/الإخْمَص

15 cartridge chamber — حُجْرَة الطلقة

16 receiver — المُسْتَقْبِل

17 magazine — المَخْزَن

18 magazine spring — نابَض المَخْزَن

19 ammunition (cartridge) — ذخيرة (خرطوش)

20 chamber — حُجْرَة

21 firing pin (striker) — إبْرَة ضرب النار (الضارب)

22 bolt handle (bolt lever) — ذِرَاع الترباس

23 triple-barrelled (triple-barreled) rifle, a self-cocking gun — بندقية ذات ثلاث مواسير/سبطانات، سلاح ذاتي التعمير

24 reversing catch; *in various guns:* safety catch — حابس سُقَّاطة الأمان؛ في أسلحة متنوعة: سُقَّاطة الأمان

25 sliding safety catch — سُقَّاطة أمان منزلقة

26 rifle barrel (rifled barrel) — ماسورة البندقية (سَبَطَانَة محززة)

27 smooth-bore barrel — ماسورة مَلْسَاء الجَوْف

28 chasing — نقوش زينية

29 telescopic sight (rifle-scope, telescope sight) — مِنْظَار تليسكوبي (ناظور البندقية)

30 graticule adjuster screws — براغي ضبط العَيْنِيَّة

31-32 graticule (sight graticule) — **سِدَادَة العَيْنِيَّة**

31 various graticule systems — أنظمة عَيْنِيَّة متنوعة

32 cross wires (*Am.* cross hairs) — السِّلْكان المتقاطعان

33 over-and-under shotgun — بندقية صَيْد ذات ماسورتين

34 rifled gun barrel — ماسورة/سَبَطَانَة بندقية مُحَزَّزَة

35 barrel casing — غلاف الماسورة/السَّبَطَانَة

36 rifling — حزوز

37 rifling calibre (*Am.* caliber) — عيار الحَزْحَزَة

38 bore axis — محْوَر جَوْف الماسورة/السَّبَطَانَة

39 land — خَدّ

40 calibre (bore diameter, *Am.* caliber) — العِيَار (قُطْر الجَوْف)

41-48 hunting equipment — **مُعِدَّات الصَّيْد**

41 double-edged hunting knife — سِكِّين صَيْد ذو نَصْلَيْن

42 [single-edged] hunting knife — سِكِّين صَيْد [ذو نصل واحد]

43-47 calls for luring game (for calling — **أدوات مُحَاكاة أصوات الطرائد لاجتذابها**

game)
43 roe call أداة مُحَاكاة صوت الرَّو
44 hare call أداة مُحَاكاة صوت الأرانب
45 quail call أداة مُحَاكاة صوت السماني
46 stag call أداة مُحَاكاة صوت الأيِّل
47 partridge call أداة مُحَاكاة صوت الحَجَل
48 bow trap (bow gin), a jaw trap فخ قَوْسِي ، فَخ فَكِي
49 small-shot cartridge خرطوش طلقات صغيرة
50 cardboard case غلاف من الورق المُقَوَّى
51 small-shot charge حَشْوَة من الطلقات الصغيرة
52 felt wad حَشْوَة من اللباد
53 smokeless powder (*different kind*: black powder) بارود عديم الدخان [نوع مختلف: بارود اسود]
54 cartridge رَصَاصَة، طلقة
55 full-jacketed cartridge رَصَاصَة بغلاف كامل
56 soft-lead core جَوْف من الرصاص اللَّيِّن
57 powder charge حَشْوَة من البارود
58 detonator cap كبسولة المُفَجِّر
59 percussion cap كبسولة القَدْح
60 hunting horn بُوق الصَّيْد
61-64 rifle cleaning kit **طاقم أدوات تنظيف البندقية**
61 cleaning rod قضيب التنظيف (المِمْرَاط/الحَرْبِي)
62 cleaning brush فرشاة التنظيف
63 cleaning tow نسالة كتانية للتنظيف
64 pull-through (*Am*. pull-thru) سِيخ التسليك
65 sights المُسَدِدة، المُوَجِّه، الناشِنْكَان
66 notch (sighting notch) فتحة التسديد/التوجيه
67 back sight leaf ورقة المُسَدِّدة الخلفية
68 sight scale division تقسيم مقياس المُسَدِّدة
69 back sight slide مِزْلاق المُسَدِّدة الخلفية
70 notch [to hold the spring] نقرة [لتثبيت النابض]
71 front sight (foresight) المُسَدِّدة الأمامية (الشَّعِيرة)
72 bead قَمْحَة (سِن نَمْلَة الدِّبانة)
73 ballistics سير المقذوف في الهواء
74 azimuth السَّمْت
75 angle of departure زَاوِيَة الخروج من الماسورة
76 angle of elevation زَاوِيَة الارتفاع
77 apex (zenith) أعلى نقطة على منحنى المَسَار
78 angle of descent زَاوِيَة السقوط
79 ballistic curve منحنى سير المقذوف

88 Game القَنَص/الطَّرائد

1-27 red deer **الأيِّل الأحمر**
1 hind (red deer), a young hind or a dam; collectively: antlerless deer, (*y.*) calf الأيِّلة ، أيِّلة صغيرة؛ اسم الجمع: الأيِّل عديم القرون، (الصغير) صغير الأيل
2 tongue لسان
3 neck رقبة
4 rutting stag أيِّل في الدَّوْرَة النَّزَوِيَّة
5-11 antlers **القرون**
5 burr (rose) منْبَت القرون بالجبهة (وردة)
6 brow antler (brow tine, brow point, brow snag) قَرْن الحاجب
7 bez antler (bay antler, bay, bez tine) قَرْن بارز
8 royal antler (royal, tray) قَرْن ملَكي
9 surroyal antlers (surroyals) قَرْن إضافي
10 point (tine) طرف القَرْن المدبب
11 beam (main trunk) فرع قرون رئيسي
12 head رَأس
13 mouth خَطْم (فم)
14 larmier (tear bag) كيس الدموع
15 eye عين
16 ear أُذن
17 shoulder كتف
18 loin خاصِرة
19 scut (tail) ذَيْل قصير (ذَيْل)
20 rump ردْف، كَفَل
21 leg (haunch) فَخْذ (إلْيَة)
22 hind leg رِجْل خلفية
23 dew claw الزُمْعَة
24 hoof حافِر
25 foreleg رِجْل أمامية
26 flank جَنْب، خاصِرة
27 collar (rutting mane) الشعر المُطَوِّق لرقبة الأيِّل
28-39 roe (roe deer) **الرَّوْ**
28 roebuck (buck) ذكر الرَّوْ (غزال الرَّوْ)
29-31 antlers (horns) **القرون**
29 burr (rose) منْبَت القرون بالجبهة (وردة)
30 beam with pearls فرع قرون رئيسي وبه بوادر القرون
31 point (tine) طرف القَرْن المدبب
32 ear أُذن
33 eye عين
34 doe (female roe), a female fawn or a barren doe أنثى الرَّوْ، أنثى غزال صغيرة أو أنثى عاقر
35 loin الخاصِرة
36 rump ردْف، كَفَل
37 leg (haunch) ورْك (إلْيَة)
38 shoulder كَتف
39 fawn, (*m.*) young buck, (*f.*) young doe ولد الرَّوْ، ذَكَر:ظبي، أنثى: ظبية
40-41 fallow deer **الأيِّل الأسمر**
40 fallow buck, a buck with palmate (palmated) antlers, (*f.*) doe ذكر الأيِّل الأسمر ذو قرون راحِيَّة، الأنثى: ظبية
41 palm راحة القَرْن
42 red fox, (*m.*) dog, (*f.*) vixen, (*y.*) cub الثعلب الأحمر (ذكر:ثعلب، أنثى:ثعْلَبَة، الصغير:شِبْل)
43 eyes عينان
44 ear أُذن
45 muzzle (mouth) خَطْم (فم)
46 pads (paws) مخالب

47 brush (tail)	ذَيْل
48 badger, (*f.*) sow	الغُرَيْر (الأنثى: أنثى الغُرَيْر)
49 tail	ذَيْل
50 paws	مخالب
51 wild boar, (*m.*) boar, (*f.*) wild sow (sow), (*y.*) young boar	خنزير بَرِّي (أنثى: خنزيرة، أنثى الرَّث، الصغير: خنوص)
52 bristles	هُلْب
53 snout	فُنْطِيسَة الخنزير
54 tusk	ناب
55 shield	دِرْع الخنزير
56 hide	جِلْد الخنزير
57 dew claw	الزَّمَعَة
58 tail	ذَيْل
59 hare, (*m.*) buck, (*f.*) doe	أرنب بَرِّي
60 eye	عيْن
61 ear	أُذُن
62 scut (tail)	ذَيْل قصير
63 hind leg	رِجْل خلفية
64 foreleg	رِجْل أمامية
65 rabbit	أرنب
66 blackcock	طائر الشَّحْرور
67 tail	ذَيْل
68 falcate (falcated) feathers	ريش معقوف
69 hazel grouse (hazel hen)	طائر طَهْيُوج البندق
70 partridge	طائر الحَجَل
71 horseshoe (horseshoe marking)	حُدْوَة حصان (علامَة)
72 wood grouse (capercaillie)	طَهْيُوج الغابة
73 beard	لحية
74 axillary marking	علامة إبطِيَّة
75 tail (fan)	ذَيْل (مِرْوَحَة)
76 wing (pinion)	جناح (جنيح سفلي)
77 common pheasant, a pheasant, (*m.*) cock pheasant (pheasant cock), (*f.*) hen pheasant (pheasant hen)	طائر التَّدْرَج (ذكر التَّدْرَج، أنثى التَّدْرَج)
78 plumicorn (feathered ear, ear tuft, ear, horn)	أُذُن مُرَيَّشَة (قَرْن)
79 wing	جناح
80 tail	ذَيْل
81 leg	رِجْل
82 spur	شَوْكة
83 snipe	طائر الشُّنْقُب
84 bill (beak)	مِنْقار

89 Fish Farming (Fish Culture, Pisciculture) and Angling — تَرْبِيَة الأسْمَاك والصَّيْد بالصِّنَّارة

1-19 fish farming (fish culture, pisciculture)	**المَزَارِع السَّمَكِيَّة** (تربية الآسماك)
1 cage in running water	قفص في ماء جار
2 hand net (landing net)	شبكَة صَيْد حديدية
3 semi-oval barrel for transporting fish	برْمِيل شِبْه بَيْضاوي لنقل السَّمك
4 vat	دَنّ، وعاء ضخم
5 trellis in the overflow	تَعْرِيشَة في فيضان الماء
6 trout pond; *sim.:* carp pond, a fry pond, fattening pond, or cleansing pond	حوض تربية سَمَك الأطْرُوط (مثله: حوض تربية سَمَك الشَّبُوط، حوض زريعة السَّمَك)
7 water inlet (water supply pipe)	أنْبُوب دخول/امداد الماء
8 water outlet (outlet pipe)	أنْبُوب خروج الماء
9 monk	صندوق غَرْبَلَة (مُونْك)
10 screen	غِرْبَال
11-19 hatchery	**مكان تربية الأسماك**
11 stripping the spawning pike (seed pike)	استخلاص البَيْض من سَمَكة الكراكي
12 fish spawn (spawn, roe, fish eggs)	بَيْض السَّمَكة
13 female fish (spawner, seed fish)	سَمَكة
14 trout breeding (trout rearing)	تربية سَمَك الأطروط
15 Californian incubator	حَضَّانة بَيْض السَّمك
16 trout fry	زريعة سَمَك الأطروط
17 hatching jar for pike	وعاء فقس بَيْض السَّمك
18 long incubation tank	خَزَّان حَضْن بَيْض السَّمك لفترة طويلة
19 Brandstetter egg-counting board	عدَّاد بَيْض السَّمك طراز "براند ستتر"
20-94 angling	**صَيْد السَّمك بالصِّنَّارة**
20-31 bottom fishing (coarse fishing)	**الصَّيْد من قاع البحر**
20 line shooting	قَذْف الصِّنَّارة
21 coils	ملفات خيط الصِّنَّارة
22 cloth (rag) or paper	خِرْقَة قماش أو ورقة
23 rod rest	مِسْنَد الصِّنَّارة
24 bait tin	عُلْبَة طُعْم الصَّيْد
25 fish basket (creel)	سَلَّة جمع السَّمك المُصْطَاد
26 fishing for carp from a boat	صَيْد سَمَك الأطروط من قارب
27 rowing boat (fishing boat)	قارِب تجديف (قارِب صَيْد)
28 keep net	شبكَة صَيْد حاجزة
29 drop net	شبكَة صَيْد اسقاطية
30 pole (punt pole, quant pole)	شَخْتُورة (عصا دفع القارب)
31 casting net	شبكَة صَيْد
32 two-handed side cast with fixed-spool reel	إلقاء صنارة ذات بكَرَة ثابتة جانبيا بكلتا اليدين
33 initial position	الوَضْع الأوَّلِي
34 point of release	نقطة الانطلاق
35 path of the rod tip	مَسَار طرَف الصِّنَّارة
36 trajectory of the baited weight	مَسَار الثِّقْل المُحمَّل بالطُّعْم
37-94 fishing tackle	**أدوات الصَّيْد**
37 fishing pliers	زرِدية صَيْد
38 filleting knife	سِكِّين تقطيع الشرائح
39 fish knife	سِكِّين سَمَك

40 disgorger (hook disgorger)	أداة تخليص الطُّعْم من خُطّاف الصِّنَّارة
41 bait needle	إبْرَة التقاط الطُّعْم
42 gag	الكمام
43-48 floats	**الطافيات/الفلِّينات**
43 sliding cork float	طافية فِلِّينية منزلقة
44 plastic float	طافية بلاستيكية
45 quill float	طافية من اللحاء المُجَفَّف
46 polystyrene float	طافية من مادة البوليسترين
47 oval bubble float	طافية بَيْضَوِيَّة الشكل
48 lead-weighted sliding float	طافية منزلقَة مثقلة بقطْعَة رصاص
49-58 rods	**قصبات الصِّنَّارة**
49 solid glass rod	قصبة صنَّارة مصنوعة من الزجاج الصلب
50 cork handle (cork butt)	مِقْبَض من الفلين
51 spring-steel ring	حلَقَة نابضية من الصلب
52 top ring (end ring)	حلَقَة علوية/طرفية
53 telescopic rod	قصبة تليسكوبية (ذات أجزاء متداخلة)
54 rod section	جزء القصبة
55 bound handle (bound butt)	مِقْبَض مُبَطَّن
56 ring	حلَقَة
57 carbon-fibre rod; *sim.:* hollow glass rod	قصبة من الألياف الكربونية (مثلها قصبة مجوَّفة من الزجاج)
58 all-round ring (butt ring for long cast), a steel bridge ring	حلَقَة حرة الحركة لتسهيل إلقاء الصِّنَّارة لمسافات بعيدة
59-64 reels	**بكرات الخيط**
59 multiplying reel (multiplier reel)	بكَرَة مضاعفة
60 line guide	دليل الخيط
61 fixed-spool reel (stationary-drum reel)	بكَرَة خيط ثابتة
62 bale arm	ذِرَاع ملف الخيط
63 fishing line	خيط الصِّنَّارة
64 controlling the cast with the index finger	التحكم في مدى رَمْي الصِّنَّارة بواسطة السَّبَّابة
65-76 baits	**أنواع طُعْم الصَّيْد**
65 fly	زريعة سَمَك
66 artificial nymph	حورية صَنْعِيَّة
67 artificial earthworm	دودة صنيعة
68 artificial grasshopper	جندب صَنْعِيَّة
69 single-jointed plug (single-jointed wobbler)	"وابلر" وحيد المفصل
70 double-jointed plug (double-jointed wobbler)	"وابلر" ذو مفصلين
71 round wobbler	"وابلر" مستدير
72 wiggler	يرَقَة حَشَرَة صَنْعِيَّة
73 spoon bait (spoon)	طُعْم ملْعَقِي
74 spinner	طُعْم دَوَّامي/دَوَّار
75 spinner with concealed hook	طُعْم دَوَّامي/دَوَّار ذو خُطَّاف مَخْفِي
76 long spinner	طُعْم دَوَّامي/دَوَّار طويل
77 swivel	وَصْلَة متراوحة
78 cast (leader)	رمية (موجِّه السمك)
79-87 hooks	**أنواع خُطَّاف الصِّنَّارة**
79 fish hook	خُطَّاف عادي
80 point of the hook with barb	طرف الخُطَّاف المدبب وبه شَوْكة
81 bend of the hook	منحنى الخُطَّاف
82 spade (eye)	عروة
83 open double hook	خُطَّاف مزدوج مفتوح
84 limerick	الليمريك
85 closed treble hook (triangle)	خُطَّاف ثلاثي مقفول
86 carp hook	خُطَّاف سَمك الشَّبُّوط
87 eel hook	خُطَّاف الأنقليس
88-92 leads (lead weights)	**أثقال الرصاص**
88 oval lead (oval sinker)	ثِقْل رصاصي بَيْضَوي
89 lead shot	كُرَيَّة رصاص
90 pear-shaped lead	ثِقْل رصاصي أجَّاصي
91 plummet	ثِقْل الفادن
92 sea lead	ثِقْل بحري
93 fish ladder (fish pass, fish way)	مَرْقَى الأسماك
94 stake net	شبكَة كيسية

90 Sea Fishing — الصَّيْد في البحَار

1-23 deep-sea fishing	**الصَّيْد في أعالي البحار**
1-10 drift net fishing	**الصَّيْد بطريقة شَبكَة صَيْد السَّمك المُنْجَرِف مع التيار**
1 herring lugger (fishing lugger, lugger)	لُغْر صَيْد الرِّنْكَة (سفينة ذات أشرِعَة معيَّنَة الشكل)
2-10 herring drift net	**شَبكَة صَيْد الرِّنْكَة المنجرفة مع التيار**
2 buoy	طافية، شَمَنْدُورَة
3 buoy rope	حبْل الطافية
4 float line	حبْل طاف
5 seizing	رباط
6 wooden float	عَوَّامَة خشبية
7 headline	الحبْل العلوي
8 net	شَبكَة
9 footrope	الحبْل السفلي
10 sinkers (weights)	غَوَاطس
11-23 trawl fishing (trawling)	**الصَّيْد بواسطة الترولة** (شَبكَة تُسحب عبر قاع البحر)
11 factory ship, a trawler	سفينة الترولة
12 warp (trawl warp)	حبْل الترولة السميك
13 otter boards	ألْوَاح خشبية
14 net sonar cable	كيبل سونار الشبَكَة
15 wire warp	حبْل سِلْكِي سميك
16 wing	جناح، جانب
17 net sonar device	جِهَاز سونار الشبَكَة
18 footrope	الحبْل السفلي
19 spherical floats	عوَّامات كُرَوِيَّة
20 belly	جزء الترولة المنتفخ
21 1,800 kg iron weight	ثِقْل حديدي زنة 1800 كجم
22 cod end (cod)	نهاية بقلية
23 cod line for closing the cod end	حبْل إقفال النهاية البقلية
24-29 inshore fishing	**الصَّيْد قرب الشاطئ**

24 fishing boat قارب صَيْد
25 ring net cast in a circle رمية شَبَكَة مستديرة في دائرة
26 cable for closing the ring net كيبل إقفال الشَبَكَة المستديرة
27 closing gear عُدَّة إقفال
28-29 long-line fishing (long-lining) **الصَّيْد باستخدام حبل طويل**
28 long line حَبْل طويل
29 suspended fishing tackle أداة صَيْد مُعلَّقَة

91 Mills الطَّواحين

1-34 windmill **الطَّاحونَة الهوائيَّة**
1 windmill vane (windmill sail, windmill arm) ريشَة الطَّاحونة الهوائيَّة (شِراع الطَّاحونة، ذِراع الطَّاحونة)
2 stock (middling, back, radius) دعامة (متوسطة، خلفية، نصف قطرية)
3 frame إطار
4 shutter غطاء متحرك
5 wind shaft (sail axle) عمود الريح (مِحْوَر الشراع)
6 sail top قمة الشراع
7 brake wheel دولاب المِكْبَح
8 brake مِكْبَح، فرملة
9 wooden cog لسان خشبي
10 pivot bearing (step bearing) مَحْمَل مِحْوَر الارتكاز
11 wallower قلابة
12 mill spindle مِحْوَر دوران الطاحونة
13 hopper قادوس
14 shoe (trough, spout) حذاء (مَجْرَى، مزراب)
15 miller عامِل الطاحونة
16 millstone حَجَر الرَحَى
17 furrow (flute) شق، ثَلَم
18 master furrow ثَلَم رئيسي
19 eye عروة
20 hurst (millstone casing) بَيْت حَجَر الرَحَى
21 set of stones (millstones) طاقم من حَجَرَيْن (حجَرا الرَحَى)
22 runner (upper millstone) حَجَر الرَحَى (الحَجَر الدَوَّار العلوي)
23 bed stone (lower stone, bedder) حَجَر الأساس (حَجَر الرَحَى السفلي)
24 wooden shovel جاروف خشبي
25 bevel gear (bevel gearing) ترس مخروطي
26 bolter (sifter) مُنْخُل آلي
27 wooden tub (wooden tun) حَوْض خشبي
28 flour طَحين، دقيق
29 smock windmill (Dutch windmill) طاحونة هوائية سَمْقيَّة (طاحونة هولندية)
30 rotating (revolving) windmill cap رَأْس الطاحونة الدَوَّارة
31 post windmill (German windmill) طاحونة عمودية (طاحونة ألمانية)
32 tailpole (pole) عمود الذيْل
33 base قاعدة
34 post دعامة عمودية

35-44 watermill **طاحونة مائيَّة**
35 overshot mill wheel (high-breast mill wheel), a mill wheel (waterwheel) ساقِيَة تدار بالدفْع العلوي
36 bucket (cavity) دَلْو
37 middleshot mill wheel (breast mill wheel) ساقِيَة تدار بالدفْع الأوسط
38 curved vane ريشَة منحنية
39 undershot mill wheel ساقِيَة تدار بالدفع السفلي
40 flat vane ريشَة مسَطحة
41 headrace (discharge flume) مَجْرَى الماء الرئيسي
42 mill weir سد الطاحونة
43 overfall (water overfall) مَسْقَط الماء الفائض
44 millstream (millrace, *Am.* raceway) تيار مائي دافق يُدير الطاحونة

92 Malting and Brewing I تَخْمير المِلْت وتَصْنيع الجُعَة (1)

1-41 preparation of malt (malting) **إعداد المِلْت** (تخمير المِلْت)
1 malting tower (maltings) برج تخمير المِلْت (التخمير)
2 barley hopper قادوس الشعير
3 washing floor with compressed-air washing unit طابق غسيل مزوَّد بوَحْدَة غسيل تعمل بالهواء المضغوط
4 outflow condenser مكثِّف الدفْق
5 water-collecting tank خَزَّان تجميع الماء
6 condenser for the steep liquor مكثِّف محلول النقع
7 coolant collecting plant مَعْمَل تجميع المُبَرِّد
8 steeping floor (steeping tank, dressing floor) طابق النقع (خَزَّان النقع)
9 cold water tank خَزَّان الماء البارد
10 hot water tank خَزَّان الماء الساخن
11 pump room حُجْرَة المِضَخَّة
12 pneumatic plant مَعْمَل يعمل بالهواء المضغوط
13 hydraulic plant مَعْمَل هيدرولي
14 ventilation shaft (air inlet and outlet) عمود التهوية (مدخل ومهرب الهواء)
15 exhaust fan مِرْوَحَة طاردة
16-18 kilning floors **طابقا التجفيف التَّنُّوري**
16 drying floor طابق تجفيف
17 burner ventilator جِهاز تهوية المَوْقِد
18 curing floor طابق المعالجة بالتخمير
19 outlet duct from the kiln منفذ خروج من التَّنُّور/القمين
20 finished malt collecting hopper قادوس المِلْت تام التجهيز
21 transformer station مَحَطَّة المحوِّل
22 cooling compressors ضواغط التبريد
23 green malt (germinated barley) مِلْت أخضر (شعير مُنَبَّت)
24 turner (plough) آلية قلابة (مِحْرَاث)
25 central control room حُجْرَة التحكم المركزي مع

with flow diagram رسم تخطيطي لسير العمليات
26 screw convẻyor ناقلة لَوْلَبِيَّة
27 washing floor طابق الغسيل
28 steeping floor طابق النقع
29 drying kiln تَنُّور التجفيف
30 curing kiln تَنُّور المعالجة بالتخمير
31 barley silo صَوْمَعَة الشعير
32 weighing apparatus جِهَاز الوزن
33 barley elevator رافعة الشعير
34 three-way chute (three-way tippler) مَجْرَى مائل ذو ثلاثة فروع
35 malt elevator رافعة المِلْت
36 cleaning machine مَاكِينَة التنظيف
37 malt silo صَوْمَعَة المِلْت
38 corn removal by suction إزالة الحبوب عن طريق الشفط
39 sacker جِهَاز تعبئة الأكياس
40 dust extractor وَحْدَة إستخراج الأتربة
41 barley reception استقبال الشعير
42-53 mashing process in the mashhouse **عملية تحويل المِلْت إلى جَرِيش بداخل وَحْدَة الجَرِيش**
42 premasher (converter) for mixing grist and water جِهَازٌ لخلط الحبوب المُعَدَّة للطحن مع الماء
43 mash tub (mash tun) for mashing the malt حوض هَرْس المِلْت
44 mash copper (mash tun, *Am.* mash kettle) for boiling the mash مِرْجَل لِغَلْي المِلْت المجروش
45 dome of the tun قبة المِرْجَل
46 propeller (paddle) رفَّاص
47 sliding door باب انزلاقي
48 water (liquor) supply pipe ماسورة إمداد الماء (محلول النقع)
49 brewer (master brewer, masher) صانع البيرة أو الجُعَّة
50 lauter tun for settling the draff (grains) and filtering off the wort حوض ترسيب الحبوب وترشيح نقيع الشعير
51 lauter battery for testing the wort for quality بطارية اختبار جودة نقيع الشعير
52 hop boiler (wort boiler) for boiling the wort مِرْجَل حشيشة الدينار لغلي نقيع الشعير
53 ladle-type thermometer (scoop thermometer) ترمومتر على شكل مِغْرَفَة

93 Brewing II تَصْنِيع الجُعَّة (2)

1-31 brewery (brewhouse) **مَصْنَع الجُعَّة**
1-5 wort cooling and break removal (trub removal) **تبريد نقيع الشعير وإزالة الهَشِيم**
1 control desk (control panel) لَوْحَة التحكم
2 whirlpool separator for removing the hot break (hot trub) فَرَّاز دَوَّامي لإزالة الهَشِيم الساخن
3 measuring vessel for the kieselguhr وعاء قياس التراب النقاعي
4 kieselguhr filter مَرْشِح التراب النقاعي
5 wort cooler مُبَرِّد نقيع الشعير
6 pure culture plant for yeast (yeast propagation plant) مَعْمَل إستنبات نقي للخميرة
7 fermenting cellar قَبْو التخمير
8 fermentation vessel (fermenter) وِعاء التخمير
9 fermentation thermometer (mash thermometer) ترمومتر التخمير (ترمومتر الجَرِيش)
10 mash جَرِيش المِلْت المنقوع
11 refrigeration system نظَام التبريد
12 lager cellar قَبْو الجُعَّة الخفيفة
13 manhole to the storage tank فتحة الدخول إلى صهريج التخزين
14 broaching tap صُنْبُور الصهريج
15 beer filter مُرَشِّح الجُعَّة
16 barrel store مَخْزَن البراميل
17 beer barrel, an aluminium (*Am.* aluminum) barrel برْمِيل جُعَّة، بِرْمِيل ألومنيوم
18 bottle-washing plant مَعْمَل غَسْل الزُجَاجَات
19 bottle-washing machine (bottle washer) مَاكِينَة غَسْل الزُجَاجَات
20 control panel لَوْحَة التحكم
21 cleaned bottles زُجَاجَات تم تنظيفها
22 bottling تعبئة الزُجَاجَات/القنينات
23 forklift truck (fork truck, forklift) عربة بمِرْفَاع شَوْكِي
24 stack of beer crates مجموعة من صناديق الجُعَّة
25 beer can عُلْبَة جُعَّة
26 beer bottle, a Eurobottle with bottled beer; *kinds of beer*: light beer (lager, light ale, pale ale or bitter), dark beer (brown ale, mild), Pilsener beer, Munich beer, malt beer, strong beer (bock beer), porter, ale, stout, Salvator beer, wheat beer, small beer زُجَاجَة/قنينة جُعَّة؛ أنواع الجُعَّة: جُعَّة خفيفة (مُعَتَّقَة، المِزْر الخفيف، المِزْر المُرّ)، الجُعَّة الدَّاكِنَة (المِزْر البُنِّيّ، متوسط)، جُعَّة بلزينر، جُعَّة ميونيخ، جُعَّة الشَّعير، الجُعَّة القَوِيَّة (جُعَّة الربيع)، جُعَّة البُرْتَر، المِزْر، جُعَّة السلفادور، جُعَّة الحِنْطَة
27 crown cork (crown cork closure) سِدَادَة فلينية تاجية
28 disposable pack (carryhome pack) عُبْوَة غير مُرْتَجَعَة
29 non-returnable bottle (single-trip bottle) زُجَاجَة غير مُرْتَجَعَة
30 beer glass كَأْس الجُعَّة
31 head رَغْوَة (رَأْس) الجُعَّة

94 Slaughterhouse (Abattoir) المَجْزَر/المَسْلَخ

1 slaughterman (*Am.* slaughterer, killer) الجَزَّار، القَصَّاب
2 animal for slaughter, an حيوان للذبح، ذبيحة

ox	
3 captive-bolt pistol (pneumatic gun), a stunning device	مسدس صَدْمِي
4 bolt	مِسْمَار
5 cartridges	خَراطيش
6 release lever (trigger)	ذِرَاع الإعتاق (زِنَاد)
7 electric stunner	صاعق كهربي
8 electrode	الكترود
9 lead	سلك كهربي
10 hand guard (insulation)	وقاء اليد
11 pig (*Am.* hog) for slaughter	خنزير ذبيح
12 knife case	عُلْبَة السكاكين
13 flaying knife	سِكِين السَّلْخ
14 sticking knife (sticker)	مدْيَة الطعن
15 butcher's knife (butcher knife)	سِكِين الجَزَّار
16 steel	مِسَن السكاكين
17 splitter	ساطور فَلْق
18 cleaver (butcher's cleaver, meat axe (*Am.* meat ax)	ساطور الجَزَّار
19 bone saw (butcher's saw)	مِنْشَار العَظْم
20 meat saw for sawing meat into cuts	مِنْشَار تقطيع اللَحْم إلى أوْصَال
21-24 cold store (cold room)	**غُرْفَة التبريد، البَرَّاد**
21 gambrel (gambrel stick)	عصا حديدية لتعليق الذبائح
22 quarter of beef	رُبْع الذبيحة
23 side of pork	جانب الخنزير المذبوح
24 meat inspector's stamp	خاتم مفتش اللحوم

95 Meat Joints أوْصَال اللَحْم

left: meat side;	يسارا: جانب اللَحْم
right: bone side	يمينا: جانب العَظْم
1-13 *animal:* **calf;** *meat:* **veal**	**الحيوان: عِجْل؛ اللَحْم: لَحْم عِجْل صَغير (بتلو)**
1 leg with hind knuckle	الرُسْغ واللَحْم المحيط به
2 flank	خاصِرة
3 loin and rib	بَيْت الكَلاوِي والضلوع
4 breast (breast of veal)	الصدر (صدر العِجْل)
5 shoulder with fore knuckle	كتف بالزَّنْد واللَحْم المحيط به
6 neck with scrag (scrag end)	الرقبة واللَحْم المحيط بها
7 best end of loin (of loin of veal)	قِطْعَة لَحْم من الخاصِرة
8 fore knuckle	الزَّنْد واللَحْم المحيط به
9 shoulder	الكتف
10 hind knuckle	الرُسْغ واللَحْم المحيط به
11 roasting round (oyster round)	شريحة سميكة للشَوْي
12 cutlet for frying or braising	كُسْتَليتة للشوى أو التسبيك بالقِدْر
13 undercut (fillet)	قِطْعَة لَحْم من داخل الخاصرة

14-37 *animal:* **ox;** *meat:* **beef**	**الحيوان: ثَوْر؛ اللَحْم: بقري**
14 round with rump and shank	الفَخْذ ولَحْم وعَظْم الساق
15-16 flank	**خاصِرة**
15 thick flank	لَحْم سميك من الخاصرة
16 thin flank	لَحْم رقيق من الخاصرة
17 sirloin	شريحة من أعلى الخاصرة
18 prime rib (fore ribs, prime fore rib)	لَحْم أعلى السلسلة
19 middle rib and chuck	الضلوع الوسطى وجزء من لَحْم الكتف
20 neck	الرقبة
21 flat rib	الضلع الأمامي
22 leg of mutton piece (bladebone) with shin	الزَّنْد وعَظْمة اللَوْح فى الضأن
23 brisket (brisket of beef)	لَحْم الصدر
24 fillet (fillet of beef)	فيليه
25 hind brisket	لَحْم الصدر الخلفي
26 middle brisket	لَحْم الضلوع
27 breastbone	عَظْم الصدر
28 shin	عَظْم الزَّنْد
29 leg of mutton piece	فَخْذ الضأن
30 bladebone [meat side]	عَظْمة اللَوْح [جانب اللَحْم]
31 part of top rib	جزء من الضلع العلوي
32 bladebone [bone side]	عَظْمة اللَوْح [جانب العَظْم]
33 shank	لَحْم عَظْم الساق
34 silverside	جزء من لَحْم الساق
35 rump	قِطْعَة من لَحْم الفَخْذ
36 thick flank	لَحْم الخاصرة السميك
37 top side	الجزء العلوي
38-54 *animal:* **pig;** *meat:* **pork**	**الحيوان: خنزير؛ اللَحْم: لَحْم خنزير**
38 leg with knuckle and trotter	عَظْم الفَخْذ واللَحْم المحيط به والكارع
39 ventral part of the belly	اللَحْم البطني
40 back fat	شَحْم الظَهر
41 belly	البطن
42 bladebone with knuckle and trotter	عَظْم الرُسْغ واللَحْم المحيط به والكارع
43 head (pig's head)	رَأس (رَأس الخنزير)
44 fillet (fillet of pork)	فيليه لَحْم الخنزير
45 leaf fat (pork flare)	دهن التجويف البطني
46 loin (pork loin)	خاصرة الخنزير
47 spare rib	الإرْب الضلعي
48 trotter	الكارع
49 knuckle	عَظْم الرُسْغ
50 butt	الجزء اللَحْمي السميك
51 fore end (ham)	الفَخْذ الأمامية
52 round end for boiling	قِطْعَة من اللَحْم السميك للسلق
53 fat end	الشَّحْم
54 gammon steak	لَحْم إعداد ستيك الخنزير المقدد

96 Butcher's Shop مَحل الجِزَارَة/القَصَّاب (الملْحَمَة)

1-30 butcher's shop	**محل الجِزَارَة، الملْحَمة**
1-4 meat	**اللحـــوم**
1 ham on the bone	فَخْذ خنزير بالعَظْم

2 flitch of bacon — قِطْعَة مُمَلَّحَة ومُقَدَّدَة من خاصِرة الخنزير
3 smoked meat — لَحْم مُدَخَّن
4 piece of loin (piece of sirloin) — قِطْعَة من لَحْم الخاصِرة
5 lard — شَحْم الخنزير
6-11 sausages — **المقانق**
6 price label — بطاقة السعر
7 mortadella — مُرْتَدِيلا
8 scalded sausage; *kinds:* Vienna sausage (Wiener), Frankfurter sausage (Frankfurter) — مقانق مسلوقة؛ أنواعها: مقانق فيينا ، مقانق فرانكفورتر
9 collared pork (*Am.* headcheese) — لَحْم خنزير ملفوف ومنقوع في الخل
10 ring of [Lyoner] sausage — حلَقَة من مقانق [الليونر]
11 pork sausages; *also*: beef sausages — مقانق لَحْم الخنزير؛ أيضاً: مقانق لَحْم بقري
12 cold shelves — رفوف اللحوم المُبَرَّدة
13 meat salad (diced meat salad) — سلطة لحوم
14 cold meats (*Am.* cold cuts) — لَحْم بارد
15 pâté — فطيرة لَحْم(باتيه)
16 mince (mincemeat, minced meat) — لَحْم مفروم
17 knuckle of pork — عَظْم رُسْغ الخنزير واللَحْم المحيط به
18 basket for special offers — سَلَّة العروض الخاصة
19 price list for special offers — قائمة أسعار العروض الخاصة
20 special offer — عَرْض خاص
21 freezer — فريزر
22 pre-packed joints — قطع لَحْم مُغَلَّفَة
23 deep-frozen ready-to-eat meal — وَجْبَة مُجَمَّدة جاهزة للأكل
24 chicken — دَجاجَة
25 canned food — طعام مُعَلَّب
26 can — عِلْبَة
27 canned vegetables — خضروات مُعلبَة
28 canned fish — أسماك مُعَلْبَة
29 salad cream — كريمة سلطة
30 soft drinks — مشروبات خفيفة
31-59 manufacturing of sausages — **تصنيع المقانق**
31-37 butcher's knives — **سكاكين الجزّار**
31 slicer — المِشْرَحة: سِكِّين تقطيع الشرائح
32 knife blade — نَصْل السكِّين
33 saw teeth — أسنان مِنْشارية
34 knife handle — مِقْبَض السكِّين
35 carver (carving knife) — سِكِّين كبيرة لتقطيع اللَحْم إلي شرائح
36 boning knife — سِكِّين إزالة اللَحْم عن العَظْم (سِكِّين التَّشْفِيَة)
37 butcher's knife (butcher knife) — سِكِّين الجَزَّار
38 butcher (master butcher) — الجَزَّار ، القَصَّاب
39 butcher's apron — مريلة الجَزَّار
40 meat-mixing trough — وعاء خلط اللحوم
41 sausage meat — لَحْم المقانق
42 scraper — مِكْحَتَة
43 skimmer — مِكْشَطَة
44 sausage fork — شَوْكة المقانق
45 scalding colander — مِصْفَاة السَّلْق
46 waste bin (*Am.* trash bin) — صفيحة الفضلات
47 cooker, for cooking with steam or hot air — جِهَاز الطبخ، الطَبَّاخ (للطهي بالبخار أو الهواء الساخن)
48 smoke house — بَيْت الدخان
49 sausage filler (sausage stuffer) — جِهَاز حَشْو المقانق
50 feed pipe (supply pipe) — أُنْبُوب الحَشْو
51 containers for vegetables — أوعية للخضروات
52 mincing machine for sausage meat — مَاكِينَة فرم لحوم المقانق
53 mincing machine (meat mincer, mincer, *Am.* meat grinder) — مَاكِينَة فرم، مفرمة اللحوم
54 plates (steel plates) — صفائح معدنية
55 meathook (butcher's hook) — خُطَّاف تعليق اللحوم
56 bone saw — مِنْشار العَظْم
57 chopping board — سَطْح تقطيع اللحوم
58 butcher, cutting meat — جَزَّار يَقْطَع اللحوم
59 piece of meat — قِطْعَة/وَصْلَة لَحْم

97 Bakery — المَخْبَز

1-54 baker's shop — **مَحل الخَبَّاز**
1 shop assistant (*Am.* salesgirl, saleslady) — البائع/البائعة
2 bread (loaf of bread, loaf) — خُبْز (رَغيف خُبْز)
3 crumb — لُبَاب الرَّغيف
4 crust (bread crust) — سَطْح الرَّغيف الخارجي المحمص
5 crust (*Am.* heel) — كعب الرَّغيف
6-12 kinds of bread (breads) — **أنواع الخُبْز**
6 round loaf, a wheat and rye bread — رَغيف مستدير، رَغيف من دقيق القمح أو الشَّيلَم
7 small round loaf — رَغيف صغير مستدير
8 long loaf (bloomer), a wheat and rye bread — رَغيف طويل، رَغيف من دقيق القمح أو الشَّيلَم
9 white loaf — رَغيف أبيض
10 pan loaf, a wholemeal rye bread — رَغيف من دقيق الشَّيلَم الأسمر
11 yeast bread (*Am.* stollen) — خُبْز يدخل في صنعه الخميرة
12 French loaf (baguette, French stick) — خُبْز فَرَنسي
13-16 rolls — **أرغفة الخُبْز الإفرنجي**
13 brown roll — رَغيف إفرنجي أسمر
14 white roll — رَغيف إفرنجي أبيض

15 finger roll	رَغِيف إفرنجي صَغِير
16 rye-bread roll	رَغِيف من دقيق الشَّيلَم
17-47 cakes (confectionery)	**الكَعْك** (الحلْوَى)
17 cream roll	رول الكريمة
18 vol-au-vent, a puff pastry (*Am.* puff paste)	نوع من الفطائر المنتفخة
19 Swiss roll (*Am.* jelly roll)	سويس رول
20 tartlet	تورتة صغيرة
21 cream slice	شريحة من كَعْكَة الكريمة
22-24 flans (*Am.* pies) **and gateaux** (torten)	**الفطائر** (الكعك) **والجاتوه**
22 fruit flan (*kinds:* strawberry flan, cherry flan, gooseberry flan, peach flan, rhubarb flan)	كَعْكَة الفاكهة؛ أنواعها: الفراولة، الكَرَز، الكِشْمِش، الخوخ، الرواند
23 cheesecake	كَعْكَة الجُبْن
24 cream cake (*Am.* cream pie) (*kinds:* buttercream cake, Black Forest gateau)	كَعْكَة الكريمة (أنواعها: كعكة بالزُّبْد، جاتوه بلاك فورست)
25 cake plate	قاعدة الكَعْكَة
26 meringue	كَعْكَة المرنغ
27 cream puff	فطائر الكريمة المنتفخة
28 whipped cream	كريمة مخفوقة
29 doughnut (*Am.* bismarck)	دونت (كَعْكَة مُحلاة مقلية بالدهن)
30 Danish pastry	كَعْكَة الدانيش
31 saltstick (Saltzstange) (*also:* caraway roll, caraway stick)	أصابع مالِحة (ساليزون) (أيضا: أصابع الكَمُّون)
32 croissant (crescent roll, *Am.* crescent)	كرواسون
33 ring cake (gugelhupf)	كَعْكَة جَرَسِيَّة الشكل
34 slab cake with chocolate icing	كَعْكَة مكعبة الشكل مغطاة بالشيكولاته
35 streusel cakes	كعك الإستريوسيل
36 marshmallow	كَعْك المارش مالو
37 coconut macaroon	معكرونة جوز الهند
38 pastry whirl	فطائر حلوة
39 iced bun	فطائر بالزبيب مكْسُوَّة بطبقة من السكر والزُّبْد
40 sweet bread	خُبْز حلو
41 plaited bun (plait)	ضفيرة بالزبيب مكْسُوَّة بطبقة من السكر والزُّبْد
42 Frankfurter garland cake	كَعْكَة إكليل فرانكفورتر
43 slices (*kinds:* streusel slices, sugared slices, plum slices)	شرائح حلوى (الأنواع: شرائح مغطاة بطبقة الاستروِيسل، شرائح مغطاة بالسُّكَّر، شرائح مغطاة بالإجَّاص)
44 pretzel	عقدية: بسكويت مُملَّح صلب
45 wafer (*Am.* waffle)	الويفر (بسكويت رقائقي هشٍّ)
46 tree cake (baumkuchen)	كَعْكَة الشَّجَرَة
47 flan case	عِلْبَة الكَعْكَة

48-50 wrapped bread	**خُبْز مُغَلَّف**
48 wholemeal bread (*also:* wheatgerm bread)	خُبْز أسمر
49 pumpernickel (wholemeal rye bread)	خُبْز الشَّيلَم الأسمر
50 crispbread	خُبْز رقاقي هش
51 gingerbread (*Am.* lebkuchen)	كَعْكَة الزنجبيل
52 flour (*kinds:* wheat flour, rye flour)	دقيق/حنطة؛ أنواعه: قمح، شَيلَم
53 yeast (baker's yeast)	خميرة (خميرة خبيز)
54 rusks (French toast)	بُقسماط، خُبْز مُحَمَّص (توست فرنسي)
55-74 bakery (bakehouse)	**المَخْبَز**
55 kneading machine (dough mixer)	خلاط العجين
56-57 bread unit	**وَحْدَة صناعة الخبز**
56 divider	وَحْدَة تقسيم
57 moulder (*Am.* molder)	وَحْدَة التشكيل
58 premixer	خلاط أوَّلي
59 dough mixer	خلاط العجين
60 workbench	سَطْح العمل
61 roll unit	وَحْدَة إعْداد الأرغفة
62 workbench	سَطْح العمل، طاولة العمل
63 divider and rounder (rounding machine)	مَاكِينَة التقسيم والتقريص
64 crescent-forming machine	مَاكِينَة تشكيل الكرواسون
65 freezers	ثلاجات تجميد
66 oven [for baking with fat]	فُرْن [للخبيز بالدهن]
67-70 confectionery unit	**وَحْدَة صناعة الحلوى**
67 cooling table	طاولة التبريد
68 sink	حَوْض غسيل
69 boiler	مِرْجَل، غلاية
70 whipping unit [with beater]	وَحْدَة خفق البَيْض أو الكريمة (مُزَوَّدة بمضرب)
71 reel oven (oven)	فُرْن
72 fermentation room	حُجْرَة التخمير
73 fermentation trolley	ترولّي التخمير
74 flour silo	صَوْمَعَة الطَحِين/الدقيق

98 Grocer's Shop (*Am.* Grocery Store) — دُكَّان البَقَّال

1-87 grocer's shop (grocer's, delicatessen shop, *Am.* grocery store, delicatessen store), a retail shop (*Am.* retail store)	**دُكَّان البَقَّال** (محل للبيع القَطَّاعِي)
1 window display	واجِهة العَرْض
2 poster (advertisement)	بُوسْتَر (إعلان)
3 cold shelves	أرْفُف المنتجات المُبَرَّدة
4 sausages	نقانق، مقانق
5 cheese	جُبْن
6 roasting chicken (broiler)	دَجَاجَة مُعَدَّة للشواء
7 poulard, a fattened hen	دَجَاجَة مُسَمَّنَة

8-11 baking ingredients	**مكونات الخبز**
8 raisins; *sim.*: sultanas	زَبيب
9 currants	كِشْمِش
10 candied lemon peel	قِشْر ليمون مُسَكَّر
11 candied orange peel	قِشْر برتقال مُسَكَّر
12 computing scale, a rapid scale	ميزان حاسِب
13 shop assistant (*Am.* salesclerk)	بائع/بائعة
14 goods shelves (shelves)	أرْفُف البضائع
15-20 canned food	**أطْعِمَة مُعلبَة**
15 canned milk	لبَن مُعلَّب
16 canned fruit (cans of fruit)	فاكِهة مُعلبَة
17 canned vegetables	خضروات معلبَة
18 fruit juice	عصير فَوَاكه
19 sardines in oil, a can of fish	سَرْدين بالزَيْت، علْبَة سردين
20 canned meat (cans of meat)	لحوم معلبَة
21 margarine	مَرْغَرين
22 butter	زُبْد
23 coconut oil, a vegetable oil	زَيْت جَوْز الهِنْد، زَيْت نباتي
24 oil; *kinds:* salad oil, olive oil, sunflower oil, wheatgerm oil, groundnut oil	زَيْت، أنواعه: زَيْت السلطة، زَيْت زيتُون، زَيْت عبَّاد/دوَّار الشمس، زَيْت أجِنَّة القمح، زَيْت الجَوْز
25 vinegar	خَلّ
26 stock cube	مُكَعبات مَرَق
27 bouillon cube	مُكَعبات مَرَق
28 mustard	زَيْت الخَرْدَل
29 pickled gherkin	خِيار صغير مُخَلَّل
30 soup seasoning	توابل الحَسَاء
31 shop assistant (*Am.* salesgirl, saleslady)	بائع، بائعة
32-34 pastas	**الباستا (المعجنات)**
32 spaghetti	اسباجيتي
33 macaroni	مكرونة
34 noodles	عصَائبية (نودلز)
35-39 cereal products	**منتجات الحبوب**
35 pearl barley	حَبُّ الشَّعير
36 semolina	السيمولينا
37 rolled oats (porridge oats, oats)	شُوفان
38 rice	أُرْز
39 sago	ساغو (نوع من نِشَاء النخيل)
40 salt	مِلْح
41 grocer (*Am.* groceryman), a shopkeeper (tradesman, retailer, *Am.* storekeeper)	البَقَّال (تاجِر، بائع تَجْزِئَة
42 capers	كَبَر مُخَلَّل
43 customer	زبون
44 receipt (sales check)	ايصال استلام نقدية
45 shopping bag	حقيبة التَّسَوُّق
46-49 wrapping material	**مَوَاد اللف/التغليف**
46 wrapping paper	وَرَق تغليف
47 adhesive tape	شَريط لاصِق
48 paper bag	كِيس وَرَقِي
49 cone-shaped paper bag	كِيس وَرَقِي مخروطي الشكل (قُرْطاس)
50 blancmange powder	مَسْحُوق مهلبية
51 whole-fruit jam (preserve)	مَرَبَّى فوَاكِه محفوظة
52 jam	مَرَبَّى
53-55 sugar	**السكر**
53 cube sugar	سُكَّر مُكَعْبات
54 icing sugar (*Am.* confectioner's sugar)	سُكَّر ناعم
55 refined sugar in crystals	سُكَّر مكَرَّر في شكل بلورات
56-59 spirits	**المشروبات الكحولية**
56 whisky (whiskey)	ويسكي
57 rum	رُوم
58 liqueur	شَرَاب مُسْكِر مُعَطَّر
59 brandy (cognac)	براندي (كونياك)
60-64 wine in bottles (bottled wine)	**نَبيذ مُعَبَّأ في زجاجات**
60 white wine	نَبيذ أبْيَض
61 Chianti	كيانتي (نوع من الخَمْر الإيطالي)
62 vermouth	فيرْمُوت (نوع من الخَمْر الأَبْيَض)
63 sparkling wine	نَبيذ فَوَّار
64 red wine	نَبيذ أحمر
65-68 tea, coffee, etc.	**الشَاي، القَهْوَة/البُن، الخ.**
65 coffee (pure coffee)	قَهْوَة (بُن خالص)
66 cocoa	كاكاو
67 coffee	قَهْوَة، بُن
68 tea bag	كيس شاي
69 electric coffee grinder	مِطْحَنَة بُن كهربائية
70 coffee roaster	مِحْمَصَة البُن
71 roasting drum	برْميل التحميص
72 sample scoop	مغرفة أخذ العينات
73 price list	قائمة الأسعار
74 freezer	ثلاجة تجميد (برَّاد)
75-86 confectionery (*Am.* candies)	**الحلويات**
75 sweet (*Am.* candy)	حَلْوَى
76 drops	حبات البونبون
77 toffees	طوفي
78 bar of chocolate	لَوْح شوكولاته
79 chocolate box	صندوق شوكولاته
80 chocolate, a sweet	شوكولاته، نوع من الحَلْوَى
81 nougat	نوغة
82 marzipan	مَرْزِيبَانِيَّة
83 chocolate liqueur	شوكَولاته بها شراب مُسْكِر
84 Turkish delight	حلقوم (مَلْبَن)
85 croquant	حلْوَى الكروكوانت
86 truffle	تُرُوفِل
87 soda water	ماء صُودا

99 Supermarket — سُوبَر مَارْكت (مَتْجَر الخِدْمَة الذَّاتِيَّة)

1-96 supermarket, a self-service food store	**سُوبَر مَارْكت** (مَتْجَر الخِدْمَة الذَّاتِيَّة)
1 shopping trolley	ترولّلي/عَرَبَة التسوق
2 customer	زبون
3 shopping bag	حَقيبة التَّسَوُّق
4 entrance to the sales area	مَدْخَل منطقة المبيعات
5 barrier	حاجز
6 sign (notice) banning dogs	لافتة تَحْظُر دخول الكلاب
7 dogs tied by their leads	كلاب مسلسلة
8 basket	سَلَّة
9 bread and cake counter (bread counter, cake counter)	قِسْم الخُبْز والكَعْك
10 display counter for bread and cakes	كاونتر عَرْض الخُبْز والكَعْك
11 kinds of bread (breads)	أنواع من الخُبْز
12 rolls	أرْغِفَة خُبْز إفرنجي
13 croissants (crescent rolls, *Am.* crescents)	كرواسون
14 round loaf	رغيف مستدير
15 gateau	جاتوه
16 pretzel [made with yeast dough]	عُقَديَّة [مصنوعة من عجينة مُخَمَّرَة]
17 shop assistant (*Am.* salesgirl, saleslady)	بائع، بائعة
18 customer	زبون
19 sign listing goods	لافتة بأسماء المعروضات
20 fruit flan	كَعْك الفاكهة
21 slab cake	كَعْكَة مكعّبة الشَّكْل
22 ring cake	كَعْكَة جَرَسِيَّة الشَّكْل
23 cosmetics gondola, a gondola (sales shelves)	أرْفُف مستحضرات التجميل
24 canopy	مظلة، تَنْدَة
25 hosiery shelf	رَفُّ الجوارب
26 stockings (nylons)	جوارب نسائية
27-35 toiletries (cosmetics)	**مستحضرات التجميل**
27 jar of cream (cream; *kinds:* moisturising cream, day cream, night-care cream, hand cream)	عُلْبَة كريم (كريم؛ الأنواع: كريم ترطيب البشرة، كريم نهار، كريم ليل، كريم لليدين)
28 packet of cotton wool	لُفافة قُطْن ماص
29 talcum powder	بُودْرَة التَّلْك
30 packet of cotton wool balls	عُبْوَة كُرَيَّات من القُطْن الماص
31 toothpaste	معجون أسنان
32 nail varnish (nail polish)	طلاء أظافر
33 shaving cream	كريم حلاقة
34 bath salts	أمْلاح الحَمَّام
35 sanitary articles	أدوات صِحِّيَّة
36-37 pet foods	**أطْعِمَة الحيوانات الأليفَة**
36 complete dog food	غذاء كلاب كامل
37 packet of dog biscuits	عُبْوَة بَسْكُوت كلاب
38 bag of cat litter	عُبْوَة مِهاد من القش للقطط
39 cheese counter	قِسْم الأجْبَان
40 whole cheese	جُبْن كامل الدسم
41 Swiss cheese (Emmental cheese) with holes	جُبْن سويسري ذو ثقوب
42 Edam cheese, a round cheese	جُبْن ايدام، قرص جُبْن مستدير
43 gondola for dairy products	قِسْم منتجات الألبان
44 long-life milk; *also:* pasteurized milk, homogenized milk	لَبَن يبقى طازجا فترة طويلة؛ أيضا: لَبَن مُبَسْتَر ولبن مُعَقَّم
45 plastic milk bag	كيس لَبَن بلاستيكي
46 cream	قِشْدَة
47 butter	زُبْد
48 margarine	مَرْغَرين
49 box of cheeses	صندوق أجْبَان
50 box of eggs	صندوق بَيْض
51 fresh meat counter (meat counter)	قِسْم اللحوم الطازجة
52 ham on the bone	فَخْذ خنزير بالعَظْم
53 meat (meat products)	لحوم (منتجات اللحوم)
54 sausages	نقانق، مقانق
55 ring of pork sausage	حلقة من نقانق الخنزير
56 ring of blood sausage	حلقة من المقانق المُدَمَّاة
57 freezer	ثلاجة تجميد (بَرَّاد)
58-61 frozen food	**أطْعِمَة مُجَمَّدَة**
58 poulard	دَجَاجَة مُسَمَّنَة
59 turkey leg (drumstick)	ورْك ديك رومي
60 boiling fowl	لحم دجاج للسلق
61 frozen vegetables	خضروات مُجَمَّدَة
62 gondola for baking ingredients and cereal products	قِسْم مكونات الخبيز ومنتجات الحبوب
63 wheat flour	دقيق القمح
64 sugar loaf	رغيف سكر
65 packet of noodles	عُبْوَة عَصَائِبِيَّة (نودلز)
66 salad oil	زَيْت السلطة
67 packet of spice	عُبْوَة توابل
68-73 tea, coffee, etc.	**الشاي والقَهْوَة، الخ.**
68 coffee	قَهْوَة (بُن)
69 packet of tea	عُبْوَة شاي
70 instant coffee	قَهْوَة سريعة التحضير
71 drinks gondola	قِسْم المشروبات
72 soft drinks	مشروبات خفيفة
73 can of beer	عُلْبَة جُعَّة
74 bottle of fruit juice	زُجَاجَة عصير فَوَاكِه
75 can of fruit juice	عُلْبَة عصير فواكه
76 bottle of wine	زُجَاجَة نَبِيذ
77 bottle of Chianti	زُجَاجَة كيانتي
78 bottle of champagne	زُجَاجَة شمبانيا
79 emergency exit	مَخْرَج الطوارئ
80 fruit and vegetable counter	قِسْم الفاكِهة والخضروات
81 vegetable basket	سلة الخضروات
82 tomatoes	طماطم
83 cucumbers	خِيَار
84 cauliflower	قنبيط

85 pineapple أناناس
86 apples تفاح
87 pears كمثرى
88 scales for weighing fruit ميزان الفواكه
89 grapes (bunches of grapes) عِنَب (عناقيد عِنَب)
90 bananas موز
91 can عُلْبَة معدنية
92 checkout دَفع الحساب والمغادرة
93 cash register مُسَجِلَة النقد
94 cashier أمين الصندوق
95 chain سلسلة
96 assistant departmental manager مُساعِد مدير المَتْجَر

100 Shoemaker (Bootmaker) الإسْكَافِي

1-68 shoemaker's workshop (bootmaker's workshop) **وَرْشَة صَانِع الأَحْذِيَة، وَرْشَة الإسْكَافِي**
1 finished (repaired) shoes أحْذِيَة تم إصلاحها
2 auto-soling machine مَاكِينَة تركيب النِعَال آليا
3 finishing machine مَاكِينَة التشطيب
4 heel trimmer آلة تشذيب الكَعْب
5 sole trimmer آلة تشذيب النَّعْل
6 scouring wheel عجلة إزالة الشحم/تنظيف
7 naum keag آلية تلميع و صقل سطح النَّعْل والكَعْب قبل التشطيب
8 drive unit (drive wheel) عجلة الإدارة
9 iron مِيْسَم
10 buffing wheel عجلة الصقل
11 polishing brush فُرْشَاة التلميع
12 horsehair brush فُرْشَاة من شعر الخيل
13 extractor grid شبكة آلة الخلع
14 automatic sole press مِكْبَس النِعَال الآلي
15 press attachment ملحق المِكْبَس
16 pad لبادة، حشية
17 press bar قضيب المِكْبَس
18 stretching machine مَاكِينَة المَط/الإطالة
19 width adjustment مِقْبَض ضَبْط العرض
20 length adjustment مِقْبَض ضَبْط الطول
21 stitching machine مَاكِينَة الخياطة
22 power regulator (power control) مُنَظِّم الطاقة الكهربائية
23 foot الطرف السفلي
24 handwheel عجلة يدوية
25 arm ذراع
26 sole stitcher (sole-stitching machine) مَاكِينَة خياطة النِعَال
27 foot bar lever ذراع قضيب الطرف السفلي
28 feed adjustment (feed setting) تعديل الإلقام
29 bobbin (cotton bobbin) بكرة، بوبينة
30 thread guide (yarn guide) دليل الخَيْط
31 sole leather جِلْد النَّعْل
32 [wooden] last قالِب أحْذِيَة [خشبي]
33 workbench طاولة الشغل
34 last قالب أحْذِيَة
35 dye spray رشاش الصبغة
36 shelves for materials أرْفُف المواد
37 shoemaker's hammer مطرقة الإسْكَافي
38 shoemaker's pliers (welt pincers) كَمَّاشَة الإسْكَافي
39 sole-leather shears مِقَصّ جِلْد النِعَال
40 small pincers (nippers) قَرَّاضة صغيرة
41 large pincers (nippers) قَرَّاضة كبيرة
42 upper-leather shears مِقَصّ الجِلْد العلوي
43 scissors مِقَصّ (عادى)
44 revolving punch (rotary punch) خَرَّامَة دَوَّارَة، مِخْرَز دَوَّار
45 punch خَرَّامَة، مِخْرَز
46 punch with handle خَرَّامَة ذات مِقْبَض
47 nail puller كَمَّاشَة المسامير
48 welt cutter سِكِّين النجَاش
49 shoemaker's rasp مِبْرَد أحْذِيَة
50 cobbler's knife (shoemaker's knife) سِكِّين أحْذِيَة
51 skiving knife (skife knife, paring knife) سِكِّين تشريح الجِلْد إلى رقائق (سِكِّين تقشير)
52 toecap remover أداة إزالة غطاء أصابع القدم بالحذاء
53 eyelet, hook, and press-stud setter أداة عمل العراوي وتركيب المشابك وكبس المسامير
54 stand (with iron lasts) حامِل ذو قوالب حديدية
55 width-setting tree قالِب ضَبْط عَرْض الحذاء
56 nail grip أداة إمساك وتثبيت المسامير
57 boot حذاء ذو رقبة
58 toecap قُرْطُوم الحذاء، بُنْطِيلَة
59 counter قطعة جِلْد قاسية داخل مؤخر الحذاء المحيط بالعقب
60 vamp وَجْه الحذاء
61 quarter جانب من أعلى الحذاء
62 hook مِشْبَك
63 eyelet عُرْوَة
64 lace (shoelace, bootlace) رباط الحذاء
65 tongue لِسَان
66 sole نَعْل
67 heel كَعْب
68 shank (waist) بَطْن النَّعْل

101 Shoes (Footwear) الأحْذِيَة

1 winter boot حذَاء شَتوي (ذو رقبة)
2 PVC sole (plastic sole) نَعْل من مادة بي في سي (نَعْل من البلاستيك)
3 high-pile lining بطانة طويلة التيلة
4 nylon نَيْلُون
5 men's boot بوت رجالي (حذَاء ذو رقبة)
6 inside zip (*Am.* zipper) سوستة داخلية
7 men's high leg boot حذَاء رجالي طويل الساق
8 platform sole (platform) نَعْل مرتفع

9	Western boot (cowboy boot)	بوت غربي (حِذَاء رعاة البقر)
10	pony-skin boot	حذَاء من جِلْد الخيل
11	cemented sole	نَعْل مثبت بالحِذَاء بمادة لاصقة
12	ladies' boot	بوت نسائي
13	men's high leg boot	بوت رجالي طويل الساق
14	seamless PVC waterproof wellington boot	بوت ولنغتون مقاوم للماء مصنوع من مادة بي في سي
15	natural-colour (*Am.* natural-color) sole	نَعْل طبيعي اللون
16	toecap	قُرْطُوم الحِذَاء
17	tricot lining (knitwear lining)	بطانة من التريكو
18	hiking boot	حذَاء (بوت) التنزه
19	grip sole	نَعْل كريب
20	padded collar	ياقة مُبَطَّنَة
21	tie fastening (lace fastening)	رباط الحذَاء
22	open-toe mule	شِبْشِب بدون كَعْب مفتوح من الأمام
23	terry upper	فَرْعَة شِبْشِب مصنوعة من نسيج وَبَري
24	polo outsole	نَعْل خارجي من الوَبَر
25	mule	شِبْشِب بدون كَعْب، مَنْتُوفلي
26	corduroy upper	فَرْعَة مصنوعة من القطيفة المُضَلَّعَة
27	evening sandal (sandal court shoe)	صَنْدَل مسائي، حِذَاء خفيف
28	high heel (stiletto heel)	كَعْب عال
29	court shoe (*Am.* pump)	حذَاء خفيف بدون رباط
30	moccasin	حذَاء الموكاسين
31	shoe, a tie shoe (laced shoe, Oxford shoe, *Am.* Oxford)	حذَاء برباط
32	tongue	لسَان
33	high-heeled shoe (shoe with raised heel)	حذَاء ذو كَعْب مرتفع
34	casual	حذَاء خفيف (كاجوال)
35	trainer (training shoe)	حذَاء رياضي للتدريب
36	tennis shoe	حذَاء رياضي خفيف للمشي
37	counter (stiffening)	قطعة جلد قاسية لتقوية الحذاء عند العقب
38	natural-colour (*Am.* natural-color) rubber sole	نَعْل مطاطي طبيعي اللون
39	heavy-duty boot (*Am.* stogy, stogie)	بوت شديد التحمل
40	toecap	قُرْطُوم الحِذَاء
41	slipper	خُفّ ، شِبْشِب
42	woollen (*Am.* woolen) slip sock	حذَاء خفيف من الصوف
43	knit stitch (knit)	غرزة حبك بالصنارة
44	clog	قبقاب، حذاء خشبي
45	wooden sole	نَعْل خشبي
46	soft-leather upper	فَرْعَة من الجِلْد الطَّري
47	sabot	حذَاء "سابوه"
48	toe post sandal	صَنْدَل ذو فاصل للإصبع الكبير
49	ladies' sandal	صَنْدَل نسائي
50	surgical footbed (sock)	حشية لإراحة القدم، فَرْشَة
51	sandal	صَنْدَل
52	shoe buckle (buckle)	إبزيم الحذَاء
53	sling-back court shoe (*Am.* sling pump)	حذَاء خفيف مقفول من الأمام وبشريط من الخلف
54	fabric court shoe	حذَاء خفيف من القماش
55	wedge heel	كَعْب إسفيني
56	baby's first walking boot	حِذَاء أطفال برقبة

102 Needlework أشْغَال الإبْرَة

1	backstitch seam	خياطة بغُرْزَة خلفية
2	chain stitch	غُرْزَة السلسلة
3	ornamental stitch	غُرْزَة زخرفية
4	stem stitch	غُرْزَة ساقية
5	cross stitch	غُرْزَة تصالبية (رِجْل غراب)
6	buttonhole stitch (button stitch)	غُرْزَة عراوي
7	fishbone stitch	غُرْزَة عَظْم السمكة
8	overcast stitch	غُرْزَة راكِبة (غُرْزَة اوفر لوك)
9	herringbone stitch (Russian stitch, Russian cross stitch)	غُرْزَة عظم سمكة الرِّنْكَة (غُرْزَة الصليب الروسي)
10	satin stitch (flat stitch)	غُرْزَة ستانية
11	eyelet embroidery (broderie anglaise)	رُكَامة
12	stiletto	ثقَّابة التَطْريز
13	French knot (French dot, knotted stitch, twisted knot stitch)	غُرْزَة فرنسية (غُرْزَة عقدية)
14	hem stitch work	تَطْريز الكُفَّة
15	tulle work (tulle lace)	زَخْرَفَة التُول
16	tulle background (net background)	خلفية التُول
17	darning stitch	غُرْزَة رَفْي
18	pillow lace (bobbin lace, bone lace); *kinds:* Valenciennes, Brussels lace	دانتيلا هونيتون
19	tatting	تخريم ذو عُقَد
20	tatting shuttle (shuttle)	مكوك حياكة تخريم ذو عُقَد
21	knotted work (macramé)	مكْرَميّة
22	filet (netting)	غُرْزَة الشَّبكة
23	netting loop	انشوطة غُرْزَة الشَّبكة
24	netting thread	خَيْط الشَّبكة
25	mesh pin (mesh gauge)	قضيب الغَزْل
26	netting needle	إبْرَة غَزْل الشَّبكة
27	open work	تَطْريز مُفَرَّغ (أجور)
28	gimping (hairpin work)	التَطْريز بدبوس الشعر
29	gimping needle (hairpin)	إبْرَة التَطْريز (دبوس الشعر)
30	needlepoint lace (point lace, needlepoint); kinds: reticella lace, Alençon lace; *sim.:* with metal thread: fili-	دانتيلا ، تَطْريز إبري؛ مثلها: تَثْقيب/تَخْريم تَزْييني

gree work	
31 braid embroidery (braid work)	كَنار تَطْرِيز

103 Dressmaker — الخَيَّاط

1-27 dressmaker's workroom	**مَشْغَل الخَيَّاط**
1 dressmaker	خَيَّاط
2 tape measure (measuring tape), a metre (*Am.* meter) tape measure	مازورة (شريط قياس)
3 cutting shears	مقَصّ القماش
4 cutting table	طاولة (بنك) قَصّ القماش
5 model dress	ثوب يستخدم كموديل
6 dressmaker's model (dressmaker's dummy, dress form)	مانيكان الخَيَّاط (دُمْيَة الخَيَّاط)
7 model coat	معْطَف معروض على المانيكان
8 sewing machine	مَاكِينَة الخِيَاطة
9 drive motor	موتور تشغيل المَاكِينَة
10 drive belt	سَيْر الإدارة
11 treadle	دَوَّاسة المَاكِينَة
12 sewing machine cotton (sewing machine thread) [on bobbin]	خَيْط مَاكِينَة الخياطة [على بوبينة]
13 cutting template	مسطرة الخَيَّاط
14 seam binding	شريط تنظيف، كُفَّة الدَّرْز
15 button box	عُلْبَة الأَزْرَار
16 remnant	قُصَاصة قماش
17 movable clothes rack	شَمَّاعة ملابس متحركة
18 hand-iron press	مِكْبَس يَدَوِي للكَيّ بالبخار
19 presser (ironer)	المكْوَجي، الكَوَّاء
20 steam iron	مِكْوَاة بالبخار
21 water feed pipe	خرطوم الإمداد بالماء
22 water container	حاوية الماء
23 adjustable-tilt ironing surface	سطح كي قابل للإمالة
24 lift device for the iron	جِهَاز رفع المِكْوَاة
25 steam extractor	جِهَاز نَفْث البخار
26 foot switch controlling steam extraction	مِفْتَاح يُشغَّل بالقَدَم للتحكم في نفث البخار
27 pressed non-woven woollen (*Am.* woolen) fabric	نسيج صوفي مكْوِيّ لم يُحاك بعد

104 Tailor — التَّرْزي

1-32 tailor's workroom	**مَشْغَل التَّرْزي**
1 triple mirror	مرآة ثلاثية الأَوْجُه
2 lengths of material	أطوال القماش
3 suiting	قماش البِدَل
4 fashion journal (fashion magazine)	مجلة أزياء
5 ashtray	مِنْفَضة رماد السجائر
6 fashion catalogue	كتالوج أزياء
7 workbench	طاولة (بنك) الشغل
8 wall shelves (wall shelf unit)	أرْفُف حائطية
9 cotton reel	بكَرَة خَيْط
10 small reels of sewing silk	بكرات صغيرة من خَيْط حريري للحياكة
11 hand shears	مقَصّ يدوي
12 combined electric and treadle sewing machine	مَاكِينَة خياطة تعمل بموتور ودَوَّاسة
13 treadle	دَوَّاسة مَاكِينَة الخياطة
14 dress guard	وقاء الثوب من عجلة المَاكِينَة
15 band wheel	عجلة بسير
16 bobbin thread	خَيْط ملفوف على بكرة المَاكِينَة
17 sewing machine table	طاولة(سطح) مَاكِينَة الخياطة
18 sewing machine drawer	درج مَاكِينَة الخياطة
19 seam binding	شريط تنظيف، كُفَّة الدَّرْز
20 pincushion	وِسادة الدبابيس
21 marking out	تعْليم القماش بالطباشير
22 tailor	تَرْزي
23 shaping pad	وِسادة التشكيل
24 tailor's chalk (French chalk)	طباشير التَّرْزِي
25 workpiece	قطعة الشغل
26 steam press (steam pressing unit)	مِكْبَس الكَيّ بالبخار
27 swivel arm	ذراع دَوَّار
28 pressing cushion (pressing pad)	وِسادة الكَيّ
29 iron	مِكْوَاة
30 hand-ironing pad	وِسَادة الكَيّ اليَدَوِي (بدون طاولة)
31 clothes brush	فُرْشَاة ملابس
32 pressing cloth	قماش الكَيّ (فُودْرَة)

105 Ladies' Hairdresser — مُصَفِّف شَعْر السَّيدات

1-39 ladies' hairdressing salon and beauty salon (*Am.* beauty parlor, beauty shop)	**صالون تصفيف شَعْر السيدات وصالون التجميل**
1-16 hairdresser's tools	**أدوات مُصَفِّف الشَّعْر**
1 bowl containing bleach	زِبْدِيَّة تحتوي على مادة التبييض/ التشقير
2 detangling brush	فُرْشَاة فَرْد الشَّعْر المتشابك
3 bleach tube	أنْبُوب مادة التبييض
4 curler [used in dyeing]	أداة لف الشَّعْر [تستخدم في صباغة الشَّعْر]
5 curling tongs (curling iron)	مكواة تجعيد الشَّعْر
6 comb (back comb, side comb)	مُشْط
7 haircutting scissors	مقَصّ تقصير الشَّعْر
8 thinning scissors (*Am.* thinning shears)	مقَصّ تخفيف الشَّعْر
9 thinning razor	شفْرَة تخفيف الشَّعْر
10 hairbrush	فُرْشَاة شَعْر
11 hair clip	دبوس شَعْر
12 roller	رول لف الشَّعْر
13 curl brush	فُرْشَاة تجعيد الشَّعْر
14 curl clip	دبوس تجعيد الشَّعْر

15 dressing comb — مُشْط تصفيف الشَّعْر
16 stiff-bristle brush — فُرْشَاة الشَّعْر الخشن
17 adjustable hairdresser's chair — كُرْسِيّ مُصَفِّف الشَّعْر القابل للتعديل
18 footrest — مِسْنَد القدمين
19 dressing table — المِزْيَنَة ، منضدة التواليت
20 salon mirror (mirror) — مِرْآة الصالون
21 electric clippers — مَاكِينَة قص الشَّعْر الكهربائية
22 warm-air comb — مُشْط الهواء الساخن
23 hand mirror (hand glass) — مرآة يدوية
24 hairspray (hair-fixing spray) — مِرَشَّة رَذَاذ تثبيت تسريحة الشَّعْر
25 drier, a swivel-mounted drier — مُجَفِّف الشَّعْر (مثبت على مِحْوَر دَوَرَاني)
26 swivel arm of the drier — ذراع دوار يحمل المُجَفِّف
27 round base — قاعدة مستديرة
28 shampoo unit — وَحْدَة غسيل الشَّعْر بالشامبو
29 shampoo basin — حَوْض غسيل الشَّعْر بالشامبو
30 hand spray (shampoo spray) — رشَّاش يدوي (للشامبو)
31 service tray — صينية الأدوات
32 shampoo bottle — قنِّينَة الشامبو
33 hair drier (hand hair drier, hand-held hair drier) — مُجَفِّف الشَّعْر (سشوار)
34 cape (gown) — مريلة، غطاء
35 hairdresser — مُصَفِّفَة الشَّعْر
36 perfume bottle — قنِّينَة عِطْر
37 bottle of toilet water — قنِّينَة ماء تواليت
38 wig — شَعْر مُسْتَعَار (باروكة)
39 wig block — حامِل الباروكة

106 Men's Hairdresser (Barber) — صَالُون حلاقَة للرِّجَال (الحلاق)

1-42 men's salon (men's hairdressing salon, (barber's shop, *Am.* barbershop) — **صالون حلاقة للرجال، صالون مُصَفِّف شَعْر الرِّجال، حلاق الرِّجال**
1 hairdresser (barber) — مُصَفِّف شَعْر (حلاق)
2 overalls (hairdresser's overalls) — مِرْيَلَة مُصَفِّف الشَّعْر
3 hairstyle (haircut) — قصَّة الشَّعْر
4 cape (gown) — مِرْيَلَة (عبَاءَة)
5 paper towel — مِنْشَفَة ورقية
6 salon mirror (mirror) — مِرْآة الصالون
7 hand mirror (hand glass) — مِرْآة يدوية
8 light — مصباح إضاءة
9 toilet water — ماء تواليت
10 hair tonic — مُقَوٍ للشَّعْر
11 shampoo unit — وَحْدَة غسيل الشَّعْر بالشامبو
12 shampoo basin — حَوْض غسيل الشَّعْر بالشامبو
13 hand spray (shampoo spray) — رشَّاش يدوي (للشامبو)
14 mixer tap (*Am.* mixing faucet) — خلاط الماء الساخن والبارد
15 sockets, e.g. for hair drier — قابس كهربي (لمُجَفِّف الشَّعْر مثلاً)
16 adjustable hairdresser's chair (barber's chair) — كُرْسِيّ مُصَفِّف الشَّعْر القابل للتعديل
17 height-adjuster bar (height adjuster) — قضيب تعديل ارتفاع الكُرْسِيّ
18 armrest — مِسْنَد الذراع
19 footrest — مِسْنَد القدمين
20 shampoo — شامبو
21 perfume spray — مِرَشَّة العطْر
22 hair drier (hand hair drier, hand-held hair drier) — مُجَفِّف الشَّعْر ، مُجَفِّف شَعْر يدوى (سشوار)
23 setting lotion in a spray can — غَسُول تثبيت الشَّعْر في مِرَشَّة
24 hand towels for drying hair — مَنَاشِف يدوية لتجفيف الشَّعْر
25 towels for face compresses — مَنَاشِف تستخدم ككمادات للوَجْه
26 crimping iron — مِكْوَاة الشَّعْر (للتجعيد أو التمويج)
27 neck brush — فُرْشَاة إزالة الشَّعْر المحلوق من على الرقبة
28 dressing comb — مُشْط تصفيف الشَّعْر
29 warm-air comb — مُشْط الهواء الساخن
30 warm-air brush — فراشة الهواء الساخن
31 curling tongs (hair curler, curling iron) — مِكْوَاة الشَّعْر (للتجعيد)
32 electric clippers — مَاكِينَة قص الشَّعْر الكهربائية
33 thinning scissors (*Am.* thinning shears) — مِقَص تخفيف الشَّعْر
34 haircutting scissors; *sim.:* styling scissors — مِقَص تقصير الشَّعْر
35 scissor-blade — نصل المِقَص
36 pivot — مِحْوَر المِقَص
37 handle — مِقْبَض المِقَص
38 open razor (straight razor) — شِفْرَة حلاقة مفتوحة
39 razor handle — مِقْبَض شِفْرَة الحلاقة
40 edge (cutting edge, razor's edge, razor's cutting edge) — حافة حادة
41 thinning razor — شِفْرَة تخفيف الشَّعْر
42 diploma — دبلوم، شهادة

107 Tobacco and Smoking Requisites — التَّبْغ ولوَازِم التَّدْخِين

1 cigar box — صندوق السيجار/السيكار
2 cigar; *kinds:* Havana cigar (Havana), Brazilian cigar, Sumatra cigar — سيجار ؛ أنواعه: سيجار هافاني، سيجار برازيلي، سيجار سُومَطْرِي
3 cigarillo — سيجارِيلُو (نوع من السيجار)
4 cheroot — شِيرُوت (سيجار مفتوح الطرفين)

5 wrapper لُفافة
6 binder غلاف
7 filler حَشْوَة
8 cigar case عُلْبَة سيجار
9 cigar cutter أداة قطع طرف لُفافة السيجار من الخلف
10 cigarette case عُلْبَة سجائر
11 cigarette packet (*Am.* pack) عُلْبَة سجائر (من الكرتون)
12 cigarette, a filter-tipped cigarette سيجارة (بفم فلتر)
13 cigarette tip; *kinds:* cork tip, gold tip فَمُ السيجارة؛ أنواعه: فِلِّيني ومُذَهَّب
14 Russian cigarette سيجارة روسي
15 cigarette roller مَاكِينَة لف السجائر
16 cigarette holder مِبْسَم سيجارة
17 packet of cigarette papers لفافة ورق سجائر
18 pigtail (twist of tobacco) تَبْغ مَجْدُول في شكل لفافة
19 chewing tobacco; *a piece*: plug (quid, chew) تَبْغ للمَضْغ؛ القطعة: مُضْغَة
20 snuff box, containing snuff صندوق سَعُوط وبه نَشُوق
21 matchbox عُلْبَة كبريت/ثقاب
22 match عود ثِقاب
23 head (match head) رأس العود
24 striking surface سطح الإشْعال (شَطَّاطة)
25 packet of tobacco; *kinds:* fine cut, shag, navy plug عُلْبَة تَبْغ؛ أنواعه : قَطْع فاخر، مفروم، قُرْص مضغوط
26 revenue stamp طابع تَمْغَة
27 petrol cigarette lighter (petrol lighter) قدَّاحة/ولاعة سجائر تعمل بالبنزين
28 flint حَجَر القدَّاحة/الولاعة
29 wick فتيل
30 gas cigarette lighter (gas lighter), a disposable lighter قدَّاحة/ولاعة سجائر تعمل بالغاز
31 flame regulator مُنَظِّم حَجْم اللهب
32 chibonk (chibonque) الشُّبُق، غَلْيُون تُرْكِي
33 short pipe غَلْيُون قصير
34 clay pipe (Dutch pipe) غَلْيُون من الصلصال (غَلْيُون هولندي)
35 long pipe غَلْيُون طويل
36 pipe bowl (bowl) رأس/دَوَايَة الغَلْيُون
37 bowl lid غِطَاء الدَّوَايَة
38 pipe stem (stem) سَاق/أُنْبُوب الغَلْيُون
39 briar pipe غَلْيُون من جذر الخَلَنْج الشجري
40 mouthpiece مِبْسَم الغَلْيُون
41 sand-blast finished or polished briar grain غَلْيُون مصقول مصنوع من جذر الخَلَنْج الشَّجَري
42 hookah (narghile, narghileh), a water pipe شيشة، نَرْجِيلة
43 tobacco pouch كيس التَّبْغ
44 smoker's companion عُدَّة المُدَخِّن
45 pipe scraper أداة كشط لتنظيف الغَلْيُون
46 pipe cleaner أداة تنظيف لتسليك الغَلْيُون
47 tobacco presser أداة كَبْس التَّبْغ
48 pipe cleaner أداة تنظيف الغَلْيُون

108 Goldsmith, Silversmith الصَّائغ (صَائِغ الذَّهَب والفضَّة)

1 wire and sheet roller مَاكِينَة لَف السلك والصفائح
2 drawbench (drawing bench) طَاوِلَة الرَّسْم
3 wire (gold or silver wire) سِلْك (سِلْك ذهب أو فضة)
4 archimedes drill (drill) مِثْقَاب أرخميدي
5 crossbar عارضة المثقاب
6 suspended (pendant) electric drilling machine آلة ثَقب كهربائية مُعلَّقَة
7 spherical cutter (cherry) قاطع كُرَوي
8 melting pot بَوْتَقة الانصهار
9 fireclay top غِطَاء من الطين الحراري
10 graphite crucible بَوْتَقة من الغرافيت
11 crucible tongs مِلْقَط البَوْتَقة
12 piercing saw (jig saw) مِنْشَار أرْكِتّ
13 piercing saw blade نصل مِنْشَار الأرْكِتّ
14 soldering gun مُسَدَّس لحام
15 thread tapper أداة حز اللوالب
16 blast burner (blast lamp) for soldering مَوْقِد لحام
17 goldsmith صائغ
18 swage block زَهْرة طرق
19 punch سُنْبُك
20 workbench (bench) طَاوِلَة الشغل
21 bench apron غِطَاء واق للطَاوِلَة
22 needle file مِبْرَد إبري
23 metal shears مِقص معادن
24 wedding ring sizing machine مَاكِينَة ضبط مقاسات خاتم الزواج
25 ring gauge (*Am.* gage) مقياس الخواتم
26 ring-rounding tool أداة تدوير الخواتم
27 ring gauge (*Am.* gage) مقياس الخواتم
28 steel set-square مثلث رَسْم معدني قائم الزاوية
29 (circular) leather pad وِسَادة جِلْدِيَّة (دائرية)
30 box of punches صندوق السنابك
31 punch سُنْبُك
32 magnet مغنطيس
33 bench brush فُرْشَاة طَاوِلَة الشغل
34 engraving ball (joint vice, clamp) كرة النقش لحفر الكليشيه (قامطَة مفصلية)
35 gold and silver balance (assay balance), a precision balance ميزان الذهب والفضة، ميزان حسَّاس
36 soldering flux (flux) صَهُور لحام
37 charcoal block قطعة فحم نباتي للحام
38 stick of solder سيخ لحام
39 soldering borax بَوْرَق لحام
40 shaping hammer مِطْرَقة تشكيل
41 chasing (enchasing) hammer مِطْرَقة ترصيع وزخرفة
42 polishing and burnishing machine مَاكِينَة صقل وتلميع
43 dust exhauster (vacuum جِهَاز طرد الأتربة

cleaner)	
44 polishing wheel	عَجلَة الصقل
45 dust collector (dust catcher)	حاجِز الأتربة
46 buffing machine	مَاكِينَة تلميع
47 round file	مِبْرَد دائرى المَقْطَع
48 bloodstone (haematite, hematite)	حَجَر الدَّم (هيماتيت)
49 flat file	مِبْرَد مسطح
50 file handle	مِقْبَض المِبْرَد
51 polishing iron (burnisher)	قضيب تلميع (مِصْقَلَة)

109 Watchmaker, Clockmaker — السَّاعَاتي

1 watchmaker; *also:* clockmaker	ساعاتي
2 workbench	طَاولَة الشغل
3 armrest	مِسْنَد للذراع
4 oiler	مِزْيَتة
5 oil stand	حامِل الزيت
6 set of screwdrivers	طاقم مفكات
7 clockmaker's anvil	سِنْدَان الساعاتي
8 broach, a reamer	مِثْقَاب، مِسْحَل، مُوَسِّع ثقوب
9 spring pin tool	أداة تركيب ونزع المسامير المزودة بنابض
10 hand-removing tool	أداة فَصْل عقارب السَّاعَة
11 watchglass-fitting tool	أداة تركيب زجاجة السَّاعَة
12 workbench lamp, a multi-purpose lamp	مصباح طَاولَة الشغل، مصباح متعدِد الأغراض
13 multi-purpose motor	موتور متعدد الأغراض
14 tweezers	ملقاط
15 polishing machine attachments	ملحقات مَاكِينَة الصقل والتلميع
16 pin vice (pin holder)	ماسك المسامير
17 burnisher, for burnishing, polishing, and shortening of spindles	مَاكِينَة صقل وتلميع وتقصير المَحَاوِر
18 dust brush	فُرْشَاة تنظيف التراب
19 cutter for metal watch straps	أداة قَطْع سُوَار السَّاعَة المعدني
20 precision bench lathe (watchmaker's lathe)	مِخْرَطة دقيقة (مِخْرَطة الساعاتي)
21 drive-belt gear	تُرْس يعمل بسير
22 workshop trolley for spare parts	تروللى قطع الغيار بالوَرْشَة
23 ultrasonic cleaner	جِهَاز تنظيف بالاهتزازات فوق الصوتية
24 rotating watch-testing machine for automatic watches	مَاكِينَة دَوَّارة لاختبار الساعات الآلية
25 watch-timing machine for electronic components	مَاكِينَة توقيت الساعات الخاصة بالأجزاء الإلكترونية
26 testing device for waterproof watches	جِهَاز اختبار الساعات المقاومة للماء
27 electronic timing machine	مَاكِينَة توقيت إلكترونية
28 vice (*Am.* vise)	مِلْزَمة
29 watchglass-fitting tool for armoured (*Am.* armored) glasses	مَاكِينَة تركيب زجاجة السَّاعَة المُدَرَّعة
30 [automatic] cleaning machine for conventional cleaning	مَاكِينَة تنظيف آليَّة للتنظيف العادي
31 cuckoo clock (Black Forest clock)	سَاعَة مُغَرِّدة
32 wall clock (regulator)	سَاعَة حائط
33 compensation pendulum	بندول السَّاعَة
34 kitchen clock	سَاعَة المطبخ
35 timer	جِهَاز توقيت

110 Clocks and Watches — السَّاعَات

1 electronic wristwatch	سَاعَة يد إلكترونية
2 digital display (a light-emitting diode (LED) display; *also:* a liquid crystal display, LCD)	شَاشَة عَرْض رَقَمِية؛ أيضاً شاشة عرض بلوري سائل
3 hour and minute button (on 6, also for setting the analogue (*Am.* analog) display)	زِرّ ضبط الساعات والدقائق (في رقم 6 يُسْتَخْدَم أيضا لضبط شاشة العرض التماثلية)
4 date and second button	زِرّ ضبط التاريخ والثواني
5 strap (watch strap)	طَوق/سوار السَّاعَة
6 multifunction electronic watch	سَاعَة إلكترونية متعددة الاستخدامات
7 analogue (*Am.* analog) display	شاشة عرض تماثلية
8 alarm button	زِرّ المنبه
9 stopwatch button	زِرّ سَاعَة الإيقاف
10 rotating bezel (time-lapse indicator ring)	قُرْص دَوَّار (قُرْص تحديد الزمن المنقضي)
11 calendar clock (alarm clock)	سَاعَة بنتيجة (سَاعَة بِجَرس منبه)
12 digital display with flip-over numerals	شاشة عَرْض رقمي بها أرقام قلابة
13 alarm indicator	مؤشِّر المنبه
14 stop button	زِرّ إيقاف جرس المنبه
15 forward and backward wind knob	ذِراع التقديم والتأخير
16 grandfather clock	سَاعَة قائمة
17 face	وَجْه السَّاعَة
18 clock case	صندوق السَّاعَة
19 pendulum	بندول السَّاعَة
20 striking weight	ثِقْل دَقَّات السَّاعَة
21 time weight	ثِقْل الوقت
22 sundial	المِزْوَلَة، سَاعَة شمسية
23 hourglass (egg timer)	سَاعَة رَمْلِيَّة
24-35 components of an automatic watch (automatic wristwatch, self-winding watch)	**مكَوِّنات سَاعَة يد آلية**
24 weight (rotor)	ثِقْل (رقَّاص)
25 stone (jewel, jewelled bearing) a synthetic	حجر كريم، ياقوت صناعي

ruby	
26 click	سقاطة
27 click wheel	تُرْس السقاطة
28 clockwork (clockwork mechanism)	آلِيَّة السَّاعَة
29 bottom train plate	اللَوْحَة السفلية لتثبيْت التروس
30 spring barrel	تُرْس زنبركي
31 balance wheel	تُرْس موازنة
32 escape wheel	تُرْس الانفلات المنتظم
33 crown wheel	تُرْس إبزيم ملء السَّاعَة
34 winding crown	إبزيم ملء السَّاعَة
35 drive mechanism	آلِيَّة الدفع/الإدارة
36 principle of the electronic quartz watch	قاعدة سَاعَة الكوارتز الإلكترونية
37 quartz	بلورة الكوارتز
38 power source (a button cell)	مَصْدَر طاقة (بطارية جافة)
39 hour hand	عقْرَب الساعات
40 minute hand	عقْرَب الدقائق
41 wheels	تروس
42 stepping motor (stepper motor)	موتور التَّدْرِيج
43 frequency divider (integrated circuit)	مُقَسِّم التردد (دائرة متكاملة)
44 decoder	ديكودر (جِهَاز فك الرموز)
111 Optician	**أخصَائي البَصَرِيَّات، النَّظَّارَاتي**
1-19 sales premises	**محل البيع**
1-4 spectacle fitting	**تَجْرِبة الإطارات لاختيار النَّظَّارة**
1 optician	أخصَائي البَصَرِيَّات، النَّظَّارَاتي
2 customer	زبون
3 trial frame	إطار التجريب
4 mirror	مِرْآة
5 stand with spectacle frames (display of frames, range of spectacles)	حامِل عرض إطارات النَّظَّارَات
6 sunglasses (sun spectacles)	نَظَّارَات شَمْسِيَّة
7 metal frame	إطار معدني (شَنْبَر معدني)
8 tortoiseshell frame (shell frame)	إطار /شَنْبَر ذَبْلي (بَاغَة)
9 spectacles (glasses)	عُوَيْنَات (نَظَّارَات)
10-14 spectacle frame	**إطار/شَنْبَر النَّظَّارَة**
10 fitting (mount) of the frame	مُثَبِّت إطار النَّظَّارَة
11 bridge	جسر الإطار (كوبري الإطار)
12 pad bridge	وِسَادة قَصَبَة الأنف
13 side	ذِرَاع النَّظَّارَة
14 side joint	مفصل ذراع النَّظَّارَة
15 spectacle lens, a bifocal lens	عَدَسَة النَّظَّارَة، عَدَسَة ازدواجية البؤرة
16 hand mirror (hand glass)	مِرْآة يدوية
17 binoculars	مِنْظَار ذو عَيْنِيَّتَيْن
18 monocular telescope (tube)	تليسكوب وحيد العَيْنِيَّة
19 microscope	ميكروسكوب، مِجْهَر
20-47 optician's workshop	**وَرْشَة النَّظَّارَاتي**
20 workbench	طَاوِلَة الشغل
21 universal centring (centering) apparatus	جِهَاز تحديد المركز عام الأغراض
22 centring (centering) suction holder	حامِل شفاط تحديد المركز
23 sucker	شَفَّاط
24 edging machine	مَاكِينَة تَحْفِيف
25 formers for the lens edging machine	قوالب التشكيل الخاصة بمَاكِينَة تحفيف العدسات
26 inserted former	قالب تشكيل مُرَكَّب بالمَاكِينَة
27 rotating printer	طابعة دَوَّارة
28 abrasive wheel combination	عَجَلَة التجليخ
29 control unit	وَحْدَة التحكم
30 machine part	جزء المَاكِينَة
31 cooling water pipe	أنْبُوب ماء التبريد
32 cleaning fluid	مَحْلُول التنظيف
33 focimeter (vertex refractionometer)	مقياس الضبط البُؤَرِي
34 metal-blocking device	جِهَاز قولبة معدنية
35 abrasive wheel combination and forms of edging	مجموعة عَجَلَة التجليخ وفورمات ضبط الحواف
36 roughing wheel for preliminary surfacing	عَجَلَة تخشين للتسوية الأولية
37 fining lap for positive and negative lens surfaces	المِصْقَلَة الدقيقة لأسطح العدسات الموجبة والسالبة
38 fining lap for special and flat lenses	المِصْقَلَة الدقيقة للعدسات الخَاصة والمستوية
39 plano-concave lens with a flat surface	عَدَسَة مُقَعَّرَة مستوية ذات سطح مستو
40 plano-concave lens with a special surface	عَدَسَة مُقَعَّرَة مستوية ذات سطح خاص
41 concave and convex lens with a special surface	عَدَسَة مُقَعَّرَة ومُحَدَّبَة ذات سطح خاص
42 convex and concave lens with a special surface	عَدَسَة مُحَدَّبَة ومُقَعَّرَة ذات سطح خاص
43 ophthalmic test stand	جِهَاز فحص العين
44 phoropter with ophthalmometer and optometer (refractometer)	فروبتر مع جِهَاز فحص قاع العين (مِكْشَاف) وجِهَاز قياس مدى الإبصار (مِبْصَار)
45 trial lens case	حقيبة عدسات التجريب
46 collimator	مُوَجِّه الأشعة، المُسَدِّدَة
47 acuity projector	بروجكتور حِدَّة الرؤية
112 Optical Instruments (I)	**الآلات البَصَرِيَّة (1)**
1 laboratory and research	ميكروسكوب المُخْتَبَر

microscope, *Leitz system* — والأبحاث، "نظام لايتز"

2 stand — حامِل

3 base — قاعدة

4 coarse adjustment — مِقْبَض الضَّبْط التقريبي

5 fine adjustment — مِقْبَض الضَّبْط الدقيق

6 illumination beam path (illumination path) — مَسَار الحِزْمَة الضوئية

7 illumination optics — بصريات ضوئية

8 condenser — مُكَثِّف

9 microscope (microscopic, object) stage — مِنَصَّة الميكروسكوب

10 mechanical stage — مِنَصَّة ميكانيكية

11 objective turret (revolving nosepiece) — بُرْج جسمية المِجْهَر (بُرْج دَوَّار متعدد العدسات لفحص العينة المِجْهَرِيَّة)

12 binocular head — رأس ذات عَيْنِيَّتَيْن

13 beam-splitting prisms — مناشير تفريق أشعة الحِزْمَة الضوئية

14 transmitted-light microscope with camera and polarizer, *Zeiss system* — مِجْهَر/ميكروسكوب الضَّوْء النافذ مزود بكاميرا ومُسْتَقْطِب (نظام "زايس")

15 stage base — قاعدة المِنَصَّة

16 aperture-stop slide — شريحة منزلقة ذات ثقوب

17 universal stage — مِنَصَّة جامعة/متعددة الأغراض

18 lens panel — لَوْحَة العدسات

19 polarizing filter — مُرَشِّح استقطابي

20 camera — كاميرا

21 focusing screen — شاشة التركيز البؤري

22 discussion tube arrangement — ترتيبة صِمَام الفحص

23 wide-field metallurgical microscope, a reflected- light microscope (microscope for reflected light) — مِجْهَر معدني واسع الحقل، مِجْهَر الضَّوْء المنعكس

24 matt screen (ground glass screen, projection screen) — حاجز مطفأ اللمعة (حاجز من الزجاج المصنفر)

25 large-format camera — كاميرا ضخمة البَيَان

26 miniature camera — كاميرا مصغَّرة

27 base plate — لَوْح القاعدة

28 lamphouse — بَيْت المصابيح

29 mechanical stage — مِنَصَّة ميكانيكية

30 objective turret (revolving nosepiece) — بُرْج جسمية المِجْهَر (بُرْج دَوَّار متعدد العدسات لفحص العينة المِجْهَرِيَّة)

31 surgical microscope — مِجْهَر جراحي

32 pillar stand — حامِل قائم

33 field illumination — إضاءة المجال

34 photomicroscope — مِجْهَر تصويري

35 miniature film cassette — كاسِيت فيلم صغير

36 photomicrographic camera attachment for large-format or television camera — وَصْلَة كاميرا تصوير مِجْهَري لكاميرا ضخمة البيان أو كاميرا تلفزيونية

37 surface-finish microscope — مِجْهَر مستوى السطح

38 light section tube — أُنْبُوب قطاع الضَّوْء

39 rack and pinion — جريدة مسننة ومسننة صغيرة

40 zoom stereomicroscope — مِجْهَر مجسِّم ذو عَدَسَة زوم

41 zoom lens — عَدَسَة زوم

42 dust counter — كاونتر الأتربة

43 measurement chamber — حجرة القياس

44 data output — خَرْج البيانات

45 analogue (*Am.* analog) output — خَرْج تماثلي

46 measurement range selector — ذراع اختيار قياس المَدَى

47 digital display (digital readout) — شاشة عرض رقمية

48 dipping refractometer for examining food — مقياس انكسار غاطس لفحص الطعام

49 microscopic photometer — فوتومتر مِجْهَري

50 photometric light source — مَصْدَر ضَوْء فوتومتري

51 measuring device (photomultiplier, multiplier phototube) — جِهَاز قياس (مُضَاعِف ضوئي إلكتروني، صِمَام ضوئي مُضَاعِف)

52 light source for survey illumination — مَصْدَر ضَوْء لإنارة المسح الحقلي

53 remote electronics — وَحْدَة إلكترونيات يتم تشغيلها عن بعد

54 universal wide-field microscope — مِجْهَر واسع الحقل متعدد الأغراض

55 adapter for camera or projector attachment — مُهايئ لوَصْلَة كاميرا أو فانوس إسقاط (بروجكتور)

56 eyepiece focusing knob — مفتاح إحكام العَيْنِيَّة

57 filter pick-up — لاقط المُرَشِّح

58 handrest — مِسْنَد اليد

59 lamphouse for incident (vertical) illumination — مقر المصابيح الخاصة بالإضاءة الساقطة (العمودية)

60 lamphouse connector for transillumination — قارنة مقر المصابيح للإضاءة المتبادلة

61 wide-field stereomicroscope — مِجْهَر مُجَسِّم واسع الحقل

62 interchangeable lenses (objectives) — عدسات (شَيْئِيَّة) قابلة للإبدال فيما بينها

63 incident (vertical) illumination (incident top lighting) — مَصْدَر الضَّوْء الساقط (ضَوْء علوي ساقط)

64 fully automatic microscope camera, a camera with photomicro mount adapter — كاميرا مِجْهَرِيَّة تعمل آليا بالكامل

65 film cassette — كاسيت الفيلم

66 universal condenser for research microscope 1 — مكثِّف متعدد الأغراض لمِجْهَر الأبحاث

67 universal-type measuring machine for photogrammetry (phototheodolite) — آلة قياس من النوع الجامع خاصة بالتصوير المِسَاحي الجَوِّي

68 photogrammetric — كاميرا فوتوجرامترية

camera	
69 motor-driven level, a compensator level	ميزان مِسَاحي يعمل بمحرك
70 electro-optical distance-measuring instrument	آلة قياس مسافات كهروبصرية
71 stereometric camera	كاميرا مُجَسِّمة
72 horizontal base	قاعدة أفقية
73 one-second theodolite	مِزْوَاة/ثيودوليت للقياس في الثانية الواحدة

113 Optical Instruments II — الآلات البَصَرِيَّة (2)

1 2.2 m reflecting telescope (reflector)	تليسكوب 2,2 ملم عاكس
2 pedestal (base)	قاعدة
3 axial-radial bearing	مَحْمَل مِحْوَري نصف قطري
4 declination gear	آلِيَّة ضبط الميل
5 declination axis	مِحْوَر الانحراف الزَّاوِيّ/الميل
6 declination bearing	مَحْمَل آلِيَّة ضبط الميل
7 front ring	الحلقة الأمامية
8 tube (body tube)	أُنْبُوب
9 tube centre (*Am.* center) section	جزء مركز الأُنْبُوب
10 primary mirror (main mirror)	المِرْآة الرئيسية
11 secondary mirror (deviation mirror, corrector plate)	المِرْآة الثانوية (مِرْآة الانحراف)
12 fork mounting (fork)	مَحْمَل شوكة
13 cover	غطاء
14 guide bearing	مَحْمَل دليلي
15 main drive unit of the polar axis	وَحْدَة الإدارة الرئيسية للمِحْوَر القطبي
16-25 telescope mountings (telescope mounts)	**مَحَامِل التليسكوب**
16 refractor (refracting telescope) on a German-type mounting	تليسكوب عاكس مثبت على قاعدة من الطراز الألماني
17 declination axis	مِحْوَر الميل
18 polar axis	المِحْوَر القطبي
19 counterweight (counterpoise)	ثِقْل موازن
20 eyepiece	عَيْنِيَّة
21 knee mounting with a bent column	مَحْمَل مرفقي ذو عمود مَحْنِي
22 English-type axis mounting (axis mount)	مَحْمَل مِحْوَري من الطراز الإنجليزي
23 English-type yoke mounting (yoke mount)	مَحْمَل مقرن من الطراز الإنجليزي
24 fork mounting (fork mount)	مَحْمَل شوكة (متشعِّب)
25 horseshoe mounting (horseshoe mount)	مَحْمَل على شكل حدوة الفرس
26 meridian circle	(جهَاز) دائرة خط الزوال
27 divided circle - (graduated circle)	دائرة مُجَزَّأة/مُدرَّجَة
28 reading microscope	مِجْهَر القراءة
29 meridian telescope	تليسكوب خط الزوال
30 electron microscope	مِجْهَر إلكتروني
31-39 microscope tube (microscope body, body tube)	**أُنْبُوب المِجْهَر** (جسم المِجْهَر)
31 electron gun	مِدْفع كَهَارِب
32 condensers	مُكَثِّفات
33 specimen insertion air lock	دِسَام هوائي لإدخال العَيِّنَات
34 control for the specimen stage adjustment	ذِرَاع التحكم فى ضبط منصة العَيِّنَات
35 control for the objective apertures	ذِرَاع التحكم الخاصة بفتحات العَدَسَة الشَّيْئِيَّة
36 objective lens	عَدَسَة الشَّيْئِيَّة
37 intermediate image screen	الشاشة المتوسطة العاكسة للصورة
38 telescope magnifier	مُكَبِّر تلسكوبي للصورة
39 final image tube	أُنْبُوب الصورة النهائية
40 photographic chamber for film and plate magazines	حُجْرَة فوتوغرافية لخزانات الأفلام والألواح

114 Photography I — التَّصْوِير (1)

1 miniature camera (35 mm camera)	كاميرا صَغيرة (كاميرا 35 ملم)
2 viewfinder eyepiece	عَيْنِيَّة رُؤْيَة المنظر
3 meter cell	خَلِيَّة مترية
4 accessory shoe	حذاء تركيب الملحقات
5 flush lens	عَدَسَة متساطحة
6 rewind handle (rewind, rewind crank)	ذِرَاع لف الفيلم
7 miniature film cassette (135 film cassette, 35 mm casette)	كاسيت (عُلْبَة) فيلم مُصَغَّر (علبة فيلم 135، علبة فيلم 35 مللم)
8 film spool	بكَرَة الفيلم
9 film with leader and perforations	فيلم ذو دليل وثقوب
10 cassette slit (cassette exit slot)	فتحة الكاسيت
11 cartridge-loading camera	كاميرا تزوَّد بلفيفة فيلم
12 shutter release (shutter release button)	زِرّ تحرير مِغْلاق العَدَسَة
13 flash cube contact	موضع توصيل مكعب الفلاش
14 rectangular viewfinder	عَيْنِيَّة رُؤْيَة مستطيلة
15 126 cartridge (instamatic cartridge)	لفيفة فيلم 126
16 pocket camera (subminiature camera)	كاميرا جيب
17 110 cartridge (subminiature cartridge)	لفيفة فيلم 110
18 film window	نافذة الفيلم
19 120 rollfilm	فيلم 120 ملفوف
20 rollfilm spool	بكرة الفيلم الملفوف
21 backing paper	ورق تغليف
22 twin-lens reflex camera	كاميرا عاكسة ذات عَدَسَة مزدوجة

23 folding viewfinder hood (focusing hood)	غطاء عَيْنِيَّة رُؤْيَة المنظر قابل للطي
24 meter cell	خَلِيَّة مترية
25 viewing lens	عَدَسَة رؤية
26 object lens	عَدَسَة شيئية
27 spool knob	مِقْبَض البكرة
28 distance setting (focus setting)	حلقة ضبط المسافة
29 exposure meter using needle-matching system	مقياس مدة التعريض للضوء باستخدام نظام مطابقة الإبرة
30 flash contact	مَوْضِع توصيل الفلاش
31 shutter release	زِرّ تحرير مِغْلاق العَدَسَة
32 film transport (film advance, film wind)	لَفُ الفيلم للأمام
33 flash switch	زِرّ تشغيل الفلاش
34 aperture-setting control	زِرّ ضبط فتحة العَدَسَة
35 shutter speed control	زِرّ التحكم في سرعة المِغْلاق
36 large-format hand camera (press camera)	كاميرا تصوير صحفي
37 grip (handgrip)	مِقْبَض مَسْك الكاميرا
38 cable release	ذِرَاع تحرير الكيبل
39 distance-setting ring (focusing ring)	حلقة ضبط المسافة
40 rangefinder window	نافذة تحديد المَدَى
41 multiple-frame viewfinder (universal viewfinder)	عَيْنِيَّة رُؤْيَة جامعة
42 tripod	حامِل ثلاثي
43 tripod leg	ساق الحامِل الثلاثي
44 tubular leg	ساق أُنْبُوبية
45 rubber foot	قَدَم مطاطية
46 central column	العمود المركزي
47 ball and socket head	رَأْس ذو كرة وحُق
48 cine camera pan and tilt head	كفَّة كاميرا تصوير سينمائي ذات رَأس مائل
49 large-format folding camera	كاميرا كبيرة البيان قابلة للطي
50 optical bench	منصة بصرية ضوئية
51 standard adjustment	ذِرَاع ضبط الحامل العمودي
52 lens standard	الحامل العمودي للعَدَسَة
53 bellows	مِنْفَاخ الكاميرا
54 camera back	ظَهْر الكاميرا
55 back standard adjustment	ذِرَاع ضبط الحامِل العمودي الخلفي
56 hand-held exposure meter (exposure meter)	مقياس يدوي لحساب مدة التعريض للضوء
57 calculator dial	قُرْص حاسِب
58 scales (indicator scales) with indicator needle (pointer)	مقياس مُدَرَّج ذو مؤشِّر
59 range switch (high/low range selector)	مِفْتَاح ضبط المَدَى
60 diffuser for incident light measurement	ناشِرة لقياس الضوء الساقط
61 probe exposure meter for large-format cameras	مقياس مِسْبَاري لمدة التعرض للضوء للكاميرات كبيرة البيان
62 meter	عدَّاد
63 probe	مِسْبار
64 dark slide	شريحة قاتمة
65 battery-portable electronic flash (battery-portable electronic flash unit)	فلاش إلكتروني محمول يعمل بالبطارية
66 power pack unit (battery)	وَحْدَة حزمة الطاقة
67 flash head	رَأْس الفلاش
68 single-unit electronic flash (flashgun)	فلاش إلكتروني من وَحْدَة مفردة
69 swivel-mounted reflector	عاكس مُثَبَّت على مِحْوَر دَوَرَاني
70 photodiode	صِمَام ثنائي ذو مُوَصِّلِيَّة ضوئية
71 foot	قدم ، قاعدة
72 hot-shoe contact	نَضْو التلامس الساخن
73 flash cube unit	وَحْدَة مكعب الفلاش
74 flash cube	مُكَعَّب الفلاش
75 flash bar (AGFA)	لَوْح الفلاشات (أجفا)
76 slide projector	جِهَاز عرض الشرائح
77 rotary magazine	عُلْبَة دَوَّارة

115 Photography II التَّصْوير (2)

1-24 system camera (fully automatic miniature single-lens reflex camera)	**نظام الكاميرا** (كاميرا آلِيَّة صغيرة عاكسة مُفْرَدَة العَدَسَة)
1 main switch	مِفْتَاح التشغيل الرئيسي
2 function adjustment button (to set exposure adjustment value, drive mode, and focus area)	زِرّ ضبط الوظيفة (لضبط قيمة تعديل تعريض الفيلم للضوء، ونمط الإدارة، ونطاق التركيز البؤري)
3 exposure mode button	زِرّ نمط تعريض الفيلم للضوء
4 accessory shoe	حذاء تركيب الملحقات
5 program reset button	زِرّ إعادة ضبط البرنامج
6 data panel (data monitor, data display)	لَوْحَة البيانات
7 card on/off key	زِرّ تشغيل/إيقاف البطاقة
8 function selector key	مِفْتَاح اختيار الوظيفة
9 chip program card	بطاقة برنامج رقائقية
10 card door	باب إدخال البطاقة
11 card window	شُبَّاك البطاقة
12 battery chamber	حجرة البطارية
13 remote control terminal	طرفية التحكم عن بعد
14 shutter release (shutter release button)	زِرّ تحرير مِغْلاق العَدَسَة
15 autofocus (AF) illuminator and self-timer light	مُؤشِّر ضوئي للإحكام الآلي للبؤرة وضوء جهاز التوقيت الذاتي
16 manual shutter control [up/down control]	التحكم يدويا في مِغْلاق العَدَسَة
17 reflex mirror	مِرْآة عاكسة
18 autofocus sensor, a CCD image converter (image sensor)	خلية استشعار آلِيَّة البؤرة

19 bayonet mounting ring	حَلَقَة توصيل على شكل حربة
20 aperture setting button	زرّ ضبط فتحة العَدَسَة
21 lens release	زرّ إطْلاق العَدَسَة
22 focus-mode switch (to switch to manual focusing)	مِفْتَاح نمط ضبط البؤرة (للتحويل إلى إحكام البؤرة يدويا)
23 autofocus zoom lens, a x3 zoom lens (35-105 mm)	عَدَسَة زوم آليَّة الإحكام البؤري (35 – 105 مم)
24 aperture and autofocus contacts	ملامسات فتحة العَدَسَة والبؤرة الآليَّة
25-35 viewfinder screen (focusing screen, matt screen), a micro-honeycombed focusing screen	**شَاشَة مُحَدِّد الرؤية** (شَاشَة الإحكام البؤري)
25 flash-on signal	إشارة تشغيل الفلاش
26 flash-ready signal	إشارة أن الفلاش جاهز للتشغيل
27 focus signals	إشارات التركيز البؤري
28 wide focus area	مِنْطَقَة واسعة البؤرة
29 shutter speed display	شَاشَة عرض سرعة مِغْلاق العَدَسَة
30 manual-exposure compensation-value indicator	مُؤَشِّر القيمة الموازنة للتعريض للضوء يدويا
31 aperture or exposure adjustment indicator	مُؤَشِّر ضبط فتحة العَدَسَة أو تعريض الفيلم للضوء
32 spot metering indicator	مُؤَشِّر القياس الفوري
33 spot metering area	مِنْطَقَة القياس الفوري
34 centre focus area	مِنْطَقَة البؤرة المركزية
35 focus area indicator	مُؤَشِّر مِنْطَقَة البؤرة
36-42 LCD data panel (data monitor)	**لَوْحَة البيانات**
36 program exposure-mode indicator	مُؤَشِّر تعريض الفيلم للضوء
37 frame counter	عَدَّاد إطاري
38 function indicators	مُؤَشِّرات الوظائف
39 aperture or exposure adjustment indicator	مُؤَشِّر ضبط فتحة العَدَسَة أو التعريض للضوء
40 shutter speed or film speed (film sensitivity) indicator	مُؤَشِّر سرعة مِغْلاق العَدَسَة أو سرعة الفيلم
41 film transport indicator	مُؤَشِّر لف الفيلم للأمام
42 function pointer	مُؤَشِّر الوظيفة
43 interchangeable lenses (autofocus lenses, AF lenses)	عدسات قابلة للإبدال فيما بينها
44 fisheye lens (fisheye)	عَدَسَة عَيْن السمكة
45 wide-angle lens (short focal-length lens)	عَدَسَة واسعة الزاوية (عَدَسَة قصيرة البعد البؤري)
46 standard lens	عَدَسَة قياسية
47 medium focal-length lens	عَدَسَة متوسطة الطول البؤري
48 telephoto lens (long focal-length lens), a zoom lens (variable focus lens, varifocal lens)	عَدَسَة تصوير عن بعد (عَدَسَة طويلة البعد البؤري)، عَدَسَة زوم (عَدَسَة متنوعة البعد البؤري)
49 long-focus lens	عَدَسَة طويلة البعد البؤري
50 mirror lens	عَدَسَة مِرآوية
51 tele converter	مُحَوِّل التصوير عن بعد
52 data back	ظهر كتابة البيانات
53 ten-metre (*Am.* ten-meter) film back (magazine back)	ظهر مخزن فيلم 10م (ظهر المخزن)
54-74 accessories for close-up and macro shots	**ملحقات تصوير المناظر القريبة واللقطات الكبيرة**
54 extension tube	أنبوب استطالة
55 adapter ring	حَلَقَة مهايئة
56 reversing ring	حَلَقَة عاكسة
57 lens in retrofocus position	عَدَسَة في وضع إحكام خلفي
58 bellows unit (extension bellows, close-up bellows attachment)	وَحْدَة منفاخ الكاميرا
59 focusing stage	مِنَصَّة التركيز البؤري
60 slide-copying attachment	ملحق شريحة نَسْخ الشرائح
61 slide-copying adapter	مُهايِئ الشريحة الناسخة
62 cable release	زرّ تحرير الكيبل
63 copying stand (copy stand)	حامِل النسخ (حامل النسخة)
64 arm of the copying stand (copy stand)	ذراع حامل النسخة
65 rifle grip	قبضة بندقية
66 table (-top) tripod (mini tripod)	حامل نضدي ثلاثي (حامِل صغير)
67 ever-ready case	حقيبة كاميرا مجهزة
68 lens case	علبة العدسات
69 soft-leather lens pouch	كيس من الجِلْد الطَّري لحفظ العدسات
70 camera bag, of metallic construction: aluminium (*Am.* aluminum) case	حقيبة الكاميرا من المعدن، صندوق من الألمونيوم
71 film container	علبة الفيلم
72 filter case	علبة المُرَشِّحات
73 second body	الجسم الثاني
74 ring flash for macro shots	فلاش حلقي للقطات الكبيرة

116 Photography III — التَّصْوير (3)

1-60 darkroom equipment	**مُعِدَّات الحجرة المظلمة**
1 developing tank	خَزَّان الإظْهار
2 spiral (developing spiral, tank reel)	حَلَزُون (حَلَزُون الإظْهار، بكَرَة الخَزَّان)
3 multi-unit developing tank	خَزَّان إظْهار متعدد الوَحدات
4 multi-unit tank spiral	حَلَزُون إظهار متعدد الوَحدات
5 daylight-loading tank	خَزَّان تعبئة الأفلام في ضوء النهار
6 loading chamber	حجرة تعبئة الفيلم

7 film transport handle	ذِرَاع تقديم الفيلم
8 developing tank thermometer	ترمومتر خَزَّان الإظْهار
9 collapsible bottle for developing solution	قنِّينَة محلول الإظْهار قابلة للطي
10 chemical bottles for first developer, stop bath, colour developer, bleach-hardener, stabilizer	قنينات تحوي مواد كيماوية للمُظْهِر الأول، حمَّام الإيقاف، مظهِر الألْوَان، مُصَلِّد مادة التقصير، والمُثَبِّت
11 measuring cylinders	أسطوانات قياس
12 funnel	قمع
13 tray thermometer (dish thermometer)	ترمومتر صينية
14 film clip	مِشْبك تثبيت الأفلام
15 wash tank (washer)	حَوْض غسيل
16 water supply pipe	أنْبُوب إمداد الماء
17 water outlet pipe	أنْبُوب خروج الماء
18 laboratory timer (timer)	جِهَاز توقيت مختبري
19 automatic film agitator	مُقَلِّب أفلام آلي
20 developing tank	خَزَّان الإظْهار
21 darkroom lamp (safe-light)	مصباح الغرفة المظلمة (ضوء آمن)
22 filter screen	ستار ترشيح
23 film drier (drying cabinet)	كابينة تجفيف الأفلام
24 exposure timer	جِهَاز توقيت ضَبْط مدة التعريض للضوء
25 developing dish (developing tray)	صينية الإظْهار
26 enlarger	آلة التكبير
27 baseboard	لَوْح القاعدة
28 angled column	عمود زاويّ
29 lamphouse (lamp housing)	دَوَاة المصباح
30 negative carrier	حَامِل النيجاتيف
31 bellows	مِنْفَاخ الكاميرا
32 lens	عَدَسَة
33 friction drive for fine adjustment	ناقل حركة احتكاكي للضَبْط الدقيق
34 height adjustment (scale adjustment)	آلِيَّة ضَبْط الارتفاع
35 masking frame (easel)	برواز الطبع التصويري
36 colour (*Am.* color) analyser	مُحَلِّل الألْوَان
37 colour (*Am.* color) analyser lamp	مصباح مُحَلِّل الألْوَان
38 probe lead	سِلْك مِسْباري
39 exposure time balancing knob	زِرّ موازنة فترة التعريض
40 colour (*Am.* color) enlarger	آلة تكبير بالألْوَان
41 enlarger head	رأس آلة التكبير
42 column	قائم عمودي
43-45 colour-mixing (*Am.* color-mixing) **knob**	**آلِيَّة خلط الألْوَان**
43 magenta filter adjustment (minus green filter adjustment)	ذِرَاع ضَبْط مُرَشِّح الماجنتا
44 yellow filter adjustment (minus blue filter adjustment)	ذِرَاع ضَبْط مُرَشِّح الصبغ الأصفر
45 cyan filter adjustment (minus red filter adjustment)	ذِرَاع ضَبْط مُرَشِّح لون السِّيَان
46 red swing filter	مُرَشِّح الصبغ الأحمر المترجِّح
47 print tongs	مِلْقَط مسك الصور المطبوعة
48 processing drum	أسْطُوَانَة مُعالَجَة
49 squeegee	ممسحة مطاطية
50 range (assortment) of papers	تشكيلة من الأوراق
51 colour (*Am.* color) printing paper, a packet of photographic printing paper	وَرَق طباعة الصور الملونة
52 colour (*Am.* color) chemicals (colour processing chemicals)	مواد كيميائية للطباعة الملونة
53 enlarging meter (enlarging photometer)	مقياس التكبير
54 adjusting knob with paper speed scale	ذِرَاع ضَبْط مُزَوَّد بمقياس سرعة الوَرَق
55 probe	مِسْبار
56 semi-automatic thermostatically controlled developing dish	طبق إظْهار نصف آلي يتم التحكم فيه ترموستاتيا
57 rapid print drier (heated print drier)	مُجَفِّف سريع للصور المطبوعة
58 glazing sheet	فَرْخ تلميع
59 pressure cloth	نسيج (قُطْنِيّ) ضاغط
60 automatic processor (machine processor)	ماكينة معالجة آلِيَّة

117 Cine Film — التَّصْوير السِّينَمائي

1 cine camera, a Super 8 sound camera	كاميرا سينمائيَّة، كاميرا سوبر 8 صوتية
2 interchangeable zoom lens (variable focus lens, varifocal lens)	عَدَسَة زوم قابلة للإبدال (عَدَسَة متغيرة البؤرة)
3 distance setting (focus setting) and manual focal length setting	ضَبْط المسافة وضَبْط الطول البؤري يدوياً
4 aperture ring (aperture-setting ring, aperture control ring) for manual aperture setting	حَلَقَة ضَبْط فتحة العَدَسَة لضَبْط الفتحة يدويا
5 handgrip with battery chamber	مِقْبَض الكاميرا وبه حجيرة البطارية
6 shutter release with cable release socket	زِرّ تحرير مِغْلاق العَدَسَة ومِقْبِس تحرير الكيبل
7 pilot tone or pulse generator socket for the sound recording equipment (with the dual film-tape system)	مِقْبِس النغمة الدليلية أو مُوَلِّد الترددات الخاص بمُعِدَّات تسجيل الصوت (في نظام شريط الفيلم الثنائي)
8 sound connecting cord for microphone or	سِلْك توصيل الصوت الخاص بالميكروفون أو

external sound source (in single-system recording)	مصدر صوت خارجي
9 remote control socket (remote control jack)	مِقْبَس التحكم من بعد (جاك التحكم من بعد)
10 headphone socket (*sim.:* earphone socket)	مِقْبَس السماعات
11 autofocus override switch	مِفْتَاح تجاوز الضَّبْط الأوتوماتي للبعد البؤري
12 filming speed selector	مِفْتَاح ضَبْط سرعة التصوير
13 sound recording selector switch for automatic or manual operation	مِفْتَاح اختيار نظام تسجيل الصوت للتشغيل الآلي أو اليدوي
14 eyepiece with eyecup	عَيْنِيَّة الكاميرا وكأس العين
15 diopter control ring (dioptric adjustment ring)	حلَقَة التحكم في ديوبتر العَدَسَة
16 recording level control (audio level control, recording sensitivity selector)	التحكم في مستوى تسجيل الصوت
17 manual/automatic exposure control switch	مِفْتَاح التحكم الخاص بتعريض الفيلم للضوء يدوياً/آلياً
18 film speed setting	ضَبْط سرعة الفيلم
19 power zooming arrangement	نظام تشغيل الزوم
20 automatic aperture control	التحكم آليا في فتحة العَدَسَة
21 sound track system	نظام مسلك الصوت
22 sound camera	كاميرا تسجيل صوت وصورة
23 telescopic microphone boom	ذِرَاع استطالة مكَبِّر صوت تليسكوبي
24 microphone	مكَبِّر صوت، ميكروفون
25 microphone connecting lead (microphone connecting cord)	سِلْك توصيل الميكروفون
26 mixing console (mixing desk, mixer)	كونسول المَزْج
27 inputs from various sound sources	مُدْخَلات من عدة مصادر للصوت
28 output to camera	خَرْج توصيل بالكاميرا
29 Super-8 sound film cartridge	خرطوش فيلم تسجيل صوتي لكاميرا سوبر 8
30 film gate of the cartridge	بوَّابة الفيلم بالخرطوش
31 feed spool	بكَرَة إلقام الفيلم
32 take-up spool	بكَرَة إلتقاط الفيلم
33 recording head (sound head)	رَأس التسجيل
34 transport roller (capstan)	أسْطُوَانَة لف الفيلم
35 rubber pinch roller (capstan idler)	أسْطُوَانَة مطاطية
36 guide step (guide notch)	درجة دليلية
37 exposure meter control step	آليَّة التحكم في مقياس تعريض الفيلم للضوء
38 conversion filter step (colour, *Am.* color, conversion filter step)	آليَّة فلتر التحويل
39 single-8 cassette	كاسيت فيلم كاميرا 8 مفرد المسلك
40 film gate opening	فتحة بوابة الفيلم
41 unexposed film	فيلم لم يُعَرَّض للضوء
42 exposed film	فيلم تم تعريضه للضوء
43 16 mm camera	كاميرا 16 مللم
44 reflex finder (through-the-lens reflex finder)	مُحَدِّد رؤية انعكاسي
45 magazine	مخزن الفيلم
46-49 lens head	**رَأس العَدَسَة**
46 lens turret (turret head)	برج العَدَسَة
47 telephoto lens	عَدَسَة التصوير من بُعْد
48 wide-angle lens	عَدَسَة واسعة الزاوية
49 normal lens (standard lens)	عَدَسَة عادِيَّة (عَدَسَة قياسية)
50 winding handle	ذِرَاع لف الفيلم
51 compact Super-8 camera	كاميرا سوبر 8 مُدْمَجَة
52 footage counter	عَدَّاد اللقطات
53 macro zoom lens	عَدَسَة زوم للتصوير الكبير
54 zooming lever	ذِرَاع تشغيل الزوم
55 macro lens attachment (close-up lens)	عَدَسَة تصوير اللقطات الكبيرة (عَدَسَة تصوير اللقطات القريبة)
56 macro frame (mount for small originals)	إطار تركيب الصور الأصلية الصغيرة المراد تكبيرها
57 underwater housing (underwater case)	عُلْبَة الكاميرا للتصوير تحت الماء
58 direct-vision frame finder	مُحَدِّد إطار الرؤية المباشرة
59 measuring rod	قضيب قياس
60 stabilizing wing	جناح تثبيت
61 grip (handgrip)	مِقْبَض صندوق الكاميرا
62 locking bolt	مِسْمَار ربط
63 control lever (operating lever)	ذِرَاع التشغيل
64 porthole	فتحة صندوق الكاميرا
65 synchronization start (sync start)	بدء التسجيل المتزامن
66 professional press-type camera	كاميرا تصوير صحافي
67 cameraman	المُصَوِّر
68 camera assistant (sound assistant)	المُصَوِّر المساعد
69 handclap marking sync start	إشارة يدوية لبدء التصوير المتزامن بالصوت والصورة
70 dual film-tape recording using a tape recorder	التسجيل الثنائي باستخدام مسجِّل بشريط فيلمي
71 pulse-generating camera	كاميرا توليد نبضي
72 pulse cable	كيبل نبضي
73 cassette recorder	جِهَاز تسجيل كاسيت
74 microphone	مكَبِّر صوت، ميكروفون
75 dual film-tape reproduction	**نسخ شريط تصوير فيلمي ثنائي المسلك**

76 tape cassette — كاسيت الشريط
77 synchronization unit — وَحْدَة المزامنة
78 cine projector — بروجكتور عرض سينمائي
79 film feed spool — بكَرَة إلقام الفيلم
80 take-up reel (take-up spool), an automatic take-up reel (take-up spool) — بكَرَة التقاط الفيلم ، بكَرَة آليَّة لالتقاط الفيلم
81 sound projector — بروجكتور صوتي
82 sound film with magnetic stripe (sound track, track) — فيلم صوتي ذو شريط مغناطيسي
83 automatic-threading button — زرّ الضَّبْط الآلى للصورة
84 trick button — زرّ ضَبْط الألوان الثلاثية
85 volume control — زَرّ التحكم في درجة ارتفاع الصوت
86 reset button — زرّ إعادة ضَبْط الشريط
87 fast and slow motion switch — مِفْتَاح العرض السريع والبطئ للشريط
88 forward, reverse, and still projection switch — مِفْتَاح تقديم وعكس وتثبيت الفيلم
89 splicer for wet splices — جِهَاز جَدْل الشرائط
90 hinged clamping plate — لَوْحة قامطة مفصلية
91 film viewer (animated viewer editor) — جِهَاز مشاهدة الفيلم للمونتاج
92 foldaway reel arm — ذِراع بكَرَة فَرْد الشريط
93 rewind handle (rewinder) — ذِراع لف الشريط
94 viewing screen — شاشة المشاهدة
95 film perforator (film marker) — آليَّة تثقيب الفيلم
96 six-turntable film and sound cutting table (editing table, cutting bench, animated sound editor) — طاولة المونتاج
97 monitor — شاشة متابعة
98 control buttons (control well) — مفاتيح التحكم
99 film turntable — سَوَّاقة الفيلم
100 first sound turntable, e.g. for live sound — سَوَّاقة اسطوانات التسجيل الصوتي الأول، التسجيل الحي مثلا
101 second sound turntable for post-sync sound — سَوَّاقة اسطوانات التسجيل الصوتي الثاني لبعد ضَبْط المزامنة
102 film and tape synchronizing head — رَأس مزامنة الصورة مع الصوت

118 Building Site (Construction Site) I — مَوْقِع البناء/الإنشاءات (1)

1-49 carcase (carcass, fabric) [house construction, carcassing] — **هَيْكل إنشاء** [هيكل منزل]
1 basement of tamped (rammed) concrete — قاعدة من الخرسانة المدكوكة
2 concrete base course — مِدْمَاك القاعدة الخرسانية
3 cellar window (basement window) — نافذة القَبْو
4 outside cellar steps — درجات القَبْو الخارجية
5 utility room window — نافذة غرفة المنافع
6 utility room door — باب غرفة المنافع
7 ground floor (*Am.* first floor) — الطابق الأرضي
8 brick wall — حائط من الطوب
9 lintel (window head) — عَتَبَة علوية للنافذة
10 reveal — المحيط البنائي حول النافذة
11 jamb — عضادة النافذة
12 window ledge (window sill) — عَتَبَة سفلية (إفريز) للنافذة
13 reinforced concrete lintel — عَتَبَة علوية من الخرسانة المسلحة
14 upper floor (first floor, *Am.* second floor) — الطابق العلوي
15 hollow-block wall — حائط من القوالب المُفَرَّغَة
16 concrete floor — أرضية خرسانية
17 work platform (working platform) — مِنَصَّة الشغل
18 bricklayer (*Am.* brickmason) — البَنَّاء
19 bricklayer's labourer (*Am.* laborer); *also:* builder's labourer — مُساعِد البَنَّاء
20 mortar trough — حَوْض الملاط
21 chimney — مدخنة
22 cover (boards) for the staircase — ألواح غطاء السُلَّم
23 scaffold pole (scaffold standard) — دعامة عمود السقالة
24 platform railing — درابزين المِنَصَّة
25 angle brace (angle tie) in the scaffold — تكتيفة زاوية في السقالة
26 ledger — اللَوْح المستعرض للسقالة
27 putlog (putlock) — جِسْر
28 plank platform (board platform) — مِنَصَّة من الألواح الخَشَبية
29 guard board — لَوْح وقاية
30 scaffolding joint with chain or lashing or whip or bond — وَصْلَة منصب السقَالة ذات سلسلة أو وِثاق أو حبل أو رِبَاط
31 builder's hoist — مِرْفاع إنشاء
32 mixer operator — عامِل/مُشَغِّل الخلاط
33 concrete mixer, a gravity mixer — خلاط الخرسانة
34 mixing drum — بَرْمِيل الخلط
35 feeder skip — قادوس التغذية
36 concrete aggregate [sand and gravel] — كِتَالَة خرسانيَّة (رَمْل وحَصَى)
37 wheelbarrow — عربة يد ذات دولاب واحد
38 hose (hosepipe) — خرطوم
39 mortar pan (mortar trough, mortar tub) — حَوْض المِلاط
40 stack of bricks — رصة من قوالب الطوب
41 stacked shutter boards (lining boards) — ألواح شدَّة خرسانية مرصوصة (ألواح تبطين)
42 ladder — سُلَّم نقال
43 bag of cement — كيس أسمنت

44 site fence, a timber fence — سُور الموقع، سُور خَشَبي
45 signboard (billboard) — لافتة
46 removable gate — بوابة قابلة للإزالة
47 contractors' name plates — لَوْحة أسماء المقاولين
48 site hut (site office) — كشك الموقع (مكتب الموقع)
49 building site latrine — مرحاض موقع البِنَاء
50-57 bricklayer's (*Am.* brickmason's) **tools** — **أدوات البَنَّاء**
50 plumb bob (plummet) — خَيْط المطمار، الشاقول
51 thick lead pencil — قلم رصاص سميك
52 trowel — مالج، مُسْطَرين
53 bricklayer's (*Am.* brickmason's) hammer (brick hammer) — مِطْرَقَة البَنَّاء
54 mallet — مِطْرَقَة خَشَبية الرَّأس
55 spirit level — ميزان تسوية
56 laying-on trowel — مُسْطَرين رص الطوب
57 float — لَوْح عجين المُونَة
58-68 masonry bonds — **أربطة البِنَاء**
58 brick (standard brick) — قالب طوبٍ عادي
59 stretching bond — رِبَاط شِنَاوى
60 heading bond — رِبَاط آديات
61 racking (raking) back — آدِيَّة مخلوفة
62 English bond — رِبَاط إنجليزي
63 stretching course — مِدْمَاك شِنَاوي
64 heading course — مِدْمَاك آديات
65 English cross bond (Saint Andrew's cross bond) — رِبَاط الصليب الإنجليزي
66 chimney bond — رِبَاط المدخنة
67 first course — المِدْمَاك الأول
68 second course — المِدْمَاك الثاني
69-82 excavation — **الحَفْر**
69 profile (*Am.* batter-board) [fixed on edge at the corner] — لَوْح عرضي [مثبت على حافة بالزاوية]
70 intersection of strings — تقاطع الحبال
71 plumb bob (plummet) — خَيْط المطمار، الشاقول
72 excavation side — جانب الحَفْر
73 upper edge board — لَوْح الحافة العلوية
74 lower edge board — لَوْح الحافة السفلية
75 foundation trench — خندق الأساس
76 navvy (*Am.* excavator) — الحَفَّار
77 conveyor belt (conveyor) — سَيْر ناقل
78 excavated earth — تراب الحَفْر
79 plank roadway — طريق مُعَبَّد بالألواح الخَشَبية
80 tree guard — وقاء الشجر
81 mechanical shovel (excavator) — مِجْرَفة ميكانيكية (حَفَّارة)
82 shovel bucket (bucket) — قادوس المِجْرَفة
83-91 plastering — **التجصيص، البياض**
83 plasterer — جصَّاص
84 mortar trough — حَوْض الملاط
85 screen — غُرْبَال
86-89 ladder scaffold — **سقالة سُلَّمية**
86 standard ladder — سُلَّم عادي
87 boards (planks, platform) — أَلْواح خَشَبية
88 diagonal strut (diagonal brace) — رِبَاط/شِكال مائل
89 railing — حاجز، درابزين
90 guard netting — شبكة واقية
91 rope-pulley hoist — مرفاع ذو حبل وبكَرَة

119 Building Site (Construction Site) II — مَوقع البناء/الإنشاءات (2)

1-89 reinforced concrete (ferroconcrete) **construction** — **إنشاءات الخرسانة المسلحة**
1 reinforced concrete (ferroconcrete) skeleton construction — إنشاء هيكل من الخرسانة المسلحة
2 reinforced concrete (ferroconcrete) frame — إطار من الخرسانة المسلحة
3 inferior purlin — مَدَّادَة/رافدة (أفقية) سفلية
4 concrete purlin — مَدَّادَة أفقية خرسانية
5 ceiling joist — جائز السقف
6 arch (flank) — عَقْد
7 rubble concrete wall — حائط خرسانة دَبْش
8 reinforced concrete (ferroconcrete) floor — أرضيَّة خرسانيَّة مسلحة
9 concreter (concretor), flattening out — عامل الخرسانة (يقوم بالتسوية)
10 projecting reinforcement (*Am.* connection rebars) — قضبان تسليح بارزة
11 column box — صندوق العمود
12 joist shuttering — شَدَّة خرسانية ذات روافد
13 shuttering strut — عمود شَدَّة خرسانية
14 diagonal bracing — رِبَاط/شِكال مائل
15 wedge — خَابور، إسفين
16 board — عارضة خَشَبية
17 sheet pile wall (sheet pile, sheet piling) — خوازيق ستارة
18 shutter boards (lining boards) — ألواح شَدَّة خرسانية (ألواح تبطين)
19 circular saw (buzz saw) — مِنْشَار دائري/قرصي
20 bending table — نضد ثَنْي قضبان المسلح
21 bar bender (steel bender) — عامل ثَنْي المسلح
22 hand steel shears — مقص صلب يدوي
23 reinforcing steel (reinforcement rods) — سيخ تسليح فولاذي
24 pumice concrete hollow block — قوالب مُفَرَّغَة من خرسانة الحجر الخَفَّاف
25 partition wall, a timber wall — جدار فاصل، جدار خَشَبي
26 concrete aggregate [gravel and sand of various grades] — كِتَالة خرسانية [حَصَى ورمل مُتَدَرِّج]
27 crane track — مَسَار الونْش
28 tipping wagon (tipping truck) — عربة نقل قلابة

29 concrete mixer — خلاط الأسمنت
30 cement silo — صَوْمَعة الأسمنت
31 tower crane (tower slewing crane) — مِرْفَاع بُرْجِي
32 bogie (*Am.* truck) — عربة نقل منخفضة
33 counterweight — ثقل موازن
34 tower — بُرْج المِرْفَاع
35 crane driver's cabin (crane driver's cage) — كابينة سائق المِرْفَاع
36 jib (boom) — ذِرَاع تطويل المِرْفَاع
37 bearer cable — كيبل الحَمْل
38 concrete bucket — قادوس الخرسانة
39 sleepers (*Am.* ties) — فلَنْكَات، أربطة
40 chock — إسفين لمنع الانزلاق/للإيقاف
41 ramp — مُنْحَدَر
42 wheelbarrow — عربة يد ذات دولاب واحد
43 safety rail — حاجز أمان
44 site hut — كُشْك الموقع
45 canteen — الكانتين
46 tubular steel scaffold (scaffolding) — سقالة أنابيب صلب
47 standard — عمود السقالة
48 ledger tube — اللَوْح المستعرض للسقالة
49 tie tube — أنْبُوبة ربط/شد
50 shoe — كعب، قاعدة (السقالة)
51 diagonal brace — ربَاط/شِكال مائل
52 planking (platform) — ألواح خَشَبية (مِنَصَّة)
53 coupling (coupler) — قارنة، ربَاط
54-76 formwork (shuttering) and reinforcement — **أعمال الشَدَّة الخرسانية والتسليح**
54 bottom shuttering (lining) — الشَّدَّة الخرسانية السفلية (بطَانة)
55 side shutter of a purlin — اللَوْح الجانبي للحائز/الرافدة
56 cut-in bottom — قاعدة
57 cross beam — كَمَرَة مستعرضة
58 cramp iron (cramp, dog) — قامطة حديد
59 upright member, a standard — عمود قائم
60 strap — طَوْق، شنبر
61 cross piece — كَمَرَة مستعرضة
62 stop fillet — عصابة، باكتَّة تلبيس
63 strut (brace, angle brace) — رِبَاط، كتف، شِكال
64 frame timber (yoke) — دعامة رابطة (مِقْرَن)
65 strap — طَوْق، شنبر
66 reinforcement binding — قضيب مسلح رابط
67 cross strut (strut) — رافدة مستعرضة
68 reinforcement — قَضِيب مسلح
69 distribution steel — قَضِيب توزيع
70 stirrup — ركَاب، طَوْق
71 projecting reinforcement (*Am.* connection rebars) — قضبان تسليح بارزة
72 concrete (heavy concrete) — خرسانة (خرسانة ثقيلة)
73 column box — صندوق العمود
74 bolted frame timber (bolted yoke) — دعامة رابطة بالمسامير الملولبة
75 nut (thumb nut) — صامولة ربط
76 shutter board (shuttering board) — لَوْح الشدة الخرسانية
77-89 tools — **أدوات**
77 bending iron — قضيب الثَّنْي
78 adjustable service girder — عارضة خدمة قابلة للضَبْط
79 adjusting screw — لَوْلَب الضَّبْط
80 round bar reinforcement — قضيب مسلَّح دائري المقطع
81 distance piece (separator, spacer) — قطعة مباعدة
82 Torsteel — فولاذ عالي المقاومة
83 concrete tamper — مِدَكُّ الخرسانة
84 mould (*Am.* mold) for concrete test cubes — قالب مكعبات اختبار الخرسانة
85 concreter's tongs — مِلْقَط/كلابة عامل الخرسانة
86 sheeting support — حَامِل ألواح الشدة الخرسانية
87 hand shears — مقص يدوي
88 immersion vibrator (concrete vibrator) — هَزَّازة غاطسة (هَزَّاز الخرسانة)
89 vibrating cylinder (vibrating head, vibrating poker) — أُسْطُوَانَة هَزَّازة (رَأْس هَزَّاز)

120 Carpenter — النَّجَّار

1-59 carpenter's yard — **ساحة النِّجَارة**
1 stack of boards (planks) — رصة من الألواح الخَشَبية
2 long timber (*Am.* lumber) — لَوْح خَشَب طويل (عِرق خَشَب)
3 sawing shed — مَنْجَر نشر الخَشَب
4 carpenter's workshop — مَنْجَرَة
5 workshop door — باب المَنْجَرَة
6 handcart — عربة يدوية
7 roof truss — جَمَلُون السقف
8 tree [used for topping out ceremony] with wreath — شجرة ذات إكليل
9 timber wall — جدار خَشَبي
10 squared timber (building timber, scantlings) — خَشَب مربع المقطع (خَشَب بنَاء)
11 drawing floor — أرضية السحب
12 carpenter — النَّجَّار
13 safety helmet — خوذة أمان
14 cross-cut saw, a chain saw — مِنْشَار قطع متعارض، مِنْشَار بسلسلة
15 chain guide — دليل السلسلة
16 saw chain — سلسلة المِنْشَار
17 mortiser (chain cutter) — أداة نقر/قطع
18 trestle (horse) — مِنْصَب (حصان)
19 beam mounted on a trestle — كَمَرَة/عارضة فوق الحصان
20 set of carpenter's tools — طاقم عُدَّة النَّجَّار
21 electric drill — مِثْقَاب كهربي

22 dowel hole — ثقب الدِّسار
23 mark for the dowel hole — علامة مَوْضِع ثقب الدِّسار
24 beams — كَمَر، عوارض خَشَبية
25 post (stile, stud, quarter) — عمود، دعامة
26 corner brace — شَدَّاد/رِبَاط الركن
27 brace (strut) — كتف/رِبَاط شَدَّاد
28 base course (plinth) — مِدْمَاك القاعدة (بَرْدُورَة)
29 house wall (wall) — جدار المنزل، حائط المنزل
30 window opening — فتحة النافذة
31 reveal — المحيط البنائي حول النافذة
32 jamb — عضادة
33 window ledge (window sill) — عَتَبَة سفلية للنافذة (طُنُف)
34 cornice — كورنيش، إفريز
35 roundwood (round timber) — لَوْح خَشَبي دائري المقطع
36 floorboards — ألواح تطبيق/الأرضية
37 hoisting rope — حبل الرفع
38 ceiling joist (ceiling beam, main beam) — علفة/كمرة السقف (كمرة السقف)
39 wall joist — رافدة/كمر الحائط
40 wall plate — لَوْح جداري
41 trimmer (trimmer joist, *Am.* header, header joist) — حائز طولي ثخين، آدِيَّة
42 dragon beam (dragon piece) — عَتَبَة مدرعة (قطعة زاوية)
43 false floor (inserted floor) — أرضية زائفة
44 floor filling of breeze, loam, etc. — حشو الأرضية من الغضار الرملي وخلافه
45 fillet (cleat) — شريحة خَشَبية (قبقاب ساند)
46 stair well (well) — بئر السُلَّم
47 chimney — مدخنة
48 framed partition (framed wall) — فاصل/حاجز/جدار إطاري
49 wall plate — لَوْح جداري
50 girt — عارضة صغيرة
51 window jamb, a jamb — عضادة نافذة
52 corner stile (corner strut, corner stud) — دعامة الركن، عمود الركن
53 principal post — الدعامة الرئيسية، العمود الرئيسي
54 brace (strut) with skew notch — رِبَاط/كتف ذو نقرة مائلة
55 nogging piece — عارضة/قطعة تثبيت
56 sill rail — قضيب عَتَبَة النافذة
57 window lintel (window head) — العَتَبَة العلوية للنافذة
58 head (head rail) — رَأس (قضيب علوي)
59 filled-in panel (bay, pan) — رقعة الحائط (فسحة بين عمودين)
60-82 carpenter's tools — **أدوات النجار**
60 hand saw — مِنْشَار يدوي
61 bucksaw — مِنْشَار قوس/عادى
62 saw blade — سلاح المِنْشَار
63 compass saw (keyhole saw) — مِنْشَار منحنيات
64 plane — فارة، مِسْحَاج
65 auger (gimlet) — مِثْقَاب بريمة
66 screw clamp (cramp, holdfast) — قامطة بلولب
67 mallet — مِطْرَقَة ذات رَأس خَشَبية
68 two-handed saw — مِنْشَار ذو مِقْبَضين
69 try square — زاوية ضَبْط قائمة، زاوية النَّجَّار
70 broad axe (*Am.* broad-ax) — بَلْطَة عريضة الشفرة
71 chisel — إزميل
72 mortise axe (mortice axe, *Am.* mortise ax) — بَلْطَة نقر
73 axe (*Am.* ax) — بَلْطَة
74 carpenter's hammer — مِطْرَقَة النَّجَّار
75 claw head (nail claw) — رَأس مخلبي
76 folding rule — مسطرة قابلة للطي
77 carpenter's pencil — قلم رصاص
78 iron square — زاوية قائمة معدنية
79 drawknife (drawshave, drawing knife) — سكين جَبْذ (للكشط)
80 shaving — قُشَارة
81 bevel — مِسْطار زوايا
82 mitre square (*Am.* miter square, miter angle) — زاوية نصف قائمة، زاوية كوستا
83-96 building timber — **خَشَب البناء**
83 undressed timber (*Am.* rough lumber) — لَوْح خَشَب غير مُجَهَّز
84 heartwood (duramen) — خَشَب القلب (الجلْب)
85 sapwood (sap, alburnum) — خَشَب النُّسْغ، خَشَب رَخْو
86 bark (rind) — لحاء، قشرة خارجية
87 baulk (balk) — كتلة خَشَبية
88 halved timber — لَوْح خَشَب مَشْطُور
89 wane (waney edge) — حافة مشطوفة
90 quarter baulk (balk) — كتلة خَشَبية رباعية التقسيم
91 plank (board) — لَوْح خَشَبي
92 end-grained timber — خَشَب ذو قطع مستعرض/ذو تَجَزُّع طَرَفي
93 heartwood plank (heart plank) — لَوْح من خَشَب القلب
94 unsquared (untrimmed) plank (board) — لَوْح خَشَبي غير مُشَذَّب
95 squared (trimmed) board — لَوْح خَشَبي مُشَذَّب
96 slab (offcut) — لُوَيْحَة خَشَب

121 Roof, Timber Joints — الأسَقْف والوَصْلات الخَشَبيَّة

1-26 styles and parts of roofs — **أشكال وَأجزاء الأسقف**
1 gable roof (saddle roof, saddleback roof) — سَقْف هَرَمِي/سَنَامِي/جَمَلُوني
2 ridge — حَرْف السَّطْح
3 verge — لَوْح مائل
4 eaves — إفريز
5 gable — واجِهَة الجَمَلُون، مِقَص جَمَلُون

6 dormer window (dormer)	شُبَّاك روش (شُبَّاك سَقْف جَمَلُوني)
7 pent roof (shed roof, lean-to roof)	سَقْف مبنى جانبي مائل
8 skylight	مَنْوَر
9 fire gable	جَمَلُون حراري
10 hip (hipped) roof	سَقْف مُسَنَّم/مُهَرَّم
11 hip end	طَرْف التهريم/التسنيم
12 hip (arris)	حرف حاد (سُوكة)
13 hip (hipped) dormer window	شُبَّاك روش مُهَرَّم
14 ridge turret	بُرْج سَرْجِي السَّقْف
15 valley (roof valley)	زَاوِيَة تقابل سَقْفين مائلين
16 hipped-gable roof (jerkin head roof)	سَقْف مُسَنَّم موشوري
17 partial-hip (partial-hipped) end	طَرْف مُسَنَّم جزئيا
18 mansard roof (*Am.* gambrel roof)	سَقْف سَنْدِي مزدوج التَّحَدُّر
19 mansard dormer window	نافذة روش فى سَقْف سَنْدِي
20 sawtooth roof	سَقْف أشْري/سن مِنْشار
21 north light	واجِهَة بحرية
22 broach roof	سَقْف مخْرَزي/برُوش
23 eyebrow	ظُلَّة حاجبيَة
24 conical broach roof	سَقْف مخْرَزي قمعي
25 imperial dome (imperial roof)	قُبَّة امبراطورية
26 weather vane	دَوَّارة الريح
27-83 roof structures of timber	**هياكل السَّقْف الخشبية**
27 rafter roof	سَقْف الرَّافِدَة
28 rafter	رَافِدَة (سَقْف مائل)
29 roof beam	كمَرَة السَّقْف
30 diagonal tie (cross tie, sprocket piece, cocking piece)	رِبَاط شدَّاد مائل
31 arris fillet (tilting fillet)	شدَّاد سُوكَة (شَرْحَة قلابة)
32 outer wall	سَطح خارجي
33 beam head	رأس الكمَرة/العَتَبَة
34 collar beam roof (trussed rafter roof)	سَقْف بعتَب شدَّاد
35 collar beam (collar)	عَتَب شدَّاد (شدَّاد)
36 rafter	رَافِدَة (لسَقْف مائل)
37 strutted collar beam roof structure	هَيْكَل سَقْف بشدَّاد وقوائم انضغاط
38 collar beams	عَتَب شدَّاد، شدَّادَات
39 purlin	رَافِدَة أفقية، مدَّادة
40 post (stile, stud)	قائم
41 brace	رِبَاط، كتف، شكال
42 unstrutted (king pin) roof structure	هَيْكَل سَقْف بقائم جَمَلُون ملك/ بعضد جَمَلُونى رئيسى
43 ridge purlin	رَافِدَة أفقية حَرْفِيَّة
44 inferior purlin	رَافِدَة أفقية سفلية
45 rafter head (rafter end)	طَرْف رَافِدَة السَّقْف المائل
46 purlin roof with queen post and pointing sill	سَقْف ذو رَافِدَة أفقية وجَمَلُون ملِكَة وعَتَبة مسننة
47 pointing sill	عَتَبة مسننة
48 ridge beam (ridge board)	كمَر حَرْفِي
49 simple tie	رِبَاط شدَّاد بسيط
50 double tie	رِبَاط شدَّاد مزدوج
51 purlin	رَافِدَة أفقية، مدَّادَة
52 purlin roof structure with queen post	هَيْكَل سَقْف ذو روافد أفقية وقائم جَمَلُون مِلكَة
53 tie beam	عَتَبة رابطة
54 joist (ceiling joist)	حائز (حائز السَّقْف)
55 principal rafter	رَافِدَة سَقْف مائل رئيسية
56 common rafter	رَافِدَة سَقْف مائل عادية
57 angle brace (angle tie)	رِبَاط/كتف زاوِيّ
58 brace (strut)	رِبَاط، كتف
59 ties	شدَّادَات، أربطة
60 hip (hipped) roof with purlin roof structure	سَقْف مُهَرَّم ذو هَيْكَل بروافد أفقية
61 jack rafter	رَافِدَة سَقْف مائل جانبية قصيرة
62 hip rafter	رَافِدَة سَقْف مائل سِنامية
63 jack rafter	رَافِدَة سَقْف مائل جانبية قصيرة
64 valley rafter	رَافِدَة سَقْف مائل ركنية/ زَاوِيَة
65 queen truss	قائم جَمَلُون ملِكَة
66 main beam	كمَر رئيسي
67 summer (summer beam)	عَتَبة علوية
68 queen post (truss post)	قائم جَمَلُون/رئيسي
69 brace (strut)	رِبَاط، كتف، شِكال
70 collar beam (collar)	عَتَبة شدَّادَة (شدَّاد)
71 trimmer (*Am.* header)	آدية، جائز طولاني ثخين
72 solid-web girder	رَافِدَة ذات وَتَرَة مُصْمَتَة
73 lower chord	وَتَر سفلي
74 upper chord	وَتَر علوي
75 boarding	لوْح تغطية
76 purlin	رَافِدَة أفقية
77 supporting outer wall	حائط الإسْناد الخارجي
78 roof truss	جَمَلُون السَّقْف
79 lower chord	وَتَر سفلي
80 upper chord	وَتَر علوي
81 post	عمود، دعامة
82 brace (strut)	رِبَاط، كتف، شِكال
83 support	مرتكز، دعامة، حامِل
84-98 timber joints	**وَصْلات خشبية**
84 mortise (mortice) and tenon joint	وَصْلة نقرة ولسان
85 forked mortise (mortice) and tenon joint	وَصْلة نقرة ولسان متشعبة
86 halving (halved) joint	وَصْلة تعشيق نصف على نصف
87 simple scarf joint	وَصْلة تراكبية بسيطة
88 oblique scarf joint	وَصْلة تراكبية مائلة
89 dovetail halving	وَصْلة غنفارِية نصفية
90 single skew notch	وَصْلة ذات ثَلْمَة مائلة
91 double skew notch	وَصْلة ذات ثَلْمَتَيْن مائلتيْن
92 wooden nail	خابور خشبي
93 pin	وَتَد
94 clout nail (clout)	مِسْمَار مربع الرأس
95 wire nail	مِسْمَار إبرة
96 hardwood wedges	أسافين من الخشب الصلب

97 cramp iron (timber dog, dog) قامِطة حديدية (كُلاّبة)
98 bolt مِسْمَار قلاووظ (مُلَوْلَب)

122 Roof and Roofer السَّقْف وأجْزَاء السَّقْف

1 tiled roof سَقْف قَرْمِيدَي
2 plain-tile double-lap roofing تسقيف مزدوج ببلاط عادي
3 ridge tile قَرْمِيدَة حَرْفية
4 ridge course tile قَرْمِيدَة مدماك حَرْفية
5 under-ridge tile بلاط حَرْفِي
6 plain (plane) tile بلاطة سَادَة (غير منقوشة)
7 ventilating tile بلاطة تهوية
8 ridge tile قَرْميد حَرْفِي
9 hip tile بلاطة تَسْنيم/تَهْريم
10 hipped end طَرْف مُسَنَّم/مُهَرَّم
11 valley (roof valley) زَاوِيَة تقابل سَقْفين مائلين
12 skylight مَنْوَر
13 chimney مِدْخَنَة
14 chimney flashing, made of sheet zinc حَشْوَة واقية بالمِدْخَنَة من صفائح الزنك لِمَنْع التسرب
15 ladder hook خُطَّاف السُلَّم
16 snow guard bracket كتيفة واقية الثلوج
17 battens (slating and tiling battens) مُورينات
18 batten gauge (*Am.* gage) مقياس المسافات بين الألواح
19 rafter رَافِدَة (لسَقْف مائل)
20 tile hammer مِطْرَقَة بلاط
21 lath axe (*Am.* ax) بَلْطة اللوَيْحَات الخشبية
22 hod حَوْض نقل الطوب والمُلاط
23 hod hook خطاف تثبيت الحَوْض
24 opening (hatch) فتحة في السَّقْف
25 gable (gable end) مقص جَمَلُون
26 toothed lath لَوْح خشبي مسنن
27 soffit بَطْنِيَّة السَّقْف
28 gutter مِزْرَاب
29 rainwater pipe (down-pipe) ماسورة تصريف ماء المطر
30 swan`s neck (swan-neck) عنق إوزي
31 pipe clip مِشْبك تثبيت ماسورة
32 gutter bracket كتيفة المِزْرَاب
33 tile cutter آلة قطع البلاط
34 scaffold سقَالة
35 safety wall جِدَار أمان
36 eaves افريز
37 outer wall جِدَار خارجي
38 exterior rendering تجصيص خارجي
39 frost-resistant brick-work بناء طوب مقاوم للصقيع
40 inferior purlin رَافِدَة أفقية سفلية
41 rafter head (rafter end) طَرْف رَافِدَة (لسَقْف مائل)
42 eaves fascia واجِهَة الافريز
43 double lath (tilting lath) قِدَّة مزدوجة (قِدَّة قلابة)
44 insulating boards ألواح عازلة
45-60 tiles and tile roofings **القَرْمِيدَة/البلاط والأسَقْف القَرْمِيدِيَّة**
45 split-tiled roof سَقْف مُغطى ببلاط مَشْطُور
46 plain (plane) tile بلاطة عادية
47 ridge course مِدْمَاك حَرْفِي/ظَهْري
48 slip شريحة مبيتة للتسمير
49 eaves course مِدْمَاك الافريز
50 plain-tiled roof سَقْف من البلاط العادي
51 nib طَرْف بلاطة مُسَنَّن
52 ridge tile قَرْمِيدَة حَرْفية/ظَهْرية
53 pantiled roof سَقْف قَرْمِيدَة مُمَوَّج متراكب
54 pantile قَرْمِيدَة مُمَوَّجة مُتَرَاكِبة
55 pointing تجميل البلاطات بالمُلاط أو المُونَة
56 Spanish-tiled roof (*Am.* mission-tiled roof) سَقْف من البلاط الأسباني
57 under tile بلاط تحتاني
58 over tile بلاط فَوْقي
59 interlocking tile بلاط تعشيق
60 flat interlocking tile بلاط تعشيق مُسطح
61-89 slate roof **السَّقْف الإردوازي**
61 roof boards (roof boarding, roof sheathing) ألواح السَّقْف الخشبية
62 roofing paper (sheathing paper); *also:* roofing felt (*Am.* rag felt) وَرَق تسقيف للعَزْل، أيضا: لباد السَّقْف
63 cat ladder (roof ladder) سُلَّم السَّقْف
64 coupling hook عقافة، خُطَّاف توصيل
65 ridge hook خُطَّاف الحافة/الظهر
66 roof trestle مِنْصَب السَّقْف
67 trestle rope حبل المِنْصَب
68 knot عُقْدَة
69 ladder hook خطاف السُلَّم
70 scaffold board لَوْح السقَالة
71 slater عامل تبليط
72 nail bag حقيبة المسامير
73 slate hammer مِطْرَقَة الإردواز
74 slate nail, a galvanized wire nail مِسْمَار إردواز، مِسْمَار إبرة مُجَلْفَن
75 slater's shoe, a bast or hemp shoe حذاء عامل التبليط، حذاء لحائي أو من القُنَّب
76 eaves course (eaves joint) مِدْمَاك الافريز
77 corner bottom slate إردواز الركن السفلي
78 roof course مِدْمَاك السَّقْف
79 ridge course (ridge joint) مِدْمَاك حَرْفي
80 gable slate إردواز الجَمَلُون
81 tail line طَرْف سفلي
82 valley (roof valley) مفرج السقف
83 box gutter (trough gutter, parallel gutter) مِزْرَاب صندوقي
84 slater's iron حديدة عامل التبليط
85 slate حَجَر إردواز
86 back الظَّهر
87 head الرأس
88 front edge الحافة الأمامية
89 tail الذَّيْل
90-103 asphalt-impregnated paper roofing and **تسقيف بالوَرَق المُشَبَّع بالأسفلت والتسقيف المُمَوَّج بالأسمنت**

corrugated asbestos cement roofing **الأمينتي**

90 asphalt-impregnated paper roof سَقْف من الوَرَق المُشَبَّع بالأسفلت
91 width [parallel to the gutter] عرض [بمُوَزاة المزراب]
92 gutter مِزْرَاب
93 ridge حرف/ظهر السَّقْف
94 join موضع تلاقي لَوْحين
95 width [at right angles to the gutter] عرض [بزوايا قائمة من المزْرَاب]
96 felt nail (clout nail) مِسْمَار لِبادي
97 corrugated asbestos cement roof سَقْف مُمَوَّج من الأسمنت الأمينتي
98 corrugated sheet لَوْح مُمَوَّج
99 ridge capping piece قطعة تغطية حَرْف السَّقْف
100 lap طية تراكب
101 wood screw مِسْمَار بريمي للخشب
102 rust-proof zinc cup كَأس زنك مقاوم للصدأ
103 lead washer صامولة من الرصاص

123 Floor, Ceiling, Staircase Construction الأرْضيَّة والسَّقْف وإنشَاءَات السَّلالِم

1 basement wall, a concrete wall حائط الأساس ، جِدَار خرساني
2 footing (foundation) أساس (قاعدة)
3 foundation base قاعدة الأساس
4 damp course (damp-proof course) طَبَقَة صامِدة للرطوبة
5 waterproofing طَبَقَة صامدة للماء
6 rendering coat طَبَقَة تجصيص
7 brick paving تبليط بالطوب
8 sand bed فَرْشَة رملية
9 ground طَبَقَة أساسية
10 shuttering شَدَّة الخرسانة
11 peg وتد خابوري
12 hardcore فَرْشَة صلدة
13 oversite concrete خرسانة قاعدية
14 cement screed طَبَقَة علوية أسمنتية للتسوية
15 brickwork base بناء قاعدي من الطوب
16 basement stairs, solid concrete stairs دَرَجات الطابق الأول
17 block step قالب دَرَجَة السلَّم
18 curtail step (bottom step) دَرَجَة السلَّم السفلية
19 top step دَرَجَة السلَّم العلوية
20 nosing بروز الأنف
21 skirting (skirting board, *Am.* mopboard, washboard, scrub board, base) إزار الحائط
22 balustrade of metal bars درابزين بِبرْمَق من القضبان الصلبة
23 ground-floor (*Am.* first-floor) landing صَدَفَة الطابق الأرضي
24 front door الباب الأمامي
25 foot scraper مِمْسَحة الأرْجُل
26 flagstone paving تبليط بالحجارة الصَّخْرِيَّة
27 mortar bed فَرْشَة مُلاطية
28 concrete ceiling, a reinforced concrete slab سَقْف خرساني
29 ground-floor (*Am.* first-floor) brick wall جِدَار الطابق الأرضي المصنوع من الطوب
30 ramp مُنْحَدر
31 wedge-shaped step طَبَقَة إسفينية الشكل
32 tread نائمة الدَرَجَة
33 riser قائمة الدرَجَة
34-41 landing **صَدَفَة السَّلالم**
34 landing beam عَتَبة الصدَفَة
35 ribbed reinforced concrete floor أرضية مُضَلَّعَة من الخرسانة المُسلَّحة
36 rib ضلع
37 steel-bar reinforcement قضيب مسلح من الصلب
38 subfloor (blind floor) أرضية تحتانية
39 level layer طَبَقَة تَسْوِيَة
40 finishing layer طَبَقَة تشطيب
41 top layer (screed) طَبَقَة علوية
42-44 dog-legged staircase, a staircase without a well **سلالم ملتوية**، سلالم بدون بئر
42 curtail step (bottom step) الدَّرَجَة السفلية
43 newel post (newel) قائم الدَرَابزين
44 outer string (*Am.* outer stringer) رَكيزة خارجية
45 wall string (*Am.* wall stringer) رَكيزة جِدَارية
46 staircase bolt مِسْمَار الدَّرَج
47 tread نائمة الدَّرَجَة
48 riser قائمة الدَّرَجَة
49 wreath piece (wreathed string) سُلَّم ذو قلبات دائرية
50 balustrade درابزين بِبرَامِق
51 baluster بَرْمَق
52-62 intermediate landing **صَدَفَة سلالم متوسطة**
52 wreath إكليل الدرابزين
53 handrail (guard rail) درابزين الدَّرَج
54 head post القائم الرئيسي
55 landing beam عَتَبة الصَّدَفَة
56 lining board لَوْح تبطين
57 fillet شَرِيحَة خشبية
58 lightweight building board لَوْح بناء خفيف الوزن
59 ceiling plaster جَصُّ السَّقْف
60 wall plaster جَصُّ الحائط
61 false ceiling سَقْف ظاهري غير حامل
62 strip flooring (overlay flooring, parquet strip) أرضية من الألواح الخشبية، أرضية بارْكيه
63 skirting board (*Am.* mopboard, washboard, scrub board, base) لَوْح إزار الحائط
64 beading حَزٌّ إطاري
65 staircase window نافذة السُلَّم
66 main landing beam عَتَبة الصَّدَفَة الرئيسية
67 fillet (cleat) قُبْقاب ساند
68-69 false ceiling **سَقْف ظاهري غير حامِل**

68 false floor (inserted floor)	أرضية زائفة
69 floor filling (plugging, pug)	حَشْو الأرضية قدَّات خشبية
70 laths	تبطين خشبي
71 lathing	جَصُّ السَّقف
72 ceiling plaster	أرضية تحتانية
73 subfloor (blind floor)	أرضية بارْكِيه من قوالب
74 parquet floor with tongued-and-grooved blocks	بحزوز وألْسِنَة
75 quarter-newelled (*Am.* quarter-neweled) staircase	سُلَّم ذو قائم درابزين ربع دائري
76 winding staircase (spiral staircase) with open newels (open-newel staircase)	سُلَّم حلزوني ذو قائم درَجِي مفتوح
77 winding staircase (spiral staircase) with solid newels (solid-newel staircase)	سُلَّم حلزوني ذو قائم درابزين مُصْمَت
78 newel (solid newel)	قائم درابزين (قائم درابزين مُصْمَت)
79 handrail	درابزين الدَّرَج

124 Glazier — الزَّجَّاج

1 glazier's workshop	وَرْشَة الزَّجَّاج
2 frame wood samples (frame samples)	عيِّنات خشب البراويز (عيِّنات براويز)
3 frame wood	خشب براويز
4 mitre joint (mitre, *Am.* miter joint, miter)	وَصْلَة مَشْطُوبَة زَاوِية
5 sheet glass; *kinds:* window glass, frosted glass, patterned glass, crystal plate glass, thick glass, milk glass, laminated glass (safety glass, shatterproof glass)	زُجَاج صَفْحِي؛ أنواعه: زُجَاج نوافذ، زُجَاج مُصَنْفَر، زُجَاج مُقَوْلَب زُجَاج، بِلَّوري، زُجَاج سميك، زُجَاج لَبَني، زُجَاج رقائقي (زُجَاج أمان)
6 cast glass; *kinds:* stained glass, ornamental glass, raw glass, bull's-eye glass, wired glass, line glass (lined glass)	زُجَاج مصبوب؛ أنواعه: زُجَاج ملون، زُجَاج مزخرف، زُجَاج خام، زُجَاج عين الثور، زُجَاج سِلْكي، زُجَاج مُخَطَّط
7 mitring (*Am.* mitering) machine	مَاكِينَة شَطْب الزُجَاج
8 glassworker (e.g. building glazier, glazier, decorative glass worker)	عامل ورشة الزُجَاج (زَجَّاج مباني، زَجَّاج، عامل الزخرفة بالزُجَاج)
9 glass holder	حامل ألواح الزُجَاج
10 piece of broken glass	قطعة زُجَاج مكسور
11 lead hammer	مِطْرَقَة ذات رأس رصاص
12 lead knife	سِكِّين ذات نصل من الرصاص
13 came (lead came)	كامة من الرصاص
14 leaded light	نافذة ذات إطار معدني من الرصاص
15 workbench	طاولة الشغل
16 pane of glass	لَوْح زُجَاجي
17 putty	معجون
18 glazier's hammer	مِطْرَقَة الزَّجَّاج
19 glass pliers	زَردية زُجَاج
20 glazier's square	زَاوِيَة الزَّجَّاج
21 glazier's rule	مِسْطَرة الزَّجَّاج
22 glazier's beam compass	فرجار ذو عاتق
23 eyelet	عروة
24 glazing sprig	مِسْمَار الزِّجَاجَة
25-26 glass cutters	**قواطع الزجاج**
25 diamond glass cutter	قاطع ماسي
26 steel-wheel (steel) glass cutter	قاطع ذو دولاب فولاذي
27 putty knife	سِكِّين المعجون
28 pin wire	سلك إبرة
29 panel pin	مِسْمَار ألواح
30 mitre (*Am.* miter) block (mitre box) [with saw]	قالب القطع المائل/ الشطب [مع المِنْشَار]
31 mitre (*Am.* miter) shoot (mitre board)	لَوْح مشطوب

125 Plumber — السَّبَّاك

1 metal shears (tinner's snips, *Am.* tinner's shears)	مِقَص الصفيح
2 elbow snips (angle shears)	قرَّاضَة زَاوية
3 gib	صفحة معدنية للتثبيت
4 lapping plate	لَوْح تجليخ بالتحضين
5-7 propane soldering apparatus	**جهَاز اللحام بالبروبين**
5 propane soldering iron, a hatchet iron	مِكْوَاة اللحام بالبروبين
6 soldering stone, a sal-ammoniac block	حَجَر اللحام
7 soldering fluid (flux)	صَهُور لحام
8 beading iron for forming reinforcement beading	أداة تحزيز لتشكيل حزوز تقوية
9 angled reamer	مِسْحَل/مِقْوَار زاويّ
10 workbench (bench)	طاولة الشغل
11 beam compass (trammel, *Am.* beam trammel)	فرجار ذو عاتق (فرجار القطع الناقص)
12 electric hand die	لُقْمَة لَوْلَبة يدوية كهربائية
13 hollow punch	سُنْبُك أجْوَف
14 chamfering hammer	مِطْرَقَة شَدْف/شَطْب
15 beading swage (beading hammer)	مِطْرَقَة تحزيز
16 abrasive-wheel cutting-off machine	مَاكِينَة قص ذات عجلة تجليخ
17 plumber	سبَّاك
18 mallet	مِطْرَقَة خشبية
19 mandrel	مَاسك العُدَّة، شِيَاق
20 socket (tinner's socket)	جِلْبَة
21 block	كتلة القاعدة
22 anvil	سِنْدَان
23 stake	وَتَد

24 circular saw (buzz saw)	مِنْشَار دائري/قرصي (مِنْشَار أزّاز)
25 flanging, swaging, and wiring machine	مَاكِينَة حف وتشكيل بالطَّرْق وتقوية بالأسلاك
26 sheet shears (guillotine)	مقص الصفائح المعدنية
27 screw-cutting machine (thread-cutting machine, die stocks)	مَاكِينَة قَطْع اللوَالِب
28 pipe-bending machine (bending machine, pipe bender)	مَاكِينَة ثَنْي المواسير
29 welding transformer	مُحَوِّل اللحام
30 bending machine (rounding machine) for shaping funnels	مَاكِينَة ثَنْي لتشكيل الأقماع

126 Plumber, Gas Fitter, Heating Engineer / السَّبَّاك، عامل تركيب أجْهِزَة الغاز، مُهَنْدِس السخَّانات

1 gas fitter and plumber	عامل تركِيب أجْهِزَة الغَاز والسَّبَّاك
2 stepladder	سُلَّم دَرَجِي
3 safety chain	سِلْسِلَة أمان
4 stop valve	مَحْبَس
5 gas meter	عدَّاد الغاز
6 bracket	كتيفة
7 service riser	أنْبُوب الخدمة
8 distributing pipe	أنْبُوب/ماسورة التوزيع
9 supply pipe	أنْبُوب الإمداد
10 pipe-cutting machine	مَاكِينَة قَطْع المواسير
11 pipe repair stand	حامل إصلاح المواسير
12-25 gas and water appliances	**الأجهزة الكهربية الخاصة بالغاز والماء**
12, 13 geyser an instantaneous water heater	سخان مياه فوري
12 gas water heater	سَخَّان ماء يعمل بالغاز
13 electric water heater	سَخَّان ماء يعمل بالكهرباء
14 toilet cistern	صندوق الطَّرْد (السِّيفُون)
15 float	عوَّامَة
16 bell	جَرَس
17 flush pipe	ماسورة اندفاع الماء
18 water inlet	ماسورة دخول الماء
19 flushing lever (lever)	ذراع تشغيل صندوق الطرد
20 radiator	المُشِعّ، ردياتير
21 radiator rib	ضلع المُشِعّ
22 two-pipe system	نظام ذو أنْبُوبتين
23 flow pipe	أنْبُوب الدفق
24 return pipe	أنْبُوب استرجاع
25 gas heater	سَخَّان يعمل بالغاز
26-37 plumbing fixtures	**تجهيزات السِّبَاكة**
26 trap (anti-syphon trap)	مِصْيَدَة
27 mixer tap (*Am.* mixing faucet) for washbasins	صُنْبُور خلاط لأحواض الغسيل
28 hot tap	صُنْبُور الماء الساخن
29 cold tap	صُنْبُور الماء البارد
30 extendible shower attachment	ذراع دُش قابل للإطالة
31 water tap (pillar tap) for washbasins	صُنْبُور ماء
32 spindle top	رأس دَوَرَاني
33 shield	غلاف واق
34 draw-off tap (*Am.* faucet)	حَنَفِيَّة تفريغ
35 supatap	حَنَفِيَّة
36 swivel tap	حَنَفِيَّة دوَّارة
37 flushing valve	صمام الدفق
38-52 fittings	**التركيبات**
38 joint with male thread	وَصْلَة ذات لَوْلَب خارجي
39 reducing socket (reducing coupler)	قارنة لَوْلَبِيَّة مُصَغِّرَة
40 elbow screw joint (elbow coupling)	قارنة مِرْفَقِيَّة
41 reducing socket (reducing coupler) with female thread	قارنة مُصَغِّرَة ذات لَوْلَب داخلي
42 screw joint	وَصْلَة لَوْلَبِيَّة
43 coupler (socket)	قارنة
44 T-joint (T-junction joint, tee)	وَصْلَة تائية
45 elbow screw joint with female thread	وَصْلَة لَوْلَبِيَّة مرفقية ذات لَوْلَب داخلي
46 bend	كوع منحني
47 T-joint (T-junction joint, tee) with female taper thread	وَصْلَة تائية ذات لَوْلَب داخلي مخروطي
48 ceiling joint	وَصْلَة سَقْفِية
49 reducing elbow	مرفق مُصَغِّر
50 cross	وَصْلَة تصالبية
51 elbow joint with male thread	وَصْلَة مرفقية ذات لَوْلَب خارجي
52 elbow joint	وَصْلَة مرفقية
53-57 pipe supports	**أجزاء تثبيت الأنابيب**
53 saddle clip	مِشْبك سَرْجِي
54 spacing bracket	كتيفة مباعدة
55 plug	خابور
56 pipe clips	مشابك أنابيب
57 two-piece spacing clip	مِشْبك مباعدة من قطعتين
58-86 plumber's tools, gas fitter's tools	**أدوات السبَّاك، أدوات عامل تركيب أجهزة الغاز**
58 gas pliers	زَرَّدِيَّة مواسير الغاز
59 alligator wrench	مفتَاح ربط تمساحي
60 combination cutting pliers	قَرَّاضة، زَرَّدِيَّة
61 water pump pliers	زَرَّدِيَّة فك وربط المواسير
62 flat-nose pliers	زَرَّدِيَّة مسَطحة الطَّرْف
63 nipple key	مفتَاح حلَمِي
64 round-nose pliers	زَرَّدِيَّة مستديرة الطَّرْف
65 pincers	كمَّاشة
66 adjustable S-wrench	مفتَاح ستلون قابل للتعديل
67 screw wrench	مفتَاح إنجليزي
68 shifting spanner	مفتَاح ربط انضباطي
69 screwdriver	مفك
70 compass saw (keyhole saw)	مِنْشَار منحنيات
71 hacksaw frame	إطار مِنْشَار المعادن
72 hand saw	مِنْشَار يدوي
73 soldering iron	مِكْوَاة لحام
74 blowlamp (blowtorch)	بُوري لِحَام

[for soldering]
75 sealing tape — شريط مانع للتسرب
76 tin-lead solder — سبيكة لحام من القصدير والرصاص
77 club hammer — مِطْرَقَة قصيرة اليد
78 hammer — شاكوش
79 spirit level — ميزان تسوية
80 steel-leg vice (*Am.* vise) — ملزَمة بقَدَم فولاذية
81 pipe vice (*Am.* vise) — ملزَمة المواسير
82 pipe-bending machine — مَاكِينَة ثَنْي المواسير
83 former (template) — أداة تشكيل (قالب)
84 pipe cutter — قاطِعة المواسير
85 hand die — لقمة يدوية
86 screw-cutting machine (thread-cutting machine) — مَاكِينَة قَطْع اللوالب

127 Electrician — الكَهْرَبَائي

1 electrician (electrical fitter, wireman) — الكَهْرَبَائي
2 bell push (doorbell) for low-voltage safety current — جَرَس باب انضغاطي يعمل بتيار أمان منخفض الفولْطِيَّة
3 house telephone with call button — هاتِف منزلي ذو زِر نِدَاء
4 [flush-mounted] rocker switch — مِفْتَاح كهربائي مُتَرَجِّح [مُرَكَّب تساطحيا]
5 [flush-mounted] earthed socket (wall socket, plug point, *Am.* wall outlet, convenience outlet, outlet) — مَقْبَس مُؤَرَّض [مُرَكَّب تساطحيا] (مَقْبَس جِداري، مَخْرَج تيار)
6 [surface-mounted] earthed double socket (double wall socket, double plug point, *Am.* double wall outlet, double convenience outlet, double outlet) — مَقْبَس مزدوج مُؤَرَّض [مثبت فوق الجدار] (مَقْبَس جِداري مزدوج، مَخْرَج تيار مزدوج)
7 switched socket (switch and socket) — مَقْبَس ذو مِفْتَاح كهربي
8 four-socket (four-way) adapter — مُهايِئ ذو أربعة مقابس
9 earthed plug — قابس مُؤَرَّض
10 extension lead (*Am.* extension cord) — وَصْلَة تمديد، سلك تمديد
11 extension plug — قابس وَصْلَة التمديد
12 extension socket — مَقْبَس وَصْلَة التمديد
13 surface-mounted three-pole earthed socket [for three-phase circuit] with neutral conductor — مَقْبَس مؤرضٌ ثلاثي الأقطاب ذو مُوَصِّل متعادل يثبت فوق الجدار
14 three-phase plug — قابس ثلاثي الأطوار
15 electric bell (electric buzzer) — جَرَس كهربي
16 pull-switch (cord-operated wall switch) — مِفْتَاح يعمل بجذب السلك
17 dimmer switch [for smooth adjustment of lamp brightness] — مِفْتَاح تخفيف شدة الإضاءة [لضبط وهج المِصْبَاح]
18 drill-cast rotary switch — مِفْتَاح دَوَّار مصبوب
19 miniature circuit breaker (screw-in circuit breaker, fuse) — قاطع تيار صغير (فيوز)
20 resetting button — زر الضبط
21 set screw [for fuses and miniature circuit breakers] — لَوْلَب ضبط [للفيوزات وقواطع التيار الصغيرة]
22 underfloor mounting (underfloor sockets) — تركيب المَقَابِس تحت الأرضية
23 hinged floor socket for power lines and communication lines — مَقْبَس أرضي مفصلي لخطوط الكهرباء والاتصالات
24 sunken floor socket with hinged lid (snap lid) — مَقْبَس أرضي غاطِس ذو غطاء مفصلي
25 surface-mounted socket outlet (plug point) box — عِلْبَة مَخْرَج المَقْبَس من النوع المثبت على الجدار
26 pocket torch, a torch (*Am.* flashlight) — مِصْبَاح بطارية جيب
27 dry cell battery — بطارية خلية جافة
28 contact spring — نابِض التماس
29 strip of thermoplastic connectors — شريط من الوصلات اللَدِنَة بالحرارة
30 steel draw-in wire (draw wire) with threading key, and ring attached — سلْك صلب للسحب ذو مِفْتَاح مَلَوْلَب وحلقة
31 electricity meter cupboard — صنْدُوق عدَّاد الكهرباء
32 electricity meter — عدَّاد الكهرباء
33 miniature circuit breakers (miniature circuit breaker consumer unit) — قاطع تيار صغير
34 insulating tape (*Am.* friction tape) — شريط عازل
35 fuse holder — حَامِل الصمام (الفيوز)
36 circuit breaker (fuse), a fuse cartridge with fusible element — قاطع تيار، فيوز ذو عنصر قابل للانصهار
37 colour (*Am.* color) indicator [showing current rating] — مؤشِّر لَوْني [يبين مُعَدَّل التيار]
38-39 contact maker — **وَصْلَة التلامس**
40 cable clip — مشبك تثبيت الكيبل
41 universal test meter (multiple meter for measuring current and voltage) — عَدَّاد اختبار للأغراض العامة (عدَّاد قياس التيار والفولطية)
42 thermoplastic moisture-proof cable — كيبل لَدِن مقاوم للرطوبة
43 copper conductor — مُوَصِّل نحاسي
44 three-core cable — كيبل ذو ثلاثة قلوب
45 electric soldering iron — مِكْوَاة لحام كهربية
46 screwdriver — مفك
47 water pump pliers — زَرَّدِيَّة فك وربط الأنابيب
48 shock-resisting safety — خوذة أمان مقاومة

helmet — للصدمات
49 tool case — صُنْدُوق العُدَّة
50 round-nose pliers — زَرَدِيَّة ذات طَرْف مستدير
51 cutting pliers — قَرَّاضة
52 junior hacksaw — مِنْشار (معادن) صغير
53 combination cutting pliers — زَرَدِيَّة قطع، قَرَّاضة
54 insulated handle — مِقْبَض معزول
55 continuity tester — جِهَاز اختبار استمرار الدائرة الكهربية
56 electric light bulb (general service lamp, filament lamp) — مِصْبَاح كهربي (مِصْبَاح بفتيلة)
57 glass bulb (bulb) — بُصَيْلَة المِصْبَاح الكهربي
58 coiled-coil filament — فتيلة ملفوفة (مِلَفِّيَة)
59 screw base — قاعدة اللوْلَبة
60 lampholder — دَوَاة المِصْبَاح
61 fluorescent tube — مِصْبَاح فلوري
62 bracket for fluorescent tubes — كتف تثبيت المصابيح الفلُوريَّة
63 electrician's knife — سِكِّين الكهربائي
64 wire strippers — زَرَدِيَّة تعرية الأسلاك
65 bayonet fitting — دَوَاة مِصْبَاح بمسمارين
66 three-pin socket with switch — مَقْبَس ثلاثة ثقوب مزود بمِفْتَاح كهربي
67 three-pin plug — قابِس ثلاثي المسامير
68 fuse carrier with fuse wire — حَامِل فيوز مزود بسلك فيوزي
69 light bulb with bayonet fitting — مِصْبَاح كهربي ذو وَصْلَة مسننة (بمسمارين)

128 Paperhanger — عامِل تَرْكِيب وَرَق الحائط

1-17 preparation of surfaces — **إعداد الأَسْطح**

1 wallpaper-stripping liquid (stripper) — سائل نَزْع وَرَق الحائط
2 plaster (plaster of Paris) — لَصُوق (جبس باريس)
3 filler — حَشْوَة
4 glue size (size) — غراء
5 lining paper, a backing paper — وَرَق تبطين، وَرَق تقوية
6 primer — بطانة، طلاء الطبقة الأساسية
7 fluate — مادة للتَّصْمِيد للماء
8 shredded lining paper — وَرَق تبطين مُقَطَّع
9 wallpaper-stripping machine (stripper) — مَاكِينَة نزع وَرَق الحائط
10 scraper — مكْشَطَة يدوية
11 smoother — مِمْلَسة
12 perforator — خَرَّامَة، أداة تخريم الوَرَق
13 sandpaper block — كتلة وَرَق السنفرة
14 sandpaper — وَرَق سنفرة
15 stripping knife — سِكِّين تقشير
16 masking tape — شريط تغطية
17 strip of sheet metal [on which wallpaper is laid for cutting] — لَوْح معدني صفائحي [يُوضع عليه الوَرَق لقطعه]

18-53 wallpapering (paper hanging) — **تركيب وَرَق الحائط**

18 wallpaper (*kinds:* wood pulp paper, wood chip paper, fabric wall-hangings, synthetic wallpaper, metallic paper,natural (*e.g.* wood or cork) paper, tapestry wallpaper) — وَرَق حائط؛ أنواعه: وَرَق من لُباب الخشب، وَرَق من نُحاتة الخشب، وَرَق نَسِيجي، وَرَق من الألياف الصناعية، وَرَق مَعْدَني، وَرَق طبيعي (خشب أو فِلِّين أو كَتَّان)
19 length of wallpaper — طول وَرَق الحائط
20 butted paper edges — أطراف وَرَق مُلْصَقَة تَنَاكُبياً
21 matching edge — طَرْف متطابق (مع الطَرْف الآخر)
22 non-matching edge — طَرْف غير متطابق
23 wallpaper paste — مَعْجُون لَصْق وَرَق الحائط
24 heavy-duty paste — مَعْجُون شديد التحمل
25 pasting machine — مَاكِينَة المَعْجَنَة
26 paste [for the pasting machine] — مَعْجُون [لمَاكِينَة المَعْجَنَة]
27 paste brush — فُرْشَاة المَعْجُون
28 emulsion paste — مَعْجُون استحلابي
29 picture rail — إفريز الصورة
30 beading pins — مسامير زخرفة
31 pasteboard (paper-hanger's bench) — طاولة دَهْن الوَرَق بالمَعْجُون
32 gloss finish — طلاء تلميع للتشطيب
33 paperhanging kit — حَقِيبَة أدوات تركيب وَرَق الحائط
34 shears (bull-nosed scissors) — مِقَص
35 filling knife — سِكِّين مَعْجُون الحَشْو
36 seam roller — رول تسوية
37 hacking knife — سِكِّين تخشين السطح
38 knife (trimming knife) — سِكِّين (تشذيب)
39 straightedge — مسطرة قويمة لاختبار الاستقامة
40 paperhanging brush — فُرْشَاة تركيب وَرَق الحائط
41 wallpaper-cutting board — لَوْح تقطيع وَرَق الحائط
42 cutter — أداة قَطْع
43 trimmer — أداة تشذيب
44 plastic spatula — جاروف بلاستيكي
45 chalked string — خَيْط طباشيري
46 spreader — أداة الفَرْش والتوزيع
47 paper roller — رول الوَرَق
48 flannel cloth — قماش (قطن)
49 dry brush — فُرْشَاة جافة
50 ceiling paperhanger — أداة تركيب وَرَق السقف
51 overlap angle — زاوية متداخلة
52 paperhanger's trestles — سُلَّم تركيب وَرَق الحائط
53 ceiling paper — وَرَق السقف

129 Painter — الصَّبَّاغ، النَّقَّاش

1 painting — الدِّهان، الطلاء
2 painter — نقّاش، دهّان
3 paintbrush — فُرْشَاة الدهان
4 emulsion paint (emulsion) — دِهان استحلابي

5 stepladder	سُلَّم دَرَجِي
6 can (tin) of paint	صفيحة الدِّهان/الطلاء
7-8 cans (tins) **of paint**	**صفائح الدِّهان/الطلاء**
7 can (tin) with fixed handle	صفيحة ذات مِقْبَض ثابت
8 paint kettle	سَطْل الطلاء
9 drum of paint	بَرْمِيل طلاء
10 paint bucket	دَلْو طلاء
11 paint roller	رول الدَّهن
12 grill [for removing excess paint from the roller]	جريل [شبكة مُصَبَّعَة لإزالة الطلاء الزائد من الرول]
13 stippling roller	رول ترقيط الطلاء
14 varnishing	الوَرْنَشَة، الدهان بالورنيش
15 oil-painted dado	جزء سفلي من الجدار مدهون بالزيت
16 canister for thinner	عِلْبَة التِّنَر (مادة مُرَقِّقَة للقوام)
17 flat brush for larger surfaces (flat wall brush)	فُرْشَاة مستوية للأسطح الكبيرة المستوية
18 stippler	فُرْشَاة الدهان المُرَقَّط
19 fitch	فُرْشَاة شَعْر
20 cutting-in brush	فُرْشَاة مزج
21 radiator brush (flay brush)	فُرْشَاة طلاء المُشِعَّات/ كشط
22 paint scraper	مِكْشَطَة طلاء
23 scraper	مِكْشَطَة يدوية
24 putty knife	سِكِّين مَعْجَنَة/المَعْجُون
25 sandpaper	وَرَق سنفرة
26 sandpaper block	كتلة وَرَق السنفرة
27 floor brush	فُرْشَاة للأرضية
28 sanding and spraying	السنفرة والرَّش
29 grinder	جَلاَّخَة
30 sander	مَاكِينَة سنفرة
31 pressure pot	وعاء ضغط
32 spray gun	مسدس رش
33 compressor (air compressor)	ضاغط هواء
34 flow coating machine for flow coating radiators, etc.	مَاكِينَة طَلْي معدني لطلاء المُشِعَّات، الخ.
35 hand spray	رشَّاش يدوي
36 airless spray unit	وحْدَة رش تعمل بدون هواء مضغوط
37 airless spray gun	مسدس رش يعمل بدون هواء مضغوط
38 efflux viscometer	مقياس درجة اللزوجة
39 seconds timer	جِهَاز توقيت الثواني
40 lettering and gilding	**نقش الحروف والتَّكْسِيَة بقشرة ذهب**
41 lettering brush (sign-writing brush, pencil)	رِيشَة كتابة الحروف (قلم)
42 tracing wheel	عجلة استشفاف
43 stencil knife	سِكِّين استنسل
44 oil gold size	مادة غَرَوِيَة من الذهب الزيتي
45 gold leaf	وَرَقَة ذهب
46 outline drawing	رَسْم تمهيدي
47 mahlstick	تُكَأَة الرَّسَّام
48 pouncing	تجفيف بالذرور
49 pounce bag	كيس الذرور
50 gilder's cushion	وِسَادة عامل الطلاء بالذهب
51 gilder's knife	سِكِّين عامل الطلاء بالذهب
52 sizing gold leaf	مُعَالَجَة وَرَق الذهب بمادة غروية
53 filling in the letters with stipple paint	مِلء الحروف بطلاء مُرَقَّط
54 gilder's mop	مِكْنَسَة عامل الطلاء بالذهب

130 Cooper and Tank Construction Engineer — مُهَنْدِس تَصْنِيع البَرَامِيل الخَشَبِيَّة والخَزَّانات

1-33 cooper's and tank construction engineer's workshops	**وَرْشَة مهندس تصنيع البراميل الخشبية والخَزَّانات**
1 tank	خَزَّان، صهريج
2 circumference made of staves (staved circumference)	جِدار خارجي مصنوع من الشرائح الخشبية
3 iron rod	قَضِيب حديد
4 turnbuckle	شدَّادَة، شكال مُلَوْلَب
5 barrel (cask)	برْمِيل (برْمِيل خشبي)
6 body of barrel (of cask)	جِسْم البرْمِيل
7 bunghole	ثقب البرْمِيل
8 band (hoop) of barrel	طَوْق البَرْمِيل
9 barrel stave	شريحة خشبية
10 barrelhead (heading)	رأس البرْمِيل
11 cooper	صانع البراميل الخشبية
12 trusser	مَاكِينَة تثبيت أطواق البرْمِيل
13 drum	أُسْطُوَانَة البرْمِيل
14 gas welding torch	حِمْلاج اللحام بالغاز
15 staining vat, made of thermoplastics	حَوْض صبغ مصنوع من اللدائن الحرارية
16 iron reinforcing bands	شرائط تقوية مصنوعة من الحديد
17 storage container, made of glass fibre (*Am.* glass fiber) reinforced polyester resin	حاوية تخزين مصنوعة من الراتِنْج المُقَوَّى بالألياف الزجاجية
18 manhole	فتحة الدخول
19 manhole cover with handwheel	غطاء فتحة دخول ذو عجلة يدوية
20 flange mount	شَفَة تركيب
21 flange-type stopcock	مِحْبَس بشَفَة
22 measuring tank	خَزَّان قياس
23 shell (circumference)	جدار، غلاف
24 shrink ring	حلَقَة انكماشية
25 hot-air gun	مُسَدَّس الهواء الساخن
26 roller made of glass fibre (*Am.* glass fiber) reinforced synthetic resin	دولفين من الراتِنْج الصناعي المُقَوَّى بألياف زجاجية
27 cylinder	أُسْطُوَانَة
28 flange	شَفَة
29 glass cloth	قماش زجاجي
30 grooved roller	دولفين مُخَدَّد

31 lambskin roller دولفين من جِلْد الغنم
32 ladle for testing viscosity مغْرَفَة لاختبار درجة اللزوجة
33 measuring vessel for hardener وعاء قياس المُقَسّى/مُعَجِّل التصليد

131 Furrier الفَرَّاء

1-25 furrier's workroom مَدْبَغَة ومصنع الملابس الفرائية

1 furrier الفَرَّاء، دبَّاغ الملابس الفرائية
2 steam spray gun مُسَدَّس رش البخار
3 steam iron مِكْوَاة بخارية
4 beating machine مَاكِينَة الضرب
5 cutting machine for letting out furskins مَاكِينَة تقطيع جلود الفِرَاء
6 uncut furskin جِلْد فِرَاء لم يقطع بعد
7 let-out strips (let-out sections) قِطَع مُطَوَّلة من الفِرَاء
8 fur worker عاملة حياكة الملابس الفرائية
9 fur-sewing machine مَاكِينَة حياكة الفِرَاء
10 blower for letting out مِرْوَحَة نفخ قطع الفِرَاء

11-21 furskins جلود الفِرَاء

11 mink skin جِلْد حيوان المِنْك
12 fur side جَانِب فرائي
13 leather side جَانِب جِلْدِي
14 cut furskin فِرَاء مُقَطَّع
15 lynx skin before letting out جِلْد حيوان الوَشَق قبل تقطيعه وتطويله
16 let-out lynx skin قطع مطوَّلة من جِلْد حيوان الوَشَق
17 fur side الجَانِب الفرائي
18 leather side الجَانِب الجِلْدِي
19 let-out mink skin قطع مطوَّلة من جِلْد حيوان المِنْك
20 lynx fur, sewn together (sewn) فِرَاء الوَشَق مُحَاك معا
21 broadtail جِلْد حَمَل القَرْكُول
22 fur marker دبابيس الفِرَاء
23 fur worker عاملة حياكة الملابس الفرائية
24 mink coat معْطَف من فِرَاء المِنْك
25 ocelot coat معْطَف من فِرَاء الأُسْلُوت

132 Joiner I نَجَّار الأثَاثَات (1)

1-73 joiner's workshop وَرْشَة نَجَّار الأثَاثَات

1-28 joiner's tools أدوات نَجَّار الأثَاثَات

1 wood rasp مِبْرَد خشب مُحَبَّب القطعية
2 wood file مِبْرَد خشب
3 compass saw (keyhole saw) مِنْشَار منحنيات (مِنْشَار تفريغ الثقوب)
4 saw handle مِقْبَض المِنْشَار
5 [square-headed] mallet مِطْرَقَة [مربعة الرَّأْس]
6 try square زَاوِيَة ضبط قائمة، زَاوِيَة النَّجَّار

7-11 chisels الأزاميل

7 bevelled-edge chisel (chisel) أَزْمِيل ذو حافة مُشْطوفة
8 mortise (mortice) chisel أَزْمِيل نقر
9 gouge أَزْمِيل مُقَعَّر، مِظْفَار
10 handle مِقْبَض
11 framing chisel (cant chisel) أَزْمِيل نقر (أَزْمِيل مُشْطوف الحافة)
12 glue pot in water bath مغراة في حمام مائي
13 glue pot (glue well), an insert for joiner's glue مِغْرَاة
14 handscrew قَامِطَة يدوية

15-28 planes المساحيج/ الفارات

15 smoothing plane مِسْحَاج/فارة تمليس
16 jack plane مِسْحَاج/فارة تخشين
17 toothing plane مِسْحَاج/فارة تسنين
18 handle (toat) مِقْبَض
19 wedge إسفين
20 plane iron (cutter) سلاح المِسْحَاج/الفارة
21 mouth فُوَّهَة
22 sole قاعدة، نَعْل
23 side جَانِب
24 stock (body) كتلة (جسم)
25 rebate (rabbet) plane مِسْحَاج / فارة افتراز
26 router plane (old woman's tooth) مِسْحَاج تخديد جناح
27 spokeshave مِسْحَاج تقعير/تسنيم ذو مِقْبَضين
28 compass plane مِسْحَاج/فارة منحنيات

29-37 woodworker's bench طاولة عامل الخشب/النَّجَّار

29 foot قاعدة
30 front vice (*Am.* vise) مِلْزَمة أمامية
31 vice (*Am.* vise) handle ذِرَاع المِلْزَمة
32 vice (*Am.* vise) screw لَوْلَب المِلْزَمة
33 jaw فَكُّ المِلْزَمة
34 bench top سطح الطاولة
35 well بئر
36 bench stop (bench holdfast) مِصَدُّ الطاولة
37 tail vice (*Am.* vise) مِلْزَمة خلفية
38 cabinet maker (joiner) نجَّار الدواليب
39 trying plane مِسْحَاج/فارة تسْوِيَة
40 shavings قُشَارَة، براية
41 wood screw برغِي خشب
42 saw set مُفلجَة مناشير
43 mitre (*Am.* miter) box صُنْدُوق القطع المائل
44 tenon saw مِنْشَار تلسين
45 thicknesser (thicknessing machine) مَاكِينَة تثخين
46 thicknessing table with rollers طاولة تثخين ذات اسيطينات
47 kick-back guard واقى الإرتداد
48 chip-extractor opening فتحة طرد النحاتة
49 chain mortising machine (chain mortiser) مَاكِينَة نقر ذات سِلْسلة
50 endless mortising chain سِلْسلة مَاكِينَة نقر متصلة
51 clamp (work clamp) قَامِطَة، ملزمة
52 knot hole moulding (*Am.* molding) machine مَاكِينَة تشكيل الأفاريز والحِلي المثقبة
53 knot hole cutter سِكِينة الثقوب الأنشوطية

54 quick-action chuck ظرف لُقَم المِثْقَب
55 hand lever عتلة يدوية
56 change-gear handle ذِرَاع تبديل السرعة
57 sizing and edging machine مَاكِينَة تحفيف ومعايرة المقاس
58 main switch مفتَاح التشغيل الرَّأسي
59 circular-saw (buzz saw) blade نَصْل مِنْشَار دائري أزاز
60 height (rise and fall) adjustment wheel عَجَلَة ضبط الارتفاع
61 V-way مَجْرَى مُثَلَّثِي المَقْطَع
62 framing table طاولة تشكيل الإطارات/البراويز
63 extension arm (arm) ذِرَاع استطالة
64 trimming table طاولة التهذيب
65 fence حاجز، مِصَد
66 fence adjustment handle ذِرَاع ضبط الحاجز
67 clamp lever ذِرَاع تثبيت
68 board-sawing machine مَاكِينَة نشر الألواح الخشبية
69 swivel motor موتور دَوَّار
70 board support حَامِل اللوح الخشبي
71 saw carriage حاضنة المِنْشَار
72 pedal for raising the transport rollers دَوَّاسة رفع أسيطينات نظام النقل
73 blockboard كتلة اللوح الخشبي

133 Joiner II نَجَّار الأثَاثَات (2)

1 veneer-peeling machine (peeling machine, peeler) مَاكِينَة تقشير الخشب
2 veneer قشرة خشبية
3 veneer-splicing machine مَاكِينَة جَدْل القشور الخشبية
4 nylon-thread cop كبَّة غزل الخيط النَيْلُون
5 sewing machine آليَّة الخياطة
6 dowel hole boring machine (dowel hole borer) مَاكِينَة ثقب فجوات الدِّسار
7 boring motor with hollow-shaft boring bit موتور ثَقْب مزود بمِثْقَاب حَفْر له عمود أجْوَف
8 clamp handle ذِرَاع القَامِطَة/المِلْزَمَة
9 clamp قَامِطَة، مِلْزَمَة
10 clamping shoe حذاء قمط/تثبيت
11 stop bar حاجز
12 edge sander (edge-sanding machine) مَاكِينَة سنفرة للحواف
13 tension roller with extension arm أسْطُوَانَة شد ذات ذِرَاع امتدادي
14 sanding belt regulator (regulating handle) مُنَظِّم سَيْر السنفرة
15 endless sanding belt (sand belt) سَيْر سنفرة متصل
16 belt-tensioning lever ذِرَاع شد السيْر
17 canting table (tilting table) طاولة إمالة
18 belt roller أسْطُوَانَة السيْر
19 angling fence for mitres (*Am.* miters) حاجز تَزْوِيَة للأسطح المَشْطوبة الزَاوِيَة
20 opening dust hood حاوية نشارة مفتوحة
21 rise adjustment of the table آليَّة ضبط ارتفاع الطاولة
22 rise adjustment wheel for the table عَجَلَة ضبط ارتفاع الطاولة
23 clamping screw for the table rise adjustment برغي تثبيت آليَّة ضبط ارتفاع الطاولة
24 console كونسول
25 foot of the machine قاعدة المَاكِينَة
26 edge-veneering machine مَاكِينَة تكْسِيَة الحواف
27 sanding wheel عَجَلَة السنفرة
28 sanding dust extractor آليَّة طرد نشارة السنفرة
29 splicing head رَأس الجَدْل/القرن بالتراكب
30 single-belt sanding machine (single-belt sander) مَاكِينَة سنفرة ذات سَيْر واحد
31 belt guard وقاء السيْر
32 band wheel cover غطاء بكرة السيْر
33 extractor fan (exhaust fan) مِرْوَحَة طاردة
34 frame-sanding pad مِسْنَد السنفرة للبراويز/للإطارات
35 sanding table طاولة السنفرة
36 fine adjustment آليَّة الضبط الدقيق
37 fine cutter and jointer جِهَاز القَطْع والجَدْل الدقيق
38 saw carriage with chain drive حَامِل المِنْشَار ذو إدارة بسلسلة
39 trailing cable hanger (trailing cable support) حَامِل الكيبل الخلفي
40 air extractor pipe أنْبُوب طرد الهواء
41 rail قضيب، درابزين
42 frame-cramping (frame-clamping) machine مَاكِينَة قَمْط الإطارات
43 frame stand حَامِل الإطار
44 workpiece, a window frame قطعة الشغل، إطار نافذة
45 compressed-air line خط هواء مضغوط
46 pressure cylinder أسْطُوَانَة الضغط
47 pressure foot قاعدة أسْطُوَانَة الضغط
48 frame-mounting device جِهَاز تثبيت الإطار
49 rapid-veneer press مِكْبَس التكسية بالقشور
50 bed فَرْشَة، سرير
51 press مِكْبَس
52 pressure piston كَبَّاس ضغط

134 Do-it-yourself مُعدَّات الإصلاحات المَنْزِليَّة

1-34 tool cupboard (tool cabinet) for do-it-yourself work **خِزَانَة أدوات** "اصنع الشيئ بنفسكَ" (دون الحاجة إلى أخصائي)
1 smoothing plane مِسْحَاج تمليس/تنعيم
2 set of fork spanners (fork wrenches, open-end wrenches) طاقم من مفاتيح الربط المُشَعَّبَة
3 hacksaw مِنْشَار معادن
4 screwdriver مِفَك

5 cross-point screwdriver	مفك ذو طَرْف متصالب
6 saw rasp	مِبْرَد شحذ مناشير مُحَبَّب القطعية
7 hammer	مِطْرَقَة، شاكوش
8 wood rasp	مِبْرَد خشب
9 roughing file	مِبْرَد تخشين
10 small vice (*Am.* vise)	مِلْزَمة صغيرة
11 corner pipe wrench	مِفْتَاح ربط الأنابيب
12 water pump pliers	زردية ربط المواسير
13 pincers	كمَّاشة
14 all-purpose wrench	مِفْتَاح ربط لجميع الأغراض
15 wire stripper and cutter	بِنْسَة تعرية الأسلاك المعزولة وقطعها
16 electric drill	مِثْقَاب (شَنْيُور) كهربي
17 hacksaw	مِنْشَار معادن
18 plaster cup	سَطْل عجن الجبس
19 soldering iron	مِكْوَاة لحام
20 tin-lead solder wire	سلك لحام مصنوع من القصدير والرصاص
21 lamb's wool polishing bonnet	خِرْقَة تلميع مصنوعة من صوف الأغنام
22 rubber backing disc (disk)	قُرْص اسناد مطاطي
23 grinding wheel	عجلة تجليخ
24 wire wheel brush	فرشاة سلك دولابية الشكل
25 sanding discs (disks)	أقراص سَنْفَرَة
26 try square	زَاوِيَة ضبط قائمة، زَاوِيَة النَّجَّار
27 hand saw	مِنْشَار يدوي
28 universal cutter	أداة قَطْع عامة
29 spirit level	ميزان تسوية
30 firmer chisel	أزْمِيل قطع بالدق
31 centre (*Am.* center) punch	سُنْبُك تعليم المركز
32 nail punch	سُنْبُك المسامير
33 folding rule (rule)	مِسْطَرَة قابلة للطى
34 storage box for small parts	صُنْدُوق حفظ القطع الصغيرة
35 tool box	صُنْدُوق العُدَّة
36 woodworking adhesive	غراء المصنوعات الخشبية
37 stripping knife	سكين تقشير
38 adhesive tape	شريط لاصق
39 storage box with compartments for nails, screws, and plugs	صُنْدُوق حفظ/تخزين له حجيرات للمسامير والبراغي والسدادات
40 machinist's hammer	شاكوش
41 collapsible workbench (collapsible bench)	طاولة شغل قابلة للطيّ
42 jig	دليل تشغيل
43 electric percussion drill (electric hammer drill)	مِثْقَب حفر بالدق يعمل بالكهرباء
44 pistol grip	قبضة مُسَدَّس
45 side grip	مِقْبَض جَانِبِي
46 gearshift switch	مِفْتَاح تبديل السرعة
47 handle with depth gauge (*Am.* gage)	ذِرَاع ذو معيار للعمق
48 chuck	ظرف لُقَم المِثْقَب
49 twist bit (twist drill)	لقمة حفر حلزونية
50-55 attachments for an electric drill	**ملحقات للمِثْقَب الكهربي**
50 combined circular saw (buzz saw) and band-saw	مِنْشَار دائري أزَّاز ومِنْشَار شريطي معاً
51 wood-turning lathe	مِخْرَطَة الخشب
52 circular saw attachment	مِنْشَار دائري
53 orbital sanding attachment (orbital sander)	مَاكِينَة سنفرة مدارية
54 drill stand	حَامِل المِثْقَب
55 hedge-trimming attachment (hedge trimmer)	مَاكِينَة تهذيب السِّيَاج
56 soldering gun	مُسَدَّس لحام
57 soldering iron	مِكْوَاة لحام
58 high-speed soldering iron	مِكْوَاة لحام عالية السرعة
59 upholstery, upholstering an armchair	التنجيد، تنجيد كرسي ذي ذِرَاعين
60 fabric (material) for upholstery	قماش تنجيد
61 do-it-yourself enthusiast	شخص يقوم بإصلاح الشيء بنفسه (دون الحاجة إلى اختصاصي)

135 Turner — الخَرَّاط

1-26 turnery (turner's workshop)	**وَرْشَة خِرَاطة**
1 wood-turning lathe (lathe)	مِخْرَطَة الخشب
2 lathe bed	فرشة المِخْرَطَة
3 starting resistance (starting resistor)	مقاومة البدء
4 gearbox	علبة تروس السرعة
5 tool rest	مِسْنَد قلم المِخْرَطَة
6 chuck	ظَرْف
7 tailstock	غراب متحرك، غراب الذيل
8 centre (*Am.* center)	ذَنَبَة المِخْرَطَة
9 driving plate with pin	قُرْص التدوير
10 two-jaw chuck	ظرف ذو فكين
11 live centre (*Am.* center)	ذنبة دَوَرَانِيَّة
12 fretsaw	مِنْشَار منحنيات / زخرفة
13 fretsaw blade	نَصْل مِنْشَار المنحنيات/ الزخرفة
14, 15, 24 turning tools	أدوات الخَرْط
14 thread chaser, for cutting threads in wood	مِمْشَط لَوْلَبَة
15 gouge, for rough turning	مِظْفَار/أزْمِيل مقعر للخَرْط الخشن
16 spoon bit (shell bit)	لقمة حفر مِلْعَقِيَّة التجويف
17 hollowing tool	أداة تجويف
18 outside calliper (caliper)	فرجار قياس خارجي
19 turned work (turned wood)	قطعة خشب مخروطة
20 master turner (turner)	رئيس الخَرَّاطين
21 [piece of] rough wood	قطعة خشب خشنة
22 drill	مِثْقَاب
23 inside calliper (caliper)	فرجار قياس داخلي
24 parting tool	قلم قَطْعِيَّة
25 glass paper (sandpaper, emery paper)	وَرَق سنفرة

26 shavings	نحاتة، قراضة، براية

136 Basket Maker — السّلال (صانع السّلال)

1-40 basket making (basketry, basketwork)	**صناعة السّلال**
1-4 weaves (strokes)	**أنسجة سلاليّة**
1 randing	أملود مَجْدُول
2 rib randing	جَدْل ضلعي
3 oblique randing	جَدْل مائل
4 randing, a piece of wickerwork (screen work)	نسيج، قطعة من الأماليد المَجْدُولة
5 weaver	نسَّاج، ناسِج
6 stake	عُود (صفصاف)
7 workboard; *also:* lapboard	سطح الشغل
8 screw block	قالب تثبيت العيدان
9 hole for holding the block	ثقب لتثبيت القالب
10 stand	حَامِل
11 chip basket (spale basket)	سَلَّة من رقاقات القش
12 chip (spale)	رقاقة من القش
13 soaking tub	حوض النقع فى الماء
14 willow stakes (osier stakes)	عيدان الصفصاف
15 willow rods (osier rods)	عصيان الصفصاف
16 basket, a piece of wickerwork (basketwork)	سَلَّة، قطعة من الأماليد المجدولة
17 border	حاشية، كنار
18 woven side	جَانِب منسوج
19 round base	قاعدة مستديرة
20 woven base	قاعدة مَنْسُوجة
21 slath	جديلة
22-24 covering a frame	**تَكْسِيَة الإطار**
22 frame	إطار
23 end	طَرْف الأملود
24 rib	ضلع
25 upsett	إطار ذو أضلع مفلطحة
26 grass; *kinds:* esparto grass, alfalfa grass	نجيل؛ أنواعه: الحلفاء والفصفصة
27 rush (bulrush, reed mace)	سمّار (نبات)
28 reed	مُشْط
29 raffia (bast)	ليف نَخْل الرافية
30 straw	قش
31 bamboo cane	خَيْزَرَان
32 rattan (ratan) chair cane	خَيْزَرَان الروطان المستخدم فى صنع الكرَاسي
33 basket maker	صانع السلال
34 bending tool	أداة ثني
35 cutting point (bodkin)	سن القطع (مخرز)
36 rapping iron	قضيب خلخلة بالدقدقة
37 pincers	كمَّاشة
38 picking knife	سِكِّين قطف
39 shave	شريحة
40 hacksaw	مِنْشَار معادن

137 Blacksmith (Smith) I — الحَدَّاد (1)

1-8 hearth (forge) **with blacksmith's fire**	**كَوْرَة الحَدَّاد**
1 hearth (forge)	مِجْمَرة، كَوْرَة
2 shovel (slice)	مِجْرَفة
3 swab	فرشاة ترطيب
4 rake	مِدَمَّة
5 poker	مِحْرَاك (الجَمْر)، سيخ تقليب الجَمْر
6 blast pipe (tue iron)	ماسورة اللفح (أقصاب الكور النقالي)
7 chimney (cowl, hood)	مدخنة
8 water trough (quenching trough, bosh)	وعاء ماء التَّسْقِيَة
9 power hammer	مِطْرَقَة آلية
10 ram (tup)	مِكْبَس، مِطْرَقَة، مِدَك
11-16 anvil	**السندان**
11 anvil	سِنْدَان
12 flat beak (beck, bick)	طَرْف السِّنْدان المفلطح
13 round beak (beck, bick)	طَرْف السِّنْدان المستدير
14 auxiliary table	نضد مساند
15 foot	قاعدة
16 upsetting block	كتلة الفلطحة بالطَّرْق على الساخن
17 swage block	زهرة طرق
18 tool-grinding machine (tool grinder)	مَاكِينَة تجليخ العدة
19 grinding wheel	عَجَلَة التجليخ
20 block and tackle	بكَّارة : بكرة وحبل
21 workbench (bench)	طاولة الشغل
22-39 blacksmith's tools	**أدوات الحَدَّاد**
22 sledge hammer	مِرْزَبَة
23 blacksmith's hand hammer	شاكوش يدوي، مِطْرَقَة يدوية
24 flat tongs	مِلْقَط مفلطح الطرْف
25 round tongs	مِلْقَط مُسْتَدِير الطرْف
26 parts of the hammer	أجزاء المِطْرَقَة/الشاكوش
27 peen (pane, pein)	حَدُّ المِطْرَقَة
28 face	وَجْه المِطْرَقَة
29 eye	عروة
30 haft	مِقْبَض
31 cotter punch	سُنْبُك سفيني
32 hardy (hardie)	مقطعة الحداد (سندان)
33 set hammer	مِطْرَقَة تسطيح
34 sett (set, sate)	أَزْمِيل قطع مطرقي الشكل
35 flat-face hammer (flatter)	مِطْرَقَة مفلَطَحة
36 round punch	سُنْبُك محدَّب (دائري المقطع)
37 angle tongs	مِلْقَط بزَاوِيَة
38 blacksmith's chisel (scaling hammer, chipping hammer)	أَزْمِيل الحَداد (مِطْرَقَة التَّقْشِير)
39 moving iron (bending iron)	قضيب الثَّني

138 Blacksmith (Smith) II (Farm Vehicle Engineering) — الحَدَّاد (2) (هندَسَة المَرْكبات الزِّراعيَّة)

1	compressed-air system	جِهَاز الهواء المضغوط
2	electric motor	مُحَرِّك كهربي
3	compressor	ضاغط
4	compressed-air tank	أسْطُوانَة الهواء المضغوط
5	compressed-air line	خُرْطُوم/خط الهواء المضغوط
6	percussion screwdriver	مفك يعمل بالصَّدْم
7	pedestal grinding machine (floor grinding machine)	مَاكِينَة تجليخ بقاعدة
8	grinding wheel	عَجَلَة التجليخ
9	guard	وقاء
10	trailer	مقطورة
11	brake drum	أسْطُوانَة الفرامل، طبلة المِكْبَح
12	brake shoe	حذاء الفرامل/المِكْبَح
13	brake lining	بطانة الفرامل/المِكْبَح
14	testing kit	صُنْدُوق أدوات الاختبار
15	pressure gauge (*Am.* gage)	مقياس الضغط
16	brake-testing equipment, a rolling road	معدات اختبار الفرامل/المِكْبَح
17	pit	بِئْر، حفرة
18	braking roller	أسْطُوانَة الفرامل/المِكْبَح
19	meter (recording meter)	عدَّاد قياس
20	precision lathe for brake drums	مخْرطَة دقيقة لضبط اسطوانات الفرامل/المِكْبَح
21	lorry wheel	دولاب شاحنة
22	boring mill	مَاكِينَة حفر عمودي
23	power saw, a hacksaw (power hacksaw)	مِنْشَار معادن كهربائي
24	vice (*Am.* vise)	مِلْزَمة، مِنْجَلة
25	saw frame	إطار المِنْشَار
26	coolant supply pipe	أُنْبُوب إمداد المحلول المُبَرِّد
27	riveting machine	مَاكِينَة برشمة
28	trailer frame (chassis) under construction	شاسيه مقطورة تحت التصنيع
29	inert-gas welding equipment	معدات اللحام في محيط من الغاز الخامل
30	rectifier	مُقَوِّم
31	control unit	وَحْدَة التحكم
32	CO_2 cylinder	أسْطُوانَة ثانى أكسيد الكربون
33	anvil	سِنْدَان
34	hearth (forge) with blacksmith's fire	كُورَة الحداد، مِجْمَرَة
35	trolley for gas cylinders	ترولى أسطوانات الغاز
36	vehicle under repair, a tractor	جرَّار تحت التصليح

139 Hammer Forging (Smith Forging) and Drop Forging — تَشْكِيل المَعَادِن بالطَّرْق

1	continuous furnace with grid hearth for annealing of round stock	فُرْن من النوع المتواصل ذو مِجْمَرَة شبكية لتخمير الخام
2	discharge opening (discharge door)	فتحة تفريغ الخامات المسخنة
3	gas burners	مواقد الغاز
4	charging door	بوابة شحن الخامات الباردة
5	counterblow hammer	مِطْرَقَة ضربات متضادة
6	upper ram	رَأس طرق علوية
7	lower ram	رَأس طرق سفلية
8	ram guide	دليل رَأس الطرق
9	hydraulic drive	إدارة هيدرولية
10	column	قائم، عمود
11	short-stroke drop hammer	مِطْرَقَة متساقطة قصيرة الشوط
12	ram (tup)	رَأس الطرق
13	upper die block	القالب العلوي
14	lower die block	القالب السفلي
15	hydraulic drive	إدارة هيدرولية
16	frame	الهيكل
17	anvil	سِنْدَان
18	forging and sizing press	مِكْبَس التشكيل وضبط المقاسات
19	standard	حَامِل عمودي
20	table	منضدة
21	disc (disk) clutch	قابض قُرْصي
22	compressed-air pipe	أُنْبُوب الهواء المضغوط
23	solenoid valve	صمام يشغل بملف لولبي
24	air-lift gravity hammer (air-lift drop hammer)	مِطْرَقَة متساقطة تعمل بالدفع الهوائي
25	drive motor	مُحَرِّك الإدارة
26	hammer (tup)	مِطْرَقَة
27	foot control (foot pedal)	آلية تحكم تعمل بالقدم
28	preshaped (blocked) workpiece	قطعة الشغل قبل تشكيلها
29	hammer guide	دليل المِطْرَقَة
30	hammer cylinder	أسْطُوانَة هواء المِطْرَقَة
31	anvil	سِنْدَان
32	mechanical manipulator to move the workpiece in hammer forging	مناول ميكانيكي لتحريك قطعة الشغل في عملية التشكيل بالمِطْرَقَة
33	dogs	كُلاَّبان، ماسِكان
34	counterweight	ثِقْل موازن
35	hydraulic forging press	مِكْبَس تشكيل هيدروليكي
36	crown	تاج
37	cross head	طربوش الوصل
38	upper die block	كتلة اللقمة العلوية
39	lower die block	كتلة اللقمة السفلية
40	anvil	سندان
41	hydraulic piston	كبَّاس هيدروليكي
42	pillar guide	دليل القائم
43	rollover device	آلية قلابة
44	burden chain (chain sling)	معلاق سلسلة
45	crane hook	خطاف المرفاع
46	workpiece	قطعة الشغل
47	gas furnace (gas-fired	فُرْن يعمل بالغاز

furnace)	
48 gas burner	موقد غازي
49 charging opening	فتحة شحن الخامات
50 chain curtain	ستارة من السلاسل
51 vertical-lift door	باب رفع رَأْسي
52 hot-air duct	مَجْرَى الهواء الساخن
53 air preheater	مُسَخِّن هواء مُتَقَدِّم
54 gas pipe	أُنْبُوب الغاز
55 electric door-lifting mechanism	آلية كهربية لرفع الباب
56 air blast	لَفْح الهواء

140 Metalworker — عامل تَشْغيل المَعَادن

1-22 metalwork shop (mechanic's workshop, fitter's workshop, locksmith's workshop)	**وَرْشَة الأشغَال المعدنيَة** (وَرْشَة الميكانيكي/البَرَّاد/ صانع الأقفال)
1 metalworker (e.g. mechanic, fitter, locksmith; form. *also:* wrought-iron craftsman)	عامل تشغيل معادن (بَرَّاد، صانع أقفال)
2 parallel-jaw vice (*Am.* vise)	ملزمة متوازية الفكين
3 jaw	فك
4 screw	لولب، مِسْمَار ملولب
5 handle	ذِرَاع
6 workpiece	قطعة الشغل
7 workbench (bench)	طاولة الشغل
8 files (*kinds:* rough file, smooth file, precision file)	مَبَارِد (أنواعها : مِبْرَد خشن، مِبْرَد أملس، مِبْرَد البَرْد الدقيق)
9 hacksaw	مِنْشَار معادن
10 leg vice (*Am.* vise), a spring vice	ملزمة قَدَميَّة
11 muffle furnace, a gas-fired furnace	فُرْن إحماء خارجي، فُرْن لافع، فُرْن يُشْعل بالغاز
12 gas pipe	أُنْبُوب الغاز
13 hand brace (hand drill)	مِثْقَاب يدوي
14 swage block	زهرة طرق
15 filing machine	مكنة بَرْد
16 file	مِبْرَد
17 compressed-air pipe	أُنْبُوب هواء مضغوط
18 grinding machine (grinder)	مكنة تجليخ (جلاخة)
19 grinding wheel	عَجَلَة تجليخ
20 guard	وقاء
21 goggles (safety glasses)	نظارات واقية من البَهْر
22 safety helmet	خوذة أمان
23 machinist's hammer	مِطْرَقَة البَرَّاد
24 hand vice (*Am.* vise)	مِلزمة يدوية
25 cape chisel (cross-cut chisel)	أَزْميل تخديد
26 flat chisel	أَزْميل مفلطح الحد
27 flat file	مِبْرَد مسطح
28 file cut (cut)	قطعية المِبْرَد
29 round file (*also:* half-round file)	مِبْرَد دائري المقطع (أيضاً: مِبْرَد نصف دائري المقطع)
30 tap wrench	مِفْتَاح ربط ذكر اللولبة
31 reamer	بَرْغَل، مُوَسِّع الثقوب
32 die (die and stock)	لقمة اللولبة
33-35 key	**مفْتاح**
33 stem (shank)	سَاق
34 bow	قوس (رَأْس)
35 bit	سن المِفْتَاح (لسان)
36-43 door lock, a mortise (mortice) lock	**قفل باب، كيلون باب**
36 back plate	اللوحة الخلفية
37 spring bolt (latch bolt)	رتاج ذو نابض، سقاطة مزلاج
38 tumbler	لسان القُفل
39 bolt	مزلاج
40 keyhole	ثقب المِفْتَاح
41 bolt guide pin	مِسْمَار دليلي للمزلاج
42 tumbler spring	نابض لسان القُفل
43 follower, with square hole	رادف ذو ثقب مربع
44 cylinder lock (safety lock)	قفل أسطواني (قفل أمان)
45 cylinder (plug)	أُسْطُوَانَة
46 spring	نابض
47 pin	مِسْمَار
48 safety key, a flat key	مِفْتَاح أمان
49 lift-off hinge	مفصلة من جزئين قابلين للفصل
50 hook-and-ride band	مفصلة خطاف وراكِب
51 strap hinge	مفصلة بجناح واحد
52 vernier calliper (caliper) gauge (*Am.* gage)	مقياس ذو قدمة وَرْنيَّة
53 feeler gauge (*Am.* gage)	مقياس تحسسي
54 vernier depth gauge (*Am.* gage)	معيار بوَرْنيَّة لتحديد العمق
55 vernier	وَرْنيَّة
56 straightedge	مِسْطَرَة تقويم
57 square	زَاوِيَة قائمة، كوس
58 breast drill	مِثْقَاب صدري
59 twist bit (twist drill)	مِثْقَاب التوائي
60 screw tap (tap)	ذَكَر لولبة
61 halves of a screw die	نصفا قالب اللولبة
62 screwdriver	مفك
63 scraper (*also:* pointed triangle scraper)	مِكْشَطَة (أيضا مِكْشَطَة مثلثة مستدقة الطَرْف)
64 centre (*Am.* center) punch	سُنْبُك تعليم المركز
65 round punch	سُنْبُك دائري المقطع
66 flat-nose pliers	زردية مسطحة الفكين
67 detachable-jaw cut nippers	قَرَّاضة ذات فك قابل للفصل
68 gas pliers	زرديَّة مواسَيْر الغاز
69 pincers	كَمَّاشة

141 Gas Welder — عامل اللحَام بالغَاز

1 gas cylinder manifold	مَجْمَع أُسْطُوَانَات الغاز
2 acetylene cylinder	أُسْطُوَانَة الأستيلين
3 oxygen cylinder	أُسْطُوَانَة الأكسجين
4 high-pressure mano-	مانومتر الضغط العالي

meter
5 pressure-reducing valve (reducing valve, pressure regulator) مُنَظِّم الضغط، صِمَام
6 low-pressure manometer مانومتر الضغط المنخفض
7 stop valve محْبَس
8 hydraulic back-pressure valve for low-pressure installations صِمَام هيدرولى للضغط الخلفي للتركيبات منخفضة الضغط
9 gas hose خُرْطُوم الغاز
10 oxygen hose خُرْطُوم الأكسجين
11 welding torch (blowpipe) مِشْعَل/حِمْلاج اللِحَام
12 welding rod (filler rod) سِيخ اللِحَام، سيخ إضافة
13 welding bench طاولة اللِحَام
14 grating حاجز مُشَبَّك
15 scrap box صُنْدُوق القراضة/الخِراطة
16 bench covering of chamotte slabs غِطَاء الطاولة المصنوع من أَلْوَاح الشاموت
17 water tank خَزَّان ماء
18 welding paste (flux) معجون اللِحَام (مُسَاعِد صهر)
19 welding torch (blowpipe) with cutting attachment and guide tractor مِشْعَل/حِمْلاج اللِحَام المزود بقَلَم القطع وجَرَّار دليلى
20 workpiece قطعة الشغل
21 oxygen cylinder أسْطُوَانَة الأكسجين
22 acetylene cylinder أسْطُوَانَة الأستيلين
23 cylinder trolley ترولى الأُسْطُوَانَات
24 welding goggles نظارات واقية من بهر اللِحَام
25 chipping hammer مِطْرَقَة جَذ/تأجين
26 wire brush فُرْشَاة سلكية
27 torch lighter (blowpipe lighter) ولاعة الحِمْلاج/المِشْعَل
28 welding torch (blowpipe) مِشْعَل/حِمْلاج اللِحَام
29 oxygen control مُنَظِّم دفق الأكسجين
30 oxygen connection وَصْلَة الأكسجين
31 gas connection (acetylene connection) وَصْلَة الغاز (وَصْلَة الاستيلين)
32 gas control (acetylene control) مُنَظِّم دفق الغاز
33 welding nozzle فُوَّهَة اللِحَام
34 cutting machine مَاكِينَة القطع
35 circular template طَبْعَة/ضبعة دائرية
36 universal cutting machine مَاكِينَة قطع عامة
37 tracing head رَأْس تتبع الطَّبْعَة/الضبعة
38 cutting nozzle رَأْس القطع

142 Arc Welder عَامِل اللحَام القَوْسِيّ

1 welding transformer مُحَوِّل اللِحَام
2 arc welder عَامِل اللِحَام القَوْسِيّ
3 arc welding helmet خَوْذَة عَامِل اللِحَام القَوْسِيّ
4 flip-up window نافذة تفتح لأعلى
5 shoulder guard واقي الكتفين
6 protective sleeve كُمّ واقٍ
7 electrode case غلاف الالكترود
8 three-fingered welding glove قُفَّاز لِحَام ذو ثلاثة أصابع
9 electrode holder حَامِل الالكترود
10 electrode الكترود
11 leather apron مريلة جلدية
12 shin guard وقاء الساق
13 welding table with fume extraction equipment طاولة اللِحَام ومعدات طرد الأدخنة
14 table top سَطْح الطاولة
15 movable extractor duct مَجْرَى جِهَاز الطرد المتحرك
16 extractor support حَامِل جِهَاز الطرد
17 chipping hammer مِطْرَقَة الرايش، مِطْرَقَة الجذ/التأجين
18 wire brush فُرْشَاة سلك
19 welding lead سلك اللِحَام
20 electrode holder حَامِل الالكترود
21 welding bench طاولة اللِحَام
22 spot welding لِحَام البقعة
23 spot welding electrode holder حَامِل الكترود لِحَام البقعة
24 electrode arm ذِرَاع الالكترود
25 power supply (lead) موصل التيار الكهربي (سلك توصيل)
26 electrode-pressure cylinder أُسْطُوَانَة ضغط الاكترود
27 welding transformer مُحَوِّل اللِحَام
28 workpiece قطعة الشغل
29 foot-operated spot welder جِهَاز لِحَام بقعة يتم تشغيله بالقدم
30 welder electrode arms ذِرَاعا الكترود جِهَاز اللِحَام
31 foot pedal for welding pressure adjustment دَوَّاسَة القدم الخاصة بتعديل ضغط اللِحَام
32 five-fingered welding glove قُفَّاز لِحَام ذو خمسة أصابع
33 inert-gas torch for inert-gas welding (gas-shielded arc welding) مِشْعَل/حِمْلاج الغاز الخامل للحَام في محيط من الغاز الخامل
34 inert-gas (shielding-gas) supply مَصْدَر إمداد الغاز الخامل
35 work clamp (earthing clamp) مِلْزَمَة/قامطة الشغل
36 fillet gauge (*Am.* gage) (weld gauge) [for measuring throat thickness] مقياس اللُحْمَة الزَاوِيَّة [لقياس ثخانة العنق الفعلية للحمة زاويّة مقعرة]
37 micrometer ميكرومتر
38 measuring arm ذِرَاع القياس
39 arc welding helmet خَوْذَة اللِحَام القَوْسِيّ
40 filter lens عدسة ترشيح
41 small turntable صِينِيَّة دَوَّارة صغيرة

143 Sections, Bolts and Machine Parts القطع والمسامير وأجْزَاء المَاكينة

[material: steel, brass, aluminium (*Am.* aluminum), [المادة : صُلْب ونحاس وألمنيوم وبلاستيك، الخ.

plastics, etc.; in the following, steel was chosen as an example] وفيما يلي اخترنا الصُلْب كمثال]
1 angle iron (angle) حَديد مُزَوَّى
2 leg (flange) شَفَة، فلانشة
3-7 steel girders **كَمرات الصُلْب**
3 T-iron (tee-iron) حَديد تائي
4 vertical leg شَفَة رَأْسية
5 flange شَفَة، فلانشة
6 H-girder (H-beam) كَمَر على شكل حرف H
7 E-channel (channel iron) قضيب ذو مَقْطَع بائى
8 round bar قضيب مستدير
9 square iron (*Am.* square stock) حَديد مربع المَقْطَع
10 flat bar قضيب مسَطح
11 strip steel صُلْب شريطي
12 iron wire سلك حَديدي
13-50 screws and bolts **البراغي والمسامير**
13 hexagonal-head bolt مِسْمَار ملَوْلَب ذو رَأْس سداسي الشكل
14 head رَأْس
15 shank ساق
16 thread حَزُّ اللَوْلَب
17 washer صامولة
18 hexagonal nut صامولة مُسَدَّسة
19 split pin دبوس خابوري
20 rounded end طَرْف مستدير
21 width of head (of flats) عرض الرَّأْس (الجوانب المسَطْحة)
22 stud الجَويط (بُرْغي ملَوْلَب عديم الرَّأْس مُلَوْلَب الطَّرْفين عادة)
23 point (end) طَرْف مستدق
24 castle nut (castellated nut) صامولة بُرْجية
25 hole for the split pin ثقب الدبوس الخابوري
26 cross-head screw, a sheet-metal screw (self-tapping screw) بُرْغي صليبي الرَّأْس، بُرْغي ألْواح معدنية
27 hexagonal socket head screw بُرْغي مجوَّف ذو رَأْس سداسي
28 countersunk-head bolt مِسْمَار ملوْلَب برأْس مُخَوَّش
29 catch ماسك
30 locknut (locking nut) صامولة زَنْق أو إحكام
31 bolt (pin) وَتَد المِسْمَار
32 collar-head bolt مِسْمَار ملَوْلَب ذو رَأْس طَوْقى
33 set collar (integral collar) طَوْق المِسْمَار
34 spring washer (washer) وَرْدَة / حلَقَة نابضية
35 round nut, an adjusting nut صامولة أُسْطُوانية، صامولة ضبط
36 cheese-head screw, a slotted screw مِسْمَار ملَوْلَب ذو رَأْس أَسْطُواني، مِسْمَار ملَوْلَب مخدود
37 tapered pin دبوس خابوري مستدق
38 screw slot (screw slit, screw groove) شق رَأْس المِسْمَار الملَوْلَب
39 square-head bolt مِسْمَار مربع الرَّأْس
40 grooved pin, a cylindrical pin دبوس مخدود، دبوس أَسْطُواني
41 T-head bolt مِسْمَار ملَوْلَب ذو رَأْس تائي
42 wing nut (fly nut, butterfly nut) صامولة مجنحة
43 rag bolt مِسْمَار مُشَوَّك (للتثبيْت)
44 barb أَشْوَاك
45 wood screw مِسْمَار بريمى للخشب
46 countersunk head رَأْس مُخَوَّش
47 wood screw thread حزوز مِسْمَار خشب بريمي
48 grub screw مِسْمَار ناخز
49 pin slot (pin slit, pin groove) شق المِسْمَار
50 round end طَرْف مستدير
51 nail (wire nail) مِسْمَار (مِسْمَار إِبْرَة)
52 head رَأْس
53 shank ساق
54 point طَرْف مستدق
55 roofing nail مِسْمَار برَأْس مسَطح
56 riveting (lap riveting) البَرْشَمَة (بَرْشَمَة متراكبة)
57-60 rivet **مِسْمَار برشام**
57 set head (swage head, die head), a rivet head رَأْس القالب، رَأْس البرشام
58 rivet shank ساق مِسْمَار البَرْشَمَة
59 closing head رَأْس البَرْشَمَة، ذيل البرشام
60 pitch of rivets خَطْوة مسامير البَرْشَمَة (المسافة بين برشام وآخر)
61 shaft عمود دوران
62 chamfer (bevel) شطبية، حد مائل، شطف
63 journal مرتكز العمود، مقعدة
64 neck عنق، رقبة
65 seat قاعدة، مستقر القاعدة
66 keyway مَجْرَى الخابور
67 conical seat (cone) قاعدة مخروطية (مخروط)
68 thread لَوْلَب، حزوز
69 ball bearing, an antifriction bearing مَحْمَل الكريات (مَحْمَل مقاوم للاحتكاك)
70 steel ball (ball) كُرَيَّة من الصُلْب
71 outer race حلَقَة مدْرَجة خارجية
72 inner race حلَقَة مدْرَجة داخلية
73-74 keys **خابوران**
73 sunk key (feather) خابور غاطس (خابور ريشي الشكل)
74 gib (gib-headed key) خابور بذقن جنيبة
75-76 needle roller bearing **مَجْرَى إسيطينات إبري**
75 needle cage قفص إبري
76 needle إبْرَة
77 castle nut (castellated nut) صامولة بُرْجية
78 split pin وَتَد خابوري
79 casing غلاف
80 casing cover غطَاء التغليف
81 grease nipple (lubricating nipple) حلَمَة التشحيم

82-96 gear wheels, cog wheels	**التروس، العجلات المُسَنَّنة**
82 stepped gear wheel	تُرْس مدرج
83 cog (tooth)	سن التُّرْس
84 space between teeth	مسافة بين الأسنان
85 keyway (key seat, key slot)	مَجْرَى خابوري
86 bore	جَوْف
87 herringbone gear wheel	تُرْس لَوْلَبي مزدوج
88 spoke (arm)	بَرْمَق
89 helical gearing (helical spur wheel)	تُرْس لَوْلَبي
90 sprocket	مُسَنَّنات التُّرْس، مضرسة
91 bevel gear wheel (bevel wheel)	تُرْس مخروطي
92-93 spiral toothing	**التسنين الحلزوني**
92 pinion	تُرْس بنيون/صغير
93 crown wheel	تُرْس رئيسي
94-96 epicyclic gear (planetary gear)	**نظام التروس التداويري**
94 planet wheels	تُروس كوكبيَّة الدَّوَران
95 internal gear	تُرْس داخلي
96 sun wheel (sun gear)	تُرْس شمسي
97-107 absorption dynamometer	**دينامومتر امتصاصي**
97 shoe brake (check brake, block brake)	فرملة حذائية
98 brake pulley	بكَرَة الفرامل/المِكْبَح
99 brake shaft (brake axle)	عمود الفرامل/المِكْبَح
100 brake block (brake shoe)	لُقْمَة الفرامل/المِكْبَح
101 pull rod	ذِرَاع الجذب
102 brake magnet	المغناطيس الرافع للفرامل
103 brake weight	وَزْن الفرامل
104 band brake	مِكْبَح طَوْقي
105 brake band	طَوْق الفرامل/المِكْبَح
106 brake lining	بِطَانَة الفرامل/المِكْبَح
107 adjusting screw, for even application of the brake	بُرْغي الضبط لتشغيل الفرامل/المِكْبَح بشكل منتظم

144 Coal Mine مَنْجَم الفَحْم

1-51 coal mine (colliery, pit)	**مَنْجَم الفَحْم**
1 pithead gear (headgear)	أجهزة فُوَّهَة المَنْجَم
2 winding engine house	بَيْت مِرْفَاع المَنْجَم
3 pithead frame (head frame)	تخشيبة فُوَّهَة المَنْجَم
4 pithead building	مَبْنَى فُوَّهَة المَنْجَم
5 processing plant	مَعْمَل التصنيع
6 sawmill	مَنْشَرَة
7-11 coking plant	**وَحْدَة تكويك**
7 battery of coke ovens	بطارية من أفران التكويك
8 larry car (larry, charging car)	شاحنة مسَطحة
9 coking coal tower	بُرْج فَحْم التكويك
10 coke-quenching tower	بُرْج إطفاء الكوك
11 coke-quenching car	عَرَبَة إطفاء الكوك
12 gasometer	مُسْتَوْدَع لخزن الغاز وقياس كميته
13 power plant (power station)	مَحَطَّة توليد الطاقة الكهربية
14 water tower	بُرْج الماء
15 cooling tower	بُرْج التبريد
16 mine fan	مِرْوَحَة تبريد المَنْجَم
17 depot	مُسْتَوْدَع
18 administration building (office building, offices)	مَبْنَى الإدارة (مكاتب إدارية)
19 tip heap (spoil heap)	رُكَام الحفر
20 cleaning plant	وَحْدَة تنظيف
21-51 underground workings (underground mining)	**أشغال جَوْفيَة** (تعدين جَوْفيّ)
21 ventilation shaft	بِئْر التهوية (مَهْوَى)
22 fan drift	سَرَب/نفق المِرْوَحَة
23 cage-winding system with cages	نظام لف الأقفاص مزود بأقفاص
24 main shaft	المَهْوَى الرئيسي
25 skip-winding system	نظام لف قواديسي
26 winding inset	قناة لف
27 staple shaft	مَهْوَى داخلي
28 spiral chute	مَجْرَى/مسقط حلزوني
29 gallery along seam	مَمَر طولي في راق فَحْم
30 lateral	مَقْطَع جانبي
31 cross-cut	مَقْطَع عرضي، طريق مختصر
32 tunnelling (*Am.* tunneling) machine	مَاكِينَة حفر الأنفاق
33-37 longwall faces	**واجهات طويلة الجدار**
33 horizontal ploughed longwall face	وَاجِهَة طويلة الجدار ذات تخديد أفقي
34 horizontal cut longwall face	وَاجِهَة طويلة الجدار ذات قطع أفقي
35 vertical pneumatic pick longwall face	وَاجِهَة طويلة الجدار ذات مِهْوَاة قائمة
36 diagonal ram longwall face	وَاجِهَة طويلة الجدار ذات مَمَر منحدر مائل
37 goaf (gob, waste)	نفاية التعدين
38 air lock	دسام هوائي
39 transportation of men by cars	نقل العمال بالعربات
40 belt conveying	النقل بالسيور/القشاطي
41 raw coal bunker	مُسْتَوْدَع الفَحْم الخام
42 charging conveyor	ناقل الشحن و التحميل
43 transportation of supplies by monorail car	نقل الإمدادات بواسطة عَرَبَة خَطّ أحادي السكة
44 transportation of men by monorail car	نقل العمال بواسطة عَرَبَة خَطّ أحادي السكة
45 transportation of supplies by mine car	نقل الإمدادات بواسطة عَرَبَة المَنْجَم
46 drainage	تصريف مياه المَنْجَم
47 sump (sink)	مَجْمَع الماء في قاع المَنْجَم
48 capping	غِطَاء لمنع تسرب الغاز
49 [layer of] coal-bearing rock	[طبقة من] الصخور الحاوية للفَحْم
50 coal seam	راق/عِرْق فَحْم
51 fault	صَدْع

145 Mineral Oil (Oil, Petroleum)	**الزَّيْت المعدني (النفط، البترول)**
1-21 oil drilling	**الحَفْر بَحْثاً عن الزيت**
1 drilling rig	جهاز الحَفْر
2 substructure	التركيبات الدنيا لجهاز الحَفْر
3 crown safety platform	مِنَصَّة أمان تاجية
4 crown blocks	بكرات تاجية
5 working platform, an intermediate platform	مِنَصَّة برج الحَفْر
6 drill pipes	أنابيب الحَفْر
7 drilling cable (drilling line)	كبل الحَفْر
8 travelling (*Am.* traveling) block	بكَرَة متحركة
9 hook	خطّاف
10 [rotary] swivel	رأس ملف [دوَّار]
11 hoist	أجهزة الرَّفْع
12 engine	مُحَرِّك
13 standpipe and rotary hose	أنْبُوب توازن وخرطوم رَحَوِيّ
14 kelly	عمود حَفْر مضلع، عمود كيلي
15 rotary table	طبلية الحَفْر الرَّحَوِيّ
16 slush pump (mud pump)	مِضَخَّة الطين الرَّخْو
17 well	بئر
18 casing	أنْبُوب تغليف
19 drilling pipe	أنْبُوب حَفْر
20 tubing	أنابيب إنتاج
21 drilling bit; *kinds:* fish-tail (blade) bit, rock (*Am.* roller) bit, core bit	لُقْمَة الحَفْر؛ أنواعها: لُقْمَة بشفرتين، لُقْمَة ذات ثلاثة دلافين مسننة، لُقْمَة التقوير
22-27 oil (crude oil) production	**إنتاج الزَّيْت الخام**
22 pumping unit (pump)	وَحْدَة الضَّخ
23 plunger	غاطس
24 tubing	أنابيب إنتاج
25 sucker rods (pumping rods)	قضبان ماصة/ضَخّ
26 stuffing box	صندوق حشو
27 polish (polished) rod	قضيب مصقول
28-35 treatment of crude oil [diagram]	**معالجة الزَّيْت الخام** [رسم تخَطيطي]
28 gas separator	فاصل الغاز/فرَّاز الغاز
29 gas pipe (gas outlet)	أنْبُوب خروج الغاز
30 wet oil tank (wash tank)	خزَّان شطف خارجي
31 water heater	سَخَّان مياه
32 water and brine separator	جهاز فصل الماء والملح
33 salt water pipe (salt water outlet)	أنْبُوب خروج الماء المالح
34 oil tank	خزَّان الزَّيْت
35 trunk pipeline for oil [to the refinery or transport by tanker lorry (*Am.* tank truck), oil tanker or pipeline]	خطّ أنابيب رئيسي لنقل الزَّيْت [إلى المصفاة أو للنقل بواسطة عربات صهريجية أو ناقلات نفطية أو خط أنابيب]
36-64 processing of crude oil [diagram]	**تصنيع الزَّيْت الخام** [رسم تخَطيطي]
36 oil furnace (pipe still)	فرن الزَّيْت
37 fractionating column (distillation column) with trays	برج تجزئة ذو أحواض
38 top gases (tops)	غازات علوية، قطافة نفطية
39 light distillation products	نواتج تقطير خفيفة
40 heavy distillation products	نواتج تقطير ثقيلة
41 petroleum	بترول
42 gas oil component	مُرَكَّب الغاز والزَّيْت
43 residue	فضالة
44 condenser (cooler)	مكثِّف (مُبَرِّد)
45 compressor	ضاغط
46 desulphurizing (desulphurization, *Am.* desulfurizing, desulfurization) plant	مَعْمَل نزع الكبريت
47 reformer (hydroformer, platformer)	المُهَذِّب الكيماوي
48 catalytic cracker (cat cracker)	وَحْدَة تكسير بالحفز
49 distillation column	برج التقطير
50 de-waxing (wax separation)	فصل الشمع
51 vacuum equipment	وَحْدَة تقطير خوائية
52-64 oil products	**منتجات الزَّيْت**
52 fuel gas	غاز الوَقُود (التدفئة)
53 liquefied petroleum gas (liquid gas)	غاز بترولي مُسال (غاز سائل)
54 regular grade petrol (*Am.* gasoline)	بنزين عادي
55 super grade petrol (*Am.* gasoline)	بنزين ممتاز
56 diesel oil	زَيْت الديزل
57 aviation fuel	وَقُود الطيران
58 light fuel oil	زَيْت وَقُود خفيف
59 heavy fuel oil	زَيْت وَقُود ثقيل
60 paraffin (paraffin oil, kerosene)	بارافين (كيروسين)
61 spindle oil	زَيْت المحاور
62 lubricating oil	زَيْت التزليق
63 cylinder oil	زَيْت الاسطوانات
64 bitumen	بيتومين
65-74 oil refinery	**مصفاة الزَّيْت**
65 pipeline (oil pipeline)	خطّ أنابيب الزيت
66 distillation plants	معامل التقطير
67 lubricating oil refinery	مصفاة زَيْت التزليق
68 desulphurizing (desulphurization, *Am.* desulfurizing, desulfurization) plant	مَعْمَل نزع الكبريت
69 gas-separating plant	مَعْمَل فصل الغاز
70 catalytic cracker plant	مَعْمَل تكسير بالحفز
71 catalytic reformer	مُهَذِّب كيماوي بالحفز
72 storage tank	صهريج تخزين
73 spherical tank	خزَّان كروي

74 tanker terminal	ميناء شحن ناقلات النفط

146 Offshore Drilling — الحَفْر البَحْري

1-39 drilling rig (oil rig)	**جِهاز الحفر** (حَفّارة الزيت)
1-37 drilling platform	**منصَّة الحفر**
1 power station	مَحَطَّة توليد الطاقة
2 generator exhausts	مواسير عادم مولد الطاقة
3 revolving crane (pedestal crane)	مِرْفَاع دوّار
4 piperack	مِنَصَّة (حمل) مواسير الحفر
5 turbine exhausts	مواسير عادم التوربين
6 materials store	مَخْزَن المواد
7 helicopter deck (heliport deck, heliport)	سَطْح هبوط الهليكوبتر
8 elevator	مصعد
9 production oil and gas separator	فرّازَة غاز وزيت الإنتاج
10 test oil and gas separators (test separators)	فرّازات اختبار الزيت والغاز
11 emergency flare stack	مِدْخَنَة شعلة الطوارئ
12 derrick	بُرْج الحفر
13 diesel tank	خزّان وَقود الديزل
14 office building	مَبْنَى المكاتب
15 cement storage tanks	خزّانات الأسمنت
16 drinking water tank	خزّان ماء الشرب
17 salt water tank	خزّان الماء المالح
18 jet fuel tanks	خزّانات الوَقود النفاث
19 lifeboats	قوارب النجاة
20 elevator shaft	بِئْر المصعد
21 compressed-air reservoir	خزّان الهواء المضغوط
22 pumping station	مَحَطَّة الضخ
23 air compressor	ضاغط هوائي
24 air lock	دِسَام هوائي
25 seawater desalination plant	مَعْمَل تحلية مياه البحر
26 inlet filters for diesel fuel	مرشحات الإدخال الخاصة بوَقود الديزل
27 gas cooler	مُبَرِّد الغاز
28 control panel for the separators	لَوْحَة تحكم الفرّازات
29 toilets (lavatories)	دَوْرات مياه (مراحيض)
30 workshop	وَرْشَة
31 pig trap [the 'pig' is used to clean the oil pipeline]	مصيدة الكاشطة [تستخدم في تنظيف خطّ أنابيب الزيت]
32 control room	غُرْفَة التحكم والمراقبة
33 accommodation modules (accommodation)	وَحْدات سكنية
34 high-pressure cementing pumps	مِضَخّات سَمْنَتَة عالية الضغط
35 lower deck	السَّطْح السفلي
36 middle deck	السَّطْح الأوسط
37 top deck (main deck)	السَّطْح العلوي (السَّطْح الرئيسي)
38 substructure	التركيبات الدنيا لجِهَاز الحفر
39 mean sea level	متوسط ارتفاع سَطْح البحر

147 Iron and Steel Works — مَصْنَع الحَدِيد والصُلْب

1-20 blast furnace plant	**وَحْدَة الفُرْن العالي، فُرْن قائم**
1 blast furnace, a shaft furnace	الفُرْن العالي
2 furnace incline (lift) for ore and flux or coke	السَّطْح المائل بالفُرْن لإدخال الخام ومساعد الصهر أو الكوك
3 skip hoist	ناقلة قلابة مزدوجة
4 charging platform	مِنَصَّة الإلقام
5 receiving hopper	قادوس استقبال
6 bell	ناقوس
7 blast furnace shaft	حلق الفُرْن العالي
8 smelting section	مِنْطَقَة الصهر، المِجْمَرَة
9 slag escape	فَتْحَة صَبّ الخبث
10 slag ladle	بَوْدَقَة الخبث
11 pig iron (crude iron, iron) runout	فَتْحَة صَبّ الحَدِيد الخام
12 pig iron (crude iron, iron) ladle	بَوْدَقَة الحَدِيد الخام
13 downtake	أُنْبُوب الهبوط
14 dust catcher, a dust-collecting machine	فاصل الأتربة
15 hot-blast stove	مُسَخِّن "كاوبر"
16 external combustion chamber	حُجْرَة الاحتراق الخارجي
17 blast main	أُنْبُوب اللفح الرئيسي
18 gas pipe	أُنْبُوب الغاز
19 hot-blast pipe	أُنْبُوب اللفح الساخن
20 tuyère	الوِدْنات
21-69 steelworks	**مَصْنَع الصُلْب**
21-30 Siemens-Martin open-hearth furnace	**فُرْن المِجْمَرَة المكشوفة لسيمنز ومارتن**
21 pig iron (crude iron, iron) ladle	بَوْدَقَة الحَدِيد الخام
22 feed runner	مَجْرَى الصَّبّ
23 stationary furnace	فُرْن ثابت
24 hearth	مِجْمَرَة، موقد
25 charging machine	آلِة الشاحن، شاحنة
26 scrap iron charging box	صُنْدُوق شحن الحَدِيد الخردة
27 gas pipe	أُنْبُوب الغاز
28 gas regenerator chamber	حُجْرَة مسترجع الغاز
29 air feed pipe	أُنْبُوب التغذية بالهواء
30 air regenerator chamber	حُجْرَة مسترجع الهواء
31 [bottom-pouring] steel-casting ladle with stopper	بَوْدَقَة صَبّ الصُلْب [من أسفل] مزودة بمِحْبَس
32 ingot mould (*Am.* mold)	قالب صَبّة الكتل (الصَّبّة)
33 steel ingot	كُتْلَة مصبوبة من الفولاذ
34-44 pig-casting machine	**مَاكِينَة صَبّ خام الحَدِيد**
34 pouring end	حَوْض الصَّبّ
35 metal runner	مَجْرَى صَبّ المعدن
36 series (strand) of moulds (*Am.* molds)	سِلْسِلَة من القوالب
37 mould (*Am.* mold)	قالب
38 catwalk	مَمَرّ ضيق

39 discharging chute	مَجْرَى تصريف
40 pig	حَدِيد خام
41 travelling (*Am.* traveling) crane	مِرْفَاع متحرك
42 top-pouring pig iron (crude iron, iron) ladle	بَوْدَقَة صَبّ علوي للخام
43 pouring ladle lip	حافة / شَفَة بَوْدَقَة الصَّبّ
44 tilting device (tipping device, *Am.* dumping device)	آلية إمالة البَوْدَقَة
45-50 oxygen-blowing converter (L-D converter, Linz-Donawitz converter)	**مُحَوِّل نفخ أكسجيني** (مُحَوِّل إل–دي)
45 conical converter top	قمة المُحَوِّل المخروطية
46 mantle	ترتيبة إمالة المُحَوِّل
47 solid converter bottom	قاع صُلْب للمُحَوِّل
48 fireproof lining (refractory lining)	بِطَانَة مقاومة للحريق (بِطَانَة حرارية)
49 oxygen lance	ماسورة الأكسجين
50 tapping hole (tap hole)	فَتْحَة صَبّ المعدن المنصهر
51-54 Siemens electric low-shaft furnace	**فُرْن سيمنز الكهربي اللافح القَصير**
51 feed	مِنَصَّة الشحن
52 electrodes [arranged in a circle]	الكترودات [في نسق دائري]
53 bustle pipe	ماسورة الهواء اللافح
54 runout	حَصِيرَة خروج المعدن المنصهر
55-69 Thomas converter (basic Beseemer converter)	**مُحَوِّل توماس** (مُحَوِّل بسمر الأساسي)
55 charging position for molten pig iron	مَوْضِع شحن خام الحَدِيد المنصهر
56 charging position for lime	مَوْضِع شحن الجير
57 blow position	مَوْضِع اللَفْح
58 discharging position	مَوْضِع التصريف
59 tilting device (tipping device, *Am.* dumping device)	جِهَاز إمالة
60 crane-operated ladle	بَوْدَقَة تعمل بمِرْفَاع
61 auxiliary crane hoist	ونش رفع إضافي
62 lime bunker	مَخْزَن الجير
63 downpipe	أنْبُوب الهبوط
64 tipping car (*Am.* dump truck)	شاحنة قلابة
65 scrap iron feed	شحن الحَدِيد الخردة
66 control desk	لَوْحَة التحكم
67 converter chimney	مِدْخَنَة المُحَوِّل
68 blast main	أنْبُوب اللفح الرئيسي
69 wind box	صُنْدُوق الهواء

148 Iron Foundry and Rolling Mill — مَسْبِك الحَدِيد و مَاكِينَة الدَلْفَنَة

1-45 iron foundry	**مَسْبِك الحَدِيد**
1-12 melting plant	**مَعْمَل الصهر**
1 cupola furnace (cupola), a melting furnace	فُرْن الدّست (كيوبلا)، فُرْن الصهر
2 blast main (blast inlet, blast pipe)	أنْبُوب اللفح الرئيسي
3 tapping spout	فَتْحَة صَبّ المعدن المنصهر
4 spyhole	فَتْحَة مراقبة
5 tilting-type [hot-metal] receiver	مُسْتَقْبِل [المعدن الساخن] من الطِراز القلاب
6 mobile drum-type ladle	بَوْدَقَة متنقلة من النوع البرْمِيلي
7 melter	عَامِل المَصْهَر
8 founder (caster)	عَامِل المَسْبَك
9 tap bar (tapping bar)	قضيب نزع السّدادة (عن فُوَّهَة الصَّبّ)
10 bott stick (*Am.* bot stick)	عصا ذات سدادة طينية لسد فَتْحَة الصَّبّ
11 molten iron	حَدِيد منصهر
12 slag spout	فُوَّهَة خروج الخبث
13 casting team	فريق عَامِلي الصَّبّ
14 hand shank	مِغْرَفَة يدوية
15 double handle (crutch)	ذِرَاع مزدوج
16 carrying bar	قضيب حمل
17 skimmer rod	قضيب الكاشطة
18 closed moulding (*Am.* molding) box	صُنْدُوق صَبّ مغلق
19 upper frame (cope)	النصف العلوي لقالب السباكة (فردة الغِطَاء)
20 lower frame (drag)	النصف السفلي لقالب السباكة (فردة القاع)
21 runner (runner gate, down-gate)	مَجْرَى صَبّ المعدن المصهور
22 riser (riser gate)	مصعد
23 hand ladle	بَوْدَقَة/مِغْرَفَة يدوية
24-29 continuous casting	**الصَّبّ المتواصل**
24 sinking pouring floor	أرضية صَبّ غاطسة
25 solidifying pig	خام حَدِيد متجمد
26 solid stage	طَوْر التجمد
27 liquid stage	طَوْر السيولة
28 water-cooling system	نظام التبريد بالمياه
29 mould (*Am.* mold) wall	جدار قالب الصَّبّ
30-37 moulding (*Am.* molding) **department** (moulding shop)	**وَرْشَة قوالب الصَّبّ**
30 moulder (*Am.* molder)	عَامِل الصَّبّ
31 pneumatic rammer	مِدَكّ يعمل بالهواء المضغوط
32 hand rammer	مِدَكّ يدوي
33 open moulding (*Am.* molding) box	صُنْدُوق صَبّ مفتوح
34 pattern	قالب صَبّ
35 moulding (*Am.* molding) sand	رَمْل قالب الصَّبّ
36 core	قلب المَسْبُوك
37 core print	طَبْعَة قلب المَسْبُوك
38-45 cleaning shop (fettling shop)	**وَرْشَة التوضيب**
38 steel grit or sand delivery pipe	أنْبُوب تصريف رواسب الصُلْب أو الرمل
39 rotary-table shot-blasting machine	مَاكِينَة سَفْع بالمساحيق الحاكة مزودة بحَصِيرَة دوّارة

40 grit guard	وقاء الرواسب
41 revolving table	حَصيرَة دوّارة
42 casting	مصَبّوبة
43 fettler	مُهَذِّب المصَبّوبات
44 pneumatic grinder	جلاخة رئوية
45 pneumatic chisel	أزميل رئوي
46-75 rolling mill	**مَاكِينَة الدَّلْفَنَة**
46 soaking pit	فُرْن غاطس
47 soaking pit crane	مِرْفَاع الفُرْن الغاطس
48 ingot	كُتْلَة معدنية مصبّوبة
49 ingot tipper	كُرْسِيّ قلاب للكتل
50 roller table	حَصيرَة مَاكِينَة دَلْفَنَة الكتل
51 workpiece	قطعة الشغل
52 bloom shears	مقص الكتل
53 two-high mill	مَاكِينَة دَلْفَنَة ثنائية
54-55 set of rolls (set of rollers)	**مجموعة من دولفينين**
54 upper roll (upper roller)	الدُّلْفين العلوي
55 lower roll (lower roller)	الدُّلْفين السفلي
56-60 roll stand	**هَيْكَل مَاكِينَة الدَّلْفَنَة**
56 base plate	قاعدة الهَيْكَل
57 housing (frame)	هَيْكَل المَاكِينَة
58 coupling spindle	عمود دوّار
59 groove	تجويف
60 roll bearing	كُرْسِيّ الدُّلْفين
61-65 adjusting equipment	**مُعَدَّة الضبط**
61 chock	كُرْسِيّ دعامة
62 main screw	الفتيل الرئيسي
63 gear	آلية مُسَنَّنَة
64 motor	موتور (مُحَرِّك)
65 indicator for rough and fine adjustment	مؤشر الضبط التقريبي والضبط الدقيق
66-75 continuous rolling mill train for the manufacture of strip [diagram]	**مَدْرَج مَاكِينَة دَلْفَنَة مستمرة لصناعة الشرائح** [رَسْم تخطيطي]
66-68 processing of semi-finished product	**تصنيع نتاج نصف تشطيب**
66 semi-finished product	نتاج نصف تشطيب
67 gas cutting installation	وَحْدَة القطع الغازي
68 stack of finished steel sheets	رَصَّة من ألْوَاح الصُّلْب كاملة التشطيب
69 continuous reheating furnaces	أفران إعادة التسخين المستمرة
70 blooming train	حَصِيرَة مَاكِينَة دَلْفَنَة الكتل
71 finishing train	حَصِيرَة التشطيب
72 coiler	مَاكِينَة لف
73 stock of coils for sale	مجموعة ملَفَّات للبيع
74 5 mm shearing train	حَصِيرَة قَص 5 مم
75 10 mm shearing train	حَصِيرَة قَص 10 مم

149 Machine Tools I — آلات الورَش (1)

1 centre (*Am.* center) lathe	مِخْرَطَة ذَنَبَة
2 headstock with gear control (geared head-stock)	غُرَاب ثابت مجهز بمسننات
3 reduction drive lever	ذِرَاع إدارة تقليل السرعة
4 lever for normal and coarse threads	ذِرَاع اللَوْلَبة العادية والخشنة
5 speed change lever	ذِرَاع تغيير السرعة
6 leadscrew reverse-gear lever	ذِرَاع عكس حركة لَوْلَب عمود السحب
7 change-gear box	صُنْدُوق تروس تبديل السرعة
8 feed gearbox (Norton tumbler gear)	صُنْدُوق تروس التغذية (آلية البرْميل الدوّار لنورتون)
9 levers for changing the feed and thread pitch	أذْرُع ضبط التغذية واللوالب
10 feed gear lever (tumbler lever)	ذِرَاع آلية التغذية (ذِرَاع حركة البرْمِيل الدوّار)
11 switch lever for right or left hand action of main spindle	ذِرَاع الضبط الخاصة بالتشغيل اليميني أو اليساري لعمود الدوران الرئيسي
12 lathe foot (footpiece)	قاعدة المِخْرَطَة
13 leadscrew handwheel for traversing of saddle (longitudinal movement of saddle)	عَجَلَة لَوْلَب عمود الجر الخاصة بحركة السرج المستعرضة
14 tumbler reverse lever	ذِرَاع عكس حركة البرْمِيل الدوار
15 feed screw	لَوْلَب التغذية
16 apron (saddle apron, carriage apron)	وقاء تُرْس المخرطة
17 lever for longitudinal and transverse motion	ذِرَاع الحركة الطولية والمستعرضة
18 drop (dropping) worm (feed trip, feed tripping device) for engaging feed mechanisms	تُرْس دودي متساقط لتعشيق آليات التغذية
19 lever for engaging half nut of leadscrew (lever for clasp nut engagement)	ذِرَاع تعشيق الصامولة النصفية للَوْلَب عمود السحب
20 lathe spindle	عمود دوران المِخْرَطَة
21 tool post	حَامِل قَلَم القطع
22 top slide (tool slide, tool rest)	حَامِل قَلَم انزلاقي
23 cross slide	مُنْزَلَقَة مستعرضة
24 bed slide	مُنْزَلَقَة الفَرْشَة
25 coolant supply pipe	أنْبُوب إمداد المُبَرِّد
26 tailstock centre (*Am.* center)	مركز الغُرَاب المتحرك
27 barrel (tailstock barrel)	برْمِيل (برْمِيل الغُرَاب المتحرك)
28 tailstock barrel clamp lever	قامطة برْمِيل الغُرَاب المتحرك
29 tailstock	الغُرَاب المتحرك
30 tailstock barrel adjusting handwheel	عَجَلَة ضبط برْمِيل الغُرَاب المتحرك
31 lathe bed	فَرْشَة المِخْرَطَة
32 leadscrew	لَوْلَب عمود السحب
33 feed shaft	عمود التغذية

34 reverse shaft for right and left hand motion and engaging and disengaging — عمود عكس الحركة اليمنى واليسرى والتعشيق والفصل
35 four-jaw chuck (four-jaw independent chuck) — ظَرْف ذو أربعة فكوك
36 gripping jaw — فك قَابِض
37 three-jaw chuck (three-jaw self-centring, *Am.* self-centering, chuck) — ظَرْف ذو ثلاثة فكوك
38 turret lathe — مخْرَطَة بُرْجِيَّة
39 cross slide — مُنْزَلِقَة مستعرضة
40 turret — بُرْج
41 combination toolholder (multiple turning head) — ماسك أقلام قطع مؤتلف
42 top slide — مُنْزَلِقَة علوية
43 star wheel — عَجَلَة نَجْمِيَّة
44 coolant tray for collecting coolant and swarf — صِينِيَّة المُبَرِّد لتجميع المحلول المُبَرِّد والخراطة
45-53 lathe tools — **أقلام المخْرَطَة**
45 tool bit holder (clamp tip tool) for adjustable cutting tips — حَامِل قَلَم قطع خاص بأسنان القطع القابلة للضبط
46 adjustable cutting tip (clamp tip) of cemented carbide or oxide ceramic — سن قطع قابل للضبط مصنوع من كربيد مُسَمْنَت أو سيراميك أكسيدي
47 shapes of adjustable oxide ceramic tips — أشكال أسنان من السيراميك الأكسيدي القابلة للضبط
48 lathe tool with cemented carbide cutting edge — عدة مخْرَطَة ذات حافة قطع من الكربيد المُسَمْنَت
49 tool shank — ساق القَلَم
50 brazed cemented carbide cutting tip (cutting edge) — سن قطع كربيدي مُسَمْنَت ملحوم بالنحاس
51 internal facing tool (boring tool) for corner work — قَلَم تسوية الأوجه الداخلية للشغل الزاويّ
52 general-purpose lathe tool — قَلَم مخْرَطَة للأغراض العامة
53 parting (parting-off) tool — عدة قطع ، قَلَم قطعية
54 lathe carrier — حَامِل (كُلاّبة المخْرَطَة)
55 driving (driver) plate — مُدوِّر (كُلاّبة المخْرَطَة)
56-72 measuring instruments — **آلات القياس**
56 plug gauge (*Am.* gage) — محدد قياس سدادي (لقياس الثقوب)
57 'GO' gauging (*Am.* gaging) member (end) — طَرْف قياس سماحي
58 'NOT GO' gauging (*Am.* gaging) member (end) — طَرْف قياس لا سماحي
59 calliper (caliper, snap) gauge (*Am.* gage) — قَدَمَة : آلة قياس ذات فكين
60 'GO' side — الجانب السماحي
61 'NOT GO' side — الجانب اللاسماحي
62 micrometer — ميكرومتر
63 measuring scale — مَدْرَج القياس
64 graduated thimble — كشتبان مدرج
65 frame — إطار
66 spindle (screwed spindle) — عمود دوران
67 vernier calliper (caliper) gauge (*Am.* gage) — قَدَمَة ذات وَرْنِيَّة
68 depth gauge (*Am.* gage) attachment rule — مِسْطَرَة وَصْلَة معيار العمق
69 vernier scale — مقياس وَرْني
70 outside jaws — فَكّان خارجيان
71 inside jaws — فَكّان داخليان
72 vernier depth gauge (*Am.* gage) — معيار عمق وَرْني

150 Machine Tools II — آلات الورَش (2)

1 universal grinding machine — جلاّخة عامة
2 headstock — غُرَاب ثابت
3 wheelhead slide — مُنْزَلِقَة رَأس العَجَلَة (لتركيب قرص التجليخ)
4 grinding wheel — عَجَلَة تجليخ
5 tailstock — غُرَاب متحرك
6 grinding machine bed — فَرْشَة الجلاخة
7 grinding machine table — صِينِيَّة الجلاخة
8 two-column planing machine (two-column planer) — مقشطة عَرَبَة ذات قائمين
9 drive motor, a direct current motor — مُحَرِّك الإدارة
10 column — قائم
11 planer table — صِينِيَّة المقشطة
12 cross slide (rail) — مُنْزَلِقَة عرضية (مَجْرَى أفقي)
13 tool box — مِرْبَط القَلَم
14 hacksaw — مِنْشَار معادن
15 clamping device — نبيطة ربط
16 saw blade — نَصْل المِنْشَار
17 saw frame — إطار المِنْشَار
18 radial (radial-arm) drilling machine — مَاكِينَة ثقب نصف قطرية (مَاكِينَة تثقيب دف)
19 bed (base plate) — قاعدة (لَوْح القاعدة)
20 block for workpiece — كُتْلَة ارتكاز قطعة الشغل
21 pillar — عمود
22 lifting motor — مُحَرِّك رفع
23 drill spindle — عمود دوران المثقب
24 arm — ذِرَاع الكتيفة
25 universal milling machine — مَاكِينَة تفريز عامة
26 milling machine table — صِينِيَّة مَاكِينَة التفريز
27 table feed drive — إدارة تغذية الصِّينِيَّة
28 switch lever for spindle rotation speed — ذِرَاع ضبط سرعة عمود الدوران
29 control box (control unit) — صُنْدُوق التحكم (وَحْدَة التحكم)
30 vertical milling spindle — عمود دوران التفريز الرَّأسي
31 vertical drive head — رَأس الإدارة الرَّأسية

32	horizontal milling spindle	عمود دوران التفريز الأفقي
33	end support for steadying horizontal spindle	دعامة طَرْفية لتثبيْت عمود دوران التفريز الأفقي
34	machine tap	ذَكَر لَوْلَبة مكَنيَّة
35	articulated robot, an industrial robot	روبوت مِفْصَلي، روبوت صناعي (إنسان آلي)
36	base plate	لَوْح القاعدة
37	rotating column (base rotating axis)	عمود دوَّار (محور قاعدة دوَّار)
38	shoulder joint	مفْصَل الكتف
39	upper arm	العضد
40	elbow joint	مفْصَل مرفقي
41	tubular forearm	ساعد أنْبُوبي
42	wrist joint	مفْصَل رسغي
43	gripper mounting flange	شَفَة تركيب القَابِض
44	gripper	القَابِض
45	fingers	أصابع
46	upright robot (linear-axis robot, rectilinear robot)	روبوت قائم (روبوت ذو محور طولي، روبوت مستقيم)
47	portal robot (gantry robot)	روبوت بابي (روبوت قنطري)

151 Drawing Office — مكْتَب الرَّسْم الهَنْدَسِيّ

1	drawing board	لَوْحَة الرَّسْم
2	drafting machine with parallel motion	جِهَاز رَسْم ذو حركة متوازية
3	adjustable knob	مِقْبَض الضبط والتعديل
4	drawing head (adjustable set square)	رَأس الرَّسْم (زاوية قائمة قابلة للتعديل)
5	drawing board adjustment	آلية ضبط لَوْحَة الرَّسْم
6	drawing table	طاولة الرَّسْم
7	set square (triangle)	زاوية قائمة (مثلث)
8	triangle	مثلث
9	T-square (tee-square)	مِسْطَرَة تائية
10	rolled drawing	رَسْم مَطْوي (ملفوف)
11	diagram	رَسْم تخَطِيطي
12	time schedule	جدول زمني
13	paper stand	حَامِل ورق الرَّسْم
14	roll of paper	لفة ورق
15	cutter	نَصْل قطع الورق
16	technical drawing (drawing, design)	رَسْم فنيّ (تصميم)
17	front view (front elevation)	مَنْظَر أمامي
18	side view (side elevation)	مَنْظَر جانبي
19	plan	تمثيل تخَطِيطي
20	surface not to be machined	سَطْح لا يصنع آلياً
21	surface to be machined	سَطْح يصنع آلياً
22	surface to be super-finished	سَطْح يتم تشطيبه تشطيباً فاخرا
23	visible edge	حافة مرئية
24	hidden edge	حافة غير مرئية
25	dimension line	خَطّ البعد
26	arrow head	رَأس سهم
27	section line	خَطّ القطاع
28	section A-B	القطاع أ–ب
29	hatched surface	سَطْح مظلل
30	centre (*Am.* center) line	خَطّ المركز
31	title panel (title block)	لَوْحَة بيانات الملكية
32	technical data	بيانات فنية
33	ruler (rule)	مِسْطَرَة
34	triangular scale	مِسْطَرَة مثلثة
35	erasing shield	شبلونة مسح
36	drawing ink cartridge	خرطوش حبر الرَّسْم
37	holders for tubular drawing pens	مِقْلَمَة أقلام الرَّسْم الأُنْبُوبية
38	set of tubular drawing pens	مجموعة من أقلام الرَّسْم الأنْبُوبية
39	hygrometer	هيجرومتر
40	cap with indication of nib size	غِطَاء موضح عليه حجم سن القَلَم
41	pencil-type eraser	مِمْحَاة على شكل قلَم رصاص
42	eraser	مِمْحَاة
43	erasing knife	سكين مَحْو
44	erasing knife blade	نَصْل سكين المحو
45	clutch-type pencil	قلَم رصاص ذو قَابِض
46	pencil lead (refill lead, refill, spare lead)	رصاص القلَم
47	glass eraser	مِمْحَاة زجاجية
48	glass fibres (*Am.* fibers)	ألياف زجاجية
49	ruling pen	قلَم تسطير
50	cross joint	وَصْلَة تقاطعية
51	index plate	قرص دليلي
52	compass with interchangeable attachments	فِرْجَار ذو ملحقات تبادلية
53	compass head	رَأس الفِرْجَار
54	needle point attachment	وَصْلَة الطَّرْف الإبْري
55	pencil point attachment	وَصْلَة طَرْف قلَم الرصاص
56	needle	إبْرَة، دبوس
57	lengthening arm (extension bar)	ذِرَاع استطالة
58	ruling pen attachment	وَصْلَة قلَم التسطير
59	pump compass (drop compass)	فِرْجَار مِضخيّ
60	piston	مِكْبَس
61	ruling pen attachment	وَصْلَة قلَم التسطير
62	pencil attachment	وَصْلَة القلَم الرصاص
63	drawing ink container	مِدْوَاة حبر الرَّسْم
64	spring bow (rapid adjustment, ratchet-type) compass	فِرْجَار ذو نابض
65	spring ring hinge	مفْصَل حلَقَة النابض
66	spring-loaded fine adjustment for arcs	وَصْلَة الرَّسْم الدقيق المحمولة على نابض لرَسْم الأقواس
67	right-angle needle	إبْرَة قائمة الزاوية
68	tubular ink unit	وَحْدَة حبر أنْبُوبية
69	stencil lettering guide (lettering stencil)	مِسْطَرَة حروف الاستنسل
70	circle template	لَوْح الدوائر

71 ellipse template — لَوْح الرَّسْم الإهليلجي

152 Power Plant (I) (Power Station) — مَحَطَّة تَوْلِيد الطَّاقَة (1)

1-28 steam-generating station, an electric power plant — **مَحَطَّة توليد البخار،** مَحَطَّة طاقة كهربية

1-21 boiler house — **مَبْنَى المِرْجَل**

1 coal conveyor — سَيْر نقل الفَحْم

2 coal bunker — مُسْتَوْدَع الفَحْم

3 travelling-grate (*Am.* traveling-grate) stoker — وقّاد آلي ذو مصبّعة متحركة

4 coal mill — طاحونة الفَحْم

5 steam boiler, a water-tube boiler (radiant-type boiler) — مِرْجَل بخاري

6 burners — مواقد

7 water pipes — أنابيب الماء

8 ash pit (clinker pit) — حفرة الرماد

9 superheater — سَخَّان فوقى

10 water preheater — سَخَّان ماء مُتَقَدِّم

11 air preheater — سَخَّان هواء مُتَقَدِّم

12 gas flue — مِدْخَنَة تصريف الغاز

13 electrostatic precipitator — مُرَسِّب الكتروستاتى

14 induced-draught (*Am.* induced-draft) fan — مِرْوَحَة سحب مستحث

15 chimney (smokestack) — مِدْخَنَة

16 de-aerator — وعاء نزع الهواء

17 feedwater tank — خَزَّان ماء التغذية

18 boiler feed pump — مِضَخَّة تغذية المرجل

19 control room — غُرْفَة التحكم

20 cable tunnel — نفق الكيبلات

21 cable vault — قبو الكيبلات

22 turbine house — مَبيت التوربين

23 steam turbine with alternator — توربين بخاري ذو مولد للتيار المتناوب

24 surface condenser — مكثِّف سَطْحي

25 low-pressure preheater — سَخَّان مُتَقَدِّم منخفض الضغط

26 high-pressure preheater (economizer) — سَخَّان مُتَقَدِّم عالي الضغط

27 cooling water pipe — ماسورة ماء التبريد

28 control room — غُرْفَة التحكم

29-35 outdoor sub-station, a substation — **مَحَطَّة فرعية خارجية**

29 busbars — موصِّلات عمومية

30 power transformer, a mobile (transportable) transformer — مُحَوِّل طاقة نقال

31 stay poles (guy poles) — قضبان تثبيت

32 high-voltage transmission line — خَطّ نقل (كهربائي) عالي الفولطية

33 high-voltage conductor — موصِّل عالي الفولطية

34 air-blast circuit breaker (circuit breaker) — قاطع الدائرة الكهربائية بالدفع الهوائي

35 surge diverter (*Am.* lightning arrester, arrester) — واقية صواعق

36 overhead line support, a lattice steel tower — حَامِل الخُطُوط الهوائية، بُرْج صُلْب تشابكي

37 cross arm (traverse) — ذِرَاع تصالبي

38 strain insulator — عازل صامد للشد (انفعالي)

39 mobile (transportable) transformer (power transformer, transformer) — مُحَوِّل نقال

40 transformer tank — خَزَّان المُحَوِّل

41 bogie (*Am.* truck) — عَرَبَة نقل منخفضة

42 oil conservator — حافظة الزيت

43 primary voltage terminal (primary voltage bushing) — طَرَف توصيل الفولطية الأولية

44 low-voltage terminals (low-voltage bushings) — أطراف توصيل الفولطية المنخفضة

45 oil-circulating pump — مِضَخَّة تدوير الزيت

46 oil cooler — مبرد الزيت

47 arcing horn — قَرْنَة إذكاء القوس الكهربائي

48 transport lug — وَصْلَة الجر بسيارة

153 Power Plant (Power Station) II — مَحَطَّة تَوْلِيد الطَّاقَة (2)

1-8 control room — **غُرْفَة التَّحكُم**

1-6 control console (control desk) — **كونسول التَّحكُم**

1 control board (control panel) for the alternators — لَوْحة التَّحكُم الخاصة بمُوَلِّدات التيَّار المُتَناوِب

2 master switch — المفتَاح الرئيسي

3 signal light — ضَوْء إرشادي

4 feeder panel — لَوْحة التَّغْذِيَة

5 monitoring controls for the switching systems — مَضَابط المراقبَة الخاصة بأنظمَة التحويل

6 controls — مَضَابط/مفاتيح التَّحكُم

7 revertive signal panel — لَوْحة الإشارات المُرْتَدَّة

8 matrix mimic board — لَوْحة المُحَاكَاة الأم

9-18 transformer — **المُحَوِّل**

9 oil conservator — حافظَة الزَّيْت

10 breather — فَتْحَة تنفيس

11 oil gauge (*Am.* gage) — مِقْيَاس الزَّيْت

12 feed-through terminal (feed-through insulator) — طَرْف تغذية

13 on-load tap changer — مُغَيِّر التفريغ

14 yoke — مقْرَن اللفائف المُمَغْنَط

15 primary winding (primary) — اللفيفة الابتدائية

16 secondary winding (secondary, low-voltage winding) — اللفيفة الثانويَّة (لفيفة منخفضة الفُولْطيَّة)

17 core — قَلْب الملَف

18 tap (tapping) — مأخَذ تفريغ، نقطة التفريغ

19 transformer connection — تَوْصِيلة المُحَوِّل

20 star connection (star network, Y-connection) — تَوْصِيلة نَجْميَّة

21 delta connection (mesh connection) — تَوْصِيلة دلتا/مثلثية

22 neutral point — نقطة التعادل/العطالة

23-30 steam turbine, a — **التوربين البخاريّ**

turbogenerator unit

23 high-pressure cylinder — أسْطُوانَة ضغط عالٍ

24 medium-pressure cylinder — أسْطُوانَة ضغط مُتَوَسِّط

25 low-pressure cylinder — أسْطُوانَة ضغط مُنْخَفض

26 three-phase generator (generator) — مُوَلِّد ثُلاثي الأطْوار

27 hydrogen cooler — مُبَرِّد هيدروجيني

28 leakage steam path — مَسَار البخار المُتَسَرِّب

29 jet nozzle — مَنْفَث نافوري

30 turbine monitoring panel with measuring instruments — لَوْحة مراقبة التوربين وبها آلات قياس

31 automatic voltage regulator — مُنَظِّم فُولْطيَّة آليّ

32 synchro — سِنكرو

33 cable box — صندوق الكيبل

34 conductor — موصِّل

35 feed-through terminal (feed-through insulator) — طَرْف تغذية

36 core — قَلْب الملَف

37 casing — غلاف خارجي

38 filling compound (filler) — مُرَكَّب حَشْو

39 lead sheath — غلاف سِلْك التوصيل

40 lead-in tube — أنْبُوب السِّلْك المَسْحُوب

41 cable — كيبل

42 high voltage cable, for three-phase current — كيبل عالي الفُولْطيَّة لتيَّار ثلاثي الأطْوار

43 conductor — مُوَصِّل

44 metallic paper (metallized paper) — وَرَق معدني

45 tracer (tracer element) — عُنْصر استشفافي

46 varnished-cambric tape — شَريط من القماش الناعِم الرَّقيق مَطْليٌّ بالوَرْنيش

47 lead sheath — غلاف سِلْك التوصيل

48 asphalted paper — وَرَق مُسَفْلَت

49 jute serving — غلاف مُقَيَّر

50 steel tape or steel wire armour (*Am.* armor) — شَريط صلب أو دِرْع معدني سِلْكيّ

51-62 air-blast circuit breaker, a circuit breaker — **قاطع دائرة بالدفع الهوائيّ** (قاطع دائرة)

51 compressed-air tank — خَزَّان هواء مضغوط

52 control valve (main operating valve) — صِمَام التَّحكُّم (صِمَام التشغيل الرئيسي)

53 compressed-air inlet — مَدْخَل الهواء المضغوط

54 support insulator, a hollow porcelain supporting insulator — عازل إسناديّ، عازل إسناديّ أجْوَف من البورسلين

55 interrupter — قاطع التيار

56 resistor — مقاوِم

57 auxiliary contacts — مُلامَسات مُساعِدة

58 current transformer — مُحَوِّل التَّيَّار

59 voltage transformer (potential transformer) — مُحَوِّل الفولطيَّة

60 operating mechanism housing — مَبيت آليَّة التشغيل

61 arcing horn — قَرْنَة إذْكاء القَوْس

الكهربائي

62 spark gap — فَرْجَة الشَّرارَة

154 Nuclear Energy — الطَّاقَة النَّوَوِيَّة

1 fast-breeder reactor (fast breeder) [diagram] — مُفَاعِل مُوَلِّد سريع [رَسْم تخطيطي]

2 primary circuit (primary loop, primary sodium system) — الدَّائرة الأوَّليَّة (نِظَام الصوديوم الأوَّليّ)

3 reactor — المُفَاعِل

4 fuel rods (fuel pins) — قضبان الوَقُود

5 primary sodium pump — مِضَخَّة الصوديوم الأوَّليَّة (نِظَام الصوديوم الثانوي)

6 heat exchanger — مُبَادِل حراري

7 secondary circuit (secondary loop, secondary sodium system) — الدائرة الثانويَّة

8 secondary sodium pump — مِضَخَّة الصوديوم الثانويَّة

9 steam generator — مُوَلِّد بُخَاريّ

10 cooling water flow circuit — دائرة دفق ماء التبريد

11 steam line — خَطّ البُخار

12 feedwater line — خَطّ مياه التغذية

13 feed pump — مِضَخَّة التغذية

14 steam turbine — توربين بُخَاريّ

15 generator — مُوَلِّد (كهربائي)

16 transmission line — خَطّ النقل

17 condenser — مكثِّف

18 cooling water — ماء التبريد

19 nuclear reactor, a pressurized-water reactor (nuclear power plant, atomic power plant) — المُفَاعِل النَّوَويّ، مُفَاعِل يعمل بالماء المضغوط (وَحْدَة توليد طاقة نَوَويَّة)

20 concrete shield (reactor building) — مَبْنًى خرسانيّ (مَبْنَى المُفَاعِل)

21 steel containment (steel shell) with air extraction vent — غلاف من الصُّلْب ذو فتْحَة لاستخلاص الهواء

22 reactor pressure vessel — وعاء المُفَاعِل الضغطي

23 control rod drive — إدارة ذراع التحكم

24 control rods — أذْرُع التحكم

25 primary coolant pump — مِضَخَّة المُبَرِّد الأوَّليَّة

26 steam generator — مُوَلِّد بُخَاريّ

27 fuel-handling hoists — مَرَافع مناولة الوَقُود

28 fuel storage — خَزَّان الوَقُود

29 coolant flow passage — مَجْرَى تدفق المُبَرِّد

30 feedwater line — خَطّ مياه التغذية

31 prime steam line — خَطّ البخار الرئيسي

32 manway — ممَر

33 turbogenerator set — جِهَاز مُوَلِّد توربيني

34 turbogenerator — مُوَلِّد توربيني

35 condenser — مكثِّف

36 service building — مَبْنَى الخدمة

37 exhaust gas stack — ماسورة غاز العادم

38 polar crane — مِرْفاع قُطْبيّ

39 cooling tower, a dry cooling tower — بُرج التبريد، بُرج تبريد جاف

40 pressurized-water — نِظَام الماء المضغوط

system — الرصاصي

41 reactor — مُفَاعِل
42 primary circuit (primary loop) — الدائرة الأوَّليَّة
43 circulation pump (recirculation pump) — مِضَخَّة التدوير (مِضَخَّة إعادة التدوير)
44 heat exchanger (steam generator) — مُبَادِل حراريّ (مُوَلِّد بخاريّ)
45 secondary circuit (secondary loop, feed-water steam circuit) — الدائرة الثانويَّة (دائرة بُخاريَّة لمياه التغذية)
46 steam turbine — توربين بُخَاريّ
47 generator — مُوَلِّد (كهربائيّ)
48 cooling system — نِظَام التبريد
49 boiling water system [diagram] — نِظَام الماء المَغْلِي [رسم تخطيطي]
50 reactor — مُفَاعِل
51 steam and recirculation water flow paths — مَمَرَّات تدفق ماء إعادة التدوير والبخار
52 steam turbine — توربين بخاري
53 generator — مُوَلِّد (كهربائي)
54 circulation pump (recirculation pump) — مِضَخَّة التدوير (مِضَخَّة إعادة التدوير)
55 coolant system (cooling with water from river) — نِظَام المُبَرِّد (تبريد بماء النَّهْر)
56 radioactive waste storage in salt mine — تخزين النفايات المُشِعَّة في مَنْجَم مِلْح
57-68 geological structure of abandoned salt mine converted for disposal of radioactive waste (nuclear waste) — **التركيب الجيولوجي لمَنْجَم مِلْح مَهْجُور يستخدم في التخلص من النفايات المُشِعَّة**
57 Lower Keuper — كيوبر سُفْلي
58 Upper Muschelkalk — سوشلاك (ترياس) عُلْوي
59 Middle Muschelkalk — سوشلاك (ترياس) أوْسَط
60 Lower Muschelkalk — سوشلاك (ترياس) سُفْلي
61 Bunter downthrow — رَمْيَة سفليَّة
62 residue of leached (lixiviated) Zechstein (Upper Permian) — فضالة ″زكستاين″ مُحْلَلَة (بِرْميَّة علوية)
63 Aller rock salt — مِلْح صَخْر ″ألير″
64 Leine rock salt — مِلْح صَخْر ″لاين″
65 Stassfurt seam (potash salt seam, potash salt bed) — طَبَقَة ستاسفورتية (طَبَقَة مِلْح بوتاسي)
66 Stassfurt salt — مِلْح ستاسفورتي
67 grenzanhydrite — جرنزانهايدريت
68 Zechstein shale — غضار، طين صَفْحي
69 shaft — مِهْوَاة المَنْجَم
70 minehead buildings — مباني رأس المَنْجَم
71 storage chamber — غُرْفَة تخزين
72 storage of medium-active waste in salt mine — تخزين نفايات متوسطة الإشْعَاعيَّة في مَنْجَم مِلح
73 511 m level — مستوى 511 م
74 protective screen (anti-radiation screen) — ستار واقٍ من الإشْعَاع
75 lead glass window — نافذة من الزُجاج
76 storage chamber — غُرْفَة تخزين
77 drum containing radioactive waste — برميل يحتوى على نفايات مُشِعَّة
78 television camera — كاميرا تليفزيونية
79 charging chamber — غُرْفَة الشحن
80 control desk (control panel) — لَوْحة التحكم
81 upward ventilator — جِهَاز تَهْوِيَة صاعِد
82 shielded container — حاوِيَة مُدَرَّعَة
83 490 m level — مستوى 490 م

155 Modern Sources of Energy — مَصَادِر الطَّاقَة الحَدِيثَة

1 heat pump system — نِظَام المِضَخَّة الحراريَّة
2 source water inlet — مَدْخَل ماء المنبع
3 cooling water heat exchanger — المُبَادِل الحراري لماء التبريد
4 compressor — ضاغِط
5 natural-gas or diesel engine — مُحَرِّك يعمل بالغاز الطبيعي أو الديزل
6 evaporator — مُبَخِّر
7 pressure release valve — صمام إعتاق الضغط
8 condenser — مكَثِّف
9 waste-gas heat exchanger — المُبَادِل الحراري لغاز العادم
10 flow pipe — أُنْبُوب الدفْق
11 vent pipe — أُنْبُوب تنفيس
12 chimney — مِدْخَنَة
13 boiler — مِرْجَل
14 fan — مِرْوَحة
15 radiator — مِشْعَاع
16 sink — بالوعة
17-36 utilization of solar energy — **استغلال الطاقة الشمسيَّة**
17 solar (solar-heated) house — مَبْنَى شمسي (يتم تدفئته بالطاقة الشمسيَّة)
18 solar radiation (sunlight, insolation) — إشعاع شمسي
19 collector — مَجْمَع الإشْعَاع الشمسي
20 hot reservoir (heat reservoir) — الخزان الساخن
21 power supply — مصدر إمداد طاقة
22 heat pump — مِضَخَّة حراريَّة
23 water outlet — مَخْرَج الماء
24 air supply — مَصْدَر إمداد الهواء
25 flue — مَصْرَف الغازات، مِدْخَنَة
26 hot water supply — مَصْدَر إمداد الماء الساخن
27 radiator heating — تسخين المِشْعَاع
28 flat plate solar collector — مَجْمَع إشْعَاع شمسي مُسَطَّح الصفائح
29 blackened receiver surface with asphalted aluminium (*Am.* aluminum) foil — سطح مُسْتَقبِل مَطْلي باللون الأسْوَد ذو رقاقة ألمونيوم مُسَفْلَتَة
30 steel tube — أُنْبُوب من الصلب
31 heat transfer fluid — سائل نقل الحرارة
32 flat plate solar collector, containing — مَجْمَع إشْعَاع شمسي مُسَطَّح الصفائح ذو خليَّة شمسيَّة

solar cell

33 glass cover	غطاء زُجاجي
34 solar cell	خليَّة شمسيَّة
35 air ducts	مَسَالك الهواء
36 insulation	طَبَقَة عازلة
37 tidal power plant [section]	وَحْدَة قُدْرَة مَدّ جَزْريَّة (مَحَطَّة توليد قدرة تَعمل بطاقة المد والجَزْر) [قطاع]
38 dam	سَدّ
39 reversible turbine	توربين انعكاسي
40 turbine inlet for water from the sea	فَتْحَة دخول ماء البحر إلى التوربين
41 turbine inlet for water from the basin	فَتْحَة دخول ماء الحوض إلى التوربين
42 wind power plant (wind generator, aero-generator)	وَحْدَة توليد الطاقة بالرياح (مُوَلِّد هوائي)
43 truss tower	بُرْج جملوني
44 guy wire	سلك شدَّاد
45 rotor	مروحة، رفَّاص
46 generator with variable pitch for power regulation	مُوَلِّد ذو خَطْوة متبادلة لتنظيم الطاقة

156 Coking Plant — وَحْدَة التَكْويك

1-15 coking plant	**وَحْدَة التَكْويك**
1 dumping of coking coal	إفْراغ فحم التَكْويك
2 belt conveyor	سَيْر نَقَّال
3 blending bunker	مُسْتودع المَزْج
4 service bunker conveyor	سَيْر نقل صَوْمَعَة الفَحْم
5 service bunker	صَوْمَعَة الفَحْم
6 larry car (larry, charging car)	عَرَبَة شحن الفرن
7 pusher ram	آليَّة دفع فَحْم الكُوك
8 battery of coke ovens	بطارية أفران الكُوك
9 coke guide	دليل الكُوك
10 quenching car, with engine	عَرَبَة نقل الكُوك لإطفائه
11 quenching tower	بُرْج إطفاء الكُوك
12 coke loading bay (coke wharf)	رصيف تحميل الكُوك
13 coke wharf conveyor	سَيْر رصيف الكُوك
14 screening of coke and breeze	غَرْبَلَة كُتَل الفَحْم وتُراب الفَحْم
15 coke loading	تحميل الكُوك
16-45 coke-oven gas processing	**معالجة غاز فرن الكُوك**
16 discharge (release) of gas from the coke ovens	تصريف الغاز من أفران الكُوك
17 gas-collecting main	الخَطّ الرئيسي لتجميع الغاز
18 coal tar extraction	استخلاص قار الكُوك
19 gas cooler	مُبَرِّد الغاز
20 electrostatic precipitator	جِهَاز ترسيب الكتروستاتي
21 gas extractor	فَرَّازَة الغاز
22 hydrogen sulphide (*Am.* hydrogen sulfide) scrubber (hydrogen sulphide wet collector)	جِهَاز غسل الغاز من كبريتيد الهيدروجين
23 ammonia scrubber (ammonia wet collector)	جِهَاز غسل الغاز من الأمونيا
24 benzene (benzol) scrubber	جِهَاز غسل الغاز من البنزين
25 gas holder	خَزَّان الغاز
26 gas compressor	ضاغط الغاز
27 debenzoling by cooler and heat exchanger	نَزْع البنزول بواسطة مُبَرِّد ومُبَادِل حراري
28 desulphurization (*Am.* desulfurization) of pressure gas	نَزْع كبريت غاز الضغط
29 gas cooling	تبريد الغاز
30 gas drying	تجفيف الغاز
31 gas meter	عدَّاد الغاز
32 crude tar tank	خَزَّان القار الخام
33 sulphuric acid (*Am.* sulfuric acid) supply	إمداد حامض الكبريتيك
34 production of sulphuric acid (*Am.* sulfuric acid)	إنتاج حامض الكبريتيك
35 production of ammonium sulphate (*Am.* ammonium sulfate)	إنتاج كبريتات الأمونيوم
36 ammonium sulphate (*Am.* ammonium sulfate)	كبريتات الأمونيوم
37 recovery plant for recovering the scrubbing agents	وَحْدَة استرجاع عَوَادِم الغسيل
38 waste water discharge	تصريف الماء الفائض/ المَهْدُور
39 phenol extraction from the gas water	استخلاص الفينول من ماء الغاز
40 crude phenol tank	خَزَّان الفينول الخام
41 production of crude benzol (crude benzene)	إنتاج البِنْزُول الخام (البنزين الخام)
42 crude benzol (crude benzene) tank	خَزَّان البِنْزُول الخام (البنزين الخام)
43 scrubbing oil tank	خَزَّان زَيْت الغسيل
44 low-pressure gas main	خَطّ الغاز الرئيسي منخفض الضغط
45 high-pressure gas main	خَطّ الغاز الرئيسي عالي الضغط

157 Sawmill — المَنْشَرَة

1 sawmill	المَنْشَرَة
2 vertical frame saw (*Am.* gang mill)	منشار إطاري قائم (مَجْمُوعة مَنَاشير جماعيَّة)
3 saw blades	أنْصَال المَنَاشير
4 feed roller	دُلْفين الإلقام
5 guide roller	دُلْفين دليلي
6 fluting (grooving, grooves)	خُدُود طوليَّة
7 oil pressure gauge (*Am.* gage)	مِقْيَاس ضغط الزَّيْت
8 saw frame	إطار المناشير
9 feed indicator	مُؤشِّر الإلقام
10 log capacity scale	مِقْيَاس سِعَة جذع الشَّجَرَة

المعَد للنَّشْر

11 auxiliary carriage — عَرَبَة مساعِدة
12 carriage — عَرَبَة
13 log grips — كُلاّبات تثبيت جِذْع الشَّجَرة
14 remote control panel — لَوْحة التحكم عن بعد
15 carriage motor — موتور العَرَبَة
16 truck for splinters (splints) — عَرَبَة لِحَمْل الشظايا والشرائح
17 endless log chain (*Am.* jack chain) — سِلْسِلَة متواصلة لدفع جذوع الشَّجَر
18 stop plate — مِصَدّ
19 log-kicker arms — أَذْرُع دفع جذوع الشَّجَر
20 cross conveyor — سَيْر نَقَّال مُتَعَاكِس
21 washer (washing machine) — مَاكِينَة غسيل
22 cross chain conveyor for sawn timber — سَيْر نَقَّال مُتَعَاكِس بسِلْسِلَة لنقل الخَشَب المَنْشُور
23 roller table — نَضُد الدلافين
24 undercut swing saw — مِنْشَار دوَّار للقطع السفلي
25 piling — تكويم الألواح
26 roller trestles — حامِل دُلفيني
27 gantry crane — مِرْفَاع قَنْطَري مُتَحَرِّك
28 crane motor — موتور المِرْفاع
29 pivoted log grips — كلابات مِحْوَرِيَّة لِمَسْك جذوع الشَّجَر
30 roundwood (round timber) — خَشَب مُسْتَدير المَقْطَع
31 log dump — كَوْمَة جذوع أشجار
32 squared timber store — مَخْزَن الخَشَب المُسَوَّى
33 sawn logs — جذوع أشجار مَنْشُورَة
34 planks — أَلْوَاح خَشَبِيَّة ثَخِينَة
35 boards (planks) — أَلْوَاح خَشَبِيَّة
36 squared timber — خَشَب مربع المقطع (مُسَوَّى)
37 stack bearer — حامِل الرَّصَّة
38 automatic cross-cut chain saw — مِنْشَار سِلْسِلَة آلي للقطع المُتَعَارِض
39 log grips — كُلاّبات تثبيت جِذْع الشَّجَرة
40 feed roller — دُلْفين الإلقام
41 chain-tensioning device — جِهَاز شد السِّلْسِلَة
42 saw-sharpening machine — ماكينة شَحْذ أَسْنَان المِنْشَار
43 grinding wheel (teeth grinder) — عَجَلَة تجليخ (لأسنان المِنْشَار)
44 feed pawl — لُسَيْن الإلقام
45 depth adjustment for the teeth grinder — ذِرَاع تعديل عمق مَاكِينَة شَحْذ أَسْنَان المِنْشَار
46 lifter (lever) for the grinder chuck — ذِرَاع ظَرْف الجَلاّخة
47 holding device for the saw blade — جِهَاز تثبيت نَصْل المِنْشَار
48 horizontal bandsaw for sawing logs — مِنْشَار شَرِيطي أُفُقِيّ لنشر جذوع الشَّجَر
49 height adjustment — آلية تعديل الارتفاع
50 chip remover — أداة إزالة القشور
51 chip extractor — فَتْحَة طرد القشور/النحاتة
52 carriage — عَرَبَة
53 bandsaw blade — نَصْل مِنْشَار شريطي
54 automatic blocking saw — مِنْشَار كتل آليّ
55 feed channel — قناة الإلقام
56 discharge opening — فَتْحَة خروج الخَشَب
57 twin edger (double edger) — مِنْشَار دائريّ مزدوج لقطع الحَوَاف
58 breadth scale (width scale) — مِقْيَاس عرض الخَشَب
59 kick-back guard (plates) — وقاء الارتداد
60 height scale — مِقْيَاس الارتفاع
61 in-feed scale — مِقْيَاس الإلقام
62 indicator lamps — لمبات إرشادية
63 feed table — طبلية الإلقام
64 undercut swing saw — مِنْشَار دوَّار للقطع السفليّ
65 automatic hold-down with protective hood — أداة تثبيت آليَّة ذات غطاء واقٍ
66 foot switch — مِفْتَاح تشغيل سفلي
67 distribution board (panelboard) — لَوْحة التوزيع
68 length stop — حاجِز الطول، مِصَدّ

158 Quarry — المَحْجَر

1 quarry, an open-cast working — المَحْجَر، مَحْجَر مكشوف
2 overburden — الغطاء الصخري/الترابي
3 working face — سطح الشغل
4 loose rock pile (blasted rock) — كَوْمَة صخور سائبة
5 quarryman (quarrier), a quarry worker — عامِل المَحْجَر
6 sledge hammer — مِرْزَبَّة
7 wedge — إسفين
8 block of stone — كتلة من الحجر
9 driller — حفَّار، ثقَّاب
10 safety helmet — خَوْذَة أمان
11 hammer drill (hard-rock drill) — مِطْرَقة ثقب (مِثْقَاب صخور)
12 borehole — ثُقْب الحَفْر
13 universal excavator — حفَّارة عامة الأغراض
14 large-capacity truck — شاحِنة كبيرة الحمولة
15 rock face — واجِهَة صخريَّة
16 inclined hoist — مِرْفع مائل
17 primary crusher — كَسَّارَة أوَّليَّة
18 stone-crushing plant — وَحْدَة تكسِيْر الحجارة
19 coarse rotary (gyratory) crusher; *sim.*: fine rotary (gyratory) crusher — كَسَّارَة لفافة للخام الخشن؛ بالمثل: كَسَّارَة لَفَّافة للخام الناعم
20 hammer crusher (impact crusher) — كَسَّارَة مِطْرَقيَّة/صَدْميَّة
21 vibrating screen — غِرْبال هَزَّاز
22 screenings (fine dust) — نفاية الغربلة (تراب ناعم)
23 stone chippings — نُحَاتة صخرية
24 crushed stone — حَجَر مُهَشَّم
25 shot firer — عامِل التفجير، مُشْعِل الطلقة
26 measuring rod — قضيب قياس
27 blasting cartridge — خرطوش متفجر
28 fuse (blasting fuse) — فيوز تفجير
29 plugging sand (stemming sand) bucket — دَلْو رمال حَشْو
30 dressed stone — حَجَر مُشكَّل

31 pick صاقُور
32 crowbar (pinch bar) عَتَلَة
33 fork شَوْكَة
34 stonemason البَنَّاء (بالحجارة)
35-38 stonemason's tools أدوات البَنَّاء بالحجارة
35 stonemason's hammer مطرقة البنَّاء
36 mallet مدَقَّة
37 drove chisel (drove, boaster, broad chisel) أزميل عريض للنحت
38 dressing axe (*Am.* ax) بَلْطَة تهذيب

159 Brickworks (Brickyard, Brickfield) مَصْنَع الطُوب

1 clay pit حُفْرَة الطين/الطُفَال
2 loam, an impure clay (raw clay) طُفَال رملي (طين خام)
3 overburden excavator, a large-scale excavator حَفَّارة الغطاء الترابي
4 narrow-gauge (*Am.* narrow-gage) track system مَسَار سكة حديدية ضيقة
5 inclined hoist مرْفَاع مائل
6 souring chambers غُرَف الحامض
7 box feeder (feeder) وَحْدَة إلقام صندوقية
8 edge runner mill (edge mill, pan grinding mill) رَحَى ذات حجر عمودي
9 rolling plant وَحْدَة الدلافين
10 double-shaft trough mixer (mixer) خلاَّط ذو مجرى له عمودين (خلاَّط)
11 extrusion press (brick-pressing machine) مَاكِينَة كبس الطُوب
12 vacuum chamber حجرة تفريغ
13 die قالب التشكيل
14 clay column عمود الطُفال
15 cutter (brick cutter) أداة قطع الطُوب
16 unfired brick (green brick) طُوب لبني (طُوب نيئ)
17 drying shed عنبر التجفيف
18 mechanical finger car (stacker truck) عَرَبَة ترصيص الطُوب
19 circular kiln (brick kiln) قَمِين دائري (قَمِين الطُوب)
20 solid brick (building brick) قالب طُوب صلب (طُوب بناء)
21-22 perforated bricks and hollow blocks قوالب طُوب مثقَّب وقوالب طُوب مُجَوَّف
21 perforated brick with vertical perforations طُوب مثقَّب ذو ثقوب رأسية
22 hollow clay block with horizontal perforations طُوب طفلي مجوف ذو ثقوب أفقية
23 hollow clay block with vertical perforations طُوب طفلي مجوف ذو ثقوب رأسية
24 floor brick طُوب الأرضية
25 compass brick (radial brick, radiating brick) طُوب أشْدف (لبناء المنحنيات)
26 hollow flooring block طُوب أرضية مجوف
27 paving brick طُوب الرصف
28 cellular brick [for fireplaces] (chimney brick) طُوب خلويّ [للمدفآت]

160 Cement Works (Cement Factory) مَصْنَع الأسْمَنْت

1 raw materials (limestone, clay, and marl) مواد خام (حجر جيري وطُفَال وطين جيري)
2 hammer crusher (hammer mill) كَسَّارَة مطرقيَّة
3 raw material store مَخْزَن المواد الخام
4 raw mill for simultaneously grinding and drying the raw materials with exhaust gas from the heat exchanger طاحونة الخام لطحن وتجفيف المواد الخام في آن واحد مع غاز العادم المنبعث من المبادل الحراري
5 raw meal silos صَوَامع الجَرِيش الخام
6 heat exchanger (cyclone heat exchanger) مُبَادِل حراري
7 dust collector (an electrostatic precipitator) for the heat exchanger exhaust from the raw mill جِهَاز ترسيب غبار عادم المبادل الحراري الناتج عن طاحونة الخام
8 rotary kiln قَمِين دوّار
9 clinker cooler مُبَرِّد مخلفات الاحتراق
10 clinker store مَخْزَن مخلفات الاحتراق
11 primary air blower نافخ هوائي أولي
12 cement-grinding mill وَحْدَة طحن الأسْمَنْت
13 gypsum store مَخْزَن الجبس (الجص)
14 gypsum crusher كَسَّارَة الجبس (الجص)
15 cement silo صَوْمَعَة أسْمَنْت
16 cement-packing plant وَحْدَة تعبئة الأسْمَنْت

161 Porcelain and China Manufacture صِنَاعَة البُورْسَلِين والصِّيني

1 grinding cylinder (ball mill) for the preparation of the raw material in water طَاحُونَة ببكَرَات لتَجْهيز المَوَاد الخَام في الماء
2 sample sagger (saggar, seggar), with aperture for observing the firing process صُنْدُوق عيِّنَات ذو ثُقْب لملاحظة عمليَّة الإشْعال
3 bottle kiln (beehive kiln) [diagram] قَمِين قنينيّ الشَّكْل [رَسْم تخطيطي]
4 firing mould (*Am.* mold) صُنْدُوق الإشْعال
5 tunnel kiln قَمِين نَفَقِيّ الشَّكْل
6 Seger cone (pyrometric cone, *Am.* Orton cone) for measuring high temperatures مَخْرُوط "زيجر" (مَخْرُوط المقياس الحراري) لقياس درجات الحرارة المرتفعة
7 de-airing pug mill (de-airing pug press), an extrusion press خَلاط مُلاط يَعْمَل بنَزْع الهَوَاء
8 clay column عمود الطين
9 thrower throwing a ball (bat) of clay خَزَّاف، عامِل تشكيل الطين يُشكِّل كُرَة طينيَّة
10 slug of clay كُتْلَة طين
11 turntable; *sim.:* potter's عَجَلَة الخَزَّاف، صينية

	wheel	دَوَّارة
12	filter press	مِكْبَس تَرْشيح
13	filter cake	قالِب تَرْشيح
14	jiggering, with a profiling tool; *sim.:* jollying	جِهَاز تثبيت القطع أثناء تشكيلها وبه أداة تشكيل الجانبية
15	plaster mould (*Am.* mold) for slip casting	قالِب جَصّ للصَّب المُنْزَلِق
16	turntable glazing machine	مَاكِينَة تلميع ذات صينيَّة دَوَّارة
17	porcelain painter (china painter)	رسَّام البورسلين (رسَّام الصيني)
18	hand-painted vase	زُهْرِيَّة (مَزْهَرِيَّة) مَرْسُومة يدوياً
19	repairer	مُصَلِّح الأشْكال المكْسُورة
20	pallet (modelling, *Am.* modeling, tool)	ظُفْرَة (سِكِّين تشكيل)
21	shards (sherds, potsherds)	شَقْفَات من الفُخَّار (قِطَع خَزَف مكْسُورة)

162 Glass Production — إنْتَاج الزُجَاج

1-20	**sheet glass production** (flat glass production)	**إنتاج ألواح الزُجَاج** (الزُجاج المُسَطَّح)
1	glass furnace (tank furnace) for the Fourcault process [diagram]	فُرْن الزُجاج الخاص بطريقة "فوركولت" [رَسْم تخطيطي]
2	filling end, for feeding in the batch (frit)	طَرَف الإلقام للتغذية بالعَجِينَة الزُجاجيَّة (مَسْحُوق مُزَجَّج)
3	melting bath	مَغْطَس الانْصِهار
4	refining bath (fining bath)	مَغْطَس تنقيَة
5	working baths (working area)	مَغَاطِس الشُغْل (منطقة الشُغْل)
6	burners	مَوَاقِد
7	drawing machines	ماكينات السَّحْب
8	Fourcault glass-drawing machine	مَاكِينَة «فوركولت» لسحب الزجاج
9	slot	حَزّ ضَيِّق
10	glass ribbon (ribbon of glass, sheet of glass) being drawn upwards	لَوْح زُجاجيّ يُسحب لأعلى
11	rollers (drawing rolls)	أُسْطُوَانات السَّحْب
12	float glass process	عملية تصنيع الزُجاج الطَوْفيَّة
13	batch (frit) feeder (funnel)	مُلَقِّم عَجِينَة الزُجاج
14	melting bath	مَغْطَس الانصهار
15	cooling tank	خَزَّان التبريد
16	float bath in a protective inert-gas atmosphere	مَغْطَس بطَوْف في محيط من الغاز الخامل
17	molten tin	قَصْدير مَصْهُور
18	annealing lehr	"لير" (فُرْن) التلْدين المستمر
19	automatic cutter	قاطع آليّ
20	stacking machines	مَاكِينَة رَصّ
21	IS (individual-section) machine, a bottle-making machine	مَاكِينَة صنع الزُجَاجَات
22-37	**blowing processes**	**عمليات نَفْخ الزُجاج**
22	blow-and-blow process	عملية تشكيل الزُجاج نَفْخاً ومَصّاً
23	introduction of the gob of molten glass	إدْخال كتلة الزُجاج المَصْهُور
24	first blowing	النَّفْخ الأوَّل
25	suction	المَصّ
26	transfer from the parison mould (*Am.* mold) to the blow mould (*Am.* mold)	النقل من قالِب العَجِينَة إلى قالِب النَّفْخ
27	reheating	إعَادَة التسخين
28	blowing (suction, final shaping)	النَّفْخ (المَصّ، التشكيل النهائيّ)
29	delivery of the completed vessel	مُناوَلَة الإناء المُكْتَمِل
30	press-and-blow process	عملية تشكيل الزُجاج كَبْساً ومَصّاً
31	introduction of the gob of molten glass	إدخال كتلة الزُجاج المَصْهُور
32	plunger	كبَّاس
33	pressing	الكَبْس
34	transfer from the press mould (*Am.* mold) to the blow mould (*Am.* mold)	النقل من قالِب العَجِينَة إلى قالِب النَّفْخ
35	reheating	إعادة التسخين
36	blowing (suction, final shaping)	النَّفْخ (المَصّ، التشكيل النهائيّ)
37	delivery of the completed vessel	مُناوَلَة الإناء المكتمل
38-47	**glassmaking** (glass-blowing, glass-blowing by hand, glass forming)	**صُنْع الزُجاج** (نَفْخ الزُجاج، نفخ الزُجاج يدوياً، تشكيل الزُجاج)
38	glassmaker (glass-blower)	نافِخ الزُجاج
39	blowing iron	أُنْبُوب النفخ
40	gob	كُتْلَة
41	hand-blown goblet	كُتْلَة صغيرة منفوخة يدوياً
42	clappers for shaping the base (foot) of the goblet	مِقْشَطَة لتشكيل قاعدة الكُتْلَة
43	trimming tool	أداة تشذيب
44	tongs	كُلاَّب، ماسِك
45	glassmaker's chair (gaffer's chair)	مَقْعَد نافِخ الزجاج
46	covered glasshouse pot	وعاء زُجاجيّ مُغَطَّى
47	mould (*Am.* mold), into which the parison is blown	قالِب الصب الذي تُنْفَخ فيه العَجِينَة
48-55	**production of glass fibre** (*Am.* glass fiber)	**إنتاج الألْيَاف الزُجاجِيَّة**
48	continuous filament process	عملية إنتاج الألْيَاف الزُجاجيَّة المستمرة
49	glass furnace	فُرْن الزُجاج
50	bushing containing molten glass	غِلاف يحتوى على زُجاج مصهور

51 bushing tips — طَرْف الغلاف
52 glass filaments — ألياف زُجاجيَّة
53 sizing — مُعَايَرَة
54 strand (thread) — خَيْط
55 spool — بَكَرَة
56-58 glass fibre (*Am.* glass fiber) **products** — **مُنْتجَات الألْيَاف الزُجاجيَّة**
56 glass yarn (glass thread) — غَزْل زُجاجيّ، خَيْط زُجاجيّ
57 sleeved glass yarn (glass thread) — خَيْط زُجاجيّ مَبْرُوم
58 glass wool — الصُوف الزُجاجيّ

163 Cotton Spinning I — غَزْل القُطْن (1)

1-13 supply of cotton — **إمداد القُطْن**
1 ripe cotton boll — نَبْتَة قُطْن يانِعَة
2 full cop (cop wound with weft yarn) — كُبٌّ كامل
3 compressed cotton bale — بالَة قُطْن مضغوطة
4 jute wrapping — غلاف من التِّيل
5 steel band — شَرِيط معدنيّ
6 identification mark of the bale — علامة تعريف البالَة
7 bale opener (bale breaker) — مَاكِينَة تفتيح البالات
8 cotton-feeding brattice — حَصِيرة التغذية بالقُطْن
9 cotton feed — صُنْدُوق التغذية بالقُطْن
10 dust extraction fan — مروحة شَفْط الغُبَار
11 duct to the dust-collecting chamber — أنْبُوبة توصيل الغُبَار إلى غرفة الأتْربَة
12 drive motor — مُحَرِّك الإدَارة
13 conveyor brattice — حصيرة ناقلة
14 double scutcher (machine with two scutchers) — مَاكِينَة الملفات المزدوجة
15 lap cradle — مِسْنَد الملف
16 rack head — رأس الحامِل
17 starting handle — يد التشغيل
18 handwheel, for raising and lowering the rack head — طَارَة رفع وخفض رأس الحامِل
19 movable lap-turner — مُحوِّل الملَف المتحرك
20 calender rollers — أسْطُوَانَات الضغط
21 cover for the perforated cylinders — غِطَاء قفص الأُسْطُوَانَات المُثَقَّبَة (غِطَاء القَفَص العلوي)
22 dust escape flue (dust discharge flue) — أنْبُوبة تصريف الغُبَار
23 drive motors (beater drive motors) — مُحَرِّكَات الإدارة
24 beater driving shaft — عمود إدارة المِضْرَب
25 three-blade beater (Kirschner beater) — مِضْرَب ذو ثلاث رِيَش
26 grid [for impurities to drop] — شَبكَة مُصَبَّعات [لفَصْل الشوائب]
27 pedal roller (pedal cylinder) — أُسْطُوَانَة دَوَّاسَة
28 control lever for the pedal roller, a pedal lever — ذراع التحكم الخاصة بأُسْطُوَانَة الدَّوَّاسة
29 variable change-speed gear — تروس تغيير السرعة
30 cone drum box — صُنْدُوق الأُسْطُوَانَات المخروطيَّة
31 stop and start levers for the hopper — أذْرُع إيقاف وبدْء جِهَاز التغذية
32 wooden hopper delivery roller — أُسْطُوَانَة المناولة الخشبيَّة لجِهَاز التغذية
33 hopper feeder — جِهَاز التغذية
34 carding machine (card, carding engine) — مَاكِينَة الكَرْد (مَاكِينَة تسريح)
35 card can (carding can), for receiving the coiled sliver — أُسْطُوَانَة لاستقبال شَرِيط الكَرْد
36 can holder — قاعدة الأُسْطُوَانَة
37 calender rollers — أسْطُوَانَات الضغط
38 carded sliver (card sliver) — شَرِيط كَرْد
39 vibrating doffer comb — مُشْط الدُوفَر الرَّعَّاش
40 start-stop lever — ذراع التشغيل
41 grinding-roller bearing — كُرْسِيّ أُسْطُوَانَة التجليخ
42 doffer — الدُوفَر
43 cylinder — أُسْطُوَانَة
44 flat clearer — مُنَظِّف الحَصَائر
45 flats — الحَصَائر
46 supporting pulleys for the flats — بَكَر حَمْل الحَصَائر
47 scutcher lap (carded lap) — الملَف
48 scutcher lap holder — مِسْنَد الملَف
49 drive motor with flat belt — مُحَرِّك إدارة بسَيْر مُسَطَّح
50 main drive pulley fast-and-loose drive pulley) — طارَة الإدارة الرئيسيَّة
51 principle of the card (of the carding engine) — رَسْم توضيحي لمَاكِينَة الكَرْد
52 fluted feed roller — دَرْفيل تغذية مُخَدَّد
53 licker-in (taker-in, licker-in roller) — دَرْفيل مُسَنَّن (المِنْشار)
54 licker-in undercasing — الغطَاء السفلي للمِنْشار
55 cylinder undercasing — الغطَاء السفلي للأُسْطُوَانَة
56 combing machine (comber) — مَاكِينَة التمشيط
57 drive gearbox (driving gear) — صُنْدُوق تروس الإدارة
58 laps ready for combing — لفائف مُعَدَّة للتمشيط
59 calender rollers — أسْطُوَانَات الضغط
60 comber draw box — صُنْدُوق السحب لمَاكِينَة التشطيب
61 counter — عَدَّاد
62 coiler top — الطَرْف العلوي للملفات
63 principle of the comber — رَسْم توضيحي لمَاكِينَة التمْشيط
64 lap — اللفافة
65 bottom nipper — المِقْبَض السفلي
66 top nipper — المِقْبَض العلوي
67 top comb — المُشْط العلوي
68 combing cylinder — أُسْطُوَانَة التمشيط

69 plain part of the cylinder	جزء أملَس بأسْطُوَانَة التمشيط
70 needled part of the cylinder	أسنان المُشْط الإبْرِيَّة بالأسْطُوَانَة
71 detaching rollers	دَرَافيل الفَصْل
72 carded and combed sliver	الخامَة المُمَشَّطة

164 Cotton Spinning II — غَزْل القُطْن (2)

1 draw frame	مَاكِينَة السَّحْب
2 gearbox with built-in motor	صُنْدُوق التروس المتصل بالمُحَرِّك المبيت
3 sliver cans	أسْطُوَانَات الشَّرِيط
4 broken thread detector roller	أسْطُوَانَة كَشَّاف انقطاع الخَيْط
5 doubling of the slivers	تَجْميع الشرائِط
6 stopping handle	يَد الإيقاف
7 draw frame cover	غطاء مَاكِينَة السَّحْب
8 indicator lamps (signal lights)	مَصَابيح إرشاديَّة
9 simple four-roller draw frame [diagram]	رَسْم توضيحي لمَاكِينَة سحب ذات أربع أسْطُوَانَات
10 bottom rollers (lower rollers), fluted steel rollers	الأسْطُوَانَات السفليَّة ، أسْطُوَانَات صلب مُخَدَّدة
11 top rollers (upper rollers) covered with synthetic rubber	أسْطُوَانَات علويَّة مُغَطَّاة بمادة لَدْنَة
12 doubled slivers before drafting	الشرائط المُجَمَّعَة قبل سحبها
13 thin sliver after drafting	شَريط رفيع بعد سحبه
14 high-draft system (high-draft draw frame) [diagram]	نظَام اللقى العالي [رَسم تخطيطي]
15 feeding-in of the sliver	تغذية الشَّرِيط
16 leather apron (composition apron)	إزار جِلْدِي
17 guide bar	قضيب دليليّ
18 light top roller (guide roller)	أسْطُوَانَة علويَّة دليليَّة
19 high-draft speed frame (fly frame, slubbing frame)	مَاكِينَة البَرْم الابتدائيّ
20 sliver cans	أسْطُوَانَات الشَّرِيط
21 feeding of the slivers to the drafting rollers	الشَّرِيط المُغَذِّي لأسْطُوَانَات السَّحْب
22 drafting rollers with top clearers	أسْطُوَانَات السَّحْب ذات المُنَظِّفَات العلويَّة
23 roving bobbins	بكَر (بوبينات) البَرْم الإبتدائي
24 fly frame operator (operative)	مُلاحِظ مَاكِينَة البَرْم
25 flyer	الفانوس
26 frame end plate	غطاء جانب المَاكِينَة
27 intermediate yarn-forming frame	مَاكِينَة البَرْم المتوسط
28 bobbin creel (creel)	حَامِل البكَر
29 roving emerging from the drafting rollers	الغزل المَبْرُوم الخارج من أسْطُوَانَات السَّحْب
30 lifter rail (separating rail)	قضيب رافع (العربة)
31 spindle drive	إدارة المَرْدَن
32 stopping handle	يَد الإيقاف
33 gearbox, with built-on motor	صُنْدُوق التروس المتصل بالمُحَرِّك
34 ring frame (ring spinning frame)	مَاكِينَة الغَزْل الحلقيّ
35 three-phase motor	مُحَرِّك ثلاثي الأطْوَار
36 motor base plate (bed-plate)	لَوْح قاعدة المُحَرِّك
37 lifting bolt [for motor removal]	حَلَقَة لرفع المُحَرِّك
38 control gear for spindle speed	مُنَظِّم للمَرْدَن ذي السرعة المتغيرة
39 gearbox	غُراب الرأس (صُنْدُوق التروس)
40 change wheels for varying the spindle speed [to change the yarn count]	تروس نقل لتغيير نِمَر الخيوط
41 full creel	حَامِل البكَر
42 shafts and levers for rising and lowering the ring rail	أعمدة وروافع لرفع وخفض العربة
43 spindles with separators	مَرَادِن مع فواصِل
44 suction box connected to the front roller underclearers	صُنْدُوق شفط متصل بالمُنَظِّفَات السفليَّة للأسْطُوَانَة الأماميَّة
45 standard ring spindle	مَرْدَن غَزْل حلَقِي نَمَطي
46 spindle shaft	عَمُود المَرْدَن
47 roller bearing	كُرْسِيّ تحميل
48 wharve (pulley)	صُرَّة المَرْدَن
49 spindle catch	ماسِك المَرْدَن
50 spindle rail	قضيب المَرْدَن
51 ring and traveller (*Am.* traveler)	الحلقة والدِّبْلَة (في مَاكِينَة الغَزْل الحلقي)
52 top of the ring tube (of the bobbin)	الطَّرَف العلوي لبكَرة الغَزْل الحلقي
53 yarn (thread)	خَيْط الغَزْل
54 ring fitted into the ring rail	الحلقة المثبتة في العربة
55 traveller (*Am.* traveler)	الدِّبْلَة
56 yarn wound onto the bobbin	خَيْط الغَزْل ملفوفاً على البكَرة
57 doubling frame	مَاكِينَة فتل الخيط
58 creel, with cross-wound cheeses	حَامِل بكَر به مجموعة من البكَر الملفوف لفاً متقاطعاً
59 delivery rollers	درافيل مناوَلَة
60 bobbins of doubled yarn	بكَر الخَيْط المفتول

165 Weaving I — النسيج (1)

1-57 processes preparatory to weaving	**العمليَّات التحضيريَّة للنسيج**
1 cone-winding frame	مَاكِينَة لَفّ المَخْرُوط
2 travelling (*Am.* traveling) blower	نافخ مُتَحَرِّك
3 guide rail, for the	قضيب دليلي للنافخ المُتَحَرِّك

travelling (*Am.* traveling) blower

4 blowing assembly تجميع النَّفْخ

5 blower aperture فتحة النَّفْخ

6 superstructure for the blower rail الحَامِل العلوي لقضيب النافخ

7 full-cone indicator مُبَيِّن المَخْرُوط الملفوف لفاً حلزونياً

8 cross-wound cone حسَّاس مَخْرُوط بحَامِل البكَر

9 cone creel حوامل المخاريط

10 grooved cylinder أُسْطُوَانَة بها تجاويف حلزونيَّة (دليل الخَيْط)

11 guiding slot for cross-winding the threads مَشْقبيَّة مُتَعَرِّجَة لمرور الخَيْط

12 side frame, housing the motor اللوح الجانبي للمَاكِينَة وبداخله المُحَرِّك

13 tension and slub-catching device مُنَظِّم الشد والمقص

14 off-end framing with filter جانِب المَاكِينَة مع مُرَشِّح

15 yarn package, a ring tube or mule cop عبوة التغذية (بكَرة غَزْل حلقي أو ماسورة غَزْل العربة)

16 yarn package container صُنْدُوق عبوات التغذية

17 starting and stopping lever ذِراع البدء والإيقاف

18 self-threading guide دليل لتسهيل مرور الخَيْط

19 broken thread stop motion وسيلة إيقاف أوتوماتيكية لإيقاف المَاكِينَة عند انقطاع الخَيْط

20 thread clearer المقصّ

21 weighting disc (disk) for tensioning the thread مُنَظِّم شد الخَيْط

22 warping machine مَاكِينَة التَّسْدِيَة

23 fan مروحة

24 cross-wound cone مخاريط بحَامِل البكَر

25 creel حَامِل البكَر

26 adjustable comb مُشْط الأشْتيك

27 warping machine frame إطار المَاكِينَة

28 yarn length recorder عَدَّاد طُول الخَيْط

29 warp beam أُسْطُوَانَة السَّدَاء

30 beam flange طارة أُسْطُوَانَة السَّدَاء

31 guard rail قضيب وقائي

32 driving drum (driving cylinder) طَنْبُور الإدارة

33 belt drive إدارة بسير

34 motor مُحَرِّك

35 release for starting the driving drum دَوَّاسة لبدء حركة طَنْبُور الإدارة

36 screw for adjusting the comb setting برغى ضَبْط المُشْط

37 drop pins, for stopping the machine when a thread breaks مسامير ساقِطَة لإيقاف المَاكِينَة عند انقطاع الخَيْط

38 guide bar قضيب دليلي

39 drop pin rollers أُسْطُوَانَات المسامير الساقِطَة

40 indigo dying and sizing machine مَاكِينَة الصباغة باللون الأزرق والتَّبْويش

41 take-off stand حَامِل مأخذ القُدْرَة

42 warp beam أُسْطُوَانَة السَّدَاء

43 warp السَّدَاء

44 wetting trough وعاء الترطيب

45 immersion roller دولفين الغَمْر

46 squeeze roller (mangle) دولفين العَصْر

47 dye liquor padding trough وعاء سائل الصبغة

48 air oxidation passage مَجْرَى هواء الأكسدة

49 washing trough وعاء الغَسْل

50 drying cylinders for pre-drying أسطوانات التجفيف المبدئي

51 tension compensator (tension equalizer) مُوَازِن الشَّدّ

52 sizing machine مَاكِينَة التَّبْويش

53 drying cylinders أُسْطُوَانَات التجفيف

54 *for cotton:* stenter; *for wool:* tenter مَاكِينَة الشد وضَبْط العَرْض

55 beaming machine مَاكِينَة التَّسْدِيَة المباشرة

56 sized warp beam أُسْطُوَانَة سداء مُبَوَّشَة

57 rollers أُسْطُوَانَات

166 Weaving II النَّسيج (2)

1 weaving machine (automatic loom) مَاكِينَة النَّسِيج (نُول أوتوماتيكي)

2 pick counter (tachometer) عَدَّاد الحَدَّافات

3 shaft (heald shaft, heald frame) guide دليل الدَّرْأ

4 shafts (heald shafts, heald frames) الدَّرْأ

5 rotary battery for weft replenishment مستودع مواسير اللُحْمَة الدّوار

6 sley (slay) cap غطاء الدَّف

7 weft pirn ماسورة اللُحْمَة

8 starting and stopping handle ذراع البدء والإيقاف

9 shuttle box, with shuttles دُرْج المواكيك وبداخله المواكيك

10 reed المُشْط

11 selvedge (selvage) بُرْسُل القُمَاش

12 cloth (woven fabric) القُمَاش المنسوج

13 temple (cloth temple) المَتِيت

14 electric weft feeler حسَّاس اللُحْمَة الكهربائى

15 flywheel الحَدَّافة

16 breast beam board مِسْنَد الصدر

17 picking stick (pick stick) ذراع القَذْف

18 electric motor مُحَرِّك كهربائي

19 cloth take-up motion جِهَاز طَي للقُمَاش

20 cloth roller (fabric roller) مِطْوَاة القُمَاش

21 can for empty pirns صُنْدُوق مواسير اللُحْمَة الفارغة

22 lug strap, for moving the picking stick سَيْر سحب لتحريك ذراع القذف

23 fuse box صُنْدُوق مُصْهِرات/ فيوزات

24 loom framing هَيْكَل النول
25 metal shuttle tip غُراب المَكوك المعدني
26 shuttle مَكوك
27 heald (heddle, wire heald, wire heddle) دَرَأة
28 eye (eyelet, heald eyelet, heddle eyelet) ثُقْب دَرَأة
29 eye (shuttle eye) زردة المَكُوك
30 pirn ماسورة اللُحْمَة
31 metal contact sleeve for the weft feeler جِلْبَة التلامس المعدنيَّة لحسَّاس اللُحْمَة
32 slot for the feeler مَشْقَبِيَّة حسَّاس اللُحْمَة
33 spring-clip pirn holder ماسِك زنبركي لكعب ماسورة اللُحْمَة
34 drop wire شريحة إيقاف، سُقَّاطَة
35 weaving machine (automatic loom) [side elevation] مَاكِينَة نسيج (نول آلي) [منظر جانبي]
36 heald shaft guiding wheels بكَر الدَّرأ الدليلي
37 backrest المِسْنَد الخلفي
38 lease rods سَمَاسِم الأشْتِيك
39 warp (warp thread) السَّدَاء
40 shed النَّفَس
41 sley (slay) ريشة الدَّف
42 race board الجَوْزَأ
43 stop rod blade for the stop motion الصَّدَّام
44 bumper steel الضفدعة
45 bumper steel stop rod بِنْز الضفدعة
46 breast beam مِسْنَد الصدر
47 cloth take-up roller أُسْطُوَانَة الصنفرة
48 warp beam أُسْطُوَانَة السَّدَاء
49 beam flange طارة أُسْطُوَانَة السَّدَاء
50 crankshaft عَمُود مِرْفَقِي
51 crankshaft wheel تُرْس العَمُود المِرْفَقِي
52 connector ذراع الدَّف
53 sley (slay) الدَّف
54 lam rods أسياخ الدَّرأ
55 camshaft wheel تُرْس عَمُود الكامات السفلي
56 camshaft (tappet shaft) عَمُود الكامات
57 tappet (shedding tappet) الكامات
58 treadle lever ذراع الدَّوَّاسة
59 let-off motion جِهَاز تنظيم انسياب السَّدَاء
60 beam motion control طارَة جِهَاز الانسياب
61 rope of the warp let-off motion حَبْل جِهَاز الانسياب
62 let-off weight lever ذِراع الثِّقْل (لجِهَاز الانسياب)
63 control weight [for the treadle] ثِقْل التحكم (للدَّوَّاسة)
64 picker with leather or bakelite pad لَطَّاشة ذات بِطانة جِلْدِيَّة
65 picking stick buffer صَدَّاد ذراع القذف
66 picking cam كامة القذف
67 picking bowl طاسة القذف
68 picking stick return spring نابِض إرجاع ذراع القذف

167 Knitting أشغال الإبرة أو التريكو

1-66 hosiery mill **مَشْغَل التريكو**
1 circular knitting machine for the manufacture of tubular fabric مَاكِينَة التريكو الدائريَّة لتصنيع القُمَاش الأُسْطواني
2 yarn guide support post (thread guide support post) عَمُود الإرتكاز لدليل الخَيْط
3 yarn guide (thread guide) دليل الخَيْط
4 bottle bobbin بكَرة على هيئة زُجاجة
5 yarn-tensioning device جِهَاز ضَبْط شد الخَيْط
6 yarn feeder المُغَذِّي
7 handwheel for rotating the machine by hand طارَة لإدارة المَاكِينَة يَدوياً
8 needle cylinder (cylindrical needle holder) أُسْطُوَانَة الإبَر (حَامِل الإبَر الأُسْطُوانيّ)
9 tubular fabric قُمَاش أُسْطواني
10 fabric drum (fabric box, fabric container) حلَّة القُمَاش (وعاء القُمَاش)
11 needle cylinder (cylindrical needle holder) [section] أُسْطُوَانَة الإبَر (حَامِل الإبَر الأُسْطُوانيّ [مقطع]
12 latch needles arranged in a circle الإبَر ذات الخُطَّاف/ سقاطة في نسق دائري
13 cam housing مَبِيت الكامات
14 needle cams كامات الإبَر
15 needle trick مشقبيات الإبَر
16 cylinder diameter (*also:* diameter of tubular fabric) قُطْر أُسْطُوَانَة الإبَر (وهو أيضا قُطْر القُمَاش الأُسْطُوانيّ)
17 thread (yarn) الخَيْط
18 Cotton's patent flat knitting machine for ladies' fully-fashioned hose مَاكِينَة تريكو لعمل جَوَارِب السيِّدات
19 pattern control chain كَتِينَة الضَّبْط
20 side frame العارضة الجانبيَّة للمَاكِينَة
21 knitting head رَأْس الغَزْل
22 starting rod عَمُود بدء التشغيل
23 Raschel warp-knitting machine مَاكِينَة تريكو راشيل
24 warp (warp beam) السَّدَاء (مِطْوَاة السَّدَاء)
25 yarn-distributing (yarn-dividing) beam مِطْوَاة التقسيم
26 beam flange طارة أُسْطُوَانَة السَّدَاء
27 row of needles صَفٌّ من الإبَر
28 needle bar قضيب (دليلي) للإبر
29 fabric (Raschel fabric) [curtain lace and net fabrics] on the fabric roll القُمَاش [دانتيلا ستائر وقماش شبكي] على مِطْوَاة القُمَاش
30 handwheel عجلة الإدارة
31 motor drive gear طارات تشغيل المُحَرِّك
32 take-down weight ثِقْل السَّحْب
33 frame هَيْكَل المَاكِينَة
34 base plate قاعدة المَاكِينَة
35 hand flat (flat-bed) مَاكِينَة تريكو مُسَطَّحَة تُشَغَّل

knitting machine — يَدوياً
36 thread (yarn) — الخَيْط
37 return spring — دليل إرْجاع الخَيْط
38 support for springs — نقطة ارتكاز دلايل ارْجاع الخَيْط
39 carriage — العَرَبة
40 feeder-selecting device — مِسْمَار اختيار المُغَذّي
41 carriage handles — أيدي التشغيل
42 scale for regulating size of stitches — مقياس ضَبْط الغرز
43 course counter (tachometer) — عدَّاد الصفوف الأفقيَّة من الغُرَز
44 machine control lever — ذراع التحكم
45 carriage rail — قضيب العربة
46 back row of needles — الصف الخلفي من الإبَرَ
47 front row of needles — الصف الأمامي من الإبَرَ
48 knitted fabric — القُمَاش التريكو
49 tension bar — قضيب الثِّقْل لتنظيم الشد على القُمَاش
50 tension weight — ثِقْل تنظيم الشد
51 needle bed showing knitting action — قضيب الإبَرَ وكيفية تكوين غرز التريكو
52 teeth of knock-over bit — الحافة العليا للمشقبيَّات
53 needles in parallel rows — الإبَرَ مُرَتَّبة في وضع متواز
54 yarn guide (thread guide) — دَليل الخَيْط
55 needle bed — قَضيب الإبَرَ
56 retaining plate for latch needles — لَوْحَة احتجاز الإبَرَ ذات السُّقَّاطَة
57 guard cam — كامة دليل علوية
58 sinker — كامة الغُرَز
59 needle-raising cam — كامة رَفْع الإبَرَ
60 needle butt — كَعْب الإبَرَة
61 latch needle — إبْرَة بسقاطة
62 loop — غُرْزَة تريكو
63 pushing the needle through the fabric — دفع الإبْرَة خلال القُمَاش
64 yarn guide (thread guide) placing yarn in the needle hook — دليل الخَيْط يُغذي خُطَّاف الإبْرَة بالخَيْط
65 loop formation — تكوين الغُرْزَة
66 casting off of loop — انزلاق الغُرْزَة بعد تكوينها

168 Finishing of Textile Fabrics — تَجْهِيز ألْيَاف النَّسْج

1-65 finishing — التَّجْهيز
1 rotary milling (fulling) machine for felting the woollen (*Am.* woolen) fabric — مَاكِينَة تَلْبيد دَوَّارَة لتَلْبيد الأقمشة الصوفيَّة
2 pressure weights — ثِقْل ضاغط
3 top milling roller (top fulling roller) — دَرْفِيل التَّلْبيد العلويّ
4 drive wheel of bottom milling roller (bottom fulling roller) — طارة التشغيل المُركَّبَة على عَمُود دَرْفِيل التَّلْبيد السفليّ
5 fabric guide roller — دَرْفيل دليليّ (الأسْطُوَانَة الأماميَّة) للقُمَاش
6 bottom milling roller (bottom fulling roller) — درفيل التَّلْبيد السفليّ
7 draft board — لَوْح السحب
8 open-width scouring machine for finer fabrics — مَاكِينَة غَسْل الألْيَاف الصوفيَّة
9 fabric being drawn off the machine — القُمَاش الخارج من المَاكِينَة
10 drive gearbox — صُنْدُوق لتروس الإدارة
11 water inlet pipe — ماسورة دخول الماء
12 drawing-in roller — دَرْفيل السَّحْب
13 scroll-opening roller — قضيب فرد القُمَاش
14 pendulum-type hydro-extractor (centrifuge), for extracting liquors from the fabric — عَصَّارَة بندولية بالطرد المركزي لنزع السوائل من القماش
15 machine base — قاعدة المَاكِينَة
16 casing over suspension — غطاء فوق التعليق
17 outer casing containing rotating cage (rotating basket) — الوِعَاء الخارجيّ وبداخله القفص الدَّوَّار
18 hydro-extractor (centrifuge) lid — غِطَاء قَفَص العَصَّارة
19 stop-motion device (stopping device) — وَسِيلة إيقاف للأمان
20 automatic starting and braking device — وَسِيلة بدء التشغيل وفرملة آليَّة
21 *for cotton:* stenter; *for wool:* tenter — مَاكِينَة الشد وضَبْط العَرْض
22 air-dry fabric — القُمَاش المُبَلَّل
23 operator's (operative's) platform — مِنَصَّة تشغيل
24 feeding of fabric by guides onto stenter (tenter) pins or clips — دلايل تغذية القُمَاش للمقابض والدبابيس
25 electric control panel — لَوْحَات تحكم كهربائية
26 initial overfeed to produce shrink-resistant fabric when dried — تغذية إضافية للسماح بالانكماش فى اتجاه السَّدَاء
27 thermometer — ترمومتر
28 drying section — غُرْفَة التجفيف
29 air outlet — مَخْرَج الهواء
30 plaiter (fabric-plaiting device) — وسيلة لتطبيق القُمَاش
31 wire-roller fabric-raising machine for producing raised or nap surface — مَاكِينَة الكَسْتَرَة
32 drive gearbox — صُنْدُوق تروس الإدارة
33 unraised cloth — قُمَاش غير مُكَسْتَر
34 wire-covered rollers — درافيل مُغطاة بالأسلاك
35 plaiter (cuttling device) — وسيلة لتطبيق القُمَاش
36 raised fabric — قُمَاش مُكَسْتَر
37 plaiting-down platform — طَبْليَّة
38 rotary press (calendering machine), for press finishing — مَاكِينَة الكَيّ الدَّوَّارة
39 fabric — القُمَاش
40 control buttons and control wheels — زرّ الإدارة ومضابط الحركة

41 heated press bowl — دَرْفِيل الكَيّ المُسَخَّن
42 rotary cloth-shearing machine — مَاكِينَة قص الوَبَرَة
43 suction slot, for removing loose fibres (*Am.* fibers) — أنبوب شفط عَوَادم الألياف
44 doctor blade (cutting cylinder) — أُسْطُوَانَة قص الوَبَرَة
45 protective guard — شبكة مُصَبَّعات واقِيَة
46 rotating brush — فُرْشَاة دَوَّارة
47 curved scray entry — طَبْلِيَّة مُنْحنِيَّة
48 treadle control — دَوَّاسة تحكم
49 [non-shrinking] decatizing (decating) fabric-finishing machine — مَاكِينَة دَكْتَرَة [لتثبيت التجهيز]
50 perforated decatizing (decating) cylinder — دَرْفِيل الدَّكْتَرَة
51 piece of fabric — قطعة القُمَاش
52 cranked control handle — عَمُود مِرْفَقِيّ
53 ten-colour (*Am.* ten-color) roller printing machine — مَاكِينَة طِبَاعَة قُمَاش ذات عشر أُسْطُوَانَات ألوان
54 base of the machine — قاعدة المَاكِينَة
55 drive motor — مُحَرِّك الإدارة
56 blanket [of rubber or felt] — غطاء [من المطّاط أو اللباد]
57 fabric after printing (printed fabric) — القُمَاش بعد طباعته
58 electric control panel (control unit) — لَوْحَة التحكم الكهربائية
59 screen printing — الطِّبَاعَة بالشَّبْلُونات
60 mobile screen frame — شَبْلُونة متحركة
61 squeegee — ضاغط لتوزيع اللون على الشَّبْلُونة
62 pattern stencil — شَبْلُونة الطِّبَاعَة
63 screen table — منضدة الطِّبَاعَة بالشَّبْلُونة
64 fabric gummed down on table ready for printing — القُمَاش المُثَبَّت على منضدة الطِّبَاعَة تمهيداً لطباعته
65 screen printing operator (operative) — عامِل الطِّبَاعَة بالشَّبْلُونة

169 Synthetic (Man-made) Fibres (*Am.* Fibers) I — الأَلْيَاف الصِّنَاعِيَّة (1)

1-34 manufacture of **continuous filament and staple fibre** (*Am.* fiber) **viscose rayon yarns** by means of the viscose process — **صناعة الأَلْيَاف المُسْتمرة وخيوط غَزْل حرير الفِسْكُوز طويلة التِّيلَة عن طريق عملية تصنيع الفِسْكُوز**
1-12 from raw material to viscose rayon — **من المَادَة الخام الى حرير الفِسْكُوز**
1 basic material [beech and spruce cellulose in form of sheets] — المَادَة الأَسَاسِيَّة [سِلِيلُوز الزَّان والرَّاتينْجِيَّات في شكل أَلْوَاح]
2 mixing cellulose sheets — مَزْج ألواح السليلوز
3 caustic soda — صودا كاوية
4 steeping cellulose sheets in caustic soda — أَلْوَاح سِلِيلُوز مَنْقُوعة في صودا كاوية
5 pressing out excess caustic soda — استخراج الصودا الكاوية الزائدة بالكَبْس
6 shredding the cellulose sheets — تقطيع أَلْوَاح السِّلِيلُوز
7 maturing (controlled oxidation) of the alkali-cellulose crumbs — إنضاج قِطَع السِّلِيلُوز القلوي
8 carbon disulphide (*Am.* carbon disulfide) — ثاني كبريتوز الكربون
9 conversion of alkali-cellulose into cellulose xanthate — تحويل السِّلِيلوز القلوي إلى سليلوز الزَّنْتَات
10 dissolving the xanthate in caustic soda for the preparation of the viscose spinning solution — إذابة الزَّنْتَات في الصودا الكاوية لإعداد مَحْلُول غَزْل الفِسْكُوز
11 vacuum ripening tanks — خَزَّانات إنضاج بالتفريغ
12 filter presses — مكابس ترشيح
13-27 from viscose to viscose rayon thread — **من الفِسْكُوز إلى خَيْط حرير الفِسْكُوز**
13 metering pump — مضَخَّة
14 multi-holed spinneret (spinning jet) — فُونِيَّة غَزْل متعددة الثقوب
15 coagulating (spinning) bath for converting (coagulating) viscose (viscous solution) into solid filaments — حَمَّام المَادَة العاقِدة لتحويل محلول الفِسْكُوز إلى خيوط صَلْبَة
16 Godet wheel, a glass pulley — بكَرَة "جوديه"
17 Topham centrifugal pot (box) for twisting the filaments into yarn — صندوق لتحويل الأَلْيَاف إلى غَزْل
18 viscose rayon cake — كَعْكَة حَرير الفِسْكُوز
19-27 processing of the cake — **مُعَالَجَة الكَعْكَة**
19 washing — الغَسِيل
20 desulphurizing (desulphurization, *Am.* desulfurizing, desulfurization) — نَزْع الكبريت
21 bleaching — التَّقْصِير (التبييض)
22 treating of cake to give filaments softness and suppleness — مُعَالَجَة الكَعْكَة لإكْسَاب الشُّعَيْرات النُّعُومَة والليُونَة
23 hydro-extraction to remove surplus moisture — نَزْع الماء لإزالة الرطُوبَة الزَّائدة
24 drying in heated room — التجفيف في حُجْرَة مُسَخَّنَة
25 winding yarn from cake into cone form — لَفّ الغَزْل من الكَعْكَة الى الشكل المَخْرُوطي
26 cone-winding machine — ماكينة لَفّ المَخْرُوط
27 viscose rayon yarn on cone ready for use — غَزْل حرير الفِسْكُوز على مَخْرُوط جاهز للاستخدام
28-34 from viscose spinning solution to viscose rayon staple fibre (*Am.* fiber) — **من محلول غَزْل الفسكوز إلى أَلياف حرير الفِسْكُوز طويلة التيلة**

28	filament tow	حَبْل أَلْيَاف
29	overhead spray washing plant	وَحْدَة غَسِيل بالرَّشّ العلوي
30	cutting machine for cutting filament tow to desired length	ماكينة قطع حَبْل الأَلْيَاف إلى الطول المرغوب
31	multiple drying machine for cut-up staple fibre (*Am.* fiber) layer (lap)	ماكينة تجفيف وقَطْع الأَلْيَاف طويلة التِّيلَة
32	conveyor belt (conveyor)	سَيْر ناقِل
33	baling press	مِكْبَس البالات
34	bale of viscose rayon ready for dispatch (despatch)	بالَة حرير الفِسْكُوز جاهزة للإرسال إلى التاجر

170 Synthetic (Man-made) Fibres (*Am.* Fibers) II — الأَلْيَاف الصِّنَاعِيَّة (2)

1-62	manufacture of **polyamide** (nylon 6, perlon) **fibres** (*Am.* fibers)	**صناعة أَلْيَاف عَدِيد الأَمْدِيد**
1	coal [raw material for manufacture of polyamide (nylon 6, perlon) fibres (*Am.* fibers)]	فَحْم [مَادَة خام لصناعة أَلْيَاف عَدِيد الأَمْدِيد (نايلون 26)]
2	coking plant for dry coal distillation	وَحْدَة التَّكْوِيك الخاصة بتقطير الفَحْم الجاف
3	extraction of coal tar and phenol	اسْتِخْلاص قار الفَحْم والفينول
4	gradual distillation of tar	تقطير القار تدريجياً
5	condenser	المُكَثِّف
6	benzene extraction and dispatch (despatch)	استخلاص البنزين
7	chlorine	الكلور
8	benzene chlorination	كَلْوَرَة البنزين
9	monochlorobenzene (chlorobenzene)	كلور بنزين أحادي (كلور بنزين)
10	caustic soda solution	مَحْلُول صودا كاوية
11	evaporation of chlorobenzene and caustic soda	تَبْخير الكلوربنزين والصودا الكاوية
12	autoclave	مِحَمٌّ مُوصَد، أوتوكلاف
13	sodium chloride (common salt), a by-product	كلوريد صوديوم (مِلْح الطعام)، مُنْتَج ثانويّ
14	phenol (carbolic acid)	الفينول (حمض الكربوليك)
15	hydrogen inlet	مَدْخَل الهيدروجين
16	hydrogenation of phenol to produce raw cyclohexanol	هَدْرَجَة الفينول لإنتاج هيكسانول حَلَقي خام
17	distillation	التقطير
18	pure cyclohexanol	هيكسانول حَلَقي نقي
19	oxidation (dehydrogenation)	الأَكْسَدة (نَزْع الهيدروجين)
20	formation of cyclohexanone (pimehinketone)	تكوين الهيكسانول الحلَقي
21	hydroxylamine inlet	مَدْخَل الهيدروزيلاين
22	formation of cyclohexanoxime	تكوين الهيكسانوكسيم الحلَقي
23	addition of sulphuric acid (*Am.* sulfuric acid) to effect molecular rearrangement	إضافة حمض الكبريتيك لإنجاز إعادة التنظيم الجُزَيْئي
24	ammonia to neutralize sulphuric acid (*Am.* sulfuric acid)	إضافة الأمونيا لمعادَلَة حمض الكبريتيك
25	formation of caprolactam oil	تكوين زَيْت الكبرولاكتم
26	ammonium sulphate (*Am.* ammonium sulfate) solution	مَحْلُول كبريتات الأمونيوم
27	cooling cylinder	أسْطُوَانَة تبريد
28	caprolactam	كبرولاكتم
29	weighing apparatus	جِهَاز الوَزْن، ميزان
30	melting pot	بَوْتَقَة انصهار
31	pump	مِضَخَّة
32	filter	مُرَشِّح، فلتر
33	polymerization in the autoclave	بلْمَرَة في الأُتُوكلاف
34	cooling of the polyamide	تبريد عَدِيد الأمْدِيد
35	solidification of the polyamide	تَصَلُّب عَدِيد الأمْدِيد
36	vertical lift (*Am.* elevator)	مِرْفاع رأسيّ
37	extractor for separating the polyamide from the remaining lactam oil	فرازة عَدِيد الأمْدِيد
38	drier	مُجَفِّف
39	dry polyamide chips	شَرَائح عَدِيد الأمْدِيد الجافة
40	chip container	حاوية الشرائح
41	top of spinneret for melting the polyamide and forcing it through spinneret holes (spinning jets)	الجزء العلوي من فُونيَّة الغَزْل المخصص لصهْر عَدِيد الأمْدِيد ودفعه خلال ثقوب الفُونيَّة
42	spinneret holes (spinning jets)	ثقوب فُونيَّة الغَزْل
43	solidification of polyamide filaments in the cooling tower	تَصَلُّب أَلْيَاف عَدِيد الأمْدِيد في بُرْج التبريد
44	collection of extruded filaments into thread form	تجميع الأَلْيَاف في شكل خَيْط
45	preliminary stretching (preliminary drawing)	الشَّد الأوَّلي للخَيْط
46	stretching (cold-drawing) of the polyamide thread to achieve high tensile strength	سَحْب خَيْط عَدِيد الأمْدِيد على البارد لإكسابه قوة لمقاومة الشد
47	final stretching (final drawing)	السَّحْب النهائي

48 washing of yarn packages — غَسِيل عبوات الخَيْط
49 drying chamber — غُرفة التجفيف
50 rewinding — إعادة لف الخَيْط
51 polyamide cone — مَخْرُوط عَدِيد الأمْدِيد
52 polyamide cone ready for dispatch (despatch) — مَخْرُوط عَدِيد الأمْدِيد جاهز لإرساله للتاجر
53 mixer — خلاط
54 polymerization under vacua — بَلْمَرَة تحت تفريغ
55 stretching (drawing) — سَحْب الخَيْط
56 washing — غَسِيل
57 finishing of tow for spinning — تجهيز حَبْل الألْيَاف للغَزْل
58 drying of tow — تجفيف حَبْل الألْيَاف
59 crimping of tow — تمويج حَبْل الألْيَاف
60 cutting of tow into normal staple lengths — قطع حَبْل الألْيَاف الى اطوال عادية
61 polyamide staple — عَدِيد الأمْدِيد طَوِيل التِّيلَة
62 bale of polyamide staple — بالة عَدِيد الأمْدِيد طَوِيل التِّيلَة

171 Weaves and Knits — النَّسْج وغُرَز التريكو

1-29 weaves [black squares: warp thread raised, weft thread lowered; white squares: weft thread raised, warp thread lowered] — **النَّسْج** [المُرَبَعات السَّوْدَاء: خَيْط السَّدَاء لأعلى، خَيْط اللحْمَة لأسفل؛ المُرَبعَات البيضاء: خَيْط اللحْمَة لأعلى، خَيْط السَّدَاء لأسفل]
1 plain weave (tabby weave) [weave viewed from above] — نَسْج سادة [منظر النَّسْج من أعلى]
2 warp thread — خَيْط السَّدَاء
3 weft thread — خَيْط اللحْمَة
4 draft (point paper design) for plain weave — باترون (ورق مربعات) للنَّسْج السادة
5 threading draft — نظام اللقْي لِلَضم الخَيْط
6 denting draft (reed-threading draft) — نِظَام اللقْي لِلَضْم المشط
7 raised warp thread — خَيْط السَّدَاء فوق خَيْط اللحْمَة
8 lowered warp thread — خَيْط اللحْمَة أسفل خَيْط السَّدَاء
9 tie-up of shafts in pairs — رَبْط النسيج زوجياً
10 treadling diagram — مُخَطَّط سَيْر الدواسة
11 draft for basket weave (hopsack weave, matt weave) — نظام لَقْي النَّسْج الشبكيّ (نَسْج سادة ممتد)
12 pattern repeat — باترون تكرار
13 draft for warp rib weave — نِظَام اللقْي الخاص بنسيج سادة ممتد في اتجاه السَّدَاء
14 section of warp rib fabric, a section through the warp — جزء من تضليعات السَّدَاء
15 lowered weft thread — خَيْط اللحْمَة أسفل السَّدَاء
16 raised weft thread — خَيْط اللحْمَة أعلى السَّدَاء
17 first and second warp threads [raised] — خَيْطَا السَّدَاء الأوَّل والثاني [فوق السَّدَاء]
18 third and fourth warp threads [lowered] — خَيْطَا السَّدَاء الثالث والرابع [أسفل اللحْمَة]
19 draft for combined rib weave — نِظَام اللقْي الخاص بالنسيج المُضَلَّع المُدْمَج
20 selvedge (selvage) thread draft (additional shafts for the selvedge) — نِظَام لَقي البُرْسُل
21 draft for the fabric shafts — نِظَام لَقْي نَسْج القماش
22 tie-up of selvedge (selvage) shafts — رَبْط نَسْج البُرْسُل
23 tie-up of fabric shafts — رَبْط نَسْج القماش
24 selvedge (selvage) in plain weave — البُرْسُل في نَسْج سادة
25 section through combination rib weave — جزء من نَسْج مُضَلَّع مُدْمَج
26 thread interlacing of reversible warp-faced cord — تداخل خيوط في كردون السَّدَاء السطحي المستعمل على الوجهين
27 draft (point paper design) for reversible warp-faced cord — باترون (ورق مربعات) كردون السَّدَاء السطحي المستعمل على الوجهين
28 interlacing points — مربعات متداخلة
29 weaving draft for honeycomb weave in the fabric — نِظَام نَسْج خلايا النَّحْل في القماش

30-48 basic knits — **غُرَز التريكو الأساسيَّة**
30 loop, an open loop — أنْشوطة ، أنْشوطة مفتوحة ، بوكليه
31 head — رأس الأنْشُوطة
32 side — جانِب الأنْشُوطة
33 neck — عُنُق الأنْشُوطة
34 head interlocking point — نقطة التعاشُق بالرأس
35 neck interlocking point — نقطة التعاشُق بالعنق
36 closed loop — أنْشُوطة مُقْفَلَة
37 mesh [with inlaid yarn] — شبكة [بغَزْل وَبَرِيّ]
38 diagonal floating yarn (diagonal floating thread) — غَزْل تشييف مائل
39 loop interlocking at the head — أنْشُوطة متعاشقة بالرأس
40 float — تشييف
41 loose floating yarn (loose floating thread) — غَزْل تشييف سائب
42 course — صَفّ غُرَز أفُقي
43 inlaid yarn — غَزْل وبري
44 tuck and miss stitch — غُرْزة مقلوبة
45 pulled-up tuck stitch — غُرْزة عدلة
46 staggered tuck stitch — غُرْزة عدلة متناثِرة
47 2 × 2 tuck and miss stitch — غُرْزة مقلوبة مزدوجة
48 double pulled-up tuck stitch — غُرْزة عدلة مزدوجة

172 Papermaking I — صناعة الوَرَق (1)

1-52 sulphate (*Am.* sulfate) **pulp mill** (kraft pulp mill) [in diagram form] — **ماكينة إعداد لبّ الكبريتات** (ماكينة إعداد لُبّ كرافت)
1 chippers with dust — وَحْدَات إعداد الجُذَاذة و

extractor	طَرْد التُّرَاب
2 rotary screen (riffler)	غُرْبَال دَوَّار (حوض فَصْل الرمال)
3 chip packer (chip distributor)	مُوَزِّع الجُذَاذة
4 blower	نَفَّاخ
5 disintegrator (crusher, chip crusher)	جَرَّاشة ، كَسَّارة
6 dust-settling chamber	حُجْرَة ترسيب الأتربة
7 digester	مِرْجَل تسخين خامات الورق
8 liquor preheater	مُسَخِّن مُتقدِّم للسائل
9 control tap	محْبَس
10 swing pipe	أنبوب تأرجحي
11 blow tank (diffuser)	خَزَّان النَّفْخ
12 blow valve	صمام النَّفْخ
13 blow pit (diffuser)	حُفْرَة النَّفْخ
14 turpentine separator	فَرَّازَة الترابنتين
15 centralized separator	فَرَّازة مركزيَّة
16 jet condenser (injection condenser)	مُكَثِّف نَفَّاث (مُكَثِّف حَقْن)
17 storage tank for condensate	خَزَّان ناتج التكثيف
18 hot water tank	خَزَّان الماء الساخِن
19 heat exchanger	مُبَادِل حراري
20 filter	فلتر ، مُرَشِّح
21 presorter	فَرَّاز مُتَقَدِّم
22 centrifugal screen	غُرْبَال نابذ
23 rotary sorter (rotary strainer)	فَرَّاز دَوَّار (مُنْخُل دَوَّار)
24 concentrator (thickener, decker)	مُغَلِّظ القَوَام
25 vat (chest)	راقود
26 collecting tank for backwater (low box)	خَزَّان تجميع الماء المُرْتَجَع/المُرْتَد
27 conical refiner (cone refiner, Jordan, Jordan refiner)	جِهَاز تنعيم مَخْروطي الشكل
28 black liquor filter	مُرَشِّح السائل الأسود
29 black liquor storage tank	خَزَّان السائل الأسود
30 condenser	مُغَلِّظ القَوَام
31 separators	فَرَّازَات
32 heaters (heating elements)	سَخَّانات
33 liquor pump	مِضَخَّة السائل
34 heavy liquor pump	مضَخَّة السائل الثقيل
35 mixing tank	خَزَّان المَزْج
36 salt cake storage tank (sodium sulphate storage tank)	خَزَّان كبريتات الصوديوم
37 dissolving tank (dissolver)	خَزَّان الإذابة
38 steam heater	سَخَّان بُخَاري
39 electrostatic precipitator	مُرَسِّب الكتروستاتي
40 air pump	مضَخَّة هوائيَّة
41 storage tank for the uncleared green liquor	خَزَّان السائل الأخضر غير النَّقِي
42 concentrator (thickener, decker)	مُغَلِّظ القَوَام
43 green liquor preheater	سَخَّان مُتقدِّم للسائل الأخضر
44 concentrator (thickener, decker) for the weak wash liquor (wash water)	مُغَلِّظ قَوَام سائل الغَسِيل الضعيف (ماء الغَسِيل)
45 storage tank for the weak liquor	خَزَّان السائل الضعيف
46 storage tank for the cooking liquor	خَزَّان سائل الطَّبْخ
47 agitator (stirrer)	محْرَاك ، آليَّة التقليب
48 concentrator (thickener, decker)	مُغَلِّظ القَوَام
49 causticizing agitators (causticizing stirrers)	مَحَارك المُعَالَجَة بالصودا الكاوية
50 classifier	آليَّة تصنيف
51 lime slaker	وَحْدَة إطفاء الجير
52 reconverted lime	جير مُسْتَرجع
53-65 groundwood mill (mechanical pulp mill) [diagram]	**ماكينة إعداد لُبّ الخشب**
53 continuous grinder (continuous chain grinder)	جلاخة مستمرة (جَلاّخة بسلسلة مقفولة)
54 strainer (knotter)	مُنْخُل ، مِصْفَاة
55 pulp water pump	مضَخَّة ماء اللب
56 centrifugal screen	غُرْبَال نابذ
57 screen (sorter)	غُرْبَال ، مُنْخُل
58 secondary screen (secondary sorter)	غُرْبَال ثانوي
59 rejects chest	صندوق الفضلات
60 conical refiner (cone refiner, Jordan, Jordan refiner)	جِهَاز تنعيم مَخْروطي الشكل
61 pulp-drying machine (pulp machine)	ماكينة تجفيف لُبّ الخشب
62 concentrator (thickener, decker)	مُغَلِّظ القَوَام
63 waste water pump (white water pump, pulp water pump)	مِضَخَّة الماء المهدور
64 steam pipe	أنبوب البخار
65 water pipe	أنبوب الماء
66 continuous grinder (continuous chain grinder)	جَلاخة مستمرة (جلاخة بِسِلْسِلَة مقفولة)
67 feed chain	حصيرة التغذية
68 groundwood	خشب شَجَر
69 reduction gear for the feed chain drive	تروس تخفيض سرعة إدارة حصيرة التغذية
70 stone-dressing device	آليَّة الصَّقْل بِحَجَر التجليخ
71 grinding stone (grindstone, pulpstone)	حَجَر تجليخ
72 spray pipe	أنبوب الرَّش
73 conical refiner (cone refiner, Jordan, Jordan refiner)	جِهَاز تنعيم مَخْرُوطيّ الشكل
74 handwheel for adjust-	دولاب ضبط المسافة بين

ing the clearance between the knives (blades)	السكاكين (الأنْصال)
75 rotating bladed cone (rotating bladed plug)	مَخْرُوط دَوَّار مُنَصَّل
76 stationary bladed shell	غِلاف مُنَصَّل ثابت
77 inlet for unrefined cellulose (chemical wood pulp, chemical pulp) or groundwood pulp (mechanical pulp)	فتحة دخول السليلوز غير المُنَقَّى (اللب الكيميائي) أو لُبّ الخشب
78 outlet for refined cellulose (chemical wood pulp, chemical pulp) or groundwood pulp (mechanical pulp)	فتحة خروج السليلوز المُنَقَّى (اللب الكيميائي) أو لُبّ الخشب
79-86 stuff (stock) preparation plant [diagram]	**عجينة اللب المروبة** [رسم تخطيطي]
79 conveyor belt (conveyor) for loading cellulose (chemical wood pulp, chemical pulp) or groundwood pulp (mechanical pulp)	سَيْر ناقل لشَحْن السليلوز (اللب الكيميائي) أو لُبّ الخشب
80 pulper	جِهَاز نَزْع اللب
81 dump chest	صندوق الإغْراق/التفريغ
82 cone breaker	كَسَّارة مخروطيَّة
83 conical refiner (cone refiner, Jordan, Jordan refiner)	جِهَاز تنعيم مَخْرُوطي الشكل
84 refiner	جِهَاز تنعيم/تنقية
85 stuff chest (stock chest)	صُنْدُوق عجينة اللب المُرَوَّبَة
86 machine chest (stuff chest)	صُنْدُوق الماكينة

173 Papermaking II — صناعَة الوَرَق (2)

1 stuff chest (stock chest, machine chest), a mixing chest for stuff (stock)	صُنْدُوق عَجِينة اللب المُرَوَّبَة
2-10 laboratory apparatus (laboratory equipment) for analysing stuff (stock) and paper	**أجْهِزَة مَعْمَليَّة لتحليل عَجِينَة اللب المُرَوَّبَة**
2 Erlenmeyer flask	مِخْبَار مَخْرُوطي
3 volumetric flask	مِخْبَار حَجْمِيّ، قارورة حَجْمِيَّة
4 measuring cylinder	مِخْبَار قياس
5 Bunsen burner	لهب/ مَوْقِد بنزن
6 tripod	حامِل ثلاثي
7 petri dish	جِفْنَة، صَحْفَة "بتْري"
8 test tube rack	حامِل أنابيب اختِبار
9 balance for measuring basis weight	ميزان لقياس الوَزْن الأساسي
10 micrometer	ميكرومتر
11 centrifugal cleaners ahead of the breastbox (headbox, stuff box) of a paper machine	وَحْدَات تنظيف العجينة قبل ذهابها إلى صُنْدُوق مَاكِينَة صُنْع الوَرَق
12 standpipe	أنْبُوب قائم
13-28 paper machine (production line) [diagram]	**مَاكِينَة صنع الوَرَق (خط إنتاج)** [مُخَطَط]
13 feed-in from the machine chest (stuff chest) with sand table (sand trap, riffler) and knotter	آليَّة تغذية من صُنْدُوق المَاكِينَة (صُنْدُوق العجينة) وبها فراز ومصفاة
14 wire (machine wire)	سِلْك (سلك المَاكِينَة)
15 vacuum box (suction box)	صُنْدُوق تفريغ
16 suction roll	دُولْفين شفط
17 first wet felt	لِبَّاد التبليل الأُوَّلي
18 second wet felt	لِبَّاد التبليل الثاني
19 first press	المِكْبَس الأول
20 second press	المِكْبَس الثاني
21 offset press	مِكْبَس أوفْسِت
22 drying cylinder (drier)	دُولْفين التجفيف (مُجَفِّف)
23 dry felt (drier felt)	لِبَّاد تجفيف
24 size press	مِكْبَس تَقْوِيم (قَلْفَنَة أو معالَجَة بالراتنجات)
25 cooling roll	دُولْفين التبريد
26 calender rolls	دلافين صَقْل الأفْرُخ
27 machine hood	غطاء المَاكِينَة
28 delivery reel	بَكَرَة سَحْب الوَرَق
29-35 blade coating machine (blade coater)	**مَاكِينَة تَكْسِيَة نَصْليَّة**
29 raw paper (body paper)	وَرَق خام
30 web	شريط الوَرَق
31 coater for the top side	آليَّة تَكْسِيَة الجانب العلوي
32 infrared drier	مُجَفِّف بالأشعة تحت الحمراء
33 heated drying cylinder	دُولْفين تجفيف مُسَخَّن
34 coater for the underside (wire side)	آلية تَكْسِيَة الجانب السفلي (جانب السلك)
35 reel of coated paper	بَكَرَة الوَرَق المكْسُوّ
36 calender (supercalender)	مَاكِينَة تشكيل وصقل الأفْرُخ
37 hydraulic system for the press rolls	نظام هيدرولي لدلافين الكَبْس
38 calender roll	أسطوانة المَاكِينَة
39 unwind station	مَحَطَّة فَكّ لَفَّة الوَرَق
40 lift platform	مِنَصَّة رَفْع
41 rewind station (rewinder, re-reeler, reeling machine, re-reeling machine)	مَحَطَّة إعَادة لَفّ الوَرَق
42 roll cutter	سكِّين لَفَّة الوَرَق
43 control panel	لَوْحة التحكم
44 cutter	سكِّين (آليَّة القطع)
45 web	شَرِيط الوَرَق
46-51 papermaking by hand	**صناعة الوَرَق يدوياً**
46 vatman	عامِل الراقود
47 vat	راقود
48 mould (*Am.* mold)	قالِب
49 coucher (couchman)	عامِل فَرْد العجينة

50 post ready for pressing	عجينة جاهِزة
51 felt	لِبَّاد

174 Typesetting Room (Composing Room) I — قِسْم الجَمْع الطباعي (1)

1 hand-setting room (hand-composing room)	قِسْم الجَمْع اليدويّ
2 composing frame	مِنْضَدَة (سيبة) صناديق الحروف
3 case (typecase)	صُنْدوق حروف
4 case cabinet (case rack)	دُولاب حِفْظ صناديق الحروف
5 hand compositor (compositor, typesetter, maker-up)	جَمَّاع يدويّ
6 manuscript (typescript)	أصْل مَخْطوط
7 sorts (types, type characters, characters)	حروف مَطْبَعيَّة
8 rack (case) for furniture (spacing material)	رَفّ (صندوق) التواضيب (الرقائق)
9 standing type rack (standing matter rack)	دُرْج الصَّفَحَات المَحْفُوظة
10 storage shelf (shelf for storing formes, *Am.* forms)	تخزين الفورمات
11 standing type (standing matter)	صَفْحَة مَحْفُوظة
12 galley	صينية "جاليه"
13 composing stick (setting stick)	المِصَفّ
14 composing rule (setting rule)	مِسْطَرَة المِصَفّ
15 type (type matter, matter)	نَصّ مَجْمُوع
16 page cord	سِلْك الصَّفْحَة
17 bodkin	مِخْرَز
18 tweezers	مِلْقاط
19 Linotype line-composing (line-casting, slug-composing, slug-casting) machine, a multi-magazine machine	مَاكِينَة جَمْع سَطْريّ (لينوتيب)، مَاكِينَة متعددة مَخازِن المتريسات
20 distributing mechanism (distributor)	مُوَزِّع الأُمَّهات (المَتْريسات)
21 type magazines with matrices (matrixes)	مَخْزَن أُمَّهات الحروف
22 elevator carrier for distributing the matrices (matrixes)	الذراع الرافعة لنقل الأُمَّهات إلى المُوَزِّع
23 assembler	صُنْدوق التجميع
24 spacebands	رَقَائق الفَصْل
25 casting mechanism	آليَّة السَّبْك
26 metal feeder	التَّغْذية بمَعْدَن الحروف
27 machine-set matter (cast lines, slugs)	صينية الأَسْطُر المَسْبُوكة
28 matrices (matrixes) for hand-setting (sorts)	أُمَّهات للإيلاج اليدوي
29 Linotype matrix	أُمّ الحَرْف (متريس) للجَمْع السَّطْري
30 teeth for the distributing mechanism (distributor)	أسنان للتحرك على مُوَزِّع أُمَّهات الحروف
31 face (type face, matrix)	وَجْه الحَرْف (السَّطْح الطِّبَاعي)
32-45 monotype single-unit composing (type-setting) **and casting machine** (monotype single-unit composition caster)	**مَاكِينَة الجَمْع الحَرْفيّ والسَّبْك**
32 monotype standard composing (typesetting) machine (keyboard)	مَاكِينَة الجَمْع الحَرْفيّ المونوتيب
33 paper tower	بُرْج بُوبينة الوَرَق (وَرَق المونوتيب)
34 paper ribbon	شَريط الوَرَق
35 justifying scale	أُسْطُوانة ضَبْط مقاس السَّطْر
36 unit indicator	وَحْدَة تحديد ثَخَانة الحَرْف
37 keyboard	لَوْحة المفاتيح
38 compressed-air hose	خُرْطُوم توصيل الهواء المَضْغُوط
39 monotype casting machine (monotype caster)	مَاكِينَة سَبْك حَرْفيّ
40 automatic metal feeder	حامِل سَبِيكَة الرصاص لتغذية حلّة الرصاص
41 pump compression spring (pump pressure spring)	نابِض لضبط ضغط مِضَخَّة الرصاص
42 matrix case (die case)	إطار أُمَّهات الحروف (كَفّ المتاريس)
43 paper tower	بُرْج بُوبينة الوَرَق
44 galley with types (letters, characters, cast single types, cast single letters)	صينية (جاليه) الحروف المَسْبُوكة
45 electric heater (electric heating unit)	وَحْدَة التسخين الكهربائيّ لحَوْض المعدن
46 matrix case (die case)	إطار الأُمَّهات
47 type matrices (matrixes) (letter matrices)	أُمَّهات الحروف (طقم متاريس بالشاسيه)
48 guide block for engaging with the cross-slide guide	مَشْقَبيَّة كَفّ المتاريس

175 Typesetting Room (Composing Room) II — قِسْم الجَمْع الطباعي (2)

1-17 composition (type matter, type)	**الجَمْع** (نَصّ مَجْمُوع)
1 initial (initial letter)	الحَرْف الإسْتِهْلالي
2 bold type (bold, bold-faced type, heavy type, boldface)	حَرْف أسْوَد (غامِق)
3 semibold type (semi-	حَرْف نصف أسْوَد (نصف

bold)	غامِق)
4 line	سطر
5 space	مسافة (بين الأسطر)
6 ligature (double letter)	حَرْف مُزْدَوَج
7 italic type (italics)	حَرْف مائل
8 light face type (light face)	حَرْف فاتح
9 extra bold type (extra bold)	حَرْف أسْوَد أكبر حجماً
10 bold condensed type (bold condensed)	حَرْف أسْوَد ضيق
11 majuscule (capital letter, capital, upper case letter)	حَرْف أجنبي كبير (حَرْف كابتال)
12 minuscule (small letter, lower case letter)	حَرْف أجنبي صغير
13 letter spacing (interspacing)	فَوْصَلَة الحروف
14 small capitals	أحَرْف كابتال صغيرة الحجم
15 break	سَطْر ناقص
16 indention	فراغ يُتْرَك في بداية الفقرة
17 space	مسافة
18 type sizes [one typographic point = 0.376 mm (Didot system), 0.351 mm (Pica system)]	أحجام الحروف الطِّبَاعية [البنط الطِّبَاعي = 0,376 مللم (نظام الديوت)، 0,351 مللم (نظام بيكا)]
19 six-to-pica (2 points)	بُنْطَان
20 half nonpareil (four-to-pica) (3 points)	ثلاثة أبْنَاط
21 brilliant (4 points); *sim.:* diamond (4 1/2 points)	"بريليانت" (4 أبْنَاط)؛ بالمثل «دايموند» (4.5 بنط)
22 pearl (5 points); *sim.:* ruby (*Am.* agate) (5 1/2 points)	"بيرل" (5 أبْنَاط)؛ بالمثل «روبي» (5.5 بنط)
23 nonpareil (6 points); *sim.:* minionette (6 1/2 points)	"نونبريل" (6 أبْنَاط)؛ بالمثل «مينيونيت» (6.5 بنط)
24 minion (7 points)	"مينيون" (7 أبْنَاط)
25 brevier (8 points)	"بريفيه" (8 أبْنَاط)
26 bourgeois (9 points)	"بورجواز" (9 أبْنَاط)
27 long primer (10 points)	"بريمر طويل" (10 أبْنَاط)
28 pica (12 points)	"بيكا" (12 بنطا)
29 English (14 points)	"إنجليزي" (14 بنطاً)
30 great primer (two-line brevier, *Am.* Columbian) (16 points)	"جريت بريمر" (16 بنطاً)
31 paragon (two-line primer) (20 points)	"باراجون" (20 بنطاً)
32-37 typefounding (type casting)	**سَبك الحروف الطِّبَاعية**
32 punch cutter	حفّار الاسْطَمْبَات
33 graver (burin, cutter)	أزْميل الحَفْر
34 magnifying glass (magnifier)	نظّارة مكَبِّرة
35 punch blank (die blank)	قالِب (إسْطَمْبَة)
36 finished steel punch (finished steel die)	إسْطَمْبَة صُلْب مُجَهَّزَة
37 punched matrix (stamped matrix, strike, drive)	أمّ الحَرْف المسبوكة
38 type (type character, character)	حَرْف مطبعي
39 head	رَأْس الحَرْف
40 shoulder	كتف الحَرْف
41 counter	تجويف الحَرْف
42 face (type face)	وَجْه الحَرْف (السَّطْح الطِّبَاعي)
43 type line (bodyline)	خَطّ القاعدة
44 height to paper (type height)	ارتفاع الحَرْف
45 height of shank (height of shoulder)	ارتفاع كتف الحَرْف
46 body size (type size, point size)	حجم جِسْم الحَرْف (البنط)
47 nick	الحزَّة
48 set (width)	العَرْض
49 matrix-boring machine (matrix-engraving machine), a special-purpose boring machine	آلة قَطْع وتشكيل الأُمَّهات والأحَرْف المطبعيَّة
50 stand	عَمُود حامِل
51 cutter (cutting head)	عُدَّة القَطْع
52 cutting table	نَضَد القَطْع
53 pantograph carriage	حامِل المِنْسَاخ (البانتوجراف)
54 V-way	دلائل منشوريَّة
55 pattern	النموذج
56 pattern table	نَضَد النموذج
57 follower	تابِع
58 pantograph	المِنْسَاخ (البانتوجراف)
59 matrix clamp	قامِطة أمّ الحَرْف/المتريس
60 cutter spindle	عَمُود القَطْع
61 drive motor	مُحَرِّك الإدارة

176 Typesetting Room III (Phototypesetting, Photocomposition, Photosetting) — قسْم الجَمْع الطباعي (الجَمْع التصويري) (3)

1-21 phototypesetting configurations	**مكَوِّنات الجَمْع التصويري**
1 off-line configuration	مكَوِّنات الجَمْع المستقلَّة
2 & 3 data capture	حَصْر البيانات
2 terminal for keying unformatted text	طرَفيَّة إدخال نص بدون هيئة
3 text capture and correction terminal	طَرَفيَّة حَصْر النص والتصحيح
4 layout terminal (page-layout terminal)	طَرَفيَّة تنسيق الصَّفْحَة
5 data carrier, a diskette (floppy disk)	حامِل البيانات، قُرْص مَرِن
6 (photo)typesetting unit (phototypesetter)	وَحْدَة الجمع التصويري

7 on-line configuration	مكَوِّنات الجَمْع المباشرة
8 make-up terminal (page make-up terminal)	طرفيَّة المونتاج
9 central processing unit (typesetting computer)	وَحْدَة معالجة مركزيَّة
10 magnetic tape unit (magnetic tape drive)	وَحْدَة الشريط المُمَغْنَط
11 disk store	وَحْدَة الأقراص المُمَغْنَطَة
12 printer, a laser printer	طابعة، طابعة بالليزر
13 phototypesetting machine (phototypesetter)	مَاكِينَة جَمْع تصويري
14 text capture (text-capture terminal)	حَصْر النص
15 typesetter (keyboarder or typographer)	جَمَّاع تصويري
16 screen (monitor)	شَاشَة
17 floppy disk drive	مُشَغِّل القُرْص المَرِن
18 computer and memory unit with central processing unit and hard disk	حاسِب آليّ ووَحْدَة ذاكِرة مع وَحْدَة معالجة مركزيَّة وقُرْص مُمَغْنَط
19 mouse, an input device	فَأْرَة
20 mouse mat	قاعدة الفَأْرَة
21 keyboard, an input device	لَوْحَة المفاتيح
22 direct-entry phototypesetter	وَحْدَة جَمْع تصويري بإدخال مباشِر
23-33 desktop publishing (DTP)	**برامج النشر المكتبيّ**
23 diskette (floppy disk) with text, layout, and graphics programs	قُرْص مَرِن وعليه برامج النصوص والتنسيق والرسوم البيانيَّة
24 scanner (flat-bed scanner)	ماسِح (سكانر) أفقيّ
25 personal computer (PC) or workstation	حاسِب آليّ شخصيّ
26 printout (computer printout)	مطبوعات (صَفْحَة مطبوعة من الحاسوب)
27 raster image processor (RIP)	وَحْدَة معالجة بشبكة خُطُوط المسح
28 laser phototypesetter	وَحْدَة جَمْع تصويري بالليزر
29 proof	بروفة
30 high-resolution graphics screen, a large-format colour monitor	شَاشَة عالية الوضوح
31 display window	نافذة عَرْض
32 typographic parameters	البرامترات الطِّبَاعية
33 (typographic) command window	نافذة الأوامر الطِّبَاعية
34 film copier	جهاز نسخ الفيلم
35-46 cathode ray tube (CRT) **typesetter**	**وَحْدَة جمع بأنبوب أشعة الكاثود**
35 scanning system	نظام المسح
36 scan-generating (scanning) cathode ray tube (CRT)	أنبوب أشعة كاثود ماسِح
37 lens	عَدَسَة
38 character grid (matrix case)	كَفُّ المتاريس
39 condenser lens	عَدَسَة مُكَثِّفَة
40 photomultiplier	مُضاعِف التيار الكهروضوئي
41 output system	نظام الإخراج
42 video amplifier	مُضَخِّم الإشارات الحاملة للصوَر
43 character-generating tube (CRT character generator)	أنبوب توليد الحروف
44 exposure plane	سَطْح التعريض للضوء
45 matrix case	كَفُّ المتاريس
46 guide claw	مَشْقَبِيَّة كَفُّ المتاريس

177 Photomechanical Reproduction — الإِسْتِنْسَاخ التَّصْوِيري

1 overhead process camera (overhead copying camera)	آلَة تَصْوير وتجميع رَأْسيَّة
2 focusing screen (ground glass screen)	شَاشَة اسْتِقبال الصورة
3 hinged screen holder	حامِل شَاشَة مفصلي
4 graticule	مقياس العَيْنِيَّة
5 control console	كونسول التحكم
6 hinged bracket-mounted control panel	لَوْحَة تحكم مُرَكَّبَة على مفصلات
7 percentage focusing charts	إيضاحات نِسْبَة التركيز البؤري
8 vacuum film holder	حامِل الفيلم
9 screen magazine	خَزَانَة الشَاشَة
10 bellows	مِنْفَاخ الكاميرا
11 standard	مُقَدَّم (واجهة) العَدَسَة
12 register device	جِهَاز عدَّاد
13 overhead gantry	حامِل علوي
14 copyboard	لَوْحَة (تَخْتَة) الأصُول المُرَاد تصويرها
15 copyholder	حامِل [ماسك] الأصْل المُرَاد تصويره
16 lamp bracket	حامِل مصابيح محوري
17 xenon lamp	مِصْباح زينون للتصوير
18 copy (original)	الأَصْل المُرَاد تصويره
19 retouching and stripping desk	نَضُد تهذيب وتقطيع الأفلام
20 illuminated screen	شَاشَة ضوئيَّة
21 height and angle adjustment	مِقْبَض تعديل ارتفاع وزاوِيَة مَيْل النضد
22 copyboard	لَوْحَة الأصْل
23 linen tester, a magnifying glass	عَدَسَة فحص الصورة
24 universal process and reproduction camera	آلة تصوير عامة للاستنساخ والتحميض
25 camera body	جِسْم الكاميرا
26 bellows	مِنْفَاخ الكاميرا
27 lens carrier	حامِل العَدَسَة
28 angled mirror	مِرْآة مائلة
29 stand	حامِل
30 copyboard	لَوْحَة الأصْل

31 halogen lamp	مِصْباح هالوجين
32 vertical process camera, a compact camera	كاميرا تحْميض رَأْسيَّة
33 camera body	جِسْم الكاميرا
34 focusing screen (ground glass screen)	شاشَة اسْتقبال الصورة
35 vacuum back	ظَهْر خوائي
36 control panel	لَوْحَة التحكم
37 flash lamp	مِصْباح الفلاش
38 mirror for right-reading images	مِرْآة لضبط وضوح الصورة
39 scanner (colour, *Am.* color, correction unit)	جِهَاز فَرْز الألْوَان (سكانر)
40 base frame	قاعدة الجِهَاز
41 lamp compartment	حُجَيْرَة المصابيح
42 xenon lamp housing	مَبِيت مِصْباح زينون
43 feed motors	مُحَرِّكات الإلْقام
44 transparency arm	ذِرَاع الشفافيَّات
45 scanning drum	أُسْطُوَانة فَرْز الألْوَان
46 scanning head	رَأْس فَرْز الألْوَان
47 mask-scanning head	رَأْس مَسْح "الماسْك"
48 mask drum	أُسْطُوَانة "الماسْك"
49 recording space	حيز التسجيل
50 daylight cassette	خَزَانَة فيلم نَهَاريَّة
51 colour (*Am.* color) computer with control unit and selective colour correction	كمبيوتر ألوان ذو وَحْدَة تحكم وتصحيح ألوان انتقائيَّة
52 engraving machine	مَاكِينَة حَفْر
53 seamless engraving adjustment	تعديل الحَفْر غير الدرزي
54 drive clutch	قابض الإدارة
55 clutch flange	شَفِير القابض
56 drive unit	وَحْدَة الإدارة
57 machine bed	قاعدة المَاكِينَة
58 equipment carrier	حامِل المعدات
59 bed slide	زلاّقة القاعدة
60 control panel	لَوْحَة التحكم
61 bearing block	قالب الحَمْل
62 tailstock	غُرَاب الذيل
63 scanning head	رَأْس فَرْز الألْوَان
64 copy cylinder	أُسْطُوَانة الأصْل
65 centre (*Am.* center) bearing	مَحْمَل مركزي
66 engraving system	آليَّة الحَفْر
67 printing cylinder	أُسْطُوَانة الطبع
68 cylinder arm	ذِرَاع الأُسْطُوَانة
69 electronics (electronic) cabinet	حُجَيْرَة الإلكترونيات
70 computers	أجهزة الكمبيوتر
71 program input	دَخْل البرامج
72 automatic film processor for scanner films	وَحْدَة معالجة آليَّة لأفلام جِهَاز فَرْز الألْوَان (سكانر)

178 Electrotyping and Block Making — إعْدَاد الأسْطح الطِّبَاعية المُجَلْفَنَة والكليشيهات

1-6 electrotyping plant	**وَحْدَة إعداد الأسْطح الطِّبَاعية المُجَلْفَنة**
1 cleaning tank	حَوْض تنظيف
2 rectifier	جِهَاز التصحيح
3 measuring and control unit	وَحْدَة التحكم والقياس
4 electroplating tank (electroplating bath, electroplating vat)	حَوْض (مَغْطَس) للطلاء بالكهرباء
5 anode rod (with copper anodes)	قضيب الأنود
6 plate rod (cathode)	قضيب الكاثود
7 hydraulic moulding (*Am.* molding) press	مِكْبَس قَوْلَبَة هيدرولي
8 pressure gauge (*Am.* gage) (manometer)	مِقْيَاس الضغط
9 apron	الفورمة التي سَيُنْسَخ منها القالب
10 round base	قاعدة جسم المِكْبَس المستديرة
11 hydraulic pressure pump	مِضَخَّة كبس هيدروليَّة
12 drive motor	مُحَرِّك الإدارة
13 curved plate casting machine (curved electrotype casting machine)	مسْبك المصبات المقوَّسة
14 motor	المُحَرِّك
15 control knobs	مفاتيح الضبط
16 pyrometer	مقياس درجات الحرارة العالية (بيرومتر)
17 mouth piece	فتحة تجويف الصَّب
18 core	غرفة الصَّب
19 melting furnace	فُرْن صَهْر سبيكة الرصاص
20 starting lever	ذراع التشغيل
21 cast curved plate (cast curved electrotype) for rotary printing	سَطْح طِبَاعي مصبوب مُقَوَّس للطباعة الدوَّارة
22 fixed mould (*Am.* mold)	إطار ثابِت للصب
23 etching machine	مَاكِينَة حَفْر
24 etching tank with etching solution (etchant, mordant) and filming agent (film former)	حَوْض الحَفْر وبه محلول الحَفْر والمادة الفيلمية
25 paddles	عَجَلات قلابة
26 turntable	نَضَد دَوَّار
27 plate clamp	قضبان تثبيت السَّطح الطِّبَاعي
28 drive motor	مُحَرِّك الإدارة
29 control unit	وَحْدَة التحكم
30 twin etching machine	مَاكِينَة حَفْر تَوْأميَّة
31 etching tank (etching bath) [in section]	حَوْض الحَفْر [مقطع]
32 photoprinted zinc plate	السَّطْح الطِّبَاعي المُصَوَّر
33 paddle	عجلة قلابة (لتقليب المَحْلُول)
34 outlet cock (drain cock, *Am.* faucet)	مِحْبَس تصريف المَحْلُول
35 plate rack	حامِل اللوح (السَّطْح الطِّبَاعي)
36 control switches	مفاتيح التشغيل
37 lid	غِطَاء الحَوْض

38 halftone photoengraving (halftone block, halftone plate), a block (plate, printing plate)	الحفْر الفوتوغرافي للصورة الظِّلِّيَّة (قالِب الهافتون)
39 dot (halftone dot), a printing element	نقطة الشبكة الطِّبَاعية
40 etched zinc plate	لَوْح زنك مَحْفُور
41 block mount (block mounting, plate mount, plate mounting)	قاعِدة الكليشيه (قاعدة السَّطْح الطِّبَاعي)
42 line block (line engraving, line etching, line plate, line cut)	قالِب (كليشيه) خَطِّي (حَفْر خَطِّي)
43 non-printing, deep-etched areas	المناطق غير المطلوب طباعتها، حَفْر غائر
44 flange (bevel edge)	الحافة المائلة (بيزو)
45 sidewall	جدار جانبي

179 Offset Platemaking — تَحْضِير سَطْح طِبَاعة الأوفْست

1 plate whirler (whirler, plate-coating machine) for coating offset plates	جِهَاز تَدوير (دوّار) لتغطية الأسْطُح المعدنية أو الزُّجاجيَّة بالمحاليل الحَسَّاسَة للضوء
2 sliding lid	غطاء منزلق
3 electric heater	وَحْدَة تسخين كهربائيَّة
4 temperature gauge (*Am.* gage)	مِقْيَاس درجة الحرارة
5 water connection for the spray unit	توصيلة مياه وحدة الرش
6 spray unit	وَحْدَة رش
7 hand spray	رشاش يدوي
8 plate clamps	قضبان تثبيت السَّطْح الطِّبَاعي
9 zinc plate (*also:* magnesium plate, copper plate)	سَطْح طِبَاعي (لوح) من الزنك (أيضا من المغنيسيوم، النحاس)
10 control panel	لَوْحَة تحكم
11 drive motor	مُحَرِّك الإدارة
12 brake pedal	دَوَّاسَة المِكْبَح
13 vacuum printing frame (vacuum frame, printing-down frame)	إطار طبع بالتفريغ
14 base of the vacuum printing frame (vacuum frame, printing-down frame)	قاعِدة الإطار
15 plate glass frame	الإطار الزجاجي للوح
16 coated offset plate	لَوْح الأوفست المُغَطَّى بالمحلول الحساس للضوء
17 control panel	لَوْحة التحكم
18 exposure timer	مُنَظِّم التعريض للضوء
19 vacuum pump switches	مفاتيح تشغيل مِضَخَّة التفريغ
20 support	حامِل
21 point light exposure lamp, a quartz-halogen lamp	مِصْبَاح التعريض للضوء، مِصْبَاح كوارتز–هالوجين
22 fan blower	نافخ المروحة
23 stripping table (make-up table) for stripping films	نَضَد تقطيع الأفلام (طاولة المونتاج)
24 crystal glass screen	لَوْح من الزجاج البلُّوري
25 light box	صندوق إضاءة
26 straightedge rules	مِسْطَرَة مستقيمة الحواف
27 vertical plate-drying cabinet	دولاب رَأْسي لتجفيف الألواح
28 hygrometer	هيجرومتر
29 speed control	مِضْبَط السرعة
30 brake pedal	دَوَّاسة الكبح
31 processing machine for presensitized plates	مَاكِينَة تحميض الألواح الحَسَّاسَة
32 burning-in oven for glue-enamel plates (diazo plates)	فُرْن أَلْوَاح الغَرَاء والمينا (فرن أَلْوَاح الديازو)
33 control box (control unit)	وَحْدَة التحكم
34 diazo plate	لَوْح الديازو

180 Offset Printing — طِبَاعَة الأُوفْست

1 four-colour (*Am.* four-color) rotary offset press (rotary offset machine, web-offset press)	مَاكِينَة طباعة أوفست دوَّارة أربعة ألوان (مَاكِينَة طبع أوفست شريطي)
2 roll of unprinted paper (blank paper)	لَفَّة الوَرَق غير المطبوع (الوَرَق الأبيض)
3 reel stand (carrier for the roll of unprinted paper)	حامِل لَفَّة الوَرَق غير المطبوع
4 forwarding rolls	طُنْبُور سحب الوَرَق
5 side margin control (margin control, side control, side lay control)	آلية التحكم في الهامشيْن الجانبييْن
6-13 inking units (inker units)	**وَحَدات** (أسْطُوَانات) **التحبير**
6, 8, 10, 12 inking units (inker units) in the upper printing unit	وَحَدَات (أسْطُوَانات) التحبير فى وَحْدَة الطباعة العلويَّة
6-7 perfecting unit (double unit) for yellow	وَحْدَة طبع على الوجهيْن للون الأصفر
7,9,11,13 inking units (inker units) in the lower printing unit	وحدات التحبير في وَحْدَة الطباعة السفليَّة
8-9 perfecting unit (double unit) for cyan	وَحْدَة طبع على الوجهيْن للون السيان
10-11 perfecting unit (double unit) for magenta	وَحْدَة طبع على الوجهيْن للون الماجنتا
12-13 perfecting unit (double unit) for black	وَحْدَة طبع على الوجهيْن للون الأسود
14 drier	وَحْدَة التجفيف
15 folder (folder unit)	مَاكِينَة الطيّ (تطبيق الوَرَق)
16 control desk	نَضَد التحكم
17 sheet	فَرْخ وَرَق
18 four-colour (*Am.* four-color) rotary offset	مَاكِينَة طباعة أوفست دوّارة أربعة ألوان (مَاكِينَة طبع

press (rotary offset machine, web-offset press) [diagram] أوفست شريطي) [رسم تخطيطي]

19 reel stand حامل لفّة الورَق

20 side margin control (margin control, side control, side lay control) آلية التحكم فى الهامشَيْن الجانبيين

21 inking rollers (ink rollers, inkers) أسْطُوانات التحبير (الحبّارات)

22 ink duct (ink fountain) المحبرة (كلمَاية)

23 damping rollers (dampening rollers, dampers, dampeners) أسْطُوانات الترطيب

24 blanket cylinder طُنْبُور الوسيط المطاطي الناقل (البلانكات)

25 plate cylinder طُنْبُور السَّطْح الطِّبَاعي

26 route of the paper (of the web) مَسَار الورَق/شريط الورَق

27 drier وَحْدَة التجفيف

28 chilling rolls (cooling rollers, chill rollers) أسْطُوانات تبريد

29 folder (folder unit) مَاكِينَة الطيّ (تطبيق الورَق)

30 four-colour (*Am.* four-color) sheet-fed offset machine (offset press) [diagram] مَاكِينَة طبع أوفست أربعة ألوان بأفرُخ [رسم تخطيطي]

31 sheet feeder (feeder) مُغَذّي أوتوماتي بأفْرُخ الورَق

32 feed table (feed board) لَوْحَة تلقيم أفرخ الورَق

33 route of the sheets through swing-grippers to the feed drum مَسَار الورَق عَبْر قوابض أرجوحيَّة إلى طُنْبُور الإلقام

34 feed drum طُنْبُور الإلقام بالورَق

35 impression cylinder طُنْبُور الطبعة/ضاغط (أسطوانة الكَبْسَة)

36 transfer drums (transfer cylinders) الطُنْبُور الناقِل

37 blanket cylinder طُنْبُور البلانكت

38 plate cylinder طُنْبُور السَّطْح الطِّبَاعي

39 damping unit (dampening unit) وَحْدَة الترطيب

40 inking unit (inker unit) وَحْدَة التحبير

41 printing unit وَحْدَة الطبع

42 delivery cylinder أسْطُوانة سحب الأفْرُخ المطبوعة

43 chain delivery سَحْب الأفْرُخ المطبوعة

44 delivery pile رَصَّة الأفْرُخ المطبوعة

45 delivery unit (delivery mechanism) وَحْدَة سحب الأفْرُخ المطبوعة

46 single-colour (*Am.* single-color) offset press (offset machine) مَاكِينَة طبع أوفست لون واحد

47 pile of paper (sheets, printing paper) رَصَّة الورَق الأبيض

48 sheet feeder (feeder), an automatic pile feeder مُغَذّي أوتوماتي لأفرخ الورَق

49 feed table (feed board) طاولة تلقيم المَاكِينَة بأفرخ الورَق

50 inking rollers (ink rollers, inkers) أسْطُوانات التحبير

51 inking unit (inker unit) وَحْدَة التحبير

52 damping rollers (dampening rollers, dampers, dampeners) أسْطُوانات الترطيب

53 plate cylinder, a zinc plate طُنْبُور السَّطْح الطِّبَاعي

54 blanket cylinder, a steel cylinder with rubber blanket طُنْبُور الوسيط المطاطي الناقل (البلانكت)

55 pile delivery unit for the printed sheets لوحة سحب الأفْرُخ المطبوعة

56 gripper bar, a chain gripper عربة قمط بجنزير

57 pile of printed paper (printed sheets) رصَّة الورَق المطبوع (أفرخ مطبوعة)

58 guard for the V-belt (vee-belt) drive وقاء إدارة السير

59 single-colour (*Am.* single-color) offset press (offset machine) [diagram] مَاكِينَة طبع أوفست لون واحد [رسم تخطيطي]

60 inking unit (inker unit) with inking rollers (ink rollers, inkers) وَحْدَة التحبير ومعها أسْطُوانات التحبير

61 damping unit (dampening unit) with damping rollers (dampening rollers, dampers, dampeners) وَحْدَة الترطيب وأسْطُوانات الترطيب

62 plate cylinder طُنْبُور السَّطْح الطِّبَاعي

63 blanket cylinder طُنْبُور البلانكت

64 impression cylinder طُنْبُور الطبعة/ضاغط

65 delivery cylinders with grippers أسْطُوانات سحب الورَق المطبوع والبِنَس

66 drive wheel ترس الإدارة

67 feed table (feed board) طاولة تلقيم المَاكِينَة بأفرخ الورَق

68 sheet feeder (feeder) آليَّة تلقيم المَاكِينَة بأفرخ الورَق

69 pile of unprinted paper (blank paper, unprinted sheets, blank sheets) رَصَّة الورَق الأبيض غير المطبوع

70 small sheet-fed offset press مَاكِينَة طبع أوفست بأفرخ صغيرة

71 inking unit (inker unit) وَحْدَة التحبير

72 suction feeder آليَّة تلقيم شفَّاطة

73 pile feeder آليَّة تلقيم أفرخ الورَق

74 instrument panel (control panel) with counter, pressure gauge (*Am.* gage), air regulator, and control switch for the sheet feeder (feeder) لَوْحَة التحكم وبها العدَّاد ومقْيَاس الضغط ومُنَظِّم الهواء ومفْتَاح التشغيل الخاصة بآليَّة التلقيم

75 flat-bed offset press (offset machine) ('Mailänder' proofing مَاكِينَة طبع تجارب أوفست ذات نحاسة مسَطّحة

press, proof press)

76 inking unit (inker unit) وَحْدَة التحبير

77 inking rollers (ink rollers, inkers) أَسْطُوَانات التحبير

78 bed (press bed, type bed, forme bed, *Am.* form bed) قاعدة السَّطْح الطِّبَاعي (النحاسة)

79 cylinder with rubber blanket طُنْبُور بوسيط مطاطي ناقل (بلانكت)

80 starting and stopping lever for the printing unit ذراع تشغيل وَحْدَة الطباعة

81 impression-setting wheel (impression-adjusting wheel) عجلة تنظيم الضغط

181 Letterpress Printing طَرِيقَة طِبَاعَة الحُرُوف (الطِباعَة البارِزَة)

1-65 presses (machines) **for letterpress printing** (letterpress printing machines) **ماكينات طباعة الحروف** (الطِّبَاعَة البَارِزَة)

1 two-revolution flat-bed cylinder press مَاكِينَة طباعة بقاعدة مُسَطحة ذات دورتَيْن

2 impression cylinder أَسْطُوَانة الكَبْسَة

3 lever for raising or lowering the cylinder ذراع رفع وخفض الأُسْطُوَانة

4 feed table (feed board)

5 automatic sheet feeder (feeder) [operated by vacuum and air blasts] طاولة التغذية بالوَرَق وَحْدَة تلقيم الوَرَق آلياً (مُغَذِّي أوتوماتي لأفرخ الوَرَق)

6 air pump for the feeder and delivery مِضَخَّة هوائيَّة لتشغيل وَحْدَة تلقيم وسحب الوَرَق

7 inking unit (inker unit) with distributing rollers (distributor rollers, distributors) and forme rollers (*Am.* form rollers) وَحْدَة التحبير أَسْطُوَانات توزيع الحبر والنحاسة

8 ink slab (ink plate) inking unit (inker unit) وَحْدَة التحبير

9 delivery pile for printed paper رَصَّة الوَرَق المطبوع

10 sprayer (anti set-off apparatus, anti set-off spray) for dusting the printed sheets رَشَّاش لتعفير الأفرخ المطبوعة

11 interleaving device جِهَاز الأفرخ البَيْنِيَّة

12 foot pedal for starting and stopping the press دَوَّاسة القدم لتشغيل وإيقاف المَاكِينَة

13 platen press (platen machine, platen) [in section] مَاكِينَة طبع بكَابِسَة مُسَطْحة [مقطع]

14 paper feed and delivery (paper feeding and delivery unit) وَحْدَة تغذية المَاكِينَة بالوَرَق وسَحْبِه بعد الطباعة

15 platen الكَبْسَة

16 toggle action (toggle-joint action) اتجاه الكَبْسَة ذهاباً وجيئة (فعل مفصلي)

17 bed (type bed, press bed, forme bed, *Am.* form bed) النحاسة (مكان الفورمة)

18 forme rollers (*Am.* form rollers) (forme-inking, *Am.* form-inking, rollers) أَسْطُوَانات تحبير النحاسة (شلندرات الفورمة)

19 inking unit (inker unit) for distributing the ink (printing ink) وَحْدَة التحبير الخاصة بتوزيع حبر الطباعة

20 stop-cylinder press (stop-cylinder machine) مَاكِينَة طبع بأُسْطُوَانة إيقاف

21 feed table (feed board) طاولة تغذية المَاكِينَة بالوَرَق

22 feeder mechanism (feeding apparatus, feeder) آليَّة تغذية المَاكِينَة بالوَرَق

23 pile of unprinted paper (blank paper, unprinted sheets, blank sheets) رَصَّة الوَرَق الأبيض (غير المطبوع)

24 guard for the sheet feeder (feeder) وقاء آليَّة التغذية بالوَرَق

25 pile of printed paper (printed sheets) رَصَّة الوَرَق المطبوع

26 control mechanism آليَّة التشغيل

27 forme rollers (*Am.* form rollers) (forme-inking, *Am.* form-inking, rollers) أَسْطُوَانات تحبير النحاسة (شلندرات الفورمة)

28 inking unit (inker unit) وَحْدَة التحبير

29 [Heidelberg] platen press (platen machine, platen) مَاكِينَة طباعة هايْدِلْبِرْج بكَابِسَة مُسَطْحة

30 feed table (feed board) with pile of unprinted paper (blank paper, unprinted sheets, blank sheets) طاولة تغذية المَاكِينَة بالوَرَق وعليها رصَّة وَرَق أبيض غير مطبوع

31 delivery table طاولة سحب الوَرَق

32 starting and stopping lever ذراع التشغيل والإيقاف

33 delivery blower نافخ سحب الوَرَق

34 spray gun (sprayer) رَشَّاش

35 air pump for vacuum and air blasts مِضَخَّة هوائيَّة لدفع الهواء

36 locked-up forme (*Am.* form) فورمة مربوطة في طَوْق (شاسيه)

37 type (type matter, matter) الصفحات المجموعة

38 chase الشاسيه

39 quoin قُفْل ربط الصفحات فى الطَّوْق (سِحلِيَّة)

40 length of furniture مواد مالئة (تواضيب ورَقائق)

41 rotary letterpress press (rotary letterpress machine, web-fed مَاكِينَة طبع الجرائد حتى 16 صَفْحَة (مَاكِينَة طباعة حروف دَوَّارة)

letterpress machine) for newspapers of up to 16 pages

42 slitters for dividing the width of the web	أسْطُوَانات لقَطْع أو شق شريط الوَرَق طولياً
43 web	شريط الوَرَق
44 impression cylinder	طُنْبُور الطبعة/ضاغط
45 jockey roller (compensating roller, compensator, tension roller)	أسْطُوَانة شد شريط الوَرَق
46 roll of paper	لفَّة (بوبينة) الوَرَق
47 automatic brake	كابِحة (فرملة) ذاتيَّة للفة الوَرَق
48 first printing unit	عجلة ضبط الكَبْسَة الطِّبَاعية الأولى
49 perfecting unit	عجلة ضبط الطبع على الوجهَيْن
50 inking unit (inker unit)	وَحْدَة التحبير
51 plate cylinder	طُنْبُور السَّطْح الطِّبَاعي (طُنْبُور الفورمة)
52 second printing unit	طُنْبُور طبع اللون الثاني
53 former	وَحْدَة تسليم شريط الوَرَق المطبوع إلى جِهَاز الطَّيّ
54 tachometer with sheet counter	تاكومتر وعدَّاد النُّسَخ المطلوبة
55 folder (folder unit)	جِهَاز الطَّيّ
56 folded newspaper	جرائد مَطْويَّة (مطبَّقة)
57 inking unit (inker unit) for the rotary press (web-fed press) [in section]	وَحْدَة التحبير فى مَاكِينَة الطبع الدوَّارة
58 web	شريط الوَرَق
59 impression cylinder	طُنْبُور الطبعة/ضاغط
60 plate cylinder	طُنْبُور السَّطْح الطِّبَاعي
61 forme rollers (*Am.* form rollers) (forme-inking, *Am.* form-inking, rollers)	أسْطُوَانات الفورمة (شلندرات الفورمة)
62 distributing rollers (distributor rollers, distributors)	أسْطُوَانات توزيع الحبر
63 lifter roller (ductor, ductor roller)	أسْطُوَانات تحبير الناقلة
64 duct roller (fountain roller, ink fountain roller)	أسْطُوَانة المَحْبَرَة (شلندر الكلماية)
65 ink duct (ink fountain)	المَحْبَرَة

182 Photogravure (Gravure Printing, Intaglio Printing) — الطِّبَاعَة بالحَفْر الضَّوْئي

1 exposure of the carbon tissue (pigment paper)	تعريض الوَرَق المُصَبَّغ (النسيج الكربوني) للضوء
2 vacuum frame	إطار طبع بالتفريغ
3 exposing lamp, a bank of quartz-halogen lamps	لَمْبات الضوء، صَفٌّ من مصابيح كوارتز–هالوجين
4 point source lamp	مِصْبَاح مصدري
5 heat extractor	جِهَاز طرد الحرارة
6 carbon tissue transfer machine (laydown machine, laying machine)	مَاكِينَة ناقلة للوَرَق المُصَبَّغ
7 polished copper cylinder	أسْطُوَانة نحاسيَّة مصقولة
8 rubber roller for pressing on the printed carbon tissue (pigment paper)	طُنْبُور مطاطي للضغط على الوَرَق المصبَّغ المطبوع
9 cylinder-processing machine	مَاكِينَة طبع بطُنْبُور ضاغط
10 gravure cylinder coated with carbon tissue (pigment paper)	طُنْبُور طبع غائر مُغَطَّى بطبقة من الوَرَق المُصَبَّغ
11 developing tank	حَوْض الإظْهار
12 staging	مرحلة
13 developed cylinder	أسْطُوَانة مُظَهَّرة
14 retoucher painting out (stopping out)	عامِل التهذيب يقوم بعمل الرُّتُوش
15 etching machine	مَاكِينَة حَفْر
16 etching tank with etching solution (etchant, mordant)	حَوْض حَفْر به محلول الحَفْر
17 printed gravure cylinder	أسْطُوَانة طبع غائر مطبوعة
18 gravure etcher	عامِل مَاكِينَة طبع من سَطْح غائر
19 calculator dial	قُرْص حاسِب
20 timer	جِهَاز توقيت
21 revising (correcting) the cylinder	تصحيح الأُسْطُوَانة
22 etched gravure cylinder	أسْطُوَانة طبع غائر مَحْفُورَة
23 ledge	رَفّ
24 multicolour (*Am.* multicolor) rotogravure press	مَاكِينَة طبع غائر شريطي متعددة الألوان (مَاكِينَة الفوتوغرافيور)
25 exhaust pipe for solvent fumes	ماسورة تصريف أبْخِرَة المُذيبات المتطايرة
26 reversible printing unit	وَحْدَة طباعة يمين ويسار
27 folder (folder unit)	جِهَاز الطَّيّ
28 control desk	مِنْضَدَة التشغيل والتحكم
29 newspaper delivery unit	وَحْدَة سحب الجرائد
30 conveyor belt (conveyor)	سَيْر ناقِل
31 bundled stack of newspapers	رَصَّة من الجرائد

183 Bookbinding I — تَجْلِيد الكُتُب (1)

1-35 hand bookbindery (hand bindery) — **تَجْلِيد الكُتُب يدوياً**

1 gilding the spine of the book	تذهيب كَعْب الكِتَاب
2 gold finisher (gilder), a bookbinder	عامِل التذهيب
3 fillet	شَرِيط
4 holding press (finishing press)	مِكْبَس تثبيت
5 gold leaf	وَرَقة ذهب

6 gold cushion — مِسْنَد تقطيع وَرَق الذهب
7 gold knife — سكين تقطيع وَرَق الذهب
8 sewing (stitching) — خِيَاطة المَلازم
9 sewing frame — إطار خياطة المَلازِم (الشَّدَّة) يدوياً
10 sewing cord — دُوبَارَة (خيط) خِيَاطة
11 ball of thread (sewing thread) — بكَرَة خَيْط
12 section (signature) — مَلْزَمَة من الكِتَاب مُعَدَّة للخياطة
13 bookbinder's knife — سكين المُجَلِّد
14 gluing the spine — تَغْرِيَة كَعْب الكِتَاب
15 glue pot — إناء الغراء
16 board cutter (guillotine) — سكينة كرتون (مقص كرتون)
17 back gauge (*Am.* gage) — مُحَدِّد قياس القص (زاوية خلفية)
18 clamp with foot pedal — قامطة تعمل بدَوَّاسة
19 cutting blade — نَصْل سكين القَطْع
20 standing press, a nipping press — مَاكِينَة قمط المَلازِم القائمة
21 head piece (head beam) — كتلة الرَّأْس
22 spindle — مِحْوَر دَوَرَان
23 handwheel — دولاب يدوي
24 platen — كَابِسَة مُسَطَّحة
25 bed (base) — قاعدة
26 gilding (gold blocking) and embossing press, a hand-lever press; *sim.:* toggle-joint press (toggle-lever press) — مَاكِينَة تذهيب وبَصْم بارِز
27 heating box — صندوق التسخين
28 sliding plate — لَوْح مُنْزَلِق
29 embossing platen — لَوْح البَصْم البارز
30 toggle action (toggle-joint action) — اتجاه الكَبْسَة ذهَاباً وجيئة
31 hand lever — ذِرَاع يَدَوِيّ
32 book sewn on gauze (mull, scrim) (book block) — كِتَاب مَخِيط على الشاشَة (كِتَاب غير مُجَلَّد)
33 gauze (mull, scrim) — شاش
34 sewing (stitching) — خِيَاطَة
35 headband — شريط الرَّأْس (حَبكَة الرَّأْس)

184 Bookbinding II — تَجْلِيد الكُتُب (2)

1-23 bookbinding machines — ماكينات تَجْلِيد الكُتُب
1 adhesive binder (perfect binder) for short runs — مَاكِينَة تَجْلِيد بالبلاستيك (مَاكِينَة تَجْلِيد كامل)
2 manual feed station — وَحْدَة التلقيم اليدوي
3 cutoff knife and roughing station — سكين القطع ووَحْدَة التجهيز الأَوَّلِي
4 gluing mechanism — آلِيَّة التغرية
5 delivery (book delivery) — سحب الكِتَاب
6 case maker (case-making machine) — مَاكِينَة صنع الأَغْلِفَة (الجِلْدَات)
7 board feed hoppers — صناديق التلقيم بالكرتون
8 pick-up suckers — شَفَّاطات الكرتون
9 glue tank — حلَّة الغراء (حلَّة)
10 cover cylinder — أسْطُوَانة تغرية
11 picker head — رَأْس اللاقط بجِهَاز الشفط
12 feed table for covering materials [linen, paper, leather] — طاولة التغذية بمَوَاد التغليف [كتان، ورق، جلد]
13 pressing mechanism — آلِيَّة الكبس
14 delivery table — لَوْحَة استقبال الأغلفة الجاهزة
15 gang stitcher (gathering and wire-stitching machine, gatherer and wire stitcher) — مَاكِينَة تجميع وتدبيس (خزم) المَلازِم
16 sheet feeder (sheet-feeding station) — مَحَطَّة التلقيم
17 folder-feeding station — مَحَطَّة تلقيم جِهَاز الطَّيّ
18 stitching wire feed mechanism — آلِيَّة التدبيس (رؤوس التدبيس، الخَزَّام)
19 delivery table — طاولة استقبال المَلازِم المُدَبَّسَة
20 rotary board cutter (rotary board-cutting machine) — مَاكِينَة قَطْع أفرخ دَوَّارة
21 feed table with cut-out section — طاولة التغذية بأفرخ الوَرَق
22 rotary cutter — مقص دَوَّار
23 feed guide — دليل التغذية

185 Bookbinding III — تَجْلِيد الكُتُب (3)

1-35 bookbinding machines — ماكينات تَجْلِيد الكُتُب
1 guillotine (guillotine cutter, automatic guillotine cutter) — مِقَصّ جيلوتين لقَطْع الوَرَق
2 control panel — لَوْحَة التشغيل والتحكم
3 clamp — كَمَرَة قَمْط
4 back gauge (*Am.* gage) — مُحَدِّد قياس القص (زاوية خلفية)
5 calibrated pressure adjustment [to clamp] — مِقْيَاس (عيار) ضغط القامطة
6 illuminated cutting scale — مِقْيَاس قص مُضَاء
7 single-hand control for the back gauge (*Am.* gage) — مِقْبَض ضبط الزاوية الخلفيَّة
8 combined buckle and knife folding machine (combined buckle and knife folder) — مَاكِينَة طَيّ (مَاكِينَة تطبيق)
9 feed table (feed board) — طاولة تلقيم الأفرخ
10 fold plates — شبابيك الطَّيّ
11 stop for making the buckle fold — مِسْطَرَة لضبط عيار الطَّيَّة الأُولى
12 cross fold knives — أسلحة الطَّيَّة العَرْضِيَّة (المتعامدة)
13 belt delivery for parallel-folded — وَحْدَة استقبال المَلازِم المَطْوِيَّة بطيات متوازية

signatures
14 third cross fold unit — وَحْدَة الطَّيَّة الثالثة (طية عَرْضِيَّة)
15 delivery tray for cross-folded signatures — صندوق استقبال المَلازم المطوية بطيَّات عَرْضِيَّة (متعامدة)
16 sewing machine (book-sewing machine) — مَاكِينَة خِيَاطة
17 spool holder — حامِل بكَرَات الخَيْط
18 thread cop (thread spool) — بكَرَة خَيْط مخروطيَّة الشكل
19 gauze roll holder (mull roll holder, scrim roll holder) — حامِل بكَرَة الشاش (حامِل بكَرَة من نسيج شفاف)
20 gauze (mull, scrim) — شاش أو نسيج شفاف لدعم كعب الكتَاب
21 needle cylinders with sewing needles — مَسَّاكات إبَر الخِيَاطة
22 sewn book — كتَاب بمَلازم مَخِيطة
23 delivery — صينية رَصّ الكتب المَخِيطة
24 reciprocating saddle — حامِل (حصان) التلقيم بالمَلازم
25 sheet feeder (feeder) — آليَّة التلقيم
26 feed hopper — كرتون التغذية
27 casing-in machine — مَاكِينَة تلبيس النُّسْخَة
28 joint and side pasting attachment — آليَّة التغرية
29 blade — سلاح لحَمْل الكتَاب
30 preheater unit — وَحْدَة التسخين الأَوَّلي
31 gluing machine for whole-surface, stencil, edge, and strip gluing — مَاكِينَة تصميغ السطح بالكامل والاستنسل والحافة والشرائط
32 glue tank — خَزَّان الصمغ
33 glue roller — أسْطُوَانة التصميغ
34 feed table — طاولة التغذية
35 delivery — طاولة استقبال
36 book — كتَاب
37 dust jacket (dust cover, book jacket, wrapper), a publisher's wrapper — سُتْرَة الكتَاب (جاكت)
38 jacket flap — لِسَان السترة/الجاكت
39 blurb — تعريف بالكِتَاب (تنويه)
40-42 binding — **التغليف**
40 cover (book cover, case) — غِلاف/جِلْدَة الكتَاب
41 spine (backbone, back) — كَعْب الكتَاب
42 tailband (footband) — حَبْكَة ذَيْل كَعْب الكتَاب
43-47 preliminary matter (prelims, front matter) — **المادة التمهيديَّة**
43 half-title — صَفْحَة العُنْوَان المختصر للكتَاب
44 half-title (bastard title, fly title) — عُنْوَان مختصر للكِتَاب
45 title page — صَفْحَة عُنْوَان الكتَاب (العُنْوَان الداخلي)
46 full title (main title) — العُنْوَان الرئيسي للكتَاب
47 subtitle — عُنْوَان ثانوي
48 publisher's imprint (imprint) — شِعَار النَّاشِر
49 fly leaf (endpaper, endleaf) — بِطَانَة الكِتَاب
50 handwritten dedication — إهداء بخَطّ اليد
51 bookplate (ex libris) — بطاقة مِلْكِيَّة الكِتَاب
52 open book — كتَاب مفتوح
53 page — صَفْحَة مطبوعة
54 fold — طَيَّة (ثنية)
55-58 margin — **الهامش**
55 back margin (inside margin, gutter) — هامِش داخلي
56 head margin (upper margin) — هامش علوي (هامِش الرَّأْس)
57 fore edge margin (outside margin, fore edge) — هامِش خارجي (جانبي)
58 tail margin (foot margin, tail, foot) — هامِش سفلي (هامِش الذيل)
59 type area — منطقة جَمْع (النص)
60 chapter heading — عُنْوَان الفَصْل أو الباب
61 asterisk — نجمة أو علامة إحالة إلى مَرْجع
62 footnote — ملاحظة أو حاشِيَة بهامِش الذيل
63 page number — رَقْم الصَّفْحَة
64 double-column page — جَمْع على عَمُودَيْن
65 column — عَمُود جَمْع
66 running title (running head) — عُنْوَان مُتكَرِّر (سيَّار)
67 caption — عُنْوَان متكرر ثانوي
68 marginal note (side note) — ملاحظة فى الهامش الخارجي (الجانبي)
69 signature (signature code) — علامة تسلسل المَلْزَمَة
70 attached bookmark (attached bookmarker) — شريط لتحديد الصَّفْحَة في الكتَاب
71 loose bookmark (loose bookmarker) — جُذَاذة لتحديد الصَّفْحَة فى الكِتَاب

186 Horse-drawn Carriages — عَرَبات تَجُرُّهَا الجِيَاد

1-54 carriages (horse-drawn vehicles) — **عَرَبات** (عَرَبَات تَجُرُّهَا الجِيَاد)
1-3, 26-39, 45, 51-54 carriages and coaches (coach wagons) — عَرَبَات وحافِلات
1 berlin — عَرَبَة البَرْلِينَة
2 wagonette; larger: brake (break) — عَرَبَة خفيفة (الأكبر حجما: البَرِيكَة)
3 coupé; *sim.:* brougham — عَرَبَة الكُوبيه (البرُهَام)
4 front wheel — عَجَلَة أماميَّة
5 coach body — جِسْم الحافِلَة (العَرَبَة)
6 dashboard (splash-board) — الحاجِبَة (وقاء من الماء والوَحْل)
7 footboard — مِسْنَد قَدَمَيّ الحَوْذِي
8 coach box (box, coachman's seat, driver's seat) — مَقْعَد الحَوْذِي
9 lamp (lantern) — مِصْبَاح (فانُوس)
10 window — نافذة
11 door (coach door) — باب الحافِلة

12 door handle (handle) مِقْبَض الباب
13 footboard (carriage step, coach step, step, footpiece) مَوْطِئ العَرَبَة
14 fixed top سَقْف ثابت
15 spring نابِض، سوستة
16 brake (brake block) مكبح، فرملة
17 back wheel (rear wheel) عَجَلَة خلفيَّة
18 dogcart, a one-horse carriage عَرَبَة الكَلْبيَّة
19 shafts (thills, poles) عَرِيش العَرَبَة
20 lackey (lacquey, footman) خادِم يرتدي بَزَّة خاصة (المُبَزَّز)
21 livery بزَّة الخادِم
22 braided (gallooned) collar ياقَة مُزَرْكَشَة
23 braided (gallooned) coat مِعْطَف مُزَرْكَش
24 braided (gallooned) sleeve كُمٌّ مُزَرْكَش
25 top hat قُبَّعَة مرتفعة
26 hackney carriage (hackney coach, cab, growler, *Am.* hack) عَرَبَة أُجْرَة
27 stableman (groom) عامِل الإسْطَبْل
28 coach horse (carriage horse, cab horse, thill horse, thiller) حصان جَرّ العَرَبَة
29 hansom cab (hansom), a cabriolet, a one-horse chaise (one-horse carriage) عَرَبَة الهَنْسُوميَّة، عَرَبَة يَجُرُّها حصان واحد
30 shafts (thills, poles) عَرِيش العَرَبَة
31 reins (rein, *Am.* line) العَنان (اللِجام)
32 coachman (driver) with inverness سائق العَرَبَة يَرْتَدي الأنفرْناسِيَّة
33 covered char-a-banc (brake, break), a pleasure vehicle أوتوبوس (للتنزه والتَّجَوُّل)
34 gig (chaise) عَرَبَة خفيفة يَجُرُّها حصان واحد (عربة الشِّيز)
35 barouche عَرَبَة البَرُوشَة
36 landau, a two-horse carriage; *sim.:* landaulet, landaulette عَرَبَة اللَنْدَويَّة
37 omnibus (horse-drawn omnibus) عَرَبَة الأومْنِيبُوس
38 phaeton عَرَبَة الفَيْتُون
39 Continental stage-coach (mailcoach, diligence); *also:* road coach مَرْكَبَة جياد عموميَّة للسفر
40 mailcoach driver حَوْذي عَرَبَة البريد
41 posthorn بُوق البريد
42 hood غِطاء العَرَبَة
43 post horses (relay horses, relays) جياد عَرَبَة البريد
44 tilbury التِلْبَريَّة
45 troika (Russian three-horse carriage) عَرَبَة التَرْيُوكَة (عَرَبَة روسيَّة يَجُرُّها ثلاثة جياد)
46 leader (wheel horse, pole horse) الجواد المُقَدَّم
47 wheeler (wheel horse, pole horse) جواد العَجَلَة
48 English buggy عَرَبَة البُوجيَّة الإنجليزيَّة
49 American buggy عَرَبَة البُوجيَّة الأمريكيَّة
50 tandem عَرَبَة التَنْدَم
51 vis-à-vis عَرَبَة مقاعدها متقابِلة
52 collapsible hood (collapsible top) سَقْف مُتَحَرِّك
53 mailcoach (English stagecoach) عَرَبَة البريد
54 covered (closed) chaise عَرَبَة شِيز مُغَطَّاة

187 Bicycle الدَّرَّاجَة الهَوَائيَّة

1 bicycle (cycle, *coll.* bike, *Am.* wheel), a gent's bicycle, a touring bicycle (touring cycle, roadster) الدَّرَّاجَة الهَوائيَّة
2 handlebar (handlebars), a touring cycle handlebar مِقْوَد الدَّرَّاجَة
3 handlebar grip (handgrip, grip) قبضة مِقْوَد الدَّرَّاجَة
4 bicycle bell جَرَس الدَّرَّاجَة
5 hand brake (front brake), a rim brake فرملة يدويَّة، فرملة أماميَّة
6 lamp bracket حامِل المِصْبَاح
7 headlamp (bicycle lamp) مِصْبَاح الدَّرَّاجَة الأمامي
8 dynamo المُوَلِّد (الدينامو)
9 pulley بَكَرَة
10-12 front forks **الشُّعَبَات الأماميَّة**
10 handlebar stem عمود مِقْوَد الدَّرَّاجَة
11 steering head رأس التَّوْجِيه
12 fork blades (fork ends) أطراف الشُّعْبَة
13 front mudguard (*Am.* front fender) وقاء الوَحْل الأماميّ
14-20 bicycle frame **إطار (جسم) الدَّرَّاجَة**
14 steering tube (fork column) أنبوب التَّوْجِيه (عمود الشُّعْبَة)
15 head badge علامة أماميَّة
16 crossbar (top tube) قضيب مُسْتَعْرَض
17 down tube أنبوب نازل
18 seat tube أنبوب المَقْعَد
19 seat stays دعامتا حَمْل المَقْعَد
20 chain stays دعامتا السِّلْسِلَة
21 child's seat (child carrier seat) مَقْعَد لحَمْل طفل
22 bicycle saddle سَرْج (مَقْعَد) الدَّرَّاجَة
23 saddle springs نَوَابِض سَرْج (مَقْعَد) الدَّرَّاجَة
24 seat pillar عمود المَقْعَد
25 tool bag صندوق الأدوات
26-32 wheel (front wheel) **العَجَلَة** (العَجَلَة الأماميَّة)
26 hub قُبُّ العَجَلَة

27 spoke	شُعاع العَجَلَة
28 rim (wheel rim)	الحافة (حافة العَجَلَة)
29 spoke nipple (spoke flange, spoke end)	طَرْف الشُّعاع
30 tyre (*Am.* tire) (pneumatic tyre, high-pressure tyre); *inside:* tube (inner tube), *outside:* tyre (outer case, cover)	الإطار(إطار مملوء بالهواء المضغوط) (من الداخل: أنبوب، من الخارج: غِلاف من المطّاط)
31 valve, a tube valve with valve tube or a patent valve with ball	بَلْف، صِمام
32 valve sealing cap	غطاء إحكام البَلْف
33 bicycle speedometer with milometer	عدّاد سُرْعَة الدَّرَّاجَة وعدّاد المسافة
34 kick stand (prop stand)	مِسْنَد للدَّرَّاجَة
35-42 bicycle drive (chain drive)	**إدارة** (سِلْسِلَة/جِنْزير دفع) **الدَّرَّاجَة**
35-39 chain transmission	**نقل الحركة بالسِّلْسِلَة/بالجنْزير**
35 chain wheel	عَجَلَة السِّلْسِلَة/الجِنْزير
36 chain, a roller chain	سِلْسِلَة(جِنْزير)
37 chain guard	وِقاء السِّلْسِلَة/الجِنْزير
38 sprocket wheel (sprocket)	قرص مُسَنَّن
39 wing nut (fly nut, butterfly nut)	صامُولة مُجَنَّحَة
40 pedal	دَوّاسَة (بَدّال)
41 crank	ذِراع تدوير
42 bottom bracket bearing	مَحْمَل الكتيفة السفليّ
43 rear mudguard (*Am.* rear fender)	وِقاء الوَحْل الخلفيّ
44 luggage carrier (carrier)	مِسْنَد الأمْتِعَة (حامل)
45 reflector	عاكِس للضوء
46 rear light (rear lamp)	مِصْبَاح خلفيّ
47 footrest	مِسْنَد القَدَم
48 bicycle pump	مِنفاخ الدَّرَّاجَة
49 bicycle lock, a wheel lock	قُفْل عَجَلَة الدَّرَّاجَة
50 patent key	مِفْتاح مُسَطَّح
51 cycle serial number (factory number, frame number)	رَقَم مسلسل الدَّرَّاجَة
52 front hub (front hub assembly)	مجموعة القُبِّ الأماميّ
53 wheel nut	صامُولة تثبيت العَجَلَة
54 locknut (locking nut)	صامُولة زَنْق
55 washer (slotted cone adjusting washer)	وردة/حلقة لإحكام الربط
56 ball bearing	مَحْمَل كُرَيّات
57 dust cap	غِطاء واقٍ من الأتْرِبَة
58 cone (adjusting cone)	مخروط
59 centre (*Am.* center) hub	القُبُّ المركزيّ
60 spindle	مِحْوَر دَوَران
61 axle	مِحْوَر
62 clip covering lubrication hole (lubricator)	مشبك تغطية المِشْحَمة
63 free-wheel hub with back-pedal brake (with coaster brake)	قُبّ دولاب حُرّ ذو فرملة بدَوّاسَة خلفيَّة
64 safety nut	صامُولة أمان
65 lubricator	مِشْحَمَة
66 brake arm	ذِراع الفرملة
67 brake arm cone	مَخْرُوط ذِراع الفرملة
68 bearing cup with ball bearings in ball race	حُقّ المَحْمَل وبه حامِل كُرَيّات في مَدْرَجَة كُرَيّات
69 hub shell (hub body, hub barrel)	غِلاف القُبّ
70 brake casing	صندوق الفرملة
71 brake cone	مَخْرُوط الفرملة
72 driver	أداة تدوير/دفع
73 driving barrel	أسطوانة الدَّفْع
74 sprocket	قُرْص مُسَنَّن
75 thread head	رأس سن اللَوْلَب
76 axle	مِحْوَر
77 bracket	كتيفة
78 bicycle pedal (pedal, reflector pedal)	دَوّاسَة (بَدّال) الدَّرَّاجَة
79 cup	حُقّ
80 spindle	مِحْوَر دَوَران
81 axle	مِحْوَر
82 dust cap	غِطاء واقٍ من الأتْرِبَة
83 pedal frame	إطار الدَّوّاسَة
84 rubber stud	وَتَد مطّاطيّ
85 rubber block (rubber tread)	كتلة مطّاطيَّة
86 glass reflector	عاكِس زُجاجيّ

188 Motorcycles, Bicycles, Scooters, Mopeds / الدَّرّاجات الناريَّة، الدراجات الهوائية، الدَّرّاجات الناريَّة الخَفيفَة

1 folding bicycle	دَرّاجَة قابلة للطَّيّ
2 hinge (*also:* locking lever)	مِفْصَلَة التوصيل
3 adjustable handlebar (handlebars)	مِقْوَد قابل للتعديل
4 adjustable saddle	سَرْج (مَقْعَد) قابل للتعديل
5 stabilizers	عَجَلات تثبيت للتوازن
6 motor-assisted bicycle	دَرّاجة بمُحَرِّك مُساعِد
7 air-cooled two-stroke engine	مُحَرِّك تبريد هواء ثنائي الأشواط
8 telescopic forks	شَوْكات تليسكوبيَّة
9 tubular frame	إطار أنبوبي
10 fuel tank (petrol tank, *Am.* gasoline tank)	خَزّان الوَقُود
11 semi-rise handlebars	مِقْوَد شِبْه قائم
12 two-speed gear-change (gearshift)	آليَّة نقل تروس ذات سرعَتَيْن
13 high-back polo saddle	سَرْج طراز "بولو" بظَهْر مرتفع
14 swinging-arm rear fork	شَوْكَة خلفيَّة بذراع تأرْجُحيّ
15 upswept exhaust	ماسورة عادِم مُصَعَّدَة
16 heat shield	غطاء واقٍ من الحرارة
17 drive chain	جِنْزِير الدفع/الإدارة
18 crash bar (roll bar)	الصَّدّاد (وِقاء السقوط)

19 speedometer (*coll.* speedo)	عَدَّاد السرعة
20 battery-powered moped, an electrically-powered vehicle	دَرَّاجَة تعمل بالبطارية
21 swivel saddle	مَقْعَد دَوَّار
22 battery compartment	حُجَيْرَة البطارية
23 wire basket	سَلَّة سِلْكِيَّة
24 touring motor (moped)	دَرَّاجَة بِمُحَرِّك صغير للتنزه
25 pedal crank (pedal drive, starter pedal)	دَوَّاسَة بدء التشغيل
26 single-cylinder two-stroke engine	مُحَرِّك ثنائيّ الأشواط ذو أسطوانة واحدة
27 spark-plug cap	غطاء شَمْعَة الشَّرَر (غطاء البُوجيه)
28 fuel tank (petrol tank, *Am.* gasoline tank)	خَزَّان الوَقُود
29 moped headlamp (front lamp)	مِصْبَاح أماميّ
30-35 handlebar fittings	**تركيبات المِقْوَد**
30 twist grip throttle control (throttle twist grip)	مِقْبَض التحكم في صمام الاختناق
31 twist grip (gear-change, gearshift)	مِقْبَض تغيير السرعة
32 clutch lever	ذراع القابض
33 hand brake lever	ذراع الفرملة اليدويَّة
34 speedometer (*coll.* speedo)	عَدَّاد السرعة
35 rear-view mirror (mirror)	مِرْآة الرؤيَة الخلفيَّة
36 front wheel drum brake (drum brake)	الفرملة الأُسطوانية للعَجَلَة الأماميَّة
37 Bowden cables (brake cables)	كيبلات الفرملة
38 stop and tail light unit	وَحْدَة المصابيح الخلفيَّة ومِصْبَاح التَّوَقف
39 light motorcycle with kickstarter	دَرَّاجَة ناريَّة خفيفة بآليَّة بدء تشغيل تعمل بالقَدَم
40 housing for instruments with speedometer and electronic rev counter (revolution counter)	مَبِيت الآلات مع عَدَّاد السرعة وعَدَّاد اللفات الالكتروني
41 telescopic shock absorber	مُمْتَص صدمات تليسكوبيّ
42 twin seat	مَقْعَد مُزْدَوَج
43 kickstarter	آليَّة بدء التشغيل بالقَدَم
44 pillion footrest, a footrest	مِسْنَد قَدَمَيْن للرَّاكِب الخلفي
45 handlebar (handlebars)	مِقْوَد
46 chain guard	وقاء الجِنْزِير/السلسلة
47 motor scooter (scooter)	دَرَّاجَة "سكوتر" بِمُحَرِّك
48 removable side panel	لَوْح جانبيّ قابل للفصل
49 tubular frame	إطار أنبوبيّ
50 metal fairings	أسطح إنسيابية
51 prop stand (stand)	مِسْنَد الدَّرَّاجَة
52 foot brake	فرملة تعمل بالقدَم
53 horn (hooter)	بُوق
54 hook for handbag or briefcase	خَطَّاف لتعليق حقيبة يد أو حقيبة خفيفة
55 foot gear-change control (foot gearshift control)	آليَّة نقل السرعة بالقَدَم
56 high-riser; *sim.:* Chopper	دَرَّاجَة مرتفعة المِقْوَد
57 high-rise handlebar (handlebars)	مِقْوَد مرتفع
58 imitation motorcycle fork	شَوْكَة شبيهة بشَوْكَة الدَّرَّاجَة الناريَّة
59 banana saddle	سَرْج (مَقْعَد) على شكل مُوزة
60 chrome bracket	كتيفة من الكُرُوم

189 Motorcycle — الدَّرَّاجَة النَّاريَّة

1 lightweight motorcycle (light motorcycle) [50 cc]	دَرَّاجَة ناريَّة خفيفة الوزن [50 سى سى]
2 fuel tank (petrol tank, *Am.* gasoline tank)	خَزَّان الوَقُود
3 air-cooled single-cylinder four-stroke engine (with overhead camshaft)	مُحَرِّك تبريد هواء رباعيّ الأشواط ذو اسطوانة واحدة (مع عمود كامة عُلويّ)
4 carburettor (*Am.* carburetor)	المكربن
5 intake pipe	أنبوب السَّحْب
6 five-speed gearbox	صندوق تروس ذو خمس سرعات
7 swinging-arm rear fork	شَوْكَة خلفيَّة ذات ذراع تأرجحيّ
8 number plate (*Am.* license plate)	لَوْحَة الرَّقَم
9 stop and tail light (rear light)	المِصْبَاح الخلفيّ ومِصْبَاح التوقف (مِصْبَاح المُؤَخِّرَة)
10 headlight (headlamp)	المِصْبَاح الأماميّ
11 front drum brake	فرملة أُسْطوانيَّة أماميَّة
12 brake cable (brake line), a Bowden cable	كيبل الفرملة
13 rear drum brake	فرملة أُسْطوانيَّة خلفيَّة
14 racing-style twin seat	مَقْعَد مُزْدَوَج
15 upswept exhaust	ماسورة عادم مُصَعَّدة
16 scrambling motorcycle (cross-country motorcycle) [125 cc], a light motorcycle	دَرَّاجَة ناريَّة خفيفة للطُّرُق الوَعِرَة [125 سى سى]
17 lightweight cradle frame	إطار حامِل خفيف الوزن
18 number disc (disk)	لَوْحَة الرقم
19 solo seat	مَقْعَد مُفْرَد
20 cooling ribs	ضلوع التبريد
21 motorcycle stand	مِسْنَد الدَّرَّاجَة النَّاريَّة
22 motorcycle chain	جِنْزِير الدَّرَّاجَة النَّاريَّة
23 telescopic shock absorber	مُمْتَص صدمات تليسكوبي
24 spokes	شُعَاع العَجَلَة
25 rim (wheel rim)	حافة العَجَلَة
26 motorcycle tyre (*Am.* tire)	إطار الدَّرَّاجَة النَّاريَّة
27 tyre (*Am.* tire) tread	مَداس الإطار
28 gear-change lever (gear	ذِراع تغيير السرعات

shift lever)
29 twist grip throttle control (throttle twist grip) — مقبَض التحكم فى صِمام الاختناق
30 rear-view mirror (mirror) — مِرآة الرؤيَّة الخلفيَّة
31-58 heavy (heavy-weight, large-capacity) **motorcycles** — **دراجات ناريَّة ثقيلة** (كبيرة السِّعَة)
31 heavyweight motor-cycle with water-cooled engine — درّاجة ناريَّة ثقيلة ذات محرك تبريد ماء
32 front disc (disk) brake — فرملة قُرْصيَّة أماميَّة
33 disc (disk) brake calliper (caliper) — الآليَّة الفكيَّة للفرملة القرصيَّة
34 floating axle — محْوَر طافٍ
35 water cooler — مُبَرِّد ماء
36 fuel tank (petrol tank, *Am.* gasoline tank) — خزّان الوَقود
37 indicator (indicator light, turn indicator light) — ضَوْء إرشاديّ للانعطاف
38 kickstarter — آليَّة بدء التشغيل بالقَدَم
39 water-cooled engine — مُحَرِّك تبريد ماء
40 speedometer — عدّاد السرعة
41 rev counter (revolution counter) — عدّاد اللفَات
42 rear indicator (indicator light) — مِصْبَاح إرشادي خلفي
43 heavy (heavyweight, high-performance) machine with fairing [1000 cc] — ماكينة ثقيلة إنسيابيَّة السطح [1000 سى سى]
44 integrated streamlining, an integrated fairing — سطح إنسيابي متكامل
45 indicator (indicator light, turn indicator light) — ضَوْء إرشادي للانعطاف
46 anti-mist windscreen (*Am.* windshield) — حاجِب ريح مقاوِم للضباب
47 horizontally-opposed twin engine with cardan transmission — مُحَرِّك مزدوج متقابل أفقيا ذو ناقل حركة كرداني
48 light alloy wheel — عَجَلَة من سبيكة خفيفة الوَزْن
49 four-cylinder machine [400 cc] — ماكينة ذات أربع أسْطوانات [400 سى سى]
50 air-cooled four-cylinder four-stroke engine — مُحَرِّك تبريد هواء رباعي الأشواط ذو أربع أسْطوانات
51 four-pipe megaphone exhaust pipe — ماسورة عادِم بُوقيَّة ذات أربعة أنابيب
52 electric starter button — زِرّ بادئ التشغيل كهربياً
53 sidecar machine — ماكينة بعَرَبَة جانبيَّة
54 sidecar body — جسم العَرَبَة الجانبيَّة
55 sidecar crash bar — صَدّاد العَرَبَة الجانبيَّة (وقاء الاصطدام)
56 sidelight (*Am.* side-marker lamp) — مِصْبَاح اشارة جانبيّ
57 sidecar wheel — عَجَلَة العَرَبَة الجانبيَّة
58 sidecar windscreen (*Am.* windshield) — حاجِب ريح العَرَبَة الجانبيَّة

190 Internal Combustion Engines — مُحَرِّكات الاحتِرَاق الدّاخليّ

1 eight-cylinder V (vee) fuel-injection spark-ignition engine (Otto-cycle engine) — مُحَرِّك ذو 8 أسْطوانات مُرَتَّبة على شكل V يعمل بنظام حَقْن الوَقود وإشْعال الشَّرَر (مُحَرِّك دَوْرَة أوتو)
2 cross-section of spark-ignition engine (Otto-cycle internal combustion engine) — مقطع عرضي لمُحَرِّك يعمل بإشْعال الشَّرَر (مُحَرِّك الاحتِرَاق الدّاخليّ بدَوْرَة أوتو)
3 sectional view of five-cylinder in-line diesel engine — منظر مَقْطَعيّ لمُحَرِّك ديزل مستقيم ذو خمس أسْطوانَات
4 cross-section of diesel engine — مَقْطَع عرضيّ لمُحَرِّك الدِّيزل
5 two-rotor Wankel engine (rotary engine) — مُحَرِّك "فانكل" (مُحَرِّك دَوّار) ذو عُضْوَيْن دَوّارَيْن
6 single-cylinder two-stroke internal combustion engine — مُحَرِّك احتراق داخليّ ثنائي الأشواط ذو أسطوانة واحدة
7 fan — مرْوَحة
8 fan clutch for viscous drive — قابِض المرْوَحة للدفع اللَزِج
9 ignition distributor (distributor) with vacuum timing control — مُوَزِّع إشْعال بآليَّة للتحكم فى توقيت الإشْعال بالخَلْخَلَة
10 double roller chain — سِلْسِلَة بدَحَاريج مُزْدَوَجَة
11 camshaft bearing — مَحْمَل عمود الكامات
12 air-bleed duct — منْزَف الهواء
13 oil pipe for camshaft lubrication — انبوب زيت لتزليق عمود الكامات
14 camshaft, an overhead camshaft — عمود الكامات
15 venturi throat — حلْق "فنتورى"
16 intake silencer (absorption silencer, *Am.* absorption muffler) — شَكْمَان السَّحْب
17 fuel pressure regulator — مُنَظِّم ضغط الوَقود
18 inlet manifold — مجمع السحب
19 cylinder crankcase — كارتير الأسْطوانة
20 flywheel — الحَدَّافة
21 connecting rod (piston rod) — ذِراع توصيل (قضيب الكباس)
22 cover of crankshaft bearing — غِطاء مَحْمَل العمود المِرْفَقي
23 crankshaft — العمود المِرْفَقِي
24 oil bleeder screw (oil drain plug) — سَدّادة تصريف الزيت
25 roller chain of oil pump drive — سلسلة بدحاريج لوَحْدَة إدارة مضخة الزيْت
26 vibration damper — مُضَائل الاهتزازات
27 distributor shaft for the ignition distributor (distributor) — عمود مُوَزِّع الإشْعال
28 oil filler neck — عنق فتحة مِلء الزيت

29 diaphragm spring — ياي رقّي
30 control linkage — أوْصَال التَّحكُم
31 fuel supply pipe (*Am.* fuel line) — أنبوب إمداد الوَقُود (خَطّ الوَقُود)
32 fuel injector (injection nozzle) — حاقِن الوَقُود
33 rocker arm — ذراع تَرَجُحِيَّة
34 rocker arm mounting — محمل الذراع التَّرَجُحِيَّة
35 spark plug (sparking plug) with suppressor — شَمْعَة شَرَر (بوجيه) ذات مانع للشرر
36 exhaust manifold — مجمع العادِم
37 piston with piston rings and oil scraper ring — كَبَّاس ذو حلقات وحلقة كَسْح الزيت
38 engine mounting — رِكُوبة المُحَرِّك
39 dog flange (dog) — شَفَّة كلابيَّة
40 crankcase — عُلْبَة المَرَافِق، كارتير
41 oil sump (sump) — الحَوْض السفليّ للزيت
42 oil pump — مِضَخَّة الزيت
43 oil filter — مُرَشِّح الزيت
44 starter motor (starting motor) — مُوتور بادئ التشغيل
45 cylinder head — رأس الأُسْطوانة
46 exhaust valve — صمام العادم
47 dipstick — قضيب قياس منسوب الزيت
48 cylinder head cover — غطاء (جوان) رأس الأُسْطوانات
49 double bushing chain — سِلْسِلَة ذات جِلْبَة مزدوجة
50 warm-up regulator — مُنَظِّم التسخين
51 tapered needle for idling adjustment — إبرة مُسْتَدَقَّة لضبط التباطؤ
52 fuel pressure pipe (fuel pressure line) — أنبوب ضغط الوَقُود
53 fuel leak line (drip fuel line) — خَطّ تنقيط الوَقُود
54 injection nozzle (spray nozzle) — فُوَّهَة الحَقْن
55 heater plug — شَمْعَة مِرْوَحَة التدفئة
56 thrust washer — حَلْقة دفْعيَّة
57 intermediate gear shaft for the injection pump drive — عمود التُّرْس المتوسط الخاص بإدارة مِضَخَّة الحَقْن
58 injection timer unit — وَحْدَة توقيت الحَقْن
59 vacuum pump (low-pressure regulator) — مِضَخَّة خَلْخَلَة (منظم الضغط المنخفض)
60 cam for vacuum pump — كامة مِضَخَّة الخَلْخَلَة
61 water pump (coolant pump) — مِضَخَّة الماء (مِضَخَّة المُبَرِّد)
62 cooling water thermostat — ترموستات ماء التبريد
63 thermo time switch — مفتَاح تَوْقيت حراري
64 fuel hand pump — مِضَخَّة يدويَّة للوَقُود
65 injection pump — مِضَخَّة الحَقْن
66 glow plug — شَمْعَة تَوَهُّج
67 oil pressure limiting valve — صمام تحديد ضغط الزيت
68 rotor — العُضْو الدَّوّار (في محرك "فانكل")
69 seal — بِرْشام
70 torque converter — مُحَوِّل العَزْم
71 single-plate clutch — قابض مُفْرَد القُرْص
72 multi-speed gearing (multi-step gearing) — صندوق تروس متعدد السرعات
73 port liners in the exhaust, manifold for emission control — بطانات المَنْفَذ فى مجمع العادِم للتحكم فى الانْبِعاث
74 disc (disk) brake — فرملة قرصيَّة
75 differential gear (differential) — ترس فَرْقي (دفرانشيه)
76 generator — مُوَلِّد كهربائي
77 foot gear-change control (foot gearshift control) — أداة التحكم السفليَّة فى نقل التروس
78 dry multi-plate clutch — قابض جاف متعدد الأقراص
79 cross-draught (*Am.* cross-draft) carburettor (*Am.* carburetor) — مكَرْبِن (كاربوراتير) سحب مُضَاد
80 cooling ribs — ضلوع التبريد
81 V-belt (fan belt) — سَيْر على شكل حَرْف v (سَيْر المرْوَحَة)

191 Motor Car (*Am.* automobile) I — السَّيَّارَة (1)

1-56 motor car (car, *Am.* automobile, auto), a passenger vehicle — **السَّيَّارَة** (مَرْكَبَة آليَّة)
1 monocoque body (unitary body) — بَدَن قِشْريّ
2 chassis, the under-structure of the body — هَيْكَل السَّيَّارَة (الشَّاسِيه)
3 front wing (*Am.* front fender) — صَدَّاد أمامي، رَفْرَف أماميّ
4 car door — بَاب السَّيَّارَة
5 door handle — مقْبَض البَاب
6 door lock — قَفْل الباب
7 boot lid (trunk lid) — غطاء صندوق السَّيَّارَة
8 bonnet (*Am.* hood) — غطاء مُحَرِّك السَّيَّارَة
9 radiator — المُشِعّ
10 cooling water pipe — أنْبُوب ماء التبريد
11 radiator grill — شَبكَة وقايَة المُشِعّ
12 badging — علامة ماركة السَّيَّارَة
13 rubber-covered front bumper (*Am.* front fender) — صَدَّاد أمامي مُغَطَّى بالمَطَّاط
14 car wheel, a disc (disk) wheel — دولاب سيَّارة
15 car tyre (*Am.* automobile tire) — إطار الدولاب (الجزء المطَّاطي من الدولاب)
16 rim (wheel rim) — الحافَة (حافة الإطار)
17-18 disc (disk) brake — **فَرْمَلَة قُرْصيَّة**
17 brake disc (disk) (braking disc) — قُرْص الفرملة
18 calliper (caliper) — آليَّة فكيَّة
19 front indicator light (front turn indicator light) — لَمْبَة إشارة أماميَّة (لمبة إشارة انعطاف أماميَّة)
20 headlight (headlamp) with main beam (high — المِصْبَاح الأمامي ذو قلاب للإضاءة القريبة والبعيدة

	beam), dipped beam (low beam), sidelight (side lamp, *Am.* side-marker lamp)	ولَمْبَة جانبيَّة
21	windscreen (*Am.* windshield), a panoramic windscreen	الزُجَاج الأمامي، حاجِب الريح
22	crank-operated car window	زُجاج يَتِمّ تحريكه بذِراع دَوَراني
23	quarter light (quarter vent)	هَوَّايَة جانبيَّة
24	boot (*Am.* trunk)	صُنْدوق السَّيَّارَة
25	spare wheel	دُولاب احْتِيَاطِيّ
26	damper (shock absorber)	مُخَمِّد الاهتزازات
27	trailing arm	ذِراع تَعْلِيق خَلْفي
28	coil spring	نابِض مُلْتَف
29	silencer (*Am.* muffler)	شَكْمَان، كاتِم الصَّوْت
30	automatic ventilation system	نِظام تَهْوِيَة آلي
31	rear seats	المَقْعَد الخلفيّ
32	rear window	الزُجاج الخلفيّ
33	adjustable headrest (head restraint)	مِسْنَد رأس قابل للضبط
34	driver's seat, a reclining seat	مَقْعَد السائق
35	reclining backrest	مِسْنَد ظَهْر قابل للبَسْط
36	passenger seat	مَقْعَد الرَّاكِب الأمامي
37	steering wheel	عَجَلَة القيادة
38	centre (*Am.* center) console containing speedometer (*coll.* speedo), revolution counter (rev counter, tachometer), clock, fuel gauge (*Am.* gage), water temperature gauge, oil temperature gauge	كونسول مركزي يَشْتَمِل على عدَّاد السُرْعَة وعدَّاد سُرْعَة الدَّوَرَان وساعة ومُؤشِّر الوَقود وعدَّاد حرارة الماء وعدَّاد حرارة الزَّيْت.
39	inside rear-view mirror	مِرْآة الرؤيَّة الخلفيَّة الداخليَّة
40	left-hand wing mirror	مِرْآة الجانب الأيسر
41	windscreen wiper (*Am.* windshield wiper)	مَسَّاحَة الزُجَاج الأمامي
42	defroster vents	فَتَحات مُزيل الصَّقيع (الدَّفَّاية)
43	carpeting	فَرْش أرضيَّة السَّيَّارة
44	clutch pedal (*coll.* clutch)	دَوَّاسَة القابِض
45	brake pedal (*coll.* brake)	دَوَّاسَة الفرملة
46	accelerator pedal (*coll.* accelerator)	دَوَّاسَة المُعَجِّل، دَوَّاسَة الوَقود
47	inlet vent	فَتْحَة السَّحْب
48	blower fan	مَرْوَحة نافخَة
49	brake fluid reservoir	خَزَّان سائل الفرامل
50	battery	بطَّاريَّة
51	exhaust pipe	ماسورة العادم
52	front running gear with front wheel drive	تُرْس أمامي دَوَّار مع إدارة العجلات الأماميَّة
53	engine mounting	مَبيت المُحَرِّك
54	intake silencer (*Am.* intake muffler)	كاتِم صَوْت السَّحْب
55	air filter (air cleaner)	مُرَشِّح الهواء
56	right-hand wing mirror	مِرْآة الجانب الأيمن
57-90	**dashboard** (fascia panel)	**لوحة التابلوه**
57	controlled-collapse steering column	عمود قيادة انضباطي محكوم
58	steering wheel spoke	ضِلْع عَجَلَة القيادة
59	indicator and dimming switch	مِفْتَاح المُبَيِّن والعاتِم
60	wiper/washer switch and horn	مفتاح تشغيل المَسَّاحَات/ الرَّشَّاش والبُوق
61	side window blower	نافخ هواء الزُجاج الجانبي
62	sidelight, headlight, and parking light switch	مِفْتَاح تشغيل المصابيح الجانبيَّة والأماميَّة ولَمْبَة الانتظار
63	fog lamp warning light	ضَوْء التحذير الخاص بمِصْبَاح الضَّبَاب
64	fog headlamp and rear lamp switch	مِفْتَاح الضوء الأمامي والخلفي الخاص بالضَّبَاب
65	fuel gauge (*Am.* gage)	عَدَّاد الوَقود
66	water temperature gauge (*Am.* gage)	عَدَّاد حرارة الماء
67	warning light for rear fog lamp	ضَوْء التحذير الخاص بمِصْبَاح الضَّبَاب الخلفي
68	hazard flasher switch	مِفْتَاح الغمَّازات في حالة الخطر
69	main beam warning light	ضَوْء التحذير الخاص بالكشَّاف الرئيسي
70	electric rev counter (revolution counter)	عدَّاد سُرْعة الدَّوَرَان (عدَّاد اللفات)
71	fuel warning light	الضَّوْء التحذيري لِنَقْص الوقود
72	warning light for the hand brake and dual-circuit brake system	الضَّوْء التحذيري الخاص بنظام فرملة اليد والفرامل مزدوجة الدائرة
73	oil pressure warning light	الضَّوْء التحذيري لضغط الزيت
74	speedometer (*coll.* speedo) with trip mileage recorder	عدَّاد السرعة وبه عدَّاد الكيلومترات (الأمْيَال)
75	starter and steering lock	قُفْل بدء التشغيل والتَّوْجيه
76	warning lights for turn indicators and hazard flashers	الأضْوَاء التحذيريَّة الخاصة بمصابيح الانعطافات وغمَّازات الخطر
77	switch for the courtesy light and reset button for the trip mileage recorder	زرّ الإضاءة الداخلية وضبط عدَّاد الكيلومترات (الأمْيَال)
78	ammeter	أميتر
79	electric clock	ساعة كهربيَّة
80	warning light for heated rear window	ضَوْء تحذيري خاص بالزُجاج الخلفي المُسَخَّن
81	switch for the leg space ventilation	مِفْتَاح تَهْوِيَة حَيِّز الأرْجُل
82	rear window heating	مِفْتَاح تسخين الزُجاج

switch	الخلفي
83 ventilation switch	مفتاح التهوية
84 temperature regulator	مُنَظِّم دَرَجَة الحرارة
85 fresh-air inlet and control	مَدْخَل الهواء الطَّلْق والتحكم في اتجاهه وكَمِيَّته
86 fresh-air regulator	مُنَظِّم الهواء الطَّلْق
87 warm-air regulator	مُنَظِّم الهواء الساخن
88 cigar lighter	قَدَّاحة السجائر
89 glove compartment (glove box) lock	قفل حُجَيْرَة التابلوه
90 car radio	راديو السيارة
91 gear lever (gearshift lever), a floor-type gear-change	ذِراع تبديل السُّرعَة (الفتيس)، فتيس أرضي
92 leather gaiter	وقاء من الجِلْد
93 hand brake lever	ذِراع الفرملة اليدويَّة
94 accelerator pedal	دَوَّاسة الوَقود/المُعَجِّل
95 brake pedal	دَوَّاسة الفرملة
96 clutch pedal	دَوَّاسة القابِض
97 seat belt (safety belt)	حِزام المَقْعَد (حزام الأمان)

192 Motor Car (*Am.* Automobile) II — السَّيَّارة (2)

1-15 carburettor (*Am.* carburetor), a down-draught (*Am.* down-draft) carburettor	**المكربن** (الردياتير)
1 idling jet (slow-running jet)	مِنْفَث التَّباطُؤ، فُوَّهَة السرعة البطيئة
2 idling air jet (idle air bleed)	منْفَث الهواء البطئ
3 air correction jet	مِنْفَث تصحيح الهواء
4 compensating airstream	تيَّار هواء التعادُل
5 main airstream	تيَّار هواء رئيسي
6 choke flap	قَلَّاب الخانق
7 plunger	غاطِس، كبَّاس
8 venturi	أنبوب فِنْتُوري
9 throttle valve (butterfly valve)	صِمَام خانِق
10 emulsion tube	أنْبوب المُسْتَحْلَب
11 idle mixture adjustment screw	بُرْغي ضبط خليط السرعة البطيئة
12 main jet	المِنْفَث الرئيسي
13 fuel inlet (*Am.* gasoline inlet) (inlet manifold)	ماسورة الإمداد بالوَقود
14 float chamber	غُرْفَة العَوَّامة
15 float	عَوَّامة
16-27 pressure-feed lubricating system	**نِظام التَّزْييت بالضغط**
16 oil pump	مِضَخَّة الزَّيْت
17 oil sump	حَوْض الزيت
18 sump filter	مُرَشِّح حَوْض الزيت
19 oil cooler	مُبَرِّد الزيت
20 oil filter	مُرَشِّح الزيت
21 main oil gallery (drilled gallery)	مَمَرّ الزيت الرئيسي
22 crankshaft drilling (crankshaft tributary, crankshaft bleed)	مِنْزَف العمود الرئيسي
23 crankshaft bearing (main bearing)	مَحْمَل العمود المِرْفَقي
24 camshaft bearing	مَحْمَل عمود الكامات
25 connecting-rod bearing	مَحْمَل قضيب التَّوْصيل
26 gudgeon pin (piston pin)	بِنْز الكَبَّاس
27 bleed	مِنْزَف
28-47 four-speed synchromesh gearbox	**صندوق تروس متزامن التعشيق رباعي السرعات**
28 clutch pedal	دَوَّاسة القابِض
29 crankshaft	عمود مِرْفَقيّ
30 drive shaft (propeller shaft)	عمود الدفْع
31 starting gear ring	حلَقَة تُرْس بدء الحركة
32 sliding sleeve for 3rd and 4th gear	كُمّ مُنْزَلِق لتعشيق السُّرْعَتَيْن الثالثة والرابعة
33 synchronizing cone	مَخْرُوط تزامني
34 helical gear wheel for 3rd gear	عَجَلَة تُرْس لَوْلَبيّ لتعشيق السرعة الثالثة
35 sliding sleeve for 1st and 2nd gear	كُمّ مُنْزَلِق لتعشيق السُّرْعَتَيْن الأولى والثانية
36 helical gear wheel for 1st gear	عَجَلَة تُرْس لَوْلَبيّ لتعشيق السرعة الأولى
37 lay shaft	عمود وَسيط
38 speedometer drive	إدارة عَدَّاد السرعة
39 helical gear wheel for speedometer drive	عَجَلَة تُرْس لَوْلَبيّ لإدارة عَدَّاد السرعة
40 main shaft	العمود الرئيسي
41 gearshift rods	قُضْبان نقل التروس
42 selector fork for 1st and 2nd gear	شَوْكَة انتقاء تعشيق السُّرْعَتَيْن الأولى والثانية
43 helical gear wheel for 2nd gear	عَجَلَة تُرْس لَوْلَبيّ لتعشيق السرعة الثانية
44 selector head with reverse gear	رأس الانتقاء مع تُرْس السرعة الخلفيَّة
45 selector fork for 3rd and 4th gear	شَوْكَة انتقاء السُّرْعَتَيْن الثالثة والرابعة
46 gear lever (gearshift lever)	ذِراع نقل السرعات (ذِراع الفيتيس)
47 gear-change pattern (gearshift pattern, shift pattern)	نمط تغيير السرعات
48-55 disc (disk) brake [assembly]	**فَرْمَلَة قُرْصيَّة** [مجموعة]
48 brake disc (disk) (braking disc)	قُرْص الفرملة
49 calliper (caliper), a fixed calliper with friction pads	آليَّة فكِّيَّة (آليَّة فكِّيَّة ثابتة ذات لقم احتكاك)
50 servo cylinder (servo unit)	وَحْدَة مُوازِرَة (سِرْفو)
51 brake shoes	حِذاء الفرملة
52 brake lining	بِطانَة الفرملة
53 outlet to brake line	فتحة تؤدي إلى خط زيت الفرملة
54 wheel cylinder	أُسْطوانة الدولاب
55 return spring	نابِض إرْجاع
56-59 steering gear	**آليَّة القيادة** (التَّوْجيه)

(worm-and-nut steering gear)

56 steering column — عمود القيادة (التَّوْجيه)

57 worm gear sector — تُرْس التَّوْجيه الدُودِيّ

58 steering drop arm — ذِراع التَّوْجيه الهابطة

59 worm — تُرْس دُودِيّ

60-64 water-controlled heater — **مُسَخِّن يتم التحكم به بالمياه**

60 air intake — سَحْب الهواء

61 heat exchanger (heater box) — مُبادِل حراري

62 blower fan — مِرْوَحة نافخة

63 flap valve — صِمام قَلّاب

64 defroster vent — فتحة دفّاية إزالة الصقيع

65-71 live axle (rigid axle) — **مِحْوَر حَيّ**

65 propeller shaft — عمود دفع

66 trailing arm — ذِراع تعليق خلفي

67 rubber bush — جِلْبَة مطّاطيَّة

68 coil spring — نابِض

69 damper (shock absorber) — مُخَمِّد الإهتزازات

70 Panhard rod — قضيب بنهارد

71 stabilizer bar — قضيب المُوازَنَة

72-84 MacPherson strut unit — **وَحْدَة دُعامَة ماكفرسون**

72 body-fixing plate — لَوْح تثبيت الجسم

73 upper bearing — مَحْمَل علوي

74 suspension spring — نابض التعليق

75 piston rod — ذِراع الكَبّاس

76 suspension damper — مُخَمِّد التعليق

77 rim (wheel rim) — حافَة (حافَة الدولاب)

78 stub axle — المِحْوَر الأبْتَر

79 steering arm — رافِعة التَّوْجيه

80 track-rod ball-joint — وَصْلَة كرَوِيَّة لعمود الدَّرْب

81 trailing link arm — ذِراع تعليق خلفيَّة للربط

82 bump rubber (rubber bonding) — مطّاط امتصاص الاهتزازات (رباط مطاط)

83 lower bearing — مَحْمَل سفلي

84 lower suspension arm — ذِراع تعليق سفليَّة

193 Motor Car (*Am.* Automobile) III — السَّيّارة (3)

1-36 car models (*Am.* automobile models) — **مُوديلات السَّيّارات**

1 four-door touring saloon (*Am.* four-door sedan) in the upper-middle range — سَيّارة صالون ذات أربعة أبواب من الفِئة فَوْق المتوَسِّطة

2 driver's door — باب السّائق

3 rear door — الباب الخلفيّ

4-10 four-door saloon (*Am.* four-door sedan) **and four-door hatchback in the middle range** — **سَيّارة صالون ذات أربعة أبواب وسَيّارة ذات أربعة أبواب مَبْتُورة المُؤخِّرَة من الفِئة المتوَسِّطة**

4 saloon (*Am.* sedan) — سَيّارة صالون

5 headrests (head restraints) — مِسْنَد رأس

6 front seat — المَقْعَد الأمامي

7 rear seat (back seat) — المَقْعَد الخلفيّ

8 fastback saloon (*Am.* fastback sedan) (stubback saloon, *Am.* stubback sedan) — سَيّارة صالون ذات مُؤخِّرَة مَبْتُورة

9 tailgate — باب المُؤخِّرَة

10 fastback (stubback) — مُؤخِّرَة تُساعِد على زيادَة السُّرْعَة (مُؤخِّرَة مَبْتُورة)

11 cross-country vehicle with all-wheel drive (four-wheel drive) — سَيّارة أسْفار نظام دَفْع بالأرْبَع عَجَلات

12 spare wheel — دُولاب احْتياطيّ

13 roll bar — قضيب أسْطوانيّ للتثبيت

14 cabriolet sports coupé (cabriolet sports car) — سَيّارة كابرْيوليه، سَيّارة مكْشوفَة

15 integral seat — مَقْعَد ثابِت

16 automatic hood (*Am.* top) (power-operated hood, *Am.* top) — سَقْف يَتَحَرَّك آليًا

17 estate car (estate, shooting brake, *Am.* station wagon) — سَيّارة ستيشن

18 boot space (luggage compartment) — صُنْدُوق الأمْتِعَة

19 small three-door car — سَيّارة صغيرة بثَلاثة أبْواب

20 back (tailgate) — المُؤخِّرَة (باب المُؤخِّرَة)

21 sill — عَتَبَة

22 folding back seat — مَقْعَد خلفي قابل للطي

23 boot (luggage compartment, *Am.* trunk) — صُنْدوق السَّيّارة

24 (sliding) sunroof (steel sliding sunroof) — سَقْف مُنْزَلِق

25 three-door hatchback — سَيّارة بثَلاثة أبْواب مَبْتُورَة المُؤخِّرَة

26 roadster (sports cabrio, sports cabriolet), a two-seater — سَيّارة خفيفة مكْشوفة (سَيّارة ذات مَقْعَدَيْن)

27 hard top — سَقْف ثابِت صَلْب

28 sports coupé, a two-plus-two (two-seater with occasional seats) — سَيّارة كُوبيه ببابَيْن

29 fastback — مُؤخِّرَة تُساعِد على زيادَة السُّرْعَة

30 occasional seat — مقعد مُعَد للاسْتِخْدام عِنْد الحاجة

31 low-profile tyre (*Am.* tire) (wide wheel) — إطار مُنْخَفِض الجانبِيَّة (دولاب عريض)

32 gran turismo car (GT car) — سَيّارة جُوتي

33 integral bumper (*Am.* integral fender) — مِصَدّ غير قابِل للفَصْل

34 rear spoiler — مُفْسِد خلفي

35 back — المؤخرة

36 front spoiler — مُفْسِد أمامي

194 Lorries (*Am.* Trucks), Vans, Buses — الشّاحنات وعَرَبات النَّقْل الخَفيفة والحافلات

1 light cross-country — شاحِنَة خَفيفة نظام دفع

lorry (light truck, pick-up truck) with all-wheel drive (four-wheel drive) بالأربع عَجَلات
2 cab (driver's cab) كابينة السائق
3 loading platform (body) صُنْدُوق التَّحْمِيل
4 spare tyre (*Am.* spare tire), a cross-country tyre دُولاب احتياطيّ
5 light lorry (light truck, pick-up truck) شاحِنَة خفيفة
6 platform truck شاحِنَة بصندوق
7 medium van عَرَبَة نقل متوسطة الحجم
8 sliding side door [for loading and unloading] باب جانبي مُنْزَلِق [للتحميل والتفريغ]
9 minibus حافِلَة صغيرة (ميني باص)
10 folding top (sliding roof) سَقْف قابِل للطي
11 rear door باب خلفي
12 hinged side door باب جانبي مُثَبَّت بمِفْصَل
13 luggage compartment حُجَيْرَة الأمْتِعَة
14 passenger seat مَقْعَد الرَّاكِب
15 cab (driver's cab) كابينة السائق
16 air inlet فتحة دخول الهواء
17 motor coach (coach, bus) حافِلَة بمُحَرِّك
18 luggage locker حُجَيْرَة الأمْتِعَة
19 hand luggage (suitcase, case) حَقِيبَة يد (حَقِيبَة مَلابِس)
20 heavy lorry (heavy truck, heavy motor truck) شاحِنَة ثقيلة
21 tractive unit (tractor, towing vehicle) وَحْدَة الجَرّ/القَطْر (الجَرَّار)
22 trailer (drawbar trailer) مَقْطُورَة
23 swop platform (body) صندوق المَقْطُورَة
24 three-way tipper (three-way dump truck) عَرَبَة قلاّبة
25 tipping body (dump body) صندوق قَلاب
26 hydraulic cylinder أُسْطُوانة هيدروليَّة
27 supported container platform حاوِيَة مَرْفُوعَة على دعامات
28 articulated vehicle, a vehicle tanker مَرْكَبَة مِفْصَليَّة
29 tractive unit (tractor, towing vehicle) وَحْدَة الجَرّ (الجَرَّار)
30-33 semi-trailer (skeletal) **نصف مقطورة**
30 tank خَزَّان
31 turntable سَطْح دَوَّار
32 undercarriage عَرَبَة سفليَّة
33 spare wheel دُولاب احتياطيّ
34 midi bus [for short-route town operations] حافِلَة متوسطة [للمسافات القصيرة داخِل المدينة]
35 outward-opening doors أَبْوَاب تُفْتَح باتجاه الخارِج
36 double-deck bus (double-decker bus) حافِلَة ذات طابِقَيْن
37 lower deck (lower saloon) الطابِق السفلي
38 upper deck (upper saloon) الطابِق العلوي
39 boarding platform منصة صعود الحافلة
40 trolley bus الترولي باص
41 current collector ذِرَاع توصيل التَّيَّار
42 trolley (trolley shoe) حِذَاء الترولي
43 overhead wires سِلْك علوي
44 trolley bus trailer مَقْطُورَة الترولي باص
45 pneumatically sprung rubber connection وَصْلَة مطَّاطِيَّة بنابِض هوائي

195 Garage (*Am.* Shop) الكَرَاج (الجَرَاج)

1-55 agent's garage (distributor's garage, *Am.* specialty shop) **كَرَاج الوَكِيل** (كَرَاج مُوَزِّع السَّيَّارات)
1-23 diagnostic test bay **حُجَيْرَة الفَحْص**
1 computer حاسِب آليّ (كمبيوتر)
2 main computer socket قابِس الحاسِب الآليّ الرئيسيّ
3 computer harness (computer cable) كيبل الحاسِب الآليّ
4 switch from automatic to manual مِفْتَاح التَّحْوِيل من التشغيل الآليّ إلى اليدويّ
5 slot for program cards فَتْحَة إدخال بِطَاقات البرامج
6 printout machine (printer) طابِعَة
7 condition report (data printout) تَقْرِير فحص السيارة
8 master selector (hand control) ذِرَاع التَّحَكُّم الرئيسيَّة
9 light read-out [green: OK; red: not OK] شَاشَة ضَوْئِيَّة [أخْضَر سَلِيم؛ أحْمَر: غير سَلِيم]
10 rack for program cards رَفّ بطاقات البرامج
11 mains button المَفَاتِيح الرئيسيَّة
12 switch for fast readout مِفْتَاح القِرَاءة السَّرِيعَة
13 firing sequence insert وَلِيجَة تَعَاقُب الإشْعَال
14 shelf for used cards رَفّ البطاقات المُسْتَعْمَلَة
15 cable boom دِعَامَة الكيبلات
16 oil temperature sensor جِهَاز إحْسَاس حرارة الزَّيْت
17 test equipment for wheel and steering alignment مُعِدَّات فَحْص الترصيص (ضبط الإسْتِقَامة)
18 right-hand optic plate لَوْحَة بَصَرِيَّة يُمْنَى
19 actuating transistors ترانزستورات التشغيل
20 projector switch مِفْتَاح البروجِكْتُور
21 check light for wheel alignment, a row of photocells ضَوْء فَحْص التَّرْصِيص، صَفّ من الخلايا الضَّوْئِيَّة
22 check light for steering alignment, a row of photocells ضَوْء فَحْص إسْتِقَامة التَّوجِيه (صَفّ من الخلايا الضَّوْئِيَّة)
23 power screwdriver مِفَكّ كهربائي
24 beam setter مُنَظِّم ذِرَاع المِيزَان
25 hydraulic lift مِرْفَاع هيدرولي

26 adjustable arm of hydraulic lift	ذِرَاع المِرْفَاع الهيدرولي القابلة للتعديل
27 hydraulic lift pad	بِطَانة المِرْفَاع الهيدرولي
28 excavation	حُفْرَة، بِئْر
29 pressure gauge (*Am.* gage)	مِقْيَاس الضغط
30 grease gun	مُسَدَّس تَشْحِيم
31 storage box for small parts	صُنْدُوق حِفْظ الأدَوَات الصَّغيرة
32 wall chart [of spare parts]	لَوْحَة حائطيَّة [تُوَضِّح قِطَع الغِيَار]
33 automatic computer test	فَحْص آليّ بالكمبيوتر
34 motor car (car, *Am.* automobile, auto), a passenger vehicle	سَيَّارَة
35 engine compartment	حُجَيْرَة المُحَرِّك
36 bonnet (*Am.* hood)	غطاء المُحَرِّك
37 bonnet support (*Am.* hood support)	مِسْنَد غِطاء المُحَرِّك
38 computer harness (computer cable)	كبل الكمبيوتر
39 main computer socket	مِقْبَس الكمبيوتر الرئيسيّ
40 oil temperature sensor	جِهَاز إحْسَاس حرارة الزَّيْت
41 wheel mirror for visual wheel and steering alignment	مِرْآة الدولاب لفحص اسْتِقَامَة الدولاب والتَّوْجِيه بَصَرِيّاً
42 tool trolley	ترولّلي الأدَوَات
43 tools	أدَوَات
44 impact wrench	مِفْتَاح رَبْط صَدْمِيّ
45 torque wrench	مِفْتَاح رَبْط يَقِيس عَزْم اللَّيّ
46 body hammer (roughing-out hammer)	مِطْرَقَة سَمكَرَة
47 vehicle under repair, a minibus	عَرَبَة تحت الإصْلاح، ميني باص
48 car location number	رَقَم مَوْقِع السَّيَّارَة
49 rear engine	مُحَرِّك خلفيّ
50 tailgate	باب المُؤَخِّرَة
51 exhaust system	نِظَام العادِم
52 exhaust repair	إصْلاح نظام العادِم
53 motor car mechanic (motor vehicle mechanic, *Am.* automotive mechanic)	ميكانيكي سيارات
54 air hose	خُرْطُوم الهواء
55 intercom	جِهَاز اتِّصَال داخليّ (انتركوم)

196 Service Station / مَحطَّة خِدْمَة السَّيَّارَات

1-29 service station (petrol station, filling station, *Am.* gasoline station, gas station), a self-service station	**مَحَطَّة خِدْمَة السَّيَّارَات** (مَحَطَّة البنزين)، مَحَطَّة الخِدْمَة الذَّاتيَّة
1 petrol (*Am.* gasoline) pump (blending pump) for unleaded (lead-free) premium grade and regular petrol (*Am.* gasoline) (*sim.:* for derv)	مِضَخَّة البنزين المُمْتَاز الخالي من الرصاص والبنزين العادي
2 hose (petrol pump, *Am.* gasoline pump, hose)	خُرْطُوم المِضَخَّة
3 nozzle	بِزْبَاز، فُوَّهَة
4 cash readout	بَيَان القيمة النقديَّة المطلوبة
5 volume readout	بَيَان عَدَّاد اللِّتْرَات المَسْحُوبَة
6 price display	بَيَان السِّعْر
7 indicator light	ضَوْء إشاريّ
8 driver using self-service petrol pump (*Am.* gasoline pump)	سائق يَسْتَخْدِم مِضَخَّة بنزين مَحطَّة الخِدْمَة الذَّاتيَّة
9 fire extinguisher	مِطْفَأة الحريق
10 paper-towel dispenser	جِهَاز المَنَاشِف الوَرَقيَّة
11 paper towel	مِنْشَفَة وَرَقيَّة
12 litter receptacle	صُنْدُوق المُهْمَلات
13 two-stroke blending pump	مِضَخَّة بنزين ثُنائيَّة الأشْواط
14 meter	عَدَّاد
15 engine oil	زَيْت المُحَرِّكَات
16 oil can	عُلْبَة زَيْت
17 tyre pressure gauge (*Am.* tire pressure gage)	مِقْيَاس ضغط الإطارات
18 air hose	خُرْطُوم الهواء
19 static air tank	خَزَّان هواء استاتيّ
20 pressure gauge (*Am.* gage) (manometer)	مِقْيَاس ضغط (مانومتر)
21 air filler neck	عُنُق جِهَاز تَعْبِئَة الهواء
22 repair bay (repair shop)	وَرْشَة الإصْلاح
23 car-wash hose, a hose (hosepipe)	خُرْطُوم غسيل السَّيَّارات
24 accessory shop	مَحَلّ بَيْع الكَمَاليَّات
25 petrol can (*Am.* gasoline can)	صَفيحَة بنزين
26 rain cape	غِطَاء واقٍ من المَطَر
27 car tyres (*Am.* automobile tires)	إطَارَات السَّيَّارات
28 car accessories	كَمَاليَّات السَّيَّارَات
29 cash desk (console)	خَزِينَة دَفْع النَّقْدِيَّة

197 Tram (*Am.* Streetcar, Trolley), Interurban Electric Train / التِّرَام، قِطَار كهربائي للخِدْمَة بَيْن الضَّوَاحِي

1 twelve-axle articulated railcar for interurban rail service	عَرَبَة سِكَك حَدِيديَّة مِفْصَليَّة ذات 12 مِحْوَراً للخِدْمَة بَيْن الضَّوَاحِي
2 current collector	قَضِيب تَوْصِيل التَّيَّار الكهربائي
3 head of the railcar	مُقَدِّمَة العَرَبَة
4 rear of the railcar	مُؤَخِّرَة العَرَبَة
5 carriage A containing the motor	العَرَبَة (أ) وتَحْمِل المُحَرِّك
6 carriage B (*also:* carriages C and D)	العَرَبَة (ب)؛ أيضاً: العربات (ج) و(د)
7 carriage E containing the motor	العَرَبَة (هـ) وتَحْمِل المُحَرِّك

8 rear controller — المُرَاقِب الخلفيّ

9 driving bogie — بُوجي الإدارة، مَجْمَع عَجَلات الإدارة

10 carrying bogie — بُوجي حَمْل

11 wheel guard — وِقَاء العَجَلَة

12 bumper (*Am.* fender) — مِصَدّ

13 six-axle articulated rail-car ('Mannheim' type) for tram (*Am.* streetcar, trolley) and urban rail services — عَرَبَة سِكَك حَدِيديَّة مِفْصَلِيَّة ذات ستة مَحَاوِر لخِدْمَة التِّرَام والخِدْمَة في المَدِينَة

14 entrance and exit door, a double folding door — باب الركوب والنزول القابل للطَّيّ

15 step — دَرَجَة

16 ticket-cancelling machine — ماكينة إلْغَاء التَّذَاكر

17 single seat — مَقْعَد مُفْرَد

18 standing room portion — الجُزْء المُخَصَّص للوقوف

19 double seat — مَقْعَد مُزْدَوَج

20 route (number) and destination sign — لافِتَة خط السَّيْر واتجاه الرِّحْلَة

21 route sign (number sign) — لافِتَة رَقَم العَرَبَة

22 indicator (indicator light) — ضَوْء إرشاديّ

23 pantograph (current collector) — بانتوجراف (ذِراع تَوْصِيل التَّيَّار)

24 carbon or aluminium (*Am.* aluminum) alloy trolley shoes — حذاء ترولّي مصنوع من سَبِيكَة الكربون أو الألومنيوم

25 driver's position — مَوْقع السائق

26 microphone — ميكروفون

27 controller — مِفْتَاح تَحَكُّم

28 radio equipment (radio communication set) — جِهَاز الراديو

29 dashboard — لَوْحَة التَّابْلُوه

30 dashboard lighting — لَمْبَات لَوْحَة التَّابْلُوه

31 speedometer — عَدَّاد السُّرْعَة

32 buttons controlling doors, windscreen wipers, internal and external lighting — أزْرَار التَّحَكُّم في الأبْوَاب والمَسَّاحَات والإضاءة الداخليَّة والخارجيَّة

33 ticket counter with change machine — عَدَّاد التذاكر وماكينة صرف

34 radio antenna — هَوَائي الراديو

35 tram stop (*Am.* street-car stop, trolley stop) — مَحَطَّة التِّرَام

36 tram stop sign (*Am.* streetcar stop sign, trolley stop sign) — لافِتَة مَحَطَّة التِّرَام

37 electric change points — نِقاط تَحْوِيل المَسَار الكهربيَّة

38 points signal (switch signal) — إشَارَة نقاط التحويل (إشَارَة التَّحْوِيل)

39 points change indicator — الأنْوَار الإشاريَّة لنقاط تَحْوِيل المَسَار

40 trolley wire contact point — نُقْطَة تَلامُس سِلْك الترولّي

41 trolley wire (overhead contact wire) — سِلْك الترولّي

42 overhead cross wire — سِلْك علويّ مُتَقَاطِع

43 electric (*also:* electro-hydraulic, electro-mechanical) points mechanism — آليَّة النقاط الكهربيَّة (أيضاً: الكهروهيدروليَّة والكهروميكانيكيَّة)

198 Cross-section of a Street — مَقْطَع عَرْضِيّ للشَّارِع

1-5 road layers — **طَبَقَات الطَّرِيق**

1 anti-frost layer — طَبَقَة مُقَاوِمَة للصقيع

2 bituminous sub-base course — طَبَقَة تَحْتَانِيَّة من البيتومين

3 base course — طَبَقَة قاعديَّة

4 binder course — طَبَقَة من مادَة لاصِقَة

5 bituminous surface — سَطْح بيتومينيّ

6 kerb (curb) — حافَة الرَّصِيف

7 kerbstone (curbstone) — حَجَر الحافَة

8 paving (pavement) — رَصْف

9 pavement (*Am.* side-walk, walkway) — الرَّصِيف

10 gutter — بالُوعة تَصْرِيف

11 pedestrian crossing (zebra crossing, *Am.* crosswalk) — عُبُور المُشَاة

12 street corner — مُنْعَطَف الشارع

13 street — الشَّارِع

14 electricity cables — كيبلات الكهرباء

15 telephone cables — كيبلات الهاتِف

16 telephone cable pipeline — أُنْبُوب كيبلات الهاتِف

17 cable manhole with cover (with manhole cover) — فَتْحَة بِئْر كيبلات ذات غطاء

18 lamp post with lamp — عَمُود النُّور وبه مِصْبَاح

19 electricity cables for technical installations — كيبلات كهرباء للتوصيلات الفنيَّة

20 subscribers' (*Am.* customers') telephone lines — خُطُوط هَوَاتِف المشتركين

21 gas main — ماسُورة الغاز الرئيسيَّة

22 water main — ماسُورة الماء الرئيسيَّة

23 drain — بالُوعَة

24 drain cover — غِطَاء البالُوعَة

25 drain pipe — ماسُورة تَصْرِيف ماء المَطَر

26 waste pipe — ماسُورة تَصْرِيف المَجَارِي

27 combined sewer — مَجْرُور مُشْتَرَك

28 district heating main — مَأْخَذ تدفئة المنطقة الرئيسي

29 underground tunnel — نَفَق مِتْرُو الأنْفَاق

199 Refuse Disposal (*Am.* Garbage Disposition), Street Cleaning — التَّخَلُّص مِن النُّفَايَات، تَنْظِيف الشَّوَارِع

1 refuse collection vehicle (*Am.* garbage truck) — عَرَبَة جَمْع النُّفَايَات

2 dustbin-tipping device (*Am.* garbage can dumping device), a — جِهَاز قَلْب صُنْدوق النُّفَايَات

dust-free emptying system

3 dustbin (*Am.* garbage can, trash can) — صُنْدوق النُّفَايَات

4 refuse container (*Am.* garbage container) — حاوِيَة النُّفَايَات

5 road sweeper (*Am.* street sweeper) — كَنَّاس الشَّارِع

6 broom — مِكْنَسَة ، مِقَشَّة

7 fluorescent armband — شَرِيط ذِرَاع فلورسنتيّ

8 cap with fluorescent band — قُبَّعَة بِشَرِيط فلورسنتيّ

9 road sweeper's (*Am.* street sweeper's) barrow — عَرَبَة كَنَّاس الشَّارِع

10 controlled tip (*Am.* sanitary landfill, sanitary fill) — مَنْطِقَة رَدْم النُّفَايَات

11 screen — حاجِز

12 weigh office — مَكْتَب الوَزْن

13 fence — سِيَاج

14 embankment — سَدّ

15 access ramp — طَرِيق مُنْحَدِر

16 bulldozer — بُلْدُوزر

17 refuse (*Am.* garbage) — نفايَات

18 bulldozer for dumping and compacting — بُلْدُوزر للردم والدَّمْج

19 pump shaft — بِئْر المِضَخَّة

20 waste water pump — مِضَخَّة الماء المَهْدُور

21 porous cover — غطاء مَسَامِيّ

22 compacted and decomposed refuse — نفَايَات مُدْمَجَة ومُتَحَلِّلَة

23 gravel filter layer — طَبَقَة تَرْشِيح الحَصَى

24 morainic filter layer — طَبَقَة تَرْشِيح رُكَامِيَّة

25 drainage layer — طَبَقَة الصَّرْف الصِّحِيّ

26 drain pipe — ماسُورة الصَّرْف

27 water tank — خَزَّان ماء

28 refuse (*Am.* garbage) incineration unit — وَحْدَة إحْرَاق النُّفَايَات

29 furnace — فُرْن

30 oil-firing system — نظام إشْعَال بالزَّيْت

31 separation plant — وَحْدَة الفَرْز

32 extraction fan — مَرْوَحَة طَرْد

33 low-pressure fan for the grate — مَرْوَحَة ضغط مُنْخَفِض للشبكة المُصَبَّعَة

34 continuous feed grate — شبكة مُصَبَّعَة للتغذية المستمرة

35 fan for the oil-firing system — مَرْوَحَة نظام الإشْعَال بالزَّيْت

36 conveyor for separately incinerated material — ناقِل المَوَاد المَحْرُوقة على حدَة

37 coal feed conveyor — ناقِل إلْقَام الفَحْم

38 truck for carrying fuller's earth — شاحِنة نقل تُراب فُوللر

39 mechanical sweeper — عَرَبَة كَنْس آلِيَّة

40 circular broom — مِكْنَسَة دَوَّارَة

41 road-sweeping lorry (street-cleaning lorry, street cleaner) — شاحِنة كَنْس الشَّوَارِع

42 cylinder broom — مِقَشَّة أسْطُوانيَّة

43 suction port — فَتْحَة الشفط

44 feeder broom — مِقَشَّة تغذية فتحة الشفط

45 air flow — تَدَفُّق الهواء

46 fan — مِرْوَحَة

47 dust collector — حاوِيَة تجميع التُّرَاب

200 Road Construction I (Road Building, Road Making) — بِنَاء الطُّرُق (1)

1-54 road-building machinery — **ماكِينَات بِنَاء/تَعْبيد الطُّرُق**

1 shovel (power shovel, excavator) — حَفَّار

2 machine housing — مَبِيت الماكِينة

3 caterpillar mounting (*Am.* caterpillar tractor) — جَرَّارَة مُزَنْجَرَة

4 digging bucket arm (dipper stick) — ذِراع حَفْر دَلْوِيَّة

5 digging bucket (bucket) — قادُوس الحَفْر

6 digging bucket (bucket) teeth — أسنان قادُوس الحَفْر

7 tipper (dump truck), a heavy lorry (*Am.* truck) — شاحِنة قلاَّبَة

8 tipping body (*Am.* dump body) — صندوق القَلاَّب

9 reinforcing rib — ضِلْع تَقْوِيَة

10 extended front — مُقَدِّمَة مُمْتَدَّة

11 cab (driver's cab) — كابينة السائق

12 bulk material — مَوَاد سائبة

13 concrete scraper, an aggregate scraper — خَلاَّط الخرسانة

14 skip hoist — مِرْفاع قادوسي

15 mixing drum (mixer drum), a mixing machine — بِرْمِيل الخلاط

16 caterpillar hauling scraper — مِكْشَطَة جَرَّارَة مُزَنْجَرَة

17 scraper blade — سلاح المِكْشَطة

18 levelling (*Am.* leveling) blade (smoothing blade) — سِلاح التَّسْوِيَة

19 grader (motor grader) — مُمَهِّدَة الطُّرُق (جريدر)

20 scarifier (ripper, road ripper, rooter) — مِخْدَشَة (لِنَبْش سطح الطريق قبل إعادة التعبيد)

21 grader levelling (*Am.* leveling) blade (grader ploughshare, *Am.* plowshare) — أسْطوانة التَّسْوِيَة بالمِخْدَشَة

22 blade-slewing gear (slew turntable) — تُرْس الإلْتِفَاف الخاص بسلاح المِخْدَشَة

23 light railway (narrow-gauge, *Am.* narrow-gage, railway) — عَرَبَة سكَّة حَدِيدِيَّة خفيفة (سِكَّة حَدِيدِيَّة ضَيِّقَة)

24 light railway (narrow-gauge, *Am.* narrow-gage) diesel — قاطِرة ديزل حَدِيدِيَّة خفيفة

locomotive
25 trailer wagon (wagon truck, skip) عَرَبَة الجَرَّار
26 tamper (rammer); heavier: frog مِدَقَّة
27 guide rods قضبان دليليَّة
28 bulldozer بُلدوزر
29 bulldozer blade سكِّينة البُلدوزر
30 pushing frame إطار دفع
31 road-metal spreading machine (macadam spreader, stone spreader) ماكينة تَعْبيد/رَصْف الطرق
32 tamping beam قضيب دَكّ
33 sole-plate لَوْحَة سفليَّة
34 side stop مِصَدّ جانبي
35 side of storage bin جانِب صندوق التخزين
36 three-wheeled roller, a road roller هَرَّاس ذو ثلاث عَجَلات
37 roller هَرَّاس
38 all-weather roof سقف لكافة الأجْوَاء
39 mobile diesel-powered air compressor ضاغِط هواء مُتَنَقِّل يعمل بالديزل
40 oxygen cylinder اسطوانة الأكسجين
41 self-propelled gritter ماكينة فَرْش حَصَى ذاتيَّة الحركة
42 spreading flap قلابة فَرْش الحَصَى
43 surface finisher ماكينة إنجاز السطح
44 side stop مِصَد جانبي
45 bin صندوق
46 tar-spraying machine (bituminous distributor) with tar and bitumen heater ماكينة فَرْش القطران مع سَخَّان القطران والبتومين
47 tar storage tank خَزَّان القطران
48 fully automatic asphalt drying and mixing plant وَحْدَة خَلْط وتجفيف الأسْفَلْت آلياً
49 bucket elevator (elevating conveyor) مِرْفاع قادوسي
50 asphalt-mixing drum (asphalt mixer drum) بِرْميل خَلْط الأسْفَلْت
51 filler hoist مِرْفَاع المادة اللاصقة
52 filler opening فتحة المادة اللاصقَة
53 binder injector حاقنَة المادة اللاصقَة
54 mixed asphalt outlet فتحة خروج الأسْفَلْت المَخْلُوط
55 typical cross-section of a bituminous road مقطع عرضي نمطي لطريق بتوميني
56 grass verge حافة الطريق
57 crossfall منحدر مستعرض
58 asphalt surface (bituminous layer, bituminous coating) السطح الأسْفَلْتي (طبقة بتومينيَّة)
59 base (base course) قاعدة (طبقة قاعديَّة)
60 hardcore sub-base course (Telford base) or gravel sub-base course, an anti-frost layer طبقة تحتيَّة صلْدَة أو طبقة تحتيَّة من الحَصَى، طبقة صامِدة للصقيع
61 sub-drainage صَرْف صحيّ تحتيّ
62 perforated cement pipe ماسورة أسمنتيَّة مُثَقَّبَة
63 drainage ditch حُفْرَة الصَّرْف الصِّحيّ
64 soil covering غِطاء التُّرْبَة

201 Road Construction II (Road Building, Road Making) بِناء الطُّرُق (2)

1-24 concrete road construction (highway construction) **إنْشاء/بِناء الطُّرُق الخرسانيَّة** (بناء الطُّرُق السَّريعة)
1 subgrade grader مُدَرِّجَة/مُمَهِّدَة الأرْضيَّة الطبيعيّة
2 tamping beam (consolidating beam) قَضِيب الدَّك/الدَّمْك
3 levelling (*Am.* leveling) beam قَضِيب التَّسْوِيَة
4 roller guides for the levelling (*Am.* leveling) beam دلايل أُسْطُوانيّة لِقَضِيب التَّسْوِيَة
5 concrete spreader فارِشة الخرسانة
6 concrete spreader box صندوق فارِشة الخرسانة
7 cable guides دلايل كيليَّة
8 control levers أذْرُع التحكم
9 handwheel for emptying the boxes عَجَلَة يدويّة لتفريغ الصناديق
10 concrete-vibrating compactor آلة دَمْك هَزَّازة للخرسانة المَصْبُوبَة
11 gearing (gears) مجموعة المُسَنَّنَات
12 control levers (operating levers) أذْرُع التحكم (أذْرُع التشغيل)
13 axle drive shaft to vibrators (tampers) of vibrating beam عمود إدارة مِحْوَرِيّ مُوَصِّل لهزَّازات قضيب هَزّ الخرسانة
14 screeding board (screeding beam) لَوْح دليلي للثخانة، لَوْح تَسْوِيَة
15 road form قالِب رَصْف الطريق
16 joint cutter قاطع الخرسانة
17 joint-cutting blade سلاح قَطْع الخرسانة
18 crank for propelling machine ذِرَاع تدوير ماكينة الدفع
19 concrete-mixing plant, a stationary central mixing plant, an automatic batching and mixing plant وَحْدَة خَلْط الخرسانة، وَحْدَة مركزيَّة ثابتة لخَلْط الخرسانة، وَحْدَة آليَّة لتحديد الدُفْعَات والخلط
20 collecting bin حَوْض تجميع
21 bucket elevator مِصْعَد القادوس
22 cement store خَزَّان الأسْمنت
23 concrete mixer خلاَّط الخرسانة
24 concrete pump hopper قادوس مِضَخَّة الخرسانة

202 Railway Line (*Am.* Railroad Track) I خَطّ السِّكَّة الحَدِيديَّة (1)

1-38 line (track) **خَطّ السِّكَّة الحَدِيديَّة**
1 rail قَضِيب السِّكَّة الحَدِيدِيَّة

2 rail head	رَأْس القَضِيب
3 web (rail web)	وَكرَة القَضِيب
4 rail foot (rail bottom)	قاعدة القَضِيب
5 sole-plate (base plate)	لَوْحَة القاعدة
6 cushion	وِسَادَة (لتلطيف الصدمة)
7 coach screw (coach bolt)	بُرْغِي ذو رأس مربَّع
8 lock washers (spring washers)	صَوَاميل زَنْق
9 rail clip (clip)	مِشْبك القَضِيب
10 T-head bolt	مِسْمَار رَبْط له رأس تائيّ الشكل
11 rail joint (joint)	وَصْلَة قَضِيب السِّكَّة الحَدِيدِيَّة
12 fishplate	لَوْح وَصْل تراكبِيّ للقُضْبَان
13 fishbolt	مِسْمَار الوَصْلات التراكبيَّة
14 coupled sleeper (*Am.* coupled tie, coupled crosstie)	فَلَنْكَتَان/رَاقِدَتَان مُقْتَرِنَتَان
15 coupling bolt	مِسْمَار رَبْط
16 manually-operated points (manually-operated switch)	خطوط تحويل تُشَغَّل يدوياً
17 switch stand	قاعدة المِحْوَال، مَوْقَف التحويل
18 weight	ثِقْل
19 points signal (switch signal, points signal lamp, switch signal lamp)	إشَارَة المِحْوَال
20 pull rod	قَضِيب جَذْب (قَضِيب مِفْتَاح التَّحْوِيل)
21 switch blade (switch tongue)	سِكِّين فَصْل، لِسَان
22 slide chair	كُرْسِيّ مُنْزَلَق
23 check rail (guard rail)	قَضِيب واقٍ
24 frog	مقص، مَفْرَق أو تقاطع السِّكَّة الحَدِيدِيَّة
25 wing rail	قَضِيب التَّحَرُّز (للقضبان الجانبيَّة الخارجيَّة لمَفْرَق أو تقاطُع)
26 closure rail	قَضِيب إغلاق
27 remote-controlled points (remote-controlled switch)	خطوط تحويل يتم تشغيلها آلياً عن بعد
28 point lock (switch lock)	قُفْل التحويلة
29 stretcher bar	قَضِيب شَدَّاد (لمِفْتَاح السِّكَّة الحَدِيدِيَّة)
30 point wire	سلك المِحْوَال
31 turnbuckle	شَدَّادة
32 channel	قناة
33 electrically illuminated points signal (switch signal)	إشَارَة مِحْوَال تُضَاء بالكهرباء
34 trough	مَجْرَى
35 points motor with protective casing	موتور خطوط التحويل داخل صندوق للحماية
36 steel sleeper (*Am.* steel tie, steel crosstie)	فَلَنْكَة من الصُّلْب
37 concrete sleeper (*Am.* concrete tie, concrete crosstie)	فَلَنْكَة من الخرسانة
38 coupled sleeper (*Am.* coupled tie, coupled crosstie)	فَلَنْكَة مُزْدَوَجَة
39-50 level crossings (*Am.* grade crossings)	**التقاطُعات المستويَة، المَزْلَقَانات**
39 protected level crossing (*Am.* protected grade crossing)	مَزْلَقان مَحْمِي
40 barrier (gate)	حاجِز (بَوَّابة)
41 warning cross (*Am.* crossbuck)	إشَارَة التَّحْذير
42 crossing keeper (*Am.* gateman)	عامِل مُرَاقَبَة المَزْلَقان
43 crossing keeper's box (*Am.* gateman's box)	كُشْك عامِل مُرَاقَبَة المَزْلَقان
44 linesman (*Am.* track-walker)	عامِل السِّكَّة الحَدِيدِيَّة
45 half-barrier crossing	مَزْلَقان للعبور فى اتجاهَيْن (مَزْلَقان بِنِصْف حاجز)
46 warning light	ضَوْء تحذيريّ
47 intercom-controlled crossing; *sim.:* telephone-controlled crossing	مَزْلَقان يتم التحكم فيه هاتفياً
48 intercom system	نِظَام التحكم هاتفياً
49 unprotected level crossing (*Am.* unprotected grade crossing)	مَزْلَقان مفتوح
50 warning light	ضَوْء تحذيريّ

203 Railway Line (*Am.* Railroad Track) II (Signalling Equipment) — خطّ السِّكَّة الحَدِيدِيَّة (2) (معدات الاشَارَة)

1-6 stop signals (main signals)	**إشَارَات التَّوَقُّف** (الإشارَات الرئيسيَّة)
1 stop signal (main signal), a semaphore signal in 'stop' position	إشَارَة التَّوَقُّف (إشَارَة رئيسيَّة)، إشَارَة السيمافور في موقع "تَوَقَّف"
2 signal arm (semaphore arm)	ذِرَاع الإشَارَة (ذِرَاع السِّيمَافُور)
3 electric stop signal (colour light, *Am.* color light, signal) at 'stop'	إشَارَة توقف كهربائية عند نقطة "تَوَقَّف" (مِصْبَاح مُلَوَّن)
4 signal position: 'proceed at low speed'	وَضْع إشَارَة: "تَقَدَّم بسرعة منخفضة"
5 signal position: 'proceed'	وَضْع إشَارَة: "تَقَدَّم"
6 substitute signal	إشَارَة بَدِيلَة
7-24 distant signals	**إشَارَات المسافات**
7 semaphore signal at 'be prepared to stop at next signal'	إشَارَة سيمافور عند "استعد للتَّوَقُّف عند الإشَارَة القادمة"
8 supplementary semaphore arm	ذراع سيمافور إضافيّ

9 colour light (*Am.* color light) distant signal at 'be prepared to stop at next signal' — إشارَة مسافة ضَوْئيَّة مُلَوَّنَة عند "استعد للتَّوَقُّف عند الإشارَة القادمة"

10 signal position: 'be prepared to proceed at low speed' — وَضْع إشارَة : "استعد للتَّقَدُّم بسرعة منخفضة"

11 signal position: 'proceed main signal ahead' — وَضْع إشارَة : "تقدم للإشارَة الرئيسيَّة فى الأمام"

12 semaphore signal with indicator plate showing a reduction in braking distance of more than 5% — إشارَة سيمافور ذات لَوْحَة توضيحيَّة تُشير إلى مسافة فَرْمَلَة مُقَلَّة تَزيد عن 5 ٪

13 triangle (triangle sign) — مُثَلَّث، لافتَة مُثَلَّثة

14 colour light (*Am.* color light) distant signal with indicator light for showing reduced braking distance — إشارَة مسافة ضَوْئيَّة مُلَوَّنَة ذات ضَوْء إرشاديّ يُوَضِّح مسافة فرملة مُقلَّلة

15 supplementary white light — ضَوْء أبْيَض إضافيّ

16 distant signal indicating 'be prepared to stop at next signal' (yellow light) — إشارَة مسافة تشير إلى : "استعد للتَّوَقُّف عند الإشارَة القادمة" (ضَوْء أصفر)

17 second distant signal (distant signal with supplementary light, without indicator plate) — إشارَة مسافة ثانية مُزَوَّدة بضَوْء إضافيّ ولا يوجد بها لَوْحَة إرشاديَّة

18 distant signal with speed indicator — إشارَة مسافة بها لَوْحَة توضيح السُرْعَة

19 distant speed indicator — مُبَيِّن سرعة المسافة

20 distant signal with route indicator — إشارَة مسافة بها لَوْحَة مُبَيِّن الطريق

21 route indicator — لَوْحَة مُبَيِّن المسار

22 distant signal without supplementary arm in position: 'be prepared to stop at next signal' — إشارَة مسافة بدون ذراع إضافيّ فى وَضْع: "استعد للتَّوَقُّف عند الإشارَة القادمة"

23 distant signal without supplementary arm in 'be prepared to proceed' position — إشارَة مسافة بدون ذراع إضافيّ في وَضْع: "استعد للتقدم"

24 distant signal identification plate — لَوْحَة تعريف إشارَة المسافة

25-44 supplementary signals — **الإشارَات الإضافيَّة**

25 stop board for indicating the stopping point at a control point — لَوْحَة التَّوَقُّف لتحديد نقطة التَّوَقُّف عند تَحْوِيلَة

26-29 approach signs — **علامات الاقتراب**

26 approach sign 100 m from distant signal — علامَة الاقتراب بمسافة 100 متر من إشارَة المسافة

27 approach sign 175 m from distant signal — علامَة الاقتراب بمسافة 175 متراً من إشارَة المسافة

28 approach sign 250 m from distant signal — علامَة الاقتراب بمسافة 250 متراً من إشارَة المسافة

29 approach sign at a distance of 5% less than the braking distance on the section — علامة الاقتراب بمسافة 5 ٪ أقل من مسافة الفرملة على قِطَاع القضيب

30 chequered sign indicating stop signals (main signals) not positioned immediately to the right of or over the line (track) — علامَة مربعاتٍ تشير إلى أن إشارَات التَّوَقُّف غير مَوْضُوعة على يمين أو فوق الخط مباشرة

31, 32 stop boards to indicate the stopping point of the front of the train — لَوْحَات تَوَقُّف تشير إلى نقطة إيقاف مُقَدِّمَة القِطَار

33 stop board indicating 'be prepared to stop' — لَوْحَة تَوَقُّف "استعد للتَّوَقُّف"

34-35 snow plough (*Am.* snowplow) **signs** — **علامتا جَرَّافات الثلوج**

34 'raise snow plough (*Am.* snowplow)' signs — علامَة "ارفع جَرَّافة الثلوج"

35 'lower snow plough (*Am.* snowplow)' sign — علامَة "اخفض جَرَّافة الثلوج"

36-44 speed restriction signs — **علامات الحَدّ من السرعة**

36-38 speed restriction sign [maximum speed 3 x 10 = 30 kph] — **علامَة الحَدّ من السرعة** [أقصى سرعة 3 × 10 = 30 كم/س]

36 sign for day running — علامَة التشغيل نهاراً

37 speed code number — رقم كود السرعة

38 illuminated sign for night running — علامَة مُضيئة للتشغيل لَيْلاً

39 commencement of temporary speed restriction — بداية الحَدّ من السرعة مؤقتاً

40 termination of temporary speed restriction — انْتِهاء الحَدّ من السرعة المؤقتة

41 speed restriction sign for a section with a permanent speed restriction [maximum speed 5 x 10 = 50 kph] — علامَة الحَدّ من السرعة لمقطع له سرعة محدودة بصفة دائمة [أقصى سرعة 5 × 10 = 50 كم/س]

42 commencement of permanent speed restriction — بداية الحَدّ من السرعة بصفة دائمة

43 speed restriction warning sign [only on main lines] — علامَة التنبيه إلى الحَدّ من السرعة [على الخطوط الرئيسيَّة فقط]

44 speed restriction sign [only on main lines] — علامة الحَدّ من السرعة [على الخطوط الرئيسيَّة فقط]

45-52 point signals (switch signals) — **إشارَات التحويلات**

45-48 single points (single switches) — **تحويلات فَرْدِيَّة**

45 route straight ahead (main line) — الطريق مستقيم أمامك (خط رئيسي)

46 [right] branch — تَفَرُّع [يمين]

47 [left] branch — تَفَرُّع [يسار]

48 branch [seen from the frog]	تَفَرُّع [كما تراه من المقص]
49-52 double crossover	**خط تحويلة مزدوج**
49 route straight ahead from left to right	الطريق مستقيم أمامك من اليسار إلى اليمين
50 route straight ahead from right to left	الطريق مستقيم أمامك من اليمين إلى اليسار
51 turnout to the left from the left	تَحْوِيلَة جِهَة اليسار عند اليسار
52 turnout to the right from the right	تَحْوِيلَة جِهَة اليمين من اليمين
53 manually-operated signal box (*Am.* signal tower, switch tower)	كُشْك تشغيل الإشَارَات يدوياً
54 lever mechanism	آلِيَّة أذْرُع التشغيل
55 points lever (switch lever) [blue], a lock lever	ذِرَاع التحويلات [أزرق]
56 signal lever [red]	ذِرَاع الإشَارَات [أحمر]
57 catch	ذِرَاع تثبيت
58 route lever	ذِرَاع المَسَار
59 block instruments	آلات البلوكَّات
60 block section panel	لَوْحَة مَقْطَع البلوك
61 electrically-operated signal box (*Am.* signal tower, switch tower)	كُشْك تشغيل الإشَارَات كهربياً
62 points (switch) and signal knobs	مَقَابِض تشغيل التحويلات والإشَارَات
63 lock indicator panel	لَوْحَة إرشاديَّة للأقْفَال
64 track and signal indicator	شاشة إرشاديَّة للإشَارَات والمَسَارات
65 track diagram control layout	تصميم التحكم فى مُخَطَّط المَسَارات
66 track diagram control panel (domino panel)	لَوْحَة التحكم في مُخَطَّط المَسَارات
67 push buttons	أزْرَار انضغاطيَّة
68 routes	المَسَارات
69 intercom system	نظام الاتصال الداخلي (انتركوم)

204 Station Concourse — صَالَة المَحَطَّة

1 parcels office	مكْتَب الطُرُود
2 parcels	طُرُود
3 basket [with lock]	سَلَّة [ذات قُفْل]
4 luggage counter	كاونتر وَزْن الأمْتِعَة
5 platform scale with dial	ميزان بمنصة للأمْتِعَة ذو مقياس مُدَرَّج
6 suitcase (case)	حقيبة ملابس
7 luggage sticker	بِطَاقة لاصِقَة تُوضَع على الأمْتِعَة
8 luggage receipt	إيصَال استلام الأمْتِعَة
9 luggage clerk	مُوَظَّف استلام الأمْتِعَة ووَزْنها
10 poster (advertisement)	إعلان حائطيّ (بوستر)
11 station post box (*Am.* station mailbox)	صُنْدُوق بَرِيد المَحَطَّة
12 station guide	دليل المَحَطَّة
13 station restaurant	مطعم المَحَطَّة
14 waiting room	غُرْفَة الانتظار
15 map of the town (street map)	خَرِيطَة المدينة
16 timetable (*Am.* schedule)	جَدْوَل
17 ticket machine	ماكينة التَّذَاكِر
18 arrivals and departures board (timetable)	لَوْحَة إعلان مواعيد الوصول والمغادرة
19 arrival timetable (*Am.* arrival schedule)	جَدْوَل مواعيد الوصول
20 departure timetable (*Am.* departure schedule)	جَدْوَل مواعيد المغادرة
21 left luggage lockers	دواليب حِفْظ الأمانات
22 change machine	ماكينة صِرَافة، ماكينة استبدال العُمْلَة
23 tunnel to the platforms	نَفَق يؤدي إلى أرْصِفَة القطارات
24 passengers	رُكَّاب
25 steps to the platforms	دَرَج يؤدي إلى أرْصِفَة القطارات
26 station bookstall (*Am.* station bookstand)	كُشْك بَيْع الكُتُب والمجلات بالمَحَطَّة
27 left luggage office (left luggage)	مكْتَب إيداع الأمْتِعَة بالأمانات
28 travel centre (*Am.* center); *also:* accommodation bureau	مَرْكَز خدمات السفر والسياحة
29 information office (*Am.* information bureau)	مكْتَب الاستعلامات
30 station clock	ساعَة المَحَطَّة
31 bank branch with foreign exchange counter	فَرْع أحَد البنوك وبه شباك صِرَافة
32 indicator board showing exchange rates	لَوْحَة إرشاديَّة تعرض أسعار الصَّرْف
33 railway map (*Am.* railroad map)	خريطة السِّكَك الحديديَّة
34 ticket office	مكْتَب بيع وحجز التذاكر
35 ticket counter	شباك التذاكر
36 ticket	تذكرة القِطَار
37 revolving tray	صينية دوَّارة
38 grill	نـافِذَة
39 ticket clerk (*Am.* ticket agent)	مُوَظَّف شباك التذاكر
40 pane of glass (window)	لَوْح من الزُّجاج (شبَّاك)
41 pocket timetable (*Am.* pocket train schedule)	جَدْوَل مواعيد القطارات للجيب
42 luggage rest	مسْنَد الأمْتِعَة
43 first aid station	مَرْكَز الإسعافات الأوَّليَّة
44 Travellers' (*Am.* Travelers') Aid	مكْتَب مُسَاعَدة المسافرين
45 railway (*Am.* railroad) information clerk	مُوَظَّف استعلامات السكة الحديد
46 official timetable (official railway guide, *Am.* train schedule)	جَدْوَل مواعيد القطارات

205 Station Platform — رَصِيف المَحَطَّة

1 platform	رَصِيف القِطَارات
2 steps to the platform	دَرَج يؤدي إلى الرَّصِيف

3 bridge جِسْر يؤدي إلى الرَّصِيف
4 platform number رَقَم الرَّصِيف
5 platform roofing سَقْف الرَّصِيف
6 passengers رُكَّاب
7-12 luggage **أمْتِعَة**
7 suitcase (case) حقيبة ملابس
8 luggage label بطاقة تُلْصَق على الأمْتِعَة
9 hotel sticker بطاقة لاصِقة تُشير إلى الفندق
10 travelling (*Am.* traveling) bag حقيبة سفر
11 hat box عِلْبَة القبعة
12 umbrella, a walking-stick umbrella مِظَلَّة، شَمْسِيَّة
13 offices مكَاتِب
14 platform الرصيف
15 crossing مَعْبَر ركوب القطار
16 news trolley ترولي بَيْع الجرائد
17 news vendor (*Am.* news dealer) بائع الجرائد
18 reading matter for the journey مَطْبُوعات للقراءة أثناء السَّفَر
19 edge of the platform حافَة الرَّصِيف
20 railway policeman (*Am.* railroad policeman) رَجُل شُرْطَة السِّكَّة الحديديَّة
21 destination board لَوْحَة بَيَان وِجْهَة القِطَار
22 destination indicator بَيَان وِجْهَة القِطَار
23 departure time indicator بَيَان وَقْت المغادرة
24 delay indicator بَيَان التأخير عن الموعد المُحَدَّد
25 suburban train, a railcar قِطَار مُخَصَّص للنقل بين الضواحي
26 special compartment حُجَيْرَة خاصة
27 platform loudspeaker مُكَبِّر صَوْت بالرَّصِيف
28 station sign علامَة المَحَطَّة
29 electric trolley (electric truck) ترولي كهربائي
30 loading foreman مُلاحِظ الشَّيَّالين
31 porter (*Am.* redcap) شيَّــال
32 barrow عَرَبَة يَدَوِيَّة
33 drinking fountain حنفيَّة مياه للشرب
34 electric Eurocity express; *also:* IC express (Intercity express) قِطَار كهربائيّ سريع للنقل بيْن مُدُن أوروبا
35 electric locomotive, an express locomotive قاطِرة كهربائية، قاطِرة سريعة (قاطرة اكسبريس)
36 collector bow (sliding bow) آليَّة توصيل التيار الكهربائي
37 secretarial compartment حُجَيْرَة السكرتارية
38 destination board لَوْحَة بيان وِجْهَة القِطَار
39 wheel tapper عامِل نَقْر العَجَلَة
40 wheel-tapping hammer مِطْرَقَة نَقْر العَجَلَة
41 station foreman مُلاحِظ المَحَطَّة
42 signal لافتة، إشَارَة
43 red cap كاب أحمر
44 inspector مُفَتِّش القِطَار
45 pocket timetable (*Am.* pocket train schedule) جَدْوَل جيب بمواعيد القطارات
46 platform clock ساعَة الرَّصِيف
47 starting signal إشَارَة بدء تحريك القِطَار
48 platform lighting مصابيح إنارة الرَّصِيف
49 refreshment kiosk كُشْك بَيْع المرطبات
50 beer bottle زُجاجة جُعَّة، زُجاجة بِيرَة
51 newspaper جَرِيدَة، صَحِيفَة
52 parting kiss قُبْلَة تَوْدِيع
53 embrace عِنَاق
54 platform seat مَقْعَد الرَّصِيف
55 litter bin (*Am.* trash bin) صندوق المُهْمَلات
56 platform post box (*Am.* platform mailbox) صندوق بريد الرَّصِيف
57 platform telephone تليفون الرَّصِيف
58 trolley wire (overhead contact wire) سِلْك الترولي، سِلْك التلامُس العلويّ
59-61 track **مَسَار السِّكَّة الحديديَّة**
59 rail قَضِيب
60 sleeper (*Am.* tie, crosstie) فَلَنْكَة، رَاقِدَة
61 ballast (bed) فَرْشَة حَصَى

206 Goods Station (Freight Depot) مَحَطَّة البَضائع (مُسْتَوْدَع الشَّحْن)

1 ramp (vehicle ramp); *sim.:* livestock ramp طريق مُنْحَدِر للعربات
2 electric truck عَرَبَة كهربائيَّة
3 trailer مَقْطُورَة
4 part loads (*Am.* package freight, less-than-carload freight); *in general traffic:* general goods in general consignments (in mixed consignments) شُحْنَة مُغَلَّفَة ؛ في النقل العام: بضائع عامَة في شُحْنَات عامَة
5 crate قَفَص/صُنْدُوق شَحْن
6 goods van (*Am.* freight car) عَرَبَة الشَّحْن (عَرَبَة البضائع)
7 goods shed (*Am.* freight house) عَنْبَر الشَّحْن
8 loading strip منطقة التَّحْمِيل
9 loading dock رَصِيف التَّحْمِيل
10 bale of peat بالَة من قماش الخُثّ
11 bale of linen (of linen cloth) بالة من الكتَّان
12 fastening (cord) رباط، حَبْل
13 wicker bottle (wickered bottle, demijohn) قنينة مُملَّدة
14 trolley ترولي
15 goods lorry (*Am.* freight truck) عَرَبَة نقل البضائع
16 forklift truck (fork truck, forklift) مِرْفَاع شَوْكيّ
17 loading siding خَطّ التَّحْمِيل
18 bulky goods بضائع ضَخْمَة
19 small railway-owned (*Am.* railroad-owned) حاوِيَة صغيرة مَمْلُوكَة للسِّكَّة الحديديَّة

container

20 showman's caravan (*sim.:* Circus caravan) — كرفان تابع للسِّيرْك

21 flat wagon (*Am.* flat freight car) — عَرَبَة شَحْن مُسَطَّحَة

22 loading gauge (*Am.* gage) — مِقْيَاس التحميل

23 bale of straw — بالَة قَشّ

24 flat wagon (*Am.* flat-car) with side stakes — عَرَبَة مُسَطَّحَة مزودة بأوْتَاد جانِبِيَّة

25 fleet of lorries (*Am.* trucks) — أسْطُول من عَرَبَات النقل

26-39 goods shed (*Am.* freight house) — **عَنْبَر البضائع**

26 goods office (forwarding office, *Am.* freight office) — مكْتَب شَحْن البضائع

27 part-load goods (*Am.* package freight) — شُحْنَات مُغلَّفَة

28 forwarding agent (*Am.* freight agent, shipper) — وَكِيل الشَّحْن

29 loading foreman — مُلاحِظ الشَّحْن

30 consignment note (waybill) — بوليصة الشَّحْن

31 weighing machine — ماكينة الوَزْن

32 pallet — منصَّة نقَّالَة

33 porter — شيَّال

34 electric cart (electric truck) — عَرَبَة نقل كهربائيَّة

35 trailer — مَقْطُورَة

36 loading supervisor — مُشْرِف الشَّحْن

37 goods shed door (*Am.* freight house door) — بابَ عَنْبَر البضائع/عَنْبَر الشَّحْن

38 rail (slide rail) — قَضِيب (قَضِيب انزلاقيّ)

39 roller — عَجَلَة أُسْطُوَانيَّة

40 weighbridge office — مكْتَب جِسْر قبَّان

41 weighbridge — جِسْر قبَّان

42 marshalling yard (*Am.* classification yard, switch yard) — ساحَة التحويل

43 shunting engine (shunting locomotive, shunter, *Am.* switch engine, switcher) — قاطِرة التحويل

44 marshalling yard signal box (*Am.* classification yard switch tower) — كُشْك إشارَات ساحَة التحويل

45 yardmaster — مسئول السَّاحَة

46 hump — حَدَبَة، سِنَام

47 sorting siding (classification siding, classification track) — خَطّ الفَرْز والتصنيف

48 rail brake (retarder) — قَضِيب فرملة

49 slipper brake (slipper) — فَرْمَلَة انزلاقيَّة

50 storage siding (siding) — خَطّ تخزين

51 buffer (buffers, *Am.* bumper) — مِصَدّ

52 wagon load (*Am.* carload) — حمولة عَرَبَة

53 warehouse — مُسْتَوْدَع

54 container station — مَرْكَز الحاوِيَات

55 gantry crane — مِرْفَاع قنطريّ مُتَحَرِّك

56 lifting gear (hoisting gear) — مَعَدَّة الرفع

57 container — حاوِيَة

58 container wagon (*Am.* container car) — عَرَبَة نقل الحاوِيَات

59 semi-trailer — نِصْف مَقْطُورَة

207 Railway Vehicles (Rolling Stock) I — عَرَبَات السِّكَك الحَدِيدِيَّة (1)

1-21 express train coach (express train carriage, express train car, corridor compartment coach), a passenger coach — **عَرَبَة رُكَّاب القِطَار السريع**

1 side elevation (side view) — مَسْقَط جانبيّ

2 coach bod — جِسْم العَرَبَة

3 underframe (frame) — الهَيْكَل السفلي، الحامِلَة

4 bogie (truck) with steel and rubber suspension and shock absorbers — مَجْمَع عَجَلات ذو تعليق صلب ومطاط ومُخَمِّدات للصدمات

5 battery containers (battery boxes) — صناديق البطَّاريَّات

6 steam and electric heat exchanger for the heating system — مُبَادِل الحرارة والبُخَار الخاص بنظام التدفئة

7 sliding window — نافذة مُنْزَلِقَة

8 rubber connecting seal — وَصْلَة مطاطيَّة مُحْكَمَة

9 ventilator — آلِيَّة تهوية

10-21 plan — **تصميم العَرَبَة**

10 second-class section — قِسْم الدرجة الثانية

11 corridor — مَمَر العَرَبَة

12 folding seat (tip-up seat) — مَقْعَد قابل للطي

13 passenger compartment (compartment) — مَقْصُورَة المسافرين

14 compartment door — باب المَقْصُورَة

15 washroom — حُجَيْرَة الغسيل

16 toilet (lavatory, WC) — دَوْرَة مياه

17 first-class section — قِسْم الدرجة الأُولى

18 swing door — باب أرْجُوحي

19 sliding connecting door — باب توصيل مُنْزَلِق

20 door — باب

21 vestibule — دهليز، رواق

22-32 dining car (restaurant car, diner) — **عَرَبَة المَطْعَم**

22-25 side elevation (side view) — **مَسْقَط جانبيّ**

22 door — باب

23 loading door — باب تحميل الأمْتِعَة

24 current collector for supplying power during stops — قَضِيب تَوْصِيل التَّيَّار الكهربائي لإمداد الطاقة أثناء التَّوَقُّفَات

25 battery boxes (battery containers) — صناديق البطَّاريَّات

26-32 plan	**تصميم عَرَبَة المَطْعَم**
26 staff washroom	غُرْفَة غسيل خاصة بالعاملين
27 storage cupboard	صُوان تخزين
28 washing-up area	منطقة غسيل الأواني والأطباق
29 kitchen	المَطْبَخ
30 electric oven with eight hotplates	مَوْقِد طَهْي كهربائي ثُمَاني الشُعْلات
31 counter	كاونتر الخدمة
32 dining compartment	مَطْعَم القِطار
33 dining car kitchen	مَطْبَخ عَرَبَة المَطْعَم
34 chef (head cook)	رئيس الطُهَاة
35 kitchen cabinet	خَزَانَة المَطْبَخ
36 sleeping car (sleeper)	عَرَبَة النَّوْم
37 side elevation (side view)	مَسْقَط جانبيّ
38-42 plan	**تصميم عَرَبَة النَّوْم**
38 two-seat twin-berth compartment (two-seat two-berth compartment, *Am.* bedroom)	مَقْصُورَة ذات مَقْعَدَيْن ومضْجَعَيْن
39 folding doors	أبْوَاب قابِلة للطيّ
40 washstand	حَوْض غسيل (مغسلة)
41 office	مَكْتَب
42 toilet (lavatory, WC)	دَوْرَة مياه
43 express train compartment	مَقْصُورَة القطار السريع
44 upholstered reclining seat	مَقْعَد مُنجَّد قابل للبَسْط
45 armrest	مِسْنَد للذِّرَاع
46 ashtray in the armrest	مَنْفَضَة سجائر مثبتة بمِسْنَد الذِّرَاع
47 adjustable headrest	مِسْنَد رأسي قابل للتعديل
48 antimacassar	غطاء ظهر المَقْعَد
49 mirror	مِرْآة
50 coat hook	عَلاّقة المعْطَف
51 luggage rack	رَفّ الأمْتِعَة
52 compartment window	نافذة المقصورة
53 fold-away table (pull-down table)	طاوِلة قابِلة للطي
54 heating regulator	مُنَظِّم التدفئة
55 litter receptacle	صندوق مهملات
56 curtain	سِتَارة
57 footrest	مِسْنَد القَدَمَيْن
58 corner seat	مَقْعَد الزاوية
59 open car	عَرَبَة مفتوحة
60 side elevation (side view)	مَسْقَط جانبيّ
61-72 plan	**تصميم العَرَبَة المفتوحة**
61 open carriage	عَرَبَة مفتوحة
62 row of single seats	صَفّ مقاعد فَرْدِيَّة
63 row of double seats	صَفّ مقاعد مزدوجة
64 reclining seat	مَقْعَد قابل للبَسْط
65 seat upholstery	وسَادة مَقْعَد
66 backrest	مِسْنَد الظَّهْر
67 headrest	مِسْنَد الرأس
68 down-filled headrest cushion with nylon cover	وِسَادة مِسْنَد رأس محشوة لها غِطاء من النايلون

69 armrest with ashtray	مِسْنَد ذراع مُزَوَّد بمَنْفَضَة سجائر
70 cloakroom	حُجْرَة تعليق العَبَاءات والمَعَاطف
71 luggage compartment	حُجَيْرَة الأمْتِعَة
72 toilet (lavatory, WC)	دَوْرَة مياه
73 buffet car (quick-service buffet car), a self-service restaurant car	عَرَبَة البُوفيه (المطعم)
74 side elevation (side view)	مَسْقَط جانبيّ
75 current collector for supplying power during stops	قَضِيب توصيل التيار الكهربائي للإمداد بالطاقة أثناء التوقف
76 plan	تصميم عَرَبَة البُوفيه
77 dining compartment	المَطْعَم (حجيرة الطعام)
78-79 buffet (buffet compartment)	**البُوفيه**
78 customer area	منطقة الزبائن
79 serving area	منطقة الخدمة
80 kitchen	المَطْبَخ
81 staff compartment	حُجَيْرَة العاملين
82 staff toilet (staff lavatory, staff WC)	دَوْرَة المياه للعاملين
83 food compartments	حُجَيْرَات الطعام
84 plates	الأطباق
85 cutlery	أدوات المائدة (السكاكين)
86 till (cash register)	ماكينة دفع النقديَّة
208 Railway Vehicles (Rolling Stock) II	**عَرَبَات السِّكَك الحَديديَّة (2)**
1-30 local train service	**خدْمَة القِطار المحلي**
1-12 local train (short-distance train)	**قِطار مَحلِّي** (للمسافات القصيرة)
1 electric locomotive	قاطِرة كهربيَّة
2 current collector	ذراع توصيل التيَّار
3 four-axled coach (four-axled car) for short-distance routes, a passenger coach (passenger car)	عَرَبَة رُباعيَّة المَحَاور للمسافات القصيرة، عربة رُكَّاب
4 bogie (truck) [with disc (disk) brakes]	مَجْمَع عَجَلات [ذو فرامل قُرْصِيَّة]
5 underframe (frame)	الهيكل السفلي
6 coach body with metal panelling (*Am.* paneling)	جِسْم العَرَبَة المكْسُوّ بألْوَاح معدنيَّة
7 double folding doors	أبْوَاب مُزْدَوَجة قابلة للطي
8 compartment window	نافذة العَرَبَة
9 open carriage	عَرَبَة مفتوحة
10 entrance	مَدْخَل
11 connecting corridor	دهليز توصيل
12 rubber connecting seal	وَصْلَة مطاطيَّة مُحكَمَة
13 light railcar, a short-distance railcar	عَرَبَة سكة حديديَّة خفيفة للمسافات القصيرة
14 cab (driver's cab, *Am.* engineer's cab)	كابينة السائق
15 carriage door	باب العربة

16	connecting hoses and coupling	خراطيم ومقَارِن توصيل
17	coupling link	وَصْلَة قارِنة
18	tensioning device (coupling screw with tensioning lever)	جِهَاز شَدّ
19	unlinked coupling	قارنة غير موصِّلة
20	heating coupling hose (steam coupling hose)	خُرْطوم توصيل هواء التدفئة
21	coupling hose (connecting hose) for the compressed-air braking system	خُرْطُوم قارِن خاص بنظام فرملة الهواء المضغوط
22	second-class section	قِسْم الدرجة الثانية
23	central gangway	مَمَر وَسَط العَرَبَة
24	compartment	مَقْصُورَة
25	upholstered seat	مَقْعَد مُنَجَّد
26	armrest	مِسْنَد الذراع
27	luggage rack	رَفّ الأَمْتِعَة
28	hat and light luggage rack	رَفّ حفظ القبعات والأَمْتِعَة الخفيفة
29	ashtray	مِنْفَضَة السجائر
30	passenger	راكِب

209 Railway Vehicles (Rolling Stock) III — عَرَبَات السِّكَك الحَدِيدِيَّة (3)

1-19 Intercity Express — **القِطَار السريع للسَّفَر بَيْنَ المُدُن**

1	German Federal Railway trainset	قِطَار السكك الحديديَّة الألمانيَّة
2	driving unit (power car)	وَحْدَة الدَّفْع (عربة الطَّاقة)
3	driving bogie with traction motors	مَجْمَع عجلات ومُحَرِّكَات السَّحْب
4	cab (driver's cab, *Am.* engineer's cab)	كابينة السائق
5	power supply (traction current filter)	إمْدَاد الطَّاقَة (فلتر تيار الجَرّ)
6	contactors (converters, inductance)	مفاتيح تلامس (مُحَوِّلات، مُحَاثَة)
7	traction motor blower	نافخ موتور السَّحْب
8	inductance protection (converter)	وقايَة المُحَاثَة (مُحَوِّل)
9	oil-cooling plant	وَحْدَة تبريد الزيت
10	converter for the auxiliaries	مُحَوِّل المُعِدَّات المُسَاعِدَة
11	electronics	أجْهِزَة إلكترونيَّة
12	control current equipment	مُعِدَّات ضَبْط التَّيَّار
13	auxiliaries (switchgear)	مُعِدَّات مُساعِدَة (مجموعة المفاتيح الكهربائية)
14	pneumatic equipment	مُعِدَّات تعمل بالهواء المضغوط
15	air-conditioning plant	وَحْدَة تكييف الهواء
16	main current converters	مُحَوِّلات التيار الرئيسيَّة
17	measuring equipment (diagnosis)	مُعِدَّات قياس
18	continuous automatic train-running control	مِضْبَط تشغيل القطار بشكل مُتَواصِل آليّاً
19	transformer	مُحَوِّل
20	TGV (Train á Grande Vitesse) of the Société Nationale des Chemins de Fer Français (SNCF)	القِطار السريع للجمعية القومية للسكك الحديدية الفرنسيَّة

210 Railway Vehicles (Rolling Stock) IV — عَرَبَات السِّكَك الحَدِيدِيَّة (4)

1-69 steam locomotives — **القاطِرَات البُخَارِيَّة**

2-37 locomotive boiler and driving gear — **مِرْجَل وتُرْس إدارَة القاطِرة**

2	tender platform with coupling	مِنَصَّة تموين ذات مِقْرَن
3	safety valve for excess boiler pressure	صِمَام أمان لضغط المِرْجَل الزائد
4	firebox	صندوق اللهب
5	drop grate	مُصَبَّعة ساقطة
6	ashpan with damper doors	مَرْمَدة بها أبواب مِقْلَب رَمَاد المِرْجَل
7	bottom door of the ashpan	الباب السفلي للمَرْمَدة
8	smoke tubes (flue tubes)	أنابيب الدخان
9	feed pump	مِضَخَّة تغذية
10	axle bearing	مَحْمَل المِحْوَر
11	connecting rod	قَضِيب توصيل
12	steam dome	قُبَّة البُخَار
13	regulator valve (regulator main valve)	صِمَام المنظِّم
14	sand dome	قُبَّة الرَّمْل
15	sand pipes (sand tubes)	مَوَاسير الرَّمْل
16	boiler (boiler barrel)	المِرْجَل
17	fire tubes or steam tubes	مَوَاسير اللهب أو مَوَاسير البُخَار
18	reversing gear (steam reversing gear)	تُرْس عاكِس
19	sand pipes	مَوَاسير الرَّمْل
20	feed valve	صِمَام تغذية
21	steam collector	آليَّة تجميع البُخَار
22	chimney (smokestack, smoke outlet and waste steam exhaust)	مِدْخَنَة (مَنْفَذ الدخان وعادم البُخَار)
23	feedwater preheater (feedwater heater, economizer)	مُسَخِّن ماء التغذية
24	spark arrester	مانِعَة الشَّرَر
25	blast pipe	ماسُورة العَصْف
26	smokebox door	باب صندوق الدخان
27	cross head	طَرْبُوش
28	mud drum	صندوق الحمأة
29	top feedwater tray	صينية ماء تغذية علويَّة
30	combination lever	رافِعة تجميعيَّة
31	steam chest	صندوق البُخَار
32	cylinder	أسْطُوَانة
33	piston rod with stuffing box (packing box)	ذِرَاع المِكْبَس وبها صندوق الحَشْو
34	guard iron (rail guard, *Am.* pilot, cowcatcher)	قَضِيب أمان
35	carrying axle (running	عَمُود حَمْل

axle, dead axle)
36 coupled axle — عَمُود مَقْرُون
37 driving axle — عَمُود الإدارة
38 express locomotive with tender — قاطِرة سريعة ذات قاطِرة تموين
39-63 cab (driver's cab, *Am.* engineer's cab) — **كابينة سائق القطار**
39 fireman's seat — مَقْعَد الوَقَّاد
40 drop grate lever — ذراع المُصَبَّعة الساقطة
41 line steam injector — حاقِن البُخَار
42 automatic lubricant pump (automatic lubricator) — مِضَخَّة تشحيم آليَّة
43 preheater pressure gauge (*Am.* gage) — مِقْيَاس ضغط المُسَخِّن المُتَقَدِّم
44 carriage heating pressure gauge (*Am.* gage) — مِقْيَاس ضغط تدفئة العَرَبَات
45 water gauge (*Am.* gage) — مِقْيَاس الماء
46 light — مِصْبَاح الإنارة
47 boiler pressure gauge (*Am.* gage) — مِقْيَاس ضغط المِرْجَل
48 distant-reading temperature gauge (*Am.* gage) — مِقْيَاس الحرارة وقراءة المسافة
49 cab (driver's cab, *Am.* engineer's cab) — كابينة السائق
50 brake pressure gauge (*Am.* gage) — مِقْيَاس ضغط الفرملة
51 whistle valve handle — مِقْبَض صِمَام الصَّافِرة
52 driver's timetable (*Am.* engineer's schedule) — جَدْوَل مواعيد السائق
53 driver's brake valve (*Am.* engineer's brake valve) — صِمَام فرملة السائق
54 speed recorder (tachograph) — مُسَجِّل السرعة (عدَّاد الدَّوْرَات)
55 sanding valve — صِمَام الرَّمْل
56 reversing wheel — عَجَلَة عاكسة
57 emergency brake valve — صِمَام فرملة الطوارئ
58 release valve — صِمَام إعتاق
59 driver's seat (*Am.* engineer's seat) — مَقْعَد السائق
60 firehole shield — وقاء ثُقْب الإشْعَال
61 firehole door — باب ثُقْب الإشْعَال
62 vertical boiler — مِرْجَل رأسيّ
63 firedoor handle handgrip — مِقْبَض باب المَوْقِد
64 articulated locomotive (Garratt locomotive) — قاطِرة مِفْصَلِيَّة
65 tank locomotive — قاطِرة صهريجيَّة
66 water tank — خزان الماء
67 fuel tender — قاطِرة تموين الوَقُود
68 steam storage locomotive (fireless locomotive) — قاطِرة بُخَارية
69 condensing locomotive (locomotive with condensing tender) — قاطِرة ذات مقطورة ماء وَوقود مُكَثَّفَة

211 Railway Vehicles (Rolling Stock) V — عَرَبَات السِّكك الحَديديَّة (5)

1 electric locomotive — قاطِرة كهربائيَّة
2 current collector — ذِرَاع توصيل التَّيَّار
3 main switch — مِفْتَاح التشغيل الرئيسي
4 high-tension transformer — مُحَوِّل عالي الضغط
5 roof cable — كيبل السقف
6 traction motor — مُوتُور جَرّ
7 inductive train control system — نظام تَحكُّم حَثِّي في القِطار
8 main air reservoir — خَزَّان الهواء الرئيسي
9 whistle — صافِرَة
10-18 plan of locomotive — **تمثيل تخطيطي للقاطرة**
10 transformer with tap changer — مُحَوِّل ذو آليَّة تغيير المَآخَذ
11 oil cooler with blower — مُبَرِّد الزَّيْت ونافخ
12 oil-circulating pump — مِضَخَّة تدوير الزَّيْت
13 tap changer driving mechanism — آليَّة إدارة مُغيِّر المَأْخَذ
14 air compressor — ضاغِط هواء
15 traction motor blower — نافخ موتور الجَرّ
16 terminal box — عُلْبَة نَهَائيَّات/مَرَابط
17 capacitors for auxiliary motors — مكثِّفات خاصة بالمُحَرِّكات الإضافيَّة
18 commutator cover — غطاء المُبَدِّل
19 cab (driver's cab, *Am.* engineer's cab) — كابينة (كابينة السائق/المهندس)
20 controller handwheel — عَجَلَة التَّحكُّم
21 dead man's handle — ذِرَاع ثابت
22 driver's brake valve (*Am.* engineer's brake valve) — صِمَام فرملة السائق
23 ancillary brake valve (auxiliary brake valve) — صِمَام فرملة تابِع
24 pressure gauge (*Am.* gage) — مِقْيَاس الضغط
25 bypass switch for the dead man's handle — مفتَاح تحويلي للذِّرَاع الثابت
26 tractive effort indicator — مُبَيِّن قُدْرَة الجَرّ
27 train heating voltage indicator — مُبَيِّن فولطيَّة تدفئة القِطَار
28 contact wire voltage indicator (overhead wire voltage indicator) — مُبَيِّن فولطيَّة ذو سِلْك تلامسيّ
29 high-tension voltage indicator — مُبَيِّن فولطيَّة عالي الضغط
30 on/off switch for the current collector — مِفْتَاح تشغيل/إيقاف ذِرَاع توصيل التَّيَّار
31 main switch — مِفْتَاح التشغيل الرئيسي
32 sander switch (sander control) — مِضْبَط مِذَرَّة الرَّمْل
33 anti-skid brake switch — مِفْتَاح فرامل مقاومة للانزلاق
34 visual display for the ancillary systems — شاشة مُتَابَعَة الأنظمة التابعة
35 speedometer — عَدَّاد السرعة
36 running step indicator — مِفْتَاح التشغيل المُتَدَرِّج

37 clock ساعة
38 controls for the inductive train control system مَضَابِط نظام التَّحكُّم الحثي في القِطَار
39 cab heating switch مفْتَاح تدفئة الكابينة
40 whistle lever ذِرَاع تشغيل الصافِرة
41 contact wire maintenance vehicle (overhead wire maintenance vehicle), a diesel railcar عَرَبَة صيانة سِلْك التلامُس
42 work platform (working platform) مِنَصَّة الشغل
43 ladder سُلَّم دَرَجِيّ
44-54 mechanical equipment of the contact wire maintenance vehicle المُعدَّات الميكانيكيَّة لعَرَبَة صيانة سِلْك التلامُس
44 air compressor ضاغط هواء
45 blower oil pump مِضَخَّة زَيْت النافخ
46 generator مُوَلِّد كهربائي
47 diesel engine مُحَرِّك ديزل
48 injection pump مِضَخَّة حَقْن
49 silencer (*Am.* muffler) كاتِم الصَّوْت، عِلْبَة العادِم
50 change-speed gear تروس تغيير السرعة
51 cardan shaft عَمُود كردان
52 wheel flange lubricator مِشْحَمَة شَفَة العَجَلَة
53 reversing gear تُرْس عاكس
54 torque converter bearing مَحْمَل مُحَوِّل عَزْم اللّيّ
55 accumulator railcar (battery railcar) عَرَبَة تسير بالمُرَكِّمَات
56 battery box (battery container) صُنْدُوق البطاريات
57 cab (driver's cab, *Am.* engineer's cab) كابينة السائق/المهندس
58 second-class seating arrangement ترتيب مَقَاعِد الدَّرَجَة الثانية
59 toilet (lavatory, WC) دَوْرَة مياه
60 fast electric multiple-unit train قِطَار كهربائيّ سريع مُتَعَدِّد الوَحْدَات
61 front railcar عَرَبَة القِطَار الأماميَّة
62 driving trailer car عَرَبَة قاطِرة الدَّفْع

212 Railway Vehicles (Rolling Stock) VI عَرَبَات السِّكَك الحَديديَّة (6)

1-84 diesel locomotives قاطِرَات تَعْمَل بالديزل
1 diesel-hydraulic locomotive, a mainline locomotive (diesel locomotive) for medium passenger and goods service (freight service) **قاطِرة ايدروليَّة تَعْمَل بالديزل** لخدمة رُكَّاب المسافات المتوسطة والشحن
2 bogie (truck) مَجْمَع عَجَلات
3 wheel and axle set طاقم من عَجَلَة ومِحْوَر
4 main fuel tank خَزَّان الوَقُود الرئيسي
5 cab (driver's cab, *Am.* engineer's cab) of a diesel locomotive كابينة قاطِرة الديزل
6 main air pressure gauge (*Am.* gage) مِقْيَاس ضغط الهواء الرئيسي
7 brake cylinder pressure gauge (*Am.* gage) مِقْيَاس ضغط أُسْطُوَانة الفرامل
8 main air reservoir pressure gauge (*Am.* gage) مِقْيَاس ضغط خَزَّان الهواء الرئيسي
9 speedometer عَدَّاد السرعة
10 auxiliary brake فرامل إضافية
11 driver's brake valve (*Am.* engineer's brake valve) صِمَام فرملة السائق
12 controller handwheel عَجَلَة التَّحكُّم
13 dead man's handle ذِرَاع ثابت
14 inductive train control system نظام تحكم حَثِّيّ في القِطَار
15 signal lights لَمْبَات الإشارة
16 clock ساعة
17 voltage meter for the train heating system مِقْيَاس فولطيَّة نظام تدفئة القطار
18 current meter for the train heating system مقياس تيار نظام تدفئة القطار
19 engine oil temperature gauge (*Am.* gage) عَدَّاد حرارة زيت المُحَرِّك
20 transmission oil temperature gauge (*Am.* gage) عَدَّاد حرارة زَيْت عَمُود نقل الحركة
21 cooling water temperature gauge (*Am.* gage) عَدَّاد حرارة ماء التبريد
22 revolution counter (rev counter, tachometer) عَدَّاد اللفَّات
23 radio telephone تليفون لاسلكي
24 diesel-hydraulic locomotive [plan and elevation] قاطِرة ايدروليَّة تَعْمَل بالديزل [تمثيل تخطيطي ومَسْقَط رأسيّ]
25 diesel engine مُحَرِّك يَعْمَل بالديزل
26 cooling unit وَحْدَة تبريد
27 fluid transmission نَقْل حركة مائعيّ
28 wheel and axle drive إدارة العَجَلَة والمِحْوَر
29 cardan shaft عَمُود كردان
30 starter motor مُحَرِّك بدء التشغيل
31 instrument panel لَوْحَة الآلات
32 driver's control desk (*Am.* engineer's control desk) لَوْحَة التَّحكُّم الخاصة بالسائق/المهندس
33 hand brake فَرْمَلَة يدويَّة
34 air compressor with electric motor ضاغط هواء ذو مُحَرِّك كهربائي
35 equipment locker خزانة المُعدَّات
36 heat exchanger for transmission oil مُبَادِل حراري لزَيْت نقل الحركة
37 engine room ventilator آليَّة تهوية غُرْفَة المُحَرِّك
38 magnet for the inductive train control system مغناطيس نظام التَّحكُّم الحثي في القِطَار
39 train heating generator مُوَلِّد كهربائي لتدفئة القطَار
40 casing of the train heating system transformer غلاف مُحَوِّل نظام تدفئة القِطَار

41 preheater — سَخَّان مُتَقَدِّم
42 exhaust silencer (*Am.* exhaust muffler) — كاتِم الصَّوْت، عِلْبَة العادِم
43 auxiliary heat exchanger for the transmission oil — مُبَادِل حراري ثانوي لزيت نقل السرعة
44 hydraulic brake — فرملة ايدروليَّة
45 tool box — صُنْدُوق الأدوات
46 starter battery — بَطَّاريَّة بدء التشغيل
47 diesel-hydraulic locomotive for light and medium shunting service — قاطِرة ايدروليَّة تَعْمَل بالديزل لخدمة تحويلات الخط الخفيفة والمتوسطة
48 exhaust silencer (*Am.* exhaust muffler) — كاتِم الصَّوْت، عِلْبَة العادِم
49 bell and whistle — جَرَس وصافِرة
50 yard radio — راديو اتصال بِسَاحَة القطارات

51-67 elevation of locomotive — **مَسْقَط رأسي للقاطِرة**

51 diesel engine with supercharged turbine — مُحَرِّك ديزل يعمل بتوربين مُزَيِّد الشحن
52 fluid transmission — نَقْل حركة مائعيّ
53 output gear box — صُنْدُوق تروس الخَرْج
54 radiator — مُشِعّ
55 heat exchanger for the engine lubricating oil — مُبَادِل حراري لزيت تزليق المُحَرِّك
56 fuel tank — خَزَّان الوَقُود
57 main air reservoir — خَزَّان الهواء الرئيسي
58 air compressor — ضاغط هواء
59 sand boxes — صناديق الرَّمْل
60 reserve fuel tank — خَزَّان الوَقُود الاحتياطي
61 auxiliary air reservoir — خَزَّان هواء إضافي
62 hydrostatic fan drive — إدارة مروحة هيدروستاتيَّة
63 seat with clothes compartment — مَقْعَد وبه حُجَيْرَة للملابِس
64 hand brake wheel — عَجَلَة الفرملة اليدويَّة
65 cooling water — ماء التبريد
66 ballast — صابُورة
67 engine and transmission control wheel — عَجَلَة التَّحَكُّم في المُحَرِّك ونقل السرعة
68 small diesel locomotive for shunting service — قاطِرة صغيرة تَعْمَل بالديزل لخدمة تحويل الخط
69 exhaust casing — غلاف عِلْبَة العادِم
70 horn — بُوق
71 main air reservoir — خَزَّان الهواء الرئيسي
72 air compressor — ضاغط هواء
73 eight-cylinder diesel engine — مُحَرِّك ديزل ثماني الأُسْطُوَانات
74 Voith transmission with reversing gear — نَقْل سرعة طراز "فويث" مع تُرْس عاكِس
75 heating oil tank (fuel oil tank) — خَزَّان زَيْت التدفئة
76 sand box — صُنْدُوق الرَّمْل
77 cooling unit — وَحْدَة التبريد
78 header tank for the cooling water — خَزَّان علويّ لماء التبريد
79 oil bath air cleaner (oil bath air filter) — مُرَشِّح هواء حَمَّام الزَّيْت
80 hand brake wheel — عَجَلة الفرمِلة اليدويَّة
81 control wheel — عَجَلَة التَّحكُّم
82 coupling — مِقْرَن، كوبلنج
83 cardan shaft — عَمُود كردان
84 louvred shutter — غِطاء ذو شَفَة للتهوية

213 Railway Vehicles (Rolling Stock) VII — عَرَبَات السِّكك الحَديديَّة (7)

1 diesel-hydraulic locomotive — قاطِرة ايدروليَّة تَعْمَل بالديزل
2 cab (driver's cab, *Am.* engineer's cab) — كابينة السائق/المهندس
3 wheel and axle set — طاقم من عَجَلَة ومِحْوَر
4 aerial for the yard radio — هوائي راديو سَاحَة القطارات
5 standard flat wagon (*Am.* standard flatcar) — عَرَبَة مُسَطَّحَة عاديَّة
6 hinged steel stanchion (stanchion) — قائم دُعامة صلب مِفْصَليّ
7 buffers — مصَدَّات
8 standard open goods wagon (*Am.* standard open freight car) — عَرَبَة بضائع عادية مفتوحة
9 revolving side doors — أبواب جانبيَّة دَوَّارة
10 hinged front — مُقَدِّمَة مفصَليَّة
11 standard flat wagon (*Am.* standard flatcar) with bogies — عَرَبَة مُسَطَّحَة عاديَّة تسير على مَجَامع عَجَلات
12 sole bar reinforcement — قَضيب تقوية القاعِدة
13 bogie (truck) — مَجْمَع عَجَلات
14 covered goods van (covered goods wagon, *Am.* boxcar) — عَرَبَة بضائع مُغَطَّاة
15 sliding door — باب انزلاقي
16 ventilation flap — قلَّابة تَهْوِيَة
17 snow blower (rotary snow plough, *Am.* snowplow), a track-clearing vehicle — عَرَبَة إزاحة الثلوج
18 wagon (*Am.* car) with pneumatic discharge — عَرَبَة تعمل بتفريغ الهواء المضغوط
19 filler hole — فتحة التعبئة
20 compressed-air supply — إمْداد الهواء المضغوط
21 discharge connection valve — صِمَام توصيل التفريغ
22 goods van (*Am.* boxcar) with sliding roof — عَرَبَة بضائع ذات سقف انزلاقي
23 roof opening — فتحة السقف
24 bogie open self-discharge wagon (*Am.* bogie open self-discharge freight car) — عَرَبَة مفتوحة ذاتيَّة التفريغ تتحرك على مَجَامع عَجَلات
25 discharge flap (discharge door) — قَلَّابة/باب التفريغ
26 bogie wagon with swivelling (*Am.* swiveling) roof — عربة ذات سقف دَوَرَانيّ تسير على مَجَامع عَجَلات
27 swivelling (*Am.* swiveling) roof — سقف دَوَرَانيّ

28 large-capacity wagon (*Am.* large-capacity car) for small livestock — عَرَبَة كبيرة الحمولة لنقل المَاشِيَة الصغيرة
29 sidewall with ventilation flaps (slatted wall) — جِدَار جانبيّ ذو قلابات تهوية
30 ventilation flap — قلابة تهوية
31 tank wagon (*Am.* tank car) — عَرَبَة صهريج
32 track inspection railcar — عَرَبَة سِكَّة حديديَّة لفحص المَسَار
33 open special wagons (*Am.* open special freight cars) — عَرَبَات شحن خاصة مفتوحة
34 lorry (*Am.* truck) with trailer — شاحِنَة ذات مقطورة
35 two-tier car carrier (double-deck car carrier) — حامِلة عَرَبَات ذات طابقَيْن
36 hinged upper deck — سطح علويّ مِفْصَليّ
37 tipper wagon (*Am.* dump car) with skips — عَرَبَة قلاّبة قادوسيَّة
38 skip — قادوس
39 general-purpose refrigerator wagon (refrigerator van, *Am.* refrigerator car) — بَرَّادَة للأغراض العامة
40 interchangeable bodies for flat wagons (*Am.* flatcars) — أجْسَام قابلة للإبدال للعربات المُسَطَّحَة

214 Mountain Railways (Am. Railroads) and Cableways — السِّكك الحَديديَّة الجَبَليَّة والسِّكَك الحَديديَّة الكيبليَّة

1-14 mountain railways (*Am.* mountain railroads) — **السِّكَك الحَديديَّة الجَبَليَّة**
1 adhesion railcar — عربة سِكَّة حديديَّة لاصقة
2 drive — إدارة
3 emergency brake — فرملة الطوارئ
4 & 5 rack mountain railway (rack-and-pinion railway, cog railway, *Am.* cog railroad, rack railroad) — سِكَّة حديديَّة ذات جَرِيدَة وتُرْس (مُسَنَّنَة)
4 electric rack railway locomotive (*Am.* electric rack railroad locomotive) — قاطرة سِكَّة حديديَّة كهربائيَّة مُسَنَّنَة
5 rack railway coach (rack railway trailer, *Am.* rack railroad car) — عَرَبَة سِكَّة حديديَّة مُسَنَّنَة
6 tunnel — نَفَق
7-11 rack railways (rack-and-pinion railways, *Am.* rack railroads) [systems] — **سِكَك حديديَّة مُسَنَّنَة**
7 running wheel (carrying wheel) — عَجَلَة التشغيل/الحَمْل
8 driving pinion — ترس الإدارة/الدفع
9 rack [with teeth machined on top edge] — جريدة [ذات أسنان بالحافة العلوية]
10 rail — قضيب سكة حديدية
11 rack [with teeth on both outer edges] — جريدة [ذات أسنان بكلتا الحافتيْن الخارجيتيْن]
12 funicular railway (funicular, cable railway) — سِكَّة حديديَّة مُعَلَّقَة
13 funicular railway car — عَرَبَة سِكَّة حديديَّة مُعلَّقَة
14 haulage cable — كيبل السحب
15-38 cableways (ropeways, cable suspension lines) — **التليفريك**
15-24 single-cable ropeways (single-cable suspension lines), endless cableways, endless ropeways — **سكَّة حديديَّة كيبليَّة مُفَرَدَة الكيبل**
15 drag lift — مِصْعَد السَّحْب
16-18 chair lift — **مَصْعَد ذو مَقْعَد**
16 lift chain, a single chain — سلسلة المصعد، سلسلة مفردة
17 double lift chair, a two-seater chair — مَقْعَد مُزْدَوَج
18 double chair (two-seater chair) with coupling — مَقْعَد مُزْدَوَج ذو مِقْرَن
19 gondola cableway, an endless cableway — سِكَّة حديديَّة كيبليَّة ذات عَرَبَات مكشوفة
20 gondola (cabin) — عَرَبَة مكشوفة (غندولا)
21 endless cable, a suspension (supporting) and haulage cable — كيبل تعليق مستمر
22 U-rail — قَضِيب على شكل حرف U
23 single-pylon support — دعامة ذات بُرْج مُفْرَد
24 gantry support — حامِل قَنْطَريّ
25 double-cable ropeway (double-cable suspension line), a suspension line with balancing cabins — سكة حديدية كبلية مزدوجة الكيبل
26 haulage cable — كيبل السحب
27 suspension cable (supporting cable) — كيبل التعليق
28 cabin — كابينة
29 intermediate support — دعامة وسطية
30 cableway (ropeway, suspension line), a double-cable ropeway (double-cable suspension line) — سِكَّة حديديَّة كيبليَّة
31 pylon — بُرْج
32 haulage cable roller — أسْطُوَانة كيبل السحب
33 cable guide rail (suspension cable bearing) — قَضِيب دليلي للكيبل
34 skip, a tipping bucket (*Am.* dumping bucket) — قادوس، قادوس قَلاّب
35 stop — ذِرَاع إيقاف

36 pulley cradle — مَحْمَل البكَرَات
37 haulage cable — كيبل السحب
38 suspension cable (supporting cable) — كيبل التعليق
39 valley station (lower station) — مَحَطَّة رُكْنِيَّة (منخفضة)
40 tension weight shaft — مِهْوَاة ثِقْل الشَّدّ
41 tension weight for the suspension cable (supporting cable) — ثِقْل شد كيبل التعليق
42 tension weight for the haulage cable — ثِقْل شد كيبل السحب
43 tension cable pulley — بكَرَة ثِقْل الشَّدّ
44 suspension cable (supporting cable) — كيبل التعليق
45 haulage cable — كيبل السحب
46 balance cable (lower cable) — كيبل مُوَازَنَة (كيبل سفليّ)
47 auxiliary cable (emergency cable) — كيبل إضافي (للطوارئ)
48 auxiliary-cable tensioning mechanism (emergency-cable tensioning mechanism) — آليَّة شد كيبل الطوارئ
49 haulage cable rollers — أسْطُوَانات كيبل السحب
50 spring buffer (*Am.* spring bumper) — مِصَد مُعَلَّق على نابِض
51 valley station platform (lower station platform) — رَصيف المَحَطَّة الرُكْنِيَّة
52 cabin (cableway gondola, ropeway gondola, suspension line gondola), a large-capacity cabin — كابينة (كبيرة السَّعَة)
53 pulley cradle — مَحْمَل البكَرَات
54 suspension gear — آليَّة التعليق
55 stabilizer — آليَّة مُوَازَنَة
56 guide rail — قَضِيب دليلي
57 top station (upper station) — مَحَطَّة علويَّة
58 suspension cable guide (supporting cable guide) — دليل كيبل التعليق
59 suspension cable anchorage (supporting cable anchorage) — إرْسَاء كيبل التعليق
60 haulage cable rollers — أسْطُوَانات كيبل السحب
61 haulage cable guide wheel — عَجَلَة دليليَّة لكيبل السحب
62 haulage cable driving pulley — بكَرَة دفع كيبل السحب
63 main drive — الإدارة الرئيسيَّة
64 standby drive — إدارة احتياطيَّة
65 control room — غرفة التحكم
66 cabin pulley cradle — مَحْمَل بكَرَات الكابينة
67 main pulley caradle — مَحْمَل البكَرَات الرئيسي
68 double cradle — مَحْمَل مزدوج
69 two-wheel cradle — مَحْمَل ذو عَجَلَتَيْن
70 running wheels — عَجَلات التشغيل
71 suspension cable brake (supporting cable brake), an emergency brake in case of haulage cable failure — فرملة كيبل التعليق ، فرملة طوارئ في حالة انقطاع كيبل السحب
72 suspension gear bolt — مِسْمَار تثبيت آليَّة التعليق
73 haulage cable sleeve — كُمّ كيبل السحب
74 balance cable sleeve (lower cable sleeve) — كُمّ كيبل المُوَازَنَة
75 derailment guard — وقاء الحيُود
76 cable supports (ropeway supports, suspension line supports, intermediate supports) — دعامات حَمْل السكة الحديديَّة الكيبليَّة
77 pylon, a framework support — بُرْج
78 tubular steel pylon, a tubular steel support — بُرْج أنبوبيّ من الصلب
79 suspension cable guide rail (supporting cable guide rail, support guide rail) — قَضِيب دليلي لكيبل التعليق
80 support truss, a frame for work on the cable — كَتِيفَة دَعْم
81 base of the support — قاعِدة الدعامة

215 Bridges — الجسُور

1 cross-section of a bridge — مقطع عَرْضيّ لجِسْر
2 orthotropic roadway (orthotropic deck) — طريق مُستقيم
3 truss (bracing) — كَتِيفَة (تقوية بالشِّكالات)
4 diagonal brace (diagonal strut) — شِكَال مائل
5 hollow tubular section — جُزْء أنبوبيّ أجْوَف
6 deck slab — بلاط السطح
7 solid-web girder bridge (beam bridge) — جِسْر برَافِدَة ذات وَتَرَة مُصْمَتَة
8 road surface — سطح الطريق
9 top flange — شَفَة علويَّة
10 bottom flange — شَفَة سفليَّة
11 fixed bearing — مَحْمَل ثابت
12 movable bearing — مَحْمَل متحرك
13 clear span — باع ، بَحْر الجِسْر
14 span — مَسَافَة ممتدة
15 rope bridge (primitive suspension bridge) — جِسْر كيبليّ/حَبْليّ
16 carrying rope — كيبل/حَبْل الحَمْل
17 suspension rope — كيبل/حَبْل التعليق
18 woven deck (woven decking) — سطح جِسْر مَنْسُوج
19 stone arch bridge, a solid bridge — جِسْر عَقْديّ/قَنْطَريّ حَجَريّ
20 arch — عَقْد ، قَنْطَرَة
21 pier — دِعَامَة جِسْر
22 statue — تمثال
23 trussed arch bridge — جِسْر عَقْديّ جَمَلُوني
24 truss element — عُضْو جَمَلُوني
25 trussed arch — عَقْد جَمَلُوني

26 arch span — باع/بحر العَقْد
27 abutment (end pier) — مُتَّكَأ الجِسْر
28 spandrel-braced arch bridge — جِسْر عَقْديّ مُقَوّى بِعُرْوَة عَقْديَّة
29 abutment (abutment pier) — مُتَّكَأ الجِسْر
30 bridge strut — رَكيزَة الجِسْر
31 crown — تاج
32 covered bridge of the Middle Ages (the Ponte Vecchio in Florence) — جِسْر مُغَطًّى من طراز العصور الوُسْطَى (جسر "بونت فيكسيو" في فلورنسا)
33 goldsmiths' shops — محلات الصَّاغَة
34 steel lattice bridge — جِسْر شبكيّ من الصلب
35 counterbrace (cross-brace, diagonal member) — تكتيف مُتَعَارِض
36 vertical member — عُضْو رأسي
37 truss joint — وَصْلَة شَدّ
38 portal frame — هَيْكل البوابة
39 suspension bridge — جِسْر مُعلَّق
40 suspension cable — كيبل التعليق
41 suspender (hanger) — قضيب تعليق، عَلاَّقَة
42 tower — بُرْج
43 suspension cable anchorage — إرْسَاء كيبل التعليق
44 tied beam [with road-way] — كَمَرَة مشدودة [مع طريق معبدة]
45 abutment — مُتَّكَأ الجِسْر
46 cable-stayed bridge — جِسْر بشدَّادات كيبليَّة
47 inclined tension cable — كيبل شد مائل
48 inclined cable anchorage — إرْسَاء الكيبل المائل
49 reinforced concrete bridge — جِسْر خرساني مسلح
50 reinforced concrete arch — عَقْد من الخرسانة المسلحة
51 inclined cable system (multiple cable system) — نظام كيبلات مائلة
52 flat bridge, a plate girder bridge — جِسْر مُسَطَّح
53 stiffener — عِضَادَة، قطعة تقوية
54 pier — دِعَامَة الجِسْر
55 bridge bearing — مَحْمَل الجِسْر
56 cutwater — دِعَامَة الجِسْر العموديَّة على مسار الماء
57 straits bridge, a bridge built of precast elements — جِسْر من أجزاء سابِقَة الصَّبّ
58 precast construction unit — وَحْدَة إنشاء سابِقَة الصَّبّ
59 viaduct — قنطرة متعددة الركائز
60 valley bottom — قاع منفرج
61 reinforced concrete pier — دِعَامَة جِسْر خرسانيَّة مسلحة
62 scaffolding — الإِسْقَالَة
63 lattice swing bridge — جِسْر شبكيّ دَوَّار
64 turntable — صينية دَوَّارة، قرص دَوَّار
65 pivot pier — دِعَامَة ارتكازية
66 pivoting half (pivoting section, pivoting span, movable half) of bridge — نصف جِسْر متحرك
67 flat swing bridge — جِسْر دَوَّار مُسَطَّح
68 middle section — الجزء الأوسط
69 pivot — مِحْوَر ارتكاز
70 parapet (handrailing) — حاجز/مِتْراس الجِسْر

216 Rivers and River Engineering — الأنْهار والهَنْدَسَة النَّهْرِيَّة

1 cable ferry (*also:* chain ferry), a passenger ferry — مُعَدِّيَّة كيبلية، مُعَدِّيَّة ركاب
2 ferry rope (ferry cable) — كيبل/حبل المُعَدِّيَّة
3 river branch (river arm) — رافد النهر
4 river island (river islet) — جزيرة نهريَّة
5 collapsed section of riverbank, flood damage — جزء مُنْهَار من ضِفَّة النهر
6 **motor ferry** — **مُعَدِّيَّة بِمُحَرِّك**
7 ferry landing stage (motorboat landing stage) — رصيف ركوب المُعَدِّيَّة
8 pile foundations — أساسات خازوقيَّة
9 current (flow, course) — تيار الماء
10 **flying ferry** (river ferry), a car ferry — **مُعَدِّيَّة سريعة** (مُعَدِّيَّة النهر)
11 ferry boat — قارب المُعَدِّيَّة
12 buoy (float) — عَوَّامَة، طافية
13 anchorage — مِرْسَاة
14 harbour (*Am.* harbor) for laying up river craft — مَرْفَأ
15 **ferry boat** (punt) — **مُعَدِّيَّة** (مَرْكِب البنط)
16 pole (punt pole, quant pole) — مُرْدِيّ (مِجْدَاف البنط)
17 ferryman — مراكبي المُعَدِّيَّة
18 blind river branch (blind river arm) — لِسَان نهريّ مسدود
19 groyne (*Am.* groin) — مِرْطَم أمواج
20 groyne (*Am.* groin) head — رأس المِرْطَم
21 fairway (navigable part of river) — العُرْض: الجزء الصالح للملاحة في النهر
22 **train of barges** — **قافلَة من الصَّنادل**
23 river tug — قارب القطر في النهر
24 tow rope (tow line, towing hawser) — حَبْل القطر
25 barge (freight barge, cargo barge, lighter) — صَنْدَل شحن
26 bargeman (bargee, lighterman) — مَرَاكبي الصَّنْدَل
27 **towing** (hauling, haulage) — **القَطْر، السحب**
28 towing mast — عمود القَطْر
29 towing engine — مُحَرِّك القَطْر
30 towing track; *form.:* tow path (towing path) — مَسَار القَطْر
31 river after river training — النهر بعد التهذيب
32 **dike** (dyke, main dike, flood wall, winter dike) — **جدار تهذيب النهر**

33 drainage ditch — خندق صرف
34 dike (dyke) drainage sluice — بوَّابَة الصرف في جدار التهذيب
35 wing wall — جِدار الجانب (حائط جناح الحائط التي تُوَجِّه مَجْرَى الماء)
36 outfall — مَخْرَج التصريف
37 drain (infiltration drain) — صَرْف، بَزْل (صَرْف الترشيح)
38 berm (berme) — مِسْطَاح
39 top of dike (dyke) — قِمَّة جدار التهذيب
40 dike (dyke) batter (dike slope) — مُنْحَدَر جدار التهذيب
41 flood bed (inundation area) — قاع فيضان النهر
42 flood containment area — منطقة حَصْر الفيضان
43 current meter — مِقْيَاس سرعة التيار
44 kilometre (*Am.* kilometer) sign — علامَة كيلومتر
45 dikereeve's (dykereeve's) house (dikereeve's cottage); *also:* ferryman's house (cottage) — كُشْك مراقِبيَّة جدار التهذيب
46 dikereeve (dykereeve) — مُرَاقِبِي جدار التهذيب
47 dike (dyke) ramp — مَمَر مُنْحَدِر لجدار التهذيب
48 summer dike (summer dyke) — سَدّ صَيْفيّ
49 levee (embankment) — سَدٌّ، حاجز، ضفة الفيضان
50 sandbags — أكياس رمل
51-55 bank protection (bank stabilization revetment) — **وقاء الضفة، جدار احتجار**
51 riprap — حِجَارة الدَّكَّة، رَدْم صَخْرِيّ
52 alluvial deposit (sand deposit) — راسِب غريني/طمي
53 fascine (bundle of wooden sticks) — شَدَّة قضبان مترابطة لِدَعْم الجدار
54 wicker fences — سِياج من الأماليد
55 stone pitching — تَكْسِيَة بالدَّبْش
56 floating dredging machine (dredger), a multi-bucket ladder dredge — **كَرَّاكَة عائمة**
57 bucket elevator chain — سلسلة مِرْفَاع قادوسيّ
58 dredging bucket — قادوس التجريف
59 suction dredger (hydraulic dredger) with trailing suction pipe or barge sucker — **كَرَّاكَة ماصَة** ذات أنبوب ماص خلفي
60 centrifugal pump — مِضَخَّة نابذة
61 back scouring valve — صِمَام تنظيف (كَسْح) خلفيّ
62 suction pump, a jet pump with scouring nozzles — مِضَخَّة ماصة، مِضَخَّة نفاثة ذات فوهات تنظيف

217 Waterway and Hydraulic Engineering — القَنَاة الملاحيَّة والهَنْدَسَة الهَيْدروليَّة

1-14 quay wall — **حائط الرصيف البحريّ**
1 road surface — سَطْح الطريق
2 body of wall — جِسْم الجِدَار
3 steel sleeper — راقِدة صُلب
4 steel pile — خازُوق صُلب
5 sheet pile wall (sheet pile bulkhead, sheet piling) — جِدَار سِتَارة خازوقيَّة
6 box pile — خازوق صُنْدُوقي
7 backfilling (filling) — رَدْم
8 ladder — سُلَّم
9 fender (fender pile) — خازوق المِصَدّ
10 recessed bollard — عَمُود غائر لِرَبْط الحِبَال على الرصيف
11 double bollard — عَمُود رَبْط حِبَال مزدوج
12 bollard — عَمُود رَبْط الحِبَال على الرصيف
13 cross-shaped bollard (cross-shaped mooring bitt) — عَمُود رَبْط حِبَال صليبي
14 double cross-shaped bollard (double cross-shaped mooring bitt) — عَمُود رَبْط حِبَال صليبي مزدوج
15-28 canal — **قناة**
15 & 16 canal entrance — مَدْخَل القناة
15 mole — بوَّابَة القناة
16 breakwater — مِلْطَم، حاجِز أمواج
17-25 staircase of locks — **سُلَّم الهَوَاويس**
17 lower level — المستوى السُفلي
18 lock gate, a sliding gate — بوَّابَة الهَوِيس
19 mitre (*Am.* miter) gate — بوَّابَة زاويَّة
20 lock (lock chamber) — هَوِيس
21 power house — مَحَطَّة الطاقة
22 warping capstan (hauling capstan), a capstan — رَحَوِيَّة حِبَال شَدّ المَرَاكِب للمرساة
23 warp — حَبْل مشدود إلى مرساة
24 offices (e.g. canal administration, river police, customs) — مكاتِب (مثال: إدارة القناة، الشُرْطَة النهريَّة، الجمارك)
25 upper level (head) — المستوَى العلوي (رأس الهَوِيس)
26 lock approach — مَدْخَل الهَوِيس
27 lay-by — مكَان التَّوَقُّف (غاطِس)
28 bank slope — مُنْحَدَر الضِّفَّة
29-38 boat lift (*Am.* boat elevator) — **مِرْفَاع القوارب**
29 lower pound (lower reach) — اللسان السفلي
30 canal bed — قاع القناة
31 pound lock gate, a vertical gate — بوَّابَة هَوِيس اللسان
32 lock gate — بوَّابَة الهَوِيس
33 boat tank (caisson) — صِهْرِيج القَوارب (قَيْسُون)
34 float — عوَّامَة، طَوْف
35 float shaft — مِهْوَاة العَوَّامَة
36 lifting spindle — عَمُود رفع دَوَرَاني

37 upper pound (upper reach) اللسان العلويّ
38 vertical gate بوّابَة رأسيَّة
39-46 pumping plant and reservoir وَحْدَة الضَّخّ والخَزَّان
39 forebay خليج أماميّ
40 surge tank صهريج الاتزان (منع التموُّر)
41 pressure pipeline خطّ أنابيب ضغط
42 valve house (valve control house) مَبْنَى الصمامات
43 turbine house (pumping station) مَحَطَّة التوربين (محطة الضخ)
44 discharge structure (outlet structure) مبنى التفريغ
45 control station مَحَطَّة التَّحكُّم
46 transformer station مَحَطَّة المُحَوِّل
47-52 axial-flow pump (propeller pump) مِضَخَّة دافِعَة
47 drive motor مُحَرِّك الإدارة
48 gear تروس الحركة
49 drive shaft عَمُود الإدارة
50 pressure pipe أنْبُوب الضغط
51 suction head رَأس المَصّ
52 impeller wheel عَجَلَة رَفَّاصَة (رفاص)
53-56 sluice valve (sluice gate) صِمام بَوَّابَة التَّحكُّم في الصَّرف
53 crank drive إدارة عَمُود المِرْفَق
54 valve housing مَبيت الصمامات
55 sliding valve (sliding gate) صِمَام منزلق
56 discharge opening فتحة الصرف
57-64 dam (barrage) سد (قنطرة)
57 reservoir (storage reservoir, impounding reservoir, impounded reservoir) خَزَّان (صهريج تخزين)
58 masonry dam سَدّ بنائي
59 crest of dam قمة السَّدّ
60 spillway (overflow spillway) قناة تصريف الفائض
61 stilling basin (stilling box, stilling pool) حَوْض تهدئة
62 scouring tunnel (outlet tunnel, waste water outlet) نَفَق تنظيف/كسح (مصرف الماء الفائض)
63 valve house (valve control house) مَبيت الصمامات
64 power station مَحَطَّة الطاقة
65-72 rolling dam (weir), a barrage; *other system:* shutterweir سَدّ دَوَّار (قنطرة احتجاز)
65 roller, a barrier حاجِز، دولفين
66 roller top قمة الحاجِز
67 flange شَفَة
68 submersible roller دولفين غاطِس
69 rack track مَمَر مُسَنَّن
70 recess تجويف
71 hoisting gear cabin كابينة مُعِدَّات الرَّفْع
72 service bridge (walkway) جِسْر خدمة (مَمْشَى)
73-80 sluice dam سَدّ بقناة تصريف ذات بوّابَة تَحكُّم
73 hoisting gear bridge جِسْر مُعِدَّات الرفع
74 hoisting gear (winding gear) مُعِدَّات الرفع
75 guide groove أُخْدُود دليلي
76 counterweight (counterpoise) ثِقْل مُوَازِن
77 sluice gate (floodgate) بوّابَة تَحكُّم (بوّابَة الهويس)
78 reinforcing rib ضِلْع تقوية
79 dam sill (weir sill) عَتَبَة السَّدّ
80 wing wall حائط جناح الحائط التي تُوَجِّه مَجْرَى الماء

218 Types of Historical Ship أنْواع القَوَارِب عَبْر العصور

1-6 Germanic rowing boat [ca. AD 400]; the Nydam boat قارب تجديف على الطراز الجِرْمانيّ [400 م]؛ قارب "النيدام"
1 stern post عَمُود الكَوْثَل
2 steersman مُوَجِّه الدَّفَّة
3 oarsman المُجَدِّف
4 stem post (stem) عَمُود الجُؤْجُؤ
5 oar, for rowing مِجْدَاف
6 rudder (steering oar), a side rudder, for steering دَفَّة التَّوْجِيه
7 dugout, a hollowed-out tree trunk **زَوْرَق شجري**، جذع شجرة مُجَوَّف
8 paddle مِجْدَاف
9-12 trireme, a Roman warship ثلاثيَّة المجاديف، سفينة حربية رومانيَّة
9 ram الرَّام: شبه منقار قوي معد لاختراق السفن المعادية
10 forecastle (fo'c'sle) السَّلُوقيَّة
11 grapple (grapnel, grappling iron), for fastening the enemy ship alongside كُلاَّب لتثبيْت سفينة الأعداء بجوار السفينة
12 three banks (tiers) of oars ثلاثة طوابق من المجاديف
13-17 Viking ship (longship, dragon ship) [Norse] **سفينة الفايكنج** [الاسكندنافيون]
13 helm (tiller) مِقْبَض دَفَّة السفينة
14 awning crutch with carved horses' heads دعامة الظُّلَّة وبها رؤوس خيل منحُوتة
15 awning ظُلَّة
16 dragon figurehead تمثال في مقدمة السفينة بشكل تنين
17 shield تُرْس، درع
18-26 cog (Hansa cog, Hansa ship) سفينة الهانسا
18 anchor cable (anchor rope, anchor hawser) حَبْل/كيبل المِرْسَاة
19 forecastle (fo'c'sle) السَّلُوقيَّة
20 bowsprit الدَّقَل المائل
21 urled (brailed-up) شراع مربع ملفوف

square sail
22 town banner (city banner) — رايَة المدينة
23 aftercastle (sterncastle) — أعلى مؤخِّرة السفينة
24 rudder, a stem rudder — دَفَّة
25 elliptical stern (round stern) — كَوْثَل مستدير/اهليلجي
26 wooden fender — وقاء خشبيّ
27-43 caravel (carvel) ['Santa Maria' 1492] — **سفينة شراعية سريعة** "[سانتا ماريًا" 1492م]
27 admiral's cabin — كابينة أمير البحر
28 spanker boom — ذِراع تطويل شِراع المؤخِّرة
29 mizzen (mizen, mutton spanker, lateen spanker), a lateen sail — شِراع المِزِّيْن
30 lateen yard — عارضة الشراع المثلث
31 mizzen (mizen) mast — صاري شِراع المِزِّيْن
32 lashing — رباط، وثاق
33 mainsail (main course), a square sail — الشِّراع الرئيسي
34 bonnet, a removable strip of canvas — وَصْلة في الشِّراع
35 bowline — الكَرُّ: حَبْل الشِّراع
36 bunt line (martinet) — حَبْل مشدود إلى أدني الشِّراع
37 main yard — العارضة الرئيسية
38 main topsail — الشِّراع الثاني الرئيسي
39 main topsail yard — عارضة الشِّراع الثاني الرئيسي
40 mainmast — الصاري الرئيسي
41 foresail (fore course) — الشِّراع الأمامي
42 foremast — الصاري الأمامي
43 spritsail — الشِّراع المنشور
44-50 galley [15th to 18th century], a slave galley — **القادس**: سفينة شراعيَّة ذات مجاديف [القرن 18- 15 م]، سفينة عبيد
44 lantern — فانوس
45 cabin — كابينة
46 central gangway — مَمَر سَطْح السفينة المركزي
47 slave driver with whip — سائق العبيد وبيده السَّوْط
48 galley slaves — عبيد القادس
49 covered platform in the forepart of the ship — منَصَّة مغطاة في الجزء الأمامي من السفينة
50 gun — مدفع
51-60 ship of the line (line-of-battle ship) [18th to 19th century], a three-decker — **سفينة حربية** [القرن 18 إلى القرن 19]، سفينة ذات ثلاثة أسطح
51 jib boom — ذراع تطويل شِراع السارِيَة الأماميَّة
52 fore topgallant sail — شِراع الدَّقَل الأعلى الأمامي
53 main topgallant sail — شِراع الدَّقَل الأعلى الرئيسي
54 mizzen (mizen) topgallant sail — شِراع الدَّقَل الأعلى المِزِّيْني
55-57 gilded stern — كَوْثَل مُزَيَّن بالذهب
55 upper stern — الكَوْثَل العلوي
56 stern gallery — شُرْفَة الكَوْثَل
57 quarter gallery, a projecting balcony with ornamental portholes — شُرْفَة الجانب القريب من المؤخِّرة ذات نوافذ زينية
58 lower stern — الكَوْثَل السفلي
59 gunports for broadside fire — فتحات المدافع لإطلاق وابِل من النيران
60 gunport shutter — مِغْلاق فتحة المدفع

219 Sailing Ship I — السُّفُن الشِّراعيَّة (1)

1-72 rigging (rig, tackle) and sails of a bark (barque) — **حبَال الأشْرعة والصواري والأشْرعة لقارب البَرْك** (قارب بثلاثة صواري)
1-9 masts — **الصواري**
1 bowsprit with jib boom — الدَّقَل المائل وذراع تطويل شِراع السارية الأماميَّة
2-4 foremast — **الصاري الأمامي**
2 lower foremast — الصاري الأمامي السفلي
3 fore topmast — الدَّقَل المتوسط الأمامي
4 fore topgallant mast — صاري الدَّقَل الأعلى الأمامي
5-7 mainmast — **الصاري الرئيسي**
5 lower mainmast — الصاري الرئيسي السفلي
6 main topmast — الدقل الرئيسي المتوسط
7 main topgallant mast — صاري الدَّقَل الأعلى الرئيسي
8 & 9 mizzen (mizen) mast — صاري المِزِّيْن
8 lower mizzen (lower mizen) — المِزِّيْن السفلي
9 mizzen (mizen) topmast — الدَّقَل المتوسط المِزِّيْنيّ
10-19 standing rigging — **حبَال الأشْرعة والصواري القائمة**
10 forestay, mizzen (mizen) stay, mainstay — الحَبْل المُثَبِّت للشِّراع الرئيسي
11 fore topmast stay, main topmast stay, mizzen (mizen) topmast stay — الحَبْل المُثَبِّت للدَّقَل المتوسط الأمامي
12 fore topgallant stay, mizzen (mizen) topgallant stay, main topgallant stay — الحَبْل المُثَبِّت للدَّقَل الأعلى الأمامي
13 fore royal stay (main royal stay) — الحَبْل المُثَبِّت للشِّراع الأمامي الصغير
14 jib stay — الحَبْل المُثَبِّت لشراع السارية الأماميَّة
15 bobstay — حَبْل تثبيْت الدَّقَل المائل
16 shrouds — حبال الصاري
17 fore topmast rigging (main topmast rigging, mizzen (mizen) topmast rigging) — حبَال الأشْرعة والصواري للدَّقَل المتوسط الأمامي
18 fore topgallant rigging (main topgallant rigging) — حبَال الأشْرعة والصواري للدَّقَل (الرئيسي) الأعلى الأمامي
19 backstays — الشِّكال الخلفي
20-31 fore-and-aft sails — **الأشْرعة الأمامية والخلفية**
20 fore topmast staysail — الشراع المثبت للدَّقَل المتوسط الأمامي

21 inner jib شراع السارية الأماميَّة الداخلي
22 outer jib شراع السارية الأماميَّة الخارجي
23 flying jib شِراع السارية الأماميَّة المُرَفرِف
24 main topmast staysail الشِّراع المُثَبَّت للدَّقَل المتوسط الرئيسي
25 main topgallant staysail الشِّراع المُثَبَّت للدَّقَل الأعلى الرئيسي
26 main royal staysail الشِّراع المُثَبَّت الرئيسي الصغير
27 mizzen (mizen) staysail الشِّراع المُثَبَّت المِزِّيْنيّ
28 mizzen (mizen) topmast staysail الشراع المثبت للدقل المتوسط
29 mizzen (mizen) topgallant staysail الشِّراع المُثَبَّت المِزِّيْنيّ للدَّقَل الأعلى
30 mizzen (mizen, spanker, driver) المِزِّيْن
31 gaff topsail الشِّراع العلوي للقَرِيَّة
32-45 spars **السَّواري**
32 foreyard عارضة الشراع الأماميَّة
33 lower fore topsail yard العارضة السفلية للدَّقَل المتوسط الأمامي
34 upper fore topsail yard العارضة العلوية للدَّقَل المتوسط الأمامي
35 lower fore topgallant yard العارضة السفلية للدَّقَل الأعلى الأمامي
36 upper fore topgallant yard العارضة العلوية للدَّقَل الأعلى الأمامي
37 fore royal yard عارضة الشِّراع الصغير الأمامي
38 main yard العارضة الرئيسية
39 lower main topsail yard العارضة السفلية للدَّقَل المتوسط الرئيسي
40 upper main topsail yard العارضة العلويَّة للدَّقَل المتوسط الرئيسي
41 lower main topgallant yard العارضة السفلية للدَّقَل الأعلى الرئيسي
42 upper main topgallant yard العارضة العلوية للدَّقَل الأعلى الرئيسي
43 main royal yard عارضة الشراع الرئيسي الصغير
44 spanker boom ذراع شِراع المؤخِّرة
45 spanker gaff قَرِيَّة شِراع المؤخِّرة
46 footrope حَبْل سفلي
47 lifts مرافع
48 spanker boom topping lift المرفاع العلوي لذراع تطويل شراع المؤخِّرة
49 spanker peak halyard كر قمة شراع المؤخرة
50 foretop مَنَصَّة في أعلى الصاري الأمامي
51 fore topmast crosstrees مَنَصَّات صاري الشِّراع العلوي الأمامي
52 maintop المَنَصَّة الرئيسية
53 main topmast crosstrees مَنَصَّات صاري الشِّراع العلوي الرئيسي
54 mizzen (mizen) top مَنَصَّة المِزِّيْن
55-66 square sails **الأشْرِعة المربعة**
55 foresail (fore course) الشِّراع الأمامي
56 lower fore topsail الشِّراع العلوي الأمامي المنخفض
57 upper fore topsail الشراع العلوي الأمامي المرتفع
58 lower fore topgallant sail الشِّراع السفلي للدَّقَل الاعلى الأمامي
59 upper fore topgallant sail الشِّراع العلوي للدَّقَل الأعلى الأمامي
60 fore royal الشِّراع الأمامي الصغير
61 mainsail (main course) الشِّراع الرئيسي
62 lower main topsail الشِّراع الرئيسي العلوي المنخفض
63 upper main topsail الشراع الرئيسي العلوي المرتفع
64 lower main topgallant sail الشِّراع السفلي للدَّقَل الأعلى الرئيسي
65 upper main topgallant sail الشراع العلوي للدَّقَل الأعلى الرئيسي
66 main royal sail الشِّراع الصغير الرئيسي
67-71 running rigging **حِبَال الأشْرِعة والصواري المتحركة**
67 braces شكَالات
68 sheets ألْوَاح
69 spanker sheet لَوْح شِراع المؤخِّرة
70 spanker vangs حبلا تثبيت القريَّة
71 bunt line خط منتصف الشِّراع
72 reef ثنية الشِّراع

220 Sailing Ship II السُفُن الشِّرَاعيَّة (2)

1-5 sail shapes **أشكَال الشِّراع**
1 gaffsail (*small:* trysail, spencer) شِراع القَرِيَّة (الصغير: شِراع العواصف)
2 jib شِراع السارية الأمامية
3 lateen sail شِراع مثلث الشكل
4 lugsail شِراع رباعي الأضلاع
5 spritsail الشِّراع المنشور (على عمود القلع)
6-8 single-masted sailing boats (*Am.* sailboats) **القوارب الشِّراعيَّة وحيدة الصاري**
6 tjalk قارب من طراز "التجاك"
7 leeboard لَوْح جانب السفينة المحجوب عن الريح
8 cutter قارب من طراز "كاتر"
9 & 10 mizzen (mizen) masted sailing boats (*Am.* sailboats) **القَوارب الشِّراعيَّة ذات الصارِي المِزِّيْنيّ**
9 ketch-rigged sailing barge صَنْدَل شِراعيّ بشراعين
10 yawl قارب طراز "يُول"
11-17 two-masted sailing boats (*Am.* sailboats) **القوارب الشِّراعيَّة ثنائية الصاري**
11-13 topsail schooner **سكُونر الدَّقَل المتوسط**
11 mainsail الشِّراع الرئيسي
12 boom foresail الشِّراع الأمامي بذراع التطويل
13 square foresail شراع أمامي مربع
14 brigantine سفينة شراعيَّة بصاريَيْن طراز "بريجانتين"

15 half-rigged mast with fore-and-aft sails	قارب شراعي بِصَاري نصف مزود بالأشرعة وله شِراع أمامي وآخر خلفي
16 full-rigged mast with square sails	صاري مزود بالأشرعة كاملة وعليه أشرعة مربعة
17 brig	سفينة شراعيَّة بصاريين طراز "بريج"
18-27 three-masted sailing vessels (three-masters)	**سفن شراعيَّة ثلاثية الصواري**
18 three-masted schooner	سكُونر ثلاثي الصواري
19 three-masted topsail schooner	سكونر ثلاثي الصواري ذو شراع علوي
20 bark (barque) schooner	سكُونر البَرْك
21-23 bark (barque) [cf. illustration of rigging and sails in plate 219]	**قارب البَرْك**
21 foremast	الصاري الأمامي
22 mainmast	الصاري الرئيسي
23 mizzen (mizen) mast	صاري المِزِّيْن
24-27 full-rigged ship	**سفينة مزودة بالأشْرعة بالكامل**
24 mizzen (mizen) mast	صاري المِزِّيْن
25 crossjack yard (crojack yard)	عارضة شِراع ذات عمود تدعيم تصالبي
26 crossjack (crojack)	عمود تصالبي لدعم الشِّراع
27 ports	فتحات السفينة
28-31 four-masted sailing ships (four-masters)	**سُفُن شراعيَّة رباعيَّة الصواري**
28 four-masted schooner	سكُونر رباعي الصواري
29 four-masted bark (barque)	بَرْك رباعي الصواري
30 mizzen (mizen) mast	صاري المِزِّيْن
31 four-masted full-rigged ship	سفينة رباعيَّة الصواري مزودة بكامل الأشْرعة
32-34 five-masted bark (barque)	**برك خماسي الصوَاري**
32 skysail	الشِّراع السماويّ
33 middle mast	الصاري الأوسط
34 mizzen (mizen) mast	صاري المِزِّيْن
35-37 development of sailing ships over 400 years	**تطور السفن الشراعيَّة طوال 400 عام**
35 five-masted full-rigged ship "Preussen" 1902–10	سفينة خماسيَّة الصواري مزودة بكامل الأشرعة طراز "بروِيسن" عام 1910–1902
36 English clipper ship "Spindrift" 1867	سفينة انجليزية طراز "سبندريفت" عام 1867
37 caravel (carvel) "Santa Maria" 1492	سفينة شراعيَّة طراز "سانتا ماريا" عام 1492

221 Types of Ship — أنْوَاع السُفُن

1 ULCC (ultra-large crude carrier) of the 'all-aft' type	ناقِلة نفط عملاقة من الطراز الخلفي
2 foremast	الصاري الأمامي
3 catwalk with pipes	ممَر ضيق وبه أنابيب
4 fire gun (fire nozzle)	مدفع إطفاء الحريق
5 deck crane	مِرْفَاع سَطْح الناقلة
6 deckhouse with bridge	بَيْت السَّطْح وبه مِنَصَّة ربَّان السفينة
7 aft signal (signalling) and radar mast	صاري الإشارات الخلفي والرادار
8 funnel	مِدْخَنَة
9 nuclear research ship "Otto Hahn", a bulk carrier	سفينة أبحاث نَوَوِيَّة طراز "اتوهان"
10 aft superstructure (engine room)	أجزاء السفينة فوق السَّطْح الرئيسي الخلفي (غرفة المُحَرِّك)
11 cargo hatchway for bulk goods (bulk cargoes)	فتحة إدخال الحمولة السائبة/ الضخمة
12 bridge	مِنَصَّة ربان السفينة
13 forecastle (fo'c'sle)	السَّلوقيَّة
14 stem	مُقَدَّم السفينة (الجُؤْجُؤ)
15 seaside pleasure boat	قارب تنزه
16 dummy funnel	مِدْخَنَة دُمْيَة
17 exhaust mast	صاري العادم
18 rescue cruiser	طَرَّاد إنقاذ
19 helicopter platform (working deck)	مِنَصَّة هبوط الهليكوبتر
20 rescue helicopter	طائرة هليكوبتر لعمليات الإنقاذ
21 all-container ship	سفينة حاوِيَات
22 containers stowed on deck	حاوِيَات مَرصوصة على السَّطْح
23 cargo ship	سفينة بضائع
24-29 cargo gear (cargo-handling gear)	**معدات الشحن**
24 bipod mast	صاري ثنائي المنصب
25 jumbo derrick boom (heavy-lift derrick boom)	ذِرَاع مِرْفَاع عملاق
26 derrick boom (cargo boom)	ذِرَاع مِرْفَاع (ذِرَاع حمل البضائع)
27 tackle	بَكَارَة (أجهزة الرفع)
28 block	بَكَرَة
29 thrust bearing	مَحْمَل دفعي
30 bow doors	أبواب الجُؤْجُؤ
31 stern loading door	باب كَوْثَل السفينة لإدخال البضائع
32 offshore drilling rig supply vessel	سفينة تموين جِهاز الحفر البحري
33 compact superstructure	أجزاء السفينة فوق السَّطْح الرئيسيّ
34 loading deck (working deck)	سَطْح التحميل
35 liquefied-gas tanker	ناقلة الغاز المُسَيَّل
36 spherical tank	خَزَّان كُرَويّ
37 navigational television receiver mast	سارِيَة استقبال تليفزيوني
38 vent mast	سارِيَة التهوية
39 deckhouse	بَيْت السَّطْح
40 funnel	مِدْخَنَة
41 ventilator	وَحْدَة التهوية
42 transom stern (transom)	كَوْثَل بعارِضة أفقيَّة
43 rudder blade (rudder)	راحة الدَّفَّة (الدَّفَّة)

44 ship's propeller (ship's screw) — رَفّاص السفينة
45 bulbous bow — جُؤْجُؤ منتفخ
46 steam trawler — ترولة بخاريَّة
47 lightship (light vessel) — مَنَارَة عائمة
48 lantern (characteristic light) — فانوس
49 smack — قارب السِّمَاك
50 ice breaker — كَسَّارة الجليد
51 steaming light mast — ساريَة الأنوار البخاريَّة
52 helicopter hangar — حظيرة الهليكوبتر
53 stern towing point, for gripping the bow of ships in tow — مَوْضِع قطر الكَوْثَل لربط مقدمة السفينة المقطورة
54 roll-on-roll-off (ro-ro) trailer ferry — مُعَدِّيَّة قَطْر
55 stern port (stern opening) with ramp — فتحة الكَوْثَل وبها مجرى مائل
56 heavy vehicle lifts (*Am.* heavy vehicle elevators) — مرافع عربات ثقيلة
57 multi-purpose freighter — سفينة شحن متعددة الأغراض
58 ventilator-type samson (sampson) post (ventilator-type king post) — دِعَامة رئيسية ذات مِهْوَاة
59 derrick boom (cargo boom, cargo gear cargo-handling gear) — ذراع المِرْفاع (أجهزة الرفع)
60 derrick mast — سارية ذراع المِرْفاع
61 deck crane — مِرْفَاع سَطْح السفينة
62 jumbo derrick boom (heavy-lift derrick boom) — ذِرَاع مِرْفاع عملاق
63 cargo hatchway — فتحة شحن/تفريغ البضائع
64 semisubmersible drilling vessel — سفينة حفر شِبْه غاطِسة
65 floating vessel with machinery — سفينة طافية وعليها المُعِدَّات
66 drilling platform — منَصَّة الحفر
67 derrick — بُرْج الحفر
68 cattleship (cattle vessel) — سفينة نقل الماشِيَة
69 superstructure for transporting livestock — أجزاء سَطْح السفينة المخصصة لنقل الماشِيَة
70 fresh water tanks — خَزَّانات ماء الشرب
71 fuel tank — خَزَّان الوقود
72 dung tank — خَزَّان الروث
73 fodder tanks — خَزَّانات العَلَف
74 train ferry [cross section] — مُعَدِّيَّة قطاريَّة [قطاع عرضي]
75 funnel — مِدْخَنَة
76 exhaust pipes — أنابيب العادم
77 mast — ساريَة
78 ship's lifeboat hanging at the davit — قارَب نجاة مُعَلَّق بالداوودي
79 car deck — سَطْح السيارات
80 main deck (train deck) — السَّطح الرئيسي
81 main engines — المحركات الرئيسية
82 passenger liner (liner, ocean liner) — عبَّارة نقل الركاب
83 stem — مُقَدَّم السفينة (الجُؤْجُؤ)
84 funnel with lattice casing — مدخنة ذات غلاف شبكي
85 flag dressing (rainbow dressing, string of flags extending over mast-heads, e.g., on the maiden voyage) — حَبْل الرايات
86 trawler, a factory ship — سفينة الترولة
87 gallows — هيكل قائم
88 stern ramp — مَمَر مُنْحَدَر بالكَوْثَل
89 container ship — سفينة حاويات
90 loading bridge (loading platform) — جِسْر الشحن
91 sea ladder (jacob's ladder, rope ladder) — سُلَّم من الحبال ذو درجات خشبية
92 barge and push tug assembly — صندل ومجموعة القَطْر الدفعي
93 push tug — قَطْر دفعي
94 tug-pushed dumb barge (tug-pushed lighter) — صَنْدَل مقطور بالدفع
95 pilot boat — زَوْرَق استطلاع
96 combined cargo and passenger liner — عَبَّارة نقل البضائع والرُكَّاب
97 passengers disembarking by boat — إنزال الرُكَّاب بالقارب
98 accommodation ladder — السُّلَّم المُدَلاَّة
99 coaster (coasting vessel) — الساحليَّة، سفينة ساحليَّة
100 customs or police launch — لانش الجمارك أو الشرطة

101-128 excursion steamer (pleasure steamer) — **سفينة رحلات ترفيهية**

101-106 lifeboat launching gear — **مُعِدَّات قارِب الإنقاذ**

101 davit — الدَّاوودي
102 wire rope span — مسافة بين حَبْلَيْن سِلْكِيَّيْن
103 lifeline — حَبْل الإنقاذ
104 tackle — بكَّارة
105 block — بكَرَة
106 fall — حَبْل الرفع
107 ship's lifeboat (ship's boat) covered with tarpaulin — قارب النجاة بالسفينة مغطى بقماش التربولين
108 stem — مُقَدَّم السفينة (الجُؤْجُؤ)
109 passenger — راكِب
110 steward — مُضِيف
111 deck-chair — كُرْسِيّ سَطْح السفينة
112 deck hand — عامِل تنظيف سَطْح السفينة
113 deck bucket — دلْو تنظيف سَطْح السفينة
114 boatswain (bo's'n, bo'sun, bosun) — عَرِّيف الملاحين
115 tunic — سترة ضيقة
116 awning — ظُلَّة، تندة
117 stanchion — دِعَامة قائمة
118 ridge rope (jackstay) — قَضِيب تشد إليه الظُلَّة

119 lashing — رباط، وثاق
120 bulwark — جانب السفينة الممتد فوق سَطْحها العلوي
121 guard rail — قَضِيب واقٍ
122 handrail (top rail) — درابزين
123 companion ladder (companionway) — دَرَج
124 lifebelt (lifebuoy) — طُوق النجاة
125 lifebuoy light (lifebelt light, signal light) — لَمْبَة طوق النجاة
126 officer of the watch (watchkeeper) — ضابط المناوبة
127 reefer (*Am.* pea jacket) — سُتْرَة ضيقة من قماش سميك
128 binoculars — نَظَّارَة مكَبِّرَة، ناظور

222 Shipbuilding — بناء السُفُن

1-43 shipyard (shipbuilding yard, dockyard, *Am.* navy yard) — **مَسْفَن، ترسانة بناء السفن**
1 administrative offices — مكاتب إدارية
2 ship-drawing office — مكتب رسم السفن
3 & 4 shipbuilding sheds — عنابر بناء السفن
3 mould (*Am.* mold) loft — علية التشكيل
4 erection shop — وَرْشَة التركيب
5-9 fitting-out quay — **رصيف تجهيز**
5 quay — رصيف
6 tripod crane — مرفاع ثلاثي القوائم
7 hammer-headed crane — مِرْفَاع كابولي عملاق
8 engineering workshop — وَرْشَة هندسية
9 boiler shop — وَرْشَة تصليح المَرَاجِل
10 repair quay — رصيف التصليح
11-26 slipways (slips, building berths, building slips, stocks) — **رصيف إنزال أو إنشاء مُنْحَدِر**
11-18 cable crane berth, a slipway (building berth) — **رصيف المِرْفَاع الكيبلي**
11 slipway portal — رصيف إنزال (أو إنشاء) قَنْطَريّ
12 bridge support — دِعامة جِسْر
13 crane cable — كِيبل المِرْفَاع
14 crab (jenny) — كبَّاش المِرْفَاع (عربة مِرْفَاع نقاليَّة)
15 cross piece — قطعة مستعرضة
16 crane driver's cabin (crane driver's cage) — كابينة سائق المِرْفَاع
17 slipway floor — أرضية رصيف الإنزال/الإنشاء
18 staging, a scaffold — سِقالَة، إسقالة
19-21 frame slipway — **رَصيف إنزال (أو إنشاء) هيكلي**
19 slipway frame — هيكل/إطار الرصيف
20 overhead travelling (*Am.* traveling) crane (gantry crane) — مِرْفَاع علوي متحرك (مِرْفَاع قَنْطَريّ)
21 slewing crab — عربة مِرْفَاع نقالية دَوَّارَة
22 keel in position — رافدة القص بعد تركيبها
23 luffing jib crane, a slipway crane — مِرْفَاع بذراع سفلي التمفصل
24 crane rails (crane track) — قضبان انزلاق المِرْفَاع المتنقل
25 gantry crane — مِرْفَاع قَنْطَريّ
26 gantry (bridge) — قَنْطَرَة
27 trestles (supports) — مساند، حوامِل
28 crab (jenny) — كَبَّاش المِرْفَاع (عربة مِرْفَاع نقالية)
29 hull frames in position — هياكل بَدَن السفينة بعد تركيبها
30 ship under construction — سفينة تحت الإنشاء
31-33 dry dock — **حَوْض الإنشاء، حَوْض جاف**
31 dock floor (dock bottom) — أرضية الحَوْض
32 dock gates (caisson) — بوابة الحوض (قيسون)
33 pumping station (power house) — مَحَطَّة الضخ (مَحَطَّة الطاقة)
34-43 floating dock (pontoon dock) — **رصيف عائم**
34 dock crane (dockside crane), a jib crane — مِرْفَاع الرصيف، مِرْفَاع ذراعي
35 fender pile — خازوق مِصَدّ
36-43 working of docks — **تشكيل الرصيف**
36 dock basin — حَوْض الرصيف
37 & 38 dock structure — هيكل الرصيف
37 side tank (side wall) — صهريج جانبي (جدار جانبي)
38 bottom tank (bottom pontoon) — صهريج سفلي (طَوْف سفلي)
39 keel block — كتلة صالب القاعدة
40 bilge block (bilge shore, side support) — كتلة الجَمَّة
41-43 docking a ship — **سحب السفينة إلى الرصيف**
41 flooded floating dock — حَوْض عائم مغمور
42 tug towing the ship — سفينة قَطْر تسحب السفينة
43 emptied (pumped-out) dock — رصيف مُفَرَّغ
44-61 structural parts of the ship — **الأجزاء الهيكلية للسفينة**
44-56 longitudinal structure — **الهيكل الطولي**
44-49 shell (shell plating, skin) — **القِشْرَة**
44 sheer strake — لَوْح طولي عمودي
45 side strake — لَوْح طولي جانبي
46 bilge strake — لَوْح طولي لِجَمَّة السفينة
47 bilge keel — رافدة الجَمَّة في السفينة
48 bottom plating — أَلْوَاح القاع
49 flat plate keel (keel plate) — لَوْح الصالِب
50 stringer (side stringer) — ضلع طولاني، عارضة
51 tank margin plate — لَوْح حافة الخَزَّان
52 longitudinal side girder — عارضة طوليَّة جانبية
53 centre (*Am.* center) plate girder (centre girder, kelson, keelson, vertical keel) — عارِضة لَوْحيَّة مركزية
54 tank top plating (tank — أَلْوَاح قمة الخَزَّان

top, inner bottom plating)
55 centre (*Am.* center) strake — لَوْح طولي مركزي
56 deck plating — أَلْوَاح السَّطْح
57 deck beam — كَمَرَات السَّطْح
58 frame (rib) — ضِلْع
59 floor plate — لَوْح أرضية
60 cellular double bottom — قاع مُضَلَّع خَلَويّ مزدوج
61 hold pillar (pillar) — عمود حامِل
62 & **63** dunnage — حشوة وقائيَّة من التلف
62 side battens (side ceiling, spar ceiling) — لُزَز جانبية
63 ceiling (floor ceiling) — سقف الأرضية
64, **65** hatchway — فتحة السفينة
64 hatch coaming — حِتَار الفتحة
65 hatch cover (hatch-board) — غِطاء الفتحة
66-72 stern — **الكَوْثَل**
66 guard rail — قَضِيب دليلي
67 bulwark — كتف السفينة العلوي
68 rudder stock — عاضِد الدَّفَّة
69, **70** Oertz rudder — دَفَّة "أورتس"
69 rudder blade (rudder) — راحة الدَّفَّة
70 & **71** stern frame — هيكل دَفَّة
70 rudder post — عَمُود الدَّفَّة
71 propeller post (screw post) — عَمُود الرفَّاص
72 ship's propeller (ship's screw) — رَفَّاص السفينة
73 draught (draft) marks — علامات الغاطس
74-79 bow — **الجُؤْجُؤ (مُقَدَّم السفينة)**
74 stem, a bulbous stem (bulbous bow) — جُؤْجُؤ
75 hawse — فتحة القَلْس
76 hawse pipe — ماسورة القَلْس
77 anchor cable (chain cable) — كيبل المِرْسَاة
78 stockless anchor (patent anchor) — مِرْسَاة مسَطحة (بدون عارِضة)
79 stocked anchor — مِرْسَاة بِكَفَّة/ بعارضة

223 Motor Ship — السُّفُن البُخاريَّة

1-71 combined cargo and passenger ship [of the older type] — **سفينة نقل البضائع والرُكَّاب** [من الطراز الأقدم]
1 funnel — مِدْخَنَة
2 funnel marking — دليل المِدْخَنَة
3 siren (fog horn) — سارينة (بُوق التحذير في حالة الضباب)
4-11 compass platform (compass bridge, compass flat, monkey bridge) — **جِسْر البُوْصُلَة**
4 antenna lead-in (antenna down-lead) — سِلْك الهوائي الهابِط
5 radio direction finder (RDF) antenna (direction finder antenna, rotatable loop antenna, aural null loop antenna) — هوائي مُحَدِّد الاتجاه اللاسِلكي
6 magnetic compass (mariner's compass) — بُوْصُلَة مغناطيسية
7 morse lamp (signalling, *Am.* signaling, lamp) — مِصْبَاح الإشارة الضوئية بنظام "مورس"
8 radar antenna (radar scanner) — هوائي الرادار (ماسِح راداري)
9 code flag signal — إشارة كود الرايات
10 code flag halyards — أحْبَال رفع/إنزال الرايات
11 triatic stay (signal stay) — دعامة الإشارات
12-18 bridge deck (bridge) — **سَطْح مِنَصَّة ربَّان السفينة**
12 radio room — غُرفة اللاسلْكي
13 captain's cabin — كابينة الربَّان
14 navigating bridge — مِنَصَّةالملاحة
15 starboard sidelight [green; port sidelight red] — ضوء جانبي بِمَيْمَنَة السفينة (أخضر؛ أحمر جانبي للميناء)
16 wing of bridge — جَنَاح المِنَصَّة
17 shelter (weather cloth, dodger) — وقاء الريح
18 wheelhouse — حُجرة مدير الدَّفَّة
19-21 boat deck — **سَطْح قَوَارِب السفينة**
19 ship's lifeboat — قَوَارِب النجاة بالسفينة
20 davit — داوودي
21 officer's cabin — كابينة الضابط البحري
22-27 promenade deck — **سَطْح النزهة**
22 sun deck (lido deck) — سَطْح التَّشَمُّس
23 swimming pool — حَمَّام/بِرْكَة سباحة
24 companion ladder (companionway) — دَرَج السفينة
25 library (ship's library) — مكْتَبَة
26 lounge — حُجْرَة جلوس، صالون
27 promenade — مُتَنَزَّه
28-30 A-deck — **سَطْح الدرجة الممتازة**
28 semi-enclosed deck space — فضاء سَطْح شبه مُغْلَق
29 double-berth cabin, a cabin — كابينة مزدوجة الأسِرَّة
30 de luxe cabin — كابينة فاخرة (ديلوكس)
31 ensign staff — سارِيَة العَلَم
32-47 B-deck (main deck) — **سَطْح الدرجة الثانية**
32 after deck — السَّطْح الخلفي (سَطْح مؤخِّرة السفينة)
33 poop — سَطْح مرتفع عند مؤخِّرة السفينة
34 deckhouse — بَيْت السَّطْح
35 samson (sampson) post (king post) — دِعامة رئيسية
36 derrick boom (cargo boom) — ذِراع المِرْفاع
37 crosstrees (spreader) — مِنَصَّة الصاري
38 crow's nest — مِنَصَّة المراقبة
39 topmast — الدَّقَل المتوسط
40 forward steaming light — ضوء بخاريّ أمامي
41 ventilator lead — مَجْرَى/قناة التهوية
42 galley (caboose, cook-room, ship's kitchen) — مطبخ السفينة

43 ship's pantry — مَخْزَن مؤن السفينة
44 dining room — قاعة الطعام
45 purser's office — مكتب مسؤول السفينة
46 single-berth cabin — كابينة بسرير مفرد
47 foredeck — السَّطح الأمامي (سَطْح مُقَدَّم السفينة)
48 forecastle (fo'c'sle) — السَّلُوقيَّة : عنبر أمامي للبَحَّارة
49-51 ground tackle — **البَكَّارَة الأرضية**
49 windlass — مِرْفَاع المِرْسَاة
50 anchor cable (chain cable) — كيبل المِرْسَاة
51 compressor (chain compressor) — ضاغِط (ضاغط سلسلي)
52 anchor — مِرْسَاة
53 jackstaff — سارِيَة العلم
54 jack — عَلَم، راية
55 after holds — العنابر/الأنْبَار الخلفية
56 cold storage room (insulated hold) — عنبر التخزين البارد (عنبر معزول حراريا)
57 store room — حُجْرَة تخزين (مخزن)
58 wake — أثَرُ المَخْر
59 shell bossing (shaft bossing) — صُرَّة عمود التدوير
60 tail shaft (tail end shaft) — عمود تدوير خلفي
61 shaft strut (strut, spectacle frame, propeller strut, propeller bracket) — كتيفة العمود (كتيفة الرفَّاص)
62 three-blade ship's propeller (ship's screw) — رفَّاص ذو ثلاث أرياش
63 rudder blade (rudder) — كَفَّة الدَّفَّة
64 stuffing box — مسيكة، صندوق حشو
65 propeller shaft — عمود الرفَّاص
66 shaft alley (shaft tunnel) — نَفَق عمود التدوير
67 thrust block — مجموعة/كتلة الدفع
68-74 diesel-electric drive — **دفع ديزل–كهربيّ**
68 electric engine room — حُجرة المُحَرِّك الكهربي
69 electric motor — مُحَرِّك كهربي
70 auxiliary engine room — حُجرة المحركات الإضافية
71 auxiliary engines — مُحَرِّكات إضافية
72 main engine room — حجرة المُحَرِّك الرئيسي
73 main engine, a diesel engine — المُحَرِّك الرئيسي، مُحَرِّك ديزل
74 generator — مُوَلِّد كهربائي
75 forward holds — العنابر/الأنْبَار الأمامية
76 tween deck — سَطْح بَيْنِيّ
77 cargo — بضائع
78 ballast tank (deep tank) for water ballast — خَزَّان الصابورة المائية
79 fresh water tank — خَزَّان ماء الشرب
80 fuel tank — خَزَّان الوقود
81 bow wave — مَوْجَة الجُؤْجُؤ

224 Navigation — الملاحَة

1 sextant — سُدْسِيَّة
2 graduated arc — قَوْس مُدَرَّج
3 index bar (index arm) — قضيب دليلي
4 decimal micrometer — ميكرومتر عَشْرِي
5 vernier — وَرْنِيَّة
6 index mirror — مِرآة دليلية
7 horizon glass (horizon mirror) — مِرآة الأُفُق
8 telescope — تليسكوب
9 grip (handgrip) — قَبْضَة، مقبض
10-13 radar equipment (radar apparatus) — **مُعِدَّات الرادار**
10 radar pedestal — قاعدة الرادار
11 revolving radar reflector — عاكِس راداري دَوَّار
12 radar display unit (radar screen) — شاشة الرادار (وَحْدَة عرض راداريَّة)
13 radar image (radar picture) — صُورَة راداريَّة
14-38 wheelhouse — **حُجرة مدير الدَّفَّة**
14 steering and control position — مَوْقع التوجيه والتَّحكُّم
15 ship's wheel for controlling the rudder mechanism — عَجَلَة التَّحكُّم في آليَّة الدَّفَّة
16 helmsman (*Am.* wheelsman) — مُوَجِّه الدَّفَّة
17 rudder angle indicator — مُبَيِّن زاوية الدَّفَّة
18 automatic pilot (autopilot) — المُرْشِد الملاحي الآلي
19 control lever for the variable-pitch propeller (reversible propeller, feathering propeller, feathering screw) — ذراع التحكم في رفَّاص الخطوة المتبادلة
20 propeller pitch indicator — مُبَيِّن خطوة الرفَّاص
21 main engine revolution indicator — مؤشر دَوْرَات المحرك الرئيسي
22 ship's speedometer (log) — عَدَّاد سرعة السفينة
23 control switch for bow thruster (bow-manoeuvring, *Am.* maneuvering, propeller) — مِفْتَاح التحكم الخاص برفَّاص الجُؤْجُؤ
24 echo recorder (depth recorder, echograph) — مُسَجِّل العمق الصوتي
25 engine telegraph (engine order telegraph) — مُبْرِقَة، تلغراف
26 controls for the anti-rolling system (for the stabilizers) — مَضَابِط نظام مقاومة التمايل
27 local-battery telephone — هاتِف ببطارية محليَّة
28 shipping traffic radio telephone — هاتِف لاسِلْكي لحركة الشحن
29 navigation light indicator panel (running light indicator panel) — لَوْحَة مؤشرات لَمْبَات المِلاحة
30 microphone for ship's address system — ميكروفون السفينة
31 gyro compass (gyroscopic compass), a compass repeater — بُوْصُلَة جيروسكوبيَّة

32 control button for the ship's siren (ship's fog horn) زرّ تشغيل سارينة السفينة
33 main engine overload indicator مُؤشِّر الحِمْل الزائد على المُحَرِّك الرئيسي
34 Decca position-finder (Decca Navigator) مُحَدِّد المواقع بطريقة "ديكا"
35 rough focusing indicator مُؤشِّر التحديد البؤري التقريبي
36 fine focusing indicator مُؤشِّر التحديد البؤري الدقيق
37 navigating officer ضابط مِلاحة
38 captain ربَّان السفينة
39 Decca navigation system نظام المِلاحة "ديكا"
40 master station المَحَطَّة الرئيسية
41 slave station مَحَطَّة تابعة
42 null hyperbola قطع زائد صِفْرِيّ
43 hyperbolic position line 1 الخط 1 لموضع القطع الزائد
44 hyperbolic position line 2 الخط 2 لموضع القطع الزائد
45 position (fix, ship fix) مَوْضِع السفينة
46-53 compasses **البوصلات**
46 liquid compass (fluid compass, spirit compass, wet compass), a magnetic compass بُوصُلَة سائلة، بوصلة مغناطيسية
47 compass card قُرْص البُوْصُلَة
48 lubber's line (lubber's mark, lubber's point) خَطّ البُوْصُلَة البحرية
49 compass bowl تجويف البُوْصُلَة
50 gimbal ring حلقة تثبيت البُوْصُلَة في وضع أفقي
51-53 gyro compass (gyroscopic compass, gyro compass unit) **بُوْصُلَة جيروسكوبيَّة**
51 master compass (master gyro compass) بُوْصُلَة رئيسية
52 compass repeater (gyro repeater) مُعيد البُوْصُلَة (للتقوية)
53 compass repeater with pelorus مُعيد البُوْصُلَة مع عِضادَة انعكاسيَّة
54 patent log (screw log, mechanical log, towing log, taffrail log, speedometer) مِقْيَاس سرعة السفينة
55 rotator دَوَّار
56 governor ضابط (سرعة) اوتوماتي
57 log clock ساعة مِقْيَاس السرعة
58-67 leads **أثقال الفادِن**
58 hand lead فادِن (ثِقْل رصاصي) يدوي لِسَبْر العمق
59 lead (lead sinker) فادِن غاطِس
60 leadline حَبْل الفادِن
61-67 echo sounder (echo sounding machine) **مِسْبار بالصدى**
61 sound transmitter مُرْسِل الصوت
62 sound wave (sound impulse) مَوْجَة صوتيَّة
63 echo (sound echo, echo signal) صَدَى (صدى صوتي)
64 echo receiver (hydrophone) مُسْتَقْبِل الصدى
65 echograph (echo sounding machine recorder) مُسَجِّل العمق الصوتي
66 depth scale مِقْيَاس العمق
67 echogram (depth recording, depth reading) قراءة العمق
68-108 sea marks (floating navigational marks) for buoyage and lighting systems **العلامات البحرية** للطافيات وأنظمة الإنارة
68-83 fairway marks (channel marks) **علامات المَجْرَى المائي**
68 light and whistle buoy طافية/شمندورة مزودة بضوء وصافرة
69 light (warning light) ضَوْء (ضوء تحذيري)
70 whistle صافِرة
71 buoy طافية، شَمَنْدُورَة
72 mooring chain سلسلة إرساء
73 sinker (mooring sinker) ثِقْل تغطيس
74 light and bell buoy طافية/شمندورة مزودة بضوء وجَرَس
75 bell جَرَس
76 conical buoy طافِيَة قُمْعِيَّة الشكل
77 can buoy طافِيَة ضخمة مخروطيَّة الشكل
78 topmark علامَة علويَّة
79 spar buoy طافية طولية
80 topmark buoy طافية بعلامَة علويَّة
81 lightship (light vessel) مَنَارة عائمة
82 lantern mast (lantern tower) صاري الفانوس
83 beam of light شُعاع ضوئي
84-102 fairway markings (channel markings) **علامات القناة المائية**
84 wreck [green buoys] حُطام [طافيات خضراء]
85 wreck to starboard حُطام إلى المَيْمَنَة
86 wreck to port حطام إلى الجانب الأيسر
87 shoals (shallows, shallow water, *Am.* flats) مياه ضحلة
88 middle ground to port يابسة وسطيَّة إلى الجانب الأيسر
89 division (bifurcation) [beginning of the middle ground; topmark: red cylinder above red ball] تشعب ذو فرعين [بداية اليابسة الوسطية؛ علامة علوية: أسطوانة حمراء فوق كُرة حمراء
90 convergence (confluence) [end of the middle ground; topmark: red St. Antony's cross above red ball] تلاق (نهاية اليابسة الوسطيَّة؛ علامة علويَّة: صليب احمر فوق كرة حمراء)
91 middle ground يابسة وسطيَّة
92 main fairway (main navigable channel) مَجْرَى مائي رئيسي

93 secondary fairway (secondary navigable channel) — مَجْرَى مائي ثانوي

94 can buoy — طافيَة ضخمة مخروطيَّة الشكل

95 port hand buoys (port hand marks) [red] — طافيات يدويَّة إلى يسار السفينة [أحمر]

96 starboard hand buoys (starboard hand marks) [black] — طافيات يدوية إلى مَيْمَنَة السفينة [أسود]

97 shoals (shallows, shallow water, *Am.* flats) outside the fairway — مياه ضحلة خارج المَجْرَى المائي

98 middle of the fairway (mid-channel) — منتصف المَجْرَى المائي

99 starboard markers [inverted broom] — علامات المَيْمَنَة

100 port markers [upward-pointing broom] — علامات الجانب الأيسر

101 & **102** range lights (leading lights) — أضْواء إرشاديَّة

101 lower range light (lower leading light) — أضْواء إرشادية سفلية

102 higher range light (higher leading light) — أضْواء إرشادية أكثر ارتفاعاً

103 lighthouse — فنار ، منارة

104 radar antenna (radar scanner) — هوائي رادار (ماسِح راداري)

105 lantern (characteristic light) — فانوس

106 radio direction finder (RDF) antenna — هوائي مُحَدِّد الاتجاه اللاسلكي

107 machinery and observation platform (machinery and observation deck) — مِنَصَّة الآلات والملاحظة

108 living quarters — وَحْدَات معيشة

225 Docks, Port, Harbour (*Am.* Harbor) (I) — أحْوَاض السُّفُن والميناء والمرْفَأ (1)

1 dock area — منطقة حَوْض السفن

2 free port (foreign trade zone) — ميناء حرة

3 free zone frontier (free zone enclosure) — حَدّ المنطقة الحرة

4 customs barrier — حاجِز المنطقة الجمركيَّة

5 customs entrance — مدخل المنطقة الجمركيَّة

6 port custom house — مَبْنَى جمارك الميناء

7 entrepôt — مستودع بضائع ، مخزن

8 barge (dumb barge, lighter) — صَنْدَل

9 break-bulk cargo transit shed (general cargo transit shed, package cargo transit shed) — عَنْبَر ترانزيت عام للبضائع

10 floating crane — مِرْفَاع عائم

11 harbour (*Am.* harbor) ferry (ferryboat) — مُعَدِّيَّة المرفأ

12 fender (dolphin) — حاجِز اصطدام

13 bunkering boat — قارب تزويد السفن بالوقود

14 break-bulk carrier (general cargo ship) — حامِلة بضائع عامة الأغراض

15 tug — سفينة قطر

16 floating dock (pontoon dock) — حَوْض سفن عائم

17 dry dock — حَوْض سفن جاف

18 coal wharf — رصيف الفحم

19 coal bunker — مُستودع الفحم

20 transporter loading bridge — جِسْر تحميل نقَّال

21 quayside railway — سكة حديدية بجانب الرصيف

22 weighing bunker — مَخْزَن الوزن

23 warehouse — مُستودع

24 quayside crane — مِرْفَاع جانب الرصيف

25 launch and lighter — لانش وصَنْدَل تفريغ /شحن الحمولة من الشاطئ للسفينة

26 port hospital — مستشفى الميناء

27 quarantine wing — جَنَاح الحَجْر الصحي

28 Institute of Tropical Medicine — معهد الطب المداريّ

29 excursion steamer (pleasure steamer) — سفينة رحلات ترفيهيَّة

30 jetty — رصيف يمتد داخل البحر

31 passenger terminal — مَحطَّة الرُكَّاب

32 liner (passenger liner, ocean liner) — عَبَّارة رُكَّاب

33 meteorological office, a weather station — مَحطَّة الأرصاد الجوية

34 signal mast (signalling mast) — صاري الإشارات

35 storm signal — إشارة هبوب عاصِفَة

36 port administration offices — المكاتب الإدارية بالميناء

37 tide level indicator — مؤشِّر مستوى المَدّ

38 quayside road (quayside roadway) — طريق جانب الرصيف

39 roll-on roll-off (ro-ro) system (roll-on roll-off operation) — نظام شحن وتفريغ

40 gantry — قَنْطَرَة

41 truck-to-truck system (truck-to-truck operation) — نظام النقل من شاحنة إلى شاحنة

42 foil-wrapped unit loads — وَحْدَات أحْمَال مُغلَّفَة بطبقة معدنية رقيقة

43 pallets — مِنَصَّات نقالة

44 forklift truck (fork truck, forklift) — شاحِنة بمرفاع شوكي

45 container ship — سفينة حاويات

46 transporter container-loading bridge — جِسْر نقال لتحميل الحاويات

47 container carrier truck — شاحنة نقل الحاويات

48 container terminal (container berth) — رصيف الحاويات

49 unit load — وَحْدَة الحَمْل
50 cold store — بَرَّادَة
51 conveyor belt (conveyor) — سَيْر ناقل
52 fruit storage shed (fruit warehouse) — عَنْبَر تخزين الفاكهة
53 office building — مَبْنَى المكاتب
54 urban motorway (*Am.* freeway) — طريق العربات
55 harbour (*Am.* harbor) tunnels — أنْفَاق المرفأ
56 fish dock — رصيف الأسماك
57 fish market — سوق الأسماك
58 auction room — صالة المزاد
59 fish-canning factory — مصنع تعليب الأسماك
60 push tow — قَطْر دفعي
61 tank farm — مركز تجميع الخزانات
62 railway siding — خط سكة حديدية جانبي
63 landing pontoon (landing stage) — رصيف النزول إلى البَرّ
64 quay — رصيف الميناء
65 breakwater (mole) — مَلْطم ، حاجز أمواج
66 pier (jetty), a quay extension — رصيف ممتد داخل البحر
67 bulk carrier — حاملة شحنات ضخمة
68 silo — صَوْمَعَة
69 silo cylinder — أسطوانة الصَوْمَعَة
70 lift bridge — جِسْر رفعي
71 industrial plant — وَحْدَة صناعية
72 storage tanks — صهاريج تخزين
73 tanker — ناقلة نفط

226 Docks, Port, Harbour (*Am.* Harbor) (II) — أحْوَاض السُفُن والميناء والمِرْفَأ (2)

1 container terminal (container berth), a modern cargo-handling berth — رصيف الحاويات
2 transporter container-loading bridge (loading bridge); *sim.:* transtainer crane (transtainer) — جِسْر نَقَّال لتحميل الحاويات
3 container — حَاوِيَة
4 truck (carrier) — عربة شَحْن
5 all-container ship — سفينة الحاويات
6 containers stowed on deck — حاويات متراصَّة على السَّطح
7 truck-to-truck handling (horizontal cargo handling with pallets) — مُنَاوَلَة من شاحنة إلى شاحنة
8 forklift truck (fork truck, forklift) — شاحنة ذات رافعة شوكيَّة
9 unitized foil-wrapped load (unit load) — وَحْدَة أحمال مُغَلَّفَة ومُجَمَّعَة
10 flat pallet, a standard pallet — مِنَصَّة نقالة مسَطحة
11 unitized break-bulk cargo — شحنة عامة مجَمَّعَة مُوَحَّدَة
12 heat sealing machine — ماكينة إحْكَام التغليف حرارياً
13 break-bulk carrier (general cargo ship) — سفينة بضائع عامة
14 cargo hatchway — فتحة إنزال البضائع من السفينة
15 receiving truck on board ship — شاحنة الاستقبال على ظهر السفينة
16 multi-purpose terminal — مَحَطَّة متعددة الاغراض
17 roll-on roll-off ship (ro-ro-ship) — سفينة تحميل وتفريغ
18 stern port (stern opening) — فتحة الكَوْثَل
19 driven load, a lorry (*Am.* truck) — بضائع منقولة في شاحنة
20 ro-ro depot — مَخْزَن تفريغ وشحن
21 unitized load (unitized package) — حمولة مُجَمَّعَة
22 banana-handling terminal [section] — مَحَطَّة مناولة الموز [قطاع]
23 seaward tumbler — برميل دَوَّار تجاه البحر
24 jib — ذِراع المِرْفَاع
25 elevator bridge — جِسْر المِرْفَاع
26 chain sling — مِعْلاق سلسلة (سلسلة تعليق)
27 lighting station — مَحَطَّة إنارة
28 shore-side tumbler for loading trains and lorries (*Am.* trucks) — برميل دَوَّار تجاه الساحل لتحميل القطارات والشاحنات
29 bulk cargo handling — مُنَاوَلَة البضائع السائبة/ الضخمة
30 bulk carrier — حامِلة البضائع السائبة/ الضخمة
31 floating bulk-cargo elevator — مِرْفَاع عائم للبضائع السائبة/ الضخمة
32 suction pipes — أنابيب ماصة
33 receiver — وَحْدَة الاستقبال
34 delivery pipe — أنبوب التوصيل
35 bulk transporter barge — صندل نقل البضائع السائبة
36 floating pile driver — مِدَقّ خوازيق عائم
37 pile driver frame — إطار مِدَقّ الخوازيق
38 pile hammer — مِطْرَقَة دق الخوازيق
39 driving guide rail — قضيب دق دليلي
40 pile — خازوق
41 bucket dredger, a dredger — كَرَّاكَة قادوسيَّة/دِلْويَّة
42 bucket chain — قطار القواديس
43 bucket ladder — سلم القواديس
44 dredger bucket — قادوس الكَرَّاكَة
45 chute — مَجْرَى مائل
46 hopper barge — صَنْدَل قادوسي
47 spoil — نفاية الحفر
48 floating crane — مِرْفَاع عائم
49 jib (boom) — ذِراع المِرْفَاع
50 counterweight (counterpoise) — ثِقْل مُوَازِن
51 adjusting spindle — مِحْوَر دَوَرَان انضباطي
52 crane driver's cabin (crane driver's cage) — كابينة سائق المِرْفَاع

53 crane framework — هيكل المِرْفَاع
54 winch house — مبَيْت الوِنْش
55 control platform — منَصَّة التَحكم
56 turntable — صِينية دَوَّارَة
57 pontoon, a pram — طَوْف
58 engine superstructure (engine mounting) — حامِل المُحَرِّك

227 Salvage (Salving) and Towage — إنْقَاذ وقَطْر السُّفُن

1 salvaging (salving) of a ship run aground — إنقاذ سفينة ارتطمت بالأرض
2 ship run aground (damaged vessel) — سفينة ارتطمت بالأرض (جانِحة)
3 sandbank; *also:* quicksand — رُكَام رَمْلِيّ؛ أيضاً رمل سريع الانهيار
4 open sea — بَحْر مفتوح
5 tug (salvage tug) — سفينة القَطْر
6-15 towing gear — **مُعِدَّات القَطْر**
6 towing gear for towing at sea — مُعِدَّات القَطْر في البحر
7 towing winch (towing machine, towing engine) — وِنْش القَطْر
8 tow rope (tow line, towing hawser) — حَبْل القَطْر
9 tow rope guide — دليل حَبْل القَطْر
10 cross-shaped bollard — عمود ربط حِبَال مُتصالِب
11 hawse hole — فتحة القَلْس في مُقَدَّم السفينة
12 anchor cable (chain cable) — كيبل مِرْسَاة
13 towing gear for work in harbours (*Am.* harbors) — مُعِدَّات القَطْر للعمل في المرفأ
14 guest rope — حَبْل نزيل
15 position of the tow rope (tow line, towing hawser) — مَوْضِع حَبْل القَطْر
16 tug (salvage tug) [vertical elevation] — سفينة القَطْر [مسقط رأسي]
17 bow fender (pudding fender) — مِصَد الجُؤْجُؤ
18 forepeak — مخزن الجُؤْجُؤ
19 living quarters — وَحَدَات معيشة
20 Schottel propeller — رفَّاص "شوتل"
21 Kort vent — منْفَس "كورت"
22 engine and propeller room — غُرفة المُحَرِّك والرفَّاص
23 clutch coupling — تقارن بقابض
24 compass platform (compass bridge, compass flat, monkey bridge) — منَصَّة البُوْصَلَة
25 fire-fighting equipment — مُعِدَّات مكافحة الحريق
26 stowage — مخزن
27 tow hook — خُطَّاف القَطْر
28 afterpeak — مخزن المؤخِّرة
29 stern fender — مِصَد الكَوْثَل
30 main manoeuvring (*Am.* maneuvering) keel — صالِب القاعدة الرئيسي للمناورة

228 Life Saving — إنْقَاذ الحَيَاة

1 rocket apparatus (rocket gun, line-throwing gun) — جهاز صاروخي (مِدْفَع رمي الحَبْل)
2 life rocket (rocket) — صاروخ حَبْل الإنقاذ
3 rocket line (whip line) — حَبْل الصاروخ
4 oilskins — ملابس من قماش مشَمَّع متين
5 sou'wester (southwester) — قبعة من المشمع لها حافة خلفية عريضة
6 oilskin jacket — سُتْرَة من قماش مشَمَّع متين
7 oilskin coat — معْطَف من قماش مشَمَّع متين
8 inflatable life jacket — سُتْرَة نجاة نفاخيَّة
9 cork life jacket (cork life preserver) — سُتْرَة نجاة فلينيَّة
10 stranded ship (damaged vessel) — سفينة جانِحة
11 oil bag, for trickling oil on the water surface — كِيس زيت لتنقيط زيت فوق سَطْح الماء
12 lifeline — حَبْل الإنقاذ
13 breeches buoy — طافية، عَوَّامَة
14 rescue cruiser — طَرَّاد الإنقاذ
15 helicopter landing deck — سَطْح هبوط الهيلوكوبتر
16 rescue helicopter — طائرة هيلوكوبتر لعمليات الإنقاذ
17 daughter boat — قارِب الطَّرَّاد
18 inflatable boat (inflatable dinghy) — قارِب نفاخي
19 life raft — طَوْف النجاة
20 fire-fighting equipment for fires at sea — مُعِدَّات مكافحة الحريق في حرائق البحر
21 hospital unit with operating cabin and exposure bath — وَحْدَة مستشفى للطوارئ بها غرفة عمليات
22 navigating bridge — جِسْر المِلاحة
23 upper tier of navigating bridge — الطابق العلوي لجِسْر المِلاحة
24 lower tier of navigating bridge — الطابق السفلي لجِسْر المِلاحة
25 messroom — ميس، غرفة الطعام
26 rudders and propeller (screw) — الدَّفَّة والرفَّاص
27 stowage — مخزن
28 foam can — عُلْبَة الرَّغْوَة
29 side engines — مُحركات جانبية
30 shower — دُشّ
31 coxswain's cabin — كابينة مُوَجِّه الدَّفَّة
32 crew member's single-berth cabin — كابينة بسرير مفرد لأحد أفراد الطاقم
33 bow propeller — رفَّاص الجُؤْجُؤ

229 Aircraft I — الطَّائِرَة (1)

1-14 wing configurations — **تشكيلات الجَنَاح**
1 high-wing monoplane (high-wing plane) — طائرة أحاديَّة السَّطْح مرتفعة الجَنَاحيْن

2 span (wing span)	مسافة امتداد الجَنَاحيْن
3 shoulder-wing monoplane (shoulder-wing plane)	طائرة أحاديَّة السَّطْح كتفيَّة الجَنَاحيْن
4 midwing monoplane (midwing plane)	طائرة أحادية السَّطْح متوسطة الجَنَاحين
5 low-wing monoplane (low-wing plane)	طائرة أحاديَّة السَّطْح منخفضة الجَنَاحيْن
6 triplane	طائرة ثلاثية الأسَطْح
7 upper wing	الجَنَاح العلوي
8 middle wing (central wing)	الجَنَاح المتوسط/المركزي
9 lower wing	الجَنَاح السفلي
10 biplane	طائرة ثنائيَّة الأسَطْح
11 strut	شكَال انضغاطي
12 cross bracing wires	أسلاك تكتيف متصالبة
13 sesquiplane	طائرة أحاديَّة نصفية
14 low-wing monoplane (low-wing plane) with cranked wings (inverted gull wings)	طائرة أحاديَّة السَّطْح منخفضة الجَنَاحيْن ذات جَنَاحيْن بمرفقيْن
15-22 wing shapes	**أشكال الجَنَاح**
15 elliptical wing	جَنَاح اهليلجي
16 rectangular wing	جَنَاح مستطيل
17 tapered wing	جَنَاح مستدق الطرف
18 crescent wing	جَنَاح هلالي
19 delta wing	جَنَاح مثلثيّ (دلتا)
20 swept-back wing with semi-positive sweep-back	جَنَاح بزاوية امتداد تراجعيّ شبه مُوجب
21 swept-back wing with positive sweepback	جَنَاح بزاوية امتداد تراجعي مُوجب
22 ogival wing (ogee wing)	جَنَاح بضلع قوسي منحرف
23-36 tail shapes (tail unit shapes, empennage shapes)	**أشْكَال الذيل** (أشكال وحدات الذيل)
23 normal tail (normal tail unit)	ذَيْل عادي
24 & 25 vertical tail (vertical stabilizer and rudder)	ذَيْل رأسي
24 vertical stabilizer (vertical fin, tail fin)	زِعْنِفَة مُوَازَنَة رأسيَّة
25 rudder	دَفَّة الطائرة
26 & 27 horizontal tail	الذيل الأفقي
26 tailplane (horizontal stabilizer)	زِعْنِفَة مُوَازَنَة أفقية
27 elevator	سَطْح رافع، سكان الارتفاع
28 cruciform tail (cruciform tail unit)	ذَيْل صليبي الشكل
29 T-tail (T-tail unit)	ذَيْل تائي الشكل
30 lobe	نتوء مستدير
31 V-tail (vee-tail, butterfly tail)	ذَيْل فراشة (على شكل حرف V)
32 double tail unit (twin tail unit)	وَحْدَة ذَيْل مزدوج
33 end plate	لَوْحَة طرفيَّة
34 double tail unit (twin tail unit) of a twin-boom aircraft	وَحْدَة ذَيْل مزدوج لطائرة ذات رافدتَيْن
35 raised horizontal tail with double booms	وَحْدَة ذَيْل افقي مرفوع ذو رافدتَيْن
36 triple tail unit	وَحْدَة ذَيْل ثلاثي
37 system of flaps	نظام القلابات
38 extensible slat	شريحة/قدَّة قابلة للامتداد
39 spoiler	جهاز تعطيل (أو تخفيف) الرفع
40 double-slotted Fowler flap	قلاب فاولر ذو شقْبَتَيْن
41 outer aileron (low-speed aileron)	جُنَيْح خارجي
42 inner spoiler (landing flap, lift dump)	جهاز تعطيل (أو تخفيف) الرفع الداخلي
43 inner aileron (all-speed aileron)	جُنَيْح داخلي
44 brake flap (air brake)	قلابة الكبح
45 basic profile	منظر جانبي أساسي
46-48 plain flaps (simple flaps)	**قلاّبات بسيطة/ مستوية**
46 normal flap	قلابة عادية
47 slotted flap	قلابة مَشْقُوبَة
48 double-slotted flap	قلابة ذات شقبتَيْن
49 & 50 split flaps	قلابتان مُجزأتان
49 plain split flap (simple split flap)	قلابة مُجزأة مستوية
50 zap flap	قلابة "زاب"
51 extending flap	قلابة امتدادية
52 Fowler flap	قلابة "فاولر"
53 slat	شريحة، قدَّة، رقيقة
54 profiled leading-edge flap (droop flap)	قلابة متدليَّة
55 Krüger flap	قلابة "كروجر"

230 Aircraft II — الطَّائِرَة (2)

1-31 cockpit of a single-engine (single-engined) racing and passenger aircraft (racing and passenger plane)	**كابينة الطاقم لطَائِرَة أحاديَّة المُحَرِّك لنقل الرُكَّاب والمسابقات**
1 instrument panel	لَوْحَة أجهزة القياس
2 air-speed (*Am.* air-speed) indicator	مُبَيِّن سرعة الهواء
3 artificial horizon (gyro horizon)	مُبَيِّن الأفُق الاصطناعي
4 altimeter	مِقْيَاس الإرتفاع، ألْتيمتر
5 radio compass (automatic direction finder)	بُوصْلَة لاسلكيَّة (مُحَدِّد اتجاه أوتوماتي)
6 magnetic compass	بُوصْلَة مغناطيسيَّة
7 boost gauge (*Am.* gage)	مِقْيَاس الضغط المُعَزِّز
8 tachometer (rev counter, revolution counter)	تاكومتر (عَدَّاد الدَّوَرَات)
9 cylinder temperature gauge (*Am.* gage)	مِقْيَاس حرارة الأُسْطُوَانة
10 accelerometer	مِقْيَاس التسارع
11 chronometer	كرونومتر، ساعة مُحكَمَة الضبط

12 turn indicator with ball — مُبَيِّن الانعطاف
13 directional gyro — حافظ الاتجاه
14 vertical speed indicator (rate-of-climb indicator, variometer) — مُبَيِّن السرعة الرأسيَّة
15 VOR radio direction finder [VOR: very high frequency omni-directional range] — مُحَدِّد اتجاه لاسلكي ذو تردد عال جدا لجميع الاتجاهات
16 left tank fuel gauge (*Am.* gage) — مُبَيِّن خَزَّان الوَقُود الأيْسَر
17 right tank fuel gauge (*Am.* gage) — مُبَيِّن خَزَّان الوَقُود الأيْمَن
18 ammeter — أميتر
19 fuel pressure gauge (*Am.* gage) — مِقْيَاس ضغط الوَقُود
20 oil pressure gauge (*Am.* gage) — مِقْيَاس ضغط الزيت
21 oil temperature gauge (*Am.* gage) — مُبَيِّن حرارة الزيت
22 radio and radio navigation equipment — معدات اللاسلكي والمِلاحة اللاسلكيَّة
23 map light — ضَوْء إنارة الخريطة
24 wheel (control column, control stick) for operating the ailerons and elevators — عصا التَّحَكُّم لتشغيل الجُنَيْحَات والأسْطُح الرَّافِعة
25 co-pilot's wheel — عصا الطَّيَّار المُسَاعِد
26 switches — مفاتيح تشغيل
27 rudder pedals — دَوَّاسَتا الدَّفَّة
28 co-pilot's rudder pedals — دَوَّاسَتا دَفَّة الطَّيَّار المُسَاعِد
29 microphone for the radio — ميكروفون اللاسلكي
30 throttle lever (throttle control) — ذراع الصمام الخانِق
31 mixture control — مِخْنَقَة تَغْيِير المزيج
32-66 single-engine (single-engined) racing and passenger aircraft (racing and passenger plane) — **طَائِرَة أحاديَّة المُحَرِّك لنقل الرُّكَّاب والمسابقات**
32 propeller (airscrew) — مِرْوَحَة
33 spinner — غطاء قُبّ المروحة
34 flat four engine — مُحَرِّك رُباعي مستو
35 cockpit — كابينة طاقم الطَّائِرَة
36 pilot's seat — مَقْعَد الطَّيَّار
37 co-pilot's seat — مَقْعَد الطَّيَّار المُسَاعِد
38 passenger seats — مَقَاعِد الرُّكَّاب
39 hood (canopy, cockpit hood, cockpit canopy) — غِطاء كابينة الطَّيَّار
40 steerable nose wheel — عَجَلَة المُقَدِّمَة القابلة للتَّوْجيه
41 main undercarriage unit (main landing gear unit) — وَحْدَة عجلات الهبوط الرئيسيَّة
42 step — دَرَجَة سُلَّميَّة
43 wing — جَنَاح
44 right navigation light (right position light) — ضَوْء المِلاحة الأيْمَن
45 spar — عَضُد الجَنَاح
46 rib — ضِلْع الجَنَاح
47 stringer (longitudinal reinforcing member) — رافِدة (عُضْو تقوية طوليّ)
48 fuel tank — خَزَّان الوَقُود
49 landing light — أضواء الهبوط
50 left navigation light (left position light) — ضَوْء المِلاحة الأيْسَر
51 electrostatic conductor — مُوَصِّل الكتروستاتيّ
52 aileron — جُنَيْح
53 landing flap — قَلَّابة الهبوط
54 fuselage (body) — جِسْم الطَّائِرَة
55 frame (former) — هَيْكَل الطَّائِرَة
56 chord — وَتَر
57 stringer (longitudinal reinforcing member) — رافِدة (عُضْو تقوية طولي)
58 vertical tail (vertical stabilizer and rudder) — ذَيْل رأسي (زعنفة مُوَازَنَة رأسية ودَفَّة)
59 vertical stabilizer (vertical fin, tail fin) — زعنفة مُوَازَنَة رأسية (زعنفة الذيل)
60 rudder — دَفَّة الطَّائِرَة
61 horizontal tail — ذيل أفقي
62 tailplane (horizontal stabilizer) — لَوْحَة الذيل (زعنفة مُوَازَنَة أفقيَّة)
63 elevator — سَطْح رافع
64 warning light (anticollision light) — أضواء تحذيريَّة (أضواء لتفادي الاصطدام)
65 dipole antenna — هوائي ثنائي القطب
66 long-wire antenna (long-conductor antenna) — هوائي بسلك توصيل طويل
67-72 principal manoeuvres (*Am.* maneuvers) of the aircraft (aeroplane, plane, *Am.* airplane) — **حركات المناورة الأساسيَّة للطائِرَة**
67 pitching — تَرَجُّح
68 lateral axis — المِحْوَر الجانبي
69 yawing — انْعِرَاج
70 vertical axis (normal axis) — المِحْوَر الرأسي
71 rolling — عُطُوف
72 longitudinal axis — المِحْوَر الطولي

231 Aircraft III — الطَّائِرَة (3)

1-33 types of aircraft (aeroplanes, planes, *Am.* airplanes) — **أنواع الطائرات**
1-6 propeller-driven aircraft (aeroplanes, planes, *Am.* airplanes) — **طَائِرَة بمِرْوَحَة**
1 single-engine (single-engined) racing and passenger aircraft (racing and passenger plane), a low-wing monoplane (low-wing plane) — طَائِرَة بمُحَرِّك واحد لنقل الرُّكَّاب والمسابقات ، طَائِرَة منخفضة الجَنَاحين
2 single-engine (single-engined) passenger aircraft, a high-wing — طَائِرَة بمُحَرِّك واحد لنقل الرُّكَّاب، طَائِرَة أحاديَّة السطح مرتفعة الجَنَاحَيْن

monoplane (high-wing plane)	
3 twin-engine (twin-engined) business and passenger aircraft (business and passenger plane)	طَائِرَة بمُحَرِّكَيْن لنقل الرُّكَّاب والأعمال
4 short/medium haul airliner, a turboprop plane (turbopropeller plane, propeller-turbine plane)	طَائِرَة رُكَّاب ضخمة للمسافات القصيرة والمتوسطة
5 turboprop engine (turbopropeller engine)	مُحَرِّك دفع توربيني
6 vertical stabilizer (vertical fin, tail fin)	وَحْدَة مُوَازَنَة رأسيَّة (زعنفة رأسيَّة، زعنفة الذيل)
7-33 jet planes (jet aeroplanes, jets, *Am.* jet airplanes)	**الطائرات النفَّاثة**
7 twin-jet business and passenger aircraft (business and passenger aircraft (business and passenger plane)	طَائِرَة بمُحَرِّكَيْن لنقل الرُّكَّاب والأعمال
8 fence	حظار
9 wing-tip tank (tip tank)	خَزَّان وَقُود بطَرَف الجَنَاح
10 rear engine	مُحَرِّك خلفيّ
11 twin-jet short/medium haul airliner	طَائِرَة رُكَّاب ضخمة بمُحَرِّكَيْن نفاثَيْن للمسافات القصيرة والمتوسطة
12 tri-jet medium haul airliner	طَائِرَة رُكَّاب ضخمة بثلاثة مُحَرِّكات نفَّاثة للمسافات المتوسطة
13 four-jet long haul airliner	طَائِرَة رُكَّاب ضخمة بأربعة مُحَرِّكات نفَّاثة للمسافات الطويلة
14 wide-body long haul airliner (jumbo jet)	طَائِرَة رُكَّاب جامبو
15 supersonic airliner [Concorde]	طَائِرَة رُكَّاب ضخمة أسرع من الصوت [كونكورد]
16 droop nose	مُقَدِّمَة مُدَلَّاة
17 twin-jet wide-body airliner for short/medium haul routes (airbus)	طَائِرَة رُكَّاب ضخمة متسعة ذات مُحَرِّكين نَفَّاثَيْن للمسافات القصيرة والمتوسطة (طَائِرَة ايرباص)
18 radar nose (radome, radar dome) with weather radar antenna	مُقَدِّمَة راداريَّة مع هوائي رادار (رصد) جَوِّي
19 cockpit	كابينة طاقم الطَّائِرَة
20 galley	مَطْبَخ الطَّائِرَة
21 cargo hold (hold , underfloor hold)	حُجَيْرَة البضائع
22 passenger cabin with passenger seats	كابينة الرُّكَّاب وبها المقاعد
23 retractable nose undercarriage unit (retractable nose landing gear unit)	وَحْدَة عَجَلات الهبوط الأماميَّة القابلة للضَّم
24 nose undercarriage flap (nose gear flap)	غطاء حجيرة عَجَلات الهبوط الأماميَّة
25 centre (*Am.* center) passenger door	باب الرُّكَّاب الأوسط
26 engine pod with engine (turbojet engine, jet turbine engine, jet engine, jet turbine)	ظَرْف المُحَرِّك وبداخله المُحَرِّك التوربيني النفَّاث
27 electrostatic conductors	مُوَصِّلات الكتروستاتيَّة
28 retractable main undercarriage unit (retractable main landing gear unit)	وَحْدَة عَجَلات الهبوط الرئيسية القابلة للضم
29 side window	نافذة جانبيَّة
30 rear passenger door	باب الرُّكَّاب الخلفيّ
31 toilet (lavatory, WC)	دَوْرَة مياه
32 pressure bulkhead	حاجِز إنشائي فاصل ضَغْطِيّ
33 auxiliary engine (auxiliary gas turbine) for the generator unit	مُحَرِّك إضافي/مُساعِد لوحدة المولِّد

232 Aircraft IV — الطَّائِرَة (4)

1 flying boat, a seaplane	طَائِرَة مائيَّة
2 hull	مُقَدَّم الطَّائِرَة
3 stub wing (sea wing)	جَنَاح أبْتَر
4 tail bracing wires	أسْلاك تقوية الذَّيْل
5 floatplane (float sea-plane), a seaplane	طَائِرَة بعَوَّامَة، طائرة بحرية
6 float	عَوَّامَة
7 vertical stabilizer (vertical fin, tail fin)	زِعْنِفَة مُوَازنة رأسيَّة
8 amphibian (amphibian flying boat)	طَائِرَة برمائيَّة
9 hull	مُقَدَّم الطَّائِرَة
10 retractable under-carriage (retractable landing gear)	عَجَلات الهبوط القابلة للضَّم
11-25 helicopters	**طائرات الهليكوبتر، الطائرات العموديَّة**
11 light multirole helicopter	هليكوبتر خفيفة مُتعدِّدة الأدوار
12, 13 main rotor	مِرْوَحَة رئيسيَّة
12 rotary wing (rotor blade)	جَنَاح المِرْوَحَة
13 rotor head	رأس المِرْوَحَة
14 tail rotor (anti-torque rotor)	دَوَّار الدَّفْع الرَّافع الخلفيّ
15 landing skids	زحافتا الهبوط
16 flying crane	مِرْفَاع طائر
17 turbine engines	مُحَرِّكات توربينيَّة
18 lifting undercarriage	هَيْكَل سفلي للرفع
19 lifting platform	مَنَصَّة الرفع
20 reserve tank	خَزَّان الوَقُود الاحتياطي
21 transport helicopter	هليكوبتر للنقل
22 rotors in tandem	مِرْوَحَتَان ترادُفيَّتان
23 rotor pylon	عمود المِرْوَحَة
24 turbine engine	مُحَرِّك توربيني

25 tail loading gate	باب الشحن الخلفي
26-32 V/STOL aircraft (vertical/short take-off and landing aircraft)	**طَائِرَة عمودية للإقلاع القصير والهبوط**
26 tilt-wing aircraft, a VTOL aircraft (vertical take-off and landing aircraft)	طَائِرَة بجَنَاح مائل (طَائِرَة إقلاع وهبوط عموديّ)
27 tilt wing in vertical position	جَنَاح مائل في وَضْع رأسيّ
28 contrarotating tail propellers	مِدْسَرَات ذيْل تدُور في اتجاه معاكس
29 gyrodyne	جيروداين ، جيروسكوب
30 turboprop engine (turbopropeller engine)	مُحَرِّك ذو رفَّاص توربيني
31 convertiplane	طَائِرَة عمودية أفقية
32 tilting rotor in vertical position	مِرْوَحَة مائلة في وَضْع رأسي
33-60 aircraft engines (aero engines)	**مُحَرِّكات الطَّائِرَة**
33-50 jet engines (turbojet engines, jet turbine engines, jet turbines)	**المُحَرِّكات النفَّاثة**
33 front fan-jet	مِنْفَث المِرْوَحَة الأمامي
34 fan	مِرْوَحَة
35 low-pressure compressor	ضاغِط ضغط منخفض
36 high-pressure compressor	ضاغِط ضغط مرتفع
37 combustion chamber	حُجْرَة الاحتراق
38 fan-jet turbine	توربين مِنْفَث المِرْوَحَة
39 nozzle (propelling nozzle, propulsion nozzle)	فُوَّهَة (فُوَّهَة الدفع)
40 turbines	توربينات
41 bypass duct	مجرى جانبي/ثانوي
42 aft fan-jet	مَنْفَث المِرْوَحَة الخلفي
43 fan	مِرْوَحَة
44 bypass duct	مَجْرَى جانبي/ثانوي
45 nozzle (propelling nozzle, propulsion nozzle)	فُوَّهَة الدفع
46 bypass engine	مُحَرِّك مُسَاعِد
47 turbines	توربينات
48 mixer	خلاط
49 nozzle (propelling nozzle, propulsion nozzle)	فُوَّهَة (فُوَّهَة الدفع)
50 secondary air flow (bypass air flow)	دفْق هواء ثانوي
51 turboprop engine (turbopropeller engine), a twin-shaft engine	مُحَرِّك دفع توربيني
52 annular air intake	مَدْخَل هواء حلَقي
53 high-pressure turbine	توربين ضغط عال
54 low-pressure turbine	توربين ضغط منخفض
55 nozzle (propelling nozzle, propulsion nozzle)	فُوَّهَة (فُوَّهَة الدفع)
56 shaft	عَمُود
57 intermediate shaft	عَمُود وَسَطي
58 gear shaft	عَمُود المُسَنَّنات
59 reduction gear	تُرْس تخفيض السرعة
60 propeller shaft	عَمُود (دوران) المِرْوَحَة

233 Airport المَطَار

1 runway	مَدْرَج إقلاع وهبوط الطائرات
2 taxiway	مَدْرَج جانبي
3 apron	حَظِيرَة الطائرات
4 apron taxiway	مَدْرَج حظيرة الطائرات
5 baggage terminal	مَحَطَّة العَفْش
6 tunnel entrance to the baggage terminal	مَدْخَل نَفَقي يؤدي إلى مَحَطَّة البضائع
7 airport fire service	مركز إطفاء المَطَار
8 fire appliance building	مَبْنَى مُعِدَّات الإطفاء
9 mail and cargo terminal	مَحَطَّة البريد والبضائع
10 cargo warehouse	مُسْتَوْدَع البضائع
11 assembly point	نُقطة التجمع
12 pier	رصيف
13 pierhead	رأس الرصيف
14 airbridge	جِسْر جَوِّي
15 departure building (terminal)	صالة/ مَبْنَى المُغادرة
16 administration building	مَبْنَى الإدارة
17 control tower (tower)	بُرْج المراقبة
18 waiting room (lounge)	صالة الانتظار
19 airport restaurant	مَطْعَم المَطَار
20 spectators' terrace	شُرْفَة الزُّوَّار/المُوَدِّعين
21 aircraft in loading position (nosed in)	طَائِرَة في وضع التحميل
22 service vehicles, e.g. baggage loaders, water tankers, galley loaders, toilet-cleaning vehicles, ground power units, tankers	عَرَبَات الخدمة، ومنها لَوَادِر العَفْش وصهاريج الماء ولَوَادِر الأطعمة إلى المطبخ وعربات تنظيف دورات المياه ووحدات الطاقة الأرضيَّة والخزانات
23 aircraft tractor (aircraft tug)	جَرَّار الطَّائِرَة
24-53 airport information symbols (pictographs)	**رموز المعلومات بالمَطَار**
24 'airport'	"مَطَار"
25 'departures'	"المُغادرون"
26 'arrivals'	"القادمون"
27 'transit passengers'	"رُكَّاب الترانزيت"
28 'waiting room' ('lounge')	"صالة الانتظار"
29 'assembly point' ('meeting point', 'rendezvous point')	"نقطة التجمع"
30 'spectators' terrace'	"شرفة الزُّوَّار/المُوَدِّعُون"
31 'information'	"استعلامات"
32 'taxis'	"سيَّارات أجرة"
33 'car hire'	"تأجير سيارات"
34 'trains'	"القطارات"
35 'buses'	"الحافلات"
36 'entrance'	"دخول"

37 'exit' — ″خروج″
38 'baggage reclaim' — ″استرجاع الأمْتِعَة″
39 'luggage lockers' — ″دواليب الأمْتِعَة″
40 'telephone – emergency calls only' — ″هاتف – للطوارئ فقط″
41 'emergency exit' — ″مَخْرَج طوارئ″
42 'passport check' — ″الجَوَازَات″
43 'press facilities' — ″تسهيلات صحافيَّة″
44 'doctor' — ″طبيب″
45 'chemist' (*Am.* 'druggist') — ″صيدلية″
46 'showers' — ″أدْشَاش استحمام″
47 'gentlemen's toilet' ('gentlemen') — ″دَوْرَة مياه للرجال″
48 'ladies toilet' ('ladies') — ″دَوْرَة مياه للسيدات″
49 'chapel' — ″كنيسة صغيرة″
50 'restaurant' — ″مَطْعَم″
51 'change' — ″صِرَافَة″
52 'duty free shop' — ″السُّوق الحُرَّة″
53 'hairdresser' — ″مُصَفِّف شَعْر″

234 Space Flight I — الطَّيَران في الفَضَاء (1)

1 Saturn V 'Apollo' booster (booster rocket) [overall view] — صاروخ تعزيز مَرْكَبَة الفضاء أبوللو ساترن V [منظر عام]
2 Saturn V 'Apollo' booster (booster rocket) [overall sectional view] — صاروخ تعزيز مَرْكَبَة الفضاء أبوللو [منظر قطاعي عام]
3 first rocket stage (S-IC) — مِنَصَّة الصاروخ الأول (S-IC)
4 F-1 engines — مُحَرِّكات F-1
5 heat shield (thermal protection shield) — دِرْع واقٍ من الحرارة
6 aerodynamic engine fairings — أسْطُح انسيابية ايروديناميَّة للمُحَرِّكات
7 aerodynamic stabilizing fins — زعانف مُوَازَنَة ايروديناميَّة
8 stage separation retro-rockets, 8 rockets arranged in 4 pairs — صواريخ كابِحَة لِفَصْل المِنَصَّات، ثَمَانِيَّة صواريخ مُرَتَّبَة في أربعة أزْوَاج
9 kerosene (RP-1) tank [capacity:811,000 litres] — خَزَّان الكيروسين [سعة 811 ألف لتر]
10 liquid oxygen (LOX, LO_2) supply lines, total of 5 — خُطُوط إمداد الأكسجين السائل، إجمالي خمسة خُطُوط
11 anti-vortex system (device for preventing the formation of vortices in the fuel) — نظام مَنْع التَّدْوِيم في الوقود
12 liquid oxygen (LOX. LO_2) tank [capacity: 1,315,000 litres] — خَزَّان الأكسجين السائل [سعة مليون و315 ألف لتر]
13 anti-slosh baffles — حَوَاجِز مَنْع الخَضْخَضَة
14 compressed-helium bottles (helium pressure bottles) — حاوِيَات الهليوم المضغوط
15 diffuser for gaseous oxygen — آليَّة نَشْر الأكسجين الغازيّ
16 inter-tank connector (inter-tank section) — آليَّة توصيل بين الخزانات
17 instruments and system-monitoring devices — الآلات وأجهزة مراقبة الأنظمة
18 second rocket stage (S-II) — مِنَصَّة الصاروخ الثاني (S-II)
19 J-2 engines — مُحَرِّكات J-2
20 heat shield (thermal protection shield) — دِرْع واقٍ من الحرارة
21 engine mounts and thrust structure — مَحَامِل المُحَرِّكات وهيكل الدفع
22 acceleration rockets for fuel acquisition — صواريخ التَّسَارُع للحصول علي الوَقُود
23 liquid hydrogen (LH_2) suction line — خَطّ شفط الهيدروجين السائل
24 liquid oxygen (LOX, LO_2) tank [capacity: 1,315,000 litres] — خَزَّان الاكسجين السائل [سعة مليون و315 ألف لتر]
25 standpipe — أنْبُوب قائم
26 liquid hydrogen (LH_2) tank [capacity: 1,020,000 litres] — خَزَّان الهيدروجين السائل [سعة مليون وعشرين ألف لتر]
27 fuel level sensor — مِكْشَاف مستوى الوَقُود
28 work platform (working platform) — منصة شغل
29 cable duct — مَجْرَى الكيبلات
30 manhole — فتحة
31 S-IC/S-II inter-stage connector (inter-stage section) — آليَّة تَوْصيل بين منصتي الصاروخَيْن الأوَّل والثاني
32 compressed-gas container (gas pressure vessel) — حاوِيَة الغاز المضغوط
33 third rocket stage (S-IVB) — مِنَصَّة الصاروخ الثالث
34 J-2 engine — مُحَرِّك J-2
35 nozzle (thrust nozzle) — فُوَّهة (فُوَّهة الدفع)
36 S-II/S-IVB inter-stage connector (inter-stage section) — آليَّة توصيل بين منصتي الصاروخَيْن الثاني والثالث
37 four second-stage (S-II) separation retro-rockets — أربعة صواريخ كابِحَة للفصل في المنصة الثانية
38 attitude control rockets — صواريخ ضبط الوجهة
39 liquid oxygen (LOX, LO_2) tank [capacity: 77,200 litres] — خَزَّان الأكسجين السائل [سعة 77 ألف و200 لتر]
40 fuel line duct — مَجْرَى خَطّ الوَقُود
41 liquid hydrogen (LH_2) tank [capacity: 253,000 litres] — خَزَّان الهيدروجين السائل [سعة 253 ألف لتر]
42 measuring probes — مِسْبَارات قياس
43 compressed-helium tanks (helium pressure vessels) — خَزَّانات الهليوم المضغوط
44 tank vent — فتحة تهوية الخَزَّان
45 forward frame section — جزء الهيكل الأمامي

46	work platform (working platform)	مِنَصَّة شغل
47	cable duct	مَجْرَى الكيبلات
48	acceleration rockets for fuel acquisition	صواريخ التسارع للحصول على الوقود
49	aft frame section	جزء الهيكل الخلفي
50	compressed-helium tanks (helium pressure vessels)	خَزَّانات الهليوم المضغوط
51	liquid hydrogen (LH_2) line	خَطّ الهيدروجين السائل
52	liquid oxygen (LOX, LO_2) line	خَطّ الأكسجين السائل
53	24-panel instrument unit	وَحْدَة آلات بها 24 لَوْحَة
54	LM hangar (lunar module hangar)	عَنْبَر الموديولات القَمَرِيَّة
55	LM (lunar module)	موديول قَمَرِيّ
56	Apollo SM (service module), containing supplies and equipment	موديول الخِدمة أبوللو وبه المُؤن والمُعِدَّات
57	SM (service module) main engine	المُحَرِّك الرئيسي لموديول الخدمة
58	fuel tank	خَزَّان الوَقُود
59	nitrogen tetroxide tank	خَزَّان رابع أكسيد النيتروجين
60	pressurized gas delivery system	نظام توصيل الغاز المضغوط
61	oxygen tanks	خَزَّانات الأكسجين
62	fuel cells	خلايا وَقُودِيَّة
63	manoeuvring (*Am.* maneuvering) rocket assembly	مجموعة صواريخ المناوَرَة
64	directional antenna assembly	مجموعة هوائي اتجاهي
65	space capsule (command section)	كبسولة فضائيَّة (جزء القيادة)
66	launch phase escape tower	بُرْج انفلات مرحلة الإطلاق

235 Space Flight II — الطَّيران في الفَضَاء (2)

1-45 Space Shuttle-Orbiter — عَرَبَة فضائيَّة مداريَّة مكوكيَّة

1	twin-spar (two-spar, double-spar) vertical fin	زِعنِفة رأسيَّة ذات عَضُدَيْن
2	engine compartment structure	هيكل حُجَيْرة المُحَرِّك
3	fin post	قَضيب الزِعْنِفَة
4	fuselage attachment [of payload bay doors]	مُلْحَق جِسْم العربة [لأبواب فرجة الحمل الآجر]
5	upper thrust mount	مَحْمَل الدفع العلوي
6	lower thrust mount	مَحْمَل الدفع السفلي
7	keel	صالب القاعدة، أرينَة
8	heat shield	دِرْع واقٍ من الحرارة
9	waist longeron	الضِلْع الطُولاني الأوسط
10	integrally machined (integrally milled) main rib	ضِلْع رئيسي مصنع آلياً
11	integrally stiffened light alloy skin	بَشْرَة من سبيكة خفيفة مُقَوَّاة
12	lattice girder	عارضة شبكيَّة
13	payload bay insulation	عازِل فُرْجَة الحِمْل الآجِر
14	payload bay door	بابَ فُرْجَة الحِمْل الآجِر
15	low-temperature surface insulation	عازِل سطح منخفض الحرارة
16	flight deck (crew compartment)	سَطْح الطيران (حُجَيْرَة الطاقم)
17	captain's seat (commander's seat)	مَقْعَد كابتن الطاقم
18	pilot's seat (co-pilot's seat)	مَقْعَد الطَّيَّار (مَقْعَد مُسَاعِد الطَّيَّار)
19	forward pressure bulk-head	حاجِز إنشائي أمامي ضغطي
20	carbon fibre reinforced nose cone	جزء المُقَدِّمَة المقوَّى بألياف كربونية
21	forward fuel tanks	خَزَّانات الوقود الأماميَّة
22	avionics consoles	كونسولات آلات الطيران
23	automatic flight control panel	لَوْحَة التَّحَكُّم في الطيران الآليّ
24	upward observation windows	نوافِذ ملاحظة علويَّة
25	forward observation windows	نوافِذ ملاحظة أمامية
26	entry hatch to payload bay	كُوَّة دخول فُرْجَة الحِمْل الآجِر
27	air lock	دِسام هوائي
28	ladder to lower deck	سُلَّم يؤدي إلى السطح السفلي
29	payload manipulator arm	ذِراع آليَّة معالجة الحِمْل الآجِر
30	hydraulically steerable nose wheel	عَجَلَة مُقَدِّمَة يتم توجيهها هيدروليّاً
31	hydraulically operated main landing gear	عَجَلَة الهبوط الرئيسيَّة التي يتم تشغيلها هيدروليّاً
32	removable (reusable) carbon fibre reinforced leading edge (of wing)	حافة أماميَّة مُقَوَّاة مصنوعة من الفِبْر قابلة للفصل
33	movable elevon sections	أجْزَاء سطح رافع عاطِف قابلة للفصل
34	heat-resistant elevon structure	هَيْكَل سطح رافع عاطِف مقاوم للحرارة
35	main liquid hydrogen (LH_2) supply	مَصْدَر إمداد الهيدروجين السائل الرئيسي
36	main liquid-fuelled rocket engine	مُحَرِّك صاروخيّ رئيسي يعمل بالوقود السائل
37	nozzle (thrust nozzle)	فُوَّهَة (فُوَّهَة الدفع)
38	coolant feed line	خَطّ تغذية المُبَرِّد
39	engine control system	نظام التحكم في المُحَرِّك
40	heat shield	وقاء الحرارة
41	high-pressure liquid hydrogen (LH_2) pump	مِضَخَّة هيدروجين سائل عالية الضغط
42	high-pressure liquid oxygen (LOX, LO_2) pump	مِضَخَّة أكسجين سائل عالية الضغط
43	thrust vector control system	نظام التحكم في كمية الدفع المُوَجَّهَة
44	electromechanically	مُحَرِّك مُنَاوَرَة مداريَّة

controlled orbital manoeuvring (*Am.* maneuvering) main engine — رئيسي يتم التحكم فيه كهروميكانيكياً
45 nozzle fuel tanks (thrust nozzle fuel tanks) — خَزَّانات الوَقُود بفُوَّهَة الدفع
46 jettisonable liquid hydrogen and liquid oxygen tank (fuel tank) — خَزَّان أكسجين سائل وهيدروجين سائل قابليْن للطَّرْح (خَزَّان وقود)
47 integrally stiffened annular rib (annular frame) — ضِلْع طرفيّ مُقَوًّى شبه كُرَوِيّ
48 hemispherical end rib (end frame) — ضلع طرفيّ شبه كُرَوِيّ
49 aft attachment to Orbiter — المُلْحَق الخلفي للعربة المداريَّة
50 liquid hydrogen (LH_2) line — خَطّ الهيدروجين السائل
51 liquid oxygen (LOX, LO_2) line — خَطّ الأكسجين السائل
52 manhole — فتحة
53 surgebaffle system (slosh baffle system) — نظام حواجز التَّمَوُّر
54 pressure line to liquid hydrogen tank — خَطّ ضغط واصِل لخزان الهيدروجين السائل
55 electrical system bus — اوتوبوس النظام الكهربائي
56 liquid oxygen (LOX, LO_2) line — خَطّ الأكسجين السائل
57 pressure line to liquid oxygen tank — خَطّ ضغط واصِل لخَزَّان الأكسجين السائل
58 recoverable solid-fuel rocket (solid rocket booster) — صاروخ قابل للاسترجاع يعمل بالوَقُود الصلب
59 auxiliary parachute bay — فُرْجَة مِظَلَّة مُسَاعِدة
60 compartment housing the recovery parachutes and the forward separation rocket motors — حُجَيْرَة مِظَلاَت الاسترجاع والمُحَرِّكات الأماميَّة لصاروخ الانفصال
61 cable duct — مَجْرَى الكيبلات
62 aft separation rocket motors — المُحَرِّكات الخلفيَّة لصاروخ الانفصال
63 aft skirt — حاشية/حافة خلفية
64 swivel nozzle (swivelling, *Am.* swiveling, nozzle) — فُوَّهَة دَوَرَانيَّة
65 **Spacelab** (space laboratory, space station) — **مُخْتَبَر فضائيّ**
66 multi-purpose laboratory (orbital workshop) — مُخْتَبَر متعدد الأغراض (وَرْشَة مداريَّة)
67 astronaut — رَجُل فضاء
68 gimbal-mounted telescope — تليسكوب على حامِل ذي محْوَرَيْن
69 measuring instrument platform — مِنَصَّة آلات القياس
70 spaceflight module — موديول فضائيّ
71 crew entry tunnel — نَفَق دخول الطاقم

236 Post Office I — مكْتَب البَريد (1)

1-30 main hall — **الصَّالة الرئيسيَّة**
1 parcels counter — شباك الطرود
2 parcels scales — ميزان الطرود
3 parcel — طَرْد
4 stick-on address label with parcel registration slip — بِطَاقة عَنَاوين لاصِقة مع كَعْب تسجيل الطرد
5 glue pot — قِنِّينَة الصَّمْغ
6 small parcel — طَرْد صغير
7 franking machine (*Am.* postage meter) for parcel registration cards — مَاكِينَة دَمْغ بطاقات تسجيل الطرود
8 telephone box (telephone booth, telephone kiosk, call box) — كُشْك الهاتِف
9 coin-box telephone (pay phone, public telephone) — هاتِف يعمل بالعُمْلَة المعدنيَّة
10 telephone directory rack — رف دليل الهاتِف
11 directory holder — حامِل الدليل
12 telephone directory (telephone book) — دليل الهاتِف
13 post office boxes — صناديق مكتب البريد
14 post office box — صُنْدُوق بريد
15 stamp counter — شباك بَيْع الطوابع
16 counter clerk (counter officer) — مُوَظَّف الشباك
17 company messenger — ساعِي شركة
18 record of posting book — سِجِلّ كتيب الإرسال
19 counter stamp machine — مَاكِينَة الطوابع بالشباك
20 stamp book — مِلَف حفظ الطوابع
21 sheet of stamps — فَرْخ طوابع
22 security drawer — دُرْج أمان
23 change rack — دُرْج الصَّرْف
24 letter scales — ميزان الخِطابات
25 paying-in (*Am.* deposit), post office savings, and pensions counter — شباك تسديد الفواتير ودفاتر توفير البريد والمَعَاشَات
26 accounting machine — مَاكِينَة حاسِبَة
27 franking machine for money orders and paying-in slips (*Am.* deposit slips) — مَاكِينَة دَمْغ أوامِر الدفع وايصالات التسديد
28 change machine (*Am.* changemaker) — مَاكِينَة صِرَافة
29 receipt stamp — خَتَّامة الايصالات
30 hatch — فَتْحَة، كُوَّة
31-44 letter-sorting installation — **قِسْم فَرْز الرسائل**
31 letter feed — إلقام الرسائل
32 stacked letter containers — حاوِيَات رسائل مُتَرَاصَة
33 feed conveyor — سَيْر الإلقام
34 intermediate stacker — جِهَاز ترصيص وَسَطِيّ
35 coding station — مَحَطَّة وَضْع الرموز البريديَّة

36 pre-distributor channel — قناة التوزيع الأوَّليّ
37 process control computer — كمبيوتر تَحكّم
38 distributing machine — مَاكِينَة تَوْزيع
39 video coding station — مَحَطَّة وَضْع الرموز البريديَّة المرئيَّة
40 screen — شاشة
41 address display — عَرْض العنوان
42 address — عنوان
43 post code (postal code, *Am.* zip code) — رَمْز بريدي
44 keyboard — لَوْحَة المفاتيح
45 handstamp — خَتَّامة يدويَّة
46 roller stamp — خَتَّامة أُسْطُوَانية
47 franking machine — مَاكِينَة دَمْغ الرسائل
48 feed mechanism — آليَّة الإلقام
49 delivery mechanism — آلية التوصيل
50-55 postal collection and delivery — **تجميع البريد وتسليمه**
50 postbox (*Am.* mailbox) — صندوق بريد
51 collection bag — حقيبة جَمْع البريد
52 post office van (mail van) — عَرَبَة مكتب البريد
53 postman (*Am.* mail carrier, letter carrier, mailman) — رَجُل البريد
54 delivery pouch (postman's bag, mailbag) — حقيبة توزيع البريد
55 letter-rate item — بند فئة الرسالة
56-60 postmarks — **أخْتام البريد**
56 postmark advertisement — خَتْم بريد إعلاني
57 date stamp postmark — خَتْم التاريخ
58 charge postmark — خَتْم الرسوم البريديَّة
59 special postmark — خَتْم بريد خاص
60 roller postmark — علامة بريد مَوْجِيَّة
61 stamp (postage stamp) — طابِع بريد
62 perforations — ثقوب

237 Post Office II (Telecommunications) — مكْتَب البَريد (2) (الإتِّصَالات السِّلكيَّة واللاسلْكيَّة)

1-41 telephone — **هاتف، تليفون**
1 dial telephone — هاتِف بقُرْص
2 handset (telephone receiver) — سمَّاعَة الهاتِف
3 receiver cord (handset cord) — سِلْك السمَّاعَة
4 telephone cable (telephone cord) — كيبل الهاتِف، سِلْك التليفون
5 telephone casing (telephone cover) — جسم الهاتِف، عُلْبَة التليفون
6 emergency numbers — أرقام الطوارئ
7 line number — رَقَم الخط
8 dial — قُرْص الهاتِف
9 compact telephone (slim line telephone), an added-feature telephone — هاتِف مُنْدَمِج
10 earpiece (receiver) — أذْنِيَّة (المستقبل)
11 keypad with number and function keys (feature keys) — لَوْحَة مفاتيح الأرقام والوظائف
12 last number redial button — زرّ تكرار آخر رقم
13 abbreviated dialling key — زرّ اتصال مختزل
14 speaker key (loudspeaker key) — زرّ مكَبِّر الصوت
15 mouthpiece — صُوَان التَّكَلُّم في الهاتِف
16 line reset button — زرّ إعادة ضبط الخط
17 speaker (loudspeaker) — مُكَبِّر صَوْت (سمَّاعة صَوْت)
18 call indicator — مؤشر الاتصال
19 push-button telephone, an added-feature telephone — هاتِف بأزْرَار انضغاطيَّة
20 display — شاشة
21 lock — قُفْل
22 novelty telephone, an added-feature telephone — هاتِف ديكور كلاسيكي
23 (telephone) cradle — مَحْمَل السمَّاعة
24 dummy crank — ذِرَاع تدوير دُمْيَة
25 detachable keypad — لَوْحَة مفاتيح قابلة للفصل
26 cordless (tele)phone (radiophone, mobile phone) — هاتِف لاسلكي
27 aerial — هوائي
28 battery strength light — ضَوْء إرشادي لقوة البطارية
29 out of signal-range indicator — مُؤشر أن الهاتِف خارج نطاق الخدمة
30 power switch — مِفْتَاح التشغيل/الإيقاف
31 cardphone — هاتِف يعمل بنظام البطاقات
32 split display showing call charges — شاشة منفصلة توضِّح رسوم المكالمة
33 language select button for the display — زرّ اختيار لغة الشاشة
34 follow-on call button — زرّ مواصلة الاتصال
35 phonecard slot — فتْحَة إدخال بطاقة الاتصال
36 phonecard (*here:* telephone credit card) — بطاقة الاتصال بالهاتف (هنا:بطاقة ائتمان للاتصالات الهاتفيَّة)
37 phonecard symbol — رَمْز بطاقة الاتصال بالهاتف
38 cardholder's name — اسم حامِل البطاقة
39 card number — رَقَم البطاقة
40 arrow indicating direction of insertion — سَهْم يشير إلى اتجاه إدخال البطاقة بالهاتف
41 chips — رقَاقَتَان
42-62 ISDN (Integrated Services Digital Network) — **شبكة رقميَّة للخدمات المتكاملة**
42 multifunction telecommunications terminal (ISDN workstation) — طَرَفيَّة اتصالات مُتَعَدِّدة الوظائف
43 screen (monitor) for viewdata, video telephone, and Teletex — شاشة للبيانات المرئيَّة، هاتِف ناقِل للصورة وتِلِكْس
44 central processing and — وَحْدَة المعالجة والذاكرة

memory unit — المركزيَّة
45 fax unit (fax) — وَحْدَة الفاكس
46 input device (keyboard) — لَوْحَة مفاتيح الإدخال
47 telephone receiver (link to the telephone network) — سمَّاعة الهاتِف
48 acoustic coupler (modem) — مُودَم (قارِنَة صَوْتيَّة)
49 telecontrol network (TEMEX network) — شبكة التَّحكُّم عن بعد
50 public telephone network (switched telephone network) — شبكة الهاتِف العمومي
51 telecontrol centres — مراكز التَّحكُّم عن بعد
52 TEMEX main control centre — مركز التَّحكُّم الرئيسي في شبكة التَّحكُّم عن بعد
53 TEMEX transmission equipment — مُعِدَّات إرسال شبكة التَّحكُّم عن بعد
54 telecommunications line (telephone line) — خط اتصالات سلكيَّة ولاسلكيَّة
55 TEMEX network termination — انتهاء شبكة TEMEX
56 slave station — مَحطَّة تابعة
57 telecontrol terminal equipment — معدات طَرَفيَّة التَّحكُّم عن بعد
58 telecontrol terminal equipment (detector, sensor, or control equipment) — مُعدَّات طَرَفيَّة التَّحكُّم عن بعد (مُعدَّات كشف أو استشعار أو تحكم)
59 glass-break detector — مكْشاف الكسر الزجاجيّ
60 temperature controller — آليَّة التَّحكُّم في درجة الحرارة
61 emergency call — آليَّة الاستدعاء في حالة الطواريء
62 meter (electricity meter) — مقْيَاس الكهرباء
63 communications satellite — قمر صناعي للاتصالات السلكية واللاسلكية
64 solar panel (solar paddle, solar array, solar generator) — صَحْفَة شَمْسِيَّة (أرْيَاش بخلايا شَمْسِيَّة)
65 antenna module — موديول الهوائي
66 receiving antenna for control commands — هوائي استقبال أوامر التَّحكُّم
67 parabolic antennas — هوائيَّات مكافئيَّة المقطع
68 communications module — موديول الاتصالات
69 propulsion module — موديول التسيير
70 broadcasting satellite (television satellite) — قَمَر صناعي خاص بالبث التليفزيوني
71 service module — موديول خدمة
72 fuel tanks — خَزَّانَات الوَقُود
73 control jets — مَنَافِث التَّحكُّم
74 earth station — مَحَطَّة أرضيَّة
75 parabolic antenna — هوائي مكافئيّ المقطع
76 main reflector — عاكِس رئيسيّ
77 feed antenna — هوائي تغذية
78 radio beams — حزم أشعَّة لاسلكية
79 satellite broadcasting, satellite television, and cable television — البَثّ عَبْر الأقْمَار الصناعية
80 broadcasting satellite — قَمَر البَثّ
81 television studio — ستوديو التليفزيون
82 television tower — بُرْج البَثّ المَرْئي
83 cablehead station — مَحَطَّة رأس كيبلية
84 terrestrial broadcasting — البَثّ الأرضيّ
85 satellite broadcasting — البَثّ من القمر الصناعي
86 line-of-sight link (microwave link) — واصِلَة خط الرؤية
87 cable network — شبكة الكيبلات
88 cable connections — وَصْلات الكيبلات

238 Broadcasting (Radio and Television) I — الإذَاعَة (الراديو والتليفزيون) (1)

1-6 central recording channel of a radio station — مَحَطَّة تسجيل مركزي بمَحَطَّة الإذاعة
1 monitoring and control panel — لَوْحَة المشاهدة والتَّحكُّم
2 data display terminal (video data terminal, video monitor) for visual display of computer-controlled programmes (*Am.* programs) — طَرَفيَّة عرض البيانات للعرض المرئي للبرامج التي يجري التَّحكُّم فيها بالحاسب الآلي
3 amplifier and mains power unit — مُضَخِّم صوت ووَحْدَة الطاقة الرئيسيَّة
4 magnetic sound recording and playback deck for 1/4" magnetic tape — جهَاز تسجيل الصوت المغناطيسي والاستماع إليه للشرائط المغناطيسية حجم رُبْع بوصة
5 magnetic tape, a 1/4" tape — شريط مغناطيسي، شريط رُبْع بوصة
6 film spool holder — حامِل بَكَرَة الفيلم
7-15 radio switching centre (*Am.* center) **control room — غُرْفَة التَّحكُّم في مركز التحويل الإذاعي**
7 monitoring and control panel — لَوْحَة المشاهدة والتَّحكُّم
8 talkback speaker — مُكبِّر صوت الانترفون
9 local-battery telephone — هاتِف ببطارية محليَّة
10 talkback microphone — ميكروفون الانترفون
11 data display terminal (video data terminal) — طَرَفيَّة عرض البيانات
12 teleprinter — طابعة عن بعد
13 input keyboard for computer data — لَوْحَة إدخال بيانات الكمبيوتر
14 telephone switchboard panel — لَوْحَة بَدَّالة الهاتِف
15 monitoring speaker (control speaker) — مكبِّر صوت للمتابعة والتَّحكُّم
16-26 broadcasting centre (*Am.* center) **— مركز الإذاعة**
16 recording room — غُرْفَة التسجيل
17 production control room (control room) — غُرْفَة مراقبة الإنتاج

18 studio ستوديو
19 sound engineer (sound control engineer) مهندس الصوت
20 sound control desk (sound control console) لَوْحَة التَّحَكُّم في الصوت
21 newsreader (newscaster) قارئ نشرة الأخبار
22 duty presentation officer مُوَظَّف التقديم المناوِب
23 telephone for phoned reports هاتِف لتلقي التقارير الهاتفيَّة
24 record turntable صينية تشغيل الأُسْطُوَانات
25 recording room mixing console (mixing desk, mixer) كونسول مكساج غُرْفَة التَّحكُّم
26 sound technician (sound mixer, sound recordist) فني الصوت

27-53 television post-sync studio **ستوديو البَثّ التليفزيوني المتزامن**
27 sound production control room (sound control room) غُرْفَة التَّحكُّم الخاصة بانتاج الصوت
28 dubbing studio (dubbing theatre, *Am.* theater) ستوديو الدبلجة
29 studio table طاولة الاستوديو
30 visual signal إشارة مرئيَّة
31 electronic stopclock ساعة وَقْف إلكترونية
32 projection screen شاشة العرض
33 monitor مِرْقَاب
34 studio microphone ميكروفون الاستوديو
35 sound effects box صندوق المؤثِّرات الصوتيَّة
36 microphone socket panel لَوْحَة مقابس الميكروفات
37 recording speaker (recording loudspeaker) مكَبِّر صوت خاص بالتسجيل
38 control room window (studio window) نافذة غُرْفَة التَّحكُّم
39 producer's talkback microphone انترفون المُنْتِج
40 local-battery telephone هاتِف ببطارية محليَّة
41 sound control desk (sound control console) كونسول التحكم في الصوت
42 group selector switch مِفْتَاح انتقاء التسجيل الجماعي
43 visual display عرض بصري
44 limiter display (clipper display) شاشة محدد الخرج
45 control modules موديولات التَّحكُّم
46 pre-listening buttons أزْرَار الاستماع المُسْبَق
47 slide control آليَّة تحكم انزلاقية
48 universal equalizer (universal corrector) مُعَادِل عام
49 input selector switches مفاتيح انتقاء الدَّخْل
50 pre-listening speaker مكَبِّر صوت للاستماع المسبق
51 tone generator مُوَلِّد النغمة
52 talkback speaker مكَبِّر صوت الانترفون
53 talkback microphone ميكروفون الانترفون

54-59 pre-mixing room for transferring and mixing 16 mm, 17.5 mm, 35 mm perforated magnetic film **غرفة المكساج المتقدم** لنقل ودبلجة فيلم مغناطيسي مثقب مقاس 16 ملم، 17.5 ملم، 35 ملم
54 sound control desk (sound control console) كونسول التَّحكُّم في الصوت
55 compact magnetic tape recording and playback equipment مُعِدَّات تسجيل وتشغيل الشرائط المغناطيسية المُنْدَمِجَة
56 single playback deck جِهَاز تشغيل مُفْرَد
57 central drive unit وَحْدَة الدفع المركزيَّة
58 single recording and playback deck جِهَاز تسجيل وتشغيل مفرد
59 rewind bench نضد اعادة لف الفيلم

60-65 final picture quality checking room **غرفة فحص جَوْدَة الصورة النهائية**
60 preview monitor شاشة العرض المُسْبَق
61 programme (*Am.* program) monitor شاشة البرامج
62 stopclock ساعَة وَقْف
63 vision mixer (vision-mixing console, vision-mixing desk) كونسول دمج الصُّوَر
64 talkback system (talk-back equipment) نظام الانترفون
65 camera monitor (picture monitor) شاشة الكاميرا

239 Broadcasting (Radio and Television) II — الإذاعَة (الراديو والتليفزيون) (2)

1-15 outside broadcast (OB) vehicle (television OB van; *also:* sound OB van, radio OB van) **عَرَبَة التسجيلات الخارجيَّة** (عربة التليفزيون؛ عربة الإذاعة)

1-4 rear equipment section of the OB vehicle **مُعدَّات الجزء الخلفي في عربة التسجيلات الخارجيَّة**
2 camera cable كيبل الكاميرا
3 cable connection panel لَوْحَة توصيل الكيبلات
4 television (TV) reception aerial (receiving aerial) for Channel I هوائي استقبال بَثْمَرْئيَّات للقناة الأولى
5 television (TV) reception aerial (receiving aerial) for Channel II هوائي استقبال بَثْمَرْئيَّات للقناة الثانية
6 interior equipment (on-board equipment) of the OB vehicle المُعدَّات الداخلية لعَربة التسجيلات الخارجيَّة
7 sound production control room (sound control room) غُرْفَة ضبط الصوت
8 sound control desk (sound control console) كونسول التَّحكُّم في الصوت

9 monitoring loudspeaker — سمَّاعة صوت للمتابعة
10 vision control room (video control room) — غُرْفَة ضبط الإشارات الحامِلة للصُّوَر (الفيديو)
11 video controller (vision controller) — مُرَاقِب وَحْدَة الفيديو
12 camera monitor (picture monitor) — شاشة متابعة الكاميرا
13 on-board telephone (intercommunication telephone) — هاتِف العربة
14 microphone cables — كيبلات الميكروفونات
15 air-conditioning plant — وَحْدَة مكيِّف الهواء

240 Broadcasting III (Television Engineering) — الإذاعة (الراديو والتليفزيون) (3)

1 colour (*Am.* color) television (TV) receiver (colour television set) of modular design — مُسْتَقْبِل بَثْمَرْئيَّات (تليفزيون) ألوان مُصَمَّم بنظام الموديولات
2 television cabinet — صُنْدُوق التليفزيون
3 television tube (picture tube) — أنْبُوب الصورة
4 IF (intermediate frequency) amplifier module — موديول مُضَخِّم الصوت ذو تردد متوسط
5 colour (*Am.* color) decoder module — موديول مُسْتَخْلِص الألوان
6 VHF and UHF tuner — مُوالِف ترددات عالية جداً وترددات منخفضة جداً
7 horizontal synchronizing module — موديول مُزَامَنَة أفقي
8 vertical deflection module — موديول الانحراف الرَّأسي
9 horizontal linearity control module — موديول ضبط الاستقامة الأفقي
10 horizontal deflection module — موديول الانحراف الأفقي
11 control module — موديول تحكم
12 convergence module — موديول الالتمام
13 colour (*Am.* color) output stage module — موديول مَخْرَج الألوان
14 sound module — موديول الصوت
15 colour (*Am.* color) picture tube — أنْبُوب الصورة الملوَّنة
16 electron beams — حزَم الكَهَارِب (الالكترونات)
17 shadow mask with elongated holes — ساتِر مُظِلّ به ثقوب مُطَوَّلَة
18 strip of fluorescent (luminescent, phosphorescent) material — مورية فلّوَريَّة
19 coating (film) of fluorescent material — تَكْسِيَة بمادة فلّوَريَّة
20 inner magnetic screen (screening) — مورية مغنطيسية داخليَّة
21 vacuum — فَرَاغ
22 temperature-compensated shadow mask mount — مَحْمَل ساتِر مُظِلّ مُعادِل التَّغَيُّر في درجة الحرارة
23 centring (*Am.* centering) ring for the deflection system — حلَقَة المركزة لنظام الانحراف
24 electron gun assembly — مجموعة مِدْفَعَة الكَهَارِب
25 rapid heat-up cathode — كاثود سريع التحارُر
26 television (TV) camera — كاميرا تصوير تليفزيوني (مُصَوِّرَة البَثْمَرْئيَّات)
27 camera head — رَأس الكاميرا
28 camera monitor — شاشة الكاميرا
29 control arm (control lever) — ذِراع تحكم
30 focusing adjustment — آليَّة ضبط التركيز البؤري
31 control panel — لَوْحَة تحكم
32 contrast control — مضْبَط التبايُن
33 brightness control — مضْبَط السطوع
34 zoom lens — عدسة زوم
35 beam-splitting prism (beam splitter) — منشور تفريق الحزمة الاشعاعيَّة
36 pick-up unit (colour, *Am.* color, pick-up tube) — وَحْدَة التقاط (أنْبُوب لاقِط)

241 Music Systems (Audio Systems) I — أنظمَة المُوسيقَى (الأنْظِمَة الصَّوْتيَّة) (1)

1-17 stereo system (hi-fi system), a midi system — **نظام الصَّوْت المُجَسَّم** (نظام الهاي فاي)
1 hi-fi stack — جِهَاز الهاي فاي
2 rack lid (rack dust cover, [housing] lid) — غِطاء واقٍ من الأتربة
3 rack (housing) with glass door — مَبِيت له باب زُجاجيّ
4 record player (record deck, analogue [*Am.* analog] record player) — مُشَغِّل الأسْطُوانات
5 tuner (receiver, radio tuner) — مُنَغِّم، مُوَالِف (مُسْتَقْبِل ، مُوَالِف راديو)
6 amplifier (power amplifier) — مُضَخِّم الصوت
7 double cassette deck (double cassette recorder) — مُسَجِّل شرائط كاسيت مزدوج
8 CD player (compact disc player) — مُشَغِّل الأقراص المُنْدَمِجَة
9 cassette rack — رَفّ تخزين الأشْرِطَة المُعَلَّبَة (الكاسيتات)
10 record and compact disc rack — حُجَيْرَة حفظ الأقراص المُنْدَمِجَة
11 castor — عَجَلَة صغيرة
12 speaker (loudspeaker), a three-way bass reflex speaker — مكبِّر الصوت
13 tweeter, a dome tweeter or piezo tweeter — مُسَقْسِق، مُسَقْسِق قُبِّيّ أو بيزو
14 mid-range speaker (squawker) — سمَّاعة متوسطة المدى
15 bass speaker (woofer) — سمَّاعة الجَهِير

16	port	فتحة
17	infrared remote control [unit] (IR remote control [unit])	وَحْدَة تحكم عن بعد تعمل بالأشِعَّة تحت الحمراء
18	record player (record deck, analogue [*Am.* analog] record player)	مُشَغِّل الأُسْطُوَانات
19	turntable with direct drive or belt drive	قُرْص الحاكي الدَّوَّار يعمل بإدارة مباشرة أو إدارة بسير
20	strobe light (strobe speed control)	ضَوْء ومضي إلكتروني
21	pitch control	ضَبْط الطبقة
22	rpm display	قراءة عدد اللفات/دقيقة
23	stop button	زِرّ إيقاف
24	auto-return button	زِرّ إعادة الأُسْطُوانة إلى البَداية تلقائياً
25	rpm selector (speed selector)	زِرّ ضبط سرعة دَوَران الأُسْطُوانة
26	cue button (down)	زِرّ إشارة البدء (لأسفل)
27	cue button (up)	زِرّ إشارة البدء (لأعلى)
28	stylus (needle)	إبْرَة الحاكي (إبرة)
29	pick-up	لاقط
30	size selector (record size selector)	مِضْبَط حجم الأُسْطُوانة
31	tone arm (pick-up arm)	ذِراع اللاقط
32	tone arm support (pick-up arm support)	مِسْنَد ذراع اللاقط
33	stylus pressure control	مِضْبَط ضغط إبْرَة الحاكي
34	anti-skate control	مِضْبَط منع الانزلاق
35	tone arm counterweight (pick-up arm counter-weight)	الثِّقْل المُوَازِن لذراع اللاقِط
36	lid (dust cover)	غطاء (وِقاء التراب)
37	tuner (receiver, radio tuner)	مُنَغِّم، مُوَالِف (مُسْتَقْبِل، مُوَالِف راديو)
38	power switch	مِفْتَاح تشغيل/قفل الجهاز
39	tuning button (tuning control)	زِر الضبط الدقيق/الموالفة
40	manual and automatic tuning selection button with muting	زِرّ انتقاء الموالفة يدوياً أو أوتوماتياً مع آليَّة إخْفات
41	stereo/mono selection button	زِرّ إنتقاء الصوت المُجَسَّم/المُفْرَد
42	strength-of-signal display button	زِرّ قراءة قوة الإشارة
43	memory button	زِرّ الذاكرة
44	station selection buttons	أَزْرَار انتقاء المحطات
45	frequency selection buttons ([wave] band selection buttons)	أَزْرَار انتقاء نطاقات التردد
46	station select display	شاشة عرض انتقاء المحطات
47	fluorescent digital display indicating wave band, frequency, and strength of signal	قراءة فلورسنت رقميَّة توضِّح نطاق المَوْجَة والتردد وقوة الإشارة
48	LED indicator for stereo and mono mode and automatic tuning	مؤشر بصمام ثنائي مضئ للتشغيل المُجَسَّم والمُفْرَد والموالفة الاوتوماتيَّة
49	amplifier (power amplifier)	مُضَخِّم صوت كهربائي
50	function select buttons for the turntable, tuner, cassette deck (tape deck), CD player, and monitor (tape monitor)	أَزْرَار انتقاء الوظيفة الخاصة بالقرص الدَّوَّار والمُوَالِف ومُشَغِّل شرائط الكاسيت ومُشَغِّل الأقراص المُدْمَجَة
51	filter buttons (high and low filter buttons)	أَزْرَار الفلاتر
52	bass control	مِضْبَط الجهير
53	treble control	مِضْبَط الثلاثي
54	balance control	مِضْبَط التَّوَازُن
55	loudness button	مِضْبَط الجَهَارَة
56	volume control	مِضْبَط حجم الصوت
57	headphone socket	مَقْبِس سمَّاعات الرَّأْس
58	speaker select buttons	أَزْرَار انتقاء سمَّاعة الصوت
59	LED display, a multi-function display	شاشة قراءة بدايود مضئ متعددة الوظائف
60	function display	قراءة وظيفة التشغيل
61	receiver, a combined tuner-amp[lifier]	مستقبل (موالف ومضخم صوت معا)
62	display select button	زِرّ انتقاء قراءة الشاشة
63	liquid crystal display (LCD), a multifunction display	شاشة قراءة بلُورِيَّة سائلة
64	[graphic] equalizer, a 2 × 7 band [graphic] equalizer	مُعَادِل [جرافيتي]
65	equalizer slide controls	مَضَابِط المُعَادِل الإنزلاقيَّة
66	LED-display spectrum analyser	مُحَلِّل طيف الشاشة متعدد الأغراض بدايود مضئ
67	headphones (stereo headphones)	سمَّاعات الرَّأْس (سمَّاعات للصوت المُجَسَّم)
68	ear pads (ear cushions)	وِسَادة الأُذُن
69, 70	microphones	ميكروفونات
69	directional microphone (stereo directional microphone)	ميكروفون اتجاهيّ
70	electret condenser microphone with omni-directional pick-up characteristic	ميكروفون بمكثِّف الكتريت له خاصيَّة التقاط الصَّوْت من جميع الاتجاهات

242 Music Systems (Audio Systems) II — أنظمة المُوسيقَى (الأنْظمة الصَّوْتيَّة) (2)

1	cassette deck (cassette recorder)	مُسَجِّل الكاسيت
2	power switch	مِفْتَاح التشغيل
3	[stop and] eject button	مِفْتَاح الإيقاف وإخراج الشريط
4	cassette holder (cassette drive, cassette transport)	حامِل الشريط المُعَلَّب (إدارة الكاسيت)
5	dust cover	غطاء واقٍ من التراب
6	counter (tape counter)	عَدَّاد الشريط
7-12	**transport buttons**	**أَزْرَار تدوير الشريط**
7	stop button	زِرّ الإيقاف
8	rewind button	زِرّ إعادة لف الشريط

9 play buttons for both directions (bi-directional play buttons)	أزْرار تشغيل الشريط لكلا الاتجاهَيْن
10 fast forward button	زرّ تقديم الشريط
11 record button	زرّ التسجيل
12 pause button	زرّ توقيف الشريط مؤقتاً
13 counter reset button	زرّ إعادة ضبط العَدَّاد
14 noise reduction buttons (Dolby select buttons)	أزْرار تقليل الضوضاء (أزْرار انتقاء نظام الدولبي)
15 auto-reverse buttons	أزْرار قلب الشريط تلقائيا
16 recording level control	مِضْبَط مستوى التسجيل
17 microphone sockets	مَقْبِسا الميكروفون
18 headphone socket	مَقْبِس سمَّاعات الرَّأس
19 level indicator display (VU meter), an LED display	شاشة دليليَّة لمستوى الصوت
20 tape type indicator (tape-bias indicator), an LED display	مؤشر نوع الشريط على الشاشة الدليليَّة
21 double cassette deck (double cassette recorder)	مُسَجِّل كاسيت مزدوج
22 play button	زرّ تشغيل الشريط
23 [stop and] eject button	زرّ الإيقاف وإخراج الشريط
24 high-speed dubbing button	زرّ دبلجة عالي السرعة
25 function select button	زرّ انتقاء وظيفة التشغيل
26 recording indicator light	ضَوْء مؤشر للتسجيل
27 on-off light (power indicator light)	لَمْبَة تشغيل/قفل الجهاز
28 CD player (compact disc player, digital compact disc player)	جِهَاز تشغيل الأقراص المُنْدَمِجَة
29 CD drawer	دُرْج القرص المُنْدَمِج
30 open/close button for the CD drawer	زر فتح/غلق دُرْج القرص المُنْدَمِج
31 search button and index search button	زرّ البحث وزرّ البحث الإرشادي
32 skip buttons (skip-track buttons)	زرّ تفويت (زِرّ قفز المسالك)
33 headphone volume control	مِضْبَط حجم صوت سماعات الرَّأس
34 function select buttons	أزْرار انتقاء وظيفة التشغيل
35 programming, track and disc repeat, and pause indicators	مؤشرات البرمجة ومسالك الصوت وتكرار القرص وتوقيف القرص مؤقتاً
36 LED display	شاشة عرض مستوى تسجيل الصوت
37 remaining time and track-index indicators	مؤشرات الوقت المتبقي ودليل المَسْلَك
38 portable radio recorder with integral CD player	جِهَاز تسجيل وراديو مَحْمُول مزود بمُشَغِّل الأقراص المُنْدَمِجَة
39 handle	مِقْبَض
40 [radio] receiver (receiver and amplifier)	مُسْتَقْبِل [الراديو] (مُسْتَقْبِل ومُضَخِّم للصوت)
41 CD player	مُشَغِّل الأقراص المُنْدَمِجَة
42 quartz clock with digital display and timer	ساعة كوارتز بشاشة رقميَّة وجهاز توقيت
43 double cassette recorder	مُسَجِّل كاسيت مزدوج
44 loudspeaker	سمَّاعة صوت
45-49 audio-cassette (cassette)	**شريط صوتي مُعلَّب** (كاسيت)
45-47 types of tape	**أنواع الشريط**
45 ferric cassette (iron oxide cassette, normal cassette)	كاسيت حديديك (كاسيت حديدي، كاسيت عادي)
46 chrome dioxide cassette (chrome cassette)	كاسيت كْرُوم
47 metal cassette (metal oxide cassette)	كاسيت معدني
48 tape type indication (indicating hole)	مُؤَشِّر نوع الشريط
49 record-protected cassettes	كاسيتات محميَّة من التسجيل عليها
50 world receiver for receiving ultra-short wave (USW), medium wave (MW), long wave (LW), and short wave (SW)	مُسْتَقْبِل عالمي لاستقبال المَوْجَات شديدة القِصَر والمَوْجَات المتوسطة والطويلة والقصيرة
51 aerial (rod aerial), a telescopic aerial	هوائي، ايريال تليسكوبيّ
52 function buttons	أزْرَار وظائف التشغيل
53 station select buttons	أزْرَار انتقاء القنوات
54 manual tuning knob	زرّ الموالفة يدوياً
55 liquid crystal display (LCD) showing waveband, frequency, and memory number	شَاشة بلورية سائلة توضح نطاق المَوْجَة والتردد ورقم الذاكرة
56 (sliding) volume control	مِفْتَاح انزلاقي لضبط الصوت
57 cassette player (Walkman® with radio)	جِهَاز تشغيل شرائط الكاسيت
58 headphones	سمَّاعات الرَّأس
59 equalizer, a 3-band equalizer	مُعَادِل، مُعَادِل 3 نطاقات
60 portable CD player (Discman®)	مُشَغِّل أقراص مُنْدَمِجَة محمول
61 compact disc (CD)	شريط مُنْدَمِج
62 lid	غِطاء
63 casing with transport, amplifier, display, and function buttons	غِلاف وبه أزْرَار التشغيل ومُضَخِّم الصوت والشاشة
64 compact hi-fi system (compact stereo system)	نظام هاي فاي (عالي الأمانة/دقيق الأداء) مُنْدَمِج (نظام صوت مُجَسَّم مُنْدَمِج)
65 amplifier section	جُزْء مُضَخِّم الصوت
66 DAT recorder (digital cassette recorder) (DAT = Digital Audio Tape)	مُسَجِّل شرائط كاسيت صوتية رقمي

67	infrared sensor (IR sensor) for the remote control	جِهَاز إحساس يعمل بالأشعة تحت الحمراء للتشغيل عن بعد
68	input selection buttons for mono, analogue (*Am.* analog), and digital signals	أزْرَار انتقاء الدَّخْل للإشارات المفردة والنظيرية والرقمية
69	index and program selection buttons	أزْرَار دليلية وأزْرَار انتقاء البرامج
70	index number display	شاشة عرض الرقم الدليلي
71	auto-scan button	زِرّ المَسْح الصوتي
72	end-record search button	زِرّ البحث عن نهاية التسجيل

243 Video Equipment — مُعدَّات الفيديو

1	camcorder (camera recorder), form: two-component system (separate camera and recorder)	كامِيرا تسجيل صوت وصورة، الشكل: نظام ثنائي المكوِّنات (كاميرا ومسجل منفصلان)
2	pocket camcorder, a video-8 camcorder	كاميرا فيديو 8 ملم للجيب
3	lens, a × 6 zoom lens (11-66 mm)	عَدَسَة زوم (11– 66ملم)
4	viewfinder (ocular)	مُحَدِّد الرؤية (عَيْنِيَّة)
5	CCD image converter (image sensor) and high-speed shutter, a half-inch chip with shutter functions	مُحَوِّل صورة بنبيطة شحنية القرن مع مِغْلاق عالي السرعة
6	video cassette	عُلْبَة شريط الفيديو
7	videotape	شريط الفيديو
8	head drum	أسْطُوَانة رَأس الفيديو
9	autofocus motor	موتور تلقائي البؤريَّة
10	built-in microphone (integral microphone)	ميكروفون داخلي
11	VHS head drum (VHS: Video Home System)	أسْطُوَانة رَأس الفيديو (نظام توجيه الإشارات الحامِلة للصُّوَر)
12	erase head	رَأس مسح الإشارات الحامِلة للصُّوَر
13	guide pin	مِسْمَار دليلي
14	tape guide	دليل الشريط
15	capstan	رَحَوِيَّة
16	audio sync head	رَأس التزامن الصوتي
17	pinch roller	أسْطُوَانة تضييق
18	video head	رَأس الفيديو
19	grooves in the wall of the head drum to promote air cushion formation	حزوز في رَأس الفيديو لتعزيز تَكَوُّن الوسادة الهوائية
20	VHS track format	تجهيز مَسْلَك الإشارات الحامِلة للصُّوَر
21	direction of tape movement	اتجاه حركة الشريط
22	direction of recording	اتجاه التسجيل
23	video track, a slant track (only a few tracks shown)	مَسْلَك الإشارات الحامِلة للصُّوَر
24	sound track (audio track)	مَسْلَك الصوت
25	sync track	مَسْلَك التزامن
26	sync head	رَأس التزامن
27	sound head (audio head)	رَأس الصوت
28	video head	رَأس الفيديو
29	video recorder	جِهَاز تسجيل الفيديو
30	infrared remote control	تحكم عن بعد بالأشِعَّة تحت الحمراء
31	program scale (program dial), a multi-display	مِقْيَاس البرامج
32	cassette compartment	حُجَيْرَة عُلْبَة شريط الفيديو
33	jog shuttle knob for forward or reverse movement of the [video] picture	مِقْبَض يعمل بالدفع الخفيف لتحريك صورة [الفيديو] للأمام أو بالعكس
34	multidisc player	جِهَاز عرض متعدد الأقراص
35	infrared remote control	جِهَاز تَحَكُّم عن بعد بالأشِعَّة تحت الحمراء
36	disc drawer	دُرْج الأقراص
37-41	**disc formats**	**أشْكَال تجهيز القرص**
37	single compact disc (single CD)	قُرْص مُنْدَمِج مُفْرَد
38	audio CD	قُرْص مُنْدَمِج صوتي
39	video CD	قُرْص مُنْدَمِج صوت وصورة
40	small laser disc (20 cm)	قُرْص ليزر صغير (20 سم)
41	large laser disc (30 cm)	قُرْص ليزر كبير (30 سم)
42	laser scanning system	نظام مَسْح بالليزر
43	[disc] spindle	عَمُود دوران [القرص]
44	laser-head tracing spindle	عَمُود تتبع رَأس الليزر
45	laser head (laser unit)	رَأس الليزر (وَحْدَة الليزر)

244 Personal Computer (PC) — الحَاسِب الآليّ الشَّخْصيّ

1	personal computer (PC; *sim.:* laptop)	الحاسب الآلي الشخصيّ
2	power switch	مفتاح التيَّار
3	power supply (power pack)	إمداد الطاقة
4	housing	مَبيت، صندوق
5	fixed-disk access light	لَمْبَة الوصول إلى القُرْص الثابت
6	main memory	الذَّاكِرَة الرئيسيَّة
7	coprocessor socket	مَقْبَس معالج مترافق
8	central processing unit (CPU), a micro-processor	وَحْدَة المعالجة المركزيَّة
9	cache memory (cache controller)	ذاكِرَة مَخْفِيَّة
10	expansion memory slot	حَيِّز تَمَدُّد الذَّاكِرَة
11	graphics card slot	حَيِّز بطاقة الأشكال البيانيَّة
12	combined fixed and floppy disk controller	مُرَاقِب قُرْص ثابت ومَرِن مُدْمَج
13	serial and parallel	بطاقة اتصال مُتَتابع–متوازٍ

communication card	
14 PC tower interior view	منظر داخلي لحافظة الحاسب الشخصي العموديّة
15-67 peripherals	**أجْهِزَة محيطيَّة**
15-32 built-in devices	**الأجْهِزَة الداخليَّة/المَبيتة**
15 keyboard	لَوْحَة المفاتيح
16 function keys	مفاتيح الوظائف
17 letter keys and number keys (numeric keys)	مفاتيح الحروف والأرقام
18 enter key (return key)	مفتاح الإدخال
19 cursor keys	مفاتيح الدَّالَّة/المُشيرَة
20 number [key] pad (numeric [key] pad)	منَصَّة أرقام
21 mouse	فأرَة
22 mouse buttons	أزرار الفأرَة
23 trackerball (trackball)	كُرَة المَسار
24 handrest	مِسْنَد اليَد
25 roller ball	كُرَة دَوَّارَة
26 digitizing tablet (digitizer; *also:* graphics tablet)	مُحَوِّل رَقمي
27 graphics area	منطقة االرسوم البيانيَّة
28 cross hairs	شعرات متقاطعة
29 receiving grids	وَحْدَات استقبال شبكيَّة
30 scanner	ماسِح، سكانر
31 control panel with function keys	لَوْحَة تحكم بها مفاتيح العمليات
32 scanning surface	سطح المَسْح
33-59 mass storage devices (magnetic stores, magnetic memories)	**أجْهِزَة تخزين ذات سعة كبيرَة** (ذاكِرات مغناطيسيَّة)
33-44 disk drives (drives, floppy disk drives)	**مُشَغِّلات الأقْراص**
33 minifloppy disk drives (5 1/4 inch [floppy] disk drive)	مُشَغِّلات القرص المَرِن المصغَّر (مشغل قرص ٥,٢٥ بوصة)
34 latch	سُقَّاطَة
35 microfloppy disk drive (3 1/2 inch [floppy] disk drive)	مُشَغِّل القرص المَرِن الصغير (مشغل قرص ٣,٥ بوصة)
36-44 diskettes (disks, floppy disks, floppies)	**الأقراص المَرِنَة الصغيرة**
36 minifloppy (minifloppy disk, 5 1/4 inch disk, flexible disk)	قُرْص مَرِن مُصغَّر (قرص ٥,٢٥ بوصة)
37 label	بطاقة العنوان
38 write-protect notch	فَرزة حماية الكتابة
39 hole for engaging the drive hub	ثُقْب لتعشيق صُرَّة بكَرة الشريط المغناطيسي
40 registration hole	ثُقْب التَّأطير
41 disk cover (envelope)	ظرف القُرْص
42 access slot for the read-write head	حيِّز الوصول إلى رأس القراءة أو الكتابة
43 microfloppy (3 1/2 inch [floppy] disk)	قُرْص مَرِن صغير (قرص ٣,٥ بوصة)
44 sliding shutter	مِغْلاق انزلاقي
45 fixed-disk drive (fixed disk, hard disk)	مُشَغِّل القُرْص الثابت (القرص الصلب)

46 base plate	لَوْح القاعدة
47 access arm (actuator)	ذراع الوصول (جِهَاز التشغيل)
48 read-write head	رأس القراءة أو الكتابة
49 drive motor for the aluminium (*Am.* aluminum) platters, a spindle drive motor	مُحَرِّك إدارة الأسطوانات الألومنيوم
50 magnetic-coated aluminium (*Am.* aluminum) platters	أسطوانات ألومنيوم مُمَغْنَطَة
51 read-write head drive motor, a linear motor or stepping motor (stepper motor)	مُحَرِّك إدارة رأس القراءة أو الكتابة
52 data, address, and control bus	ناقل البيانات والعناوين وأوامر التحكم
53 magnetic tape unit (magnetic tape drive, streamer)	وَحْدَة الشريط المُمَغْنَط
54 magnetic tape	شريط مُمَغْنَط
55 magnetic tape reel	بكَرَة الشريط المُمَغْنَط
56 magnetic tape cassette (magnetic tape cartridge)	كاسيت الشريط المُمَغْنَط
57 drive post	عمود إدارة
58 drive band	شريط إدارة
59 drive motor	مُحَرِّك إدارة
60-65 output devices	**أجْهِزَة الإخراج**
60 screen (monitor, display), a high-resolution colour (*Am.* color) monitor	شاشة، شاشة مُلَوَّنَة عالية الوضوح
61 printer, a dot-matrix printer (here: laser printer; also: inkjet printer, needle printer)	طابِعَة، طابعة نُقَطيَّة (هنا: طابِعة بالليزر؛ أيضاً: طابعة بحبر نفَّاث وطابعة إبريَّة)
62 control panel with function keys and display	لَوْحَة تحكم مزودة بمفاتيح الوظائف وشاشة عرض المعلومات
63 paper tray (paper cassette)	كاسيت الوَرَق
64 paper feed path	مسار إلقام الوَرَق
65 paper output tray	صينية خروج الوَرَق
66, 67 devices for long-distance data transmission	أجْهِزَة نقل البيانات عن بُعْد
66 acoustic coupler	قارِن صَوْتي
67 modem	مُودِم

245 Office I — المكْتَب (1)

1-33 receptionist's office (secretary's office)	**مَكْتَب موظف الاستقبال** (مَكْتَب السكرتير)
1 fax machine	جِهَاز الفاكسميلي
2 transmitted copy or received copy	رسالة مُرْسَلَة أو مُسْتَقْبَلَة
3 wall calendar	نتيجة/روزْنَامة حائط
4 filing cabinet	خِزَانَة الملفات
5 tambour door (roll-up	باب دُفِّيّ

door)

6 file (document file) — مَلَف (حافظة مستندات)

7 transfer-type addressing machine — مَاكِينَة طباعة استنسل

8 vertical stencil magazine — مَخْزَن استنسل عمودي

9 stencil ejection — خروج الاستنسل

10 stencil storage drawer — درج تخزين الاستنسل

11 paper feed — إلقام الوَرَق

12 stock of notepaper — رَصَّة وَرَق الكتابة

13 switchboard (internal telephone exchange) — بدالة، سنترال داخلي

14 push-button keyboard for internal connections — لَوْحَة مفاتيح انضغاطيَّة للتوصيلات الداخليَّة

15 handset — سمَّاعة يدويَّة

16 dial — قُرْص الهاتف

17 internal telephone list — قائمة أرقام الهاتِف الداخلية

18 master clock (main clock) — ساعة حائط (الساعة الرئيسيَّة)

19 folder containing documents, correspondence, etc. for signing (to be signed) — حافِظة أوراق وبها مستندات ومراسلات الخ. للتوقيع

20 intercom (office intercom) — جِهَاز اتصال داخلي (انتركوم مكتبي)

21 pen — قلم حبر

22 pen and pencil tray — مِقْلَمَة

23 card index — فهرس البطاقات

24 stack (set) of forms — رَصَّة استمارات (نماذج)

25 typing desk — مكتب الطباعة على الآلة الكاتبة

26 electronic memory typewriter — آلة كاتبة إلكترونية بذاكرة

27 keyboard — لَوْحَة المفاتيح

28 function keys — مفاتيح العمليات

29 shorthand pad (*Am.* steno pad) — اضْمَامَة وَرَق الاختزال

30 letter tray — صينية الخطابات

31 office calculator — آلة حاسِبة بشريط / مكتبية

32 printer — طابعة

33 business letter — خطاب تجاري

246 Office II — المكْتَب (2)

1-36 executive's office — **مكتب المسؤول التنفيذي**

1 swivel chair — كُرْسيّ دَوَّار

2 desk — مكْتَب

3 desk top — سطح المكْتَب

4 desk drawer — دُرْج المكْتَب

5 cupboard (storage area) with door — صوان له باب، الدرج الكبير

6 desk mat (blotter) — نَشَّافة المكْتَب

7 business letter — خطاب تجاري

8 appointments diary — يَوْميَّة تسجيل المواعيد

9 desk set — طاقم المكْتَب

10 intercom (office intercom) — جِهَاز اتصال داخلي (انتركوم مكتبيّ)

11 desk lamp — مِصْبَاح المكْتَب

12 pocket calculator (electronic calculator) — آلة حاسبة للجيب

13 telephone, an executive-secretary system — تليفون، هاتف

14 dial; *also:* push-button keyboard — قُرْص؛ أيْضاً: لَوْحَة أزْرَار انضغاطيَّة

15 call buttons — أزْرَار الاتصال

16 receiver (telephone receiver) — سمَّاعة (سمَّاعة الهاتف)

17 dictating machine — المِمْلاة، الدكتافون

18 position indicator — مُبيِّن المَوْقع

19 control buttons (operating keys) — مفاتيح التشغيل

20 cabinet — خِزَانَة

21 visitor's chair — كُرْسيّ الزائر

22 safe — خَزِينَة

23 bolts — آليَّة قفل الخزينة (ترابيس)

24 armour-plated (*Am.* armor-plated) lock area — منطقة قُفْل مُدَرَّعَة

25 confidential documents — مستندات سِرِّيَّة

26 patent — براءة اختراع

27 petty cash — نَقْد النثريَّات

28 picture — صورة

29 bar (drinks cabinet) — بار (صُوَان المشروبات)

30 bar set — طاقم أكواب البار

31-36 conference grouping — **طاقم حجرة الاجتماعات**

31 conference table — طاولة الاجتماعات

32 pocket-sized dictating machine, a micro-cassette recorder — مِمْلاة صغيرة للجيب، جِهَاز تسجيل صغير

33 ashtray — مِنْفَضَة السجائر

34 corner table — طاولة الزاوية

35 table lamp — مصباح الطاولة (أباجورة)

36 two-seater sofa [part of the conference grouping] — كَنَبَة ذات مِقْعَدَيْن [جزء من طاقم حجرة الاجتماعات]

247 Office III — المكْتَب (3)

1-44 office equipment (office supplies, office materials) — **المستلزمات المكتبيَّة**

1, 2 paper clips — مَشَابك وَرَق

3 punch — خَرَّامَة الوَرَق

4 stapler (stapling machine) — دبَّاسَة

5 anvil — سِنْدَان

6 spring-loaded magazine — مَخْزَن محمول على نابض

7 type-cleaning brush — فرشاة تنظيف حروف الآلة الكاتبة

8 type cleaner (type-cleaning kit) — طاقم تنظيف أحرف الآلة الكاتبة

9 fluid container (fluid reservoir) — وِعاء السائل

10 cleaning brush — فُرْشَاة تنظيف

11 felt tip pen — قلم حبر ذو سن لبادي

12 correcting paper [for typing errors] — وَرَق تصحيح [الأخطاء الطباعيَّة]

13 correcting fluid [for typing errors] — سائل تصحيح [الأخطاء الطباعية]

14 electronic pocket calculator — آلة حاسبة الكترونيَّة للجيب
15 eight-digit fluorescent display — شاشة عرض مضيئة سعة ثمانية أرقام
16 on/off switch — مِفْتاح التشغيل/الإيقاف
17 function keys — مفاتيح العمليات
18 number keys — مفاتيح الأرقام
19 decimal key — مِفْتاح العلامة العشرية
20 'equals' key — مِفْتاح علامة =
21 instruction keys (command keys) — مفاتيح التعليمات/الأوامر
22 memory keys — مفاتيح الذاكرة
23 percent key (percentage key) — مِفْتاح النسبة المئويَّة
24 π-key (pi-key) for mensuration of circles — مفاتيح حساب مساحة وأحجام الدوائر
25 pencil sharpener — مبراة الأقلام الرصاص
26 typewriter rubber — مِمْحاة الآلة الكاتبة
27 adhesive tape dispenser — أداة سحب الشريط اللاصق
28 adhesive tape holder (roller-type adhesive tape dispenser) — حامِل الشريط اللاصق
29 roll of adhesive tape — بكَرَة شريط لاصق
30 tear-off edge — حافة قطع الشريط اللاصق
31 moistener — وعاء إسفنجة الترطيب
32 desk diary — يَوْميَّة مكتب
33 date sheet (calendar sheet) — وَرَقة التاريخ، وَرَقة تقويم
34 memo sheet — وَرَقة كتابة المُذَكِّرات
35 ruler — مسطرة
36 centimetre and millimetre (*Am.* centimeter and millimeter) graduations — تدريج السنتيمتر والمِلِّيمتر
37 file (document file) — حافظَة مستندات
38 spine label (spine tag) — بطاقة كعب الحافظَة
39 finger hole — فتحة إصبع
40 arch board file — حافظَة ذات لَوْح قَوْسيّ
41 arch unit — وَحْدَة قَوْسيَّة
42 release lever (locking lever, release/lock lever) — ذراع اعتاق / قفل المشبك القَوْسيّ
43 compressor — لَوْح ضاغط
44 bank statement (statement of account) — كشف حساب من البَنْك

248 Office IV — المكْتَب (4)

1-48 open plan office — **مكْتَب مفتوح المساحات**

1 partition wall (partition screen) — جدار فاصل، حاجز
2 filing drawer with suspension file system — دُرْج حفظ الملفات مزود بنظام لتعليق الملفات
3 suspension file — مِلَف علاّقي
4 file tab — لِسان الملف
5 file (document file) — حافظة مستندات
6 filing clerk — كاتبة الملفات
7 clerical assistant — مُساعدة كاتبة الملفات
8 note for the files — مُذَكِّرَة يتم وضعها بالملف
9 telephone — تليفون، هاتف
10 filing shelves — رَفّ حفظ الملفات
11 clerical assistant's desk — مكْتَب مُساعدة الكاتبة
12 office cupboard — صُوَان مكتبي
13 plant stand (planter) — حامِل النباتات، حوض نباتات
14 indoor plants (house-plants) — نباتات ظِلّ (نباتات منزليَّة)
15 programmer — مُبَرْمِج الكمبيوتر
16 data display terminal (visual display unit) — طَرَفيَّة عرض البيانات (وَحْدَة عرض مرئيّ)
17 customer service representative — ممثل خدمة العملاء
18 customer — عميل (زبون)
19 computer-generated design — تصميم على الكمبيوتر
20 sound-absorbing partition — حاجِز ماصّ للصوت
21 typist — طابعة على الآلة الكاتبة
22 typewriter — آلة كاتبة
23 filing drawer — دُرْج حفظ الملفات
24 customer card index — فهرس بطاقات العملاء
25 office chair, a swivel chair — كُرْسيّ المكْتَب، كُرْسيّ دَوَّار
26 typing desk — مكْتَب الطباعة على الآلة الكاتبة
27 card index box — صندوق فهرس البطاقات
28 multi-purpose shelving — أرْفُف متعددة الأغراض
29 proprietor — مالك/صاحب المؤسسة
30 business letter — خطاب تجاري
31 proprietor's secretary — سكرتير صاحب المؤسسة
32 shorthand pad (*Am.* steno pad) — إضْمَامة وَرَق الاختزال
33 audio typist — طابعة صوتيَّة
34 dictating machine — المِمْلاة، الدكتافون
35 earphone — سمَّاعة الأذن
36 statistics chart — مُخَطَّط إحصائي
37 pedestal containing a cupboard or drawers — قطعة أثاث تحتوي على خزانة أو أدْرَاج
38 sliding-door cupboard — خِزَانَة ذات باب انزلاقي
39 office furniture arranged in an angular configuration — أثاث مكتبي في ترتيب زاويّ
40 wall-mounted shelf — رَفّ مُعلَّق بالجدار
41 letter tray — صينية الخطابات
42 wall calendar — روزنامة حائط، نتيجة حائط
43 data centre (*Am.* center) — مركز المعلومات
44 calling up information on the data display terminal (visual display unit) — استدعاء المعلومات على طَرَفيَّة عرض البيانات
45 waste paper basket — سلة المهملات
46 sales statistics — إحصائيات المبيعات
47 EDP print-out, a continuous fan-fold sheet — وَرَق طباعة للكمبيوتر مطوي على شكل مروحة
48 connecting element — قطعة توصيل

249 Office V (Office Machinery) — المكْتَب (5) (مُعدَّات مكْتَبيَّة)

1 electric typewriter, a — آلة كاتبة كهربائية

golf ball typewriter	
2-6 keyboard	**لَوْحَة المفاتيح**
2 space bar	قضيب المباعدة بين الحروف والكلمات
3 shift key	مفاتيح الحروف العليا
4 line space and carrier return key	مِفْتَاح المسافة بين الأسْطُر والانتقال إلى أول السطر التالي
5 shift lock	مفاتيح قفل مفتاح الحروف العليا
6 margin release key	مفتاح إطلاق الهامش الجانبيّ
7 tabulator key	مِفْتَاح الجَدْوَلَة
8 tabulator clear key	مِفْتَاح إلغاء الجَدْوَلَة
9 on/off switch	مفتاح التشغيل/الإيقاف
10 striking force control (impression control)	أداة التحكم في درجة (حبر)الطباعة
11 ribbon selector	أداة اختيار الشريط
12 margin scale	مِقْيَاس مُدَرَّج لتحديد الهامش
13 left margin stop	أداة إيقاف الهامش الأيسر
14 right margin stop	أداة إيقاف الهامش الأيمن
15 golf ball (spherical typing element) bearing the types	كُرَة الطباعة وتحمل الحروف الطباعية
16 ribbon cassette	عُلْبَة الشريط
17 paper bail with rollers	مُثَبِّتَة الوَرَق على أسْطُوَانَة الآلة الكاتبة وعليها الأسطوانات
18 platen	أُسْطُوَانَة الآلة الكاتبة
19 typing opening (typing window)	نافذة الطباعة
20 paper release lever	ذِراع تحرير الوَرَقة
21 carrier return lever	ذِراع إعادة العربة
22 platen knob	مِقْبَض أُسْطُوَانَة الطباعة
23 line space adjuster	أداة ضبط المسافة بين الأسْطُر
24 variable platen action lever	ذِراع تشغيل أُسْطُوَانَة الآلة الكاتبة
25 push-in platen variable	أُسْطُوَانَة آلة كاتبة انضغاطية
26 erasing table	نَضُد المَحْوَ
27 transparent cover	غطاء شفاف
28 exchange golf ball (exchange typing element)	كُرَة الطباعة
29 type	حَرْف طباعي
30 golf ball cap (cap of typing element)	غطاء كُرَة الطباعة
31 teeth	أسنان
32 photocopier (copier, photocopying machine)	مَاكِينَة تصوير
33 copyboard cover with single-copy (single-sheet) delivery tray	غِطاء سطح التصوير وبه صينية خروج وَرَقة واحدة
34 universal paper cassette	كاسيت وَرَق عام
35 adjustable paper cassettes	كاسيتات وَرَق انضباطية
36 front door	باب أمامي
37 dual vertical transport unit	وَحْدَ نقل رأسيَّة مزدوجة
38 sorter	آليَّة فَرْز
39 copy delivery bins	صفائح خروج النُّسَخ المصورة
40-43 control panel displays and control keys	**شاشات لوحة التحكم ومفاتيح التحكم**
40 enlargement, reduction, and program selection keys	مفاتيح التكبير والتصغير وانتقاء البرامج
41 sort mode and two-sided copy keys	مفاتيح انتقاء وظيفة الفَرْز وتصوير صفحتي الكتاب
42 display with colour, exposure, format,and copy number selection keys	شاشة عرض مزودة بمفاتيح انتقاء الألوان والتعريض للضوء وعدد النُّسَخ
43 start key (copy start key)	مفتاح بدء التصوير
44 letter-folding machine	مَاكِينَة طيّ الخطابات
45 paper feed	إلقام الوَرَق
46 folding mechanism	آليَّة الطي
47 receiving tray	لَوْحَة إستقبال الوَرَق المطبوع
48 small offset press	مَاكِينَة طباعة أوفست صغيرة
49 paper feed	لَوْحَة تلقيم المَاكِينَة بالوَرَق
50 lever for inking the plate cylinder	ذِراع تحبير أُسْطُوَانَة السطح الطباعي
51-52 inking unit (inker unit)	**وَحْدَة تحبير**
51 distributing roller (distributor)	طنبور توزيع الحبر
52 ink roller (inking roller, fountain roller)	أُسْطُوَانَة التحبير
53 pressure adjustment	آليَّة ضبط طنبور الطبعة (الطنبور الضاغط)
54 sheet delivery (receiving table)	وَحْدَة استقبال الوَرَق المطبوع
55 printing speed adjustment	آليَّة تعديل سرعة الطباعة
56 jogger for aligning the piles of sheets	آليَّة ترصيص الوَرَق
57 pile of paper (pile of sheets)	رَصَّة وَرَق
58 folding machine	مَاكِينَة طي الوَرَق
59 gathering machine (collating machine, assembling machine) for short runs	مَاكِينَة تجميع مَلازِم
60 gathering station (collating station, assembling station)	مَحَطَّة التجميع
61 adhesive binder (perfect binder) for hot adhesives	مَاكِينَة تغليف كامل
62 magnetic tape dictating machine	مِمْلاة ذات شريط مغناطيسي
63 headphones (headset, earphones)	سمَّاعة الأذن
64 on/off switch	مفتاح التشغيل/الإيقاف

65 microphone cradle	حامِل الميكروفون
66 foot control socket	مَقْبَس تحكم سفلي
67 telephone adapter socket	مَقْبَس مهايئ الهاتف
68 headphone socket (earphone socket, head-set socket)	مَقْبَس سمَّاعة الأذن
69 microphone socket	مَقْبَس الميكروفون
70 built-in loudspeaker	مكبِّر صوت داخلي
71 indicator lamp (indicator light)	لَمْبَة إرشادية
72 cassette compartment	حُجَيْرَة شريط التسجيل
73 forward wind, rewind, and stop buttons	أزْرَار لف وتقديم وإيقاف الشريط
74 time scale with indexing marks	مِقْيَاس زمني مُدَرَّج
75 time scale stop	أداة إيقاف المقياس الزمنيّ

250 Bank — البَنْك/المصْرَف

1-11 main hall	**القاعة الرئيسيَّة**
1 cashier's desk (cashier's counter)	شباك الصَّرَّاف
2 teller (cashier)	الصَّرَّاف
3 bullet-proof glass	زُجاج مقاوم للرصاص
4 service counters (for service and advice on savings accounts, private and company accounts, personal loans)	مكتب خدمة العملاء (لتقديم الخدمات المصرفية والاستشارات الخاصة بالحسابات الادخاريَّة وحسابات الأفراد والشركات والقروض الشخصية)
5 bank clerk	مُوَظَّفَة بالبَنْك
6 customer	عميل
7 brochures	كُتَيِّبَات
8 stock list (price list, list of quotations)	قائمة أسعار الأسْهُم والأوراق الماليَّة بالبورصة
9 information counter	كاونتر الاستعلامات
10 foreign exchange counter	كاونتر صرف النقد الأجنبي (استبدال العُمْلَة)
11 entrance to strong room	مدخل الغرفة المنيعة (غرفة حفظ النفائس والأموال)
12 bill of exchange (bill); *here:* a draft, an acceptance (bank acceptance)	وَرَقة تجارية؛ هنا : كمبيالة، قبول مصرفي
13 place of issue	مكان الإصدار
14 date of issue	تاريخ الإصدار
15 place of payment	مكان السداد
16 date of maturity (due date)	تاريخ الاستحقاق
17 bill clause (draft clause)	شَرْط الكمبيالة
18 value	القيمة
19 payee (remittee)	المَدْفُوع له (المستفيد)
20 drawee (payer)	المَسْحُوب عليه (دافع الكمبيالة)
21 drawer	السَّاحِب
22 domicilation (paying agent)	الوكيل الدافع
23 acceptance	قبول
24 Eurocheque card	بطاقة ائتمان "يوروتشك"
25 issuing bank (drawee bank)	بَنْك الإصْدار (البَنْك المسحوب عليه)
26 account number	رقم الحساب
27 card number	رقم البطاقة
28 hologram, a white light hologram (rainbow hologram)	هولوجرام، صورة مجسمة
29 (*on the back:*) magnetic strip	شريط مُمَغْنَط (من الخلف)

251 Stock Exchange — بُورْصَة الأوْرَاق المَاليَّة

1-10 stock exchange	**بُورْصَة الأوْرَاق المَاليَّة**
1 exchange hall (exchange floor)	قاعة البُورْصَة
2 market for securities	سُوق الأوْرَاق المَاليَّة
3 broker's post	مكْتَب السِّمْسَار
4 sworn stockbroker (exchange broker, stockbroker, *Am.* specialist), an inside broker	سِمْسَار معتمد بالبُورْصَة
5 kerbstone broker (kerb-stoner, curbstone broker, curbstoner, outside broker), a commercial broker dealing in unlisted securities	سِمْسَار سوق غير رسميَّة، سِمْسَار تجاري يتعامل في الأوراق غير المُدْرَجَة بالبُورْصَة
6 member of the stock exchange (stockjobber, *Am.* floor trader, room trader)	وسيط في البُورْصَة
7 stock exchange agent (boardman), a bank employee	وكيل بالبُورْصَة، موظف بنك
8 quotation board	لَوْحَة عرض الأسعار
9 index curve	مُنْحَنَى إرْشاديّ
10 telephone box (telephone booth, telephone kiosk, call box)	كُشْك التليفون (كُشْك الهاتِف)
11-19 securities; *kinds:* share (*Am.* stock), fixed-income security, annuity, bond, debenture bond, municipal bond (corporation stock), industrial bond, convertible bond	**الأوراق الماليَّة**؛ أنواعها: أسْهُم، شهادات الدَّخْل الثابت، شهادات الدَّخْل السنويّ، صكوك، صكوك أسهم، صكوك تجاريَّة، صكوك صناعيَّة، صكوك قابلة للتحويل
11 share certificate (*Am.* stock certificate); *here:* bearer share (share warrant)	شهادة أسْهُم، هنا: سَهْم لحامله (ضمان أسْهُم)
12 par (par value, nominal par, face par) of the share	سِعْر التعادل أو السِّعْر الاسمي للسَّهْم
13 serial number	رقم مسلسل
14 page number of entry	رقم صفحة القيد في سجل

in bank's share register (bank's stock ledger) — الأسهم بالبنك

15 signature of the chairman of the board of governors — تَوْقيع رئيس مجلس المحافظين

16 signature of the chairman of the board of directors — تَوْقيع رئيس مجلس الإدارة

17 sheet of coupons (coupon sheet, dividend coupon sheet) — فَرْخ كوبونات أرباح الأَسْهُم

18 dividend warrant (dividend coupon) — كوبون رِبْح الأَسْهُم

19 talon — كَعْب فَرْخ كوبونات الأرباح

252 Money (Coins and Notes, *Am.* Coins and Bills) — النقود (العُمْلات المَعْدَنيَّة والأَوْرَاق المَاليَّة)

1-29 coins (coin, coinage, metal money, specie, *Am.* hard money); *kinds:* gold, silver, nickel, copper, or aluminium, *Am.* aluminum, coins — **العُمْلات المَعْدَنيَّة؛** أنواعها: ذَهَب، فِضَّة، نيكل، نحاس، ألومنيوم

1 Athens: tetradrachm (tetradrachmon, tetradrachma) — أثينا: الدراخمة الرباعيَّة

2 the owl [emblem of the city of Athens] — البُومة [رمز مدينة أثينا]

3 aureus of Constantine the Great — إكْليل قسطنطين الأعْظَم

4 bracteate of Emperor Frederick I Barbarossa — عملة الإمبراطور فريدريك الأول الأعْظَم

5 Louis XIV louis-d'or — لويس الرابع عشر

6 Prussia: 1 reichstaler (speciestaler) of Frederick the Great — برُوسْيَا: 1 رايخستولر يحمل صورة فردريك الأعْظَم

7 Federal Republic of Germany: 5 Deutschmarks (DM); 1 DM = 100 pfennigs — جمهورية ألمانيا الاتحاديَّة: 5 ماركات ألمانيَّة؛ 1 مارك = 100 فنيش

8 obverse — وَجْه القِطْعَة النَّقْديَّة

9 reverse (subordinate side) — الجانب الآخَر للعُمْلَة (ظَهْر القِطْعَة النَّقْديَّة)

10 mint mark (mintage, exergue) — النَّقْش المضروب على العُمْلَة المعدنيَّة

11 legend (inscription on the edge of a coin) — نَقْش (نَقْش حافة العُمْلَة)

12 device (type), a provincial coat of arms — شِعار، شِعار نَبَالة محلي

13 Austria: 25 schillings; 1 sch = 100 groschen — النمسا: 25 شلناً؛ 1 شلن = 100 جرُوشن

14 provincial coats of arms — شِعار نَبَالة محلي

15 Switzerland: 5 francs; 1 franc = 100 centimes — سويسرا: 5 فرنكات؛ 1 فرنك = 100 سنتيم

16 France: 1 franc = 100 centimes — فرنسا: 1فرنك = 100 سنتيم

17 Belgium: 100 francs — بلجيكا: 100 فرنك

18 Luxembourg (Luxemburg): 1 franc — لكسمبورج: 1فرنك

19 Netherlands: 2 1/2 guilders; 1 guilder (florin, gulden) = 100 cents — هولندا: 2 1/2 جلدر؛ 1جلدر = 100سنت

20 Italy: 200 lire (*sg.* lira) — إيطاليا: 200 ليرة

21 Vatican City: 100 lire (*sg.* lira) — مدينة الفاتيكان: 100 ليرة

22 Spain: 1 peseta = 100 céntimos — أسبانيا: 1 بزيتا = 100 سنتيمو

23 Portugal: 1 escudo = 100 centavos — البرتغال: 1سكودو= 100سنتافو

24 Denmark: 1 krone = 100 öre — الدانمارك: 1كرون = 100 أور

25 Sweden: 1 krona = 100 öre — السويد: 1 كرونة = 100 أور

26 Norway: 1 krone = 100 öre — النرويج: 1 كرون = 100 أور

27 Czechoslovakia: 1 koruna = 100 heller — تشيكوسلوفاكيا: 1 كورونا 100 هيلر

28 Yugoslavia: 1 dinar = 100 paras — يوغسلافيا: 1 دينار = 100 بارا

29 United Kingdom of Great Britain and Northern Ireland: 1 pound sterling (£1) = 100 new pence (100 p); (*sg.* new penny, new p) — المملكة المتحدة لبريطانيا العظمى وأيرلندا الشماليَّة: 1جنيه إسترليني = 100 بنس

30-39 banknotes (*Am.* bills) (paper money, notes, treasury notes) — **الأوراق الماليَّة** (النقود الورقيَّة وأذون الخزانة)

30 Federal Republic of Germany: 100 DM — جمهورية ألمانيا الاتحاديَّة: 100 مارك ألماني

31 bank of issue (bank of circulation) — بنك الإصْدار

32 watermark [a portrait] — العلامَة المائيَّة (صورة شخص)

33 denomination — قيمة العُمْلَة

34 USA: 1 dollar ($1) = 100 cents — الولايات المتحدة الأمريكيَّة: 1 دولار أمريكي = 100 سنت

35 facsimile signatures — صورة طِبْق الأصْل من التَّوْقيع

36 impressed stamp — خاتم مطبوع بالضغط

37 serial number — الرقم المسلسل

38 Greece: 1,000 drachmas (drachmae); 1 drachma = 100 lepta (*sg.* lepton) — اليونان: 1000 دراخمة؛ 1 دراخمة = 100 لبتون

39 portrait — صورة لشَخْص

40-44 striking of coins (coinage, mintage) — **سَكُّ العُمْلات المعدنيَّة** (سَكُّ العُمْلَة)

40-41 coining dies (minting dies) — **قالبا سك العُمْلَة**

40 upper die — القالِب العلوي

41 lower die — القالِب السفلي

42 collar — طَوْق

43 coin disc (flan, planchet, blank) قُرْص العُمْلَة
44 coining press (minting press) مِكْبَس سَكُّ العُمْلَة

253 Flags الأعْلام

1-3 flag of the United Nations **عَلَم الأُمَم المتحدة**
1 flagpole (flagstaff) with truck صاري العَلَم يعلوه قرص الحبال
2 halyard (halliard, haulyard) الكَرّ : حَبْل رفع العَلَم أو إنزاله
3 bunting قماش راية مُلَوَّن
4 flag of the Council of Europe عَلَم المجلس الأوروبي
5 Olympic flag العَلَم الأوليمبي
6 flag at half-mast (*Am.* at half-staff) [as a token of mourning] عَلَم مُنكَّس [رمز للحِداد]
7-11 flag **العَلَم**
7 flagpole (flagstaff) صاري العَلَم
8 ornamental stud نقوش زخرفيَّة
9 streamer شَريط طويل مُلَوَّن
10 pointed tip of the flagpole الطَّرْف المدبب لصاري العَلَم
11 bunting قماش الرَّاية المُدَبَّب
12 banner (gonfalon) راية ، بيرق
13 cavalry standard (flag of the cavalry) راية سِلاح الفرسان
14 standard of the German Federal President [ensign of head of state] راية رئيس ألمانيا الاتحاديَّة
15-21 national flags **الأعْلام القوميَّة**
15 the Union Jack (Great Britain) العَلَم البريطاني (بريطانيا العظمى)
16 the Tricolour (*Am.* Tricolor) (France) العَلَم الفرنسيّ (فرنسا)
17 the Danebrog (Dannebrog) (Denmark) علم الدانمارك
18 the Stars and Stripes (Star-Spangled Banner) (USA) عَلَم الولايات المتحدة الأمريكيَّة
19 the Crescent (Turkey) الهلال (تُرْكيَا)
20 the Rising Sun (Japan) الشمس المُشْرِقَة (اليابان)
21 the Hammer and Sickle (USSR) المِطْرَقَة والمِنْجَل (علم اتحاد الجمهوريَّات الاشتراكيَّة السوفيتيَّة)

22-34 signal flags, a hoist **رايَات الإشارات**
22-28 letter flags **رايَات الحروف**
22 letter A, a burgee (swallow-tailed flag) الحَرْف A، علم مَرْكب تجاريّ
23 G, pilot flag الحَرْف G، علم إرشاد السفن في المرافئ
24 H ('pilot on board') الحَرْف H (" المُرْشِد على مَتْن السفينة")
25 L ('you should stop, I have something important to communicate') الحَرْف L (" يجب أن تتوقف ، هناك رسالة هامة لك")
26 P, the Blue Peter ('about to set sail') الحَرْفP، عَلَم الإبحار ("على وَشَك الإبحار")
27 W ('I require medical assistance') الحَرْف W ("أطلب مساعدة طبيَّة")
28 Z, an oblong pennant (oblong pendant) الحَرْف Z، راية بحريَّة مستطيلة
29 code pennant (code pendant), used in the International Signals Code راية كودية ، تستخدم فى نظام الإشارات الدوليّ
30-32 substitute flags (repeaters), triangular flags (pennants, pendants) **الرايات البديلة**، الرايات المثلثة
33-34 numeral pennants (numeral pendants) **الرايات البحريَّة الرقميَّة**
33 number 1 رقم 1
34 number 0 رقم صفر
35-38 customs flags **أعْلام الجمارك**
35 customs boat pennant (customs boat pendant) راية قارب الجمارك
36 'ship cleared through customs' "السفينة أنهت الإجراءات الجمركيَّة"
37 customs signal flag راية إشارة الجمارك
38 powder flag ['inflammable (flammable) cargo'] راية البارود ["شُحنة قابلة للاشتعال"]

254 Heraldry, Crowns and Coronets شعَارَات النَّبَالَة وَالتِّيجَان والتُّوَيْجَات

1-36 heraldry (blazonry) **شعَارَات النَّبَالَة**
1, 11, 30-36 crests **شارَات**
1-6 coat-of-arms (achievement of arms, hatchment, achievement) **رَمْز الإمارة أو المُلك**
1 crest شارة
2 wreath of the colours (*Am.* colors) إكْليل الألوان
3 mantle (mantling) غطاء
4, 7-9 helmets (helms) **خَوْذات**
4 tilting helmet (jousting helmet) خَوْذَة مائلة (خَوْذَة المبارزة على ظهر الخيل)
5 shield درْع
6 bend sinister wavy تَمَوُّج أيْسَر مُنْحَني
7 pot-helmet (pot-helm, heaume) خَوْذَة معدنيَّة كُرَويَّة
8 barred helmet (grilled helmet) خَوْذَة شبكيَّة
9 helmet affronty with visor open خَوْذَة ذات فتحة أماميَّة لها جزء متحرك
10-13 marital achievement (marshalled, *Am.* marshaled, coat-of-arms) **الشِّعَارَات الزَّيجيَّة**
10 arms of the baron (of the husband) شِعَار نَبَالَة الزَّوْج
11-13 arms of the family of the femme (of the wife) **شِعَار نَبَالَة أُسْرَة الزَّوْجَة**

11 demi-man; *also:* demi-woman	نصف رجل؛ أيضا: نصف إمرأة
12 crest coronet	تُوَيْج، إكْلِيل
13 fleur-de-lis	شِعَار ملُوك فرنسا (قديماً)
14 heraldic tent (mantling)	غطاء شعار النَّبالَة
15-16 supporters (heraldic beasts)	**حامِلا الشِّعَار**
15 bull	ثَوْر
16 unicorn	أحادي القَرْن (حصان خُرافيّ)
17-23 blazon	**شِعَار نَبالَة**
17 inescutcheon (heart-shield)	دِرْع المنتصف (دِرْع القلب)
18-23 quarterings one to six	**أقسام التُّرْس من 1 إلي 6**
18, 20, 22 dexter (right)	الجزء الأيمن من التُّرْس
18-19 chief	**الجزء العلوي من التُّرْس**
19, 21, 23 sinister (left)	الجزء الأيْسَر من شِعَار النَّبالَة
22-23 base	قاعِدة
24-29 tinctures	الأَصْبَاغ
24-25 metals	المَعَادِن
24 or (gold) [yellow]	ذهبيّ [أصفر]
25 argent (silver) [white]	فضِّيّ [أبيض]
26 sable	أَسْوَد، غامق
27 gules	أحْمَر
28 azure	سماوي، لازوردي
29 vert	أخْضَر
30 ostrich feathers (treble plume)	ريش النَّعَام
31 truncheon	صَوْلَجان، عصا
32 demi-goat	نصف ماعِز
33 tournament pennons	رايات مبارزات الفرسان
34 buffalo horns	قَرْنا الجاموس
35 harpy	الخَطَّاف (مخلوق خُرافيّ)
36 plume of peacock's feathers	مجموعة ريش الطاووس
37, 38, 42-46 crowns and coronets [continental type]	**التِّيجان والتويجات/الأكاليل** [طراز قاري]
37 tiara (papal tiara)	تاج البابا المُرصع بالجواهِر
38 Imperial Crown [German, until 1806]	التاج الإمبراطوري [في ألمانيا حتى عام 1806]
39 ducal coronet (duke's coronet)	تُوَيْج الدوق
40 prince's coronet	تُوَيْج الأمير
41 elector's coronet	تُوَيْج الناخب
42 English Royal Crown	التاج الملكيّ الإنجليزيّ
43-45 coronets of rank	**تُوَيْجات الرُتَب**
43 baronet's coronet	تُوَيْج البارونيتيَّة
44 baron's coronet (baronial coronet)	تُوَيْج البارونيَّة
45 count's coronet	تُوَيْج الكونتيَّة
46 mauerkrone (mural crown) of a city crest	تاج قمة سور المدينة

255 Armed Forces I (Army) — القُوَّات المُسَلَّحَة (1) (الجَيْش)

1-96 army armament (army weaponry)	**أسْلِحَة الجَيْش**
1-28 hand weapons	**الأسلحة اليدويَّة**
1 P1 pistol	مسدس بي 1
2 barrel	سَبَطَانَة، ماسورة
3 front sight (foresight)	مُسدِّدة أمامية
4 hammer	الطارق، التتك
5 trigger	الزناد
6 pistol grip	قبضة المسدس
7 magazine holder	حابس المَخْزَن
8 MP2 submachine gun	الرشاش الخفيف إم بي 2
9 shoulder rest (butt)	مِسْنَد الكتف (الإخْمَص، الدبشك)
10 casing (mechanism casing)	غلاف آلية التعمير والإطلاق
11 barrel clamp (barrel-clamping nut)	جِلْبَة تثبِيْت السبطانة/ الماسورة
12 cocking lever (cocking handle)	ذراع التعمير
13 palm rest	مِسْنَد اليد
14 safety catch	ذراع سقاطة الأمان
15 magazine	مَخْزَن الذخيرة
16 G3-A3 self-loading rifle	البندقية "جي 3 إيه 3" ذاتية التعمير
17 flash hider (flash eliminator)	كاتم الوميض
18 trigger mechanism	آلية الزناد
19 notch (sighting notch, rear sight)	فتحة المُسدِّدَة/الناشنكاة الخلفية
20 front sight block (foresight block) with front sight (foresight)	مجموعة المُسَدِّدَة الأمامية والشعيرة
21 rifle butt (butt)	إخْمَص/دبشك البندقية
22 44 2A1 light anti-tank rocket launcher	قاذف صواريخ خفيفة طراز 44 2 إيه 1 مضادة للدبابات
23 rocket (projectile)	صاروخ (مقذوف)
24 telescopic sight (telescope sight)	سدَّادَة تليسكوبيَّة
25 cheek rest	مِسْنَد الخَدّ
26 MG3 machine gun (Spandau)	مِدْفَع رشاش "إم جي 3" (سبانداو)
27 recoil booster	مُخَفِّف الارتداد
28 belt-changing flap	قلابة تغيير الحمَّالة
29-61 artillery weapons mounted on self-propelled gun carriages	**أسْلِحَة مدْفَعيَّة محمولة على عربات مَدَافِع متحركة**
29 SFM 110 A2 self-propelled howitzer	مدفع هويتزر متحرك طراز "إس إف إم 110 إيه 2
30-32 gun carriage	**عَرَبَة المدْفَع**
30 drive wheel	عَجَلَة الدفع
31 track	جنزير
32 road wheel	عَجَلَة السير على الطريق
33 hull	بَدَن العَرَبَة
34 spade	غارز الحاضن
35 spade piston	مِكْبَس غارز الحاضن
36 hydraulic system	نظام هيدرولي

37 elevating piston	مِكْبَس ضبط الارتفاع
38 breech ring	حلقة الترباس
39 barrel	ماسورة، سبطانة
40 muzzle	فوهة الماسورة
41 buffer (buffer recuperator)	مُخَفِّف الارتداد
42 M 109 A3 G self-propelled howitzer	مِدْفَع هاوتزر متحرك طراز "إم 109 إيه 3 جي"
43 armoured (*Am.* armored) turret	بُرْج مدرع
44 fighting compartment	حجيرة القتال
45 barrel clamp	جِلْبَة تثبيْت الماسورة
46 fume extractor	آلية إطلاق الدخان
47 barrel recuperator	جِهَاز ارتداد الماسورة
48 light anti-aircraft (AA) machine gun	رشاش خفيف مضاد للطائرات
49 SF Lance missile launch system (missile launcher)	نظام إطلاق صواريخ "إس إف لانس"
50 skirt	وقاء
51 tracked vehicle	عَرَبَة مجنزرة
52 missile (guided missile)	صاروخ (صاروخ مُوَجَّه)
53 elevating gear	ترس ضبط الارتفاع
54 launching ramp	مِنَصَّة إطلاق
55 110 SF 2 rocket launcher	قاذف صواريخ طراز "110 إس إف 2"
56 fire control system	نظام ضبط النيران
57 launching tubes	مواسير الإطلاق
58 tube bins	صناديق المواسير
59 turntable	صينية دوَّارَة
60 jack	دعامة تثبيْت رأسية
61 driver's cab	كابينة السائق
62-87 armoured (*Am.* armored) **vehicles**	**عربات مدرعة**
62 Leopard 2 tank	دبابة "ليوبارد 2"
63 smooth-barrelled gun	مِدْفَع بماسورة ملساء
64 driver's hatch	حجيرة السائق
65 commander's periscope	بريسكوب القائد
66 smoke canister (smoke dispenser)	حاوية الدخان
67 Luchs armoured (*Am.* armored) reconnaissance vehicle, an amphibious vehicle	عَرَبَة استطلاع مدرعة طراز "لوكس"، عَرَبَة برمائية
68 cannon	مِدْفَع
69 hatch	حجيرة
70 antenna	هوائي
71 propeller (for propulsion in water)	رفَّاص (للدفع في الماء)
72 Jagdpanzer Jaguar 1 ATGW vehicle (HOT)	عَرَبَة طراز "جادبنزر جاجوار 1 إيه تي جي دبليو"
73 guidance system (upper part) with guidance unit	نظام توجيه (الجزء العلوي) وبه وحدة التوجيه
74 HOT guided-missile launcher	قاذف صواريخ "هوت" موجهة
75 firing mechanism (upper part)	آلية الإطلاق (الجزء العلوي)
76 commander's cupola	قبة القائد
77 Marder armoured (*Am.* armored) personnel carrier	ناقلة جنود مدرعة طراز "ماردر"
78 searchlight	ضوء كاشف
79 MILAN anti-tank guided-missile system	نظام "ميلان" للصواريخ الموجهة المضادة للدبابات
80 Fuchs armoured (*Am.* armored) personnel and load carrier, an amphibious vehicle	ناقلة جنود وأحمال مدرعة طراز "فوكس"، عَرَبَة برمائية
81 rear door	باب خلفي
82 Gepard anti-aircraft tank	دبابة "جيبارد" مضادة للطائرات
83 surveillance radar	رادار مراقبة
84 tracking radar for fire control	رادار التتبع الخاص بضبط النيران
85 twin 35 mm cannon	مِدْفَع مزدوج عيار 35 مللم
86 M113 A1 G armoured (*Am.* armored) personnel carrier	ناقلة جنود مدرعة طراز "إم 113 إيه 1"
87 machine gun on a traversing mount	مِدْفَع رشاش على محمل التنشير
88-96 helicopters	**طائرات الهليكوبتر**
88 CH-53 G transport helicopter	طائرة هليكوبتر للنقل طراز "سي إتش 53"
89 single rotor	مِرْوَحَة مفردة
90 turbine	توربين
91 stabilizing tail rotor	مِرْوَحَة ذَيْل للموازنة
92 fuselage	بَدَن الطائرة
93 cockpit	كابينة الطائرة
94 BO-105P anti-tank helicopter	صائدة دبابات طراز "بي أو 105 بي"
95 skid	زلاقة هبوط
96 HOT anti-tank guided-missile launcher	قاذف صواريخ "هوت" موجهة مضادة للدبابات

256 Armed Forces II (Air Force I) / القُوَّات المُسَلَّحَة (2) (القُوَّات الجَوِّيَّة 1)

1 *McDonnell-Douglas F-4F Phantom II* interceptor and fighter-bomber	طائرة مُعْتَرِضَة ومُقَاتِلَة قاذفة قنابل طراز "ماكدونل ـ دوجلاس إف 4 إف فانتوم 2"
2 squadron marking	رمز السِّرْب
3 aircraft cannon	مِدْفَع الطائرة
4 wing tank (underwing tank)	مَخْزَن ذخيرة الجَنَاح (مَخْزَن ذخيرة أسفل الجَنَاح)
5 air intake	ممَص هواء
6 boundary layer control flap	قلابة تَحكُّم الطبقة المتاخمة
7 in-flight refuelling (*Am.* refueling) probe (flight refuelling probe, air refuelling probe)	وَحْدَة التزود بالوَقُود فى الجَوّ
8 *Panavia 2000 Tornado* multirole combat aircraft (MRCA)	طائره قتالية طراز "بنافيا 2000 تورنادو" مُتَعَدِّدة المَهَام
9 swing wing	جَنَاح تأرجحي

10 radar nose (radome, radar dome) مُقَدِّمَة رادارِيَّة (قُبَّة رادارِيَّة)
11 pitot-static tube (pitot tube) أُنْبُوب التَّوْجيه والإرشاد
12 brake flap (air brake) قَلابة فرملة هوائيَّة
13 afterburner exhaust nozzles of the engines فُوَّهات عادِم المُحَرِّكات
14 *C160 Transall* medium-range transport aircraft طائرة نقل متوسطة المدى طراز "سي 160 ترنسال"
15 undercarriage housing (landing gear housing) مَبَيْت عَجَلات الهبوط
16 propeller-turbine engine (turboprop engine) مُحَرِّك توربينيّ الدفع
17 antenna هوائي
18 *Bell UH-ID Iroquois* light transport and rescue helicopter طائرة هليكوبتر للإنقاذ والنقل الخفيف طراز "بل يو إتش - آى دى إروكوا"
19 main rotor المِرْوَحَة الرئيسيَّة
20 tail rotor مِرْوَحَة الذَّيْل
21 landing skids مِزْلَقات الهبوط
22 stabilizing fins (stabilizing surfaces, stabilizers) زَعانِف المُوازَنَة الجانبيَّة
23 tail skid مِزْلَقَة الذَّيْل
24 *Dornier DO 28 D-2 Skyservant* transport and communications aircraft طائرة إتصالات ونقل طراز "دورنيير دو 28 دي أو سكاى سرفنت"
25 engine pod مقر المُحَرِّك
26 main undercarriage unit (main landing gear unit) وَحْدَة آليَّة الهبوط الرئيسيَّة
27 tail wheel عَجَلَة المؤخِّرة (عَجَلَة الذَّيْل)
28 sword antenna هوائي سيفيّ

257 Armed Forces III (Air Force II) القُوَّات المُسَلَّحَة (3) (القُوَّات الجَوِّيَّة 2)

1-41 *Dornier-Dassault-Breguet Alpha Jet* Franco-German jet trainer طائرة تدريب نفاثة طراز دورنيير - دو سولت - بريجيت ألفا جيت فرانكو - جرمان
1 pitot-static tube (pitot tube) أُنْبُوب التَّوْجيه والإرشاد (أُنْبُوب بيْتوت)
2 oxygen tank خَزَّان الأكسجين
3 forward-retracting nose wheel عَجَلَة المُقدمة قابلة للطي
4 cockpit canopy (cockpit hood) قبَّة كابينة الطَّيَّار
5 canopy jack مِرْفاع القُبَّة
6 pilot's seat (student pilot's seat), an ejector seat (ejection seat) مَقْعَد الطَّيَّار، مَقْعَد قاذِف
7 observer's seat (instructor's seat), an ejector seat (ejection seat) مَقْعَد المُراقِب (مَقْعَد المُدَرِّب)، مَقْعَد قاذِف
8 control column (control stick) عصا التَّحكُم
9 thrust lever عتلة الدفع
10 rudder pedals with brakes دوَّاسات الدفة وبها المكابح
11 front avionics bay حُجَيْرة إلكترونيَّات الطيران الأماميَّة
12 air intake to the engine مدخل الهواء إلى المُحَرِّك
13 boundary layer control flap قلابة تحكم الطبقة المتاخمة
14 air intake duct فتحة دخول الهواء (الممَص)
15 turbine engine مُحَرِّك توربينيّ
16 reservoir for the hydraulic system خَزَّان النظام الهيدرولي
17 battery housing حُجَيْرة البطاريات
18 rear avionics bay حُجَيْرة إلكترونيّات الطيران الخلفيَّة
19 baggage compartment حُجَيْرة الأمتعة
20 triple-spar tail construction عَضُد الذَّيْل الثلاثيّ
21 horizontal tail ذَيْل أفقيّ
22 servo-actuating mechanism for the elevator آليَّة تشغيل مُوازِرَة لجِهَاز الإرتفاع
23 servo-actuating mechanism for the rudder آليَّة تشغيل مُوازِرَة للدَّفَّة
24 brake chute housing (drag chute housing) حجيرة مِظَلَّة الكبح
25 VHF (very high frequency) antenna (UHF antenna) هوائي تردد عال جداً (هوائي تردد فائق العُلُوّ)
26 VOR (very high frequency omnidirectional range) antenna هوائى لجميع الاتجاهات ذو تردد عال جداً
27 twin-spar wing construction جَنَاح ذو عَضُد ثنائيّ
28 former with integral spars قلاب ذو أعْضَاد متكامِلة
29 integral wing tanks خزَّانات ثابتة بالجَنَاح
30 centre-section (*Am.* center-section) fuel tank خزَّان وَقُود بوَسَط الطائرة
31 fuselage tanks خزَّانات جسم الطائرة
32 gravity fuelling (*Am.* fueling) point نقطة تزود بوَقُود الجاذبيَّة
33 pressure fuelling (*Am.* fueling) point نقطة تزود بوَقُود الضغط
34 inner wing suspension تعليق الجَنَاح الداخلي
35 outer wing suspension تعليق الجَنَاح الخارجيّ
36 navigation lights (position lights) أضواء المِلاحة (أضواء توضِّح موقع الطائرة)
37 landing lights أضواء الهبوط
38 landing flap قلابة الهبوط
39 aileron actuator مُشَغِّل الجُنَيْح
40 forward-retracting main undercarriage unit (main landing gear unit) وَحْدَة آليَّة الهبوط الرئيسيَّة
41 undercarriage hydraulic الأُسْطُوانة الهيدروليَّة لآليَّة

cylinder (landing gear hydraulic cylinder) — الهبوط

258 Warships I — السُّفُن الحَرْبيَّة (1)

1 Hamburg class guided-missile destroyer — مُدَمِّرَة طراز "هامبورج" تحمل صواريخاً موَجَّهَة
2 hull of flush-deck vessel — بدَن السفينة المستوية السَّطْح
3 bow (stem) — مُقدَّم السفينة (الجُؤْجُؤ)
4 flagstaff (jackstaff) — صاري العلم (الراية)
5 anchor, a stockless anchor (patent anchor) — مِرْسَاة
6 anchor capstan (windlass) — رَحَوِيَّة المِرْساة (مرفاع المِرْساة)
7 breakwater (*Am.* manger board) — حائل الأمْوَاج
8 chine strake — صَفيفة ألواح ذات حافة
9 main deck — السَّطْح الرئيسي
10-28 superstructures — **أجزاء السفينة فوق السَّطْح الرئيسي**
10 superstructure deck — سَطْح التجهيزات العلويَّة
11 life rafts — أطْوَاق النجاة
12 cutter (ship's boat) — زَوْرَق سريع
13 davit (boat-launching crane) — الداوودِيّ (ونْش رفع أو إنزال قوارب النجاة)
14 bridge (bridge superstructure) — مَنَصَّة ربَّان السفينة (برج القيادة)
15 side navigation light (side running light) — ضوء مِلاحة جانبي
16 antenna — هوائي
17 radio direction finder (RDF) frame — مُحَدِّد اتجاه اللاسلكي
18 lattice mast — صاري شبكي
19 forward funnel — مدْخَنَة أماميَّة
20 aft funnel — مدْخَنَة خلفيَّة
21 cowl — طربوش المدْخَنَة
22 aft superstructure (poop) — أجزاء السفينة الخلفية فوق السَّطْح الرئيسي
23 capstan — رَحَوِيَّة
24 companion ladder (companionway, companion hatch) — سُلَّم داخلي
25 ensign staff — صاري الراية
26 stern, a transom stern — الكَوْثَل: مؤخِّرة السفينة
27 waterline — خط الماء
28 searchlight — أنوار كاشفة
29-37 armament — **التسليح**
29 100 mm gun turret — بُرْج مدْفَع عيار 100 ملم
30 four-barrel anti-submarine rocket launcher (missile launcher) — قاذف صواريخ مضادة للغواصات رباعي
31 40 mm twin anti-aircraft (AA) gun — مِدْفَع مُزْدَوَج مُضاد للطائرات عيار 40 ملم
32 MM 38 anti-aircraft (AA) rocket launcher (missile launcher) in launching container — قاذف صواريخ إم إم 38 مُضادة للطائرات فى حجيرة الإطلاق
33 anti-submarine torpedo tube — ماسورة طوربيد مُضاد للغوَّاصات
34 depth-charge thrower — قاذف قنابل الأعماق
35 weapon system radar — رادار نظام التسليح
36 radar antenna (radar scanner) — هوائي المَسْح الراداري
37 optical rangefinder — جِهَاز تحديد المدى البصريّ
38 Lütjens class guided-missile destroyer — مُدَمِّرَة فئة "لوتشن" محملة بصواريخ مُوَجَّهَة
39 bower anchor — مِرْساة مُقدَّم السفينة
40 propeller guard — وقاء الرفَّاص
41 tripod lattice mast — صاري شبكي على حامل ثلاثي
42 pole mast — عمود الصاري
43 ventilator openings (ventilator grill) — فتحات تهوية (شبكة التهوية)
44 exhaust pipe — ماسورة العادم
45 ship's boat — قارب السفينة
46 antenna — هوائي
47 radar-controlled 127 mm all-purpose gun in turret — مِدْفَع بُرْجي لجميع الأغراض عيار 127 ملم ذو تحكم راداري
48 127 mm all-purpose gun — مِدْفَع عيار 127 ملم لجميع الأغراض
49 launcher for Tartar missiles — قاذف صواريخ " تارتر "
50 anti-submarine rocket (ASROC) launcher (missile launcher) — قاذف صواريخ مُضادة للغوَّاصات (أسروك)
51 fire control radar antennas — هوائيَّات رادار ضبط النيران
52 radome (radar dome) — الرادوم (قبة الرادار)
53 Bremen class frigate — فُرْقَاطَة فئة "بريمن"
54 radar-controlled 76 mm rapid-fire gun — مِدْفَع سريع النيران عيار 76 مللم يتم التَّحَكُّم فيه رادارياً
55 Sea Sparrow surface-to-air missiles — صواريخ سَطْح– جو طراز "سي سبارو"
56 radar and fire control system — نظام الرادار و ضبط النيران
57 Harpoon surface-to-surface missiles — صواريخ سَطْح–سَطْح طراز "هاربون"
58 funnel — مدْخَنَة
59 cowl — طربوش المدخنة
60 air/surface search radar — رادار تفَقُّد جو/أرض
61 cutter — زَوْرَق سريع
62 close-range surface-to-air missiles — صواريخ سَطْح–جو للمدى القريب
63 helicopter deck — سَطْح هبوط الهليكوبتر
64 type 206 submarine — غوَّاصة فئة 206
65 flooded foredeck — سَطْح أمامي غاطِس
66 pressure hull — بدَن يتحمل ضغط المياه
67 turret — بُرْج الغوَّاصة
68 retractable instruments — آلات قابلة للطي
69 type 148 missile-firing fast attack craft — زَوْرَق صواريخ هجومي سريع فئة 148
70 76 mm all-purpose gun with turret — مِدْفَع عيار 76 ملم لكافة الأغراض محمول على بُرْج
71 missile-launching housing — حامِل إطلاق الصواريخ
72 deckhouse — بَيْت سَطْح السفينة

73 40 mm anti-aircraft (AA) gun	مِدْفَع عيار 40 ملم مُضاد للطائرات
74 propeller guard moulding (*Am.* molding)	قالب وقاء الرفَّاص
75 type 143 missile-firing fast attack craft	زَوْرَق صواريخ هجومي سريع فئة 143
76 breakwater (*Am.* manger board)	حائل الأمْوَاج
77 radome (radar dome)	الرادوم (قبَّة الرادار)
78 torpedo tube	ماسورة الطوربيد
79 exhaust escape flue	مسْرَب خروج العادم
80 type 331 mine hunter	صائدة ألْغَام طراز 331
81 reinforced rubbing strake	ألْوَاح احتكاك مُقوَّاة
82 inflatable boat (inflatable dinghy)	قارب نُفاخي
83 davit	الداوودي
84 type 341 minesweeper	كاسِحَة ألغام طراز 341
85 cable winch	مرفاع كيبلي
86 towing winch (towing machine, towing engine)	مرفاع ماكينة السحب/ القطر
87 mine-sweeping gear (paravanes)	جرَّافة الألغام (جِهَاز كسح الألغام)
88 crane (davit)	مرفاع كيبلي (داوودي)
89 Barbe class landing craft	صَنْدَل إنزال فئة "بارب"
90 bow ramp	سُلَّم الإنزال الأمامي
91 stern ramp	سُلَّم الإنزال الخلفي
92 Rhein class tender	سفينة تموين صغيرة طراز "راين"
93 Lüneberg class support ship	سفينة إسناد فئة "لونيبرْج"
94 Sachsenwald class mine transport	ناقلة ألغام فئة "زاكسنفالد"
95 Helgoland class salvage tug	سفينة قطر للإنقاذ طراز "هلجولاند"
96 replenishing tanker "Eifel"	سفينة الإمداد بالمؤن والوقود "إيفيل"

259 Warships II (Modern Fighting Ships) — السُفُن الحَرْبيَّة (2) (السُفُن الحَرْبيَّة الحَديثَة)

1 nuclear-powered aircraft carrier *Nimitz ICVN 68* (USA)	حامِلَة الطائرات النَّوَويَّة "نيمتز آي سي في إن 68" (الولايات المتحدة الأمريكية)
2-11 body plan	**مُخَطَّط الجِسْم**
2 flight deck	سَطْح الطيران
3 island (bridge)	منَصَّة الربَّان (بُرْج القيادة)
4 aircraft lift (*Am.* aircraft elevator)	مِرْفاع الطائرات
5 eight-barrel anti-aircraft (AA) rocket launcher (missile launcher)	قاذف صواريخ مضادة للطائرات ثُماني المواسير
6 pole mast (antenna mast)	عمود الصاري (صاري الهوائي)
7 antenna	هوائي
8 radar antenna (radar scanner)	هوائي راداري
9 fully enclosed bow	جُؤْجُؤ مُغْلَق بالكامل
10 deck crane	مرفاع السَّطْح
11 transom stern	كَوْثَل برافدة أفقيَّة
12-20 deck plan	**مُخَطَّط السَّطْح**
12 angle deck (flight deck)	سَطْح زاوِيّ (سَطْح الطيران)
13 aircraft lift (*Am.* aircraft elevator)	مِرْفاع الطائرات
14 twin launching catapult	مِجْنَقَة مزدوجة
15 hinged (movable) baffle board	لَوْح حاجز مفصليّ متحرِّك
16 arrester wire	سِلك كابح/مُوقِف
17 emergency crash barrier	حاجِز ارتطام للطوارئ
18 safety net	شبكة أمان
19 caisson (cofferdam)	قَيْسُون
20 eight-barrel anti-aircraft (AA) rocket launcher (missile launcher)	قاذف صواريخ مضادة للطائرات ثماني المواسير
21 *Kara class* rocket cruiser (missile cruiser) (USSR)	زَوْرَق صواريخ فئة "كارا" (الاتحاد السوفيتي)
22 hull of flush-deck vessel	بَدَن سفينة بسَطْح مستوٍ
23 sheer	مُنْحَدَر
24 twelve-barrel underwater salvo rocket launcher (missile launcher)	قاذف صَليات صواريخ تحت الماء ذو 12 ماسورة
25 twin anti-aircraft (AA) rocket launcher (missile launcher)	قاذف صواريخ مضادة للطائرات مزدوج
26 launching housing for 4 short-range rockets (missiles)	مبَيْت إطلاق أربعة صواريخ قصيرة المدى
27 baffle board	لَوْح حاجِز
28 bridge	منَصَّة الربَّان (بُرْج القيادة)
29 radar antenna (radar scanner)	هوائي الرادار
30 twin 76 mm anti-aircraft (AA) gun turret	بُرْج مِدْفَع مزدوج مضاد للطائرات عيار 76 ملم
31 turret	بُرْج
32 funnel	مِدْخَنَة
33 twin anti-aircraft (AA) rocket launcher (missile launcher)	قاذف صواريخ مضادة للطائرات مزدوج
34 automatic anti-aircraft (AA) gun	مِدْفَع آلي مضاد للطائرات
35 ship's boat	قارب السفينة
36 underwater 5-torpedo housing	مبَيْت تحت الماء لعدد خمس قذائف طوربيد
37 underwater 6-salvo rocket launcher (missile launcher)	قاذف صواريخ تحت الماء لعدد ست صَلْيَات
38 helicopter hangar	حظيرة الهليكوبتر
39 helicopter landing platform	مَنَصَّة هبوط الهليكوبتر

40 variable depth sonar (VDS) سونار سَبْر الأعماق
41 *California class* rocket cruiser (missile cruiser) (USA) زَوْرَق صواريخ طراز "كاليفورنيا" (الولايات المتحدة الأمريكية)
42 hull بَدَن القارب
43 forward turret بُرْج أماميّ
44 aft turret بُرْج خلفي
45 forward superstructure أجزاء السفينة الأماميَّة
46 landing craft زَوْرَق الإنزال
47 antenna هوائي
48 radar antenna (radar scanner) هوائي راداري
49 radome (radar dome) قُبَّة راداريَّة
50 surface-to-air rocket launcher (missile launcher) قاذف صواريخ سَطْح–جَوّ
51 underwater rocket launcher (missile launcher) قاذف صواريخ تحت الماء
52 127 mm gun with turret مِدْفَع بُرْجيّ عيار 127 مللم
53 helicopter landing platform مِنَصَّة هبوط الهليكوبتر
54 nuclear-powered fleet submarine غَوَّاصَة أسطول نَوَويَّة
55-74 middle section [diagram] **القِسْم الأوْسَط** [رسم تخطيطي]
55 pressure hull بَدَن يتحمَّل الضغط
56 auxiliary engine room غرفة المُحَرِّك المُساعِد
57 rotary turbine pump مضَخَّة توربينيَّة دَوَّارَة
58 steam turbine generator مُوَلِّد توربيني بُخاري
59 propeller shaft عمود الرفَّاص
60 thrust block كُتْلَة الدَّفْع
61 reduction gear تروس تقليل السرعة
62 high and low pressure turbine توربين ضغط عال ومنخفض
63 high-pressure steam pipe for the secondary water circuit (auxiliary water circuit) ماسورة بخار ضغط عال لدائرة الماء الثانوية
64 condenser مُكَثِّف
65 primary water circuit دائرة الماء الرئيسيَّة
66 heat exchanger مُبادِل حراري
67 nuclear reactor casing (atomic pile casing) غلاف مفاعِل نووي
68 reactor core قلب المفاعِل النووي
69 control rods قضبان تحكم
70 lead screen ستَار رصاص
71 turret بُرْج
72 snorkel (schnorkel) سنُورْكِل
73 air inlet فتحة دخول الهواء
74 retractable instruments مُعدَّات قابلة للضم
75 patrol submarine with conventional (diesel-electric) drive غَوَّاصَة دَوريَّة بإدارة دَفْع تقليديَّة
76 pressure hull بَدَن يتحمَّل الضغط
77 flooded foredeck سَطْح أمامي غاطِس
78 outer flap (outer doors) [for torpedoes] أبْوَاب خارجية [للطوربيد]
79 torpedo tube أنْبُوب الطوربيد
80 bow bilge جَمَّة الجُؤْجُؤ
81 anchor مِرْسَاة
82 anchor winch وِنْش المِرْسَاة
83 battery بطَّاريَّة
84 living quarters with folding bunks عنابر معيشة بها أسِرَّة قابلة للطي
85 commanding officer's cabin كابينة ضابط القيادة
86 main hatchway فتحة أرضيَّة القارب الرئيسيَّة
87 flagstaff عمود الراية
88-91 retractable instruments **مُعدَّات قابلة للضم**
88 attack periscope بريسكوب الهجوم
89 antenna هوائي
90 snorkel (schnorkel) سنُورْكِل
91 radar antenna (radar scanner) هوائي رادار
92 exhaust outlet ماسورة خروج العادم
93 heat space (hot-pipe space) مكان أنْبُوب التدفئة
94 diesel generators مُوَلِّدات تعمل بالديزل
95 aft diving plane and vertical rudder سَطْح الغَوْص الخلفي والدَّفَّة الرأسيَّة
96 forward vertical rudder الدَّفَّة الرأسيَّة الأماميَّة

260 School I (Primary School) المَدْرَسَة (1) (المَدْرَسَة الإبْتدائيَّة)

1-85 primary school **مَدْرَسَة إبْتدائيَّة**
1-45 classroom **حُجْرَة الدِّرَاسَة**
1 arrangement of desks in a horseshoe ترتيب المقاعد على شكل حُدْوَة فَرَس
2 double desk مَقْعَد مزدوَج
3 pupils (children) in a group (sitting in a group) تلاميذ يَجْلِسُون كمجموعة
4 exercise book كتاب التمارين
5 pencil قَلَم رصاص
6 wax crayon قَلَم ألْوَان شَمْع
7 school bag حقيبة المَدْرَسَة
8 handle يَدّ الحقيبة
9 school satchel (satchel) حقيبة الكُتُب
10 front pocket جيب أماميّ
11 strap (shoulder strap) حِزَام (حِزَام الكَتِف)
12 pen and pencil case مِقْلَمَة
13 zip (*Am.* zipper) سَوسْتَة
14 fountain pen (pen) قَلَم حِبْر سائل
15 loose-leaf file (ring file) دُوسيه بحَلَقَة
16 reader كِتاب تعليم القراءة
17 spelling book كِتاب تعليم الكِتَابَة
18 exercise book (note-book) كِتَاب التمارين
19 felt tip pen قَلَم طَرْفه من اللباد
20 pupil raising her hand تلميذة ترفَع يَدَها
21 teacher مُدَرِّس
22 teacher's desk مكْتَب المُدَرِّس
23 register سِجِل، دفتر

24 pen and pencil tray صينية الأقلام الحبر والرصاص
25 desk mat (blotter) نشَّافة المكتَب
26 window painting with finger paints (finger painting) طِلاء النافذة بأقلام ملَوَّنَة
27 pupils' (children's) paintings (watercolours, *Am.* watercolors) رسومات التلاميذ
28 cross صَليب
29 three-part blackboard سَبُورَة ثُلاثيَّة
30 bracket for holding charts كَتيفة حمْل الرُسوم البيَانيَّة
31 chalk ledge حافة وَضْع الطباشير
32 chalk طباشير
33 blackboard drawing رَسْم على السَّبُورَة
34 diagram رَسْم تخطيطي
35 reversible side blackboard سَبُورَة قلاّبَة
36 projection screen شاشَة فانوس الإسقاط
37 triangle مُثَلَّث
38 protractor مِنْقَلَة
39 divisions تَدْريج المِنْقَلَة
40 blackboard compass فرْجَار السَّبُورَة
41 sponge tray صينية إسْفِنْجَة مَسْح السَّبُورَة
42 blackboard sponge (sponge) إسْفِنْجَة مَسْح السَّبُورَة
43 classroom cupboard خزانَة حُجْرَة الدِّرَاسَة
44 map (wall map) خَريطَة (خَريطَة حائط)
45 brick wall حائط من قَوَالِب الطُوب
46-85 craft room **حُجْرَة المهارات الفنيَّة**
46 workbench طاولة الشُغْل
47 vice (*Am.* vise) مِلْزَمَة
48 vice (*Am.* vise) bar ذِرَاع المِلْزَمَة
49 scissors مِقَصّ
50-52 working with glue (sticking paper, cardboard, etc.) **الشُغْل بالصَّمْغ**
50 surface to be glued سَطْح سيتم تصميغه
51 tube of glue أنْبوب الصَّمْغ
52 tube cap غطاء الأنْبوب
53 fretsaw مِنْشَار زَخْرَفَة/أرْكِت
54 fretsaw blade (saw blade) نَصْل مِنْشَار الزَخْرَفَة/ الأرْكِت
55 wood rasp (rasp) مِبْرَد الخَشَب
56 piece of wood held in the vice (*Am.* vise) قطعة خشب مُثَبَّتَة بالمِلْزَمَة
57 glue pot قنِّينَة الصَّمْغ
58 stool كُرْسيّ بدون مِسْنَد للظَهْر
59 brush فُرْشَاة
60 pan (dustpan) صفيحة النفايات
61 broken china قِطَع خَزَف مكْسُورَة
62 enamelling (*Am.* enameling) الطلاء بالمينا
63 electric enamelling (*Am.* enameling) stove فُرْن الطلاء بالمينا الكهربي
64 unworked copper نحاس لم يُشَكَّل بَعْد
65 enamel powder مسحوق المينا
66 hair sieve مُنْخُل شَعْري
67-80 pupils' (children's) work أشْغَال التلاميذ
67 clay models (models) نماذج من الصلصال
68 window decoration of coloured (*Am.* colored) glass زَخْرَفَة نافذة من الزُجاج الملَوَّن
69 glass mosaic picture (glass mosaic) فُسَيْفِساء زُجاج
70 mobile لُعْبَة تعليق
71 paper kite (kite) طائرة وَرَقيَّة
72 wooden construction بناء خَشَبي
73 polyhedron مُجَسَّم مُتعدِّد الأسَطْح
74 hand puppets دُمْيَات يدويَّة
75 clay masks أقْنِعَة من الصلصال
76 cast candles (wax candles) شمعدان مصبوب
77 wood carving نَحْت خشبيّ
78 clay jug إبريق من الصلصال
79 geometrical shapes made of clay أشكال هندسيَّة مصنوعة من الصلصال
80 wooden toys لُعَب خشبيَّة
81 materials مَوَاد
82 stock of wood رَصَّة أخْشَاب
83 inks for wood cuts حِبْر للمصنوعات الخشبيَّة
84 paintbrushes فُرَش التَلْوين
85 bag of plaster of Paris جُوَال جصّ باريس

261 School II (Secondary School, High School) المَدْرَسَة (2) (المَدْرَسَة الثَّانويَّة)

1-45 grammar school; *also:* upper band of a comprehensive school (*Am.* alternative school) مَدْرَسَة متوسِّطَة، مدرسة ثانوية
1-13 chemistry **الكيمياء**
1 chemistry lab (chemistry laboratory) with tiered rows of seats مَعْمَل الكيمياء مُجَهَّز بصفوف تصاعديَّة من المقاعد
2 chemistry teacher مُدَرِّس الكيمياء
3 demonstration bench (teacher's bench) طَاولَة الشروح المعمليَّة
4 water pipe أنْبُوب ماء
5 tiled working surface سطح شغل مُبَلَّط
6 sink حَوْض
7 television monitor, a screen for educational programmes (*Am.* programs) شاشة عرض تليفزيونية، شاشة عرض البرامج التعليمية
8 overhead projector بروجكتور الإسقاط الرأسي
9 projector top for skins السطح العلوي للبروجكتور المخصص لوضع الشرائح الشفافة
10 projection lens with right-angle mirror عدسة إسقاط ذات مرآة قائمة الزاوية
11 pupils' (*Am.* students') bench with experimental apparatus دكَّة التلاميذ المزودة بأجهزة التجارب
12 electrical point (socket) مَقْبَس كهربائي
13 projection table نَضَد الإسقاط

14-34 biology preparation room (biology prep room) — **حُجْرَة الإعداد لمادة الأحْيَاء**

14 skeleton — هَيْكَل عظميّ

15 casts of skulls — رُتَب الجماجِم

16 calvarium of Pithecanthropus erectus — جُمْجُمَة إنسان جاوة

17 skull of Steinheim man — جُمْجُمَة إنسان شتاينهايم

18 calvarium of Peking man (of Sinanthropus) — جُمْجُمَة إنسان بكِين

19 skull of Neanderthal man, a skull of primitive man — جُمْجُمَة الإنسان البدائي

20 Australopithecine skull (skull of Australopithecus) — جُمْجُمَة إنسان استراليا البدائي

21 skull of present-day man — جُمْجُمَة إنسان العصر الحديث

22 dissecting bench — طَاوِلَة التشريح

23 chemical bottles — زُجاجات تحوي مواداً كيميائيَّة

24 gas tap — صُنْبُور غاز

25 petri dish — صَحْفَة بِتْري : صحن زجاجي صغير ذو غطاء مَرِن

26 measuring cylinder — أُسْطُوَانة قياس

27 work folder containing teaching material — حافِظة المواد التعليمية

28 textbook — كتاب مَدْرَسيّ

29 bacteriological cultures — مَزَارِع بكتيريَّة

30 incubator — الحاضِن : جِهَاز لحضانة البكتريا

31 test tube rack — رَفّ أنابيب الاختبار

32 washing bottle — قنينة غسيل

33 water tank — خَزَّان ماء

34 sink — حَوْض

35 language laboratory — مَعْمَل اللغات

36 blackboard — سَبُّورَة

37 console — كونسول

38 headphones (headset) — سمَّاعات الرأس

39 microphone — ميكروفون

40 earcup — كَأْس الأذن

41 padded headband (padded headpiece) — عِصابة رأسية مُبطَّنة

42 programme (*Am.* program) recorder, a cassette recorder — جِهَاز تسجيل البرامج

43 pupil's (*Am.* student's) volume control — زِرّ التحكم في ارتفاع صوت التلميذ

44 master volume control — زر التحكم الرئيسي بارتفاع الصوت

45 control buttons (operating keys) — مفاتيح التشغيل

262 University — الجَامِعَة

1-28 university (college) — **الجامعَة** (الكليَّة)

1 lecture — مُحاضَرَة

2 lecture room (lecture theatre, *Am.* theater) — مُدَرَّج المحاضرات

3 university lecturer (lecturer, college lecturer, *Am.* assistant professor) — مُحاضِر (المُدَرِّس الجامعي)

4 lectern — منضدة المُحاضِر

5 microphone — ميكروفون

6 remote-controlled blackboard — سَبُّورَة يتم التحكم فيها من بُعْد

7 overhead projector — فانوس الإسقاط الرأسي

8 projection screen for projecting pictures by means of a film projector, slide projector, or an epidiascope — شاشة عرض الصُّوَر عن طريق فانوس عرض الأفلام أو فانوس الشرائح الشفافة

9 student — طالِب

10 student — طالِبة

11-28 university library; *sim.:* national library, regional or municipal scientific library — **مكْتَبة الجامعة**؛ بالمثل: المكتبة الوطنية، المكتبة الإقليمية أو البلدية العلمية

11 stack (book stack) with the stock of books — رَفُّوف متراصة تحمل كميات من الكُتُب

12 bookshelf, a steel shelf — رَفّ الكُتُب، رَفّ معدنيّ

13 reading room — قاعة القراءة

14 member of the reading room staff, a librarian — مُوَظَّف قاعة القراءة، أمين مكْتَبة

15 periodicals rack with periodicals — رَفّ الدوْرِيَّات

16 newspaper shelf — رَفّ الجرائد

17 reference library with reference books (handbooks, encyclopedias, dictionaries) — مكْتَبة المَرَاجِع (الكتب الإرشاديَّة والمَوْسُوعات والمعاجِم)

18 lending library and catalogue (*Am.* catalog) room — مكْتَبة الإعارة وحُجْرَة الفهرس

19 librarian — أمِين مكْتَبة

20 issue desk — مكْتَب الاستعارة

21 main catalogue (*Am.* catalog) — الفهرس الرئيسي

22 card catalogue (*Am.* catalog) — فهرس البطاقات

23 card catalogue (*Am.* catalog) drawer — دُرْج فهرس البطاقات

24 library user — مُسْتَخْدِم المكْتَبة

25 borrower's ticket (library ticket) — بطاقة المستعير

26 issue terminal — طَرَفيَّة الصرَفّ

27 microfiche (fiche) — ميكروفيش

28 microfiche reader — جِهَاز قراءة الميكروفيش

263 Election — الانْتخَابَات

1-15 election meeting, a public meeting — **اجتمَاع انتخابيّ**، اجتماع عام

1-2 committee — **لَجْنَة**

1 chairman — رئيس اللَجْنَة

2 committee member — عضو اللَجْنَة

3 committee table — طَاولَة اللَجْنَة

4 pamphlet — مَنْشور

5 election speaker (speaker) — المتحدث الانتخابي
6 rostrum — مِنْبَر الخَطَابَة
7 microphone — ميكروفون
8 meeting (audience) — جمهور الحاضرين
9 man distributing leaflets — رجل يقوم بتوزيع منشورات
10 stewards — المضيفون
11 armband (armlet) — شريط الذراع
12 banner — لافتة بأحْرُفٍ ضخمة
13 placard — إعلان
14 proclamation — بَيَان
15 heckler — شخص يقاطع المتحدِّث بكَثْرَة أسئلته

16-29 election — **الانتخاب**
16 polling station (polling place) — مقر انتخابي
17 polling officers — مَسْئُولا الانتخاب
18 electoral list — قائِمَة انتخابيَّة
19 polling card with registration number (polling number) — بطاقة انتخابيَّة ذات رقم انتخابي
20 ballot paper with the names of the parties and candidates — وَرَقَة انتخابيَّة تحمل أسماء الأحزاب والمرشَّحين
21 ballot envelope — مَظْرُوف الاقتراع
22 voter — مُصَوِّت، ناخب
23 polling booth — حُجَيْرَة الانتخاب
24 elector (qualified voter) — ناخِب (مُصَوِّت مؤهل)
25 election regulations — لوائح العملية الانتخابية
26 electoral register — سِجِلّ انتخابيّ
27 election supervisor — مُشْرِف الانتخابات
28 ballot box — صُنْدُوق الاقتراع
29 slot — فتحة الصُّنْدُوق

264 Police — الشُّرْطَة

1-33 police duties — **مَهام الشُّرْطَة**
1 police helicopter (traffic helicopter) for controlling traffic from the air — طائرة هليكوبتر تابعة للشُّرْطَة لتنظيم حركة المرور من الجو
2 cockpit — كابينة قيادة الطائرة
3 rotor (main rotor) — مِرْوَحَة (المِرْوَحَة الرئيسية)
4 tail rotor — مِرْوَحَة الذيل
5 use of police dogs — استخدام الكلاب البوليسيَّة
6 police dog — كلب بوليسي
7 uniform — زيّ رسمي
8 uniform cap, a peaked cap with cockade — قبعة الزيّ الرسميّ
9 traffic control by a mobile traffic patrol — تنظيم المرور بواسطة دَوْرِيَّة مرور متحركة
10 patrol car — سيارة الدَّوْرِيَّة
11 blue light — مصباح أزرق
12 loud hailer (loudspeaker) — مُكَبِّر صوت
13 patrolman (police patrolman) — رَجُل الدَّوْرِيَّة
14 police signalling (*Am.* signaling) disc (disk) — قرص إعطاء الإشارات الخاص بالشرطة
15 riot duty — مُكافحة الشغب
16 special armoured (*Am.* armored) car — عَرَبَة عمليات خاصة مُدَرَّعة
17 barricade — ساتر، حاجز
18 policeman (police officer) in riot gear — رجل شرطة مجهز بعتاد مكافحة الشغب
19 truncheon (baton) — هُراوة
20 riot shield — دِرْع مكافَحَة الشغب
21 protective helmet (helmet) — خَوْذَة واقية
22 service pistol — مُسدَّس الخدمة (مُسدَّس ميري)
23 pistol grip — قبضة المُسدَّس
24 quick-draw holster — جِرَاب سهل الفتح لسحب السلاح بسرعة
25 magazine — مَخْزَن الذخيرة
26 police identification disc (disk) — شارة هَوِيَّة الشُّرْطَة المعدنيَّة
27 police badge — شارة الشُّرْطَة
28 fingerprint identification (dactyloscopy) — التعرّف على بَصَمَات الأصابع
29 fingerprint — بَصْمَة إصبع
30 illuminated screen — شاشة ضوئية
31 search — التفتيش
32 suspect — مُشْتَبَه فيه، مشبوه
33 detective (plainclothes policeman) — رَجُل شرطة سِرِّيّ (رَجُل شرطة يرتدي ملابس عادية)
34 English policeman — رجل شرطة إنجليزي
35 helmet — خَوْذَة
36 pocket book — دفتر المُخالَفات
37 policewoman — شُرْطِيَّة
38 police van — عَرَبَة الشُّرْطَة

265 Café — المَقْهَى

1-31 café; *sim.:* espresso bar, tea room, ice-cream parlour (*Am.* parlor) — **مَقْهَى**؛ بالمثل: صالة الشاي، صالة المُرَطِّبات
1 counter (cake counter) — كاونتر الكعك
2 coffee urn — غلايَّة إعداد القَهْوَة
3 tray for the money — صينية النقود
4 gateau — جاتوه
5 meringue with whipped cream — حلوى المرنغ وعليها كريمة مَخْفُوقة
6 trainee pastry cook — حلواني تحت التدريب
7 counter assistant — مُضيفة الكاونتر
8 newspaper shelves (newspaper rack) — أرَفُف الجرائد
9 wall lamp — مصباح جداريّ
10 corner seat, an upholstered seat — مَقْعَد الزاوية، مَقْعَد مُنَجَّد
11 café table — طَاوِلَة المَقْهَى
12 marble top — سطح رُخامي
13 waitress — نادلة، جرسونة، مُضيفة
14 tray — صينية
15 bottle of lemonade — زُجاجة عصير الليمون
16 lemonade glass — كوب عصير الليمون
17 chess players playing a — لاعِبان يلعبان مباراة

game of chess شطرنج
18 coffee set طاقم القَهْوَة
19 cup of coffee فنجان القَهْوَة
20 small sugar bowl سُكَّرِيَّة صغيرة
21 cream jug (*Am.* creamer) إناء مُبَيِّض القهوة
22-24 café customers **زبائن المَقْهَى**
22 gentleman رَجُل
23 lady سيِّدة
24 man reading a newspaper رَجُل يقرأ جريدة
25 newspaper جَريدَة
26 newspaper holder حامِل الجريدة
27 espresso قَهْوَة اكسبرسو
28 ice cream in assorted flavours (*Am.* flavors) آيس كريم مُشَكَّل
29 ice-cream dish (sundae dish) طبق الآيس كريم (طبق آيس كريم صَنْدَاي)
30 iced coffee قَهْوَة مُثَلَّجَة
31 (drinking) straw شارُوقة

266 Restaurant المَطْعَم

1-27 restaurant **المَطْعَم**
1-11 bar (counter) **البار** (الكاونتر)
1 beer pump (beerpull) ماكينة صب الجُعَة
2 drip tray صينية تصريف القطرات المتساقطة
3 beer glass كُوب الجُعَة
4 froth (head) رَغْوَة الجُعَة
5 spherical ashtray for cigarette and cigar ash منْفضَة السجائر والسيجار كروية الشكل
6 beer glass (beer mug) كُوب الجُعَة (كُوز الجُعَة)
7 beer warmer سيخ تدفئة الجُعَة
8 bartender (barman, *Am.* barkeeper, barkeep) الساقي
9 shelf for glasses رَفّ الأكْوَاب
10 shelf for bottles رَفّ الزُجاجات
11 stack of plates رَصَّة من الأطباق
12 coat stand حامِل المعاطِف (شماعة رأسية)
13 hat peg شمّاعة القبعات
14 coat hook خُطّاف تعليق المعْطَف
15 wall ventilator مِرْوَحَة تهوية مثبتة بالجدار
16 bottle زجاجة، قنينة
17 complete meal وَجْبَة كاملة
18 waitress مضيفة، نادِلة، جرسونة
19 tray صينية
20 dessert, a slice of cake حلوَى، شطيرة كيك
21 menu (menu card) قائمة الطعام
22 cruet stand حامِل إبريق الزيْت/الخلّ
23 toothpick holder حامِل خِلال الأسنان
24 matchbox holder حامِل الكبريت/أعواد الثِّقَاب
25 customer زبون
26 beer mat مفرش كوب الجُعَة
27 meal of the day طبق اليَوْم
28-44 wine restaurant (wine bar) **بار الخُمُور**
28 tablecloth مفْرش الطَّاوِلَة
29 glass of water كُوب ماء
30 wine waiter, a head waiter نادِل تقديم الخمور
31 wine list قائمة الخمور
32 wine carafe دَوْرَق الخمور
33 wineglass كَأس الخمر
34 tiled stove مَوْقد قرميدي
35 stove tile قرميدة المَوْقِد
36 stove bench أريكة المَوْقد
37 wooden panelling (*Am.* paneling) كسوة جدار خشبيَّة
38 corner seat مقْعَد الزاوية
39 table reserved for regular customers طَاولَة محجوزة للزبائن الدائمين
40 regular customer زبون دائم
41 cutlery chest صُوان فضِّيَّة (أدوات المائدة
42 wine cooler مُبَرِّد الخمر
43 bottle of wine زُجاجة خمر
44 ice cubes (ice, lumps of ice) مكعَّبات الثلج
45-78 self-service restaurant **مَطْعَم الخدمة الذاتيَّة**
45 stack of trays رَصَّة من الصواني
46 drinking straws (straws) الشاروقات، مصَّاصات
47 serviettes (napkins) مناشِف ورقيَّة
48 cutlery holders حوامِل فضِّيَّة المائدة
49 cool shelf رَفّ الأطعمة البارِدَة
50 slice of honeydew melon شريحة من كُوز العَسل
51 plate of salad طبق سلطة
52 plate of cheeses طبق جبن
53 fish dish طبق سمك
54 filled roll لفائف
55 meat dish with trimmings طبق لحوم والطعام المصاحب لها
56 half chicken نصف دَجاجة
57 basket of fruit سَلَّة فواكه
58 fruit juice عصير فواكه
59 drinks shelf رَفّ المشروبات
60 bottle of milk زُجاجة لَبَن
61 bottle of mineral water زُجاجة مياه معدنيَّة
62 vegetarian meal (diet meal) وَجْبَة نباتيَّة
63 tray صينية
64 tray counter طَاولَة الصواني
65 food price list قائمَة أسعار الطعام
66 serving hatch بوَّابة الخدمة
67 hot meal وَجْبَة ساخنة
68 beer pump (beerpull) ماكينة صب الجُعَّة
69 cash desk مكْتَب دفع النقدية
70 cashier أمين الصُّنْدُوق
71 proprietor مالك المطعم
72 rail درابزين، حاجز
73 dining area منطقة تناول الطعام
74 table طَاولَة، مائدة
75 open sandwich شَطِيرَة
76 ice-cream sundae آيس كريم صاندي

77 salt cellar and pepper pot	المَلاّحة ووعاء الفلفل
78 table decoration (flower arrangement)	زينة المائدة (باقة أزْهار)

267 Hotel — الفُنْدُق

1-26 vestibule (foyer, reception hall)	رُدْهَة (صالة، قاعة استقبال)
1 doorman (commissionaire)	بَوَّاب
2 letter rack with pigeon holes	رَفّ الخطابات وبه صناديق حفظ البريد
3 key rack	لَوْحَة مفاتيح الغُرَف
4 globe lamp, a frosted glass globe	مِصْباح كُرَوِيّ، مِصْباح كُرَوِيّ مصنفر
5 indicator board	لَوْحَة إرشاديَّة
6 indicator light	ضوء إرشاديّ
7 chief receptionist	رئيس موظفي الاستقبال
8 register (hotel register)	المُسَجِّل (مُسَجِّل الفندق)
9 room key	مِفْتَاح غُرَفَة
10 number tag (number tab) showing room number	بطاقة رقم الغُرَفَة
11 hotel bill	فاتورة الفندق
12 block of registration forms	مجموعة من نماذج تسجيل النُّزَلاء
13 passport	جواز سفر
14 hotel guest	نزيل بالفندق
15 lightweight suitcase [for air travel]	حقيبة ملابس خفيفة
16 wall desk	مكْتَب مُثَبَّت بالجدار
17 porter (*Am.* baggage man)	شَيّال، حمّال
18-26 lobby (hotel lobby)	**بَهْو الفندق**
18 page (pageboy, *Am.* bell boy)	وصيف (خادم يرتدي بزَّة خاصة)
19 hotel manager	مُدير الفندق
20 dining room (hotel restaurant)	قاعة تناول الطعام (مَطْعَم الفندق)
21 chandelier	ثُرَيّا (نَجَفَة)
22 fireside	جانب المدْفَأة/المستوقد
23 fireplace	المدْفَأة، المُسْتَوقد
24 mantelpiece (mantelshelf)	رَفّ المدفأة/المستوقد
25 fire	نار
26 armchair	كُرْسِيّ ذو مِسْنَد للذراع
27-38 hotel room, a double room with bath	**غُرْفَة الفندق**، غُرَفَة مزدوجة بحَمَّام
27 double door	باب مزدوج
28 service bell panel	لَوْحَة جرس استدعاء موظف خدمة الغُرَف
29 wardrobe (*Am.* clothes closet)	صُوَان الملابس
30 clothes compartment	ضَلْفَة الملابس
31 linen compartment	ضلفة المفروشات
32 double washbasin	حَوْض غسيل مزدوج
33 room waiter	مُضيف خدمة الغُرَف
34 room telephone	تليفون الغرفَة
35 velour (velours) carpet	بساط/سجادة مخملية
36 flower stand	حامِل الزهور
37 flower arrangement	باقة زهور
38 double bed	سَرير مزدوج لفَرْدَيْن
39 function room (banqueting hall)	صَالة المأدُبَات/المُنَاسَبَات
40-43 private party	**حفلة خاصة**
40 speaker proposing a toast	مُتَحَدِّث يقترح نخباً
41 42's neighbour (*Am.* neighbor)	الجالس جوار رقم 42
42 43's partner	رَفيق الجالس رقم 43
43 42's partner	رَفيقة الجالس رقم 42
44 bar trio	ثلاثي عازفي البار
45 violinist	عازِف الكَمَان
46 couple dancing (dancing couple)	شاب وفتاة يرقصان
47 waiter	النادل، الجرسون
48 napkin	مِنْشَفَة ورقيَّة
49 cigarette	سيجارة
50 ashtray	مِنْفَضَة السجائر
51 hotel bar	بار الفندق
52 foot rail	مِسْنَد القَدَم
53 bar stool	كُرْسِيّ البار
54 bar	بار
55 bar customer	زبون البار
56 cocktail glass (*Am.* highball glass)	كَأس الكوكتيل
57 whisky (whiskey) glass	كَأس الويسكي
58 champagne cork	فلينة زجاجة الشمبانيا
59 champagne bucket (champagne cooler)	دِلْو تبريد زُجاجة الشمبانيا
60 measuring beaker (measure)	إناء قياس حجم المشروب (عيار)
61 cocktail shaker	رَجّاجَة الكوكتيل
62 bartender (barman, *Am.* barkeeper, barkeep)	الساقي
63 barmaid	الساقِيَة
64 shelf for bottles	رَفّ زُجاجات
65 shelf for glasses	رَفّ الكؤوس
66 mirrored panel	لَوْح زُجاجي عاكِس
67 ice bucket	دلو الثلج
68 hotel foyer	رُوَاق الفُنْدُق

268 Town (Town Centre, *Am.* Downtown) — المَدينَة (وَسَط المَدينَة)

1 parking meter	عدَّاد انتظار السيارات
2 map of the town (street map)	خريطة المدينة (خريطة الشوارع)
3 illuminated board	لَوْحَة ضوئيَّة
4 key	مِفْتَاح، زِر
5 litter bin (*Am.* trash bin)	صُنْدُوق المهملات
6 street lamp (street light)	فانوس الشارع
7 street sign showing the name of the street	لافتة اسْم الشارع
8 drain	بالُوعة
9 clothes shop (fashion	مَتْجَر/مَحل ملابس (دار

house) أزياء)
10 shop window واجهة المحل، فترينة
11 window display (shop window display) معروضات الفترينة
12 window decoration (shop window decoration) ديكور الفترينة
13 entrance مَدْخَل
14 window نافذة
15 window box أصيص النافذة
16 neon sign لافتة نِيُون
17 tailor's workroom مَشْغَل الخيَّاط
18 pedestrian أحَد المارة
19 shopping bag حقيبة التَّسَوُّق
20 road sweeper (*Am.* street sweeper) كنّاس الشارع
21 broom مِكْنَسَة
22 rubbish (litter) نفايات (مهملات)
23 tramlines (*Am.* streetcar tracks) قضبان التِّرَام (سكة التِّرَام)
24 pedestrian crossing (zebra crossing, *Am.* crosswalk) عبور المشاة
25 tram stop (*Am.* streetcar stop, trolley stop) مَحَطَّة الترام (مَحَطَّة الترولي)
26 tram stop sign (*Am.* streetcar stop sign. trolley stop sign) لافتة مَحَطَّة التِّرَام
27 tram timetable (*Am.* streetcar schedule, trolley schedule) جدول بمواعيد التِّرَام
28 ticket machine ماكينة التذاكر
29 'pedestrian crossing' sign لافتة "عبور المشاة"
30 traffic policeman on traffic duty (point duty) رجل المرور أثناء المناوبة
31 traffic control cuff كُمّ المرور (كُمّ خاص يرتديه رجل المرور)
32 white cap كاب أبيض
33 hand signal إشارة يدويَّة
34 motorcyclist راكب درَّاجة ناريَّة
35 motorcycle درَّاجة ناريَّة
36 pillion passenger (pillion rider) راكب على المَقْعَد الخلفي للدرَّاجة
37 bookshop مكْتَبَة
38 hat shop (hatter's shop); *for ladies' hats:* milliner's shop محل القُبَّعَات؛ للسيدات: محل بائعة القُبَّعَات النسائية
39 shop sign لافتة المحل
40 insurance company office مكْتَب شركة تأمين
41 department store مَتْجَر ذو أقسام متنوِّعَة
42 shop front الواجهَة الأماميَّة للمحل
43 advertisement إعلان
44 flags رايات
45 illuminated letters حروف ضوئيَّة
46 tram (*Am.* streetcar, trolley) ترام (ترولي)
47 furniture lorry (*Am.* furniture truck) شاحِنَة نقل الأثاث
48 flyover كوبري عبور المشاة
49 suspended street lamp مِصْبَاح مُعلَّق لإنارة الشارع
50 stop line خط وقوف العربات لعبور المُشاة
51 pedestrian crossing (*Am.* crosswalk) عبور المُشاة
52 traffic lights أضواء إشارة المرور
53 traffic light post عمود إشارة المرور
54 set of lights مجموعة الأضواء
55 pedestrian lights أضواء عبور المُشاة
56 telephone box (telephone booth, telephone kiosk, call box) كُشْك التليفون
57 cinema (*Am.* movie) advertisement (film poster, *Am.* movie poster) إعلان عن فيلم سينمائيّ
58 pedestrian precinct (paved zone) منطقة تَرَجُّل المُشاة (منطقة مُعَبَّدَة)
59 street café مَقْهَى بالشارع
60 group seated (sitting) at a table مجموعة جالِسة إلى طَاولَة
61 sunshade ظُلَّة، تندة
62 steps to the public lavatories (public conveniences) سلم يؤدي إلى المراحيض العامة
63 taxi rank (taxi stand) مَوْقَف سيارات الأجرة
64 taxi (taxicab, cab) سيَّارة أُجْرَة
65 taxi sign علامَة سيارة الأجرة
66 'taxi rank' ('taxi stand') sign لافتة تحمل عِبَارة "موقف سيارات أجرة"
67 taxi telephone تليفون استدعاء سيارة أجرة
68 post office مكْتَب البريد
69 cigarette machine ماكينة بيع السجائر
70 advertising pillar عمود لَصْق الإعلانات
71 poster (advertisement) إعلان (بوستر)
72 white line خط أبيض
73 lane arrow for turning left سَهْم الإشارة للانعطاف يساراً من الحارة
74 lane arrow for going straight ahead سَهْم الإشارة لمواصلة السير في خط مستقيم
75 news vendor (*Am.* news dealer) بائع الصُّحُف

269 Water Supply إمْدَاد المِيَاه

1-66 drinking water supply **إمداد مياه الشرب**
1 water table (groundwater level) مستوى الماء الباطني (منسوب الماء الجوفي)
2 water-bearing stratum (aquifer, aquafer) طبقة حامِلة للماء
3 groundwater stream (underground stream) مَجْرَى مياه جوفيَّة
4 collector well for raw water بِئْر تجميع الماء الخام
5 suction pipe أُنْبُوب ماص

6 pump strainer with foot valve — مُنْخَل مِضَخَّة ذو صمام سفلي
7 bucket pump with motor — مِضَخَّة دلوية ذات مُحَرِّك
8 vacuum pump with motor — مِضَخَّة خوائية بمُحَرِّك
9 rapid-filter plant — وَحْدَة ترشيح سريع
10 filter gravel (filter bed) — حَصَى ترشيح (طبقة ترشيح)
11 filter bottom, a grid — قاع الترشيح
12 filtered water outlet — مَخْرَج الماء المرشح
13 purified water tank — خَزَّان ماء نقي
14 suction pipe with pump strainer and foot valve — أُنْبُوب ماص ذو مصفاة ترشيح مِضَخِّيَّة وصمام سفلي
15 main pump with motor — مِضَخَّة رئيسية بمحرك
16 delivery pipe — أُنْبُوب توصيل الماء
17 compressed-air vessel (air vessel, air receiver) — وعاء هواء مضغوط
18 water tower — بُرْج الماء
19 riser pipe (riser) — أُنْبُوب قائم (أُنْبُوب عمودي)
20 overflow pipe — أُنْبُوب الفائض
21 outlet — مَخْرَج
22 distribution main — ماسورة التوزيع الرئيسية
23 excess water conduit — مَجْرَى الماء الزائد
24-39 tapping a spring — **سحب المياه**
24 chamber — غُرْفَة
25 chamber wall — جدار الغُرْفَة
26 manhole — فتحة دخول
27 ventilator — فتحة تهوية
28 step irons — قضبان حديدية دَرَجِيَّة
29 filling (backing) — حَشْوَة
30 outlet control valve — صِمَام التحكم في خروج الماء
31 outlet valve — صِمَام خروج الماء
32 strainer — مُنْخَل
33 overflow pipe (overflow) — أُنْبُوب الفائض
34 bottom outlet — فتحة خروج سفليَّة
35 earthenware pipes — أنابيب من الفخار
36 impervious stratum (impermeable stratum) — طبقة غير مُنْفِذَة (طبقة كتيمة)
37 rough rubble — حَصَى خشن
38 water-bearing stratum (aquifer, aquafer) — طبقة حامِلة للماء (طبقة خازنة للماء)
39 loam seal (clay seal) — طبقةَ لُوميّة مانعة للتسرب
40-52 individual water supply — **إمداد المياه للأفراد**
40 well — بِئْر
41 suction pipe — أُنْبُوب شفط
42 water table (ground-water level) — مستوى الماء الباطني (منسوب الماء الجوفي)
43 pump strainer with foot valve — مُنْخُل مِضَخَّة ذو صمام سفلي
44 centrifugal pump — مِضَخَّة طرد مركزي
45 motor — موتور
46 motor safety switch — مفتاح أمان الموتور
47 manostat, a switching device — مانوستات، جِهَاز تشغيل
48 stop valve — مِحْبَس
49 delivery pipe — أُنْبُوب توصيل
50 compressed-air vessel (air vessel, air receiver) — وعاء هواء مضغوط
51 manhole — فتحة دخول
52 delivery pipe — أُنْبُوب توصيل
53 water meter, a rotary meter — عَدَّاد الماء
54 water inlet — مَدْخَل الماء
55 counter gear assembly — مجموعة تروس العَدَّاد
56 cover with glass lid — غِطاء ذو سطح زجاجي
57 water outlet — مَخْرَج الماء
58 water-meter dial — قُرْص عَدَّاد الماء
59 counters — عَدَّادات
60 driven well (tube well, drive well) — بِئْر مُغلَّفَة/أنبوبية
61 pile shoe — كعب الخازوق
62 filter — مُرَشِّح
63 water table (ground-water level) — مستوى الماء الباطني (منسوب الماء الجوفي)
64 well casing — قميص البِئْر
65 well head — رأس البِئْر
66 hand pump — مِضَخَّة يدوية

270 Fire Service (*Am.* Fire Department) — الإطْفَاء (المَطَافِئ)

1-46 fire service drill (extinguishing, climbing, ladder, and rescue work) — **تدريب الإطفاء** (أعمال الإطفاء والتسلق والسُّلَّم والإنقاذ)
1-3 fire station — **مَحَطَّة الإطفاء**
1 engine and appliance room — غُرْفَة عَرَبَة الإطفاء ومعدات الإطفاء
2 firemen's (*Am.* fire-fighters') quarters — سَكَن رِجال الإطفاء
3 drill tower — بُرْج التدريب
4 fire alarm (fire alarm siren, fire siren) — إنذار الحريق
5 fire engine — عَرَبَة الإطْفَاء
6 blue light (warning light), a flashing light (*Am.* flashlight) — مصباح أزرق (ضوء تحذيري، ضوء وميضي)
7 horn (hooter) — بُوق، نفير
8 motor pump, a centrifugal pump — مِضَخَّة بمحرك، مِضَخَّة نابِذة
9 motor turntable ladder (*Am.* aerial ladder) — سُلَّم دوّار بمحرك
10 ladder, a steel ladder (automatic extending ladder) — سُلَّم معدني (سُلَّم امتدادي آلي)
11 ladder mechanism — آليَّة تشغيل السلَّم
12 jack — رافعة
13 ladder operator — مُشَغِّل السلَّم
14 extension ladder — سُلَّم امتدادي
15 ceiling hook (*Am.* preventer) — خُطَّاف السقف
16 hook ladder (*Am.* pompier ladder) — سُلَّم خطافيّ
17 holding squad — مجموعة مَسْك الشبكة لالتقاط القافزين

18 jumping sheet (sheet) شبكة القفز
19 ambulance car (ambulance) عَرَبَة الإسعاف
20 resuscitator (resuscitation equipment), oxygen apparatus جِهَاز إنعاش القلب والرئتَيْن، جِهَاز أكسجين
21 ambulance attendant (ambulance man) رَجُل الإسعاف
22 armband (armlet, brassard) شريط/شارة الذراع
23 stretcher نقَّالَة
24 unconscious man شخص فاقد الوَعْي
25 pit hydrant حنفية حريق داخل حفرة
26 standpipe (riser, vertical pipe) أنْبُوب قائم
27 hydrant key مفتاح حنفية الحريق
28 hose reel (*Am.* hose cart, hose wagon, hose truck, hose carriage) بكَرَة خرطوم الحريق (عَرَبَة خرطوم الحريق)
29 hose coupling مقْرن الخرطوم
30 soft suction hose خرطوم طَري ماص
31 delivery hose خرطوم دفق الماء
32 dividing breeching طوق توزيع
33 branch مسدس خرطوم الإطفاء
34 branchmen رَجُلا مسدس خرطوم الإطفاء
35 surface hydrant (fire plug) حنفية حريق فوق سطح الأرض
36 officer in charge الضابط المسئول
37 fireman (*Am.* firefighter) رَجُل إطفاء، إطفائي
38 helmet (fireman's helmet, *Am.* fire hat) with neck guard (neck flap) خَوْذَة (خَوْذَة الإطفائي) مُزَوَّدَة بواقٍ للرقبة
39 breathing apparatus جِهَاز التنفس
40 face mask قناع واقٍ، كمَّامة
41 walkie-talkie set جِهَاز اتصال لاسلكي
42 hand lamp مصباح يدوي
43 small axe (*Am.* ax, pompier hatchet) بلْطَة صغيرة
44 hoot belt حزام خطافي
45 beltline حَبْل الحزام
46 protective clothing of asbestos (asbestos suit) or of metallic fabric لِبَاس واق مصنوع من مادة الأسبستوس أو نسيج معدني
47 breakdown lorry (*Am.* crane truck, wrecking crane) شاحنة ونْشيَّة
48 lifting crane ونْش رَفْع
49 load hook (draw hook, *Am.* drag hook) خُطَّاف الأحمال
50 support roll أُسْطُوَانة تثبيت
51 water tender عَرَبَة المياه
52 portable pump مضَخَّة محمولة
53 hose layer عَرَبَة الخراطيم
54 flaked lengths of hose أطْوَال من الخراطيم مكسوة برقائق
55 cable drum أُسْطُوَانة الكيبل
56 winch ونْش
57 face mask filter مُرَشِّح الكمَّامة/قناع الوجه
58 active carbon (activated carbon, activated charcoal) كربون نَشِط (كربون مُنَشَّط)
59 dust filter مُرَشِّح الغبار
60 air inlet مَدْخَل الهواء
61 portable fire extinguisher طفاية حريق محمولة
62 operating valve صمام التشغيل
63 hose with spray nozzle خَرْطُوم ذو فُوَّهَة رَشّ
64 foam-making branch (*Am.* foam gun) مُسَدَّس الرَّغْوَة
65 fireboat قارب إطفاء
66 monitor (water cannon) مِدْفَع الماء
67 suction hose خرطوم شفط

271 Department Store المَتْجَر التَّنْويعي

1 cashier أمين الصُّنْدُوق
2 electronic cash register (till) (scanner till) آلة حاسِبة إلكترونية
3 number keys مفاتيح الأرقام
4 scanner (light pen) سكانر (قَلَم ضَوْئيّ)
5 cash drawer (till) دُرْج النقديَّة
6 compartments (money compartments) for coins and notes (*Am.* bills) حُجَيْرَات للعملة المعدنيَّة والأوراق النقديَّة
7 receipt (sales check) إيصال (قسيمة مبيعات)
8 amount [to be paid] المبلغ [المطلوب دفعه]
9 function keys مفاتيح العمليَّات
10 goods بضائع، سِلَع
11 glass-roofed well بئْر ذو سقف زجاجيّ
12 men's wear department قسم الملابس الرجالي
13 showcase (display case, indoor display window) واجِهَة عرض، فترينة (واجِهَة عرض داخلية)
14 wrapping counter كاونتر لف البضائع
15 tray for purchases صينية المشتريات
16 customer زبون، عميل
17 hosiery department قسم الجَوَارِب
18 shop assistant (*Am.* salesgirl, saleslady) بائع/بائعة
19 price card بطاقة الأسعار
20 glove stand حامِل القفازات
21 duffle coat, a three-quarter length coat معْطَف "دوفيل"
22 escalator سُلَّم متحرك
23 fluorescent light (fluorescent lamp) مصباح فلورسنتي
24 office (e.g. customer accounts office, travel agency, manager's office) مكْتَب (مثلا: مكْتَب حسابات العملاء، وكيل سياحي، مكْتَب المدير)
25 poster (advertisement) إعلان (بوستر)
26 theatre (*Am.* theater) and concert booking office (advance booking office) مكْتَب حجز تذاكر المسرح والحفلات الموسيقية (مكْتَب الحجز المُسْبَق)
27 shelves أرْفُف
28 ladies' wear department قسم الملابس النِّسَائيَّة

29 ready-made dress (ready-to-wear dress, *coll.* off-the-peg dress) ثوب/فستان جاهز

30 dust cover غطاء واقٍ من الغبار

31 clothes rack شمَّاعة الملابس

32 changing booth (fitting booth) حجيرة قياس الملابس

33 mirror مرآة

34 dummy دُمْيَة

35 seat (chair) مَقْعَد (كُرْسيّ)

36 fashion journal (fashion magazine) مجلة أزياء

37 tailor marking a hemline خيَّاط يضع علامة على كُفَّة الثوب

38 measuring tape (tape measure) شريط قياس

39 tailor's chalk (French chalk) طباشيرة الخيَّاط

40 hemline marker أداة تعليم كفَّة الثوب

41 loose-fitting coat معْطَف واسع

42 sales counter كاونتر المبيعات

43 warm-air curtain ستارة الهواء الدافئ

44 stairs سُلَّم، دَرَج

45 lift (*Am.* elevator) مِصْعَد

46 lift cage (lift car, *Am.* elevator car) صَنْدُوق المِصْعَد (عَرَبَة المِصْعَد)

47 direction indicators لمْبَات إرْشاديَّة للطَوَابِق

48 controls (lift controls, *Am.* elevator controls) مفاتيح التحكم

49 floor indicator مؤشِّر الطابق

50 sliding door باب منزلق

51 lift shaft (*Am.* elevator shaft) بِئْر المِصْعَد

52 bearer cable كبل حمل

53 control cable كبل التحكم

54 guide rail مسار دليلي

55 customer زبون، عميل

56 hosiery الملابس الداخليَّة والجوارب

57 linen goods (table linen and bed linen) مفروشات (مفروشات المائدة والسرير)

58 fabric department قسم الأقمشة

59 roll of fabric (roll of material, roll of cloth) ثوب/ لفافة قماش

60 head of department (department manager) رئيس القسم (مدير القسم)

61 sales counter كاونتر المبيعات

62 jewellery (*Am.* jewelry) department قسم الحُلِيّ والمجوهرات

63 customer assistant بائعة لمُسَاعَدَة الزبائن

64 special counter (extra counter) كاونتر خاص (كاونتر إضافي)

65 placard advertising special offers لَوْحَة إعلانات تعلن عروضاً خاصة

66 curtain department قسم الستائر

67 display on top of the shelves معروضات فوق الأرَفّ

272 Park المُنْتَزَه

1-40 formal garden **حَدِيقة فرنسيَّة** (حَدِيقة باروكيَّة)
(French Baroque garden), palace gardens

1 grotto (cavern) مَغَارَة (كَهْف طبيعي أو صناعي)

2 stone statue, a river nymph تِمْثَال حَجَري على شكل حوريَّة الماء

3 orangery (orangerie) دَفيئَة البرتقال: بَيْت زجاجي لزراعة البرتقال في المناطق البارِدَة

4 boscage (boskage) أيكَة، أجمة

5 maze (labyrinth of paths and hedges) مَتَاهَة (مَتَاهَة من الممرات والسياجات)

6 open-air theatre (*Am.* theater) مَسْرَح مكشوف

7 Baroque palace قَصْر باروكي

8 fountains نافورات

9 cascade (broken artificial waterfall, artificial falls) شلال (مسقط مياه صناعي)

10 statue, a monument تِمْثَال

11 pedestal قاعدة التِّمْثَال

12 globe-shaped tree شَجَرَة مُقَلَّمَة بشكل كُرَويّ

13 conical tree شَجَرَة مُقَلَّمَة بشكل مخروطيّ

14 ornamental shrub شُجَيْرَة زينة

15 wall fountain نافورة جداريَّة

16 park bench أريكة الحَدِيقة

17 pergola (bower, arbour, *Am.* arbor) تَعْرِيشَة، تكعيبة

18 gravel path (gravel walk) مَمَر من الحصى

19 pyramid tree (pyramidal tree) شَجَرَة هرميَّة الشكل

20 cupid (cherub, amoretto, amorino) تِمْثَال كيوبيد (إلَه الحب)

21 fountain نافورة

22 fountain نَفْث من الماء

23 overflow basin حَوْض الماء الفائض

24 basin حَوْض

25 kerb (curb) حافة ناتئة

26 man out for a walk شخص خرج للتَّرَجُّل

27 tourist guide مُرْشِد سياحي

28 group of tourists مجموعة من السائحين

29 park by-laws (bye-laws) تعليمات الحَدِيقة

30 park keeper حارس الحَدِيقة

31 garden gates made of wrought iron بوَّابات الحَدِيقة مصنوعة من الحَدِيد المطاوع

32 park entrance مَدْخَل الحَدِيقة

33 park railings سُور الحَدِيقة

34 railing (bar) قضبان

35 stone vase زُهْرِيَّة حجريَّة

36 lawn أرْض عُشْبِيَّة

37 border, a trimmed (clipped) hedge حَدّ، سياج شجريّ مُشَذَّب

38 park path مَمْشَى الحَدِيقة

39 parterre أرْض مُعَشَّبَة بها أحواض للزهور

40 birch (birch tree) شَجَرَة البتولا أو السَّنْدَر

41-72 landscaped park (jardin anglais) **حَدِيقة على الطراز الإنجليزي**

41 flower bed	حَوْض زهور
42 park bench (garden seat)	أريكة الحَدِيقة
43 litter bin (*Am.* trash bin)	صفيحة/سلة المهملات
44 play area	منْطَقَة اللعب
45 stream	جَدْوَل مائي
46 jetty	رصيف مائي
47 bridge	جِسْر، كوبري
48 park chair	كُرْسيّ الحَدِيقة
49 animal enclosure	حظيرة حيوانات
50 pond	بِرْكَة ماء، بُحَيْرَة صغيرة
51-54 waterfowl	**طيور مائيَّة**
51 wild duck with young	بَطَّة بَرِّيَّة مع صغارها
52 goose	إوزة
53 flamingo	طائر البشروش، طائر الفلامنجو
54 swan	بَجَعَة
55 island	جزيرة
56 water lily	زهرة زَنْبَق الماء
57 open-air café	مَقْهَى مكشوف
58 sunshade	مِظَلَّة، تندة
59 park tree (tree)	شَجَرَة المنتزه (شَجَرَة)
60 treetop (crown)	تاج الشَّجَرَة
61 group of trees	مجموعة أشجار
62 fountain	نافورة
63 weeping willow	أشجار الصفصاف
64 modern sculpture	تِمْثَال على نمط الفن الحَدِيث
65 hothouse	دَفيئَة: مستنبت زجاجي مرتفع الحرارة
66 park gardener	بستاني الحَدِيقة
67 broom	مِكْنَسَة
68 minigolf course	مَلْعَب جولف صغير
69 minigolf player	لاعب جولف
70 minigolf hole	حفرة كُرَة الجولف
71 mother with pram (baby carriage)	أمّ تدفع عَرَبَة طفل
72 courting couple (young couple)	حبيبان

273 Children's Playground — مَلْعَب الأطْفَال

1 table tennis	تنس الطَّاولة
2 table	طاولة
3 table tennis net	شبكة تنس الطاولة
4 table tennis racket (raquet) (table tennis bat)	مِضْرَب تنس الطاولة
5 table tennis ball	كُرَة تنس الطاولة
6 badminton game (shuttlecock game)	لُعْبَة الريشة الطائرة
7 shuttlecock	الريشة الطائرة
8 maypole swing	أرْجُوحَة سارية نوَّار
9 child's bicycle	درَّاجة أطفال
10 football (soccer)	كُرَة القَدَم
11 goal (goalposts)	المَرْمَى
12 football	الكُرَة
13 goal scorer	الهدَّاف
14 goalkeeper	حارس المَرْمَى
15 skipping (*Am.* jumping rope)	قفز الحَبْل
16 skipping rope (*Am.* skip rope, jump rope, jumping rope)	حَبْل القفز
17 climbing tower	بُرْج التسلق
18 rubber tyre (*Am.* tire) swing	أرْجُوحَة من دولاب مطاطي
19 lorry tyre (*Am.* truck tire)	دولاب شاحنة
20 bouncing ball	كُرَة نطَّاطة
21 adventure playground	ملعب المغامرات
22 log ladder	سُلَّم من جذوع الشَّجَر
23 lookout platform	مِنَصَّة المراقبة
24 slide	زُحْلُوقَة
25 litter bin (*Am.* trash bin)	صندوق المهملات
26 teddy bear	دُبّ لُعْبَة
27 wooden train set	طاقم قطار خشبي
28 paddling pool	بِرْكَة ماء
29 sailing boat (yacht, *Am.* sailboat)	قارب شراعي
30 toy duck	بَطَّة لُعْبَة
31 pram (baby carriage)	عَرَبَة طفل
32 high bar (bar)	جِهاز العُقْلَة (عُقْلَة)
33 go-cart (soap box)	عَرَبَة تتحرك بالبدَّال
34 starter's flag	راية اعلان بداية السباق
35 seesaw	نَوَّاسَة (أرْجُوحَة)
36 robot	إنسان آلي، روبوت
37 flying model aeroplanes (*Am.* airplanes)	نماذج طائرات
38 model aeroplane (*Am.* airplane)	نموذج طائرة
39 double swing	أرْجُوحَة مزدوجة
40 swing seat	مَقْعَد الأرْجُوحَة
41 flying kites	طائرات ورقيَّة
42 kite	طائرة ورقيَّة
43 tail of the kite	ذيل الطائرة الورقيَّة
44 kite string	خيط الطائرة الورقيَّة
45 revolving drum	بِرْميل دَوَّار
46 spider's web	بَيْت العنكبوت
47 climbing frame	إطار التسلق
48 climbing rope	حَبْل التسلق
49 rope ladder	سُلَّم من الحبال
50 climbing net	شبكة التسلق
51 skateboard	لَوْح التزلج
52 up-and-down slide	زحلوقة متعرجة ارتفاعاً وهبوطاً
53 rubber tyre (*Am.* tire) cable car	عَرَبَة كيبلية ذات دولاب مطاطي
54 rubber tyre (*Am.* tire)	دولاب مطاطي
55 tractor, a pedal car	جرَّار، عَرَبَة تسير بالبدَّال
56 den	مَخْبَأ
57 presawn boards	ألواح خشبية جاهزة للتركيب
58 seat (bench)	مَقْعَد (أريكة)
59 Indian hut	كوخ هندي
60 climbing roof	سقف التسلق
61 flagpole (flagstaff)	صاري الراية
62 toy lorry (*Am.* toy truck)	شاحنة لُعْبَة

63 walking doll دُمْيَة متحركة
64 sandpit (*Am.* sandbox) حفرة مملوءة بالرمل
65 toy excavator (toy digger) حفّارة لُعْبَة
66 sandhill تَلّ رمليّ

274 Spa مُنْتَجَع المِيَاه المَعْدَنيَّة

1-21 spa gardens حَدَائق مَنتجع المياه المعدنية

1-7 salina (salt works) **المَلاّحة**
1 thorn house (graduation house) بَيْت الزعرور
2 thorns (brushwood) الزعرور: شُجَيْرَات شائكة من الفصيلة الورقيَّة
3 brine channels قَنَوَات الماء المالح
4 brine pipe from the pumping station أنْبُوبَة الماء المالح الواصِل من مَحَطَّة الضخ
5 salt works attendant عامِل المَلاّحة
6-7 inhalational therapy العلاج الاستنشاقي
6 open-air inhalatorium (outdoor inhalatorium) منْطَقَة العلاج الاستنشاقي المفتوحة
7 patient inhaling (taking an inhalation) مريض يقوم بالاستنشاق (يأخذ شهيقا)
8 hydropathic (pump room) with kursaal (casino) مبنى العلاج المائي (غرفة المِضَخَّة) وملحق به كازينو
9 colonnade صف أعمدة، رُوَاق مُعَمَّد
10 spa promenade التنزه في منتجع المياه المعدنية
11 avenue leading to the mineral spring طريق مؤدية إلى نبع المياه المعدنية
12-14 rest cure العلاج بالاستلقاء في الشمس
12 sunbathing area (lawn) منْطَقَة أخذ حمامات الشمس
13 deck-chair كرسيّ قماش
14 sun canopy مظَلَّة، تندة
15 pump room حُجْرَة المضَخَّة
16 rack for glasses رف للأكواب
17 tap حنفية، صنبور
18 patient taking the waters مريضة تتناول المياه
19 bandstand تَخْت الفرقة الموسيقيَّة (في الحدَائق العامة)
20 spa orchestra giving a concert الفرقة الموسيقيَّة التابعة للمنتجع وهى تعزف
21 conductor قائد الفرقة الموسيقيَّة

275 Roulette الرُوليت

1-33 roulette, a game of chance (gambling game) **لُعْبَة الروليت**، لُعْبَة حظ
1 gaming room in the casino (in the gambling casino) حجرة اللعب بالملْهَى (ملْهَى لعب القمار)
2 cash desk مكْتَب النقديَّة
3 tourneur (dealer) موظف تدوير عجلة الروليت (موظف بالكازينو)
4 croupier مدير الطاولة
5 rake ممْشَاط: آلة جمع النقود والفيش
6 head croupier رئيس مديري الطاولة
7 hall manager مدير القاعة
8 roulette table (gaming table, gambling table) طاولة الروليت
9 roulette layout رُقْعَة الروليت
10 roulette wheel عَجلَة الروليت
11 bank بنك
12 chip (check, plaque) فيشة
13 stake مال مُراهنَة
14 membership card بطاقة عضويَّة
15 roulette player لاعب الروليت
16 private detective (house detective) رَجُل أمن سري خاص (رَجُل أمن تابع للكازينو)
17 roulette layout رُقْعَة الروليت
18 zero (nought, 0) صفر
19 passe (high) [numbers 19 to 36] عابِر [الأرقام من 19 إلى 36]
20 pair (even numbers) زَوْج (الأرقام الزوجيَّة)
21 noir (black) أسود
22 manque (low) [numbers 1 to 18] مُخْفِق [الأرقام من 1 إلى 18]
23 impair [odd numbers] الأرقام الفرديَّة
24 rouge (red) أحمر
25 douze premier (first dozen) [numbers 1 to 12] الدستة الأولى [من رقم 1 إلى 12]
26 douze milieu (second dozen) [numbers 13 to 24] الدستة الثانية [من رقم 13 إلى 24]
27 douze dernier (third dozen) [numbers 25 to 36] الدستة الثالثة [من رقم 25 إلى 36]
28 roulette wheel (roulette) عَجلَة الروليت
29 roulette bowl إطار الروليت
30 fret (separator) زخرفة
31 revolving disc (disk) showing numbers 0 to 36 قرص دَوَّار يحمل الأرقام من صفر إلى 36
32 spin دَوَّارة
33 roulette ball كُرَة الروليت

276 Board Games and Party Games ألْعَاب الرقْعَات والألْعَاب الجَمَاعيَّة

1-16 chess, a game involving combinations of moves, a positional game **الشَطَرَنْج**
1 chessboard (board) with the men (chessmen) in position رُقْعَة الشطرنج وعليها القِطَع في مواضعها
2 white square (chessboard square) مربع أبيض
3 black square مربع أسود
4 white chessmen (white pieces) [white = W] قطعة من قطع الشطرنج البيضاء
5 black chessmen (black قطعة من قطع الشطرنج

pieces) [black = B]	السوداء
6 letters and numbers for designating chess squares in the notation of chess moves and chess problems	حروف وأرقام تحدّيد مربعات الشطرنج عند التنبيه إلى تحركات الشطرنج والمآزق
7 individual chessmen (individual pieces)	قطع الشطرنج الفردية
8 king	الملك
9 queen	الملِكَة (الوزير)
10 bishop	الفيل
11 knight	الحصان
12 rook (castle)	الطابية (الرخ)
13 pawn	البيدق
14 moves of the individual pieces	تحركات القطع الفرديَّة
15 mate (checkmate), a mate by knight	إماتة الملك بالحصان
16 chess clock, a double clock for chess matches (chess championships)	ساعة الشطرنج، ساعة مزدوجة لمباريات الشطرنج (بطولات الشطرنج)
17-19 draughts (*Am.* checkers)	**لُعْبَة الداما** (الضامة)
17 draughtboard (*Am.* checkerboard)	رقعة الداما
18 white draughtsman (*Am.* checker, checkerman); *also:* piece for backgammon and nine men's morris	قُشَاط أبيض؛ أيضاً: قشاط للطاولة ولُعْبَة المرية
19 black draughtsman (*Am.* checker, checkerman)	قُشاط أسود
20 salta	لُعْبَة السالتا (القفز)
21 salta piece	قطعة القفز
22 backgammon board	رُقْعَة الطاولة
23-25 nine men's morris	**لُعْبَة المرية**
23 nine men's morris board	رُقْعَة لُعْبَة المرية
24 mill	المِلّ
25 double mill	مِلّ مزدوج
26-28 halma	**لُعْبَة الهالما**
26 halma board	رُقْعَة الهالما
27 yard (camp, corner)	ساحة (معسكر، زاوية)
28 halma pieces (halma men) of various colours (*Am.* colors)	قِطَع الهالما مختلفة الألوان
29 dice (dicing)	النَّرْد
30 dice cup	كأس النَّرْد
31 dice	زهر النَّرْد
32 spots (pips)	نقط حَجَر الدومينو
33 dominoes	أحجار لعبة الدمينو
34 domino (tile)	دومينو (حَجَر)
35 double	حَجَر زَوْجي
36 playing cards	ورق اللعب (الكوتشينة)
37 playing card (card)	ورقة الكوتشينة (كارت)
38-45 suits	**نقوش ورق اللعب** (الكوتشينة)
38 clubs	السباتي
39 spades	البستوني
40 hearts	القلب (الكوبة)
41 diamonds	الديناري (الكاروه)
42-45 German suits	**نقوش الورق الألمانيَّة**
42 acorns	جوزة البلوط
43 leaves	ورقة الشجر
44 hearts	القلب
45 bells (hawkbells)	الجرس

277 Billiards — البلْيَارْدُو

1-19 billiards	**لُعْبَة البلْيَارْدُو**
1 billiard ball, an ivory or plastic ball	كُرَة البلْيَارْدُو، كُرَة من العاج أو البلاستيك
2-6 billiard strokes	**ضربات البلْيَارْدُو**
2 plain stroke (hitting the cue ball dead centre, *Am.* center)	ضَرْبَة عاديَّة (ضرب الكُرَة في مركزها الميت)
3 top stroke [promotes extra forward rotation]	ضَرْبَة علويَّة [لتوليد دوران أمامي إضافي]
4 screw-back [imparts a direct recoil or backward motion]	ضَرْبَة اللوْلبة العكسيَّة [تؤدي إلى حركة حلزونيَّة مباشرة أو حركة خلفيَّة]
5 side (running side, *Am.* English)	ضَرْبَة الجانب الأيسر
6 check side	ضَرْبَة الجانب الأيمن
7-19 billiard room (*Am.* billiard parlor, billiard saloon, poolroom)	**صالة البلْيَارْدُو**
7 billiards (English billiards); *sim.* pool, carrom (carrom billiards)	البلْيَارْدُو؛ (البلْيَارْدُو الإنجليزي)؛ بالمِثْل: البُولة
8 billiards player	لاعب البلْيَارْدُو
9 cue (billiard cue)	عصا البلْيَارْدُو
10 leather cue tip	طرف العصا المصنوع من الجلْد
11 white cue ball	الكُرَة البيضاء المدفوعة
12 red object ball	الكُرَة الحمراء المُسْتَهْدَفَة
13 white spot ball (white dot ball)	كُرَة النقطة البيضاء
14 billiard table	طاولة البلْيَارْدُو
15 table bed with green cloth (billiard cloth, green baize covering)	أرْضيَّة الطاولة ذات غطاء قماش أخضر
16 cushions (rubber cushions, cushioned ledge)	بطانة حافة طاولة البلْيَارْدُو
17 billiard clock, a timer	ساعة البلْيَارْدُو، جهاز توقيت
18 billiard marker	لوحة تسجيل نتائج البلْيَارْدُو
19 cue rack	رَفّ عصى البلْيَارْدُو

278 Camping and Caravanning (*Am.* Trailering) — إقامة المُخَيَّمات والكَرَفانات

1-59 camp site (camping site, *Am.* campground)	**مَوْقع المُخَيَّم/المُعَسْكَر**
1 reception (office)	قاعة الاستقبال

2 site warden	مُراقِب مَوْقع المُخَيَّم
3 folding trailer (collapsible caravan, collapsible trailer)	قطيرة قابلة للطي
4 hammock	أُرْجُوحَة شبكيَّة للنَّوْم
5-6 washing and toilet facilities	**مَرَافِق الغسيل والمراحيض**
5 toilets and washrooms (*Am.* lavatories)	المراحيض ودَوْرَات الغسيل
6 washbasins and sinks	أحواض الغسيل والبالوعات
7 bungalow (chalet)	البنغل (شاليه)
8-11 scout camp	**مُعَسْكَر الكشافة**
8 bell tent	خيمة ناقوسية الشكل
9 pennon	راية
10 camp fire	نار المُعَسْكَر
11 boy scout (scout)	صبي كشافة (كَشَّاف)
12 sailing boat (yacht, *Am.* sailboat)	قارب شراعي (يخت)
13 landing stage (jetty)	رصيف الإرساء (المَرْسَى)
14 inflatable boat (inflatable dinghy)	قارب نُفاخي
15 outboard motor (outboard)	مُحَرِّك خارجي بمؤخرة القارب
16 trimaran	زَوْرَق
17 thwart (oarsman's bench)	مَقْعَد المُجَدِّف
18 rowlock (oarlock)	مِسْنَد المِجْدَاف
19 oar	مِجْدَاف
20 boat trailer (boat carriage)	قَطِيرة القارب (عَرَبَة القارب)
21 ridge tent	خَيْمَة جبليَّة الشكل
22 flysheet	غطاء الخيمة الخارجي
23 guy line (guy)	شَدَّادة : حَبْل تثبيْت
24 tent peg (peg)	وَتَد نَصْب الخَيْمَة
25 mallet	مِطْرَقَة خشبية
26 groundsheet ring	حلقة تثبيْت فرش الأرْضية
27 bell end	طَرْف ناقوسي
28 erected awning	ظُلَّة منصوبة
29 storm lantern, a paraffin lamp	مِصْبَاح برافين
30 sleeping bag	كِيْس النوم
31 air mattress (inflatable air-bed)	مَرْتَبَة هوائيَّة
32 water carrier (drinking water carrier)	إناء الماء
33 double-burner gas cooker for propane gas or butane gas	جِهَاز طهي ذو مَوْقدَيْن يعمل بغاز البروبين أو البوتان
34 propane or butane gas bottle	أُسْطُوَانة غاز البروبين أو البوتان
35 pressure cooker	طَنْجَرَة طهي بالضغط
36 frame tent	خَيْمَة إطاريَّة
37 awning	ظُلَّة ، تندة
38 tent pole	قائم الخَيْمَة
39 wheelarch doorway	مدخل قوسي الشكل
40 mesh ventilator	فتحة تهوية شبكية الشكل
41 transparent window	نافذة شفافة
42 pitch number	رقم الخَيْمَة
43 folding camp chair	كرسي مخيم قابل للطي
44 folding camp table	طاولة مُخَيَّم قابلة للطي
45 camping eating utensils	لَوَازِم تناول الطعام في المُخَيَّم
46 camper	فَرْدٌ في المُخَيَّم
47 charcoal grill (barbecue)	شَوَّايَة تعمل بالفحم
48 charcoal	فَحْم
49 bellows	مِنْفَاخ
50 roof rack	شبكة سقف السيارة
51 roof lashing	حَبْل ربط أحمال فوق سقف السيارة
52 caravan (*Am.* trailer)	كَرَفَان (قطيرة)
53 box for gas bottle	صندوق أسطوانة الغاز
54 jockey wheel	عجلة القطيرة
55 drawbar coupling	مَقْرَن قضيب الجَرّ
56 roof ventilator	فتحة تهوية سقفيَّة
57 caravan awning	ظلة الكَرَفَان
58 inflatable igloo tent	خَيْمَة قُبِّيَّة قابلة للتمدد
59 camp bed (*Am.* camp cot)	سرير سَفَري يمكن طَيُّه

279 Surf Riding (Surfing), Skin Diving — رُكُوب الأمْوَاج ، الغَوْص

1-6 surf riding (surfing)	**ركوب الأمْوَاج المُتَكَسِّرَة**
1 plan view of surfboard	منظر أفقي للوح ركوب الأمْوَاج المُتَكَسِّرَة
2 section of surfboard	مقطع عرضي للوح ركوب الأمْوَاج المُتَكَسِّرَة
3 skeg (stabilizing fin)	زعنفة مُوَازَنَة
4 big wave riding	ركوب الأمْوَاج العالية
5 surfboarder (surfer)	راكب الأمْوَاج المُتَكَسِّرَة
6 breaker	مَوْجَة عارِمة
7-27 skin diving (underwater swimming)	**الغَوْص**
7 skin diver (underwater swimmer)	غوَّاص/غطاس
8-22 underwater swimming set	**طاقم جِهَاز السباحة تحت الماء**
8 knife	سكين
9 neoprene wetsuit	لِبَاس غَوْص مطاطيّ (من مادة النيوبرين)
10 diving mask (face mask, mask), a pressure-equalizing mask	قِنَاع الغوص
11 snorkel (schnorkel)	الشنركل: أُنْبُوب التنفس أثناء السباحة تحت الماء
12 harness of diving apparatus	أحْزِمَة تثبيْت جِهَاز الغوص
13 compressed-air pressure gauge (*Am.*gage)	مقياس ضغط الهواء المضغوط
14 weight belt	حزام الثِّقْل
15 depth gauge (*Am.* gage)	مِقْيَاس العمق
16 waterproof watch for checking duration of dive	ساعة ضد الماء لمتابعة فترة الغوص

17 decometer for measuring stages of ascent — ديكومتر لقياس مراحل الصعود
18 fin (flipper) — زعنفة
19 diving apparatus (aqualung, scuba) with two cylinders (bottles) — جِهَاز غوص ذو أسطوانتيْن
20 two-tube demand regulator — مُنَظِّم دفق الهواء ذو أنْبُوبتيْن
21 compressed-air cylinder (compressed-air bottle) — أُسْطُوَانة هواء مضغوط
22 on/off valve — صمام الفتح/القفل
23 underwater photography — التصوير تحت الماء
24 underwater camera — كاميرا للتصوير تحت الماء
25 underwater flashlight — فلاش للتصوير تحت الماء
26 exhaust bubbles — فُقَاعَات الهواء المُسْتَنْفَذ
27 inflatable boat (inflatable dinghy) — قارب نُفَّاخي

280 Bathing Beach — شَاطِيء الاسْتِحْمَام

1 lifesaver (lifeguard) — غَطَّاس/سَبَّاح (مُنْقِذ المشرفين على الغرَق)
2 lifeline — حَبْل الانقاذ
3 lifebelt (lifebuoy) — طَوْق النجاة من الغرَق
4 storm signal — إشارة العاصفة
5 time ball — كُرَة الوقت
6 warning sign — لافتة تحذير
7 tide table, a notice board showing times of low tide and high tide — لَوْحة إعلان أوقات المَدّ والجَزْر
8 board showing water and air temperature — لَوْحة اعلان درجتي حرارة المياه والجَوّ
9 bathing platform — لسان الاستحمام
10 pennon staff — صاري الراية
11 pennon — راية
12 paddle boat (pedal boat) — قَارِب بعجلات تجديف
13 surf riding (surfing) behind motorboat — ركوب الأمْوَاج المُتَكَسِّرَة خلف قَارب بمُحَرِّك
14 surfboarder (surfer) — راكِب الأمْوَاج المُتَكَسِّرَة
15 surfboard — لَوْح ركوب الأمْوَاج المُتَكَسِّرَة
16 water ski — التزحلق فوق الماء
17 inflatable beach mattress — مَرْتَبَة شاطئ نُفَّاخية
18 beach ball — كُرَة البحر
19-23 beachwear — **لِبَاس الشاطئ**
19 beach suit — بِذْلة شاطئ
20 beach hat — قُبَّعَة شاطئ
21 beach jacket — سُتْرَة شاطئ
22 beach trousers — سِرْوَال شاطئ
23 beach shoe (bathing shoe) — حذاء شاطئ
24 beach bag — حقيبة شاطئ
25 bathing gown (bathing wrap) — عَبَاءة الاستحمام (البُرنس)
26 bikini (ladies' two-piece bathing suit) — مايوه بكيني: لباس استحمام من قطعتيْن للسيدات
27 bikini bottom — القطعة السفليَّة من البكيني
28 bikini top — القطعة العلويَّة من البكيني
29 bathing cap (swimming cap) — طاقية الاستحمام
30 bather — سابح، مُسْتَحِم
31 deck tennis (quoits) — لُعْبَة الكُتّ
32 rubber ring (quoit) — حلقة مطاطيَّة (الكُتّ)
33 inflatable rubber animal — لُعْبَة مطاطيَّة بشكل حيوان قابلة للنفخ
34 beach attendant — مراقب الشاطئ
35 sand castle — قلعة من الرمال
36 roofed wicker beach chair — كُرْسيّ شاطئ مَسْقُوف مصنوع من الأمْلُود
37 underwater swimmer — غَوَّاص
38 diving goggles — نظارات الغَوْص
39 snorkel (schnorkel) — الشنركل
40 hand harpoon (fish spear, fish lance) — حَرْبَة يدويَّة (رُمْح لاصطياد السمك)
41 fin (flipper) for diving (for underwater swimming) — زِعْنِفَة الغَوْص
42 bathing suit (swimsuit) — لِباس الاستحمام، مايوه
43 bathing trunks (swimming trunks) — لِباس بحر للرِّجَال
44 bathing cap (swimming cap) — طاقيَّة الاستحمام
45 beach tent, a ridge tent — خَيْمَة الشاطئ
46 lifeguard station — مركز انقاذ الغَرْقَى

281 Swimming Bath (Leisure Centre, *Am.* Center) — حَمَّام السباحة (مَرْكَز تَرْفيهي)

1-9 wave pool, an indoor pool — **حَمَّام سَبَّاحة ذو أمْوَاج اصطناعية**، حَمام سباحة مُغطًّى
1 artificial waves — أمْوَاج اصطناعية
2 beach area — مِنْطَقَة الشاطئ
3 edge of the pool — حافة حَمَّام/بِرْكَة السباحة
4 swimming pool attendant (pool attendant, swimming bath attendant) — مُراقب حَمَّام/بِرْكَة السباحة
5 sun bed — مَقْعَد الاستلقاء في الشمس، مَقْعَد الحَمَّام الشمسي
6 lifebelt — طَوْق نجاة
7 water wings — عوَّامتان لمساعدة المبتدىء على السباحة
8 bathing cap — طاقية الإستحمام
9 channel to outdoor mineral bath — قناة تؤدي الى بركة مياه معدنية خارجية (مكشوفة)
10 solarium — المَشْمَس
11 sunbathing area — مِنْطَقَة تعريض الجسم للشمس (الحَمَّام الشمسي)
12 sunbather — أحد المستلقين في الحَمَّام الشمسي
13 sun ray lamp — طاقة دخول الأشعة الشمسية
14 bathing towel — مِنْشَفَة استحمام، بَشْكِير
15 nudist sunbathing area — مِنْطَقَة الحمام الشمسي

	للعُرَاة
16 nudist (naturist)	شخص عار
17 screen (fence)	حاجز (سياج)
18 mixed sauna	حمَّام ساونا مُخْتَلَط
19 wood panelling (*Am.* paneling)	تكسية من الألواح الخشبية
20 tiered benches	نضد متعدد الدَّرَجَات
21 sauna stove	مَوْقِد الساونا
22 stones	حِجَارَة
23 hygrometer	هايجرومتر: جهاز قياس الرطوبة النسبيَّة في الجَوّ
24 thermometer	ترمومتر : مقياس الحرارة
25 towel	منْشَفَة
26 water tub for moistening the stones in the stove	حَوْض خشبي لترطيب حجارة المَوْقِد
27 birch rods (birches) for beating the skin	عيدان من خشب السندر لضرب البشرة
28 cooling room for cooling off (cooling down) after the sauna	حُجْرَة تبريد الجسم بعد الساونا
29 lukewarm shower	دُشّ دافئ
30 cold bath	حمام بارد
31 hot whirlpool (underwater massage bath)	حَمَّام تدليك دوامي ساخن (حَمَّام تدليك تحت الماء)، جاكوزي
32 step into the bath	عتبة الحَمَّام
33 massage bath	حَمَّام التدليك
34 jet blower	نافورة نفَّاثة
35 hot whirlpool (diagram)	رسم تخطيطي لحَمَّام التدليك الدوَّامي الساخن
36 section of the bath	قطاع من الحَمَّام
37 step	دَرَجَة (عتبة)
38 circular seat	مَقْعَد دائري
39 water extractor	فتحة خروج الماء
40 water jet pipe	أنْبُوب نفث الماء (نافورة)
41 air jet pipe	أنْبُوب نفث الهواء

282 Swimming — السِّباحة

1-32 swimming pool, an open-air swimming pool	**حَمَّام السباحة**، حَمَّام سَبَّاحة مكشوف
1 changing cubicle	مقصورة تغيير الملابس
2 shower (shower bath)	الدُشّ
3 changing room	غرفة تغيير الملابس
4 sunbathing area	منْطَقَة الحَمَّام الشمسي
5-10 diving boards (diving apparatus)	**منَصَّات/ألواح الغطس** (جهاز الغَطْس)
5 diver (highboard diver)	غاطس
6 diving platform	منَصَّة الغَطْس
7 ten-metre (*Am.* ten-meter) platform	منَصَّة الغَطْس من ارتفاع عشرة أمتار (سُلَّم ثابت)
8 five-metre (*Am.* five-meter) platform	منَصَّة الغَطْس من ارتفاع خمسة أمتار (سُلَّم ثابت)
9 three-metre (*Am.* three-meter) springboard (diving board)	لَوْحة الغَطْس من ارتفاع ثلاثة أمتار (سُلَّم متحرك)
10 one-metre (*Am.* one-meter) springboard	منَصَّة الغَطْس من ارتفاع متر واحد (سُلَّم متحرك)
11 diving pool	حمَّام الغَطْس
12 straight header	القَفْز والجسم في وضع الاستقامة (قَفْزة مستقيمة)
13 feet-first jump	قَفْزة دخول الماء بالقدمين أولاً
14 tuck jump (haunch jump)	قَفْزة مكَوَّرَة
15 swimming pool attendant (pool attendant, swimming bath attendant)	مُراقب حمَّام السباحة
16-20 swimming instruction	**تعليم السباحة**
16 swimming instructor (swimming teacher)	مُدَرِّب السباحة
17 learner-swimmer	شخص يتعلم السباحة
18 float; *sim.:* water wings	طَوْف، عوَّامتان لمساعدة المبتدىء على السباحة
19 swimming belt (cork jacket)	حِزَام السباحة (سترة فلينية)
20 land drill	تدريب على الأرض
21 non-swimmers' pool	حَمَّام سباحة للتعليم فقط
22 footbath	مَمْشى
23 swimmers' pool	حَمَّام سباحة للسَبَّاحين
24-32 freestyle relay race	**سباق السباحة الحرة**
24 timekeeper (lane timekeeper)	الميقاتي
25 placing judge	قاضي الوصول
26 turning judge	قاضي الدَّوَرَان
27 starting block (starting place)	مِنَصَّة البدء
28 competitor touching the finishing line	مُنَافِس يلمس خَطّ النهاية
29 starting dive (racing dive)	قَفْزة الغَطْس في بدء السباق
30 starter	حكَم الانطلاق
31 swimming lane	حارة السباحة
32 rope with cork floats	حَبْل مزوَّد بطوافات فلينية
33-39 swimming strokes	**الضربات المنتظمة للذراعين في السباحة**
33 breaststroke	ضَرْبَة سباحة الصدر
34 butterfly stroke	ضَرْبَة سباحة الفراشة
35 dolphin butterfly stroke	ضَرْبَة سباحة الفراشة الدولفينية
36 side stroke	ضَرْبَة السباحة الجانبيَّة
37 crawl stroke (crawl); *sim.:* trudgen stroke (trudgen, double overarm stroke)	ضَرْبَة سباحة الكرول، السباحة الحرة
38 diving (underwater swimming)	الغَوْص (السباحة تحت الماء)
39 treading water	المَشْي في الماء
40-45 diving (acrobatic diving, fancy diving, competitive diving, highboard diving)	**الغَطْس** (الغَطْس الاكروباتي /مسابقات الغَطْس)
40 standing take-off pike dive	قَفْزة من وضع الوقوف ثم الارتقاء
41 one-half twist isander	قَفْزة مع نصف دَوْرَة (قَفْزة

(reverse dive) عكسيَّة)
42 backward somersault (double backward somersault) قَفْزة السمرسولت الخلفيَّة (دَوْرَة ونصف خلفية مكَوَّرَة)
43 running take-off twist dive قَفْزة مع لفة كاملة من وضع الجري والارتقاء
44 screw dive قَفْز مع اللف حول المِحْوَر
45 armstand dive (handstand dive) القَفْز من وضع الوقوف على اليدَيْن

6-50 water polo **كُرَة الماء**
46 goal المَرْمَى
47 goalkeeper حارس المرمى
48 water polo ball الكُرَة (كُرَة الماء)
49 back مُدَافع، ظهير
50 forward مُهاجِم

283 Rowing and Canoeing التَّجْديف وسِبَاقَات التَّجْديف

1-18 taking up positions for the regatta **أخذ الأماكن استعداداً لبدء السباق**
1 punt, a pleasure boat البُنْط ، قَارِب للتنزه ذو قاع مُسَطَّح يُدْفَع بواسطة عصا طويلة تمس قاع النهر
2 motorboat قَارِب بمُحَرِّك
3 Canadian canoe قَارِب الكَنُو الكندي
4 kayak (Alaskan canoe, slalom canoe), a canoe قَارِب الكَيَّاك
5 tandem kayak كَيَّاك زَوْجِيّ
6 outboard motorboat (outboard speedboat, outboard) قَارِب بمُحَرِّك خارجي (في مؤخرته)
7 outboard motor (outboard) مُحَرِّك خارجي بمؤخرة القَارِب
8 cockpit كابينة القيادة
9-16 racing boats (sportsboats) **قَوَارِب السباق**
9-15 shells (rowing boats, *Am.* rowboats) **قَوَارِب التجديف**
9 coxless four, a carvel-built boat قَارِب رباعي بدون قائد دَفَّة
10 eight (eight-oared racing shell) قَارِب ثماني مع قائد دَفَّة
11 cox قائد الدَّفَّة
12 stroke, an oarsman فَرْد جدَّاف، مُجَدِّف
13 bow ('number one') المُجَدِّف الأمامي
14 oar مِجْدَاف
15 coxless pair قَارِب زَوْجي بدون قائد دَفَّة
16 single sculler (single skuller, racing sculler, racing skuller, skiff) قَارِب فَرْدي
17 scull (skull) مِجْدَاف صغير
18 coxed single, a clinker-built single قَارِب فَرْدي بقائد دَفَّة
19 jetty (landing stage) مَنَصَّة إرساء، رصيف
20 rowing coach مدرِّب تجديف
21 megaphone ميجافون : مكبر صوت
22 quayside steps درجات سُلَّم الرصيف
23 clubhouse (club) مَبْنَى النادي
24 boathouse عنبر القَوَارِب
25 club's flag راية النادي
26-33 four-oared gig, a touring boat **قَارِب الجيغ الرباعي**
26 oar مِجْدَاف
27 cox's seat مَقْعَد قائد الدَّفَّة
28 thwart (seat) مَقْعَد متحرك للمُجَدِّف
29 rowlock (oarlock) ماسك المِجْدَاف (الشكرمة)
30 gunwale (gunnel) الشَّفير : الحافة العليا لجانب القَارِب
31 rising لَوْح عمودي لربط الضلوع
32 keel رافدة القص، صالب القاعدة
33 skin (shell, outer skin) [clinker-built] القشرة الخارجية للقَارِب
34 single-bladed paddle (paddle) مِجْدَاف ذو كَفَّة واحدة
35-38 oar (scull, skull) **مِجْدَاف**
35 grip مَقْبَض
36 leather sheath غلاف جِلْدِيّ
37 shaft (neck) ساق (عنق)
38 blade كَفَّة المِجْدَاف
39 double-bladed paddle (double-ended paddle) مِجْدَاف ذو كفتيْن
40 drip ring حلقة ناتئة لِرَدّ قطرات الماء
41-50 sliding seat **مَقْعَد منزلق/متحرك**
41 rowlock (oarlock) ماسك المِجْدَاف (الشكرمة)
42 outrigger ذراع امتداد عرضي
43 saxboard حافة مستوية
44 sliding seat مَقْعَد منزلق/متحرك
45 runner مَجْرَى انزلاق المَقْعَد
46 strut دعامة انضغاطية
47 stretcher عارضة ممتدة
48 skin (shell, outer skin) القشرة الخارجية للقَارِب
49 frame (rib) هيكل (ضِلْع)
50 kelson (keelson) الكلسون:عارضة طولية تشد فوق رافدة القص
51-53 rudder (steering rudder) **الدَّفَّة** (دفة توجيه القَارِب)
51 yoke مِقْرن
52 lines (steering lines) حَبْلان (حَبْلا التوجيه)
53 blade (rudder blade, rudder) راحَة الدَّفَّة (الدَّفَّة)
54-66 folding boats (foldboats, canoes) **قَوَارِب قابلة للطي**
54 one-man kayak كيَّاك فَرْدي
55 canoeist مُجَدِّف قَارِب الكَنُو
56 spraydeck سطح احتجاز رذاذ الماء
57 deck ظهر القَارِب
58 rubber-covered canvas hull بَدَن القَارِب مصنوع من قماش القَنَب مُغطى بالمطاط
59 cockpit coaming (coaming) حِتَار القَارِب
60 channel for rafts alongside weir قناة الأطْوَاف بامتداد سد
61 two-seater folding kayak, a touring kayak كيَّاك زَوْجي قابل للطي، قَارِب كيَّاك للتنزه
62 sail of folding kayak شراع الكيَّاك القابل للطي
63 leeboard لَوْح جانب القَارِب

	المحجوّب من الريح
64 bag for the rods	حقيبة القضبان
65 rucksack	حقيبة الظهر
66 boat trailer (boat carriage)	عربة قطر القارِب
67 frame of folding kayak	إطار كياك قابل للطي
68-70 kayaks	**قَوارِب الكيَّاك**
68 Eskimo kayak	كيَّاك الاسكيمو
69 wild-water racing kayak	كيَّاك السباق في المياه المضطربة
70 touring kayak	كيَّاك التَّنَزُّه

284 Sailing I — الإبْحَار الشِّرَاعيّ (1)

1-9 windsurfing	**الركْمَجَة الرِّيَاحيَّة**
1 windsurfer	راكِب الركْمَجَة الرِّيَاحيَّة
2 sail	شِرَاع
3 transparent window (window)	نافذة شفَّافة
4 mast	صاري
5 surfboard	لَوْح الركْمَجَة
6 universal joint (movable bearing) for adjusting the angle of the mast and for steering	وَصْلَة عامة لتعديل زاوية الصاري والتَّوْجيه
7 wishbone	تُرْقُوَة
8 retractable centreboard (*Am.* centerboard)	لَوْح مركزي قابل للضمّ
9 rudder	دَفَّة
10-48 yacht (sailing boat, *Am.* sailboat)	**اليَخْت** (قارِب شِرَاعي)
10 foredeck	سطح أمامي
11 mast	صاري
12 trapeze	شِرَاع مُعَيَّنيّ الشكل
13 crosstrees (spreader)	منَصَّات الصاري
14 hound	مَرْبط حَبْل التثبيت الأمامي بالصاري
15 forestay	الحَبْل الأمامي لتثبيت الصاري
16 jib (Genoa jib)	شِرَاع السارية الأماميَّة
17 jib downhaul	مِنْكاس ذراع السارية الأماميَّة
18 side stay (shroud)	سناد جانبي
19 lanyard (*also:* turnbuckle)	شَدَّادَة
20 foot of the mast	قاعدة الصاري
21 kicking strap (vang)	شريط المقاومة
22 jam cleat	مَرْبط تثبيت
23 foresheet (jib sheet)	حَبْل ذراع السارية الأماميَّة
24 centreboard (*Am.* centerboard) case	صندوق اللَوْح المركزي
25 bitt	مَرْبط الحِبَال
26 centreboard (*Am.* centerboard)	اللَوْح المركزي
27 traveller (*Am.* traveler)	قَضيب المُتَرَحِّلَة
28 mainsheet	حَبْل الشِّرَاع الرئيسي
29 foresheet fairlead (jib fairlead)	دليل حَبْل الشِّرَاع الأمامي
30 toestraps (hiking straps)	سيُور الرَّفْع
31 tiller extension (hiking stick)	امتداد ذراع الدَّفَّة
32 tiller	ذراع الدَّفَّة
33 rudderhead (rudder stock)	عاضِد الدَّفَّة
34 rudder blade (rudder)	راحَة الدَّفَّة
35 transom	رافِدة أُفُقيَّة
36 drain plug	سدادة تصريف
37 gooseneck	عُنُق إوزَّة
38 window	نافذة، شبَّاك
39 boom	ذراع تطويل قاعدة الشِّرَاع
40 foot	قاعدة الشِّرَاع
41 clew	الكظامَة
42 luff (leading edge)	حَافَة الشِّرَاع الأماميَّة
43 leech pocket (batten cleat, batten pocket)	جيب الضلع العمودي في الشِّرَاع
44 batten	شريحة خَشَبية
45 leech (trailing edge)	ضِلْع حَافَة الشِّرَاع
46 mainsail	الشِّرَاع الرئيسي
47 headboard	اللَوْحة الرأسية بالشِّرَاع
48 racing flag (burgee)	راية السباق
49-65 yacht classes	**فئات اليخُوت**
49 Flying Dutchman	فلاينج داتشمان
50 O-Joller	أو–جوللر
51 Finn dinghy (Finn)	الفِنّ
52 pirate	البايْرَات
53 12.00 m^2 sharpie	شارْبي 12 م²
54 tempest	تمْبِسْت
55 star	ستَار
56 soling	سُولِنغ
57 dragon	دراجُون
58 5.5-metre (*Am.* 5.5-meter) class	يَخْت فئة 5ر5 م
59 6-metre (*Am.* 6-meter) R-class	يَخْت فئة آر–6 أمتار
60 30.00 m^2 cruising yacht (coastal cruiser)	يَخْت ساحلي 30 م²
61 30.00 m^2 dinghy cruiser	زَوْرَق تَنَزُّه 30 م²
62 25.00 m^2 one-design keelboat	زَوْرَق الكَلْبَت 25 م²
63 KR-class	فئة كيه آر
64 catamaran	القَطْمَران
65 twin hull	بَدَن مزدوج

285 Sailing II — الإبْحَار الشِّرَاعيّ (2)

1-13 points of sailing and wind directions	**الإبْحار بمحاذاة الريح واتجاهات الريح**
1 sailing downwind (running)	الإبْحار تجاه الريح
2 mainsail	الشِّرَاع الرئيسي
3 jib	شِرَاع السارية الأماميَّة
4 sails set goose-winged	أشرِعة منشورة بشكل جناح إوزة
5 centre (*Am.* center) line	خَطّ المنتصف
6 wind direction	اتجاه الريح
7 yacht stopped head to wind	يَخْت مُتوَقف ومقدمته قبالة الريح
8 sail, shivering	شِرَاع يَرْتَجِف
9 luffing	إدارة رأس القارب نحو

الريح

10 sailing close-hauled — الإبْحار في اتجاه مُعاكِس للريح جَهْدَ الإمكان

11 sailing with wind abeam — الإبْحار والريح مقابلة لمنتصف جانب القارب

12 sailing with free wind — الإبْحار في رياح حرة الاتجاه

13 quartering wind (quarter wind) — ريح تهُب على جزء من جانب القارب قريب من مُؤخَّرته

14-24 regatta course — **مضْمار سباق القوارب**

14 starting and finishing buoy — عوَّامة بدء وانهاء السباق

15 committee boat — قارب لجنة السباق

16 triangular course (regatta course) — مِضْمار مُثَلَّثي (مِضْمار السباق)

17 buoy (mark) to be rounded — عوَّامة يتم الدوران حولها

18 buoy to be passed — عوَّامة يتم اجتيازها

19 first leg — المرحلة الأولى

20 second leg — المرحلة الثانية

21 third leg — المرحلة الثالثة

22 windward leg — مرحلة مواجهة هبوب الريح

23 downwind leg — مرحلة في اتجاه هبوب الريح

24 reaching leg — مرحلة بلوغ منتصف المسافة

25-28 tacking — **تغيير اتجاه القارب**

25 tack — وجْهَة القارب

26 gybing (jibing) — انحراف الشِّراع من جانب إلى آخر فجأة

27 going about — انطلاق القارب

28 loss of distance during the gybe (jibe) — فقدان المسافة أثناء انحراف الشِّراع

29-41 types of yacht hull — **أنواع بدَن اليَخْت**

29-34 cruiser keelboat — **كَلْبَت التَّنَزُّه**

29 stern — كَوْثَل

30 spoon bow — مُقَدَّم مِلْعَقي

31 waterline — خَطّ الماء

32 keel (ballast keel) — رافدة القص

33 ballast — صابورة

34 rudder — دَفَّة

35 racing keelboat — كَلْبَت سباق

36 lead keel — رافدة قص متقدمة

37-41 keel-centreboard (*Am.* centerboard) **yawl** — **يَوْل برافدة قص ولَوْح مركزي**

37 retractable rudder — دَفَّة قابلة للضَّمّ

38 cockpit — كابينة القيادة

39 cabin superstructure (cabin) — أجزاء الكابينة

40 straight stem — جُؤْجُؤ مستقيم

41 rectractable centre-board (*Am.* center-board) — لَوْح مركزي قابل للضَّم

42-49 types of yacht stern — **أنواع كَوْثَل اليَخْت**

42 yacht stern — كَوْثَل يَخْت

43 square stern — كَوْثَل مُرَبَّع

44 canoe stern — كَوْثَل الكنْو

45 cruiser stern — كَوْثَل زَوْرَق التَّنَزُّه

46 name plate — لَوْحة الاسم

47 deadwood — خَشَب يابِس

48 transom stern — كَوْثَل برافدة أفقيَّة

49 transom — رافدة أفقيَّة

50-57 timber planking — **التَّلْويح**

50-52 clinker planking (clench planking) — **تَلْويح مُتَراكِب**

50 outside strake — صفيفة ألواح طوليَّة خارجيَّة

51 frame (rib) — ضِلع

52 clenched nail (riveted nail) — مِسمار مُثَبَّت بإحكام

53 carvel planking — تَلْويح انسيابي

54 ribband-carvel construction — تَلْويح انسيابي مع ضِمامَة

55 ribband, a stringer — ضِمامَة

56 diagonal carvel planking — تَلْويح انسيابي مائل

57 inner planking — تَلْويح داخلي

286 Motorboats (Powerboats), Water Skiing — القَوَارِب البُخَارِيَّة، رياضة الانزلاقَ على سطح الماء

1-5 motorboats (power-boats, sportsboats) — **القَوَارِب البُخَارِيَّة**

1 inflatable sportsboat with outboard motor (outboard inflatable) — قَارب نُفَّاخي ذو موتور خارِجي بالمؤخرة

2 Z-drive motorboat (outdrive motorboat) — قَارب بُخاري بمُحَرِّك زودياك خارجي

3 cabin cruiser — طَوَّاف ذو كابينة قيادة

4 motor cruiser — طَوَّاف ذو مُحَرِّك

5 30-metre (*Am.* 30-meter) oceangoing cruiser — طَوَّاف للإبحار في المحيطات طوله 30مترا

6 association flag — راية الرابطة/النقابة

7 name of craft (*or:* registration number) — اسم القَارب (أو رقم التسجيل)

8 club membership and port of registry (*Am.* home port) — عضوية النادي وميناء التسجيل

9 association flag on the starboard crosstrees — راية الرابطة فوق منصة الصاري الأيمن

10-14 navigation lights of sportsboats in coastal and inshore waters — **أضْواء الملاحة بالقَوَارِب في المياه الساحلية وقرب الساحل**

10 white top light — ضَوْء أبيض علوي

11 green starboard side-light — ضَوْء أخضر جانبي في الميمنة

12 red port sidelight — ضَوْء أحمر جانبي

13 green and red bow light (combined lantern) — ضَوْء مقدمة القَارب الأخضر والأحمر (فانوس مزدوج)

14 white stern light — ضَوْء مؤخرة السفينة الأبيض

15-18 anchors — **أنواع المِرْسَاة**

15 stocked anchor (Admiralty anchor), a — مِرسَاة هِلْبِيَّة

bower anchor	
16-18 lightweight anchor	**مِرْسَاة خفيفة الوزن**
16 CQR anchor (plough, *Am.* plow, anchor)	مِرْسَاة مِحْراثيَّة
17 stockless anchor (patent anchor)	مِرْسَاة بدون عاضِد/ عارضة
18 Danforth anchor	مِرْسَاة دانفورث
19 life raft	طَوْف النجاة
20 life jacket	سُتْرَة النجاة
21-44 powerboat racing	**سباق القَوَارِب البُخَاريَّة**
21 catamaran with outboard motor	القَطَمَرَان: طَوَّاف ذو مُحَرِّك بالمؤخرة
22 hydroplane	الطائرة المائية : زَوْرَق بُخاري سريع
23 racing outboard motor	مُحَرِّك المؤخرة لقَارِب السباق
24 tiller	ذراع الدفة
25 fuel pipe	أُنْبُوب الوقود
26 transom	رافدة مستعرضة
27 buoyancy tube	أُنْبُوبة الطَّفْو
28 start and finish	البداية والنهاية
29 start	البداية
30 starting and finishing line	خَطّ البداية والنهاية
31 buoy to be rounded	طافِيَة يُدَار حولها
32-37 displacement boats	**قَوَارِب تعمل بنظام إزاحة الماء**
32-34 round-bilge boat	**قَارِب مستدير الجَوَف**
32 view of hull bottom	منظر قاع بَدَن القَارِب
33 section of fore ship	قطاع مقدمة القَارِب
34 section of aft ship	قطاع مؤخرة القَارِب
35-37 V-bottom boat (vee-bottom boat)	**قَارِب ذو قاع على شكل v**
35 view of hull bottom	منظر قاع بَدَن القَارِب
36 section of fore ship	قطاع مُقَدِّمَة القَارِب
37 section of aft ship	قطاع مؤخِّرة القَارِب
38-44 planing boats (surface skimmers, skimmers)	**القَوَارِب السريعة**
38-41 stepped hydroplane (stepped skimmer)	**طائرة مائية دَرَجيَّة** (قَارِب سريع دَرَجي)
38 side view	منظر جانبي
39 view of hull bottom	منظر قاع بَدَن القَارِب
40 section of fore ship	قطاع مُقَدِّمَة القَارِب
41 section of aft ship	قطاع مؤخِّرة القَارِب
42 three-point hydroplane	**طائرة مائية ثلاثية النقط**
43 fin	زِعْنِفَة
44 float	طَوْف
45-62 water skiing	**التزلُّج على الماء**
45 water skier	ممارس رياضة التزلج على الماء
46 deep-water start	البداية في الماء العميق
47 tow line (towing line)	حَبْل السَّحْب
48 handle	مِقْبَض
49-55 water-ski signalling (code of hand signals from skier to boat driver)	**إشارات التزلُّج على الماء** (إشارات اليد من المتزلِّج إلى قائد القَارِب)
49 signal for 'faster'	إشارة "اسرِع"
50 signal for 'slower' ('slow down')	إشارة "خَفِّف السُّرْعَة"
51 signal for 'speed OK'	إشارة "السرعة مضبوطة "
52 signal for 'turn'	إشارة " انْعَطِف"
53 signal for 'stop'	إشارة "قف"
54 signal for 'cut motor'	إشارة " أَوْقِف المُحَرِّك "
55 signal for 'return to jetty' ('back to dock')	إشارة "عُد إلى المرسى "
56-62 types of water ski	**أنواع الزلاجات**
56 trick ski (figure ski), a monoski	زَلاَّجَة الحركات، زَلاَّجَة منفَرِدة
57-58 rubber binding	**الأربطة المطاطيَّة**
57 front foot binding	رباط القَدَم الأماميَّة
58 heel flap	حاشية الكعب
59 strap support for second foot	سناد الرباط الخاص بالقَدَم الثانية
60 slalom ski	زَلاَّجَة التَّعَرُّج
61 skeg (fixed fin, fin)	زِعْنِفَة ثابتة
62 jump ski	زَلاَّجَة القَفْز
63 hovercraft (air-cushion vehicle)	حَوَّامَة (مركبة بوسادة هوائية)
64 propeller	رفَّاص، مروحة
65 rudder	الدَّفَّة
66 skirt enclosing air cushion	غلاف يحيط بالوسادة الهوائية

287 Gliding (Soaring) — الطَّيَرَان الشِّرَاعيّ

1 aeroplane (*Am.* airplane) tow launch (aerotowing)	القَطْر الجَوّيّ بالطائرة
2 tug (towing plane)	طائرة القَطْر
3 towed glider (towed sailplane)	طائرة شراعيَّة مقطورة
4 tow rope	حَبْل القَطْر
5 winched launch	الإطلاق الونْشيّ
6 motor winch	ونْش ذو مُحَرِّك
7 cable parachute	مَظَلَّة كيلية
8 motorized glider (powered glider)	طائرة شراعيَّة بمُحَرِّك
9 high-performance glider (high-performance sailplane)	طائرة شراعيَّة عالية الأداء
10 T-tail (T-tail unit)	ذيل تائي الشكل
11 wind sock (wind cone)	مخروط الريح
12 control tower (tower)	بُرْج المراقبة
13 glider field	حقل الطائرات الشراعية
14 hangar	عَنْبَر الطائرات
15 runway for aeroplanes (*Am.* airplanes)	مَدْرَج الطائرات
16 wave soaring	التحليق المَوْجيّ
17 lee waves (waves, wave system)	أمْوَاج مع اتجاه الريح
18 rotor	طيران دوامي
19 lenticular clouds (lenticulars)	سُحُب عَدَسِيَّة الشكل
20 thermal soaring	التحليق بواسطة الكتل الهوائية الصاعدة
21 thermal	تيار هوائي دافئ صاعد

22 cumulus cloud (heap cloud, cumulus, wool-pack cloud) سُحُب رُكامية
23 storm-front soaring التحليق بصَدْر العاصفة
24 storm front صَدْر العاصفة
25 frontal upcurrent تيَّار هوائي جَبْهي صاعِد
26 cumulonimbus cloud (cumulonimbus) رُكَام مَزْنيّ
27 slope soaring التحليق المُنْحَدِر
28 hill upcurrent (orographic lift) تيَّار هوائي جبليّ صاعد
29 multispar wing جَنَاح متعدد العُضُد
30 main spar, a box spar العَضُد الرئيسي
31 connector fitting تركيبة توصيليَّة
32 anchor rib ضِلْع تثبيت
33 diagonal spar عَضُد أفقي
34 leading edge الحافة الأماميَّة
35 main rib الضِّلْع الرئيسي
36 nose rib (false rib) ضِلْع أمامي (ضِلْع زائف)
37 trailing edge الحافة الخلفية
38 brake flap (spoiler) قلابة الكَبْح
39 torsional clamp قامِطة التوائيَّة
40 covering (skin) غلاف خارجي
41 aileron جنيح
42 wing tip طَرْف الجَنَاح
43 hang gliding الطيران بشراع التحليق
44 hang glider شِراع التحليق
45 hang glider pilot ربَّان شراع التحليق
46 control frame إطار التحكم في شراع التحليق

288 Aerial Sports (Airsports) الرِّيَاضَات الجَوِّيَّة

1-9 aerobatics (aerobatic manoeuvres, *Am.* maneuvers) **بهلوانيات جَوِّيَّة**
1 loop انقلاب، تَحلُّق
2 horizontal eight شكل 8 أفُقيَّة
3 rolling circle دائرة عُطُوف
4 stall turn (hammer head) عُطُوف انهياري
5 tail slide (whip stall) انزلاق بالذيل (انهيار سَوْطي)
6 vertical flick spin دوران لَوْلَبي رأسي صاعِد
7 spin هبوط لَوْلَبي سريع
8 horizontal slow roll تَرَجُّح أفقي بطيء
9 inverted flight (negative flight) طَيَرَان مقلوب (طَيَرَان سَالِب)
10 cockpit **كابينة القيادة**
11 instrument panel لَوْحَة الآلات
12 compass بُوْصُلَة
13 radio and navigation equipment مُعِدَّات اللاسلكي والمِلاحَة
14 control column (control stick) عصا القيادة
15 throttle lever (throttle control) ذِراع التحكم في الخانِق
16 mixture control مِضْبَط المَزْج
17 radio equipment مُعِدَّات اللاسلكي
18 two-seater plane for racing and aerobatics طائرة ذات مَقْعَدَيْن للسبَاقات والبهلوانيات الجَوِّيَّة
19 cabin كابينة
20 antenna هوائي
21 vertical stabilizer (vertical fin, tail fin) زعنفة مُوَازَنَة رأسيَّة
22 rudder دَفَّة
23 tailplane (horizontal stabilizer) لَوْحَة الذَّيْل (زعنفة مُوَازَنَة أفقيَّة)
24 elevator سَطْح رافع
25 trim tab (trimming tab) سُطَيْح توازن إضافي
26 fuselage (body) بَدَن الطائرة
27 wing جناح
28 aileron جُنَيْح
29 landing flap قلابة الهبوط
30 trim tab (trimming tab) سُطَيْح توازن إضافي
31 navigation light (position light) [red] لَمْبَة ضَوْء المِلاحَة [احمر]
32 landing light لَمْبَة ضَوْء الهبوط
33 main undercarriage unit (main landing gear unit) وَحْدَة عَجَلات الهبوط الرئيسيَّة
34 nose wheel عَجلة المُقَدِّمَة
35 engine مُحَرِّك
36 propeller (airscrew) مِرْوَحَة
37-62 parachuting (sport parachuting) **رياضَة القَفْز بالمِظَلَّة**
37 parachute مِظَلَّة، براشوت
38 canopy قُبَّة المِظَلَّة
39 pilot chute مِظَلَّة دَليليَّة
40 suspension lines أحْبَال التعليق
41 steering line حَبْل التَّوْجيه
42 riser ماسورة صاعِدة
43 harness أحْزِمَة
44 pack حِمْل
45 system of slots of the sports parachute نظام الشُّقَبَات في المِظَلَّة الرياضيَّة
46 turn slots شُقْبَات الدَّوَرَان
47 apex قِمَّة القُبَّة
48 skirt حافة
49 stabilizing panel لَوْحَة مُوَازَنَة
50, 51 style jump أسْلُوبَا القَفْز
50 back loop قَفْزة دورانية إلى الخلف
51 spiral قَفْزة لَوْلَبيَّة
52-54 ground signals **الإشارات الأرضيَّة**
52 signal for 'permission to jump' ('conditions are safe') (target cross) إشارة "الإذن للقَفْز" ("الظروف آمنة")
53 signal for 'parachuting suspended - repeat flight' إشارة "القَفْز بالمِظَلَّة مُعلَّق – أعِد الطَّيَرَان"
54 signal for 'parachuting suspended - aircraft must land' إشارة "القَفْز بالمِظَلَّة مُعلَّق – يجب هبوط الطائرة"
55 accuracy jump قَفْزة الدِّقَّة
56 target cross الهدف المُحَدَد
57 inner circle [radius 25 m] دائرة داخليَّة [نصف القُطْر 25 متراً]

58 middle circle [radius 50 m]	دائرة وَسَطيَّة [نصف القُطْر 50 متراً]
59 outer circle [radius 100 m]	دائرة خارجيَّة [نصف القُطْر 100 متر]
60-62 free-fall positions	**أوضاع السقوط الحرّ**
60 full spread position	وَضْع فتْح الذراعيْن والساقيْن
61 frog position	وَضْع الضُّفْدَع
62 T position	الوَضْع التَّائي
63-84 ballooning	**ركوب المُنْطاد**
63 gas balloon	مُنْطاد غاز
64 gondola (balloon basket)	عَرَبَة مُستطيلة (سَلَّة المُنْطاد)
65 ballast (sandbags)	ثِقْل مُوَازَنة (أكياس رَمْل)
66 mooring line	حَبْل المرساة
67 hoop	طَوْق
68 flight instruments (instruments)	مُعِدَّات الطَّيَران
69 trail rope	حَبْل خلفي
70 mouth (neck)	عُنُق المُنْطاد
71 neck line	حَبْل عُنُق المُنْطاد
72 emergency rip panel	لَوْحَة إطلاق غاز المُنْطاد في حالة الطوارئ
73 emergency ripping line	حَبْل إطلاق غاز المُنْطاد في حالة الطوارئ
74 network (net)	شَبكَة
75 rip panel	لَوْحَة إطلاق غاز المُنْطاد
76 ripping line	حَبْل إطلاق غاز المُنْطاد
77 valve	صمام
78 valve line	حَبْل الصِّمام
79 hot-air balloon	مُنْطاد الهواء الساخِن
80 burner platform	مِنصَّة المَوْقِد
81 mouth	فُوَّهَة
82 vent	فتحة تهوية
83 rip panel	لَوْحَة إطلاق غاز المُنْطاد
84 balloon take-off	انطلاق المُنْطاد
85-91 flying model aeroplanes (*Am.* airplanes)	**نماذج الطائرات الطائرة**
85 radio-controlled model flight	نَمُوذَج طَيَران يتم التحكم فيه عن بُعْد باللاسلكي
86 remote-controlled free flight model	نَمُوذَج طَيَران حُرّ يتم التحكم فيه عن بُعْد
87 remote control radio	لاسلكي التحكم عن بُعْد
88 antenna (transmitting antenna)	هوائي
89 control line model	نَمُوذَج يتم التحكم فيه بواسطة حَبْل
90 mono-line control system	نظام تحكم أحادي الحَبْل
91 flying kennel, a K9-class model	بيت صغير طائر

289 Horsemanship, Equestrian Sport — الفرُوسيَّة، رِياضَة الفرُوسيَّة

1-7 dressage	**تَرْويض الخَيْل**
1 arena (dressage arena)	مِضْمار تَرْويض الخَيْل
2 rail	سِياج
3 school horse	فَرَس تعليم
4 dark coat (black coat)	مِعْطَف غامِق
5 white breeches	بنْطال أبيض
6 top hat	قُبَّعَة رسميَّة
7 gait (*also:* school figure)	مِشْيَة الفرس
8-14 show jumping	**القَفْز الاستعراضي**
8 obstacle (fence), an almost-fixed obstacle; *sim.:* gate, gate and rails, palisade, oxer, mound, wall	حاجز، بوَّابَة، مانع
9 jumper	فَرَس قَفْز
10 jumping saddle	سَرْج قَفْز الحواجِز
11 girth	حِزام السَّرْج
12 snaffle	شَكِيمَة
13 red coat (hunting pink, pink; *also*: dark coat)	سُتْرة حمراء (أيضاً: سوداء)
14 hunting cap (riding cap)	كاب فروسيَّة
15 bandage	عِصَابَة
16-19 three-day event	**مُسابقة الأيام الثَّلاثة**
16 endurance competition	مُسابَقة قوَّة التحمُّل
17 cross-country	الضَّاحِيَة
18 helmet (also: hard hat, hard hunting cap)	خَوْذَة
19 course markings	رايَة تحديد المضمار
20-22 steeplechase	**سِبَاق الحَواجِز**
20 water jump, a fixed obstacle	قفْز المانع المائي
21 jump	قَفْزة
22 riding switch	سَوْط الفَرَس
23-40 harness racing (harness horse racing)	**سِبَاق الخَيْل بكامل عُدَّتها**
23 harness racing track (track)	مِضْمَار سِبَاق الخَيْل بكامل عُدَّتها
24 sulky	عربة الصُّلْكيَّة
25 spoke wheel (spoked wheel) with plastic wheel disc (disk)	دولاب مُبَرْمَق ذو قرص بلاستيكي
26 driver in trotting silks	سائق العربة بزيِّه المُلَوَّن باللَّوْن الخاص بالإسْطَبْل الذي ينتمي إليه
27 rein	عِنَان الفرس
28 trotter	فَرَسٌ يَخُبُّ
29 piebald horse	فَرَسٌ أَرْقَط/ أَبْقَع
30 shadow roll	شريط تحكُّم
31 elbow boot	وقاء المِرْفَق
32 rubber boot	وقاء مطَّاطي
33 number	رَقَم
34 glass-covered grandstand with totalizator windows (tote windows) inside	مُدَرَّج مَسْقُوف مُغَطَّى بالزُّجاج به شبابيك المُراهنات المشتَرَكَة
35 totalizator (tote)	شباك المُراهنات المشتَرَكَة
36 number	رَقَم
37 odds (price, starting price, price offered)	سِعْر مُراهَنَة (السِّعْر المعروض)
38 winners' table	لَوْحة الفائز
39 winner's price	سِعْر الفائز
40 time indicator	مُبَيِّن الوَقْت

41-49 hunt, a drag hunt; *sim.:* fox hunt, paper chase (paper hunt, hare-and-hounds) — **الصَّيْد، الصَّيْد باقتفاء الأثر**
41 field — حَقْل
42 hunting pink — سُتْرَة الصَّيْد
43 whipper-in (whip) — السَّوَّاط (مُساعِد الصَّيَّاد)
44 hunting horn — بُوق الصَّيْد
45 Master (Master of fox-hounds, MFH) — السَّيِّد (مالِك كِلاب صَيْد الثَّعالِب)
46 pack of hounds (pack) — فريق من كلاب الصَّيْد
47 staghound — كَلْب الأيائل
48 drag — سَحَّابَة تَرْك الأثَر
49 scented trail (artificial scent) — أثَر ذو رائحَة
50 horse racing (racing) — سِبَاق الخيول
51 field (racehorses) — مِضْمَار (خيول السِّبَاق)
52 favourite (*Am.* favorite) — الفَرَس المُرَشَّح للفوز
53 outsider — فَرَس خارج المنافسة (غير مرشح للفوز)

290 Cycle Racing and Motorsports — سِبَاق الدَّرَّاجَات والسَّيَّارات

1-23 cycle racing — **سِبَاق الدَّرَّاجَات**
1 cycling track (cycle track); *here:* indoor track — مِضْمَار سِبَاق الدَّرَّاجَات
2-7 six-day race — **سِبَاق الأيام السِّتَّة**
2 six-day racer, a track racer (track rider) on the track — مُتَسابِق مُشارِك في سِبَاق الأيام السِّتَّة يُنافِس بالمِضْمَار
3 crash hat — خُوْذَة واقية
4 stewards — المُشْرِفون
5 judge — القاضي
6 lap scorer — مُسَجِّل الدَّوْرات المُفردة
7 rider's box (racer's box) — صُندوق راكِب الدَّرَّاجة
8-10 road race — **السِّبَاق على الطريق**
8 road racer, a racing cyclist — مُتَسابِق على الطريق
9 racing jersey — قَميص السِّبَاق
10 water bottle — زُجاجة ماء
11-15 motor-paced racing (long-distance racing) — **سِبَاق المسافات الطويلة بالدراجات النارية الصغيرة**
11 pacer, a motorcyclist — مُتَسابِق بالدراجات النارية الصغيرة
12 pacer's motorcycle — دَرَّاجَة صغيرة سريعة
13 roller, a safety device — آلِيَّة أمان
14 stayer (motor-paced track rider) — مُتَسابِق بالمضمار
15 motor-paced cycle, a racing cycle — دَرَّاجَة صغيرة سريعة
16 racing cycle (racing bicycle) for road racing (road race bicycle) — دَرَّاجَة سِبَاق الطُّرُق
17 racing saddle, an unsprung saddle — مَقْعَد دَرَّاجَة السِّبَاق
18 racing handlebars (racing handlebar) — مِقْوَد دَرَّاجَة السِّبَاق
19 tubular tyre (*Am.* tire) (racing tyre) — دولاب أنبوبي
20 chain — جنزير، سِلْسِلَة
21 toe clip (racing toe clip) — كُلاَّبَة تثبيت القَدَم بالبدَّال
22 strap — رباط/شريط تثبيت
23 spare tubular tyre (*Am.* tire) — إطار أنْبُوبي احتياطي
24-38 motorsports — **الرياضات الموتورية**
24-28 motorcycle racing; *disciplines:* grasstrack racing, road racing, sand track racing, cement track racing, speedway [on ash or shale tracks], mountain racing, ice racing (ice speedway), scramble racing, trial, moto cross — **سِبَاق الدَّرَّاجَات النَّارِيَّة؛** أنواعه: سِبَاق المِضْمَار العُشْبي، سِبَاق الطُّرُق البرِّيَّة، سِبَاق المِضْمَار الرَّمْلِيّ، سِبَاق المِضْمَار الأسمنتيّ، سِبَاق الطُّرُق السريعة، سِبَاق الطُّرُق الجبلِيَّة، سِبَاق المُرْتَفَعات، السِّبَاق التجريبي
24 sand track — مِضْمار رَمْلِيّ
25 racing motorcyclist (rider) — مُتَسابِق الدراجات النارية
26 leather overalls (leathers) — أوفرول من الجِلْد
27 racing motorcycle, a solo machine — دَرَّاجة سِبَاق نارِيَّة
28 number (number plate) — لَوْحَة رَقَم الدَّرَّاجَة
29 sidecar combination on the bend — تَوَافُق العربة الجانبية عند المُنْعَطَف
30 sidecar — عَرَبَة جانبية
31 streamlined racing motorcycle [500 cc.] — دَرَّاجة سِبَاق نارِيَّة إنسيابيَّة السطح [500 سي سي]
32 gymkhana, a competition of skill; *here:* motorcyclist performing a jump — حفلة رياضِيَّة، مُسابقة إظهار المهارات؛ هنا: راكِب دَرَّاجة نارِيَّة يؤدي قَفْزة
33 cross-country race, a test in performance — سِبَاق الضاحية، اختبار الأداء
34-38 racing cars — **سيَّارات السِّبَاق**
34 Formula One racing car (a mono posto) — سَيَّارَة سِبَاق فورميولا 1
35 rear spoiler (aerofoil, *Am.* airfoil) — مُفْسِد خلفي
36 Formula Two racing car — سَيَّارَة سِبَاق فورميولا 2
37 Super-Vee racing car — سَيَّارَة سِبَاق سوبر في
38 prototype, a racing car — نَمُوذَج أوَّلي لسَيَّارَة السِّبَاق

291 Ball Games I (Football, Association Football, Soccer) — ألْعَاب الكُرَة (1) (كُرَة القَدَم)

1-16 football pitch — **مُستطيل مَلْعَب كُرَة القدم**
1 field (park) — المَلْعَب
2 centre (*Am.* center) circle — دائرة المَرْكَز
3 half-way line — خَطّ منتصف المَلْعَب
4 penalty area — مِنْطَقَة الجَزاء

5 goal area منطَقَة المَرْمَى
6 penalty spot نقطة ركلة الجَزاء
7 goal line (by-line) خَطّ المَرْمَى
8 corner flag راية الزاوِيَة
9 touch line خَطّ التَّماس
10 goalkeeper حارس المَرْمَى
11 sweeper (libero) مُدافع/ظَهير مُتَأخِّر (قَشَّاش)
12 inside defender مُدافع/ظَهير أوْسَط
13 outside defender مُدافع/ظَهير أوَّل (أيْمَن/أيْسَر)
14 midfield players لاعِبا المنتصف
15 inside forward (striker) مُهَاجِم (أيْمَن/أيْسَر)
16 outside forward (winger) جناح (أيْمَن/أيْسَر)
17 football كُرَة القَدَم
18 valve بِلْف
19 goalkeeper's gloves قُفَّازا حارس المَرْمَى
20 foam rubber padding حشوة من المطاط الرَّغَوي
21 football boot حذاء كُرَة القَدَم
22 leather lining بطانَة من الجِلْد
23 counter كُونْتَر الحذاء: قطعة جِلْد قاسية داخل مؤخر الحذاء المحيط بالعقب
24 foam rubber tongue لِسان الحذاء مصنوع من المطاط الرغوي
25 bands أشْرِطَة
26 shaft جانِب الحذاء الأمامي الخارجي
27 insole باطن الحذاء
28 screw-in stud مِسْمار، وَتَد معدني مُقَلْوَظ
29 groove أُخْدُود
30 nylon sole نَعْل من النَيْلُون
31 inner sole نعل داخلي
32 lace (bootlace) رباط الحذاء
33 football pad with ankle guard حَشْوَة خاصة ذات واقٍ للكاحلَيْن
34 shin guard شنكار، وقاء الساق
35 goal المَرْمَى
36 crossbar عارِضَة المَرْمَى
37 post (goalpost) قائم المَرْمَى
38 goal kick رَكْلَة مَرْمَى
39 save with the fists صَدُّ الكُرَة بالقَبْضَتَيْن
40 penalty (penalty kick) رَكْلَة جزاء
41 corner (corner kick) رَكْلَة زاوية
42 offside تَسَلُّل
43 free kick رَكْلَة حرة
44 wall حائط
45 bicycle kick (overhead bicycle kick) رَكْلَة مزدوجة خلفية
46 header لاعِب يضرب الكُرَة برأسه
47 pass (passing the ball) تَمْرِيرة
48 receiving the ball (taking a pass) استقبال الكُرَة
49 short pass (one-two) تَمْرِيرة قصيرة (واحِد–اثْنَيْن)
50 foul (infringement) خَطَأ، مُخالَفَة
51 obstruction إعاقة
52 dribble مُراوَغَة
53 throw-in رَمْيَة تماس
54 substitute بَدِيل
55 coach مُدَرِّب
56 shirt (jersey) قميص، فانلة
57 shorts سِرْوَال قصير، شورت
58 sock (football sock) شَرَاب، جَوْرَب
59 linesman مُرَاقِب الخَطّ
60 linesman's flag رايَة مراقب الخَطّ
61 sending-off طَرْد من المَلْعَب
62 referee الحَكَم
63 red card; *also:* yellow card بطاقة حمراء؛ أيضاً: بطاقة صَفْراء
64 centre (*Am.* center) flag راية منتصف المَلْعَب

292 Ball Games II أَلْعَاب الكُرَة (2)

1 handball (indoor handball) كُرَة اليَدّ
2 handball player, a field player لاعِب كُرَة اليَدّ
3 attacker, making a jump throw مُهاجِم يقوم بقَفْزَة للتسديد
4 defender مُدافِع
5 penalty line خَطّ منْطَقَة الجَزَاء
6 hockey الهُوكي
7 goal المَرْمَى
8 goalkeeper حارس المَرْمَى
9 pad (shin pad, knee pad) وقاء (واقٍ للساق، واقٍ للرُكْبَة)
10 kicker حذاء ثقيل لِرَد الكُرَة
11 face guard قناع واقٍ
12 glove قُفَّاز
13 hockey stick عصا لُعْبَة الهُوكي
14 hockey ball كُرَة الهُوكي
15 hockey player لاعِب الهُوكي
16 striking circle دائرة الهَدَف
17 sideline الخَطّ الجَانِبي
18 corner رُكْن المَلْعَب
19 rugby (rugby football) الروكبي
20 scrum (scrummage) وَضْع التشابك
21 rugby ball كُرَة الروكبي
22 American football (*Am.* football) كُرَة القَدَم الأمريكيَّة
23 player (football player) carrying the ball لاعب يحمل الكُرَة
24 helmet خَوْذَة
25 face guard وقاء الوجه
26 padded jersey قميص مُبَطَّن
27 ball (pigskin) كُرَة (من جلد الخنزير)
28 basketball لُعْبَة كُرَة السَّلَّة
29 basketball كُرَة السَّلَّة
30 backboard اللَوْحة الخلفية
31 backboard support حامِل لَوْحة السَّلَّة
32 basket سلَّة
33 basket ring حلقة السَّلَّة
34 target rectangle مُستطيل التهديف
35 basketball player shooting لاعِب يصوِّب الكُرَة في السَّلَّة
36 end line الخَطّ الخَلْفِيّ
37 restricted area المنْطَقَة المَحْظُورَة
38 free-throw line خَطّ الرَّمْيَة الحُرَّة

39 substitute	لاعِب بديل
40-69 baseball	**البيسبول** (كُرَة القاعدة)
40-58 field (park)	**الملعَب**
40 spectator barrier	حاجِز المتفرجين
41 outfielder	لاعِب في اقصى الملعب، جناح
42 short stop	منْطَقة تَوَقُّف وَجيْز
43 second base	القاعدة الثانية
44 baseman	لاعِب القاعدة
45 runner	عدَّاء
46 first base	القاعدة الأولى
47 third base	القاعدة الثالثة
48 foul line (base line)	خَطّ المخالَفة (خَطّ القاعدة)
49 pitcher's mound	رابيَة اللاعِب القاذِف
50 pitcher	اللاعِب القاذِف
51 batter's position	موقع اللاعب الضارِب
52 batter	اللاعب الضارِب
53 home base (home plate)	موقع الضرب
54 catcher	اللاعب اللاقِط
55 umpire	الحكَم
56 coach's box	مقصورة/كشك المُدَرِّب
57 coach	مُدَرِّب
58 batting order	ترتيب لاعبي المِضْرَب
59-60 baseball gloves (baseball mitts)	**قُفَّازات البيسبول**
59 fielder's glove (fielder's mitt)	قُفَّاز لاعِب الحقل
60 catcher's glove (catcher's mitt)	قُفَّاز اللاعب اللاقط
61 baseball	كُرَة البيسبول
62 bat	عصا الضَّرْب
63 batter at bat	الضَّارِب في وَضْع استعداد لضرب الكُرَة
64 catcher	اللاقِط
65 umpire	الحكم
66 runner	العدَّاء
67 base plate	لَوْحة القاعدة
68 pitcher	القاذِف
69 pitcher's mound	رابيَة القاذِف
70-76 cricket	**الكريكيت**
70 wicket with bails	الكريكيت بقوائمه الخشبيَّة
71 bowling crease	خَطّ الرَّمْي الخلفي
72 popping crease	خَطّ ضرب الكُرَة بالمِضْرَب
73 wicket keeper of the fielding side	حارس الويكيت
74 batsman	الضارِب
75 bat (cricket bat)	مِضْرَب (مِضْرَب الكريكيت)
76 fielder (bowler)	لاعِب أو رامي الكرة
77-82 croquet	**الكروكيه**
77 winning peg	وَتَد الفوز
78 hoop	قنطرة
79 corner peg	وَتَد الرُكْن
80 croquet player	لاعِب الكروكيه
81 croquet mallet	عصا (مِضْرَب) الكروكيه
82 croquet ball	كُرَة الكروكيه

293 Ball Games III / أَلْعَاب الكُرَة (3)

1-42 tennis	**كُرَة التِّنس، كُرَة المِضْرَب**
1 tennis court	ملْعَب التِّنس
2 to **3** doubles sideline (sideline for doubles matches); *kinds of doubles:* men's doubles, women's doubles, mixed doubles	خَطّ جَانِبي لمباريات الزَّوْجي؛ أنواع الزَّوْجي: زَوْجي الرجال، زَوْجي السيدات، زَوْجي مختلط
3 to **10** base line	خَطّ القاعدة
4 to **5** singles sideline (sideline for singles matches); *kinds of singles:* men's singles, women's singles	الخَطّ الجَانِبي للفَرْدي؛ أنواع الفَرْدي: فردي الرجال، فَرْدي السيدات
6 to **7** service line	خَطّ الإرْسَال
8 to **9** centre (*Am.* center) line	خَطّ الإرْسَال الأوْسَط
11 centre (*Am.* center) mark	علامة منتصف خَطّ القاعدة
12 service court	حرم الإرْسَال
13 net (tennis net)	شَبكَة (شَبكَة التِّنس)
14 net strap	شَريط الشبكة
15 net post	قائِم الشبكة
16 tennis player	لاعِب التِّنس
17 smash	ضربة إرْسَال هجومية
18 opponent	المُنافِس
19 umpire	الحكَم
20 umpire's chair	مَقْعَد الحكَم
21 umpire's microphone	ميكروفون الحكَم
22 ball boy	صَبي جمع الكُرَات
23 net-cord judge	حكَم الشبكة
24 foot-fault judge	حكَم مخالفة وَضْع القدم
25 centre (*Am.* center) line judge	حكَم خَطّ الإرسال الأوسط
26 base line judge	حكَم خَطّ القاعدة
27 service line judge	حكَم خَطّ الإرسال
28 tennis ball	كُرَة التنس
29 tennis racket (tennis racquet, racket, racquet)	مِضْرَب التنس
30 racket handle (racquet handle)	مِقْبَض المِضْرَب
31 strings (striking surface)	أوتار المِضْرَب (سطح ضرب الكُرَة)
32 press (racket press, racquet press)	ضاغِط
33 tightening screw	بُرْغي الإحكَام
34 scoreboard	لَوْحة النتائج
35 results of sets	نتائج المجموعات
36 player's name	اسْم اللاعب
37 number of sets	عدد المجموعات
38 state of play	حالة سير المجموعة
39 backhand stroke	ضَرْبَة خلفيَّة
40 forehand stroke	ضَرْبَة أماميَّة
41 volley (forehand volley at normal height)	ضرب الكُرَة قبل أن تمس الأرض مباشرة
42 service	ضَرْبَة الإرْسَال
43-44 badminton	**البادمنتون (الريشة الطائرة)**
43 badminton racket (badminton racquet)	مِضْرَب البادمنتون

44 shuttle (shuttlecock)	ريشة البادمنتون
45-55 table tennis	**كُرَة الطاولة**
45 table tennis racket (racquet) (table tennis bat)	مِضْرَب كُرَة الطاولة
46 racket (racquet) handle (bat handle)	مِقْبَض المِضْرَب
47 blade covering	طبقة مطاطيَّة لتغطية المِضْرَب
48 table tennis ball	كُرَة الطاولة
49 table tennis players; *here:* mixed doubles	لاعبو كُرَة الطاولة؛ هنا: زَوْجي مختلط
50 receiver	مُسْتَقْبِل الكُرَة
51 server	ضارِب الإرسال
52 table tennis table	طاولَة كُرَة الطاولة
53 table tennis net	شبكة كُرَة الطاولة
54 centre (*Am.* center) line	خَطّ المنتصف
55 sideline	الخَطّ الجانِبي
56-71 volleyball	**الكُرَة الطّائِرَة**
56-57 correct placing of the hands	**الوَضْع الصحيح لليَدَيْن على الكُرَة**
58 volleyball	الكُرَة الطائرة
59 serving the volleyball	رَمْيَة الإرسال
60 blocker	لاعِب حائط الصد
61 service area	مِنْطَقَة الإرسال
62 server	لاعب الإرسال
63 front-line player	لاعِب الخَطّ الأمامي
64 attack area	مِنْطَقَة الهجوم
65 attack line	خَطّ الهجوم
66 defence (*Am.* defense) area	مِنْطَقَة الدفاع
67 referee	الحكَم
68 umpire	القاضي (المُساعِد)
69 linesman	مُراقِب الخَطّ
70 scoreboard	لَوْحة النتائج
71 scorer	الهدّاف
72-78 faustball	**لعبة كُرَة الفاوست**
72 base line	خَطّ القاعدة
73 tape	شَريط
74 faustball	كُرَة الفاوست
75 forward	مُهاجِم
76 centre (*Am.* center)	لاعِب المنتصف
77 back	ظَهير
78 hammer blow	ضربة مِطْرَقيَّة
79-93 golf	**الغُولْف**
79-82 course (holes)	**ملْعَب الغُولْف**
79 teeing ground	مكان البدء
80 rough	مِنْطَقَة وَعِرَة
81 bunker (*Am.* sand trap)	مطب رملي
82 green (putting green)	المِنْطَقَة الخضراء
83 golfer, driving	لاعب الغُولْف يضرب الكُرَة
84 follow-through	متابعة الحَرَكَة
85 golf trolley	ترولّي (عربة) الغُولْف
86 putting (holing out)	ضَرْب الكُرَة إلى داخل الحفرة
87 hole	حفرة أو ثقب
88 pin (flagstick)	عمود العَلَم
89 golf ball	كُرَة الغُولْف
90 tee	مَوْضِع البدء
91 wood, a driver; *sim.:* brassie (brassy, brassey)	العصا الخشبيَّة
92 iron	العصا المعدنيَّة
93 putter	عصا الإدخال

294 Fencing — الشَّيْش، المُسَايَفَة

1-33 fencing (modern fencing)	**الشَّيْش، المُسَايَفَة**
1-18 foil	**شَيْش المُبارَزَة**
1 fencing master (fencing instructor)	مُدَرِّب الشَّيْش
2 piste	الحلبة
3 on guard line	خَطّ الاستعداد
4 centre (*Am.* center) line	خَطّ المنتصف
5-6 fencers (foil fencers, foilsmen, foilists) in a bout	**مُتبارِزان في أحد الأشواط**
5 attacker (attacking fencer) in lunging position (lunging)	مُهاجِم في وَضْع طعن الخصم
6 defender (defending fencer), parrying	مُدافع في وَضْع دفاع
7 straight thrust, a fencing movement	طعنة مستقيمة، إحدى حركات الشَّيْش
8 parry of the tierce	دفاع ثلاثي
9 line of fencing	خَطّ المُبارَزَة
10 the three fencing measures (short, medium, and long measure)	خَطْوات المُبارَزَة الثلاث (قصيرة، متوسطة، طويلة)
11 foil, a thrust weapon	شَيْش المُبارَزَة
12 fencing glove	قُفَّاز المُبارَزَة
13 fencing mask (foil mask)	قِناع المُبارَزَة
14 neck flap (neck guard) on the fencing mask	وقاء الرقبة المُثَبَّت بالقِناع
15 metallic jacket	واقي الصدر (سُتْرَة المبارزة)
16 fencing jacket	قميص لُعْبَة الشَّيْش
17 heelless fencing shoes	حذاء خفيف بدون كعب
18 first position for fencer's salute (initial position, on guard position)	الوَضْع الأوَّلي لتحية المُبارِز (وَضْع الاستعداد)
19-24 sabre (*Am.* saber) **fencing**	**المُبارَزَة بالسَّيْف**
19 sabreurs (sabre fencers, *Am.* saber fencers)	مُبَارِز بالسَّيْف
20 (light) sabre (*Am.* saber)	سَيْف (خفيف)
21 sabre (*Am.* saber) glove (sabre gauntlet)	قُفَّاز سيف المُبارَزَة
22 sabre (*Am.* saber) mask	قِناع المُبارَزَة
23 cut at head	فَتْحة في أعلى الرأس
24 parry of the fifth (quinte)	دفاع الخُماسي
25-33 épée, with electrical scoring equipment	**سلاح سيف المُبارَزَة مُزَوَّد بجِهاز تسجيل كهربائي**
25 épéeist	لاعب سيف المُبارَزَة

26	electric épée; *also:* electric foil	سلاح سيف المُبارَزَة الكهربائي؛ أيضاً: شَيْش كهربائي
27	épée point	نقطة الإصابة باللمس
28	scoring lights	مصابيح تسجيل الإصابة
29	spring-loaded wire spool	بكُرَة سلك مُثبتة على نابض
30	indicator light	مصباح إشاري
31	wire	سِلْك كهربي
32	electronic scoring equipment	جِهَاز التسجيل الإلكتروني
33	on guard position	وَضْع الاستعداد
34-45	**fencing weapons**	**أسلحة المُبارَزَة/الشَّيْش**
34	light sabre (*Am.* saber), a cut and thrust weapon	سَيْف خفيف
35	guard	واقي اليد
36	épée, a thrust weapon	سَيْف المُبارَزَة، سلاح طاعِن
37	French foil, a thrust weapon	الشَّيْش الفرنسي، سلاح طاعِن
38	guard (coquille)	واقي اليد
39	Italian foil	الشَّيْش الإيطالي
40	foil pommel	رُمَّانَة السَّيْف
41	handle	مِقْبَض
42	cross piece (quillons)	قطعة مستعرضة
43	guard (coquille)	واقي اليَد
44	blade	نَصْل السلاح
45	button	زرّ اللمس
46	engagements	اشتباكات بالسيوف
47	quarte (carte) engagement	اشتباك "كوارت"
48	tierce engagement (*also:* sixte engagement)	اشتباك ثلاثي (ايضا: سداسي)
49	circling engagement	اشتباك دائري
50	seconde engagement (*also:* octave engagement)	اشتباك "اوكتاف"
51-53	**target areas**	**المناطق المستهدفة**
51	the whole body in épée fencing (men)	الجسم بالكامل في سَيْف المُبَارَزَة (رجَال)
52	head and upper body down to the groin in sabre (*Am.* saber) fencing (men)	الرأس والجِذْع حتى الأربية في المُبَارَزَة بالسَّيْف (رِجال)
53	trunk from the neck to the groin in foil fencing (ladies and men)	الجِذْع من العنق حتى الأربية في سلاح الشَّيْش (سيدات ورِجال)

295 Free Exercise التَّمْرينات الحُرَّة

1	basic position (starting position)	الوَضْع الأساسي (وَضْع البداية)
2	running posture	وَضْع الجري
3	side straddle	فتْح الساقَيْن جَانِباً
4	straddle (forward straddle)	فتْح الساقَيْن (للأمام)
5	toe stand	وقوف علي أصابع القدمَيْن
6	crouch	وَضْع "كروش" (التكوُّر)
7	upright kneeling position	جلوس على الرُكْبَتَيْن والجسم منتصب
8	kneeling position, seat on heels	جلوس على الرُكْبَتَيْن، الجلوس على الكعبيْن
9	squat	قُرْفُصَاء
10	L seat (long sitting)	وَضْع الجلوس والساقيْن مفرودتيْن للأمام (وَضْع على شكل حرف L)
11	tailor seat (sitting tailor-style)	وَضْع مَقْعَد الخياط
12	hurdle (hurdle position)	وَضْع "هردل"
13	V-seat	جلوس حرف v
14	side split	وَضْع فرجارى جانبي أيمن
15	forward split	وَضْع فرجارى أمامي
16	L-support	الارْتِكَاز على شكل حرف L
17	V-support	الارْتِكَاز على شكل حرف v
18	straddle seat	وَضْع "سترادل"
19	bridge	حَرَكَة الجسر
20	kneeling front support	وَضْع الارْتِكَاز الأمامي مع الجلوس على الركبتيْن
21	front support	وَضْع الارْتِكَاز الأمامي
22	back support	وَضْع الارْتِكَاز الخلفي
23	crouch with front support	وَضْع "كروش" مع الارْتِكَاز الأمامي
24	arched front support	الارْتِكَاز الأمامي المُقَوَّس
25	side support	الارْتِكَاز الجَانِبي
26	forearm stand (forearm balance)	الوقوف على الذراعَيْن
27	handstand	وقوف على اليدين
28	headstand	وقوف على الرأس
29	shoulder stand (shoulder balance)	وقوف على الكتفيْن
30	forward horizontal stand (arabesque)	حَرَكَة الأرابيسك
31	rearward horizontal stand	وقوف أفقي خلفي
32	trunk-bending sideways	ثَنْي الجذع للجَانِب
33	trunk-bending forwards	ثَنْي الجذع للأمام
34	arch	قَوْس
35	astride jump (butterfly)	قَفْزة الفَرَاشَة
36	tuck jump	قَفْزة مكَوَّرَة
37	astride jump	القَفْز عالياً مع فتْح الساقيْن
38	pike	القَفْز عالياً مع فرْد الساقيْن والذراعيْن للأمام
39	scissor jump	قَفْزة المقص
40	stag jump (stag leap)	قَفْزة الظبي
41	running step	خَطْوة الجري للاقتراب
42	lunge	وَضْع الوثْب
43	forward pace	خَطْوة أماميَّة
44	lying on back	الرقود على الظهر
45	prone position	وَضْع الانبطاح
46	lying on side	الرقود على الجَانِب
47	holding arms downwards	فَرْد الذراعَيْن لأسفل
48	holding (extending) arms sideways	فَرْد الذراعَيْن جَانِباً
49	holding arms raised upward	فَرْد الذراعَيْن لأعلى
50	holding (extending)	فَرْد الذراعَيْن للأمام

arms forward
51 arms held (extended) backward — فَرْد الذراعَيْن للخلف
52 hands clasped behind the head — مَسْك اليدَيْن خلف الرأس

296 Apparatus Gymnastics I — جُمْبَاز الأجْهِزَة (1)

1-11 gymnastics apparatus in men's Olympic gymnastics — **أجهزة الجُمْبَاز في مسابقات الجُمْبَاز الأوليمبية للرجال**
1 long horse (horse, vaulting horse) — حِصَان الوَثْب
2 parallel bars — المتوازيان
3 bar — عَارِضَة خشبية
4 rings (stationary rings) — جِهَاز الحلَق
5 pommel horse (side horse) — حِصَان الحلَق
6 pommel — حلَقَة
7 horizontal bar (high bar) — العُقْلَة
8 bar — عَارِضَة العُقْلَة
9 upright — قائم العُقْلَة
10 stay wires — الشَّدَّادات
11 floor (12m × 12m floor area) — مِنْطَقَة الحركات الأرضيَّة (12م×12م)
12-21 auxiliary apparatus and apparatus for school and club gymnastics — **الأجهزة التكميليَّة وأجهزة الجُمْبَاز الخاصة بالمدارس والأندية**
12 springboard (Reuther board) — سُلَّم الوَثْب
13 landing mat — فَرْشَة الهبوط
14 bench — دكَّة، بنش
15 box — صُنْدُوق
16 small box — صُنْدُوق صغير
17 buck — حِصَان صغير (البك)
18 mattress — مَرْتَبَة، حشية
19 climbing rope (rope) — حَبْل التسلق
20 wall bars — جِهَاز عوارض جداريَّة
21 window ladder — سُلَّم تسلُّق
22-39 positions in relation to the apparatus — **الأوْضَاع بالنسبة للأجهزة**
22 side, facing — جَانِب المواجهة الأماميَّة
23 side, facing away — جَانِب المواجهة في الاتجاه المعاكس
24 end, facing — طرف المواجهة الأماميَّة
25 end, facing away — طرف المواجهة في الاتجاه المعاكس
26 outside, facing — المواجهة الخارجيَّة
27 inside, facing — المواجهة الداخليَّة
28 front support — ارْتكَاز أمامي
29 back support — ارْتكَاز خلفي
30 straddle position — وَضْع فَتْح الساقين
31 seated position outside — وَضْع الجلوس للخارج
32 riding seat outside — وَضْع الركوب للخارج
33 hang — التعلق
34 reverse hang — التعلق العكسي
35 hang with elbows bent — التعلق مع ثَنْي المِرْفقَيْن
36 piked reverse hang — وَضْع الحربة العكسي
37 straight inverted hang — التعلق المقلوب مع استقامة الجسم
38 straight hang — التعلق المستقيم
39 bent hang — التعلق مع ثَنْي الذراعين
40-46 grasps (kinds of grasp) — **أنواع المَسْكَات**
40 overgrasp on the horizontal bar — مَسْكَة العُقْلَة واليَدَيْن للامام
41 undergrasp on the horizontal bar — مَسْكَة العُقْلَة واليَدَيْن للخلف
42 combined grasp on the horizontal bar — مَسْكَة مُرَكَّبة على العُقْلَة
43 cross grasp on the horizontal bar — مَسْكَة متقاطعة على العُقْلَة
44 rotated grasp on the horizontal bar — مَسْكَة اليَدَيْن المستديرة على العُقْلَة
45 outside grip on the parallel bars — مَسْكَة المتوازي من الخارج
46 rotated grasp on the parallel bars — مَسْكَة المتوازي من الداخل
47 leather handstrap — شَرِيط من الجِلْد لليد
48-60 apparatus exercises — **تمَارين الأجهزة**
48 long-fly on the horse — الطيران الطويل فوق حِصَان الوَثْب
49 rise to straddle on the parallel bars — الارتفاع لفَتْح الساقَيْن على المتوازي
50 crucifix on the rings — وَضْع التصالب على جِهَاز الحلَق
51 scissors (scissors movement) on the pommel horse — وَضْع المقص على حِصَان الحلَق
52 legs raising into a handstand on the floor — رَفْع الساقَيْن للوقوف على اليَدَيْن على الأرض
53 squat vault on the horse — الشقْلَبَة في وَضْع القرفصاء على الحِصَان
54 double leg circle on the pommel horse — دائرة مزدوجة بالساقَيْن على حِصَان الحلَق
55 hip circle backwards on the rings — دائرة خلفيَّة بالخصر على جِهَاز الحلَق
56 lever hang on the rings — تعليق الرافعة على جِهَاز الحلَق
57 rearward swing on the parallel bars — المَرْجَحَة الخلفيَّة على المتوازي
58 forward kip into upper arm hang on the parallel bars — حَرَكَة كيب أماميَّة للتعلق بالذراعَيْن على المتوازي
59 backward underswing on the horizontal bar — مَرْجَحَة سفلية للخلف على العُقْلَة
60 backward grand circle on the horizontal bar — دائرة واسعة خلفيَّة على العُقْلَة
61-63 gymnastics kit — **طاقم ملابس الجُمْبَاز**
61 singlet (vest, *Am.* undershirt) — فانلة
62 gym trousers — بنطلون/سروال جُمْبَاز لاصِق
63 gym shoes — حذاء جُمْبَاز

64 wristband — رباط للرسغ

297 Apparatus Gymnastics II (Women's Gymnastics) — جُمْبَاز الأجْهِزَة (2) (جُمْبَاز السَّيِّدَات)

1-6 gymnastics apparatus in women's Olympic gymnastics — **أجهزة الجُمْبَاز في مسابقات الجُمْبَاز الأوليمبية للسيدات**

1 horse (vaulting horse) — حِصَان الوَثْب
2 beam — عَارِضَة التوازن
3 asymmetric bars (uneven bars) — العارِضتان
4 bar — عَارِضَة خشبية
5 stay wires — الشَّدادات
6 floor (12m × 12m floor area) — مِنْطَقَة الحركات الأرضيَّة (12م×12م)

7-14 auxiliary apparatus and apparatus for school and club gymnastics — **الأجهزة التكميلية وأجهزة الجُمْبَاز الخاصة بالمدارس والأندية**

7 landing mat — فَرْشَة الهبوط
8 springboard (Reuther board) — سلم الوثب
9 small box — صُنْدُوق صغير
10 trampoline — الترامبولين
11 sheet (web) — قماش مشدود
12 frame — اطار ، مِنْصَب معدني
13 rubber springs — نوابض ، زنبركات
14 springboard trampoline — مِقْفَز ترامبولين

15-32 apparatus exercises — **تمارين الأجهزة**

15 backward somersault — حَرَكَة سمرسولد خلفيَّة (الشقلبة الخلفية)
16 spotting position (standing-in position) — وَضْع النقاط القافز
17 vertical backward somersault on the trampoline — حَرَكَة سمرسولد رأسيَّة خلفيَّة على الترامبولين
18 forward somersault on the springboard trampoline — حَرَكَة سمرسولد أماميَّة على مِقْفَز ترامبولين
19 forward roll on the floor — دَحْرَجَة أماميَّة على الأرض
20 long-fly to forward roll on the floor — حَرَكَة طيران طويل لدَحْرَجَة أماميَّة على الأرض
21 cartwheel on the beam — حَرَكَة عجلة على عَارِضَة التوازن
22 handspring on the horse — القفْز على اليدين على حِصَان الوَثْب
23 backward walkover — دَوَرَان خلفي
24 back flip (flik-flak) on the floor — قَفْزَة خلفية على الأرض
25 free walkover forward on the floor — دَوَرَان حر للأمام على الأرض
26 forward walkover on the floor — دَوَرَان أمامي على الأرض
27 headspring on the floor — دَوَرَان على الرأس للأمام
28 upstart on the asymmetric bars — قَفْزَة البدء على العارِضَتَيْن
29 free backward circle on the asymmetric bars — دائرة خلفية حرة على العارِضَتَيْن
30 face vault over the horse — وَثْبَة أمامية على حِصَان الوَثْب
31 flank vault over the horse — وَثْبَة جَانِبية على حِصَان الوَثْب
32 back vault (rear vault) over the horse — وَثْبَة خلفية على حِصَان الوَثْب

33-50 gymnastics with hand apparatus — **الجُمْبَاز والأجهزة اليدويَّة**

33 hand-to-hand throw — قذف الكُرَة من يد إلى الأخرى
34 gymnastic ball — كُرَة جُمْبَاز
35 high toss — قذف الكُرَة عالياً
36 bounce — تنطيط الكُرَة على الأرض
37 hand circling with two clubs — عمل دائرة باليدَيْن وبهما هِرَاوَتَيْن
38 gymnastic club — هِرَاوَة الجُمْبَاز
39 swing — مَرْجَحَة
40 tuck jump — قَفْزَة مكوَّرَة
41 bar — عصا خشبية
42 skip — نَطُّ الحَبْل
43 rope (skipping rope) — حَبْل
44 criss-cross skip — نَطُّ الحَبْل مع تقاطع اليديْن
45 skip through the hoop — القَفْز خلال الطَّوْق
46 gymnastic hoop — طَوْق الجُمْبَاز
47 hand circle — دائرة باليد
48 serpent — شكل ثعباني
49 gymnastic ribbon — شَريط جُمْبَاز
50 spiral — حَرَكَة لَوْلَبيَّة

51-52 gymnastics kit — **طاقم ملابس الجُمْبَاز**

51 leotard — لِباس الجُمْبَاز
52 gym shoes — حذاء جُمْبَاز

298 Athletics (Track and Field Events) — ألْعَاب القُوَى (مُسابَقات المِضْمَار والحَقْل)

1-8 running — **الجَرْيَ**

1-6 start — **بداية الجري**

1 starting block — مكعب بدء السباق
2 adjustable block (pedal) — دواسة قابلة للتعديل
3 start — بداية السباق
4 crouch start — بداية "كروش"
5 runner, a sprinter; *also:* middle-distance runner, long-distance runner — عَدَّاء؛ أيضاً: عدَّاء مسافات متوسطة وعدَّاء مسافات طويلة
6 running track (track), a cinder track or synthetic track — مِضْمَار الجري

7-8 hurdles (hurdle racing); *sim.:* steeple-chase — **سباق الحواجز**

7 clearing the hurdle — تَخَطّي الحاجز
8 hurdle — حاجز

9-41 jumping and vaulting — **الوَثْب والقَفْز**

9-27 high jump **الوَثْب العالي**
9 Fosbury flop (Fosbury, flop) "فوسبري"، سَقْطَة فوسبري
10 high jumper لاعب الوَثْب العالي
11 body rotation (rotation on the body's longitudinal and latitudinal axes) دَوَرَان الجسم
12 shoulder landing الهبوط على الكتفَيْن
13 upright قائم عَارِضَة الوَثْب
14 bar (crossbar) عَارِضَة الوَثْب
15 Eastern roll اللف الشرقي
16 Western roll اللف الغربي
17 roll لَفّ
18 rotation دَوَرَان
19 landing هبوط
20 height scale مقياس الارتفاع
21 Eastern cut-off حَرَكَة اللف الشرقيَّة أعلى العَارِضَة
22 scissors (scissor jump) قَفْزَة المقص
23 straddle (straddle jump) القَفْز مع فَتْح الساقَيْن
24 turn الانعطاف
25 vertical free leg حَرَكَة القَفْز بالساق المستقيمة الحرة
26 take-off الارتقاء في الهواء
27 free leg ساق حرة
28-36 pole vault **القَفْز بالزَّانَة**
28 pole (vaulting pole) الزَّانَة
29 pole vaulter (vaulter) in the pull-up phase لاعب القَفْز بالزَّانَة في مرحلة جذب الجسم عالياً
30 swing مَرْجَحَة
31 crossing the bar تَخَطِّي العَارِضَة
32 high jump apparatus (high jump equipment) جِهَاز الوَثْب العالي
33 upright قائم
34 bar (crossbar) عَارِضَة
35 box صُنْدُوق
36 landing area (landing pad) مِنْطَقَة الهبوط
37-41 long jump **الوثب الطويل**
37 take-off الارتقاء
38 take-off board لَوْحَة الارتقاء
39 landing area مِنْطَقَة الهبوط، الحفرة
40 hitch-kick رَفْسَة لدفع الجسم للأمام
41 hang تعلق في الهواء
42-47 hammer throw **رَمْي المِطْرَقَة**
42 hammer المِطْرَقَة
43 hammer head رأس المِطْرَقَة
44 handle ذراع المِطْرَقَة
45 grip قَبْضَة
46 holding the grip مسكة المِطْرَقَة
47 glove قُفَّاز
48 shot put قذف الكُلَّة/الجِلَّة
49 shot (weight) الكُلَّة/الجِلَّة
50 O'brien technique أسلوب "اوبريان" في قذف الكُلَّة/الجِلَّة
51-53 javelin throw **رَمْي الرمح**
51 grip with thumb and index finger القَبْضَة بالإبهام والسبَّابة
52 grip with thumb and middle finger القَبْضَة بالإبهام والوُسْطَى
53 horseshoe grip قَبْضَة حدوة الفرس
54 binding بطانة

299 Weightlifting and Combat Sports رياضَات رَفْع الأثْقَال والقِتَال

1-5 weightlifting **رَفْع الأثقال**
1 squat-style snatch رَفْعة الخَطْف
2 weightlifter رَبَّاع، رافع أثقال
3 disc (disk) barbell طارة الثِّقْل
4 jerk with split النَّتْر مع مباعدة السَّاقَيْن
5 maintained lift حِفْظ تَوَازُن الرَّفْعة
6-12 wrestling **المصارعة**
6-9 Greco-Roman wrestling **المصارعة اليونانية–الرومانية**
6 standing wrestling (wrestling in standing position) المصارعة في وَضْع الوقوف
7 wrestler مُصارِع
8 on-the-ground wrestling (*here:* the referee's position) المصارعة على الأرض (هنا: الوَضْع الإغريقي)
9 bridge قنطرة
10-12 freestyle wrestling **المصارعة الحرة**
10 bar arm (arm bar) with grapevine تكتيف الذراع مع حَرَكَة الكَرْمَة
11 double leg lock قفل مزدوج لحَرَكَة الساق
12 wrestling mat (mat) بُسَاط المصارعة
13-17 judo (*sim.:* ju-jitsu, jiu-jitsu, ju-jutsu) **الجُودُو**
13 drawing the opponent off balance to the right and forward جذب الخصم لإفقاده التوازُن
14 judoka (judoist) لاعب الجُودُو
15 coloured (*Am.* colored) belt, as a symbol of Dan grade حزام مُلَوَّن يشير إلى رتبة الدرجة
16 referee الحكَم
17 judo throw رَمْيَة الجُودُو
18-19 karate **الكاراتيه**
18 karateka لاعب الكاراتيه
19 side thrust kick, a kicking technique رَكْلَة طاعنة جَانِبية
20-50 boxing (boxing match) **المُلاكَمَة**
20-24 training apparatus (training equipment) **مُعدات التدريب**
20 spring-supported punch ball كُرَة اللكْم المثبتة على نابض
21 punch bag (*Am.* punching bag) كيس اللكم
22 speed ball كُرَة السرعة
23 suspended punch ball كُرَة لَكْم مُعلَّقة
24 punch ball كُرَة لَكْم
25 boxer, an amateur boxer (boxes in a singlet, vest, *Am.* مُلاكِم، مُلاكِم هاو (مُلاكِم يرتدي قميصاً بلا أكمام وسروالاً قصيراً)، أو ملاكم

undershirt) or a professional boxer (boxes without singlet) — محترف

26 boxing glove — قُفّاز المُلاكِم

27 sparring partner — مُلاكِم يتناوَش

28 straight punch (straight blow) — لَكْمَة مستقيمة

29 ducking and side-stepping — الميل بالجذع والتحرك جَانباً

30 headguard — واقي الرأس

31 infighting; *here:* clinch — إلْتِحام

32 uppercut — ضربة صاعدة

33 hook to the head; *here:* right hook — ضربة خَطّافيَّة إلى الرأس؛ هنا: خَطّافيَّة يُمْنَى

34 punch below the belt, a foul punch (illegal punch, foul) — لَكْمَة أسفل الحزام، لَكْمَة خاطئة

35-50 boxing match (boxing contest), a title fight (title bout) — **مُبَارَاة مُلاكَمَة**، منازَلَة على اللقب

35 boxing ring (ring) — حلقة المُلاكَمَة

36 ropes — أحْبَال

37 stay wire (stay rope) — سلْكٌ شدَّاد

38 neutral corner — الرُكْن المحايد

39 winner — الفائز

40 loser by a knockout — خاسِر بالضربة القاضية

41 referee — حكَم الحلقة

42 counting out — العَدّ حتى عشر ثوان

43 judge — قاضي

44 second — مساعد المُلاكِم

45 manager — مدير أعمال المُلاكِم

46 gong — جرس (عبارة عن قرص معدني)

47 timekeeper — الميقاتي

48 record keeper — المُسَجِّل

49 press photographer — مُصوِّر صحفي

50 sports reporter (reporter) — مُرَاسِل/مندوب صحفي لأخبار الرياضة

300 Mountaineering — تَسَلُّق الجِبَال

1-57 mountaineering (mountain climbing, Alpinism) — **تَسَلُّق الجِبَال** (تَسَلُّق جِبَال الألْب)

1 hut (Alpine Club hut, mountain hut, base) — كُوخ جَبَلي (كُوخ النَّادي الألْبي)

2-13 climbing (rock climbing) [rock climbing technique] — **التَّسَلُّق**

2 rock face (rock wall) — جدار صَخْريّ

3 fissure (vertical, horizontal, or diagonal fissure) — شَقّ (رأسي، أفقي، مائل)

4 ledge (rock ledge, grass ledge, scree ledge, snow ledge, ice ledge) — حَيْد، إفْريز

5 mountaineer (climber,mountain climber, Alpinist) — مُتَسَلِّق

6 anorak (high-altitude anorak, snowshirt, padded jacket) — قُلُنْسُوَة البَرْكَة

7 breeches (climbing breeches) — سِرْوَال قصير

8 chimney — مِنَصَّة

9 belay (spike, rock spike) — صَخْرَة ناتئة لتثبيت الحَبْل

10 belay — صَخْرَة وَتَد

11 rope sling (sling) — علاّقَة الحَبْل

12 rope — حَبْل

13 spur — مِهْمَاز

14-21 snow and ice climbing [snow and ice climbing technique] — **تَسلُّق الثلوج والجليد**

14 ice slope (firn slope) — مُنْحَدَر ثلجي

15 snow and ice climber — مُتَسَلِّق الثلوج والجليد

16 ice axe (*Am.* ax) — فَأس الجليد

17 step (ice step) — خطوة

18 snow goggles — نظّارات واقية من وهج الشمس

19 hood (anorak hood) — قُلُنْسُوَة

20 cornice (snow cornice) — إفْريز (طُنُف جليدي)

21 ridge (ice ridge) — حافة مرتفعة (حافة جليدية)

22-27 rope (roped party) — **حَبْل** (مجموعة مرتبطة معاً بحَبْل)

22 glacier — مَثْلَجَة

23 crevasse — شقّ

24 snow bridge — جسر جليدي

25 leader — قائد

26 second man (belayer) — الرَّجُل الثاني (فَرْد ربط الحَبْل)

27 third man (non-belayer) — الرَّجُل الثالث

28-30 roping down (abseiling, rapelling) — **الهبوط بالحَبْل**

28 abseil sling — علاّقَة الهبوط بالحَبْل

29 sling seat — مَقْعَد العلاّقَة

30 Dülfer seat — مَقْعَد "دولفر"

31-57 mountaineering equipment (climbing equipment, snow and ice climbing equipment) — **مُعدَّات تَسَلُّق الجِبَال والجليد**

31 ice axe (*Am.* ax) — فَأس تسلُّق الجليد

32 wrist sling — حمَّالَة الرسغ

33 pick — مِعْوَل

34 adze (*Am.* adz) — قَدُوم

35 karabiner hole — عُرْوَة

36 short-shafted ice axe (*Am.* ax) — فَأس جليد قصيرة الذراع

37 hammer axe (*Am.* ax) — فَأس مِطْرَقيَّة

38 general-purpose piton — رُزَّة عامة الأغراض

39 abseil piton (ringed piton) — رُزَّة حلَقيَّة

40 ice piton (semi-tubular screw ice piton, corkscrew piton) — رُزَّة جليد مَلْوَلَبَة

41 drive-in ice piton — رُزَّة جليد دَفْعيَّة

42 mountaineering boot — حذاء تسلق الجبال

43 corrugated sole — نَعْل مموج

44 climbing boot — حِذاء التسلُّق

45 roughened stiff rubber upper	فرْعَة حِذاء مطاطيَّة مُقوَّاة
46 karabiner	كُلاّبَة
47 screwgate	بوابة بُرْغيَّة
48 crampons (lightweight crampons, twelve-point crampons, ten-point crampons)	خُفّ مِسْماريّ
49 front points	المسامير الأماميَّة
50 point guards	وقاء المسامير
51 crampon strap	شريط الخُفّ المِسْماريّ
52 crampon cable fastener	أداة كيلية لتثبيت الخُفّ المِسْماريّ
53 safety helmet (protective helmet)	خَوْذَة أمان
54 helmet lamp	لَمْبَة الخَوْذَة
55 snow gaiters	الغَيْتَر: وقاء يُلْبَس فوق الحذاء
56 climbing harness	طقم لِجَام التسلق
57 sit harness	لِجَام جلوس

301 Winter Sports I (Skiing) — الرِّيَاضَات الشِّتْوِيَّة (1) (التَّزَلُّج على الجَلِيد)

1-72 skiing	**التَّزَلُّج على الجَلِيد**
1 compact ski	مِزْلاج
2 safety binding (release binding)	رِبَاط أمان
3 strap	شَرِيط
4 steel edge	حافَة صُلب
5 ski stick (ski pole)	عَصَا التَّزَلُّج على الجليد
6 grip	مِقْبَض
7 loop	أُنْشُوطَة
8 basket	سَلَّة
9 ladies' one-piece ski suit	سالوبيت نسائي للتَّزَلُّج على الجليد
10 skiing cap (ski cap)	كاب التَّزَلُّج على الجَلِيد
11 skiing goggles	نظارات واقِيَة للتَّزَلُّج على الجليد
12 cemented sole skiing boot	حِذاء تَزَلُّج ذو نَعْل مُسَمْنَت
13 crash helmet	خَوْذَة واقية
14-20 cross-country equipment	**مُعِدَّات سِبَاق الضَّاحِيَة**
14 cross-country ski	مِزْلاج سِبَاق الضَّاحِيَة
15 cross-country rat trap binding	رباط على شكل مصيدة الفأر
16 cross-country boot	حِذَاء سِبَاق الضَّاحِيَة
17 cross-country gear	لِبَاس سِبَاق الضَّاحِيَة
18 peaked cap	كاب ذو حافة ناتئة
19 sunglasses	نَظَّارات شَمْسِيَّة
20 cross-country poles made of bamboo	أعمدة سباق الضاحية مصنوعة من الخيزران
21-24 ski-waxing equipment	**مُعِدَّات تشميع المِزْلاج**
21 ski wax	شَمْع المِزْلاج
22 waxing iron (blowlamp, blowtorch)	أداة التشميع
23 waxing cork	فِلِّينَة تشميع
24 wax scraper	مِكْشَطَة شَمْع
25 downhill racing pole	عصا التَّزَلُّج المُنْحَدِر
26 herringbone, for climbing a slope	طريقة المقص لِصُعُود المُنْحَدَر
27 sidestep, for climbing a slope	طريقة السُّلَّم لِصُعُود المُنْحَدَر
28 ski bag	حقيبة التَّزَلُّج
29 slalom	التَّزَلُّج المُتَعَرِّج
30 gate pole	عمود البَوَّابة
31 racing suit	بذلة السِّبَاق
32 downhill racing	سِبَاق الانْحِدَار
33 'egg' position, the ideal downhill racing position	وَضْع "البَيْضَة"، الوَضْع المثالي لسِبَاق الانْحِدَار
34 downhill ski	مِزْلاج الانْحِدَار
35 ski jumping	القَفْز بالمِزْلاج
36 lean forward	الانْحِنَاء للأمام
37 number	رَقَم
38 ski jumping ski	مِزْلاج القَفْز
39 grooves (3 to 5 grooves)	حزوز (3–5 حزوز)
40 cable binding	رباط كيبلي
41 ski jumping boots	حذاء القَفْز بالمِزْلاج
42 cross-country	سِبَاق الضَّاحِيَة
43 cross-country stretch-suit	سالوبيت سِبَاق الضَّاحِيَة
44 course	مِضْمَار
45 course-marking flag	رايَة تحديد المِضْمَار
46 layers of a modern ski	طبقات مِزْلاج حديث
47 special core	لُبّ من مادة خاصة
48 laminates	صفائح رقيقة
49 stabilizing layer (stabilizer)	طبقة مُوَازِنَة
50 steel edge	حافَة من الصُلب
51 aluminium (*Am.* aluminum) upper edge	شفْرَة علويَّة من الألومنيوم
52 synthetic bottom (artificial bottom)	قاعدة من مادة صناعيَّة
53 safety jet	إطَار أمان
54-56 parts of the binding	**أجْزَاء الرِّبَاط**
54 automatic heel unit	وَحْدَة الكَعْب الأتُوماتِيَة
55 toe unit	وَحْدَة أصابع القَدَم
56 ski stop	مِكْبَح المِزْلاج
57-63 ski lift	**مِصْعَد التَّزَلُّج**
57 double chair lift	مِصْعَد ذو مَقْعَد مزدوج
58 safety bar with footrest	قضيب أمان مُزَوَّد بمِسْنَد للقَدَمَيْن
59 ski lift	مِصْعَد التَّزَلُّج
60 track	مَسَار، سِكَّة
61 hook	خُطَّاف
62 automatic cable pulley	بَكَرَة كيبليَّة أتُوماتِيَة
63 haulage cable	كيبل السَّحْب
64 slalom	التَّزَلُّج المُتَعَرِّج
65 open gate	باب مفتوح
66 closed vertical gate	باب عمودي مغلق
67 open vertical gate	باب عمودي مفتوح
68 transversal chicane	عَقَبَة مفتوحة
69 hairpin	مُنْعَطَف حاد
70 elbow	مُنْعَطَف مِرْفَقي

71 corridor	دهلِيز
72 Allais chicane	عَقَبَة " أليــز "، تَعَرُّج

302 Winter Sports II — الرِّيَاضَات الشِّتْوِيَّة (2)

1-26 ice skating	**التَّزَحْلُق على الجلِيد**
1 ice skater, a solo skater	مُتَزَحْلِق على الجلِيد
2 tracing leg	رِجْل تابعة
3 free leg	رِجْل حرة
4 pair skaters	زَوْج من المُتَزَحْلِقين
5 death spiral	حَرَكَة حَلَزُون الموت
6 pivot	حَرَكَة المِحْوَر
7 stag jump (stag leap)	وَثْبَة المُهْر
8 jump-sit-spin	دَوَرَان القَفْز والجلوس
9 upright spin	الدَّوَرَان المنتصب
10 holding the foot	مَسْك القَدَم
11-19 compulsory figures	**حركات إجبارِيَّة**
11 curve eight	مُنْحَنَى على شكل 8
12 change	تغيير الاتجاه
13 three	شكل 3
14 double-three	شكل 3 مُزْدَوَجَة
15 loop	أُنْشُوطة
16 change loop	الأُنْشُوطة المتغيِّرَة مع تغيير الاتجاه
17 bracket	قَوْس
18 counter	الدائرة العكْسِيَّة
19 rocker	المِهَزَّة
20-25 ice skates	**زَلاَّجَات الجليد**
20 speed skating set (speed skate)	زَلاَّجة سريعة
21 edge	حافة
22 hollow grinding (hollow ridge, concave ridge)	شفْرَة الحذَاء
23 ice hockey set (ice hockey skate)	زَلاَّجة هوكي الجليد
24 ice skating boot	حذَاء التزحلق على الجليد
25 skate guard	وِقَاء الزَّلاَّجَة
26 speed skater	مُتَزَحْلِق سِبَاق السرعة
27-28 skate sailing	**التَّزَحْلُق الشِّرَاعي**
27 skate sailor	مُتَزَحْلِق شراعي
28 hand sail	شِرَاع يدوي
29-37 ice hockey	**هوكي الجليد**
29 ice hockey player	لاعِب هوكي الجليد
30 ice hockey stick	عصا هوكي الجليد
31 stick handle	مِقْبَض العصا
32 stick blade	رَاحَة العصا
33 shin pad	وِقَاء السَّاق
34 headgear (protective helmet)	خَوْذَة لحماية الرَّأس
35 puck, a vulcanized rubber disc (disk)	البَكّ: قُرْص مطاطي يُسْتَخْدَم فى هوكي الجليد
36 goalkeeper	حارِس المَرْمَى
37 goal	المَرْمَى
38-40 ice-stick shooting (Bavarian curling)	**رِمَايَة الكرَة** (الكيرلِنْغ البَافاري)
38 ice-stick shooter (Bavarian curler)	لاعِب الكيرلِنْغ
39 ice stick	عصا الكرَة (عصا الجليد)
40 block	كُتْلَة
41-43 curling	**الكيرلِنْغ**
41 curler	لاعب الكيرلِنْغ
42 curling stone (granite)	كرة الكيرلِنْغ (من الجرانيت)
43 curling brush (curling broom, besom)	عصا (فرشاة) الكيرلِنْغ
44-46 ice yachting (ice-boating, ice sailing)	**الانزلاق بمَرَاكِب الجَمْد**
44 ice yacht (iceboat)	مَرْكِب الجَمْد
45 steering runner	مِزْلاق طولي للتوجيه
46 outrigged runner	مِزْلاق طولي للإسْناد

303 Winter Sports III — الرِّيَاضَات الشِّتْوِيَّة (3)

1 toboggan (sledge, *Am.* sled)	تُبُوغَان (مِزْلَقة)
2 toboggan (sledge, *Am.* sled) with seat of plaid straps	تُبُوغَان ذو مَقْعَد من أَشْرِطَة النسيج المَجْدُولَة
3 junior luge toboggan (junior luge, junior toboggan)	تُبُوغَان صغير بِحَبْل توجيه
4 rein	العِنَان (حَبْل التوجيه)
5 bar (strut)	قضِيب، سِناد
6 seat	مَقْعَد
7 bracket	كتيفة
8 front prop	دعامة أماميَّة
9 rear prop	دعامة خلفيَّة
10 movable runner	مِزْلاق قابِل للفصل
11 metal face	واجِهَة معدنية
12 luge tobogganer	راكِب تُبُوغَان بحبل توجيه
13 luge toboggan (luge, toboggan)	تُبُوغَان بِحَبْل توجيه
14 crash helmet	خَوْذَة واقية
15 goggles	نَظَّارات واقية
16 elbow pad	وِقاء المِرْفَق
17 knee pad	وِقاء الرُّكْبَة
18 Nansen sledge, a polar sledge	مِزْلَقة قُطْبِيَّة
19-21 bobsleigh (bob-sledding)	**الانْزِلاق بمِزْلَقة مُزْدَوَجَة**
19 bobsleigh (bobsled), a two-man bobsleigh (a boblet)	مِزْلَقة مزدوجة لشَخْصَيْن
20 steersman	فَرْد توجيه المِزْلَقة
21 brakeman	فَرْد مكَبِّح المِزْلَقة
22-24 skeleton tobogganing (Cresta tobogganing)	**ركوب التُبُوغَان الهَيْكَلي**
22 skeleton (skeleton toboggan)	هَيْكَل التُبُوغَان
23 skeleton rider	راكِب هَيْكَل التُبُوغَان
24 rake, for braking and steering	حافة مُسَنَّنَة للكَبْح والتوجيه

304 Countryside in Winter — الرِّيف في الشِّتَاء

1 avalanche (snow	

avalanche, *Am.* snowslide); *kinds:* wind avalanche, ground avalanche — هَيَار جليدي؛ أنواعه: هَيَار ريحي، هَيَار أرضي
2 avalanche wall, a deflecting wall (diverting wall); *sim.:* avalanche wedge — جِدار حارِف للهَيَار الجليدي
3 avalanche gallery — رُواق الهَيَار الجليدي
4 snowfall — سقوط الثلوج
5 snowdrift — مَجْرُوف ثلجي
6 snow fence — سياج احتجاز الثلوج
7 avalanche forest [planted as protection against avalanches] — غابة هَيَاريَّة [تُزْرَع كَوِقَاء من الهيارات الجليديَّة]
8 street-cleaning lorry (street cleaner) — شاحنة تنظيف الشوارع
9 snow plough (*Am.* snowplow) attachment — جَرَّافة الثلج
10 snow chain (skid chain, tyre chain, *Am.* tire chain) — سلسلة للوقاية من الانزلاق في الثلج
11 radiator bonnet (*Am.* radiator hood) — غِطَاء المُشِعّ
12 radiator shutter and shutter opening (louvre shutter) — غِطَاء مِغْلاق المُشِعّ وفتحة المِغْلاق
13 snowman — رَجُل جليدي
14 snowball fight — التقاذُف بِكُرَات الثلج
15 snowball — كُرَة ثلجيَّة
16 ski bob — دَرَّاجَة الثلج
17 slide — التَّزَحْلُق على الجليد
18 boy, sliding — صَبِي يتزحلق
19 icy surface (icy ground) — سَطْح جليدي (أرض جليدية)
20 covering of snow (on the roof) — غطاء جليدي (فوق السطح)
21 icicle — دلاة جليديَّة
22 man clearing snow — رَجُل يزيح الثلج
23 snow push (snow shovel) — جاروف إزاحة الثلج
24 heap of snow — كَوْمة ثلج
25 horse-drawn sleigh (horse sleigh) — مِزْلَقة يجرها حصان
26 sleigh bells (bells, set of bells) — أجْرَاس المِزْلَقة
27 foot muff (*Am.* foot bag) — مُوْفَة تدفئة القَدَمَيْن
28 earmuff — مُوْفَة تدفئة الأذنين
29 handsledge (tread sledge); *sim.:* push sledge — مِزْلَقَة يدويَّة
30 slush — وَحْل جليدي

305 Various Sports — رِيَاضَات مُتَنَوِّعَة

1-13 skittles — **لُعْبَة القناني الخشبية**
1-11 skittle frame — **إطار لُعْبَة القناني الخشبية**

1 front pin (front) — القَارُورَة الخشبية الأماميَّة
2 left front second pin (left front second) — القَارُورَة الخشبية الأماميَّة اليسرى
3 running three [left] — المسافة ثلاثة [يساراً]
4 right front second pin (right front second) — القَارُورَة الخشبية الأماميَّة اليُمنى الثانيَّة
5 running three [right] — المسافة ثلاثة [يميناً]
6 left corner pin (left corner), a corner (copper) — قَارُورَة الزَّاوية اليُسرى
7 landlord — القَارُورَة المركزيَّة
8 right corner pin (right corner), a corner (copper) — قَارُورَة الزَّاوية اليُمنى
9 back left second pin (back left second) — القَارُورَة الخشبية الخلفية اليُسرى الثانيَّة
10 back right second pin (back right second) — القَارُورَة الخشبية الخلفية اليُمنى الثانيَّة
11 back pin (back) — القَارُورَة الخلفيَّة
12 pin — قَارُورَة خشبيَّة
13 landlord — القَارُورَة المركزيَّة
14-20 tenpin bowling — لُعْبَة البولنج العشريَّة
14 frame — إطار
15 bowling ball (ball with finger holes) — كُرَة البولنج
16 finger hole — ثقب الإصْبَع
17-20 deliveries — **أساليب قذف الكرة**
17 straight ball — كُرَة مستقيمة
18 hook ball (hook) — كُرَة خطَّافيَّة
19 curve — كُرَة مُنحنيَّة
20 back-up ball (back-up) — كُرَة مائلة
21 **boules**; *sim.:* Italian game of boccie, green bowls (bowls) — البُولِنْغ الإيطالي
22 boules player — لاعب البُولِنْغ الإيطالي
23 jack (target jack) — كُرَة الهَدَف البيضاء
24 grooved boule — كُرَة البُولِنْغ الإيطالي المُخدَّدة
25 group of players — مجموعة من اللاعبين
26 **rifle shooting** — **الرماية بالبندقية**
27-29 shooting positions — أوضاع الرماية
27 standing position — وَضْع الوقوف
28 kneeling position — وَضْع البروك/الركوع
29 prone position — وَضْع الانبطاح/الامتداد
30-33 targets — الأهداف
30 target for 50 m events (50 m target) — هَدَف مُسابقات الرماية من مسافة 50 متراً
31 circle — دائرة
32 target for 100 m events (100 m target) — هَدَف مُسابقات الرماية من مسافة 100 متر
33 bobbing target (turning target, running-boar target) — هَدَف حرامي/متحرك
34-39 ammunition — الذخيرة
34 air rifle cartridge — خرطوش بندقية تعمل بضغط الهواء
35 rimfire cartridge for zimmerstutzen (indoor target rifle), a small-bore German single-shot rifle — خرطوش بندقية قصيرة الماسورة للرماية في الصالات المغلقة
36 case head — رَأس ظرف الطَّلْقَة

37 caseless round — طَلْقَة بدون ظرف
38 .22 long rifle cartridge — خرطوش بندقية طويل عيار 22ر مللم
39 .222 Remington cartridge — خرطوش رمينجتون عيار 222ر
40-49 sporting rifles — **بنادق المسابقات الرياضيَّة**
40 air rifle — بندقية تعمل بضغط الهواء
41 optical sight — سدَّادة بصريَّة
42 front sight (foresight) — سدَّادة أماميَّة ، ناشنكاة أماميَّة
43 smallbore standard rifle — بندقية قياسيَّة قصيرة الماسورة
44 international smallbore free rifle — بندقية دوليَّة قصيرة الماسورة للرماية الحُرَّة
45 palm rest for standing position — مِسْنَد اليَد في وَضْع الوقوف
46 butt plate with hook — كُتْلَة الدَّبْشِك/الإخْمَص وبها عقيفة
47 butt with thumb hole — الدَّبْشِك/الإخْمَص وثقب الإصبع
48 smallbore rifle for bobbing target (turning target) — بندقية قصيرة الماسورة للأهداف المتحركة
49 telescopic sight (rifle-scope, telescope sight) — سدَّادة تليسكوبيَّة
50 optical ring sight — سدَّادة بصريَّة حلقية
51 optical ring and bead sight — سدَّادة بصريَّة بحلَقَة وَقَمْحَة
52-66 archery (target archery) — **الرَّمْيَ بالسَّهْم**
52 shot — الرَّمْيّ نحو الهَدَف
53 archer — رامي السِّهام
54 competition bow — قَوْس الرماية في المسابقات
55 riser — شَد القَوْس
56 point-of-aim mark — علامة نقطة التصويب
57 grip (handle) — قبضة
58 stabilizer — أداة موازنة
59 bow string (string) — وَتَر السهم
60 arrow — سَهْم
61 pile (point) of the arrow — رَأس السَّهْم
62 fletching — ترييش السَّهْم
63 nock — ثُلم طرف السهم
64 shaft — قصبة السهم
65 cresting — زخرفة
66 target — الهَدَف
67 Basque game of pelota (jai alai) — لُعْبَة البلُّوتة الباسكيَّة
68 pelota player — لاعب البلُّوتة
69 wicker basket (cesta) — سَلَّة من الأماليد المجدولة
70-78 skeet (skeet shooting), a kind of clay pigeon shooting — **رَمي الحَمَام**
70 skeet over-and-under shotgun — بندقية رَشّ لِرَمْيّ الحَمَام
71 muzzle with skeet choke — فُوَّهَة بها خانِق
72 ready position on call — وَضْع الاستعداد عند سماع النداء
73 firing position — وَضْع الإطلاق
74 shooting range — ميدان الرماية
75 high house — مَبْنَى مرتفع
76 low house — مَبْنَى منخفض
77 target's path — مَسَار الهَدَف
78 shooting station (shooting box) — مَحَطَّة الرماية (صندوق الرماية)
79 aero wheel — **العجلة الهوائيَّة**
80 handle — مقبَض
81 footrest — مِسْنَد القَدَم
82 go-karting (karting) — **ركوب العربات الصغيرة المكشوفة**
83 go-kart (kart) — عَرَبَة صغيرة مكشوفة
84 number plate (number) — لَوْحة الرقم
85 pedals — دوَّاسَات
86 pneumatic tyre (*Am.* tire) — دولاب مملوء بالهواء المضغوط
87 petrol tank (*Am.* gasoline tank) — خزان الوقود
88 frame — إطار
89 steering wheel — عجلة القيادة
90 bucket seat — مَقْعَد دلْويّ
91 protective bulkhead — حاجز واقٍ
92 two-stroke engine — محرك ثنائي الأشواط
93 silencer (*Am.* muffler) — شكمان ، مخمد الصوت

306 Carnival — الكَرْنَفَال

1-48 masked ball (masquerade, fancy-dress ball) — **حَفْلَة تَنَكُّرِيَّة**
1 ballroom — صالة المَرْقَص
2 dance band — فريق مُوسيقي ، فريق راقِص
3 pop musician — عازف موسيقي البوب
4 paper lantern — فانوس وَرَقي
5 festoon (string of decorations) — الفِسْطون : حَبْل من الزينات
6-48 disguise (fancy dress) at the masquerade — **الأزْيَاء التَّنَكُّريَّة فى الحفلة التَّنَكُّرِيَّة**
6 witch — ساحِرَة
7 mask — قناع
8 fur trapper (trapper) — صائد الدِّبَبَة
9 Apache girl — فتاة الأبَاشي
10 net stocking — جَوْرَب شَبَكِيّ
11 first prize in the tombola (raffle), a hamper — الجائزة الأُولى في الطمبولا
12 pierette — مُهَرِّجَة
13 half mask (domino) — قناع نصفيّ
14 devil — شَيْطان
15 domino — بُرْنُس تَنَكُّري
16 hula-hula girl (Hawaii girl) — فتاة رَقْصَة البَحْشَلَة
17 garland — إكْلِيل زهور
18 grass skirt (hula skirt) — تَنُّورَة رَقْصَة البَحْشَلَة
19 pierrot — مُهَرِّج

20 ruff	الرّاف: طوق رقبة مكَشْكَش
21 midinette	ميدينيت
22 Biedermeier dress	ثَوْب سَهْرَة عاري الصدر والكتفيْن
23 poke bonnet	بوكيَّة
24 décolletage with beauty spot	ديكولْتَاج مع شامَة حُسْن
25 bayadère (Hindu dancing girl)	راقِصَة هِنْدُوسِيَّة
26 grandee	نبيل أسباني
27 Columbine	كولومبين
28 maharaja (maharajah)	مهْرَاجا
29 mandarin, a Chinese dignitary	مُوَظَّف صيني
30 exotic girl (exotic)	فتاة شاذة المَظْهَر
31 cowboy; *sim.:* gaucho (vaquero)	راعي البَقَر
32 vamp, in fancy dress	إمْرأة لَعُوب، مِغْناج
33 dandy (fop, beau)	غنْـدُور
34 rosette	حلْيَة وَرْدِيَّة الشكل
35 harlequin	بلياتشو، مُهَرِّج
36 gipsy (gypsy) girl	فتاة الغجَر
37 cocotte (demi-monde, demi-mondaine, demi-rep)	مُومِس (امْرَأة مَشْبُوهَة)
38 owl-glass, a fool (jester, buffoon)	بَهْلُول
39 foolscap (jester's cap and bells)	طُرْطُور البَهْلُول
40 rattle	خُشْخَيْشَة
41 odalisque, Eastern female slave in Sultan's seraglio	محْظِيَّة (جارِيَة في حريم السلطان في بلاد الشرق)
42 chalwar (pantaloons)	بنطلون/بنطال
43 pirate (buccaneer)	قُرْصَان
44 tattoo	وَشْم
45 paper hat	قُبَّعَة وَرَقِيَّة
46 false nose	أنف زائفَة
47 clapper (rattle)	خُشْخَيْشَة
48 slapstick	مقْرَعَة
49-54 fireworks	**الألعاب الناريَّة**
49 percussion cap	كبسولة القَدْح
50 cracker	مُفَرْقَعَة ناريَّة
51 banger	مُفَرْقَعَة ناريَّة
52 jumping jack	الدُّمْيَة الوَثَّابة
53 cannon cracker (maroon, marroon)	مُفَرْقَعَة مِدْفَعِيَّة
54 rocket	صاروخ
55 paper ball	كُرَة ورقيَّة
56 jack-in-the-box	عفْريت العُلْبَة
57-70 carnival procession	**مَوْكِب الكرنفال**
57 carnival float (carnival truck)	عَرَبَة الكرنفال
58 King Carnival	الملك كرنفال
59 bauble (fool's sceptre, *Am.* scepter)	صَوْلَجَان
60 fool's badge	شارَة
61 Queen Carnival	الملِكَة كرنفال
62 confetti	نِثار: قصاصات من الورق المُلَوَّن تنثر في الاحتفالات
63 giant	عمْلاق
64 beauty queen	مَلِكَة الجمال
65 fairy-tale figure	شخصيَّة خُرافيَّة (من الحواديت)
66 paper streamer	رايَة مُلَوَّنة خَفَّاقة من الورق
67 majorette	فتاة من فتيات المَوْكب
68 king's guard	حارس الملك
69 buffoon, a clown	بهلول، مُهَرِّج
70 lansquenet's drum	طَبْلَة مَوْكِب الكرنفال

307 Circus — السِّيرْك

1-63 travelling (*Am.* traveling) **circus**	**سِيرْك مُتَجَوِّل**
1 circus tent (big top), a four-pole tent	خَيْمَة السِّيرْك
2 tent pole	عمود الخَيْمَة
3 spotlight	أضواء كاشِفَة
4 lighting technician	فنيّ الإضاءة
5 trapeze platform	منَصَّة أرْجُوحَة السِّيرْك
6 trapeze	أرْجُوحَة السِّيرْك
7 trapeze artist	لاعب أرْجُوحَة السِّيرْك
8 rope ladder	سُلَّم من الحِبَال
9 bandstand	تَخْت الفرقة الموسيقيَّة
10 circus band	فِرْقَة السِّيرْك الموسيقيّة
11 ring entrance (arena entrance)	مَدْخَل الحلَبَة
12 wings	جِنَاحان
13 tent prop (prop)	سَناد الخيمة
14 safety net	شبكة الأمان
15 seats for the spectators	مقاعِد المشاهدين
16 circus box	مقصورة السِّيرْك
17 circus manager	مدير السِّيرْك
18 agent	وكيل
19 entrance and exit	باب الدخول والخروج
20 steps	دَرَجَات سُلَّميَّة
21 ring (arena)	حلَبَة
22 ring fence	سياج الحلَبَة
23 musical clown (clown)	مُهرِّج موسيقي
24 clown	مُهرِّج
25 comic turn (clown act), a circus act	فَقْرَة كوميديَّة
26 circus riders (bareback riders)	راكبو حصان السيرك
27 ring attendant, a circus attendant	عامِل السِّيرْك
28 pyramid	تشكيل هرَمي
29 support	لاعب ارْتِكاز
30-31 performance by liberty horses	**عَرْض الخيول البَرِّيَّة**
30 circus horse, performing the levade (pesade)	حصانِ السِّيرْك يقوم بالتَّوَثُّب
31 ringmaster	سَيِّد الحلَبَة، مُدَرِّب
32 vaulter	قافِز
33 emergency exit	مَخْرَج الطوارئ
34 caravan (circus caravan, *Am.* trailer)	قَطِيرَة (كرفان السِّيرْك)
35 springboard acrobat	بهلوان لَوْح الوَثْب

(springboard artist)
36 springboard — لَوْح الوَثْب
37 knife thrower — قاذف السَّكَاكِين
38 circus marksman — رامي السِّيرْك
39 assistant — مُسَاعِدة
40 tightrope dancer — راقِص الحَبْل المشدود
41 tightrope — حَبْل مشدود
42 balancing pole — قضيب حفظ التَّوَازُن
43 throwing act — حَرَكَة قَذْف
44 balancing act — حَرَكَة تَوَازُن
45 support — لاعِب ارْتِكَاز
46 pole (bamboo pole) — عصا (عصا من الخيزران)
47 acrobat — بهلوان
48 equilibrist (balancer) — لاعِب تَوَازُن
49 wild animal cage, a round cage — قفَص الحَيَوَانات المُتَوَحِّشة
50 bars of the cage — قضبان القفص
51 passage (barred passage, passage for the wild animals) — مَمَر (مَمَر مَسَيَّج بالقضبان لمُرُور الحَيَوَانات المُتَوَحِّشة)
52 tamer (wild animal tamer) — مرَوِّض (مدرِّب الحَيَوَانات المُتَوَحِّشة)
53 whip — كُرْبَاج، سَوْط
54 fork — شَوْكَة
55 pedestal — قاعدة
56 wild animal (tiger, lion) — حيوان مُتَوَحِّش (نمر، أسد)
57 stand — حامِل
58 hoop (jumping hoop) — طَوْق (طَوْق القفْز)
59 seesaw — نوَّاسَة (أرجوحة)
60 ball — كُرَة
61 camp — مُخَيَّم
62 cage caravan — كرفان الأقفاص
63 menagerie — مَعْرَض للوُحوش

308 Fair, Fairground — السُّوق المَوْسِميَّة، أَرْضُ السُّوق

1-69 fair (annual fair) — **سُوق** (السُّوق السَّنَوِيَّة)
1 fairground — أرْض السُّوق
2 children's merry-go-round, (whirligig), a roundabout (*Am.* carousel) — أرْجُوحَة دَوَّامَة الخيل
3 refreshment stall (drinks stall) — كُشْك المُرَطِّبَات
4 chairoplane — الكرَاسي الطائرة
5 up-and-down roundabout — أرْجُوحَة دوَّارَة
6 show booth (booth) — حُجَيْرَة الاستعراض
7 box (box office) — شُبَّاك التذاكر
8 barker — مُنَاد
9 medium — الوَسِيطَة الرُّوحَانيَّة
10 showman — رَجُل الاستعراض
11 try-your-strength machine — ماكينة اسْتِعْرَاض القوَّة
12 hawker — بائع مُتَجَوِّل
13 balloon — بالُونة
14 paper serpent — ثُعْبَان وَرَقي
15 windmill — دوَّراة الرِّيَاح
16 pickpocket (thief) — نشَّال
17 vendor — بائع
18 nougat — نُوجَة
19 ghost train — قطَار الأشْباح
20 monster — وَحْش
21 dragon — تِنِّين
22 monster — وَحْش
23 beer marquee — سُرَادِق
24 sideshow — استعراض جانبي
25-28 travelling (*Am.* traveling) **artistes** (travelling show people) — **الفَنَّانُون الجَوَّالُون**
25 fire eater — آكِل النَّار
26 sword swallower — بالِع السُّيُوف
27 strong man — الفُتُوَّة
28 escapologist — لاعِب التَّخَلُّص من الأغْلال
29 spectators — المُشَاهِدون، النُّظَّارَة
30 ice-cream vendor (ice-cream man) — بائع الآيس كريم/البوظة
31 ice-cream cornet, with ice cream — بَسْكُوتة آيس كريم
32 sausage stand — منَصَّة بيع المقانق
33 grill (*Am.* broiler) — مِشْوَاة
34 bratwurst (grilled sausage, *Am.* broiled sausage) — مَقَانِق مَشْوية
35 sausage tongs — ماسك المقانق
36 fortune teller — العَرَّافة
37 big wheel (Ferris wheel) — أرْجُوحَة السَّاقِيَة
38 orchestrion (automatic organ), an automatic musical instrument — أرْغَن آليّ
39 scenic railway (switch-back) — أرْجُوحَة سكة حديديّة صغيرة تجري بين مناظر اصطناعيّة
40 toboggan slide (chute) — زُحْلُوقَة التوبوغان
41 swing boats — أرْجُوحَة القَوَارِب
42 swing boat, turning full circle — قارب أرْجُوحَة يدور دَوْرَة كامِلَة
43 full circle — دَوْرَة كاملة
44 lottery booth (tombola booth) — كشك اللوتارية/الطمبولا
45 wheel of fortune — عَجلَة الحظ
46 devil's wheel (typhoon wheel) — عَجلَة الشَّيْطان
47 throwing ring (quoit) — حلَقَة القَذْف (الكَتّ)
48 prizes — جوائز
49 sandwich man on stilts — بائع سندوتشات يسير فوق طُوَّالَتَيْن
50 sandwich board (placard) — إعْلان عن السندوتشات
51 cigarette seller, an itinerant trader (a hawker) — بائع سجائر مُتَجَوِّل
52 tray — صينية
53 fruit stall — كُشْك الفاكهة
54 wall-of-death rider — لاعب جِدَار الموت
55 hall of mirrors — قاعَة المَرَايا (الضاحِكَة)
56 concave mirror — مِرْآة مُقَعَّرَة

57 convex mirror — مِرْآة مُحَدَّبة
58 shooting gallery — رُكْن لعبة الرماية
59 giant swing boat — أُرْجُوحَة القارب العملاق
60 junk stalls (second-hand stalls) — أكْشاك بَيْع البَضائع المستعملة
61 first aid tent (first aid post) — خَيْمَة الإسعافات الأوَّليَّة
62 dodgems (bumper cars) — لعبة سيارات التصادم
63 dodgem (bumper car) — سيارة تصادم
64-66 pottery stand — **منَصَّة بَيْع الفُخَّاريَّات**
64 barker — المنادي على المعروضات
65 market woman — بائعة السوق
66 pottery — أوانٍ فُخَّاريَّة
67 visitors to the fair — زُوَّار السوق
68 waxworks — مَشْغُولات من الشَّمْع
69 wax figure — تمثال من الشَّمْع

309 Flea Market — سُوق السِّلَع الرَّخِيصَة أو المُسْتَعْمَلَة

1 treadle sewing machine — ماكينة خِياطة بدَوَّاسَة
2 flower vase — زُهَرِيَّة ، مَزْهَرِيَّة
3 wall mirror — مِرْآة حائط
4 cylindrical stove — مَوْقِد أُسْطُواني
5 stovepipe — ماسورة المَوْقِد
6 stovepipe elbow — مرفق ماسورة المَوْقِد
7 stove door — باب المَوْقِد
8 stove screen — سِتَار المَوْقِد
9 coal scuttle — دَلْو الفَحْم
10 firewood basket — سَلَّة حَطَب
11 doll — دُمْيَة
12 teddy bear — دُبّ لُعْبَة
13 barrel organ — أرْغَن يدوي
14 orchestrion — أرْغَن آليّ
15 metal disc (disk) — قُرْص معدني
16 radio (radio set, *joc.:* 'steam radio'), a super heterodyne (superhet) — مِذْيَاع ، راديو
17 baffle board — لَوْح حَجْز المَوْجَات الصوتيَّة
18 'magic eye', a tuning indicator valve — "عَيْن سِحْرِيَّة"، صمام دليلي للضبط الدقيق
19 loudspeaker aperture — فتحة مكَبِّر الصوت
20 station selector buttons (station preset buttons) — مفاتيح انتقاء القنوات
21 tuning knob — مِفْتَاح المُوَالَفَة
22 frequency bands — نطاقات التردد
23 crystal detector (crystal set) — كَشَّاف كريستالي
24 headphones (headset) — سمَّاعات الرَّأس
25 folding camera — كاميرا قابلة للطي
26 bellows — مِنْفَاخ الكاميرا
27 hinged cover — غطاء مفصَلي
28 spring extension — وَصْلَة امتداديَّة نابضيَّة
29 salesman — بائع
30 box camera — كاميرا صندوقيَّة
31 gramophone — الفونوغراف
32 record (gramophone record) — أُسْطُوانة فونوغراف
33 needle head with gramophone needle — رَأس إبْري وبه إبْرَة الفونوغراف
34 horn — بُوق
35 gramophone box — صُنْدُوق الفونوغراف
36 record rack — حامِل الأُسْطُوَانات
37 portable tape recorder — مُسَجِّل شرائط نقَّالي
38 flashgun — مِصْبَاح وميضي
39 flash bulb — لَمْبَة وميضيَّة
40-41 electronic flash (electronic flashgun) — **مِصْبَاح وميضي إلكتروني**
40 flash head — رَأس المِصْبَاح الوميضي
41 accumulator — مَرْكَم
42 slide projector — فانوس عَرْض الشرائح (السلايدات)
43 slide holder — حامِل الشرائح
44 lamphouse — مَبِيت المِصْبَاح
45 candlestick — شَمْعَدَان
46 scallop shell — صَدَفَة مَحَّارة
47 cutlery — لَوَازِم مائدة
48 souvenir plate — دِرْع تذكاري
49 drying rack for photographic plates — رف تجفيف ألْوَاح التصوير
50 photographic plate — لَوْح تصوير
51 delayed-action release — زِرّ الفعل المُؤَخَّر
52 tin soldiers (*sim.:* lead soldiers) — تماثيل على شكل جنود من الصفيح
53 beer mug (stein) — كوب الجُعَّة
54 bugle — نَفِير ، بُوق ، صُور
55 second-hand books — كُتُب مستعملة
56 grandfather clock — ساعة دَقَّاقَة قائمة
57 clock case — صُنْدُوق الساعة
58 pendulum — بندول الساعة
59 time weight — ثِقْل الوقت
60 striking weight — ثِقْل دَقَّات الساعة
61 rocking chair — كُرْسي هَزَّاز
62 sailor suit — بذلة بَحَّار
63 sailor's hat — قُبَّعَة بَحَّار
64 washing set — طقم غسيل
65 washing basin — حَوْض غسيل
66 water jug — إبْرِيق الماء
67 washstand — حامِل حَوْض الغسيل
68 dolly — المِضْرَبَة : أداة لتقليب الملابس أثناء الغسيل
69 washtub — وعَاء غسيل (طِشْت)
70 washboard — لَوْح غسيل
71 humming top — نَحْلَة طَنَّانَة أو خُذْروف (لعبة)
72 slate — لَوْح أرْدُوَاز للكتابة
73 pencil box — علبة أقلام رصاص
74 adding machine — ماكينة جَمْع
75 paper roll — بكَرَة ورق
76 number keys — مفاتيح الأرقام
77 abacus — مِعْداد (عَدَّاد)
78 inkwell, with lid — دَوَاة حِبْر ذات غِطاء
79 typewriter — آلَة كاتِبَة
80 [hand-operated] calculating machine (calculator) — آلة حاسِبَة يدويَّة
81 operating handle — ذِراع تشغيل
82 result register (product — مُسَجِّل نتائج العمليات

register) الحسابيَّة
83 rotary counting mechanism (rotary counter) آليَّة حِسَاب دَوَّارة
84 kitchen scales ميزَان مَطْبَخ
85 waist slip (underskirt) جيبونة (تَنُّورة تحتيَّة)
86 wooden handcart عَرَبة يد خشبيَّة
87 wall clock ساعَة حائط
88 bed warmer جِهَاز تدفئة السَّرير
89 milk churn قِسْط اللبن

310 Films (Motion Pictures) I — الأفْلام السِّينَمَائيَّة (1)

1-13 film studios (studio complex, *Am.* movie studios) **استوديوهات التصوير السينمائي**
1 lot (studio lot) أرْض الاستديو
2 processing laboratories (film laboratories, motion picture laboratories) مَعَامِل تَحْمِيض الأفلام
3 cutting rooms حُجُرَات تنقيح الأفلام السينمائيَّة والأشرطة المُسَجَّلة
4 administration building (office building, offices) مَبْنَى الإدارة
5 film (motion picture) storage vault (film library, motion picture library) مكتبة الأفلام
6 workshop وَرْشة
7 film set (*Am.* movie set) منظر سينمائي
8 power house وَحْدَة توليد الطاقة
9 technical and research laboratories المَعَامِل الفنيَّة ومَعَامِل البحث
10 groups of stages مجموعات من المِنَصَّات/ المسارح
11 concrete tank for marine sequences خَزَّان خرساني لأخذ سلسلة لقطات بحرية متعاقِبَة
12 cyclorama ستارة سَيكْلُورَاميَّة
13 hill تَـلّ
14-60 shooting (filming) **تصوير اللقطات**
14 music recording studio (music recording theatre, *Am.* theater) ستوديو تسجيل الموسيقى
15 'acoustic' wall lining بِطَانة جِدَار صَوْتيَّة
16 screen (projection screen) شَـاشـة (شاشة إسْقَاط الصورة)
17 film orchestra أوركسترا موسيقى الفيلم التصويريَّة
18 exterior shooting (outdoor shooting, exterior filming, outdoor filming) تصوير مناظر خارجيَّة
19 camera with crystal-controlled drive كاميرا ذات مِقْوَد تَحَكُّم بلَّوري
20 cameraman المُصَوِّر
21 assistant director مُسَاعِد المُخْرِج
22 boom operator (boom swinger) مُشَغِّل ذِراع الميكروفون
23 recording engineer (sound recordist) مُهَنْدِس تسجيل الصوت
24 portable sound recorder with crystal-controlled drive جِهَاز تسجيل صوت مَحْمُول ذو مِقْوَد تَحَكُّم بلّوري
25 microphone boom ذِراع الميكروفون
26-60 shooting (filming) **in the studio** (on the sound stage, on the stage, in the filming hall) **التصوير داخل الاستديو**
26 production manager مدير الإنتاج
27 leading lady (film actress, film star, star) بَطَلَة الفيلم
28 leading man (film actor, film star, star) بَطَل الفيلم
29 film extra (extra) كُومْبَارس الفيلم
30 arrangement of microphones for stereo and sound effects مجموعة مُرَتَّبة من الميكروفونات للصوت المُجَسَّم والمؤثرات الصوتيَّة
31 studio microphone ميكروفون الاستوديو
32 microphone cable كيبل الميكروفون
33 side flats and background الأسْطُح الجانبية وخلفية المَنْظَر
34 clapper boy عامِل "الكلاكيت"
35 clapper board (clapper) with slates (boards) for the film title, shot number (scene number), and take number لَوْح "الكلاكيت" ويحمل اسم الفيلم ورقم اللقطة ورقم المنظر
36 make-up artist (hair-stylist) الماكيير (مُصَفِّف الشَّعْر)
37 lighting electrician (studio electrician, lighting man, *Am.* gaffer) فني الإضاءة
38 diffusing screen سِتَار نَشْر الضوء
39 continuity girl (script girl) فتاة السيناريو
40 film director (director) مُخْرِج الفيلم
41 cameraman (first cameraman) المُصَوِّر (مُصَوِّر أوَّل)
42 camera operator, an assistant cameraman (camera assistant) مُساعَد المُصَوِّر ، مُشَغِّل الكاميرا
43 set designer (art director) مُصَمِّم المناظر (المدير الفني)
44 director of photography مدير التصوير
45 filmscript (script, shooting script, *Am.* movie script) سيناريو الفيلم
46 assistant director مُخْرِج مُسَاعِد
47 soundproof film camera (soundproof motion picture camera), a wide screen كاميرا تصوير سينمائي بعازِل للصوت

camera (cinemascope camera)	
48 soundproof housing (soundproof cover, blimp)	مَبِيت كاميرا عازِل للصوت
49 camera crane (dolly)	مِنَصَّة تحريك الكاميرا
50 hydraulic stand	حامِل هيدرولي
51 mask (screen) for protection from spill light (gobo)	سِتَار للحماية من الضوء الزائد
52 tripod spotlight (fill-in light, filler light, fill light, filler)	ضَوْء كَشَّاف على حامِل ثلاثي
53 spotlight catwalk	مَمَر الأضواء الكاشِفة
54 recording room	حُجْرَة التسجيل
55 recording engineer (sound recordist)	مُهَنْدِس (تسجيل) الصوت
56 mixing console (mixing desk)	كونسول المكْسَاج (الدَّمْج)
57 sound assistant (assistant sound engineer)	مُسَاعِد مُهَنْدِس الصوت
58 magnetic sound recording equipment (magnetic sound recorder)	مُسَجِّل صوت مغناطيسي
59 amplifier and special effects equipment, e.g. for echo and sound effects	مُضَخِّم الصوت ومُعِدَّات المؤثِّرات الخاصة
60 sound recording camera (optical sound recorder)	كاميرا تسجيل صوتي (مُسَجِّل صوت ضَوْئي)

311 Films (Motion Pictures) II — الأفْلام السِّينْمَائيَّة (2)

1-46 sound recording and re-recording (dubbing)	**تَسْجِيل الصَّوْت والدُّوبْلاج**
1 magnetic sound recording equipment (magnetic sound recorder)	معدات تَسْجيل صوت مغناطيسي
2 magnetic film spool	بكَرَة الشَّريط المغناطيسي
3 magnetic head support assembly	مَجْمُوعَة حامِل الرَّأس المغناطيسي
4 control panel	لَوْحة التَّحَكُّم
5 magnetic sound recording and playback amplifier	مُجَسِّم الصوت الخاص بتَسْجيل الصوت المغناطيسي وتشغيله
6 optical sound recorder (sound recording camera, optical sound recording equipment)	مُسَجِّل الصوت الضَّوْئي
7 daylight film magazine	مَخْزَن حفظ الفيلم في ضَوْء النهار
8 control and monitoring panel	لَوْحة التَّحَكُّم والمراقبة
9 eyepiece for visual control of optical sound recording	عَيْنِيَّة للتحكم البصري في تَسْجيل الصوت الضوئي
10 deck	غلاف
11 recording amplifier and mains power unit	مُضَخِّم تَسْجيل الصوت ووحْدة الطاقة الرئيسيَّة
12 control desk (control console)	كونسول التحكم
13 monitoring loudspeaker (control loudspeaker)	مكبِّرُ صوت للتحكم
14 recording level indicators	مؤشرات مستوى تَسْجيل الصوت
15 monitoring instruments	آلات المتابعة
16 jack panel	لَوْحة المقَابِس
17 control panel	لَوْحة التَّحكُّم
18 sliding control	زِرّ تحكم انزلاقي
19 equalizer	المُوَازِن
20 magnetic sound deck	جِهَاز الصَّوْت المغناطيسي
21 mixer for magnetic film	جِهَاز مكْسَاج الفيلم المغناطيسي
22 film projector	بروجكتور عَرْض الفيلم
23 recording and playback equipment	مُعِدَّات التَّسْجيل والاستماع
24 film reel (film spool)	بكَرَة الفيلم
25 head support assembly for the recording head, playback head, and erase head	مجموعة حامِل رؤوس التَّسْجيل والاستماع والمَسْح
26 film transport mechanism	آليَّة نَقْل الفيلم
27 synchronizing filter	مُرَشِّح تزامني
28 magnetic sound amplifier	مُجَسِّم صوت مغناطيسي
29 control panel	لَوْحة تَحكُّم
30 film-processing machines (film-developing machines) in the processing laboratory (film laboratory, motion picture laboratory)	مُعِدَّات مُعَالَجَة الفيلم في مَعْمَل مُعَالَجَة الأفلام
31 echo chamber	غُرْفَة الصَّدَى
32 echo chamber loudspeaker	مكبِّر صوت غُرْفَة الصَّدَى
33 echo chamber microphone	ميكروفون غُرْفَة الصَّدَى
34-36 sound mixing (sound dubbing, mixing of several sound tracks)	**الدُّوبْلاج** (مَزْج الأصْوَات)
34 mixing room (dubbing room)	حُجْرَة الدوبلاج
35 mixing console (mixing desk) for mono or stereo sound	كونسول دَبْلَجَة الصوت العادي أو المُجَسَّم
36 dubbing mixers (recording engineers, sound recordists) dubbing (mixing)	مُهَنْدِسو الدوبلاج
37-41 synchronization	**الدَّبْلَجَة**

(syncing, dubbing, . post-synchronization, post-syncing)

37 dubbing studio (dubbing theatre, *Am.* theater) — ستديو الدَّبْلَجَة

38 dubbing director — مدير الدوبلاج

39 dubbing speaker (dubbing actress) — المُتَحَدِّث المُرَاد دَبلَجَة صَوْتِه

40 boom microphone — ميكروفون ذو ذِراع

41 microphone cable — كبل الميكروفون

42-46 cutting (editing) — **تنقيح الأفلام وشرائط التَّسْجيل** (المونتاج)

42 cutting table (editing table, cutting bench) — طاولة المونتاج

43 film editor (cutter) — المونتير

44 film turntables for picture and sound tracks — أقْراص الفيلم الدَّوَّارة الحامِلة لِمَسَارات الصورة والصوت

45 projection of the picture — عَرْض الصورة

46 loudspeaker — مكبِّر صوت

312 Films (Motion Pictures) III — الأفْلام السِّينَمَائيَّة (3)

1-23 film projection (motion picture projection) — **عَرْض الفيلم**

1 cinema (picture house, *Am.* movie theater, movie house) — دار السينما (الخيَّالة)

2 cinema box office (*Am.* movie theater box office) — شُبَّاك التذاكر

3 cinema ticket (*Am.* movie theater ticket) — تَذْكَرَة السينما

4 usherette — دليل النَّظَّارَة إلى مقاعدهم

5 cinemagoers (filmgoers, cinema audience, *Am.* moviegoers, movie audience) — زائر السينما

6 safety lighting (emergency lighting) — ضَوْء مَخْرَج الطوارئ

7 emergency exit — مَخْرَج الطوارئ

8 stage — مَسْرَح

9 rows of seats (rows) — صفوف من المقاعد

10 stage curtain (screen curtain) — ستارة المَسْرَح (ستَارة الشاشة)

11 screen (projection screen) — شاشة (شاشة العرض)

12 projection room (projection booth) — حُجَيْرَة إسقاط الفيلم على الشاشة

13 lefthand projector — جِهَاز الإسقاط الأيْسَر

14 righthand projector — جِهَاز الإسقاط الأيْمَن

15 projection room window with projection window and observation port — نافذَة حُجَيْرَة الإسقاط ذات نافِذة الإسقاط وكُوَّة المراقبة

16 reel drum (spool box) — عُلْبَة بكَرَة الفيلم

17 house light dimmers (auditorium lighting control) — أجهزَة التحكم في خَفْت إضاءة دُور العَرْض

18 rectifier, a selenium or mercury vapour rectifier for the projection lamps — مُقَوِّم التيار المتردد

19 amplifier — مُضَخِّم الصوت

20 projectionist — فني أجهزة العرض

21 rewind bench for rewinding the film — طاولة لَفّ الفيلم إلى بدايَتِه

22 film cement (splicing cement) — مادة لاصِقة للأفلام

23 slide projector for advertisements — جِهَاز عَرْض السلايدات الخاص بالإعلانات

24-52 film projectors — **أجهزة عرض الفيلم**

24 sound projector (film projector, cinema projector, theatre projector, *Am.* movie projector) — جِهَاز الصوت

25-38 projector mechanism — **آليَّة جِهَاز العرض**

25 fireproof reel drums (spool boxes) with circulating oil cooling system — أُسْطُوانَتَا البكَرَتَيْن المقاوِمَتَان للحريق المُزَوَّدَتان بنظام تبريد زيتي

26 feed sprocket (supply sprocket) — ضرس التلقيم

27 take-up sprocket — ضرس التقاط الفيلم

28 magnetic head cluster — عنقود الرَّأس المغناطيسي

29 guide roller (guiding roller) with framing control — دولفين دليلي ذو تَحكُّم إطاري

30 loop former for smoothing out the intermittent movement; *also*: film break detector — آليَّة تشكيل أنشوطية لتسوية الحركة المُقَطَّعة؛ أيضا: جِهَاز كَشْف انقطاع الفيلم

31 film path — مَسَار الفيلم

32 film reel (film spool) — بكَرَة الفيلم

33 reel of film — لُفَافَة الفيلم

34 film gate (picture gate, projector gate) with cooling fan — بَوَّابة فيلم بمرْوَحَة تبريد

35 projection lens (projector lens) — عدَسَات جِهَاز العَرْض

36 feed spindle — مِحْوَر تلقيم دَوَّار

37 take-up spindle with friction drive — مِحْوَر التقاط الفيلم ذو إدارة احتكاكيَّة

38 maltese cross mechanism (maltese cross movement, Geneva movement) — آليَّة صليب مالطة

39-44 lamphouse — **مَبيت المصْباح**

39 mirror arc lamp, with aspherical (nonspherical) concave mirror and blowout magnet for stabilizing the arc (*also:* high- — مصْبَاح قوسي ذو مرآة لاكُرَويَّة مُقَعَّرَة ومغناطيس لتثبيت القَوْس (مِصْبَاح زينون قوي عالي الضغط)

pressure xenon arc lamp)

40 positive carbon (positive carbon rod) — قضيب كربون مُوجَب

41 negative carbon (negative carbon rod) — قضيب كربون سالِب

42 arc — قَوْس

43 carbon rod holder — حامِل قضيب الكربون

44 crater (carbon crater) — حُفْرَة الكربون

45 optical sound unit [also designed for multi-channel optical stereophonic sound and for push-pull sound tracks] — وَحْدَة الصوت الضَّوْئي (مصممة أيضاً للصوت المجسم البصري متعدد القنوات ولمسارات الصوت الدفعية الجذبية)

46 sound optics — بصريَّات صوتيَّة

47 sound head — رَأْس صوتي

48 exciter lamp in housing — مِصْبَاح مُسْتَثِير في مَبيته

49 photocell in hollow drum — خَلِيَّة كهروضوئيَّة في أسطوانة مُجَوَّفَة

50 attachable four-track magnetic sound unit (penthouse head, magnetic sound head) — وَحْدَة صوت مغناطيسيَّة ذات أربعة مسالِك قابِلة للفصل والتركيب

51 four-track magnetic head — رَأْس مغناطيسي ذات أربع مَسَارَات

52 narrow-gauge (*Am.* narrow-gage) cinema projector for mobile cinema — جِهَاز عَرْض سينمائي ذو مِقْيَاس ضيق للسينما المتنقلة

313 Films (Motion Pictures) IV — الأفْلام السِّينْمَائيَّة (4)

1-39 motion picture cameras (film cameras) — **كاميرات الصُّوَر المتحركة**

1 standard-gauge (*Am.* standard-gage) motion picture camera (standard-gauge, *Am.* standard gage, 35 mm camera) — كاميرا تصوير سينمائي ذات مِقْيَاس قياسي 35 مللم

2 lens (object lens, taking lens) — عَدَسَة

3 lens hood (sunshade) with matte box — غطاء عَدَسَة ذو صندوق مُطْفِأ اللمْعَة

4 matte (mask) — سَطْح مُطْفِأ اللمْعَة (مُصَنْفَر)

5 lens hood barrel — أُسْطُوَانة غطاء العَدَسَة

6 viewfinder eyepiece — عَيْنِيَّة مُحَدِّد الرؤية

7 eyepiece control ring — حَلَقَة ضبط العَيْنِيَّة

8 opening control for the segment disc (disk) shutter — ذِراع ضبط الفتحة الخاص بمِغْلاق القُرْص

9 magazine housing — مَبيت عُلْبَة الفيلم

10 slide bar for the lens hood — القَضيب المنزلق الخاص بغِطَاء العدسة

11 control arm (control lever) — ذِراع الضبط

12 pan and tilt head — رَأْس التدوير الفوتوغرافي والإمالَة

13 wooden tripod — حامِل ثلاثيّ خشبي

14 degree scale — مقياس مُدَرَّج

15 soundproof (blimped) motion picture camera (film camera) — كاميرا تصوير سينمائي مزودة بعازِل للصوت

16-18 soundproof housing (blimp) — **مَبيت عازِل للصوت**

16 upper section of the soundproof housing — الجُزْء العلوي للمَبيت العازِل للصوت

17 lower section of the soundproof housing — الجُزْء السفلي للمَبيت العازِل للصوت

18 open sidewall of the soundproof housing — السَّطْح الجانبي المفتوح للمَبيت العازِل للصوت

19 camera lens — عَدَسَة الكاميرا

20 lightweight professional motion picture camera — كاميرا تصوير سينمائي خفيفة الوَزْن

21 grip (handgrip) — قَبْضَة الكاميرا

22 zooming lever — ذِراع عَدَسَة الزوم

23 zoom lens (variable focus lens, varifocal lens) with infinitely variable focus — عَدَسَة زوم ذات بُعْد بؤري لانهائي متنوِّع

24 handgrip with shutter release — قَبْضَة اليد وَزِرّ اعتاق المِغْلاق

25 camera door — باب الكاميرا

26 sound camera (newsreel camera) for recording sound and picture — كاميرا صوتيَّة لتَسْجيل الصوت والصورة

27 soundproof housing (blimp) — مَبيت عازِل للصوت

28 window for the frame counters and indicator scales — نافذة عدَّادات الإطار والقياسات الإرشاديَّة

29 pilot tone cable (sync pulse cable) — كيبل النغمة الدليليَّة

30 pilot tone generator (signal generator, pulse generator) — مُوَلِّد النغمة الدليليَّة

31 professional narrow-gauge (*Am.* narrow-gage) motion picture camera, a 16 mm camera — كاميرا تصوير سينمائي عيار 16 ملم

32 lens turret (turret head) — بُرْج العَدَسَة

33 housing lock — حَابِس المبيت

34 eyecup — كَأْس العَيْنِيَّة

35 high-speed camera, a special narrow-gauge (*Am.* narrow-gage) camera — كاميرا عالية السرعة، كاميرا خاصة بمقياس ضيق

36 zooming lever — ذِراع الزوم

37 rifle grip — قبضة بندقية

38 handgrip with shutter release — قبضة اليد وَزِرّ اعتاق المِغْلاق

39 lens hood bellows — مِنْفَاخ غِطاء العَدَسَة

314 Ballet — البَاليه

1-6 the five positions — **الأَوْضَاع الخَمْسَة للباليه**

(ballet positions)	
1 first position	الوَضْع الأوَّل
2 second position	الوَضْع الثاني
3 third position	الوَضْع الثالِث
4 fourth position [open]	الوَضْع الرابِع [مفتوح]
5 fourth position [crossed; extended fifth position]	الوَضْع الرابِع [متقاطع؛ الوَضْع الخامِس المُمْتَدّ]
6 fifth position	الوَضْع الخامِس
7-10 ports de bras (arm positions)	**أوْضاع الذِّرَاعَيْن**
7 port de bras à coté	وَضْع الذِّرَاعَيْن جانباً
8 port de bras en bas	وَضْع الذِّرَاعَيْن إلى أسفل
9 port de bras en avant	وَضْع الذِّرَاعَيْن للأمام
10 port de bras en haut	وَضْع الذِّرَاعَيْن لأعلى
11 dégagé á la quatrième devant	وُقوف على طَرْف القَدَم اليسرى إلى الأمام والقَدَم اليمنى ثابتة
12 dégagé á la quatrième derrière	وُقوف على طَرْف القَدَم اليسرى إلى الخلف والقَدَم اليمنى ثابتة
13 effacé	وُقوف على طَرْف القَدَم اليمنى إلى الجانب والقَدَم اليسرى ثابتة
14 sur le cou-de-pied	وُقوف على طَرْف القَدَم اليسرى وضمها إلى القَدَم اليمنى
15 écarté	وُقوف على القَدَم اليسرى ورفع الرِّجْل اليمنى مستقيمة إلى الجانب
16 croisé	وَقْفَة تَصالُبِيَّة
17 attitude	الوُقوف على طَرْف القَدَم ورَفْع الأخرى مستقيمة إلى الخلف
18 arabesque	أرابيسك
19 à pointe (on full point)	طَرْف القَدَم
20 splits	انفِراج الساقَيْن بزاوية قائمة مع الجِذْع
21 cabriole (capriole)	وَثْبَة
22 entrechat (entrechat quatre)	وَثْبَة تَصالُبِيَّة
23 préparation [e.g. for a pirouette]	الإعداد [للدوران البَرْوَتَة مثلاً]
24 pirouette	بَرْوَتَة (دوران على قدم واحدة أو أصابع القدم)
25 corps de ballet	فريق الباليه
26 ballet dancer (ballerina)	راقِصة الباليه (باليرينا)
27-28 pas de trois	**الرقصة الثلاثية**
27 prima ballerina	الباليرينا الأولى (الراقِصة الأولى)
28 principal male dancer (leading soloist)	الراقِص الأوَّل
29 tutu	تَنُّورة منتفخة قصيرة
30 point shoe, a ballet shoe (ballet slipper)	حِذاء الباليه (حِذاء مستدق الطَرْف)
31 ballet skirt	تَنُّورة الباليه

315 Theatre (*Am.* Theater) I — المَسْرَح (1)

1-4 types of curtain operation	**أنواع تَشْغيل الستارة**
1 draw curtain (side parting)	سِتَارَة تُسْحَب إلى الجانب
2 tableau curtain (bunching up sideways)	سِتَارَة التابلوه : تنفتح في الوسط ولها جناحان يمكن رفعهما لأعلى أو سحبهما يميناً ويساراً
3 fly curtain (vertical ascent)	سِتَارَة رَأْسِيَّة
4 combined fly and draw curtain	سِتَارَة رَأْسِيَّة تنسحب إلى الجانب
5-11 cloakroom hall (*Am.* checkroom hall)	**رَدْهَة حُجْرَة إيداع المَعَاطِف والقُبَّعَات**
5 cloakroom (*Am.* checkroom)	حُجْرَة إيداع المَعَاطِف والقُبَّعَات مؤقتاً
6 cloakroom attendant (*Am.* checkroom attendant)	عامِلة حُجْرَة إيداع المَعَاطِف
7 cloakroom ticket (*Am.* check)	بطاقة حُجْرَة إيداع المَعَاطِف
8 playgoer (theatregoer, *Am.* theatergoer)	زائر المَسْرَح
9 opera glass (opera glasses)	مِنْظَار الأوبرا
10 commissionaire	بَوَّاب ببذلة رسمية
11 theatre (*Am.* theater) ticket, an admission ticket	تذكرة دخول المَسْرَح
12-13 foyer (lobby, crush room)	**بَهْو/رُوَاق المَسْرَح**
12 usher; *form.*: box attendant	دليل النُّظَّارة إلى مقاعدهم
13 programme (*Am.* program)	البرنامج
14-27 auditorium and stage	**القاعة وخشبة المَسْرَح**
14 stage	خَشَبَة المَسْرَح
15 proscenium	ستارة المَسْرَح وإطارها
16-20 auditorium	**القاعة**
16 gallery (balcony)	البَلَكُون
17 upper circle	الشُّرْفَة العلويَّة
18 dress circle (*Am.* balcony, mezzanine)	الشُّرْفَة الرسميَّة
19 front stalls	المقاعِد الأماميَّة
20 seat (theatre seat, *Am.* theater seat)	مَقْعَد
21-27 rehearsal (stage rehearsal)	**البروفات المسرحية**
21 chorus	كورال
22 singer	مُغَنِّي
23 singer	مُغَنِّيَة
24 orchestra pit	مَوْضِع الأوركسترا أمام خَشَبَة المسرح
25 orchestra	الأوركسترا
26 conductor	قائد الأوركسترا
27 baton (conductor's	عصا قائد الأوركسترا

baton)

28-42 paint room, a workshop **حُجْرَة الطلاء، وَرْشَة**

28 stagehand (scene shifter) مُبَدِّل المناظر

29 catwalk (bridge) مَمَر (كوبري)

30 set piece قطعة مَنْظَر في المسرحيَّة

31 reinforcing struts دعامتا تقوية

32 built piece (built unit) قطعة مَبْنِيَّة

33 backcloth (backdrop) ستارة المَسْرَح الخلفية

34 portable box for paint containers صندوق عُلَب الطلاء

35 scene painter عامِل طلاء المناظر

36 paint trolley تروللى الطلاء

37 stage designer (set designer) مُصَمِّم المناظر

38 costume designer مُصَمِّم الملابس

39 design for a costume تصميم ملابس

40 sketch for a costume رسم تخطيطي لزيّ

41 model stage نموذج مسرح

42 model of the set نموذج منظر مسرحي

43-52 dressing room **حُجْرَة الملابس**

43 dressing room mirror مِرآة حُجْرَة الملابس

44 make-up gown مريلة الماكياج

45 make-up table طاولة المكياج

46 greasepaint stick قلم مكياج شَحْميّ

47 chief make-up artist (chief make-up man) الماكيير الرئيسي

48 make-up artist (hair-stylist) مُصَفِّف الشَّعْر

49 wig شَعْر مُسْتَعار (باروكة)

50 props (properties) مُقْتَنَيَات

51 theatrical costume زيّ مسرحي

52 call light ضَوْء الاستدعاء

316 Theatre (*Am.* Theater) II المَسْرَح (2)

1-60 stagehouse with machinery (machinery in the flies and below stage) **دار المَسْرَح والماكينات** (الماكينات أعلى وأسفل خشبة المَسْرَح)

1 control room غرفة التحكم

2 control console (lighting console, lighting control console) with preset control for presetting lighting effects كونسول التحكم ومفاتيح ضبط المؤثِّرات الضوئيَّة مُسبقاً

3 lighting plot (light plot) دليل الإضاءة

4 grid (gridiron) شبكة قضبان متصالبة

5 fly floor (fly gallery) طابق علوي

6 sprinkler system for fire prevention (for fire protection) نظام رش لمقاومة الحريق

7 fly man عامِل الطابق العلوي

8 fly lines (lines) أحْبَال الطابق العلوي

9 cyclorama السَّيْكْلُورَاما

10 backcloth (backdrop, background) ستارة المَسْرَح الخلفيَّة

11 arch, a drop cloth قَوْس

12 border حَدّ

13 compartment (compartment-type, compartmentalized) batten (*Am.* border light) عارِضة خشبيَّة

14 stage lighting units (stage lights) وَحْدَات إضاءة خشبة المَسْرَح

15 horizon lights (backdrop lights) أضواء الستارة الخلفيَّة

16 adjustable acting area lights (acting area spot-lights) أضواء كاشفة خاصة بمنطقة التمثيل على المَسْرَح

17 scenery projectors (projectors) أجهزة عرض المناظر

18 monitor (water cannon) (piece of safety equipment) مِدْفَع المياه (معدة سلامة)

19 travelling (*Am.* traveling) lighting bridge (travelling lighting gallery) جِسْر إضاءة مُتَحَرِّك

20 lighting operator (lighting man) مُشَغِّل الإضاءة

21 portal spotlight (tower spotlight) ضَوْء كاشِف بُرْجيّ

22 adjustable proscenium ستارة المَسْرَح وإطارها (قابلة للضبط)

23 curtain (theatrical curtain) سِتَارة

24 iron curtain (safety curtain, fire curtain) سِتَارة حديديَّة (ستارة أمان، ستارة حريق)

25 forestage (apron) مقدمة خشبة المَسْرَح أمام الستارة

26 footlight (footlights, floats) إضاءة سفليَّة

27 prompt box صندوق المُلَقِّن

28 prompter المُلَقِّن

29 stage manager's desk مكتب مدير خشبة المَسْرَح

30 stage director (stage manager) مدير خشبة المَسْرَح

31 revolving stage مَسْرَح دَوَّار

32 trap opening باب مَسْحُور

33 lift (*Am.* elevator) مصعد

34 bridge (*Am.* elevator), a rostrum كوبري، جِسْر

35 pieces of scenery قِطَع المناظر

36 scene مَشْهَد

37 actor مُمَثِّل

38 actress مُمَثِّلة

39 extras (supers, supernumeraries) كومبارس

40 director (producer) المُخْرِج (المُنْتِج)

41 prompt book (prompt script) سيناريو التَّلْقِين

42 director's table (producer's table) طاولة المُخْرِج (طاولة المُنْتِج)

43 assistant director (assistant producer) المُخْرِج المُسَاعِد (المُنْتِج المُسَاعِد)

44 director's script (producer's script)	نَصُّ المُخْرِج (نَصُّ المُنْتِج)
45 stage carpenter	نجَّار المسرح
46 stagehand (scene shifter)	مُبَدِّل المناظر
47 set piece	قطعة مَنْظَر
48 mirror spot (mirror spotlight)	ضَوْء كاشِف مزود بمرآة
49 automatic filter change (with colour filters, colour mediums, gelatines)	غيار مُرَشِّح آليّ (مع فلاتر وأوساط الألوان والهيلامين)
50 hydraulic plant room	حُجْرَة الوَحدَة الهيدروليَّة
51 water tank	خَزَّان ماء
52 suction pipe	أنبوب ماص
53 hydraulic pump	مضَخَّة هيدروليَّة
54 pressure pipe	أنبوب ضغط
55 pressure tank (accumulator)	خَزَّان ضغط
56 pressure gauge (*Am.* gage)	مِقْيَاس الضغط
57 level indicator (liquid level indicator)	مؤشر مستوى السائل
58 control lever	ذراع التحكم
59 operator	مُشَغِّل
60 rams	مكْبَسَا المِضَخَّة

317 Discotheque — صَالَة الدِّيسْكُو

1 bar	البار
2 barmaid	ساقِيَة البار
3 bar stool	مَقْعَد البار
4 shelf for bottles	رَفُّ الزجاجات
5 shelf for glasses	رَفُّ الأكْوَاب
6 beer glass	كُوب الجُعَّة
7 wine and liqueur glasses	أكْوَاب الخمور والمُسْكِرات
8 beer tap (tap)	صُنْبُور الجُعَّة
9 bar	بار
10 refrigerator (fridge, *Am.* icebox)	ثلاجة
11 bar lamps	مصابيح البار
12 indirect lighting	إضاءة غير مباشرة
13 colour (*Am.* color) organ (clavilux)	أرْغَن مُلَوَّن
14 dance floor lighting	إضاءة أرضيَّة المَرْقَص
15 speaker (loudspeaker)	مُكَبِّر صوت
16 dance floor	أرضيَّة المَرْقص
17-18 dancing couple	**ثنائي يرقصان**
17 dancer	رَاقِصة
18 dancer	رَاقِص
19 record player	جِهَاز تشغيل الأسطوانات
20 microphone	ميكروفون
21 tape recorder	مُسَجِّل شرائط
22-23 stereo system (stereo equipment)	**نظام تجسيم الصوت**
22 tuner	جِهَاز الضبط الدقيق
23 amplifier	مُضَخِّم الصوت
24 records (discs)	أسْطُوَانات (أقراص)
25 disc jockey	مشغل الأسْطُوَانات (دي جيه)
26 mixing console (mixing desk, mixer)	كونسول الدَّمْج
27 tambourine	رِقٌّ، دُفٌّ صغير
28 mirrored wall	حَائط مكْسُو بالمرايات
29 ceiling tiles	قرميد السقف
30 ventilators	فتحات التهوية
31 toilets (lavatories, WC)	دورات المياه
32 long drink	كَأْس طويلة للشراب
33 cocktail (*Am.* highball)	كوكتيل

318 Nightclub — المَلْهَى الليْلِي

1-33 nightclub (night spot)	**المَلْهَى الليْلِي**
1 cloakroom (*Am.* check-room)	غرفة إيداع القُبَّعَات والمَعَاطِف
2 cloakroom attendant (*Am.* checkroom attendant)	عامِل غرفة إيداع القُبَّعَات والمَعَاطِف
3 band	فِرْقَة موسيقيَّة
4 clarinet	كلارنيت
5 clarinettist (*Am.* clarinetist)	عازف الكلارنيت
6 trumpet	البُوق
7 trumpeter	عازف البُوق
8 guitar	الجيتار
9 guitarist (guitar player)	عازف الجيتار
10 drums	الطَّبْلَة
11 drummer	عازف الطَّبْلَة
12 speaker (loudspeaker)	مكبِّر صوت
13 bar	البار
14 barmaid	ساقية البار
15 bar	بار
16 bar stool	مَقْعَد البار
17 tape recorder	جِهَاز تَسْجيل
18 receiver	مُسْتَقْبِل
19 spirits	مَشْرُوبات رَوْحيَّة
20 cine projector for porno films (sex films, blue movies)	جِهَاز عرض سينمائي للأفلام الجِنْسِيَّة
21 box containing screen	صندوق يحتوى على شاشة
22 stage	مَسْرَح
23 stage lighting	إضاءة المَسْرَح
24 spotlight	ضَوْء كاشف
25 festoon lighting	إضاءة فُسْطُونيَّة
26 festoon lamp (lamp, light bulb)	مِصْبَاح فُسْطُوني
27-32 striptease act (striptease number)	**رقصة التجرد من الملابس** (استربتيز)
27 striptease artist (stripper)	رَاقِصة الاستربتيز
28 suspender (*Am.* garter)	حَمَّالة
29 brassière (bra)	صُدَيْريَّة الثديين
30 fur stole	دِثَار من الفرو
31 gloves	قُفَّازان
32 stocking	جَوْرَب نسائيّ
33 hostess	النادِلَة، المضيفة

319 Bullfighting, Rodeo — مُصَارَعَة الثِّيرَان

1-33 bullfight (corrida,	**مُصَارَعَة الثِّيرَان**

corrida de toros)
1 mock bullfight مُصَارَعَة ثيران زائفة
2 novice (aspirant matador, novillero) متمرِّن، مُتَدَرِّب
3 mock bull (dummy bull) ثَوْر زائف
4 novice banderillero (apprentice banderillero) مُصَارِع ثيران تحت التدريب
5 bullring (plaza de toros) [diagram] حلَبَة مُصَارَعَة الثيران [رسم تخطيطي]
6 main entrance المَدْخَل الرئيسي
7 boxes مقصورات
8 stands منَصَّات
9 arena (ring) حَلَبَة
10 bullfighters' entrance مَدْخَل مُصَارِع الثيران
11 torril door باب دخول الثَّوْر إلى الحَلَبَة
12 exit gate for killed bulls باب خروج الثيران القتيلة
13 slaughterhouse المَجْزَر
14 bull pens (corrals) حظائر الثيران
15 paddock اصطبل عرض الثيران قبل تباريها
16 lancer on horseback (picador) رَمَّاح يمتطي صهوة الحصَان
17 lance (pike, pole, javelin) رُمْح
18 armoured (*Am.* armored) horse حِصَان مُدَرَّع
19 leg armour (*Am.* armor) دِرْع الساق
20 picador's round hat قُبَّعَة البيكادور المستديرة
21 banderillero, a torero مُصَارِع الثيران
22 banderillas (barbed darts) سِهَام مُرَيَّشَة
23 shirtwaist بلوزة تصل إلى الخصر
24 bullfight مُصَارَعَة الثيران
25 matador (swordsman), a torero الماتادور، مُصَارِع الثيران
26 queue, a distinguishing mark of the matador ضفيرة، علامة مميزة للمُصَارِع
27 red cloak (capa) عباءة حمراء
28 fighting bull ثَوْر المُصَارَعَة
29 montera [hat made of tiny black silk chenille balls] المونتيرا [قبعة مصنوعة من كريات صغيرة من الحرير الأسود]
30 killing the bull (kill, estocada) قَتْل الثَّوْر
31 matador in charity performances [without professional uniform] المَتَادُور في عروض خيْريَّة [بدون الزيّ الرسمي]
32 estoque (sword) سَيْف
33 muleta عباءة (الميوليتا)
34 rodeo الروديـو
35 young bull ثَوْر صغير
36 cowboy راعي البقر
37 stetson (stetson hat) قُبَّعَة راعي البقر
38 scarf (necktie) منديل، رباط عنق
39 rodeo rider فارس الروديُو
40 lasso وَهَق: حَبْل في طَرَفه أنشوطة

320 Musical Notation I — النُّوتَات المُوسِيقيَّة (1)

1-2 medieval (mediaeval) **notes** **النوتات القروسطية**
1 plainsong notation (neumes, neums, pneumes, square notation) التَّنْويت لعدد من الأصوات
2 mensural notation التَّنْويت القياسي
3-7 musical note (note) **النُّوتَة الموسيقية**
3 note head رَأس النُّوتَة
4 note stem (note tail) ذَيْل النُّوتَة
5 hook خطّاف
6 stroke شَرْطَة
7 dot indicating augmentation of note's value نُقْطَة تفيد مضاعفة قيمة النُّوتَة
8-11 clefs **المفاتيح**
8 treble clef (G-clef, violin clef) مِفْتَاح "صول"
9 bass clef (F-clef) مِفْتَاح "فا" (باص)
10 alto clef (C-clef) مِفْتَاح "دو" (ألتو)
11 tenor clef مِفْتَاح تينور
12-19 note values **قِيَم النوتات**
12 breve (brevis, *Am.* double-whole note) نُوتَة بسرعة مضاعفة
13 semibreve (*Am.* whole note) [المستديرة] نُوتَة بقيمة "روند"
14 minim (*Am.* half note) [البيضاء] نُوتَة بقيمة "بلانش"
15 crotchet (*Am.* quarter note) [السوداء] نُوتَة بقيمة "نوار"
16 quaver (*Am.* eighth note) [ذات السِّن] نُوتَة بقيمة "كروش"
17 semiquaver (*Am.* sixteenth note) [ثُنَائيَّة الأَسْنَان] نُوتَة بقيمة "دوبل كروش"
18 demisemiquaver (*Am.* thirty-second note) [ثُلاثيَّة الأَسْنَان] نُوتَة بقيمة "تربل كروش"
19 hemidemisemiquer (*Am.* sixty-fourth note) [رُبَاعِيَّة الأَسْنَان] نُوتَة بقيمة "كوادربل كروس"
20-27 rests **راحة، سَكْتَة**
20 breve rest سَكْتَة موجزة
21 semibreve rest (*Am.* whole rest) سَكْتَة بقيمة "روند" [الراحة]
22 minim rest (*Am.* half rest) سَكْتَة بقيمة "بلانش" [نِصْف الراحة]
23 crotchet rest (*Am.* quarter rest) سَكْتَة بقيمة "نوار" [زمن التنفس]
24 quaver rest (*Am.* eighth rest) سَكْتَة بقيمة "كروش" [نِصْف زمن التنفس]
25 semiquaver rest (*Am.* sixteenth rest) سَكْتَة بقيمة "دوبل كروش" [رُبْع زمن التنفس]
26 demisemiquaver rest (*Am.* thirty-second rest) سَكْتَة بقيمة "تربل كروش" [اللميحة]
27 hemidemisemiquaver rest (*Am.* sixty-fourth rest) سَكْتَة بقيمة "كوادربل كروش" [الومضة]
28-42 time (time signatures, measure, *Am.* meter) **المِيزَان، دليل المِيزَان**

28 two-eight time — ميزَان 2–8
29 two-four time — ميزَان 2–4
30 two-two time — ميزَان 2–2
31 four-eight time — ميزَان 4–8
32 four-four time (common time) — ميزَان 4–4 (الميزَان العادي)
33 four-two time — ميزَان 4–2
34 six-eight time — ميزَان 6–8
35 six-four time — ميزَان 6–4
36 three-eight time — ميزَان 3–8
37 three-four time — ميزَان 3–4
38 three-two time — ميزَان 3–2
39 nine-eight time — ميزَان 9–8
40 nine-four time — ميزَان 9–4
41 five-four time — ميزَان 5–4
42 bar (bar line, measure line) — حاجز
43-44 staff (stave) — **المدْرَج**
43 line of the staff — خَطّ المَدْرَج
44 space — فراغ
45-49 scales — **السُلَّم**
45 C major scale naturals: c, d, e, f, g, a, b, c — علامات سُلَّم الـ "دو" الكبير: دو، ري، مي، فا، صول، لا، س، دو
46 A minor scale [natural] naturals: a, b, c, d, e, f, g, a — علامات السُلَّم الصغير "لا": لا، سي، دو، ري، مي، فا، صول، لا
47 A minor scale [harmonic] — سُلَّم "لا" الصغير [توافقي]
48 A minor scale [melodic] — سُلَّم "لا" الصغير [لَحْنِيّ]
49 chromatic scale — سُلَّم ملَوَّن
50-54 accidentals (inflections, key signatures) — **علامات تحويل النَّغمَة عرضياً**
50-51 signs indicating the raising of a note — **علامات رَفْع النَّغمَة**
50 sharp (raising the note a semitone or half-step) — علامة الزيادة (رَفْع النَّغمَة نِصْف درجة)
51 double sharp (raising the note a tone or full-step) — علامة الزيادة مرتين (رَفْع النَّغمَة درجة كاملة)
52-53 signs indicating the lowering of a note — **علامات خَفْض النَّغمَة**
52 flat (lowering the note a semitone or half-step) — علامة التنقيص (خَفْض النَّغمَة نِصْف درجة)
53 double flat (lowering the note a tone or full-step) — علامة التنقيص مرتين (خَفْض النَّغمَة درجة كاملة)
54 natural — [علامة الغناء]، علامة الطبيعة
55-68 keys (major keys and the related minor keys having the same signature) — **المفاتيح** (المفاتيح الكبيرة والمفاتيح الصغيرة المرتبطة بها ولها نفس الدليل)
55 C major (A minor) — "دو" كبير ("لا" صغير)
56 G major (E minor) — "صول" كبير ("مي" صغير)
57 D major (B minor) — "ري" كبير ("سي" صغير)
58 A major (F sharp minor) — "لا" كبير ("فا" زائدة صغير)
59 E major (C sharp minor) — "مي" كبير ("لا" زائدة صغير)
60 B major (G sharp minor) — "سي" كبير ("صول" زائدة صغير)
61 F sharp major (D sharp minor) — "فا" زائدة كبير ("ري" صغير)
62 C major (A minor) — "دو" كبير ("لا" صغير)
63 F major (D minor) — "فا" كبير ("ري" صغير)
64 B flat major (G minor) — "سي" ناقصة كبير ("صول" صغير)
65 E flat major (C minor) — "مي" ناقصة كبير ("دو" صغير)
66 A flat major (F minor) — "لا" ناقصة كبير ("فا" صغير)
67 D flat major (B flat minor) — "ري" ناقصة كبير ("سي" ناقصة صغير)
68 G flat major (E flat minor) — "صول" ناقصة كبير ("مي" ناقصة صغير)

321 Musical Notation II — النُوتَات المُوسِيقيَّة (2)

1-5 chord — **ائتلاف**
1-4 triad — مُثَلَّث
1 major triad — مُثَلَّث كبير
2 minor triad — مُثَلَّث صغير
3 diminished triad — مُثَلَّث محسوم
4 augmented triad — مُثَلَّث مضاف
5 chord of four notes, a chord of the seventh (seventh chord, dominant seventh chord) — ائتلاف من أَرْبَع نغمات (ائْتِلاف سُباعي)
6-13 intervals — الفواصل
6 unison (unison interval) — تطابق النغمات
7 major second — ثنائي كبير، مسافة صوتية ببعد ثان كبير
8 major third — ثلاثي كبير، مسافة صوتية ببعد ثلاثي كبير
9 perfect fourth — رباعي تام، مسافة صوتية رُبَاعيَّة تامة
10 perfect fifth — خماسي تام، مسافة صوتية خُمَاسيَّة تامة
11 major sixth — سداسي كبير، مسافة صوتية سُدَاسِيَّة كبيرة
12 major seventh — سباعي كبير، مسافة صوتية سباعية كبيرة
13 perfect octave — ثُمَاني تام، مسافة صوتية ببعد ثامن تام
14-22 ornaments (graces, grace notes) — **الزخارف** (النوافل)
14 long appoggiatura — نَافلَة طويلة
15 acciaccatura (short appoggiatura) — نَافلَة قصيرة
16 slide — انزلاق
17 trill (shake) without turn — زغردة بدون التفاف
18 trill (shake) with turn — زغردة بالتفاف
19 upper mordent — زغردة قصيرة علوية

(inverted mordent, pralltriller)

20 lower mordent (mordent) — زغردة قصيرة سفلية

21 turn — التفاف

22 arpeggio — ائتلاف منفصل

23-26 other signs in musical notation — **علامات أخرى في التنويت الموسيقي**

23 triplet: corresponding groupings: duplet (couplet), quadruplet, quintuplet, sextolet (sextuplet), septolet (septuplet, septimole) — ثُلْثيَّة: المجموعات المقابلة: ثُنْئيَّة، رُبْعيَّة، خُمْسيَّة، سُدْسيَّة، سُبْعيَّة

24 tie (bind) — رباط

25 pause (pause sign) — راحة، سَكْتَة (علامة السَكْتَة)

27 marcato (marcando, markiert, attack, strong accent) — مُشَدَّد، مُنَبَّر

28 presto (quick, fast — سريع جداً

29 portato (lourer, mezzo staccato, carried) — مَحْمُول (نِصْف متقطِّع)

30 tenuto (held) — مُطَوَّل، مُمْتَد

31 crescendo (increasing gradually in power) — [التَّصَعُّد] (تزايد الوقع تدريجيا)

32 decrescendo (diminuendo, decreasing or diminishing gradually in power) — [التَّنَزُّل] (يزخَّم تدريجياً)

33 legato (bound) — مربوط

34 staccato (detached) — مُتقطع

35 piano (soft) — رَخيم

36 pianissimo (very soft) — رَخيم جداً، خافت جداً

37 pianissimo piano (as soft as possible) — رَخيم للغاية

38 forte (loud) — قوي، جَهير

39 fortissimo (very loud) — شديد الوقع، بمنتهي الشدة

40 forte fortissimo (double fortissimo, as loud as possible) — قوي أو شديد الوقع للغاية

41 forte piano (loud and immediately soft again) — قوي ثم رَخيم ثانية فجأة

42-50 divisions of the compass — **أقسام المدى**

42 subcontra octave (double contra octave) — أوكْتَاف دُبْل كونتر

43 contra octave — أوكْتَاف كونتر

44 great octave — أوكْتَاف كبير

45 small octave — أوكْتَاف صغير

46 one-line octave — أوكْتَاف خَطّ واحد

47 two-line octave — أوكْتَاف خَطَّيْن

48 three-line octave — أوكْتَاف ثلاثة خَطُوط

49 four-line octave — أوكْتَاف اربعة خَطُوط

50 five-line octave — أوكْتَاف خمسة خَطُوط

322 Musical Instruments I — الآلات المُوسِيقيَّة (1)

1 lur, a bronze trumpet — ترامبيت برونزي

2 panpipes (Pandean pipes, syrinx) — المِصْفَار

3 aulos, a double shawm — آلة الشَّوْم الخشبية المزدوجة

4 aulos pipe — مِزْمَار آلة الشَّوْم

5 phorbeia (peristomion, capistrum, mouth band) — رباط الفم

6 crumhorn (crummhorn, cromorne, krumbhorn, krummhorn) — بُوق الكرومهورن

7 recorder (fipple flute) — مِزْمَار خشبي

8 bagpipe; *sim.:* musette — مِزْمَار القِرَب

9 bag — القِرْبَة

10 chanter (melody pipe) — مِزْمَار اللحن

11 drone (drone pipe) — مِزْمَار القِرْبَة

12 curved cornett (zink) — السَّيَاع، كورنه

13 serpent — بُوق السربنت

14 shawm (schalmeyes); larger: bombard (bombarde, pommer) — آلة الشَّوْم

15 cythara (cithara); *sim. and smaller:* lyre — القِيثَارَة؛ مثلها ولكن أصغر حجما: قيثارة اللير

16 arm — ذِرَاع القِيثَارَة

17 bridge — مُشْط القِيثَارَة

18 sound box (resonating chamber, resonator) — صُنْدُوق الصوت، حجيرة الرنين

19 plectrum, a plucking device — رِيشَة العازِف

20 kit (pochette), a miniature violin — كَمَان صغير

21 cittern (cithern, cither, cister, citole), a plucked instrument; *sim.:* pandora (bandora, a bandore) — قانون إفرنجي، سيتار؛ مثله: البَنْدُور

22 sound hole — فتحة خروج الصوت

23 viol (descant viol, treble viol, a viola da gamba); *larger:* tenor viol, bass viol (viola da gamba, gamba), violone (double bass viol) — الكَمَان، [الفيولون]؛ الحجم الكبير: الكَمَان الأَجْهَر/الصَّادِح

24 viol bow — قَوْس الكَمَان

25 hurdy-gurdy (vielle à roue, symphonia, armonie, organistrum) — أَرْغَن يدوي

26 friction wheel — عجلة الاحتكاك

27 wheel cover (wheel guard) — وقاء العجلة

28 keyboard (keys) — لَوْحة المفاتيح

29 resonating body (resonator, sound box) — صُنْدُوق الصوت

30 melody strings — أَوْتَار الألحان

31 drone strings (drones, bourdons) — أَوْتَار الدندنة

32 dulcimer — قانون، سنطير، سنْطور

33 rib (resonator wall) — ضِلْع (جدار الرنين)

34 beater for the Valasian dulcimer — أداة عزف القانون الفالصي

35 hammer (stick) for the Appenzell dulcimer	مِقرْعة القانون الأبنزلي
36 Clavichord; *kinds:* fretted or unfretted clavichord	كلافيكورد؛ أنواعه: ذو عتب أو بدون عتب
37 clavichord mechanism	آلية عمل الكلافيكورد
38 key (key lever)	مِفْتَاح
39 balance rail	قضيب توازن
40 guiding blade	لِسَان دليلي
41 guiding slot	شقّة دليلية
42 resting rail	قضيب إسناد
43 tangent	قطعة مماس
44 string	وَتَر
45 harpsichord (clavicembalo, cembalo), a wing-shaped stringed keyboard instrument; *sim.:* spinet (virginal)	الهاربسيكورد؛ السبنيت، بيان صغير
46 upper keyboard (upper manual)	لَوْحة المفاتيح العلوية
47 lower keyboard (lower manual)	لَوْحة المفاتيح السفلية
48 harpsichord mechanism	آلية عمل الهاربسيكورد
49 key (key lever)	مِفْتَاح
50 jack	عمود
51 slide (register)	قطعة منزلقة
52 tongue	لِسَان
53 quill plectrum	رِيشَة عاجية لنقر الوَتَر
54 damper	دَوَّاسَة منع اهتزاز الأَوْتَار
55 string	وَتَر
56 portative organ, a portable organ; *larger:* positive organ (positive)	أَرْغَن نقالي
57 pipe (flue pipe)	مِصْفَار
58 bellows	مِنْفَاخ الأَرْغَن

323 Musical Instruments II — الآلات المُوسِيقيَّة (2)

1-62 orchestral instruments	**آلات الأوركسترا**
1-27 stringed instruments, bowed instruments	**آلات وَتَرِيَّة**
1 violin	الكَمَان
2 neck of the violin	عُنُق الكَمَان
3 resonating body (violin body, sound box of the violin)	جسم الكَمَان
4 rib (side wall)	ضِلْع (الجدار الجانبي)
5 violin bridge	مُشْط الكَمَان
6 F-hole, a sound hole	فتحة علي شكل F
7 tailpiece	قطعة الذَّيْل
8 chin rest	مِسْنَد ذقن العازف
9 strings (violin strings, fiddle strings): G-string, D-string, A-string, E-string	أَوْتَار الكَمَان: وَتَر "صول" وَتَر "ري" وَتَر "لا" وَتَر "مي"
10 mute (sordino)	مِخْفَات
11 resin (rosin, colophony)	رَاتنج القلْفونيَّة
12 violin bow (bow)	قَوْس الكَمَان
13 nut (frog)	صامولة
14 stick (bow stick)	عصا القَوْس
15 hair of the violin bow (horsehair)	شعر القَوْس
16 violoncello (cello), a member of the da gamba violin family	فيولونسيل (الكَمَان الجَهير)
17 scroll	رَأْس الكَمَان المعقوف
18 tuning peg (peg)	مِلْوَى الدَّوْزَنَة
19 pegbox	صُنْدُوق المِلْوَى
20 nut	صامولة
21 fingerboard	لَوْح الأصابع
22 spike (tailpin)	مِلْوَى الذَّيْل
23 double bass (contrabass, violone, double bass viol, *Am.* bass)	كونتر باص (الكَمَان الأجْهَر)
24 belly (top, soundboard)	لَوْحة الصوت
25 rib (side wall)	ضِلْع (جدار جانبي)
26 purfling (inlay)	ترصيع، تطعيم
27 viola	فيولا (الكَمَان الأوسط)
28-38 woodwind instruments (woodwinds)	**آلات نفخيَّة خشبية**
28 bassoon; *larger:* double bassoon (contrabassoon)	باصون (الزَّمْخَر)؛ الكبير: كونتر باصون
29 tube with double reed	أنبوب ذو مِزْمَارين
30 piccolo (small flute, piccolo flute, flauto piccolo)	بيكولو (سرناي)
31 flute (German flute), a cross flute (transverse flute, side-blown flute)	فلوت (ناي افرنجية)
32 key	مِفْتَاح
33 fingerhole	فتحة الاصبع
34 clarinet; *larger:* bass clarinet	الكلارينت؛ الأكبر حجماً: الكلارينت باص
35 key (brille)	مِفْتَاح
36 mouthpiece	قطعة الفم (المبسم)
37 bell	طَرْف الكلارينت المتسع (جرسي الشكل)
38 oboe (hautboy); *kinds:* oboe d'amore; tenor oboes: oboe da caccia, cor anglais; heckelphone (baritone oboe)	أبوا
39-48 brass instruments (brass)	**الآلات النُّحاسيَّة**
39 tenor horn	بُوق تينور
40 valve	صمام
41 French horn (horn, waldhorn), a valve horn	بُوق فرنسي
42 bell	طَرْف جرسي الشكل
43 trumpet; *larger:* Bb cornet; *smaller:* cornet	ترامبيت؛ الأكبر: كورنه سي؛ الأصغر: كورنه
44 bass tuba (tuba, bombardon); *sim.:* helicon (pellitone), contrabass	توبا؛ توبا كونتر باص

tuba

45 thumb hold ماسك الإصبع

46 trombone; *kinds:* alto trombone, tenor trombone, bass trombone ترومبون [المترددة]؛ أنواعه: ترومبون التو، ترومبون تينور، ترومبيون باص

47 trombone slide (slide) منزلقة الترومبون

48 bell طَرْف جرسي الشكل

49-59 percussion instruments **آلات القَرْع**

49 triangle المُثَلَّث

50 cymbals صنوج

51-59 membranophones **الآلات الغشائية**

51 side drum (snare drum) طَبْل مطوَّق، طَبْل جانبي صغير

52 drum head (head, upper head, batter head, vellum) رَأْس الطَّبْل

53 tensioning screw برغي شد الغشاء

54 drumstick عصا الطَّبْل

55 bass drum (Turkish drum) طَبْل قراري

56 stick (padded stick) عصا مبطنة

57 Kettledrum (timpano), a screw-tensioned drum; *sim.:* machine drum (mechanically tuned drum) نَقَّارِيَّات

58 kettledrum skin (kettle-drum vellum) جِلْد/غشاء النقاريَّات

59 tuning screw برغي الضَّبْط

60 harp, a pedal harp هارب، هارب ذو دَوَّاسَة

61 strings أَوْتَار

62 pedal دَوَّاسَة

324 Musical Instruments III الآلات المُوسِيقيَّة (3)

1-46 popular musical instruments (folk instruments) **الآلات الموسيقية الشائعة**

1-31 stringed instruments **الآلات الوَتَرية**

1 lute; *larger:* theorbo, chitarrone العُود؛ الأكبر حجماً: أَلْوَنُ

2 resonating body (resonator) جسم الرنين، صُنْدُوق الصوت

3 soundboard (belly, table) لَوْحة الصوت

4 string fastener (string holder) مُشْط تثبيت الأَوْتَار

5 sound hole (rose) فتحة خروج الصوت (وردة)

6 string, a gut (catgut) string وَتَر

7 neck عُنُق

8 fingerboard لَوْح الأصابع

9 fret دستان، زَخْرَفَة

10 head (bent-back pegbox, swan-head pegbox, pegbox) صُنْدُوق مِلْوَى العُود، رَأْس العُود

11 tuning peg (peg, lute pin) مِلْوَي الدَّوْزَنَة

12 guitar جيتار

13 string holder مُشْط تثبيت الأَوْتَار

14 string, a gut (catgut) or nylon string وَتَر

15 resonating body (resonating chamber, resonator, sound box) صُنْدُوق الصوت، جسم الرنين

16 mandolin (mandoline) ماندولين

17 sleeve protector (cuff protector) وقاء الكُم

18 neck عُنُق

19 pegdisc قرص المِلْوَى

20 plectrum رِيشَة العازف

21 zither (plucked zither) القَانون

22 pin block (wrest pin block, wrest plank) لَوْحة مفاتيح ضَبْط الأَوْتَار

23 tuning pin (wrest pin) مِفْتَاح الضَّبْط

24 accompaniment strings (bass strings, unfretted strings, open strings) أَوْتَار مصاحبة

25 melody strings (fretted strings, stopped strings) أَوْتَار الألحان

26 semicircular projection of the resonating sound box (resonating body) صُنْدُوق صوت نِصْف دائري

27 ring plectrum رِيشَة عزف حلقية

28 balalaika البَلالايكة

29 banjo البانجو

30 tambourine-like body جسم شبيه بالدُف (الرِّق)

31 parchment membrane رقٌ من البرشمان

32 ocarina, a globular flute الأَكْرِيْنَة

33 mouthpiece قطعة الفَمّ، المِبْسَم

34 fingerhole فتحة الأصابع

35 mouth organ (harmonica) الهرمونيكا

36 accordion; *sim.:* piano accordion, concertina, bandoneon الأكورديون

37 bellows مِنْفَاخ الأكورديون

38 bellows strap سَيْر المِنْفَاخ

39 melody side (keyboard side, melody keys) جانب مفاتيح الألحان

40 keyboard (keys) لَوْحة المفاتيح

41 treble stop (treble coupler, treble register) آلية إيقاف السوبرانو

42 stop lever ذِرَاع ضَبْط الأنابيب في الأكورديون

43 bass side (accompaniment side, bass studs, bass press-studs, bass buttons) جانب الباص (أزرار الباص)

44 bass stop (bass coupler, bass register) آلية إيقاف الباص

45 tambourine الرِّق

46 castanets صنَّاجات

47-78 jazz band **آلات فريق الجاز**

instruments (dance band instruments)

47-58 percussion instruments آلات القَرْع

47-54 drum kit (drum set, drums) طاقم الطَّبْل

47 bass drum طَبْل قراري

48 small tom-tom طَبْلَة "توم توم" صغيرة

49 large tom-tom طَبْلَة "توم توم" كبيرة

50 high-hat cymbals (choke cymbals, Charleston cymbals, cup cymbals) صنوج "تشارلستون"

51 cymbal صَنْج

52 cymbal stand (cymbal holder) حامل الصَّنْج

53 wire brush فُرْشَاة سلكية

54 pedal mechanism آلية الدَّوَّاسَة

55 conga drum (conga) طَبْل نقارية ، طَبْل الكونجا

56 tension hoop طوق شد الغشاء

57 timbales نقاريَّة ، تمبال

58 bongo drums (bongos) البُونْجز

59 maracas; *sim.:* shakers القَرْعية ، ماراكاس

60 guiro الجيرو

61 Xylophone; *form.:* straw fiddle; *sim.:* marimbaphone (steel marimba), tubaphone زَيْلُوفُون

62 wooden slab شريحة خشبية

63 resonating chamber (sound box) صندوق الصوت

64 beater عصا قَرْع الزَّيْلُوفُون

65 jazz trumpet ترامبيت الجاز

66 valve صمام

67 finger hook خطّاف الإصبع

68 mute (sordino) مخْفَات

69 saxophone ساكسوفون

70 bell طَرْف جرسي الشكل

71 crook انعقاف ، انحناء

72 mouthpiece المِبْسَم

73 struck guitar (jazz guitar) جيتار الجاز

74 hollow to facilitate fingering تجويف لسهولة حركة الأصابع

75 vibraphone (*Am.* vibraharp) الفيبرافون

76 metal frame إطار معدني

77 metal bar قطعة معدنية

78 tubular metal resonator مِرْنَان تضخيم صوت معدني أنبوبي الشكل

325 Musical Instruments IV الآلات المُوسِيقيَّة (4)

1 piano (pianoforte, upright piano, upright, vertical piano, spinet piano, console piano), a keyboard instrument (keyed instrument); *smaller form:* cottage piano (pianino); *earlier forms:* pantaleon, celesta, with steel bars instead of strings بيَانُو (بيَانُوفورت ، بيَانُو قائم ، بيَانُو رأسي) ، بيانه؛ الأشكال الأولية: بنتاليون ، سَلَستة ، بقضبان من الصلب بدلا من الأوتار

2-18 piano action (piano mechanism) آلية عمل البيَانُو

2 iron frame إطار معدني

3 hammer; *collectively:* striking mechanism مِطْرَقَة (جماعياً: آلية القَرْع)

4-5 keyboard (piano keys) لَوْحة المفاتيح

4 white key (ivory key) مفْتَاح أبْيَض/عاج

5 black key (ebony key) مفْتَاح أسْوَد/ابنوس

6 piano case صُنْدُوق البيَانُو

7 strings (piano strings) أوْتَار (أوْتَار البيَانُو)

8-9 piano pedals دوَّاستا البيَانُو

8 right pedal (sustaining pedal, damper pedal; *loosely:* forte pedal, loud pedal) for raising the dampers الدَّوَّاسَة اليمنى لرَفْع المخْفَات

9 left pedal (soft pedal; *loosely:* piano pedal) for reducing the striking distance of the hammers on the strings الدَّوَّاسَة اليسرى لتقليل مسافة قَرْع المطارق على الأوْتَار

10 treble strings الأوْتَار عالية الطَّبَقة

11 treble bridge (treble belly bridge) جِسْر الأوْتَار عالية الطَّبَقة

12 bass strings أوْتَار الباص

13 bass bridge (bass belly bridge) جِسْر أوْتَار الباص

14 hitch pin مِسْمَار رَبْط الأوْتَار

15 hammer rail قضيب المطارق

16 brace دعامة ، شكَال

17 tuning pin (wrest pin, tuning peg) مِسْمَار الدَّوْزَنَة

18 pin block (wrest pin block, wrest plank) لَوْحة مسامير الضَّبْط

19 metronome مترونوم بندول الإيقاع

20 tuning hammer (tuning key, wrest) مِفْتَاح الضَّبْط/الدَّوْزَنَة

21 tuning wedge إسفين الضَّبْط/ الدَّوْزَنَة

22-29 key action (key mechanism) آلية عمل المفاتيح

22 beam عارضة خشبية

23 damper-lifting lever ذِرَاع رَفْع المخْفَات

24 felt-covered hammer head رَأْس مِطْرَقَة مكسوَّة باللباد

25 hammer shank رِجْل المِطْرَقَة

26 hammer rail قَضيب المِطْرَقَة

27 check (back check) محكّ

28 check felt (back check felt) لِبَادَة المحكّ

29 wire stem of the check (wire stem of the back check) ساق المحك السلكية

30 sticker (hopper, hammer jack, hammer مرفاع المِطْرَقَة

lever)

31 button — زرّ

32 action lever — آلَيَّة التشغيل

33 pilot — دليل

34 pilot wire — سلك الدليل

35 tape wire — سلك الشريط

36 tape — شريط

37 damper (damper block) — المخْفَات (كتلة المخْفَات)

38 damper lifter — ذِرَاع رَفْع المخْفَات

39 damper rest rail — قضيب اسناد المفخات

40 grand piano (horizontal piano, grand, concert grand; *smaller:* baby grand piano, boudoir piano; *sim.:* square piano, table piano) — بِيَانُو أفقي/مربّع

41 grand piano pedals: right pedal for raising the dampers; left pedal for softening the tone (shifting the keyboard so that only one string is struck 'una corda') — دوَّاستا البِيَانُو الأفقي: الدَّوَّاسَة اليمنى لرَفْع المفْخَات؛ الدَّوَّاسَة اليسرى لترَخِيم النَّغَمَة

42 pedal bracket — كتيفة الدوَّاستان

43 harmonium (reed organ, melodium) — هارمنيوم

44 draw stop (stop, stop knob) — مِقْبَض ضَبْط أنابيب الأَرْغَن

45 knee lever (knee swell, swell) — أداة ضَبْط حجم الصوت

46 pedal (bellows pedal) — دَوَّاسَة (دَوَّاسَة بمِنْفَاخ)

47 harmonium case — صُنْدُوق آلة الهارمنيوم

48 harmonium keyboard (manual) — لَوْحة مفاتيح آلة الهارمنيوم

326 Musical Instruments V — الآلات المُوسِيقيَّة (5)

1-52 organ (church organ) — **الأَرْغَن** (أَرْغَن الكنيسة)

1-5 front view of organ (organ case) [built according to classical principles] — **منظر أمامي للأَرْغَن** [مُصنَّع طَبَقاً للمبادئ الكلاسيكية]

1-3 display pipes (face pipes) — **مزامير أمامية**

1 Hauptwerk — الأَرْغَن الكبير

2 Oberwerk — الأَرْغَن الضخم

3 pedal pipes — مزامير الدَّوَّاسَة

4 pedal tower — برج الدَّوَّاسَة

5 Rückpositiv — الروكبوزيتيف

6-16 tracker action (mechanical action); *other systems:* pneumatic action, electric action — **آليَّة التشغيل الميكانيكية**؛ أنظمة أخرى: تشغيل بالهواء المضغوط، تشغيل كهربي

6 draw stop (stop, stop knob) — مِقْبَض ضَبْط مزامير الأَرْغَن

7 slider (slide) — قطعة منزلقة

8 key (key lever) — مِفْتَاح (ذِرَاع المِفْتَاح)

9 sticker — مرفاع المِطْرَقَة

10 pallet — سقاطة

11 wind trunk — خرطوم الهواء المضغوط

12-14 wind chest, a slider wind chest; *other types:* sliderless wind chest (unit wind chest), spring chest, kegellade chest (cone chest), diaphragm chest — صُنْدُوق الهواء المضغوط؛ أنواع أخرى: صُنْدُوق هواء مضغوط بدون منزلقة، صُنْدُوق بنابض، صُنْدُوق مخروطي، صُنْدُوق رِقّي

12 wind chest (wind chest box) — صُنْدُوق الهواء المضغوط

13 groove — أخدود

14 upper board groove — أخدود اللَوْح العلوي

15 upper board — اللَوْح العلوي

16 pipe of a particular stop — مِزْمَار له مِقْبَض ضَبْط خاص

17-35 organ pipes (pipes) — **مزامير الأَرْغَن**

17-22 metal reed pipe (set of pipes: reed stop), a posaune stop — **مِزْمَار معدني** (مجموعة من المزامير: مِضْبَط قصبات المزامير)

17 boot — غطاء واقٍ

18 shallot — قُفْلُوط

19 tongue — لِسَان

20 block — كتلة

21 tuning wire (tuning crook) — سلك الضَّبْط

22 tube — مِزْمَار

23-30 open metal flue pipe, a salicional — **مِزْمَار معدني مفتوح ذو مجرى هوائي**

23 foot — قَدَم

24 flue pipe windway (flue pipe duct) — فتحة مرور الهواء بالمِزْمَار

25 mouth (cutup) — فم

26 lower lip — شَفَة سفلي

27 upper lip — شَفَة علوية

28 languid — أداة تخفيت

29 body of the pipe (pipe) — جسم المِزْمَار

30 tuning flap (tuning tongue), a tuning device — جِهَاز الضَّبْط

31-33 open wooden flue pipe (open wood), principal (diapason) — مِزْمَار خشبي مفتوح ذو قناة هوائية (شوكة الدَّوْزَان)

31 cap — غطاء

32 ear — وِدْنَة

33 tuning hole (tuning slot), with slide — فتحة دَوْزَنَة ذات قطعة منزلقة

34 stopped flue pipe — مِزْمَار ذو قناة هوائية بعد ضَبْطه

35 stopper — أداة الضَّبْط

36-52 organ console (console) of an electric action organ — كونسول أَرْغَن كهربائي

36 music rest (music stand) — مِنَصَّة

37 crescendo roller indicator — مؤشر تزايد الوقع تدريجياً

38 voltmeter — فولتامتر

39 stop tab (rocker) — ذِرَاع مِقْبَض الضَّبْط

40 free combination stud (free combination knob) مِقْبَض ائْتِلافي حر

41 cancel buttons for reeds, couplers etc. أزرار الإلغاء الخاصة بالمزامير، الخ.

42 manual I, for the Rückpositiv مِفْتَاح 1 لضَبْط "الروكبوزيتيف" (أرْغَن المرتلين بالكنيسة)

43 manual II, for the Hauptwerk مِفْتَاح 2 لضَبْط "الهاوبتفرك"

44 manual III, for the Oberwerk مِفْتَاح 3 لضَبْط "الاوبرفرك"

45 manual IV, for the Schwellwerk مِفْتَاح 4 لضَبْط "الشويلفرك"

46 thumb pistons controlling the manual stops (free or fixed combinations) and buttons for setting the combinations صمامات الإبهام للتحكم في توقفات المفاتيح وأزرار ضَبْط الائْتِلافات

47 switches for current to blower and action مفاتيح تيار المِنْفَاخ وآلية التشغيل

48 toe piston, for the coupler صمام إصبع القَدَم لآلية القارنة

49 crescendo roller (general crescendo roller) أُسْطُوَانَة التَّصَعُد

50 balanced swell pedal دَوَّاسَة متوازنة

51 pedal key [natural] مِفْتَاح الدَّوَّاسَة [طبيعي]

52 pedal key [sharp or flat] مِفْتَاح الدَّوَّاسَة [حاد أو ناقص]

53 cable (transmission cable) كبل (كبل الإرسال)

327 Fabulous Creatures (Fabled Beings) المَخْلُوقَات الخُرَافيَّة (المَخْلُوقات الأُسْطُوريَّة)

1-61 fabulous creatures (fabulous animals), mythical creatures **المَخْلُوقَات الخُرَافيَّة** (المَخْلُوقَات الأُسْطُوريَّة)

1 dragon التِّنِّين

2 serpent's body جِسْم ثُعْبَان

3 claws (claw) مَخَالِب

4 bat's wing جَنَاح خُفَّاش

5 fork-tongued mouth فَمٌ به لِسَان مُشَعَّب

6 forked tongue لِسَان مُشَعَّب

7 unicorn [symbol of virginity] أَحَادِي القَرْن [رَمْز العُذْرِيَّة]

8 spirally twisted horn قَرْن مَلْفُوف حلزونياً

9 Phoenix العنقاء

10 flames or ashes of resurrection أَلْسِنَة لَهَب أو رَمَاد البَعْث

11 griffin (griffon, gryphon) الغِرْفين

12 eagle's head رَأْس نِسْر

13 griffin's claws مَخَالِب الغِرْفين

14 lion's body جِسْم أَسَد

15 wing جَنَاح

16 chimera (chimaera), a monster الكِمِيْر

17 lion's head رَأْس أَسَد

18 goat's head رَأْس عَنْزَة

19 dragon's body جِسْم تِنِّين

20 sphinx, a symbolic figure أَبُو الهَوْل

21 human head رَأْس آدَمِيّ

22 lion's body جِسْم أَسَد

23 mermaid (nix, nixie, water nixie, sea maid, sea maiden, naiad, water nymph, water elf, ocean nymph, sea nymph, river nymph); *sim.:* Nereids, Oceanids (sea divinities, sea deities, sea goddesses); male: nix (merman, seaman) حُورِيَّة الماء؛ النارِيدة: حورية البحر؛ الذكر: نكس

24 woman's trunk جِذْع امْرَأة

25 fish's tail (dolphin's tail) ذَيْل سمكة (ذَيْل دولفين)

26 Pegasus (favourite, *Am.* favorite, steed of the Muses, winged horse); *sim.:* hippogryph الفَرَس المُجَنَّح (بيغاسوس)؛ الهيبوغريف

27 horse's body جِسْم حصان

28 wings جَنَاحان

29 Cerberus (hellhound) سَيْربيروس (الكَلْب الحارس لباب الجحيم)

30 three-headed dog's body جِسْم كَلْب له ثلاث رؤوس

31 serpent's tail ذَنَب ثُعْبَان

32 Lernaean (Lernean) Hydra العُدار

33 nine-headed serpent's body جِسْم ذو تسع رؤوس ثعابين

34 basilisk (cockatrice) البازِيليق

35 cock's head رَأْس ديك

36 dragon's body جِسْم تِنِّين

37 giant (titan) المارد

38 rock صَخْرَة

39 serpent's foot قَدَم على شكل ثُعْبان

40 triton, a merman (demigod of the sea) تريتون (أحد أنصاف آلهة البَحر عند الإغريق)

41 conch shell trumpet بُوق من صَدَف المَحَّار

42 horse's hoof حافِر حصان

43 fish's tail ذَيْل سمكة

44 hippocampus مارد البحر

45 horse's trunk جِذْع حصان

46 fish's tail ذَيْل سمكة

47 sea ox, a sea monster ثَوْر البَحْر

48 monster's body جسم وحشي

49 fish's tail ذَيْل سمكة

50 seven-headed dragon of St. John's Revelation (Revelations, Apocalypse) تِنِّين سِفْر الرُّؤيَا للقديس يوحنا ذو السبع رؤوس

51 wing جَنَاح

52 centaur (hippocentaur), half man and half beast — القَنْطُور ، نصف رَجُل ونصف وَحْش
53 man's body with bow and arrow — جِسْم إنسان يحمل قوساً وسهماً
54 horse's body — جِسْم حصان
55 harpy, a winged monster — الخَطّاف
56 woman's head — رَأس إمْرَأة
57 bird's body — جِسْم طائر
58 siren, a daemon — السِّيْرانة ، شَيْطان
59 woman's body — جِسْم إمْرَاة
60 wing — جَنَاح
61 bird's claw — برْثَن طائر

328 Prehistory — ما قَبْلَ التَّاريخ

1-40 prehistoric finds — **لُقْيَات تَعُود إلى ما قَبْلَ التَّاريخ**

1-9 Old Stone Age (Palaeolithic, Paleolithic, period) **and Mesolithic period** — **العَصْر الحَجَري القديم والحِقْبة الميزوليتيّة**

1 hand axe (*Am.* ax) (fist hatchet), a stone tool — فأس يدوي
2 head of throwing spear, made of bone — رَأس رُمْح مصنوع من العَظْم
3 bone harpoon — حَرْبُون عَظْميّ
4 head — رَأس
5 harpoon thrower, made of reindeer antler — قاذفة حربون مصنوعة من قرن الوَعْل
6 painted pebble — حَصْوَة مُلَوَّنة
7 head of a wild horse, a carving — رَأس حصان بَرِّيّ، رَأس مَنْحُوت
8 Stone Age idol, an ivory statuette — وَثَن من العَصْر الحَجَري، تمثال صغير من العاج
9 bison, a cave painting (rock painting) [cave art, cave painting] — رَسْم البيسون بداخل أحد الكهوف [فَنّ رَسْم الكهوف]

10-20 New Stone Age (Neolithic period) — **العَصْر الحَجَري الحديث**

10 amphora [corded ware] — الأمْفُورَة
11 bowl [menhir group] — قَصْعَة خَزَفِيَّة [مجموعة المَنْهير]
12 collared flask [Funnel-Beaker culture} — قارورة ذات عُنُق
13 vessel with spiral pattern [spiral design pottery] — إناء ذو زخارف لَوْلبيَّة الشكل
14 bell beaker [bell beaker culture] — آنِيَة خزفيَّة جَرَسِيَّة الشكل
15 pile dwelling (lake dwelling, lacustrine dwelling) — مَسْكَن يرتفع على عِضادات، مَسْكَن بُحَيْريّ
16 dolmen (cromlech), a megalithic tomb (*coll.*: giant's tomb); *other kinds:* passage grave, gallery grave (long cist); when covered with earth: tumulus (barrow, mound) — الدُولْمَن ، قَبْر ميجاليتي؛ أنواعه: مَمَرّيّ ودِهلْيزيّ، إذا كان مُغَطًى بالتراب فهو جُثْوَة
17 stone cist, a contracted burial — ضَريح حَجَريّ
18 menhir (standing stone), a monolith — المَنْهير: نُصُب حَجَريّ عموديّ
19 boat axe (*Am.* ax), a stone battle axe — فأس حَجَريّ للقتال
20 clay figurine, an idol — وَثَن من الصلصال

21-40 Bronze Age and Iron Age; epochs: Hallstatt period, La Tène period — **العَصْر البرونزيّ والعَصْر الحديديّ**

21 bronze spear head — رَأس رُمْح برونزيّ
22 hafted bronze dagger — خنْجَر برونزيّ ذو مِقْبَض
23 socketed axe (*Am.* ax), a bronze axe with haft fastened to rings — فأس برونزيّ ذو مِقْبَض مُثَبَّت إلى حلقات
24 girdle clasp — دلاية مِدالية ذات حِزام
25 necklace (lunula) — قلادَة، عِقْد
26 gold neck ring — حَلَقَة العُنُق المصنوعة من الذهب
27 violin-bow fibula (safety pin) — مِشْبك أمان على شكل قوس الكَمَان
28 serpentine fibula; other *kinds:* boat fibula, arc fibula — مِشْبك سربنتيني الشكل؛ نوعان آخران: قاربي وقوسي
29 bulb-head pin, a bronze pin — دبوس ذو رَأس مُنْتَفِخ
30 two-piece spiral fibula; *sim.:* disc (disk) fibula — مِشْبك حلزونيّ من قطعتيْن
31 hafted bronze knife — سكين برونزيّ ذو مِقْبَض
32 iron key — مِفْتاح من الحديد
33 ploughshare (*Am.* plowshare) — شفرة مِحْرَاث
34 sheet-bronze situla, a funerary vessel — آنِيَة مَأتَمِيَّة من ألْوَاح البرونز
35 pitcher [chip-carved pottery] — إبريق خزفيّ مُزَخْرَف بالنَّحْت
36 miniature ritual cart (miniature ritual chariot) — عَرَبَة طقوس مُصَغَّرَة
37 Celtic silver coin — عُمْلَة سَلْتِيَّة من الفضة
38 face urn, a cinerary urn; *other kinds:* domestic urn, embossed urn — جَرَّة (لحفظ رماد المَوْتَى) على شكل وَجْه؛ أنواعها : جَرَّة منزلية وجَرَّة ذات نَقْش ناتئ
39 urn grave in stone chamber — قَبْر على شكل جَرَّة في حُجْرَة حجرية
40 urn with cylindrical neck — جَرَّة ذات عُنُق أسْطُواني

329 Chivalry — الفرُوسيَّة

1 knight's castle (castle) — قَلْعَة الفارس (قلعة)
2 inner ward (inner bailey) — الفناء الداخلي
3 draw well — بِئْر
4 keep (donjon) — بُرْج مُحَصَّن
5 dungeon — بُرْج الحِصْن الرئيسي
6 battlements (crenellation) — شُرُفَات

7 merlon — المَارْلُون: الجدار الفاصل بين شرفات الحصن

8 tower platform — مِنَصَّة البُرْج

9 watchman — حارس (خفير)

10 ladies' apartments (bowers) — مَنْزِل السَّيِّدات

11 dormer window (dormer) — نافذة ناتئة (شباك جملون بارز)

12 balcony — بلكون

13 storehouse (magazine) — مستودع (مخزن)

14 angle tower — بُرْج الزاوِيَة

15 curtain wall (curtains, enclosure wall) — جُزْء الجدار بين البُرْجَيْن

16 bastion — البَسْتِين: جُزْء ناتئ من الحِصْن

17 angle tower — بُرْج الزاوِيَة

18 crenel (embrasure) — كُوَّة في جِدار الحِصْن

19 inner wall — جدار داخلي

20 battlemented parapet — حاجِز به شرفات

21 parapet (breastwork) — حاجِز، متراس

22 gatehouse — البَوَّابة

23 machicolation (machicoulis) — شرفة مكوَّاة

24 portcullis — شَعْرِيَّة التحصين

25 drawbridge — جِسْر متحرك

26 buttress — دِعَامَة الجدار

27 offices and service rooms — مَكَاتِب وحُجُرات الخدمة

28 turret — بُرَيْج

29 chapel — كَنِيسَة صغيرة

30 great hall — القاعة الكبرى

31 outer ward (outer bailey) — الفِنَاء الخارجي

32 castle gate — بَوَّابة الحِصْن

33 moat (ditch) — خَنْدَق مائي حَوْل الحِصْن

34 approach — طريق الاقتراب

35 watchtower (turret) — بُرْج المراقبة

36 palisade (pallisade, palisading) — حَسَيكَة الحِصْن

37 moat (ditch, fosse) — خندق مائي حول الحِصْن

38-65 knight's armour (*Am.* armor) — **دِرْع الفارِس**

38 suit of armour (*Am.* armor) — بذلة الدِّرْع

39-42 helmet — **الخَوْذَة**

39 skull — الجُمْجُمَة

40 visor (vizor) — مُقَدَّم الخَوْذَة المتحرك

41 beaver — لِفاع الخَوْذَة: جُزْء متحرك في أسفلها

42 throat piece — غطاء الرقبة

43 gorget — دِرْع العُنُق

44 épaulière — الكَتِيفِيَّة

45 pallette (pauldron, besageur) — صفيحة الإبط

46 breastplate (cuirass) — دِرْع الصدر

47 brassard (rear brace and vambrace) — العِضَاد: دِرْع للذراع أو عصابة للعضد

48 cubitière (coudière, couter) — حِلْيَة تشير إلى فارس البَلاط

49 tasse (tasset) — الجُزْء السفلي من سُتْرَة الدرع

50 gauntlet — قُفَّاز واقٍ

51 habergeon (haubergeon) — دِرْع واقٍ للمنطقة أسفل البطن

52 cuisse (cuish, cuissard, cuissart) — دِرْع الفَخْذ

53 knee cap (knee piece, genouillère, poleyn) — غِطاء الرُّكْبَة

54 jambeau (greave) — درع الرِّجْل

55 solleret (sabaton, sabbaton) — حذاء فولاذيّ

56 pavis (pavise, pavais) — تُرْس مستطيل

57 buckler (round shield) — تُرْس مستدير

58 boss (umbo) — حلْيَة مُحَدَّبَة في التُّرْس

59 iron hat — خَوْذَة فولاذية

60 morion — المَرْيُون (خوذة عالية)

61 light casque — خَوْذَة خفيفة

62 types of mail and armour (*Am.* armor) — أنواع الزَّرَدِيَّات والدروع

63 mail (chain mail, chain armour, *Am.* armor) — زَرَدِيَّة (زَرَدِيَّة سلسليّة)

64 scale armour (*Am.* armor) — دِرْع مُصَفَّح

65 plate armour (*Am.* armor) — دِرْع صَفَحَاني

66 accolade (dubbing, knighting) — حفلة الاحتضان: حفلة تقام عند منح شخص رتبة فارس

67 liege lord, a knight — المَوْلَى

68 esquire — المُرَشَّح لِرُتْبَة الفارِس

69 cup bearer — حامِل الكَأس

70 minstrel (minnesinger, troubadour) — مُغَنِّي القِيثَارَة

71 tournament (tourney, joust, just, tilt) — مباراة في المُسَايَفَة بين الفرسان

72 crusader — مُبَارِز صَلِيبيّ

73 Knight Templar — الدَّاوِي: أحد فرسان الهيكل

74 caparison (trappings) — غطاء مزركش لِسَرْج الفرس

75 herald (marshal at tournament) — حَكَم المبارزة

76 tilting armour (*Am.* armor) — دِرْع المُثَاقَفَة

77 tilting helmet (jousting helmet) — خَوْذَة المُثَاقَفَة

78 panache (plume of feathers) — بَنَاش: حزْمَة زينيّة من الريش أعلى الخَوْذَة

79 tilting target (tilting shield) — تُرْس المُثَاقَفَة

80 lance rest — مِسْنَد الرمح

81 tilting lance (lance) — رُمْح المُثَاقَفَة

82 vamplate — دِرْع واقٍ لليد

83-88 horse armour (*Am.* armor) — **دِرْع الفَرَس**

83 neck guard (neck piece) — وقاء العُنُق

84 chamfron (chaffron, chafron, chamfrain, chanfron) — دِرْع رَأْس الفَرَس

85 poitrel — غطاء مُقَدَّم الفَرَس

86 flanchard (flancard) غطاء البطن
87 tournament saddle سَرْج المبارزة
88 rump piece (quarter piece) غِطاء الكَفَل

330 Church I الكَنِيسَة (1)

1-30 Protestant church الكَنِيسَة البروتاستينيّة

1 chancel الهَيْكَل
2 lectern المقْرَأ: منضدة تلاوة الكتاب المقدس
3 altar carpet بِسَاط المَذْبَح
4 altar (communion table, Lord's table, holy table) المَذْبَح
5 altar steps دَرَج المَذْبَح
6 altar cloth غطاء/مفرش المَذْبَح
7 altar candle شَمْعَدان المَذْبَح
8 pyx (pix) حُقُّ القُرْبَان المُقَدَّس
9 paten (patin, patine) طَبَق القُرْبَان المُقَدَّس
10 chalice (communion cup) كأس القُرْبَان
11 Bible (Holy Bible, Scriptures, Holy Scripture) الكتاب المُقَدَّس
12 altar crucifix صَلِيب المَذْبَح (يُمَثِّل المَسِيح مصلوباً)
13 altarpiece نَقْش خلف مذبح الكَنِيسَة (أو فوقه)
14 church window نافذة الكَنِيسَة
15 stained glass زجاج ملون
16 wall candelabrum شَمْعَدان الجدار
17 vestry door (sacristy door) باب مجلس الكَنِيسَة
18 pulpit steps دَرَج المِنْبَر
19 pulpit مِنْبَر الوَعْظ
20 antependium غِطاء الجُزْء الأمامي من المِنْبَر
21 canopy (soundboard, sounding board) ظُلَّة (فوق شخص ذو منزلة أو مُقَدَّس)
22 preacher (pastor, vicar, clergyman, rector) in his robes (vestments, canonicals) واعِظ في ردائه
23 pulpit balustrade درابزين المِنْبَر
24 hymn board showing hymn numbers لَوْحة التراتيل وهي توضح أعداد التراتيل
25 gallery شرفة خارجية
26 verger (sexton, sacristan) حامِل الصَّوْلَجان (أمام الأُسْقُف)
27 aisle مَمَرّ بين صَفَّيّ المقاعد
28 pew; *collectively:* pews (seating) مقعد في الكَنِيسَة
29 churchgoer (worshipper); *collectively:* congregation إلْف الكَنِيسَة (مُصَلِّي بالكنيسة)؛ المجموعة: جماعة مصلين
30 hymn book كتاب التراتيل

31-62 Roman Catholic church الكَنِيسَة الكاثوليكيّة الرومانيّة

31 altar steps دَرَج المَذْبَح
32 presbytery (choir, chancel, sacrarium, sanctuary) هَيْكَل: الجُزْء المخصص للقساوسة القائمين بالقداس
33 altar المَذْبَح
34 altar candles شَمْعَدان المَذْبَح
35 altar cross صَلِيب المَذْبَح
36 altar cloth غطاء (مفرش) المَذْبَح
37 lectern المقْرَأ
38 missal (mass book) كتاب القداس
39 priest قسيس، كاهِن
40 server مُسَاعد القسيس
41 sedilia مقاعد الجهة الجنوبية من المذبح
42 tabernacle وعاء خُبْز القربان
43 stele (stela) عمود حَجَري يحمل نَقْشاً تذكارياً
44 paschal candle (Easter candle) شمعة الفِصْح
45 paschal candlestick (Easter candlestick) شَمْعَدان الفِصْح
46 sanctus bell ناقوس القداس
47 processional cross صَلِيب زيَّاحي
48 altar decoration (foliage, flower arrangement) زينة المَذْبَح
49 sanctuary lamp مصباح المَقْدِس
50 altarpiece, a picture of Christ نَقْش خلف المَذْبَح (صورة المَسِيح)
51 Madonna (statue of the Virgin Mary) السيدة العَذْراء، تمثال مريم العَذْراء
52 pricket مَغْرَز الشموع بالكنيسة
53 votive candles شموع نَذْريَّة
54 station of the Cross مراحل الصَّلْب (14 صورة تمثل مراحل صَلْب المَسِيح)
55 offertory box صُنْدُوق جَمْع الصدقات أثناء القداس
56 literature stand حامِل المطبوعات
57 literature (pamphlets, tracts) مطبوعات (نشرات وكتيبات)
58 verger (sexton, sacristan) حامِل الصولجان (أمام الأُسْقُف)
59 offertory bag كيس جمع الصدقات
60 offering إعَانة للكنيسة
61 man praying رَجُل يُصَلِّي
62 prayer book كتاب الصَّلَوات

331 Church II الكَنِيسَة (2)

1 Church الكَنِيسَة
2 steeple بُرْج الكَنِيسَة
3 weathercock دوارة الرِّيَاح
4 weather vane (wind vane) دليل اتجاه الرِّيح
5 spire ball كُرَة قِمَّة البُرْج المُسْتَدَقَّة
6 church spire (spire) قِمَّة مُسْتَدَقَّة
7 church clock (tower clock) ساعة الكَنِيسَة (ساعة البُرْج)
8 belfry window كُوَّة بُرْج الجرس
9 electrically operated جَرَس يُشَغَّل كهربياً

bell
10 ridge cross — صَلِيب حرف السطح
11 church roof — سطح الكَنِيسَة
12 memorial chapel — كنيسة صغيرة تذكارية
13 vestry (sacristy), an annexe (annex) — مَجْلِس الكَنِيسَة ، حجرة للاجتماعات والصفوف الكنسيَّة
14 memorial tablet (memorial plate, wall memorial, wall stone) — لَوْح تذكاريّ
15 side entrance — مَدْخَل جانبي
16 church door (main door, portal) — باب الكَنِيسَة (الباب الرئيسي)
17 churchgoer — إلْف الكنيسة ، مُصَلٍّي
18 graveyard wall (churchyard wall) — سور المدافنّ/المقابر الملحقة بالكَنِيسَة
19 graveyard gate (churchyard gate, lichgate, lychgate) — مدخل المدافنّ الملحقة بالكَنِيسَة
20 vicarage (parsonage, rectory) — مقر القِسّ
21-41 **graveyard** (churchyard, God's acre, *Am.* burying ground) — **فِنَاء المقابر/المدافنّ**
21 mortuary — مستودع الجُثَث: تحفظ فيه لحين دفنها
22 grave digger — حَفَّار القبور
23 grave (tomb) — قَبْر
24 grave mound — رابِيَة القبر
25 cross — صَلِيب
26 gravestone (headstone, tombstone) — شاهِد القَبْر
27 family grave (family tomb) — مَدْفَنّ عائلي
28 graveyard chapel — مُصَلَّى المقابر
29 child's grave — قَبْر طِفْل
30 urn grave — مَدْفَنّ جِرَار حفظ رماد المَوْتى
31 urn — جَرَّة (لحفظ رماد الموتى)
32 soldier's grave — قَبْر جُنْدي
33-41 **funeral** (burial) — **الجَنَازَة** (الدفن)
33 mourners — المُنْتَحِبُون
34 grave — قَبْر
35 coffin (*Am.* casket) — كَفَنّ
36 spade — جاروف الحَفْر
37 clergyman — كاهِن ، رجل الدين
38 the bereaved — أهْل المَيِّت
39 widow's veil, a mourning veil — بُرْقُع الأرْمَلَة
40 pallbearers — حاملو بُسَاط الرحمة
41 bier — نَعْش ، تابوت
42-50 **procession** (religious procession) — **مَوْكِب الجنازة**
42 processional crucifix — صَلِيب الجنازة يُصَوِّر المَسِيح مصلوباً
43 cross bearer (crucifer) — حامِل الصَّلِيب
44 processional banner, a church banner — رايَة المَوْكِب الجنائزيّ
45 acolyte — مُسَاعِد الكاهن
46 canopy bearer — حامِل الظُلَّة
47 priest — القِسّ
48 monstrance with the Blessed Sacrament (consecrated Host) — وِعاء القُرْبَان المُقَدَّس وبه القُرْبَان المُقَدَّس
49 canopy (baldachin, baldaquin) — ظُلَّة
50 nuns — راهبات
51 participants in the procession — مشاركون في الجنازة
52-58 **monastery** — **الدَّيْر**
52 cloister — رِوَاق مُعَمَّد مسقوف
53 monastery garden — حديقة الدَّيْر
54 monk, a Benedictine monk — راهِب ، راهِب بنيديكتي
55 habit (monk's habit) — رِداء الراهب
56 cowl (hood) — قلنسوة الراهب
57 tonsure — الجُزْء الحَلِيق من رَأْس الراهب
58 breviary — كتاب الصَّلَوَات اليوميّة
59 catacomb, an early Christian underground burial place — سِرْدَاب المَوْتَى
60 niche (tomb recess, arcosolium) — مِشْكَاة
61 stone slab — بلاطة حَجَرِيَّة

332 Church III — الكَنِيسَة (3)

1 Christian baptism (christening) — المَعْمُودِيّة المَسِيحيّة
2 baptistery (baptistry) — بَيْت المَعْمُودِيّة
3 Protestant clergyman — كاهن بروتستانتي
4 robes (vestments, canonicals) — رِداء الكاهن
5 bands — شَرِيطَان
6 collar — ياقَة
7 child to be baptized (christened) — طفل سيتم تعميده
8 christening robe (christening dress) — رداء التعميد
9 christening shawl — شال التعميد
10 font — جُرْن المَعْمُودِيّة
11 font basin — حَوْض جُرْن المَعْمُودِيّة
12 baptismal water — ماء التعميد
13 godparents — العَرَّابان
14 church wedding (wedding ceremony, marriage ceremony) — إكْلِيل ، عَقْد القِرَان بالكنيسة
15-16 **bridal couple** — **العَرُوسَان**
15 bride — العروس
16 bridegroom (groom) — العريس
17 ring (wedding ring) — خاتم الزواج
18 bride's bouquet (bridal bouquet) — باقة وَرْد العروس
19 bridal wreath — تاج العروس
20 veil (bridal veil) — طَرْحَة العروس
21 [myrtle] buttonhole — عُرْوَة [لِوَضْع زَهْرَة الآس]
22 clergyman — الكاهن
23 Witnesses [to the — شهُود [الزيجة]

marriage]
24 bridesmaid إشبينة العروس
25 kneeler مَوْطِئ الركوع
26 Holy Communion العَشاء الإلهي أو الرَّبَّاني
27 communicants متناولو العَشَاء الرَّبَّاني
28 Host (wafer) خُبْز القُرْبَان المُقَدَّس
29 communion cup كأس العَشَاء الرَّبَّاني
30 rosary مِسْبَحَة
31 paternoster الصلاة الربانيّة، الصيغة المكْرُورة (رُقْيَة)
32 Ave Maria; set of 10: decade السلام المرْيَمي؛ مجموعة من ١٠: عَقْد
33 crucifix صَليب يمثل المَسيح مصلوباً، المصلوب

34-54 liturgical vessels (ecclesiastical vessels) **الأوْعِيَة الكَنَسِيَّة**
34 monstrance وعاء القُرْبَان المُقَدَّس
35 Host (consecrated Host, Blessed Sacrament) خُبْز القُرْبَان المُقَدَّس
36 lunula (lunule) علامة هلاليّة
37 rays إشعاعات
38 censer (thurible), for offering incense (for incensing) مِبْخَرَة لحَرْق البخور
39 thurible chain سلسلة المِبْخَرَة
40 thurible cover غطاء المِبْخَرَة
41 thurible bowl سلطانية المِبْخَرَة
42 incense boat قارب البخور
43 incense spoon مِلْعَقَة البخور
44 cruet set طاقم أوعية الماء المقدس
45 water cruet وعاء الماء
46 wine cruet وعاء الخَمْر
47 holy water basin حَوْض الماء المقدس
48 ciborium containing the sacred wafers وعاء خُبْز القُرْبَان
49 chalice كأس خمر القُرْبَان
50 dish for communion wafers طَبَق خُبْز العشاء الربانيّ
51 paten (patin, patine) طَبَق القُرْبَان المقدس
52 altar bells أجْرَاس المذبح
53 pyx (pix) حُق القُرْبَان المقدس
54 aspergillum مِرَشَّة الماء المقدس

55-72 forms of Christian crosses **أشكال الصَّلِيب المَسِيحي**
55 Latin cross (cross of the Passion) الصَّليب اللاتيني (صَليب الآلام)
56 Greek cross الصَّليب اليوناني
57 Russian cross الصَّليب الروسي
58 St. Peter's cross صَليب القديس بطرس
59 St. Anthony's cross (tau cross) صَليب القديس أنطونيوس (الصَّليب التائي)
60 St. Andrew's cross (saltire cross) صَليب القديس أندروس
61 Y-cross صَليب على شكل حرف Y
62 cross of Lorraine صَليب اللورين
63 ansate cross صَليب الأنسيت
64 patriarchal cross الصَّليب البطريركي
65 cardinal's cross الصَّليب الكاردينالي
66 papal cross الصَّليب الباباوي
67 Constantinian cross, a monogram of Christ (CHR) الصَّليب القسطنطيني
68 crosslet صَليب صغير
69 cross moline أطْراف صَليب رؤوسها ثُنائيَّة مُنْحَنِيَة
70 cross of Jerusalem صَليب أورشليم
71 cross botonnée (cross treflée) أطْراف صَليب ثُلاثيَّة الرؤوس
72 fivefold cross (quintuple cross) صَليب خماسي
73 Celtic cross الصَّليب السَّلْتي

333 Art I الفَنّ (1)

1-18 Egyptian art **الفَنّ المصْريّ**
1 pyramid, a royal tomb هَرَم، قبر مَلَكِي
2 king's chamber حُجْرَة الملك
3 queen's chamber حُجْرَة الملِكَة
4 air passage مَمَرّ الهواء
5 coffin chamber حُجْرَة التابوت
6 pyramid site مَوْقع الهرم
7 funerary temple مَعْبَد جنائزي
8 valley temple مَعْبَد الوادي
9 pylon, a monumental gateway بوابة الهَيْكل الفرعوني
10 obelisks مَسَلَّتان
11 Egyptian sphinx أبو الهَوْل المِصْريّ
12 winged sun disc (sun disk) قرص الشمس المُجَنَّح
13 lotus column عمود لوتسيّ الزخارف
14 knob-leaf capital (bud-shaped capital) تاج عمود على شكل بُرْعُم
15 papyrus column عمود برديّ الزخارف
16 bell-shaped capital تاج عمود جرسيّ الشكل
17 palm column عمود نخيليّ
18 ornamented column عمود مُزَيَّن بالزخارف والرسومات

19-20 Babylonian art **الفَنّ البابليّ**
19 Babylonian frieze إفريز بابليّ
20 glazed relief tile قرميد بارز مُمَوَّه بالميناء

21-28 art of the Persians **الفَنّ الفارسيّ**
21 tower tomb قبر بُرْجِيّ
22 stepped pyramid هَرَم مُدَرَّج
23 double bull column عمود الثَّوْرَيْن
24 projecting leaves أوراق شجر بارزة
25 palm capital تاج عمود نخلي
26 volute (scroll) زخارف حلزونية (لَوْحة مرسومة رمزية)
27 shaft جذع العمود
28 double bull capital تاج عمود الثَّوْرَيْن

29-36 art of the Assyrians **الفَنّ الآشوري**
29 Sargon's Palace, palace buildings قصر سرجون، مباني القصر
30 city wall سور المدينة
31 castle wall سور الحِصْن
32 temple tower (ziggurat), a stepped بُرْج المَعْبَد، بُرْج مدرج

(terraced) tower
33 outside staircase دَرَج خارجيّ
34 main portal البَوّابة الرئيسيّة
35 portal relief النقوش البارزة بالبوابة
36 portal figure نَقْش بارز بالبوابة
37 art of Asia Minor فَنّ آسيا الصُغْرَى
38 rock tomb مَقْبَرَة صَخْرِيَّة

334 Art II الفَنّ (2)

1-48 Greek art الفَنّ اليوناني
1-7 the Acropolis الاكروبول، الاكروبوليس
1 the Parthenon, a Doric temple بارثنون، معبد دوريّ
2 peristyle رُوَاق مُعَمَّد
3 pediment جبهة، تاج البناء
4 crepidoma (stereobate) قاعدة المبنى
5 statue تمثال
6 temple wall سور المَعْبَد
7 propylaea مداخل المَعْبَد
8 Doric column عمود دوريّ
9 Ionic column عمود أيونيّ
10 Corinthian column عمود كورنتي
11-14 cornice طُنُف
11 cyma سِيمَة
12 corona الجُزْء الناتيء من طُنُف كلاسيكي
13 mutule زَخْرَفَة افريزية
14 dentils الدَّنْطِيل
15 triglyph الطَّرْغليف
16 metope, a frieze decoration المَيْتُوب
17 regula نَقْش أسفل الطَّرْغليف
18 epistyle (architrave) أُسْكُفَة
19 cyma (cymatium, kymation) سِيمَة
20-25 capital تاج العمود
20 abacus وسادة حجريّة
21 echinus صَلْب مائل
22 hypotrachelium (gorgerin) عُنُق العمود
23 volute (scroll) زخارف حلزونيّة (لَوْحة مرسومة رمزية)
24 volute cushion وسادة الزخارف الحلزونيّة
25 acanthus أقَنْثَة، الأكانث
26 column shaft جِذْع العمود
27 flutes (grooves, channels) أخاديد، حزوز
28-31 base قاعدة العمود
28 [upper] torus قَوْصَرَة [علويّة]
29 trochilus (concave moulding, *Am.* molding) تجويف
30 [lower] torus قَوْصَرَة [سفلية]
31 plinth وَطِيدَة، وَزرَة
32 stylobate أساس/قاعدة العمود
33 stele (stela) نُصَيْب، مِسَلَّة صغيرة
34 acroterion (acroterium, acroter) اكروتير (زينة سَعْفِيَّة)
35 herm (herma, hermes) تمثال عطارد ذي الغمد
36 caryatid; *male:* Atlas كارياتيد؛ مُذَكَّر: أطلس
37 Greek vase مَزْهَرِيَّة يونانية
38-43 Greek ornamentation (Greek decoration, Greek decorative designs) **الزخارف اليونانيّة**
38 bead-and-dart moulding (*Am.* molding), an ornamental band شريط زخرفيّ مُرَصَّع باللؤلؤ الزجاجيّ
39 running dog (Vitruvian scroll) زخارف حلزونيّة دارجَة
40 leaf ornament زخارف على شكل ورقة شجر
41 palmette نُخَيْلَة
42 egg and dart (egg and tongue, egg and anchor) cyma سِيمَة بيضاوية وهِلْبِيَّة الزَخْرَفَة
43 meander تَمَعُّج زخرفيّ
44 Greek theatre (*Am.* theater) المسرح اليونانيّ
45 scene مَشْهَد
46 proscenium خشبة المسرح
47 orchestra الأوركسترا، الفرقة الموسيقية
48 thymele (altar) المَذْبَح
49-52 Etruscan art الفَنّ الإتروسكيّ
49 Etruscan temple مَعْبَد إتروسكيّ
50 portico رُوَاق
51 cella حُجْرَة التمثال المقدس
52 entablature المَحْمُول، الطِّبان
53-60 Roman art الفَنّ الرومانيّ
53 aqueduct قناة ماء عالية
54 conduit (water channel) قناة ماء
55 centrally-planned building (centralized building) مبنى مركزيّ
56 portico رواق
57 reglet حلْيَة معماريّة مُسَطَّحَة
58 cupola قُبَّة صغيرة
59 triumphal arch قَوْس النَّصْر
60 attic العلِّيَّة
61-71 Early Christian art الفَنّ المَسِيحي البِدْئي
61 basilica بازيليك
62 nave صَحْن الكنيسة
63 aisle الجَنَاح: جُزْء جانبي مفصول عن الصحن بصف من الأعمدة
64 apse مِحْرَاب، حنْيَة
65 campanile بُرْج جَرَس الكنيسة
66 atrium أتريوم (فنَاء الكنيسة)
67 colonnade صَفّ الأعمدة
68 fountain نافورة، فَسْقِيَّة
69 altar المَذْبَح
70 clerestory (clearstory) منْوَر الكنيسة
71 triumphal arch قَوْس النَّصْر
72-75 Byzantine art الفَنّ البيزنطيّ
72-73 dome system نظام القِبَاب
72 main dome القُبَّة الرئيسيّة
73 semidome نِصْف قُبَّة

74 pendentive — مُثَلَّث القُبَّة، ركن القُبَّة
75 eye, a lighting aperture — كُوَّة لدخول الضوء

335 Art III — الفَنّ (3)

1-21 Romanesque art — **الفَنّ الروميّ**
1-13 Romanesque church, a cathedral — **الكنيسة الروميَّة، كاتدرائيَّة**
1 nave — صحن الكنيسة
2 aisle — الجَنَاح : جُزْء جانبي مفصول عن الصحن بصف من الأعمدة
3 transept — جَنَاح مَدْخَل الكنيسة
4 choir (chancel) — جُزْء الكنيسة المخصص للمُرَتِّلين والكَهَنَة
5 apse — حنية، مِحْرَاب
6 central tower (*Am.* center tower) — البرج المركزي
7 pyramidal tower roof — سقف برج هرمي
8 arcading — مُقَنْطَرَات، سلسلة قناطر
9 frieze of round arcading — طُنُف من القناطر المستديرة
10 blind arcade (blind arcading) — قناطر مُصْمَتَة
11 lesene, a pilaster strip — طِبْر، كتف
12 circular window — نافذة/طاقة دائريَّة
13 side entrance — مَدْخَل جانبي
14-16 Romanesque ornamentation (Romanesque decoration, Romanesque decorative designs) — **الزخارف الروميَّة**
14 chequered (*Am.* checkered) pattern (chequered design) — نموذج الزخارف المربعة
15 imbrication (imbricated design) — نموذج الزخارف المُتَرَاكِبة
16 chevron design — نموذج الحِلْيَات الشارية
17 Romanesque system of vaulting — الطراز الروميّ في إقامة العقود
18 transverse arch — قَوْس مستعرض
19 barrel vault (tunnel vault) — عَقْد مَهْدي
20 pillar — رُكن، عِضادة
21 cushion capital — تاج عمود مسطح
22-41 Gothic art — **الفَنّ القُوطي**
22 Gothic church [westwork, west end, west façade], a cathedral — الكنيسة القُوطيَّة [الواجهة الغربية]، كاتدرائيَّة
23 rose window — زَهْرِيَّة، نافذة زَهْرِيَّة
24 church door (main door, portal), a recessed portal — باب الكنيسة (الباب الرئيسي)
25 archivolt — واجِهَة العَقْد
26 tympanum — قلب القَوْصَرَة
27-35 Gothic structural system — **النظام الهيكلي للبناء القوطيّ**
27-28 buttresses — **دعامات المبنى**
27 buttress — دعامة، كتف
28 flying buttress — زافِرَة: نِصْف قنطرة يدعم بها جدار
29 pinnacle — بناء مُدَبَّب
30 gargoyle — ميزاب، مِزْران
31-32 cross vault (groin vault) — **عَقْد متصالب مُنْكَسِر**
31 ribs (cross ribs) — ضلوع (ضلوع متصالبة)
32 boss (pendant) — حِلْيَة مُحَدَّبة
33 triforium — عَقْد ثلاثي الأقواس
34 clustered pier (compound pier) — عمود مُرَكَّب
35 respond (engaged pillar) — عمود داعِم لِقَوْس
36 pediment — الجبهة، تاج البناء
37 finial — قمة البرج المزَخْرَفَة
38 crocket — تخريم نباتي على الخشب، حلية ناتئة منقوشة تشبه ورق النبات
39-41 tracery window, a lancet window — **نافذة الزَّخْرَفَة التشجيرية، نافذة رُمْحيَّة**
39-40 tracery — **الزَّخْرَفَة التشجيرية**
39 quatrefoil — زَخْرَفَة رُبَاعيَّة الأوراق
40 cinquefoil — زَخْرَفَة خُمَاسيَّة الأوراق
41 mullions — عَمَد النافذة
42-54 Renaissance art — **فَنّ عصر النهضة**
42 Renaissance church — كنيسة عصر النهضة
43 projection, a projecting part of the building — نتوء، بروز
44 drum — رقبة القُبَّة
45 lantern — مَنْوَر السقف
46 pilaster (engaged pillar) — طِبْر، كتف
47 Renaissance palace — قصر عصر النهضة
48 cornice — طُنُف، كورنيش
49 pedimental window — نافذة الجبهة
50 pedimental window with round gable — نافذة واجِهَة ذات جبهة مُثَلَّثَة
51 rustication (rustic work) — طراز ريفي
52 string course — مِدْمَاك خَطّيّ
53 sarcophagus — ناووس
54 festoon (garland) — فسطون (إكليل)

336 Art IV — الفَنّ (4)

1-8 Baroque art — **الفَنّ الباروكيّ**
1 Baroque church — كنيسة باروكيَّة
2 bull's eye — كُوَّة
3 bulbous cupola — قُبَّة صغيرة بَصَلِيَّة الشكل
4 dormer window (dormer) — نافذة ناتئة
5 curved gable — جَبْهَة مُثَلَّثة منحنية على واجهة المبنى
6 twin columns — أعْمِدة مزدوجة
7 cartouche — إطار مزخرف
8 scrollwork — زَخْرَفَة
9-13 Rococo art — **فَنّ الروكوكو/الفَنّ الحَصَوي**
9 Rococo wall — جدار روكوكو
10 coving, a hollow moulding (*Am.* — ناتئة زخرفية مُفَرَّغَة

molding)	
11 framing	تأطِير
12 ornamental moulding (*Am.* molding)	ناتئة زخرفيَّة زينيَّة
13 rocaille, a Rococo ornament	زَخْرَفَة روكوكيَّة
14 table in Louis Seize style (Louis Seize table)	طاولة طراز لويس سايز
15 neoclassical building (building in neo-classical style), a gateway	مبنى على الطراز الكلاسيكي المُحدَّث
16 Empire table (table in the Empire style)	طاولة على الطراز الإمبراطوري
17 Biedermeier sofa (sofa in the Biedermeier style)	أريكة طراز "بيدرميير"
18 Art Nouveau easy chair (easy chair in the Art Nouveau style)	مقعد على طراز الفَنّ المُحدَّث
19-37 types of arch	**أنواع القناطر/العقود**
19 arch	قنطرة، عَقْد
20 abutment	كتف قنطرة
21 impost	وسادة حجرية، مُسْتَقَر القَوْس
22 springer, a voussoir (wedge stone)	حَجَر خَصْر العَقْد
23 keystone	مِفْتَاح العَقْد/القَوْس
24 face	وَجْه
25 intrados	مُنْحَنَى القَوْس الداخليّ
26 extrados	ظاهِر القَوْس
27 round arch	قَوْس مستدير، قنطرة مستديرة
28 segmental arch (basket handle)	قَوْس مَوْتُور
29 parabolic arch	قَوْس على شكل قطع مكافئ
30 horseshoe arch	قَوْس حَدَوِيّ
31 lancet arch	قَوْس سهمي
32 trefoil arch	قَوْس نَفْلي (ثلاثي فصوص الزخارف)
33 shouldered arch	قَوْس كتفي
34 convex arch	قَوْس مُحَدَّب
35 tented arch	قَوْس خَيْمي
36 ogee arch (keel arch)	عَقْد ذو قَوْسَيْن متعاكسَيْن "اوجي"
37 Tudor arch	قَوْس مُفَلْطَح
38-50 types of vault	**أنواع العقود** (الأسقف المقوسة)
38 barrel vault (tunnel vault)	عَقْد مَهْدي
39 crown	تاج البناء
40 side	الجانب
41 cloister vault (cloistered vault)	عَقْد مُعَمَّد
42 groin vault (groined vault)	عَقْد متصالب أو متقاطع
43 rib vault (ribbed vault)	عَقْد مُضلع
44 stellar vault	عَقْد نَجْمِيّ
45 net vault	عَقْد شبكي
46 fan vault	عَقْد مروحي
47 trough vault	عَقْد صُنْدُوقي
48 trough	صُنْدُوق
49 cavetto vault	عَقْد رُبْع دائري
50 cavetto	حلْيَة مقعرة

337 Art V — الفَنّ (5)

1-6 Chinese art	**الفَنّ الصينيّ**
1 pagoda (multi-storey, multistory, pagoda), a temple tower	باغود (معبد صيني ذو طوابق متعددة)
2 storey (story) roof (roof of storey)	سقف من طابق واحد
3 pailou (pailoo), a memorial archway	قنطرة تذكارية
4 archway	مَدْخَل مُقَنْطَر
5 porcelain vase	مَزْهَرِيَّة من البورسلين
6 incised lacquered work	شكل فخاري مَطْلي بورنيش اللَّك
7-11 Japanese art	**الفَنّ اليابانيّ**
7 temple	مَعْبَد
8 bell tower	برج جرسيّ
9 supporting structure	هيكل الإسْنَاد
10 Bodhisattva (boddhisattva), a Buddhist saint	كاهن بوذيّ
11 torii, a gateway	مَدْخَل ذو حلْيَة مُحَدَّبَة
12-18 Islamic art	**الفَنّ الإسلامي**
12 mosque	مَسْجِد، جامع
13 minaret, a prayer tower	مِئْذَنَة
14 Mihrab	اتجاه القِبْلَة، مِحْرَاب
15 minbar (minibar, pulpit)	المِنْبَر
16 mausoleum, a tomb	ضَرِيح
17 stalactite vault (stalactitic vault)	عَقْد مُقَوْنَص
18 Arabian capital	تاج عمود عربي
19-28 Indian art	**الفَنّ الهنديّ**
19 dancing Siva (Shiva), an Indian god	الإله "سيفا" الراقص
20 statue of Buddha	تمثال بوذا
21 stupa (Indian pagoda), a mound (dome), a Buddhist shrine	أسْطُبَة
22 umbrella	مظلة
23 stone wall (*Am.* stone fence)	جدار/سور حَجَري
24 gate	بَوَّابة
25 temple buildings	مباني المَعْبَد
26 shikara (sikar, sikhara, temple tower)	بُرْج المَعْبَد الهندي
27 chaitya hall	بَهْو الأُسْطُبَة الصغيرة
28 chaitya, a small stupa	أُسْطُبَة صغيرة

338 Artist's Studio — مَرْسَم، ستوديو الرسام

1-43 studio	**مَرْسَم، مَنْحَت**
1 studio skylight	منور المَرْسَم/المَنْحَت

2 painter, an artist	رَسَّام
3 studio easel	مِسْنَد المَرْسَم
4 chalk sketch, rough draft	رسم أوَّلي بالطباشير
5 crayon (piece of chalk)	قلَم طباشير/ ملون
6-19 painting materials	**مواد التلوين**
6 flat brush	فُرْشَاة مسطحة
7 camel hair brush	فُرْشَاة من شَعْر الجَمَل
8 round brush	فُرْشَاة مستديرة
9 priming brush	فُرْشَاة التحضير
10 box of paints (paint-box)	صُنْدُوق الألوان
11 tube of oil paint	أنبوب لون زيتي
12 varnish	برنيق، طلاء شفاف
13 thinner	الثنر: مادة الترقيق
14 palette knife	سكين الملْوَنَة/المِوْشَاة
15 spatula	المِلْوَق: أداة مزج الألوان
16 charcoal pencil (charcoal, piece of charcoal)	قلَم فحم
17 tempera (gouache)	أنبوب ألوان غواش
18 watercolour (*Am.* watercolor)	ألوان مائية
19 pastel crayon	قلَم ألوان بَسْتِل
20 wedged stretcher (canvas stretcher)	إطار شد قماش اللَوْحة
21 canvas	قماش اللَوْحة، الخيش
22 piece of hardboard, with painting surface	قطعة من لَوْح صلد وعليها سطح التلوين
23 wooden board	لَوْح خشبي
24 fibreboard (*Am.* fiberboard)	رقاقة ليفيّة
25 painting table	طاولة الألوان
26 folding easel	مِسْنَد قابل للطي
27 still life group, a motif	مجموعة طبيعة صامتة، عنصر
28 palette	مِلْوَنَة، مِوْشَاة
29 palette dipper	مغْرَفة المِلْوَنَة
30 platform	مَنَصَّة، تخت
31 lay figure (mannequin, manikin)	شاخِص، مانيكان
32 nude model (model, nude)	موديل عارٍ
33 drapery	غطاء فضفاض
34 drawing easel	مِسْنَد الرَسْم (بدون ألوان)
35 sketch pad	لَوْحة الرَسْم الأوَّلي
36 study in oils	رسم إعدادي من ألوان الزيت
37 mosaic (tessellation)	الفسيفساء
38 mosaic figure	صورة من الفسيفساء
39 tesserae	فصوص الفسيفساء
40 fresco (mural)	فريسك
41 sgraffito	اسجرافيت
42 plaster	جصٌ، كِلْس
43 cartoon	كرتون

339 Sculptor's Studio — مَنْحَت، ستوديو النحات

1 sculptor	نَحَّات
2 proportional dividers	مُقَسِّم النِّسَب/الأبعاد
3 calliper (caliper)	مِسْمَاك
4 plaster model, a plaster cast	نموذج/موديل من الجص
5 block of stone (stone block)	كتلة من الحَجَر
6 modeller (*Am.* modeler)	المَثَّال، ناسخ التماثيل
7 clay figure, a torso	شكل من الصلصال، جذع تمثال
8 roll of clay, a modelling (*Am.* modeling) substance	لفيفة من الصلصال، مادة قَوْلَبَة
9 modelling (*Am.* modeling) stand	حامِل القَوْلَبَة
10 wooden modelling (*Am.* modeling) tool	أداة قَوْلَبَة خشبية
11 wire modelling (*Am.* modeling) tool	أداة قَوْلَبَة سلكية
12 beating wood	عصا الدَّكّ
13 claw chisel (toothed chisel, tooth chisel)	مِنْحَت مُسَنَّن
14 flat chisel	مِنْحَت مسطح
15 point (punch)	شُنْبُك
16 iron-headed hammer	مِطْرَقَة برأْس حديديَّة
17 gouge (hollow chisel)	مِظْفَار، مِنْحَت مُجَوَّف
18 spoon chisel	مِنْحَت مِلْعَقي
19 wood chisel, a bevelled-edge chisel	مِنْحَت خشبي
20 V-shaped gouge	مِظْفَار على شكل حرف V
21 mallet	مِطْرَقَة النَحَّات
22 framework	إطار، هيكل خشبي
23 baseboard	لَوْح القاعدة
24 armature support (metal rod)	مِسْنَد الهيكل المعدني
25 armature	هيكل معدني (لتسليح التماثيل)
26 wax model	نموذج/موديل شَمْعي
27 block of wood	كتلة من الخشب
28 wood carver (wood sculptor)	نَحَّات الخشب
29 sack of gypsum powder (gypsum)	شوال من الجص الناعم
30 clay box	صُنْدُوق الصلصال
31 modelling (*Am.* modeling) clay	صلصال القَوْلَبَة
32 statue, a sculpture	تمثال، شكل منحوت
33 low relief (bas-relief)	نَحْت نافِر
34 modelling (*Am.* modeling) board	لَوْح القَوْلَبَة
35 wire frame, wire netting	إطار سلكي
36 circular medallion (tondo)	رصيعة مستديرة
37 mask	قناع
38 plaque	لَوْحة منقوشة، أبلَكيه

340 Graphic Art — فَنُ الجرافيك

1-13 wood engraving (xylography), a relief printing method (a	**النَقْش على الخشب،** إحدى طرق النَقْش النافِر

letterpress printing method)

1 end-grain block for wood engravings, a wooden block — كتلة خشبية للحفر

2 wooden plank for woodcutting, a relief image carrier — لَوْح خشبي ثخين للنَقْش على الخشب ، حامِل صورة ناتئة

3 positive cut — نَقْش النسخة الإيجابيَّة

4 plank cut — نَقْش اللَوْح الخشبي

5 burin (graver) — مِنْقَاش ، مِحْفَار

6 U-shaped gouge — مِظْفَار على شكل حرف U

7 scorper (scauper, scalper) — مِكْشَاط ، مِنْحات

8 scoop — مِغْرَفَة النقاش

9 V-shaped gouge — مِظْفَار على شكل حرف V

10 contour knife — سكين النطاق

11 brush — فُرْشَاة

12 roller (brayer) — مِطْبَع التضريس

13 pad (wiper) — ناتئة زخرفية زينية

14-24 copperplate engraving (chalcography), an intaglio process; kinds: etching, mezzotint, aquatint, crayon engraving — **النَقْش على النحاس**؛ أنواعه: بالحفر ، تظليلي ، ملون بالقَلَم

14 hammer — مِطْرَقَة

15 burin — مِنْقَاش ، مِحْفَار

16 etching needle (engraver) — إبرة الحَفْر

17 scraper and burnisher — مِكْشَاط ومِصْقَال

18 roulette — الدُحْرُوجة

19 rocking tool (rocker) — مِحْفَار للنَقْش على الصخر

20 round-headed graver, a graver (burin) — مِنْقَاش ذو رَأس مستديرة

21 oilstone — المِسَنّ الزيتي: حجر السن بالزيت

22 dabber (inking ball, ink ball) — كُرَة التحبير

23 leather roller — مِطْبَع جِلْدِيّ

24 sieve — مُنْخُل

25, 26 lithography (stone lithography), a planographic printing method — الطباعة الحَجَرِيَّة ، إحدى طرق الطباعة على الأسطح المستوية

25 sponge for moistening the lithographic stone — إسفَنْجة لترطيب حجر الطباعة الحجرية

26 lithographic crayons (greasy chalk) — أقلام الطباعة الحَجَرِيَّة (طباشير شحمي)

27-64 graphic art studio, a printing office (*Am.* printery) — **مَرْسَم الفَنُون الترسيميَّة** ، ستوديو فن الجرافيك

27 broadside (broadsheet, single sheet) — لَوْحة عريضة

28 full-colour (*Am.* full-color) print (colour print, chromolithograph) — طباعة مُلَوَّنة بالكامل

29 platen press, a hand press — ماكينة طبع بكبسة مسطحة

30 toggle — آليَّة الفعل المفصليّ

31 platen — كَبْسَة مسطحة

32 type forme (*Am.* form) — فورمة الحروف المطبعية

33 feed mechanism — آليَّة التغذية

34 bar (devil's tail) — ذِرَاع الماكينة

35 pressman — عامِل ماكينة الطبع

36 copperplate press — ماكينة طباعة ذات رَوْسَم نحاسي

37 tympan — التمبان

38 pressure regulator — مُنَظِّم الضغط

39 star wheel — عجلة نَجْمِيَّة

40 cylinder — طنبور ، أُسْطُوَانَة

41 bed — فَرْشَة

42 felt cloth — لِبَادَة

43 proof (pull) — بروفة الطباعة

44 copperplate engraver — عامِل طباعة بالرَّوْسَم النحاسي

45 lithographer (litho artist), grinding the stone — عامِل طباعة ليثوغرافية يصقل حجراً

46 grinding disc (disk) — قُرْص الصقل/التجليخ

47 grain (granular texture) — حُبَيْبَات

48 pulverized glass — زُجاج مَسْحُوق

49 rubber solution — سائل مطاطي

50 tongs — كُلاّبة

51 etching bath for etching — حَوْض الحَفْر

52 zinc plate — لَوْح زنك

53 polished copperplate — لَوْح نحاسي مصقول

54 cross hatch — حزوز متقاطعة

55 etching ground — أرضيَّة الحَفْر

56 non-printing area — منطقة اللاطباعة

57 lithographic stone — حَجَر الطباعة الليثوغرافية

58 register marks — علامات تطابق (علامات تسجيل)

59 printing surface (printing image carrier) — سطح الطبع

60 lithographic press — ماكينة طبع ليثوغرافي

61 lever — ذِرَاع الماكينة

62 scraper adjustment — مَضْبَط المكشطة

63 scraper — مِكْشَطَة

64 bed — فَرْشَة

341 Script I — أشكال الكتَابَة (1)

1-20 scripts of various peoples — **أشكال كتابَات شعوب مختلفة**

1 ancient Egyptian hieroglyphics, a pictorial system of writing — الكِتَابَة المصريَّة القديمة: الهيروغليفيَّة ، نظام كتابة بالرُسوم

2 Arabic — الكِتَابَة العربية

3 Armenian — الكِتَابَة الأرْمِينيَّة

4 Georgian — الكِتَابَة الجُورْجِيَّة

5 Chinese — الكِتَابَة الصينيَّة

6 Japanese — الكِتَابَة اليابانيَّة

7 Hebrew (Hebraic) — الكِتَابَة العِبْرِيَّة

8 cuneiform script — الكِتَابَة المِسْمَارِيَّة

9 Devanagari, script employed in Sanskrit — الكِتَابَة السَّنسكْرِيتيَّة

10 Siamese — الكِتَابة السيامية

11 Tamil الكِتَابَة التاميليَّة
12 Tibetan الكِتَابَة التبتيَّة
13 Sinaitic script الكِتَابَة السِّينيتكيَّة
14 Phoenician الكِتَابَة الفينيقيَّة
15 Greek الكِتَابَة اليونانيَّة
16 Roman capitals الحُرُوف الرومانية الاستهلالية/التاجية
17 uncial (uncials, uncial script) الحُرُوف الإنْشِيَّة
18 Carolingian (Carlovingian, Caroline) minuscule الحُرُوف الكارُولينيَّة الصَّغيرة
19 runes الحُرُوف الرُونيَّة
20 Cyrillic الحُرُوف السِّيرِيْليَّة
21-26 ancient writing implements **أدوات الكِتَابَة في قديم الزمان**
21 Indian steel stylus for writing on palm leaves مِرقَم هندي من الصُّلْب للكتابة على سَعَف النخيل
22 ancient Egyptian reed pen قصبة كتابة استخدمها المصريون القدماء
23 writing cane بوصة الكتابة
24 brush فُرْشَاة
25 Roman metal pen (stylus) مِرقَم معدني روماني
26 quill (quill pen) ريشة
27 Korean الكِتَابَة الكُوريَّة

342 Script II أشكال الكِتَابَة (2)

1-15 types (type faces) **أنواع الحُرُوف الطباعيَّة**
1 Gothic type (German black-letter type) الحُرُوف القُوطيَّة
2 Schwabacher type (German black-letter type) فونط شوابشر (حُرُوف سوداء ألمانيَّة)
3 Fraktur (German black-letter type) فُونط فراكتور (حُرُوف سوداء ألمانيَّة)
4 Humanist (Mediaeval) فونط هيومانيست
5 Transitional فونط ترانزيشنال
6 Didone فونط ديدون
7 Sanserif (Sanserif type, Grotesque) فونط سانسريف
8 Egyptian فونط مِصْري
9 typescript (typewriting) خط الآلَة الكاتبة
10 English hand (English handwriting, English writing) الفونط الإنجليزي اليدوي
11 German hand (German handwriting, German writing) الفونط الألماني اليدوي
12 Latin script الكتابة اللاتينيَّة
13 shorthand (shorthand writing, stenography) اختزال
14 phonetics (phonetic transcription) الصَّوْتِيَّات (الرموز الصوتية)
15 Braille طريقة برايْل
16-29 punctuation marks (stops) **علامات التنصيص والترقيم**
16 full stop (period, full point) النقطة (علامة الوقف)
17 colon النقطتان
18 comma الفاصِلَة
19 semicolon الفاصِلَة المَنْقُوطَة
20 question mark (interrogation point, interrogation mark) علامة الاستفهام
21 exclamation mark (*Am.* exclamation point) علامة التأثُّر/التعجب
22 apostrophe الفاصِلَة العليا
23 dash (em rule) الشَّرْطَة
24 parentheses (round brackets) القَوْسان
25 square brackets المعْقفان
26 quotation mark (double quotation marks, paired quotation marks, inverted commas) علامة الاقتباس
27 guillemet (French quotation mark) علامة الاقتباس الفرنسيَّة
28 hyphen الواصِلَة
29 marks of omission (ellipsis) علامات الحذف
30-35 accents and diacritical marks (diacritics) **العلامات النُطْقيَّة والصوتيَّة**
30 acute accent (acute) نَبْرَة حادة
31 grave accent (grave) نَبْرَة خفيضة
32 circumflex accent (circumflex) نَبْرَة فوق حُرُوف العِلَّة تشير إلى طريقة نطقها
33 cedilla [under c] السَّدِيلَة [تحت حرف c]
34 diaeresis (*Am.* dieresis) [over e] علامة تُوضَع على الحرف الثاني من حُرُوف العلَّة إشارة إلى أن يلفظ كمقطع مستقل [فوق حرف e]
35 tilde [over n] التِّلدة : علامة توضع فوق حرف في الإسبانية
36 section mark علامة فَصْل
37-70 newspaper, a national daily newspaper **الجريدة، الصحيفة،** جريدة قوميَّة يَوْميَّة
37 newspaper page صفحة الجريدة
38 front page الصفحة الأولى
39 newspaper heading اسم الجريدة
40 contents المحتويات
41 price السِّعْر
42 date of publication تاريخ طبعة الجريدة
43 place of publication مكان الطَّبْع
44 headline عُنْوَان الخَبَر
45 column عمود
46 column heading عُنْوَان العمود
47 column rule خط فاصِل بين الأعمدة
48 leading article (leader, editorial) المقال الرئيسي
49 reference to related article إشارة إلى المقال المعنيّ
50 brief news item خَبَر مُوجَز
51 political section قسم الأخبار السياسيَّة
52 page heading اسم الصفحة
53 cartoon كاريكاتير

54 report by newspaper's own correspondent — تَقْرِير من مُرَاسِل الجريدة
55 news agency's sign — رَمْز وكالة الأنباء
56 advertisement (*coll.* ad) — إعْلان
57 sports section — قسم أخبار الرياضة
58 press photo — صورة صحفية
59 caption — تعليق الصورة
60 sports report — تَقْرير الأنشطة الرياضية
61 sports news item — خَبَر رياضي
62 home and overseas news section — قسم الأخبار المحلّيّة والخارجية
63 news in brief (miscellaneous news) — أخبار قصيرة
64 television programmes (*Am.* programs) — برامج التليفزيون
65 weather report — تَقْرير حالة الطقس
66 weather chart (weather map) — خريطة الطقس
67 arts section (feuilleton) — قسم الأخبار الفنية
68 death notice — إشْعَار وفاة
69 advertisements (classified advertising) — إعْلانات مُبَوَّبة
70 job advertisement, a vacancy (a situation offered) — إعْلان وظائف شاغِرة

343 Colour (*Am.* Color) — الألْوَان

1 red — أحْمَر
2 yellow — أصْفَر
3 blue — أزْرَق
4 pink — قُرَمْزي
5 brown — بُنّي
6 azure (sky blue) — سَمَاوي
7 orange — بُرْتُقَالي
8 green — أخْضَر
9 violet — بَنَفْسجي
10 additive mixture of colours (*Am.* colors) — مزيج جَمْعي من الألوان
11 white — أبْيَض
12 subtractive mixture of colours (*Am.* colors) — مزيج طَرْحي من الألوان
13 black — أسْوَد
14 solar spectrum (colours, *Am.* colors, of the rainbow) — الطَّيْف الشمسيّ (ألوان قوس قزح)
15 grey (*Am.* gray) scale — مُدَرَّج اللون الرَّمَادي
16 heat colours (*Am.* colors) — الألْوَان الساخِنَة

344 Mathematics I — الرِّياضيَّات (1)

1-26 arithmetic — **الحســاب**
1-22 numbers — **الأعْدَاد**
1 Roman numerals — الأعْدَاد الرومانية
2 Arabic numerals — الأعْدَاد العربية
3 abstract number, a four-figure number [8: units; 5: tens; 6: hundreds; 9: thousands] — عدد معنوي؛ عدد رباعي [8: أحاد؛ 5: عشرات؛ 6: مئات؛ 9: آلاف]
4 concrete number (physical quantity consisting of the numerical value and the unit or unit symbol) — عدد مادي (قيمة مادية تتكون من القيمة الرقمية ورمز الوحدة/الوحدات)
5 cardinal number (cardinal) — عدد أصلي
6 ordinal number (ordinal) — عدد ترتيبي
7 positive number [with plus sign] — عدد موجب [+]
8 negative number [with minus sign] — عدد سالب [−]
9 algebraic symbols — رموز جَبْرية
10 mixed number [3: whole number (integer); $^1/_3$: fraction] — عدد كَسْري [3: عدد صحيح؛ $^1/_3$: كَسْر]
11 even numbers — أعْدَاد زوجية
12 odd numbers — أعْدَاد فردية
13 prime numbers — أعْدَاد أولية
14 complex number [3: real part; $2\sqrt{-1}$: imaginary part] — عدد مُرَكَّب [3: عدد حقيقي؛ $2\sqrt{-1}$: عدد تخيلي]
15-16 vulgar fractions — **الكسور الإعتيادية**
15 proper fraction [2: numerator, horizontal line; 3: denominator] — كَسْر حقيقي [2: بسط ؛ 3: مقام]
16 improper fraction, also the reciprocal of item 15 — كَسْر غير حقيقي
17 compound fraction (complex fraction) — كَسْر مُرَكَّب
18 improper fraction [when cancelled down produces a whole number] — كَسْر غير حقيقي [عند الاختزال ينتج عدد صحيح]
19 fractions of different denominations [35: common denominator] — كسور مختلفة المقام [35: مقام مشترك]
20 proper decimal fraction with decimal point and decimal places [3: tenths; 5: hundredths; 7: thousandths] — كَسْر عَشْري حقيقي بفاصلة عَشْريَّة [3:عشرات؛ 5: مئات؛ 7: آلاف]
21, 22 recurring decimal — كَسْر عَشْري دائري
23-26 fundamental arithmetical operations — **العمليات الحسابية الأساسية**
23 addition (adding) [3 and 2: the terms of the sum; +: plus sign; =: equals sign; 5: the sum] — الجَمْع [3 و2: رَقْما الجَمْع؛ +: زائد (علامة الجَمْع)؛ =: تساوي؛ 5: حاصل الجَمْع]
24 subtraction (subtracting); [3: the minuend; –: minus sign; 2: the subtrahend; 1: the remainder (difference)] — الطَّرْح [3: المطروح منه؛ –: ناقص (علامة الطَّرْح)؛ 2: المطروح؛ 1: الباقي]

25 multiplication (multiplying); [3: the multiplicand; ×: multiplication sign; 2: the multiplier; 2 and 3: factors; 6: the product] — الضَّرْب [3: المضروب؛ ×: في (علامة الضرب)؛ 2: المضروب فيه؛ 2 و3 : عاملا الضرب؛ 6: ناتج الضرب]

26 division (dividing); [6: the dividend; ÷: division sign; 2: the divisor; 3: the quotient] — القِسْمَة [6: المقسوم؛ ÷: على (علامة القِسْمَة)؛ 2: المقسوم عليه؛ 3: خارج القِسْمَة]

345 Mathematics II — الرِّياضيَّات (2)

1-24 arithmetic — **الحساب**

1-10 advanced arithmetical operations — **العمليات الحسابية المتقدمة**

1 raising to a power [three squared (3^2): the power; 3: the base; 2: the exponent (index); 9: value of the power] — الرفع إلى قوة [3 تربيع (3^2): القوة؛ 3: الأساس؛ 2: الأُس؛ قيمة القوة]

2 evolution (extracting a root); [cube root of 8: cube root; 8: the radical; 3: the index (degree) of the root; $\sqrt{\ }$: radical sign; 2: value of the root] — طَرْح الجذور؛ [الجَذْر التكعيبي لعدد 8 : جَذْر تكعيبي؛ 8: الأساس؛ 3: درجة الجَذْر؛ $\sqrt{\ }$: علامة جَذْرية؛ 2: قيمة الجَذْر]

3 square root — جَذْر مربع

4-5 algebra — **الجَبْر**

4 simple equation [3, 2: the coefficients; x: the unknown quantity] — مُعَادَلَة بسيطة [2، 3: مُعَامِلان؛ x: كمية غير معروفة]

5 identical equation; [a, b, c: algebraic symbols] — مُعَادَلَة متطابقة؛ [أ، ب، جـ رموز جَبْرية]

6 logarithmic calculation (taking the logarithm, log); [log: logarithm sign; 3: number whose logarithm is required; 10: the base; 0: the characteristic; 4771: the mantissa; 0.4771: the logarithm] — حساب اللوغاريتم [لو: رَمْز اللوغاريتم؛ 3: العدد المطلوب حساب اللوغاريتم له؛ 10: الأساس؛ صفر: العدد البياني؛ 4771: الجزء العَشْري من اللوغاريتم؛ 0,4771 اللوغاريتم]

7 simple interest formula [P: the principal; R: rate of interest; T: time; I: interest (profit);%: percentage sign] — صيغة مبسطة لحساب الفائدة [P : المبلغ الأساسي؛ R: نسبة الفائدة؛ T: الزمن؛ I: الفائدة؛ %: علامة النسبة المئوية]

8-10 rule of three (rule-of-three sum, simple proportion) — **قاعدة الثلاثة** (التناسب البسيط)

8 statement with the unknown quantity x — بيان بكمية غير معروفة x

9 equation (conditional equation) — مُعادَلَة (مُعَادَلَة شرطية)

10 solution — الحَلّ

11-14 higher mathematics — **الرياضيات الأعلى**

11 arithmetical series with the elements 2, 4, 6, 8 — مُتَوَالِيَة حسابية من العوامل 2، 4، 6، 8

12 geometrical series — مُتَوَالِيَة هندسية

13-14 infinitesimal calculus — **التَّفَاضُل والتَّكَامُل اللانهائي**

13 derivative [dx, dy: the differentials; d: differential sign] — المشتق [dx، dy: أرقام تَفَاضُلية؛ d:علامة التَّفَاضُل]

14 integral (integration) [x: the variable; C: constant of integration; ∫: the integral sign; dx: the differential] — تَكَامُل [x: المتغير؛ C: ثابت التَّكَامُل؛ ∫ : علامة التَّكَامُل؛ dx رَقْم التَّفَاضُل]

15-24 mathematical symbols — **الرموز الحسابية**

15 infinity — لانهائي

16 identically equal to (the sign of identity) — مطابق لـ

17 approximately equal to — مساو تقريبا لـ

18 unequal to — لا يساوي

19 greater than — أكبر من

20 less than — أقل من

21-24 geometrical symbols — **الرموز الهندسية**

21 parallel (sign of parellelism) — يوازي (علامة التوازي)

22 similar to (sign of similarity) — يماثل (علامة التماثل)

23 angle symbol — رَمْز الزَّاوِيَة

24 triangle symbol — رَمْز المثلث

346 Mathematics III (Geometry I) — الرِّياضيَّات (3) (الهَنْدَسَة 1)

1-58 plane geometry (elementary geometry, Euclidian geometry) — **الهَنْدَسَة المستوية**

1-23 point, line, angle — **نُقْطَة ، خَط ، زَاوِيَة**

1 point [point of intersection of g_1 and g_2], the angular point of 8 — نُقْطَة [نُقْطَة تقاطع g1 مع g2]

2, 3 straight line g_2 — المُسْتَقِيم g2

4 the parallel to g_2 — المُسْتَقِيم الموازي للمُسْتَقِيم g2

5 distance between the straight lines g_2 and g_3 — المسافة بين المُسْتَقِيمين g2 وg3

6 perpendicular (g_4) on g_2 — العمود g4 المتعامد على g2

7, 3 the arms of **8** — ضلعا الزَّاوِيَة **8**

8,13 vertically opposite angles — زاويتان متقابلتان

8 angle — زَاوِيَة

9 right angle [90°] — زَاوِيَة قائمة [90 درجة]

10, 11, 12 reflex angle — زَاوِيَة منعكسة

10 acute angle, also the alternate angle to **8** — زَاوِيَة حادة، أيضا زَاوِيَة تبادلية مع زَاوِيَة **8**

11 obtuse angle — زَاوِيَة مُنْفرِجة

12 corresponding angle to **10** — زَاوِيَة مطابقة لزَاوِيَة **10**

13, 9, 15 straight angle — زَاوِيَة مُسْتَقِيمة [180

[180°] — درجة]

14 adjacent angle; *here:* supplementary angle to **13** — زَاوِيَة مجاورة؛ هنا: الزَّاوِيَة المكمِّلة لزَاوِيَة **13**

15 complementary angle to **8** — زَاوِيَة متممة لزَاوِيَة **8**

16 straight line AB — المُسْتَقِيم AB

17 end A — الطرف A

18 end B — الطرف B

19 pencil of rays — حُزْمَة أشِعَّة

20 ray — شُعَاع

21 curved line — خَطّ منحني

22 radius of curvature — نِصْف قطر التقَوس/ الانحناء

23 centre (*Am.* center) of curvature — مَرْكَز التقَوس/الانحناء

24-58 plane surfaces — **أسَطح مستوية**

24 symmetrical figure — شكل تناظري

25 axis of symmetry — محْوَر التناظر

26-32 plane triangles — **مُثَلَّثات مستوية**

26 equilateral triangle [A, B, C: the vertices; a, b, c: the sides; α (alpha), β (beta), γ (gamma): the interior angles; α′, β′, γ′: the exterior angles; S: the centre (*Am.* center)] — مُثَلَّث متساوى الأضلاع [A، B، C: رؤوس المُثَلَّث؛ a، b، c الأضلاع؛ α (ألفا)، β (بيتا)، γ (جاما) : زوايا داخلية؛ ألفا، بيتا، جاما : زوايا خارجية؛ S: المَرْكَز]

27 isosceles triangle [a, b: the sides (legs); c: the base; h: the perpendicular, an altitude] — مُثَلَّث متساوى الساقين [a، b : ضلعان؛ c: القَاعِدَة؛ h: عمود]

28 acute-angled triangle with perpendicular bisectors of the sides — مُثَلَّث حاد الزَّاوِيَة ذو أعمدة تنصيف للضلوع

29 circumcircle (circumscribed circle) — دائرة مُحيطية

30 obtuse-angled triangle with bisectors of the angles — مُثَلَّث مُنْفَرِج الزَّاوِيَة ذو منصفات للزوايا

31 inscribed circle — دائرة داخلية

32 right-angled triangle and the trigonometrical functions of angles [a, b: the catheti; c: the hypotenuse; γ: the right angle; $^a/_c = \sin\alpha$ (sine); $^b/_c = \cos\alpha$ (cosine); $^a/_b = \tan\alpha$ (tangent); $^b/_a = \cot\alpha$ (cotangent)] — مُثَلَّث قائم الزَّاوِيَة ودالات حساب المُثَلَّثات الخاصة بالزاويا؛ [a،b: ضلعا الزَّاوِيَة القائمة؛ c : الوتر؛ γ (جاما): الزَّاوِيَة القائمة؛ $^a/_c$: جا ألفا؛ $^b/_c$: جتا ألفا؛ $^a/_b$: ظا ألفا؛ $^b/_a$: ظتا ألفا]

33-39 quadrilaterals — **الأشكال الرباعية**

33-36 parallelograms — **المُتَوَازِيات**

33 square [d: a diagonal] — مُرَبَّع [d : خَطّ قطري]

34 rectangle — مستطيل

35 rhombus (rhomb, lozenge) — معيَّن

36 rhomboid — متوازى أضلاع

37 trapezium — معيَّن منحرف

38 deltoid (kite) — منحرف الأضلاع

39 irregular quadrilateral — شكل رباعي غير منتظم

40 polygon — مُضَلَّع

41 regular polygon — مُضَلَّع منتظم

42 circle — دائرة

43 centre (*Am.* center) — مَرْكَز الدائرة

44 circumference (periphery) — مُحيط الدائرة

45 diameter — قُطْر الدائرة

46 semicircle — نصْف دائرة

47 radius (r) — نِصْف قُطْر

48 tangent — مَمَاس

49 point of contact (P) — نُقْطَة التماس

50 secant — قاطع

51 the chord AB — الوتر AB

52 segment — قطْعة

53 arc — قَوْس

54 sector — قطَاع

55 angle subtended by the arc at the centre (*Am.* center) (centre, *Am.* center, angle) — الزَّاوِيَة المَرْكَزية المقابلة للقَوْس

56 circumferential angle — زَاوِيَة مُحيطية

57 ring (annulus) — حلقَة

58 concentric circles — دائرتان متحدتا المَرْكَز

347 Mathematics IV (Geometry II) — الرِّياضيَّات (4) (الهَنْدَسَة 2)

1 system of right-angled coordinates — نِظَام الإحْدَاثيَّات قائمة الزوايا

2-3 axes of coordinates (coordinate axes) — **مَحَاوِر الإحْدَاثيَّات**

2 axis of abscissae (x-axis) — محْوَر الإحداثى السيني (الأفقي)

3 axis of ordinates (y-axis) — محْوَر الإحْدَاثي الصادي (الرأسي)

4 origin of ordinates — مَنْشَأ الإحْدَاثيَّات

5 quadrant [I–IV: 1st to 4th quadrant] — قطَاع ربعي [I–IV: من الربع الأول إلى الرابع]

6 positive direction — اتجاه موجب

7 negative direction — اتجاه سالب

8 points [P_1 and P_2] in the system of coordinates; x_1 and y_1 [and x_2 and y_2 respectively] their coordinates — النقطتان [P1 وP2] في النظام الإحداثي]؛ إحْدَاثيا النقطتين x1 وy1 [وx2 وy2 على التوالي]

9 values of the abscissae [x_1 and x_2] (the abscissae) — قيمتا الإحْدَاثي السيني [x1 وx2]

10 values of the ordinates [y_1 and y_2] (the ordinates) — قيمتا الإحْدَاثي الصادي [y1 وy2]

11-29 conic sections — **القطاعات المَخْرُوطية**

11 curves in the system of coordinates — الانحناءات فى نِظَام الإحْدَاثيَّات

12 plane curves [a: the gradient (slope) of the curve; b: the ordinates' intersection of the curve; c: the root of the — منحنيان مستويان [a: ميل المنحنى؛ b: تقاطع الإحْدَاثي الصادي مع المنحنى؛ c: جذر المنحنى]

curve]

13 inflected curves — منحنيات منقلبة

14 parabola, a curve of the second degree — قَطْع مكافِئ، منحنى من الدرجة الثانية

15 branches of the parabola — فَرْعَا القَطْع المكَافِئ

16 vertex of the parabola — رأس القَطْع المكَافِئ

17 axis of the parabola — مِحْوَر القَطْع المكَافِئ

18 a curve of the third degree — منحنى من الدرجة الثالثة

19 maximum of the curve — أعلَى نُقْطَة فى المنحنى

20 minimum of the curve — أدْنَى نُقْطَة فى المنحنى

21 point of inflexion (of inflection) — نُقْطَة الإنْقِلاب

22 ellipse — قَطْع ناقص

23 transverse axis (major axis) — المِحْوَر المستعرض

24 conjugate axis (minor axis) — مِحْوَر متزاوج

25 foci of the ellipse [F_1 and F_2] — بؤرتا القَطْع الناقص [F1 وF2]

26 hyperbola — القَطْع الزائد

27 foci [F_1 and F_2] — بؤرتان [F1 وF2]

28 vertices [S_1 and S_2] — رأسا القَطْع المكَافِئ [S1 وS2]

29 asymptotes [a and b] — خَطّان مقاربان [a وb]

30-46 solids — **المُجَسَّمات**

30 cube — مكعَّب

31 square, a plane (plane surface) — مُرَبَّع ، سَطْح مستوٍ

32 edge — حافة

33 corner — زَاوِيَة، رُكْن

34 quadratic prism — مَنْشُور رباعي

35 base — قَاعِدَة

36 parallelepiped — متوازى السطوح

37 triangular prism — مَنْشُور ثلاثى الزوايا

38 cylinder, a right cylinder — أسْطُوَانَة، أسْطُوَانَة قائمة

39 base, a circular plane — قَاعِدَة ، سَطْح مستوٍ دائري

40 curved surface — سَطْح منحني

41 sphere — كُرَة

42 ellipsoid of revolution — مُجَسَّم إهليلجي

43 cone — مَخْرُوط

44 height of the cone (cone height) — ارتفاع المَخْرُوط

45 truncated cone (frustum of a cone) — مَخْرُوط مقطوع

46 quadrilateral pyramid — هَرَم رباعى الأسَطْح

348 Mathematics V (Sets) — الرِّياضيَّات (5) (المَجْمُوعَات)

1 the set A, the set {a, b, c, d, e, f, g} — المَجْمُوعَة A، المَجْمُوعَة {a ،b ،c ،d ،e ،f ،g}

2 elements (members) of the set A — عناصر المَجْمُوعَة A

3 the set B, the set {u, v, w, x, y, z} — المَجْمُوعَة B، المَجْمُوعَة {u ،v ،w ،x ،y ،z}

4 intersection of the sets A and B, A ∩ B = {f, g, u} — تقاطع المَجْمُوعَتَيْن A, B A ∩ B = {f, g, u}

5-6 union of the sets A and B, A ∪ B = {a, b, c, d, e, f, g, u, v, w, x, y, z} — اتحاد المَجْمُوعَتَيْن A ،B A ∪ B = {a, b, c, d, e, f, g, u, v, w, x, y, z}

7 complement of the set B, B′ = {a, b, c, d, e} — مكمِّل المَجْمُوعَة B, B′ = {a, b, c, d, e}

8 complement of the set A, A′ = {v, w, x, y, z} — مكمِّل المَجْمُوعَة A, A′ = {v, w, x, y, z}

9-11 mappings — **الإسْقَاطات**

9 mapping of the set M onto the set N — إسْقَاط المَجْمُوعَة M على المَجْمُوعَة N

10 mapping of the set M into the set N — إسْقَاط المَجْمُوعَة M في المَجْمُوعَة N

11 one-to-one mapping of the set M onto the set N — إسْقَاط المَجْمُوعَة M على المَجْمُوعَة N نقطة لنقطة

349 Chemistry Laboratory I — مَعْمَل الكِيمْيَاء (1)

1-38 laboratory apparatus (laboratory equipment) — **الأجْهِزَة المُخْتَبَرِيَّة**

1 Scheidt globe — كُرَة شمايت

2 U-tube — أنْبُوب نُونِيّ/على شكل U

3 separating funnel — قُمْع فاصِل

4 octagonal ground-glass stopper — سِدَادَة ثُمَانِيَّة من الزُجَاج المصنفر

5 tap (*Am.* faucet) — حَنَفِيَّة ، صنبور

6 coiled condenser — مكَثِّف حلزونيّ

7 air lock — دِسَام هوائي

8 wash-bottle — قنِّينَة غَسْل

9 mortar — هاوِن

10 pestle — مدَقَّـة

11 filter funnel (Büchner funnel) — قُمْع ترشيح

12 filter (filter plate) — مُرَشِّح

13 retort — مُعْوَجَّـة

14 water bath — حَمَّام مائي

15 tripod — حامِل ثلاثي

16 water gauge (*Am.* gage) — مِقْيَاس مستوى الماء

17 insertion rings — حَلَقَات الإيلاج

18 stirrer — مِحْرَاك ، أداة تقليب

19 manometer for measuring positive and negative pressures — مانومتر قياس الضغط الموجب والضغط السالب

20 mirror manometer for measuring small pressures — مانومتر ذو مِرْآة لقِيَاس الضغط المنخفض

21 inlet — مَدْخَل

22 tap (*Am.* faucet) — حَنَفِيَّة، صنبور

23 sliding scale — مِقْيَاس مُدرَّج مُنْزَلِق

24 weighing bottle — قارُورة وَزْن

25 analytical balance — ميزان تحليليّ

26 case — صُنْدُوق

27 sliding front panel — لَوْح أمامي مُنْزَلِق

28 three-point support — حامِل ثلاثيّ النقاط

29 column (balance column) — عمود قائم (عمود الميزان)

30 balance beam (beam) — عاتِق الميزان

31 rider bar — قضيب المِثْقَال الرَّاكِب

32 rider holder — حامل المثْقَال الرَّاكِب
33 rider — مثْقَال راكِب للوَزْن الدقيق
34 pointer — مُؤَشِّر
35 scale — مقْيَاس مُدَرَّج
36 scale pan — كَفَّة الميزان
37 stop — حاجِز، مِصَد
38 stop knob — مِقْبَض المِصَد / الحاجِز

350 Chemistry Laboratory II — مَعْمَل الكِيمْيَاء (2)

1-63 laboratory apparatus (laboratory equipment) — **الأجْهِزَة المختبريَّة**
1 Bunsen burner — لَهَب بنْزن، مَوْقِد بنْزن
2 gas inlet (gas inlet pipe) — أنْبُوبَة دخول الغاز
3 air regulator — مُنَظِّم الهواء
4 Teclu burner — مَوْقد تكلو
5 pipe union — وَصْلَة الأنابيب
6 gas regulator — مُنَظِّم الغاز
7 stem — جِذْع
8 air regulator — مُنَظِّم الهواء
9 bench torch — مِصْبَاح نَضَدِيّ
10 casing — غلاف، عُلْبَة
11 oxygen inlet — مَدْخَل الأكسجين
12 hydrogen inlet — مَدْخَل الهيدروجين
13 oxygen jet — منفث الأكسجين
14 tripod — حامِل ثلاثي
15 ring (retort ring) — حَلَقَة المُعْوَجَّات
16 funnel — قُمْع
17 pipe clay triangle — مُثَلَّث أنْبُوبِيّ من الصلصال
18 wire gauze — شَبكَة سِلْكِيَّة
19 wire gauze with asbestos centre (*Am.* center) — شَبكَة سِلْكِيَّة مركزها من الأسبستوس
20 beaker — كأس، مِخْبار
21 burette (for measuring the volume of liquids) — سَحَّاحَة (مقياس حَجْم السوائل)
22 burette stand — حامِل السَّحَّاحَات
23 burette clamp — ماسِك السحَّاحَة
24 graduated pipette — ماصَة مُدَرَّجَة
25 pipette — ماصة
26 measuring cylinder (measuring glass) — أسْطُوانَة قياس (مِخْبَار قياس)
27 measuring flask — قارُورة قِيَاس
28 volumetric flask — قارُورة حجْمِيَّة
29 evaporating dish (evaporating basin), made of porcelain — جفْنَة، طَبَق التبخير (من البورسلين)
30 tube clamp (tube clip, pinchcock) — ماسِك أنابيب
31 clay crucible with lid — بَوْتَقَة صَلْصَاليَّة ذات غطاء
32 crucible tongs — مِلْقَط البَوْتَقَة
33 clamp — ماسِك
34 test tube — أنْبُوب اختبار
35 test tube rack — حامِل أنابيب الاختبار
36 flat-bottomed flask — قارُورة مُسَطَّحَة القاعدة
37 ground glass neck — عُنُق من الزُّجاج المصنفر
38 long-necked round-bottomed flask — قارُورة طويلة العنق مستديرة القاعدة
39 Erlenmeyer flask (conical flask) — قارُورة مخروطيَّة الشكل
40 filter flask — قارُورة ترشيح
41 fluted filter — مُرَشِّح مُخَدَّد
42 one-way tap — حَنَفِيَّة تسمح بمرور السائل من اتجاه واحد فقط
43 calcium chloride tube — أنْبُوب كلوريد الكالسيوم
44 stopper with tap — سِدادَة ذات حَنَفِيَّة
45 cylinder — أُسْطُوَانَة
46 distillation apparatus (distilling apparatus) — جِهَاز التقطير
47 distillation flask (distilling flask) — قارورة التقطير
48 condenser — مُكَثِّف
49 return tap, a two-way tap — حَنَفِيَّة مُرْجِعَة
50 distillation flask (distilling flask, Claisen flask) — قارُورة تقطير
51 desiccator — مُجَفِّف، وعاء تجفيف
52 lid with fitted tube — غطاء ذو أنْبُوب مُحكم التثبيت
53 tap — حَنَفِيَّة
54 desiccator insert made of porcelain — وَلِيجَة المُجَفِّف (مصنوعة من البورسلين)
55 three-necked flask — قارُورة ثُلاثيَّة الأعناق
56 connecting piece (Y-tube) — قطعة توصيل (أنْبُوب ذات فَرْعَيْن)
57 three-necked bottle — قنِّينَة ثُلاثيَّة الأعناق
58 gas-washing bottle — قنِّينَة غسيل الغاز
59 gas generator (Kipp's apparatus, *Am.* Kipp generator) — مُوَلِّد الغاز (مُوَلِّد كِب)
60 overflow container — وعاء الفائض
61 container for the solid — وعاء المواد الصلبة
62 acid container — وعاء الأحماض
63 gas outlet — أنْبُوب خروج الغاز

351 Crystals, Crystallography — البلُّورَات وعِلْم التَّبَلُّور

1-26 basic crystal forms and crystal combinations [structure of crystals] — **الأشكال الأساسيَّة للبلُّورات وتركيبات البلُّورات**
1-17 regular (cubic, tesseral, isometric) **crystal system** — **النِّظَام البلُّورِي العادي** (مكَعَّب، متساوي الأبعاد، متساوي المَحَاور)
1 tetrahedron (four-faced polyhedron) [tetrahedrite, fahlerz, fahl ore] — رُبَاعِيّ الأَوْجُه [تتراهيدريت]
2 hexahedron (cube, six-faced polyhedron), a holohedron [rock salt] — سُدَاسِيّ الأَوْجُه، بلُّورَة تامة التماثُل [ملح صخريّ]
3 centre (*Am.* center) of symmetry (crystal centre) — مركز التناظر (مركز البلُّور)
4 axis of symmetry (rotation axis) — محْوَر التناظر (مِحْوَر الدوران)

5 plane of symmetry	مستوى التناظر
6 octahedron (eight-faced polyhedron) [gold]	مُجَسَّم ثماني الأوْجُه [ذهب]
7 rhombic dodecahedron [garnet]	المُجَسَّم المُعَيَّنِيّ ذو الإثنى عشر وَجْهاً [عقيق أحمر، غرينيت]
8 pentagonal dodecahedron [pyrite, iron pyrites]	المُجَسَّم الخماسي ذو إثنى عشر وجهاً [بريت الحديد]
9 pentagon (five-sided polygon)	مضلع مُخَمَّس
10 triakis-octahedron [diamond]	مُجَسَّم ثلاثيّ ثماني الأوجه [الماس]
11 icosahedron (twenty-faced polyhedron), a regular polyhedron	المُجَسَّم المنتظم ذو العشرين وجهاً
12 icositetrahedron (twenty-four-faced polyhedron) [leucite]	مُجَسَّم ذو أربعة وعشرين وجهاً [لوسيت]
13 hexakis-octahedron (hexoctahedron, forty-eight-faced polyhedron) [diamond]	مُجَسَّم ذو ثمانية وأربعين وجهاً [الماس]
14 octahedron with cube [galena]	ثماني الأوجه ذو مكعَّب [كبريتيد الرصاص الطبيعي]
15 hexagon (six-sided polygon)	مضلع مُسَدَّس
16 cube with octahedron [fluorite, fluorspar]	مكعَّب ذو أوْجُه ثُمانيَّة الأضلاع [فلوريت، حجر فلوري]
17 octagon (eight-sided polygon)	سَطْح ثُمانيّ الأضلاع
18-19 tetragonal crystal system	**النِّظَام البلُّوري الرُّبَاعيّ**
18 tetragonal dipyramid (tetragonal bipyramid)	هَرَم ثنائي رُبَاعيّ الأوْجُه
19 protoprism with protopyramid [zircon]	مَنْشُور أوَّلي مع هَرَم أوَّلي [زركون]
20-22 hexagonal crystal system	**النِّظَام البلُّوري السُّداسيّ**
20 protoprism with protopyramid, deuteropyramid and basal pinacoid [apatite]	مَنْشُور أوَّلي مع هَرَم أوَّلي وبناكويد سفلي [أباتيت]
21 hexagonal prism	مَنْشُور سُدَاسيّ
22 hexagonal (ditrigonal) biprism with rhombohedron [calcite]	مَنْشُور ثنائي سُداسيّ ذو سَطْح مُعَيَّنِيّ [كالسيت]
23 orthorhombic pyramid (rhombic crystal system) [sulphur, *Am.* sulfur]	هَرَم مُعَيَّنِيّ مستقيم [كبريت]
24-25 monoclinic crystal system	**النِّظَام البلُّوري أحادى المَيْل**
24 monoclinic prism with clinoprinacoid and hemipyramid (hemihedron) [gypsum]	مَنْشُور أحادى المَيْل ذو مسطوح مائل وسَطْح نصف هَرَمي [الجبس]
25 orthopinacoid (swallow tail twin crystal) [gypsum]	مُسَطَّح أمامي (أورتوبناكويد) [الجبس]
26 triclinic pinacoids (triclinic crystal system) [copper sulphate, *Am.* copper sulfate]	مُسَطَّح ثلاثي المَيْل [كبريتات النحاس]
27-33 apparatus for measuring crystals (for crystallometry)	**جهَاز قياس البلُّورات** (المِقْيَاسيَّة البلُّورِيَّة)
27 contact goniometer	مقْيَاس زوايا التماس
28 reflecting goniometer	مِنْقَل [غنيومتر] انعكاس
29 crystal	بلُّورَة
30 collimator	كوليماتور (مُوَجِّه الأشعة)
31 observation telescope	تليسكوب الرَّصْد
32 divided circle (graduated circle)	دائرة مُدرَّجة
33 lens for reading the angle of rotation	عدسة قراءة زاوية الدَّوَرَان

352 Ethnology I — عِلْم الأعْرَاق البَشَرِيَّة (1)

1 totem pole	العمود الطَّوْطَميّ
2 totem, a carved and painted pictorial or symbolic representation	طَوْطَم: شيْ منحوت وملون يُتَّخَذ رمزاً لأسرة أو عشيرة
3 plains Indian	هنْدي أحْمَر، هندي السهول الأمريكيَّة
4 mustang, a prairie horse	المُسْتَنْغ: فَرَس السهول الأمريكيَّة البريّ أو نصف البريّ
5 lasso, a long throwing-rope with running noose	الوَهَق: حَبْل بآخره أنشوطة لصيد الخيول وما شابهها
6 pipe of peace	غليون هنديّ: غليون طويل
7 wigwam (tepee, teepee)	الوَغْم، التِّيبة (خَيْمَة مخروطيَّة من الجِلْد)
8 tent pole	عمود الخَيْمَة
9 smoke flap	فَتْحَة خروج الدخان
10 squaw, an Indian woman	هِنْدِيَّة حَمْرَاء أمريكيَّة
11 Indian chief	زعيم الهنود الحُمْر
12 headdress, an ornamental feather headdress	غِطاء الرأس، غطاء رأس زيني من الرِّيش
13 war paint	طلاء الحَرْب
14 necklace of bear claws	عِقْد من مخالب الدُّبَبَة
15 scalp (cut from enemy's head), a trophy	فَرْوَة رأس (منزوعة من رأس أحد الأعداء)
16 tomahawk, a battle axe (*Am.* ax)	التَّمْهُوك: فأس الهنود الحمر
17 leggings	الطِّمَاق: غطاء للساق
18 moccasin, a shoe of leather and bast	المُقْسِين: حذاء من الجِلْد بدون كعب
19 canoe of the forest Indians	الكَنُوّ: قارب صغير يستخدمه الهنود الحمر سكان الغابات
20 Maya temple, a stepped pyramid	مَعْبَد المايا، هَرَم مُدَرَّج

21 mummy مُومْيَاء
22 quipa (knotted threads, knotted code of the Incas) ذات العُقَد: أداة مؤلفة من حَبْل وعُقَد صغيرة مختلفة الألْوَان كان أهْل بيرو القدماء يستخدمونها في الحسابات
23 Indio (Indian of Central and South America); *here:* high-land Indian هندي أحمر من أمريكا الوسطى والجنوبيَّة
24 poncho, a blanket with a head opening used as an armless cloak-like wrap عباءة البُنْش
25 Indian of the tropical forest هِنْدي أحْمَر من سُكَّان الغابات الاستوائيَّة
26 blowpipe أنْبُوب نفخ
27 quiver جُعْبَة
28 dart سَهْم مُرَيَّش
29 dart point سِنُّ السَّهْم المُرَيَّش
30 shrunken head, a trophy رأس مفصول مُنْكَمِش
31 bola (bolas), a throwing and entangling device البُولا: سلاح مكوَّن من كُرَتَيْن يُرْشَق به الحيوان لأسْره
32 leather-covered stone or metal ball حَجَر أو كُرَة معدنيَّة مُغَطًّى بالجِلْد
33 pile dwelling مَسْكَن مصنوع من الخوازيق
34 duk-duk dancer, a member of a duk-duk (men's secret society) راقص "الداك داك" (جمعية سِرِّيَّة للرِّجَال)
35 outrigger canoe (canoe with outrigger) كَنُو ذو ذراع امتداديّ
36 outrigger ذراع امتداديّ
37 Australian aborigine أرومي أسترالي: أحد سكان أستراليا الأصليين
38 loincloth of human hair ستار عَوْرَة (مِئْزَر) من شَعْر آدميّ
39 boomerang, a wooden missile بَمَرَنْغ: قذيفة خشبية معقوفة
40 throwing stick (spear thrower) with spears عصا للقذف ذات حِرَاب

353 Ethnology II علْم الأعْرَاق البَشَرِيَّة (2)

1 Eskimo فرْد من الإسكيمو
2 sledge dog (sled dog), a husky كلب جَرّ المِزْلَجَة
3 dog sledge (dog sled) مِزْلَجَة يجرها الكلاب
4 igloo, a dome-shaped snow hut كوخ قِبابيّ من الجليد
5 block of snow كُتْلَة من الجليد
6 entrance tunnel نَفَق الدخول
7 blubber-oil lamp مِصْبَاح يُضاء بزيت دُهْن الحوت
8 wooden missile قذيفة خشبيَّة
9 lance حَرْبَة، رُمْح
10 harpoon حَرْبُون لصَيْد الحيتان
11 skin float طَوْف من الجِلْد
12 kayak, a light one-man canoe زَوْرَق الكياك
13 skin-covered wooden or bone frame إطار خشبيّ أو عظميّ مكْسُو بالجِلْد
14 paddle مِجْذَاف
15 reindeer harness لِجام حيوان الرِّنَّة
16 reindeer حيوان الرِّنَّة
17 Ostyak (Ostiak) استياك
18 passenger sledge مِزْلَجَة رُكَّاب
19 yurt (yurta), a dwelling tent of the western and central Asiatic nomads اليورتة: خَيْمَة جِلْديَّة أو لباديَّة من خيام بدو سَيْبِرْيَا المنغوليين
20 felt covering غطاء من اللباد
21 smoke outlet فَتْحَة تهوية لخروج الدخان
22 Kirghiz فَرْد قرغيزي: من العِرْق المغولي الذي يقطن سهول آسيا الوسطى
23 sheepskin cap قُبَّعَة من جِلْد الغنم
24 shaman الشَّامان: كاهِن يستخدم السِّحْر لمعالجة المرضى ومعرفة المُخَبَّأ
25 decorative fringe شراشيب زينة
26 frame drum طَبْلَة إطاريَّة
27 Tibetan فَرْد من التيبت
28 flintlock with bayonets المُصَوَّنَة: بندقية ذات زند مُصَوَّن
29 prayer wheel عجلة العبادة
30 felt boot حذاء (بُوت) من اللباد
31 houseboat (sampan) مَرْكَب مُعَدّ للسُّكْنَى، بَيْت في مَرْكَب
32 junk اليُنْك: سفينة شِرَاعية صينية
33 mat sail شِرَاع
34 rickshaw (ricksha) جِنْرِكْشَة: عربة صغيرة لشخص واحد تستخدم في اليابان
35 rickshaw coolie (cooly) الكُولي: حمال الجِنْرِكْشَة
36 Chinese lantern فانوس ورق
37 samurai ساموراي: أحد المحاربين اليابانيين من الطبقة الأرستقراطية
38 padded armour (*Am.* armor) دِرْع مُبَطَّن
39 geisha فتاة الجيشا
40 kimono رداء الكيمونو
41 obi الأوبي: زِنَار عريض يُشَد فوق ثوب ياباني
42 fan مِرْوَحَة
43 coolie (cooly) حمَّال، شيَّال
44 kris (creese, crease), a Malayan dagger الكريس: خنجر إندونيسي
45 snake charmer حاوي الأفاعي
46 turban عِمَامَة
47 flute فلُوت
48 dancing snake حيَّة راقِصة

354 Ethnology III علْم الأعْرَاق البَشَرِيَّة (3)

1 camel caravan قافلة الإبل
2 riding animal حيوان الرُّكُوب
3 pack animal حيوان حَمْل الأمتعة

4 oasis — وَاحَة
5 grove of palm trees — بُسْتَان من النخيل
6 bedouin (beduin) — بَدَوِي
7 burnous — بُرْنُس
8 Masai warrior — مُحارِب من الماساي
9 headdress (hairdress) — غِطاء الرأس
10 shield — درع
11 painted ox hide — جِلْد ثَوْر مَطْلِي
12 long-bladed spear — رُمْح طويل النَّصْل
13 negro — زِنْجِي
14 dance drum — طَبْلَة رقص
15 throwing knife — سِكِّين للرَّشْق
16 wooden mask — قناع خشبيّ
17 figure of an ancestor — تمثال لأحَد الأسْلاف
18 slit gong — طَبْلَة قُرْصِيَّة الشكل مشقوقة
19 drumstick — عصا الطَّبْلَة
20 dugout, a boat hollowed out of a tree trunk — زَوْرَق شجريّ
21 negro hut — كُوخ الزِّنُوج
22 negress — امْرَأة زِنْجِيَّة
23 lip plug (labret) — الشَّفِيهة: حِلْيَة تُعلَّق في الشفة بعد ثقبها
24 grinding stone — حَجَر التجليخ
25 Herero woman — إمْرَأة من الهيريرو
26 leather cap — كاب من الجِلْد
27 calabash (gourd) — قَرْعَة
28 beehive-shaped hut — كُوخ على شكل خَلِيَّة النَّحْل
29 bushman — البُشْمان: أحد سكان الأدغال
30 earplug — حِلْيَة أُذُنِيَّة
31 loincloth — مِئْزَر (سِتار للعورة)
32 bow — قَوْس
33 knobkerry (knob-kerrie), a club with round, knobbed end — نَبُوت
34 bushman woman making a fire by twirling a stick — امرأة البُشْمان: وهى تُشْعِل النار بواسطة تدوير عصا
35 windbreak — حاجِز الريح
36 Zulu in dance costume — أحد أفراد الزولو يرتدي زيّ الرقص
37 dancing stick — عصا الرَّقْص
38 bangle — سِوَار
39 ivory war horn — بُوق من العَاج: يُنْفَخ فيه لإعلان الحرب
40 string of amulets and bones — خَيْط من التعاويذ والعِظام
41 pigmy — قزم
42 magic pipe for exorcising evil spirits — مِزْمَار سحريّ لطَرْد الأرواح الشريرة
43 fetish — صَنَم

355 Historical Costumes — اللبَاس عَبْرَ العصُور

1 Greek woman — امرأة إغريقيَّة
2 peplos — بِبْلُوس
3 Greek — رَجُل إغْريقي
4 petasus (Thessalonian hat) — قُبَّعَة البتاسوس
5 chiton, a linen gown worn as a basic garment — عَبَاءة إغريقيَّة (للرِجال والنساء)
6 himation, woollen (*Am.* woolen) cloak — شَمْلَة
7 Roman woman — امرأة رومانيَّة
8 toupee wig (partial wig) — خصلة من شَعْر مُستعار تعلو قمة الرأس
9 stola — بَطْرَشِيل
10 palla, a coloured (*Am.* colored) wrap — دِثار مُلَوَّن
11 Roman — رومانيّ
12 tunica (tunic) — التُّنْك: رداء روماني طويل
13 toga — التُّوجَة: ثَوْب روماني فضفاض
14 purple border (purple band) — كَنَار أرجواني (رمز للمَنْزِلَة الرفيعة)
15 Byzantine empress — إمبراطورة بيزنطيَّة
16 pearl diadem — إكْلِيل مُرَصَّع باللؤلؤ
17 jewels — جَوَاهِر
18 purple cloak — عَبَاءة أُرجوانيَّة
19 long tunic — تُنْك طويل
20 German princess [13th cent.] — أميرة ألمانيَّة [القرن الثالث عشر]
21 crown (diadem) — تاج (إكْلِيل)
22 chinband — شريط الذَّقْن
23 tassel — شُرَّابة
24 cloak cord — حبْل العباءة
25 girt-up gown (girt-up surcoat, girt-up tunic) — ثَوْب نسائي بحزام
26 cloak — عَبَاءة، معْطَف فضفاض
27 German dressed in the Spanish style [ca. 1575] — ألماني يرتدي زيّاً أسبانياً، [1575]
28 wide-brimmed cap — قُبَّعَة بحافة عريضة
29 short cloak (Spanish cloak, short cape) — عَبَاءة قصيرة (عَبَاءة أسبانيَّة، كاب قصير)
30 padded doublet (stuffed doublet, peasecod) — صُدْرَة ضيِّقَة مُبَطَّنَة
31 stuffed trunk-hose — بِنْطَال قصير محشوّ
32 lansquenet (German mercenary soldier) [ca. 1530] — جُنْدي ألماني مُرْتَزَق [1530]
33 slashed doublet (paned doublet) — صُدْرَة ضيقة مشقوقة بحيث يُظْهِر ما تحتها
34 Pluderhose (loose breeches, paned trunk-hose, slops) — سِرْوَال مُنْتَفِخ
35 woman of Basle [ca. 1525] — امرأة البازل [1525]
36 overgown (gown) — ثَوْب خارجي
37 undergown (petticoat) — ثَوْب تحتاني (تَنُّورَة تحتانيَّة)
38 woman of Nuremberg [ca. 1500] — امرأة نورمبرج [1500]
39 shoulder cape — عَبَاءة للكتفيْن
40 Burgundian [15th cent.] — بُرْغندي [القرن الخامس عشر]
41 short doublet — صُدْرَة ضيقة صغيرة

42 piked shoes (peaked shoes, copped shoes, crackowes, poulaines)	حِذاء طويل مُسْتَدَقّ الطرف
43 pattens (clogs)	نَعْل من الخشب
44 young nobleman [ca. 1400]	شابٌ نبيل [1400]
45 short, padded doublet (short, quilted doublet, jerkin)	صُدْرَة ضيقة قصيرة مُبطَّنة
46 dagged sleeves (petal-scalloped sleeves)	كُمٌ واسع متدلٍ
47 hose	بنْطَال ضيِّق
48 Augsburg patrician lady [ca. 1575]	سيِّدة نبيلة من العصر الأُغْسُطْسيّ [1575]
49 puffed sleeve	كُمّ مُنْتَفِخ
50 overgown (gown, open gown, sleeveless gown)	ثَوْب خارجي، عباءة
51 French lady [ca. 1600]	امرأة فرنسيَّة [1600]
52 millstone ruff (cart-wheel ruff, ruff)	طَوْق رقبة دائري مكَشْكَش
53 corseted waist (wasp waist)	خَصْر نحيل مشدود بمِشَد
54 gentleman [ca. 1650]	رَجُل نبيل المَحْتِد [1650]
55 wide-brimmed felt hat (cavalier hat)	قُبَّعَة لباديَّة عريضة الحافة
56 falling collar (wide-falling collar) of linen	ياقة ساقطة من الكتَّان
57 white lining	بطَانة بيضاء
58 jack boots (bucket-top boots)	بُوت بِوَاقيَة للرُكْبَة
59 lady [ca. 1650]	سيِّدَة نبيلة المَحْتِد [1650]
60 full puffed sleeves (puffed sleeves)	كُمٌ مُنتفخ بالكامِل
61 gentleman [ca. 1700]	رَجُل نبيل المَحْتِد [1700]
62 three-cornered hat	قُبَّعَة بثلاثة قرون
63 dress sword	سَيْف الثَّوْب
64 lady [ca. 1700]	سيِّدَة نبيل المَحْتِد [1700]
65 lace fontange (high headdress of lace)	غطاء رأس بشريط زيني
66 lace-trimmed loose-hanging gown (loose-fitting housecoat, robe de chambre, negligée, contouche)	عَبَاءة فضفاضة مُزيَّنَة بأشْرِطَة
67 band of embroidery	شَريط تطريز
68 lady [ca. 1880]	سيِّدَة نبيلة المَحْتِد [1880]
69 bustle	أَرْدَاف مُستعَارَة
70 lady [ca. 1858]	سيِّدَة نبيلة المَحْتِد [1858]
71 poke bonnet	بَوْكِيَّة
72 crinoline	تَنُّورَة نافخَة
73 gentleman of the Biedermeier period	رَجُل نبيل المَحْتِد من العصر البيدرميري
74 high collar (choker collar)	ياقة مرتفعة
75 embroidered waistcoat (vest)	صُدَيْريَّة مُطرَّزَة
76 frock coat	معْطَف الفراك/ قصير حتى الركبتين
77 pigtail wig	شَعْر مُستعار
78 ribbon (bow)	شريط (بابيون)
79 ladies in court dress [ca. 1780]	سيِّدات نبيلات المَحْتِد في لباس البلاط [1780]
80 train	ذَيْل الثَّوْب
81 upswept Rococo coiffure	تسريحة شَعْر روكوكو لأعْلَى
82 hair decoration	زينة للشعْر
83 panniered overskirt	تَنُّورَة خارجيَّة منفوخة

356 Zoo (Zoological Gardens) حَديقَة الحَيَوَان

1 outdoor enclosure	حَظيرة مُسَيَّجة في الهواء الطَّلْق
2 rocks	صخور
3 moat	خَنْدَق مائيّ
4 enclosing wall	جِدَار سياجي
5 animals on show; *here:* a pride of lions	حيوانات مَعْرُوضَة؛ في الصورة: قطيع من الأسُود
6 visitor to the zoo	زائر حديقة الحيوان
7 notice	لافتَة
8 aviary	قفص طُيُور كبير
9 elephant enclosure	حظيرة الفيلة
10 animal house (e.g. carnivore house, giraffe house, elephant house, monkey house)	بَيْت الحيوانات (مِثال بَيْت آكِلات اللحوم، أو الزَّراف، أو الفيلَة، أو القُرُود)
11 outside cage (summer quarters)	قفص حيوانات خارجي (البَيْت الصَّيْفي للحيوانات)
12 reptile enclosure	بَيْت الزَّوَاحِف
13 Nile crocodile	تِمْسَاح النيل
14 terrarium and aquarium	مَرْبَى الأحْيَاء البريَّة ومَرْبَى الأحْيَاء المائيَّة
15 glass case	صندوق زُجاجي
16 fresh-air inlet	فَتْحَة دخول الهواء الطَّلْق
17 ventilator	فَتْحَة التهويَّة
18 underfloor heating	جِهَاز تدفئة سفلي
19 aquarium	مَرْبَى أحْيَاء مائيَّة
20 information plate	لَوْحة المعلومات
21 flora in artificially maintained climate	نباتات في مَنَاخ صناعي

357 Invertebrates الفَقَاريَّات

1-12 unicellular (one-celled, single-celled) animals (protozoans)	**الحيوانات وَحيدة الخليَّة**
1 amoeba, a rhizopod	الأميبا
2 cell nucleus	نَوَاة الخليَّة
3 protoplasm	البروتوبلازم
4 pseudopod	الشَّواة الكاذبة
5 excretory vacuole (contractile vacuole, an organelle)	حُوَيْصِلَة إفرازيَّة
6 food vacuole	حُوَيْصِلَة الطعام
7 Actinophrys, a heliozoan	أكتونيفريس: حيوان من الشَّمْسِيَّات
8 radiolarian; *here:* siliceous skeleton	حيوان بحري شعَوْعي؛ في الصورة: هيكل سيليكوني
9 slipper animalcule, a	حُيَيْوِيْن (حيوان

Paramecium (ciliate infusorian)	ميكروسكوبي زَلِق لا يُرى بالعين المُجَرَّدَة)
10 cilium	هُدْب
11 macronucleus (meganucleus)	نَوَاة كبيرة
12 micronucleus	نَوَاة ميكرسكوبيَّة
13-39 multicellular animals (metazoans)	**الحيوانات مُتَعَدِّدَة الخلايا**
13 bath sponge, a porifer (sponge)	إسْفِنْج الحَمَّام
14 medusa, a discomedusa, a coelenterate	رِئَة البَحر ، قنديل البحر
15 umbrella	مِظَلَّة
16 tentacle	مِجَس
17 red coral (precious coral), a coral animal (anthozoan, reef-building animal)	مَرْجَان أحمر
18 coral colony	مجموعة مَرْجَانيَّة
19 coral polyp	بُولِب مَرْجاني
20-26 worms (Vermes)	**الديدان**
20 leech, an annelid	عَلَقَة ، دُودَة حَلَقِيَّة
21 sucker	مِمَصّ ، عضو المَصّ
22 Spirographis, a bristle worm	دُودَة الإسبيروجرافيس ، دُودَة هُلْبِيَّة
23 tube	أُنْبُوب
24 earthworm	الخُرْطُون: دُودَة الأرض
25 segment	فَصّ
26 clitellum [accessory reproductive organ]	عُضْو التناسُل [عضو تناسل إضافي]
27-36 molluscs (*Am.* mollusks)	**الرَّخَوِيَّات**
27 edible snail, a snail	حَلَزُون/قَوْقَع صالح للأكْل
28 creeping foot	قَدَم زاحِفة
29 shell (snail shell)	صَدَفَة
30 stalked eye	عَيْن ذُنَيْبِيَّة
31 tentacles (feelers)	قرون استشعار ، مِجَسَّات
32 oyster	مَحَّارة
33 freshwater pearl mussel	مَحَّار لُؤْلُؤ المياه العَذْبَة
34 mother-of-pearl (nacre)	أُمّ اللُؤْلُؤ
35 pearl	لُؤْلُؤة
36 mussel shell	صَدَفَة المَحَّارة
37 cuttlefish, a cephalopod	الحَبَّار ، الصَّبِّيْد
38-39 echinoderms	**القُنْفُذِيَّات**
38 starfish (sea star)	نَجْمَة البَحْر
39 sea urchin (sea hedgehog)	قُنْفُذ البَحْر

358 Arthropods — المفْصَلِيَّات

1-2 crustaceans	**القِشْرِيَّات**
1 mitten crab, a crab	سَرَطَان البَحْر
2 water slater	دُوَيْبَة البَحْر
3-39, 48-56 insects	**الحَشَرات**
3 water nymph (dragonfly), a homopteran (homopterous insect)	يَعْسُوب ، سُرْمان
4 water scorpion (water bug), a rhynchophore	عَقْرَب الماء (بَقُّ الماء)
5 raptorial leg	ساق كاسِرَة/جارِحَة
6 mayfly (dayfly, ephmerid)	ذُبَابَة نَوَّار ، ابنة يَوْم
7 compound eye	عَيْن مُرَكَّبَة
8 green grasshopper (green locust, meadow grasshopper), an orthopteron (orthopterous insect)	الجُنْدُب الأخْضَر
9 larva (grub)	يَرَقَانَة ، يَرَقَة
10 adult insect, an imago	حَشَرَة كاملة النمو
11 leaping hind leg	ساق خلفيَّة للقَفْز
12 caddis fly (spring fly, water moth), a neuropteran	ذُبَابَة الكادِس (حَشَرَة شَعْرِيَّة الجَنَاح)
13 aphid (greenfly), a plant louse	إرْقَة المَنَّة: حَشَرَة تمتص عصارة النبات
14 wingless aphid	مَنَّة عديمة الأجنحة
15 winged aphid	مَنَّة مُجَنَّحَة
16-20 dipterous insects (dipterans)	**الحَشَرات مزدوجة الجَنَاح**
16 gnat (mosquito, midge), a culicid	قِرْس (بَعُوضَة صغيرة)
17 proboscis (sucking organ)	خرطوم (عضو المَصّ)
18 bluebottle (blowfly), a fly	ذُبَابَة اللحم الزرقاء
19 maggot (larva)	يَرَقَة قَطْعاء
20 chrysalis (pupa)	خادِرَة
21-23 Hymenoptera	**الحَشَرات غشائيَّة الأجنحة**
21-22 ant	**النَّمْل**
21 winged female	أُنْثى مُجَنَّحَة
22 worker	شَغَّالَة
23 bumblebee (humblebee)	النَّحْلَة الطَّنَّانَة
24-39 beetles (Coleoptera)	**الخنافس**
24 stag beetle, a lamellicorn beetle	خُنْفِسَاء الحُنْظُب
25 mandibles	فَكَّان
26 trophi	فَتْحَة تغذية
27 antenna (feeler)	قَرْن استشعار (مِجَسّ)
28 head	رأس
29-30 thorax	**الصَّدْر**
29 thoracic shield (prothorax)	الدرع الصَّدْري
30 scutellum	حَرْشَفَة ، صفيحة قَرْنيَّة
31 tergites	ظَهْر حَلَقِيّ
32 stigma	علامَة
33 wing (hind wing)	جَنَاح (جَنَاح خلفي)
34 nervure	عِرْق جَنَاح الحَشَرَة
35 point at which the wing folds	الجُزْء الذي ينطوي عنده الجَنَاح
36 elytron (forewing)	الجنيح الغِمْدِيّ
37 ladybird (*Am.* ladybug), a coccinellid	الدُعْسُوقَة
38 Ergates faber, a longicorn beetle (longicorn)	القرنبي: خُنْفُسَاء طويلة القَرْنَان ، خُنْفُس أقْرَن
39 dung beetle, a lamellicorn beetle	خُنْفِسَاء الرَّوْث

40-47 arachnids	**العَنْكَبُوتيات**
40 Euscorpius flavicandus, a scorpion	عقرب
41 cheliped with chelicer	كُلاّب
42 maxillary antenna (maxillary feeler)	قَرْن استشعار فَكّي
43 tail sting	إبْرَة الذَّيْل
44-46 spiders	**العناكب**
44 wood tick (dog tick)	قُرَادَة الخشب
45 cross spider (garden spider), an orb spinner	عَنْكَبُوت الحدائق
46 spinneret	المِغْزَال: العضو الناسِج للخيوط
47 spider's web (web)	نسيج العَنْكَبُوت
48-56 Lepidoptera (butterflies and moths)	**قشْرِيَّات الأجنحة**
48 mulberry-feeding moth (silk moth), a bombycid moth	فَرَاشَة الحرير
49 eggs	بَيْض
50 silkworm	دُودَة القَزّ
51 cocoon	شَرْنَقَة
52 swallowtail, a butterfly	مُذَنَّبَة ، فراشة خطافيَّة
53 antenna (feeler)	قَرْن استشعار
54 eyespot	تَبَقُّع عَيْنِيّ
55 privet hawkmoth, a hawkmoth (sphinx)	فَرَاشَة هَوْلِيَّة
56 proboscis	خرطوم الفَرَاشَة

359 Birds I — الطُّيُور(1)

1-3 flightless birds	**طُيُور لا تطير**
1 cassowary; *sim.:* emu	الشَّبْنَم
2 ostrich	النَّعَام
3 clutch of ostrich eggs [12-14 eggs]	حَضْنَة من بَيْض النَّعَام [12–14 بيضة]
4 king penguin, a penguin, a flightless bird	البَطْرِيق
5-10 web-footed birds	**الطُّيُور ذات الأقْدام الوتريَّة**
5 white pelican	البَجَع الأبْيَض
6 webfoot (webbed foot)	قدم ذات وَتَرَة
7 web (palmations) of webbed foot (palmate foot)	وَتَرَة
8 lower mandible with gular pouch	فك سفلي ذو جراب
9 northern gannet (gannet, solan goose), a gannet	الأطْيَش الشمالي
10 green cormorant (shag), a cormorant displaying with spread wings	الغاق الأخضر
11-14 long-winged birds (seabirds)	**الطُّيُور طويلة الأجنحة** (طيور بحرية)
11 common sea swallow, a sea swallow (tern), diving for food	طائِر سُنُوْنُو الماء يَغُوص بحثاً عن الطعام
12 fulmar	طائر الفُلْمار
13 guillemot, an auk	طائر الغلموت: من طُيُور البِحَار الشماليَّة
14 black-headed gull (mire crow), a gull	النَّوْرَس ذو الرأس الأسود
15-17 Anseres	**رُتْبَة الإوَز**
15 goosander (common merganser), a sawbill	بَطَّة البَلَقْشَة
16 mute swan, a swan	البَجَعَة الصامتة
17 knob on the bill	زائدة جِلْدِيَّة فَوْق المِنْقَار
18 common heron, a heron	مالِك الحزين ، البَلَشُون
19-21 plovers	**الطُّيُور الزَّقْزَاقة**
19 stilt (stilt bird, stilt plover)	طائر الطُّوَّل
20 coot, a rail	الغُرَّة
21 lapwing (green plover, peewit, pewit)	الزقزاق الشامي ، أبو طيط
22 quail, a gallinaceous bird	السُّمانَى ، السَّلْوَى
23 turtle dove, a pigeon	القُمْرِيَّة
24 swift	السَّمَامة
25 hoopoe, a roller	الهُدْهُد
26 erectile crest	عُرْف إنتصابي
27 spotted woodpecker, a woodpecker; related: wryneck	نَقَّار الخشب المُرَقَّط
28 entrance to the nest	مَدْخَل العُشّ
29 nesting cavity	تجويف العُشّ
30 cuckoo	الوَقْوَاق

360 Birds II (European Birds) — الطُّيُور (2) (الطُّيُور الأورُوبيَّة)

1, 3, 4, 5, 7, 9, 10 song-birds	**طُيُور مُغَرِّدَة**
1 goldfinch, a finch	الحَسُّون ، نقَّار الشَّوْك
2 bee eater	الوَرْوَار ، الخُضَّار
3 redstart (star finch), a thrush	الحُمَيراء ، هزَّاز الحائط
4 bluetit, a tit (titmouse), a resident bird (non-migratory bird)	العُصْفُور الأزْرَق (طائر غير مُهَاجِر)
5 bullfinch	الدُّغْنَاش
6 common roller (roller)	الشُّقِرَّاق
7 golden oriole, a migratory bird	الصُّفَارية ، طائر مُهَاجِر
8 kingfisher	الرَّفْرَاف ، مُلاعِب ظلِّه
9 white wagtail, a wag-tail	الذُّعْرَة
10 chaffinch	الشُّرْشُور

361 Birds III (Passerines) — الطُّيُور (3) (الجَوَاثم)

1-20 songbirds	**الطُّيُور المُغَرِّدَة**
1-3 Corvidae (corvine birds, crows)	**فَصِيلَة الغُرَابيَّات**
1 jay (nutcracker)	أبو زُرَيْق
2 rook, a crow	غُدَاف ، غُرَاب القَيْظ
3 magpie	العَقْعَق ، كُنْدُش

4 starling (pastor, shepherd bird)	الزرزور
5 house sparrow	عُصْفُور معروف
6-8 finches	**طُيُور الشُّرْشُور**
6-7 buntings	**الدُّرَّاسات**
6 yellowhammer (yellow bunting)	اليَلْمَر: الدُّرَّاسَة
7 ortolan (ortolan bunting)	الأرطلان (بلبل الشعير)
8 siskin (aberdevine)	السِّسْكِن
9 great titmouse (great tit, ox eye), a titmouse (tit)	القُرْقُف
10 golden-crested wren (goldcrest); *sim.:* firecrest, one of the Regulidae	النُّمْنِمة ذو العُرْف الذهبي
11 nuthatch	خَازِن البندق
12 wren	النُّمْنُمَة ، الصَّعْو
13-17 thrushes	**طُيُور السُّمْنَة**
13 blackbird	الشُّحْرُور
14 nightingale (*poet.:* philomel, philomela)	العَنْدَليب
15 robin (redbreast, robin redbreast)	أبو الحِنَّاء
16 song thrush (throstle, mavis)	سُمْنَة الدَّبق
17 thrush nightingale	العَنْدَليب المُطْرِب
18-19 larks	**القَنَابر**
18 woodlark	قُنْبُرَة الغابة
19 crested lark (tufted lark)	القُنْبُرَة ذات القُنْزُعَة
20 common swallow (barn swallow, chimney swallow), a swallow	السِّنُوْنُو

362 Birds IV (Birds of Prey) — الطُّيُور (4) (الجَوَارِح)

1-13 diurnal birds of prey	**الجَوَارِح النَّهَارِيَّة**
1-4 falcons	**الصقور**
1 merlin	جلَم ، يُوْيُوْ (صَقْر صغير)
2 peregrine falcon	باز جَوَّال ، شاهين
3 leg feathers	ريش السَّاق
4 tarsus	ساق الصَّقْر
5-9 eagles	**العُقْبان**
5 white-tailed sea eagle (white-tailed eagle, grey sea eagle, erne)	الأرن: عُقَاب بحريّ أبْيَض الذَّيْل
6 hooked beak	منْقَار مَعْقُوف
7 claw (talon)	بُرْثُن
8 tail	ذَيْل
9 common buzzard	صَقْر حَوَّام ، سَقَاوَة
10-13 accipiters	**الأبْوَاز** (جَمْع باز)
10 goshawk	باز
11 common European kite (glede, kite)	الحَدَأة الأوروبيَّة الشائعة
12 sparrow hawk (sparhawk)	الباشِق
13 marsh harrier (moor buzzard, moor harrier, moor hawk)	مُرْزَة البطائح ، عُقَيِّب
14-19 owls	**البُوم**
14 long-eared owl (horned owl)	بُومَة أذْناء ، بُومَة الحراج
15 eagle-owl (great horned owl)	البُومَة الصخَّابَة (البُومَة القَرْناء)
16 plumicorn (feathered ear, ear tuft, ear, horn)	ريشة أذن مُرَيَّشَة
17 barn owl (white owl, silver owl, yellow owl, church owl, screech owl)	بُومَة الهامَة (البُومَة البيضاء ، البُومَة الفضِّيَّة ، البُومَة الصفراء ، بُومَة الكنيسة ، البُومَة الصَّيَّاحَة/الصَّمْعَاء)
18 facial disc (disk)	قُرْص الوَجْه
19 little owl (sparrow owl)	بُومَة صغير ة (صَدَى)

363 Birds V (Exotic Birds) — الطُّيُور (5) (الطُّيُور النَّادِرَة)

1 sulphur-crested cockatoo, a parrot	كوكَاتة: ببغاء ذو عُرْف أصْفَر
2 blue-and-yellow macaw	المَقْو: ببغاء أمريكي ضخم طويل الذيْل ظَهْره أزرق وبطْنه أصفر
3 blue bird of paradise	عُصْفُور الجنة الأزرق
4 sappho	الصَّبْهو
5 cardinal (cardinal bird)	كردينال: طائر أمريكي مُغَرِّد
6 toucan (red-billed toucan), one of the Piciformes	طُوقان

364 Fish, Amphibia, and Reptiles — الأسْماك ، البَرْمائيَّات ، والزَّوَاحِف

1-18 fishes	**الأسْمَاك**
1 man-eater (blue shark, requin), a shark	آكِل الإنْسَان (القِرْش الأزْرَق)
2 nose (snout)	خَطْم (أنف)
3 gill slit (gill cleft)	فَتْحَة الخَيْشُوم
4 mirror carp	سَمكَة الشَّبُّوط
5 gill cover (operculum)	غطَاء الخَيْشُوم
6 dorsal fin	زَعْنفَة الظَّهْر
7 pectoral fin	زَعْنفَة صَدْرِيَّة
8 pelvic fin (abdominal fin, ventral fin)	زَعْنفَة حَوْضِيَّة
9 anal fin	زعْنفَة شَرَجِيَّة
10 caudal fin (tail fin)	زَعْنفَة الذَّيْل
11 scale	حَرْشَفَة ، قشْرَة
12 catfish (sheatfish, sheathfish, wels)	سَمكَة السِّلَّوْر ، سَمكَة القط
13 barbel	البَرْبَل: زائدة استشعاريَّة رفيعة
14 herring	الرِّنْكَة
15 brown trout	السَّلْمون المُرَقَّط
16 pike (northern pike)	سَمكَة الكراكي
17 freshwater eel (eel)	ثُعْبَان المياه العَذْبَة ، الأنقليس
18 sea horse (Hippocampus, horsefish)	حصان البَحْر/النهر

19 tufted gills	خَيْشوم مُخَصَّل
20-26 Amphibia (amphibians)	**البَرْمَائيَّات**
20-22 salamanders	**الضُفْدَعيَّات**
20 greater water newt (crested newt), a water newt	سَمَنْدَل الماء
21 dorsal crest	قمَّة ظَهْرِيَّة
22 fire salamander, a salamander	سَمَنْدَر النَّار
23-26 salientians (anurans, batrachians)	**القَفَّازات ، القَوَافِز**
23 European toad, a toad	ضُفْدَع الطين الأوروبي
24 tree frog (tree toad)	ضُفْدَع الشجر
25 vocal sac (vocal pouch, croaking sac)	كيس النقيق
26 adhesive disc (disk)	قُرْص لاصِق
27-41 reptiles	**الزَّوَاحف**
27, 30-37 lizards	**العَظَاءات/السَّحَالي**
27 sand lizard	عَظَاءة الرِّمَال
28 hawksbill turtle (hawksbill)	سُلَحْفَاة بحريَّة
29 carapace (shell)	درقة السُّلَحْفَاة (دِرْع قَرْني)
30 basilisk	البازيليق (عَظَاءة أمريكيَّة)
31 desert monitor, a monitor lizard (monitor)	الوَرَل
32 common iguana, an iguana	الإغوانة: عظاءة أمريكيَّة إستوائيَّة عاشِبَة
33 chameleon, one of the Chamaeleontidae (Rhiptoglossa)	الحِرباء
34 prehensile foot	قَدَم إمْسَاكِيَّة
35 prehensile tail	ذيل إمْسَاكي
36 wall gecko, a gecko	البُرْص، أبو بريص
37 slowworm (blindworm), one of the Anguidae	العَظَاءة العَمْيَاء
38-41 snakes	**الأفاعي**
38 ringed snake (ring snake, water snake, grass snake), a colubrid	أفْعى الماء
39 collar	ياقة
40-41 vipers (adders)	**أفاعي سامة**
40 common viper, a poisonous (venomous) snake	أفعى سامة شائعة
41 asp (asp viper)	الصِّل المِصْري: أفعى صغيرة سامة

365 Lepidoptera (Butterflies and Moths) / قشْريَّات الأجْنحَة (الفَرَاشَات و البَشَّارَات)

1-6 butterflies	**الفَرَاشَات**
1 red admiral	الأميرة الحمراء
2 peacock butterfly	الفَرَاشَة الطاووسيَّة
3 orange tip (orange tip butterfly)	الفَرَاشَة البرتقاليَّة
4 brimstone (brimstone butterfly)	كَبْرِيتِيَّة
5 Camberwell beauty (mourning cloak, mourning cloak butterfly)	فَرَاشَة نَهَارِيَّة
6 blue (lycaenid butterfly, lycaenid)	الفَرَاشَة الزرقاء
7-11 moths (Heterocera)	**البَشَّارات : فَرَاشَات ليليَّة** (مختلفات القرون)
7 garden tiger	نمر الحديقة
8 red underwing	ذات الجناح الخلفي الأحمر
9 death's-head moth (death's-head hawkmoth), a hawkmoth (sphinx)	فَرَاشَة جُمْجُمِيَّة
10 caterpillar	يُسْرُوع ، سُرْفَة
11 chrysalis (pupa)	خادِرَة

366 Mammals I / الثَّدْيِيَّات (1)

1 platypus (duck-bill, duck-mole), a monotreme (oviparous mammal)	البلاتّبوس ، مِنْقَار البَطَّة
2-3 marsupial mammals (marsupials)	**الثَّدْيِيَّات الجِرابيَّة**
2 New World opossum, a didelphid	الأبوسوم: حيوان أمريكي يتظاهر بالمَوْت عندما يحدق به خطر
3 red kangaroo (red flyer), a kangaroo	الكَنْغَر الأحْمَر
4-7 insectivores (insect-eating mammals)	**آكِلات الحشرات**
4 mole	الخُلْد
5 hedgehog	القُنْفُذ
6 spine	شَوْكَة
7 shrew (shrew mouse), one of the Soricidae	الزَّبَابَة
8 nine-banded armadillo (peba)	المُدَرَّع
9 long-eared bat (flitter-mouse), a flying mammal (chiropter, chiropteran)	الخُفَّاش طويل الأذنَيْن
10 pangolin (scaly ant-eater), a scaly mammal	البنغول ، أم قِرْفة
11 two-toed sloth (unau)	الكسلان ذو الإصبعَيْن
12-19 rodents	**القوارض**
12 guinea pig (cavy)	خنزير غينيا ، الخنزير الهندي
13 porcupine	الشَّيْهَم ، النَّيْص
14 beaver	القُنْدُس
15 jerboa	الجَرْبُوع
16 hamster	الهمستر
17 water vole	فَأْر الماء
18 marmot	المرموط
19 squirrel	السِّنْجَاب
20 African elephant, a proboscidean (proboscidian)	الفيل الأفريقي

21 trunk (proboscis) خُرْطُوم
22 tusk ناب
23 manatee (manati, lamantin), a sirenian خَرُوف البحر
24 South African dassie (das, coney, hyrax), a procaviid الأرنب الأوروبي، الزَّلَم
25-31 ungulates ذَوات الحَوَافر
25-27 odd-toed ungulates ذوات الحَوَافِر فَرْدِيَّة الأصابع
25 African black rhino, a rhinoceros (nasicorn) وَحِيد القَرْن، الكركدن
26 Brazilian tapir, a tapir التبير : حيوان أمريكي استوائي شبيه بالخنزير
27 zebra الحِمَار الوحشي المُخَطَّط
28-31 even-toed ungulates ذوات الحَوَافِر زَوْجِيَّة الأصابع
28-30 ruminants الحيوانات المُجْتَرَّة
28 llama اللاما
29 Bactrian camel (two-humped camel) الجَمَل ذو السَّنَامَيْن
30 guanaco الغَوْنَاق
31 hippopotamus فَرَس النَّهْر

367 Mammals II — الثَّدْيِيَّات (2)

1-10 ungulates, ruminants ذوات الحَوَافِر، مُجْتَرَّات
1 elk (moose) الإلْكَة
2 wapiti (*Am.* elk) الوَبِيت: الأيِّل الأمريكي
3 chamois الشمواة
4 giraffe الزَّرَافة
5 black buck, an antelope الظَّبْي الأسْوَد
6 mouflon (moufflon) المَفْلُون
7 ibex (rock goat, bouquetin, steinbock) الوَعْل، تَيْس الجَبَل
8 water buffalo (Indian buffalo, water ox) جامُوسة الماء
9 bison الثَّوْر الأمريكي (البيسون)
10 musk ox ثَوْر المِسْك
11-22 carnivores (beasts of prey) **آكِلات اللحوم** (الكواسِر)
11-13 Canidae ذوات الأنياب
11 black-backed jackal (jackal) ابن آوى ذو الظَّهْر الأسْوَد
12 red fox الثعلب الأحْمَر
13 wolf الذئب
14-17 martens الفرائيَّات
14 stone marten (beach marten) الدَّلَق
15 sable السَّمُّور
16 weasel ابن عِرْس
17 sea otter, an otter ثعلب البحر
18-22 seals (pinnipeds) **زعنفيات الأقدام**
18 fur seal (sea bear, ursine seal) الفُقْمَة
19 common seal (sea calf, sea dog) كَلْب البَحْر المعروف
20 walrus (morse) عِجْل البَحْر
21 whiskers شوارب
22 tusk ناب

23-29 whales الحيتان
23 bottle-nosed dolphin (bottle-nose dolphin) دولفين قنينيّ الخطم
24 common dolphin دولفين معروف
25 sperm whale (cachalot) حُوت العَنْبَر
26 blowhole (spout hole) أحد مَنْخَارَي الحوت
27 dorsal fin زِعْنِفَة ظَهْرِيَّة
28 flipper زِعْنِفَة الحوت
29 tail flukes (tail) فصا ذَنَب الحوت

368 Mammals III — الثَّدْيِيَّات (3)

1-11 carnivores (beasts of prey) **آكِلات اللحوم** (الكواسِر)
1 striped hyena, a hyena الضَّبْع المُخَطَّط
2-8 felines (cats) **السِّنَّوْرات**
2 lion أسَد
3 mane (lion's mane) عُرْف الأسد
4 paw مِخْلَب
5 tiger نمر، بَبْر
6 leopard ضَبْع، فَهْد
7 cheetah (hunting leopard) فَهْد هِنْدِيّ
8 lynx وَشَق
9-11 bears الدُّبَبَة
9 raccoon (racoon, *Am.* coon) الراكون
10 brown bear الدُّبُ البُنِّيّ
11 polar bear (white bear) الدُّبُ القطبيّ (الدُّبُ الأبْيَض)
12-16 primates الرَّئيسَات
12-13 monkeys القرود
12 rhesus monkey (rhesus, rhesus macaque) قِرْد الرِّيص
13 baboon الرُّبَّاح، قرد البابون
14-16 anthropoids (anthropoid apes, great apes) **أشباه الإنسان**
14 chimpanzee الشمبانزي
15 orang-utan (orang-outan) إنسان الغاب
16 gorilla الغوريلا

369 Deep-sea Fauna — أحْيَاء أعْمَاق البحَار

1 Gigantocypris agassizi شَبُوط عملاق
2 Eupharynx pelecanoides (pelican eel, pelican fish) ثُعْبَان بَجَعِيّ
3 Metacrinus (feather star), a sea lily, an echinoderm نَجْم رِيشِيّ
4 Lycoteuthis diadema (jewelled squid), a cuttlefish [luminescent] حَبَّار، صَبَّيْد، سِبْيَا [مضئ]
5 Atolla, a deep-sea medusa, a coelenterate قَنْدِيل البَحْر، رِئَة البَحْر
6 Melanocetes, a pediculate [luminescent] أبُو الشصّ، نَوْع من العَظْمِيَّات [مضئ]
7 Lophocalyx philippensis, a glass إسْفِنْج كِلْسِيّ

sponge

8 Mopsea, a sea fan [colony] — مِرْوَحَة البَحْر [مُسْتَعْمَرَة]

9 Hydrallmania, a hydroid polyp, a coelenterate [colony] — زَهْر البَحْر، عُدَار رِئَوِيّ، بَوْلِب هِدْرِيّ [مُسْتَعْمَرَة]

10 Malacosteus indicus, a stomiatid [luminescent] — سَمَكَة مَلاكُوسْتِيُوس المُسَوَّطَة [مضيئة]

11 Brisinga endecacnemos, a sand star (brittle star), an echinoderm [luminescent only when stimulated] — نَجْم الرِّمَال، حَيَوان شَوْكِيّ الجِلْد [مضيئ عند حَفْزِه]

12 Pasiphaea, a shrimp, a crustacean — إرْبيان، بُرْغُوث البَحْر، جَمْبَري، حيوان قِشْرِيّ

13 Echiostoma, a stomiatid, a fish [luminescent] — سَمَكَة الاكْيُسْتُوما [مضيئة]

14 Umbellula encrinus, a sea pen (sea feather). a coelenterate [colony, luminescent] — انْكرِينُوس خَيْمِيّ، رِيشَة البحر، حيوان لامِعَوِيّ [مستعمرة، مضيئ]

15 Polycheles, a crustacean — أمّ الإرْبيَان، حيوان من القشْرِيَّات

16 Lithodes, a crustacean, a crab — سَرَطَان الليثُودس، حيوان قِشْرِيّ

17 Archaster, a starfish (sea star), an echinoderm — كَوْكَب البَحْر، نَجْم البَحْر، حيوان شَوْكِيّ الجِلْد

18 Oneirophanta, a sea cucumber, an echinoderm — أونَايْرُوفَنْتا، خِيَار البَحْر، حيوان شَوْكِيّ الجِلْد

19 Palaeopneustes niasicus, a sea urchin (sea hedgehog), an echinoderm — قُنْفُذ البَحْر، حيوان شَوْكِيّ الجِلْد

20 Chitonactis, a sea anemone (actinia), a coelenterate — شُقَّار البَحْر، شَقِيق البَحْر، حَيَوان لامِعَوِيّ

370 General Botany — عِلْم النَّبَات

1 tree — شَجَرَة

2 bole (tree trunk, trunk, stem) — جِذْع

3 crown of tree (crown) — تاج الشَّجَرَة

4 top of tree (treetop) — أعلى الشَّجَرَة

5 bough (limb, branch) — فَرْع شَجَرِي، غُصْن كبير

6 twig (branch) — غُصْن، فنَد

7 bole (tree trunk) [cross section] — جِذْع [مقطع عرضيّ]

8 bark (rind) — لِحَاء

9 phloem (bast sieve tissue, inner fibrous bark) — لِحَاء داخليّ

10 cambium (cambium ring) — قَلْب، قِلْب

11 medullary rays (vascular rays, pith rays) — أشعة لُبِّيَّة

12 sapwood (sap, alburnum) — خَشَب أبْيَض، خَشَب النُّسْغ

13 heartwood (duramen) — جِلْب، خَشَب القَلْب

14 pith — نُخَاع، لُبّ

15 plant — نَبْتَة

16-18 root — **جَذْر**

16 primary root — جَذْر رئيسيّ، عِرْقَة

17 secondary root — جَذْر ثانَوِيّ

18 root hair — شُعُور جَذْرِيَّة

19-25 shoot (sprout) — **فَرْخ، رَكْزَة، فَسِيلَة**

19 leaf — وَرَقَة

20 stalk — عُنَيْق

21 side shoot (offshoot) — فَرْع جانبي

22 terminal bud — بُرْعُم انتهائيّ

23 flower — زَهْرَة

24 flower bud — بُرْعُم الزَّهْرَة

25 leaf axil with axillary bud — مِحْوَر الوَرَقة مع بُرْعُم إضافيّ

26 leaf — وَرَقة

27 leaf stalk (petiole) — عُنَيْق الوَرَقة

28 leaf blade (blade, lamina) — نَصْل الوَرَقة

29 venation (veins, nervures, ribs) — تَعَرُّق، تَعْرِيق

30 midrib (nerve) — عَيْر، ضِلْع

31-38 leaf shapes — **أشكال الوَرَقة**

31 linear — خَطِّيَّة

32 lanceolate — سِنَانِيَّة

33 orbicular (orbiculate) — دائرِيَّة

34 acerose (acerous, acerate, acicular, needle-shaped) — إبْرِيَّة

35 cordate — قَلْبِيَّة

36 ovate — بَيْضَوِيَّة

37 sagittate — سَهْمِيَّة

38 reniform — كُلْوِيَّة

39-42 compound leaves — **أوْرَاق مُرَكَّبَة**

39 digitate (digitated, palmate, quinquefoliolate) — وَرَقة مُصَبَّعَة

40 pinnatifid — وَرَقة ريشيَّة الإنشقاق

41 abruptly pinnate — وَرَقة ريشيَّة مَبْتُورَة

42 odd-pinnate — وَرَقة ريشيَّة مُفْرَدَة

43-50 leaf margin shapes — **أشكال حافة الوَرَقة**

43 entire — كاملة/مَلْساء

44 serrate (serrulate, saw-toothed) — مِنْشَارِيَّة

45 doubly toothed — زَوْجِيَّة الأسْنان

46 crenate — مُفَرَّضَة/مُشَرَّفَة

47 dentate — مُسَنَّنَة

48 sinuate — مُتَمَعِّجَة

49 ciliate (ciliated) — هُدْبِيَّة

50 cilium — هُدْب

51 flower — زَهْرَة

52 flower stalk (flower stem, scape) — عُنَيْق الزهرة

53 receptacle (floral axis, thalamus, torus) — قُرْص/كُرْسِيّ الزهرة

54 ovary مبْيَض
55 style قلم السِّمة ، حامل السِّمَة
56 stigma سِمَة ، مِيْسَم
57 stamen سَدَاة
58 sepal كَأْسِيَّة ، فِصْلَة
59 petal تُوَيْجِيَّة
60 ovary and stamen [section] المِبْيَض والسداة [مقطع]
61 ovary wall جدار المِبْيَض
62 ovary cavity تجويف المِبْيَض
63 ovule بُيَيْضَة ، بُوَيْضَة
64 embryo sac كِيْس الجنين
65 pollen غُبَار الطَّلْع ، لَقَاح
66 pollen tube أنبوب اللقاح
67-77 inflorescences **أشكال الإزهرار ، النَّوْرات**
67 spike (racemose spike) سُنْبُلَة ، سَبلَة ، سُبُولَة
68 raceme (simple raceme) عُنْقُود
69 panicle عُثْكُول
70 cyme سَنَمَة ، قِمَّة
71 spadix (fleshy spike) طَلْع
72 umbel (simple umbel) خَيْمَة
73 capitulum رؤيس
74 composite head (discoid flower head) رأس مُرَكَّب
75 hollow flower head رأس زهرة مجوَّف
76 bostryx (helicoid cyme) سَنَمَة حلَزُونيَّة
77 cincinnus (scorpioid cyme, curled cyme) سَنَمَة مُقَوَّسَة
78-82 roots **الجذور**
78 adventitious roots جَذْر عَرَضيّ/طارئ
79 tuber (tuberous root, swollen taproot) عَسْقَل ، عُسْقُول
80 adventitious roots (aerial roots) جذور عَرَضِيَّة
81 root thorns شَوْك الجَذْر
82 pneumatophores حَوامِل رئويَّة
83-85 blade of grass **نَصْل النَّجيليَّات**
83 leaf sheath قاعدة مِعْلَاق الوَرَقة
84 ligule (ligula) لُسَيْن
85 leaf blade (lamina) نَصْل الوَرَقة
86 embryo (seed, germ) جَنين
87 cotyledon (seed leaf, seed lobe) فِلْقَة ، فَلْقَة
88 radicle جُذَيْر
89 hypocotyl سُوَيْق الجنين
90 plumule (leaf bud) ساق جنينيَّة
91-102 fruits **الثِّمار**
91-96 dehiscent fruits **ثمار مُتفتِحة**
91 follicle ثَمَرَة جرابيَّة
92 legume (pod) سِفْنَة ، قَرْن ، حبُلَة
93 siliqua (pod) خَرْدَلِيَّة
94 schizocarp ثَمَرَة مُشَقَّقَة الخِبَاء
95 pyxidium (circumscissile seed vessel) عُلْبَة
96 poricidal capsule (porose capsule) عُلَيْبَة مَسَاميَّة
97-102 indehiscent fruits **ثمار مُطْبَقَة**
97 berry عِنَبِيَّة
98 nut جَوْزَة
99 drupe (stone fruit) (cherry) نَوَوِيَّة
100 aggregate fruit (compound fruit) (rose hip) ثَمَرَة عُلَيْقِيَّة
101 aggregate fruit (compound fruit) (raspberry) ثَمَرَة مُتَضاعِفَة (تُوت شَوْكيّ)
102 pome (apple) ثَمَرَة تفاحيَّة

371 Deciduous Trees أشجَار نَفْضيَّة

1-73 deciduous trees **أشجَار نَفْضِيَّة**
1 oak (oak tree) البلوط
2 flowering branch فَرْع مُزْهِر
3 fruiting branch فَرْع مُثْمِر
4 fruit (acorn) ثَمَرَة
5 cupule (cup) كُوَيْس (كأس)
6 female flower زَهْرَة مُؤنَّثَة
7 bract قنَابة
8 male inflorescence ازهار ذَكَري
9 birch (birch tree) بَتُولا ، شَجَرَة القُضْبان
10 branch with catkins, a flowering branch فَرْع وعليه القِدَّات
11 fruiting branch فَرْع مُثْمِر
12 scale (catkin scale) حَرْشَفَة
13 female flower زَهْرَة مُؤنَّثَة
14 male flower زَهْرَة مُذَكَّرَة
15 poplar حَوْرَة
16 flowering branch فَرْع مُزْهِر
17 flower زَهْرَة
18 fruiting branch فَرْع مُثْمِر
19 fruit ثَمَرَة
20 seed حَبَّة ، بَذْرَة
21 leaf of the aspen (trembling poplar) وَرَقة حَوَر رَجْرَاج
22 infructescence عُنْقُود ثَمَر
23 leaf of the white poplar (silver poplar, silverleaf) وَرَقة حَوَر أبيض
24 sallow (goat willow) صَفْصَاف المَعْز
25 branch with flower buds فَرْع وعليه براعم الزهور
26 catkin with single flower قِدَّه وحيدة الزَّهْرَة
27 branch with leaves فَرْع مُورق
28 fruit ثَمَرَة
29 osier branch with leaves فَرْع صَفْصَاف السَّلاّلين مُورق
30 alder جار الماء
31 fruiting branch فَرْع مُثْمِر
32 branch with previous year's cone فَرْع وبه صَنَوْبَريَّات العام السابق
33 beech (beech tree) شَجَرَة الزَّان
34 flowering branch فَرْع مُزْهِر
35 flower زَهْرَة
36 fruiting branch فَرْع مُثْمِر
37 beech nut ثَمَرَة الزَّان

38 ash (ash tree)	شَجَرة المُرَّان
39 flowering branch	فَرْع مُزْهِر
40 flower	زَهْرَة
41 fruiting branch	فَرْع مُثْمِر
42 mountain ash (rowan, quickbeam)	شَجَرة السَّمَّن
43 inflorescence	نظام الإِزْهِرَار
44 infructescence	عُنْقُود ثَمَر
45 fruit [longitudinal section]	ثَمَرَة [مَقْطَع طولي]
46 lime (lime tree, linden, linden tree)	شَجَرة الزيزفون
47 fruiting branch	فَرْع مُثْمِر
48 inflorescence	نظام الإِزْهِرَار
49 elm (elm tree)	بُوقِيْصا، شَجَرة البَقّ
50 fruiting branch	فَرْع مُثْمِر
51 flowering branch	فَرْع مُزْهِر
52 flower	زَهْرَة
53 maple (maple tree)	شَجَرة القَيْقَب
54 flowering branch	فَرْع مُزْهِر
55 flower	زَهْرَة
56 fruiting branch	فَرْع مُثْمِر
57 maple seed with wings (winged maple seed)	بَذْرَة قَيْقَب جناحيَّة
58 horse chestnut (horse chestnut tree, chestnut, chestnut tree, buckeye)	قَسْطَلَة الهند، قَسْطَل الحصان
59 branch with young fruits	فَرْع وبه بَوَادِر الثِّمَار
60 chestnut (horse chestnut)	قَسْطَل، كَسْتَنَة
61 mature (ripe) fruit	ثَمَرَة يانعَة
62 flower [longitudinal section]	زَهْرَة [مَقْطَع طولي]
63 hornbeam (yoke elm)	شَجَرة النِّير، نَيرِيَّة شائعة
64 fruiting branch	فَرْع مُثْمِر
65 seed	حَبَّة، بَذْرَة
66 flowering branch	فَرْع مُزْهِر
67 plane (plane tree)	دُلْب، صِنار
68 leaf	وَرَقة
69 infructescence and fruit	عُنْقُود ثَمَر وثَمَرَة
70 false acacia (locust tree)	رُوْبِينِيَّة شائعة، سَنْط كاذِب
71 flowering branch	فَرْع مُزْهِر
72 part of the infructescence	جزء من عُنْقُود الثَّمَر
73 base of the leaf stalk with stipules	قاعدة ساق الوَرَقة وبها أُذَنات

372 Conifers — الصَّنَوْبَرِيَّات

1-71 coniferous trees (conifers)	**الأَشْجَار الصَنوبَرِيَّة**
1 silver fir (European silver fir, common silver fir)	تَنُّوب مُسْتَحَب، تَنُّوب مِشْطي
2 fir cone, a fruit cone	صَنَوْبَرَة التَّنُّوب
3 cone axis	محْوَر الصَّنَوْبَرَة
4 female flower cone	صَنَوْبَرَة زَهْرَة مُؤَنَّثَة
5 bract scale (bract)	قِنابَة
6 male flower shoot	فَسِيلَة زَهْرَة مُذَكَّرَة
7 stamen	سَدَاة
8 cone scale	حَرْشَفَة الصَّنَوْبَرَة
9 seed with wing (winged seed)	بَذْرَة جناحيَّة
10 seed [longitudinal section]	بَذْرَة (حبة) [مَقْطَع طولي]
11 fir needle (needle)	وَرَقة التَّنُّوب الخَيْطِيَّة
12 spruce (spruce fir)	راتِنْجِيَّة عالية
13 spruce cone	صَنَوْبَرَة الرَّاتِنْجِيَّة العالية
14 cone scale	حَرْشَفَة الصَنَوْبَرَة
15 seed	بَذْرَة، حبة
16 female flower cone	صَنَوْبَرَة زَهْرَة مُؤَنَّثَة
17 male inflorescence	شكل إِزْهِرَار ذَكَري
18 stamen	سَدَاة
19 spruce needle	وَرَقة الرَّاتِنْجِيَّة الخَيْطِيَّة
20 pine (Scots pine)	صَنَوْبَر (صَنَوْبَر اسكتلندي)
21 dwarf pine	صَنَوْبَر قِزَمي
22 female flower cone	صَنَوْبرة زَهْرَة مُؤَنَّثَة
23 short shoot with bundle of two leaves	فَسِيلَة قصيرة ذات وَرَقَتَيْن
24 male inflorescences	أشكال إِزْهِرَار ذَكَري
25 annual growth	نَمَاء سَنَوِيّ
26 pine cone	صَنَوْبَرَة الصَّنَوْبَر
27 cone scale	حَرْشَفة الصنَوْبَرَة
28 seed	بَذْرَة، حَبَّة
29 fruit cone of the arolla pine (Swiss stone pine)	صَنَوْبَرَة ثَمَرَة الصَّنَوْبَر السويسري
30 fruit cone of the Weymouth pine (white pine)	صَنَوْبَرَة ثَمَرَة الصَّنَوْبَر الأبيض
31 short shoot [cross section]	فَسِيلَة قصيرة [مقْطَع عرضي]
32 larch	أَرْزِيَّة
33 flowering branch	فَرْع مُزْهِر
34 scale of the female flower cone	حَرْشَفَة صَنَوْبَرَة زَهْرَة مُؤَنَّثَة
35 anther	مِئْبَر، مئبار
36 branch with larch cones (fruit cones)	فرع وعليه صَنَوْبَرَات الأَرْزِيَّة
37 seed	بَذْرَة، حبة
38 cone scale	حَرْشَفَة الصَّنَوْبَرَة
39 arbor vitae (tree of life, thuja)	شَجَرة الحياة، عَفْصِيَّة
40 fruiting branch	فَرْع مُثْمِر
41 fruit cone	صَنَوْبَرَة الثَّمَرَة
42 scale	حَرْشَفَة
43 branch with male and female flowers	فَرْع وبه أزهار مُذَكَّرَة ومُؤَنَّثَة
44 male shoot	فَسِيلَة مُذَكَّرَة
45 scale with pollen sacs	حَرْشَفَة وعليها أكياس اللقاح
46 female shoot	فَسِيلَة مُؤَنَّثَة
47 juniper (juniper tree)	شَجَرة العَرْعَر
48 female shoot [longitudinal section]	فَسِيلَة مُؤَنَّثَة [مَقْطَع طولي]
49 male shoot	فَسِيلَة مُذَكَّرَة
50 scale with pollen sacs	حَرْشَفَة وعليها أكياس اللقاح

51 fruiting branch فَرْع مُثْمِر
52 juniper berry ثَمَرَة العَرْعَر
53 fruit [cross section] ثَمَرَة [مَقْطَع عرضي]
54 seed بَذْرَة، حبة
55 stone pine صَنَوْبَر مُثْمِر
56 male shoot فَسِيلَة مُذَكَّرَة
57 fruit cone with seeds [longitudinal section] صنوبره الثَّمَرَة وبها البذور [مَقْطَع طولي]
58 cypress السَّرْو
59 fruiting branch فَرْع مُثْمِر
60 seed بَذْرَة، حبة
61 yew (yew tree) الطَّقْسُوس
62 male flower shoot and female flower cone فَسِيلَة زَهْرَة مُذَكَّرَة وصَنَوْبَرَة زَهْرَة مُؤَنَّثَة
63 fruiting branch فَرْع مُثْمِر
64 fruit ثَمَرَة
65 cedar (cedar tree) شَجَرَة الأَرْز
66 fruiting branch فَرْع مُثْمِر
67 fruit scale حَرْشَفة الثَّمَرَة
68 male flower shoot and female flower cone فَسِيلَة زَهْرَة مُذَكَّرَة وصَنَوْبرة زَهْرَة مؤنثة
69 mammoth tree (Wellingtonia, sequoia) جَبَّارة، سَكُوْيَة
70 fruiting branch فَرْع مُثْمِر
71 seed بَذْرَة، حبة

373 Ornamental Shrubs and Trees I جَنْبَات وأَشْجَار الزِّينَة (1)

1 forsythia فِرْسِيثِيَّة
2 ovary and stamen المِبْيَض والسَّدَاة
3 leaf وَرَقَة
4 yellow-flowered jasmine (jasmin, jessamine) اليَاسِمِيْن الأصفر
5 flower [longitudinal section] with styles, ovaries, and stamens زَهْرَة [مَقْطَع طولي] وبها أقلام السِّمة والمبايض والأَسْدِيَة
6 privet (common privet) جَنْبَة الرِّبَاط، لِيغُسْطْرُوم
7 flower زَهْرَة
8 infructescence عُنْقُود ثَمَر
9 mock orange (sweet syringa) فِيلادَلْفُس إكليلي
10 snowball (snowball bush, guelder rose) كُرَة الثَّلج، خَمَان الماء
11 flower زَهْرَة
12 fruits ثمار
13 oleander (rosebay, rose laurel) دِفْلَى، ألاء
14 flower [longitudinal section] زَهْرَة [مَقْطَع طولي]
15 red magnolia مَغْنُوْلِيَة حمراء
16 leaf وَرَقَة
17 japonica (japanese quince) يابانيَّة
18 fruit ثَمَرَة
19 common box (box, box tree) بَقْس شائع
20 female flower زَهْرَة مؤنثة
21 male flower زَهْرَة مذكرة
22 fruit [longitudinal section] ثَمَرَة [مَقْطَع طولي]
23 weigela (weigelia) ويغِيلَة
24 yucca [part of the inflorescence] يَكَّة
25 leaf وَرَقَة
26 dog rose (briar rose, wild briar) نِسْرِيْن بري
27 fruit ثَمَرَة
28 kerria كَرِيَّة
29 fruit ثَمَرَة
30 cornelian cherry قَرانيا معروفة
31 flower زَهْرَة
32 fruit (cornelian cherry) ثَمَرَة
33 sweet gale (gale) شَمْعِيَّة عِطْرِيَّة

374 Ornamental Shrubs and Trees II جَنْبَات وأَشْجَار الزِّينَة (2)

1 tulip tree (tulip poplar, saddle tree, whitewood) شَجَرَة الزَّنْبَق
2 carpels أَخْبِيَة
3 stamen سَدَاة
4 fruit ثَمَرَة
5 hyssop زُوْفا، أشْنَان داود
6 flower [front view] زَهْرَة [مَنْظَر أمامي]
7 flower زَهْرَة
8 calyx with fruit كأس مع ثَمَرَة
9 holly بَهْشِيَّة، إِيلَكْس
10 androgynous (hermaphroditic, hermaphrodite) flower زَهْرَة خنثى
11 male flower زَهْرَة مُذَكَّرَة
12 fruit with stones exposed ثَمَرَة وأَنْوِيَة مكشوفة
13 honeysuckle (woodbine, woodbind) سلطان الجبل، شبر فايد
14 flower buds بَرَاعِم الزهور
15 flower [cut open] زَهْرَة [مشقوقة]
16 Virginia creeper (American ivy, woodbine) لَبْلابة عذراء
17 open flower زَهْرَة مُفَتَّحة
18 infructescence عُنْقُود ثَمَر
19 fruit [longitudinal section] ثَمَرَة [مَقْطَع طولي]
20 broom قُوطيسون، رَتَم المكانس
21 flower with the petals removed زَهْرَة نُزِعَت منها البَتَلات/التُوَيْجِيَّات
22 immature (unripe) legume (pod) بَقْلَة لم تنضج بعد
23 spiraea إكْلِيل، إسْبِيْرِيَة
24 flower [longitudinal section] زَهْرَة [مَقْطَع طولي]
25 fruit ثَمَرَة
26 carpel خِبَاء
27 blackthorn (sloe) بُرقوق شائك
28 leaves أوراق
29 fruits ثمار

30 single-pistilled hawthorn (thorn, may)	زُعْرُور وحيد المِدَقَّة
31 fruit	ثَمَرَة
32 laburnum (golden chain, golden rain)	سِيتِيسس ، قُوْطِيسُوس
33 raceme	عُنْقُود
34 fruits	ثمار
35 black elder (elder)	خَمَان أسود
36 elder flowers	زهور الخمان
37 elderberries	عِنَبِيَّات الخمان

375 Meadow Flowers and Wayside Flowers (Wild Flowers) I — أزْهار المراعي والأزهار البَرِّيَّة (1)

1 rotundifoliate (rotundifolious) saxifrage (rotundifoliate breakstone)	كاسِر الحَجَر المستدير الوَرَق
2 leaf	وَرَقة
3 flower	زَهْرَة
4 fruit	ثَمَرَة
5 anemone (windflower)	شقائق النعمان
6 flower [longitudinal section]	زَهْرَة [مَقْطَع طولي]
7 fruit	ثَمَرَة
8 buttercup (meadow buttercup, butterflower, goldcup, king cup, crowfoot)	حَوْذان
9 basal leaf	وَرَقة قاعدية
10 fruit	ثَمَرَة
11 lady's smock (ladysmock, cuckoo flower)	حُرْفُ الماء ، حُرْفُ المروج
12 basal leaf	وَرَقة قاعدية
13 fruit	ثَمَرَة
14 harebell (hairbell, bluebell)	جُرَيْس مستدير الوَرَق
15 basal leaf	وَرَقه قاعدية
16 flower [longitudinal section]	زَهْرَة [مَقْطَع طولي]
17 fruit	ثَمَرَة
18 ground ivy (ale hoof)	لَبْلاب أرضي
19 flower [longitudinal section]	زَهْرَة [مَقْطَع طولي]
20 flower [front view]	زَهْرَة [مَنْظَر أمامي]
21 stonecrop	سِيدُوم ، حَيُّ العالم
22 speedwell	زَهْرَة الحَوَاشِي ، وَيْرُونِيكَة
23 flower	زَهْرَة
24 fruit	ثَمَرَة
25 seed	بَذْرَة ، حبة
26 moneywort	لُوْسِيمَاخُوس نقدىّ
27 dehisced fruit	ثَمَرَة متفتحة
28 seed	بَذْرَة ، حبة
29 small scabious	إسْكَبْيُوزَة ، زَهْرَة الجَرَب
30 basal leaf	وَرَقة قاعدية
31 ray floret (flower of outer series)	زُهَيْرة شعاعيَّة (زَهْرَة ذات نسق خارجي)
32 disc (disk) floret (flower of inner series)	زُهَيْرة قُرصيَّة (زَهْرَة ذات نسق داخلي)
33 involucral calyx with pappus bristles	كأس قُنَّابي مع شعيرات شوكية مظلية
34 ovary with pappus	مِبْيَض وظلة ، شعيرات ناشرة
35 fruit	ثَمَرَة
36 lesser celandine	عُشْبَة البواسير
37 fruit	ثَمَرَة
38 leaf axil with bulbil	مِحْوَر وَرَقة ذو بصيلة
39 annual meadow grass	عُشْبَة الكلأ
40 flower	زَهْرَة
41 spikelet [side view]	سُنَيْبِلَة [مَنْظَر جانبي]
42 spikelet [front view]	سُنَيْبِلَة [مَنْظَر أمامي]
43 caryopsis, an indehiscent fruit	بُرَّة
44 tuft of grass (clump of grass)	حزمة عُشْبيَّة
45 comfrey	سَنْفِيتُون
46 flower [longitudinal section]	زَهْرَة [مَقْطَع طولي]
47 fruit	ثَمَرَة

376 Meadow Flowers and Wayside Flowers (Wild Flowers) II — أزْهار المراعي والأزهار البَرِّيَّة (2)

1 daisy (*Am.* English daisy)	زَهْرَة الربيع ، مَرْغرِيتا
2 flower	زَهْرَة
3 fruit	ثَمَرَة
4 oxeye daisy (white oxeye daisy, marguerite)	أقْحُوان المُرُوج
5 flower	زَهْرَة
6 fruit	ثَمَرَة
7 masterwort	بَقْلَة الرئيس ، هِرَقْلِيَّة صُوفيَّة
8 cowslip	آذريون الماء ، زَهْرَة الربيع المَرْجيَّة
9 great mullein (Aaron's rod, shepherd's club)	آذان الدُب ، بُوصير
10 bistort (snakeweed)	جُنْجَر مِلْتو (عُشْبَة الأفْعى)
11 flower	زَهْرَة
12 knapweed	قَنْطَريون أسود
13 common mallow	خُبَّازة بَرِّيَّة
14 fruit	ثَمَرَة
15 yarrow	أخلِيَّة ذات ألف وَرَقة
16 self-heal	زَهْرَة إلتئام ذاتي
17 bird's foot trefoil (bird's foot clover)	قَرْن الغزال ، لُوْطَس قُرَيْنِيّ
18 horsetail (equisetum) [a shoot]	كُنْباث ، ذَنَب الخيل [فسيلة]
19 flower (strobile)	زَهْرَة (مخروط)
20 campion (catchfly)	سلَيُوس ، مَنْثُور بريّ (لُخْنَيس الذُباب)
21 ragged robin (cuckoo flower)	زَهْرَة الوقواق
22 birthwort	زَرَاوَنْد
23 flower	زَهْرَة

24 crane's bill	إبرة الراعي
25 wild chicory (witloof, succory, wild endive)	هِنْدِبا برِّيَّة
26 common toadflax (butter-and-eggs)	كَتَّانيَّة شائعة
27 lady's slipper (Venus's slipper, *Am.* moccasin flower)	خفّ السَّيِّدة، مِجْزَاعَة الحدائق
28 orchis (wild orchid), an orchid	سَحْلَب (خُصى الثَّعْلَب)

377 Plants of Forest, Marsh, and Heathland — نَبَاتات الأحْرَاج والمُسْتَنْقَعات والبَرَاحات

1 wood anemone (anemone, windflower)	شُقَّار حَرَجي
2 lily of the valley	زَنْبَق الوادي
3 cat's foot (milkwort); *sim.:* sandflower (everlasting)	رِجْل الهِرّ (مُسْتَدرَّة)؛ مثلها: زَهْرَة الرِّمال (مُخَلِّدَة)
4 turk's cap (turk's cap lily)	زَنْبَق مُرْتَاغون
5 goatsbeard (goat's beard)	لِحْيَة التَّيْس
6 ramson	ثُوم الدُّبَيَة
7 lungwort	حشيشة الرِّئة
8 corydalis	قُبَّرِيَّة
9 orpine (livelong)	مُخَلِّدة
10 daphne	دَفْنَة
11 touch-me-not	زَهْرَة لا تَمَسَّني، المستحية
12 staghorn (stag horn moss, stag's horn, stag's horn moss, coral evergreen)	قرن الأيِّل
13 butterwort, an insectivorous plant	نبات آكِل للحشرات
14 sundew; *sim.:* Venus's flytrap	دوروسيِرَة
15 bearberry	عِنَب الدب
16 polypody (polypod), a fern; *sim.:* male fern, brake (bracken, eagle fern), royal fern (royal osmund, king's fern, ditch fern)	بَسْفايَج ، نوع من السرخسيات؛ مثله: سَرْخَس ذَكَر ، أَسْمُنْدة مُلُوكيَّة
17 haircap moss (hair moss, golden maiden-hair), a moss	طحْلَب شعري
18 cotton grass (cotton rush)	كَتَّان المناقع
19 heather (heath, ling); *sim.:* bell heather (cross-leaved heather)	خَلَنْج؛ مثله: زَهْرَة الخَلَنْج
20 rock rose (sun rose)	زَهْرَة الشَّمْس
21 marsh tea	شاي المناقع
22 sweet flag (sweet calamus, sweet sedge)	وَجّ، عِرْق أَكَر ، أَقْوَرُون
23 bilberry (whortleberry, huckleberry, blue-berry); *sim.:* cowberry (red whortleberry), bog bilberry (bog whortle-berry), crowberry (crakeberry)	عِنَب الأحْرَاج ، أُوَيْسة؛ ومثله: عنبيَّة جبليَّة ، وعنبيَّة المناقع والحَجَريَّة

378 Alpine Plants, Aquatic Plants (Water Plants), and Marsh Plants — النَّبَاتَات الألْبِيَّة ونَبَاتَات الماءَ ونَبَاتَات المُسْتَنْقَعَات

1-13 alpine plants	**النَّبَاتَات الألْبِيَّة**
1 alpine rose (alpine rhododendron)	ورد ألْبي
2 flowering shoot	فَرْع مُزْهِر
3 alpine soldanella (soldanella)	سولدانيلا ألْبية
4 corolla opened out	تويج مفتَّح
5 seed vessel with the style	وعاء البَذْرَة والمِيْسم
6 alpine wormwood	أفسَنْتين ألْبي
7 inflorescence	شكل إزْهِرَار
8 auricula	زَهْرَة الربيع الأذْنِيَّة
9 edelweiss	بَرْسيَّة ألْبيَّة
10 flower shapes	أشكال الزَّهْرَة
11 fruit with pappus tuft	ثَمَرَة ذات حزمة خيوط شعريَّة مظليَّة
12 part of flower head (of capitulum)	جزء من رأس زَهْرَة
13 stemless alpine gentian	جَنْطِيَانا ألْبيَّة عديمة الساق
14-57 aquatic plants (water plants) **and marsh plants**	**النباتات المائية ونباتات المناقِع**
14 white water lily	نَيْلَوْفَر أبيض
15 leaf	وَرَقة
16 flower	زَهْرَة
17 Queen Victoria water lily (Victoria regia water lily, royal water lily, Amazon water lily)	زَنْبَق فكتوريا ، فِكْتُوريَّة ملَكيَّة ، ذُرَة الماء
18 leaf	وَرَقة
19 underside of the leaf	الجانب السفلي للوَرَقة
20 flower	زَهْرَة
21 reed mace bulrush (cattail, cat's tail, cat-tail flag, club rush)	تيفا عريضة الوَرَق ، عُشْبة البِرَك
22 male part of the spadix	الجزء الذَّكَري للطَّلْع
23 male flower	زَهْرَة مذكرة
24 female part	جزء مؤنث
25 female flower	زَهْرَة مؤنثة
26 forget-me-not	أذن الفأر
27 flowering shoot	فَرْع مُزْهِر
28 flower [section]	زَهْرَة [مَقْطَع]
29 frog's bit	كَلْوَة الماء
30 watercress	قُرَّة العين
31 stalk with flowers and immature (unripe) fruits	ساق عليها أوراق وثمار غير ناضجة
32 flower	زَهْرَة
33 siliqua (pod) with	خَرْدَلِيَّة بها حبوب

seeds
34 two seeds حَبَّتان
35 duckweed (duck's meat) عَدَس الماء
36 plant in flower نَبْتَة فى زَهْرَة
37 flower زَهْرَة
38 fruit ثَمَرَة
39 flowering rush أَسَل مُزْهِر ، سَمار مُزْهِر
40 flower umbel خيمة الزَّهْرَة
41 leaves أوراق
42 fruit ثَمَرَة
43 green alga طُحلُب أخضر ، أُشْنَة خضراء
44 water plantain مِزْمار الرَّاعي ، آذان العَنْز
45 leaf وَرَقة
46 panicle عُثْكُول
47 flower زَهْرَة
48 honey wrack, a brown alga طُحلُب الفَوْقَس ، طُحلُب أسمر
49 thallus (plant body, frond) مَشْرَة، ثالوس
50 holdfast مُثبِّت
51 arrow head سَهْمِيَّة
52 leaf shapes أشكال الوَرَقة
53 inflorescence with male flowers [above] and female flowers [below] شكل إزْهِرار مع زهور مذكرة [أعلى] وزهور مؤنثة [أسفل]
54 sea grass كَلأ البحر
55 inflorescence شكل إزْهِرار
56 Canadian waterweed (Canadian pondweed) عُشْب مائي كندي
57 flower زَهْرَة

379 Poisonous Plants نَبَاتَات سَامَّة

1 aconite (monkshood, wolfsbane, helmet flower) أقُونِيطُن ، بِيْش
2 foxglove (Digitalis) قمعِيَّة ، دِيجِيْتَالِيس
3 meadow saffron (naked lady, naked boys) سُورَنْجان الخريف ، أصابع هِرْمِس
4 hemlock (Conium) شَوْكَرَان كبير
5 black nightshade (common nightshade, petty morel) مَغْد أسود ، ثَلْثَان
6 henbane بَنْج أسود
7 deadly nightshade (belladonna, banewort, dwale), a solanaceous herb بِلاَدونا سامة
8 thorn apple (stramonium, stramony, *Am.* jimson weed, jimpson weed, Jamestown weed, stinkweed) دَاتُورَة ، دَاتُورَة مُنْتِنَة ، عُشْبَة جيمْس
9 cuckoo pint (lords-and-ladies, wild arum, wake-robin) لُوف أبْقَع
10-13 poisonous fungi (poisonous mushrooms, toadstools) **طحالب سامة** (عش غراب سام)
10 fly agaric (fly amanita, fly fungus), an agaric غارِيْقون الذباب (أمانيت الذباب)
11 amanita أمانيت
12 Satan's mushroom فُطْر الشَّيْطان
13 woolly milk cap قُبَّعَة اللبن الصُّوفِيَّة

380 Medicinal Plants نَبَاتَات طبِّيَّة

1 camomile (chamomile, wild camomile) البابونج ، بَهَار نبيل
2 arnica زَهْرَة العُطاس
3 peppermint نَعْنَع بُسْتانيّ
4 wormwood (absinth) أفْسَنْتين ، شِيْح
5 valerian (allheal) ناردِيْن ، سُنْبُل
6 fennel شَمَار ، شُمْرة
7 lavender خُزَامَى
8 coltsfoot حَشِيْشَة السُّعال
9 tansy حَشِيْشَة الدُّود/الشِّفاء
10 centaury قَنْطُرْيون صغير
11 ribwort (ribwort plantain, ribgrass) لِسَان الحَمَل السِّناني
12 marshmallow خطميّ مَخْزَنَي ، غَسُول
13 alder buckthorn (alder dogwood) جَلْهَم ، عَوْسَج أسود
14 castor-oil plant (Palma Christi) خِرْوَع مَعْرُوف
15 opium poppy خَشْخَاش مُنَوِّم
16 senna (cassia); *the dried leaflets:* senna leaves سَنَا ، سَنَي ؛ الوُرَيْقات المُجففَة: أوراق السَّنا
17 cinchona (chinchona) كينا
18 camphor tree (camphor laurel) كافُور
19 betel palm (areca, areca palm) فَوْفَل ، كَوْثَل
20 betel nut (areca nut) ثَمَرَة الفَوْفَل ، ثَمَرَة الكَوْثَل

381 Edible Fungi (Esculent Fungi) فُطْرِيَّات صالحة للأكل

1 meadow mushroom (field mushroom) فُطْر زراعي
2 mycelial threads (hyphae, mycelium) with fruiting bodies غَزْل فُطْري بجسيمات مُثْمِرة
3 mushroom [longitudinal section] فُطْر ، غاريقون [مَقْطَع طُولي]
4 cap (pileus) with gills قبعة فُطْر ذات خياشيم
5 veil (velum) برقع
6 gill [section] خَيْشُوم [مَقْطَع]
7 basidia [on the gill with basidiospores] دُعَامَات [على الخيشوم ولها أبْوَاغ دعامية]
8 germinating basidiospores (spores) أبواغ دعامية نابِتَة
9 truffle كَمْء
10 truffle [external view] كَمْء [منظر خارجي]
11 truffle [section] كَمْء [مَقْطَع]
12 interior showing asci [section] زِقَاق من الداخل [مَقْطَع]

13 two asci with the ascospores (spores) زِقَاقان بأبواغ زِقّيَّة
14 chanterelle (chantarelle) الإنائيَّة : فُطْر يؤكل
15 Chestnut Boletus فُطْر بُولِيطُس
16 cep (cepe, squirrel's bread, Boletus edulis) خبز السنجاب (بُولِيطُس مأكول)
17 layer of tubes (hymenium) طبقة من الأنابيب (غشَيّ)
18 stem (stipe) عنق (سُوَيق)
19 puffball (Bovista nigrescens) فُقْع الذئب
20 devil's tobacco pouch (common puffball) فُقْع شائع
21 Brown Ring Boletus (Boletus luteus) فُطْر بُولِيطُس ذو الحلقة البُنّيَّة
22 Birch Boletus (Boletus scaber) بُولِيطُس قاس
23 Russula vesca إنائية معروفة
24 scaled prickle fungus فُطْر ابري حَرْشَفي
25 slender funnel fungus فُطْر قِمْعي نحيل
26 morel (Morchella esculenta) غوشنة (فُطْر صالح للأكل)
27 morel (Morchella conica) غوشنة (فُطْر مخروطيّ الشكل)
28 honey fungus فُطْر الجذور العسليّ
29 saffron milk cap لبَنيَّة لذيذة
30 parasol mushroom فُطْر مظَلّي
31 hedgehog fungus (yellow prickle fungus) فُطْر قنفذيّ
32 yellow coral fungus (goatsbeard), goat's beard, coral Clavaria) دَبُّوسيَّة مَرْجانيَّة
33 little cluster fungus فُطْر عنقودي

382 Tropical Plants used as Stimulants, Spices, and Flavoring نباتات مداريَّة تستخدم كمُنَبِّهات وتوَابل ومُكسِبات نَكْهَة

1 coffee tree (coffee plant) شَجَرَة البُنّ
2 fruiting branch فَرْع مُثْمِر
3 flowering branch فَرْع مُزْهِر
4 flower زَهْرَة
5 fruit with two beans [longitudinal section] ثَمَرَة من فلقتيْن [مَقْطَع طُوليّ]
6 coffee bean; *when processed:* coffee حبَّة البُنّ، عند تصنيعها: بُن، قهوة
7 tea plant (tea tree) شَجَرَة الشاي
8 flowering branch فَرْع مُزْهِر
9 tea leaf; *when processed:* tea وَرَقَة الشاي؛ عند تصنيعها: شاي
10 fruit ثَمَرَة
11 maté shrub (maté, yerba maté, Paraguay tea) شاي برغواي
12 flowering branch with androgynous (hermaphroditic, hermaphrodite) flowers فَرْع مُزْهِر ذو أزهار خُنْثَى
13 male flower زَهْرَة ذكر
14 androgynous (hermaphroditic, hermaphrodite) flower زَهْرَة خُنْثَى
15 fruit ثَمَرَة
16 cacao tree (cacao) شَجَرَة الكاكاو
17 branch with flowers and fruits فَرْع ذو أزهار وثمار
18 flower [longitudinal section] زَهْرَة [مَقْطَع طُوليّ]
19 cacao beans (cocoa beans); *when processed:* cocoa, cocoa powder حبَّة الكاكاو؛ عند تصنيعها: كاكاو
20 seed [longitudinal section] بذرة [مَقْطَع طُوليّ]
21 embryo جنين
22 cinnamon tree (cinnamon) شَجَرَة القِرْفَة
23 flowering branch فَرْع مُزْهِر
24 fruit ثَمَرَة
25 cinnamon bark; *when crushed:* cinnamon لحاء القِرْفَة؛ عند طحنه: قِرْفَة
26 clove tree شَجَرَة القَرَنْفُل
27 flowering branch فَرْع مُزْهِر؛
28 flower bud; *when dried:* clove برعم الزَهْرَة؛ عند تجفيفه: قَرَنْفُل
29 flower زَهْرَة
30 nutmeg tree جَوْز الطِّيب، بَسْبَاسة
31 flowering branch فَرْع مُزْهِر
32 female flower [longitudinal section] زَهْرَة أُنثَى [مَقْطَع طُوليّ]
33 mature (ripe) fruit ثَمَرَة ناضجة
34 nutmeg with mace, a seed with laciniate aril جَوْزَة الطِّيب ذات زيت
35 seed [cross section]; *when dried:* nutmeg حبَّة، بزرة [مَقْطَع عَرْضيّ]؛ عند تجفيفها: جَوْز الطِّيب
36 pepper plant فلفل
37 fruiting branch فَرْع مُثْمِر
38 inflorescence شكل الازْهرَار
39 fruit [longitudinal section] with seed (peppercorn); *when ground:* pepper ثَمَرَة [مَقْطَع طُوليّ] ذات بزرة؛ عند طحنها: فلفل
40 Virginia tobacco plant تَبْغ فرجينيَّة
41 flowering shoot غصن مُزْهِر
42 flower زَهْرَة
43 tobacco leaf; *when cured:* tobacco وَرَقَة تَبْغ؛ عند معالجتها : تَبْغ
44 mature (ripe) fruit capsule جِرْو ثَمَرَة ناضجة
45 seed حبَّة
46 vanilla plant فانيلا ، وَنِيلِيَّة
47 flowering shoot غصن مُزْهِر
48 vanilla pod; *when cured:* stick of vanilla قرن الفانيلا؛ عند معالجته: عصا فانيلا
49 pistachio tree شجرة فُسْتُق
50 flowering branch with female flowers فَرْع مُزْهِر ذو أزهار أُنْثَى

51 drupe (pistachio, pistachio nut)	نَوَوِيَّة
52 sugar cane	قَصَب السُّكَّر
53 plant in bloom	نَبْتَة مُزْهِرة
54 panicle	عُنْكُول
55 flower	زَهْرَة

383 Plants used in Industry — نباتات تستخدم في الصناعة

1 rape (cole, coleseed)	لفت
2 basal leaf	وَرَقَة أساسية
3 Flower [longitudinal section]	زَهْرَة [مَقْطَع طُولِيّ]
4 mature (ripe) siliqua (pod)	سنفة ناضجة
5 oleiferous seed	بزرة زيتية
6 flax	كتان
7 peduncle (pedicel, flower stalk)	مِعْلاق ، زَنْد
8 seed vessel (boll)	لوزة
9 hemp	قنَّب هندي
10 fruiting female (pistillate) plant	نَبْتَة أُنْثَى مُثْمِرة
11 female inflorescence	ازْهِرَار أنثى
12 flower	زَهْرَة
13 male inflorescence	ازْهِرَار ذكري
14 fruit	ثَمَرَة
15 seed	حبَّة
16 cotton	قُطْن
17 flower	زَهْرَة
18 fruit	ثَمَرَة
19 lint [cotton wool]	خيوط القُطْن
20 silk-cotton tree (kapok tree, capoc tree, ceiba tree)	شَجَرَة القَابُوق أو القُطْن الحريري
21 fruit	ثَمَرَة
22 flowering branch	فَرْع مُزْهِر
23 seed	بزرة، حبَّة
24 seed [longitudinal section]	حبَّة [مَقْطَع طُولِيّ]
25 jute	جُوْتَة، جوت، قِنَّب كَلْكَتَّة
26 flowering branch	فَرْع مُزْهِر
27 flower	زَهْرَة
28 fruit	ثَمَرَة
29 olive tree (olive)	شَجَرَة الزَّيْتُون
30 flowering branch	فَرْع مُزْهِر
31 flower	زَهْرَة
32 fruit	ثَمَرَة
33 rubber tree (rubber plant)	شَجَرَة المَطَّاط (تين المَطَّاط)
34 fruiting branch	فَرْع مُزْهِر
35 fig	تِينَة
36 flower	زَهْرَة
37 gutta-percha tree	شَجَرَة الغاتابرشا
38 flowering branch	فَرْع مُزْهِر
39 flower	زَهْرَة
40 fruit	ثَمَرَة
41 peanut (ground nut, monkey nut)	فُول سوداني ، فُسْتُق العبيد
42 flowering shoot	فَسِيلَة مُزْهِرة
43 root with fruits	جذر وبه ثمار
44 nut (kernel) [longitudinal section]	جَوْزَة (نواة)
45 sesame plant (simsim, benniseed)	شَجَرَة السمسم
46 flowers and fruiting branch	ازهار فَرْع مُثْمِر
47 flower [longitudinal section]	زَهْرَة [مَقْطَع طُولِيّ]
48 coconut palm (coconut tree, coco palm, cocoa palm)	شَجَرَة جَوْزَة الهند
49 inflorescence	نظام الازْهِرَار
50 female flower	زَهْرَة أُنْثَى
51 male flower [longitudinal section]	زَهْرَة ذكر [مَقْطَع طُولِيّ]
52 fruit [longitudinal section]	ثَمَرَة [مَقْطَع طُولِيّ]
53 coconut (cokernut)	جَوْزَة الهند
54 oil palm	نَخْل الدُّهْن
55 male spadix	طَلْع ذكر
56 infructescence with fruit	عُنْقُود ثَمَر به ثمرة
57 seed with micropyles (foramina) (foraminate seed)	بزرة ذات بُوَيْبَات
58 sago palm	نَخْل الدقيق
59 fruit	ثَمَرَة
60 bamboo stem (bamboo culm)	جذع خَيْزَران
61 branch with leaves	فَرْع ذو أوراق
62 spike	سُنْبُلَة ، سَبَلَة
63 part of bamboo stem with joints	جزء من جذع خَيْزَران له وصلات
64 papyrus plant (paper reed, paper rush)	بَرْدي
65 umbel	خَيْمَة
66 spike	سُنْبُلَة ، سَبَلَة

384 Southern Fruits (Tropical, Subtropical, and Mediterranean Fruits) — ثمار جنوبية (مداريَّة وشبه مداريَّة وبَحْر أوْسَطيَّة)

1 date palm (date)	نَخْلَة
2 fruiting palm	نَخْلَة مُثْمِرة
3 palm frond	سَعَفَة النَخْل
4 male spadix	طَلْع ذكري
5 male flower	زَهْرَة ذكر
6 female spadix	طَلْع أُنْثَي
7 female flower	زَهْرَة أُنْثَى
8 stand of fruit	حامل الثمر
9 date	رُطْبَة ، تَمْرَة
10 date kernel	نواة التمرة
11 fig	تِيْنَة
12 branch with pseudocarps	فَرْع به أخبية كاذبة
13 fig with flowers	تِيْنَة ذات أزهار [مَقْطَع

[longitudinal section]	طُولي]
14 female flower	زَهْرَة أُنْثَى
15 male flower	زَهْرَة ذكر
16 pomegranate	رُمَّانَة، ثَمَرَة الرُّمَّان
17 flowering branch	فَرْع مُزْهِر
18 flower [longitudinal section, corolla removed]	زَهْرَة [مَقْطَع طُولي، بدون تُوَيْج]
19 fruit	ثَمَرَة
20 seed [longitudinal section]	بزرة، حبَّة [مَقْطَع طُولي]
21 seed [cross section]	بزرة، حبَّة [مَقْطَع عَرْضي]
22 embryo	جنين
23 lemon; *sim.:* tangerine (mandarin), orange, grapefruit	لَيْمُون؛ مثلها اليوسفي والبرتقال والجريب فروت
24 flowering branch	فَرْع مُزْهِر
25 orange flower [longitudinal section]	زَهْرَة البرتقال [مَقْطَع طُولي]
26 fruit	ثَمَرَة
27 orange [cross section]	برتقالة [مَقْطَع عَرْضي]
28 banana plant (banana tree)	شَجَرَة المَوْز
29 crown	تاج
30 herbaceous stalk with overlapping leaf sheaths	ساق عُشْبِيَّة بها أغْماد أوراق متداخلة
31 inflorescence with young fruits	نظام ازْهِرَار به ثمار نامية
32 infructescence (bunch of fruit)	عُنْقُود ثَمَر
33 banana	مَوْزَة
34 banana flower	زَهْرَة المَوْز
35 banana leaf [diagram]	وَرَقَة المَوْز
36 almond	لوز
37 flowering branch	فَرْع مُزْهِر
38 fruiting branch	فَرْع مُثْمِر
39 fruit	ثَمَرَة
40 drupe containing seed	نووية تحتوي على بزور
[almond]	[لوزة]
41 carob	خَرُّوب
42 branch with female flowers	فَرْع به أزهار أُنْثَى
43 female flower	زَهْرَة أُنْثَى
44 male flower	زَهْرَة ذكر
45 fruit	ثَمَرَة
46 siliqua (pod) [cross section]	خَرْدلِيَّة [مَقْطَع عرضي]
47 seed	بزرة، حبَّة
48 sweet chestnut (Spanish chestnut)	قَسْطَل
49 flowering branch	فَرْع مزهر
50 female inflorescence	ازْهِرَار أُنْثَى
51 male flower	زَهْرَة ذكر
52 cupule containing seeds	قِمْع، كُوَيْس
53 Brazil nut	بُنْدق برازيلي
54 flowering branch	فَرْع مُزْهِر
55 leaf	وَرَقَة
56 flower [from above]	زَهْرَة [مِن أعلى]
57 flower [longitudinal section]	زَهْرَة [مَقْطَع طُولي]
58 opened capsule containing seeds	جِرْو مفتوح وبه بزور
59 Brazil nut [cross section]	بُنْدق برازيلي [مَقْطَع عَرْضي]
60 nut [longitudinal section]	جَوْزَة [مَقْطَع طُولي]
61 pineapple plant (pineapple)	نبات الأناناس
62 pseudocarp with crown of leaves	خِبَاء كاذب له تاج من الأوراق
63 syncarp	ثَمَرَة متحدة الأخبية
64 pineapple flower	زَهْرَة الأناناس
65 flower [longitudinal section]	زَهْرَة [مَقْطَع طُولي]

ENGLISH-ARABIC INDEX

مسرد إنجليزي - عربي

تسلية وثقافة وفن

حيوانات ونباتات

المكتب والمصرف وبورصة الأوراق المالية

مجتمع

ترفيه وألعاب ورياضة

مهن وحرف وصناعة

صناعة الطباعة

النقل والاتصالات وتكنولوجيا المعلومات

المحتويات

الأرقام العربية هي أرقام الصور

المحتويات

دليل استعمال القاموس

القاموس الإنجليزي المصور والمسرد الإنجليزي ـ العربي والمحتويات الكاملة مرتبة تحت رؤوس الموضوعات التالية:

- الذرة ـ الكون ـ الأرض
- الإنسان وبيئته الاجتماعية
- الطبيعة: البيئة والزراعة والحراجة
- مهن وحرف وصناعة
- صناعة الطباعة
- النقل والاتصالات وتكنولوجيا المعلومات
- المكتب والمصرف وبورصة الأوراق المالية
- مجتمع
- ترفيه وألعاب ورياضة
- تسلية وثقافة وفن
- حيوانات ونباتات

للعثور على الترجمة الإنجليزية لإحدى المفردات، عليك أولا أن تتصفح مجالات الموضوعات المدرجة في ″المحتويات″ (صفحة 967–970). اختر الموضوع ذا العلاقة، ثم حدد الرقم المتوافق معه في ″القاموس الإنجليزي المصور″ (الأرقام مثبتة في الركن العلوي من كل صفحة). وإذا ما عثرت على المادة المصورة المطلوبة، ابحث عن الرقم المتوافق معها في ″المسرد الإنجليزي ـ العربي″ تحت رأس الموضوع نفسه.

قاموس أوكسفورد - دودن الإنجليزي المصور مع مسرد إنجليزي - عربي

المسرد الإنجليزي - العربي من إعداد
مصطفى محمد جبر